PRINCIPLES OF MACRO-
ECONOMICS
AND THE CANADIAN ECONOMY

JOSEPH E. STIGLITZ
STANFORD UNIVERSITY

ROBIN W. BOADWAY
QUEEN'S UNIVERSITY

W · W · NORTON & COMPANY · NEW YORK · LONDON

To Andrew

Cover painting: Laszlo Moholy-Nagy, *LIS*, 1922
Oil on canvas, 131 × 100 centimetres
Courtesy of the Kunsthaus, Zurich
Special thanks to Hattula Moholy-Nagy
Cover design: Antonina Krass and Jay J. Smith

The text of this book is set in Electra with display set in Kabel and Binner Gothic.
Composition by TSI Graphics and Manufacturing by Arcata Graphics.
Book design and Interior Graphics by Antonina Krass.
The Interior Graphics were inspired by the cover painting, *LIS* by Moholy-Nagy.

ISBN 0-393-96570-8

W.W. Norton & Company, Inc., 500 Fifth Avenue, New York, N.Y. 10110
W.W. Norton & Company Ltd., 10 Coptic Street, London WCIA IPU

1 2 3 4 5 6 7 8 9 0

Contents in Brief

CONTENTS

CHAPTER 2   THINKING LIKE AN
ECONOMIST • 28

CHAPTER 3   EXCHANGE AND
PRODUCTION • 55

CHAPTER 6 TIME AND RISK • 139

CHAPTER 7 THE PUBLIC SECTOR • 166

PART TWO

AGGREGATE MARKETS

CHAPTER **12**   AGGREGATE DEMAND • 320

CHAPTER **13**   CONSUMPTION AND INVESTMENT • 350

CHAPTER **14** GOVERNMENT EXPENDITURES
AND TRADE • 384

CHAPTER **15** AGGREGATE DEMAND AND
SUPPLY • 416

CHAPTER **16** STICKY PRICES • 448

PART THREE

MONEY'S ROLE

CHAPTER **19**   MONETARY POLICY: THE
INTERNATIONAL SIDE • 530

CHAPTER **20** PRICE STABILITY • 554

PART FOUR

POLICIES FOR GROWTH AND STABILITY

CHAPTER **21** GROWTH AND
PRODUCTIVITY • 583

CHAPTER **22** THE PROBLEM OF THE TWIN DEFICITS • 619

CHAPTER **25** DEVELOPMENT • 706

PREFACE

The last fifty years have been an exciting time for economics. The world has changed in so many fundamental ways. And the discipline of economics has changed in fundamental ways too, partly to reflect these changes.

In the years immediately following World War II, the world economy was dominated by the United States. International trade was relatively unimportant for many countries, in part because of the prevalence of trade barriers. International capital flows were dominated by those from the United States, especially to Europe to rebuild economies that had been devastated by the war, but also to most other corners of the world, including to Canada. The Cold War put the market economies of North America and Western Europe in military and economic competition with the Soviet Union with its very different form of economy. Countries in Asia and Africa, freed from their colonial status, looked forward as well to rising living standards that they believed would accompany their newly acquired freedom.

These postwar years saw the Canadian economy growing vigourously and living standards rising rapidly as we took advantage of our position next door to the largest and most vibrant economy in the world. Indeed, given our seemingly boundless natural resources, our young, educated labour force, and an ability to attract foreign capital to put both of these to good use, the future seemed to belong to Canada.

All of this has changed. The economies of the nations of the former Soviet Union have collapsed, along with their political systems. International trade has grown in importance as trade barriers have been reduced and markets have become globalized through the revolution in communications and transportation; Japan and other countries of East Asia and Europe now provide formidable competition for North American firms. While the rates of growth in East Asia have been phenomenal, virtually unprecedented in the history of mankind, the rate of increase in productivity in Canada, the United States, and Western Europe has slowed down markedly. Indeed, wages of less-skilled workers in these Western countries have actually fallen during the past two decades. The dream that each generation would be better off than its parents has been lost. The United States is even losing its lead in the wealth sweepstakes: it has gone from being the largest creditor nation in the world—foreigners owed it billions of dollars—to being the largest debtor nation.

International capital markets have played an important role in the globalization of the world economy, with hundreds of billions of dollars moving daily from one country to another. Multinational companies have grown beyond belief, to the point where the largest are now larger than many small countries. In the battles for the control of some of these large companies, the capital markets have provided the large sums of money required by the different contestants.

It is not only that the world has changed; expectations have changed as well. While there has been enormous improvement in the quality of air in our major cities, and while Lake Erie has been rescued from becoming polluted to the point where life could not survive, our expectations about the environment have grown even faster; we have become increasingly aware of environmental costs. Longevity has increased, but our knowledge of how to prolong life has grown more rapidly, and rising health care costs have become a major political issue. The economic role of women has changed: not only have they taken a more active part in the labour force, there has been a revolution in expectations concerning the kinds of jobs women can hold.

And in virtually every one of the major issues facing the economy, there is a debate about the role of government. Government at all levels in Canada has grown enormously, largely due to the rapid growth of social programs and of cash transfers to various groups in the economy. Before World War II, government took about one out of every six dollars; today it takes more than one out of every three. There are differing views of government responsibility. For instance, people expect, even demand, that government do something about unemployment and provide free health care and education to all. But at the same time, there is a wider understanding of the limitations of government in an increasingly globalized economy. The increasing government deficits over the past decade, the largest in Canada's peacetime history, have meant that one of the wealthiest countries in the world seems short of money to maintain basic public programs. Issues concerning the responsibility, capabilities, and strategies of government in the economy have come to the centre of the political debates. Analysts and policy makers now openly question the role of governments in such fundamental areas as the provision of health care and education, while at the same time others argue that governments should do more for children, the elderly, and the disadvantaged.

These are exciting issues and events, and they fill the front pages of our newspapers and the evening television news shows. Yet in the recent past, teachers of the introductory course in economics have felt frustrated: none of the textbooks really conveyed this sense of excitement. Try as they might, none seemed to prepare the student adequately for interpreting and understanding these important economic events.

On reflection, one of the reasons for this becomes clear: the principles expounded in the classic textbook of Alfred Marshall of a hundred years ago, or that of Paul Samuelson, now almost fifty years old, are not the principles for today. The way we economists understand our discipline has changed to reflect the changing world, but the textbooks have not kept pace. Our professional discourse was built on a *modern* economics, but these new developments simply are not adequately reflected in any of the vast array of textbooks that are available to us as teachers.

Indeed, changes in the economics discipline over the past half century have been as significant as the changes in world events. The basic competitive model of the economy was perfected in the 1950s. Since then, economists have gone beyond that model in several directions as they have come to understand better its limitations. Earlier researchers had paid lip service to the importance of incentives and to problems posed by limited information. However, it was only in the last two decades that real progress was made in understanding these issues, and the advances have found extensive application. The collapse of the Soviet bloc economies, the debt crisis facing many less-developed countries, the rash of major bankruptcies in the financial sector, and the escalating costs of health and unemployment insurance programs can all be viewed as consequences of the failure to provide appropriate incentives. Thus, a central question in the debate over growth and productivity should be: How can an economy provide stronger incentives for innovation? The debate over pollution and the environment centers around the relative merits of regulation and providing incentives not to pollute and to conserve resources.

The past fifty years have also seen a reexamination of the boundary between economics and business. Subjects like finance and management used to be relegated to business schools, where they were taught without reference to economic principles. Today we know that to understand how market economies actually work, we have to understand how firms finance and manage themselves. Tremendous insights can be gleaned through the application of basic economic principles, particularly those grounded in an understanding of incentives. Stories of corporate takeovers have been replaced on the front page by stories of bankruptcies as acquiring corporations have found themselves overextended. The 1990 Nobel Prize was awarded to three economists who had contributed most to the endeavour to integrate finance and economics. Yet the introductory textbooks had not yet built in the basic economics of finance and management.

We have also come to appreciate better the virtues of competition. We now understand, for instance, how the benefits of competition extend beyond price to competition for technological innovation. At the same time, we have come to see better why, in so many circumstances, competition appears limited. Again, none of the available textbooks seemed to provide students with a sense of this new understanding.

Samuelson's path-breaking textbook is credited with being the first to integrate successfully the (then) new insights of Keynesian economics with traditional microeconomics. Samuelson employed the concept of the neoclassical synthesis—the view that once the economy was restored to full employment, the old classical principles applied. In effect, there were two distinct regimes to the economy. In one, when the economy's resources were underemployed, macroeconomic principles applied; in the other, when the economy's resources were fully employed, microeconomic principles were relevant. That these were distinct and hardly related regimes was reflected in how texts were written and courses were taught; it made no difference whether micro was taught before macro, or vice versa. In the last decades, economists came to question the split that had developed between microeconomics and macroeconomics. The profession as a whole came to believe that macroeconomic behaviour had to be related to underlying microeconomic principles; there was one set of economic principles, not two. But this view simply was not reflected in any of the available texts.

Thus, none of the books seemed to provide students with an understanding of the *principles* of *modern* economics—both the principles that are necessary to understand how modern economists think about the world and the principles that are required to understand current economic issues. As we approach a new century, we need principles that go beyond those of Marshall and Samuelson. To be sure, *some*, even much, of what was contained in these older texts remains in this book. Demand curves and supply curves are tools that have continued to be useful. A thorough understanding of concepts such as comparative advantage, opportunity costs, and marginal analysis is necessary if students are to understand adequately the problems facing market economies. One of the challenges was how to integrate the new principles with the old.

Economics is often characterized as the science of choice. Writing a textbook involves many choices; there is limited space, and the subject matter is vast. The textbook writer must continually ask, "What are the basic principles every student of economics should know? What are the most relevant, current applications with which to illustrate each of these principles?" Let us illustrate some of our answers by mentioning several ways in which this text is different.

- The macroeconomic analysis is based on sound microeconomic principles, and the microeconomics is presented in a way that builds a foundation for macroeconomics. Many textbooks develop their material in microeconomics and macroeconomics independently, leading to a false dichotomy. We have attempted to provide a completely integrated view of the entire subject, and to show how each part throws light on the other.

- Finance is recognized as an important part of economics, in both the microeconomic and macroeconomic discussions. Chapter 6 introduces the basic ideas of time and risk, and Chapter 9 raises the question of investment by households and firms. This new understanding of the microeconomics of finance is then reflected in the macroeconomic discussions, in the analysis of investment in Chapter 13 and in the analysis of monetary economics in Chapters 17–20.

- Problems of growth and international competitiveness are discussed at length. Chapter 21, for instance, discusses explanations for the slowdown of productivity in Canada.

- The importance of international trade and finance is recognized, and not just by adding more chapters or pages. For instance, the role of trade and exchange, including the gains from trade, is developed in Chapter 3. Exports and imports and capital flows are an integral part of the analysis throughout the book. And a separate chapter (22) is devoted to the relationship between the current-account deficit and the government's budget deficit.

- Throughout, issues of incentives and the problems posed by incomplete information are given prominence. Chapter 11 discusses how firms' concerns about providing incentives for their workers may lead to wage rigidities, while Chapters 13 and 21 discuss how governments can attempt to alter households' incentives to save and firms' incentives to invest. The consequences of incomplete information for the capital market, including the possibility of credit rationing, and the resulting implications for investments and for how monetary policy works are discussed in Chapters 13 and 18.

• As our understanding of the limitations of markets has increased, so has our understanding of the limitations of government, and the age-old questions of the appropriate balance between government and the private sector have to be reexamined. This book looks at a wide range of policy issues, including whether, or how, the government should try to promote economic growth and stabilize economic fluctuations (Chapter 21) and how the deficit arose and what should be done about it (Chapter 22).

ACKNOWLEDGMENTS

When I was approached by Norton to consider doing a Canadian edition of an introductory textbook by Joe Stiglitz, I was neither aware nor surprised to hear that he had done such a book. I barely had to see the manuscript to know that I would be interested. Over the years, the writings of Joe Stiglitz in so many fields have served as valuable learning devices for my cohort of teachers. By the clarity and breadth of his writings, Joe served not only to define individual fields of economics (including risk and uncertainty, asymmetric information, tax and public expenditure theory, technological innovation, product diversity and market structure, capital theory, the operation of labour markets in both industrialized and developing countries, and decision making within institutions and bureaucracies, to name a few), but in many cases showed the common features of these various subfields and the important role that incentives and information play in determining economic outcomes. In particular, his application of economic analysis was always motivated by explaining important real-world phenomena. While he wrote his technical articles as a teacher of teachers would do, he was obviously not satisfied that this went far enough. His role in bringing about the *Journal of Economic Perspectives* is well known. This journal has succeeded in making available the most abstract of advances in our discipline to a very wide audience of economists. It was only a matter of time before he would turn his attention from educating economists to educating students.

My role in this venture was necessarily a modest one. It was to direct the textbook to the interests of Canadian students, drawing on special features of the Canadian economy and particular policy problems facing it. This was not a difficult task. The principles of analysis are universal and apply to any market economy. It was simply a matter of showing their relevance to the various issues of Canadian interest. These include our special industrial structure, which results from the combination of a relatively small population for our size, a rich endowment of natural resources, and an historic reliance on inflows of capital from abroad for our development; the importance of trade and financial flows with the rest of the world; the special relationship we have with our giant neighbour to the south, a relationship that has resulted in a sequence of negotiated trading arrangements; the role our government has assumed in providing an array of social programs and programs for regional development; and the importance of our relatively decentralized federal system of government. Not surprisingly, many of the current policy problems facing Canada are similar to those facing the United States as well as other developed economies, including lagging productivity growth, difficulties in balancing our trade in the face of increased international competition, and concerns about the way our governments go about their business, both in terms of the services they provide and the difficulty of covering their costs. These issues are all reflected in the Canadian edition of this book.

In addition to my obvious deep debt to Joe Stiglitz for giving me the opportunity to participate in this venture, I have also received some exceptional help in preparing the Canadian edition. I am grateful to Drake McFeely of Norton for approaching me and encouraging me to take it on at a time when I, like most others, had plenty to keep me busy. He stayed with the project from start to finish, and his continuous advice and suggestions for improvement were always right on the mark without ever compromising the traditional independence of an author. When I got down to work, I was provided with valuable research assistance by three persons, each of whom brought their unique expertise to the task—Louise Affleck, whose Prairie roots matched my own and who was particularly helpful in putting together some of the macroeconomics material; Sean Heincke, who formed the Upper Canadian part of the team and whose knowledge of the industrial organization scene in Canada was particularly helpful; and Josée Voizard, whose Québec roots and experience in research served particularly well in covering many of the applied policy topics in the book. And, lest the Atlantic provinces feel slighted, my wife Bernie, a Maritimer, helped put together the material and prepare the manuscript for the publisher.

Once the draft manuscript was completed, it was placed in the very capable hands of Sandy Lifland, who is as careful and thoughtful an editor as I have seen. Though not an economist by training, she very quickly came to understand the outline of the book and its arguments, and was able to improve significantly on my sometimes dry and other times terse presentation. As well, her precise editing served to enhance the chances that my statements were factually correct as well as timely.

A number of other individuals also deserve mention for their part in the production process. Rich Rivellese gathered the photographs and assisted in the editorial process in a variety of other ways; Roberta Flechner did the layout; Antonina Krass designed the book; Roy Tedoff coordinated its production; and Susan Gaustad did the manuscript editing for the U.S. edition. Their work was timely and efficient and, I think the reader will agree, resulted in a splendidly produced book.

One other person deserves a great deal of credit for the way in which the ideas are presented in the book and exemplified by real-world examples. That is Tim Taylor of Stanford University, who is well known in his role as managing editor of the *Journal of Economic Perspectives*. Tim worked closely with Joe Stiglitz through the various drafts of the U.S. edition and contributed greatly to both the content and exposition of both the U.S. and the Canadian editions. In particular, he drafted many of the close-ups for the U.S. edition, some of which also found their way into this book.

Necessary and valuable adjuncts to the book are the Study Guide for students, the Instructor's Manual for teachers, the test bank, and the computer tutorials. The Study Guide was very capably revised for the Canadian edition by Alan Harrison of McMaster University. It was based on the U.S. edition prepared by Lawrence Martin of Michigan State. I took on the Instructor's Manual with the careful and helpful assistance of Travis Armour. Also available on computer diskette, it follows closely that for the U.S. edition by Glenn Harrison and Elisabet Rutström of the University of South Carolina. Alan Harrison also adapted for this edition the test bank by Dale Bails of Iowa Wesleyan University. This test item file is also available on the highly regarded Norton TestMaker software system. Stephen R. King and Rick M. McConnell are responsible for the unusual and effective computer tutorials.

Finally, though I tried to complete this task with minimal disruption to my family, I am sure that is not the way it seemed to them. At least, they know that if it were not this, it would have been something else. In any case, they showed characteristic patience with my preoccupations. My only defence is to suggest that a good understanding of the principles of economics by whoever should study it at colleges and universities in Canada can only help to serve the interests of my sons' generation.

I especially dedicate this book to Andrew, who has struggled with a disease that few can, or try to, understand. May the Canadian economy afford him the opportunities that its resources should allow it to do.

SUGGESTED OUTLINE FOR A SHORT COURSE

The following is our suggestion for an abbreviated course. We would cover all of the chapters in Part One. In Part Two, Chapter 8 introduces the basic macroeconomic measures: unemployment, inflation, and growth. Chapter 9 reviews some technical microeconomics from which macroeconomic analysis stems. While it enriches the discussion that follows, it can be skipped if time is short. Likewise, Chapters 13, 14, and 15 may be dropped without the loss of continuity. In Part Three, Chapter 19, which presents monetary theory in an open economy, may be dropped, though we recommend against it, since we do not believe that monetary policy can be adequately understood today from the more traditional closed economy perspective. Finally, Part Four provides wide scope for choice: although each of the chapters draws upon ideas presented in earlier chapters, any may be dropped without impeding the understanding of subsequent chapters.

INTRODUCTION

These days economics is big news. If we pick up a newspaper or turn on the television for the prime-time news report, we are likely to be bombarded with statistics on unemployment rates, inflation rates, exports, and imports. How well are we doing in competition with other countries, such as Japan? Everyone seems to want to know. Political fortunes as well as the fortunes of countries, firms, and individuals depend on how well the economy does.

What is economics all about? That is the subject of Part One. Chapter 1 uses the story of the automobile industry to illustrate many of the fundamental issues with which economics is concerned. The chapter describes the four basic questions at the heart of economics, and how economists attempt to answer these questions.

Chapter 2 introduces the economists' basic model and explains why notions of property, profits, prices, and cost play such a central role in economists' thinking.

A fact of life in the modern world is that individuals and countries are interdependent. Even a wealthy country like Canada is dependent on foreign countries for vital imports. Chapter 3 discusses the gains that result from trade; why trade, for instance, allows greater specialization, and why greater specialization results in increased productivity. It also explains the patterns of trade—why each country imports and exports the particular goods it does.

Prices play a central role in enabling economies to function. Chapters 4 and 5 take up the question of what determines prices. Also, what causes prices to change over time? Why is water, without which we cannot live, normally so inexpensive, while diamonds, which we surely can do without, are very expensive? What happens to the prices of beer and cigarettes if the government imposes a tax on these goods? Sometimes the government passes laws requiring firms to pay wages of at least so much, or forbidding landlords to charge rents that exceed a certain level. What are the consequences of these government interventions?

Chapter 6 introduces two important realities: economic life takes place not in a single moment of time but over long periods, and life is fraught with risk. Decisions today have effects on the future, and there is usually much uncertainty about what those effects will be. How do economists deal with problems posed by time and risk?

Finally, Chapter 7 turns to the pervasive role of the government in modern economies. Its focus is on why the government undertakes the economic roles it does and on the economic rationale for government actions. It also describes the various forms that government actions might take and the changing roles of the government over time.

1

THE AUTOMOBILE AND ECONOMICS

F or a teenager, an automobile can symbolize status, freedom of movement, and adventure. For a mechanic, a car can seem like a sick creature to be healed. For a commuter stuck in traffic, a car can feel like a padded prison. For an assembly-line worker, an automobile may be only a partially completed collection of loose pieces, and a job. For a bank robber or a race car driver, a car is a modernized mechanical horse. In the lives of each of these different people—and their example could be multiplied indefinitely—the combination of metal and rubber and plastic that we call an automobile plays an important role, whose nature varies from the grease and grit of utmost practicality to the romanticism of an open convertible on a moonlit highway.

For an economist, the automobile can serve as a starting place for illustrating almost any part of economics. By looking at this familiar subject from the perspective of economics, we can learn a great deal about the economic way of thinking.

1. What *is* economics? What are the basic questions it addresses?

2. In economies such as that of Canada, what are the respective roles of government and the private, or "market," sector?

3. What are markets, and what are the principal markets that make up the economy?

4. Why is economics called a science?

5. Why, if economics is a science, do economists so often seem to disagree?

THE AUTOMOBILE: A BRIEF HISTORY

After nearly one hundred years of automobile production, it is hard to imagine a time when cars did not exist. But just like any other new product, the automobile had to start with an idea. Of course, ideas by themselves are not enough. Ideas must be translated into marketable products and produced at affordable prices, and the production process must be financed. Before investors will provide financial support, they have to be convinced that the proposed idea is not only feasible, but likely to be profitable enough to compensate them for the risks of the investment.

No single discovery led to the development of the automobile, and the idea of a motorized carriage occurred to many individuals in the United States, Germany, France, and Great Britain in the late nineteenth century. The technical problems that had to be solved were easy to state, if difficult to tackle. For instance, unlike a steam locomotive, a horseless carriage could not carry its fuel in a separate car, so the development of a powerful but relatively light internal combustion engine was critical.

If you visit a museum of early cars, you will see that the technical problems were resolved independently in a variety of ways. At the end of the nineteenth and beginning of the twentieth centuries, the area around Detroit was full of innovators developing their various cars—Ransom E. Olds, the Dodge brothers, and Henry Ford, ultimately the most successful of them all. The spirit must have been much like that of "Silicon Valley" (the area in California between San Francisco and San Jose) in the past quarter century, which has been at the center of the development of new computer technologies: a spirit of excitement and of important breakthroughs being made and new milestones being reached. The various automobile innovators could draw upon a stock of ideas that were "floating in the air." Then too they had the help of specialized firms that had developed a variety of new technologies and skills unusual for that time: for example, new alloys that enabled lighter motors to be constructed and new techniques for machining that allowed for greater power, precision, and durability. Innovators could draw upon these new technologies to supplement their own ideas.

Henry Ford is generally given credit for having recognized the potential value of a vehicle that could be made available at a reasonable price. Before Ford came along, automobiles were luxuries, affordable only by the very rich. He saw the potential benefit from providing inexpensive transportation. Even after he introduced the Model T in 1909 at a seeming "bargain" price of U.S. $900, he subsequently cut the price in half, to U.S. $440, in 1914 and then reduced the price by almost a fifth again, to U.S. $360, by 1916. The public responded: sales skyrocketed from 58,000 in 1909 to 730,000 in 1916. Ford's prediction of a mass market for inexpensive cars had proved correct.

There was more to Ford's success than simply putting a lower price tag on his cars. He also devised a way to produce cars less expensively. His major innovation was the assembly line, which allowed mass production; this was the key to his lower car prices. Furthermore, Ford managed to obtain the needed financial resources to hire and train a labour force that could produce the automobiles. Underlying all his other successes was the creation of the organization—Ford Motor Company—within which the production, financing, and marketing took place.

The riskiness of the venture was great. Would Ford be successful in developing his automobile? Would someone else beat him to it? Would the price of a car be low enough for many people to buy it? If he was successful, would imitators copy his invention and produce so many cars that he could not make any money?

Investors in Ford's venture contemplated these risks as they thought about whether to provide him with the funds he needed. As it turned out, the investors should have anticipated—but probably did not—a further problem. Ford formed a partnership to develop his first car. He was primarily to supply the ideas and work, while his partners supplied the funds. But the partnership went broke before production began, and Ford's critics claimed that the reason was that he spent all his time and energy thinking about his next set of ideas, rather than actually making any cars.

On the basis of his more developed ideas, Ford then persuaded a new set of investors to finance him. The previous experience should, perhaps, have made them suspicious, but they went ahead. Again the partnership failed, and again Ford seemed to be spending his time developing new ideas.

In his third partnership, Ford finally succeeded in producing cars. Were Ford's first two sets of partners treated unfairly? Ford might well have argued that he entered each of the partnerships in good faith, but he simply was not able to pull off the feat of producing cars until the third time around. Besides, Ford might say, the success of that venture was more attributable to his ideas and efforts than to the money supplied by his partners. Whatever the truth of Ford's particular case, this general sort of problem—one or more partners feels he has contributed proportionately more than his share of profits indicates, or one or more partners tries to "cheat" the others of what they consider their due—occurs over and over again.

Ford's success was due as much to his ability to come up with innovative ways of providing incentives and organizing production as to his skill in solving technical problems. He demonstrated this ability with his original labour policies. Instead of trying to hold down worker pay, he offered more than double the going wage and paid his workers the then princely sum of U.S. $5 a day. In exchange, though, Ford worked his employees hard: the moving assembly line he invented enabled him to set his workers a fast pace and push them to keep up. The amount produced per worker increased enormously. Still, it was clear that the high wages were ample compensation for the extra effort. In fact, riots almost broke out as workers clamoured for the jobs being offered. Ford had rediscovered an old truth: by paying workers more than they could earn elsewhere, it is possible to obtain a labour force that is harder working and more loyal, with less quitting and absenteeism. In some cases, higher wages for employees can repay the employer in higher productivity.

Ford's success in using incentives to compensate his workers for increasing productivity meant that he could sell his cars far more cheaply than his rivals could. The lower prices and the high level of sales that accompanied them made it possible for him to take full advantage of the mass production techniques he had developed. At one point, however, Ford's plans were almost thwarted when a lawyer-inventor named George Baldwin Selden claimed that Ford had infringed on his patent.

Governments grant patents to enable inventors to reap the rewards of their innovative activity. These are generally for specific inventions, like a new type of braking system or transmission mechanism. A patent gives the inventor the exclusive right to produce his invention for a limited time, thus helping to assure that inventors will be able to make some money from their successful inventions. Patents may lead to higher prices for these new products, since there is no competition from others making the same product, but the presumption is that the gains to society from the stimulation to innovative activity more than compensate for the losses to consumers from the temporarily higher prices.

To obtain a patent, one has to meet certain criteria. Ford's idea of an assembly line, for example, was not an invention that could be patented, and it was imitated by other car manufacturers. One of the criteria for granting a patent (and judging whether someone else is infringing on that patent) is a standard of "novelty." Ideas cannot, in general, be patented; only specific innovations can. Selden had applied for, and been granted, a patent for a horseless, self-propelled carriage. He demanded that other car manufacturers pay him a royalty, which is a payment for the right to use a patented innovation. Simultaneously, he established an association that would ensure that prices of automobiles remained high.

Ford challenged Selden's patent in court on the grounds that the concept of a "horseless, self-propelled carriage," which Selden claimed he had patented, was too vague to be patentable. Ford won and became a national hero. Providing cars to the masses at reasonably low prices made Ford millions of dollars and made many millions of North Americans better off, by enabling them to go where they wanted to go more easily, cheaply, and speedily. In time, automobile production spread to Canada, largely through foreign investment. It became the heart of the manufacturing industry in central Canada, providing thousands of high-paying jobs both directly and indirectly to Canadian workers.

THE REBIRTH OF THE NORTH AMERICAN AUTOMOBILE INDUSTRY

Today people think of computers and gene-splicing, not automobiles, as the new technologies. The story of the automobile is no longer emblematic of the latest technological breakthroughs. The changing fortunes of the automobile industry during the past two decades reflect a redefinition of Canadian industry.

There were more than a hundred automobile manufacturers in the fall of 1903, twenty-seven of which accounted for more than 70 percent of the total sales of the industry. By the early 1960s, however, only three companies (General Motors, Ford, and Chrysler—known as the Big Three) were responsible for 88 percent of North American auto sales. Of the car manufacturers that existed at the beginning of the century, many had gone bankrupt or left for more profitable businesses, and the remainder had been agglomerated into or taken over by the dominant firms. In the 1960s, with only one or two exceptions, foreign car manufacturers simply could not make cars of a quality and price that many North Americans wanted to buy. Without the spur of competition pitting many companies against one another, the prices of North American–made automobiles were relatively high, and the industry's rate of innovation was relatively low.

The most serious problems faced by the auto industry in the 1960s involved the quality of the environment and automobile safety. It became recognized that the automobile was contributing significantly to air pollution. The American and Canadian governments regulated the kind of exhaust fumes a car could produce, and design changes followed. On the safety front, automobile companies quickly responded to demands for increased safety by providing seat belts. They balked, however, at supplying air bags that would inflate automatically if a car crashed.

This relatively rosy picture changed dramatically in 1973. That year, the Organization of Petroleum Exporting Countries (OPEC)—mainly countries in the Middle East—combined forces to hold down the supply of oil, create a scarcity, and thus push up its price. In fact, OPEC actually cut off all oil exports for a few tense weeks late in 1973. The power of OPEC was a surprise to many, including the automobile industry. North American cars then tended to be bigger and heavier than those in Japan and Europe. This was easily explained: incomes in the United States and Canada were higher, which meant that consumers could afford larger cars and the gasoline they guzzled. Also, Japan and Europe imposed heavy taxes on gasoline, thus encouraging consumers in the countries to buy smaller and more fuel-efficient cars.

The North American auto industry had expected that this taste for large, gas-guzzling cars would continue, which left them ill-prepared for the shock of the higher gas prices caused by OPEC's move. But other countries, especially Japan, stood ready to gain, with smaller, cheaper, and more fuel-efficient cars. By 1990, more than a quarter of cars sold in Canada were imports. Figure 1.1 shows the value of the imports of new passenger

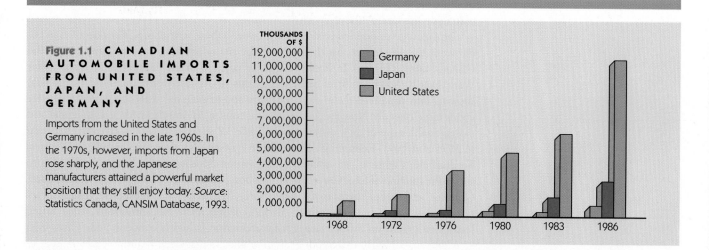

Figure 1.1 CANADIAN AUTOMOBILE IMPORTS FROM UNITED STATES, JAPAN, AND GERMANY

Imports from the United States and Germany increased in the late 1960s. In the 1970s, however, imports from Japan rose sharply, and the Japanese manufacturers attained a powerful market position that they still enjoy today. *Source*: Statistics Canada, CANSIM Database, 1993.

cars from the United States, Japan, and Germany from 1965 to 1990. The figure immediately tells a story: car imports from Japan increased quickly, both absolutely and in comparison with those from other countries. To an economist, such a sudden change from a past trend can be the trigger for a deeper investigation of causes.

It was clear that the Japanese firms were supplying what was wanted by consumers, but the explosion of imports had a devastating effect on the North American automobile industry. Profits fell and workers were laid off. Whereas Henry Ford had believed that by paying workers higher wages one could obtain a more productive labour force, the high price of North American–made cars in the 1970s was blamed, in large part, on the high wages that the auto industry was paying. The wages could not be justified by the level of productivity of the workers.

PROTECTION FROM FOREIGN COMPETITION

In the early 1980s, the Big Three began to make a recovery from the hard times of the 1970s, for several reasons. The unions dramatically reduced their wage demands. Smaller and more fuel-efficient cars were developed. And while these changes were occurring, the government again stepped in, this time to help protect the industry from foreign competition. Again there was concern about layoffs in the domestic automobile industry. But rather than imposing a tariff (a tax) on car imports, the Canadian and American governments negotiated with the Japanese government to restrain Japan's automobile exports. Although the export limits were called voluntary, they were actually negotiated under pressure. If the Japanese had not taken the "voluntary" step of limiting exports, Parliament and Congress probably would have passed laws forcing them to do so involuntarily.

In any event, the reduced supply of Japanese cars led not only to increased sales of North American cars, but to higher prices, for both Japanese and domestic cars. The domestic industry was subsidized, not by the taxpayers in general but by those who bought cars, through these higher prices. Even the Japanese car manufacturers had little to complain about, since they too benefited from the higher prices. Indeed, had a group of Canadian manufacturers gotten together and agreed to reduce their production and raise prices, it would have been viewed as a violation of Canadian anti-combines laws, which were designed to enforce competition. But here the government itself was encouraging less competition!

The Japanese responded in still another way to these restrictions. They decided to circumvent the limitations on their exports by manufacturing cars in Canada and the United States. This was an ironic reversal of pattern. In the decades immediately after World War II, American firms had set up plants all over the world, including in Canada, showing how American technical knowledge and managerial skills could produce better goods more cheaply. Now the Japanese were coming to America with technological and managerial lessons of their own to teach. Table 1.1 shows who produced cars in Canada in 1971 and 1991. Economists often like to translate numbers into graphs and figures. To illustrate, Figure 1.2 summarizes some of the information in Table 1.1. The figure shows the fraction of total Canadian production accounted for by General Motors, Ford, Chrysler, and "other" firms in 1971 and 1991. While in 1971, most other-firm production was by American-owned firms, in 1991 it was all by non-American firms. Three lessons emerge from this picture. First, production is highly concentrated. Thus, GM

Table 1.1 WHO MAKES CARS IN CANADA

	1971	1991
General Motors	406,186	444,213
Ford	392,527	321,886
Chrysler	232,749	18,042
American Motors	42,908	—
Honda	—	99,080
Volvo	8,281	7,661
Total production	1,094,631	890,952

Source: Statistics Canada, CANSIM Database, 1993.

with about 37 percent of total production is shown as having over one-third of the pie. Second, by 1991, "other" American-owned firms had been obliterated. Third, the production of at least one Japanese-owned firm exceeded that of the smallest American-owned producer, Chrysler.

CANADA'S PLACE IN THE AUTOMOBILE INDUSTRY

More than any other industry, the automobile industry typifies the "openness" of the Canadian economy—its reliance on foreign investment and technology, and its inter-relationship with its American counterpart. The same companies that came to dominate

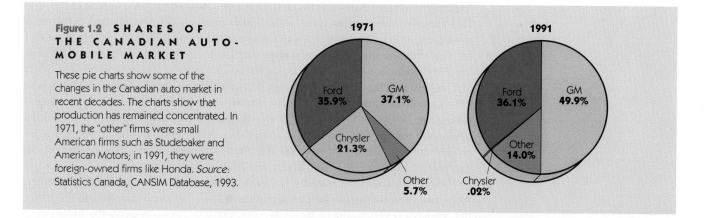

Figure 1.2 SHARES OF THE CANADIAN AUTO-MOBILE MARKET

These pie charts show some of the changes in the Canadian auto market in recent decades. The charts show that production has remained concentrated. In 1971, the "other" firms were small American firms such as Studebaker and American Motors; in 1991, they were foreign-owned firms like Honda. *Source*: Statistics Canada, CANSIM Database, 1993.

1971: Ford 35.9%, GM 37.1%, Chrysler 21.3%, Other 5.7%

1991: Ford 36.1%, GM 49.9%, Other 14.0%, Chrysler .02%

the American industry also dominated the Canadian one, largely through branch plants or subsidiaries of U.S. firms. Automobiles and parts produced in each country served the entire North American market. The fortunes of the Canadian automobile industry were interwoven with those of the U.S. automobile industry; these were formalized with the signing of the so-called Auto Pact in 1965 (technically called the Canada-U.S. Automotive Products Trade Agreement).

By the end of the 1980s, Canadian vehicle production was close to 2 million units and employed more than 40,000 workers. Under the Auto Pact, as discussed below, the allocation of production was rationalized between Canada and the United States, with each country specializing in certain vehicle lines. In Canada, most activity is in light vehicle production (automobiles, mini-vans, and light trucks) and is dominated by the Big Three. But as a result of the relative ease of entry, efficient and competitive foreign automobile producers have been able to set up production facilities and gain a substantial share of the North American market. Asian-owned production from companies such as Toyota, Hyundai, and Suzuki has been growing rapidly and is now over 30 percent of industry output. Part of the reason for setting up plants in Canada is to avoid the tariff levied on imported vehicles coming into Canada and the United States. In Canada, the tariff ranges from 6.0 to 9.2 percent of the value of vehicles, while the U.S. tariff rates are slightly lower.

Foreign producers have put considerable pressure on the Canadian industry, and they are likely to continue to do so. For example, Japanese corporations are moving towards the production of more specialized and expensive mid-range automobiles from the traditional smaller ones. As well, Japanese parts manufacturers are poised to begin making parts in Canada. The Big Three are responding partly by adapting to Japanese methods, such as building stronger ties to component manufacturers, and partly by closing down existing plants and investing in modernization.

The development of the Canadian automobile industry has been heavily influenced by the Canada-U.S. Auto Pact of 1965, whose provisions were maintained intact by the Canada-U.S. Free Trade Agreement of 1988. The Auto Pact essentially stipulates that there be limited duty-free movement of automobile products across the Canadian-U.S. border. That is, it provides for free trade in the products of a particular industry, referred to as **sectoral free trade.** Its two main goals are to integrate the North American auto industry to bring about more efficient patterns of investment, production, and trade, and to strengthen trade relations between the two countries. The main provision of the Auto Pact concerns the circumstances under which products can be imported duty-free. A manufacturer may import vehicles and original parts into Canada free of duty, provided the manufacturer maintains a ratio of production to sales in Canada at least as great as the 1964 production-to-sales ratio and at least 0.75.

The Auto Pact has apparently served Canada well as attested by the relative success of the automotive industry. The Canadian industry attracted over $12 billion of investment during the 1980s and is preparing to face the challenges of the 1990s. These include continued competition from Asian automobile producers plus the prospects for increased competition from Mexico as the North American Free Trade Agreement encompassing Canada, the United States, and Mexico takes effect.

Though the Canadian industry has been dominated by foreign-owned companies, there have been attempts in the past to produce a made-in-Canada car. Back in the 1950s, the Studebaker was produced in Walkerville, Ontario, largely to serve the British market. It produced up to 15,000 cars per year but was unable to compete against the larger U.S.-based companies. A more spectacular case was that of the Bricklin car, a dream car intended to capture some of the uppermost end of the luxury market. These cars were to be produced in New Brunswick, though with franchises in the United States. The New Brunswick government agreed to provide financial support for the enterprise in the hope of creating permanent jobs in the province. As it turned out, the corporation declared bankruptcy in 1975 after two years in operation and after producing 2,800 cars. The New Brunswick government lost a total of $23 million in the venture.

More recently, some independence was achieved on the labour side of the industry. In 1985, the Canadian Autoworkers Union (CAW) split from the International Union of United Automobile, Aerospace, and Agricultural Implement Workers of America (UAW), and now represents most automobile workers in Canada. At the time of the split, the CAW had about 140,000 workers, making it the sixth largest union in Canada.

WHAT IS ECONOMICS?

This short narrative illustrates many facets of economics, but now a definition of our subject is in order. **Economics** studies how individuals, firms, governments, and other organizations within our society make choices, and how those choices determine how the resources of society are used. **Scarcity** figures prominently in economics: choices matter because resources are scarce. Imagine an enormously wealthy individual who can have everything he wants. We might think that scarcity is not in his vocabulary—until we consider that time is a resource, and he must decide what expensive toy to devote his time to each day. Taking time into account, then, scarcity is a fact in everyone's life.

To produce a single product, like an automobile, thousands of decisions and choices have to be made. Since any economy is made up not only of automobiles but of millions of products, it is a marvel that the economy functions at all, let alone functions as well as it does most of the time. This marvel is particularly clear if you consider instances when things do not work so well: the worldwide Great Depression in the 1930s, when almost 20 percent of the Canadian work force could not find a job; the countries of the former Soviet Union today, where ordinary consumer goods like carrots or toilet paper or boots are often simply unavailable; the less-developed economies of many countries in Africa, Asia, and Latin America, where standards of living have remained stubbornly low, or have even been declining in some places.

The fact that choices must be made applies to the economy as a whole as well as it does to each individual. Somehow, decisions are made—by individuals, households, firms, and government—that together determine how the economy's limited resources, including its land, labour, machines, oil, and other natural resources, are used. Why is it that land used at one time for growing crops may, at another time, be used for an automobile plant? How was it that over the space of a couple of decades, resources were transferred from making horse carriages to making automobile bodies? that blacksmiths were replaced by auto mechanics? How do the decisions of thousands of consumers, workers, investors, managers, and government officials all interact to determine the use of the scarce resources available to society? Economists reduce such matters to four basic questions concerning how economies function:

1. *What is produced, and in what quantities?* There have been important changes in consumption over the past fifty years. Spending for medical care, for example, was only 3.5 percent of total personal consumption in 1950. By 1990, more than one out of every eight dollars was spent on medical care, virtually all of it by the public sector. In 1950, more than one out of every four dollars was spent on food. By the late 1980s, the figure was only one out of seven dollars. In the past twenty years, consumers have switched from gas guzzlers to more fuel-efficient cars. What can account for changes like these? The economy seems to spew out new products like videocassette recorders and new services like automated bank tellers. What causes this process of innovation? The overall level of production has also shifted from year to year, often accompanied by large changes in the levels of employment and unemployment. How can economists explain these changes?

In Canada, the question of what is produced, and in what quantities, is answered largely by the private interaction of firms and consumers, but government also plays a role. Prices are critical in determining what goods are produced. When the price of some good rises, firms are induced to produce more of that good, to increase their profits. A central question with which economists have thus been concerned is, why are some goods more expensive than others? And why is it that the price of some good has increased or decreased?

2. *How are these goods produced?* There are often many ways of making something. Textiles can be made with hand looms. Modern machines enable fewer workers to produce more cloth. Very modern machines may be highly computerized, allowing one worker to monitor many more machines than was possible earlier. The better machines generally cost more, but they require less labour. Which technique will be used, the advanced technology or the labour-intensive one? Henry Ford introduced a new way of making cars, the assembly line. More recently, car manufacturers have begun using robots. What determines how rapidly technology changes?

In the Canadian economy, firms answer the question of how goods are produced, again with help from the government, which sets regulations and enacts laws that affect everything from the overall organization of firms to the ways they interact with their employees and customers.

3. *For whom are these goods produced?* With goods produced, the issue of distribution arises. Who gets to consume the goods that are produced in any society? In Canada, individuals who have higher incomes can consume more goods. But that answer only pushes the question back one step: What determines the differences in income and wages? What is the role of luck? of education? of inheritance? of savings? of experience and hard work? These questions are difficult to answer. For now, suffice it to say that while, again, incomes are primarily determined by the private interaction of firms and households, government also plays a strong role, with taxes as well as programs that redistribute income and education and health programs that enhance the ability of persons to earn income.

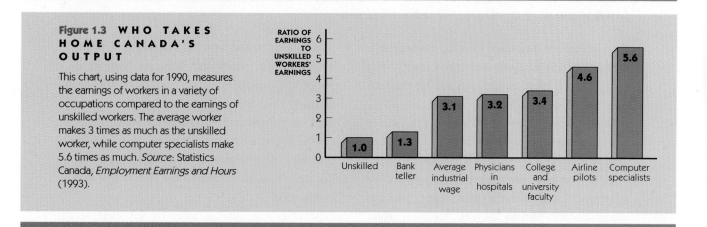

Figure 1.3 WHO TAKES HOME CANADA'S OUTPUT

This chart, using data for 1990, measures the earnings of workers in a variety of occupations compared to the earnings of unskilled workers. The average worker makes 3 times as much as the unskilled worker, while computer specialists make 5.6 times as much. *Source*: Statistics Canada, *Employment Earnings and Hours* (1993).

Figure 1.3 shows the relative pay in a variety of different occupations. To judge by income, each computer specialist receives almost twice as much of the economy's output as the average worker, and over four times as much as a bank teller.

4. Who takes economic decisions, and by what process? In a **centrally planned economy,** as the Soviet Union used to be, the government takes responsibility for virtually every aspect of economic activity. The first three questions, as well as the fourth, are thus answered by the government. A central economic planning agency works through a bureaucracy to say what will be produced and by what method, and who shall consume it.

At the other end of the spectrum are economies that rely primarily on the free interchange of producers and their customers to determine what, how, and for whom. Canada, which lies towards this latter end, is said to have a **mixed economy;** that is, there is a mix between public (governmental) and private decision making. Four-fifths of all goods and services are produced in the private sector. Within limits, producers make what they want to make; they use whatever method of production seems appropriate to them; and the collective output is distributed to consumers according to their income. When economists examine an economy, they want to know to what extent economic decisions are taken by the government, and to what extent they are taken by private individuals. In Canada, while individuals are allowed for the most part to take their own decisions about what kind of car to purchase, the government has intruded in a number of ways: it has taken actions that affect the imports of Japanese cars, that restrict the amount of pollutants a car can produce, and that promote fuel efficiency and automobile safety.

A related question is whether economic decisions are taken by the individuals for their own interests or for the interests of an employer such as a business firm or government agency. This is an important distinction. We can expect people acting on their own behalf to take decisions that benefit themselves. When they act on behalf of organizations, however, a conflict of interest may arise. Observers often refer to corporations

CLOSE-UP: RUSSIA AND EASTERN EUROPE TRY NEW ANSWERS TO OLD QUESTIONS

For most of the twentieth century, the centrally planned economic system of the former Soviet Union gave straightforward answers to the four basic economic questions.

What was produced in such an economy, and in what quantities? Government planners set the targets, which firms then struggled to fulfill.

How were these goods produced? Again, since government planners decided what supplies would be delivered to each factory, they effectively chose how production occurred.

For whom were these goods produced? The government made decisions about what people on each job were paid, which affected how much people could consume. In principle, individuals could choose what to buy at government-operated stores, at prices set by the government. But in practice, many goods were unavailable at these stores. Those who held positions of power and influence could find alternate sources of goods, but average consumers could not. The government also directly controlled many goods like apartments, deciding who could live where.

Who made economic decisions, and by what process? The government planners decided, basing the decisions on their view of national economic goals.

At one time, all this planning sounded very sensible, but as former Soviet premier Nikita Khrushchev once said, "Economics is a subject that does not greatly respect one's wishes." By the time that Mikhail Gorbachev rose to power in the mid-1980s, it was clear to Soviet citizens and outsiders alike that some change was needed. Many examples of Soviet economic woes could be cited, but two will suffice. In the shoe market, the Soviet

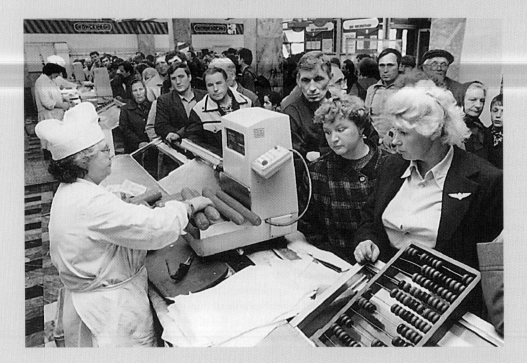

Union was the largest national producer in the world. However, the average shoe was of such low quality that it fell apart in a few weeks, and inventories of unwanted shoes rotted in warehouses. In agriculture, the Soviet government had traditionally allowed small private agricultural plots. Although the government limited the amount of time that farmers could spend on these plots, publicly run farming was so unproductive that the 3 percent of Soviet land that was privately run usually produced about 25 percent of the total farm output.

Today the standard of living in the former Soviet Union is not only below that in industrialized nations like the United States and those of Western Europe, but it is barely ahead of developing nations like Brazil and Mexico. Workers in the Soviet Union shared a grim one-liner: "We pretend to work and they pretend to pay us."

Gorbachev came to power promoting the ideas of *perestroika* (restructuring) and *glasnost* (openness). In political terms, these ideas had very rapid and powerful consequences. In the countries of Eastern Europe, the Communist leaders were overthrown in 1989 and 1990. The Soviet Union itself disintegrated at the end of 1991, breaking up into Russia, Ukraine, and a number of other independent states. Many of these countries held elections to determine, at least in part, who would hold the power of government.

Deciding to hold an election, however, is relatively easy compared with the job of restructuring an entire economy. The political desires of people striving for freedom often seemed to overshadow economic considerations. Yet by early in the 1990s, some general pathways towards economic reform of these economies were becoming clear. Workers need increased incentives to work hard, even if that means greater inequality of wages. Firms need greater incentives to become more efficient and produce what people want, even if that occasionally means unemployment and bankruptcy. It seems evident that the role of government planners must be reduced. Programs along these lines were instituted in many Eastern European nations in 1989 and 1990, and in Russia under Boris Yeltsin at the start of 1992.

But after seven decades of central economic planning, making the transition to an economy in which market forces have greater power promises to be excruciatingly difficult. Things may very well become worse before they get better. The eventual payoff may be years or even decades in the future.

and governments as if they were a single individual. Economists point out that organizations consist, by definition, of a multitude of individuals and that the interests of these individuals do not necessarily coincide with one another or, for that matter, with the interests of the organization itself. This is but one example of the fact that organizations bring a number of distinctive problems to the analysis of choice.

As you can see by their concern with decision making, economists are concerned not only with *how* the economy answers the four basic questions but also with *how well*. They ask, is the economy efficient? Could it produce more of some goods without producing fewer of others? Could it make some individuals better off without making some other individuals worse off?

MARKETS AND GOVERNMENT IN THE MIXED ECONOMY

The large reliance on private decision making in Canada reflects economists' belief that this reliance is appropriate and necessary for economic efficiency; however, economists also believe that certain kinds of interventions by the government are desirable. Finding the appropriate balance between the public and the private sectors of the economy is one of the central issues of economic analysis.

MARKETS

When economists argue for a basic reliance on private decision making, they often say that economic decisions should be left "to the market." The modern concept of the **market** is an extension of the traditional village market, where buyers and sellers came together to exchange goods by barter. This kind of market still exists in many less-developed countries, and in most cities some farmers still bring their produce to sell in a farmers' market, though barter has been replaced by cash sales. In modern economies, some markets exist in well-defined locations: shares, for instance, are mostly traded on the "stock market" at locations like the Toronto Stock Exchange, the New York Stock Exchange, the American Stock Exchange, and the Pacific Stock Exchange.

Today the concept of markets is used to include any situation where exchange takes place, though this exchange may not necessarily resemble the village market. In department stores and shopping malls, customers rarely haggle over the price. When manufacturers purchase the materials they need for production, they exchange money for them, not other goods. Most goods, from cameras to clothes, are not sold directly from producers to consumers. They are sold from producers to distributors, from distributors to retailers, from retailers to consumers. All of these transactions are embraced by the concept of the **market economy.**

In market economies with competition, individuals make choices that reflect their own desires. And firms make choices that maximize their profits; to do so, they must produce the goods that consumers want, and they must produce them at lower cost than other firms. As firms compete against one another in the quest for profits, consumers are benefited, both in the kinds of goods produced and the prices at which they are supplied. The market economy thus provides answers to three of the four basic economic questions—what is produced, how it is produced, and how these decisions are made—and on the whole, the answers ensure the efficiency of the economy.

The market economy also provides an answer to the remaining question—for whom goods are produced—but it is an answer that not everyone finds acceptable. Markets allocate goods to those who are willing and able to pay the most for them. Like bidders at an auction, the market participants willing and able to pay the highest price take home the goods. But what people are willing and able to pay depends on their income. It is possible that some groups of individuals—including those without skills that are valued by the market—may receive such a low income that they could not survive or feed and educate their children without outside assistance. Government provides the assistance by taking steps to increase income equality. These steps, however, often blunt economic incentives. While welfare payments provide an important safety net for the poor, they may also discourage work effort by the recipient, and the high taxation required to finance them may discourage work and savings by taxpayers. After all, if the government takes one out of three or even two dollars that a high-income individual earns, she may not be inclined to work so hard. She may decide not to work every Saturday and to take a longer vacation. And if the government takes one out of two or three dollars a person earns from interest on savings, she may decide to spend more now and save less. Like the question of the appropriate balance between the public and private sectors, the question of the appropriate balance between concerns about equality, often referred to as **equity concerns,** and efficiency is one of the central issues of modern economics.

THE ROLE OF GOVERNMENT

While the market provides, *on the whole*, answers to the basic economic questions that ensure efficiency, there are certain areas in which the solutions are inadequate, or appear to be so to many people. When the market is not working well, or is not perceived to be working well, societies often turn to government. This, however, is only part of government's function.

The government plays a major role in modern economies, and we need to understand both what that role is and why government undertakes the activities that it does. Historically, governments have always taken an active role in economic affairs in Canada. The construction of the trans-Canadian railroad in the 1880s, which was instrumental in unifying the country, was only accomplished with the active financial support of the government. The system of tariff protection for manufacturing under the National Policy implemented by the 1889 Conservative government of Sir John A. Macdonald formed the basis of industrial policy for most of the twentieth century. The encouragement of large amounts of immigration in the early 1900s was instrumental in developing the agricultural economy of the Prairie provinces. Government-owned corporations have been important in such industries as transportation, communications, and energy. Government has virtually taken over the provision of services in the areas of health, education, and welfare, services that were originally offered either by the private sector or by charitable organizations such as the churches. By tax and subsidy policies, governments have changed the fortunes of entire industries or segments of the nation. The National Energy Policy of the 1970s had an enormous impact on the oil and gas industry. Federal transportation policies have helped farmers to economize on the costs of getting grain to foreign markets. And an active program of regional development subsidies has attempted to encourage industry to settle in high employment regions of the Atlantic provinces and parts of Quebec. Many observers have noted the seemingly greater tendency to resort to government intervention in the Canadian economy than in the U.S. economy.

As well as intervening in particular industries, the government also sets the legal structure under which all private firms and individuals operate. It regulates businesses to ensure that they do not discriminate by race or sex, that they do not mislead customers, that they are careful about the safety of their employees, that they do not pollute the air and water. In some cases, such as telecommunications, even the prices that firms can charge are regulated. In many industries, government firms (**Crown corporations**) operate as private businesses, sometimes in competition with private firms: examples include PETRO Canada in the gas and oil industry, Air Canada and Canadian National Railways in transportation, the Canadian Broadcasting Corporation in entertainment, Canada Post, several provincial electrical utilities, as well as telephone companies and even automobile insurance in some provinces. Most schools as well as virtually all universities and hospitals are government-owned. In other cases, such as providing for the national defence, building roads, and printing money, the government supplies goods and services that the private sector does not. Government programs provide for the elderly through Old Age Security (which pays income to retired individuals) and health care (which is fully funded by the government). The government helps those who have suffered some sort of economic dislocation through unemployment insurance for those temporarily unemployed and disability insurance for those who are no longer able to work. The government also attempts to provide a "safety net" of support for the poor through various welfare programs.

One can, however, easily imagine a government controlling the economy more directly. In countries where decision-making authority is centralized and concentrated in the government, government bureaucrats might decide what and how much a factory should produce and pass laws on the level of wages that should be paid. At least until recently, governments in countries like the former Soviet Union and China attempted to control practically all major decisions regarding resource allocation.

THE THREE MAJOR MARKETS

In simple form, the market economy revolves around exchange between individuals (or households), who buy goods and services from firms, and firms, which take **inputs,** the various materials of production, and produce **outputs,** the goods and services that they sell. In thinking about a market economy, economists focus their attention on three broad categories of markets in which individuals and firms interact. The markets in which firms sell their outputs to households are referred to collectively as the **product market,** or the market for goods and services. Many firms also sell their products to other firms; the outputs of the first firm become the inputs of the second. These transactions too are said to occur in the product market.

On the input side, firms need (besides the materials that they buy in the product market) some combination of labour and machinery with which their goods can be produced. They purchase the services of workers in the **labour market.** They raise funds with which to buy inputs in the **capital market.** Traditionally, economists have also highlighted the importance of a third input, land, but in modern industrial economies, land is of secondary importance, except to a few industries like agriculture and forestry. Hence, for most purposes, it suffices to focus attention on the three major markets listed here, and this text will follow this pattern.

As Figure 1.4 shows, individuals participate in all three markets. When individuals buy goods or services, they act as **consumers** in the product market. When people act as **workers,** economists say that they "sell their labour services" in the labour market. When individuals buy shares of stock in a firm or lend money to a business, economists note that they are participating in the capital market, and refer to them as **investors.**

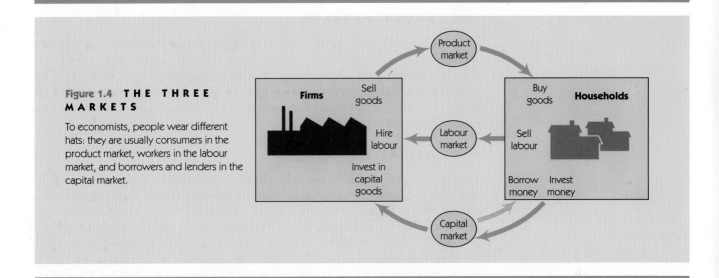

Figure 1.4 THE THREE MARKETS

To economists, people wear different hats: they are usually consumers in the product market, workers in the labour market, and borrowers and lenders in the capital market.

THE PRODUCT MARKET

Economists use the term "product market" to refer to the sale of goods by firms to households and to other firms. Among the most important characteristics of the product market is the degree of competition. This is, in turn, influenced by the extent to which the product is traded on international markets. One of the key features of the Canadian economy is the extent to which it relies on trade with the rest of the world, particularly with the United States. Products that are traded tend to be characterized by more competition than those that are not, except to the extent that policies are undertaken to protect the domestic market from international competition. The automobile industry is an interesting case in point. Although it has been dominated by U.S. producers, the North American market has been highly integrated. In the early 1900s, it was dominated by a large number of auto companies competing against one another and based in the United States. In the 1910s, one company, Ford, became dominant; in the 1960s, three U.S.-owned companies dominated the industry and produced automobiles in both Canada and the United States in accordance with the Auto Pact, which provided for free trade in both autos and parts as well as production sharing between the two countries; today strong competition is provided in the North American market by various foreign firms, particularly Japanese ones.

Economic competition, however, is only one of several important economic concerns. Patent rights provide one case where society is willing to risk a lack of competition for a limited amount of time in exchange for an incentive to inventors to produce new products. As well, numerous examples exist in which governments have acted to prevent the collapse of firms where the consequences of market competition would have resulted in a major bankruptcy that was judged to be unacceptable by the political system, for example, because of the dependence of towns or regions on the firm. An example of this is the Sydney Steel Corporation in Sydney, Nova Scotia, which eventually had to be taken over and operated by the government in order to keep it going.

THE LABOUR MARKET

Economists use the term "labour market" to refer to the transactions in which workers are hired or labour services are purchased. Firms not only must hire and train workers, they must provide them with incentives to work hard and not to quit. Henry Ford discovered that it might be profitable to pay higher wages than competitors, and auto companies in the early 1980s found that excessively high wages might prevent them from competing against imported cars.

THE CAPITAL MARKET

The term "capital" is used in two different but closely related ways in economics. The first refers to machines and buildings, what are sometimes called **capital goods.** The second refers to the money used to buy and sell capital goods, or to buy and sell firms (which may, in turn, own capital goods). When economists refer to the "capital market," they generally mean the markets in which funds are raised and transferred, including all the institutions involved in borrowing and lending money. Care is taken in this book to use the term "capital goods" whenever it is just the machines and buildings themselves that are of concern.

The capital market includes the whole array of institutions by which firms (and individuals) raise money from other firms and individuals. From the economist's perspective, people have two choices about what to do with their money: they can spend it or they can save it. What they save goes into bank accounts, stock brokerage accounts, and a variety of other forms by which funds enter the market for capital. The capital market plays an important role not only in financing new ventures and new investment—as when Henry Ford sought out investors, with whom he was supposed to share the proceeds from his innovative activity—but also in sustaining established firms when they face hard times. In the recession of 1991–1993, many firms survived reductions in their revenues through bank loans, especially firms in the real estate industry such as Olympia and York.

Capital markets play a critical role in determining how Canada's savings are allocated. Individual investors and companies like banks or pension funds that collect and hold the savings of individuals must decide not only which industries look most promising, but which firms within those industries look most likely to be profitable. As with the product market, Canadian capital markets are highly integrated with world capital markets. The financial assets that Canadian savings are used to purchase may well be foreign assets, either loans to foreign borrowers or acquisitions of equity (that is, shares) in foreign companies. Conversely, foreigners' savings may be used to acquire Canadian assets, including ownership in Canadian companies. With the advent of computer and information technology, world capital markets have become highly integrated. We will see how this internationalization of capital markets provides both opportunities and constraints to the Canadian economy.

Yet another important participant in capital markets is the public sector. Governments from time to time have to borrow money in order to meet planned or unplanned shortfalls of their revenues from their expenditures. In this case, savings that otherwise would be lent to the private sector will be used by the public sector instead. The consequences of government borrowing is a matter of some policy importance.

MICROECONOMICS AND MACROECONOMICS

Economics is a broad subject. Understanding even the development of a single industry, such as the automobile industry, requires studying economics from several different perspectives.

The detailed study of product, labour, and capital markets is called **microeconomics.** Microeconomics ("micro" is derived from the Greek word meaning "small") focuses on the behaviour of the units—the firms, households, and individuals—that make up the economy. It is concerned with how the individual units make decisions and what affects those decisions. By contrast, **macroeconomics** ("macro" comes from the Greek word meaning "large") looks at the behaviour of the economy as a whole, in particular the behaviour of such aggregate measures as overall rates of unemployment, inflation, economic growth, and the balance of trade. The aggregate numbers do not tell us what any firm or household is doing. They tell us what is happening in total, or on average.

It is important to remember that these economic perspectives are just two ways of looking at the same thing. Microeconomics is the bottom-up view of the economy; macroeconomics is the top-down view. The behaviour of the economy as a whole is dependent on the behaviour of the units that make it up; for example, the overall unemployment rate is, in part, the result of the employment decisions of the thousands of firms that make up the economy; the inflation rate is the result of thousands of decisions about what prices should be charged; the rate of economic growth is determined by thousands of decisions about investment, research and development, and new products.

The automobile industry is a story of both micro- and macroeconomics. In part, it is a story of microeconomic interactions of individual companies, investors, and labour unions. In part, it is a story of global macroeconomic forces like oil shortages and a surge in foreign competition. When auto companies laid off workers in the late 1970s, their problems boosted the overall unemployment rate. The recession of the early 1990s brought heavy reductions in car sales.

THE SCIENCE OF ECONOMICS

Economics is a **social science.** It studies the social problem of choice from a scientific viewpoint, which means that it is built on a systematic exploration of the problem of choice. This systematic exploration involves both the formulation of theories and the examination of data.

A **theory** consists of a set of assumptions (or hypotheses), and conclusions derived from those assumptions. Theories are logical exercises: *if* the assumptions are correct, *then* the conclusions follow. If all university graduates have a better chance of getting jobs and Ellen is a university graduate, then Ellen has a better chance of getting a job than a nongraduate. Economists make predictions with their theories. They might use a theory to predict what will happen if a tax is increased, or if some regulation is removed, or if imports of foreign cars are limited. The predictions of a theory are of the form "If a tax is increased and if the market is competitive, then output will decrease and prices will increase."

In economics, another word for theory is **model.** To understand how economists use models, consider a modern car manufacturer trying to design a new automobile. It is extremely expensive to construct a new car. Rather than creating a separate, fully developed car for every engineer's or designer's conception of what she would like to see the new car be, the company uses models. The designers might use a plastic model to study the general shape of the vehicle and to assess reactions to the car's aesthetics. The engineers might use a computer model to study the air resistance, from which they can calculate fuel consumption. Another major question concerns the comfort of the passengers; engineers might construct a separate model for the interior of the car. And the interior designers may have little interest in details of the exterior shape, and use an interior model of their own.

Just as the engineers construct different models to study a particular feature of a car, so too an economist constructs a model of the economy—in words or equations—to depict the particular features of the economy with which he is concerned. An economic model might describe a general relationship ("When incomes rise, the number of cars purchased increases"), describe a quantitative relationship ("When incomes rise by 10 percent, the number of cars purchased rises, on average, by 12 percent"), or make a general prediction ("An increase in the tax on gasoline will decrease the demand for cars").

AN ECONOMIC EXAMPLE: CHOOSING HOW TO GET TO WORK

Traffic congestion is a major problem in almost all of Canada's major cities. Urban planners would like to encourage more commuters to use public transport. In thinking about how best to do this, they have found simple models of how commuters decide on how to get to work extremely useful. While recognizing that there are a wide variety of considerations in deciding whether to take a bus or subway versus driving, planners might focus on two: cost and time. But as the expression goes, time is money. The planners thus add up the actual transportation cost plus the value of the time. Again, while recognizing that different people value their time differently, the planners might simplify by saying that time is valued at the wage a person receives.

To see how such a model can be used, consider the city of Urbania, contemplating replacing its current slow rail service to Idyllic Park with a high-speed train line, which would reduce travel time by 30 minutes. The train ride currently takes 1 hour, and the car commute takes 45 minutes. The current cost of a train ride is $1; for driving, the estimated cost of gasoline plus wear and tear on the car is $1.25. The average commuter in Idyllic Park makes $20 an hour, so the value of the extra quarter of an hour is $5. The total cost of going by car is $15 (value of time) + $1.25 = $16.25, and by train is $20 (value of time) + $1 (fare) = $21. The model predicts that few commuters will take the current, slow train.

The high-speed train will necessitate raising the fare to $2. The total cost of a train ride will then be $2 (fare) + $10 (value of time) = $12, considerably cheaper than the

$16.25 cost of going by car. The model predicts that many commuters will switch, and argues that considerable attention should be placed on speed.

While this example is hypothetical, similar considerations arose in discussions concerning the construction of the Metro subway system in Montreal and the Island airport in Toronto. And they arise repeatedly as cities consider whether to extend or improve their subway systems.

DISCOVERING AND INTERPRETING RELATIONSHIPS

A **variable** is any item that can be measured and that changes. Prices, wages, interest rates, quantities bought and sold, are all variables. The price of bread changes over time, as does the quantity sold. So does the price of wheat, the number of people who have jobs, the interest rate your bank pays. What interests economists is the connection among variables. When economists see what appears to be a systematic relationship among variables, they ask, could it have arisen by chance, or is there indeed a relationship? This is the question of **correlation.**

Economists use statistical tests to measure and test correlations. For instance, consider the problem of deciding whether a coin is biased. If you flip a coin 10 times and get 6 heads and 4 tails, is the coin a fair one? Or is it weighted to heads? Statistical tests will say that the result of 6 heads and 4 tails could easily happen by chance, so the evidence does not prove that the coin is weighted. Of course, it does not prove that it is *not* slightly weighted either. The evidence is just not strong enough for either conclusion. On the other hand, if you flip a coin 100 times and get 80 heads, then statistical tests will tell you that the possibility of this happening by blind chance with a fair coin is extremely small. Thus, the evidence would support the assertion that the coin is weighted.

A similar logic can be used on questions about correlations in economic data. People with more education tend to earn higher wages. Is the connection merely one of chance? Statistical tests show whether the evidence is too weak for a conclusion, or whether it supports a particular answer.

CAUSATION VERSUS CORRELATION

Economists would like to accomplish more than just asserting that different variables are indeed correlated. They would like to conclude that changes in one variable *cause* the changes in the other variable. This distinction between correlation and **causation** is an important one. If one variable "causes" the other, then changing one variable necessarily will change the second. If the relationship is just a correlation, this may not be true.

For instance, Figure 1.5 shows the relationship between years of schooling completed and annual income. There is no doubt that those with more years of schooling receive a higher income. But there are at least two possible explanations. One is that firms are willing to pay more for workers who are more productive and that education increases individuals' productivity. In this explanation, there is causation. More education "causes" greater productivity, which "causes" higher wages. The other explanation is that firms are willing to pay higher wages to those who are smarter even though they

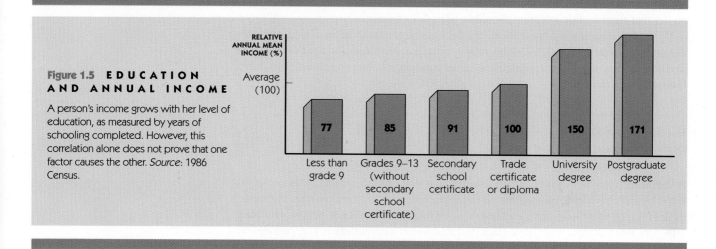

Figure 1.5 EDUCATION AND ANNUAL INCOME

A person's income grows with her level of education, as measured by years of schooling completed. However, this correlation alone does not prove that one factor causes the other. *Source*: 1986 Census.

may not yet have many productive skills (and what skills they have may have little to do with what they have learned in school), and those who are smarter survive longer in school. In this view, more able individuals stay in school longer and receive higher wages, but the schools do not cause increased productivity. There is a correlation, but no causation.

Sometimes there are systematic relationships between variables in which it is difficult to tell which variable is the cause, which the effect. For example, there is a systematic relationship between the number of children a woman has and the wages she earns. But the explanation for this relationship is not clear. Low wages mean that the income the woman must give up when she takes off work to have a child is less; in a sense, children are "less expensive." Do low wages, then, induce women to have more children? Or does having more children distract a woman from pursuing her career as avidly, and thus lead to low wages? Or is there a third factor, accounting for both the level of wages and the number of children?

EXPERIMENTS IN ECONOMICS

Many sciences use experiments to test alternative explanations, since experiments allow the scientist to change one factor at a time and see what happens. But the economy is not a chemistry lab. Instead, economics is like astronomy, in that both sciences must use the experiments that nature provides. Economists look for situations in which only one factor changes, and study the consequences of changing that factor. A change in the income tax system is an example of a natural experiment. But nature is usually not kind to economists; the world does not hold still. As the tax system changes, so do other features of the economy, and economists often have a difficult time deciding whether changes that they perceive are the result of the new tax system or of some other economic change. Sometimes they can use what is called **econometrics,** the branch of statistics that has developed to analyze the particular sorts of measurement problems that arise in economics.

In a few cases, economists have engaged in social experiments. For example, they have given a selected group of individuals a different income tax schedule or a different welfare program. They have tried experiments with alternative ways of providing housing or education to the poor. Also, in recent years, economists have studied certain aspects of economic behaviour in "laboratory" situations. One way of seeing how individuals respond to risk is to construct an artificially risky situation in the form of a game, and see how people react when they play it. One way of seeing how buyers respond to various ways of organizing an auction is to simulate different kinds of auctions in a controlled laboratory setting. Both social and laboratory experiments have provided economists with valuable insights concerning economic behaviour.

But even using all available tools, the problem of finding a variety of correlations between several different types of data and having to discern which connections are real and which are only apparent is obviously a difficult one. Economists' interest in these questions is motivated by more than just curiosity—though this plays an important role. Often important policy questions depend on what one believes is really going on. Whether a country thinks it worthwhile to pour more resources into higher education may depend on whether it believes that the differences in wages observed between those with and without a university education are largely due to the skills and knowledge acquired while at university, or whether they are mainly related to differences in ability between those who make it through university and those who do not.

The important lessons to remember here are: (1) the fact of a correlation does not prove a causation; (2) the way to test different explanations of causation is to hold all of the factors constant except for one, and then allow that one to vary; (3) data do not always speak clearly, and sometimes they just do not allow any conclusions to be drawn.

WHY ECONOMISTS DISAGREE

Economists are frequently called upon to make judgments on matters of public policy. Should the government reduce the deficit? Should inflation be reduced? If so, how? In these public policy discussions, the disagreements among economists often get considerable attention. But disagreement can be a productive way of learning more, if approached properly. Economists try carefully to define the sources and reasons for their differences.

Two major sources of disagreement exist within the scientific realm of economics. First, economists may differ over what is the appropriate model of the economy. They may disagree about how well people and firms are able to perceive and calculate their self-interest, and whether their interactions take place in a competitive or a noncompetitive market. Different models will often produce different results. Often the data that we currently have available do not allow us to say which of two competing models provides a better description of some market.

Second, even when they agree about the appropriate theoretical model, economists may disagree about quantitative magnitudes, and accordingly their predictions will differ. They may agree, for instance, that reducing the tax on interest income will encourage individuals to save more. But some economists may claim, on the basis of their studies, that individuals will increase their savings only a little; others, that people will increase their savings a lot. Again, many of these disagreements arise because of the lack of relevant data. We may have considerable data concerning savings in Canada over the past century. But institutions and economic conditions today are markedly different from those of fifty or even ten years ago.

There is another source of disagreement, but this one lies outside the scientific realm. It is common for economists to be asked questions like "Should the government cut the capital gains tax to encourage savings?" "Should the government cut taxes to stimulate the economy and reduce unemployment?" To answer such questions, economists must determine the consequences of the policy in question, which makes it necessary first to formulate a model of the economy or the market. Even if the goals of the policy are clear, disagreements may occur for either of the reasons given above. But if the goals are unclear, then the economist's own values may intrude, and this is where the third source of disagreement comes in.

There are generally many consequences of any policy, some beneficial, some harmful. In comparing two policies, one may benefit some people more, another may benefit others. One policy is not unambiguously better than another. It depends on what you care about. A cut in the tax on the profits from the sale of stocks might encourage savings, but at the same time, most of the benefits accrue to the very wealthy; hence, it increases inequality. A reduction in taxes to stimulate the economy may reduce unemployment, but it may also increase inflation. Even though two economists agree about the model, they may make different recommendations. In assessing the effect of a tax cut on unemployment and inflation, for instance, an economist who is worried more about unemployment may recommend in favour of the tax cut, while the other, concerned about inflation, may recommend against it. In this case, the source of the disagreement is a difference in values.

POSITIVE AND NORMATIVE ECONOMICS

Economists try to identify carefully the points in their analysis where values are brought in. When they describe the economy, and construct models that predict either how the economy will change or the effects of different policies, they are engaged in what is called **positive economics.** When they attempt to evaluate alternative policies, weighing up the various benefits and costs, they are engaged in what is called **normative economics.** Positive economics is concerned with what "is," with describing how the economy functions; normative economics deals with what "should be," with making judgments about the desirability of various courses of action. Normative economics makes use of positive economics. We cannot make judgments about whether a policy is desirable unless we have a clear picture of its consequences. Good normative economics also tries to be explicit about precisely what values or objectives it is incorporating. It tries to couch its statements in the form "If these are your objectives . . . , then this is the best possible policy."

Consider the positive and normative aspects of a proposal to levy a $1-per-case tax on beer. Positive economics would describe what effect the tax would have on the price of beer—would the price rise by the full $1, or would producers absorb some of the price rise? On the basis of that analysis, economists would go on to predict how much beer consumption would be reduced, and who would be affected by the tax. They might find, for instance, that since lower-income individuals spend a larger fraction of their income on beer, these people would be affected proportionately more. Studies may have indicated that there is a systematic relationship between the quantity of beer consumed and road accidents. Using this information, economists might attempt to estimate how the beer tax would affect the number of accidents. These steps are all part of describing the full consequences of the tax, without making judgments. In the end, however, the question is, *should* the tax be adopted? This is a normative question, and in responding to it, economists will weigh the benefits of the tax revenue, the distortions it induces in consumption, the inequities caused by the fact that proportionately more of the tax is borne by lower-income individuals, and the lives saved in road accidents. Furthermore, in evaluating the tax, economists will also want to compare it with other ways of raising similar amounts of revenue.

REVIEW AND PRACTICE

SUMMARY

1. Economics is the study of how individuals, firms, and governments within our society make choices. Choices are unavoidable because desired goods, services, and resources are inevitably scarce.

2. There are four basic questions that economists ask about any economy: (1) What is produced, and in what quantities? (2) How are these goods produced? (3) For whom are these goods produced? (4) Who makes economic decisions, and by what process?

3. Canada has a mixed economy; there is a mix between public and private decision making. The economy relies primarily on the private interaction of individuals and firms to answer the four basic questions, but government plays a large role as well. A central question for any mixed economy is the balance between the public and private sectors.

4. The term "market" is used to describe any situation where exchange takes place. In Canada's market economy, individuals, firms, and government interact in product markets, labour markets, and capital markets.

5. Economists use models to study how the economy works and to make predictions about what will happen if something is changed. A model can be expressed in words or equations, and is designed to mirror the essential characteristics of the particular phenomena under study.

6. A correlation exists when a change in one variable leads to a predictable change in another variable. However, the simple existence of a correlation does not prove that one factor causes the other to change. Additional outside factors may be influencing both.

7. Economists may disagree for three main reasons: they differ on the appropriate model of the economy or market; they differ about the value of some important empirical estimate, and thus about the quantitative magnitudes of the consequences of a change; and they differ in values, in how they weigh the various costs and benefits resulting from change.

KEY TERMS

sectoral free trade	product market	theory
mixed economy	labour market	model
centrally planned economy	capital market	correlation
	capital goods	causation
market economy	microeconomics	positive economics
Crown corporations	macroeconomics	normative economics

REVIEW QUESTIONS

1. Why are choices unavoidable?

2. How are the four basic economic questions answered in the Canadian economy?

3. What is a mixed economy? Describe some of the roles government might play, or not play, in a mixed economy.

4. Name the three main economic markets, and describe how an individual might participate in each one as a buyer and seller.

5. Give two examples of economic issues that are primarily microeconomic, and two examples that are primarily macroeconomic. What is the general difference between microeconomics and macroeconomics?

6. What is a model? Why do economists use models?

7. When causation exists, would you also expect a correlation to exist? When a correlation exists, would you also expect causation to exist? Explain.

8. "All disagreements between economists are purely subjective." Comment.

PROBLEMS

1. Characterize the following events as microeconomic, macroeconomic, or both.

    (a) Unemployment increases this month.
    (b) A drug company invents and begins to market a new medicine.
    (c) A bank loans money to a large company but turns down a small business.
    (d) Interest rates decline for all borrowers.
    (e) A union negotiates for higher pay.
    (f) The price of oil increases.

2. Characterize the following events as part of the labour market, the capital market, or the product market.

(a) An investor tries to decide which company to invest in.

(b) With practice, the workers on an assembly line become more efficient.

(c) The opening up of the economies in Eastern Europe offers new markets for Canadian products.

(d) A big company that is losing money decides to offer its workers a special set of incentives to retire early, hoping to reduce its costs.

(e) A consumer roams around a shopping mall, looking for birthday gifts.

(f) The federal government needs to borrow more money to finance its level of spending.

3. Discuss the incentive issues that might arise in each of the following situations. (Hint: Remember the history of the automobile industry at the start of this chapter.)

(a) You have some money to invest, and your financial adviser introduces you to a couple of software executives who want to start their own company. What should you worry about as you decide whether to invest?

(b) You are running a small company, and your workers promise that if you increase their pay, they will work harder.

(c) A large industry is going bankrupt and appeals for government assistance.

4. Name ways in which government intervention has helped the automobile industry in the last two decades, and ways in which it has injured the industry.

5. The back of a bag of cat litter claims, "Cats that use cat litter live three years longer than cats that don't." Do you think that cat litter actually causes an increased life expectancy of cats, or can you think of some other factors to explain this correlation? What evidence might you try to collect to test your explanation?

6. Life expectancy in Sweden is 78 years; life expectancy in India is 57 years. Does this prove that if an Indian moved to Sweden he would live longer? That is, does this prove that living in Sweden causes an increase in life expectancy, or can you think of some other factors to explain these facts? What evidence might you try to collect to test your explanation?

CHAPTER 2

THINKING LIKE AN ECONOMIST

In Chapter 1, economics was defined as the science that studies how individuals, firms, governments, and other organizations make choices, and how those choices determine how the resources of society are used. We also learned how economists formulate models to study these questions. This chapter begins with a basic model of the economy. We follow this with a closer look at how the basic units that comprise the economy—individuals, firms, and governments—make choices in situations where they are faced with scarcity. In Chapters 3 through 5, we study ways in which these units interact with one another, and how those interactions "add up" to determine how society's resources are allocated.

1. What is the basic competitive model of the economy?

2. What are incentives, property rights, prices, and the profit motive, and what roles do these essential ingredients of a market economy play?

3. What alternatives for allocating resources are there to the market system, and why do economists tend not to favour these alternatives?

4. What are some of the basic techniques economists use in their study of how people make choices? What are the various concepts of costs that economists use?

THE BASIC COMPETITIVE MODEL

Though different economists employ different models of the economy—and as a result sometimes reach markedly different conclusions—they all commonly use a basic set of assumptions as a point of departure. This is the economist's basic model, and it has three components: assumptions about how consumers behave, assumptions about how firms behave, and assumptions about the markets in which these consumers and firms interact. The model ignores government, not because government is not important, but because before we can understand the role of government we need to see how an economy without a government might function.

RATIONAL CONSUMERS AND PROFIT-MAXIMIZING FIRMS

The fact of scarcity, which we encountered in Chapter 1, implies that individuals and firms must make choices. Underlying much of economic analysis is the basic assumption of **rational choice,** that people weigh the costs and benefits of each possibility. This assumption is based on the expectation that individuals and firms will act in a consistent manner, with a reasonably well-defined notion of what they like and what their objectives are, and with a reasonable understanding of how to attain those objectives.

In the case of an individual, the rationality assumption is taken to mean that he makes choices and decisions in pursuit of his own self-interest. Different people will, of course, have different goals and desires. Sally may want to drive a Porsche, own a yacht, and have a large house; to attain those objectives, she knows she needs to work long hours and sacrifice time with her family. Andrew prefers a less harried life-style; he is willing to accept a lower income for longer vacations and more leisure throughout the year.

Economists make no judgments about whether Sally's preferences are "better" or "worse" in some sense than Andrew's. They do not even spend much time asking why it is that different individuals have different views on these matters, or why tastes change over time. These are important questions, but they are more the province of psychology, sociology, and other social sciences. What economists are concerned about are the consequences of these different preferences. What decisions can they expect Sally and Andrew, rationally pursuing their respective interests, to make?

In the case of firms, the rationality assumption is taken to mean that firms operate to maximize either their profits or stock market value. If a company pays adequate attention to profits in the long run as well as the short, it turns out that profit maximization and maximization of stock market value are essentially the same. We will therefore stick to profit maximization as the firm's goal.

Individuals and firms often have to make choices without being sure about the consequences. Fred has to decide on Monday whether to buy a ticket for Saturday's football game. He knows it may rain. He also knows that if he waits until Saturday to decide he wants to go to the game and it is a beautiful day, it will be too late to get a ticket. The assumption of rationality implies that individuals think through the consequences, forming judgments about the likelihood of various possibilities. Thus, Fred decides to buy the ticket on Monday. When it rains on Saturday, he has no regrets about his decision; he wishes it hadn't rained, but he knows his decision was made rationally. He felt it was fairly likely that it would not rain, and he knew he would be much unhappier not being able to go to the game if the sun shone on Saturday than he would be if he lost the $10 on an unused ticket. Given the information he had about the likelihood of rain, he made the best possible decision.

The principle of rationality applies to decisions about gathering information as well. Rational individuals and firms decide whether to spend money and time to become more informed—say, about whether it will rain on Saturday—by weighing the costs and benefits. Fred looked up the week's weather forecast in Monday's newspaper, but he did not bother to go to the library to look up the forecast in the *Farmers Almanac*. The *Almanac's* track record in predicting weather accurately, he felt, was sufficiently weak that the cost, in terms of time, was not worth the possible benefit, in terms of improved accuracy of forecast.

While rational choices involve the careful balancing of costs and benefits, economists spend more time discussing costs than benefits. This is largely because individuals and firms often see clearly the benefits of each alternative; where they make mistakes is in evaluating the costs. In later sections of this chapter, we will see how economists think systematically about costs.

COMPETITIVE MARKETS

To complete the model, economists make some assumptions about the places where self-interested consumers and profit-maximizing firms meet: markets. Economists often begin by focusing on the case where there are many buyers and sellers, all buying and selling the same thing. You might picture a crowded farmers' market to get a sense of the number of buyers and sellers—except that you have to picture everyone buying and selling just one good. Let's say we are in Ontario, and the booths are all full of peaches.

Each of the farmers—our profit-maximizing firm—would like to raise his prices. That way, if he can still sell his peaches, his profits go up. Yet with a large number of sellers, each is forced to charge close to the same price, since if any farmer charged much more, he would lose business to the farmer next door. Firms are in the same position. In an extreme case, it may even be expected that if a firm charged any more than the going price, it would lose *all* of its sales. Economists label this case **perfect competition.** In perfect competition, each firm is a **price taker,** which simply means that because it cannot influence the market price, it must accept that price. The firm takes the market price as given because it cannot raise its price without losing all sales, and at the market price it can sell as much as it wishes. Even if it multiplied sales by a factor of ten, this would have a negligible effect on the total quantity marketed. The various markets for agricultural goods are perhaps the best example of real markets that, in the absence of government intervention, would probably be perfectly competitive. There are so many wheat farmers, for instance, that each farmer believes that he can grow and sell as much wheat as he wishes and have essentially no effect on the price of wheat. (Later in the book, we will encounter markets with limited or no competition, like monopolies, where firms can raise prices without losing all their sales. Firms with such market power are called **price makers.**)

On the other side of our farmers' market are rational individuals, each of whom would like to pay as little as possible for her peaches. Why can't she pay less than the going price? Because the seller sees another buyer in the crowd who will pay the going price. Thus, the consumers take the market price as given, and focus their attention on other factors—their taste for peaches, primarily—in deciding how many to buy.

Even though all participants in the market—the buyers and the sellers—take the price as given, the interaction of all buyers and sellers determines the price that will eventually prevail. The price is said to be exogenous (outside their control) to each of the individuals and firms in the market, but endogenous to (determined by) the market as a whole. Economists use the notion of **market equilibrium** to describe the level to which the market price settles down. Suppose, for example, that at the beginning of the day, the price of peaches is set quite low, say $2 per dozen. Buyers will find this price very attractive and will want to buy large quantities. On the other hand, at this low price, sellers will not be willing to offer many for sale. The result is that buyers will want to buy more than sellers are willing to sell, and the market will be out of equilibrium. In these circumstances, the price will be bid up and this will simultaneously reduce the amount that buyers want to buy and increase the amount that sellers want to sell. Conversely, when the price is too high, supply will exceed demand and the price will be bid down. In either case, the price will converge to the level at which demand and supply are equal. Here the market is in equilibrium, and the price will have no further tendency to change. The process by which market prices converge to equilibrium as well as the speed will differ from market to market and in fairly complicated ways. Economic reasoning usually focuses on markets that are in equilibrium. Most important insights can be gained from those circumstances.

This description of the farmers' market is an economic model. It pulls together the assumptions of self-interested consumers, profit-maximizing firms, and perfectly competitive markets in a combination that has predictive power. These predictions can be tested against empirical observation. As we just saw, for instance, the model predicts that when there are many firms, they will not be able to charge more than their competitors, and if we went to a farmers' market, we could check to see if this is true.

This model of consumers, firms, and markets is the **basic competitive model.** Economists generally believe that, to the extent that it can be duplicated by market systems in the real world, the competitive model will provide answers to the basic economic questions of what is produced and in what quantities, how it is produced, and for whom it is produced, resulting in the greatest economic efficiency. Resources are not wasted: it is not possible to produce more of one good without producing less of another, and indeed it is not even possible to make anyone better off without making someone else worse off. In the basic competitive model, these results are obtained without any help from the government. Unfortunately, the model is not and cannot be fully duplicated, and governments frequently intervene. Nevertheless, it is a convenient benchmark. Some economists believe that the competitive model describes many markets well, even if it does not describe them exactly. Even those who do not think real markets can be described by the competitive model nonetheless often find that the model is a useful jumping-off point. By observing the difference between its predictions and the observed outcomes, they know what other models to employ.

INGREDIENTS IN THE BASIC COMPETITIVE MODEL

1. Rational, self-interested consumers

2. Rational, profit-maximizing firms

3. Competitive markets with price-taking behaviour

PROPERTY RIGHTS AND INCENTIVES

A healthy economy depends on people who work and firms that are as efficient as possible. What, then, makes self-interested individuals get out of bed in the morning? How can we expect that profit-maximizing firms will invest their hard-earned profits trying to find more efficient ways to produce goods? The government could pass a law, perhaps, requiring that individuals and firms behave properly. However, market economies, like that of Canada, accomplish this with a carrot rather than a stick.

The carrot that provides incentives to firms in a market economy is profits. The carrot for households is income. Economists assume that individuals would prefer not to work hard, at least beyond a certain point. But they also assume that people would prefer more goods to fewer goods. If you want more goods, you have to work harder or longer. For business firms, the goal of more profits gives them an incentive to produce efficiently, develop new products, discover unmet needs, and find better production techniques.

For the profit motive to be effective, firms need to be able to keep at least some of their profits. Households, in turn, need to be able to keep at least some of what they earn or receive as a return on their investments. (The return on their investments is simply what they receive back in excess of what they invested. If they receive back less than they invested, the return is negative.) There must, in short, be **private property,** with its at-

CLOSE-UP: ECONOMISTS AGREE!

Try the following seven statements out on your classmates or your family to see whether they, like the economists surveyed, disagree, agree with provisos, or agree:

| | Percentage of economists who | | |
	Disagree	Agree with provisos	Agree
1. Tariffs and import quotas usually reduce general economic welfare.	6.5%	21.3%	71.3%
2. A minimum wage increases unemployment among young and unskilled workers	20.5%	22.4%	56.5%
3. A ceiling on rents reduces the quantity and quality of housing available.	6.5%	16.6%	76.3%
4. If the federal budget is to be balanced, it should be done over the business cycle rather than yearly.	13.4%	24.8%	60.1%
5. The cause of the rise in gasoline prices that occurred in the wake of the Iraqi invasion of Kuwait is the monopoly power of large oil companies.	67.5%	20.3%	11.4%
6. The trade deficit is primarily a consequence of the inability of domestic firms to compete.	51.5%	29.7%	18.1%
7. Cash payments increase the welfare of recipients to a greater degree than do transfers-in-kind of equal cash value.	15.1%	25.9%	58.0%

Among the general population, these are controversial questions. You will find many people who believe that restricting foreign imports is a good thing; that government regulation of wages and rents has few ill effects; that the federal budget should be balanced every year; that the trade deficit is mainly caused by the inability of domestic companies to compete; that government should avoid giving cash to poor people (because they are likely to waste it); and that oil companies are the cause of higher oil prices.

But when professional economists are surveyed, there is broad agreement that many of those popular answers are misguided. The percentage listed above are from a survey carried out in the United States in 1990. Notice that healthy percentages of economists apparently believe that most import quotas are economically harmful; that government control of wages and rents does lead to adverse consequences; that thinking about an annually balanced budget is improper; that oil companies are not to blame for higher oil prices; that the trade deficit is not caused by the competitive problems of individual companies; that cash payments benefit the poor more than direct (in-kind) transfers of food, shelter, and medical care.

Sources: Richard M. Alston, J. R. Kearl, and Michael B. Vaughan, "Is There a Consensus Among Economists in the 1990s?" *American Economic Review* (May 1992); J. R. Kearl, Clayne L. Pope, Gordon C. Whiting, and Larry T. Wimmer, "A Confusion of Economists?" *American Economic Review* (May 1979): 28–37.

tendant **rights.** Property rights include both the right of the owner to use the property as she sees fit and the right to sell it.

These two attributes of property rights give individuals the incentive to use property that is under their control efficiently. The owner of a piece of land tries to figure out the most profitable use of the land; for example, whether to build a store or a restaurant. If he makes a mistake and opens a restaurant when he should have opened a store, he bears the consequences: the loss in income. The profits he earns if he makes the right decisions—and the losses he bears if he makes the wrong ones—give him an incentive to think carefully about the decision and do the requisite research. The owner of a store tries to make sure that her customers get the kind of merchandise and the quality of service they want. She has an incentive to establish a good reputation, because if she does so, she will do more business and earn more profits.

The store owner will also want to maintain her property—which is not just the land anymore, but includes the store as well—because she will get more for it when the time comes to sell her business to someone else. Similarly, the owner of a house has an incentive to maintain *his* property, so that he can sell it for more when he wishes to move. Again, the profit motive combines with private property to provide incentives.

HOW THE PROFIT MOTIVE DRIVES THE MARKET SYSTEM

In market economies, incentives are supplied to individuals and firms by the chance to own property and to retain some of the profits of working and producing.

WHEN PROPERTY RIGHTS FAIL

The fact of property rights and the profit motive is so pervasive in our society that most of us take it for granted. To see why economists hold this idea in such high esteem, it is worth examining a few cases where property rights are interfered with.

ILL-DEFINED PROPERTY RIGHTS

Fish are a valuable resource. Not long ago, the area southeast of Newfoundland, called the Grand Banks, was teeming with fish, especially cod. Not surprisingly, it was also teeming with fishermen, who saw an easy livelihood scooping out the fish from the sea. Since there were no property rights, everyone tried to catch as many fish as he could. Canadian and American fishermen were joined by Europeans and, more recently, by large vessels from Japan and the Soviet Union. They failed not only to consider that as they fished more, others would find it harder to catch fish, but even to consider that if they caught too many fish, the number of fish in future years would decline. A self-interested fisherman would rationally reason that if he did not catch the fish, someone else would. The result was a tragedy: the Grand Banks was overfished, to the point where not only was it not teeming with fish, but commercial fishing became unprofitable. In 1977, foreign fishing was reduced by the extension of Canada's offshore jurisdiction to include most of the Grand Banks. As well, Canada and the United States have a treaty limiting the amount of fish that fishermen from each country can take. Only by limiting the quantity that can be taken can the fish stocks be restored.

Similar problems arise in the use of fresh waters. For many years, industrial firms flushed waste containing harmful chemicals into the lakes, rivers, and streams of the country, essentially treating water as a free resource. The result was a deterioration of the quality of water to an extent that was harmful to other users. Again, the problem arose because of a lack of definition of property rights. Governments have gradually intervened with a variety of regulatory measures to attempt to redress the costs that have been imposed by pollution.

The problem of ill-defined property rights is more general than the situation of fishermen and fresh water users, however. *Any* time society fails to define the owners of its resources and does not allow the highest bidder to use them, we can expect inefficiencies to result. Resources will be wasted or will not be used in the most productive way.

In Canada, much of the timberland is provincial Crown land that is leased to firms wishing to cut down trees for profit. The sale of licences combined with taxes imposed based on the number of trees cut down (stumpage fees) was a valuable and seemingly inexhaustible source of revenue to provincial governments. Leases were only temporary, however, thus conferring only partial property rights to the leaseholders. The value of timber as a resource depends upon the extent to which reforestation is undertaken. But the benefit of reforestation will accrue sometime in the future, perhaps far in the future. Since leasehold only confers temporary property rights on the logging industry, the incentive does not exist to engage in reforestation practices that generate the largest long-term benefit from the forests, and the forests may be inefficiently used. When forest resources seem endless, insufficient reforestation may not have been perceived as a great problem. Recent concern, however, has led governments to attempt to regulate reforestation practices on Crown lands held in leasehold by timber firms.

ENTITLEMENTS AS PROPERTY RIGHTS

Property rights do not always mean that you have full ownership or control. A **legal entitlement,** such as the right to occupy an apartment for life, common in some large cities, is viewed by economists as a property right. Individuals do not own the apartment, and thus cannot sell it, but they cannot be thrown out, either.

A similar situation exists with the use of frequencies on the airwaves. In principle, these are scarce resources that are valuable to radio stations, but that are not allocated by the market. Instead, they are allocated by a federal regulatory agency, the Canadian Radio-television and Telecommunications Commission (CRTC). The result is that those who value the slots most are not necessarily those to whom they are allocated. Thus, for example, a large commercial station would be willing to pay a great deal of money for the frequency held by a nonprofit organization, such as a university. But the latter are not allowed to sell their entitlement to the frequency. The result is that frequencies are allocated in a way that is different than a market would allocate them.

Economists found legal entitlements even in countries like the former Soviet Union, which claimed to have abolished private property. Economists argue that such countries changed, but did not eliminate, property rights. The manager of a Soviet firm had considerable discretion over who got his products, which were often in very short supply. This right was much like a property right. He exchanged "favours" with other managers who had the right to decide on who got their own products. Thus, a market emerged even in an economic system where free markets were outlawed.

In market economies, these partial and restricted property rights result in many inefficiencies. Because the individual in a rent-controlled apartment cannot (legally) sell the right to live in her apartment, as she gets older she may have limited incentives to maintain its condition, let alone improve it. (In the Soviet example, these restricted property rights may have had the opposite effect, improving the economy's efficiency from what it would have been in the absence of *any* market.)

INCENTIVES VERSUS EQUALITY

One way to provide incentives, whether for an individual or a company, is to relate compensation to performance. There are some problems, however, with tying compensation closely to performance. Commission plans for sales representatives, for instance, link compensation to sales. But a salesperson's sales may be up, not because he did a better job of selling, but because more customers wanted to buy the product. The salesperson will claim it was superior skill and effort, while his colleague may argue that it was dumb luck.

Providing incentives by tying compensation to performance also means that those who are successful will earn a higher income. Thus, if there are incentives, there must be some inequality. This is called the **incentive-equality trade-off.** The inequality may arise not just because one individual has worked harder than another, but also because she has been luckier than another, as the sales commission story makes clear.

If society provides greater incentives, total output is likely to be higher, but there will also probably be greater inequality. The relationship is depicted in Figure 2.1, whose vertical axis shows a measure of equality and whose horizontal axis shows some measure of output. At a point such as A, incentives are strong because taxes are low and government welfare programs are limited, so how hard a person works determines how well off

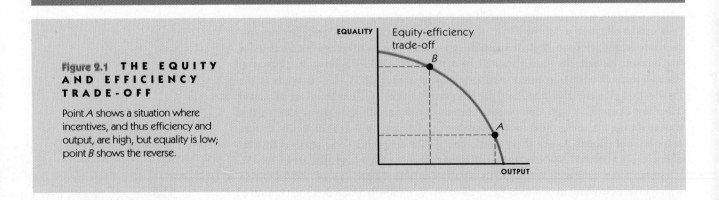

Figure 2.1 THE EQUITY AND EFFICIENCY TRADE-OFF

Point *A* shows a situation where incentives, and thus efficiency and output, are high, but equality is low; point *B* shows the reverse.

he is. Thus, output is high, but equality is low (inequality is high). At point *B*, by contrast, there are weak incentives; taxes are high and government welfare programs are generous, so that the differences in the levels of consumption someone can enjoy, whether he works hard or not, are small. So there is not much incentive to work hard. Output is low, but equality is high.

One of the basic questions facing members of society in their choice of tax rates and welfare systems is, how much would incentives be diminished by an increase in tax rates to finance a better welfare system and thus reduce inequality? What would be the results of those reduced incentives.

RATIONING

In a market economy, goods go to those individuals who are most willing and able to pay for them. Thus, the market economy is called a **price system.** But the price system is only one of several ways of allocating resources, and a comparison with other systems will help to clarify the advantages of markets. When individuals get less of a good than they would like at the terms being offered, the good is said to be **rationed.** Different rationing schemes are different ways of deciding who get society's scarce resources.

RATIONING BY QUEUES

Rather than supplying goods to those most willing and able to pay the most for them, a society could give them instead to those most willing to wait in line. This system is called **rationing by queues.** Tickets are often allocated by queues, whether they are for movies, sporting events, or rock concerts. A price is set, and it will not change no matter how many people line up to buy at that price. (The high price that scalpers can get for "hot" tickets is a good indication of how much more than the ticket price individuals would have been willing to pay.)

Rationing by queues is thought by many to be a more desirable way of supplying medical services than the price system. Why, it is argued, should the rich—who are most able to pay for medical services—be the ones to get better or more medical care? Using this reasoning, Britain, in the 1940s, decided to provide free medical care to everyone on its soil. Many other countries have followed suit, including Canada in the 1960s. To see a doctor, all you have to do is wait in line. Rationing medicine by queues turns the allocation problem around: since the value of time for low-wage workers is lower, they are more willing to wait, and therefore they get a disproportionate share of (government-supplied) medical services.

In general, rationing by queues is an inefficient way of distributing resources. The time spent in line is a wasted resource. There are usually ways of achieving the same goal within a price system that can make everyone better off. Again using the medical example, if some individuals were allowed to pay for doctors' services and could obtain them without waiting in line, more doctors could be hired, and the lines for those who are unable or unwilling to pay could actually be reduced.

RATIONING BY LOTTERIES

Lotteries allocate goods by a random process, like picking a name from a hat. University dormitory rooms are usually assigned by lottery. So might seats be in popular courses; when more students want to enroll in a section of a principles of economics course than the size of the section allows, there may be a lottery to determine the lucky ones who get to enroll. Certain mining rights and licences to radio airwaves used to be allocated by lottery. Like queue systems, lotteries are thought to be fair because everyone has an equal chance. For example, the Ontario Ministry of Natural Resources conducted public meetings to determine how to rehabilitate the moose population by controlling the annual moose harvest. The results of the meetings showed that the public preferred the lottery draw to the first-come-first-served technique on the grounds that it would provide an equal chance for all residents. But lotteries are also inefficient, because the scarce resources do not go to the individual or firm who is willing and able to pay the most.

RATIONING BY COUPONS

Most governments in wartime use systems of **coupon rationing.** People are allowed so many gallons of gasoline, so many pounds of sugar, so much meat, and so much flour each month. To get the good, you have to pay the market price *and* produce a coupon. The reason this system of rationing is used is that it is thought that without coupons prices would soar, and these extremely high prices would inflict a hardship on poorer individuals.

Coupon systems take two forms, depending on whether coupons are tradable or not. Systems in which coupons are not tradable give rise to the same inefficiency that occurs with most of the other nonprice systems—goods do not in general go to the individuals who are willing and able to pay the most. There is generally room for a deal, a trade that will make all parties better off. For instance, I might be willing to trade some of my flour ration for some of your sugar ration. But in a nontradable coupon system, the law prohibits such transactions. Usually when coupons cannot be legally traded, there are strong incentives for the establishment of a **black market,** an illegal market in which the goods or the coupons for goods are traded.

RATIONING BY GOVERNMENT REGULATION

Sometimes direct **government regulation** is used to ration the amounts that can be bought or sold. There are numerous examples of this. Many countries have operated capital controls that restrict the amount of foreign currency that can be purchased. The amount of game that can be taken by recreational hunters is also often subject to regulation. Some communities limit the number of bags of garbage that each household can leave out for collection. Quantity controls are often used to restrict the amounts of pollutants emitted by firms. In each of these cases, the quantity restriction typically bears no direct relation to the value put on the item by the various users of it. As a result, the item is likely to be inefficiently allocated among users.

In some cases this inefficiency is overcome by allowing persons to trade their quotas. This is typically the case with agricultural and fishing quotas, and has been suggested by economists for pollution controls. Being able to buy and sell quotas will ensure that those who value the restricted item most will have the opportunity to use it.

OPPORTUNITY SETS

We have covered a lot of ground so far in this chapter. We have seen the economist's basic model, which relies on competitive markets. We have seen how the profit motive and private property supply the incentives that drive a market economy. And we have gotten our first glimpse at why economists believe that market systems, which supply goods to those who are willing and able to pay the most, provide the most efficient means of allocating what the economy produces. They are far better than the variety of nonprice rationing schemes that have been employed. It is time now to return to the question of choice. Market systems leave to individuals and firms the question of what to consume. How are these decisions made?

For a rational individual or firm, the first step in the economic analysis of any choice is to identify what is possible, what economists call the **opportunity set,** which is simply the group of available options. If you want a sandwich and you have only roast beef and tuna fish in the refrigerator, then your opportunity set consists of a roast beef sandwich, a tuna fish sandwich, a strange sandwich combining roast beef and tuna fish, or no sandwich. A ham sandwich is out of the question. Defining the limitations facing an individual or firm is a critical step in economic analysis. One can spend time yearning after the ham sandwich, or anything else outside the opportunity set, but when it comes to making choices, only what is within the opportunity set is relevant.

BUDGET AND TIME CONSTRAINTS

What limits choices are **constraints.** Constraints define the opportunity set. In most economic situations, the constraints that limit a person's choices—that is, those constraints that actually are relevant—are not sandwich fixings, but time and money. Money can be used to buy anything in the economy. Opportunity sets whose constraints are imposed by money are referred to as **budget constraints;** opportunity sets whose constraints are prescribed by time are called **time constraints.** A billionaire may feel that his choices are limited not by money but by time; while for an unemployed worker, time hangs heavy—it is the lack of money rather than time that limits his choices.

The budget constraint defines a typical opportunity set. Consider the budget constraint of Alfred, who has decided to spend $100 on either cassette recordings or compact discs. A CD costs $10, a cassette $5. So Alfred can buy either 10 CDs or 20 cassettes. Or he can buy 9 CDs and 2 cassettes; or 8 CDs and 4 cassettes. The various possibilities are set forth in Table 2.1, and they are depicted graphically in Figure 2.2. Along the vertical axis, we measure the number of cassettes purchased, and along the horizontal axis, we measure the number of CDs. The line marked $B_1 B_2$ is Alfred's budget constraint. The extreme cases, where Alfred buys only CDs or cassettes, are repre-

Table 2.1 ALFRED'S OPPORTUNITY SET

Cassettes	CDs
0	10
2	9
4	8
6	7
8	6
10	5
12	4
14	3
16	2
18	1
20	0

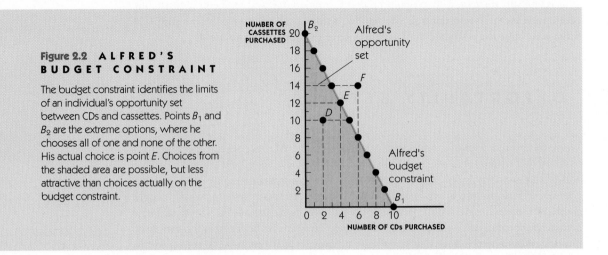

Figure 2.2 ALFRED'S BUDGET CONSTRAINT

The budget constraint identifies the limits of an individual's opportunity set between CDs and cassettes. Points B_1 and B_2 are the extreme options, where he chooses all of one and none of the other. His actual choice is point E. Choices from the shaded area are possible, but less attractive than choices actually on the budget constraint.

sented by the points B_1 and B_2 in the figure. The dots between these two points, along the budget constraint, represent the other possible combinations. The cost of each combination of CDs and cassettes must add up to $100. The point actually chosen by Alfred is labelled E, where he purchases 4 CDs (for $40) and 12 cassettes (for $60).

While Alfred's budget constraint is the line that defines the outer limits of his opportunity set, the whole opportunity set is larger. It also includes all points below the budget constraint. This is the shaded area in the figure. The budget constraint shows the maximum number of cassettes Alfred can buy for each number of CDs purchased, and vice versa. Alfred is always happiest when he is on (chooses a point on) his budget constraint. To see why, compare the points E and D. At point E, he has more of both goods than at point D. He would be even happier at point F, where he has still more cassettes and CDs; but that point, by definition, is unattainable.

Figure 2.3 depicts a time constraint. The most common time constraint simply says

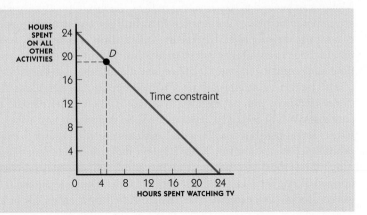

Figure 2.3 AN OPPORTU- NITY SET FOR WATCHING TV AND OTHER ACTIVITIES

This opportunity set is limited by a time constraint, which shows the trade-off a person faces between spending time watching television and spending it on other activities. At 5 hours of TV time per day, point D represents a typical choice for a Canadian.

that the sum of what an individual spends her time on each day—including sleeping—must add up to 24 hours. The figure plots the hours spent watching television on the horizontal axis and the hours spent on all other activities on the vertical axis. People—no matter how rich or how poor—have only 24 hours a day to spend on different activities. The time constraint is quite like the budget constraint. A person cannot spend more than 24 hours or fewer than zero hours a day watching TV. The more time she spends watching television the less time she has available for all other activities. Point *D* (for dazed) has been added to the diagram at 5 hours a day—this is the amount of time the typical Canadian chooses to spend watching TV.

THE PRODUCTION POSSIBILITIES CURVE

Business firms and whole societies face constraints. They too must make choices limited to opportunity sets. The amounts of goods a firm or society could produce, given a fixed amount of land, labour, and other inputs, are referred to as its **production possibilities.**

As one commonly discussed example, consider a simple description of a society in which all economic production is divided into two categories, military spending and civilian spending. Of course, each of these two kinds of spending has many different elements, but for the moment, let's discuss the choice between the two broad categories. For simplicity, Figure 2.4 refers to military spending as "guns" and civilian spending as "butter." The production of guns is given along the vertical axis, the production of butter along the horizontal. The possible combinations of military and civilian spending—of guns and butter—is the opportunity set. Table 2.2 sets out some of the possible combinations: 90 million guns and 40 million tonnes of butter, or 40 million guns and 90 million tonnes of butter. These various possibilities are depicted in the figure. In the case of a choice involving production decisions, the boundary of the opportunity set—giving the maximum amount of guns that can be produced for each amount of butter and vice versa—is called the **production possibilities curve.**

Table 2.2 PRODUCTION POSSIBILITIES FOR THE ECONOMY

Guns (millions)	Butter (millions of tonnes)
100	0
90	40
70	70
40	90
0	100

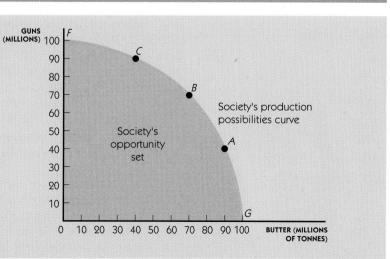

Figure 2.4 THE GUNS AND BUTTER TRADE-OFF

A production possibilities curve can show society's opportunity set. This one describes the trade-off between military spending ("guns") and civilian spending ("butter"). Points *F* and *G* show the extreme choices, where the economy produces all guns or all butter. Notice that unlike the budget and time constraints, the production possibilities line curves, reflecting diminishing returns.

When we compare the individual's opportunity set and that of society, reflected in its production possibilities curve, we notice one major difference. The individual's budget constraint is a straight line, while the production possibilities curve bows outwards. There is a good reason for this. An individual typically faces fixed **trade-offs:** if Alfred spends $10 more on CDs (that is, he buys one more CD), he has $10 less to spend on cassettes (he can buy two fewer cassettes).

On the other hand, the trade-offs faced by society are not fixed. If a society produces only a few guns, it will use those resources—the men and machines—that are best equipped for gun making. But as society tries to produce more and more guns, it finds that doing so becomes more difficult; it will increasingly have to rely on those who are less and less good at producing guns. It will be drawing these resources out of the production of other goods, in this case, butter. This means that for each successive increment in gun production, society will have to reduce the production of butter more. Thus, when the economy increases its production of guns from 40 million a year (point A) to 70 million (B), butter production falls by 20 million tonnes, from 90 million tonnes to 70 million tonnes. But if production of guns is increased further, to 90 million (C), butter production has to decrease not by 20 million tonnes but by 30 million tonnes, to only 40 million tonnes. The change in the number of tonnes of butter produced, for each increase in the number of guns, does not stay constant. That is why the production possibilities line is curved.

The importance of the guns-butter trade-off was seen dramatically during World War II when car production plummeted almost to zero as the automobile factories were diverted to the production of tanks and other military vehicles.

In another example, assume that a firm owns land that can be used for growing wheat but not corn, and land that can grow corn but not wheat. In this case, the only way to increase wheat production is to move workers from the cornfields to the wheat fields. As more and more workers are put into the wheat fields, production of wheat goes up, but each successive worker increases production less. The first workers might pick the largest and most destructive weeds. Additional workers lead to better weeding, and better weeding leads to higher output. But the additional weeds rooted up are smaller and less destructive, so output is increased by a correspondingly smaller amount. This is an example of the general principle of **diminishing returns.** Adding successive units of any input such as fertilizer, labour, or machines to a fixed amount of other inputs—seeds or land—increases the output, or amount produced, but by less and less.

Table 2.3 shows the output of the corn and wheat fields as labour is increased in each field. Assume the firm has 6,000 workers to divide between wheat production and corn production. Thus, the second and fourth columns together give the firm's production possibilities, which are depicted in Figure 2.5.

There is no reason to assume that a firm or an economy will always be on its production possibilities curve. Any inefficiency in the economy will result in a point such as A in Figure 2.5, below the production possibilities curve, where society could obtain more of everything, both more wheat and corn. One of the major quests of economists is to look for instances in which the economy is inefficient in this way.

Whenever the economy is operating below the production possibilities curve, it is possible for us to have more of every good—more wheat and more corn, more guns and more butter. No matter what goods we like, we can have more of them. That is why we can unambiguously say that points below the production possibilities curve are undesirable. But this does not mean that every point on the production possibilities curve is bet-

Table 2.3 DIMINISHING RETURNS

Labour in cornfield (no. of workers)	Corn output (bushels)	Labour in wheat field (no. of workers)	Wheat output (bushels)
1,000	60,000	5,000	200,000
2,000	110,000	4,000	180,000
3,000	150,000	3,000	150,000
4,000	180,000	2,000	110,000
5,000	200,000	1,000	60,000

ter than any point below it. Compare points A and C in Figure 2.5. Corn production is higher at C, but wheat production is lower. If people do not like corn very much, the increased corn production may not adequately compensate them for the decreased wheat production.

There are many reasons why the economy may be below the production possibilities curve. If land that is better suited for the production of corn is mistakenly devoted to the production of wheat, the economy will operate below its production possibilities curve. If some of society's resources—its land, labour, and capital goods—are simply left idle, as happens when there is a depression, the economy operates below the production possibilities curve. The kinds of problems discussed earlier in the chapter with inadequately or improperly defined property rights also give rise to inefficiencies.

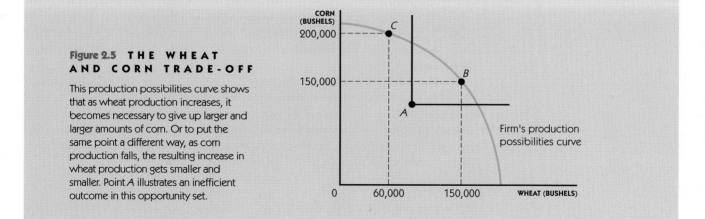

Figure 2.5 THE WHEAT AND CORN TRADE-OFF

This production possibilities curve shows that as wheat production increases, it becomes necessary to give up larger and larger amounts of corn. Or to put the same point a different way, as corn production falls, the resulting increase in wheat production gets smaller and smaller. Point A illustrates an inefficient outcome in this opportunity set.

COST

The beauty of a well-defined opportunity set like the budget constraint, the time constraint, or the production possibilities curve is that it specifies the cost of one option in terms of another. If the individual, the firm, or the society is operating on the constraint or curve, then it is possible to get more of one thing only by sacrificing some of another. The "cost" of one more unit of one good is how much you have to give up of the other.

Economists thus think about cost in terms of trade-offs within opportunity sets. Let's go back to Alfred choosing between CDs and cassettes in Figure 2.2. The trade-off is given by the **relative price,** the ratio of the prices of CDs and cassettes. In our example, a CD costs $10, a cassette $5. The relative price is $10 ÷ $5 = 2; for every CD Alfred gives up, he can get two cassettes. Likewise, societies and firms face trade-offs along the production possibilities curve, like the one shown in Figure 2.4. There, point A is the choice where 40 million guns and 90 million tonnes of butter are produced. The trade-off can be calculated by comparing points A and B. Society can have 30 million more guns by giving up 20 million tonnes of butter.

Trade-offs are necessary because resources are scarce. If you want something, you have to pay for it; you have to give up something. If you want to go to the library tomorrow night, you have to give up going to the movies. If you want to have more income to spend, you have to work more; that is, you have to give up some of your leisure. If a sawmill wants to make more two-by-four beams from its stock of wood, it will not be able to make as many one-by-four boards.

Noneconomists, particularly politicians, sometimes ignore trade-offs. During the 1970s, government expenditures of various sorts grew very rapidly. The liberalization of the Unemployment Insurance system increased the federal government's costs dramatically. Provincial expenditures on health, education, and welfare rose rapidly, causing an increase in federal shared-cost transfers to the provinces. The oil price shock of 1973 (discussed in Chapter 1) increased federal government liabilities to provide equalization payments to the poorer provinces that had no oil revenues. As well, the federal government undertook to subsidize oil imports into the eastern part of the country. But the government neglected to increase tax revenues to finance these increases in its expenditures. It preferred not to cut back private-sector consumption to release resources for its own expenditures. The increased expenditures were financed by government borrowing.

Even a nodding acquaintance with economics should explain why it is not possible to have higher government expenditures without some cost. In this case, the cost emerged as a rapid increase in the size of the government debt. The increase in debt was so dramatic that by the 1990s one-quarter of all federal tax revenues was going to pay the interest costs of the debt alone. In other words, the cost of the increased government expenditures of the 1970s was only postponed for future taxpayers, not avoided.

OPPORTUNITY COSTS

If someone were to ask you right now what it costs to go to a movie, you would probably answer, "Seven dollars," or whatever you paid the last time you went to the movies. But with the concept of trade-offs, you can see that a *full* answer is not that simple. To begin with, the cost is not so much the $7 as it is what that $7 could otherwise buy. Furthermore, your time is a scarce resource that must be figured into the calculation. Both the money and the time represent opportunities forgone in favour of going to the movie, or what economists refer to as the **opportunity cost** of the movie. To apply a resource to one use means that it cannot be put to any other use. Thus, we should consider the next-best, alternative use of any resource when we think about putting it to use. This next-best use is the formal measurement of opportunity cost.

Some examples will help to clarify the idea of opportunity cost. Consider a student, Sarah, who enrolls in university. She thinks that the cheque for tuition and room and board represents the costs of her education. But the economist's mind immediately turns to the job she might have had if she had not enrolled in university. If Sarah could have earned $15,000 from September to June, her next-best choice of what to do this year, then this is the opportunity cost of her time, and this forgone income must be added to the university bills in calculating the total economic cost of the school year.

Now consider a business firm that has bought a building for its headquarters that is bigger than necessary. If the firm, by renting out the space that is not needed, could receive $3 per month for each square foot, then this is the opportunity cost of leaving the space idle. The firm would be wise to pretend it has to pay itself rent for all the space it owns, and to balance the benefits of using space against this cost.

The analysis can be applied to the government level as well. The federal government owns a vast amount of northern wilderness. In deciding whether it is worthwhile to convert some of that land into a national park, the government needs to take into account the opportunity cost of the land. The land might be used for growing timber or for mining. Whatever the value of the land in its next-best use, this is the economic cost of the national park. The fact that the government does not have to buy the land does not mean that the land should be treated as a free good.

Thus, in the economist's view, when rational firms and individuals make decisions—whether to undertake one investment project rather than another, whether to buy one product rather than another—they take into account *all* of the costs, the full opportunity costs, not just the direct expenditures.

SUNK COSTS

Economic cost includes costs, as we have just seen, that noneconomists often exclude, but it also ignores costs that noneconomists tend to include. If an expenditure has already been made and cannot be recovered no matter what choice is made, a rational person would ignore it. Such expenditures are called **sunk costs.**

To understand sunk costs, let's go back to the movies, assuming now that you have spent $7 to buy a movie ticket. You were skeptical about whether the movie was worth $7. Half an hour into the movie, your worst suspicions are realized: the movie is a disaster. Should you leave the movie theatre? In making that decision, the $7 should be ignored. It is a sunk cost; your money is gone whether you stay or leave. The only relevant choice now is how to spend the next 90 minutes of your time: watch a terrible movie or go do something else.

We can also return to Fred, who at the beginning of the chapter was deciding whether to buy a nonrefundable ticket to a football game for Saturday. He decides to buy it, knowing that if he waits until Saturday, there is a good chance that all the tickets will be

CLOSE-UP: OPPORTUNITY COSTS AND SMOKING

Since the 1970s when evidence began to accumulate that smoking is potentially harmful to one's health, governments have used regulations and tax policy both to discourage smoking and to raise revenues to cover the costs imposed on society by smokers. Not surprisingly, this has given rise to a battle of rights between smokers and nonsmokers. Nonsmokers claim that smokers impose large external costs on the rest of society which are not reflected in the price paid for cigarettes. On the other hand, smokers argue that the price and taxes they pay are more than enough compensation for any costs they impose on society, and that these policies unnecessarily interfere with their freedom to choose the amount they should consume of perfectly legal products.

The concept of opportunity cost can help us evaluate the net costs imposed on society by smokers. The question is whether the price paid by smokers covers all the costs to society of the activity. In the case of cigarettes, in addition to the production costs and the costs voluntarily assumed by smokers in deciding to smoke, there are certain external costs imposed on society at large. These include especially the health services provided to smokers and nonsmokers alike for smoking-related diseases. In addition, some economists count as part of social costs the opportunity cost of potential output (GDP) lost due to the premature death of some smokers. On the other hand, smokers compensate society over and above the costs of producing cigarettes. This compensation takes two forms. One is the substantial government revenues from taxes on tobacco products. The other is the reduction in transfer payments that results from the fact that early death results in a reduction in public pension benefits that would otherwise accrue to elderly persons. In addition,

premature death also economizes on certain types of public services used by the elderly, especially health services and residential care facilities.

A recent study by economists André Raynauld and Jean-Pierre Vidal of the University of Montreal attempted to place dollar values on these various amounts. They estimated that, using 1986 data, the social costs attributable to smoking were $669 million for all of Canada. These include both the total hospitalization and medical services costs, and the cost to properties of accidental fires blamed on smokers' negligence. Against this, however, reductions in future hospital, medical, and residential care costs amounted to $462 million, leaving a net cost of $207 million. Note that the authors assume that smokers know that smoking is bad for their health and that they internalize this risk of premature death in their decision to smoke. Therefore, loss of years of a smokers' life is not an

extra cost. The authors also state that there is no evidence that smoking is a cause of death for nonsmokers.

These costs are more than made up for by the taxes paid by smokers, estimated to be $3.17 billion and the savings in pension plan payments of $1.42 billion. When set against the net external costs imposed on nonsmokers, this leads Raynauld and Vidal to conclude that it is a myth that smokers impose a cost on society. Of course, many persons will dispute the choice of items to include in the costs of smoking and the way in which they are measured. Because of the difficulty of computing some costs, other economists may differ in their conclusions about the net costs of smoking.

Source: André Raynauld and Jean-Pierre Vidal, "Smokers' Burden on Society: Myth and Reality in Canada," *Canadian Public Policy* XVIII, no. 3 (September 1992): 300–17.

sold. When Saturday arrives, it is raining. Fred hates sitting out in the rainy weather. But he feels that since he has already spent the money on the ticket, it would be a waste not to go to the game. Is this rational?

An economist would ask Fred, "What if someone had offered you a free ticket to the game on Saturday?" Fred hates sitting in the rain so much that he would have said, "Thanks, but no thanks." The economist would then say that if he feels this way, it would be irrational for him to go the game even if he had already paid for the ticket. The money he paid for it is gone, and the decision to buy it is a bygone; Monday's expenditures on the ticket are sunk costs, and should be ignored in Saturday's decision about whether to go to the game.

Or assume you have just purchased a fancy laptop computer for $2,000. You are feeling very pleased with your purchase. But then the next week, the manufacturer announces a new computer with twice the power for $1,000; you can trade in your old computer for the new one by paying an additional $400. You are angry. You feel you have just paid $2,000 for a computer that is now almost worthless, and you have gotten hardly any use out of it. You decide not to buy the new computer for another year, until you have gotten some return for you investment. Again, an economist would say that you are not approaching the question rationally. The past decision is a sunk cost. The only question you should ask yourself is whether the extra power of the fancier computer is worth the additional $400. If it is, buy it. If not, do not.

MARGINAL COSTS

The third aspect of cost that economists emphasize is the extra costs and extra benefits, or what economists call the **marginal costs** and **marginal benefits.** The most difficult decisions we make are not whether to do something or not. They are whether to do a little more or a little less of something. Few of us waste much time deciding whether or not to work. We have to work; the decision is whether to work more or fewer hours. When we need an apartment or a house, the tough question is whether to buy (or rent) a bigger or a smaller place. A country does not consider whether or not to have an army; it decides whether to have a larger or smaller army.

Jim has just obtained a job for which he needs a car. He must decide how much to spend on the car. By spending more, he can get a newer, bigger, and more luxurious car. But he has to decide whether it is worth a few hundred (or thousand) marginal dollars for extra items like cute hubcaps, power windows, a stereo system, a model that is a year newer, and so on.

Similarly, Polly is thinking about flying to Banff for a ski weekend. She has three days off from work. The air fare is $200, the hotel room costs $100 a night, and the ski ticket costs $35 a day. Food costs the same as at home. She is trying to decide whether to go for two or three days. The *marginal* cost of the third day is $135, the hotel cost plus the cost of the ski ticket. There are no additional transportation costs involved in staying the third day. She needs to compare the marginal cost with the additional enjoyment she will have from the third day.

Marginal analysis can be addictive. You are at a refreshment stand, trying to decide what size drink to order. A small 300 ml cup costs $.75, a 600 ml cup costs $1.00, and a big 1,000 ml cup costs $1.25. In going from the small to the medium size, the marginal cost for the extra 300 ml is $.25. In deciding whether to buy a small or medium Coke, you have to decide whether the benefit of an additional (marginal) 300 ml is worth the $.25 cost. In deciding whether to buy a medium or large Coke, you have to decide whether the benefit of an additional (marginal) 400 ml is worth an extra quarter.

People, consciously or not, think about the trade-offs at the margin in most of their decisions. Economists, however, bring them into the foreground. Like opportunity costs and sunk costs, marginal analysis is one of the critical concepts that enable economists to think systematically about the costs of alternative choices.

REVIEW AND PRACTICE

SUMMARY

1. The economists' basic model consists of rational, self-interested individuals and profit-maximizing firms, interacting in competitive markets.

2. The profit motive and private property provide incentives for rational individuals and firms to work hard and efficiently. Ill-defined or restricted property rights can lead to inefficient or counterproductive behaviour.

3. Society often faces choices between equality, which means allowing people more or less equal amounts of consumption, and efficiency, which requires incentives that enable people or firms to receive different benefits depending on their behaviour.

4. The price system in a market economy is one way of allocating goods and services. Other methods include rationing by queue, by lottery, by coupon, and by government regulation.

5. An opportunity set illustrates what choices are possible. Budget constraints and time constraints define individuals' opportunity sets. Both show the trade-offs of how much of one thing a person must give up to get more of another.

6. A production possibilities curve defines a firm or society's opportunity set, representing the possible combinations of goods that the firm or society can produce. If a firm or society is producing below its production possibilities curve, it is said to be inefficient, since it could produce more of either good (or both goods) without producing less of the other.

7. The opportunity cost is the cost of using any resource. It is measured by looking at the next-best, alternative use to which that resource could be put.

8. A sunk cost is a past expenditure that cannot be recovered, no matter what choice is made in the present. Thus, rational decision makers ignore them.

9. Most economic decisions concentrate on choices at the margin, where the marginal (or extra) cost of a course of action is compared with its extra benefits.

KEY TERMS

perfect competition
market equilibrium
basic competitive
  model
rationing systems
opportunity sets

budget constraints
time constraints
production possibili-
  ties
trade-offs
diminishing returns

relative price
opportunity cost
sunk cost
marginal costs and
  benefits

REVIEW QUESTIONS

1. What are the goals of individuals and of firms in economists' basic competitive model?

2. Consider a lake in a provincial park where everyone is allowed to fish as much as he wants. What outcome do you predict? Might this problem be averted if the lake were privately owned and fishing licences were sold?

3. Why might government policy to make the distribution of income more equitable lead to less efficiency?

4. List advantages and disadvantages of rationing by queue, by lottery, by coupon, and by government regulation. If the government permitted a black market to develop, might some of the disadvantages of these systems be reduced?

5. What are some of the opportunity costs of going to university? What are some of the opportunity costs a province should consider when deciding whether to widen a highway?

6. Give two examples of a sunk cost, and explain why they should be irrelevant to current decisions.

7. How is the decision to purchase a good such as a car or a house different from the marginal decisions involved in that purchase?

PROBLEMS

1. Imagine that many businesses are located beside a river, into which they discharge industrial waste. There is a city downstream, which uses the river as a water supply and for recreation. If property rights to the river are ill-defined, what problems do you predict will occur?

2. Suppose an underground reservoir of oil may reside under properties owned by several different individuals. As each well is drilled, it reduces the amount of oil that others can take out. Compare how quickly the oil is likely to be extracted in this situation with how quickly it would be extracted if one person owned the property rights to drill for the entire pool of oil.

3. In some provinces, hunting licences are allocated by lottery; if you want a licence, you send in your name to enter the lottery. If the purpose of the system is to ensure that those who want to hunt the most get a chance to do so, what are the flaws of this system? How would the situation improve if people who won licences were allowed to sell them to others?

4. Imagine that during time of war, the government imposes coupon rationing. What are the advantages of allowing people to buy and sell their coupons? What are the disadvantages?

5. Kathy, a university student, has $20 a week to spend: she spends it either on junk food at $2.50 a snack, or on gasoline at $.50 per litre. Draw Kathy's opportunity set. What is the trade-off between junk food and gasoline? Now draw each new budget constraint she would face if
   (a) a kind relative started sending her an additional $10 per week;
   (b) the price of a junk food snack fell to $2;
   (c) the price of gasoline rose to $.60 per litre
In each case, how does the trade-off between junk food and gasoline change?

6. Why is the opportunity cost of going to medical school likely to be greater than the opportunity cost of going to university? Why is the opportunity cost of a woman with a university education having a child greater than the opportunity cost of a woman with just a secondary education having a child?

APPENDIX: READING GRAPHS

Whether the old saying that a picture is worth a thousand words under- or overestimates the value of a picture, economists find graphs extremely useful.

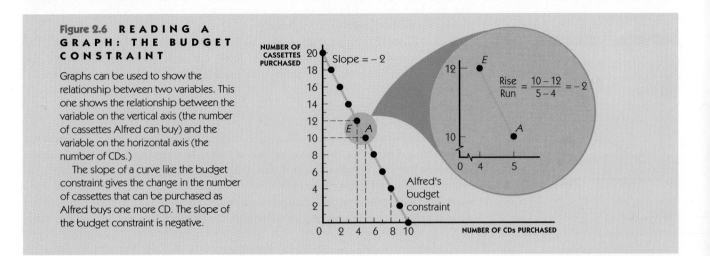

Figure 2.6 READING A GRAPH: THE BUDGET CONSTRAINT

Graphs can be used to show the relationship between two variables. This one shows the relationship between the variable on the vertical axis (the number of cassettes Alfred can buy) and the variable on the horizontal axis (the number of CDs.)

The slope of a curve like the budget constraint gives the change in the number of cassettes that can be purchased as Alfred buys one more CD. The slope of the budget constraint is negative.

For instance, look at Figure 2.6; it is a redrawn version of Figure 2.2, showing the budget constraint—the various combinations of CDs and cassettes he can purchase—of an individual, Alfred. More generally, a graph shows the relationship between two variables, here, the number of CDs and the number of cassettes that can be purchased. The budget constraint gives the maximum number of cassettes that can be purchased, given the number of CDs that have been bought.

In a graph, one variable (here, CDs) is put on the horizontal axis and the other variable on the vertical axis. We read a point such as E by looking down to the horizontal axis and seeing that it corresponds to 4 CDs, and by looking across to the vertical axis and seeing that it corresponds to 12 cassettes. Similarly, we read point A by looking down to the horizontal axis and seeing that it corresponds to 5 CDs, and by looking across to the vertical axis and seeing that it corresponds to 10 cassettes.

In the figure, each of the points from the table has been plotted, and then a curve has been drawn through those points. The "curve" turns out to be a straight line in this case, but we still use the more general term. The advantage of the curve over the individual points is that with it, we can read off from the graph points on the budget constraint that are not in the table.

Sometimes, of course, not every point on the graph is economically meaningful. You cannot buy half a cassette or half a CD. For the most part, we ignore these considerations when drawing our graphs; we simply pretend that any point on the budget constraint is actually possible.

SLOPE

In any diagram, the amount by which the value along the vertical axis increases from a change in a unit along the horizontal axis is called the **slope,** just like the slope of a

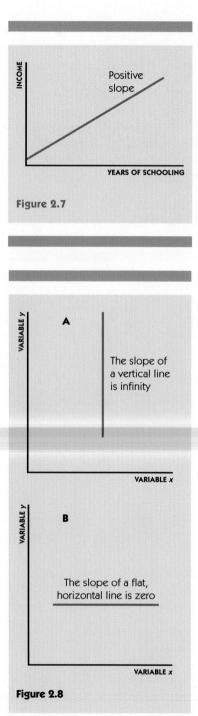

Figure 2.7

Figure 2.8

mountain. Slope is sometimes described as "rise over run," meaning that the slope of a line can be calculated by dividing the change on the vertical axis (the "rise") by the change on the horizontal axis (the "run").

Look at Figure 2.6. As we move from E to A, increasing the number of CDs by 1, the number of cassettes purchased falls from 12 to 10. For each additional CD bought, the feasible number of cassettes that can be purchased falls by 2. So the slope of the line is

$$\frac{\text{rise}}{\text{run}} = \frac{10 - 12}{5 - 4} = \frac{-2}{1} = -2.$$

When, as in Figure 2.6, the variable on the vertical axis falls when the variable on the horizontal axis increases, the curve, or line, is said to be **negatively sloped.** A budget constraint is always negatively sloped. But when we describe the slope of a budget constraint, we frequently omit the term "negative." We say the slope is 2, knowing that since we are describing the slope of a budget constraint, we should more formally say that the slope is negative 2. Alternatively, we sometimes say that the slope has an absolute value of 2.

Figure 2.7 shows the case of a curve that is **positively sloped.** (Figure 1.5 in Chapter 1 suggested such a relationship between the number of years of schooling and income.) The variable along the vertical axis, income, increases as schooling increases, giving the line its upward tilt from left to right.

In later discussions, we will encounter two special cases. A line that is very steep has a very large slope; that is, the increase in the vertical axis for every unit increase in the horizontal axis is very large. The extreme case is a perfectly vertical line, and we say then that the slope is infinite (Figure 2.8, panel A). At the other extreme is a flat, horizontal line; since there is no increase in the vertical axis no matter how large the change along the horizontal, we say that the slope of such a curve is zero (panel B).

Figures 2.6 and 2.7 both show straight lines. Everywhere along the straight line, the slope is the same. This is not true in Figure 2.9, which repeats the production possibilities curve shown originally in Figure 2.4. Look first at point E. Panel B of the figure blows up the area around E, so that we can see what happens to the output of guns when we increase the output of butter by 1. From the figure, you can see that the output of guns decreases by 1. Thus, the slope is

$$\frac{\text{rise}}{\text{run}} = \frac{69 - 70}{71 - 70} = -1.$$

Now look at point A, where the economy is producing more butter. The area around A has been blown up in panel C. Here, we see that when we increase butter by 1 more unit, the reduction in guns is greater than before. The slope at A is

$$\frac{\text{rise}}{\text{run}} = \frac{38 - 40}{91 - 90} = -2.$$

With curves such as the production possibilities curve, the slope differs as we move along the curve.

INTERPRETING CURVES

Look at Figure 2.10. Which of the two curves has a larger slope? The one on the top appears to have a slope that has a larger absolute value. But look carefully at the axes. No-

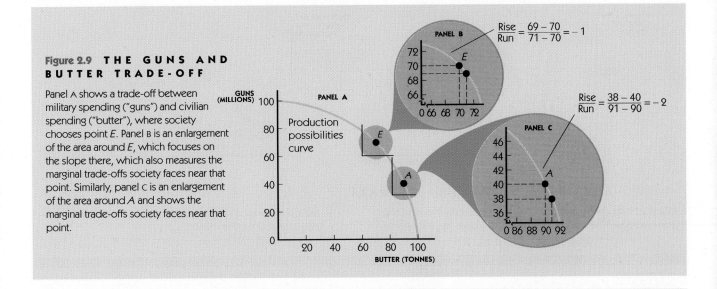

Figure 2.9 THE GUNS AND BUTTER TRADE-OFF

Panel A shows a trade-off between military spending ("guns") and civilian spending ("butter"), where society chooses point E. Panel B is an enlargement of the area around E, which focuses on the slope there, which also measures the marginal trade-offs society faces near that point. Similarly, panel C is an enlargement of the area around A and shows the marginal trade-offs society faces near that point.

tice that in panel A, the vertical axis is stretched relative to panel B. The same distance that represents 20 cassettes in panel B represents only 10 cassettes in panel A. In fact, both panels represent the same budget constraint. They have exactly the same slope.

This kind of cautionary tale is as important in looking at the graphs of data that were common in Chapter 1 as it is in looking in this chapter at the relationships that produce

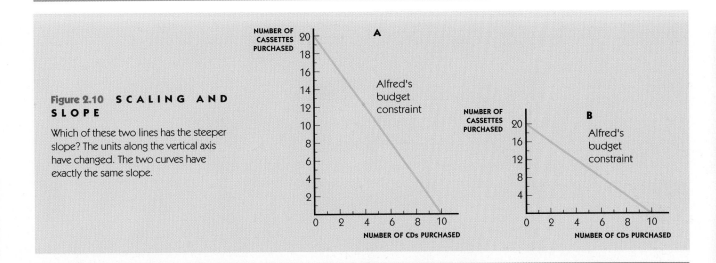

Figure 2.10 SCALING AND SLOPE

Which of these two lines has the steeper slope? The units along the vertical axis have changed. The two curves have exactly the same slope.

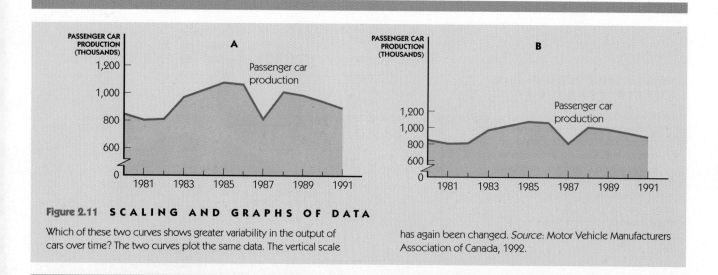

Figure 2.11 SCALING AND GRAPHS OF DATA

Which of these two curves shows greater variability in the output of cars over time? The two curves plot the same data. The vertical scale has again been changed. *Source*: Motor Vehicle Manufacturers Association of Canada, 1992.

smooth curves. Compare, for instance, panels A and B of figure 2.11. Which of the two curves exhibits more variability? Which looks more stable? Panel B appears to show that car production does not change much over time. But again, a closer look reveals that the axes have been stretched in panel A. The two curves are based on exactly the same data, and there is really no difference between them.

EXCHANGE AND PRODUCTION

A creature on another planet looking down at a developed modern economy on earth might compare human activity to an enormous ant colony. Each ant seemingly has an assigned task. Some stand guard. Some feed the young. Some harvest food and others distribute it. Some of these peculiar human ants also spend a lot of time shuffling paper, scribbling notes in books, and keyboarding at computer consoles. Others work in factories, tightening screws, running machines, and so on. Still others move goods from one place to another. How is all of this activity coordinated? Who decides who does what? No dictator or superintelligent computer is giving instructions. Yet somehow an immense amount is accomplished in a reasonably coordinated way. Understanding how a complex economy operates—how it is that certain individuals do one task, others do another, how information is communicated and decisions are made—is a central objective of economics.

This chapter discusses the problem of economic interdependence at two levels: of individuals and firms within a country, and of countries within the world economic community. Many of the same principles apply at both levels. Economic interdependence has its benefits—and its costs.

KEY QUESTIONS

1. Why is trade (exchange) mutually beneficial?

2. What are the similarities and differences between trade (exchange) between individuals within a country and trade between countries?

3. What determines what any particular country produces and sells on the international market? What is meant by comparative advantage, and why does it play such an important role?

4. What are the gains from specialization?

5. How valid is the argument, so often heard in political circles, that trade should be restricted?

THE BENEFITS OF ECONOMIC INTERDEPENDENCE

We begin by considering the benefits of trade, specifically the exchange of those goods that are already available in the economy.

THE GAINS FROM TRADE

When individuals own different goods, have different desires, or both, there is an opportunity for mutually beneficial trades: trades that benefit all parties to the trade. Kids trading hockey cards learn the basic principles of exchange. One has two Wayne Gretzky cards, the other has two Mario Lemieux cards. A trade will probably benefit both of them. The same lesson applies to countries. Canada has more natural gas than it can possibly use, but it does not produce enough fruit to feed its populace. The United States has more fruit than Americans can possible consume, but needs natural gas. Trade can benefit both countries.

Voluntary trade between two individuals involves not a winner and loser, but only two winners. After all, if the trade would make a loser of either party, that party would choose not to trade. Thus, a fundamental consequence of voluntary exchange is that it benefits everyone involved.

"FEELING JILTED" IN TRADE

In spite of the seemingly persuasive argument that individuals only voluntarily engage in a trade if they think they will be better off as a result, people often walk away from a deal believing they have been hurt. It is important to understand that when economists say that a voluntary trade makes the two traders better off, they do not mean that it makes them both happy.

Imagine, for example, that Frank brings an antique rocking chair to a flea market to sell. He is willing to sell it for $100—at any lower price, he would rather keep it himself—but he hopes to sell it for $200. Helen comes to the flea market planning to buy such a chair, hoping to spend only $100, but willing to pay as much as $200. They argue and negotiate, eventually settle on a price of $150, and make the deal. But when they go home, they both complain. Frank complains the price was too low, and Helen that it was too high. It is common to hear people complain that a product cost "too much," but that they went ahead and bought it anyway.

From an economist's point of view, such complaints are self-contradictory. If Frank *really* thought $150 was too low, he should not have sold at that price. If Helen *really* thought $150 was too high, she should not have paid the price. Of course, sellers always wish they could have received more money, and buyers always wish they could have paid less. But economists argue that people reveal their preferences not by what they say, but by what they do. If one voluntarily agrees to make a deal, one also agrees that the deal is, if not perfect, at least better than the alternative of not making the deal.

There are two common objections to this line of reasoning. Both of them involve the idea of Frank or Helen "taking advantage" of the other. The implication, of course, is that if a buyer or a seller can take advantage, then the other party may be a loser rather than a winner.

The first objection is that either Frank or Helen may not really know what is being agreed to. Perhaps Helen recognizes that the chair is actually a rare antique, worth $5,000, but by neglecting to tell Frank this fact, manages to buy it for only $150. Perhaps Frank knows that the rockers fall off the chair if one rocks in it for ten minutes, but sells the chair anyway without telling Helen, thus keeping the price high. In either case, by keeping hidden information a secret, the party without this information becomes a loser after the trade, rather than a winner.

The second objection concerns the division of the **gains from trade.** Since Helen would have been willing to pay as much as $200, anything she pays less than that is **surplus,** the term economists use for a gain from trade. Similarly, since Frank would have been willing to sell the chair for as little as $100, anything he receives more than that is also surplus. The total dollar value of the gain from trade is $100—the difference between the maximum price Helen would have been willing to pay and the minimum price at which Frank would have been willing to sell. At a price of $150, they split the gain in half; each gets a surplus of $50. But if the price had been $125, $25 of the gain would have gone to Frank, $75 to Helen. The split would thus not have been an equitable one.

Economists do not have much patience with these objections. Like most people, they favour making as much information public as possible, and they think vendors and customers should be made to stand behind their promises. Thus, many economists support laws against selling defective products or misrepresenting products. But economists also point out that second thoughts and the "If only I had known" arguments are just not relevant. If Frank sells his antique at a flea market instead of taking it around to several different reputable antique dealers and asking them what it might be worth, he has made a voluntary decision to save his time and energy. If Helen buys an antique at a flea market instead of going to a reputable dealer who will guarantee that the product is in good condition, she knows she is taking a risk. Maybe both Frank and Helen would like to go back and do things differently. Maybe they acted prematurely or foolishly. As for the negotiations, it is only natural that both would like to get more of the gains from trade.

The logic of free exchange, however, does not say that everyone must express great happiness with the result either at the time of the sale or forever after. It simply says that when people choose to make a deal, they prefer making the deal to not making the deal. And if they prefer making the deal, they are by definition better off *in their own minds* making the deal, at the time the transaction takes place.

The objections to trade nonetheless carry an important message: exchanges that happen in the real world tend to be considerably more complicated than swapping hockey cards. They involve problems of information, problems of estimating risks, and problems of forming expectations about what will happen in the future. These complications will be discussed throughout the book. So without going into too much detail at the moment, let's just say that if you are worried that you do not have the proper information to make a trade, then shop around, or get a guarantee or an expert opinion, or buy insurance; such precautions are a legitimate part of voluntary exchange. If you feel there is too much risk even taking these steps, don't go through with the trade. But if you choose to plunge ahead without any of these precautions, you can't pretend you didn't have other choices. Like those who buy a ticket in a lottery, you know you are taking chances.

ECONOMIC RELATIONS AS EXCHANGES

Individuals in our economy can be thought of as involved in a multiplicity of voluntary trades. They "trade" their labour services (their time and skills) to their employer in exchange for dollars. They then trade some of those dollars with a multitude of merchants for goods, like gasoline and groceries; other dollars they trade for services, like those of plumbers and hair stylists. The firm for which an individual works trades the goods it produces for dollars, and then it turns around and trades dollars for labour services. Even your savings account at a bank can be viewed as a trade: you give the bank $100 today, and in exchange, the bank promises to give you $105, for example, at the end of the year (your original deposit plus 5 percent interest).

While voluntary exchanges necessarily make people better off, there are some economic transactions that are not voluntary. Some of the money you earn from supplying your labour services *must* be paid to the government in taxes. Presumably you would not pay those taxes voluntarily, so they must make you worse off. At the same time, part of the taxes go to provide public services that may provide benefits for you. But there is no guarantee that on balance you are better off as a result of the transactions with the government.

TRADE BETWEEN COUNTRIES

Why is it that people engage in this complex set of economic relations with others? Wouldn't life be easier and simpler if all people were self-sufficient and relied on their own resources? The answer is that people are better off as a result of trading. And this applies not just to trade and economic relations between individuals but to trade and economic relations between countries as well. Just as individuals *within* a country find it advantageous to trade with one another, so too do countries find trade advantageous. Just as it is virtually impossible for any individual to be self-sufficient, it is almost impossible for any country to be completely self-reliant without sacrificing a great deal of its standard of living. Canada has long been part of an international economic community, and this participation has grown in recent decades. Let's look at how interdependence has affected the three main markets in the Canadian economy.

INTERDEPENDENCE IN THE PRODUCT MARKET

Foreign-produced goods are commonplace in Canadian markets. In the late 1980s, for instance, over a fifth of the goods and services sold in Canada were **imports** (goods produced abroad but sold domestically). Roughly two-thirds of motor vehicles sold in Canada were imported, along with a third of the oil, and virtually all of the CDs and VCRs, as well as some basic foodstuffs like bananas, coffee, and tea. Not surprisingly, two-thirds of the imports into Canada came from the United States, and that number may rise as a result of the Canada-U.S. Free Trade Agreement of 1988. At the same time, Canadian producers sell a quarter of everything they produce as **exports** (goods produced domestically but sold abroad), almost three-quarters of it to the United States. Fully 70 percent of motor vehicles produced in Canada are exported, along with 30 percent of the oil and gas produced, as well as even higher proportions of wheat and forest products.

The Canadian economy has always been heavily dependent on trade, though the extent of dependency has changed over time. The share of both exports and imports plummeted dramatically during the Great Depression and rose rapidly during World War II. Figure 3.1 shows how exports and imports have varied as a proportion of national income, known as gross domestic product (GDP), over the postwar period. The proportion initially declined from the immediate postwar level of just over one-quarter of GDP to less than one-fifth in the mid-1950s. It has been on an upward trend for much of the postwar period, reaching almost 30 percent, with temporary declines during major recessions. Canadian trade as a share of GDP is comparable to that of Britain and France, and over twice as high as that of the United States. This reflects the fact that smaller countries tend to be more dependent than larger ones on international trade.

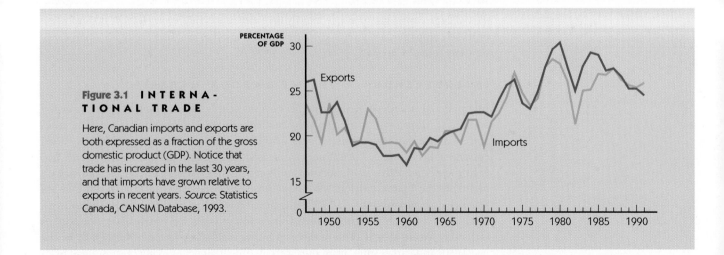

Figure 3.1 INTERNA- TIONAL TRADE

Here, Canadian imports and exports are both expressed as a fraction of the gross domestic product (GDP). Notice that trade has increased in the last 30 years, and that imports have grown relative to exports in recent years. *Source*: Statistics Canada, CANSIM Database, 1993.

Table 3.1 EXPORT-DEPENDENT BIG COMPANIES

Company and product	Rank by export sales	Exports as % of sales
Chrysler Canada (automobiles)	3	85
Pratt & Whitney Canada (aerospace)	14	75
Ford Canada (automobiles)	2	70
General Motors Canada (automobiles)	1	65
Magna (automobile parts)	13	63
Fletcher Challenger Canada (forest products)	12	62
Mobil Oil Canada (energy)	16	59
Bombardier (engineering)	11	54
Falconbridge (mining)	19	50
Inco (nickel)	10	45
Nova (energy, chemicals)	7	42
Noranda (resources)	4	40
Honda Canada (automobiles)	20	38
IBM Canada (computers)	8	38
Abitibi-Price (forest products)	18	32
Amoco Canada (energy)	15	26

Source: The Globe and Mail Report on Business, April 1992, p. 42.

Earnings from abroad constitute a major source of income for some of our largest corporations. Exports account for 85 percent of sales for Chrysler Canada, 75 percent for Pratt and Whitney Canada, and 45 percent for Inco. Table 3.1 gives some other examples of large companies that rely heavily on exports. It is interesting to note that over half of these companies are foreign-owned, which is another feature of a highly open economy like that of Canada.

INTERDEPENDENCE IN THE LABOUR MARKET

International interdependence extends beyond simply the shipping of goods between countries. More than 98 percent of Canadian citizens either immigrated here from abroad or are descended from people who did so. The flow of immigrants has varied considerably over time. The numbers increased rapidly from the 1850s until World War I. In the period 1910–1914, about 3 million settlers arrived from Europe and Britain mainly to the Prairie provinces. Immigration fell dramatically during the war and did not pick up again until the mid-1920s, again largely from European and British sources. It fell off considerably after the Great Depression of 1929 and was virtually nonexistent until after World War II. The number of immigrants started to increase rapidly in the late 1940s and early 1950s; again they were mainly Europeans many of whom had been displaced by the war. By the end of the 1950s, the kinds of immigrants started to change considerably, from rural to urban workers and from European to more diverse sources. The number of immigrants tripled from 1961 to 1967, when it reached 220,000. It then fell off and averaged about 140,000 per year until the early 1980s. With the recession of 1981–1982, immigration began to fall to less than 100,000, but it has gradually recovered to 200,000 since then. By 1989, the proportion of immigrants coming from different sources had changed—almost one-half of all immigrants came from Asia, about one-quarter from Europe, a further one-eighth from North and Central America, and the remainder mostly from Africa and South America. The numbers are expected to rise even further in the 1990s.

The nations of Europe have increasingly recognized the benefits that result from the international movement of workers. One of the important provisions of the treaty establishing the Common Market, an agreement among most countries within Western Europe—the European Community (EC)—allows for the free flow of workers within the Common Market.

INTERDEPENDENCE IN THE CAPITAL MARKET

Canada has always borrowed heavily from abroad, but the country also invests heavily overseas. In 1990, for example, Canadians invested approximately $18 billion of assets (factories, businesses, buildings, loans, etc.) in foreign countries, while foreigners invested about $20 billion in Canada. A number of Canadian companies have sought out profitable opportunities abroad, where they can use their special skills and knowledge to earn high returns. They established branches and built factories in the United States, Europe, Latin America, and elsewhere in the world.

Just as the nations of Western Europe have recognized the advantages that follow from the free flow of goods and labour among their countries, so too they have recognized the gains from the free flow of capital. Funds can be invested where they yield the highest returns. Knowledge and skills from one country can be combined with capital from another to produce goods that will be enjoyed by citizens of all countries. The process of liberalizing the flow of goods, labour, and capital among the countries of the European Common Market has been going on for more than twenty years, with the removal of tariff and tax barriers and more recently of border controls. Nevertheless, the worldwide recession of the early 1990s has slowed the final steps in the elimination of the remaining barriers to free trade.

BENEFITS OF MULTILATERAL TRADE

Many of the examples thus far have emphasized two-way trade between individuals or nations. Trade between two individuals or countries is called **bilateral trade.** But in most cases, exchanges between two parties may be less advantageous than **multilateral trade,** which is trade among several parties. Sometimes such trades are observed between sports teams. The Toronto Blue Jays send a catcher to the St. Louis Cardinals, the Cardinals send a pitcher to the Montreal Expos, and the Expos send an outfielder to the Blue Jays (see Figure 3.2A). No two of the teams might have been willing to make a two-way trade, but all can benefit from the three-way swap.

Countries may function in a similar way. Japan has no domestic sources of oil; it imports oil from Arabian countries. The Arabian countries want to sell their oil, but they

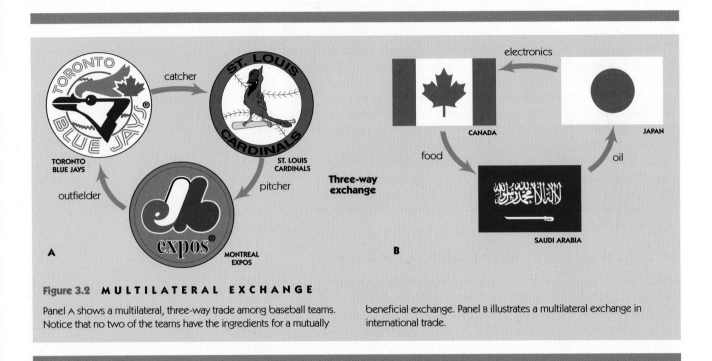

Figure 3.2 MULTILATERAL EXCHANGE

Panel A shows a multilateral, three-way trade among baseball teams. Notice that no two of the teams have the ingredients for a mutually beneficial exchange. Panel B illustrates a multilateral exchange in international trade.

want wheat and food, not only the cars and television sets that Japan can provide. Canada can provide the missing link by buying cars and televisions from Japan and selling food to the Arab nations. Again, this three-way trade, shown in Figure 3.2B, offers gains that two-way trade cannot. The scores of nations active in the world economy create patterns far more complex than these simplified examples.

Figure 3.3 illustrates the construction of a Ford Escort in Europe, and dramatizes the importance of multilateral and interconnected trade relations. The parts that go into an Escort come from all over the world. Similar diagrams could be constructed for many of the components in the diagram; the aluminum alloys may contain bauxite from Jamaica, the chrome plate may use chromium from Africa, the copper for wiring may come from Chile.

Multilateral trade means that trade between any two participants may not balance. In Figure 3.2B, the Arab countries send oil to Japan to get no goods (only yen) in return. No one would say that the Arab countries have an unfair trade policy with Japan. Yet some politicians, newspaper columnists, and business executives complain that since Canada imports more from a particular country (often Japan) than it exports to that country, the trade balance is "unfair." A misguided popular cliché says that "trade is a two-way street." But trade in the world market involves hundreds of possible streets between different nations. Canada runs a trade deficit not only with Japan, but also with the United Kingdom, and with other European Community countries taken together. In fact, Canada runs a trade deficit with the non-U.S. world. At the same time, the trade surplus with the United States is enough to ensure that overall Canadian trade is in surplus, and that is really all that matters. There is no particular reason that exports and imports with any particular country should be balanced.

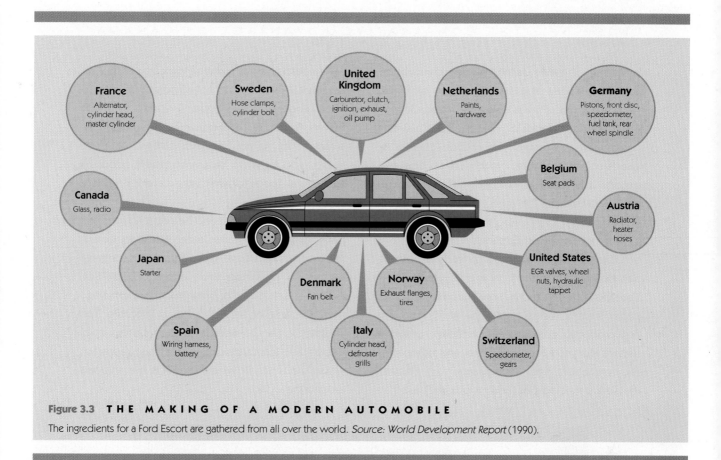

Figure 3.3 THE MAKING OF A MODERN AUTOMOBILE

The ingredients for a Ford Escort are gathered from all over the world. *Source: World Development Report* (1990).

COMPARATIVE ADVANTAGE

Up to this point, it has been assumed that exchange occurs with existing goods, and no new goods are produced. But clearly, most of what is exchanged must be produced. Another advantage of trade is that it allows individuals and countries to concentrate on what they produce best. As a result, the gains from trade are even larger when production is allowed for.

Some countries are more efficient at producing almost all goods than are other countries. The possession of superior production skills is called having an **absolute advantage,** and these advanced countries are said to have an absolute advantage over the others. How can the countries with disadvantages successfully engage in trade? The answer lies in the principle of **comparative advantage,** which states that individuals and countries specialize in producing those goods in which they are *relatively*, not absolutely, more efficient.

To see what comparative advantage means, let's say that both Canada and Japan produce two goods, TV sets and wheat. The amount of labour needed to produce these

CLOSE-UP: THE COMPARATIVE ADVANTAGE OF CANADA

Three lists of goods define Canada's comparative advantage today. The first are those of which Canada exports a great deal and imports little—presumably the goods in which we have a strong comparative advantage. The second consists of goods of which Canada imports a great deal and exports little, in which we have a strong comparative disadvantage. The third are goods of which Canada is both a high importer and high exporter, in which we have neither a comparative advantage nor disadvantage, and in which trade is presumably based on the gains from specialization.

Category 1: High Exports, Low Imports Pulp and paper, lumber, wheat and other grains, fish and fish products, ores and concentrates, precious metals, aluminum, copper, nickel and other metals, nonmetallic minerals, fertilizers, coal, electricity. Notice that most of these goods are based on natural resources, as might be expected.

Category 2: High Imports, Low Exports Communications and electronics equipment, fruit and vegetables, cotton, wool and textiles, chemicals, consumer goods. In contrast with category 1, these goods tend either to be manufactured goods or agricultural goods for which the Canadian climate is unsuited.

Category 3: High Imports and Exports Vehicles and parts, aircraft and parts, other transport equipment, oil and natural gas, industrial machinery, agricultural machinery, iron and steel, plastics, food products. Some of these goods are exported from one area of the country and imported into another, so transport costs play an important role. Others are manufactured goods that represent global industries in which products are shipped around the world.

Table 3.2 LABOUR COST OF PRODUCING TV SETS AND WHEAT (WORKER HOURS)

	Canada	Japan
Labour required to make a TV set	100	120
Labour required to make a tonne of wheat	5	8

goods is shown in Table 3.2. In Canada, say that it takes 100 worker hours to make a TV set (that is, if we add up all the time spent by all the people working to make a TV set, the sum is 100 hours); in Japan, it takes 120 worker hours. In Canada, it takes 5 man hours to make a tonne of wheat; in Japan, it takes 8 man hours. Canada is more efficient at making both products. Even though Canada is more efficient at making TV sets, it imports them from Japan. Why? The answer is comparative advantage. The cost of making a TV set (in terms of labour used) in Japan *relative* to the cost of producing a tonne of wheat is low, compared with the cost of making them in Canada. That is, in Japan, it takes 15 times as many hours (120/8) to produce a TV set as it does to produce a tonne of wheat; in Canada, it takes 20 times as many hours (100/5) to produce a TV set as it does to produce a tonne of wheat. While Japan has an absolute *dis*advantage in producing TV sets, it has a *comparative* advantage.

The principle of comparative advantage applies to individuals as well as countries. The president of a company might type faster than her secretary, but it still pays to have the secretary type her letters, because the president may have a comparative advantage at bringing in new clients, while the secretary has a comparative (but not absolute) advantage at typing.

A CLOSER LOOK AT THE GAINS FROM COMPARATIVE ADVANTAGE

When two countries exploit their comparative advantage, the gains from trade that result can benefit both countries. Assume that in both Canada and Japan, 120,000 worker hours are spent altogether making TV sets, and 120,000 worker hours are spent growing wheat. So, according to the information given in Table 3.2, Japan produces 1,000 TV sets and 15,000 tonnes of wheat; Canada produces (with the same amount of labour) 1,200 TV sets and 24,000 tonnes of wheat. There is no reason that all 240,000 worker hours have to be divided equally between the two products, however. Table 3.3 shows what happens when each country changes its level of production to benefit from its comparative advantage.

Suppose Canada devotes 200,000 worker hours to producing wheat, and the remaining 40,000 worker hours to producing TV sets. Japan concentrates on producing TV sets and shifts 100,000 worker hours from producing wheat to producing TV sets. Japan then produces 1,833 (220,000 ÷ 120) TV sets, and output of TV sets goes up by 833; but wheat production has fallen, to 2,500 tonnes. Meanwhile, the shift of 80,000 man hours from TV sets to wheat in Canada has reduced TV set output by 800 and increased wheat

Table 3.3 HOW TRADE INCREASES OUTPUT FROM THE SAME LABOUR FORCE

Canada		Japan		Combined output	
Labour devoted to wheat (worker hours)	Labour devoted to TV sets (worker hours)	Labour devoted to wheat (worker hours)	Labour devoted to TV sets (worker hours)	Wheat (tonnes)	TV sets
120,000	120,000	120,000	120,000	39,000	2,200
200,000	40,000	20,000	220,000	42,500	2,233

output by 16,000 tonnes; Canada now produces 400 TV sets and 40,000 tonnes of wheat. The total combined production of the two countries of both wheat and TV sets has gone up: TV sets from 2,200 to 2,233, and wheat from 39,000 tonnes to 42,500 tonnes. There are clearly gains from trade and specialization—an extra 33 TV sets and an extra 3,500 tonnes of wheat. By focusing on their comparative advantages and then trading, Japan and Canada can both be better off.

HOW COMPARATIVE ADVANTAGE IMPROVES PRODUCTION POSSIBILITIES

The wheat-TV set example can also be illustrated with production possibility curves, developed in Chapter 2. Consider Figure 3.4, which shows the trade-off between TV sets and wheat for Canada and Japan. The trade-offs are pictured as straight lines in this case because we are assuming that the two goods are produced by labour alone, and in each country a given amount of labour is required to produce each unit of each good. Thus,

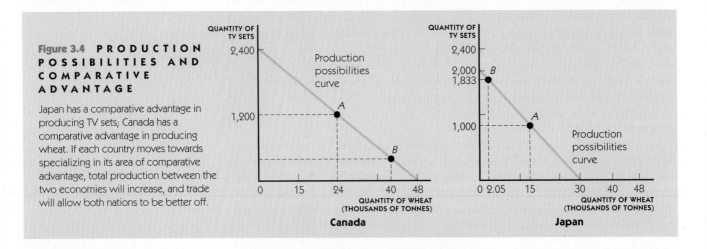

Figure 3.4 PRODUCTION POSSIBILITIES AND COMPARATIVE ADVANTAGE

Japan has a comparative advantage in producing TV sets; Canada has a comparative advantage in producing wheat. If each country moves towards specializing in its area of comparative advantage, total production between the two economies will increase, and trade will allow both nations to be better off.

every time 100 worker hours in Canada are switched from producing TV sets to producing wheat, 1 less TV set and 20 more tonnes of wheat are produced. The trade-off between TV sets and wheat is determined by their *relative* costs—in terms of the labour required. In the figure, both countries start at A and then move to B.

Notice that the production possibilities curve for Canada is sloped less sharply downwards than the line for Japan. If Japan wants to produce 1 more TV set, it must reduce its wheat production by 15 tonnes. If Canada wants to produce 1 less TV set, it can produce 20 tonnes more of wheat.

The differences in trade-offs facing the two countries reflect their differences in comparative advantage. Because Canada has a comparative advantage in wheat, the increase in the wheat it produces (20 tonnes) when it reduces its TV set production by 1 is much greater than the increase in wheat Japan produces (15 tonnes) when it reduces its TV set production by 1. When Canada focuses on its comparative advantage, net world production of wheat is increased by 5 tonnes.

The figure also shows what happens when production moves all the way from A to B: the output of both products goes up. Both countries—including Canada, with its absolute advantage in both products—gain from the increased production.

The principle of comparative advantage implies that trade can always provide mutual benefits to both countries, even trade between countries where one is more efficient in producing every single individual product than its trading partner. Generally speaking, economies that are smaller tend to specialize more than do those that are larger. For example, some developing countries rely heavily on a single product (for example, sugar in Cuba, cocoa in Ghana, or rubber and palm oil in Malaysia). Larger countries like the United States tend to produce a large variety of products, though even here there are some products that, because of comparative advantage, it does not pay to produce, such as VCRs and many other electronic gadgets. Canada's economy is large enough such that many manufactured goods are still produced, despite competition from imports. Examples include textiles and footwear, both of which are also heavily imported from Asia.

The same general principles of comparative advantage that apply to countries also apply to individuals: from an economic standpoint, individuals as well as nations should play to their comparative strengths.

COMPARATIVE ADVANTAGE AND SPECIALIZATION

Both nations and individuals frequently wind up specializing in the goods in which they have a comparative advantage, producing little or none of the goods in which they have a comparative disadvantage. Comparative advantage thus leads to specialization, and specialization leads to increased competence in those specialized activities, reinforcing the original comparative advantage.

To see the benefits of specialization, consider the lowly pencil. It is a simple tool, but there may be no single person in the world who knows how to make all that goes into a pencil. Some tree, containing the right kind of wood, must be felled somewhere; it must be transported somehow to a sawmill, and there cut into pieces that can be further processed in the shape of the casings. The graphite that runs through the pencil's center, the eraser at its tip, the metal that holds the two together, are all relatively simple materials, yet it takes specially trained people to produce each one of them.

Why Specialization Increases Productivity Specialization increases productivity, thus enhancing the benefits of trade, for three reasons. First, specializing avoids the time it takes a worker to switch from one production task to another. Second, by repeating the same task, the worker becomes more skilled at it. And third, specialization creates a fertile environment for invention.

Workers may possess roughly equal skills before they begin specializing in their jobs. The choice of who specializes in what particular job could be made at random. But after workers have begun specializing, switching them back and forth between jobs will tend to make production less efficient.

Note the immense productive power that can result from the division of labour. Dividing jobs so that each worker can practice a particular skill may increase productivity hundreds or thousands of times. Almost anyone who practices simple activities like sewing on a button, shooting a basketball, or adding a column of numbers for a week or two will be quite a lot better than someone who has not practiced. Similarly, a country that specializes in producing sports cars may develop a comparative advantage, because with its relatively large scale of production, it can divide tasks into separate assignments for different people; as each becomes better at his own tasks, productivity is increased.

At the same time, the division of labour often leads to invention. As someone learns a particular job extremely well, she might figure out ways of doing the job better. Also, a simple job may be a job that a machine can be invented to do. One can argue over whether necessity or laziness is the mother of this sort of invention, but whatever its cause, such an invention is more likely to occur with specialization. Specialization and invention reinforce each other. A slight initial advantage in some good leads to greater production of that good, thence to more invention, and thence to even greater production and further specialization.

Limits of Specialization   The extent of division of labour, or specialization, that is possible is limited by the size of the market. There is greater scope for specialization in mass-produced manufactured goods like picture frames than in custom-made items like the artwork that goes into picture frames. That is one of the reasons why the costs of production of mass-produced goods have declined so much. Similarly, there is greater scope for specialization in a big city than a small town. That is why in any big city, one will find small stores that specialize in a particular food or sport or type of clothing. The size of a market in a city provides an opportunity for dividing the labour of retail sales, and owners of specialty shops take advantage of that opportunity.

The gains from specialization also may be limited. The repetition of specialized jobs sometimes leads to bored, sloppy, and unproductive workers. Also, new insights and ideas can often arise from the cross-fertilization of disciplines, rather than from single-tracked specialization. Still, even in these cases, a certain degree of specialization adds greatly to productivity.

WHAT DETERMINES COMPARATIVE ADVANTAGE?

A close look at what each country in the world exports and imports presents a complex picture of trade. For example, Canada imports bananas from Central America, cars, TVs, and personal computers from Japan, cloth from Taiwan and Hong Kong; it exports automobiles and parts, wheat, and lumber. Earlier we learned that comparative advantage determines the pattern of trade. But what determines comparative advantage? In the modern world, this turns out be a fairly complex matter.

Natural Endowments   In first laying down the principle of comparative advantage in the early 1800s, the great British economist David Ricardo used the example of Portugal's trade with Britain. In Ricardo's example, Portugal had an absolute advantage in producing both wool and wine. But it had a comparative advantage in producing wine, because it could produce wine better than it could produce wool, compared with Britain. Thus, Britain had a comparative advantage in producing wool.

In this and other early examples, economists tended to assume that a nation's comparative advantage was determined largely by its **natural endowments.** Countries with soil and climate that are *relatively* better for grapes than for pasture will produce wine; countries with soil and climate that are relatively better for pasture than for grapes will produce sheep (and hence wool). In the modern economy, Canada's abundance of arable farmland gives the country a comparative advantage in agriculture. Countries that have an abundance of low-skilled labour relative to other resources, such as South Korea and Hong Kong, have a comparative advantage in producing goods like textiles, which require a lot of handwork.

While this theory, called **geographical determinism,** can still be applied in some places, it has clearly been outdated by developments in the modern world economy. Rather than searching for whatever comparative advantage nature has bestowed, nations in today's technological age can act to acquire a comparative advantage.

Acquired Endowments   A nation's endowments need not be limited by accidents of geography. The Japanese have little in the way of natural resources, yet they are a major player in international trade, in part because they have **acquired endowments.** Their case underscores the principle that by saving and accumulating capital and building large factories, a nation can acquire a comparative advantage in goods, like steel, that require large amounts of capital in their production. And by devoting resources to education, a nation can develop a comparative advantage in those goods that require a skilled labour force. Thus, the resources—human and physical—that a country has managed to acquire for itself can also give rise to comparative advantage.

Superior Knowledge   In the modern economy, what is important is not only possessing resources, but having the knowledge to use those resources productively. Switzerland's comparative advantage in watches is not based on a larger store of capital goods or better-educated labourers, nor does it have a better natural endowment of the materials that go into making watches. It is simply that over the years, the country has accumulated superior knowledge and expertise in watch making. In some cases, such as with Swiss watches, the knowledge that one country accumulates is largely a matter of historical accident. Belgium has a comparative advantage in fine lace; its workers have developed the requisite skills. A quirk of fate might have led Belgium to acquire a comparative advantage in watches and Switzerland in lace.

While sometimes patterns of specialization occur almost as an accident of history, in modern economies they are more likely to be a consequence of deliberate decisions. One of the principal ways that countries acquire a comparative advantage is by establishing or increasing their technological knowledge in a particular area. The U.S. semiconductor industry is a case in point. This industry manufactures the tiny silicon brains that control computers. Semiconductors were invented by an American, Robert Noyce, and in the 1970s, the United States had a powerful comparative advantage in manufacturing semiconductors; but Japan managed to become a close competitor (some would say the dominant producer) in the 1980s. The rise of the U.S. semiconductor industry was built in part on decisions by the federal government to fund the necessary research (usually so the semiconductors could be used in guided missiles and other weapons), and the rise of the Japanese industry was similarly based on decisions by that government to subsidize and support its semiconductor industry.

Thus, the semiconductor industry provides an example where a comparative advantage was first gained, then equalled by another competitor, and now may be lost, through the cumulative effect of many business and government decisions taken in Japan and the United States. If U.S. producers today concede the comparative advantage of Japanese producers and leave the market, the United States will be in an even worse position for competing in the future, as still more sophisticated computer chips are developed.

Stories like that of the semiconductor industry have led some economists to argue that government should encourage certain industries, in order for them to gain a technological advantage. This would happen either through trade protection, through support of research, through government financial assistance to domestic firms, or through the provision of infrastructure. Some observers have pointed to the success with which the Quebec government has encouraged industrial activity through its tax system and through the use of extensive investment in hydroelectricity. Firms such as Bombardier and Lavalin in the transportation sector have flourished in such an environment, referred to as Quebec Inc.

Specialization   Earlier we saw how comparative advantage leads to specialization. At the same time, specialization may lead to comparative advantage. The Swiss make fine watches, and have a comparative advantage in that market based on years of unique experience. Such superior knowledge, however, does not explain why Britain, Germany, Canada, and the United States, which are at roughly the same level of technological expertise in building cars, all trade cars with one another. How can each country have a comparative advantage in making cars? The answer lies in specialization.

Both Britain and Germany may be better off if Britain specializes in producing sports cars and Germany in producing luxury cars, or conversely, because specialization increases productivity. Countries enhance, or simply develop, a comparative advantage by specializing just as individuals do. As a result, similar countries enjoy the advantages of specialization even when they specialize in different but similar products.

THE FOUR BASES OF COMPARATIVE ADVANTAGE

Natural endowments, which consist of geographical determinants such as land, natural resources, and climate

Acquired endowments, which are the physical capital and human skills a nation has developed

Superior knowledge, including technological advantages, which may be acquired either by the accident of history or through deliberate policies

Specialization, which may create comparative advantages between countries that are similar in all other respects

THE PERCEIVED COSTS OF INTERNATIONAL INTERDEPENDENCE

The argument that voluntary trade must be mutually beneficial seems so compelling that one wonders why there has been, from time to time, such strong antitrade sentiment in Canada and many other countries. This antitrade feeling is often labelled **protectionism,** because it calls for "protecting" the economy from the effects of trade. Those who favour protectionism raise a number of concerns: (1) trade leads to a loss of jobs; (2) dependence on trade makes a country vulnerable, particularly in times of war; (3) *fair* trade may be good, but foreign countries subsidize their producers, and thus trade unfairly; (4) trade imbalances make a country indebted to foreigners; and (5) weak countries can be hurt by trade. Most of these objections make little sense to economists, as we will see in the following paragraphs.

LOSS OF DOMESTIC JOBS

The Canadian economy relies very heavily on international trade. Over one-quarter of our total output is exported, and we spend over one-fifth of our income on imports from other countries. Developments in the world economy can have an important effect on Canadian industry. In recent years, our manufacturing industries have come under considerable pressure as a result of several factors. The onslaught of Japanese imported cars beginning in the mid-1970s caused a dramatic reduction in sales of North American cars. The Japanese manufacture of electronics virtually displaced the domestic manufacture of television sets and VCRs. The rapid development of the so-called Newly Industrialized Countries (NICs) of Asia has resulted in a rapid increase in the importation of low-cost consumer goods at the expense of domestic production. As well, there has been some relocation of manufacturing firms from Canada to the United States in the aftermath of the Canada-U.S. Free Trade Agreement of 1988. All of these factors have caused losses of jobs in the manufacturing sector, particularly in Ontario, many of which are feared to be permanent losses. The reaction in many circles was to advocate increased protection from foreign imports. From an economic point of view, that would be wrong.

One of the dangers in drawing analogies between individuals and countries is that countries as a whole do not actually trade or make decisions. Instead, some person or company within one country makes a beneficial trade with some person or company from another country. Perhaps a Canadian consumer buys an automobile from a Japanese company, or a Canadian pharmaceutical manufacturer makes a sale to a German company. Those making the trade are, by definition, better off, but others in the country may feel disadvantaged. A Canadian autoworker may say, "If only those Canadian consumers were buying cars from us, this company would not be losing money." Similarly, a German pharmaceutical manufacturer might say, "If only those Canadian pharmaceutical companies were forbidden to sell in Germany, then German pharmaceutical companies would benefit."

For this reason, trade between people from different countries will often create a situation in which the country as a whole is better off, but particular groups within the country may be worse off. Canadian consumers benefit greatly from being able to buy

CLOSE-UP: THE PROVINCES PROTECT BEER

Despite the fact that the Canadian Constitution gives the federal government jurisdiction over international and interprovincial trade, the provinces have effectively been able to undertake policies that protect their own producers of some products within provincial borders. Beer is a case in point. Until very recently, Ontario residents were unable to purchase Moosehead beer in Ontario, despite the fact that this Maritime brand is the most popular Canadian beer sold in the United States. The Ontario government did this by restricting distribution of beer to government-regulated outlets operated by the Ontario breweries, and these outlets only sold beer brewed in Ontario plants. Other provinces with breweries accomplished the same thing by other means, such as by selling the beer in provincially owned retail stores. The effect of this was not only to restrict the number of brands available, but also to increase the cost of beer to the consumer and to induce inefficient methods of production. Thus, the major breweries were forced to operate small-scale plants in many provinces rather than concentrating their efforts in larger plants that could produce at lower costs.

The signing of the Canada–U.S. Free Trade Agreement in 1988 signalled the beginning of the end of this form of protection of the Canadian breweries. The practice has also been found to be in contravention of the General Agreement on Tariffs and Trade (GATT), which establishes rules of conduct for international trade with most other countries in the world. Provinces such as Ontario were forced to admit imported beer for sale in order to comply with these rules. They have begun to do so only gradually, recognizing that large-scale producers in the United States could under-

Some record history. We bottle it.

price inefficient Canadian producers by a considerable margin, at least until the latter have a chance to rationalize their operations.

In fact, the provinces have found other ways to provide implicit protection to domestic breweries. In Ontario, a significant "handling" charge was imposed on imported beers. As well, a large "environmental tax" was imposed on beer cans and not on beer bottles (and not on soft-drink cans either). Since beer imported from the United States tends to be canned rather than bottled, this effectively imposed a differential cost on imported beer. (It also incidentally hurt Ontario can producers.) More recently, the Ontario government has imposed a "minimum price" on beer, allegedly for social reasons. This also tends to eliminate the cost advantage of imported beer.

As is often the case, entrepreneurs will find ways to skirt regulations that artificially keep prices high. In Ontario, firms have sprung up in most cities that specialize in assisting consumers to brew their own beer. Not only can this be done at relatively low cost, it can also avoid the punitive taxes imposed on alcoholic beverages by the federal and provincial governments.

quality imported products at a good price. Many Canadian workers benefit because their companies export products abroad. But certain industries within the country that are facing stiffer competition may be hurt. And when companies are struggling and people are losing their jobs, those who are suffering will get a lot of attention. Nevertheless, while trade costs some workers their jobs, it creates jobs for others. Beyond that, consumers benefit because trade enables them to buy those goods that foreigners can make less expensively and better than Canadians can.

When economic circumstances change, it may be desirable for the government to help those in industries that have been hurt by imports to get jobs in other sectors of the economy, and to provide them support during the transition process. Government assistance may be particularly valuable when jobs are lost in import-competing industries faster than jobs are created in export industries. Several countries (including Canada) have programs to provide such assistance. By its nature such assistance is temporary rather than permanent as in the case of protective tariffs.

Canada's economic dealings with the rest of the world go far beyond trade in goods and services, however. We import and export capital on international financial markets. As well, labour moves into and out of the country by immigration and emigration. Protective sentiments arise in these contexts as well, but they are of a different form.

The Canadian economy has developed largely through the use of foreign capital. In the nineteenth century and the early part of the twentieth century, much of the investment took the form of borrowing (portfolio investment), particularly from the United Kingdom. The capital was needed to finance the costly infrastructure required to establish a transportation system as well as to develop the capital-intensive resource industries. As time has passed, the source of foreign capital gradually has changed from the United Kingdom to the United States. And more important, the form has changed to direct investment, that is, the establishment of subsidiaries and branch plants of American firms in Canada. Unlike portfolio investment, however, direct investment carries with it control of the company. This has given rise to a considerable amount of concern in Canada that management decisions in Canada will be made by those abroad and that desirable forms of employment, such as in research and development, will be retained in the home country rather than in the country of the subsidiary. Nonetheless, foreign direct investment also brings with it a number of benefits. The capital it brings creates job opportunities that might otherwise not exist and thereby improves the wages and working conditions of those involved. Some of these job opportunities include managerial ones. It brings forms of technology that would otherwise be available only elsewhere, thus contributing to the growth and productivity of the Canadian economy. Since foreign investment tends to be done by corporations that operate worldwide **(multinational corporations),** these corporations are in a good position to see to it that goods are produced in accordance with the comparative advantages of the countries involved. Thus, they help exploit the nation's gains from trade. Nonetheless, the control of foreign investment remains an important issue in economic policy; we will return to it later in the book.

The effect that immigration has on Canadian jobs has also played an important role in shaping immigration policy. Many immigrants are unskilled. Because they are willing to take low-wage jobs, wages in those jobs can stay low. The lower wages mean that consumers can buy goods and services such as food products and transportation at lower prices. The country as a whole thus benefits. The immigrants also benefit; after all, though the wages are low by Canadian standards, they are very high in comparison with the wages these workers would earn in their own countries. But low-skilled Canadian workers who are in direct competition with the immigrants lose. Thus, there is considerable public pressure to restrict immigration to those who would take jobs where shortages of workers exist.

VULNERABILITY

Another objection to free trade has to do with the vulnerability of a nation that depends on other nations for critical resources. Countries should treasure their independence, critics argue, and this requires a degree of self-sufficiency. There is some merit to this line of reasoning, although not as much as the special interests who seek trade protection would have us believe.

Some open economies, especially less-developed ones, are heavily dependent on the production of a small number of commodities, especially primary products such as an agricultural product or a mineral resource. Since the prices of these products can fluctuate widely, the fortunes of the economy are subject to considerable risk. This risk can be avoided by diversification. This argument does not apply with much force to Canada as a whole, but some provincial economies are quite dependent on a small number of commodities (e.g., wheat in Saskatchewan, fish in Newfoundland, timber in British Columbia). It would make little economic sense for each province to try to become more self-sufficient. These provinces obtain the benefits from the national economy being diversified. The risks of a downturn in the wheat market are spread across the country by federal transfer programs as well as by the free movement of labour and capital.

A more fundamental concern includes the shifting away from manufacturing and certain high-technology fields to traditional resource-based activities and to the growing service sector, including financial services, education, and health. Were Canada to become involved in a war, unless it maintains a technological capability in these areas, it could be at a marked disadvantage in producing steel, tanks, and ships. But antitrade proposals couched in terms of vulnerability should be eyed with caution. The costs of maintaining complete self-sufficiency are enormous, partly because they require forgoing the mutual benefits of trade. Maintaining the country's technological capabilities for defence purposes usually does not require the abandonment of trade.

UNFAIR TRADE

Another objection to trade holds that foreign governments subsidize their producers, and thus compete unfairly. If foreign governments subsidized their products continually, then there would be no problem. After all, if the Japanese government wants to provide an endless parade of subsidized products for Canadian consumers, enabling them to buy those goods more cheaply than they otherwise could, why should the Canadian government complain? More difficult issues arise if one believes that the subsidies are temporary, and will only persist long enough to drive Canadian producers from desirable markets. After forcing out the Canadian competition, foreign firms will be in a position to exploit Canadian consumers by charging higher prices. This argument makes theoretical sense, but in most industries, competition among the several foreign and Canadian firms is sufficiently keen that it does not appear to be a serious threat in practice.

INDEBTEDNESS

Historically, Canada has exported more goods than it imported, that is, it has had a **trade surplus.** At the same time, the imports of services exceed exports, giving rise to a deficit on what is called the **invisible account.** The relative size of imports and exports of both goods and services can be seen in Figure 3.5. This figure shows that the balance between exports and imports has varied considerably over the years. The large trade surpluses of the 1980s have given way to **trade deficits** in the 1990s, reflecting in part the effects of the worldwide recession.

Exports and imports are not the only transactions that occur between Canadians and the rest of the world, however. Canada receives far less investment income from the rest of the world than it pays out (primarily interest and dividends). The combination of the merchandise trade, invisible, and investment accounts makes up the **current account** of the Canadian **balance of payments.** (The balance of payments summarizes transactions of all types between Canadians and the rest of the world—payments by foreigners to Canadians less payments by Canadians to foreigners.) Given the above facts, the current account is in substantial deficit and has been since 1985. The deficit on the current account is offset by net borrowing from abroad, that is, by a **capital account surplus.** In other words, Canada is becoming more indebted to the rest of the world. Close to 5 percent of domestic income is now devoted to servicing the debt owed to foreigners. In other words, with an average per capita GDP of about $25,000 in the 1990s, every person in the country would, on average, be sending a check for $1,250 abroad every year *just to pay the interest.*

But to blame foreigners for Canada's current-account deficit is a bit like blaming the owner of a candy store for the stomachache that results from eating too much candy. The problem, as will be explained in later chapters, is that over the past several years Canada has spent more than it has produced, not that nasty foreigners are snookering virtuous Canadians. Furthermore, to the extent that the excess spending represented investment financed by foreign capital, that investment itself should be yielding a return great enough to cover the cost involved in repaying foreigners. In any case, the deficit cannot be used as an argument for discriminating against foreigners.

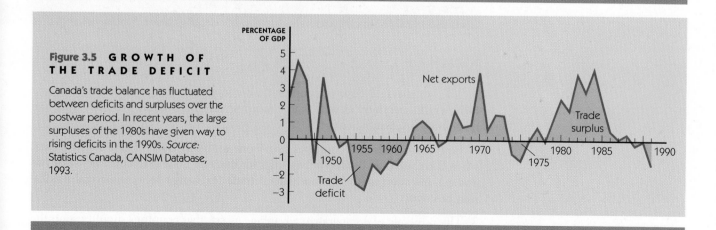

Figure 3.5 GROWTH OF THE TRADE DEFICIT

Canada's trade balance has fluctuated between deficits and surpluses over the postwar period. In recent years, the large surpluses of the 1980s have given way to rising deficits in the 1990s. *Source:* Statistics Canada, CANSIM Database, 1993.

WEAK COUNTRIES HURT BY TRADE

The final objection to trade is that poorer countries are exploited by richer countries, and therefore they should protect themselves. Again, this political rhetoric misses the basic point of trade: both sides gain from exchanges that are entered into voluntarily. The relative strength of the trading partners may determine how the mutual gains from trade are shared. The weaker trading partner may wind up just a little bit better off than it was without trade, with most of the advantages of trade reaped by the stronger partner. This may seem unfair, but it does not contradict the result that both sides gain.

This conclusion, however, is predicated on the assumption that countries rationally pursue their self-interest in making their decisions to trade, and that they take into account the long-term consequences. Weaker nations may not be so farsighted, particularly if those who are making the trading decisions do not adequately reflect the interests of the country. In the long run, for instance, Brazil may not be better off cutting down its rain forests because it will take generations to replace the trees. Wealthy landowners might view it as privately profitable to sell their trees, knowing there is a good chance that within a decade or two the government may seize the land from them.

WHY PROTECTIONISM SURVIVES

Given all of these seemingly persuasive arguments against protectionism, why does it have such a popular appeal? Why have almost all countries enacted trade restrictions? The answer is simple. While the country as a whole may benefit from trade, particular groups may be hurt. Because the gainers gain more than the losers lose, the gainers could, in principle, compensate the losers. This seldom happens, however. The gains to society come in the form of a slight reduction in the prices consumers pay. But the losses—the lower wages and lost jobs that result in industries facing competition—are often more visible than the gains. Unless people who suffer such losses receive some compensation, they will fight free trade.

REVIEW AND PRACTICE

SUMMARY

1. The benefits and costs of economic interdependence apply to individuals and firms within a country as well as to countries within the world. No individual and no country is self-sufficient.

2. Both individuals and countries gain from voluntary trade. There may be cases when there are only limited possibilities for bilateral trade (exchange between two parties), but the gains from multilateral trade (exchange between several parties) may be great.

3. The principle of comparative advantage asserts that countries should export the goods in which their production costs are *relatively* low.

4. Specialization tends to increase productivity for three reasons: specializing avoids the time it takes a worker to switch from one production task to another; workers who repeat a task become more skilled at it; specialization creates a fertile environment for invention.

5. A country's comparative advantage can arise from natural endowments, or as a result of acquired endowments, superior knowledge, or specialization.

6. Those who favour protectionism say that trade leads to a loss of domestic jobs, makes a country vulnerable, gives foreign nations the chance to trade unfairly, creates foreign debt, and hurts weak countries. Most of these objections are of doubtful validity, and even when there is some truth to the problem, protectionist policies are usually a costly and inappropriate response.

KEY TERMS

gains from trade	comparative advan-	trade surplus
imports	tage	invisible account
exports	natural endowments	current account
bilateral trade	acquired endowments	balance of payments
multilateral trade	protectionism	capital account sur-
absolute advantage	trade deficit	plus

REVIEW QUESTIONS

1. Why are all voluntary trades mutually beneficial?

2. Describe a situation (hypothetical, if need be) where bilateral trade does not work, but multilateral trade is possible.

3. What are some of the similarities of trade between individuals and trade between countries? What is a key way in which they differ?

4. Does a country with an absolute advantage in a product necessarily have a comparative advantage in that product? Does a country with an absolute disadvantage in a product necessarily not have a comparative advantage in that product? Explain.

5. Does specialization tend to increase or decrease productivity? Explain.

6. "A country's comparative advantage is dictated by its natural endowments." Discuss.

7. "If trade with a foreign country injures anyone in this country, the government should react by passing protectionist laws to limit or stop that particular trade." Comment.

PROBLEMS

1. Four players on a Bantam hockey team discover that they have each been collecting hockey cards, and they agree to get together and trade. Is it possible for

everyone to benefit from this agreement? Does the fact that one player starts off with many more cards than any of the others affect your answer?

2. Leaders in many less-developed countries of Latin America and Africa have often argued that because they are so much poorer than the wealthy nations of the world, trade with the more-developed economies of North America and Europe will injure them. They maintain that they must first become self-sufficient before they can benefit from trade. How might an economist respond to these claims?

3. If Canada changes its immigration quotas to allow many more unskilled workers into the country, who is likely to gain? Who is likely to lose? Consider the impact on consumers, on businesses that hire low-skilled labour, and on low-skilled labour in both Canada and the workers' countries of origin.

4. David Ricardo illustrated the principle of comparative advantage in terms of the trade between England and Portugal in wine and wool. Suppose that in England it takes 120 labourers to produce a certain quantity of wine, while in Portugal it takes only 80 labourers to produce that same quantity. Similarly, in England it takes 100 labourers to produce a certain quantity of wool, while in Portugal it takes only 90. Draw the opportunity set for each country, assuming that each has 72,000 labourers. Assume that each country commits half its labour to each product in the absence of trade, and designate that point on your graph. Now describe a new production plan, with trade, that can benefit both countries.

5. In 1981, the Canadian government prodded Japanese automakers to limit the number of cars they would export to Canada. Who benefited from this protectionism in Canada and in Japan? Who was injured in Canada and in Japan? Consider companies that produce cars (and their workers) and consumers who buy cars.

6. For many years, an international agreement called the Multifiber Agreement has limited the amount of textiles that the developed economies of North America and Europe can buy from poor countries in Latin America and Asia. Textiles can be produced by relatively unskilled labour with a reasonably small amount of capital. Who benefits from the protectionism of the Multifiber Agreement, and who suffers?

APPENDIX: ORGANIZATIONS AND THE REAL COSTS OF INTERDEPENDENCE

Almost everyone has reflected at one time or another that life would be simpler if we did not have to depend on others. Emerging from their reveries, however, most individuals decide that the gains from interdependence exceed the costs; so too in the realm of economics.

Many of the problems of economic interdependence are similar to those that arise in daily life. You rely on someone to pick you up at a particular time to go to a concert. He is late, and you find that the tickets are sold out. Two friends are trying to decide how to spend the day. One wants to go biking, the other hiking. There are conflicts that have to be resolved. Two couples want to go on summer vacation together, but they find it difficult coordinating their schedules. Think of the time it takes for a group of more than five people to decide on what restaurant to go to or what movie to see!

Individuals who specialize in doing what they have a comparative advantage in have to rely on others for everything else. The frustrations of interdependence often make one recall the old adage "If you want anything done right, do it yourself." Someone you hire to do a task for you seldom has the incentive to do it with the care that you would exercise.

Beyond misplaced incentives, economic interdependence also introduces problems of communication and coordination, of selecting individuals to perform different tasks, and of collective decision making. In our economy, these problems are addressed in a variety of ways. Each has its costs. Much of this book will discuss how the price system provides appropriate incentives, how it communicates information about scarcity, how it guides individuals and countries in their choices of specializations, and how it serves to coordinate economic activity.

Even the price system has its costs, however. When a firm wants to buy some input, it has two alternatives. For example, when Ford needed steel, it could have bought the steel from another firm or it could have produced the steel itself. In the first case, we say that the firm is using the market. But there are costs involved. The steel producers have to hire salespeople and set prices. Ford would have to hire buyers to search among alternative suppliers and to negotiate the best price. The costs of engaging in transactions are called, quite naturally, **transactions costs.** In some markets, transactions costs may be quite high, motivating firms to produce the goods they need themselves. Thus, Ford decided to produce its own steel. Or to take another example, a large builder may employ plumbers, electricians, and carpenters directly rather than buying these services from other firms. These workers' activities are then controlled not by prices, primarily, but by the orders of the firm's managers. Within organizations, managers, not markets, take on the role of coordinating the workers and supervising them to make sure that they work hard.

There are real costs associated with addressing such problems, whether within organizations or markets; and while the benefits of economic interdependence far outweigh the costs, it is important to bear these costs in mind. When we think about technological progress, we often have a picture of lasers and transistors, computers and VCRs. No less important for the economy, however, have been those advances that have reduced the costs of economic interdependence and allowed markets and organizations to function more efficiently.

FOUR ECONOMIC PROBLEMS WITHIN ORGANIZATIONS

Most production takes place inside organizations; in fact over one-fourth of Canadian manufacturing takes place inside the fifty largest manufacturing corporations. Most consumption takes place in households, which can be viewed as small organizations. Local, provincial, and federal governments are nothing more than large organizations. In fact, the whole economy can be thought of as an organization—an organization made up of smaller organizations. The following sections explore four common economic problems that these different kinds of organizations face.

INCENTIVES

When you do something for yourself, you know the costs (both in materials and effort) and the benefits. If you own a car and you get a thrill out of screeching the tires, both the benefit (the feeling of going fast) and the cost (the wear and tear on the tires) are yours to consider. Because you reap the benefits and pay the costs yourself, you have the right economic incentives: you only burn rubber if the benefits exceed the costs. However, the teenager driving the family car may be able to enjoy the benefits while letting her parents pay the costs. As this simple example illustrates, *whenever costs and benefits do not accrue to the same person, there is an incentive problem.*

Incentive problems arise in every economic organization, from families to households to government, because the interests of the individual and those of the organization are rarely identical. People must be motivated to exert effort and do high-quality work. But many workers are paid an agreed-upon salary. Even when a company makes an attempt to link pay to overall levels of performance, there is no close connection between any particular action and the worker's pay. A sales representative may know that if he drives a company car too hard, it will shorten the life of the car; but he may enjoy driving it hard, and doing so will enable him to get his job done more quickly and get home to watch his favourite TV show. The sales representative has no incentive to take care of the car. He knows that his supervisor has no way to tell whether he drove the car too hard; even if the car actually breaks down while he is hot-rodding, it will be almost impossible to tell whether it was his fault or a mechanical defect in the car.

There is an obvious solution to this incentive problem—make the salesperson provide his own car. But many incentive problems do not have such an easy answer. A store's employee may know that if all the windows of the store are not double-locked, the probability of a break-in increases. But it takes effort to go around to check whether they are locked, and the employee may feel he has no incentive to exert that effort. Even the owner herself may not exert much effort if she has purchased insurance against burglary for the store.

Those in decision-making positions must also be motivated to make good decisions, decisions that benefit not just themselves but the organization. The retiring manager of a firm may know that one of two candidates for the job as his successor is better than the other; but it may require some effort to convince the others who are involved in the decision. Since the manager is retiring, there may not be a sufficient incentive to induce him to exert that effort.

In Chapter 2, we learned that prices play a central role in providing incentives in market economies. Within organizations, prices rarely play this role. The Production Department does not pay the Personnel Department for its services. One manager does not charge another for the value of her time used in a consultation on whether to go ahead on a project. When the manager of a division calls a meeting, she often does not weigh carefully the opportunity cost of those attending the meeting—what their time is worth on other tasks. Finding substitutes for prices as the basis of incentives is a key problem within many organizations.

COMMUNICATION AND COORDINATION

When you are on your own, you do not have to communicate with anyone; you do not have to coordinate what you do with anyone else. But as soon as there is economic interdependence, communication and coordination become extremely important—and there are considerable costs involved, both in communicating and coordinating and in failing to communicate and coordinate.

Communication and coordination are essential in any team play, if each individual is to do his part. Any organization can be viewed as a team. Information is divided and dispersed throughout the divisions of the firm, and throughout the people in those divisions. If the organization is to get its job done, there has to be communication and coordination. Individuals within the organization must have incentives to communicate essential information.

A dramatic example where information was not collected and communicated properly was the explosion of the space shuttle *Challenger* in 1987, which killed the seven astronauts aboard. The source of the problem turned out to be a defective "O-ring," which performed badly in the low temperatures that Florida was experiencing at the time of the launch. Some of the engineers had had concerns about the O-ring, but the managers to whom they communicated their concerns did not pay attention. The managers' concern was to get the project done on schedule.

After the tragedy, the concerns of the engineers finally reached the ears of the late physicist Richard Feynman, who was part of a committee appointed to investigate the disaster. In a simple but dramatic experiment, Feynman dropped the O-ring in a glass of ice water and pointed out that it became less flexible. The failure to incorporate such simple but vital information was an obvious organizational failure. Those building the space shuttle had had insufficient incentives to obtain the requisite information, and indeed were motivated to press ahead without the vital information.

SELECTION

When an individual is on her own, not only does she avoid the costs of communication and coordination, she also avoids the costs of deciding who should do what tasks. She does everything herself!

We saw earlier that there are gains from specialization, and that it pays to have individuals do the tasks for which they have a comparative advantage. But knowing what is each individual's comparative advantage is no easy matter. A central problem facing any organization is deciding whom to hire, whom to assign to what job, whom to promote to the company presidency, and whom to fire.

STRUCTURING DECISION MAKING

All organizations must make decisions, just as individuals do. Organizations have to decide what to produce and how to produce it, and what investment projects to undertake. It used to be thought that decision making could be reduced to a simple formula: decide on your objectives; find out what the alternative possible actions are; ascertain the consequences of each action; evaluate the extent to which each action meets your goals; and choose the action that most clearly meets your objective. Life, unfortunately, is not so simple.

This formula may actually do more to reveal the problems of decision making than to solve them. In most organizations, different individuals may have different objectives. Even when they agree on the firm's objectives, such as maximizing its profits, they may disagree about the best way of accomplishing these objectives. They may disagree because of different information or different beliefs about the consequences of certain policies.

In the final analysis, individual interests and those of the organization may not precisely coincide. The manager of one division may truly believe that the best way for the firm to make money is to expand his division, but it surely does not escape his attention that if his division is expanded, his status within the firm and probably his salary will also increase.

Even after the event, it is often difficult to judge whether a decision made was the correct one, and whether it was made for the right reason. With the perspective of twenty-twenty hindsight, we can say that a wrong (or a right) decision was made. The investors in Henry Ford's first two enterprises undertook great risks, for which they never received a return. In the 1960s, the managers of North American automobile firms had to forecast what kinds of cars consumers would want in the 1970s. They predicted that consumers would continue to want big cars. In both of these cases, wrong decisions were made. But relying on the benefits of hindsight is not fair. The real question is whether those making the decisions gathered the necessary amount of information, and whether their decisions were appropriate given the information that was available to them at the time.

Thus, a central problem facing all organizations is how to structure decision making. All organizations face a general choice between **centralized systems,** where a lot of control is vested in those at the top, and **decentralized systems,** where considerable discretion remains with subordinates. In the former Soviet Union, a single government ministry decided on how much steel each steel mill should produce. Economic decisions in that country were highly centralized. By contrast, in Canada, these decisions are made by many different firms.

Centralized systems are sometimes better than decentralized ones for making substantial changes, but such changes can turn out to be big mistakes as well as successes. When Communist China, under the direction of Mao Tse-tung, decided that more land should be converted from growing rice to growing wheat, the economy responded quickly, with disastrous consequences. Land that was ill-suited for wheat was converted, erosion set in, and by the time the decision was reversed, some of the land had been largely ruined—not even rice could be grown on it.

Centralized systems also have greater problems of collecting information and providing incentives to all the members of the organization. The economic ills that plagued the centralized economy of the former USSR were largely attributed to the country's failure to provide incentives, to its inability to elicit information about what was going on in the economy, and to its consequent inability to coordinate economic activity. For instance, hospitals wanting to give an impression of their effectiveness had an incentive *not* to report the number of babies that died. And schools had an incentive to overreport the number of children in attendance, so they would get bigger budgets. As a result, phantom children passed through the school system. It was not until these children were drafted into the military—and failed to report for duty—that the mistakes became evident. Thus, the inaccuracy of Soviet statistics on population (as in other areas) was not just a matter of distortions by the leaders at the top. The information on which those statistics were compiled, supplied by those beneath, was simply inaccurate. Worse still, the system provided incentives for inaccurate reporting.

The issue of centralization versus decentralization also arises within firms. Many companies have several divisions, each of which operates almost autonomously, with only general oversight provided by the central headquarters. Some firms, such as Hewlett-Packard (a major U.S. computer and high-tech electronics firm with a wholly owned subsidiary in Canada), decentralize even further, allowing a large number of project managers to decide for themselves what research projects to pursue.

There are several advantages to decentralization: firms can respond quickly to current conditions, avoid the bureaucracies almost always associated with centralized control, and provide greater incentives and motivation by allowing more employees to participate in decision making. Advocates of centralization, on the other hand, cite the advantages of the stronger sense of control, which at times (such as war) may allow the organization to respond more quickly, and the greater ability to coordinate. Whether or not this greater sense of control, ability to respond quickly, and ability to coordinate are illusory remains controversial. While those at the top might be able to control matters better *if* they had all the information that those under them have, they never do have all such information, and this puts them at a disadvantage.

Of course, when, say, a manager delegates responsibility to a subordinate, the subordinate may not do exactly what the manager would have done in that situation; she may make a mistake (though the manager too may have made a mistake). The possibility of mistaken judgments drives many organizations to try to retain more central control. But again, there are trade-offs. Mistakes will occur under any system. And the subordinate may have more of the detailed information required to make a good decision; she may see more of what goes on in the workplace than the manager, who cannot be everywhere at once. The manager may indeed make better decisions when he has the requisite information and time. But as we saw earlier, there are advantages to specialization; it pays him to spend his time making the bigger decisions. The manager needs to stick to his comparative advantage too.

Direct versus Indirect Control   Issues of centralization and decentralization are closely related to issues of *how* control is exercised. When one individual attempts to affect or control the behaviour of another individual by "ordering" her to do something, with an implicit or explicit threat of dire consequences if the order is not followed, he is using a direct control mechanism. Many politicians have argued that the government should control automobile pollution by issuing regulations. Some old-style management textbooks suggested that the managers of a firm should decide what they want, and then order their employees to carry out those decisions.

But economists argue that better results are often obtained by using incentive systems as indirect control mechanisms, where individuals are *motivated* to act in the desired manner by the rewards they receive from doing so, rather than as a result of being told or ordered to do something. Noneconomists frequently fail to recognize the power of indirect control mechanisms, of incentives, and of the limitations of direct control.

Imperfect and Costly Information   If information were perfect—complete and accurate—problems of how to allocate resources would be relatively easy to solve. If consumers had perfect information, they would know the prices of each seller's products, all the characteristics of each product, and thus whether a price was lower because the product was shoddier or simply because it was a better deal. Firms would know precisely what the skills of every employee were, so that each could be assigned to an appropriate job. But information is imperfect—less than complete and accurate—and costly to acquire. It is, for instance, costly, even to administer tests that give only an imperfect assessment of each worker's skills.

All four of the organizational problems named above can be viewed as largely resulting from the fact that information is imperfect and costly. Even the problem of incentives is essentially an information problem. If an employer could costlessly observe everything the worker does, and if he could easily ascertain what it is that the worker should do, then he would simply tell the worker what to do and pay her if and only if she complied. The questions of communication and coordination are quite clearly information problems; how to convey, for instance, information about the scarcity, measured by their opportunity costs, of the various raw materials used in production. If an employer had perfect (complete and accurate) information about the skills of a worker as well as the characteristics making for success on the job, the selection problem would be trivial.

Finally, if all decision makers had perfect information concerning the consequences of their decisions, decision making would be a relatively easy matter. But they have imperfect and often contradicting information, and different decision makers come to different conclusions about the desirability of a project. These information problems are at the core of understanding how economics and economic organizations function. As a result, the "economics of information" has become one of the most active areas of research in economics during the past two decades.

ECONOMIC ORGANIZATION AND POLITICAL FREEDOM

There is a widespread feeling that there is a relationship between the economic and the political organization of a society. Totalitarian regimes, such as the former Soviet Union under Stalin, centralized economic as well as political power at the top. They restricted the rights of individuals to engage in economic activities just as they restricted people's political rights.

Among the former Soviet bloc economies during the 1980s, there was growing recognition of the importance of increased economic decentralization if these economies were to improve their dismal records. Finally, at the end of the decade, these countries openly embraced the idea of a market economy. The notion that any central authority could run an economy efficiently was abandoned. With these economic changes has come a further benefit: the rights to make economic decisions, to enter a business, to make a new product, to hire workers, have been accompanied by greater political rights.

Today in Canada and the other industrialized democracies, there is a widespread consensus in favour of the mixed economy, where government's economic power is limited. But even given this consensus, there is considerable debate over precisely what role the government should take. Frequently concerns have been raised that a particular government program would represent an unreasonable aggrandizement of power on the part of the government. The debate over the role of the government in providing medical services is one example, though there is little evidence that countries in which the government dominates the medical sector, including Canada, are any less democratic on that account. In the discussions of economic policy in this book, we will focus our attention more narrowly on economic costs and benefits, but many of the policy controversies touch on broader issues—such as the consequences for the Canadian political system.

4

DEMAND, SUPPLY, AND PRICES

E conomics, as we have seen, is concerned with choice in the face of scarcity. This chapter is about prices. **Price** is defined as what is given in exchange for a good or a service. When the forces of supply and demand are permitted to operate freely, price measures scarcity. As such, prices are a thing of beauty to economists, for they convey critical economic information. When the price of a resource used by a firm is high, the company has a greater incentive to economize on its use. When the price of a good that the firm produces is high, the company has a greater incentive to produce more of that good, and its customers have an incentive to economize on its use. In these ways and others, prices provide our economy with incentives to use scarce resources efficiently.

K E Y   Q U E S T I O N S

1. What is meant by demand? Why do demand curves normally slope downwards? On what variables, other than price, does the quantity demanded depend?

2. What is meant by supply? Why do supply curves normally slope upwards? On what variables, other than price, does the quantity supplied depend?

3. Why do economists say that the equilibrium price occurs at the intersection of the demand and supply curves?

4. How do shifts in the demand and supply curves affect the equilibrium price?

THE ROLE OF PRICES

Prices are the way that the participants in the economy communicate with one another. Assume a drought hits the country, reducing drastically the supply of corn. Households will consequently need to reduce their consumption of corn. But how will they know this? Suppose newspapers across the country ran an article informing people that they would have to eat less corn. Would it be read? If so, would people pay attention to it? Why should they? What incentive do they have? How would each family know how much it ought to reduce its consumption? As an alternative to the newspaper, consider the effect of an increase in the price of corn. The higher price quickly and effectively conveys all of the relevant information. Households do not need to know why the price is high. They do not need to know the details of the drought. All they need to know is that there is a greater scarcity of corn, and that they would be wise to reduce their consumption. The higher price tells them that corn is scarce at the same time that it encourages families to consume less of it.

Prices present interesting problems and puzzles. In the late 1980s, while the price of an average house in Toronto went up by over 20 percent, the price of a house in Regina increased by only about 2 percent. Why? During the same period, the price of computers fell dramatically, while the price of bread rose, but at a much slower rate than the price of housing in Toronto. Why? The "price" of labour is just the wage or salary that is paid. Why does a physician earn twice as much as a university professor, though the university professor may have performed better in the university courses they took together? Why do women, on average, earn two-thirds the amount that men do? Why did average wage rates rise in Canada in the postwar period? Why is the price of bread, which provides some of the essential nutrients of life, very low in most cases, but the price of diamonds, which we can surely live without, very high? The simple answer to all of these questions is that in market economies like that of Canada, price is determined by supply and demand. Changes in prices are determined by changes in supply and demand.

Noneconomists see much more in prices than the impersonal forces of supply and demand. One of the events that precipitated the French Revolution was the rise in the price of bread, for which the people blamed the government. More recently, large price changes have given rise to political turmoil in several countries, including Morocco, the Dominican Republic, Russia, and Poland.

On a personal level, individuals tend to blame the owner of an enterprise for the higher prices he charges. It was the landlord who raised the rent on the apartment; it was the oil company or the owner of the gas station who raised the price of gasoline; it was the owner of the movie theatre or movie studio who raised the price of the movie tickets. These people and companies *chose* to raise their prices, says the noneconomist, in moral indignation. True, replies the economist, but there must be a reason why they decided to raise their prices at this particular time. After all, it is not plausible to say that the landlord or the oil company or the movie theatre just had a brainstorm one day and decided to charge more. There must be some factor that made these people and companies believe that a higher price was not a good idea yesterday, but is today.

When all the gas stations in a province or all the landlords in a town start charging roughly the same amount more at the same time, economists argue that there must be a reason. And economists point out that at a different time, these same impersonal forces often oblige these same landlords and oil companies and movie theatres to cut their prices. Economists see prices, then, as symptoms of underlying causes, and they encourage those who are outraged by higher prices to focus on the forces of supply and demand behind the price changes.

DEMAND

Economists use the concept of **demand** to describe the quantity of a good or service that a household or firm chooses to buy at a given price. It is important to understand that economists are concerned not just with what people desire, but with what they choose to buy given the spending limits imposed by their budget constraint and given the prices of various goods. Of course, the total demand for a good in the economy depends on more than price. Demand for a product at any price may change with the population (more babies result in a higher demand for diapers) or with the style (demand for miniskirts changes over the years) or with broad social trends (Canadians drink more wine and less whiskey now than they did several decades ago).

If analyzing demand meant analyzing all the possible influences on the demand for all possible products, the job of economists would be hopelessly complex. Economists deal with this problem of complexity and multiple factors by focusing on one variable at a time, while keeping all of the other factors fixed. They focus their attention particularly on factors that are most important in causing *changes* in demand. Of these, the factor that receives the most attention is price. When other changes are important, such as changes in people's income or the structure of the population, then economists take these changes, as well as the effect of these changes on prices, into account.

THE INDIVIDUAL DEMAND CURVE

Think about what happens as the price of candy bars changes. At a price of $5.00, you might never buy one. At $3.00, you might buy one as a special treat. At $1.25, you might buy a few, and if somehow the price declined to $.50, you might buy a lot. Table 4.1 summarizes the weekly demand of one individual, Roger, for candy bars at these different prices. We can see that the lower the price, the larger the quantity demanded.

We can also summarize the information in this table in a graph that shows the quantity Roger demands at each price. By convention, the quantity demanded is measured along the horizontal axis, and the price is measured along the vertical axis. Figure 4.1 plots the points in Table 4.1.

A smooth curve can be drawn to connect the points. This curve is called the **demand curve.** The demand curve gives the quantity demanded at each price. Thus, if we want to know how many candy bars a week Roger will demand at a price of $1.00, we simply look along the vertical axis at the price $1.00, find the corresponding point A along the demand curve, and then read down to the horizontal axis. At a price of $1.00, Roger buys 6 candy bars each week. Alternatively, if we want to know at what price he will buy just 3 candy bars, we look along the horizontal axis at the quantity 3, find the corresponding point B along the demand curve, and then read across to the vertical axis. Roger will buy 3 candy bars at a price of $1.50.

The fact that as the price of candy bars increases the quantity demanded decreases can be seen in Table 4.1, or from the fact that the demand curve in Figure 4.1 slopes downwards from left to right. This relationship is typical of most demand curves, and it makes common sense: the cheaper a good is (the lower down we look on the vertical axis), the more of it a person will buy (the farther right on the horizontal axis); the more expensive, the less a person will buy.

Table 4.1 ROGER'S DEMAND FOR CANDY BARS AT VARIOUS PRICES

Price	Quantity demanded
$5.00	0
$3.00	1
$2.00	2
$1.50	3
$1.25	4
$1.00	6
$ .75	9
$ .50	15

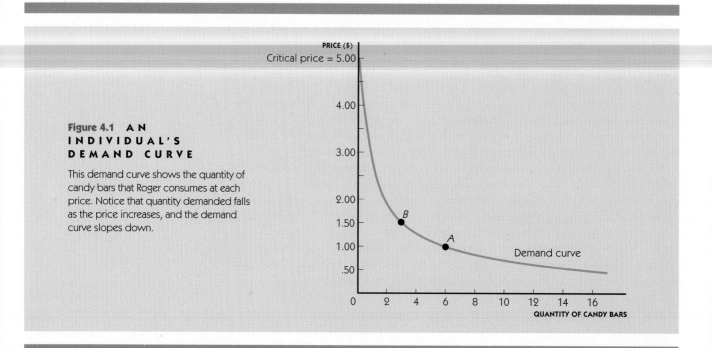

Figure 4.1 AN INDIVIDUAL'S DEMAND CURVE

This demand curve shows the quantity of candy bars that Roger consumes at each price. Notice that quantity demanded falls as the price increases, and the demand curve slopes down.

DEMAND CURVE

The demand curve gives the quantity of the good demanded at each price.

THE MARKET DEMAND CURVE

Table 4.1 gave the quantity of candy bars Roger demanded each week at various prices, while Figure 4.1 presented his demand curve. Table 4.2 gives the total quantity of candy bars demanded by everybody in the economy at various prices. If we had a table like Table 4.1 for each person in the economy, we would construct Table 4.2 simply by adding up, at each price, the total quantity of candy bars purchased. Table 4.2 tells us, for instance, that at a price of $3.00 per candy bar, the total market demand for candy bars is .1 million candy bars, and that lowering the price to $2.00 increases market demand to .3 million candy bars.

Figure 4.2 depicts in a graph the information from Table 4.2. As with Figure 4.1, price lies along the vertical axis, but now the horizontal axis measures the quantity demanded by everyone in the economy. Joining the points in the figure together, we get

Table 4.2 TOTAL MARKET DEMAND FOR CANDY BARS AT VARIOUS PRICES

Price	Quantity demanded (millions)
$5.00	0
$3.00	.1
$2.00	.3
$1.50	.4
$1.25	.8
$1.00	1.3
$ .75	2.0
$ .50	3.0

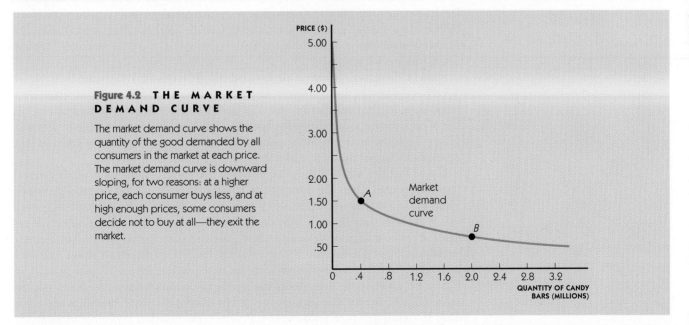

Figure 4.2 THE MARKET DEMAND CURVE

The market demand curve shows the quantity of the good demanded by all consumers in the market at each price. The market demand curve is downward sloping, for two reasons: at a higher price, each consumer buys less, and at high enough prices, some consumers decide not to buy at all—they exit the market.

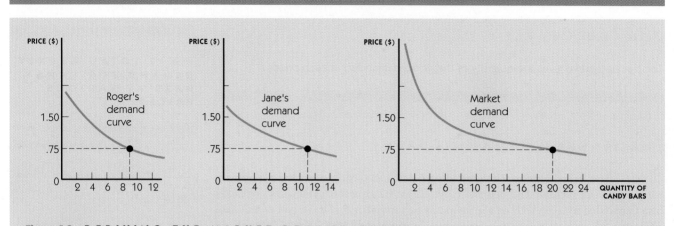

Figure 4.3 DERIVING THE MARKET DEMAND CURVE

The market demand curve is constructed by adding up, at each price, the total of the quantities consumed by each individual. It shows what market demand would be if there were only two consumers. Actual market demand, as depicted in Figure 4.2, is much larger because there are many consumers.

the **market demand curve.** The market demand curve gives the total quantity demanded by all individuals. For instance, if we want to know what the total demand for candy bars will be when the price is $1.50 per candy bar, we look on the vertical axis at the price $1.50, find the corresponding point A along the demand curve, and read down to the horizontal axis; at that price, total demand is .4 million candy bars. If we want to know what the price of candy bars will be when the demand equals 2 million, we find 2 million along the horizontal axis, look up to find the corresponding point B along the market demand curve, and read across to the vertical axis; the price at which 2 million candy bars are demanded is $.75.

Suppose there was a simple economy made up of two people, Roger and Jane. Figure 4.3 illustrates how to add up the demand curves of these two individuals to obtain a demand curve for the market as a whole. We "add" the demand curves horizontally by taking, at each price, the quantities demanded by Roger and by Jane and adding the two together. Thus, in the figure, at the price of $.75, Roger demands 9 candy bars and Jane demands 11, so that the total market demand is 20 candy bars.

Notice that just as when the price of candy bars increases, the individual's demand decreases, so too when the price of candy bars increases, market demand decreases. Thus, the market demand curve also slopes downwards from left to right. This general rule holds both because each individual's demand curve is downward sloping and because as prices change, some individuals will decide to enter or exit the market. We have already examined the first of these reasons, but the second deserves a closer look. At a high enough price, consumers may drop out of the market for a particular product. In Figure 4.1, for example, Roger **exits the market**—consumes a quantity of zero—at the price of $5.00, at which the demand curve hits the vertical axis. Similarly, when prices drop low enough, more consumers will **enter the market** and thus increase the demand.

SUPPLY

Economists use the concept of **supply** to describe the quantity of a good or service that a household or firm would like to sell at a particular price. They use the concept to refer to such seemingly disparate choices as the number of candy bars that firms want to sell and the number of hours that a worker is willing to work. As with demand, the quantity supplied can change according to a variety of factors. A drought can reduce the supply of farm products dramatically. A better production technique may increase the amount supplied of a product. The birth of a child may lead one parent to supply less labour, as that parent takes time off to raise the child, while the other parent may supply more. As in the case of demand, economists focus on price first, while keeping other factors like weather, technology, and so on, constant for the moment.

Table 4.3 shows the number of candy bars that the Melt-in-the-Mouth Chocolate Company would like to sell, or supply to the market, at each price. Below $1.00, the firm finds it unprofitable to produce. At $2.00, it would like to sell 85,000 candy bars. As the price rises, so does the quantity supplied—at $5.00, the firm would like to sell 100,000.

Figure 4.4 depicts these points in a graph. The curve drawn by connecting the points is called the **supply curve.** It shows the quantity that Melt-in-the-Mouth will supply at each price, holding all other factors constant. As with the demand curve, we put the price on the vertical axis. The quantity supplied is on the horizontal axis. Thus, we can

Table 4.3 MELT-IN-THE-MOUTH'S SUPPLY OF CANDY BARS AT VARIOUS PRICES

Price	Supply
$5.00	100,000
$3.00	95,000
$2.00	85,000
$1.50	70,000
$1.25	50,000
$1.00	25,000
$ .75	0
$ .50	0

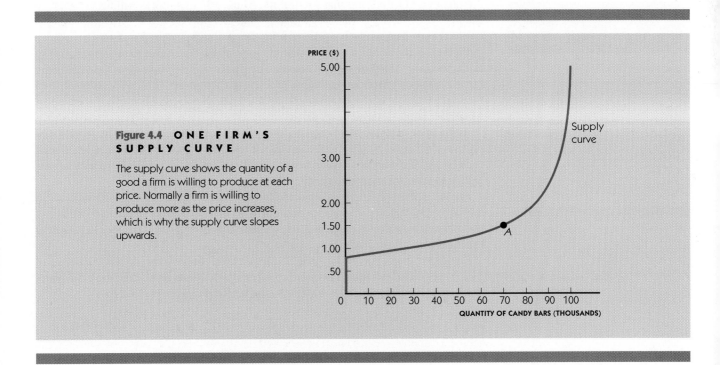

Figure 4.4 ONE FIRM'S SUPPLY CURVE

The supply curve shows the quantity of a good a firm is willing to produce at each price. Normally a firm is willing to produce more as the price increases, which is why the supply curve slopes upwards.

read point A on the curve as indicating that at a price of $1.50 the firm would like to supply 70,000 candy bars.

Unlike the demand curve, the typical supply curve slopes upwards from left to right; at higher prices, firms will supply more.[1] This is because suppliers find it more profitable to produce the goods with higher prices; the higher prices provide them with an incentive to do so.

SUPPLY CURVE

The supply curve gives the quantity of the good supplied at each price.

Table 4.4 TOTAL MARKET SUPPLY FOR CANDY BARS AT VARIOUS PRICES

Price	Total market supply (millions)
$5.00	8.2
$3.00	8.0
$2.00	7.0
$1.50	5.9
$1.25	4.7
$1.00	3.4
$ .75	2.0
$ .50	.5

MARKET SUPPLY

The **market supply** of a good is simply the total quantity that all the firms in the economy are willing to supply at a given price. Similarly, the market supply of labour is simply the total quantity of labour that all the households in the economy are willing to supply at a given wage. As with market demand, market supply is calculated by adding up the quantities of the good that each of the firms or households is willing to supply at each price. Table 4.4 tells us, for instance, that at a price of $2.00, firms will supply 7 million candy bars, while at a price of $.50, they will supply only .5 million.

Figure 4.5 shows the same information graphically. The curve joining the points in the figure is the **market supply curve.** The market supply curve gives the total quantity of a good that firms are willing to produce at each price. Thus, we read point A on the market supply curve as showing that at a price of $.75, the firms in the economy would like to sell 2 million candy bars.

As the price of candy bars increases, the quantity supplied increases. The market supply curve generally slopes upwards from left to right for two reasons: at higher prices, each firm in the market is willing to produce more; and at higher prices, more firms are willing to enter the market to produce the good.

The market supply curve is calculated from the supply curves of the different firms in the same way that the market demand curve is calculated from the demand curves of the different households: at each price, we add horizontally the quantities that each of the firms is willing to produce.

Figure 4.6 shows how this is done in a market with only two producers. At a price of $1.25, Melt-in-the-Mouth Chocolate produces 50,000 candy bars, while the Chocolates of Choice Company produces 40,000. So the market supply is 90,000 bars.

---

[1]Chapter 11 will describe some unusual situations where supply curves may not be upward sloping.

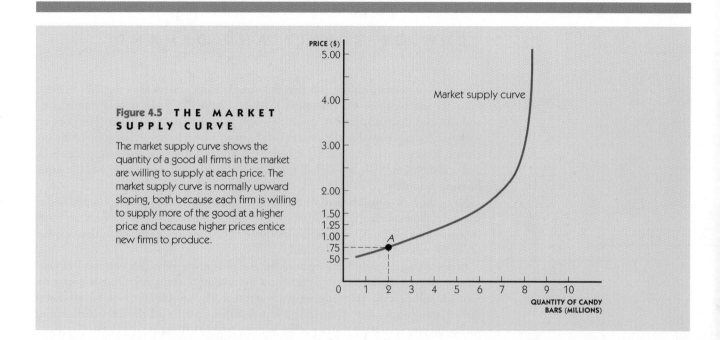

Figure 4.5 THE MARKET SUPPLY CURVE

The market supply curve shows the quantity of a good all firms in the market are willing to supply at each price. The market supply curve is normally upward sloping, both because each firm is willing to supply more of the good at a higher price and because higher prices entice new firms to produce.

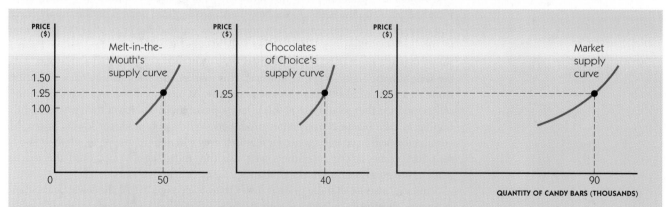

Figure 4.6 DERIVING THE MARKET SUPPLY CURVE

The market supply curve is constructed by adding up the quantity that each of the firms in the economy is willing to supply at each price. It shows what market supply would be if there were only two producers. Actual market supply, as depicted in Figure 4.5, is much larger because there are many producers.

LAW OF SUPPLY AND DEMAND

This chapter began with the assertion that supply and demand work together to determine the market price in competitive markets. Figure 4.7 puts a market supply curve and a market demand curve on the same graph to show how this happens. The price actually paid and received in the market will be determined by the intersection of the two curves. This point is labelled E_0, for equilibrium, and the corresponding price ($.75) and quantity (2 million) are called, respectively, the **equilibrium price** and the **equilibrium quantity.**

Since the term **equilibrium** will recur throughout the book, it is important to understand the concept clearly. Equilibrium describes a situation where there are no forces (reasons) for change. No one has an incentive to change the result—the price or quantity in the case of supply and demand.

In describing a weight hanging from the end of a spring, physicists also speak of equilibrium. There are two forces working on the weight. Gravity is pulling it down; the spring is pulling it up. When the weight is at rest, it is in equilibrium, with the two forces just offsetting each other. If the weight is pulled down a little bit, the force of the spring will be greater than the force of gravity, and the weight will spring up. In the absence of any further intrusions, the weight will eventually bob back and forth to its equilibrium position.

An economic equilibrium is established in roughly the same way. At the equilibrium price, consumers get precisely the quantity of the good they are willing to buy at that price, and producers sell precisely the quantity they are willing to sell at that price. Thus, neither producers nor consumers have an incentive to alter the price or quantity. At any other price, there is an incentive for either buyers or sellers to change the price.

Consider the price of $1.00 in Figure 4.7. There is no equilibrium quantity here. First find $1.00 on the vertical axis. Now look across to find point A on the supply curve, and read down to the horizontal axis; point A tells you that at a price of $1.00, firms want to supply 3.4 million candy bars. Now look at point B on the demand curve. Point B shows that at a price of $1.00, consumers only want to buy 1.3 million candy bars. Like the weight bobbing on a spring however, this market will work its way back to equilibrium. At a price of $1.00, there is **excess supply.** As producers discover that they cannot sell as much as they would like at this price, some of them will lower their prices slightly, hoping to take business from other producers. When one producer lowers prices, his competitors will have to respond, for fear that they will end up unable to sell their goods. As prices come down, consumers will also buy more, and so on, until the market reaches the equilibrium price and quantity.

Similarly, assume that the price is lower than $.75, say $.50. At the lower price, there is **excess demand:** individuals want to buy 3.0 million candy bars (point C), while firms only want to produce .5 million (point D). Consumers unable to purchase all they want will offer to pay a little bit more; other consumers, afraid of having to do without, will match these higher bids or raise them. As prices start to increase, suppliers will also have a greater incentive to produce more. Again the market will tend towards the equilibrium point.

At equilibrium, no purchaser and no supplier has an incentive to change the price or quantity. The observation that in competitive market economies actual prices tend to be

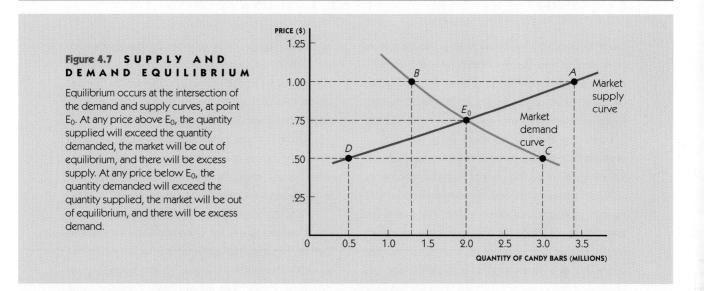

Figure 4.7 SUPPLY AND DEMAND EQUILIBRIUM

Equilibrium occurs at the intersection of the demand and supply curves, at point E_0. At any price above E_0, the quantity supplied will exceed the quantity demanded, the market will be out of equilibrium, and there will be excess supply. At any price below E_0, the quantity demanded will exceed the quantity supplied, the market will be out of equilibrium, and there will be excess demand.

the equilibrium prices, at which demand equals supply, is called the **law of supply and demand.** It is important to note that this law does not mean that at every moment of time the price is precisely at the intersection of the demand and supply curves. As with the example of the weight and the spring, the market may bounce around a little bit when it is in the process of adjusting. The law of supply and demand does say that when a market is out of equilibrium, there are predictable forces for change.

PRICE, VALUE, AND COST

As noted above, price is easily defined in the economist's impersonal language as what is given in exchange for a good or service. Price is determined by the forces of supply and demand. Adam Smith called our notion of price "value in exchange," and contrasted it to the notion of "value in use":

> The word VALUE, it is to be observed, has two different meanings, and sometimes expresses the utility of some particular object, and sometimes the power of purchasing other goods which the possession of that object conveys. The one may be called "value in use"; the other, "value in exchange." The things which have the greatest value in use have frequently little or no value in exchange; and, on the contrary, those which have the greatest value in exchange have frequently little or no value in use. Nothing is more useful than water, but it will purchase scarce any thing; scarce any thing can be had in exchange for it. A diamond, on the contrary, has scarce any value in use; but a very great quantity of other goods may frequently be had in exchange for it.[2]

[2]Adam Smith, *The Wealth of Nations* (1776), Book I, Chapter IV.

CLOSE-UP: THE STRUCTURE OF ECONOMIC MODELS

Every economic model, including the model of how supply and demand determine the equilibrium price and quantity in a market, is constructed of three kinds of relationships: identities, behavioural relationships, and equilibrium relationships. Recognizing these component parts will help in understanding how economists think and understanding the source of many of their disagreements.

As described in the text, the demand curve represents a relationship between the price and the quantity demanded. The statement that normally, as prices rise, the quantity of a good demanded decreases is a description of how individuals behave. It is called a behavioural relationship. The supply curve for each firm is also a behavioural relationship.

Economists disagree over behavioural relationships in at least two ways. First, they may differ over the strength of the connection. For any given product, does a change in price lead to a large change in the quantity demanded or a small one? Second, economists may sometimes even disagree over the direction of the effect. There are some special cases where a higher price may actually lead to a *lower* quantity supplied.

The statement that the market demand is equal to the sum of the individual demands is an identity. An identity is a statement that is true according to the definition of the terms; in other words, market demand is *defined* to be the sum of the demands of all individuals. Similarly, it is an identity that market supply is equal to the sum of the supplies of all firms; the terms are defined in that way. Economists rarely disagree over identities, since disagreements over definitions are pointless.

Finally, an equilibrium relationship exists when there are no forces for change. In the supply and demand model, the equilibrium occurs when the quantity demanded is equal to the quantity supplied. An equilibrium relationship is not the same as an identity. It is possible for the economy to be out of equilibrium, at least for a time. Of course, being out of equilibrium implies that there are forces for change pushing towards equilibrium. But an identity must always hold true at all times, as a matter of definition.

Economists usually agree about what an equilibrium would look like, but they often differ on whether the forces pushing the markets towards equilibrium are strong or weak, and thus on whether the economy is usually fairly close to equilibrium or sometimes rather far from it.

Why is it that water, which is a basic necessity for life, has a lower price than diamonds or other luxuries that most people could easily live without? The law of supply and demand can help to explain the diamond-water paradox, and many similar examples where "value in use" seems very different from "value in exchange." Figure 4.8 presents a demand and a supply curve for water. Individuals are willing to pay a high price for the water they need to live, as illustrated by point A on the demand curve. But above some quantity, B, people will pay almost nothing more for additional water. In most of the inhabited parts of the world, water is readily available, so it gets supplied in plentiful quantities at low prices. Normally, the supply curve of water intersects the demand curve to the right of B, as in the figure; hence the low equilibrium price. Of course, in

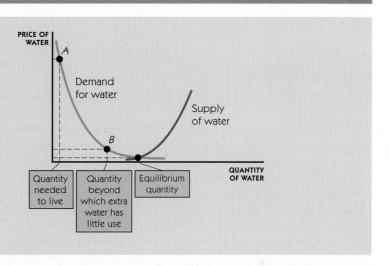

Figure 4.8 SUPPLY AND DEMAND FOR WATER

Point A shows that people are willing to pay a relatively high price for the first few units of water. But to the right of B, people have plenty of water already and are not willing to pay much for an additional amount. The price of water will be determined at the point where the supply curve crosses the demand curve. In most cases, the resulting price is extremely low.

the desert, the water supply may be very limited, and then the price may rise to very high levels.

To an economist, the statements that the price of diamonds is high and the price of water is low are statements about supply and demand conditions, not a deep philosophical assertion that diamonds are "more important" than water or "better" than water. They are not statements about value in use. Similarly, the fact that many writers or artists make no money, while a few make fortunes, does not necessarily mean that those who make more money are "better," just that the conditions of supply and demand allow them to receive more money.

Price is related to the *marginal* value of an object, that is, the value of an additional unit of the object. Water has a low price not because the *total* value of water is low—it is obviously high, since we could not live without it—but because the marginal value, what we would be willing to pay to be able to drink one more glass of water a year, is not very high.

Supply and demand analysis provides an organized and logical framework for searching for an explanation of both the level of prices and their changes. When confronted by a question about prices, economists think about what the shape of the demand and supply curves look like, and where they might intersect. For example, why do lawyers get paid so much, and why have their salaries been declining relative to salaries in other professions?

In the short run, the supply of lawyers is relatively fixed; it can only be augmented gradually, as more lawyers are trained. If the supply is low, relative to the demand, the price for legal services will be high, and lawyers' incomes will be high. For many years the supply of lawyers was kept low because of the limited number of places in approved law schools. The demand for legal services increased rapidly as a result of such things as increased housing and real estate transactions as the baby boom generation became adults, increased divorce rates, and rapid development of urban areas. Civil litigation has also been on the rise. These increases in demand caused lawyers' salaries to increase, making the profession a relatively attractive one. Supply began to respond as the number of law school graduates rose and as the proportion of women law students increased dramatically. The result was an increase in the number of practicing lawyers and a decline in their relative income. As in any other real-life example, there are numerous other factors that may partially account for the changing income of lawyers too. But almost all of them can be analyzed, compared, and accommodated within the framework of supply and demand.

Just as economists take care to distinguish the words "price" and "value," they also distinguish the *price* of an object (what it sells for) from its *cost* (the expense of making the object). The two are distinct concepts. The costs of producing a good affect the price at which firms are willing to supply that good. An increase in the costs of production will normally cause prices to rise. While under some conditions, *in equilibrium*, the price of an object will equal its cost of production, this need not be the case.

Normally, we think of land as something that cannot be produced, so its cost of production can be considered infinite (though, admittedly, there are situations where land can be produced, as when Holland filled in part of the sea to expand its usable land). Yet there is an equilibrium price of land—where the demand for land is equal to its fixed supply.

SHIFTS IN DEMAND CURVES

One of the uses of the law of supply and demand is to be able to explain changes in prices; for instance, why it is that in one year the price of wheat rises and in another year it falls. The explanation lies in changes in the market demand curve, changes in the market supply curve, or both. We will take up changes in demand first.

The analysis so far has focused on one major determinant of how much will be demanded of a good: its price. Changes in the price of a good move us up and down the existing demand curve; they do not *shift* it. But what about the other factors that affect the quantity demanded, like income, the price of other goods, style, and season? Changes in any of these will lead to shifts in the demand curve.

Figure 4.9 shows hypothetical demand curves for candy bars in 1960 and in 1990. The 1960 curve replicates the demand curve in Figure 4.7. As Canadians become more health conscious, the demand curve for candy bars has shifted to the left, which means that the demand for candy bars at each price is less in 1990. We can see from the figure, for instance, that the demand for candy bars at a price of $.75 has decreased from 2 million candy bars (point E_0, the original equilibrium) to 1 million (point F).

Figure 4.9 also shows the supply curve for candy bars, which by assumption is unchanged from 1960 to 1990. For simplicity, we assume that the overall price level has remained unchanged over that period. The equilibrium is at the intersection of the demand and supply curve. The leftward shift in the demand curve thus has had two effects: the equilibrium price is lower and the equilibrium quantity is lower. Price is lowered from $.75 to $.62, and quantity is lowered from 2 million candy bars to 1.25 million. The new equilibrium is E_1. Notice that the reduction in quantity sold (from 2 million to 1.25 million) is less than would have occurred if the price had not fallen from $.75 to $.62 (in which case only 1 million candy bars would have been bought).

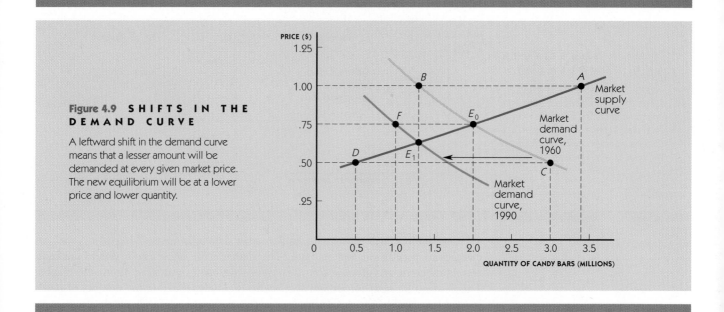

Figure 4.9 SHIFTS IN THE DEMAND CURVE

A leftward shift in the demand curve means that a lesser amount will be demanded at every given market price. The new equilibrium will be at a lower price and lower quantity.

SOURCES OF SHIFTS IN DEMAND CURVES

Of the various factors that shift the demand curve, two—changes in income and in the price of other goods—are specifically economic factors. As an individual's income increases, she normally purchases more of any good. As we see in Figure 4.10, rising incomes shift the demand curve to the right. At each price, she consumes more of the good.

Changes in the price of other goods, particularly closely related goods, will also shift the demand curve for a good. For example, when the price of margarine increases, some individuals will substitute butter. Butter and margarine are thus **substitutes.** When people choose between butter and margarine, one important factor is the relative price, that is, the ratio of the price of butter to the price of margarine. An increase in the price of butter and a decrease in the price of margarine both increase the relative price of butter, and thus both induce individuals to substitute margarine for butter.

Candy bars and granola bars can also be considered substitutes, as the two goods satisfy a similar need. As shown in Figure 4.11A, an increase in the price of granola bars makes candy bars relatively more attractive, and hence leads to a rightward shift in the demand curve for candy bars. (At each price, the demand for candy is greater.) Two goods are substitutes if an increase in the price of one *increases* the demand for the other.

Sometimes, however, an increase in a price of other goods has just the opposite effect. Consider an individual who insists on having sugar in her coffee. In deciding on how much coffee to demand, she is concerned with the price of a cup of coffee *with* sugar. If sugar becomes more expensive, she will demand less coffee. For this person, sugar and coffee are **complements;** that is, an increase in the price of one *decreases* the demand for the other. As shown in Figure 4.11B, the price increase of sugar shifts the demand curve of coffee to the left. (At each price, the demand for coffee is less.)

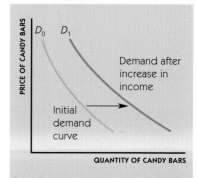

Figure 4.10 HOW INCOME SHIFTS THE DEMAND CURVE

Normally, an increase in income leads to a higher quantity demanded of a good at each price. This is shown as a rightward shift of the demand curve.

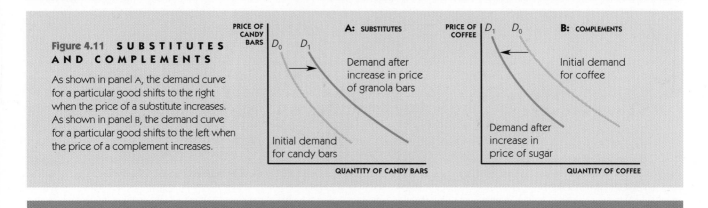

Figure 4.11 SUBSTITUTES AND COMPLEMENTS

As shown in panel A, the demand curve for a particular good shifts to the right when the price of a substitute increases. As shown in panel B, the demand curve for a particular good shifts to the left when the price of a complement increases.

Noneconomic factors can also shift market demand curves. The major ones are changes in population and in taste. The demand for many goods differs markedly among different age groups. Young families with babies purchase disposable diapers. The demand for new houses and apartments is closely related to the number of newly formed households, which in turn depends on the number of individuals of marriage-able age. The population of Canada has been growing older, on average, both because life expectancies are increasing and because birthrates fell somewhat after the baby boom that followed World War II; so there has been a shift in demand away from diapers and new houses. Economists working for particular firms and industries spend a consid-erable amount of energy ascertaining the population effects, called **demographic ef-fects,** on the demand for the goods their firms sell.

Sometimes demand curves shift simply because of a shift in tastes. Since the 1970s, Canadians have changed their drinking habits; they now consume more wine and less hard liquor than they did previously. There has been a shift in taste towards yogurt and away from buttermilk, towards low-cholesterol foods and away from fatty meats. Each of these changes has shifted the demand curve for the good in question.

SOURCES OF SHIFTS IN MARKET DEMAND CURVES

A change in income

A change in the price of a substitute

A change in the price of a complement

A change in the composition of the population

A change in tastes

A change in information

A change in the availability of credit

A change in expectations

Sometimes demand curves shift as the result of a change in information. Part of the change in the demand for alcohol may be due to improved consumer information about the dangers of alcohol. Certainly the shift in the demand for cigarettes is largely the result of heightened awareness of the effects of smoking.

People typically borrow to buy goods like cars and houses. At times, they may simply not be able to borrow from their usual sources, such as the bank. This reduced availability of credit may also give rise to a shift in the demand curve.

What households demand today depends not only on current income and prices but also on their expectations about the future. If people think they may become unemployed, they will reduce their spending in general, and the demand curve for certain goods like cars will shift. In this case, economists say that their demand curve depends on expectations.

SHIFTS IN A DEMAND CURVE VERSUS MOVEMENTS ALONG A DEMAND CURVE

It is important to distinguish between changes that result from a shift in the demand curve and changes that result from a *movement* along the demand curve. A movement along a demand curve is simply the change in the quantity demanded as the price changes, holding all other factors constant. Figure 4.12A illustrates a movement along the demand curve from point A to point B; *given a demand curve*, at lower prices, more

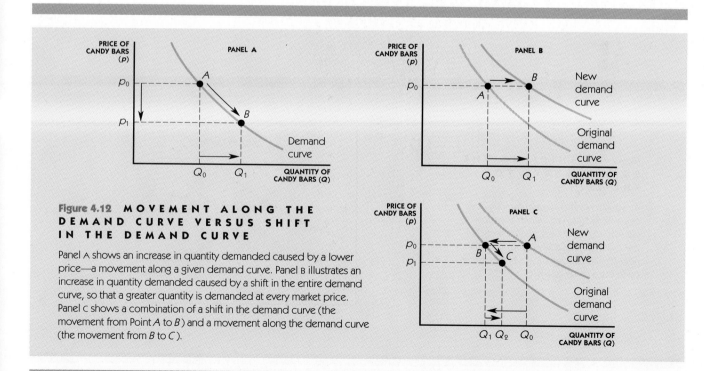

Figure 4.12 **MOVEMENT ALONG THE DEMAND CURVE VERSUS SHIFT IN THE DEMAND CURVE**

Panel A shows an increase in quantity demanded caused by a lower price—a movement along a given demand curve. Panel B illustrates an increase in quantity demanded caused by a shift in the entire demand curve, so that a greater quantity is demanded at every market price. Panel C shows a combination of a shift in the demand curve (the movement from Point A to B) and a movement along the demand curve (the movement from B to C).

is consumed. Figure 4.12B illustrates a shift as the result of a change in some factor other than price; the demand curve has shifted to the right, so that at a *given price*, more is consumed. Quantity again increases from Q_0 to Q_1, but the price stays the same.

In practice, both effects are often present. Thus, in panel C, the movement from point A to point C—where the quantity demanded has been reduced from Q_0 to Q_2—can be thought of as consisting of two parts: a change in quantity demanded resulting from a shift in the demand curve (the reduction of output from Q_0 to Q_1) and a movement along the demand curve (the change from Q_1 to Q_2).

SHIFTS IN SUPPLY CURVES

Supply curves too can shift. Suppose a drought hits the breadbasket provinces of Manitoba, Saskatchewan, and Alberta. Figure 4.13 illustrates the predictions of the law of supply and demand in this situation. The supply curve for wheat shifts to the left, which means that at each price of wheat, the quantity firms are willing to supply is smaller. The shift in the supply curve results in a lower equilibrium quantity (Q_3) and a higher equilibrium price (p_3). Notice that if the price had remained unchanged, the quantity produced would have fallen from Q_1 to Q_2. The increase in the price induces farmers to produce more. Thus, the equilibrium reduction in quantity from Q_1 to Q_3 is somewhat smaller than it would have been had price remained unchanged.

Figure 4.13 SHIFTING THE SUPPLY CURVE TO THE LEFT

A drought or other disaster (among other possible factors) will cause the supply curve to shift to the left, so that at each price, a smaller quantity is supplied. The new equilibrium will be at a higher market price but a lower quantity.

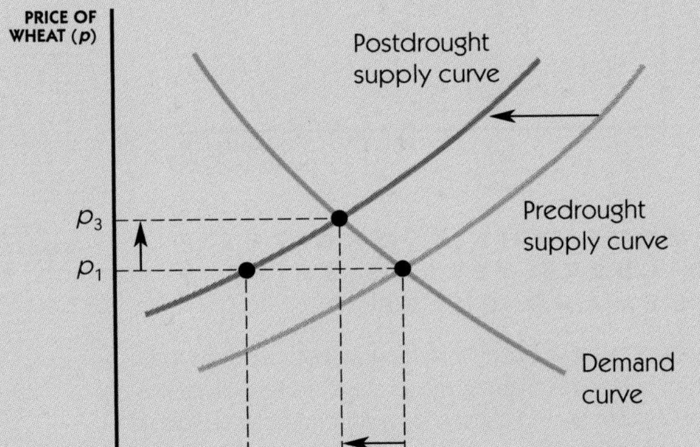

Close-up: The Drought of 1988 as a Supply Shock

For the Canadian prairies and the midwestern United States, 1988 brought one of the worst droughts ever recorded. Wheat production was down 40 percent in Canada and 10 percent in the United States; corn production fell by 24 percent in Canada and 35 percent in the United States; soybean production was down 9 percent in Canada and 20 percent in the United States; and oats and barley were down 13 percent in Canada and 40 percent in the United States.

The examples could go on and on. From an economist's perspective, an unpredictable event like a severe drought is a good example of a shift in the supply curve. The drought reduced the amount of any crop that could be supplied at any given price, which means that the supply curve itself shifted to the left.

As an economist would predict, this shift in the supply curve led to higher prices for these farm products. To cite some examples from the Winnipeg Commodity Exchange, feed wheat prices rose by almost 50 percent between 1987 and 1988, corn prices by 43 percent, and soybeans by 50 percent. Overall, crop prices rose by about 12 percent.

The drought also had a number of predictable side effects on substitute and complement goods. For example, higher prices in North America stimulated foreign agricultural production. Canadian farmers planted many more hectares in 1989, to make up for some of their lost production the previous year. Since much grain is fed to cattle, the higher price of grain led many farmers to slaughter their cattle sooner than they had originally planned. As a result, meat production rose slightly in 1988, and meat prices (adjusted for inflation) dropped slightly. Supermarket prices increased sharply for consumers in the middle of the summer; fruit and vegetable prices were up 5 percent in July 1988.

Despite these many side effects, the drought of 1988 had only a temporary effect on prices and quantities. Because of stockpiles of goods and the possibility of buying farm products from other nations, the agricultural system has enough flexibility to live through a bad year.

SOURCES OF SHIFTS IN SUPPLY CURVES

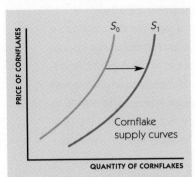

There are several sources of shifts in market supply curves. One is lower prices of the inputs used to produce a good. Figure 4.14 shows that as corn becomes less expensive, the supply curve for cornflakes shifts to the right. Producing cornflakes costs less, so at every price, firms are willing to supply a greater quantity. That is why the quantity supplied along the curve S_1 is greater than the quantity supplied, at the same price, along the curve S_0.

Improvements in technology, such as have occurred in the computer industry over the past two decades, will also lead to a rightward shift in the market supply curve. Another source of shifts is nature. The supply curve for agricultural goods may shift to the right or left depending on whether nature is kind or unkind, in the form of weather conditions, insect infestations, or animal diseases. Some economists would even categorize these changes in the natural environment as technology shifts, but this blurs an important distinction between changes in the known technology of farming and the vagaries to which these technologies are subjected.

Just as changed expectations concerning future income and prices can lead to a shift in the demand curve, changed expectations concerning new technologies or prices of inputs can lead to a shift in the supply curve. If firms believe that a new technology for making cars will become available in two years' time, this belief will discourage investment today and will lead to a temporary leftward shift in the supply curve. By the same token, a reduction in the availability of credit may curtail firms' ability to borrow to obtain inputs needed for production, and this too will induce a leftward shift in the supply curve.

Figure 4.14 SHIFTING THE SUPPLY CURVE TO THE RIGHT

An improvement in technology or a reduction in input prices (among other possible factors) will cause the supply curve to shift to the right, so that at each price, a larger quantity is supplied.

SOURCES OF SHIFTS IN MARKET SUPPLY CURVES

A change in the prices of inputs

A change in technology

A change in the natural environment

A change in expectations

A change in the availability of credit

SHIFTS IN A SUPPLY CURVE VERSUS MOVEMENTS ALONG A SUPPLY CURVE

The same care that is taken in distinguishing between a movement along a demand curve and a shift in the demand curve must be taken with market supply curves. In Fig-

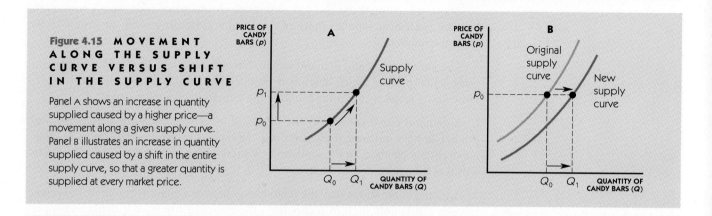

Figure 4.15 MOVEMENT ALONG THE SUPPLY CURVE VERSUS SHIFT IN THE SUPPLY CURVE

Panel A shows an increase in quantity supplied caused by a higher price—a movement along a given supply curve. Panel B illustrates an increase in quantity supplied caused by a shift in the entire supply curve, so that a greater quantity is supplied at every market price.

ure 4.15A, the price of candy bars has gone up, with a corresponding increase in quantity supplied. There has been a movement along the supply curve. The increase in price may itself have arisen from a rightward shift in the market demand curve.

By contrast, in Figure 4.15B, the supply curve has shifted to the right, perhaps because a new production technique has made it cheaper to produce candy bars. Now, even though the price does not change, the quantity supplied increases. The quantity supplied in the market can increase either because the price of the good has increased—and at a higher price, for a *given supply curve*, the quantity produced is higher—or because the supply curve has shifted, so that at a *given price*, the quantity supplied has increased.

REVIEW AND PRACTICE

SUMMARY

1. An individual's demand curve gives the quantity demanded of a good at each possible price. It normally slopes down, which means that the person demands a greater quantity of the good at lower prices and a lesser quantity at higher prices.

2. The market demand curve gives the total quantity of a good demanded by all individuals in an economy at each price. As the price rises, demand falls, both because each person demands less of the good and because some people exit the market.

3. A firm's supply curve gives the amount of a good the firm is willing to supply at each price. It is normally upward sloping, which means that firms supply a greater quantity of the good at higher prices and a lesser quantity at lower prices.

4. The market supply curve gives the total quantity of a good that all firms in the economy are willing to produce at each price. As the price rises, supply rises, both because each firm supplies more of the good and because some additional firms enter the market.

5. The law of supply and demand says that in competitive markets, the equilibrium price is that price at which quantity demanded equals quantity supplied. It is represented on a graph by the intersection of the demand and supply curves.

6. A demand curve shows *only* the relationship between quantity demanded and price. Changes in tastes, in demographic factors, in income, in the prices of other goods, in information, in the availability of credit, or in expectations are reflected in a shift of the entire demand curve.

7. A supply curve shows *only* the relationship between quantity supplied and price. Changes in factors such as technology, the prices of inputs, the natural environment, expectations, or the availability of credit are reflected in a shift of the entire supply curve.

8. It is important to distinguish movements along a demand curve from shifts in the demand curve, and movements along a supply curve from shifts in the supply curve.

KEY TERMS

price	market supply curve	law of supply and
demand curve	equilibrium price	demand
market demand	equilibrium quantity	substitute
curve	excess supply	complement
supply curve	excess demand	demographic effects

REVIEW QUESTIONS

1. Why does an individual's demand curve normally slope down? Why does a market demand curve normally slope down?

2. Why does a firm's supply curve normally slope up? Why does a market supply curve normally slope up?

3. What is the significance of the point where supply and demand curves intersect?

4. Explain why, if the price of a good is above the equilibrium price, the forces of supply and demand will tend to push the price towards equilibrium. Explain why, if the price of the good is below the equilibrium price, the market will tend to adjust towards equilibrium.

5. Name some factors that could shift the demand curve out to the right.

6. Name some factors that could shift the supply curve in to the left.

PROBLEMS

1. Imagine a company lunchroom that sells pizza by the slice. Using the following data, plot the points and graph the demand and supply curves. What is the equilibrium price and quantity? Find a price at which excess demand would exist and a price at which excess supply would exist, and plot them on your diagram.

Price per slice	Demand (number of slices)	Supply (number of slices)
$1	420	0
$2	210	100
$3	140	140
$4	105	160
$5	84	170

2. Suppose a severe drought hit the sugarcane crop. Predict how this would affect the equilibrium price and quantity in the market for sugar and the market for honey. Draw supply and demand diagrams to illustrate your answers.

3. Imagine that a new invention allows each mine worker to mine twice as much coal. Predict how this will affect the equilibrium price and quantity in the market for coal and the market for heating oil. Draw supply and demand diagrams to illustrate your answer.

4. Canadians' tastes have shifted away from beef and towards chicken. Predict how this change affects the equilibrium price and quantity in the market for beef, the market for chicken, and the market for roadside hamburgers. Draw supply and demand diagrams to illustrate your answer.

5. During the 1970s, the postwar baby boomers reached working age, and it became more acceptable for married women with children to work. Predict how this increase in the number of workers is likely to affect the equilibrium wage and quantity of employment. Draw supply and demand curves to illustrate your answer.

CHAPTER 5

USING DEMAND AND SUPPLY

The concepts of demand and supply are among the most useful in economics. The demand and supply framework explains why dentists are paid more than lawyers, or why the income of unskilled workers has increased less than that of skilled workers. It can also be used to predict what the demand for condominiums or disposable diapers will be fifteen years from now, or what will happen if the government increases the tax on cigarettes. Not only can we predict that prices will change, we can predict by how much they will change.

This chapter has two purposes. The first is to develop some of the concepts required to make these kinds of predictions, and to illustrate how the demand and supply framework can be used in a variety of contexts.

The second is to look at what happens when people interfere with the workings of competitive markets. Rents may seem too high for poor people to afford adequate housing. The wages of unskilled workers may seem too low for people to live on. Prices of wheat may seem unfairly low, not adequate to compensate farmers for their work. With such hardship, it is only natural that political pressures develop to intervene on behalf of the disadvantaged. (Political pressures do not come only from the disadvantaged, however. Voters in Ontario, for instance, prevented Metropolitan Toronto from introducing market value assessment for property taxation.) In the second part of this chapter, we explore the consequences of these interventions.

KEY QUESTIONS

1. What is meant by the concept of elasticity? Why does it play such an important role in predicting market outcomes?

2. What happens when market outcomes are interfered with, as when the government imposes price floors and ceilings? Why do such interferences give rise to shortages and surpluses?

SENSITIVITY TO PRICE CHANGES

If tomorrow supermarkets across the country were to cut the price of bread or milk by 50 percent, the quantity demanded of these items would not change much. If stores offered the same reduction on ice cream, however, demand would increase substantially. Why do price changes sometimes have small effects and at other times large ones? The answer lies in the shape of the demand and supply curves.

The demand for ice cream is more sensitive to price changes than is the demand for milk, and this is reflected in the shape of the demand curves as illustrated in Figure 5.1.

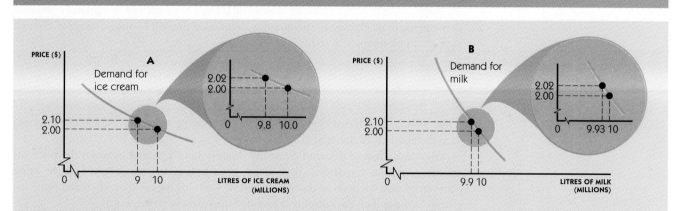

Figure 5.1 ELASTIC VERSUS INELASTIC DEMAND CURVES

Panel A shows a hypothetical demand curve for ice cream. Note that quantity demanded changes rapidly with fairly small price changes, indicating that demand for ice cream is elastic. The telescoped portion of the demand curve shows that a 1 percent rise in price leads to a 2 percent fall in quantity demanded. Panel B shows a hypothetical demand curve for milk. Note that quantity demanded changes very little, regardless of changes in price, meaning that demand for milk is inelastic. The telescoped portion of the demand curve shows that a 1 percent rise in price leads to a .7 percent fall in quantity demanded.

The demand curve for ice cream (panel A) is flatter than the one for milk (panel B). When the demand curve is very flat, it means that a change in price, say by 5 percent from $2.00 a litre to $2.10, has a large effect on the quantity consumed. In panel A, the demand for ice cream decreases from 10 million litres at a price of $2.00 a litre to 9 million litres at a price of $2.10 per litre.

By contrast, when the demand curve is very steep, it means that a change in price has little effect on quantity. In panel B, the demand for milk decreases from 10 million litres at $2.00 per litre to 9.9 million litres at $2.10 per litre. But saying that the demand curve is steep or flat just pushes the question back a step: why are some demand curves steeper than others?

The answer is that though substitutes exist for almost every good or service, substitution will be more difficult for some goods and services than for others. When substitution is difficult, then even when the price increases, the quantity demanded will not decrease by very much. Similarly, when the price falls, demand will not increase very much. The typical consumer does not substitute milk for beer—or for anything else— even if milk becomes a good deal cheaper.

When substitution is easy, on the other hand, a fall in price may lead to a very large increase in quantity demanded. For instance, there are many very good substitutes for ice cream, including sherbets and frozen yogurts. The price decrease for ice cream means that these close substitutes have become relatively more expensive, and the demand for ice cream would thus increase significantly.

THE PRICE ELASTICITY OF DEMAND

For many purposes, economists need to be more precise about how steep or how flat the demand curve is. They use the concept of the **price elasticity of demand** (for short, the price elasticity or the elasticity of demand). The price elasticity of demand is defined as the percentage change in the quantity demanded divided by the percentage change in price. In mathematical terms,

$$\text{elasticity of demand} = \frac{\text{percent change in quantity demanded}}{\text{percent change in price}}.$$

If the quantity demanded changes 8 percent in response to a 2 percent change in price, then the elasticity of demand is 4.

(Price elasticities of demand are really *negative* numbers; that is, when the price increases, quantities demanded are reduced. Usually, however, we simply write the price elasticity of, say, tobacco as .6, understanding that this means that when the price increases by 1 percent, the quantity demanded decreases by .6 percent.)

It is easiest to calculate the elasticity of demand when there is just a 1 percent change in price. Then the elasticity of demand is just the percent change in the quantity demanded. In the telescoped portion of Figure 5.1A, we see that increasing the price of ice cream from $2.00 a litre to $2.02—a 1 percent increase in price—reduces the demand from 10 million litres to 9.8 million, a 2 percent decline. So we say the price elasticity of demand for ice cream is 2.

By contrast, assume that the price of milk increases from $2.00 a litre to $2.02 (again a 1 percent increase in price), as shown in the telescoped portion of Figure 5.1B. This reduces demand from 10 million litres per year to 9.93 million. Demand has gone down by .7 percent, so the price elasticity of demand is therefore .7. Larger numerical values for price elasticity indicate that demand is more sensitive to changes in price, while smaller values indicate that demand is less sensitive to price changes.

It behooves business firms to pay attention to the price elasticity of demand for their products. Suppose that a cement producer, the only one in town, is considering a 1 percent price increase and wants to know what that will do to revenues. The firm hires an economist to estimate the elasticity of demand, so that it will know what will happen to sales when it raises its price. The economist tells the firm that its demand elasticity is 2. This means that if the price of cement rises by 1 percent, the quantity sold will decline by 2 percent.[1]

The firm's executives will not be pleased by the findings. To see why, assume that initially the price of cement was $1,000 per tonne and 100,000 tonnes were sold. To calculate revenues, you multiply the price times the quantity sold. So initially revenues were $1,000 × 100,000 = $100 million. With a 1 percent increase, the price will be $1,010. If the elasticity of demand is 2, then a 1 percent price increase results in a 2 percent decrease in the quantity sold. With a 2 percent quantity decrease, sales are now 98,000 tonnes. Revenues are down to $98.98 million ($1,010 × 98,000), just slightly over 1 percent. Because of the high elasticity figure, this cement firm's price *increase* leads to a *decrease* in revenues.

The price elasticity of demand works the same way for price decreases. Suppose the cement producer decided to decrease the price of cement 1 percent, to $990. With an elasticity of demand of 2, sales would then increase 2 percent, to 102,000 tonnes. Thus, revenues would *increase* to $100,980,000 ($990 × 102,000), that is, by almost 1 percent.

In the case where the price elasticity is **unity,** or 1, the decrease in the quantity demanded just offsets the increase in the price, so price increases have no effect on revenues. If the price elasticity is less than unity, then when the price of a good increases by 1 percent, the quantity demanded is reduced by less than 1 percent. Since there is not much reduction in demand, elasticities in this range, between 0 and 1, mean that price increases will also increase revenues. And price decreases will decrease revenues. We say that the demand for that good is **relatively inelastic,** or *insensitive* to price changes.

On the other hand, if the price elasticity for a good is greater than unity, then when the price increases by 1 percent, the quantity demanded is reduced by more than 1 percent. Thus, price increases mean that total revenues for that good will be reduced. Price decreases will increase revenues. The increase in sales more than offsets the decreased price. We say that the demand for that good is **relatively elastic,** or *sensitive* to price changes.

There are two extreme cases that deserve attention. One is that of a flat demand curve, a curve that is perfectly horizontal. We say that such a demand curve is perfectly elastic, or has **infinite elasticity,** since even a slight increase in the price results in demand dropping to zero. The other case is that of a steep demand curve, a curve that is perfectly vertical. We say that such a demand curve is perfectly inelastic, or has zero elasticity, since no matter what the change in price, demand remains the same.

---

[1]There is a simple relationship between price elasticity and revenue. Revenue is just price times quantity. If prices go up by 1 percent and quantity remains unchanged, then revenue rises by 1 percent. But normally, the quantity sold decreases. The amount it decreases depends on the elasticity of demand. Thus, percentage change in revenues from a 1 percent change in price = 1 − elasticity of demand.

Table 5.1 SOME PRICE ELASTICITIES IN THE CANADIAN ECONOMY

Commodity group	Elasticity
Elastistic demands	
Household expenses	1.28
Transportation	1.37
Inelastic demands	
Tobacco and alcohol	.54
Clothing	.52
Food	.47
Shelter	.38
Miscellaneous	.67

Source: Alan Powell, "Post-War Consumption in Canada: A First Look at the Aggregates," *Canadian Journal of Economic and Political Science* 31 (November 1965), pp. 559–65.

The elasticity of demand for most foods is low (an increase in price will not affect demand much), while the elasticity of demand for most luxuries, such as perfume, ski trips, and Mercedes cars, is relatively high (an increase in price will lead to much less demand). Table 5.1 gives one set of estimates of the elasticities of demand for broad commodity groups in Canada. The price elasticity of demand for food is .47, in contrast to the price elasticity for transportation, which is 1.37. These are for broad commodity groups. One might expect that for specific goods within these broad categories, the price elasticity of demand would be much higher. For example, the price elasticity of purchased meals or snack foods would be higher than that for food broadly defined. More generally, goods for which it is easy to find substitutes will have high price elasticities; goods for which substitutes cannot easily be found will have low price elasticities.

SMALL VERSUS LARGE PRICE CHANGES

So far, we have focused our attention on small price changes. If the elasticity of demand for apples is 2 (a 1 percent increase in price will lead to a 2 percent decrease in quantity demanded), then an increase in the price of apples by 1 percent will decrease the quantity demanded by 2 percent (2 × 1). A decrease in the price of apples by 3 percent will increase the quantity demanded by 6 percent (2 × 3).

But what about large price changes? With a price elasticity of 2, will a 25 percent price increase reduce demand by 50 percent? The answer is, in general, no, and the reason is illustrated in Figure 5.2. For high prices, such as at point A, the demand curve is very inelastic, while for low prices, demand is very elastic. Many demand curves have this shape. At low prices, such as at point B, there are many substitutes for the product. For example, when the price of aluminum is low, it is used as a food wrap (aluminum foil), for cans, and for airplanes. As the price increases, customers constantly seek out more and more substitutes. At first, substitutes are easy to find, and the demand for the product is greatly reduced. For example, plastic wrap can be used instead of aluminum foil. As the price rises still further, tin is used instead of aluminum for cans. At very high prices, say near point A, aluminum is used only where its lightweight properties are es-

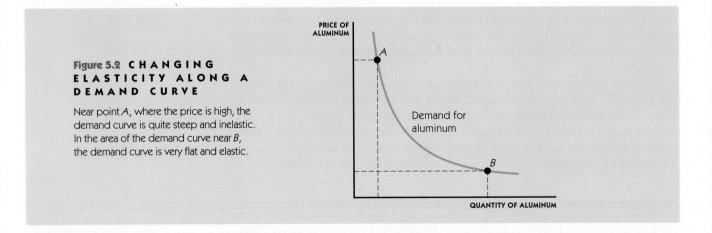

Figure 5.2 CHANGING ELASTICITY ALONG A DEMAND CURVE

Near point A, where the price is high, the demand curve is quite steep and inelastic. In the area of the demand curve near B, the demand curve is very flat and elastic.

sential, such as in airplane frames. At this point, a price increase will not affect the demand for aluminum very much; it may take a *huge* price increase before steel or some other material becomes an economical substitute.[2]

USING THE PRICE ELASTICITY OF DEMAND

Using the elasticity of demand to predict the consequences of price changes is a fairly straightforward process. Assume prices of oil are expected to rise by 10 percent over the next two years. What will this do to the consumption of oil in Canada, if the elasticity of demand is 1?

An elasticity of demand of 1 means that a 1 percent increase in price will reduce demand by 1 percent. So a 10 percent increase in price will reduce demand by 10 percent. If the initial consumption was 10 million barrels, then the 10 percent increase in price will result in a reduction in demand by 1 million barrels, to 9 million.

What happens to total revenues from oil consumption? The price has gone up by 10 percent, the consumption down by 10 percent. The two effects are just offsetting. Total revenues remain virtually unchanged.

What will happen to the consumption of oil in Canada if the elasticity of demand is .7? An elasticity of demand of .7 means that a 1 percent increase in price reduces de-

PRICE ELASTICITY OF DEMAND

ELASTICITY	DESCRIPTION	EFFECT ON QUANTITY DEMANDED OF 1% INCREASE IN PRICE	EFFECT ON REVENUES OF 1% INCREASE IN PRICE
Zero	Perfectly inelastic (vertical demand curve)	Zero	Increased by 1%
Between 0 and 1	Inelastic	Reduced by less than 1%	Increased by less than 1%
1	Unitary elasticity	Reduced by 1%	Unchanged
Greater than 1	Elastic	Reduced by more than 1%	Reduced; the greater the elasticity, the more revenue is reduced
Infinite	Perfectly elastic (horizontal demand curve)	Reduced to zero	Reduced to zero

[2]It is important to note that even along a straight-line demand curve, the elasticity changes, as explained in the appendix to this chapter.

mand by .7 percent. So a 10 percent increase in price will reduce demand by 7 percent. Demand will fall from 10 million barrels to 9.3 million.

What happens to total revenues? If the initial price was $20 a barrel, total revenues initially were $200 million. Now, with a price of $22 a barrel (a 10 percent increase from $20), they have gone up to $22 × 9.3 million = $204 million.

SHORT RUN VERSUS LONG RUN

It is always easier to make adjustments when you have a longer time to make them. Economists distinguish between the long run, the period in which all adjustments can be made, and the short run, in which at least some adjustments cannot be made. As a result, demand is likely to be less elastic (less sensitive to price changes) in the short run than in the long run, when consumers have time to adapt. Figure 5.3 illustrates the difference in shape between short-run and long-run demand curves.

The sharp increase in oil prices in the 1970s provides an outstanding example. The short-run price elasticity of gasoline was .2 (a 1 percent increase in price led to only a .2 percent decrease in quantity demanded), while the long-run elasticity was .7 or more; the short-run elasticity of fuel oil was .2, and the long-run elasticity was 1.2. In the short run, consumers were stuck with their old gas-guzzling cars, their draughty houses, and their old fuel-wasting habits. In the long run, however, consumers bought smaller cars, became used to houses with slightly lower temperatures, installed better insulation in their homes, and turned to wood-burning stoves, electricity, natural gas, and other alternative energy sources. The long-run demand curve was therefore much more elastic (flatter) than the short-run curve; and indeed, the long-run elasticity turned out to be much larger than anticipated.

How long is the long run, and how short is the short run? The example of the response to the oil price increases shows that there is no simple answer to that question. It will vary from product to product. In some cases, adjustments can occur rapidly; in other cases, they are very gradual. As old gas guzzlers wore out, they were replaced with fuel-economy compact cars. As furnaces wore out, they were replaced with more efficient ones. New homes are now constructed with more insulation, so that gradually, over time, the fraction of houses that are well insulated is increasing. Thus, two decades after the initial increase in the price of oil, the adjustments are not yet completed.

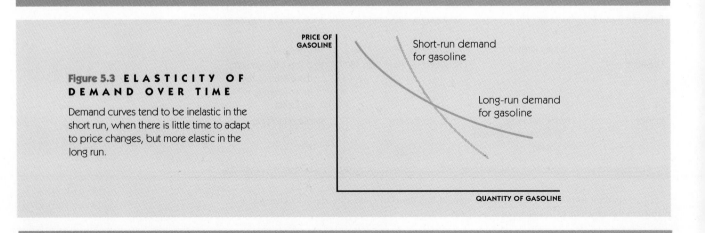

Figure 5.3 ELASTICITY OF DEMAND OVER TIME

Demand curves tend to be inelastic in the short run, when there is little time to adapt to price changes, but more elastic in the long run.

THE PRICE ELASTICITY OF SUPPLY

Supply curves normally slope upwards, but they are very steep in some cases and very flat in others. As with demand curves, the degree of steepness reflects sensitivity to price changes. A steep supply curve, like the one for oil in Figure 5.4A, means that a very large change in price generates only a small change in the quantity firms would like to produce. By contrast, a flatter curve, like the one for chicken in Figure 5.4B, means that a small change in price generates a large change in supply. Just as with demand, economists have developed a more precise way of representing the sensitivity of supply to prices. They use a concept that parallels the one already introduced: the **price elasticity of supply** is defined as the percentage change in quantity supplied divided by the percentage change in price (or the percentage change in quantity supplied corresponding to a price change of 1 percent).

The elasticity of supply of crude oil is very high as the federal government found after it held the price of oil to domestic producers well below the world price under the Petroleum Administration Act of 1985. The result was an increasing gap between what was demanded domestically and what could be supplied. This gap was made up by a large increase in imports into eastern Canada. By the time the price controls were eliminated in the 1980s, the world price had fallen again.

As is the case with demand, if a 1 percent increase in price results in more than a 1 percent increase in supply, we say that the supply curve is elastic, and if a 1 percent increase in price results in less than a 1 percent increase in supply, we say that the supply curve is inelastic. In the extreme case of a vertical supply curve—where the amount supplied does not depend at all on price—the curve is said to be perfectly inelastic, or to have zero elasticity; and in the extreme case of a horizontal supply curve, the curve is said to be perfectly elastic, or to have infinite elasticity.

Just as the demand elasticity differs at different points of the demand curve, so too for the supply curve. Figure 5.5 shows a typical supply curve in manufacturing. An example might be ball bearings. At very low prices, plants are just covering their operating costs. Some plants shut down. In this situation, a small increase in price elicits a large increase

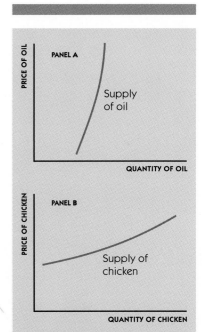

Figure 5.4 DIFFERING ELASTICITIES OF SUPPLY

Panel A shows a supply curve for oil. It is inelastic: quantity supplied increases only a small amount with a rise in price. Panel B shows a supply curve for chicken. It is elastic: quantity supplied increases substantially with a rise in price.

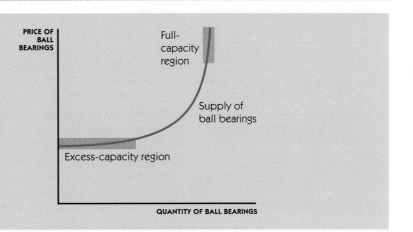

Figure 5.5 CHANGING ELASTICITY ALONG A SUPPLY CURVE

When output is low and many machines are idle, a small change in price can lead to a large increase in quantity produced, so the supply curve is flat and elastic. When output is high and all machines are working close to their limit, it takes a very large price change to induce even a small change in output; the supply curve is steep and inelastic.

in supply. The supply curve is relatively flat (elastic). But eventually, not only are all machines being worked, factories are working all three shifts. In this situation, it may be hard to increase supply further, so that beyond some point, the supply curve becomes close to vertical (inelastic); that is, however much the price increases, the supply will not change very much.

USING THE PRICE ELASTICITY OF SUPPLY

Again, it is easy to use the concept of price elasticity of supply to predict what will happen to the quantity produced when prices increase. Assume that prices of oil are expected to rise by 10 percent over the next two years. What will this do to the supply of oil in Canada, if the elasticity of supply is .5?

An elasticity of supply of .5 means that a 1 percent increase in price results in a .5 percent increase in quantity produced. Thus, a 10 percent increase in price will result in a 5 percent (10 × .5) increase in quantity produced. (Note that with elasticity of demand, a price increase leads to a decrease in quantity demanded, but with elasticity of supply, a price increase leads to an *increase* in supply.)

SHORT RUN VERSUS LONG RUN

Just as economists distinguish between the responsiveness of demand to price in the short run and in the long run, so too with supply. The fact that firms can respond to an increase in prices in the long run in ways that they cannot in the short run means that the long-run supply elasticity is greater than the short-run supply elasticity. We define the short-run supply curve as the supply response *given the current stock of machines and buildings*; by contrast, in the long run, we assume that the stock of machines and buildings can adjust.

Farm crops are a typical example of a good whose supply in the short run is not very sensitive to changes in price; that is, the supply curve is steep (inelastic). After farmers have done their spring planting, they are committed to a certain level of production. If the price of their crops goes up, they cannot go back and plant more. If the price falls, theoretically farmers could decide to cut the supply by not harvesting their crops, but the price would have to fall very, very low to justify that sort of waste. Thus, in this case, the supply curve is relatively close to vertical, as illustrated by the steeper curve in Figure 5.6.

On the other hand, the long-run supply curve for many crops is very flat (elastic). A relatively small change in price can lead to a large change in the quantity supplied. A small increase in the price of soybeans relative to the price of corn may induce many farmers to shift their planting from corn and other crops to soybeans, generating a large increase in the quantity of soybeans. This is also illustrated in Figure 5.6.

Earlier, we noted the response of consumers to the marked increase in the price of oil in the 1970s. The long-run demand elasticity was much higher than the short-run. So too for supply. The higher prices drove firms, both in Canada and abroad in places like the United States, Mexico, and the North Sea off the coast of Great Britain, to explore for more oil. Though the alternative supplies could only be increased to a limited extent in the short run (the short-run supply curve was inelastic, or steep), the long run had greater potential for increasing supply. Because new supplies were found, the long-run supply elasticity was much higher (the supply curve was flatter) than the short-run supply elasticity.

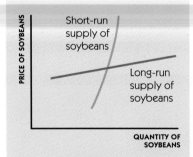

Figure 5.6 ELASTICITY OF SUPPLY OVER TIME

Supply curves may be inelastic in the short run and very elastic in the long run, as in the case of agricultural crops like soybeans.

PRICE ELASTICITY OF SUPPLY

ELASTICITY	DESCRIPTION	EFFECT ON QUANTITY SUPPLIED OF 1% INCREASE IN PRICE
Zero	Perfectly inelastic (vertical supply curve)	Zero
Between 0 and 1	Inelastic	Increased by less than 1%
1	Unitary elasticity	Increased by 1%
Greater than 1	Elastic	Increased by more than 1%
Infinite	Perfectly elastic (horizontal supply curve)	Infinite increase

To know when long-run effects set in, we need to know the industry. Consider truck transportation. In the short run, we can increase the "supply" (kilometers driven) simply by having existing drivers drive all night and on weekends. In the long run, we can increase the number of trucks and drivers on the road. This will only take a few months, at most; it does not take long to increase the supply of trucks. The long run for other industries, on the other hand, can be a longer time. It takes years to build a new electric power-generating station.

IDENTIFYING PRICE AND QUANTITY ADJUSTMENTS

When the demand curve for a good such as wine shifts to the right—when, for instance, wine becomes more popular, so that at each price the demand is greater—there is an increase in both the equilibrium price of wine and the quantity demanded, or consumed. Similarly, when the supply curve for a good such as corn shifts to the left—because, for instance, of a drought that hurt the year's crop, so that at each price farmers supply less—there is an increase in the equilibrium price of corn and a decrease in quantity. Knowing that the shifts in the demand or supply curve will lead to an adjustment in both price *and* quantity is helpful, but it is even more useful to know whether most of the impact of a change will be on price or on quantity. For this, we have to consider the price elasticity of both the demand and supply curves.

SOME EXTREME CASES

At the extreme, all of the effect of a change in supply or demand will be translated fully into either price changes or quantity changes. These extreme cases are somewhat hypothetical, but they should help in understanding what happens in the more usual cases.

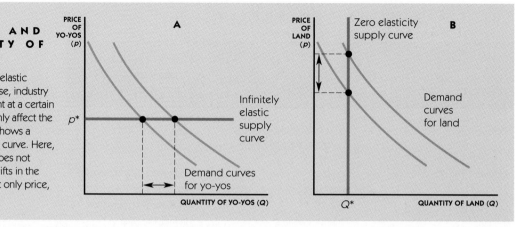

Figure 5.7 INFINITE AND ZERO ELASTICITY OF SUPPLY

Panel A shows a flat, infinitely elastic supply curve. Since, in this case, industry is willing to supply any amount at a certain price, shifts in demand will only affect the equilibrium quantity. Panel B shows a vertical, zero-elasticity supply curve. Here, since the quantity supplied does not change regardless of price, shifts in the demand curve will now affect only price, not quantity.

Figure 5.7 depicts the two extreme cases for a shift in the demand curve. In panel A, the supply curve is perfectly flat. A situation where this might be the case is in the yo-yo industry. Each yo-yo manufacturer could easily increase its output just by buying more machines and hiring proportionately more workers. If the firm doubled the number of machines and doubled its work force, its output would double. Because the industry is so small, if the producers of yo-yos doubled or even quadrupled their output, it would have little effect on what they have to pay either for machines or workers. In short, a small change in the price would elicit an enormous increase in quantity supplied. If yo-yos sold for a price just above what it costs to produce them, producers would rush in to supply more; at a lower price, firms would rather shut down than incur losses.

In the extreme case depicted in Figure 5.7A, below p^*, firms are not willing to supply any of the good, but at or above p^*, they are willing to supply an unlimited quantity. Since a small change in the price around p^* leads to an **infinite** rise or fall in the quantity supplied, this is a case where the price elasticity of supply is infinite. A *shift in demand is reflected only in a change in quantity purchased*; since the firms are willing to produce any amount at the price p^*, the market equilibrium price remains unchanged.

In Figure 5.7B, the supply curve is vertical. The supply curve of natural resources, such as land, is generally vertical. Nature, not prices, determines the quantity available. Likewise, the supply of paintings by van Gogh—or for that matter, any painter who has passed on—is also vertical, or inelastic. Firms simply cannot increase the quantity produced beyond Q^*; but they are willing to produce Q^* regardless of the price. Here, the supply curve has **zero elasticity,** because no change in price, no matter how large, will change the quantity produced. In that case, as eager consumers bid more for the fixed supply, *the shifts in the demand are reflected only in price changes*.

Similarly, different demand elasticities lead to very different consequences of a shift in the supply curve. Figure 5.8 depicts two special cases. When the demand curve for a good is horizontal (perfectly elastic)—that is, consumers are willing to consume an indefinite amount at the price p^*, but nothing at a price beyond p^*—the market equilibrium price remains unchanged, and *the shift in the supply curve simply increases the quantity purchased*. The demand curve will be horizontal if there exists a *perfect* substi-

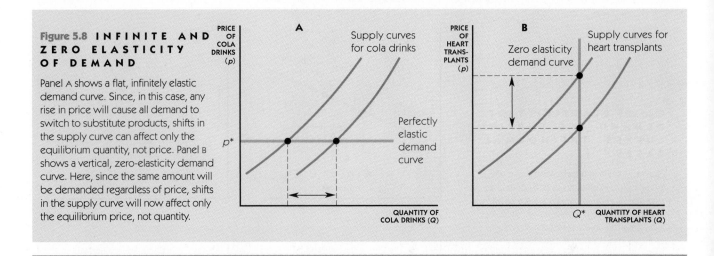

Figure 5.8 INFINITE AND ZERO ELASTICITY OF DEMAND

Panel A shows a flat, infinitely elastic demand curve. Since, in this case, any rise in price will cause all demand to switch to substitute products, shifts in the supply curve can affect only the equilibrium quantity, not price. Panel B shows a vertical, zero-elasticity demand curve. Here, since the same amount will be demanded regardless of price, shifts in the supply curve will now affect only the equilibrium price, not quantity.

tute for the good. If two goods are perfect substitutes, consumers will choose the cheapest. If Coca-Cola and Pepsi were perfect substitutes, then if the price of Coke were a penny higher than the price of Pepsi, everyone would switch to Pepsi; everyone would drink Coke if its price were a penny lower. Thus, a small change in the price causes a very large change in quantity demanded. Figure 5.8A depicts the extreme case where the demand curve is horizontal.

The other extreme is where the demand curve is vertical, as shown in Figure 5.8B. Here the elasticity of demand is zero. Consumers demand the quantity Q^*; they are unwilling, even at a zero price, to consume any more, and even at very high prices they refuse to consume any less. The demand for heart transplants provides an example of an almost perfectly inelastic demand curve. People who need them will buy them at any price they are able to pay. In that case, *the shift in the supply curve is completely reflected in price.*

THE MORE USUAL IN-BETWEEN CASES

Panels A and B of Figures 5.7 and 5.8 depict the extreme cases, but it should be clear how the results generalize to in-between examples, as illustrated in Figure 5.9. If the supply curve is highly elastic (horizontal), then shifts in the demand curve will be mostly reflected in changes in quantities; if the supply curve is *relatively* inelastic (vertical), then shifts in the demand curve will be *mostly* reflected in changes in price. If the demand curve is highly elastic, then shifts in the supply curve will be mostly reflected in changes in quantities; if the demand curve is relatively inelastic, then shifts in the supply curve will be mostly reflected in changes in price.

LONG-RUN VERSUS SHORT-RUN ADJUSTMENTS

Because demand and supply curves are likely to be less elastic (more vertical) in the short run than in the long run, shifts in the demand and supply curves are more likely to be reflected in price changes in the short run, but in quantity changes in the long run.

Figure 5.9 ELASTICITY OF DEMAND AND SUPPLY CURVES: THE NORMAL CASES

Normally, shifts in the demand curve will be reflected in changes in both price and quantity, as seen in panels A and B. When the supply curve is highly elastic, shifts in the demand curve will result mainly in changes in quantities; if it is relatively inelastic, shifts in the demand curve will result mainly in price changes. Likewise, shifts in the supply curve will be reflected in changes in both price and quantity, as seen in panels C and D. If the demand curve is highly elastic, shifts in the supply curve will result mainly in changes in quantities; if it is relatively inelastic, shifts in the supply curve will result mainly in price changes.

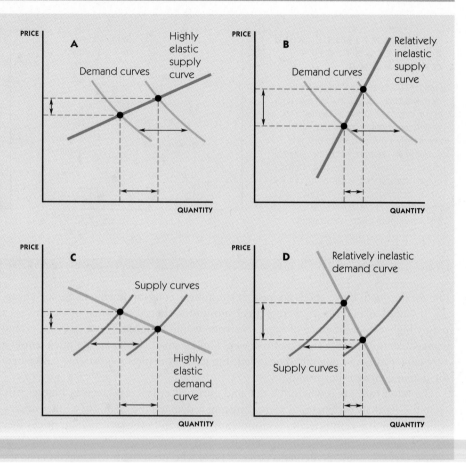

In fact, the increases in prices that take place in the short run provide the signals to firms to increase their production. Short-run price increases can be thought of as being responsible for the output increases that occur in the long run.

USING MARKET DATA TO DERIVE DEMAND AND SUPPLY CURVES

In the real world, it is sometimes not as easy to draw demand and supply curves as it is in textbooks. Because the shapes of the demand and supply curves are so important for understanding how the market behaves, economists have put an enormous effort into calculating their position and shapes precisely. In some cases, this can be relatively easy. For instance, consider the case where economists *know* that the demand for some crop has not shifted over several years, but that supply has varied (as a result of rainfall). They also know that each year the price is determined at the intersection of the demand and

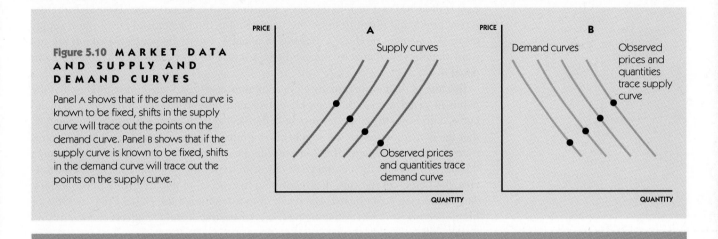

Figure 5.10 MARKET DATA AND SUPPLY AND DEMAND CURVES

Panel A shows that if the demand curve is known to be fixed, shifts in the supply curve will trace out the points on the demand curve. Panel B shows that if the supply curve is known to be fixed, shifts in the demand curve will trace out the points on the supply curve.

supply curves. Economists draw the supply curve for each year, as shown in Figure 5.10A. They plot the equilibrium point for each year. This point, which represents a price and a quantity, is the intersection where demand and supply meet. Therefore, by taking the intersections of price and quantity for several years, economists can trace out the demand curve, as illustrated in the figure. The market data thus provide a basis for determining precisely how steep the demand curve is. Conversely, if the supply curve of Popsicles is *known* to be fixed, but demand varies, say with the weather, then as the demand curve shifts, the prices and quantities observed indicate equilibrium points—the intersections of demand and supply. Thus, they trace out the supply curve, as shown in Figure 5.10B.

The more common case, however, is where every year there are some disturbances to both the demand and supply curves, as illustrated in Figure 5.11. For instance, the de-

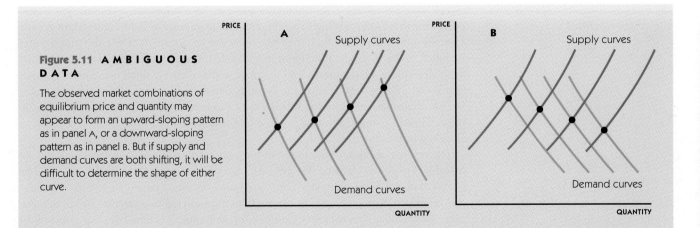

Figure 5.11 AMBIGUOUS DATA

The observed market combinations of equilibrium price and quantity may appear to form an upward-sloping pattern as in panel A, or a downward-sloping pattern as in panel B. But if supply and demand curves are both shifting, it will be difficult to determine the shape of either curve.

mand curve for yogurt may shift as health consciousness changes, and the supply curve may shift as the cost of milk changes with different farm programs. Note that the observed prices and quantities now are tracing out neither a demand curve nor a supply curve. They might produce a shape as in panel A, where the points traced out are upward sloping. Alternatively, the points traced out might be downward sloping, as in panel B.

Because of their shapes, many a noneconomist has been fooled into thinking that the points in panel A trace out a supply curve, and those in panel B trace out a demand curve. This is not the case. Because both demand and supply are shifting, identifying either the demand curve or the supply curve from the set of observed equilibrium points is, to say the least, difficult if not impossible. Devising mathematical methods for doing this has been one of the central goals of research over the past fifty years in **econometrics,** the branch of statistics that focuses on the special problems arising in economics. The Norwegian economist Trygve Haavelmo was awarded the Nobel Prize in 1989 for his pioneering work in developing methods for separating out the effects of demand and supply shifts.

TAX POLICY AND THE LAW OF SUPPLY AND DEMAND

For many questions of public policy, understanding the law of supply and demand is vital. One of the important ways economists use this law is to help them understand what will happen if the government imposes a tax, say, on cigarettes. Assume that the tax on a pack of cigarettes is increased by 10 cents, and that the tax is imposed on cigarette manufacturers. Let's assume that all the companies try to pass on the cost increase to consumers, by raising the price of a pack by 10 cents. At the higher price, fewer cigarettes will be consumed, with the decrease in demand depending on the price elasticity of demand. With lower demand, firms may reduce their price; but by how much depends on the price elasticity of supply. The new equilibrium is depicted in Figure 5.12A.

The new tax on cigarette manufacturers can be thought of as shifting the supply curve. For firms to be willing to produce the same amount as before, they must receive 10 cents more per pack (which they pass on to the government). Thus, the supply curve is shifted up by 10 cents. If demand is relatively inelastic (as demand for cigarettes is), this will result in a large increase in the price and a relatively small decrease in quantity demanded. Notice that because the quantity demanded is reduced slightly, prices paid by consumers do not rise by the full 10 cents. Producers receive a slightly lower after-tax price. Therefore, most of the tax is borne by consumers, but a small fraction of the tax is absorbed by producers.

The results would be quite different for a tax imposed on a good for which the demand is very elastic. Assume, for instance, that the government decided to tax cheddar cheese (but not other cheeses). There are many cheeses that are almost like cheddar, and fewer people are addicted to cheese than are addicted to cigarettes, so the demand curve for cheddar cheese is very elastic. Now, as Figure 5.12B makes clear, most of the tax is absorbed by the producer, who receives (net of tax) a lower price. Production of cheddar cheese is reduced drastically.

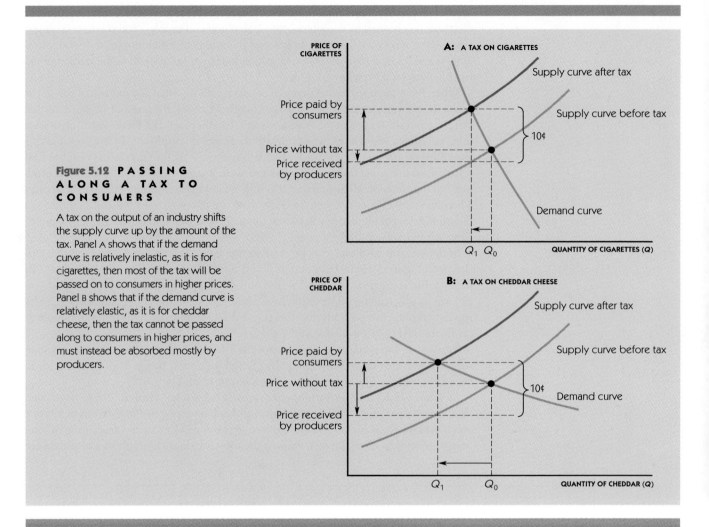

Figure 5.12 PASSING ALONG A TAX TO CONSUMERS

A tax on the output of an industry shifts the supply curve up by the amount of the tax. Panel A shows that if the demand curve is relatively inelastic, as it is for cigarettes, then most of the tax will be passed on to consumers in higher prices. Panel B shows that if the demand curve is relatively elastic, as it is for cheddar cheese, then the tax cannot be passed along to consumers in higher prices, and must instead be absorbed mostly by producers.

When, as in the case of a tax on cigarettes, a tax on producers results in consumers paying a higher price, economists say the tax is "passed on" or "shifted" to consumers. The fact that the consumer bears the tax (even though it is collected from the producers) does not mean that the producers are "powerful" or have conspired together. It is simply the reflection of the workings of supply and demand.

SHORTAGES AND SURPLUSES

Most of the time, the law of supply and demand works so well in a developed modern economy that everyone can take it for granted. Canadians rarely stop to marvel that they can walk into a shopping mall or grocery store and select what they want from a dizzying array of products. If you are willing to pay the "market price"—the prevailing price of the good, determined by the intersection of demand and supply—you can obtain almost any good or service, without needing access to some powerful politician or friend. Similarly, if a seller of a good or service is willing to charge no more than the market price, he can always sell what he wants to.

When the price is set so that demand equals supply—so that any individual can get as much as she wants at that price, and any supplier can sell the amount he wants at that price—economists say that the market **clears.** But there are also times when the market does not clear, when there are dramatic shortages or surpluses. To an economist, a **shortage** means that people would like to buy something, but they simply cannot find it for sale at the going price. A **surplus** means that sellers would like to sell their product, but they cannot sell as much of it as they would like at the going price. These cases where the market does not seem to be working are often the most forceful reminders of the importance of the law of supply and demand. The problem is that the "going price" is not the market equilibrium price.

Shortages and surpluses can be seen in the standard supply and demand diagram shown in Figure 5.13. In both panels A and B, the market equilibrium price is p^*. In panel A, the going price, p_1, is below p^*. At this low price, demand exceeds supply; you can see this by reading down to the horizontal axis. Demand is Q_d; supply is Q_s. The gap between the two points is the "shortage." With the shortage, consumers scramble to get the limited supply available at the going price.

In panel B, the going price, p_1, is above p^*. At this high price, demand is less than supply. Again we denote the demand by Q_d and the supply by Q_s. There is a surplus in the market of $Q_s - Q_d$. Now sellers are scrambling to find buyers.

At various times and for various goods, markets have not cleared. There have been shortages of apartments in Toronto; farm surpluses have plagued both Western Europe and North America; in 1973, there was a shortage of gasoline, with cars waiting in long lines outside of gasoline stations. Perhaps the most important example of a surplus is un-

Figure 5.13 SHORTAGES AND SURPLUSES

In panel A, the actual price p_1 is below the market-clearing price p^*. At a price of p_1, quantity demanded exceeds quantity supplied, and a shortage exists. In panel B, the actual price p_1 is above the equilibrium price p^*. In this case, quantity supplied exceeds quantity demanded, and there is a surplus, or glut, in the market.

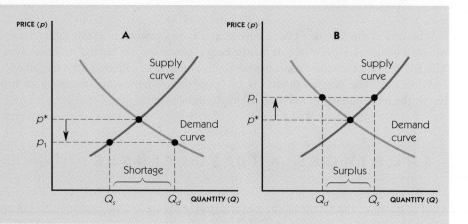

employment: at some times, significant fractions of the labour force find that they cannot sell their labour services at the going wage.

In some markets, like the stock market, the adjustment of prices to shifts in the demand and supply curves tends to be very rapid. In other cases, such as in the housing market, the adjustments tend to be very sluggish. Decreased demand for housing translates slowly into lower housing prices. When price adjustments are sluggish, shortages or surpluses may appear as prices adjust. Houses tend not to sell quickly, for instance, during periods of decreased demand.

When the market does not seem to be adjusting quickly towards equilibrium, economists say that prices are **sticky.** Even in these cases, the analysis of market equilibrium is useful. It indicates the direction of the changes—if the equilibrium price exceeds the current price, prices will tend to rise. Moreover, the rate at which prices fall or rise is often related to the gap, at the current market price, between the quantity demanded and supplied.

INTERFERING WITH THE LAW OF SUPPLY AND DEMAND

Many of the complaints about market economies and the law of supply and demand, which governs how prices are set, are not that they do not work, but that they produce results that some individuals or groups do not like. For example, a reduced supply of oil may lead to a higher equilibrium price for oil. The higher price is not a malfunction of the law of supply and demand, but this is little comfort to those who use gasoline to power their cars and oil to heat their homes. Increased farm productivity during this century has led to a rightward shift in the supply curve; at any price, farmers are willing to produce more. While the demand for agricultural products has also increased with the increase in population and income, the shifts in the supply curve have outpaced those in the demand curve. This shift in the supply curve results in lower farm prices— an unhappy prospect for farmers.

Low demand for unskilled labour may similarly lead to very low wages for unskilled workers. By the same token, an increase in the demand for apartments in Toronto leads, in the short run (with an inelastic supply), to an increase in rents—to the delight of landlords, but an unfortunate development for renters.

In each of these cases, dissatisfaction with the outcome of market processes has led to government actions. The price of oil and natural gas was, at one time, regulated; minimum wage laws set a minimum limit on what employers can pay their workers, even if the workers would be willing to work for less; and rent control laws limit rents that can be charged. The concerns behind these interferences with the market are understandable, but the agitation for government action is based on two errors.

First, someone (or some group) was assigned blame for the change in the price (wages, rents): the oil price rises were blamed on the oil companies, wages on the employer, and rent increases on the landlord. As already explained, economists emphasize the role of anonymous market forces in determining these prices. After all, if landlords or oil companies are basically the same people today as they were last week, there must be some reason that they started charging different prices this week. To be sure, sometimes the price increase is the result of producers colluding to raise prices. This was the case in 1973, when the oil-exporting countries got together to raise the price of oil. The more common situation, however, is illustrated by the increase in the price of oil in August 1990, after Iraq's invasion of Kuwait. The higher price simply reflected the anticipated reduction in the supply of oil.

The second error was to forget that as powerful as governments may be, they can no more repeal the law of supply and demand than they can repeal the law of gravity. When they attempt to interfere with its working, the forces of supply and demand will not be balanced. There will either be excess supply or excess demand. Shortages and surpluses create problems of their own, often far worse than the original problem the government policy was supposed to resolve.

This is precisely what happened in the former Soviet Union and other former socialist economies. In those countries, governments did not allow the law of supply and demand to work. The government set prices by decree. In some cases, the government tried to figure out what the prices would have been had the law of supply and demand been allowed to function naturally. This may seem a little pointless—after all, why not just let the market work? Even if the government was successful in deciding on an appropriate price, it could do so only after a lengthy bureaucratic process. But economic conditions were changing while the bureaucrats were deliberating, which means that the government-announced price was rarely the same as the market price. Moreover, the government-announced price was usually inflexible.

In some cases, the government set prices to assure that important products were "affordable." The result of government price setting was that in those socialist countries, shortages became the rule rather than the exception. Consumers in Russia and Poland spent hours each day waiting in line to buy the foods they needed. They waited months or years to get a car or an apartment.

Two of the more straightforward examples of government overruling the law of supply and demand are **price ceilings,** which are attempts to impose a maximum price that can be charged for a product, and **price floors,** which are attempts to impose a minimum price. Rent control laws are price ceilings, and minimum wage laws are price floors. A closer look at each will help to highlight the perils of interfering with the law of supply and demand.

PRICE CEILINGS: THE CASE OF RENT CONTROL

Price ceilings are always tempting to governments because they seem an easy way to assure that everyone will be able to afford a particular product. Thus, in the last couple of decades in Canada, price ceilings have been set for various goods, from natural gas to oil to rental accommodation. In each case where the government has attempted to set a price ceiling, the result has been to create shortages at the controlled price; more people want to buy the product than there are products, because producers have no incentive to produce more of the good. Those who can buy at the cheaper price benefit; producers and those unable to buy suffer.

Rent control is one example of a price ceiling. The effect of rent control laws—setting the maximum rent that a landlord can charge for a one-bedroom apartment, for example—is illustrated by Figure 5.14. In panel A, R^* is the market equilibrium rental

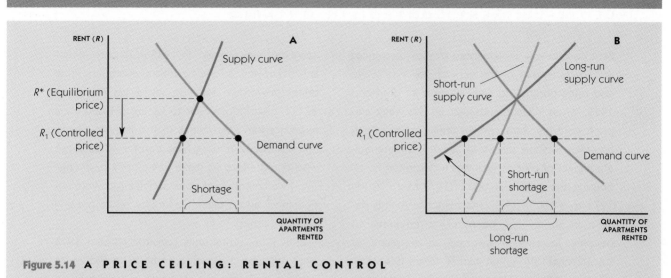

Figure 5.14 **A PRICE CEILING: RENTAL CONTROL**

Rent control laws limit the rents apartment owners may charge. If rents are held down to R_1, below the market-clearing level R^*, as in panel A, there will be excess demand for apartments. Panel B shows the long-run response. The supply of rental housing is more elastic in the long run, since landlords can refuse to build new apartment buildings, or they can sell existing apartments as condominiums. The price ceiling eventually leads to the quantity supplied being even farther below the quantity demanded.

rate at which the demand for housing equals the supply. However, the provincial government is concerned that at R^*, many poor people cannot afford housing in the cities, so it imposes a law that says that rents may be no higher than R_1. At R_1, there is an excess demand for apartments. While the motives behind the government action may well have been praiseworthy—after all, making sure that everyone can afford housing is a laudable goal—the government has created an artificial scarcity.

The problems caused by rent control are likely to be worse in the long run than in the short run. In the short run, the quantity of apartments does not change much; in other words, the supply of apartments is inelastic in the short run. But in the long run, the quantity of apartments can decline for several reasons. They may be abandoned as they deteriorate; they can be converted to condominiums and sold instead of rented; and apartment owners may not wish to construct new ones if they cannot charge enough in rent to cover their costs. As argued earlier, long-run supply curves are likely to be more elastic than short-run supply curves.

Panel B illustrates the probable result. Rent control leads to a housing shortage that is likely to increase over time. Rent control results in all *existing* renters being better off, whether they are poor or rich, at least as long as the landlord stays in the business. But the quantity of available rental housing will decrease, so that many would-be residents will be unable to find rental housing in the market. Since renters tend to be poorer than those who can buy a home, a shortage of rental housing will tend to hurt the poor most.

These predicted results have been confirmed by the experience of Toronto. The Ontario government has had some form of rent control since 1975, but it was extended to cover virtually all rental units in 1986. At the time, rents were rising rapidly and there

CLOSE-UP: RENT CONTROL IN ONTARIO

Rent control was implemented by most provinces in Canada as part of the general policy of wage and price controls to fight inflation in 1974 and 1975. When inflation subsided, so did wage and price controls. Rent control remained in effect, however, in some places. In Ontario, the immediate impact of rent control was a decline in rental housing starts, from 26,000 in 1973 to 15,000 in 1974 to 3,800 in 1975. The response to this decline in supply has been for governments to become increasingly involved as suppliers or subsidizers in the rental market. Given this subsidization and the social and political opposition to rent decontrol, rent control has become entrenched since 1974 in Ontario.

Although the rationale behind rent control is to give lower-income persons access to affordable housing, other economic classes often benefit most from the system. The decreased supply of rental units reduces the turnover rate and thus the availability of rental housing. The original occupiers of the regulated housing are the initial winners.

Contributing to this allocation problem is the existence of "key money." In 1985 in Toronto, a tenant occupying a one-bedroom apartment in a prime downtown location might be offered a $2,000 cash inducement to vacate ($5,000 for a two-bedroom apartment). In this manner, cheap rent-controlled housing was transferred to those who could afford to make key-money payments. The government's rent-control objectives were undermined, and a black market for rental housing was established.

Until 1986, rental units constructed after 1975 were not subject to rent control. Since middle- to upper-income persons could more easily gain access to the limited number of regulated units becoming available (through the black market), lower-income persons were left either to scramble for a place in the newer, uncontrolled, and more expensive units, or were forced into run-down areas or even onto the street.

In 1986, several changes to the Ontario system of rent control were enacted in order to enhance equity and efficiency. Landlords were allowed to cover maintenance costs in their yearly rent in-

creases, thereby reducing the incentive to allow rent-controlled units to become run down. And, post-1975 construction was included in the rent-control scheme. Still, in 1987, the vacancy rate of rental units in Toronto was only 0.1 percent. In the early 1980s, the four western provinces and New Brunswick all removed the rent controls that had been in existence since the 1970s. Vacancy rates in 1987 for Vancouver, Edmonton, and St. John were 2.3 percent, 5.5 percent, and 5.4 percent, respectively.

It appears that rent controls have not been effective in providing low-cost housing to the poor. In addition to the effects on the rental market itself, there have also been effects on the owner-occupied housing market and on labour mobility. The severe shortage of rental housing is seen by some economists as a problem that only decontrol and a freely functioning market can solve.

Sources: Lawrence B. Smith, "An Economic Assessment of Rent Controls: The Ontario Experience," in Richard J. Arnott and Jack M. Mintz, eds., *Rent Control: The International Experience* (Kingston, Ontario: The John Deutsch Institute for the Study of Economic Policy), pp. 57–72; R. Andrew Muller, "Ontario's Options in the Light of the Canadian Experience with Decontrol," in Richard J. Arnott and Jack M. Mintz, eds., *Policy Forum on Rent Controls in Ontario* (Kingston, Ontario: The John Deutsch Institute for the Study of Economic Policy), pp. 21–38.

was a fear that rental accommodation would become unaffordable to the less well-off. In fact, the high rents reflected a shortage of rental accommodation, caused in part by the rapid growth in the population of Toronto. Rent control served to increase the shortage of accommodation even further by discouraging the building of rental units at a time when the demand for them was growing more rapidly than ever. The shortage made it even more difficult for low-income persons to find suitable accommodation. It also gave rise to a whole set of questionable practices as apartment owners tried to find alternative ways of obtaining revenues or reducing costs (such as imposing incidental charges, neglecting needed repairs, imposing an up-front charge for leasing an apartment, and subletting at a higher price), some legal and some not. In addition, landlords could be more selective in choosing to whom they rented their properties, resulting in discrimination by income, family size, gender, or race.

The reason why rent control has such deleterious effects in the long run is that it is typically imposed as a permanent measure. In contrast to this, governments have occasionally resorted to price ceilings to alleviate the adverse effects that would arise from temporary shortages. During World War II, there was a need to divert enormous amounts of resources from consumer goods to military equipment and supplies. The result was a temporary shortage of consumer goods that would have resulted in rapid increases in their prices. The chief beneficiaries of this would have been the suppliers of consumer goods, who would have gained at the expense of consumers. Rationing was introduced as a temporary measure to restrict artificially the excess demand that otherwise would have developed and caused prices to rise. This was, however, recognized to be a temporary measure introduced explicitly to prevent the windfall gain that would have accrued to the producers and also to preclude them from increasing output in response to the rise in prices. In other words, creating shortages was perceived to be part of the solution. In the case of rent control, it is part of the problem.

PRICE FLOORS:
THE CASE OF THE MINIMUM WAGE

To many Canadians, it has long seemed fair that if you work full-time fifty-two weeks a year at some job, you ought to earn enough to support yourself and a family. Yet, there are some jobs, especially those demanding low-level skills, for which this may not be the case. In the absence of government intervention, the wage rates on such jobs might be so low as to leave the worker and the worker's family living in poverty. The result is either that other members of the family are forced to go to work or all are forced to live in poverty. Given this possibility it is easy to see the source of the sentiment for governments to interfere with the market and attempt to force firms to pay a decent wage. In Canada, all provinces and territories have enacted **minimum wages** at rates ranging from $4.75 per hour in Newfoundland and Prince Edward Island to $6.00 in Ontario and $6.50 in the Northwest Territories. Rates have tended to be raised periodically to keep pace with the cost of living, and have tended to be about half the average wage for all workers.

The minimum wage is an example of a price floor. While price ceilings are meant to help demanders (buyers), price floors are meant to help suppliers (sellers). With a price floor such as the minimum wage, buyers (employers) cannot pay less than the government-set minimum price.

Price floors have predictable effects too. The reasoning is simply the reverse of the reasoning for price ceilings. If the government attempts to raise the minimum wage higher than the equilibrium wage, the demand for workers will be reduced and the supply increased. There will be an excess supply of labour. Of course, those who are lucky enough to get a job will be better off at the higher wage than at the market equilibrium wage; but there are others, who might have been employed at the lower market equilibrium wage, who cannot find employment and are worse off. These tend to be among the least-skilled workers.

How much unemployment does the minimum wage create? That depends on the level at which the minimum wage is set and on the elasticity of demand and supply for labour. If the minimum wage is set low enough, then it has little effect, either on wages or on unemployment. Panel A of Figure 5.15 shows a market in which an equilibrium wage is above the minimum wage. A small increase in the minimum wage thus has no effect on either the wage rate or the employment level. With the current level of minimum wages, only the very unskilled individuals—those whose wages would have been below the minimum wage—are affected. In Canada, perhaps the major unemployment effect of minimum wages is on teenagers. Most other workers, even the unskilled, get paid more than the minimum wage.

Panel B of Figure 5.15 shows a case where the demand and supply for unskilled labour are very inelastic, so that wages can be increased significantly, with little increase in unemployment. In panel C, the demand and supply for unskilled labour are both very elastic, and the minimum wage has been set substantially above the market equilibrium price. As a result, substantial unemployment is generated with an increase in the minimum wage.

Recent policy discussions on minimum wages have focused on whether the original intent of minimum wage legislation—to ensure that those who work earn enough to support a family—makes any sense. While it may have been reasonable back in the 1930s to assume that one man needed to earn a certain minimum wage to support a wife

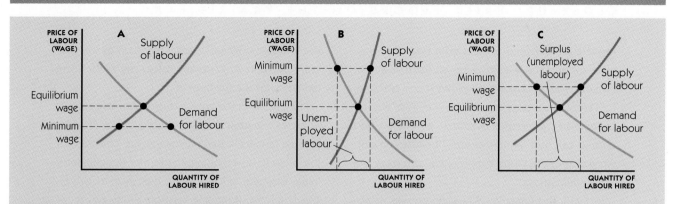

Figure 5.15 EFFECTS OF MINIMUM WAGES

In panel A, the minimum wage is below the equilibrium wage. However, since the minimum wage is a price floor, there is nothing to stop the market from paying the higher equilibrium wage, and any increase in the minimum wage will have no effect so long as the minimum wage remains below the equilibrium wage. In panel B, an increase in the minimum wage will result in very little increase in unemployment, as the demand and supply curves for labour are inelastic. In panel C, the demand and supply curves are more elastic; the minimum wage is above the equilibrium wage, creating a large surplus of workers who would like to work but cannot find jobs. Increases in the minimum wage in this case will increase unemployment significantly.

and family, today's labour market often has both spouses and even a teenage child or two working. Surely they do not *all* need to earn enough to support their own family. In addition, a higher minimum wage does not seem a particularly useful way to help the poor. Most poor people earn more than the minimum wage *when they are working*; their problem is not low wages. The problem comes when they are not working. And this may be either because they cannot find a job, in which case the problem is the level of unemployment, not the level of wages, and increasing wages may make it even more difficult to find a job; or because they are not well enough to work. Only about 10 percent of people in poverty work at jobs that pay at or near the minimum wage. Thus, the minimum wage is not a good way of trying to deal with problems of poverty. Other government programs need to be designed to address those problems.

ALTERNATIVE SOLUTIONS

Widespread unhappiness with the workings of the law of supply and demand is understandable because large changes in prices cause distress. It is natural to try to find scapegoats and to look to the government for a solution. Such situations call for compassion, and the economists' caution against the use of scapegoats and government action can seem coldhearted. But the fact remains that in competitive markets, the price changes are simply the impersonal workings of the law of supply and demand; without the price changes, there will be shortages and surpluses. The examples of government attempts to interfere with the workings of supply and demand provide an important cautionary tale: one ignores the workings of the law of supply and demand only at one's peril. It is a les-

CLOSE-UP: PRICE FLOORS ON THE PRAIRIE FARM

Farmers are exposed to risks from both the environment and the market. After all the investment of hard work and money in plowing and planting, bad weather or bugs can decimate a crop. But unexpectedly wonderful weather at home and abroad can hurt farmers as well: it causes an outward shift of the world supply curve, driving down equilibrium prices.

In 1935, the Canadian Wheat Board was established by the federal government as the marketing agent for Prairie farmers. But the Wheat Board is more than a middleman in the grain trade. Its other role is to provide a kind of price insurance to farmers. Every year, the federal government sets "initial payments" for all grades of wheat and barley, based on grains market analysis. These initial payments represent price floors for the farmer, since they are guaranteed minimum prices for his crops. If market prices for grains, net of appropriate costs, are lower than the initial payments, the loss to the Wheat Board is made up by the federal government. If market prices are higher, the farmer reaps the full benefit.

Price floors in the grain industry can have consequences, whether they are binding or not. They influence farmers in two main ways. For one thing, if the price floor is binding, the farmer benefits from initial payment prices higher than market prices. This is a form of income support or insurance for the farmer. But it is more than pure insurance. Since price floors prevent the price from falling but not from rising, the insurance is one-sided. It should cause the average or expected price to rise. (Ordinary insurance would reduce price fluctuations, but would not change the average around which prices fluctuate.) This increase in the average price of grain would encourage farmers to supply more than they would otherwise. Thus, it is similar in effect to a subsidy to grain farmers on their output.

At international trade negotiations and conferences, grain traders typically object to policies in other countries that introduce supply distortions and flood the market with produce. Indeed, most countries, including the United States and the nations of Europe, have some form of agricultural subsidy programs, whether by price support or by more direct means. The question is: How effective have different types of policies been at subsidizing grain supplies and leading to a glut on world markets, as opposed simply to protecting farmers from the vagaries of weather and the world market?

Some recent studies in Canada have suggested that the initial payment policy of the Canadian Wheat Board has not had a significant effect on Prairie grain supplies but has operated more to protect farmers' incomes after the fact. The argument is that uncertainty about the market price means that the initial payment policy does not necessarily reduce uncertainty faced by farmers and may not even cause the average price they expect to receive to rise. Part of the uncertainty arises because of the fact that at the time of seeding the farmer does not know what grades of grain he will harvest. The authors of the studies conclude that the initial payment policy has a minimal supply effect and in their view should not have been treated as an agricultural subsidy in the multilateral trade negotiations that took place under the General Agreement on Tariffs and Trade (GATT). Abolition of the policy would eliminate a form of insurance to farmers without necessarily having any significant effect on grain supplies. Since initial payments are no longer announced prior to seeding, but just prior to harvest, the value of this price insurance is even lower than determined in these studies.

Sources: J. Stephen Clark, Jonalyn K. Siemens, and Catherine S. Fleming, "Effects of Initial Payment Policy on the Welfare of Saskatchewan Wheat and Barley Producers," *Canadian Journal of Agricultural Economics* 38 (1990): 385–404; J. Stephen Clark and Catherine S. Fleming, "Estimating Price Distortions Caused by Canadian Wheat Board Initial Payment Policy," *Canadian Journal of Agricultural Economics* 38 (1990): 923–30.

son that politicians seem to need to learn over and over again. This does not mean, however, that the government should simply ignore the distress caused by large price and wage changes. It only means that government must take care in addressing the problems; price controls, including price ceilings and floors, are unlikely to be effective instruments.

Later chapters will discuss some of the ways in which the government can try to address the problems that arise from dissatisfaction with the consequences of the law of supply and demand, by making use of the power of the market rather than trying to fight against it. For example, if the government is concerned with low wages paid to unskilled workers, it can try to increase the demand for these workers. A shift to the right in the demand curve will increase the wages these workers receive. The government can do this either by subsidizing firms that hire unskilled workers or by providing more training to these workers and thus increasing their productivity.

If the government wants to increase the supply of housing to the poor, it can provide housing subsidies for the poor, which will elicit a greater supply. If government wants to conserve on the use of gasoline, it can impose a tax on gasoline. Noneconomists often object that these sorts of economic incentives have other distasteful consequences, and sometimes they do. But government policies that take account of the law of supply and demand will tend to be more effective, with fewer unfortunate side effects, than policies that try to ignore the predictable economic consequences that follow from disregarding the law of supply and demand.

REVIEW AND PRACTICE

SUMMARY

1. The price elasticity of demand describes how sensitive the quantity demanded of a good is to changes in the price of the good. When demand is inelastic, an increase in the price has little effect on quantity demanded; when demand is elastic, an increase in the price has a large effect on quantity demanded.

2. If price changes do not induce much change in demand, the demand curve is very steep and is said to be inelastic, or insensitive to price changes. If the demand curve is very flat, indicating that the price changes induce large changes in demand, demand is said to be elastic, or sensitive to prices changes. Demand for necessities is usually quite inelastic; demand for luxuries is elastic.

3. The price elasticity of supply describes how sensitive the quantity supplied of a good is to changes in the price of the good.

4. If price changes do not induce much change in supply, the supply curve is very steep and is said to be inelastic. If the supply curve is very flat, indicating that price changes cause large changes in supply, supply is said to be elastic.

5. The extent to which a shift in the supply curve is reflected in price or quantity depends on the shape of the demand curve. The more elastic the demand, the more a given shift in the supply curve will be reflected in changes in equilibrium quantities and the less it will be reflected in changes in equilibrium prices. The more inelastic the demand, the more a given shift in the supply curve will be reflected in changes in equilibrium prices and the less it will be reflected in changes in equilibrium quantities.

6. Likewise, the extent to which a shift in the demand curve is reflected in price or quantity depends on the shape of the supply curve.

7. Demand and supply curves are likely to be more elastic in the long run than in the short run. Therefore a shift in the demand or supply curve is likely to have a larger price effect in the short run and a larger quantity effect in the long run.

8. Elasticities can be used to predict to what extent consumer prices rise when a tax is imposed on a good. If the demand curve for a good is very inelastic, consumers in effect have to pay the tax. If the demand curve is very elastic, the quantities produced and the price received by producers are likely to decline considerably.

9. Government regulations may prevent a market from moving towards its equilibrium price, leading to shortages or surpluses. Price ceilings lead to excess demand. Price floors lead to excess supply.

KEY TERMS

price elasticity of
  demand
price elasticity of
  supply
infinite elasticity of
  demand

infinite elasticity of
  supply
zero elasticity of
  demand
zero elasticity of
  supply

market clearing
shortage
surplus
sticky prices
price ceiling
price floor

REVIEW QUESTIONS

1. What is meant by the elasticity of demand and the elasticity of supply? Why do economists find these concepts useful?

2. Is the slope of a perfectly elastic demand or supply curve horizontal or vertical? Is the slope of a perfectly inelastic demand or supply curve horizontal or vertical? Explain.

3. If the elasticity of demand is unity, what happens to total revenue as the price increases? What if the demand for a product is very inelastic? What if it is very elastic?

4. Under what condition will a shift in the demand curve result mainly in a change in quantity? in price?

5. Under what condition will a shift in the supply curve result mainly in a change in price? in quantity?

6. Why do the elasticities of demand and supply tend to change from the short run to the long run?

7. Under what circumstances will a tax on a product be passed along to consumers?

8. Why do price ceilings tend to lead to shortages? Why do price floors tend to lead to surpluses?

PROBLEMS

1. Suppose the price elasticity of demand for gasoline is .2 in the short run and .7 in the long run. If the price of gasoline rises 28 percent, what effect on quantity demanded will this have in the short run? in the long run?

2. Imagine that the short-run price elasticity of supply for a farmer's corn is .3, while the long-run price elasticity is 2. If prices for corn fall 30 percent, what are the short-run and long-run changes in quantity supplied? What are the short- and long-run changes in quantity supplied if prices rise by 15 percent? What happens to the farmer's revenues in each of these situations?

3. Assume that the demand curve for hard liquor is highly inelastic and the supply curve for hard liquor is highly elastic. If the tastes of the drinking public shift away from hard liquor, will the effect be larger on price or on quantity? If the federal gov-

ernment decides to impose a tax on manufacturers of hard liquor, will the effect be larger on price or on quantity? What is the effect of an advertising program that succeeds in discouraging people from drinking? Draw diagrams to illustrate each of your answers.

4. Imagine that wages (the price of labour) are sticky in the labour market, and that a supply of new workers enters that market. Will the market be in equilibrium in the short run? Why or why not? If not, explain the relationship you would expect to see between the quantity demanded and supplied, and draw a diagram to illustrate. Explain how sticky wages in the labour market affect unemployment.

5. For each of the following markets, explain whether you would expect prices in that market to be relatively sticky or not:

(a) the stock market;
(b) the market for autoworkers;
(c) the housing market;
(d) the market for cut flowers;
(e) the market for pizza-delivery people.

6. Suppose a government wishes to assure that its citizens can afford adequate housing. Consider three ways of pursuing that goal. One method is to pass a law requiring that all rents be cut by one-quarter. A second method offers a subsidy to all builders of homes. A third provides a subsidy directly to renters equal to one-quarter of the rent they pay. Predict what effect each of these proposals would have on the price and quantity of rental housing in the short run and the long run.

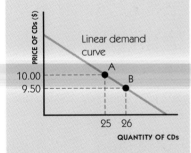

Figure 5.16 LINEAR DEMAND CURVE

The slope of this linear demand curve, the change in price divided by the change in quantity (rise over run), is the same at all points on the curve. But the elasticity of demand, the percentage change in quantity divided by the percentage change in price, changes as we move along the curve. At point A, elasticity of demand is higher than it is at B.

APPENDIX: ALGEBRAIC DERIVATION OF ELASTICITIES

The association of the steepness of demand curves with their elasticities implies some relationship between the elasticity and the slope of a demand curve. But while the two concepts are related, there are also important differences.

In the appendix to Chapter 2, the slope of a line was defined as the change in the vertical axis resulting from a change of one unit along the horizontal axis—the rise over the run. Figure 5.16 shows a demand curve for CDs; it is called a **linear demand curve** because it is a straight line. We write the slope as

$$\text{slope} = \frac{\Delta p}{\Delta Q} \quad ,$$

where the symbol Δ, the Greek letter delta, is used to represent change. Thus, the above expression reads, "Slope equals delta p divided by delta Q" or, "Slope equals the change in price divided by the change in quantity." At point A, the slope is −$0.50 per CD, because an increase in the quantity by 1 reduces the price from $10.00 to $9.50. In fact, the slope is −$.50 all along this demand curve, a result of the general rule that the slope of a straight line is the same at all points along the line.

The elasticity of demand, as stated in this chapter, is the percentage change in quantity demanded corresponding to a 1 percent change in price or, more generally in mathematical terms,

$$\text{elasticity of demand} = \frac{\text{percentage change in quantity demanded}}{\text{percentage change in price}}.$$

When there is a 1 percent change in price, then the elasticity is equal to the percentage change in quantity demanded.

The percentage change in price is taken as the change in the price divided by the price,[3] and likewise for quantity:

$$\text{percentage change in price} = \frac{\Delta p}{p}\quad,$$

$$\text{percentage change in quantity demanded} = \frac{\Delta Q_d}{Q_d},$$

where Q_d is the quantity demanded. Thus, the elasticity of demand is defined as

$$\text{elasticity of demand} = \frac{\Delta Q_d/Q_d}{\Delta p/p} = \frac{\Delta Q_d}{\Delta p} \times \frac{p}{Q_d},$$

the percentage change in the quantity demanded divided by the percentage change in price.[4]

If the price of a CD decreases by $.50 and the price initially is $10.00, that represents a decrease in price of 5 percent ($.50/$10.00 × 100). The quantity increase of 1, from 25 CDs to 26 CDs, represents an increase in quantity demanded of 4 percent (1/25 × 100). So in our example, the elasticity of demand for CDs would be .8 (.04/.05) at Point A.

The equation for elasticity is closely related to the one above for slope, with two important differences. First, the elasticity equation puts quantity on top and price on the bottom, while slope does the opposite. This reflects, in the case of slope, a mathematical convention (price is usually on the vertical axis) and, in the case of elasticity, the economist's focus on quantity changes induced by price changes.

Second, elasticity is stated in percentage terms, which means that it is free of the units (in this case, number of CDs) that carry over in the calculation of slope. The reason percentages are used is that they mean elasticities will be the same no matter what units are used. If the good in question is eggs, it will not matter if we measure them singly or by

---

[3]This raises a slight technical problem: do we express the change as a percentage of the initial price, the final price, or a price somewhere in between? If the change is small enough, the percentages we calculate each of these ways will be approximately the same; it makes little difference. In our example, if we had calculated the change as a percentage of final price, we would have obtained $.50/$9.50 = .052 rather than .050.

[4]Students familiar with calculus will note that the elasticity can be written in a simple form. We simply substitute the expression dQ/dp for the expression $\Delta Q_d/\Delta p$.

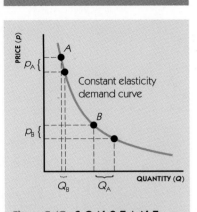

Figure 5.17 CONSTANT ELASTICITY DEMAND CURVE

The elasticity of demand is the same for every price along this demand curve; the slope, however, is not constant.

the dozen. But the calculation of the slope of a linear demand curve for eggs will change if we change our unit of measurement from eggs to dozens of eggs.

Note that even though the slope of a linear demand curve is constant, the elasticity changes as we move along the curve. In Figure 5.16, the slopes at A and B are the same, but at A the ratio of price to quantity, p/Q, is much higher than at B: price is higher and quantity is lower. Hence the elasticity of demand at A is higher than at B. Figure 5.17 shows a demand curve for which the elasticity is the same at every price. This demand curve is called the **constant elasticity demand curve.** (Note that the slope in this case is not constant.)

The fact that the elasticity of demand is constant means that we can take any two points along the curve, such as A and B, and calculate the elasticity, and it would be the same. At A, the elasticity is

$$\frac{\Delta Q_A}{\Delta p_A} \times \frac{p_A}{Q_A},$$

and at B, it is

$$\frac{\Delta Q_B}{\Delta p_B} \times \frac{p_B}{Q_B}.$$

Because the curve has constant elasticity, the two numbers are the same.

The analysis for elasticity of supply proceeds in an analogous fashion. The elasticity of supply is the percentage change in quantity supplied corresponding to a 1 percent increase in price or, more generally,

$$\text{elasticity of supply} = \frac{\text{percentage change in quantity supplied}}{\text{percentage change in price}}.$$

Again, when there is a 1 percent change in price, the elasticity of supply is equal to the percentage change in quantity supplied. As before, we can write the percentage change in price as $\Delta p/p$ and the percentage change in quantity supplied as $\Delta Q_s/Q_s$, where Q_s denotes the quantity supplied. Thus, the elasticity of supply is defined as

$$\text{elasticity of supply} = \frac{\Delta Q_s/Q_s}{\Delta p/p}.$$

CHAPTER 6

TIME AND RISK

T he discussion of markets in Chapters 4 and 5 might lead an astute observer to ask two questions. First, how do markets take account of the future? The litre of ice cream you buy today is for consumption in the present and has no value five years down the road, but real estate, gold coins, and other goods may retain their value or even increase in value over time. The first part of this chapter shows how prices in the present are linked to expectations of prices in the future.

Since we never know for sure what the future will bring, we can never be sure what future prices will be. This raises the second question, that of risk. How does uncertainty affect markets? Firms build new plants; they also fund projects designed to produce new products or new techniques of production. In both cases, they cannot know with certainty what the future value of the plant or product will be. When individuals face risk, sometimes they can buy insurance, as when a home owner buys fire insurance. But sometimes they cannot. They cannot buy insurance against the risk of not graduating from university. Nor can a firm buy insurance against the risk that its newest product will be a failure. How well market economies handle the problems posed by risk has much to do with their successes. Conversely, shortcomings in their ability to handle risk will have much to do with their failures. In the latter part of this chapter, we investigate insurance and other markets for risk.

KEY QUESTIONS

1. How do we compare a dollar received next year or in five years' time with a dollar received today?

2. What determines the demand for an asset like gold, which is purchased mainly with the intent of selling it at some later date? What determines shifts in the demand curve for assets?

3. Why do people buy insurance?

4. Why are there many risks for which insurance is not available?

5. How do the different ways that firms raise funds in the capital market affect the risks borne by the investors who provide those funds? Why do some firms have to pay a higher interest rate on what they borrow than do others?

INTEREST

The simplest future-oriented transaction occurs when you put money into a bank account. In effect, you have loaned your money to the bank, and the bank has promised to pay you back whenever you say. But banks offer more than security; they offer you a *return* on your savings. This return, like the return on any loan, is called **interest.** If you put $1,000 in the bank at the beginning of the year, and the interest rate is 10 percent per year, you will receive $1,100 at the end of the year. The $100 is the payment of interest, while the $1,000 is the repayment of the **principal,** the original amount lent to the bank.

To an economist, the interest rate is like a price. Normally, we express prices in terms of dollars. If the price of an orange is $1.00, that means we must give up $1.00 to get one orange. Economists talk about the relative price of two goods as the amount of one good you have to give up to get one more unit of the other. The relative price is just the ratio of the "dollar" prices.

For example, if the price of an apple is $.50 and the price of an orange is $1.00, then the relative price (that is, the ratio of the prices) is 2. If we wish to consume one more orange, we have to give up two apples. The relative price is thus just a way of describing a trade-off. Similarly, if the interest rate is 10 percent, by giving up $1.00 worth of consumption today, a saver can have $1.10 worth of consumption next year.

Thus, the rate of interest tells us how much additional future consumption we can get by giving up $1.00 worth of current consumption. It allows us to determine the relative price between the present and the future.

THE TIME VALUE OF MONEY

Interest rates are normally positive. This means that *$1.00 today is worth more than $1.00 in the future.* If you have $1.00 today, you can put it into the bank and, if the interest rate is 5 percent, receive $1.05 at the end of next year. Similarly, if you wanted $1.00 today, you could borrow it and promise to pay $1.05 in a year. In short, $1.00 today is worth, in this example, $1.05 next year.

Economists use the concept of **present discounted value** to calculate and express how much less $1.00 in the future is worth than $1.00 today. The present discounted value of $100 a year from now is what you would pay today for $100 a year from now. Suppose the interest rate is 10 percent. If you put $90.91 in the bank today, at the end of the year you will receive $9.09 interest, which together with the original amount will total $100. Thus, $90.91 is the present discounted value of $100 a year from now, if the interest rate is 10 percent.

There is a simple formula for calculating the present discounted value of any amount to be received a year from now: just divide the amount by 1 plus the annual rate of interest. The annual rate of interest is often denoted by r.

To check this formula, consider the present discounted value of $100. According to the formula, it is $100/(1 + r)$. That means that if you put $100 in the bank today, at the end of the year you will have the principal ($100) *times* $(1 + r)$. Thus, if you take the present discounted value, $100 / (1 + r)$, and put it in the bank, at the end of the year you will have

$$\frac{\$100}{1 + r} \times (1 + r) = \$100,$$

confirming our conclusion that $100 / (1 + r)$ today is the same as $100 one year from now.

A similar calculation can be performed to figure the present discounted value of $100 to be received two years from now. The problem now is to take **compound interest** into account. In the second year, you earn interest on the interest you earned the first year. (By contrast, simple interest does not take into account the interest you earn on

---

PRESENT DISCOUNTED VALUE

Present discounted value of $1.00 next year $= \dfrac{\$1.00}{1 + \text{interest rate}}$.

Often the annual interest rate is denoted by r, so the right-hand side of the equation

becomes $\dfrac{\$1.00}{1 + r}$.

Table 6.1 PRESENT DISCOUNTED VALUE OF $100

Year received	Present discounted value
Next year	$\dfrac{1}{1+r} \times 100 = \dfrac{100}{1+r}$
Two years from now	$\dfrac{1}{1+r} \times \dfrac{100}{1+r} = \dfrac{100}{(1+r)^2}$
Three years from now	$\dfrac{1}{1+r} \times \dfrac{100}{(1+r)^2} = \dfrac{100}{(1+r)^3}$

interest you have previously earned.) If the rate of interest is 10 percent and is compounded annually, $100 today is worth $110 a year from now and $121 (*not* $120) in two years' time. Thus, the present discounted value today of $121 two years from now is $100. Table 6.1 shows how to calculate the present discounted value of $100 received next year, two years from now, and three years from now.

We can now see how to calculate the value of an investment project that will yield a return over several years. We look at what the returns will be each year, adjust them to their present discounted values, and then add these values up. Table 6.2 shows how this is done for a project that yields $10,000 next year and $15,000 the year after, and that you plan to sell in the third year for $50,000. The second column of the table shows the return in each year. The third column shows the discount factor—what we multiply the return by to obtain the present discounted value of that year's return. The calculations assume an interest rate of 10 percent. The fourth column multiplies the return by the discount factor to obtain the present discounted value of that year's return. In the bot-

Table 6.2 CALCULATING PRESENT DISCOUNTED VALUE OF A THREE-YEAR PROJECT

Year	Return	Discount factor ($r = 0.10$)	Present discounted value ($r = 0.10$)
1	$10,000	$\dfrac{1}{1.10}$	$ 9,091
2	$15,000	$\dfrac{1}{(1.10)^2} = \dfrac{1}{1.21}$	$12,397
3	$50,000	$\dfrac{1}{(1.10)^3} = \dfrac{1}{1.331}$	$37,566
Total	$75,000	—	$59,054

tom row of the table, the present discounted values of each year's return have been added up to obtain the total present discounted value of the project. Notice that it is much smaller than the number we obtain simply by adding up the returns, the "undiscounted" yield of the project.

EFFECTS OF CHANGES IN THE INTEREST RATE

If the interest rate increases, the present discounted value of $100 a year from now will decrease. If the interest rate should rise to 20 percent, for example, the present discounted value of $100 a year from now becomes $83.33 (100/1.2).

Thus, if the interest rate rises, the present discounted value of the returns from any investment project will be diminished. This can be seen in Table 6.3, where the value of the project shown in Table 6.2 has been calculated at a 20 percent as well as a 10 percent interest rate. The present value, $47,685, is now even lower.

The concept of present discounted value is an important one because so many decisions in economics are oriented to the future. Whether the decision is made by a person buying a house or saving money for retirement or a company building a factory or making an investment, it is necessary to be able to calculate how to value money that will be received one, two, five, or ten years in the future. Economists say that it is necessary to remember the time value of money. The concept of present discounted value tells us precisely how to do that.

Table 6.3 CHANGING THE INTEREST RATE

Year	Return	Present discounted value ($r = 0.10$)	Present discounted value ($r = 0.20$)
1	$10,000	$ 9,091	$ 8,333
2	$15,000	$12,397	$10,417
3	$50,000	$37,566	$28,935
Total	$75,000	$59,054	$47,685

THE MARKET FOR LOANABLE FUNDS

The previous section explained how the interest rate is a price, similar to the price of any other good, like apples and oranges. The price of borrowing a dollar is the dollar plus the annual rate of interest. How is the interest rate determined? Like other prices, the interest rate is determined by the law of supply and demand.

At any given time, there are some people and companies who would like to borrow, so they can spend more than they currently have. Rachel has her first job and knows she needs a car for transportation; George needs kitchen equipment, tables, and chairs to open his sandwich shop. Others would like to save, or spend less than they currently have. John is putting aside money for his children's university education and for his retirement; Sandy's Sauces has become a huge success, and Sandy cannot spend the money as fast as it is coming in.

The gains from trade, discussed in Chapter 3, apply equally well to what economists call **intertemporal** trades, which are exchanges that occur over time. When one individual lends money to another, both gain. John and Sandy can lend money to Rachel and George. John and Sandy will get paid interest in the future, to compensate them for letting Rachel and George use their funds now. Rachel and George are willing to pay the interest because to them, having the funds today is particularly valuable. The borrower may be a business firm like the one owned by George, who believes that with these funds he will be able to make an investment that will yield a return far higher than the interest rate charged. Or the borrower may be an individual facing some emergency, such as a medical crisis, that requires funds today. The borrower may even simply be a free spirit, wishing to consume as much as he can (as much as lenders are willing to give him), and letting the future take care of itself.

How is the supply of funds to be equated with the demand? Those who wish to borrow will have to pay interest, while those who save will receive interest. As the interest rate rises, some borrowers will be discouraged from borrowing. Rachel may decide to ride her bicycle to work and postpone buying a new car until she can save up the money herself (or until interest rates come down). At the same time, as the interest rate rises, some savers may be induced to save more. Their incentives for savings have increased. John realizes that every extra dollar he saves today will produce more money in the future, so he may put more aside.[1] Figure 6.1 shows the supply and demand curves for loanable funds. Here the interest rate is the "price," and the amount of money loaned and borrowed is the quantity. At r^*, the demand for funds equals the supply of funds.

Below r^*, the demand for funds exceeds the supply. The would-be borrowers who cannot get loans bid up the interest rate; those least desirous of borrowing drop out of the competition for the scarce funds. At the higher interest rates, savers save more, so there are more funds to go around. The process goes on until the interest rate is bid up to the level where supply equals demand. Exactly the converse process goes on if initially the interest rate is above r^*, where the supply of funds exceeds the demand.

We can now explain why the equilibrium interest rate is normally positive. If it were zero percent or negative, prospective borrowers would demand more funds than prospective savers would be willing to supply. Indeed, negative interest rates would mean that people could borrow to consume today and pay back less in the future, and that savers would receive less in the future than the amount they saved. Only at a positive interest rate can the demand for loans be equated to the supply.

In our economy, borrowers and lenders do not usually meet face to face. Instead, banks and other financial institutions serve as intermediaries, collecting savings from those who want to save and disbursing money to those who want to borrow. These inter-

---

[1]In Chapter 9, we will see that there is some controversy about whether higher interest rates really induce people to save more. Under some circumstances, increasing the interest rates can have even the perverse effect of reducing the supply of savings.

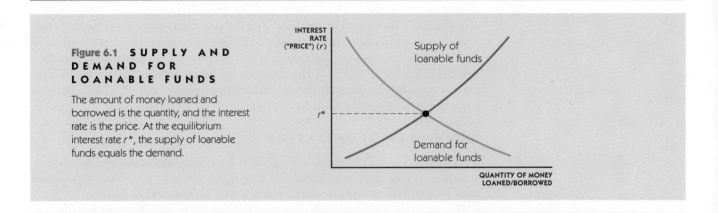

Figure 6.1 SUPPLY AND DEMAND FOR LOANABLE FUNDS

The amount of money loaned and borrowed is the quantity, and the interest rate is the price. At the equilibrium interest rate r^*, the supply of loanable funds equals the demand.

mediaries help make the market for loans work smoothly. For their services, the intermediaries charge fees, which can be measured as the difference between the interest rate they pay savers and the interest rate they charge borrowers.

TWO PROBLEMS IN INTERPRETING INTEREST RATES

When borrowers look at loan options and when savers look at investment options, they are confounded with an array of possibilities. Borrowers can pay back the money they borrow in two years or three years. One bank offers 9.5 percent interest compounded monthly; another offers 10 percent, compounded annually. These are exchanges, and as in any other exchanges, individuals should take care that what they are trading for matches their needs and expectations. Economists encourage people to consider two, often hidden, issues: the effect of compounding, and the effect of inflation on the true cost of borrowing or on the true return from investing.

THE EFFECT OF COMPOUNDING

The rate of compounding affects the total interest received or paid. We have already seen the benefits to the saver of interest compounded annually. Interest compounded monthly is even better because you start earning interest on interest more quickly, and most banks now have accounts that compound interest on a daily basis.

To see the advantage of more frequent compounding, consider the choice between an account that pays 10 percent compounded annually and one that pays 9.6 percent compounded daily. If you put $1,000 in the first account, at the end of the year you will get $1,100, and $1,210 at the end of two years. At 9.6 percent compounded daily, you will have $1,100.75 at the end of the year and $1,211.64 at the end of two. The faster rate of compounding makes the 9.6 percent rate better than the 10 percent rate.

The same story holds in reverse for borrowers. If you borrow $1,000 for two years at 10 percent annual interest, then with simple interest, you will pay the bank $1,200 at the end of two years. With annual compounding, at the end of the first year, you will owe the bank $1,100. At the end of two years, you will owe interest on the $100 interest you already owe, for a total of $1,210. With *daily* compounding, matters are worse—you will owe $1,221.37. Banks used to offer loans with the rate of compounding in the fine print. The confusion this caused led Parliament to enact a law requiring lenders to express all interest and charges as a rate per annum as well as an amount in dollars and cents (Section 243 of the Bank Act, 1980). This provision has been helpful to borrowers; savers too are wise to make the same conversion. For simplicity, in this book we will normally assume that interest is compounded annually.

THE EFFECT OF INFLATION

Borrowers and savers are also wise to consider the effect of **inflation** on loans and investments. Goods and services generally have higher prices this year than they did last year. This general upward creep of all prices is what economists call inflation.

Consider the case of an individual who decides to deposit $1,000 in a savings account. At the end of the year, at a 10 percent interest rate, she will have $1,100. But prices meanwhile have risen by 6 percent. That means that a good that cost $1,000 in the beginning of the year now costs $1,060. In terms of "purchasing power," she has only $40 extra to spend ($1,100 – $1,060)—4 percent more than she had at the beginning of the year. This is her real return. On the other hand, a borrower knows that if he borrows money, the dollars he gives back to repay the loan will be worth less than the dollars he receives today. Thus, what is relevant for individuals to know when deciding either how much to borrow or how much to lend (save) is the *real* interest rate, which takes account of inflation. It is the real interest rate that should appear on the vertical axis of Figure 6.1.

Economists separate interest rate measures into **nominal interest rates,** which name the amount you are paid in dollars, and **real interest rates,** which give the nominal interest rate minus the rate of inflation. The real interest rate tells how much extra *consumption*, or goods, you can get next year if you give up some consumption today. If the nominal interest rate is 10 percent and the rate of inflation is 6 percent, then the real interest rate is 4 percent. By lending out (or saving) a dollar today, you can increase the amount of goods that you can get in one year's time by 4 percent.

REAL INTEREST RATE

Real interest rate = nominal interest rate – rate of inflation

THE MARKET FOR ASSETS

Gardeners today would have been shocked at the price of tulip bulbs in seventeenth-century Holland, which rose to the point where one bulb sold for the equivalent of $16,000 in today's dollars. The golden age of tulips did not last long, however, and in

1637, prices of bulbs fell by over 90 percent. Such a dramatic price swing is by no means a quirk of history. Between 1973 and 1980, the price of gold rose from $98 to $613, or by 525 percent; then from 1980 to 1985, it fell to $318. Between 1975 and 1980, the price of farmland and capital increased by two and one-half times, only to fall by 15 percent from 1980 to 1989. In yet another example, on October 19, 1987, prices plummeted in stock markets around the world. In that single day, referred to as Black Monday, the total value of stock in Canadian companies decreased by almost 25 percent. Even a major war would be unlikely to destroy a quarter of the Canadian capital stock in a day. But there was no war or any other external event sufficient to explain the 1987 drop.

Just how large these price swings have been can be seen graphically in Figure 6.2, which shows how the prices of four assets have risen and fallen. If you bought at the low points and sold at the high, you could have made a fortune, but if you bought at the high points and sold at the low, you could have easily lost a fortune.

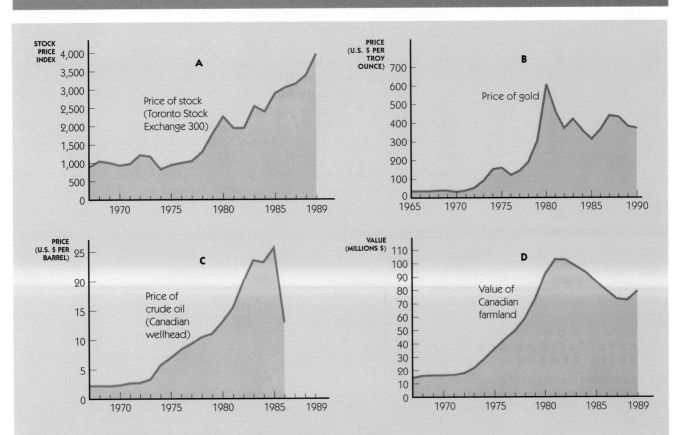

Figure 6.2 SWINGS IN PRICES OF FOUR ASSETS

Prices for some assets—such as stocks, gold, oil, and farmland— changed dramatically between 1965 and 1990. *Sources*: (A) Statistics Canada, CANSIM Database, 1993; (B) *Mineral Commodity Summaries* (1991); (C) John F. Helliwell, Mary E. MacGregor, Robert N. McRae, *Oil and Gas in Canada: Domestic Policies and World Events* (Toronto: Canadian Tax Foundation, 1988), p. 293; (D) Statistics Canada, CANSIM Database, 1993.

How can the demand and supply model of Chapters 4 and 5 explain these huge price swings? Surely the supply curves for these goods did not shift dramatically in such short intervals. Nor is it plausible that the uses to which the goods could be put suddenly expanded and then contracted, causing some fantastic shifts in demand. The solution to this puzzle lies in shifts of the demand curve, but not directly for the reasons we saw in Chapter 4.

The first step in the solution is to recognize that the goods in the examples above are unlike ice cream cones, newspapers, or any other goods that are valued by the consumer mainly for their present use. Gold, land, stock, and even tulips in seventeenth-century Holland are all examples of **assets.** Assets are long-lived and thus can be bought at one date and sold at another. For this reason, the price individuals are willing to pay for them today depends not only on today's conditions, the immediate return or benefits, but also on some expectation as to what tomorrow's conditions will be; in particular, on what the assets will be worth in the future, what they can be sold for.

The concept of present discounted value tells us how to measure and compare returns anticipated in the future. Changes in present discounted value shift demand curves, as shown in Figure 6.3, because the amount that someone is willing to pay today depends on the present discounted value of what she can get for it in the future. There are two sources of changes in present discounted value. The first is changes in the interest rate: an increase in the interest rate reduces the present discounted value of the dollars you expect to receive in the future. This is the explanation of much of the volatility of the stock markets in recent years (although not the October 1987 crash). For instance, increases in the interest rate are often accompanied by drops in the price of shares on the stock market, and vice versa. Smart investors thus try to forecast interest rates.

Second, since expectations of future prices are important in determining what individuals are willing to pay today, a change in the expected price of an asset at the time

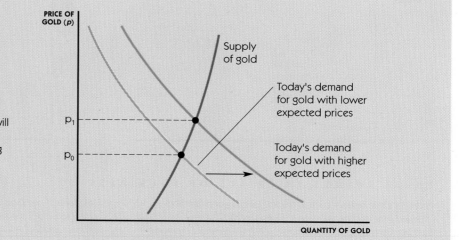

Figure 6.3 HOW EXPECTATIONS CAN SHIFT DEMAND

Expectations that the price of an asset will rise in the future can cause the demand curve to shift out to the right, thus raising the current price.

PRICE OF GOLD (p)

Supply of gold

Today's demand for gold with lower expected prices

Today's demand for gold with higher expected prices

p_1

p_0

QUANTITY OF GOLD

one expects to sell it will change the present discounted value. Again, this will lead to a shift in the demand curve. Expectations can be quite volatile, and this volatility in expectations explains a great deal of the volatility in asset prices.

To see how expectations concerning future events affect *current* prices, consider a hypothetical example. People suddenly realize that, ten years from now, a new rapid transit system will make certain parts of Toronto much more attractive as a place to live. As a result, future-oriented individuals will think that ten years from now, the price of land in those areas will be much higher, say $1 million per hectare. But, they think, nine years from now surely it will be recognized that in one short year one hectare will be worth $1 million. Hence, nine years from now investors will be willing to pay almost $1 million for the land; even if, at that date (nine years from now), the transit system has not yet been completed. But then, these same individuals think, eight years from now investors will realize that in one short year the price will rise to almost $1 million and will pay close to that amount. So working backwards, it becomes apparent that if people are confident that land is going to be much more valuable in ten years, its price rises today.

Thus, while changes in tastes or technology or incomes or the prices of other goods *today* could not account for some of the sharp changes in asset values described at the start of this section, changes in expectations concerning any of these variables in the future will have an effect *today* on the demand. Markets for assets are linked together over time. An event that will happen—or is expected to happen—ten or fifteen or even fifty years hence can have a direct bearing on today's market.

FORMING EXPECTATIONS

Changes in expectations of the future, about either returns or interest rates, thus can be reflected today in large changes in asset prices. How do individuals and firms form expectations? Partly by looking at past experience. If a company has steadily grown more valuable, investors may come to expect that pattern to continue. If every time inflation rates increase rapidly the banking authorities act to slow down the economy by raising interest rates, people come to expect inflation to be followed by higher interest rates.

Psychologists and economists have extensively studied how individuals form their expectations. Sometimes people are **myopic,** or short-sighted. They simply expect what is true today to be true tomorrow. The price of gold today is what it will be tomorrow. Sometimes they are **adaptive,** extrapolating events of the recent past into the future. For instance, if the price of gold today is 5 percent higher than it was last year, they expect its price next year to be 5 percent higher than it is today.

When people make full use of all the relevant available past data to form their expectations, economists say that their expectations are **rational.** While the price of gold rises during an inflationary period, the individual also knows that the price of gold goes down when inflation subsides. Thus, if a person knows that economic analysts are predicting lower inflation, he will not expect the gold price increases to continue. When individuals form their expectations rationally, they will not be right all the time. Sometimes they will be overly optimistic, sometimes overly pessimistic (although in making their decisions, they are aware of these possibilities), but the assumption of rational expectations is that on average they will be right.

The 1970s were a period when adaptive expectations reigned. Many investors came to expect prices to continue to rise at a rapid rate. The more you invested, the more money you made. The idea that the price of a house or of land might actually fall seemed beyond belief—in spite of the fact that historically there had been a number of episodes (most recently during the 1930s) when prices fell dramatically. The weak real estate markets of the 1980s in many regions became a reminder of the importance of incorporating more historical data in forming expectations.

The problem in all types of fortune-telling, however, is that history never repeats itself exactly. Since the situation today is never precisely like any past experience, it is never completely clear which facts will turn out to be the relevant ones. The last fifty years have seen a variety of gradual changes as corporations have expanded and diversified, governments have taken on new responsibilities, tax rates have bounced up and down, and the world economy has become more integrated. Indeed, all of society's institutions are in a state of flux that can be gradual or violent in turn. Even the best-informed experts are likely to disagree on which changes are likely to be most relevant. When it comes to predicting the future, everyone has a cloudy crystal ball.

FORECASTING: A FIRST LOOK

Despite the difficulty of making good forecasts, they are in great demand. Many economists have grown rich on the basis of a good forecasting record, and a whole industry has developed trying to provide better forecasts of everything—from the number of babies in ten years' time to the size of the economy to the demand for steel to the price of various shares on the stock market. There is money to be made if you can tell which stocks are going to do better in the market. If you know when the demand for your product is going to drop, you can make a better investment decision.

Forecasters often construct statistical models of an industry or of the economy to predict what will happen. Thus, a model of the industry will include an estimate of the demand curve and the supply curve (including an estimate of the price elasticity of demand and supply), and an analysis of the major factors that are likely to shift either the demand curve or the supply curve. These models can incorporate more of the relevant information than a "seat of the pants" guess about the future.

Some forecasters seem to predict a new Great Depression every other year, while others seem perpetually to believe that the Canadian economy is about to enter a golden age of unparalleled prosperity. Many of the forecasts are reminiscent of newspaper advertisements of long ago that promised to predict the sex of a child, with a money-back guarantee. Even if these seers had always predicted a boy, they would have been right half the time. So too—thanks to blind chance—practically all economic forecasters, no matter how incompetent, eventually have a day when they can crow, "I told you so!"

The real test of forecasters, of course, is not whether they are ever correct, but whether they are correct more consistently than mere chance can explain, and correct when it really counts. Despite the many jokes made about economic forecasters—for example, the claim that economists have predicted twelve out of the last five recessions—they have actually done a fairly credible job. The main failure has been in attempting to forecast turning points, when the economy switches from growth to stagnation, or stagnation to growth. But because one of the predicaments of business is to plan for turning points and one of the main objectives of government policy is to forestall downturns, this inability to predict turning points has been a major limitation.

THE MARKET FOR RISK

Risk accompanies most future-oriented economic activity, and most of us do not like this uncertainty about outcomes. We might spend a few dollars on some lottery tickets or playing the horses at the local racetrack, but for the most part, we try to avoid or minimize serious risks. Psychologists have extensively studied this "risk-avoidance behaviour," focusing, for instance, on the anxiety to which uncertainty gives rise. Economists refer to risk-avoidance behaviour by saying that individuals are **risk averse.**

Individuals are risk averse, and yet our economy needs to encourage risk taking. New ventures are risky, but they are the engine of economic growth. Our economy has developed a number of ways by which risks are transferred, transformed, and shared. The collection of institutions and arrangements by which this is done is known as the **market for risk.**

INSURANCE

Among the most important parts of the market for risk is the insurance market, in which people buy security from the financial risk of specified events—fires, car accidents, and other misfortunes. A look at the insurance market will supply us with some of the general issues and concerns in the market for risk.

When an individual takes out an insurance policy, she pays a fixed amount to the insurance company, the **premium,** in return for which she receives a promise that some payment will be made if the insured-against event occurs. Thus, the individual transfers the risk (at least the financial part of it) to the insurance firm. The insurance firm is able to absorb this risk for two reasons. First, it spreads the risk among a large number of people. If the insurance firm has many owners, as most do, the risks it takes are effectively carried by all of them.

Second, the insurance firm can predict risk quite accurately because it insures a large pool of individuals who face similar risks. The company may be looking at a population of a million people, all of whom want fire insurance. It can estimate with a fair degree of accuracy the number of individuals who will have a fire in a given year. If there is a 1 in 100 chance of a fire, with 1 million people insured, the firm can be fairly sure that approximately 10,000 will have fires. In a lucky year, 9,000 may have fires; in an unlucky year, 11,000. If the firm sets the premium at just slightly greater than the amount it expects to pay out on each policy, it can be quite confident that the premiums it collects will cover its disbursements.

Unfortunately, while individuals and firms can divest themselves of many risks through insurance, there are many important risks for which they cannot buy insurance. A business cannot buy insurance that protects it against the risk that the demand for its product will fall, or the risk that a competitor will develop a better product that will drive the company into bankruptcy. Economists have identified two inherent problems that limit the use of insurance as a mechanism for handling risk: adverse selection and moral hazard.

CLOSE-UP: ADVERSE SELECTION AND DISCRIMINATION IN THE AUTO INSURANCE MARKET

Private automobile insurers do not have complete information about the risk level of their clients, but they know that, as a group, young, single males demonstrate the highest claim frequency. Insurers would like to segment their market by charging higher premiums to high-risk individuals. But they cannot monitor the driving of automobile insurance buyers to see who drives too fast or who drives when tired or when drinking. The problem of adverse selection arises because the insurers cannot identify the individuals who are high risks. Pricing based on gender discrimination partially solves this problem.

In 1983, at the time when some provincial courts were addressing the issue of gender discrimination in auto insurance, Beverly Dahlby of the University of Alberta conducted a study evaluating the relative riskiness of male versus female drivers. He used Canadian auto insurance statistics for 1975–1978. These show that the claim frequency on collision insurance was:

0.142 for single males aged 21–22,

0.123 for single males aged 23–24,

0.109 for married males aged 21–24, and

0.0998 for females aged 21–24.

Interestingly enough, of single males aged 21–22, the riskiest group, only 47.9 percent purchased collision insurance, as opposed to 74.7 percent of females aged 21–24. This was presumably due to the fact that insurance companies charged the males much higher premiums in light of their collective accident record.

The policy of discriminating by gender is bound to be an imperfect way to overcome the adverse selection problem. There will undoubtedly be some young males who are cautious drivers but who have to pay high premiums because of the accident record of others of their gender. In 1978,

the Alberta Board of Industry responded to the complaints of gender discrimination made by numerous male drivers. The board ruled that the premiums policies of insurance companies in the province contravened the Individual's Rights and Protection Act, which guards against discrimination based on race, religion, colour, gender, ancestry, or place of origin.

In the case of collision insurance, Dahlby demonstrates that the equalization of premiums between males and females causes young females to face much higher premiums. The effect is largest for single females aged 21–22 whose premiums would increase by 61 percent. Approximately 10 percent of females in this category would be expected to stop purchasing collision coverage.

The end result is that young females are less insured than they would like to be, because of high prices. Is this the most efficient economic outcome, or can it be argued that this is an instance where gender discrimination is more fair?

Source: B.G. Dahlby, "Adverse Selection and Statistical Discrimination: An Analysis of Canadian Automobile Insurance," *Journal of Public Economics* 20 (1983): 121–130.

ADVERSE SELECTION

Some individuals are more likely to have an accident than others. Consider, for example, the issues posed by automobile insurance. Some people may frequently drink before they drive. They may drive when they are tired. They may drive carelessly. An insurance company can ask what sort of car you drive and how far a typical commute is, but many accident-related attributes are hard or impossible for an insurance firm to detect. A firm certainly does not expect an individual to admit that he is an accident-prone driver, which would practically beg the company to charge him a higher rate.

Insurance companies do make some effort to divide people into better and worse risk categories. This general problem—knowing that there are differences among individuals, differences in their likelihood of collecting on insurance, but not knowing which people are high risk and which are low—is an example of what is called a selection problem. The insurance company would like to select the best risks to insure, just as the employer would like to select the most productive employees to hire. Before selling life insurance, insurance firms often ask an individual to submit to a medical exam. Before selling fire or theft insurance, they may send around a building inspector to inspect the premises and make suggestions for greater security and safety. But although these examinations will gather some information, they will not reveal everything.

If an insurance company knows an individual is a bad risk, it may still be willing to provide insurance but only at a higher premium, such as automobile insurance for drivers who have had a recent accident. Not surprisingly, then, people who are bad risks and are attempting to purchase insurance do not readily tell the insurance company that they are bad risks. For example, the prospective buyer of life insurance may try to hide any malady from the doctor examining him; he is certainly unlikely to draw any problems to the attention of the doctor. Someone thinking of buying fire or theft insurance is not likely to point out faulty electrical wiring or unlocked back windows to the insurance company's building inspector.

Worse still for the insurance company is the general rule that those who are most likely to collect from insurance—for example, those who are most accident-prone—are often among the most eager to purchase it. Those who are least likely to collect—for example, those who are most safety conscious—may still want to buy some insurance; but since they know they are relatively safe, they will not be willing to pay too much for the insurance.

To understand the insurance firm's problem, we need to see how insurance markets work. In simple terms, firms collect premiums from a pool of customers to cover those customers against a specified risk. As long as the average losses and the costs of doing business match up with the premiums, an insurance market is viable. To keep the story simple, we can ignore wages and the other costs of doing business, and say the premiums must be at least as high as average losses for the market to be viable. The 45-degree line in Figure 6.4A shows the points where premiums equal average losses: on the line and below it, the market is viable, while above the line, the market is not viable because the firm is paying out more than it is taking in.

As premiums rise, the "best" risks decide not to buy insurance, so the *average* loss per policy increases. Panel B shows a curve relating average losses per policy to the level of the premium. At very low premiums, the market is not viable because the firm is simply not charging enough to cover losses. At some level of premiums, the market passes into the viable side of the 45-degree line. The question is, why does it not remain viable forever as premiums get higher and higher? The answer is that higher premiums drive low-

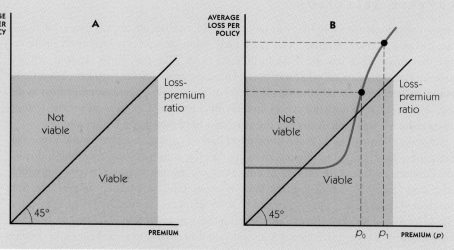

Figure 6.4 ADVERSE SELECTION

The 45-degree line in panel A divides an insurance market into viable and nonviable regions. Above the 45-degree line, the average loss per policy exceeds the premium, and the policy is not viable. The typical pattern of losses and premiums overlaid in panel B shows how as premiums rise, a market becomes viable but then may again become nonviable.

risk customers from the market, leaving a smaller pool with a higher fraction of customers who will have an accident.

The fact that the insurance company cannot completely discern between good risks and bad risks presents it with a serious dilemma. Consider an insurance firm that finds that the current premiums on its policies, p_0 in panel B, do not pay for the losses covered by these policies. The natural response if premiums are failing to pay for losses is to raise the premiums to p_1. But if the insurance firm raises its premiums, those who are not very accident-prone will decide that the price is too high, and they will demand less insurance. As they drop out of the market, however, the change in the proportion of "bad" customers may swamp the direct effect of the increase in premiums. Rather than reducing the insurance firm's gap between losses and premiums, the price increase will widen the gap. The company could raise the price of its insurance further in another attempt to make up the difference, but it will lose still more of the remaining safety-conscious people.

The effect is called **adverse selection:** those who tend to buy insurance tend to be those most at risk, and charging higher prices for insurance will discourage those at less risk from buying insurance at all. This adverse selection effect is a consequence of the limited information available to the insurance firm. The firm knows that among its customers, some people are better risks than others, but it does not know who are the better risks. The insurance firm knows less about the individual than the individual knows about herself, and the person has no incentive to supply possibly damaging information to the insurance firm.

For many kinds of insurance, such as fire insurance, adverse selection problems may not be too bad. The critical information (determining the likelihood of a fire) can easily enough be observed—for instance, by building inspectors. But for many of the kinds of risks against which individuals would like to buy insurance, adverse selection effects are important. With life or automobile insurance, for instance, an insurance firm is likely to find it difficult to determine any particular individual's risk. Even worse, consider the problem of measuring the risk that a firm's new product will fail to meet expectations. It would be nearly impossible for an insurance company to decide what the prospects for the product are. The business firm itself is certainly more likely to be better informed about the markets in which it is trying to sell the product. Not surprisingly, then, because of their disadvantage in obtaining crucial information, insurance firms do not supply insurance against such business risks.

Sometimes governments do not allow firms to use all the information available to "discriminate" among persons of different risks. For example, the Charter of Rights and Freedoms enacted by Parliament in 1982 precludes discrimination by age and gender. Thus, even though young males may have systematically higher risks of automobile accidents than older females, insurance companies are not permitted to use these demographic factors to differentiate the premiums they charge. This results in a form of adverse selection whose disadvantages must be weighed against the perceived social advantages of disallowing such discrimination.

MORAL HAZARD

A second problem faced by insurance companies is an incentive problem: insurance affects people's incentives to avoid whatever contingencies they are insured against. A person who has no fire insurance on a house, for example, may choose to limit the risk of fire by buying smoke alarms and home fire extinguishers and being especially cautious. But if that same person had fire insurance, he might not be so careful. Indeed, if the insurance would pay more than the house's market value, he might even be tempted to burn his own house down. This would be rational but, most people would say, immoral.

This general feature of insurance, that it reduces the individual's incentives to avoid the insured-against accident, is called **moral hazard.** Of course, from an economist's point of view, what is at issue is not a question of morality, but only a question of incentives. If a person bears only a portion, or none, of the consequences of his actions—as he does when he has purchased insurance—then his incentives are altered.

In 1971, the unemployment insurance system was liberalized extensively: the number of workers covered was increased, benefits were raised, and the number of weeks of work required for eligibility was reduced. Not surprisingly, work patterns adjusted to take advantage of the system. Workers left their current jobs more frequently, the duration of unemployment spells increased, the number of workers taking repeated claims increased, and more persons entered the work force temporarily in order to qualify for unemployment insurance benefits. A somewhat similar response has been observed in the use of health services, such as visits to the doctor, laboratory tests, and cosmetic surgery, since universal public health insurance was introduced in the mid-1960s.

Moral hazard concerns may not be too important for many kinds of insurance; an individual who buys a large life insurance policy and thus knows that her children will be well cared for in the event of her demise is hardly likely to take much bigger risks with her life. (There was, however, a grisly case in California some years ago in which a person cut off one foot with an axe to try to collect on disability insurance.) But for many kinds of risks against which a firm's managers would *like* to buy insurance, moral hazard concerns are important. For example, if a company could buy insurance to guarantee a minimum level of profit, managers would have less incentive to exert effort. When moral hazard problems are strong, insurance firms will offer limited—or even no—insurance.

THE CAPITAL MARKET: SHARING RISKS AND RAISING CAPITAL

The insurance market is concerned with risks: risks are transferred from an individual to an insurance firm, which is better able to bear those risks. Other markets are concerned with time: an individual gives up consumption today in return for more consumption in the future. Bank accounts illustrate in simple form the time aspect of markets. When we look more generally at the broad class of markets called the capital market—the general set of institutions involved in lending and borrowing and in raising funds—we can see that generally both the risk and time aspects arise at the same time.

Trades in the capital market are intertemporal: they occur over time. For this reason, there is also risk: individuals and households who give up funds today to other individuals and firms face uncertainty about how much will be repaid in the future and in what circumstances. Because most of the important risks cannot be insured through an insurance company, in the capital market issues of time and risk are intricately interconnected. How the capital is raised determines who bears what risks.

In modern capital markets, there are two principal ways in which capital is raised: through debt (also referred to as credit or loans) and through equity (also referred to as shares). In loan markets, the borrower promises to pay back certain fixed amounts of money at certain times in the future. Firms can obtain loans not only from banks, but also by issuing **bonds,** which are purchased by households and other firms. A bond is a promise the firm makes to pay a certain amount, say thirty years from now, and to make regular interest payments on the amount borrowed, say twice a year. Just as it does with a bank, the firm thus receives money today in return for a promise to repay a certain amount in the future (to whoever owns the bond at the time). Economists often lump bonds and bank credit (outstanding loans) together, and refer to funds raised in this way as **debt.** Alternatively, firms raise **equity capital,** which is the money the firm's owners supply directly to the firm. The most popular form of ownership in Canada is the corporation, on which we will focus for now. Ownership of the corporation is established through the sale of **shares,** also called **stock.** The initial owner of a company gives up a fraction of her company to people who supply her with capital. Those who provide the capital are then said to have a "share" in the company; they are the firm's **shareholders.** If a company issues 2,000,000 shares, for example, an individual who owns 100,000 shares then is entitled to 100,000/2,000,000 = 5 percent of the firm's profits, and to cast 5 percent of the votes in deciding who should run the company. Thus, Henry Ford may have had the ideas that led to the success of Ford Motor Company, but he needed capital, and he received much of the capital by giving a fraction of his company to those who provided it. If a company's new shareholders own 50 percent of the shares, that means they get 50 percent of the profits. If the value of the firm goes up, they receive 50 percent of the gains.

RISKS OF STOCKS

With shares, investors (shareholders) do not receive back a fixed amount. What they get depends on how well the firm does. If it fails, they may receive nothing. If it is a roaring success, they may make a fortune. For example, there is the case of Bombardier, the Montreal-based transportation company known for its snowmobiles. If you had bought $1,000 worth of stock in 1976, by 1990 the stock would have been worth $4,000, a return of 300 percent, or a rate of return of nearly 50 percent per year. But there are other transportation firms whose shareholders have received no returns at all.

There are thus considerable risks associated with investing in stocks. But the risks are limited, a feature that sets the corporate form of ownership apart from other, less popular forms. The investor in a corporation can lose all the money he invests in shares, but no more. He is said to have **limited liability.** By contrast, owners who do not protect themselves with the corporate form may be personally liable for the firm's debts and thus may lose *more* than the amount they have invested in their firm.

RISKS OF LOANS

There are risks associated with any investment, loans as well as stocks. In the case of a loan, as we have seen, the borrower promises to pay back a certain amount of money. But promises are sometimes broken. Sometimes a borrower may **default;** that is, fail to make a promised payment. Indeed, about 2 to 3 percent of all bank loans to consumers go into default every year, and every year thousands of firms—including several major firms—go bankrupt. They find themselves in a situation in which they cannot fulfill their obligations to creditors, including the banks that have lent them money and the stipulation that payments be made in thirty to sixty days. Novatel Communications (a company in Alberta specializing in cellular telephones and heavily financed by the provincial government) and Olympia and York (one of the largest real estate developers in the world, with office buildings in Toronto, New York, and London) are among the large Canadian companies that have recently gone "belly-up."

The fact that there is some risk of default explains why some borrowers must pay higher rates of interest than others. The Canadian government, which borrows money just as individuals and firms do, can usually borrow what it wants by promising to pay a relatively low interest rate. That is because the government is generally thought of as having an extremely low risk of defaulting, practically zero. Well-established, healthy companies like Inco and Bell Canada pay a slightly higher rate than the government, because even big companies like these, although their risk of defaulting is low, are slightly more likely to default than the federal government. The rate of interest these firms and others judged to have a low risk of default are charged is called the **prime rate.** Other borrowers pay even higher rates.

The law of supply and demand explains how these differences in interest rates are determined. The discussion of interest rates early in this chapter ignored default. It implicitly assumed that the amount borrowed was so low that the default risk was negligible. A more realistic scenario is one where lenders are aware that there are differences between the default rates on, say, loans made to people for the purpose of buying a car and on loans to major corporations. Figure 6.5 shows the demand and supply curves for car loans and loans to major corporations. The equilibrium interest rate in panel A (car loans) is higher than in panel B (loans to major corporations). The difference in interest rates reflects the difference in default risks. It is not that lenders discriminate against car buyers or in favour of large corporations. It is just that they must receive a higher return from the car loan to compensate them for bearing the greater risk. This higher return is sometimes referred to as a **risk premium.**

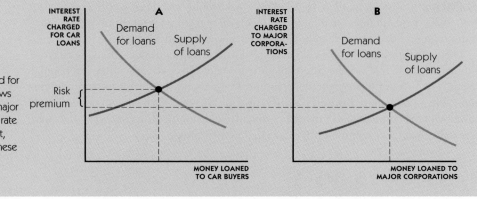

Figure 6.5 RISK AND EQUILIBRIUM INTEREST RATES

Panel A shows the supply and demand for loans to buy automobiles. Panel B shows the supply and demand for loans to major corporations. The equilibrium interest rate is higher in the automobile loan market, which reflects the higher riskiness of these loans.

Even though there is some chance of loans not being repaid, lending money to a firm is much less risky than giving money to a firm by buying shares of stock. The only risk lenders bear is that of default. Otherwise, the lender gets back the promised amount regardless of how well the firm does. By contrast, not only do shareholders bear the risk of getting back nothing if the firm goes bankrupt, but how much they get back depends completely on the vagaries of how well the firm does. Stock must therefore yield a higher return to shareholders in order to compensate them for the extra risk.

But what may be an advantage from the perspective of a lender may be a disadvantage from the perspective of a borrower. The higher return on stocks, while an advantage to shareholders, who provide capital, is a disadvantage for firms trying to raise capital; these firms, on average, have to pay more to get equity capital. On the other hand, investors share the risk; this is an advantage for firms trying to raise capital, but generally viewed as a disadvantage by shareholders. How these advantages and disadvantages are weighed out in determining the mix of debt (outstanding loans and bonds) and stocks we see in the market is a question we will turn to in later chapters.

THE TWO PRINCIPAL WAYS FIRMS RAISE FUNDS

Debt: issuing bonds, taking out loans, and otherwise obtaining funds with a commitment to repay

Equity: selling ownership shares (stock)

THE RISK-INCENTIVE TRADE-OFF

Those who supply capital share with insurance companies the problem that risk sharing distorts incentives. Indeed, it is a general rule that as we reduce risk, we also reduce incentives. A store manager whose salary is guaranteed faces little risk but also has little incentive. If his pay depends on the store's sales, he has stronger incentives but faces greater risk. Sales may be low because of an economic downturn or because buyers have simply turned away from his products; in either case, his income will be low.

In many cases, the market reaches a compromise: partial insurance, providing the purchaser of insurance with some incentives, but making her also bear some risk. With automobile insurance, for example, it is common for an insurance company to require that an individual pay some fixed amount (like $100) before the insurance policy covers the rest of accident costs. The fixed amount is referred to as a **deductible.** As well, future insurance premiums may rise as a result of an accident. In other cases, insurance policies may be such that only some percentage (like 80 percent) of expenses are covered; the remainder must be paid by the insured individual. This is called **co-insurance.** In all these cases, the individual will have a financial motivation to exercise care and prevention, but still be protected against the risk of large payments.

Similarly, a firm that borrows money for a project is generally required to invest some of its own funds in the project, or to supply the lender with collateral; that is, provide the lender with an asset that the firm forfeits if it fails to repay the loan. Lenders know that with more of their own money at stake, borrowers will have better incentives to use the funds wisely.

Figure 6.6 shows the trade-off between risks and incentives. Along the horizontal axis, we have some measure of risk; along the vertical, some measure of incentives. It is a general rule that as we reduce the proportion of the accident costs the insurance policy pays, we move along the risk-incentive trade-off from point A, where the individual faces little risk and has little incentive to economize on accident costs, to point B, where she faces considerable risk but has strong incentives for keeping costs down.

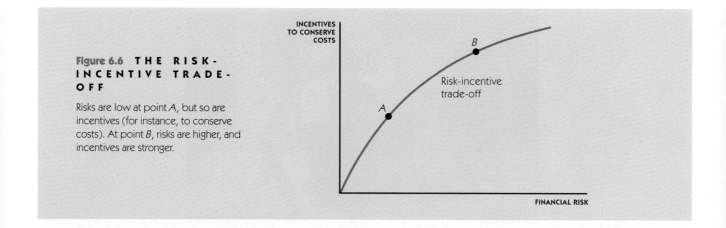

Figure 6.6 THE RISK-INCENTIVE TRADE-OFF

Risks are low at point A, but so are incentives (for instance, to conserve costs). At point B, risks are higher, and incentives are stronger.

INCENTIVES TO CONSERVE COSTS

B

Risk-incentive trade-off

A

FINANCIAL RISK

CLOSE-UP: CRISES IN THE BANKING SECTOR

Banking can be a risky business. This was amply illustrated in the aftermath of the 1980–1981 recession in both Canada and the United States. In the latter, the so-called S & L crisis resulted in hundreds of savings and loan associations (S & L's for short) going bankrupt at a cost of well over U.S. $100 billion to the U.S. government. In Canada, two western banks, Canadian Commercial Bank (CCB) of Edmonton and Northlands of Calgary collapsed in 1985, the first bank failures since 1923. This followed the bankruptcies of some smaller trust companies a bit earlier. The contrast between the Canadian and U.S. cases is interesting both for its similarities and its differences.

The S & L's are banks whose traditional function is to accept deposits from savers, and to use this money to make mortgage loans to home buyers. They have been successful in this purpose. The United States is a nation of home owners, with almost two-thirds of families owning their own homes compared with less than half in 1920. Yet, the S & L system began to collapse in the mid-1980s. Economists argued that the S & L crisis resulted from a combination of bad economic luck and bad government incentives.

The U.S. government has long been involved with savings and loans, both as a regulator and as a provider of insurance. In the past, if an S & L went bankrupt, a government agency, the Federal Savings and Loan Insurance Corporation (FSLIC), stepped in and paid off the depositors. The savings and loan crisis occurred because so many of them had gone bankrupt that the FSLIC did not have the money to pay off the depositors. Either people would lose their savings, or taxpayers had to step in.

These bankruptcies were rooted in the economic problems of the late 1970s and early 1980s. Until the 1970s, S & L's mainly loaned money for home mortgages at an interest rate of about 6 percent and were allowed by law to pay only 5 percent interest to depositors.

But interest rates skyrocketed in the late 1970s and early 1980s. The value of home mortgages—the principal asset of the S & L's—fell. The value of a mortgage is the present discounted value of the money that borrowers promise to pay back (interest and principal). Those promises were based on mortgage interest rates often fixed at around 6 percent or even lower. When interest rates

jumped to 14 percent or higher, the present discounted value of these mortgages was cut by half or more. This is just another example of the principle that when interest rates rise, the present discounted value of future income is reduced.

In the early 1980s, the federal government was forced to react, or else the entire savings and loan industry might have gone bankrupt. The government allowed S & L's to invest in many things besides mortgages. Many S & L's worked themselves back to financial stability.

But for a smaller group of S & L's, matters went from bad to worse. Some S & L managers tried a strategy of making high-risk loans, for which they could charge high interest rates. If the loans worked out, these S & L's could make a lot of money.

Incentives were all awry. Depositors had no reason to worry about this high-risk strategy; if the loans failed, as high-risk loans have a nasty tendency to do, government insurance would pay them off. Money poured into these high-risk S & L's, which offered depositors' higher interest rates.

The situation was a classic example of a moral hazard problem. Because of depositor insurance, the owners not only lacked incentives to invest in safe investments, they actually had incentives to undertake quite risky investments. Since if they did not take these risks they would almost surely have gone bankrupt, they were in a no-lose situation.

If the government had simply shut down all the bankrupt savings and loans in 1984 or 1985, it might have cost U.S. $20 billion or so to pay off the depositors. But by the end of the 1980s, the total bill was estimated at well over U.S. $100 billion in present discounted value. Together with accumulated interest payments, the undiscounted value of the payments over forty years could run as high as U.S. $500 billion.

The analog of the S & L crisis did not occur in Canada, partly because there is no institution quite like the S & L's in Canada. The mortgage market tends to be spread between the banks and the trust companies, and these institutions are more concentrated as large firms in Canada. Nonetheless, the collapse of the CCB and Northlands banks bore some similarities to the S & L failures. These two banks started up in the mid-1970s when the Alberta "oil patch" was booming, and the government wanted to encourage diversification and decentralization of the banking sector to respond better to local needs. The two banks' operations were concentrated heavily in the energy and real estate sectors, and their assets were both more concentrated in the hands of relatively few lenders and were more risky than those of the other large banks. When the recession and the decline in the fortunes of the oil and gas industry hit in the early 1980s, the banks found themselves very exposed. Earlier in 1985, the federal and Alberta governments, along with the six major banks, attempted to prevent the failure of CCB by providing financial assistance. Even that was insufficient, however, to preclude it from failing. In the end, the damage was limited to the collapse of these two banks.

As in the United States, depositors were protected by deposit insurance provided by the Canadian Deposit Insurance Corporation, but the limit was $60,000 per depositor. The government decided to extend support to noninsured depositors after the fact. As well, the regulation of banks was tightened up as a result of these failures. As in the U.S. case, it could be argued that moral hazard played a role in the decision of the banks to engage in what were risky investments. But the extent of the damage and the cost to the government was much less in the Canadian case.

ENTREPRENEURSHIP

Innovation gives life to a capitalist economy. It also demonstrates the vital roles played by time and risk. Consider for a moment the many new products and new processes of production that have so enriched (or at least altered) everyone's life in the last century: fast food, transistors, computers, airplanes, cars, televisions—the list is endless. Each of these innovations required more than just an idea. It needed people willing to follow the advice of David Lloyd George, once prime minister of Great Britain, who said: "Don't be afraid to take a big step if one is indicated. You can't cross a chasm in two small jumps."

Innovations require people and businesses to take risks. Innovators need capital too, since those who have innovative ideas, like Henry Ford, often do not have the capital to carry them out. They must turn to others to supply them with resources, generally in exchange for a fraction of the return. After all, someone who lends to an innovator bears a risk, and he must receive compensation to be willing to undertake these risks.

In forming judgments about whether to pursue a possible innovation, innovators and investors must form expectations about the future. But because they are dealing with new ideas, products, and processes, the expectations of reasonable men and women may well differ. When the returns are in and the project has proved to be a success or a failure, it is often difficult to ascertain the reasons why, even with the wisdom of hindsight. Thus, those whose jobs require them to make decisions—the lending officers of banks, the managers of pension funds and other financial institutions, the leaders of corporations—face a difficult task. But the lack of any simple formula does not mean that there are not better and worse ways of going about making these decisions. Forming expectations and evaluating risks are like trying to play football in a heavy fog; you cannot always tell what is going on, but skilled players with good foresight still have an advantage.

Thus, **entrepreneurs**—the individuals responsible for creating new businesses, bringing new products to market, developing new processes of production—face all the problems we have discussed. While all business decision making involves risk taking, entrepreneurs who take the responsibility for managing a new business generally face more risk than do those in well-established companies. Businesses frequently require additional financing for new projects, but new enterprises almost always require extensive outside financing. The problem of selection, of determining which of a set of potential investment projects and entrepreneurs ought to receive funds, is particularly acute, since because these projects are new, they have yet to establish a reputation. Lenders may be reluctant to provide funds for fear of default. Equity financing may be difficult too, since prospective buyers may wonder why, if this company is such a great opportunity, the entrepreneur is sharing the profits by selling stock, rather than borrowing the money and keeping all the profit.

The entrepreneur cannot buy insurance to cover most of the risks he faces. Thus, entrepreneurs must be willing to bear the risks themselves. Entrepreneurs need a return to compensate them for their efforts and the risks they undertake. Similarly, those who provide these new enterprises with capital must receive a return greater than they might receive elsewhere, to compensate them for the additional risks they have to bear. There has been ongoing concern about the effect of a variety of public policies, especially tax policy, on the returns. Does the current tax system discourage entrepreneurship? Are there policies that can be designed to encourage it? These questions will be addressed later in the book.

REVIEW AND PRACTICE

SUMMARY

1. Much of economics is future-oriented, which means that households and firms must form expectations about the future and cope with problems of risk and uncertainty.

2. The interest rate is a price. It equates the supply of funds by savers and the demand by borrowers. Savers receive interest for deferring consumption, and borrowers pay interest so that they can consume or invest now and pay later.

3. The fact that the market interest rate is positive means that a dollar received today is worth more than a dollar received in the future; this is the time value of money. The present discounted value of a dollar in the future is the amount that, if received today, is equal to what a dollar will be worth in the future, given the prevailing rate of interest.

4. The real interest rate, which measures a person's actual increase in buying power when she saves money, is equal to the nominal interest rate (the amount paid in dollars) minus the inflation rate.

5. What investors are willing to pay today for an asset depends largely on what they believe they can sell it for in the future. Changes in expectations can thus shift the demand curve for an asset and change current prices.

6. Most people are risk averse. Insurance is one way they attempt to reduce the risks they face. Insurance companies face two problems. One is that people who buy insurance tend to be those most at risk, and charging higher prices for insurance will discourage those less at risk from buying insurance at all. This effect is called adverse selection. The second problem is that insurance reduces the incentives individuals have to avoid whatever they are insured against. This is called the moral hazard problem.

7. Firms can raise money through either debt (issuing bonds or taking out loans) or equity (selling stock, or shares). Purchasers of equities share the firm's risks, its losses as well as gains.

8. With every loan, there is a risk the borrower will default. This risk explains why some borrowers must pay higher rates of interest than others.

9. Entrepreneurial innovation plays a central role in modern economies.

KEY TERMS

interest	nominal interest	debt
principal	rate	equity, shares, stock
present discounted	real interest rate	limited liability
value	asset	default
compound interest	risk averse	risk premium
simple interest	adverse selection	deductible
time value of money	moral hazard	co-insurance
inflation	bonds	entrepreneurs

REVIEW QUESTIONS

1. Who is on the demand side and who is on the supply side in the market for loanable funds? What is the price in that market?

2. Would you prefer to receive $100 one year from now, or five years from now? Why? Does your answer change if the rate of inflation is zero?

3. How does compound interest differ from simple interest?

4. What is the relationship between the nominal interest rate and the real interest rate?

5. True or false: "Demand curves depend on what people want now, not on their expectations about the future. " Explain your answer.

6. What is meant by risk aversion? What are some consequences of the fact that most people are risk averse?

7. Why do people pay insurance premiums if they hope and expect that nothing bad is going to happen to them?

8. Would you expect a borrower's rate of interest to be higher if the borrower was a large automobile company or a small restaurant owner? Why?

9. Why is there a trade-off between risk and incentives? Give an example of this trade-off.

PROBLEMS

1. Imagine that $1,000 is deposited in an account for five years; the account pays 10 percent interest per year, compounded annually. How much money will be in the account after five years? What if the rate of interest is 12 percent? What if the annual rate of interest is 12 percent, but the interest is compounded monthly?

2. Suppose you want to buy a car three years from now, and you know that the price of a car at that time will be $10,000. If the interest rate is 7 percent per year, how much would you have to set aside today to have the money ready when you need it? If the interest rate is 5 percent, how much would you have to set aside today?

3. Many states in the United States have passed laws that put a ceiling on the rate of interest that can be charged; these laws are called usury laws. Using a supply and demand framework, diagram the effect of interest rate ceilings on the quantity (supply) of lending. Who is better off as a result of usury laws? Who is worse off?

4. Imagine that you win the lottery, but find that your $10 million prize is paid out in five chunks: a $2 million payment right away, and then $2 million every five years until you have received the total. Calculate the present discounted value of your winnings if the interest rate is 10 percent. What would it be if the interest rate were 15 percent? How does a higher interest rate affect the present discounted value?

5. Suppose the workers at a particular company have been complaining that their prescription drug insurance does not cover enough items. To help build loyalty among the staff, the company agrees to cover more items. However, it finds that the number of sick days taken and its expenses for prescription drugs both rise sharply. Why might this happen? What is the name for it?

6. You hire someone to paint your house. Since it is a large job, you agree to pay him by the hour. What moral hazard problem must you consider? Explain the trade-off between risk and incentives in this situation.

CHAPTER 7

THE PUBLIC SECTOR

M ost Canadians have a great deal of faith in our economic system, with its primary reliance on private markets. In earlier chapters, we have seen how the profit system provides firms with the incentive to produce the goods that consumers want. Prices give firms the incentive to economize on scarce resources, and serve to coordinate economic activity and to signal changes in economic conditions. Private property provides incentives for individuals to invest in and to maintain buildings, machines, land, cars, and other possessions. Chapter 3 demonstrated the incentives individuals and countries have to engage in mutually advantageous trades and to specialize in areas of comparative advantage. Chapters 4 and 5 showed how, in free markets, prices are determined by the interaction of demand and supply.

We have thus seen how the private market provides answers to the four basic questions set out in Chapter 1: what is produced and in what quantities, how it is produced, for whom it is produced, and who makes the decisions. What is produced is determined by the interaction of demand and supply, reflecting both the goods consumers want and what it costs firms to produce those goods. Firms, competing against one another, produce the goods in the least expensive way possible. The answer to the "for whom" question is given by the incomes of individuals in the economy. Those with high incomes get more of the economy's goods and services, and those with low incomes receive less. These incomes, in turn, are established by the demand and supply for labour, which determines what workers are paid, and the demand and supply for capital, which determines the return people get on their savings. The answer to the "who decides" question is "everyone." Decisions about which goods are produced are the result of millions of decisions made in households and firms throughout the economy. Moreover, firms, competing against one another, have incentives to choose as managers those most able to make the hard decisions—whether to enter some new market or develop some new product—that every firm must face if it is to survive.

Yet in spite of this basic faith in the market economy, Canada has an enormous public, or governmental, sector, reaching out into all spheres of economic activity. Why is this? What role do economists see for the government? Economists tend to look hard at any function government serves, not because they are antigovernment, but because they are pro-market. They recognize that the government must set and enforce the basic laws of society, and provide a framework within which firms can compete fairly against one another. Beyond this, however, economists' understanding of the market's ability to answer the basic economic questions leads them to wonder at any additional function the government serves: why is it that private markets do not serve this function? This chapter will explore the roles the government has undertaken, and how and why it carries out those roles.

KEY QUESTIONS

1. What distinguishes the private from the public sector?

2. What explains the economic roles the government has undertaken?

3. What are externalities and public goods, and why do they imply that markets may not work well?

4. What are the various ways the government can affect the economy and attempt to achieve its economic objectives?

5. How has the role of government changed in recent decades? And how does the role of government in Canada compare with its role in other industrial countries?

6. What are some of the current controversies concerning the roles of government? Why do failures of the market system not necessarily imply that government action is desirable?

THE PUBLIC AND PRIVATE SECTORS

Most countries of the world have an ongoing debate over what the appropriate balance between the public and private sectors should be, and different countries have supplied different answers to this question. In some nations, like Switzerland, the public sector is small and government economic activities are severely limited. In the former Soviet Union and China, the government tried to control virtually all aspects of economic activity, though the difficulty of doing this created increasing pressures for change.

There is a wide spectrum between these extremes: free market economies like Hong Kong, where businesses are free from most of the regulations that they encounter in

North America and Western Europe; welfare state economies like Sweden, where the government takes major responsibilities for health care, child care, and a host of other social services, but where there is also a large private sector; a number of European economies, like Great Britain, where the government has dominated major industries like steel, coal, railroads, airlines, and public utilities; and the United States where heavier reliance is placed on the private sector than in most other countries with industrialized, developed economies. Canada falls within the spectrum somewhere between the United States and Western Europe. There is a mixture of public and private enterprises in such industries as transportation, telecommunications, utilities, broadcasting, and petroleum. As well, the government plays a more active role in the provision of services such as health and postsecondary education in Canada than in the United States.

The balance between government and the private sector seems to swing over time. From 1930 to 1970, for example, government took on an increasing role in most countries. Many private industries were **nationalized** in this period, or taken over and run by the government, and social services expanded rapidly, especially in the postwar period. Since 1970, there has been a time for retrenchment for the public sector and a reevaluation of its role. This is true no less for communist countries like China and the former Soviet Union, which have recently begun to allow a greater degree of private enterprise, than it is of the Western industrialized countries. Some of these countries have been selling off their government enterprises to the private sector; this is known as **privatization.** Similarly, government regulations that were in force in many industries, such as airlines, railroads, and trucking, have been reduced or eliminated, a process called **deregulation.** In Canada, for example, many Crown corporations have been privatized, though they have tended to be smaller ones that did not monopolize entire industries. There are still over fifty federal Crown corporations in existence, ranging from the Bank of Canada to the Canadian Broadcasting Corporation to the Canadian Wheat Board. As well, the provinces have their own sets of provincial Crown corporations.

THE FEDERAL GOVERNMENTAL STRUCTURE

In Canada, decisions concerning taxes, expenditures, and regulations are made by thousands of different governmental bodies. Canada has a **federal governmental structure,** which means that government activities take place at several levels: national, provincial, territorial, and local. This federal structure is the reason that the national government is generally referred to as the federal government; it is the only government with jurisdiction across the entire federation. The British North America (BNA) Act of 1867, subsequently amended various times (most recently in 1982), sets out the responsibilities of the federal and provincial levels of government. The federal government is responsible for matters of national interest such as defence and foreign affairs, currency and the banking system, international trade, competition policy, and criminal law. As well, the federal government delivers some important social programs, including unemployment insurance, family allowances, and payments to the elderly. The provinces are responsible for the important areas of health, education, and welfare; natural resources within their boundaries; civil and property rights; and civil law. As well, the provinces determine the role of municipalities within their jurisdictions. Some areas—such as agriculture and regional development—are the joint responsibility of the federal government and the provinces, but residual powers (those not explicitly assigned to either level) rest with the federal government. In addition, although both levels of government can levy most taxes, the federal government has historically raised much more revenue than it needs for its own purposes and transferred the excess to the provinces through a system of grants intended to make the financial capacities of the various provinces more equal.

Other governing units exist within Canada alongside the federal government and the provinces. Yukon and the Northwest Territories have a unique status in Canada. Both are within the jurisdiction of the federal government, but the latter has devolved many provincial-type expenditure responsibilities to them. Also, some native communities, which are historically within the federal jurisdiction, have negotiated various degrees of self-government with the federal government, and others are in the process of doing so.

Despite the fact that the division of powers is spelled out in some detail, the BNA Act has proven to be a flexible-enough document that the exact boundaries between govern-ing units are ambiguous and the degree of decentralization of responsibilities has varied considerably over the years. For example, the federal government has exercised varying amounts of influence in provincial areas of jurisdiction such as health, welfare, and transportation through shared-cost programs with the provinces. There is some strain within the existing federal system, especially with respect to the federal government's role vis-à-vis Quebec. Whether the existing federal structure will continue to be flexible enough to accommodate the concerns of various constituencies remains to be seen.

Moreover, there is no single entity that can be called "the government" at any of the levels. At the federal level, budgetary matters are all legislated by the Parliament at the initiative of the governing party. But the implementation of spending is decentralized to the various departments of the public sector, who have considerable responsibility for economic decision making. Furthermore, many economic decisions, particularly regu-latory ones, are delegated to agencies responsible for particular functions. Investment Canada reviews foreign takeovers of Canadian firms; the Competition Tribunal reviews anticompetitive practices of firms that may violate the Competition Act; the Canadian Transport Commission regulates all modes of transportation that fall under federal juris-diction; Health and Welfare Canada (a department of the federal government) regulates human health and safety standards for products produced and sold in Canada; the Su-perintendent of Financial Institutions regulates the chartered banks; the Human Rights Commission administers the Canadian Human Rights Act, which prohibits discrimina-tion by employers under federal jurisdiction; the Immigration and Refugee Board of Canada (the largest administrative tribunal) reviews applications for immigration and refugee status; and so on. The judiciary itself may occasionally take decisions that have economic ramifications, especially those that involve cases brought under the Charter of Rights and Freedoms.

At the local level, there are a large number of separate governmental bodies. Munici-palities of all sizes may have elected councils, elected school boards, elected public util-ities commissions, and elected police commissions, each with the right to set policies and levy taxes. As well, separate regional governments exist in some provinces.

What Distinguishes the Private and Public Sectors?

Private institutions include not only profit-maximizing firms but a large number of not-for-profit organizations like churches, hospitals, cooperatives, and private schools. What

CLOSE-UP: THE DIVISION OF FEDERAL AND PROVINCIAL RESPONSIBILITIES

You often hear federal politicians talking about how they will fight to maintain social programs or to improve education. The sanctity of social programs arose as a concern in the debate over free trade, first with the United States and subsequently with Mexico. It was also prominent in the prolonged debate over the Constitution; some participants thought it important that the federal government be able to enforce national standards for such things as health care and to implement major new programs like day care and a national education initiative.

In fact, according to the BNA Act, jurisdiction in the areas of health, education, and other social programs is in the hands of the provinces. In fact, health, education, and welfare are the three largest expenditure items at the provincial level, and the most rapidly growing ones as well. As shown in the chart, they take up over one-half of provincial and municipal expenditures. Other important categories are debt charges and transportation and communications. The remaining provincial and municipal expenditures include police and fire protection, natural resources, parks and recreation, housing, public buildings, prisons, libraries, sewerage and garbage, and more. In all, provincial and municipal spending is actually larger than that of the federal government, and is growing rapidly.

Federal spending is also concentrated in a few areas. Although you often hear about federal initiatives in areas like international affairs, science policy, housing, energy, the environment, natural resources, agriculture, fishing, and the administration of justice, all of those categories take up a very small proportion of the federal budget.

There are four big ticket items for the federal government: transfers to persons (unemployment

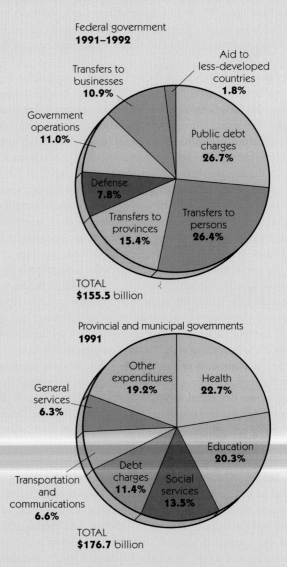

Federal government
1991–1992

Transfers to businesses
10.9%

Government operations
11.0%

Aid to less-developed countries
1.8%

Public debt charges
26.7%

Defense
7.8%

Transfers to provinces
15.4%

Transfers to persons
26.4%

TOTAL
$155.5 billion

Provincial and municipal governments
1991

Other expenditures
19.2%

General services
6.3%

Health
22.7%

Education
20.3%

Debt charges
11.4%

Social services
13.5%

Transportation and communications
6.6%

TOTAL
$176.7 billion

insurance, payments to the elderly and to families), transfers to the provinces, defence, and interest on the public debt. Any attempt to reduce the size of the federal budget must come to grips with reducing spending in these categories.

Sources: Department of Finance, *The Budget 1992* (February 25, 1992), Table 3.3, p. 79; Canadian Tax Foundation, *Provincial and Municipal Finances, 1991,* Table 3.8, p. 3:13.

distinguishes those institutions that are labelled as "government" from private institutions?

In a democracy, there are two important differences between private and public institutions. First, the people responsible for running public institutions are elected or appointed by someone who is elected (or appointed by someone who is appointed by someone who is elected . . .). The legitimacy of the person holding the position is derived directly or indirectly from the electoral process.

Second, the government is endowed with certain rights of compulsion that private institutions do not have. For instance, the Canadian government has the right to force its citizens to pay taxes; if they fail to do so, it can confiscate their property and even imprison them. The government even has the right to force its young people to serve in the armed forces at wages below those that would induce them to volunteer and has exercised that right during wartime. The government also has the right of **eminent domain,** which is the right to seize private property for public use, provided it compensates the owner fairly.

Private institutions and individuals do not have these rights. Moreover, the government restricts such coercion by private institutions, even if the individuals involved agree to it; for instance, the government does not allow you to sell yourself into slavery. Private exchanges are voluntary. One person may want another to work for him, but he cannot coerce that person into doing so. One person may need another's property to construct an office building, but she cannot force the owner to sell. You may think that some deal is advantageous to the person you are proposing the deal to, but you cannot legally force him to engage in the deal.

Because the government can use compulsion it is able to do some things that private institutions cannot do. Once a decision has been made to build a public road, for instance, a local government can make sure that everyone in town helps to pay for it. On the other hand, governments sometimes create rules to bind their own hands, so that they cannot do *anything* they wish. For instance, the government has established elaborate hiring procedures for government organizations that private firms generally do not find worthwhile. The owner of a private firm can decide whom she wants to hire; if she hires someone incompetent, she and her firm suffer. If the manager of a public enterprise hires someone incompetent, however, the public pays. The government's strict hiring procedures help avoid bad hiring, but they may also result in rigidities that often make it difficult for government enterprises to compete against private firms for the most talented individuals.

The government of the day does not have absolute power, however. It is constrained to act according to the rules set out in the Canadian constitution. For example, the government cannot discriminate on the basis of race, religion, or gender. Nor can it interfere with the rights of individuals to live where they choose. The ultimate constraint on government, of course, comes from the threat of being voted out of office at the next election.

Economists, concerned with the most efficient solutions to economic problems, focus on government's powers of compulsion, including its power to tax, when they try to find a role for government. They focus on its limitations, such as its limited flexibility and the special problems posed by the political processes that govern its behaviour, when they try to delineate the extent of that role. Before looking more closely at the economic role of government, it is instructive to observe how governmental and private solutions are combined in Canada.

THE PERVASIVENESS OF GOVERNMENT

Canada, as we saw in Chapter 1, has a mixed economy; this means that like most countries, it combines private and public solutions to its economic problems. The emphasis is on private solutions, but to think that Canada has a simple market economy is to ignore the pervasiveness of government.

From the moment Canadians are born to the moment they die, government touches their lives. They are born in a government-financed hospital. Births are recorded by a government bureau to aid in establishing citizenship, and a variety of rights (and obligations) of citizenship follow. Most children attend publicly run schools as they grow up. Many then go on to attend public postsecondary institutions such as universities or community colleges; some obtain government-subsidized loans to pay their tuition. Throughout their lives Canadians receive publicly funded medical care. The currency in their pockets is printed by the government. Canadians travel on a transportation system that is publicly built and maintained, with publicly provided roads and publicly run airports. Air safety is supervised by a federal agency, and national rail passenger service is run by VIA Rail, a government enterprise.

The elderly have been increasingly supported by government. Much of what they live upon is provided by the government, through Old Age Security and the Canada Pension Plan; all of their medical expenses are covered through a government program called Medicare; and even the pensions they receive from private companies are affected by government regulations, with the government ensuring that the private firms actually pay what they promise. Government issues death certificates for Canadians when they die, and government rules oversee inheritances by and property settlements for the next generation.

In all of these activities, the government plays a variety of roles. First, it sets the legal framework within which all private actions take place. Second, it acts as a producer: most of elementary and secondary education and a large fraction of higher education is produced publicly, as are police and fire services; and in most communities, water and garbage collection lie within the public sector. Government is also a "consumer," buying goods and services that it then provides freely to the public. Expenditures on national defence and the highway system are examples. Much of government production goes directly to consumption—education, for example—but the two roles of producer and consumer are distinct. The government buys, but does not produce, airplanes and tanks; it also pays for, but does not itself produce, medical services for the aged.

Equally as important as these direct roles of the government are its indirect roles, in affecting how households and firms behave. The government regulates and it subsidizes. There are regulations designed, for instance, to restrict anticompetitive practices, to protect consumers, and to promote general social objectives, such as the elimination of discrimination. Subsidies too are directed at a multitude of objectives, from the drilling of oil to the construction of low-income housing to the encouragement of investment in depressed areas. Perhaps the most important type of subsidies are transfer payments to households for redistributive purposes. These include unemployment insurance, payments to families with children, welfare support, and payments to the elderly.

The functions of government have been changing during the past century. Consider railroads, for example. During the nineteenth century, the federal government became involved in the construction and operation of the railways not only as a matter of industrial policy, but more importantly as a matter of nation building. The construction of a transcontinental railway joining existing lines in the Maritimes with the Grand Trunk in central Canada, and extending the Grand Trunk westward was an important part of the Confederation. New Brunswick and Nova Scotia joined Ontario and Quebec partly on the promise of a system to link the two railway systems. Later, Prince Edward Island joined when the federal government agreed to absorb the debt of constructing their railway. As early as 1871, the federal government agreed to construct a railway that would link the Pacific with the rest of Canada, partly in response to the rapid expansion of the American rail system, which threatened to divert trade (and loyalties) from the Canadian west to the United States. In 1880, the government contracted with the Canadian Pacific Railway Company to complete the project, thus assuring British Columbia's membership in the new nation. The government provided assistance to the project, primarily by donating the land on which the railway was built and also assisting in obtaining financing. By 1885, the "last spike" was driven as the world's longest railway was completed at Craigellachie, British Columbia. In 1923, the government absorbed two bankrupt lines—the Grand Trunk and Intercolonial—to form the Canadian National Railway.

The coexistence of a Crown corporation and a private firm in the same industry became a common form of government intervention in key sectors of the economy, to be repeated in the broadcasting, airlines, and oil industries. The railways remained a heavily regulated sector, both as regards the routes they could use and the rates they could charge customers, and the public part of the system was heavily subsidized. Along with the tariff, this was one of the major forms of industrial policy in Canada, contributing to the east-west flow of trade in manufactured goods, agricultural products, and resources as well as to the settlement and development of western Canada. In recent years, following the example of the United States and culminating in the National Transportation Act of 1987, the government has moved to deregulate the entire transport sector by allowing unprofitable rail lines to close and prices to reflect costs and competitive forces. The passenger component of the rail system was separated off into a separate publicly owned corporation (VIA Rail), and its subsidy was reduced considerably. From being a major instrument for building a national economy, the railways now must compete for their business with the trucking, airline, bus, and shipping industries.

Just because government today customarily provides certain goods and services does not mean that it must do so; and the fact that government customarily does not provide some good or service does not mean that it should not. There are other dramatic examples of the changing role of the government besides railroads. Take currency, for instance. Today, it is hard to imagine private firms producing bills and coins. But private banks in Canada issued their own "bank notes" alongside those of the government until well into the twentieth century, and these notes circulated just like currency. Indeed, it was well after the creation of the Bank of Canada in 1934 that bank notes were phased out. Even today, in Scotland, private banks provide currency.

Or consider the Canadian mail. By law, first-class mail is restricted to Canada Post, which is a Crown corporation of the federal government. But private firms have happily jumped at the chance to provide other mail services. Today courier firms deliver over half of all parcels and dominate the market in providing overnight mail delivery.

Finally, consider health care. Originally, hospitals were largely supported by charitable organizations, and the costs of medical care were recovered from the users. But gov-

CLOSE-UP: INEFFICIENCY IN THE POST OFFICE: MYTH OR REALITY

Canada Post has a monopoly on the delivery of first-class mail. In fact, mail delivery almost anywhere in the world is a government-run monopoly. It is debatable whether this is a natural monopoly. If competition were allowed, rival companies might well deliver mail between major cities, particularly business mail, but it is not clear whether more than one firm would service smaller communities.

The Canadian postal service has not been popular in recent years, and griping about its shortcomings is a great Canadian tradition. Critics point to a deterioration in service, including reductions in the number of home deliveries and in the number of postbox pickups per week, the increase in the average delivery time and in its variance, the inability to receive home delivery in new suburbs, and the disruptions caused by frequent strikes.

How much of this distrust does Canada Post deserve? About three-quarters of total expenditures

goes to paying employees, so measuring the productivity of these employees is the real test of the postal service. In 1968–1969, Canada Post delivered 106,000 pieces of mail per employee. By 1985–1986, this rose to 146,000, an increase of over 2 percent per year. This measure is a rather crude approximation to productivity, however, since service standards and the composition of the mail have changed as well. For example, over the same period, total operating costs per unit of mail delivered (as measured in constant dollars) more than doubled. Furthermore, while Canada Post had the same unit costs in 1972 as the U.S. Postal Service, the costs of the latter were 50 percent less by 1985. Economic studies of productivity in the post office relative to other sectors have shown that labour productivity was roughly constant in Canada Post over the period 1950 to 1965, and then it actually began to decline until the end of the 1970s. Over the same time frame, productivity in the commercial non-agricultural sector more than doubled.

The figures make clear that the complaint about the productivity of the postal service might have some justification. In recent years, post office management has embarked on a program of cost reduction and service improvement. New managerial controls and mechanization have been introduced, and Canada Post has been instructed to cover its own costs. It remains to be seen whether this can be translated into actual productivity gains, comparable to those achieved in the U.S. Postal Service.

Source: Figures are reported in Adie, *The Mail Monopoly* (Vancouver: The Fraser Institute, 1990).

ernments gradually took over the full financing, first of hospitalization, then of medical care, so that today virtually all basic health costs are publicly funded. This might be contrasted with the United States, where the financing of health care is largely a private responsibility, with the exception of the elderly and the least well off.

AN ECONOMIC ROLE FOR GOVERNMENT

The previous section teaches us that we cannot simply look at the services and goods provided by government and assume that only government can provide them. The economist does not say that grade school education or currency or postal service has to be provided by the government. Economists ask how societies can supply these and any other needs most efficiently. The tax, expenditure, and regulatory policies of government have a profound effect on how the basic economic questions are answered. If economic models of the private market are accurate, and the general faith in market solutions is justified, then a good question to ask would be, why is there *any* economic role for government? Another visit with Adam Smith is a good place to start answering this question.

ADAM SMITH'S "INVISIBLE HAND" AND THE CENTRAL ROLE OF MARKETS

Most of the time, private markets provide the best way of maintaining economic efficiency, of ensuring that goods are produced at least cost and that the goods produced are in fact those consumers want. The modern economic faith in private markets can be traced back to Adam Smith's 1776 masterpiece *The Wealth of Nations*. Smith argued that workers and producers, interested only in helping themselves and their families, were the root of economic production. The public interest would best be promoted by individuals pursuing their own self-interest. As Smith put it:

> Man has almost constant occasion for the help of his brethren, and it is in vain for him to expect it from their benevolence only. He will be more likely to prevail if he can interest their self-love in his favour, and show them that it is for their own advantage to do for him what he requires of them. . . . It is not from the benevolence of the butcher, the brewer, or the baker, that we expect our dinner, but from their regard to their own interest. We address ourselves, not to their humanity but to their self-love, and never talk to them of our own necessities but of their advantages.[1]

Smith's insight was that individuals work hardest to help the overall economic production of society when their efforts help themselves. He argued that an "obvious and simple system of liberty" provided the greatest opportunities for people to help themselves and thus, by extension, to create the greatest wealth for a society.

In another famous passage, Smith used the metaphor of the **"invisible hand"** to describe how self-interest led to social good: "He intends only his own gain, and he is in

[1]Adam Smith, *The Wealth of Nations*, Book 1, Chapter 2.

this as in many other cases, led by an invisible hand to promote an end which was no part of his intention. Nor is it always the worse for the society that it was no part of it. By pursuing his own interest he frequently promotes that of the society more effectually than when he really intends to promote it."

Economics has progressed a long way since Adam Smith, but his fundamental argument has had great appeal over the past two centuries. In practice, although there are certainly exceptions, greater liberty for individuals in country after country has indeed led to huge increases in production that have benefited if not everyone, almost everyone. The general belief in the productivity of a market system can largely be considered a legacy from Adam Smith.

While today's economists stress the central place of private firms in modern economies, most also believe that government must play a role as well, because there are certain problems with which the market does not deal well.

GOVERNMENT AS A RESPONSE TO DISAPPOINTMENTS WITH THE MARKET

It is not difficult to find complaints about and discontent with the market. There is concern that markets produce too much of some things, like air and water pollution, and too little of other things, such as support for the arts or child-care facilities. Much of the growth in government this century has stemmed from a concern that private markets fail to achieve the social goals of high levels of employment, economic stability, growth, and income security for citizens. Indeed, in Canada, the past two hundred years have been marked by periodic episodes of high unemployment. In the Great Depression of the 1930s, the unemployment rate reached almost 20 percent and national output fell by 25 percent from its pre-Depression peak in 1929. The Depression brought to the fore problems that, in less severe form, had existed for a long time. Many individuals lost virtually all of their money when banks failed and the stock market crashed. Many elderly people did not have the resources on which to survive. Many farmers found that the prices they received for their products were so low that they could not make their mortgage payments, and defaults became commonplace.

In response to the Depression, the federal government not only took a more active role in attempting to stabilize the level of economic activity, it also passed legislation aimed at alleviating many of the specific problems, including Unemployment Insurance, Old Age Security, federal housing programs, and federal programs aimed at supporting agricultural prices and marketing agricultural products.

After World War II, the economy recovered, and the country experienced an unprecedented level of prosperity. But it became clear that the fruits of that prosperity were not being enjoyed by all. Many people faced a life of poverty and insecurity; they could not afford to purchase the basic necessities of a comfortable life; they received inadequate medical care; and their prospects for obtaining good jobs were bleak. These inequities provided the impetus for the rapid growth of the welfare state in the 1960s parallelling what was occurring in the United Kingdom and other European countries. Provinces began implementing hospital insurance and then medical insurance programs, and ultimately the federal government entered into shared-cost programs in the health insurance area, which made the coverage virtually universal and accessible to all. Welfare assistance and social services were expanded rapidly, again with the financial assistance of the federal government. Unemployment insurance was made much more generous. Other programs, such as job training and regional development initiatives, were introduced in an attempt to improve the economic opportunities of the disadvantaged.

In the late 1980s, a new set of concerns emerged having to do with the competitiveness of the Canadian economy. The rapid growth of the economies of Europe and of the newly industrialized nations in Asia, along with the Free Trade Agreement with the United States, was forcing a rapid restructuring of the economy. The high rates of increases in productivity that marked the 1950s and early 1960s seemed to have come to an end. Canadians were saving and investing less than some competitors. There were new calls for government to take the initiative, both in cushioning the adjustment to the new realities and in improving the amount of research and development activity and in training the labour force. To these concerns have been added those of protection of the environment.

Anyone who follows the news can come up with many other examples of discontent with the outcome of private markets. The concerns listed here, as well as many others, can be placed into three broad categories: those that are based on an ignorance of the laws of economics, those having to do with redistribution of income, and those having to do with genuine failures of private markets.

GOVERNMENT AND THE LAWS OF ECONOMICS

Some of the complaints about markets are of the "Wouldn't the world be a better place if we still lived in the Garden of Eden?" variety. Things have a price because they are scarce. The price of oil may be high, not because oil companies are trying to take advantage of consumers, but simply because oil is scarce, and the high prices reflect that scarcity. In Chapter 4, we saw that economists regard these situations not as market failures but as the hard facts of economic life. Much as everyone would like to live in a world where all individuals could have almost everything they wanted at a price they could afford, this is simply unrealistic. Some pretend that the government can "solve" the problem of scarcity by passing laws about prices; but this simply shifts the problem around, leading to reduced prices for some and shortages for everyone else.

GOVERNMENT AND REDISTRIBUTION

A second category of complaints against the market represents a dissatisfaction with the distribution of income. Market economies may be productive and efficient at producing wealth, but they may also yield a distribution of income where some people become very rich and others starve. Someone who has a rare and valuable skill will, by the laws of supply and demand, receive a high income. Someone else who has few skills, and common ones at that, will find his wage to be low—perhaps even too low for survival. Furthermore, someone who is unlucky enough to be of ill health or to have a disability will incur larger expenditures to meet the basic needs of living than a healthy person.

Most economists see an important role for the government in income redistribution, taking income from those who have more and giving it to those who have less. In their view, society does not need to sit passively by the side and accept whatever distribution of income results from the workings of private markets. Government income taxes on the rich and welfare programs for the poor can be seen as part of the government's role in redistribution. More generally, social programs such as Medicare, Unemployment Insurance, and Old Age Security can be viewed as largely redistributive in nature.

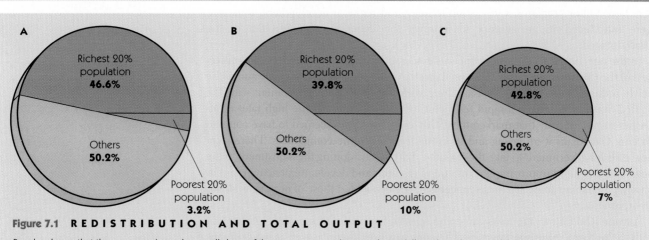

Figure 7.1 **REDISTRIBUTION AND TOTAL OUTPUT**

Panel A shows that the poor receive only a small share of the economy's output. Plans for redistribution often assume that they will create the situation in panel B, where the poor simply receive a larger share. But if the redistribution is poorly managed or too great, it may substantially reduce the size of the overall pie, as in panel C, making all groups worse off. *Source: Income Distribution by Size in Canada* (1980), Statistics Canada Catalogue 13-207, p. 147.

While concern for greater economic equality is a generally accepted role for government, there is still room for much disagreement about the benefits and costs of programs aimed at reducing inequality. Also, if the government does want to reduce inequality, economists will disagree as to what is the best method. Redistributive tax systems and welfare programs often interfere with economic incentives. Questions of redistribution are often posed as: How should the economy's pie be divided? What size slice should each person get?

By looking at the pie in panel A of Figure 7.1, you can see that the poorest 20 percent of the population get a relatively small slice—that is, 20 percent only receive 3.2 percent of the economy's income—while the richest 20 percent of the population get a relatively large slice, 46.6 percent of the economy's income. Often redistribution is viewed as simply cutting the pie differently, giving the poor somewhat larger slices and the rich somewhat smaller, as in panel B. But if the process of redistributing income makes the economy less productive, the size of the whole pie will shrink, as illustrated in panel C. There the poor get a larger share of a smaller pie. The rich are much worse off now—they get a smaller share of a smaller pie. If the size of the pie has shrunk enough, even the poor may be worse off. By designing government redistribution programs appropriately, it may be possible to limit the size of these effects on productivity.

GOVERNMENT AND MARKET FAILURES

The final category of discontent with private markets represents cases where the market does indeed fail in its role of producing economic efficiency. Economists refer to these problems as **market failures,** and have studied them closely. When there is a market failure, there may be a role for government if it can correct the market failure and enhance the economy's efficiency. The correction of market failures leads to two main functions for government: stabilization of the aggregate economy and reallocation of its resources.

Stabilization of the Economy   The most dramatic example of market failures is the periodic episodes of high unemployment that have plagued capitalist economies. It is hard to tout the virtues of an efficient market when a fifth of the industrial labour force and capital stock sits idle, as it did in the Great Depression of the 1930s. While many economists believe there are forces that might eventually restore the economy to full employment, the costs of waiting for the economy to correct itself—in terms of both forgone output and human misery—are enormous, and today virtually all governments take it as their responsibility to stabilize the economy. They *try* to avoid the extreme fluctuations in economic activity—both the downturns, when much of the economy's resources, its workers and machines, remain idle, and the booms, which may result in high inflation. The causes of these fluctuations, and how and whether the government can succeed in significantly reducing them, are among the main topics discussed in macroeconomics, to which Parts Four to Six of this book are devoted.

When the economy's scarce resources are idle, the economy is operating below its production possibilities curve, as shown in Figure 7.2. As usual, the curve has been simplified to two goods, guns and butter, which represent the general output levels in the public and private sectors. The government attempts to move the economy from point E to a point closer to the production possibilities curve, E'.

Reallocation of Resources   Even when an economy's resources are fully utilized, they may not be utilized well. Socialist countries such as the former Soviet Union used to brag that they had developed an economic system in which there was no unemployment, but the economies were extremely inefficient. They even had trouble getting food from the rural sector where it was produced to the cities where it was needed. During the past quarter century, economists have come to understand much better the circumstances under which market economies are efficient. There must be competition, and government has taken it as a responsibility to ensure that there is at least some level of competition in most markets. But even when there is competition, the market may supply too much of some goods and too little of others.

One of the most important instances of this kind of market failure occurs when there are **externalities.** These are present whenever an individual or a firm can take an action that directly affects others and for which it neither pays nor is paid compensation. It therefore does not bear all the consequences of its action. (The effect of the action is "external" to the individual or firm.) Externalities are pervasive. Someone who litters, a driver whose car emits pollution, a child who leaves a mess behind after he finishes playing, a person who smokes a cigarette in a crowded room, all create externalities. In each case, the actor is not the only one who must suffer the consequences of his action; others suffer them too. Externalities can be thought of as instances when the price system works imperfectly. The individual is not "charged" for the litter she creates, nor does the car owner pay for the pollution the car makes.

Externalities can be negative or positive. A common example of a negative externality is a factor that emits air pollution. The factory benefits from emitting the pollution, since by doing so, the company can make its product more cheaply than it could if it put in pollution-control devices. However, society as a whole bears the negative external costs. If the factory had to pay for its pollution, it would find ways to produce less of it. And indeed, government environmental regulations are often aimed at just that goal.

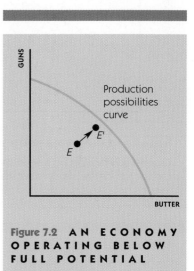

Figure 7.2 AN ECONOMY OPERATING BELOW FULL POTENTIAL

The economy is at point E, below the edge of its production possibilities curve. The government seeks to have it operate closer to the curve, at point E', for instance.

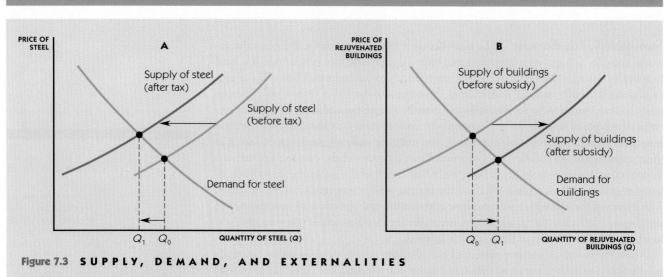

Figure 7.3 **SUPPLY, DEMAND, AND EXTERNALITIES**

The steel industry produces a negative externality of pollution. In panel A, a tax on steel production shifts the supply curve to the left, reducing both steel production and pollution. In panel B, a subsidy for rejuvenated buildings, which create the positive externality of neighbourhood beautification, shifts the supply curve to the right, causing more buildings and neighbourhoods to be renovated.

A common example of a positive externality is a new invention. Almost always, when someone makes a new discovery that leads to greater economic productivity, other people (or companies) benefit. The inventor receives, through the prices he charges, only a fraction of the total gains to society from the invention. Other firms, for instance, will copy it and learn from it. Inventions like the laser and the transistor have benefited consumers, both by providing new products and allowing other products to be made less expensively. While the individual researcher bears the cost of making a discovery, society receives positive external benefits. If everyone who benefited from an invention had to pay money to the inventor, there would be far higher incentives for research and development. And indeed, patents and other government laws enable the investors to get a larger return than they otherwise would.

With externalities present, the market's allocation of goods is inefficient. When the production of a good such as steel entails a negative externality—like smoke and its effect on the air—the level of production is too high. This is because the producer fails to take into account the "social costs" in deciding how much to produce. To put it another way, the price of steel determined in competitive markets by the law of supply and demand only reflects *private* costs, the costs actually faced by firms. If firms do not have to pay *all* of the costs (including the costs of pollution), equilibrium prices will be lower and output higher than they would be if firms took social costs into account.

The government can try to offset this effect in several ways. For instance, it might impose a tax. Panel A of Figure 7.3 shows the demand and supply curves for steel, and depicts the market equilibrium at the intersection of the two curves, Q_0. With a tax on the production of steel, the supply curve will shift to the left—the quantity produced at each price will be lower—and the equilibrium level of production will be less, Q_1.

Similarly, there is an undersupply of goods that produce positive externalities, and the government can try to enlarge the supply. The rejuvenation of an apartment building in a decaying part of a city is an example of a positive externality; it will probably enhance the value of buildings around it. Panel B of Figure 7.3 shows the demand and supply curve for rejuvenated buildings. A government subsidy to rejuvenation shifts the supply curve to the right, increasing the number of rejuvenated buildings from Q_0 to Q_1.

Public Goods   There is a category of goods, called **public goods,** that can be viewed as an extreme case of positive externalities. Public goods are goods that it costs nothing extra for an additional individual to enjoy (their consumption is **nonrivalrous**), and that it costs a great deal to exclude any individual from enjoying (they are **nonexcludable**). The standard example of a public good is defence. Once Canada is protected from attack, it costs nothing extra to protect each new baby from foreign invasion, nor would it be possible to exclude a newborn baby from this protection.

Public parks along the sides of a highway are another example. Anyone driving along the highway enjoys the view; the fact that one person is enjoying the view does not exclude others from enjoying it; and it would in fact be expensive to stop anyone who is driving along the highway from benefiting from the view. A lighthouse to guide ships around dangerous shoals or rocks is still another example of a public good. There are no additional costs incurred as an additional ship navigates near the lighthouse, and it would be difficult to shut off the light in the lighthouse at just the right time to prevent a ship passing by from taking advantage of the lighthouse.

A **pure public good** is one where the marginal costs of providing it to an additional person are strictly zero and where it is impossible to exclude people from receiving the good. Many public goods that government provides are not *pure* public goods in this sense. It is possible, but relatively expensive, to exclude people from (or charge people for) using an uncrowded interstate highway; the cost of an additional person using an uncrowded interstate highway is very, very small, but not zero.

Figure 7.4 compares some examples of publicly provided goods against the strict definition of a pure public good. It shows the ease of exclusion along the horizontal axis and the (marginal) cost of an additional individual using the good along the vertical axis. The lower left-hand corner represents a pure public good. Of the major public expendi-

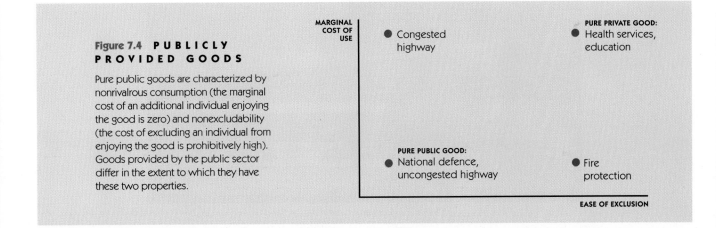

Figure 7.4 PUBLICLY PROVIDED GOODS

Pure public goods are characterized by nonrivalrous consumption (the marginal cost of an additional individual enjoying the good is zero) and nonexcludability (the cost of excluding an individual from enjoying the good is prohibitively high). Goods provided by the public sector differ in the extent to which they have these two properties.

MARGINAL COST OF USE

● Congested highway

PURE PRIVATE GOOD:
● Health services, education

PURE PUBLIC GOOD:
● National defence, uncongested highway

● Fire protection

EASE OF EXCLUSION

CLOSE-UP: GET WHAT YOU PAY FOR AND PAY FOR WHAT YOU GET

How much should the government finance inter-city transportation systems? Today, the government heavily subsidizes most forms of transportation directly or indirectly. Three-quarters of the cost of intercity passenger transportation by train is borne by the taxpayer and only one-quarter by the user. Other major modes of transportation, such as air, car, bus, and ferry, are subsidized by the taxpayer to the extent of 18 percent, 9 percent, 5 percent, and 41 percent, respectively. The cost breakdown differs across modes. In the case of car and air travel, the costs borne by the taxpayer mainly represent infrastructure and environmental costs, whereas for train travel, taxpayers directly subsidize the cost of the ticket. Bus travel, the least expensive mode of intercity transportation per passenger-kilometer and also the mode most used by lower-income persons, however, is the least-subsidized mode. In aggregate, taxpayers pay 12 percent of intercity travel costs, so that users pay only 88 percent of the costs they incur. By subsidizing air, car, and train travel, the government is effectively encouraging more expensive modes of transportation.

The Royal Commission on National Passenger Transportation (which was appointed in 1989) recommended in 1991 that the role of government in intercity transportation should be significantly modified and reduced. It recommended that all travellers be charged the full costs of their travel. If drivers paid full highway repair, environmental damages, and safety/accident costs, presumably more people would take the bus, at an average cost of 9.5 cents per passenger-kilometer as opposed to 17.4 cents by car.

In the opinion of the commission, the public would be best served if the market for bus, train, and air services were more open to private suppli-

ers. The government should not engage in unprofitable ventures. For instance, if it cannot make a profit, the government should get out of passenger train travel and should sell shares of Canada's international air carriers to individual Canadians. (In addition, the government should refrain from assisting uncompetitive airlines to survive with cash infusions.) The market should dictate which public transportation routes are viable and thus where services are supplied.

According to the commission, the government's role in intercity transportation should be severely limited. Its main responsibilities should be ensuring fair competition practices by suppliers, establishing a fund for infrastructural and environmental maintenance, paid into by drivers, and ensuring passenger safety and accessibility to transportation services for disabled persons. The objectives thus met would be safety, protection of the environment, fairness to taxpayers (and travellers and carriers), and efficiency. These are far-reaching recommendations indeed for a nation that has been largely developed with the assistance of a government-supported transportation sector. Whether they will be acted upon remains to be seen.

Source: Directions: The Final Report of the Royal Commission on National Passenger Transportation (Ottawa: Minister of Supply and Services, 1992).

tures, only national defence is close to a pure public good. Uncongested highways, to the extent that they exist, are also an example. The upper right-hand corner represents a pure private good (health services or education), where the cost of exclusion is low and the marginal cost of an additional individual using the good is high.

There are many goods that are not pure public goods but that have one or the other property to some degree. Fire protection is a good for which exclusion is relatively easy—individuals who refuse to contribute to the fire department could simply not be helped in the event of a fire. But fire protection is like a public good in that the marginal cost of covering an additional person is low. Most of the time, firefighters are not engaged in fighting fires but are waiting for calls. Protecting an additional individual has little extra cost. Only in that rare event when two fires break out simultaneously will there be a significant cost to extending the protection to an additional person.

Sometimes the marginal cost of using a good to which access is easy (a good that possesses the property of nonexcludability) will be high. When an uncongested highway turns congested, the costs of using it rise dramatically, not in terms of wear and tear on the road but in terms of time lost by drivers using the road then. It is costly to exclude by charging for road use—as a practical matter, this can only be done on toll roads, and, ironically, the toll booths often contribute to the congestion.

Many of the goods that are publicly provided, such as education and health services, have high costs associated with providing the service to additional individuals. For most of these goods, exclusion is also relatively easy. In fact, many of these goods and services are provided privately in some countries, or provided both publicly and privately. Though they are publicly provided, they are not *pure* public goods, in the technical sense in which the term is defined.

Private markets undersupply public goods. If there were a single shipowner using the port near which a lighthouse is constructed, he could weigh the costs and benefits of the lighthouse. But if there were one large shipowner and many smaller owners, it would not pay any one of the small owners to build the lighthouse; and the large shipowner, in deciding whether to construct the lighthouse, would only take into account the benefits he would receive, not the benefits to the small shipowners. If the costs of construction exceeded the benefits that he alone would receive, he would not build the lighthouse. But at the same time, if the benefits accruing to *all* the shipowners, large and small, were taken into account, those benefits would exceed the costs; it would then be desirable to build the lighthouse.

One can imagine a voluntary association of shipowners getting together to construct a lighthouse in this situation. But what happens if some small shipowner refuses to contribute, thinking that even if he does not contribute, the lighthouse will be built anyway? This is the **free-rider** aspect of public goods; because it is difficult to preclude anyone from using them, those who benefit from the goods have an incentive to avoid paying for them. Every shipowner has an incentive to "free ride" on the efforts of others. When too many decide to do this, the lighthouse will not get built.

Governments bring an important advantage to bear on the problem of public goods. They have the power to coerce citizens to pay for them. It is true that there might be *some* level of purchase of public goods—lighthouses, highway parks, even police or fire services—in the absence of government intervention. But society would be better off if the level of production were increased, and citizens were forced to pay for the increased level of public services through taxes.

ECONOMIC ROLES FOR THE GOVERNMENT

Redistributing income

Stabilizing the economy

Reallocating resources

GOVERNMENT'S OPTIONS

Once it has been decided that government should do something, there is a second question: how can government accomplish society's ends most efficiently? The government will have to choose among several courses of action. It could do something directly; it could provide incentives for the private section to do something; it could mandate that the private sector do something; or it could take some combination of these three courses of action.

TAKING DIRECT ACTION

Faced with a market failure, the government could simply take charge itself. If it believes there is a market failure in the provision of medical care, for instance, it can nationalize the medical sector, as Britain did after World War II. If the government believes there is a market failure in the airline or railroad industry, it can nationalize the industry, or the part of the industry with which it is discontent, and run the industry itself. Thus, in Canada, government-owned firms have operated in the airline industry (Air Canada), in the rail transport industry (Canadian National) and in the oil industry (PETRO Canada), to give only three of many examples. If the government believes there is a failure in the provision of housing for the poor, it can build government housing projects, as the provinces have done.

Sometimes, the direct action the government takes is not to produce the good itself, but to purchase the good from the private sector, including the nonprofit sector. Thus, the military purchases virtually all of the equipment it uses from the private sector. While the government operates a comprehensive medical insurance system, the hospitals are not run by the government, nor are doctors members of the public service. And those provinces that operate public automobile insurance schemes use the services of independent firms to administer them.

PROVIDING INCENTIVES TO THE PRIVATE SECTOR

Another alternative is for the government to operate at a distance, providing incentives that attempt to alter the workings of private markets in desirable ways. It can provide incentives directly through subsidies, as it does for agriculture, or, as is commonly done in Canada, indirectly through the tax system. The government has used energy tax credits to encourage energy conservation. It has also used an investment tax credit, which gives firms a tax break for investing in new machines, to encourage investment, and tax credits to induce research and development. Moreover, special provisions of the income tax encourage employers to provide disability insurance and pensions for their employees.

Both of these strategies, subsidies and taxes, put the government in the position of manipulating the price system to achieve its ends. If the government is worried about the supply of adequate housing for the poor, for example, it can provide incentives for builders to construct low-income housing in inner cities—it can provide the builders with direct payments, or it can grant tax reductions for those who make investments in slum areas. If the government wants to encourage oil conservation, it can impose a tax on oil or gasoline, which will encourage conservation by raising the price. Similarly, the government can impose a tax on cars that are not energy efficient.

MANDATING ACTION IN THE PRIVATE SECTOR

Sometimes, however, there is concern about whether the private sector will respond to incentives, or uncertainty about what effect particular incentives will have. Or there is concern that providing subsidies is too costly. In these circumstances, the government often mandates the desired action, which means that it forces the private sector to do something, under threat of some legal punishment. The government may mandate, for instance, that private firms provide safe work environments for their employees. The government may mandate that automobile manufacturers produce fuel-efficient cars, specifying particular standards for kilometers per litre of gas. In some localities, real estate developers who want to get a permit for a large housing project may be required to provide a certain number of units for low-income individuals, or to help improve a local road or build a local school. In all these cases, the fact that the government requirement does not show up on the government's budget does not mean that there is not a cost to such a requirement. The costs—borne indirectly by workers, firms, and consumers—can be very high.

COMBINING INSTRUMENTS

The government often combines two or more courses of action in its attempts to achieve some objectives. Consider, for instance, the concern over living standards of the elderly. The government provides a basic pension to all persons sixty-five years of age and older; it provides a supplementary pension for low-income persons; it operates a contributory pension scheme based on past earnings; and it offers a tax incentive to save for one's own retirement either through a company pension plan or through one's own retirement savings plan. As well, it regulates some of the terms of private pension plans, for example, to ensure that they do not discriminate by gender. And it provides some public services that are directed specifically to the needs of the elderly. Different countries have chosen different mixes of these policies, but most provide some such services. For example, in the United States, much more emphasis is placed on the contributory pension component rather than the general pension scheme.

GOVERNMENT'S OPTIONS

Taking direct action
   Production of a good or service
   Purchase of a good or service
Providing incentives to the private sector
   Subsidies
   Taxes
Mandating private-sector action

OTHER PERSPECTIVES

Debates over the role of government are an ongoing part of political life. Changes in economic circumstances lead to new demands for government action. These new demands, combined with the scarce resources that government has available, force a reevaluation of old programs, often leading to cutbacks in or restructuring of these programs. Sometimes government programs have been around so long that people forget about alternative, and perhaps better, ways of accomplishing the same objectives.

Each of these debates has many facets. In areas such as health, banking, and housing for the poor, where there already is extensive government involvement, people disagree about whether there should be more or less government involvement, and whether the form of government involvement should be changed. While some claim that the presently perceived problems are the result of, or are at least exacerbated by, government programs, others believe that the main problem is too little government, or misdirected government programs.

A central issue in all of these debates is how resources are to be allocated. These are economic issues. But behind the economic issues are value judgments. Is it more important to spend an extra dollar trying to prolong the life of an octogenarian, or trying to improve the life opportunities of an underprivileged child from one of the nation's inner cities? These are hard choices, and it would be nice to say, let's do both. The fact of scarcity means that we cannot have everything we want.

Another set of noneconomic issues relates to how much government *should* intervene in the lives of its citizens, and the rights of individuals to make decisions for themselves, for better or worse. The principle that individuals are the best judges of what is in their own interests, and that their preferences should be respected, is called the **principle of consumer sovereignty.** Thus, critics of public education argue that "forcing" people to participate in government-run schools violates the principle of consumer sovereignty. Society's basic concern—that the nation's youth receive the best possible education— can, it is argued, be taken care of with *less* intrusion by the government.

Some claim that a major responsibility of government is establishing a just and humane society. John Rawls, professor of philosophy at Harvard and widely regarded as one of the world's leading moral philosophers, has argued in his book A *Theory of Justice* that a society is to be judged on how well it treats its worst-off members. Others, such as Harvard philosopher Robert Nozick, question the moral right of government to take away the fruits of any individual's labour. The conflicting views of the role of government in our society lead, quite naturally, to conflicting views about the role of government in the economy.

THE SIZE OF GOVERNMENT

The impact of government today is far larger than it was a half century ago. The government produces more, it regulates more, it taxes more, and it spends more. The growth in expenditures is the easiest of these to quantify. A standard measure of the size of the economy is the **gross domestic product** (GDP), which measures the value of all the goods and services produced in an economy. In Canada today, expenditures by all levels of government are about 44 percent of GDP. This compares with about 20 percent in 1939 immediately before World War II. The comparable figure for the United States is 36 percent, and in the industrialized countries overall it is 40 percent. Furthermore, roughly $2.00 out of every $5.00 earned goes to the government in taxes to pay for the expenditures. Much of these expenditures include pure transfers rather than expenditures on the goods and services represented by GDP. Government expenditures on goods and services are about 23 percent of GDP. This means that almost one-quarter of the output produced in the economy is used by the government.

SOURCES OF GROWTH IN GOVERNMENT EXPENDITURES

Canada, as was noted earlier, has a federal government structure in which many important economic functions are decentralized to the lower levels of government. The provinces and territories and their municipalities are responsible for health, education, welfare, and natural resources within their boundaries, for the regulation of labour markets and nonbank financial institutions, and for the provision of services of a local nature. The federal government is responsible for defence and foreign affairs, money and banking, international trade and investment, communications, pensions and unemployment insurance. Joint federal-provincial responsibility has been exercised in the areas of agriculture, housing, and environmental protection. Through the use of grants to the provinces and territories, the federal government has been able to influence the provision of basic services by the provinces, especially in the areas of health, welfare, and transportation.

Expenditures at both the federal and provincial/municipal levels have increased over the past two decades, as shown in Figure 7.5. And they have increased much more rapidly than the nation's output, so that the *fraction* of the nation's output that is spent by each level of government has grown much larger.

Figure 7.6, which shows the relative importance of different categories of federal expenditures in 1950, 1970, and 1990, helps us to see what accounts for this increase at the federal level. Interestingly, none of it is due to expenditures on goods and services. These have actually fallen as a percentage of GDP, largely owing to a decline in the importance of defence expenditures. Transfers to persons have increased rapidly reflecting especially the growing importance of two categories of transfers—unemployment insurance and payments to the elderly. Grants to other levels of governments have also increased significantly. In the 1960s, the federal government instituted some significant shared-cost programs with the provinces in the areas of health (Medicare) and welfare (Canada Assistance Plan). As well, the equalization scheme whereby the federal government transfers funds to the less-well-off provinces increased in importance, especially in the 1970s when resource revenues of the western provinces increased dramatically. But

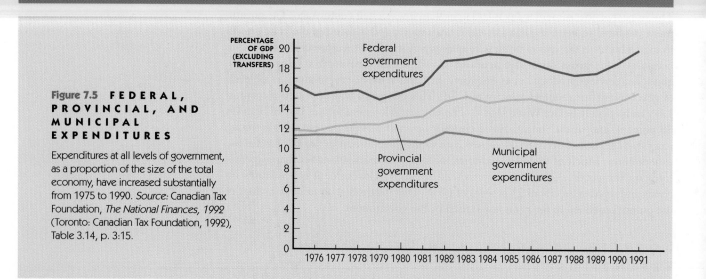

Figure 7.5 FEDERAL, PROVINCIAL, AND MUNICIPAL EXPENDITURES

Expenditures at all levels of government, as a proportion of the size of the total economy, have increased substantially from 1975 to 1990. *Source:* Canadian Tax Foundation, *The National Finances, 1992* (Toronto: Canadian Tax Foundation, 1992), Table 3.14, p. 3:15.

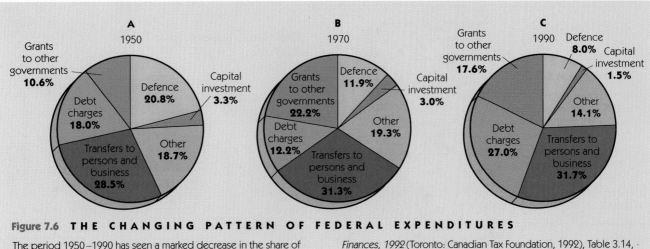

Figure 7.6 THE CHANGING PATTERN OF FEDERAL EXPENDITURES

The period 1950–1990 has seen a marked decrease in the share of defence expenditures. Interest expenses declined from 1950 to 1970, but then rose. *Source:* Canadian Tax Foundation, *The National Finances, 1992* (Toronto: Canadian Tax Foundation, 1992), Table 3.14, p. 3:15.

more recently the growth of transfers to the provinces have declined relative to GDP as the federal government has made reforms to the major programs so as to make them less open-ended.

Another factor contributing to the growth in federal government expenditures in the last decade has been the interest the government must pay on the huge debt it has been accumulating. During the 1970s and 1980s, the government spent more than it collected in taxes and had to borrow to finance the difference; it consequently had to pay interest on that debt. These interest payments grew significantly during the 1980s, and they now account for over one-quarter of the federal budget.

The expenditures of the provinces and their municipalities have grown even more dramatically. In 1982, they stood at about 10 percent of GDP. By 1990, they had risen to about 22 percent of GDP, comparable to the size of the federal government. This increase reflects the rapid growth of provincial expenditures in the areas of health, welfare, and education, as the government has taken more and more responsibility for providing these services on a comprehensive and accessible basis.

COMPARISON WITH OTHER COUNTRIES

The increase of government expenditures in the postwar period has been dramatic in most industrialized countries. And those in Canada have risen much more than most. As Figure 7.7 illustrates, the share of total government expenditures in Canada from 1960–1973 was comparable to that of the OECD countries (the OECD, or Organization for Economic Cooperation and Development, includes most industrialized countries of the non-Communist world) and to the so-called G-7 countries (the G-7, or

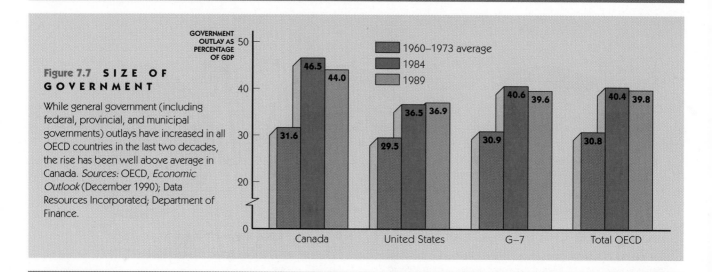

Figure 7.7 SIZE OF GOVERNMENT

While general government (including federal, provincial, and municipal governments) outlays have increased in all OECD countries in the last two decades, the rise has been well above average in Canada. *Sources*: OECD, *Economic Outlook* (December 1990); Data Resources Incorporated; Department of Finance.

Group of Seven, includes Canada, France, Germany, Italy, Japan, the United Kingdom, and the United States, and meets regularly to discuss the coordination of economic policies). But in the 1980s, Canada's expenditures were well above average. There were some individual countries for which government expenditures were more important. For example, government expenditures are roughly half of GDP in the Western European countries. But American government expenditures are about 37 percent of GDP, while in Japan they are closer to 33 percent of GDP.

These figures are broad aggregates and do not reflect differences in the types of expenditures across countries. For example, a large proportion of U.S. federal expenditures go to defence; the relative size of U.S. nondefence expenditures is comparable to that of Japan, which has the lowest federal expenditures of the industrialized countries.

Naturally, these foreign comparisons mean different things to different persons. Opponents of more government spending argue that Japan, with its low level of expenditures, is a better model to emulate than the slow-growing countries of Western Europe. On the other hand, advocates of government spending worry about the pressure that exists to follow the American model, where low government spending has not resulted in rapid growth lately and where difficult social problems persist. Concern over freer trade with the United States and Mexico has focused more than anything else on the pressures that it would entail for maintaining social programs in the face of competitive pressures from these lower-tax countries.

THE SIZE OF GOVERNMENT DEBATE

A central question of debate in Canada and in other mixed economies is what the appropriate size of the public sector should be. Some believe that the government should have a greater role in the economy, and hence that government should be larger in size. In their view, government spending could ameliorate some problems, like blighted cities and inadequate schools. Others believe that government should have less of a role and that the public sector should be smaller. They believe that the public sector is too large for two reasons: they are skeptical of government's ability to solve social and economic problems, and they fear that bigger government undermines economic and political freedom. Finally, others believe that private-sector principles should be used by the public sector and that the use of such market principles will make the public sector more efficient and hence smaller.

MORE GOVERNMENT

Given the need for technological innovation and training, as well as the necessity of trading with countries that finance and encourage national industrial policies, many in Canada see the need for a greater role for government.

Canadian Competitiveness   Some believe Canada is falling behind in competition with some of our major industrial competitors, particularly Japan. These people advocate more government action to direct the nation's energies towards maintaining Canada's competitiveness in industries it has dominated in the past, and establishing its technological leadership in new areas.

One reflection of changes in Canada's competitive position is the increased imports of industrial goods, from steel to automobiles to advanced electronics. Besides the positive response—how can Canada become more productive?—there is the negative response that government should protect Canada from competition. The competition from which protection is wanted is usually labelled "unfair."

It is widely thought that research and development is a major contributor to technological innovation and thus to economic growth and competitiveness. Companies do less research and development in Canada than in many other industrialized nations. Part of this is due to the fact that much of Canadian industry consists of foreign-owned corporations that may prefer to consolidate their R & D activities in the home country. Governments have been urged to take the initiative in encouraging firms to undertake R & D in Canada, for example, by using tax breaks or subsidies to encourage R & D expenditures or by direct government participation in R & D.

Environment   The public has become more and more concerned about the state of the environment as more and more information becomes available about the long-term consequences of acid rain, automobile pollution, the greenhouse effect, the disposal of garbage, and the loss of valuable resources from the forests and fisheries. Governments have been urged to institute strict measures to arrest the growth of pollution so that a clean environment can be passed on to future generations.

Education   Almost all formal education now is provided by the public sector. But deficiencies in the educational system are easy to find. Teenage dropout rates are high, the system is said not to produce the basic skills needed for the technological age, and advanced education does not prepare the student for the job market. This has given rise to a call for more resources to be put into education, for more effort to be put into skill development, possibly with the cooperation of the private sector, and for national standardized methods of testing to be introduced. One difficulty is that the federal government is restricted in its ability to act since education is the sole responsibility of the provinces.

LESS GOVERNMENT

In recent years, there has been increasing concern about the efficiency of the government as a producer, and growing willingness to explore the possibility of the private production of publicly provided goods. Thus, today many towns rely on private garbage collection services, which the municipality pays for. Similarly, it has been suggested that market-based principles could be introduced into the provision of public services, especially in such areas as health care.

Health Care   The costs of providing health care have risen dramatically as a result of such things as increased longevity and improved medical technology. Many also argue that costs have risen on account of the Medicare system itself, which guarantees free access by all citizens to a comprehensive list of health services. They argue that costs could be contained by introducing some elements of pricing into the financing of medical care so as to induce users to be more prudent in the use of costly health care resources.

Agriculture   The government has intervened in the agricultural industry more than it has interfered with any other industry. In part, this has been out of a desire to protect farmers from the unexpected, and sometimes wild, fluctuations in their products. As well, governments have responded to competitive pressures induced by governments in competing countries, especially in the European Community, where agriculture is heavily subsidized. But a more fundamental reason concerns the gradual decline in the size of the work force. The ability to produce more efficiently has caused a reduction in agricultural prices and incomes as the market attempts to induce a reallocation of workers out of agriculture and into other industries. Governments have responded with a bewildering variety of programs such as marketing boards, supply management schemes, and outright subsidies. The persistence of such policies has introduced permanent distortions into the agricultural sector.

BETTER GOVERNMENT

The debate over the appropriate role and size of government has also extended to ways to make government programs more efficient. Some suggestions include subjecting government, where possible, to competitive pressures; decentralizing, which would allow more of the decisions to occur at the local level and enable government programs thus to be more responsive to the needs of those they are intended to benefit; and strengthening the incentives provided to public employees, providing greater rewards for good performance and making it easier to dismiss employees who do not perform well.

Unemployment Insurance   Unemployment Insurance became one of the biggest programs operated by the federal government when the program was liberalized in 1971. It collects premiums from all workers and then pays them out to the eligible unemployed, that is, to those who have worked a minimum number of weeks. The amount and length of the payment period depend upon amount of income earned as well as upon the region of the country (provisions are much more generous to high-unemployment regions like the Atlantic provinces than to other areas). Economists have argued that the program has incentives built into it that inhibit the productivity of the market economy. The low eligibility requirements are said to encourage excessive job quits and prolonged unemployment spells; the regional incentives inhibit the efficient allocation of labour among regions; and the fact that the premiums do not differentiate by industry means that seasonal industries and those that are prone to demand fluctuations are favoured relative to more stable industries. Many have suggested that the program has become more of a scheme for redistribution than for insurance. Economists argue that the scheme should have more features of insurance built into it, such as premiums that vary with risk (referred to as experience rating), so that it is operated more as a proper insurance scheme than as a redistributive device. Then, goals of redistribution could be pursued with policies more suited to the purpose.

Public Pensions   The system of payments to the elderly is a bit of a patchwork system consisting of a mixture of equal per capita pensions with income-tested payments and an occupational pension scheme. In addition, many provinces provide supplements to pensions received by their residents from the federal government. There is some concern that as the population ages, it will be more and more costly to maintain the existing system. Some observers call for a rationalization of the system in two ways. One would be to make the pensions paid out of general government revenues more selective so that those who really need them obtain more benefits. This would entail abandoning the principle of **universality,** which many people feel strongly about. The other would be to put the contributory component of the public pension system on a purely self-financing basis, or as it is put in insurance circles, to make it **actuarially fair.**

Welfare   Government welfare policies have two main goals: to provide the poor with a basic level of subsistence and to help the poor become economically independent members of society. It is clear that they have only met with limited success. Welfare expenditures continue to increase, especially in the larger cities. Many critics have pointed to the fact that welfare schemes by their design tend to discourage recipients from taking jobs, and they do little to help the working poor. Reformers have argued that the system should be changed from one of welfare to **workfare;** that is, in return for receiving welfare benefits, poor people would be required to look for jobs, participate in job training, or take government-provided jobs.

GOVERNMENT ACTION AND PUBLIC FAILURES

The call for government action is a natural one. Individuals feel powerless to correct broad social problems. If such problems are to be addressed, collective action will be required, and the government is the one collective institution to which all of us, in some sense, belong. But the fact that a market failure exists does not necessarily mean that the government should do something. It has to be shown that government action could improve matters.

When demanding that the government take action, individuals often forget the budget constraints facing society as a whole; sometimes observed deficiencies are merely the reflection of scarcity. If members of society wish to guarantee first-rate nursing home care to all of the elderly, it will be expensive. It is no less expensive—and, indeed, it may be more expensive—when it is paid for collectively than when the families of the elderly have to pay for it as individuals. The funds for increased expenditures must come from somewhere, either from reallocating current expenditures or by increasing taxes (that is, increasing the size of the public sector at the expense of the private). Clearly, if it were costless, everyone would favour providing first-rate nursing home care for all of the elderly who want or need it. Given the costs, people may choose not to do so.

Some calls for government programs may simply be slightly veiled attempts to redistribute income. Those who want the government to pay for nursing care for the aged or child care for the young know that it takes resources to provide these services. They want someone else—the anonymous taxpayer—to pick up the bill.

In recent years, there has been increasing awareness of government failures, that it is not sufficient simply for government programs to have lofty objectives to redress the inadequacies of the market. For example, while inner-city slums represent a serious social problem, many government housing projects have proved to be little if any better.

Thus, an analysis of the role of the government requires an understanding of the strengths and weaknesses of governments as well as those of markets. Governments can fail just as markets can. Careful analysis is required to determine whether the government should actually take action, and what form that action should take. What is the cause of the problem? Is there reason to believe the government can do a more effective job? What will it cost in the short and long run? Where will the funds come from?

An understanding of the basic tools and techniques economists use in making evaluations about the benefits or costs of particular government interventions can help greatly to put contemporary economic issues in perspective. Subsequent chapters will develop these tools and techniques.

REVIEW AND PRACTICE

SUMMARY

1. The government plays a pervasive role in the economy of almost every industrialized country. Government expenditures in Canada are over 40 percent of national output—a much larger proportion than thirty years ago, and a significantly larger proportion than that of the United States.

2. In a democracy, the public sector differs from the private in two main ways. First, its legitimacy and authority are derived from the electoral process. Second, it has certain powers of compulsion, such as requiring households and firms to pay taxes and obey laws.

3. By and large, economists believe that private markets allocate resources efficiently. But there are a number of areas in which they do not, as is the case with externalities and public goods. Moreover, at times, when the economy fails to use the available resources fully, there may be idle industrial capacity and unemployed workers. And even when the economy is efficient, there may be dissatisfaction with the distribution of income.

4. Individuals and firms tend to produce too much of a good with a negative externality, such as air or water pollution, since they do not need to bear all the costs. On

the other hand, they tend to produce too little of a good with a positive externality, such as a new invention, since they cannot receive all the benefits.

5. Public goods are goods that it costs little or nothing for an additional individual to enjoy, and that it costs a great deal to exclude any individual from enjoying. National defence and lighthouses are two examples. Free markets tend to underproduce public goods, since it is (by definition) difficult to prevent anyone from using them without paying for them.

6. Government has a variety of instruments it can use to attain its objectives. It can take direct action, provide incentives to the private sector, or mandate action by the private sector.

7. The proper balance between the public and private sectors is a major concern of economics. Recent years have seen an increased reliance on the private sector, with movements towards deregulation and privatization.

8. Government expenditures have grown in the past few decades, as a result of increased spending on programs for the aged and the unemployed, and the growing interest government must pay on the national debt, among other reasons. Provincial government expenditures have grown more rapidly than those of the federal government in recent years, mainly due to the rapid increase in health, education, and welfare responsibilities.

9. There is much debate over what the role of government should be, in areas such as trade, education, agriculture, banking, and social programs. Careful analysis is required to determine whether the government should take action in these areas, with the recognition that governments can fail just as markets can.

KEY TERMS

nationalization	Smith's "invisible hand"	principle of consumer sovereignty
privatization	market failure	gross domestic product (GDP)
deregulation	externality	
federal governmental structure	public good	actuarially fair
eminent domain	free-rider problem	workfare

REVIEW QUESTIONS

1. Name some of the ways government touches the lives of all citizens, both in and out of the economic sphere.

2. "Since democratic governments are elected by the consent of a majority of the people, they have no need for compulsion." Comment.

3. How can individual selfishness end up promoting social welfare?

4. Name areas in which market failure can occur.

5. Why do goods with negative externalities tend to be overproduced and goods with positive externalities tend to be underproduced? Give an example for each.

6. What two characteristics define a public good? Give an example.

7. What three broad types of instruments does government have to try to achieve its goals?

8. Does the presence of a market failure necessarily mean that government action is desirable? If not, why not?

9. Describe some of the major economic roles of government.

10. How has the size of government changed over time? How does the size of the Canadian government compare with that of other industrialized countries?

PROBLEMS

1. In each of the following areas, specify how the government is involved, either as a direct producer, a regulator, a purchaser of final goods and services distributed directly to individuals or used within government, or in some other role:
   (a) education
   (b) mail delivery
   (c) health care
   (d) air travel
   (e) national defence.
In each of these cases, can you think of ways that part of the public role could be provided by the private sector?

2. Can you explain why even a benevolent and well-meaning government may sometimes have to use the power of eminent domain? (Hint: Consider the incentives of one person who knows that her property is the last obstacle to building a highway.)

3. Explain why government redistribution programs involve a trade-off between risk and incentives for *both* rich and poor.

4. Each of the situations below involves an externality. Tell whether it is a positive or negative externality, or both, and explain why free markets will overproduce or underproduce the good in question:
   (a) a business performing research and development projects;
   (b) a business that discharges waste into a nearby river;
   (c) a concert given in the middle of a large city park;
   (d) an individual who smokes cigarettes in a meeting held in a small, unventilated room.

5. When some activity causes a negative externality like pollution, would it be a good idea to ban the activity altogether? Why or why not? (Hint: Consider marginal costs and benefits.)

6. Highways are often referred to as public goods. That designation is basically fair, but not perfect. What are the costs of "exclusion"? Can you describe a case where the marginal cost of an additional driver on a highway might be relatively high? How might society deal with this problem?

PART TWO

AGGREGATE MARKETS

P eace and prosperity" is the slogan on which many political candidates have run for office, and the failure to maintain prosperity has led to many a government's defeat. There is widespread belief among the citizenry that government is responsible for maintaining the economy at full employment, with stable prices, and for creating an economic environment in which growth can occur.

Although most economists agree with these sentiments, there are dissenting views. Some claim that the government has relatively little power to control most of the fluctuations in output and employment; some argue that, apart from isolated instances such as the Great Depression of the 1930s, neither inflation nor unemployment is a major *economic* problem (though they obviously remain political problems); and some believe that government has been as much a cause of the problems of unemployment, inflation, and slow growth as part of their solution. We will explore these various interpretations in greater depth in the chapters that follow.

The problems of unemployment, inflation, and growth relate to the performance of the entire economy. Earlier in the book, we learned how the law of supply and demand operates in the market for oranges, apples, or other goods. At any one time, one industry may be doing well, another poorly. Yet to understand the forces that determine how well the economy as a whole is doing, we want to see beyond the vagaries that affect any particular industry. This is the domain of macroeconomics. Macroeconomics focuses not on the output of single products like orange juice or peanut butter, nor on the demand for masons or bricklayers or computer programmers. Rather, it is concerned with the characteristics of an entire economy, such as the overall level of output, the total level of employment, and the stability of the overall level of prices. What accounts for the "diseases" that sometimes affect the economy—the episodes of massive unemployment, rising prices, or economic stagnation—and what can the government do, both to prevent the onset of these diseases and to cure them once they have occurred?

Macroeconomic *theory* is concerned with what determines the level of employment and output as well as the rate of inflation and the overall growth rate of the economy; while macroeconomic *policy* focuses on what government can do to stimulate employment, prevent inflation, and increase the economy's growth rate.

We begin our study of macroeconomics in Chapter 8 by learning the major statistics used to measure the economy—rates of unemployment, inflation, and growth—and the major macroeconomic goals. Modern macroeconomic theory is grounded in an understanding of how the basic units that make up the economy, households and firms, behave. Chapter 9 provides an overall picture of the economy, based on the competitive model first introduced in Chapter 2. It also explains why, under some conditions, that model may not provide a good description of the economy. One of its failings is that it cannot account for unemployment, one of the principal concerns of this book. Chapter 10 presents the main schools of macroeconomics and the major analytical issues as they relate to the three aggregate markets—labour, product, and capital. It introduces the key concepts of *aggregate* demand and *aggregate* supply curves, with which we can analyze price and output levels for the economy as a whole.

Chapter 11 looks in detail at the aggregate labour market and the reasons it might not clear. When the demand for labour decreases, real wages may not fall and unemployment is the result. But what causes the demand curve for labour to shift? The answer lies in the product market, to which Chapters 12–16 are devoted. Chapter 12 introduces the concept of aggregate expenditures, the total of what households, firms, and government, in Canada and abroad, would like to spend on goods produced in Canada. Chapters 13 and 14 examine each of the components of aggregate expenditures—consumption, investment, government spending, and net exports—to learn why aggregate expenditures fluctuate and how government policy can affect these fluctuations.

In Chapter 15, we learn how the aggregate demand and supply curves are derived, in order to understand what causes them to shift, how government policies can affect them, and why they have the shape they do. Finally, Chapter 16 explores why it is that prices may not adjust in the speedy way envisioned by the basic competitive model, as well as the consequences for the behaviour of the economy and the role of government intervention. The third aggregate market, the capital market, is the subject of Part Three.

8

MACROECONOMIC GOALS AND MEASURES

J ust as doctors find it useful to take a patient's temperature to help them determine just how sick the patient is, economists use statistics to get a quantitative measure of the economy's performance. This chapter introduces the major statistics that summarize the overall condition of the economy. In studying these measures, economists look for patterns. Are good years regularly followed by lean years? Does inflation usually accompany high employment levels? If they find patterns, they ask why.

This chapter also discusses problems of measurement that affect almost every economic variable. It often does not mean much when the rate of unemployment or inflation changes by a few tenths of a percent, just as there is rarely cause for alarm when a person's temperature changes by a tenth of a degree. But over time, the statistics describing the economy may change more dramatically. When unemployment statistics show an increase from 5 percent to 10 percent (that is, a change from one out of twenty workers without jobs to one out of ten), few would doubt that there has been a sizable increase in unemployment.

The sections below discuss the issues of unemployment, inflation, and growth and explain how each is measured.

KEY QUESTIONS

1. What are the main objectives of government macroeconomic policy?

2. How are unemployment, output, growth, the cost of living, and inflation measured?

3. What problems arise in measuring these variables?

4. What are some of the different forms of unemployment?

UNEMPLOYMENT

High on the list of economic goals the government sets for itself is maintaining full employment. Everyone who wants to get a job and is capable of working should be able to find gainful employment.

To an economist, unemployment represents an underutilization of resources: people who are willing and able to work are not being productively employed. To the unemployed individuals and their families, unemployment represents economic hardship and changes in their way of life: vacations will have to be given up, and children may have to forgo their dreams of going to university. If a person is unemployed for a long time, he will no longer be able to ignore the notices for missed rent or mortgage payments, and the family will have to find less expensive housing.

Unemployment not only costs individuals a pay-cheque, it can deal a powerful blow to their self-respect. Unemployed workers in today's urban Canada cannot fall back on farming or living off the land as they might have done in colonial times. Instead, they and their families may be forced to choose between poverty and the bitter taste of welfare or private charity. And many of these families may break up.

Unemployment presents different problems for each age group of workers. For the young, having a job is necessary for developing job skills, whether they are technical skills or such basic work prerequisites as punctuality and responsibility. Thus, persistent unemployment among the youth (and other workers too, to a lesser extent) not only wastes valuable human resources today but may also reduce the future productivity of the labour force. Furthermore, young people who remain unemployed for an extended period of time seem especially prone to becoming alienated from society and turning to antisocial activities such as crime and drugs.

For the middle-aged or elderly worker, losing a job poses particular problems as well. Despite various prohibitions on age discrimination enacted at the provincial and federal levels, employers are often hesitant to hire older workers. They wonder why such a worker lost her previous job and fear she is more likely to become sick or disabled than a younger person is. They may worry about being able to "teach old dogs new tricks." When the unemployed older worker succeeds in getting a job, it often entails a reduction in wages and status from her previous job and may make limited use of previously acquired skills. Even if the new job is challenging and interesting, these changes impose a heavy burden of stress on the newly reemployed worker and her family.

In addition to these personal losses, unemployment poses heavy costs for communities. If a number of people in a particular town are thrown out of work—say, because a big employer closes down or decides to move—then everyone else in town is likely to suffer as well, since there will be fewer dollars circulating around town to buy everything from cars and houses to gasoline and groceries. As more unemployment results in fewer people paying local taxes, it means downgrading the schools, libraries, parks, and police.

The existence of unemployment may also reinforce racial or ethnic tensions that persist in society as a whole. The unemployment rate for aboriginal persons is more than twice that of whites, and that for blacks is almost as high. The differential is even higher for younger persons in these groups. Even among white groups, those of different ethnic backgrounds have quite different unemployment rates. For example, according to the 1986 Census, the unemployment rate of persons of French origin was 11.77 percent, compared with 8.06 percent for those from other Western European backgrounds.

Unemployment is thus often a tragedy for the individual, a source of dislocation and stress for a community, and a waste of productive resources for society as a whole.

THE MAGNITUDE OF THE PROBLEM

One shorthand description of the Canadian economy is that the economy is what happens when 12 million people get up and go to work. But living in the midst of those who have jobs is a fluctuating group of several million healthy people who do not. During the recession year of 1991, 1.3 million people were out of a job, and one-fourth of those people were out of work for fifteen weeks or more. As recently as the recession of 1983, 1.4 million potentially productive workers were looking for jobs. From the standpoint of the economy as a whole, these potentially productive workers who cannot find jobs are a major loss. Not only do the rest of the workers need to pay the costs of supporting the unemployed and their families, but even more important, the rest of society is deprived of the contributions the unemployed are capable of making.

During the 1980s, an average of 9.3 percent of those willing to work were unable to find jobs. Roughly speaking, that figure represents a loss of one worker in every eleven. A simple calculation, based on the difference in the unemployment rate from between 1982 and 1985 and the average rate in the surrounding years, puts the loss in GDP (Gross Domestic Product) from the high unemployment of the early 1980s at roughly $15 billion per year, for a per capita loss of about $800. That means that every man, woman, and child in Canada would have had (on average) an additional $800 to spend if the extra unemployed workers had been gainfully employed. Clearly, society has many good reasons to be concerned with reducing the level of unemployment.

UNEMPLOYMENT STATISTICS

In Canada, unemployment data is collected by Statistics Canada, which surveys a representative mix of households and asks each whether a member of the household is currently seeking employment. The **unemployment rate** is the ratio of the number of

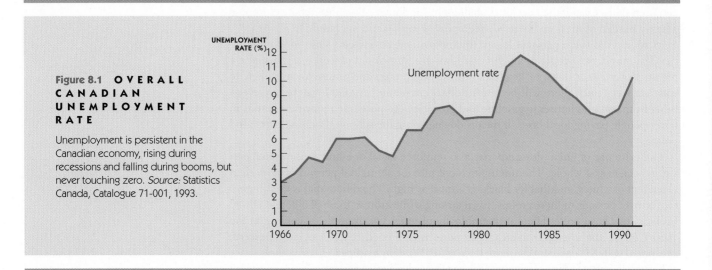

Figure 8.1 OVERALL CANADIAN UNEMPLOYMENT RATE

Unemployment is persistent in the Canadian economy, rising during recessions and falling during booms, but never touching zero. *Source:* Statistics Canada, Catalogue 71-001, 1993.

those seeking employment to the total labour force. If there are 12 million Canadians employed and 1 million say they are looking for a job but cannot find one, then the total labour force is 13 million, and the

$$\text{unemployment rate} = \frac{\text{number unemployed}}{\text{labour force}}$$

$$= \frac{\text{number unemployed}}{\text{number employed} + \text{number unemployed}}$$

$$= \frac{1 \text{ million}}{12 \text{ million} + 1 \text{ million}} = 7.7 \text{ percent.}$$

Figure 8.1 plots the unemployment rate for Canada since 1966. The figure illustrates two facts. First, unemployment is clearly persistent; it never touches zero. Indeed, Canadian unemployment rates are quite high relative to those in the United States, and reach levels comparable to those in some European countries. As Figure 8.2 shows, unemployment in Canada was more than 10 percent in the early part of the 1980s. Moreover, some regions in eastern Canada face unemployment rates in excess of 20 percent, which is similar to the rates in some cities in the less-developed countries.

The second fact we can observe from Figure 8.1 is that the level of unemployment can fluctuate dramatically. In the worst days of the Great Depression, almost 20 percent of the Canadian labour force was unemployed. As recently as March 1983, the unemployment rate reached 13.9 percent before declining to about 7 percent at the end of the decade.

Underlying the overall unemployment rates plotted in Figure 8.1 is the important fact referred to earlier: there are marked differences in the unemployment rates of different groups. Unemployment among natives and youths has been persistently larger—sometimes significantly so—than unemployment among adult white males. Economists

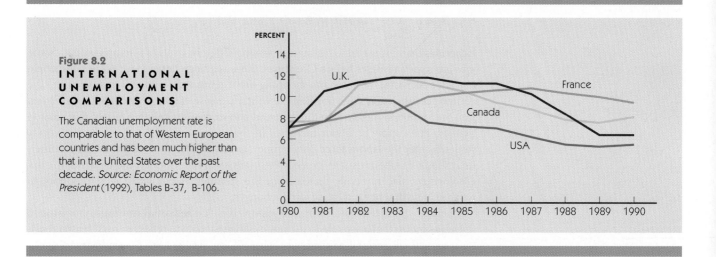

Figure 8.2

INTERNATIONAL UNEMPLOYMENT COMPARISONS

The Canadian unemployment rate is comparable to that of Western European countries and has been much higher than that in the United States over the past decade. *Source: Economic Report of the President* (1992), Tables B-37, B-106.

seek to explain these differences in unemployment rates and how they change with varying economic circumstances.

PROBLEMS WITH UNEMPLOYMENT STATISTICS

Some economists believe that the answers to the Statistics Canada survey provide too high an estimate of the true unemployment rate; some believe the estimate is too low. Some individuals who say they are actively seeking a job may not really be doing so in any meaningful way. Even if an unemployed person is actively looking for work, he may have turned down several reasonable job offers, hoping (unrealistically) for a job that is beyond his ability. Should an unskilled worker who turns down all job offers, insisting on waiting for a corporate vice-presidency or some other top executive job, be viewed as "actively seeking employment"?

Other people may have given up all hope of finding a job. They are referred to as **discouraged workers.** If some workers who want jobs have given up looking, the statistics will not count them as unemployed, and thus the reported rate may provide an underestimate of the number of people who would choose to work if a job were available.[1] The fraction of the working-age population that is employed or seeking employment is called the **labour force participation rate.** Because of discouraged workers, the labour force participation rate tends to decline in recessions.

Despite these ambiguities, there is little doubt that substantial changes in the unemployment rate reflect changes in the rest of the economy. When the unemployment rate increases, it is usually because the economy has slowed down. Some individuals have probably been laid off and have not found new jobs, and firms may have slowed down the pace at which they hire new workers.

---

[1] There are other problems with the unemployment data. It has been suggested that the number of households reporting an unemployed worker depends on who is asked, which in turn depends in part on what time of day the household is surveyed. If the mother of a teenager is asked, she may report that her teenage son is seeking a job, while the teenager may not view himself as actively seeking employment.

FORMS OF UNEMPLOYMENT

Economists find it useful to distinguish among different kinds of unemployment. Some jobs are seasonal. Right before Christmas, there is a huge demand for retail salespeople to work in department stores and shopping malls across the country. In many parts of the country, construction slows down in the winter because of the climate. For the same reason, tourism often increases in the summer, and so does the number of jobs that cater to tourists. The supply of labour increases in the summer, as high school and university students enter the labour force on a temporary basis. Since the increase in the summertime supply of labour usually exceeds the increase in the summertime demand, the unemployment rate normally increases in the summer. Accordingly, it is important to make an adjustment for these seasonal changes.

Unemployment that varies with the seasons is called **seasonal unemployment,** and the adjustments that are made to the unemployment data to reflect normal seasonal patterns are called seasonal adjustments. Thus, if, on average, the unemployment rate is normally .4 percent higher in the summer than at other times, the seasonally adjusted unemployment rate will be the actually measured unemployment rate minus .4 percent. If between May and July the unemployment rate increases by much more than .4 percent, then there is something to worry about.

While workers in construction, agriculture, and tourism regularly face seasonal unemployment, still others are unemployed only as part of a normal transition from one job to another. This kind of unemployment is referred to as **frictional unemployment.** An individual who has grown sick of her job and has quit to look for a new one is among the frictionally unemployed. If people could move from job to job instantaneously, there would be no frictional unemployment. In a dynamic society such as Canada's, with some industries growing and others declining, there will always be movements from one job to another, and hence there will always be frictional unemployment.

Young people tend to switch jobs more often than older people, as they search for a job that matches their skills and interests. Thus, in periods in which there are an unusually large number of individuals entering the labour force, there is likely to be a higher level of frictional unemployment. In the late 1960s and early 1970s, when the post–World War II baby boomers reached working age, the level of frictional unemployment rose substantially.

Most bouts of unemployment are short-lived; the average person who loses a job is out of work for only three months. However, approximately 10 percent of the jobless have been unemployed for more than six months. This kind of long-term unemployment often results from structural change in the economy, and so it is called **structural unemployment.** Quite often substantial structural unemployment is found side by side with job vacancies because the unemployed lack the skills required for the newly created jobs. For example, there may be vacancies for computer programmers, while construction workers are unemployed. By the same token, there may be job shortages in those parts of the economy that are expanding (as in the West during much of the 1980s) and unemployment in areas that are suffering declines (as in southern Ontario during the period of decline in the demand for North American cars). Older individuals, in particular, may find it difficult to adapt to structural change; and employers may be reluctant to spend the money required to retrain a fifty-five-year-old whose job has disappeared. Structural unemployment poses a particularly significant problem for society, since those who are unemployed for long periods of time become disaffected and can lose their work habits.

The kind of unemployment with which we will be most concerned in this part of the book is called **cyclical unemployment,** the unemployment that increases when the economy goes into a slowdown and decreases when the economy goes into a boom. Government policy is particularly concerned with reducing both the frequency and magnitude of this kind of unemployment, by reducing the frequency and magnitude of the recessions that give rise to it; and with reducing its impact, by providing unemployment compensation for those temporarily thrown out of work.

INFLATION

In the 1920s, the years of silent pictures, a movie ticket cost a nickel. By the late 1940s, in the heyday of Hollywood, the price was up to $.50. By the 1960s, the price of a movie was $2.00, and now it is well over $7.00. This steady price rise is no anomaly; most other goods have undergone similar increases over time. This increase in the general level of prices is called inflation, as we learned in Chapter 6. While unemployment tends to be concentrated in certain groups within the population, *everyone* is affected by inflation. Thus, it is not surprising that when inflation becomes high, it almost always rises to the top of the political agenda.

It is not inflation if the price of only one good goes up; it *is* inflation if the prices of *most* goods go up. The **inflation rate** is the rate at which the *general level* of prices increases.

MEASURING INFLATION

If the prices of all goods rose by the same proportion, say by 5 percent, over a period of a year, measuring inflation would be easy: the rate of inflation for that year would be 5 percent. The difficulties arise from the fact that the prices of different goods rise at different rates, and some goods may even decline in price. Over the past twenty years, while the price of fruit and vegetables has increased by 380 percent, the price of gasoline by 384 percent, and the price of health care by 310 percent, the price of computers has declined. To determine the change in the overall price level, economists calculate the *average* percentage increase in prices. But in making this calculation, more importance must be placed on the change in the price of any goods that loom large in the budget (such as housing) than on the change in price of a relatively unimportant item, such as pencils. If the price of pencils goes down 5 percent but the price of housing goes up by 5 percent, the overall measure of the price level should go up.

Economists have a straightforward way of measuring the price level. They ask, what would it cost consumers to purchase the same bundle of goods this year that they bought last year? If, for example, it cost $22,000 in 1991 to buy what it cost consumers only $20,000 to purchase in 1990, then we say that prices, *on average*, have risen by 10 percent. Such results are frequently expressed in the form of a **price index,** which measures the price level in any given year relative to a common base year.

The price index for the base year is, by definition, 100. The price index for any other year is calculated by taking the ratio of the price level in that year to the price level in the base year and multiplying it by 100. For example, if 1990 is our base year and we want to know the price index for 1991, we first calculate the ratio of the cost of a certain bundle of goods in 1991 ($22,000) to the cost of the same bundle of goods in 1990 ($20,000), which is 1.1. The price index in 1991 is therefore $1.1 \times 100 = 110$. This does not mean that average prices are $1.10 or $110—whatever that would mean. The index of 110, using 1990 as a base, means that prices are 10 percent higher, on average, in 1991 than in 1990. In using price indices, one has to be careful to keep in mind both how they are calculated and the base year.

There are several different indices, each using a different bundle of goods. When the government, in calculating the price index, uses the bundle of goods that represents how the average Canadian household spends its income, this index is called the **consumer price index,** or CPI. To determine this bundle, the government, through Statistics Canada, conducts a Family Expenditure Survey, which is updated once a decade or so.

The consumer price index tells us how much more the basket of goods that represents goods purchased by the average household costs today than it did at some earlier time. In Figure 8.3, 1986 is the base year and thus represents 100. Suppose in 1986 it took $887 to buy the basket of goods purchased by the average Canadian family in a month. Assume in 1991 it cost $1,130 to buy the same basket. Then the price index for 1991 is just the ratio of the cost in 1991 to the cost in 1986, times 100; that is,

$$\text{CPI for 1991} = (1{,}130/887) \times 100 = 127.$$

The CPI rose 27 percent between 1986 and 1991.

Similarly, if the same basket cost $416 in 1976, then the consumer price index for 1976 (again, using 1986 as the base year) compares this figure with what the goods would have cost at 1986 prices:

$$\text{CPI for 1976} = (416/887) \times 100 = 47.$$

The CPI was 53 percent lower in 1976 than in 1986.

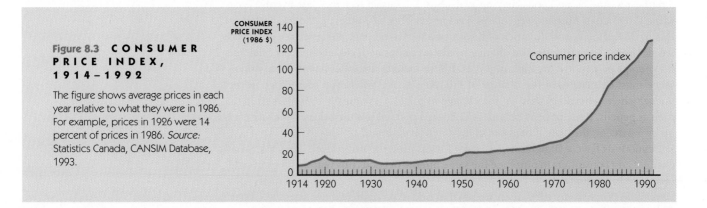

Figure 8.3 CONSUMER PRICE INDEX, 1914–1992

The figure shows average prices in each year relative to what they were in 1986. For example, prices in 1926 were 14 percent of prices in 1986. *Source:* Statistics Canada, CANSIM Database, 1993.

The advantage of an index is that once we have an index number for any year, we can compare it with any other year. The CPI for 1976 was 47, and for 1989 it was 114. Between those years, it rose by 67, so the increase was

67/47 = 143 percent.

On average, prices rose by 143 percent from 1976 to 1989.

THE CANADIAN EXPERIENCE WITH INFLATION

As we have learned, the inflation rate is the percentage increase of the price level from one year to the next. Figure 8.4 shows the inflation rate for Canada since 1915. Three interesting features about inflation emerge from the figure.

First, the rate of inflation was relatively low for most of the period, with three exceptions: around World War I, after World War II, and during the period 1973–1982. Indeed, from the early 1920s until the early 1960s, inflation averaged only about 1 percent per year.

Second, the figure also shows that prices may actually come down. During the recession that followed World War I, prices fell by more than 25 percent, and in the Great Depression of the 1930s, prices fell by more than 20 percent. It may seem hard to believe, but just as today inflation seems an ever-present threat, at the end of the nineteenth century, there was great concern about **deflation,** which is a steady decline of the price level. Borrowers at that time who were in debt and had not anticipated the fall in prices found that the real value of the dollars they had to pay back was far more than the value of the dollars that they had borrowed. They were as upset about this as investors today are about the fact that with inflation, the value of the dollars they get back from an investment is worth less than the value of the dollars they originally spent.

Finally, while prices on average have been stable and there have even been periods of price decline, there have also been a few periods of high inflation, when prices in-

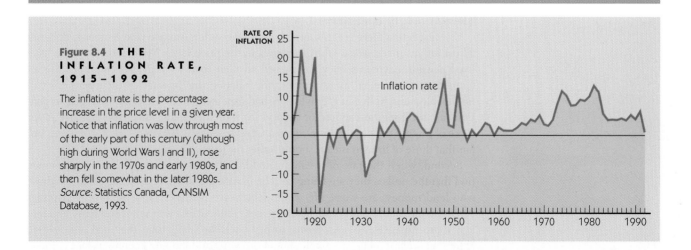

Figure 8.4 THE INFLATION RATE, 1915–1992

The inflation rate is the percentage increase in the price level in a given year. Notice that inflation was low through most of the early part of this century (although high during World Wars I and II), rose sharply in the 1970s and early 1980s, and then fell somewhat in the later 1980s. *Source:* Statistics Canada, CANSIM Database, 1993.

creased rapidly. The most notable recent episode was in the late 1970s and early 1980s; in 1981, prices rose by more than 12 percent. Moreover, concern about inflation getting out of control led to government attempts to control prices in two instances: during World War II, when the rate rose to 5.8 percent in 1941, and in the early 1970s, when inflation went over 10 percent. In the latter instance, the Trudeau government was concerned enough to implement a freeze on wages and prices; that is, a declaration that wages and prices could not increase under penalty of federal law. Price controls are now widely regarded as counterproductive; as the simple supply and demand model would predict, they resulted in shortages of some products. Furthermore, when the controls were lifted, inflation shot up again, moving beyond 10 percent by the beginning of the 1980s.

Even the high level of inflation Canada (and the United States) experienced in the late 1970s and early 1980s—so-called "double-digit" inflation—is only the little brother of inflation that has occurred at other times and places. In Germany in the 1920s, for example, prices were increasing so rapidly that people rushed from the pay window to the market, fearful that prices would go up before they could get there. More recently, in Israel from 1980 to 1990, prices increased by over 100 percent each year. In Bolivia, prices rose by nearly 400 percent per year for the same period. On the other hand, some countries have managed to contain inflation quite well. In Japan, for example, the average rate of inflation over the 1980–1990 period was only 1.3 percent.

THE IMPORTANCE OF INFLATION

In modern economies, much has been done to ease the pain of inflation. For workers, rising levels of prices are usually accompanied by higher wages, and if a worker faces higher prices but has commensurately more money in his pocket, he is just as well off. Many unions now often negotiate contracts with cost-of-living adjustments (COLAs); and nonunion firms often give bigger raises in inflationary times to keep up with the rising cost of living. Most significantly, Old Age Security payments and other transfer programs go up automatically as prices increase; so do income tax credits. We say that they are "indexed" to the cost of living.

Why, then, does fighting inflation rank so high as a priority in economic policy? There seem to be three answers.

The first is that there are still some groups who suffer. Anyone whose income does not adjust fully is made worse off by increases in the price level. Many retired people have fixed pension payments; they have saved all their lives with an expectation of the income they would need in retirement, but inflation may mean that their pensions will not enable them to live in the style they had expected to. To the extent that public pensions are an important source of support for the elderly, and this is particularly so for those of limited means, the importance of this problem is lessened. But it still seems unfair that those of limited means should suffer for reasons beyond their control.

Second, when the rate of inflation suddenly increases, those who have lent money find that the dollars they are being paid back with are worth less. Thus, creditors (those who lend money) are worse off, while debtors are better off. Just the reverse happens when the rate of inflation suddenly decreases. Those who owe money suddenly find that it is more expensive, in real terms, to pay back the loans than they had anticipated. When the inflation rate is variable, both borrowing and lending become riskier.

Third, many feel that something is fundamentally wrong with the economy when what cost $1 five years ago costs $2 today. Sometimes these observers are right: the inflation is often a reflection of gross errors in government economic policy, such as spending that is far in excess of revenues, or excessive provision of credit. Frequently inflation gets the blame when something else is the underlying problem. The steep increase in oil prices in 1973 set off a worldwide inflationary spiral. With eastern Canadians paying more to the oil-exporting countries, that part of the country was, in a sense, poorer. Someone had to take a cut. Furthermore, the worldwide economic downturn set off by the 1973 oil price rise made the cut that had to be taken that much larger. Thus, workers' real wages fell. They blamed inflation for their declining standard of living. But inflation was not really the culprit—higher oil prices were.

As the economy has adapted to inflation, economists have increasingly debated about how concerned we should be about moderate rates of inflation, the 3 to 6 percent inflation that has occurred regularly during the past few decades. They worry that in trying to stop the inflation, the cures may be worse than the disease. Still, most economists think that double-digit inflation levels, at the very least, are symptomatic of some kind of malfunction in the economy. Certainly there is a consensus that the kind of rapid rates of inflation experienced in Israel and some Latin American countries are extremely disruptive to the economy.

ALTERNATIVE PRICE INDICES

Other price indices besides the consumer price index can be calculated using different market baskets. One of them, the **producer price index,** measures the average level of prices of the goods sold by producers to wholesalers. The **wholesale price index** measures the average level of prices of the goods sold by wholesalers to retailers. These indices are useful because they give us an inkling of what will happen to consumer prices in the near future. Usually, if producers are receiving higher prices from their sales to wholesalers, in a short while wholesalers will have to charge higher prices to retailers; this will be reflected in a higher wholesale price index. A short while later, retailers will have to charge higher prices, and this will be reflected in an increase in the consumer price index.

GROWTH

For more than a century, Canadians had become used to the idea that their children would have a higher standard of living than their own, and their grandchildren a still higher standard of living. Wages were increasing, so much so that each successive generation could enjoy both higher incomes and more leisure than the previous generation. Growth in Canada was rapid in the first half of the twentieth century, with the discovery and exploitation of natural resources and with westward expansion fueled by high levels of immigration. The resource-based growth spread into the manufacturing sectors as well, largely financed by foreign investment. Compared to most European and Asian countries, rates of growth were high. Rising living standards came to be expected. There was a widely held feeling among Canadians that "the future belonged to Canada." The benefits of high growth were spread among all segments of society including the poorest by a combination of rising wages and the institution of many social programs.

All of this has changed. In the 1970s and much of the 1980s, wages stagnated. Family incomes continued to increase, but only because of an increase in hours spent by family members in the workplace, as more and more women joined the labour force. Canada's economic performance, which had relied heavily on the exploitation and processing of natural resources for export and on the protection of domestic manufacturing industries, was overtaken by the rapid industrial growth of Japan and some European countries. A major objective of macroeconomic policy today is to increase the economy's rate of growth. This, along with maintaining full employment and stable prices, constitutes the third major area of concern for macroeconomists.

If an economy is to compete effectively and grow rapidly, it must use its resources efficiently and it must invest in increasing its productive potential. To accomplish the first task—using resources efficiently—the economy must operate along its production possibilities curve. This concept was first introduced in Chapter 2, and it is fundamental to our thinking about macroeconomics. Figure 8.5A shows a production possibilities curve, which represents the *maximum* amount of one good that can be produced, given the amounts of other goods that are produced. In the figure, we focus on only two goods. The horizontal axis measures the amount of "consumption" goods that are produced, and the vertical axis measures the amount of capital goods (machines and buildings). If the economy is at point E, it is not using all of its resources, or at least not using them efficiently. Workers may be unemployed; machines may be idle. Production could be expanded to a point on the curve such as F, where the economy would be producing as efficiently as it possibly could. Here people would have more to consume, and there would be a higher level of investment.

The second task of an economy, increasing its productive potential, is illustrated in panel B of Figure 8.5: economic policy also seeks to move the production possibilities curve outward. The economy moves from point F to point G; there are both more consumption goods and more investment goods. (One has to be somewhat careful in interpreting what it means for the economy to be on its production possibilities curve. It does not mean that there is zero unemployment, or that all machines are fully used. There is, for instance, always some frictional unemployment, as workers move from one job to another. Normally, some machines may be idle, simply because they are being repaired or because they are being held in reserve for an emergency.)

MEASURING OUTPUT

The problem of measuring changes in output is similar to the problem of measuring changes in the price level. We could report how much of each good the economy produced: 1,362,478 hammers, 473,562,382 potatoes, 7,875,342 wristwatches, and so forth. Such data may be useful for some purposes, but they do not provide us with the information we want. If next year the output of hammers goes up by 5 percent, the output of potatoes goes down by 2 percent, and the output of wristwatches rises by 7 percent, has total output gone up or down? And by how much?

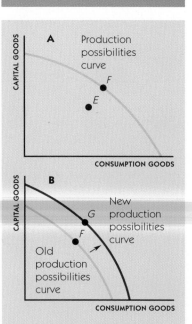

Figure 8.5 ECONOMIC EFFICIENCY AND GROWTH

In panel A, if the economy made efficient use of its resources, it could move from point E to F on the production possibilities curve. Panel B shows that the economy can also expand if the production possibilities curve is shifted outwards.

For many purposes, it is convenient to have a single number that summarizes the output of the economy. But how do we add up the hammers, potatoes, wristwatches, and billions of other products produced in the economy? We do this by adding the money value of all the final goods (goods that are not used to make other goods) produced and arriving at a single number that encapsulates the production of the economy. This number is called the **gross domestic product,** or **GDP.** It is the standard measure of the output of an economy, and sums up the total money value of the goods and services produced by the residents of a nation during a specified period. Thus, GDP includes everything from buttons to air travel, and from haircuts to barrels of oil. It makes no difference whether the production takes place in the public or private sector, or whether the goods and services are purchased by households or by the government.[2]

There is one problem with using money as a measure of output. Inflation means that money changes in value over time. Candy bars, books, movie tickets, hammers, all cost more today than they did ten years ago. Another way of saying this is that a dollar does not buy as much as it did ten years ago. We do not want to be misled into believing that the output is higher when in fact all that has happened is that the price level has risen.

To keep the comparisons of different years straight, economists adjust GDP for inflation. Unadjusted GDP is known as **nominal GDP.** The term **real GDP** is used for inflation-adjusted GDP figures, which are truer year-to-year measures of what the economy actually produces. To calculate real GDP, economists simply take the nominal value of GDP—the money value of all the goods and services produced in the economy—and divide it by a measure of the price level. Thus, real GDP is defined by the equation

$$\text{real GDP} = \frac{\text{nominal GDP}}{\text{price level}}.$$

If nominal GDP has risen 3 percent in the past year but inflation has also increased prices by 3 percent, then real GDP is unchanged. If nominal GDP has risen 3 percent in the past year but prices have increased by 6 percent, real GDP has actually decreased.

Earlier in the chapter, we learned how to measure the price level by analyzing how the cost of a particular bundle of goods changes over time. The measure of the price level that we use to adjust our GDP measure for inflation is the **GDP deflator,** which represents a comparison between what it would cost to buy the total mix of goods and services within the economy today and in a base year. In other words, the GDP deflator is a weighted average of the prices of different goods and services, where the weights represent the importance of each of the goods and services in GDP.

Between 1989 and 1990, nominal GDP rose by 2.8 percent, but the GDP deflator (using 1986 as a base year) went up from 114.9 to 118.6. Thus, the price level (measured this way) increased by 3.2 percent ($118.6 \div 114.9 = 1.032$); this is just the inflation rate. The percentage change in real GDP equals the percentage change in nominal GDP minus the inflation rate. Therefore, the percentage change in real GDP was $2.8 - 3.2 = -0.4$.

---

[2]We use prices not only because they are a convenient way of making comparisons, but also because prices reflect how consumers value different goods. If the price of an orange is twice that of an apple, it means an orange is worth twice as much (at the margin) as an apple.

INSIDE THE PRODUCTION POSSIBILITIES CURVE

While GDP provides a measure of how much the economy actually produces, it is also useful to know what the economy *could* produce if labour and machines were used fully to their capacity. Another measure, **potential GDP,** does just this. The gap between potential GDP and actual GDP is a measure of how far inside the production possibilities curve the economy is operating.

Figure 8.6 shows how potential (real) GDP and actual (real) GDP have increased over the past twenty years. Two features stand out.[3] First, output does not grow smoothly, and there have been periods in which actual output has been far below potential output. The jagged progression in the figure shows the effect of short-term fluctuations around an upward trend. Sometimes these fluctuations represent only a slow-down in the rate of growth; sometimes output actually falls. The dips in real GDP from 1981 to 1982 and from 1990 to 1991 represent periods when Canada's economic output actually declined. Strong upward fluctuations are called **booms,** and downward ones are called **recessions.** Severe downturns are referred to as **depressions.** The last depression, called the Great Depression because of its length and depth, began in 1929. The economy did not fully recover from it until World War II. While there is no technical definition of a boom, a recession is said to have occurred when GDP falls for at least two consecutive quarters. (For statistical purposes, the year is divided into quarters. GDP

[3]Figure 8.6 shows actual GDP exceeding potential GDP in a few years. How is this possible, if potential GDP really measures what the economy *could* produce? The answer is that the estimates of potential GDP are based on assumptions about "normal" levels of frictional unemployment and on the fact that even when the economy is quite strong, some capacity is not fully utilized. In fact, for short spurts of time, such as when a country goes to war, actual GDP can exceed estimates of potential GDP by a considerable amount.

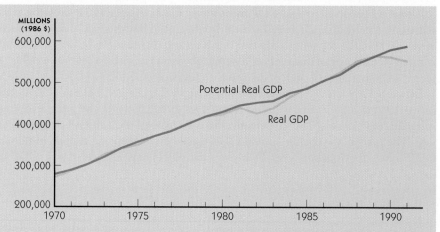

Figure 8.6 POTENTIAL AND REAL GDP

Potential GDP measures how much the economy would produce if it used all its resources efficiently. Real GDP shows what the economy actually produces. Notice that both have been growing over time. *Source:* Department of Finance, *Quarterly Economic Review,* March 1992.

data are reported at the end of each quarter.) An economic slowdown occurs when the rate of growth of the economy slows to the point where unemployment starts increasing. The economy suffers such a slowdown every few years. A notable exception to this is the period from 1983 to 1990, one of the longest upswings in peacetime history.

Because the ups and downs seem to occur with such regularity, the economy's fluctuations are sometimes referred to as **business cycles.** Businessmen have a great interest in being able to predict when the cycle will **peak,** that is, when the economy will stop growing as rapidly and start turning down; by the same token, they want to know when the bottom or **trough** of a recession will occur. While economists have used sophisticated statistical models to try to predict output and employment over the next few months or next year or two, they have found it particularly difficult to predict these turning points in the business cycle.

There are some variables that usually (but not always) signal a downturn; a decline in producers' orders for new machines is an indicator of a lack of confidence in the future and the decline in orders may itself contribute to a slowdown in the economy, as fewer machines are built. Variables that anticipate a downturn or an upswing are called **leading indicators.**

Recessions are marked by the fact that the economy operates well below its potential; there are high levels of unemployment and a large fraction of its machines remain idle. Figure 8.7 shows the percentage of Canada's industrial capacity that was utilized for the past several decades. The figures vary from slightly more than 70 percent of industrial capacity being used when the economy is in a recession to over 85 percent of industrial capacity being used when the economy is in a boom. Again, notice the pattern. Capacity is never fully utilized—just as there is frictional and structural unemployment, which keeps unemployment rates from ever reaching zero, so too some machines, which are part of the nation's capacity statistics, are being repaired and maintained, while others are not suited for the economy's current structure. But there are fluctuations in how much goes unused. Low-capacity utilization can be thought of as unemployment of machines. Like unemployment of workers, it represents an economic waste, although it lacks the element of human loss. And, of course, the government does not have to make unemployment or welfare payments to an unused machine.

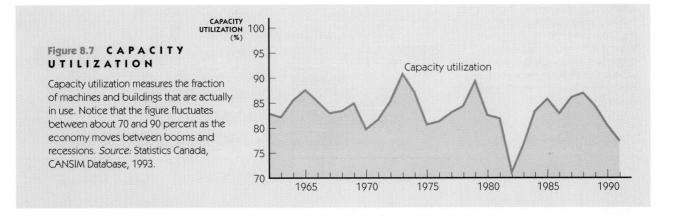

Figure 8.7 **CAPACITY UTILIZATION**

Capacity utilization measures the fraction of machines and buildings that are actually in use. Notice that the figure fluctuates between about 70 and 90 percent as the economy moves between booms and recessions. *Source:* Statistics Canada, CANSIM Database, 1993.

GROWTH IN CANADA AND ELSEWHERE

The second important feature of output illustrated in Figure 8.6 is that it has risen over time; it has increased by two and a half since 1965 (and by sixfold since 1947). However, different countries grow at different rates, as Figure 8.8 shows. During the past quarter century, Japan's output has been growing much faster than that of Canada. During the fifteen years from 1965 to 1980, Canada was around the middle of the pack, faring much better than the United States or the United Kingdom, but worse than Japan and some of the faster-growing developing countries. But as panel B shows, in more recent years, Canada's growth rate has slipped, although its position relative to other countries has changed little. While both Canada and the United States grew at slightly more than 3 percent during the 1980s, Japan grew at 3.7 percent and the Western European countries at rates of between 1.3 percent and 2.3 percent.

The difference between 3 percent and 3.7 percent may seem small, but these slight differences have large effects over time, just as compound interest rates do. If two countries had the same levels of output in 1900 but one country grew at .7 percent rate faster per year, at the end of the century its output would be twice that of the other. The persistent gap between the rates of growth in Canada and Japan has given rise to alarm and concern. Chapter 21 will discuss some of the causes of the differences in growth rates, some of the reasons for concern, and some of the proposed solutions.

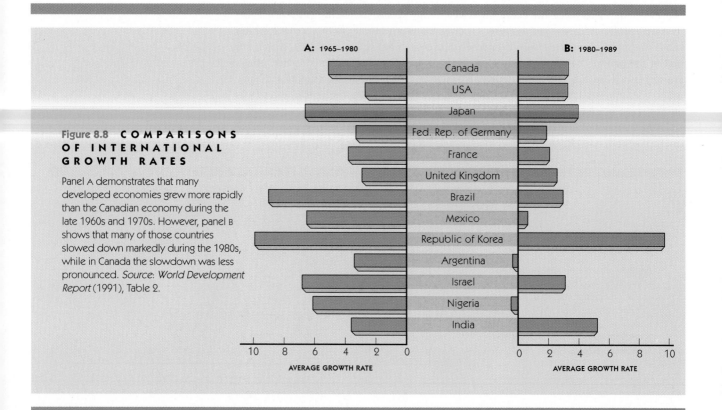

Figure 8.8 COMPARISONS OF INTERNATIONAL GROWTH RATES

Panel A demonstrates that many developed economies grew more rapidly than the Canadian economy during the late 1960s and 1970s. However, panel B shows that many of those countries slowed down markedly during the 1980s, while in Canada the slowdown was less pronounced. *Source: World Development Report* (1991), Table 2.

MEASURING GDP: THE VALUE OF OUTPUT

There are three approaches to measuring GDP (whether real or nominal), each of which yields the same result. Two concentrate on output data. The third relies on the fact that the value of output all becomes income to someone, and uses income figures to obtain a measure of output.

THE FINAL GOODS APPROACH

On the face of it, measuring GDP is a straightforward task, albeit massive. One gathers together the dollar values of all goods and services sold in a country, and then adds them up. Unfortunately, matters are not this simple, because it is first necessary to distinguish between final goods and intermediate goods. Final goods are those that are sold to consumers, like automobiles, books, bread, and shoes. Intermediate goods are those that are used to produce outputs, such as coal when it is used to make steel, or apples when they are used to make applesauce. A good such as an apple can be either a final or an intermediate good, depending on how it is used.

The reason it is so important to distinguish between final and intermediate goods is that the value of final goods includes the value of the intermediate goods that went into making them. When Ford Canada sells a car for $20,000, that figure may include $400 worth of Uniroyal tires, and it would be double counting to list in GDP the revenues of both the car maker and the tire producer. Likewise for the steel, plastic, and other components that go into the car. In fact, cases where some intermediate goods are used to produce other intermediate goods could even lead to triple or quadruple counting.

The **final goods approach** to GDP adds up the total dollar value of goods and services as they are purchased by their ultimate users. One way of calculating the value of the final goods of the economy is to consider where those goods go. There are four possibilities. Some final goods are consumed by individuals—we call this aggregate **consumption** (and we include all consumption goods, regardless of where they are produced). Some are used by firms to build buildings and make machines—this is called aggregate **investment** (again, we include all investment goods, regardless of where they are produced). Some are purchased by government, and are called **government spending.** Finally, some of the goods go abroad; but at the same time, some outputs that we consume or invest or that the government uses are imported from abroad. Thus, the fourth category we refer to as **net exports,** the difference between exports and imports. We can also categorize goods by their "type"—whether they are consumption, investment, or government goods. There are some simple relationships between these two perspectives.

Let's say C = aggregate consumption, C_d = domestic production of consumption goods, M_C = imports of consumption goods, and X_C = exports of consumption goods. Consumption goods are either exported or purchased at home; and total purchases at home of domestically produced consumption goods consist of all purchases of consumption goods *minus* what is imported. Hence,

$$C_d = X_C + C - M_C.$$

Similarly, let I = aggregate investment, I_d = domestic production of investment goods,

M_I = imports of investment goods, and X_I = exports of investment goods. Then, as for consumption goods,

$$I_d = X_I + I - M_I.$$

Finally, let G = total government expenditures, G_d = government expenditures on domestically produced goods, M_G = imports for government expenditures, and X_G = exports of "government goods." Then

$$G_d = X_G + G - M_G.$$

All of the goods produced in the economy, GDP, can be thought of as either (private) consumption goods, (private) investment goods, or government goods, so

$$GDP = C_d + I_d + G_d.$$

By the same token, aggregate imports, M, and aggregate exports, X, can be broken into the same three categories:

$$X = X_C + X_I + X_G;$$
$$M = M_C + M_I + M_G.$$

Using the expression for C_d, I_d, and G_d that we have derived, we have the equation

$$GDP = X_C + X_I + X_G + C + I + G - (M_C + M_I + M_G)$$
$$= C + I + G + (X - M),$$

where $(X - M)$ is net exports.

Breaking down final goods this way is particularly useful for analyzing how the macroeconomy works, as we will see in Chapter 10.

THE VALUE-ADDED APPROACH

A second way to calculate the value of GDP is to study the intermediate goods directly. The production of most items occurs in several stages. Consider the automobile. At one stage in its production, iron ore, coal, and limestone are mined. At a second stage, these raw materials are shipped to a steel mill. A third stage finds a steel company combining these ingredients to make steel. Finally, the steel and other inputs, such as rubber and plastics, are combined by the automobile firm to make a car. The difference in value between what the automaker pays for intermediate goods and what it receives for the finished cars is called the firm's **value added.**

Value added = firm's revenues − cost of intermediate goods. GDP can be measured by calculating the value added at each stage of production.

GDP = sum of value added of all firms.

THE INCOME APPROACH

The third method used to calculate GDP involves measuring the income generated by selling products, rather than the value of the products themselves; this is known as the

income approach. Firms do five things with their revenues: they pay for labour, they pay interest, they buy intermediate goods, they pay indirect taxes such as excise taxes, and what is left over they enjoy as profits.

Revenues = wages + interest payments + cost of intermediate inputs + taxes + profits.

But we already know that the firm's value added is its revenue minus the cost of intermediate goods. Therefore, value added = wages + interest payments + taxes + profits. And since the value of GDP is equal to the sum of the value added of all firms, GDP must also equal the sum of the value of all wage payments, interest payments, taxes, and profits for all firms:

GDP = wages + interest payments + taxes + profits.

People receive income from wages, from capital, and from profits of the firms they own (or own shares in). Thus, the right-hand side of this identity is just the total income of all individuals plus government revenue from indirect taxes. This is an extremely important result, one economists use frequently, so it is worth highlighting: *aggregate output equals aggregate income*. A final way to measure output, then, is to add up the income of all the individuals in the society, whether received as wages, interest, or profits and add to that indirect taxes.

Differences between Individual Incomes and National Income   The notion of income used above to calculate GDP differs slightly from the way individuals commonly perceive income, and it is important to be aware of some of the distinctions.

First, people are likely to include in their view of income any capital gains they earn. Capital gains are the increase in value of assets, and accordingly do not represent production (output) in any way. The national income accounts used to calculate GDP, which are designed to focus on the production of goods and services, do not include capital gains.

Second, profits that are retained by a firm are included in national income, but individuals may not perceive these retained profits as part of their own income. Again, this is because the GDP accounts measure the value of production, and profits are part of the value of production, whether those profits are actually distributed to shareholders or retained by firms.

Third, and most conspicuous, people tend to concentrate on their **disposable income,** or what they have available to spend. To calculate disposable income, people subtract from their income the taxes they have to pay. Part of the value of production that GDP measures is the taxes collected at all stages. For instance, part of the value added of a firm is the total costs of its workers. But not all of what the firm spends for workers is actually received by the workers; the government takes part in the form of taxes. Thus, GDP exceeds the total disposable income of households by the value of taxes paid.

COMPARISON OF THE FINAL GOODS AND INCOME APPROACHES

Earlier we learned how to break down the output of the economy into four categories—consumption, investment, government expenditures, and net exports. Similarly, we typi-

Table 8.1 TWO APPROACHES TO CANADIAN GDP, 1990

Final outputs	Billions $	Income	Billions $
Consumption	403.0	Employee compensation	382.2
Investment	122.6	Profits, rents, interest	219.2
Government expenditures	149.3	Indirect taxes	76.5
Net exports	3.0		
Total	677.9	Total	677.9

cally break down the income of the economy into three categories—wages and other payments to workers; profits, interest, rents, and other payments to owners of capital; and taxes. Table 8.1 shows that the value of GDP calculated in both ways is the same: in 1990, Canadian GDP was approximately $678 *billion.*

The fact that the value of output is equal to the value of income—that GDP measured either way is identical—is no accident. It is a consequence of what Chapter 14 described as the circular flow of the economy. What each firm receives from selling its goods must go back somewhere else into the economy—as wages, profits, interest, or taxes. The income to households flows back in turn to firms, either in the form of the consumption goods households purchase or in the form of savings, which eventually are used to purchase plant and equipment by firms; or it flows to the government, in the form of taxes or newly issued government bonds. Similarly, the money spent by the government must have come from somewhere—either from households or corporations in the form of taxes, or through borrowing.

THE THREE APPROACHES TO GDP: AN EXAMPLE

Each of the three approaches to measuring GDP has its uses. When studying how much income individuals and households receive from wages and profits, the income approach is natural. When studying the changing composition of national output, the final goods approach is used. Sometimes it is easier to obtain the numbers used in one approach than those used in another. For example, a large fraction of the value added is produced in large corporations, from whom reliable numbers can be obtained, while final goods are sold by a myriad of small retail establishments whose actual proceeds are much more difficult to track. One advantage of having three different approaches, in fact, is that they provide a check on one another. There will always be small statistical discrepancies, but if the work is done right, all three approaches should produce very close to the same number.

A numerical example will help to illustrate the basic principles. Consider an economy that produces only automobiles, and the automobiles are made entirely from steel. Automakers buy steel from steel companies and transform this steel into cars. They then sell the cars to retailers, who sell them to consumers. The steel industry has revenues of $100 billion, $80 billion of which it pays to its workers and $15 billion of which it pays

Table 8.2 INCOME AND EXPENDITURE ACCOUNTS (billions)

Steel industry Expenditures		Receipts	Automobile industry Expenditures		Receipts	Automobile retail industry Expenditures		Receipts
Wages	$80	$100	Wages	$ 60	$200	Purchases of cars	$200	$200
Dividends	$ 5		Purchases of steel	$100		Wages	$ 10	
Interest	$15		Dividends	$ 20		Dividends	$ 10	
			Interest	$ 20				

in interest to creditors. The rest it pays out as dividends to its shareholders. The steel industry's accounts are given in Table 8.2.

The automobile industry pays the steel industry $100 billion for steel, pays its workers $60 billion, and sells it automobiles to the car dealers for $200 billion. It pays out $20 billion in interest. The difference—$200 billion minus the costs of $160 billion minus the $20 billion in interest—is the profits, which it pays out to shareholders. The automobile industry's accounts are also given in the table.

Finally, the car dealers sell the cars for $220 billion. For the sake of simplicity, we will assume that their only other costs are the wages they pay their workers, $10 billion.

Now let's use these accounts to calculate GDP. Using the final goods approach, we look only at the receipts of the automobile retailers and find that GDP is equal to $220 billion. (We do not also add the revenues of the steel or automobile industry because that would be double counting.) With the value-added approach, GDP is equal to the value of the sales of each industry, minus the value of inputs purchased from other industries. The value added of the three industries is given in Table 8.3.

Table 8.3 APPLYING THE VALUE-ADDED APPROACH TO GDP

	Value of output		Less cost of Intermediate goods		Value added
Steel	$100 billion	–	0	=	$100 billion
Automobile	$200 billion	–	$100 billion	=	$100 billion
Car retailers	$220 billion	–	$200 billion	=	$ 20 billion
			Total value added:		$220 billion

Table 8.4 APPLYING THE INCOME APPROACH TO GDP

Wages	
Steel	$ 80 billion
Automobile	$ 60 billion
Car retailers	$ 10 billion
Total wages:	$150 billion

Interest payments	
Steel	$ 15 billion
Automobile	$ 20 billion
Total interest paid:	$ 35 billion

Dividends	
Steel	$ 5 billion
Automobile	$ 20 billion
Car retailers	$ 10 billion
Total dividends:	$ 35 billion

GDP	
Total wages	$150 billion
Total interest	$ 35 billion
Total dividends	$ 35 billion
Total GDP:	$220 billion

Last, with the income approach, GDP is measured by the income received by households. Table 8.4 shows the different steps. First we add up all the wages received. Next we add the interest payments. Then we add the profits, which are paid out as dividends. GDP according to the income approach is $220 billion, the same total we reached using the first two approaches.

ALTERNATIVE MEASURES OF OUTPUT

The above examples omit an important dimension in an economy like Canada's: a substantial proportion of our purchases and sales are with foreigners. Different ways of taking account of this lead to different measures of output. Since GDP includes exports but excludes imports, it is a measure of all goods and services produced by Canadians wherever they are eventually used. Quite naturally, this has been the standard measure of output used in Canada as well as in most European countries. But until 1991 the United States, for which international trade has been far less important, used as its main statistical measure of output **gross national product (GNP).** This is a measure that includes imports and excludes exports.

The basic difference between GDP and GNP is that GNP includes income that residents of a country receive from abroad (wages, returns on investment, interest payments), but excludes similar payments made by residents of a country to those abroad. By contrast, GDP ignores income received from or paid overseas. Thus, in the example of Table 8.1, the category of profits, rents, and interest includes all such amounts earned in Canada, regardless of whether they accrue to Canadians or foreigners. Similarly, on the final outputs side, exports are included and imports deducted through the item net exports. The deduction of imports is needed since consumption, investment, and government expenditures measures will include in them some imported goods.

The treatment of machines and other capital goods (buildings) is a vexing problem in measuring national output. As machines are used to produce output, they wear out. Worn-out machines are a cost of production that should be balanced against total output.

As an example, consider a firm that has a machine worth $1,000 and that uses the machine, with $600 of labour, to produce $2,000 worth of output. Furthermore, assume that at the end of the year the machine is completely worn out. The firm then has a *net* output of $400: $2,000 minus the labour costs *and* minus the value of the machine, which has been worn out.

The reduction in the value of the machine is called the machine's **depreciation.** But machines wear out at all sorts of different rates, and accounting for how much the machines in the economy have depreciated is an extremely difficult problem. The GDP figures take the easy road, and make no allowance for depreciation. But in fact, the term "gross" in "gross domestic product" should serve as a reminder that the statistic covers all production. Economists sometimes use a separate measure that includes the effects of depreciation, called **net domestic product (NDP),** which subtracts an estimate of the value of depreciation from GDP:

$$NDP = GDP - depreciation.$$

But most economists and statisticians have little confidence in the estimates of depreciation, and usually use the GDP (or GNP) figure as a measure of the economy's output.

CLOSE-UP: HUMAN DEVELOPMENT AND GDP

Nobel laureate Robert Solow once wrote: "If you have to be obsessed by something, maximizing real national income is not a bad choice." Indeed, it is common among economists to rank the nations of the world according to the absolute or per capita size of their economies. But as Solow would be the first to admit, the size of the economy taken alone does not capture many important elements of the standard of living of the population. As a result, different groups have proposed alternatives to GDP or GDP per capita that make adjustments for changes to the environment, access to medical care, literacy, life expectancy, and so on.

The United Nations Development Program offers one example of an alternate index, called the Human Development Index (HDI), which includes in its measurement life expectancy, literacy, and the purchasing power of an average income. Canada fares extremely well by either index, having the highest HDI index and the second highest GDP per capita. The United States is the richest country in the world measured by GDP per capita. But on the HDI, it falls behind five other countries, including Japan, Norway, Switzerland, and Sweden, all of whom exceed the United States in life expectancy.

At the other end of the scale, Zaire and Ethiopia are the two poorest countries in the world measured by GDP per capita. But measured by the HDI, Zaire is the thirty-fourth poorest and Ethiopia is the twenty-third poorest. The two poorest countries in the world measured by the HDI are Guinea and Sierra Leone, where life expectancy is less than 44 years and the literacy rate is less than 25 percent.

But no alternate method of measuring national well-being seems likely to replace calculations based on GDP. The main difficulty of measurements like those of the U.N. Development Program is the difficulty of placing weights on the different elements. Is literacy just as important as life expectancy? only 90 percent as important? How should the value of an extra $1,000 of purchasing power compare with the value of life expectancy increasing by, say, two years? In the face of imponderable questions like these, calculations of GDP look relatively value-free and straightforward.

Sources: United Nations Development Program, *Human Development Report (1992)* (Oxford: Oxford University Press, 1992), pp. 127–29; Robert M. Solow, "James Meade at Eighty," *Economic Journal* (December 1987): 986–88.

GDP, GNP, and NDP go up and down together. For most purposes, it does not much matter which one you use. This book generally uses GDP, only switching to GNP when referring to statistics for foreign countries that use it.

MEASURING THE STANDARD OF LIVING

While the data on GDP or GNP tell something about the overall level of economic activity, ultimately economists are interested in how increases in the economy's output translate into increases in the standards of living of citizens of the nation.

One indicator of the standard of living is **GDP per capita,** which is found by dividing real GDP by population. Figure 8.9 shows the pattern of GDP per capita in Canada from 1965 to 1991. Over this period, the Canadian economy has gone from producing roughly $11,000 for every man, woman, and child to producing $20,500 (measured in 1986 dollars). Figure 8.10 shows that while per capita income in Canada has not increased as rapidly as it has in Japan and other countries, still the Canadian level remains higher. In fact, of the countries shown, only the United States has a higher level of per capita GDP.

There are, to be sure, a number of difficulties in making international comparisons, partly resulting from the fact that people in different countries consume different goods. One should not make too much out of small differences, but large differences usually mean something.[4] GDP per capita in Sweden in 1990 was measured as roughly 3 per-

[4]A particularly vexing problem is caused by changes in exchange rates, the rate at which the currencies used in different countries are exchanged for one another. In recent years, exchange rates have changed considerably. When the value of the dollar is low relative to that of the Swedish kronor—that is, $1 can be exchanged for, say, 5 kronor rather than 6—then if we translate per capita income in Sweden into dollars, Swedish per capita income looks very high. But the exchange rate may not accurately reflect purchasing power—what you can buy with the currency in each country. Even though the exchange rate between the dollar and the kronor is 5 kronor to the dollar, you can buy more in Canada with a dollar than you can buy in Sweden with 5 kronor. Making adjustments for differences in purchasing power makes Canada look better off.

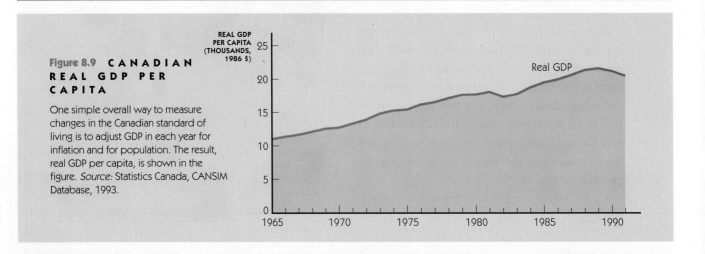

Figure 8.9 CANADIAN REAL GDP PER CAPITA

One simple overall way to measure changes in the Canadian standard of living is to adjust GDP in each year for inflation and for population. The result, real GDP per capita, is shown in the figure. *Source:* Statistics Canada, CANSIM Database, 1993.

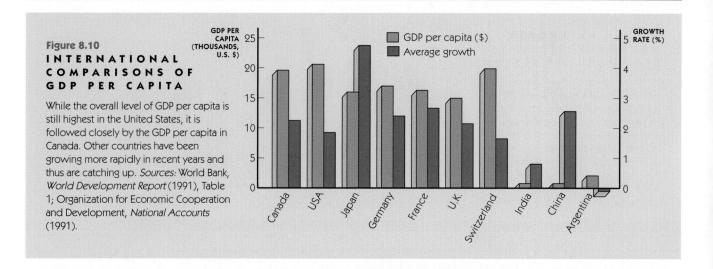

Figure 8.10

INTERNATIONAL COMPARISONS OF GDP PER CAPITA

While the overall level of GDP per capita is still highest in the United States, it is followed closely by the GDP per capita in Canada. Other countries have been growing more rapidly in recent years and thus are catching up. *Sources:* World Bank, *World Development Report* (1991), Table 1; Organization for Economic Cooperation and Development, *National Accounts* (1991).

cent lower than that of the United States. These figures are sufficiently close that it would be difficult to tell whether the standard of living in Sweden is really higher or lower than in the United States. But when GDP per capita is measured as U.S. $340 in India and U.S. $19,840 in the United States, it is fair to infer a big difference in the standard of living. The output of Canada, for example, with a population of about 27 million, is $670 billion. This is two and a half times the GDP of India ($250 billion), which has over 800 million people. Output in Canada is also more than 50 percent larger than the GDP ($400 billion) shared by over 1.1 billion citizens of China. These figures reflect large differences in standards of living.

There are marked differences not only in the levels of GDP per capita, but also in the rates of change. From 1965 to 1990, GDP per capita grew at 1.6 percent per year in Canada, 4.3 percent per year in Japan, but not at all in Argentina. Before World War II, Great Britain was one of the great powers of the world, while Japan's per capita income was below that of any of the major European countries. By 1990, Japan had a per capita income that was two-thirds higher than that of Great Britain. If per capita income continues to grow faster in Japan than in North America and Europe, in the near future Japan's living standards will become the highest in the world.

There are other measures of the standard of living, such as how long individuals live, or the number of infants who die. These different measures are correlated—that is, in general, in countries with higher GDP per capita, people live longer and infant mortality (the number of babies who die per 100,000 live births) is lower. But looking at Figure 8.11, we see that Canada does not fare appreciably better on these measures than do countries with lower per capita incomes. Life expectancy is not much different from that in several other countries, some of which, such as Ireland and Greece, have substantially lower per capita incomes. In the case of infant mortality, Canada's rate is higher than those of Japan, Sweden, and Ireland. Life expectancies in the United States are not much different from the average, and infant mortality rates are significantly above those of several countries, including Canada. This is perhaps explained by the fact that inequality is greater in the United States than in many other developed countries.

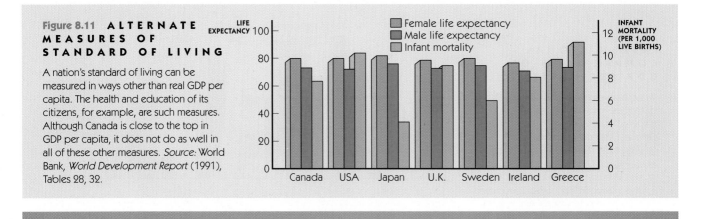

Figure 8.11 ALTERNATE MEASURES OF STANDARD OF LIVING

A nation's standard of living can be measured in ways other than real GDP per capita. The health and education of its citizens, for example, are such measures. Although Canada is close to the top in GDP per capita, it does not do as well in all of these other measures. *Source:* World Bank, *World Development Report* (1991), Tables 28, 32.

MEASURING PRODUCTIVITY

Increases in the average standard of living are brought about by increases in the average productivity of workers. Economists calculate **productivity,** or **GDP per hour worked,** by dividing real GDP by an estimate of the number of hours worked in the economy. Increases in productivity will be reflected in either higher GDP per capita or more leisure, or both.

Figure 8.12 plots productivity in Canada for recent years. Two facts emerge. First, there are fluctuations. Output per hour climbs in boom times and grows more slowly, or sometimes even declines, in recessions. Second, there has been a slowdown in the growth of productivity during recent years. In the 1960s, for example, productivity increased by 4.0 percent per year. In the 1970s, it rose by 2.0 percent per year. In the 1980s, it rose by only 1.4 percent per year.

One of the consequences of the slowdown of productivity increases is that wage rates

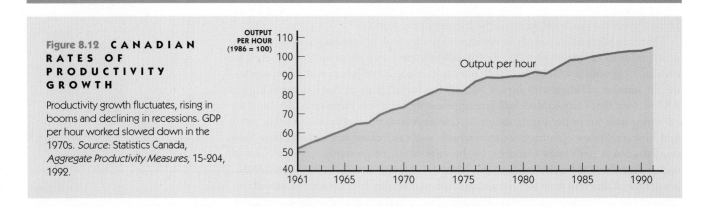

Figure 8.12 CANADIAN RATES OF PRODUCTIVITY GROWTH

Productivity growth fluctuates, rising in booms and declining in recessions. GDP per hour worked slowed down in the 1970s. *Source:* Statistics Canada, *Aggregate Productivity Measures,* 15-204, 1992.

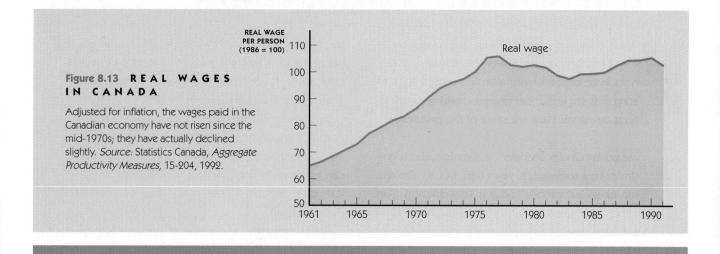

Figure 8.13 REAL WAGES IN CANADA

Adjusted for inflation, the wages paid in the Canadian economy have not risen since the mid-1970s; they have actually declined slightly. *Source:* Statistics Canada, *Aggregate Productivity Measures,* 15-204, 1992.

have failed to grow. Figure 8.13 shows that real wages (wages taking into account inflation) were actually lower in 1991 than they were fifteen years earlier.

These statistics on productivity and real wages, perhaps more than any others, have given rise to concern about the long-run prospects for the country; they have obvious implications for the future living standards of Canadians.

RELATIONSHIP BETWEEN PRODUCTIVITY AND STANDARDS OF LIVING

There has been a marked slowdown in the growth of productivity—output per hour—and real wages have been virtually unchanged during the past decade. At the same time, as Figure 8.14 shows, real family income has increased over the 1980s, though it took a

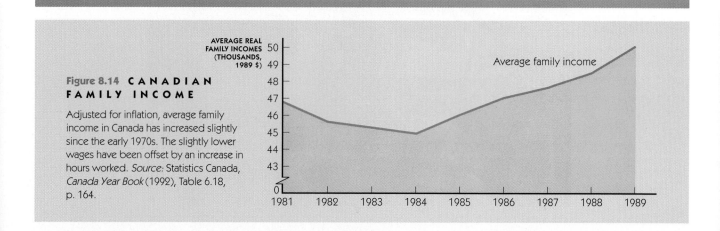

Figure 8.14 CANADIAN FAMILY INCOME

Adjusted for inflation, average family income in Canada has increased slightly since the early 1970s. The slightly lower wages have been offset by an increase in hours worked. *Source:* Statistics Canada, *Canada Year Book* (1992), Table 6.18, p. 164.

CLOSE-UP: PROBLEMS IN MEASURING OUTPUT

Gross domestic product is an approximation, a way of adding up the millions of goods and services in an economy into a single number. But creating that single number requires making some difficult decisions. Here are some of the problems:

Measuring Quality Changes   A tomato today is very similar to a tomato fifty years ago, but an airplane trip or an automobile today is very different than either was even twenty years ago. With some products, the quality (and the price) changes almost every year.

Consider the problem posed by the rapid improvement in computers. If those calculating GDP simply use market prices, they might get the idea that the output of computers is rising only slowly or perhaps even declining, since the price has fallen so rapidly. But one would not want simply to compare the *number* of computers, for that would not allow for how much more powerful the new computers are than the old. A measure of the *real*

output of the computer industry must take into account the improvement in quality. If insufficient adjustment is made, it will appear as if output is growing more slowly than it really is.

Or consider the problem posed by the improvement in the quality of medical care. Given the new medical technologies that are available today, how can economists compare the output of the medical care industry today with that of several decades ago?

GDP statisticians are aware of these problems and try to make some adjustments for changes in quality. For example, when antipollution devices were first required in automobiles in the early 1970s, the price of cars rose. Statisticians had to decide whether the increased cost should be counted as a simple price rise and thus a contributor to inflation, or whether it was a quality improvement and effectively adding to real output, since consumers were buying a "better" car. They decided on the second approach. Users of the

statistics need to bear in mind, however, that all such adjustments are necessarily imperfect.

Measuring Government Services The standard GDP calculation measures price and quantity at the point of sale. But what about goods that are not sold, at least not directly?

One important category of such goods is government-produced services. Imagine that provincial government bureaucrats become more efficient and are able to process automobile registrations faster. This might mean that the province can hire fewer workers to do the same job. But the price of registrations is not determined in a competitive market. Taxpayers pay taxes for the salaries of these government workers. And the GDP statistics simply reflect the number of hours worked by government officials. If the government becomes more efficient, measured GDP might go down, even though actual output—the number of registrations—increases.

Measuring Nonmarketed Goods Nonmarketed goods and services, like housework done by family members, present similar problems for the national income statistician. The statistics underestimate the true level of production in the economy, because they ignore such economic activity. For example, if one spouse stays at home and cleans and cooks, that would not be measured in GDP. However, if that spouse leaves home to take a job and hires someone else to do the cleaning and cooking, then both the spouse and the housekeeper would be measured in the GDP.

The Magnitude of Statistical Problems How important are these difficulties in measurement? One indication may be obtained from estimates that have been made by Statistics Canada analysts of the value of household work in Canada. Since household work does not involve any market transactions, its economic value cannot be measured directly using wage payments. Instead, studies of the value of work done in the household typically obtain indirect measures by one of two methods.

The first is called the *replacement cost* method. It estimates the value of household work by using the hourly wage rates for specific forms of household work that are performed as paid jobs. Examples include food preparation, cleaning, child care, and the like. This method assumes that household work and market replacements are equally productive. The second is called the *opportunity cost* method. It assumes that paid work is given up when one chooses to do household work, and uses the average hourly employment earnings to evaluate household work.

The aggregate value of household work in 1986 was estimated to be $198,845 million when the replacement cost method was used, and $159,438 million when the opportunity cost method was used. These values represent, respectively, 39.3 and 31.5 percent of GDP. In 1981, the figures were $146,653 using the replacement cost method and $120,330 using the opportunity cost method, representing 41.2 and 33.8 percent, respectively. This decline in value is not unique to the 1980s. Such a decline was also found for both the 1961–1971 and the 1971–1981 periods in previous Statistics Canada studies. They may be attributed to the increased labour force participation of married women—from 20.8 percent in 1961 to 52 percent in 1981 to 57.4 percent in 1986.

Source: Chris Jackson, "The Value of Household Work in Canada, 1986," *Canadian Economic Observer* (June 1992): 3.1–3.19.

big dip during the first few years of the decade when the country entered a major recession. How do we account for the discrepancy between these two statistics?

The answer has largely to do with the increased fraction of women who are working. To put it another way, while pay per hour has declined slightly, when we add up the working time of the husband and wife, the average *family* now works more hours. This is but one example of several that demonstrates that GDP per capita may not adequately reflect either changes in standards of living over time or differences in standards of living across countries. If incomes go up simply because people work more, does this really represent an improvement in standards of living?

Most of the changes in our environment—which can have enormous effects on standards of living, including life spans—are not reflected well in GDP statistics. For instance, if the government requires steel producers to install devices that reduce their smoke emissions, and the steel producers pass on the price increases to customers, it will appear as if the steel industry has become less productive; more resources are required to produce a tonne of steel. The benefits—the improvement in the quality of air—do not show up anywhere in the statistics.

CONNECTING THE VARIABLES

Often the three major macroeconomic variables move together. For example, when the economy is in a recession, as it was in 1982, unemployment tends to be higher and inflation tends to be lower. These connections should make some sense; after all, when the economy is suffering tough times, businesses reduce their output, lay off workers, and do not hire new workers. In addition, businesses that are having a hard time selling products in a competitive market are less likely to raise prices.

FLOWS AND STOCKS

GDP, GNP, and NDP are all measures of output *per year*. Rate measurements such as these are called **flows.** When a news report says, "The quarterly GDP statistic, just released, shows that GDP was $700 billion per year," it does not mean that $700 billion of goods and services was produced during the quarter; rather, it means that $175 billion was produced during the quarter, so that if that rate of production were maintained for a whole year, the total value of goods and services would be $700 billion.

Stock statistics measure some item at a single point in time. Among the most important stocks is the capital stock, the total value of all the buildings and machines that underlie the productive potential of the economy.

There are simple relationships between stocks and flows. The stock of capital at the end of 1993 consists of the stock of capital at the end of 1992 plus or minus the flows into or out of this stock. Investment is just the flow into the capital stock, and depreciation is the measure of the flow out of the capital stock.

Similarly, we can look at the *number* of unemployed individuals as a stock. This number at the end of 1993 consists of the number at the end of 1992 plus or minus the flows into or out of the unemployment pool. New hires represent flows out of the unemployment pool; layoffs, firings, and resignations represent flows into the unemployment pool.

MACROECONOMIC POLICY AND INCOME DISTRIBUTION

This chapter has focused on the macroeconomic objectives of the government—full employment, stable prices, and rapid growth—and discussed how performance in each area is measured. But these macroeconomic goals have to be kept in perspective with other goals and objectives of government, such as the distribution of income and reducing poverty. To a large extent, the successful pursuit of the macroeconomic goals will have important side effects in reducing poverty. When there are more jobs, there are fewer people in poverty. When the economy grows rapidly, there are more goods to go around; the size of the pie is larger, and normally even the poorest segments in society get a larger piece.

But sometimes conflicts do arise. In 1992, faced with a persistent slowdown and a burgeoning budget deficit, the federal government decided to tighten up on the rules applying to unemployment insurance recipients. One specific measure taken involved denying benefits to persons who quit their jobs rather than being laid off. At the same time, the federal government cut back on transfer payments to the provinces in support of health, education and, especially, welfare programs. This forced the provinces to find ways to cut expenditure in these areas. At the same time, the federal government was proceeding with revisions to the income tax system that would allow better-off persons to save more for their retirement in tax-sheltered vehicles such as Registered Retirement Savings Plans and Registered Pension Plans. Critics argued that the government was forcing the most vulnerable and least-well-off persons in society to take on a disproportionate share of the burden of the recession. The government responded that economizing on social expenditures in the short run was necessary in order to encourage growth in the economy so that the income could be created to support generous social programs.

Thus, while in this part of the book we focused on aggregates—on output, employment, and inflation—behind those aggregate statistics are individuals, and how different individuals are affected by different government actions is a central concern of macroeconomic policy.

REVIEW AND PRACTICE

SUMMARY

1. The three central macroeconomic policy objectives of the government are low unemployment, low inflation, and high growth. Macroeconomics studies how these aggregate variables change as a result of household and business behaviour, and how government policy may affect them.

2. Unemployment imposes costs both on individuals and on society as a whole, which loses what the unemployed workers could have contributed and ends up supporting them in other ways.

3. Seasonal unemployment, such as construction in the winter months, occurs regularly depending on the season. Frictional unemployment results from people being in transition between one job and another. Structural unemployment refers to the unemployment generated as the structure of the economy changes, with the new jobs being created having requirements different from the old jobs being lost. Cyclical unemployment increases or decreases with the level of economic activity.

4. The inflation rate is the percentage increase of the price level from one year to the next. Canadian inflation was low through most of the early part of this century, rose sharply in the 1970s and early 1980s, and then fell somewhat in the later 1980s. In different countries at different times, inflation has sometimes been very high, with prices increasing by factors of tens or hundreds in a given year.

5. The amount of inflation between two years is measured by the percentage change in the amount it would cost to buy a given basket of goods in those years. Different baskets define different price indices, such as the consumer price index, the producer price index, and the wholesale price index.

6. Gross domestic product (GDP) is the typical way of measuring national output. To derive real GDP, we simply divide nominal GDP by the price index.

7. GDP can be calculated in three ways: the final goods approach, which adds the value of all final goods produced in the economy; the value-added approach, which adds the difference between firms' revenues and costs of intermediate goods; and the income approach, which adds together all income received from domestic production. All three methods should reach the same answer.

8. One indicator of the standard of living is real GDP per capita, which is found by dividing real GDP by population. Productivity, or GDP per hour worked, is found by dividing real GDP by an estimate of the number of hours worked in the economy.

9. Economists seek to understand why many macroeconomic variables seem to move together. For example, in a boom, unemployment tends to fall, inflation tends to rise, productivity tends to rise. In a recession, the reverse happens.

KEY TERMS

unemployment rate	structural unemployment	producer price index
discouraged workers	cyclical unemployment	wholesale price index
labour force participation rate	inflation rate	gross domestic product (GDP)
seasonal unemployment	price index	nominal GDP
frictional unemployment	consumer price index	real GDP
	deflation	GDP deflator
		potential GDP

boom
recession
business cycle
net exports
value added
disposable income

gross national prod-
   uct (GNP)
depreciation
net domestic prod-
   uct (NDP)

GDP per capita
productivity, or GDP
   per hour worked
flow statistics
stock statistics

REVIEW QUESTIONS

1. What are the three main goals of macroeconomic policy?

2. What is the difference between frictional unemployment, seasonal unemployment, and structural unemployment?

3. When there is a reduction in the number of hours worked in the economy, is this normally shared equally by all workers? Are workers in some groups more impacted by increased unemployment than those in other groups?

4. When the prices of different goods change at different rates, how do we measure the rate of inflation?

5. Are all groups of people affected equally by inflation? Why or why not?

6. What is the difference between nominal GDP, real GDP, and potential GDP?

7. What is the difference between the final outputs approach to measuring GDP, the value-added approach, and the income approach?

8. Why is real GDP per capita a better indicator of a country's standard of living than real GDP alone?

9. How is productivity growth related to growth in a nation's standard of living? Will growth in real GDP per hour worked and growth in GDP per capita be identical? Why might a decline in the rate of growth of productivity be of concern?

10. What is the difference between GDP, GNP, and NDP?

PROBLEMS

1. Which would you expect to fall fastest in a recession, real GDP or potential GDP? Could potential GDP rise while real GDP fell?

2. Explain how these two factors would have different effects on real GDP per capita and real GDP per hour worked:
    (a) people working longer weeks;
    (b) a larger proportion of adults holding jobs.

3. Geoffrey spends his allowance on three items: candy, magazines, and renting VCR movies. He is currently receiving an allowance of $30 per month, which he is using to rent 4 movies at $2 apiece, buy 10 candy bars at $1 apiece, and purchase 4

magazines at $3 apiece. Calculate a Geoffrey price index (GPI) for this basket of goods, with the current price level equal to 100, in the following cases.

(a) The price of movies rises to $3.

(b) The price of movies rises to $3, and the price of candy bars falls by $.20.

(c) The price of movies rises to $3, the price of candy bars falls by $.20, and the price of magazines rises to $4.

What is the rate of inflation from the original price level to each of the new situations?

4. An increase in the consumer price index will often affect different groups in different ways. Think about how different groups will purchase items like housing, travel, or education in the CPI basket, and explain why they will be affected differently by increases in the overall CPI. How would you calculate an "urban CPI" or a "rural CPI"?

5. Given the information below about the Canadian economy, how much did real Canadian GDP grow between 1965 and 1975? between 1975 and 1985?

	1965	1970	1975	1980	1985	1990
Nominal GDP (billions)	$58	$89	$172	$310	$478	$668
Consumer price index	26.1	31	46	70.5	97.8	121.8

6. Much of this chapter has discussed how economists often adjust the data to find what they want to know—for example, by adjusting for inflation or dividing by the population level. What adjustments might you suggest for analyzing education expenditures? Old Age Security payments?

Microfoundations

Chapter 8 took up the key objectives of macroeconomic policy—growth, full employment, and stable prices—and the way in which success in reaching each of these objectives is gauged. In Chapter 10, we begin to look specifically at what determines such aggregate variables as the economy's output and employment levels. The behaviour of these macroeconomic variables is determined by the actions of the millions of households and firms that make up the economy. Accordingly, an understanding of macroeconomics begins with microeconomics. Earlier chapters discussed how prices are determined in competitive markets by the intersection of demand and supply curves (for goods, for labour, and for loans). This chapter rounds out that discussion.

In approaching macroeconomic questions, it is useful to think of the economy as divided into three groups of markets: markets for labour, for products, and for capital. The term "market" is used loosely here. There is not a single kind of labour, since different workers have a myriad of different skills; there is a wide variety of products; and, as we saw in Chapter 6, various kinds of loans and investments differ significantly in the risks with which they are associated. In approaching macroeconomics, however, we pay less attention to these differences. We talk, for instance, about the number of people who have jobs and the number who are unemployed. (To be sure, in a more refined analysis, we would want to know more details about *who* are unemployed, whether skilled or unskilled workers, whether they are concentrated in one industry or in one part of the country.)

This chapter takes a brief look at how households and firms interact in these three groups of markets. It then surveys the economy as a whole, from the perspective of the basic competitive model first introduced in Chapter 2. By and large, the market system envisioned in that model is the most efficient way to coordinate an economy. In fact, if the real world matched this microeconomic vision, macroeconomic problems such as unemployment would not exist, and macroeconomics would probably not have the prominence it does.

Many economists, however, believe that the basic competitive model provides an incomplete description of the economy. Most important, the model assumes that in every market, demand equals supply. When applied to the labour market, this assumption means that there is no unemployment. Since one of the main concerns in macroeconomics is what determines the unemployment rate and why there are periods in which it seems to be persistently high, we must go beyond the basic competitive model. Accordingly, the final section of this chapter points out the discrepancies between modern economies and the basic competitive model, thus laying the groundwork for the analysis of such central macroeconomic phenomena as unemployment and economic instability.

KEY QUESTIONS

1. How are the demand and supply curves for goods and services derived? for labour? for capital?

2. How does the basic competitive model provide answers to the questions of what will be produced and in what quantities, how it will be produced, and for whom it will be produced?

3. How are the various parts of the economy tied together?

4. What are the most important limitations of the basic competitive model? Why may markets by themselves not result in economic efficiency?

HOUSEHOLDS IN THE BASIC COMPETITIVE MODEL

In the basic competitive model, rational households interact with profit-maximizing firms in competitive markets. The supply and demand curves introduced in Chapter 4 give us a framework for analyzing this interaction. Here and in the next section, we explore the determinants of the demand and supply curves—why they have the shapes economists postulate that they do, and what causes the curves to shift. This section takes the perspective of households, while the next one gives the firm's viewpoint. The principles developed here will be applied to each of the markets that make up the economy: product, labour, and capital. After looking at the decisions of households and firms, we will look at the market equilibrium, how firms and households interact in all three markets, and the implications for the economy as a whole of these interactions.

THE HOUSEHOLD'S CONSUMPTION DECISION

As we saw in Chapter 2, individuals face a budget constraint. They have a certain amount of money to spend; they can only consume more of one good by consuming less of another. The trade-off is given by relative prices. If the price of apples is twice that of oranges, by giving up one apple, an individual can get two oranges.

Chapter 4 suggested that normally demand curves are downward sloping, as shown in Figure 9.1; that is, as the price rises, people consume less of a good. There are two reasons for this. First, as the price of apples increases, apples become less attractive relative to oranges and other goods. To get one more apple, Alfred must give up more oranges, so Alfred substitutes oranges (and other fruits) for apples. The reduction in demand resulting from the change in the relative price—the fact that to get one more apple, Alfred must give up more oranges—is called the **substitution effect.**

Second, if Alfred spends all or even part of his income on apples, he is worse off when the price of apples increases. He simply cannot buy what he bought before. He is, in this sense, poorer, just as he would be if his income had been reduced. If we define **real income** as what an individual's income will buy (rather than simply the money received), Alfred's real income has been reduced. When this happens, he spends less on almost every good.[1] The reduction in Alfred's demand for apples resulting from the reduction in real income is called the **income effect.** Both the income and substitution effects lead Alfred to demand fewer apples when the price increases. This is why the demand curve for apples is depicted as downward sloping: at higher prices, fewer apples are demanded.

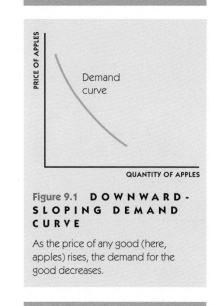

Figure 9.1 DOWNWARD-SLOPING DEMAND CURVE

As the price of any good (here, apples) rises, the demand for the good decreases.

SUBSTITUTION AND INCOME EFFECTS

Substitution effect: The reduction in demand resulting from the change in the relative price; the individual substitutes less expensive products for more expensive ones.

Income effect: The reduction in demand resulting from the reduction in real income that occurs when the price of any good rises.

Chapter 4 also discussed *shifts* in the demand curve; Figure 9.2 shows a rightward shift. What causes the demand curve to shift? There is a change in the amount of apples, at each price, that Alfred demands; he demands more. There are many factors that might cause this shift, some of them noneconomic. For instance, Alfred's tastes may change; he may simply decide that he likes apples better. Or Alfred may find apples more refreshing in hot weather, and when the weather turns warm, his demand for apples at each price increases.

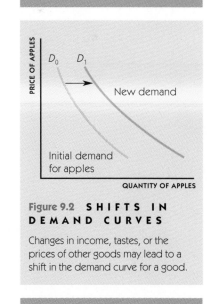

Figure 9.2 SHIFTS IN DEMAND CURVES

Changes in income, tastes, or the prices of other goods may lead to a shift in the demand curve for a good.

[1]There are some exceptions. A good for which the demand decreases as income increases is said to be *inferior*, while goods for which demand increases as income increases are said to be *normal*.

There are also important economic variables that can cause the demand curve to shift. The first is Alfred's income. When his income increases, he spends more on all goods, including apples. His demand curve shifts to the right.

A second variable is an increase in the price of another good, such as oranges. This has two effects on Alfred's demand for apples. On the one hand, higher-priced oranges reduce his real income, which in turn implies a reduction in his demand for apples. Thus, the income effect of an increase in the price of oranges leads to a decrease in the demand for apples. On the other hand, the increase in the relative price of oranges encourages the consumption of apples; that is, the substitution effect leads to an *increase* in the demand for apples. The two effects work in opposite directions. When the income effect is larger than the substitution effect, so that the demand for one product decreases when the price of another product increases, the two products are complements; when the substitution effect is larger than the income effect, so that the demand for one product increases when the price of another product increases, the two products are substitutes. Skis and ski boots are complements; Coke and Pepsi are substitutes.

SUBSTITUTES AND COMPLEMENTS

Complements: Two goods are complements if the demand for one product decreases when the price of another product increases; the substitution effect is less than the income effect.

Substitutes: Two goods are substitutes if the demand for one product increases when the price of another product increases; the substitution effect is larger than the income effect.

There is one basic lesson that emerges from this discussion: what occurs in one market can have effects in other markets. If something happens in the labour market that makes Alfred's income go down, his demand for apples, oranges, and other goods will be reduced. The interrelations among markets will play an important role in this book.

THE HOUSEHOLD'S SAVING DECISION

The same kind of analysis applies to Alfred's decision about how much to save. We can think of a decision about how much to save as a decision about how much to consume now and how much to consume in the future. If Alfred reduces his consumption (with a fixed income), he has money left over, which he saves. He takes this savings and puts it in the bank (or invests it some other way), and receives a return of r (the interest rate). If r is 10 percent, then for every dollar of reduced consumption today, he gets $1.10 in the future. Thus, $1.10 is the *relative* price of consumption today versus consumption in the future.

What is the effect of an increase in the interest rate? If Alfred saves nothing—he takes his current income and simply consumes it—then the interest rate has no effect. If he does save, he has more to consume in the future. He is better off. When an individual's income goes down, she normally consumes less of all goods. When Alfred is better off, he normally consumes more of every good; this means, in our example, that he consumes more now and more in the future. This is the income effect of higher interest rates. Alfred consumes more now, which implies that he saves less.

On the other hand, an increase in the interest rate means that for each dollar of consumption Alfred gives up today, he gets more consumption in the future; the trade-off has changed. This is the substitution effect, and the substitution effect of higher interest rates leads Alfred to consume less today and more in the future. Thus, an increase in the interest rate has an income effect leading to lower savings and a substitution effect leading to more savings. The net effect is ambiguous, though most studies indicate that on average, the substitution effect slightly outweighs the income effect: savings increase slightly. Figure 9.3 shows the supply of savings as a slightly upward-sloping curve.

In Chapter 6, we saw that what is expected to happen in the future can have effects on markets today. An increase in the demand for land ten years from now will cause its current price to go up. The principle that expectations about the future can have effects on markets today is quite general. Assume Alfred expects to receive a bequest from his rich uncle next year. This means that he does not need to save as much for the future. The expected bequest increases his current consumption. It increases his consumption for every good at each price level; that is, it shifts his demand curve for apples to the right.

INVESTING

Having decided how much to save, Alfred now faces a new problem: what to do with his savings. He has a number of choices. For instance, he could put his money in a bank account. Alternatively, he could buy a certificate of deposit, which is a promise from the bank to pay him, in addition to the money he has invested—the principal—a specified interest in, say, six months or a year. Other options include corporate stocks and corporate or government bonds. In evaluating his alternatives, Alfred looks at several characteristics of each asset: the **expected return** (what he expects to get on average), the risk, the tax advantages, and how costly it would be for him to sell the asset quickly, should he need to do so (technically called the **liquidity**). Alfred is risk averse, so he decides to put most of his savings in government bonds, which are very safe. But he knows he pays a price: assets that are less risky tend to have lower expected returns. In general, he knows that financial markets are efficient, although there are no bargains to be had. If he wants higher returns, the cost to him is that he has to bear greater risk.

THE HOUSEHOLD'S LABOUR SUPPLY DECISION

We can use the same basic reasoning that we have employed to analyze the demand for apples and savings to discuss how much Alfred decides to work. Of course, in some jobs, Alfred may have no choice; if he wants to work for Grinding Grinders, he may have to work a sixty-hour week, while if he wants to work for Easy Riding Stables, his work week may be only thirty hours. But the number of hours he wants to work will affect which

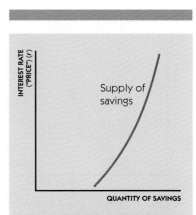

Figure 9.3 THE SUPPLY CURVE FOR SAVINGS

The supply of savings rises slightly with increases in the interest rate. The substitution effect slightly exceeds the income effect.

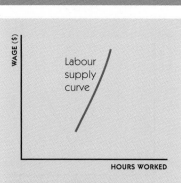

Figure 9.4 THE LABOUR SUPPLY CURVE

The supply of labour increases with the wage, but only slightly. The income and substitution effects are almost just balanced.

job he chooses; and economists believe that by and large, employers respond to preferences of workers. If workers, on average, want shorter work weeks, then over time, work weeks will get shorter. In fact, the work week is considerably shorter today than it was at the beginning of the century.

The question is, what determines how much Alfred would like to work? Again, we need to look at Alfred's opportunity set. If he works less, his income will be lower; he will not be able to consume as much as he otherwise could. In making his decision, he looks at the trade-off, the benefit of the extra leisure and the cost of the reduced amount of goods he can buy. This trade-off is given by the wage he receives. The wage is the price of labour. The **real wage** is the nominal wage divided by the average price of the goods a person buys (as reflected, for instance, in the consumer price index). Thus, the real wage tells us how much extra consumption Alfred can have if he works an hour more.

What happens when real wages increase? Again, there is an income effect. Alfred is better off and so would like to consume more of every good; viewing leisure as a "good," he wants more leisure—that is, he wants to work less. On the other hand, the higher wage has changed the trade-off. For every hour of leisure he gives up, he now gets, for example, $20 of extra consumption rather than $10. The substitution effect causes him to want to work more. Again, the net effect is ambiguous. Most studies show that the income and substitution effects are almost precisely balanced, so that the labour supply curve appears to be fairly steep, as depicted in Figure 9.4.

FIRMS IN THE BASIC COMPETITIVE MODEL

Competitive firms maximize their profits.[2] Profits are just revenues minus costs. Revenues are the price of a good times the quantity sold of the good. The firm in the basic competitive model believes that it has no effect on price—it takes the market price as given. For instance, any wheat farmer believes that the price of wheat will be unaffected by the amount of wheat he sells.

THE FIRM'S SUPPLY DECISION

In deciding how much to produce, the firm in the competitive model compares the extra revenue it receives from producing one more unit of output—the price—with the extra cost, which is called the **marginal cost.** When price exceeds marginal cost, the firm gains more than the increased costs; it pays to expand output. By contrast, if marginal cost exceeds price, it pays to contract output. What the firm does is produce at the level where price equals marginal cost. This is the profit-maximizing level of output.

Here is another way of looking at the firm's decision. Figure 9.5 shows the firm's total costs of producing each level of output. Total costs increase as the firm produces more. The figure also shows the company's total revenue curve. The firm's profit at any level of

[2]Alternatively, we can describe firms as maximizing their market value; to do that, they must maximize their profits. They may, of course, be willing to give up some profits today if they think profits in the future will be increased by enough to compensate.

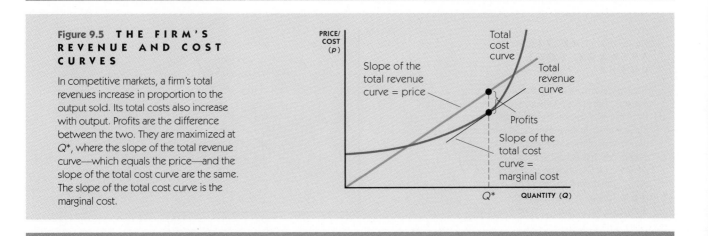

Figure 9.5 THE FIRM'S REVENUE AND COST CURVES

In competitive markets, a firm's total revenues increase in proportion to the output sold. Its total costs also increase with output. Profits are the difference between the two. They are maximized at Q^*, where the slope of the total revenue curve—which equals the price—and the slope of the total cost curve are the same. The slope of the total cost curve is the marginal cost.

output is simply the difference between the two at that level of output. The slope of the total revenue curve measures the increase in revenues when output increases by a unit, called the **marginal revenue.** It is a fundamental feature of the basic competitive model that the firm's total revenue increases in proportion to output. The total revenue curve is thus a straight line through the origin, with a slope equal to the market price: marginal revenue equals price. The slope of the total cost curve is the marginal cost. As long as marginal revenue is higher than marginal cost, profits are increasing. Profits are maximized when the two curves have the same slope; that is, when marginal revenue (price) equals marginal cost.

We learn more about the firm's production decision by looking more closely at its costs. The firm's **average costs,** total costs divided by output, are shown in Figure 9.6. The average cost curve is U-shaped. It heads downward at low levels of output because there are certain costs a firm must pay just to remain in operation. It has to pay rent, pay its top management, and so forth. These are referred to as **fixed** or **overhead costs.** If these were the *only* costs, then average costs would decline rapidly as output increases. There are other costs, however, called **variable costs,** and not only do these increase, but they often increase faster than output, at least beyond a certain point. In the short run, the firm cannot immediately expand the number of machines and workers. To produce more, it has to work two or three shifts, and must work its machines and workers at full speed. This is expensive. Thus, its average costs start to increase. This explains why the typical firm has a U-shaped average cost curve.

Figure 9.6 also shows the firm's marginal costs. In the figure, marginal costs are initially relatively flat. If the firm wishes to expand production, it simply hires more workers and buys more raw materials. But as we just saw, after some point it becomes more expensive to produce an extra unit. Marginal costs start to increase. Eventually the firm may find that it simply cannot increase its output beyond a certain level. The marginal cost curve in the figure intersects the average cost curve at its lowest price. This is no accident. When marginal costs—the costs of producing an extra unit—exceed the average costs, the marginal costs are pulling up the average, so average costs are rising. When marginal costs are below average costs, marginal costs are pulling down the average, so average costs are falling.

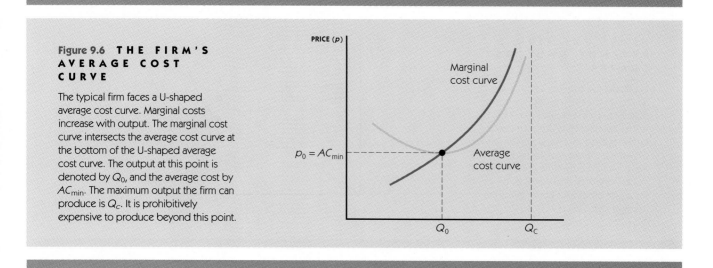

Figure 9.6 THE FIRM'S AVERAGE COST CURVE

The typical firm faces a U-shaped average cost curve. Marginal costs increase with output. The marginal cost curve intersects the average cost curve at the bottom of the U-shaped average cost curve. The output at this point is denoted by Q_0, and the average cost by AC_{min}. The maximum output the firm can produce is Q_c. It is prohibitively expensive to produce beyond this point.

Once we understand the average cost curve, we can add an important qualification to the statement above that the firm in the competitive model produces at the point where price equals marginal cost. It does so only *so long as it covers costs*—that is, so long as price equals or exceeds average costs. If price is below average costs, the firm shuts down. Thus, the firm's supply curve is its marginal cost curve in the region where price exceeds minimum average costs; otherwise, the firm supplies zero.

THE FIRM'S SUPPLY DECISION

Competitive firms produce at the output at which price equals marginal costs, provided price equals or exceeds average costs. If price is below average costs, the firm shuts down.

THE MARKET SUPPLY CURVE

The collection of firms making the same product is called an **industry.** The industry or market supply curve, as we saw in Chapter 4, is found simply by adding up the supply curves of each of the firms in the industry. Figure 9.7 shows a typical shape, with a horizontal portion at price p_0 and an upward-sloping portion beyond that. In the figure, the industry simply cannot produce at an output beyond Q_c^M; this point is referred to as the total **capacity** of the industry.

The reason that the market supply curve has this shape can be seen if we return to the U-shaped cost curves illustrated in Figure 9.6. Assume all firms have the same average

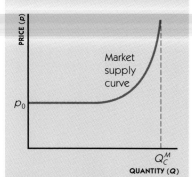

Figure 9.7 THE MARKET SUPPLY CURVE

The figure illustrates a typical shape, with a horizontal portion at price p_0 and an upward-sloping portion beyond that. There is some total capacity of the industry: it simply cannot produce at output beyond Q_c^M.

cost curves, with minimum average cost equal to AC_{min} and the corresponding output equal to Q_0. Then, when the price is $p_0 = AC_{min}$, each firm is indifferent between not operating and operating at Q_0. If there are N firms, then industry output at price p_0 is somewhere between 0, when all shut down, and $N \times Q_0$, when all operate. Above p_0, the market supply is simply the sum of the amounts supplied by each of the firms, all of which will be operating.

The Effect of Wage Increases on the Market Supply Curve   The amount the industry is willing to supply depends, of course, not just on the price it receives, but on what it must pay for labour and other inputs. Implicitly, we have assumed throughout the analysis so far that those are fixed.

An increase in wages (or the price of any other input) shifts *all* of the cost curves—total, average, and marginal—upwards. Figure 9.8A illustrates the effects on average and marginal costs. As a result, the supply curve of the industry shifts, as depicted in panel B.

THE FIRM'S DEMAND FOR LABOUR AND CAPITAL

The firm's production decision is intimately tied to its demand for labour. At each level of wages and prices, we can calculate the amount firms are willing to supply. But we can also calculate their demand for labour. As the wage increases at a given price level, firms' demand for labour will decrease, for two reasons. First, the upward shift in the marginal cost curve means that firms will wish to produce less. With lower levels of production, they will demand less labour. But in addition, if wages increase, labour becomes more expensive relative to other inputs. Firms will thus substitute, where possible, other inputs for labour. In some cases, this may be easy; for instance, some industries can use more machines, or more expensive machines, which require fewer workers to run them. In other cases, it is more difficult.

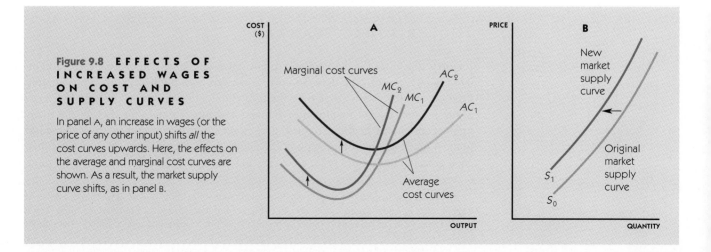

Figure 9.8 EFFECTS OF INCREASED WAGES ON COST AND SUPPLY CURVES

In panel A, an increase in wages (or the price of any other input) shifts *all* the cost curves upwards. Here, the effects on the average and marginal cost curves are shown. As a result, the market supply curve shifts, as in panel B.

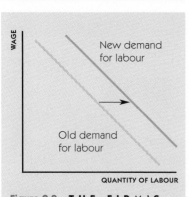

Figure 9.9 THE FIRM'S DEMAND CURVE FOR LABOUR

As wages increase, the amount of labour demanded by firms decreases. The demand curve for labour shifts to the right when the price of the good produced by the firm increases.

We can immediately extend this analysis to the industry, and then to the whole economy: as wages increase (at fixed prices), the total amount of labour demanded by all firms together—the market demand for labour—decreases.

Figure 9.9 shows a firm's demand curve for labour, which is downward sloping. It is drawn under the assumption of a given price of output. If the price of output increases, firms will want to produce more; and at the higher level of output, they will want more labour. The demand curve for labour will shift to the right, as depicted in the figure.

Exactly the same kind of analysis applies to the demand for capital.[3] As the interest rate—the price of using capital—increases, firms' demand for capital decreases; each firm produces less and each firm substitutes other inputs, such as labour, for capital, which has become more expensive.

MARKET EQUILIBRIUM IN THE BASIC COMPETITIVE MODEL

Now that we have analyzed the behaviour of firms and households, we need to put these results together, to analyze equilibrium in each of the major markets of the economy.

THE LABOUR MARKET

Figure 9.10A shows the demand and supply curves for labour (which take prices and interest rates as given). We find the demand curve for labour through the analysis of the behaviour of the firm, as described above, and the supply curve of labour through an analysis of the household's labour supply decision. The intersection gives the equilibrium wage. When the demand for labour equals the supply of labour, we say that the labour market **clears.** By definition, in the basic competitive model, there is no unemployment, since the wage is set at the level at which the demand for labour equals the supply.

THE PRODUCT MARKET

Figure 9.10B shows the demand and supply curves for goods (which take wages and interest rates as given). The demand curve is derived from the household's consumption decision, and the supply curve from the firm's production decision. This aggregate view of the product market incorporates demand and supply curves for each of the many products produced in the economy, and closer inspection would reveal a myriad of product markets. The intersection of the demand and supply curves for any individual good gives its equilibrium price, as we saw in Chapter 4. When we talk about the prod-

---

[3]Recall the discussion of Chapter 2, which pointed out that the term "capital" is used in two different ways: it refers to capital goods—plant and equipment—and to the funds used to purchase these capital goods. Here, we are referring to the latter, to the supply of "funds" made available to firms by households and to the demand for funds by firms to finance their investment.

uct market as a whole, with an aggregate demand and supply curve, we say that the intersection of the demand and supply curves gives the equilibrium **price level.**

THE CAPITAL MARKET

Figure 9.10C shows the demand and supply curves for capital, derived from the supply of savings by households and the demand for funds by firms to finance new investment. As we saw earlier, we can think of the interest rate as the price of funds; for instance, higher interest rates mean that households have to give up more future consumption if they wish to increase current consumption by a dollar. The intersection of the demand and supply curves gives the equilibrium interest rate.

GENERAL EQUILIBRIUM

The **general equilibrium** of the economy is the situation in which *all* markets are in equilibrium (or all markets clear); that is, the demand for each good equals its supply, the demand for each kind of labour equals its supply, and the demand for capital equals its supply. We call such a situation an equilibrium because when all markets clear, there is no incentive for prices—including the price of labour (the wage) and the price of capital (the interest rate)—in any market to change.

THE INTERRELATEDNESS OF MARKETS

It is important to recognize that all markets are interrelated: what goes on in one market may have repercussions throughout the economy. Consider, for instance, a tax that firms must pay on each worker hired. Figure 9.11 shows the initial effect of the tax. The tax means that the wage received by a worker is less than the cost of labour to the firm, which includes both the wage and tax. At each wage received by the worker, w, the cost of the worker to the firm has gone up (to $w_1 + t$), so the demand for labour decreases. The demand curve shifts to the left. As the figure illustrates, the wage received by the worker accordingly goes down, from w_0 to w_1, and the total cost of the worker to the firm, $w_1 + t$, goes up. But this is not the end of the story.

Lower wages received by households result in their demanding fewer goods; the demand curve for each product shifts to the left. Higher wages paid by firms result in firms' being willing to supply less output at any given price; the supply curve for each product shifts to the left. Output is reduced, and normally the price will change.

If, for instance, the price level increases, this will have ramifications back on the labour market. At higher prices, households' real wages—the extra goods workers can buy as a result of working an hour more—will be lower, and they will be willing to supply less labour. At higher prices, firms will, at each wage, be willing to produce more, and hence will demand more labour. The wage rate—both the wage paid by firms and the wage received by workers—will thus increase. We then need to trace the effect of this wage increase back on the product market.

The labour market is not the only market to be disturbed. The capital market will also be affected. As firms expand or contract production, they will demand more or less

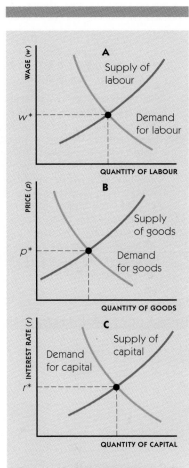

Figure 9.10 MARKET EQUILIBRIUM

In panel A, the equilibrium wage is at the intersection of the demand and supply curves for labour (which take prices and interest rates as given). In panel B, the equilibrium price level is given by the intersection of the demand and supply curves for goods (which take wages and interest rates as given). Panel C shows the equilibrium interest rate at the intersection of the demand and supply curves for capital (which take wages and prices as given.)

Figure 9.11 EFFECT OF A TAX ON LABOUR

The tax means that the wage received by a worker is less than the cost of labour to the firm, which includes the tax. As a result of the tax, the wage received by the worker normally goes down, and the total cost of labour to the firm normally goes up. These are, however, only the initial effects. These wage changes give rise to changes in the product and capital markets, and the resulting changes in interest rates and prices have reverberations back on the demand and supply curves for labour, and hence on the equilibrium wage rate.

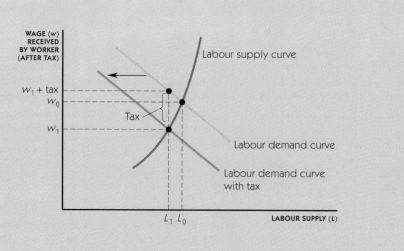

capital. As wages increase, firms will substitute capital for labour, since labour has become relatively more expensive. Accordingly, the demand curve for capital shifts. At the same time, if workers' income is reduced, they are likely to reduce their savings, so the supply curve of capital also shifts. As the demand and supply curves of capital shift, the interest rate changes, and this too has effects, both on the product market (since households' incomes and firms' cost curves are thereby affected) and on the labour market (for the same reasons).

The process continues. Eventually the economy settles down to a new equilibrium. General equilibrium analysis takes all of these interactions into account.

GENERAL EQUILIBRIUM

The general equilibrium of the economy occurs when all markets clear. The demand for labour equals the supply; the demand for each good equals its supply; and the demand for capital equals the supply.

All markets are interrelated; disturbances to one market have consequences for the equilibrium in other markets.

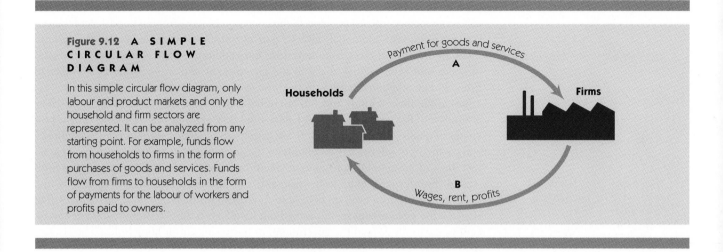

Figure 9.12 A SIMPLE CIRCULAR FLOW DIAGRAM

In this simple circular flow diagram, only labour and product markets and only the household and firm sectors are represented. It can be analyzed from any starting point. For example, funds flow from households to firms in the form of purchases of goods and services. Funds flow from firms to households in the form of payments for the labour of workers and profits paid to owners.

Payment for goods and services

A

Households

Firms

B

Wages, rent, profits

CIRCULAR FLOWS

The relationships among the various parts of the economy are sometimes illustrated by means of a **circular flow** diagram. Households buy goods and services from firms. Households supply labour and capital to firms. The income individuals receive, whether in the form of wages or the return on their savings, is spent to buy the goods that firms produce.

Figure 9.12 depicts this circular flow for a simplified economy in which there are no savings (and therefore no capital), no government, and no foreign trade. Firms hire labour from households and sell goods and services to households. The income they receive from selling their products goes to pay their workers, and anything left over is paid out to households as profits.

A circular flow can be analyzed from any starting point, but let's start on the upper arrow (at point A), moving from left to right. Consumers pay money to firms to buy their goods and services, and this money then flows back through the firms to households at B in the form of wages, rents on land, and profits. Not only is the circular flow diagram useful in keeping track of how funds flow through the economy, it also enables us to focus on certain balance conditions, which must always be satisfied. Thus, in the figure, the income of households (the flow of funds from firms) must equal the expenditures of households (the flow of funds to firms).

Figure 9.13 expands the depiction of circular flow in several ways. First, savings and capital are included. Here, some of the funds that flow from the firm to the household are a return on capital (interest on loans, dividends on equities), while some of the funds that flow from the household to the firm are savings, which go to purchase machines and buildings. In addition, firms retain some of their earnings and use them to finance investment.

The diagram is expanded further to include funds flowing into and out of the government. Now households and firms have both additional sources of funds and additional places where funds go. Some households receive money from the government (like unemployment insurance from the federal government and welfare payments from the provinces); some sell their labour services to the government rather than private firms; and some receive interest on loans to the government (government bonds). And there is now an important additional outflow: part of household income goes to the government, in the form of taxes. Similarly, firms have additional sources of inflow in the sales of goods and services they make to the government and in government subsidies to firms, and an additional outflow in the taxes they must pay to the government.

Just as the flow of funds into and out of households and firms must balance, the flow of funds into the government must balance the flow of funds out.[4] Funds go out as purchases of goods and services from firms, purchases of labour services from households, and payments of interest to households on the government debt. Funds also go out as direct flows to households, for unemployment insurance, welfare payments, and so forth (called "transfer payments" in the diagram), and to firms as subsidies. Funds flow into the government from taxes on both households and firms. When there is a deficit—that is, when the government spends more than it collects in taxes—as there has been in recent years, funds go into the government as borrowings from households. The government finances the difference between what it spends and what it raises in taxes by borrowing (in our diagram, from households).

Figure 9.13 also includes the flow to and from foreign countries. Firms sell goods to foreigners (exports) and borrow funds from foreigners. Households buy goods from foreigners (imports) and invest funds in foreign firms. Again, there must be a balance in the flow of funds: Canadian exports plus what the country borrows and receives as investment income from abroad (the flow of funds from abroad) must equal its imports plus what it lends and pays as investment income abroad (the flow of funds to other countries).[5]

The flow of funds diagram is useful as a way of keeping track of the various relationships in the economy. The various balance conditions that make up the diagram are basically identities. Identities, as we know, are statements that are always true; they follow from the basic definitions of the concepts involved. Household income, for example, must equal expenditures on goods plus savings (the flow of funds to firms).

The interconnections and balance conditions making up circular flow analysis are the same as those that arise in the competitive equilibrium model discussed earlier in the chapter. Even if the economy were not competitive, however, the interrelationships and balance conditions of the circular flow diagram would still be true. The circular flow diagram is useful, for it reminds us that whether the economy is competitive or not, if one element of a balance changes, some other element *must* change.

Let's put the circular flow diagram to work. Consider an increase in the personal income tax, such as occurred in 1992 under the Conservatives. The flow of funds into the government was increased. The circular flow diagram reminds us that if flows in and out are to remain balanced, then either some other flow into the government must be reduced or some flow out of the government must be increased. That is, either some other tax must be reduced, government borrowing must decrease, or government expenditures must increase. In this instance, the intent was to reduce government borrowing.

---

[4]We ignore here the possibility that the government can simply pay for what it obtains by printing money. In Canada, the government always finances any shortfall in revenue by borrowing.

[5]This condition will play an important role in the discussion of Chapter 22. It can be put another way: the difference between Canadian imports and exports must equal the net flow of funds from abroad (the difference between what the country borrows from abroad and what it lends net of investment income received less that paid).

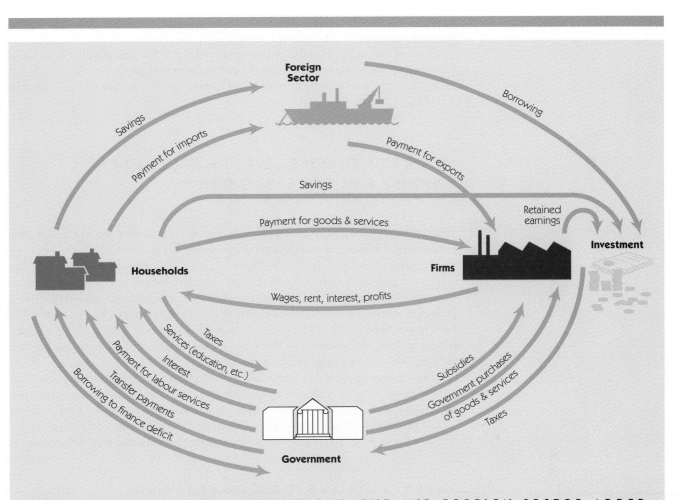

Figure 9.13 CIRCULAR FLOW WITH GOVERNMENT AND FOREIGN SECTOR ADDED

This expanded circular flow diagram shows the labour, capital, and product markets along with households, firms, government, and foreign countries; it too can be analyzed from any starting point. The flow of funds into each sector must balance the flow of funds out of each sector.

THE EFFICIENCY OF THE BASIC COMPETITIVE MODEL

Chapter 7 explained one of the reasons why economists are so interested in the basic competitive model: in the model, resources are allocated efficiently. The economy operates along its production possibilities curve. The economy cannot produce more of one good without producing less of another. It produces the goods that consumers want. That is, production simultaneously takes into account the trade-offs individuals are willing to make (how many apples they are willing to give up to get one more orange) and the trade-offs the production possibilities curve gives the economy (how many apples have to be given up to get one more orange).

Moreover, competitive markets ensure that goods get to the right people. As we saw in Chapter 3, if individuals do not like the particular mix of goods they have, they can trade; exchange will continue in competitive markets until no further mutually advantageous trades are feasible.

LIMITATIONS OF THE BASIC COMPETITIVE MODEL

While the basic model provides a good starting point for economic analysis, under some circumstances it may not provide a good description of the economy. In this book, we will be particularly concerned with the problem of unemployment. Periodically, the economy is plagued with high levels of unemployment. In the Great Depression, which began in 1929, unemployment in Canada reached almost 20 percent, and in the United States it reached 25 percent. Ireland in recent years has faced unemployment rates of 20 percent and Spain, rates of 15 percent or more. With so many people unable to find a job for so long, the assumption that all markets—including the labour market—are clearing seems, at least at times, inappropriate.

In the remaining chapters of this book, we will spend considerable time understanding the causes of large-scale unemployment and related macroeconomic market failures. Many of the explanations for unemployment are related to other ways in which market economies differ from the assumptions of the competitive equilibrium model. The remaining pages of this chapter take up the most important of these differences.

IMPERFECTIONS OF COMPETITION

The basic competitive model begins with the assumption that there are so many buyers and sellers in each market that each firm and each individual believes that it has no effect on the equilibrium price. We say that firms and households are **price takers.** In particular, the amount produced by any firm has a negligible effect on the market price.

In many markets, firms do seem to have an effect on the price. They are **price makers.** This is true of many of the goods we buy—from automobiles to film, brand-name cereals, beer, and soft drinks. The production decision of a price maker determines the price it receives; alternatively, such a firm picks a price, and the price it picks determines how much it can sell. The difference between the price-taking firms of the basic competitive model and the price-making firms of imperfect competition can be represented by the demand curves they face. With perfect competition, firms face a horizontal demand curve. They can sell as much as they want at the going market price. With imperfect competition, firms face a downward-sloping demand curve.

The basic rule for determining how much firms produce is still that firms produce more if the extra (or marginal) revenue of producing one more unit exceeds the marginal cost. Profit maximizing entails setting marginal revenue equal to marginal cost. The important difference between perfect and imperfect competition is that with its

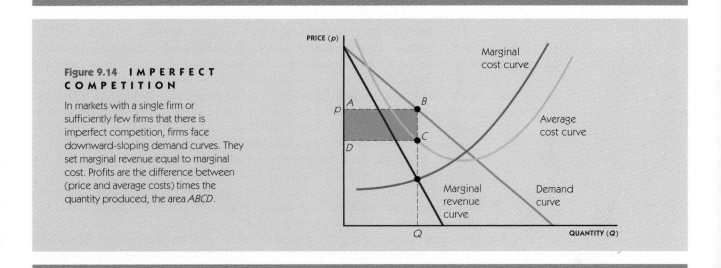

Figure 9.14 IMPERFECT COMPETITION

In markets with a single firm or sufficiently few firms that there is imperfect competition, firms face downward-sloping demand curves. They set marginal revenue equal to marginal cost. Profits are the difference between (price and average costs) times the quantity produced, the area *ABCD*.

downward-sloping demand curve, if the imperfectly competitive firm increases its output, price falls. The extra revenue the firm receives (its marginal revenue) is less than the price at which it sells the last unit, because in order to sell that last unit, the firm had to lower the price on all the other units it sold.

Thus, in Figure 9.14, the marginal revenue curve is below the demand curve, and the equilibrium output is that at which marginal revenue equals marginal cost. The profits per unit sold are the difference between the price and average costs. Total profits are shown in the figure as the rectangle *ABCD*, the difference between (price and average costs) times the quantity produced.

The extreme case of imperfect competition is no competition. A firm that faces no competitors is called a **monopolist.** There are relatively few industries with only one firm. At one time, Kodak was a virtual monopolist in the photographic film industry, as was Inco in the nickel industry.

When there are a few firms in an industry, it is called an **oligopoly.** The analysis of oligopolies is complicated by the fact that the extra revenue a firm receives from selling an extra unit depends in part on how the company's rivals react. Firms must consider rivals' possible reactions when they make decisions such as whether to produce more or to advertise more.

In between oligopolies and perfect competition is a situation called **monopolistic competition,** where there are sufficiently many firms that no firm worries about the reactions of rivals to any action it takes. At the same time, however, there are sufficiently few firms that each one faces a downward-sloping demand curve for its product. With monopolistic competition, barriers to entry (such as the cost of entering a market) are low enough that profits may be driven to zero, but still firms are not price takers.

In most markets in modern economies, competition is not perfect. A firm that raises its price does not lose all of its customers, as would be the case in the perfectly competitive model. There are several reasons for this, the most important of which is the fact that the products of different firms are slightly different from one another. There is **product differentiation.** The automobile made by Ford Canada is slightly different from the one made by General Motors Canada, and likewise throughout most of the major industries in Canada.

The differences may be real or simply perceived. They may be as simple as the differences in location of several gasoline stations, or as complex as the differences between two separate computers. The differences may be related to differences in the quality of products, or they may arise from brand loyalty or firm reputations. As will be discussed briefly later in this chapter, developing new and better products, different from those produced by other firms, is one of the main ways in which firms compete in modern economies. In the basic competitive model, however, firms only compete on price.

In labour markets, competition is also often limited. In many industries, workers do not compete actively against one another but rather work together, through unions. Together, they threaten to refuse to work for a firm unless the firm raises its wages; that is, they use their market power to extract higher wages by threatening a strike. Of course, their market power is limited to the extent that the employer may turn to nonunion workers. However, that option has been curtailed in British Columbia, Ontario, and Quebec, all of which have passed legislation outlawing the hiring of replacement workers.

For the present purposes, it is important to note that the ability of unions to extract higher wages depends on the ability of firms to pay higher wages. When a firm has profits resulting from monopoly power, then it can pay higher wages. When the firm operates in a highly competitive industry, if it pays higher wages, it cannot compensate by charging higher prices.

The growth in union membership began to level off in 1975, as illustrated in Figure 9.15. In fact, within the private sector, there has been a marked decline; the major area of growth of unionization is among public employees. Part of this decline is attributed to the increased competition faced by such traditionally highly unionized sectors as automobiles and steel. These sectors have grown smaller, some claim, partly as a result of the high wages the unions have won for their workers. In most European countries, however, unions remain powerful and play a major role in setting wages.

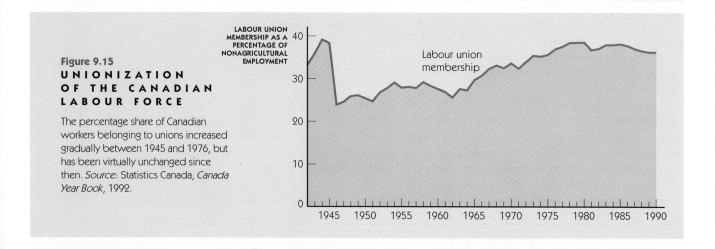

Figure 9.15

UNIONIZATION OF THE CANADIAN LABOUR FORCE

The percentage share of Canadian workers belonging to unions increased gradually between 1945 and 1976, but has been virtually unchanged since then. *Source*: Statistics Canada, *Canada Year Book*, 1992.

LABOUR UNION MEMBERSHIP AS A PERCENTAGE OF NONAGRICULTURAL EMPLOYMENT

Labour union membership

CLOSE-UP: THE NATIONAL ENERGY PROGRAM AND GENERAL EQUILIBRIUM

Oil products permeate virtually every sector of the economy. Any major change in their price inevitably has general equilibrium consequences. One significant such change occurred in the mid-1970s when the Organization of Petroleum Exporting Countries (OPEC) cartel caused oil prices to soar by restricting the rates of production of its members. Since we produce more oil than we consume in Canada (that is, we are net exporters), the OPEC price rise might have had a positive effect here. But most of the producers of oil are concentrated in Alberta while the users are spread across the country, so the gains would have been concentrated in Alberta.

In response to this, the federal government introduced the National Energy Program (NEP) in 1980 in an effort to spread the benefits around the country. The NEP restricted the price of oil in Canada to be well below the world price. This was partly accomplished by a tax imposed on exports

sold from the West to foreigners, and by a subsidy paid on imports coming into eastern Canada. As well, the federal government imposed a tax on the production of oil, effectively reducing the ability of the Alberta government to do so. Finally, tax incentives were offered to encourage production by Canadian-owned firms in the oil industry.

The federal government had three main objectives in implementing the NEP. The first was energy self-sufficiency. It was hoped that oil imports for Canadian consumption could be eliminated by 1990. Secondly, the government envisioned Canadianization of the oil and gas industry. Domestic ownership and control were encouraged over foreign interests. The third objective of the NEP was fairness in energy pricing and revenue sharing across Canada.

To the extent that the NEP was successful both at keeping oil prices lower than they would otherwise have been, and at spreading across the coun-

try the revenues from the price increase that did occur, certain general equilibrium consequences could be avoided. For one thing, if the windfall profits from the OPEC oil price rise had been allowed to accrue to Alberta firms and the Alberta treasury, that province would have been able to offer fiscal benefits such as lower taxes and better public services that would have attracted labour and capital out of neighbouring provinces. The NEP was partly intended to reduce this so-called fiscally induced migration by sharing the revenues from the oil price increase across the country as well as reducing the size of the price increase.

Quite apart from that are the ramifications that a large oil price rise would have had for industries in other parts of the country. A major study conducted for Transport Canada in 1982 found that the NEP could be important for the survival of Maritime producers who export to central Canada and the United States. For some Maritime goods the energy cost of transportation is a large component of the product price. In the case of New Brunswick green lumber, the cost of (trucking) diesel fuel accounted for 4.8 percent of the product price in 1982. This cost was not nearly as high for the competing firms in Ontario, Quebec, and the northern states in the United States where the Maritime products were sold. More generally, it was estimated that rising energy prices could have a "significant negative impact on the competitive position" of Maritime producers of canned fruits and vegetables as well as lumber. (Less sensitive to energy prices were the canned and frozen fish industries since oil inputs make up a much smaller proportion of their costs.) In a general equilibrium sense, then, the NEP was seen to benefit seemingly remote Maritime sectors by keeping energy prices low.

Sources: Edward A. Carmichael and J.K. Stewart, *Lessons from the National Energy Program* (Toronto: C.D. Howe Institute, 1983); E.H.M. Jagoe and A.D. Fiander, *Assessment of the Impact of the NEP on the Long-Haul Freight Movements from the Maritime Provinces,* for Transport Canada Strategic Planning, Group Project No. 59–86, June 1982.

IMPERFECT INFORMATION

An important assumption of the basic competitive model is that households are well informed. They have good information about the products they buy. They know the prices at which they can acquire each good at each store. They have good information about the firms in which they invest. Similarly, firms have good information about potential employees. Firms know each worker's abilities. They can costlessly monitor what workers are doing and ensure that they do as they are told. It is clear that these assumptions are not quite correct; households and firms both face limited or, as economists say, **imperfect information.** This fact has important implications for how each of the markets in the economy functions.

In the product market, imperfect information provides an additional reason why each firm faces a downward-sloping demand curve. If firm A lowers its prices below that of its rival, firm B, it does not instantly garner for itself all of B's customers. Customers may not know that firm A has lowered its prices; even if they do, they may not be sure that the product being sold by A, or the services it provides in conjunction with the product, are of the same quality as the product sold by B. Thus, imperfect information leads to imperfect competition.

In the labour market, a firm must spend considerable resources trying to screen various applicants, to find out which are best suited for the firm. Even then, it will not be perfectly successful. Some of the workers it hires will turn out to be unsuitable. Thus, in many jobs, hiring and training workers is extremely costly. Firms often find that by paying higher wages, they can get a larger and better-quality applicant pool from which to choose workers, and the workers they hire are less likely to quit.

Also, firms spend considerable energy in trying to motivate workers. They realize that low morale leads to low productivity. They may provide economic incentives for hard work: the carrot, higher pay or increased promotion possibilities with better performance, and the stick, the threat of being sacked for bad performance. The theory that by paying workers higher wages one can obtain a higher-quality labour force, one that works harder and quits less frequently, is called the **efficiency wage theory,** and will be discussed more extensively in Chapter 11.

Just as managers may have trouble getting workers to do what they want, owners of the firms may have trouble getting their managers to act in the interests of the owners. The owners would, of course, like the managers simply to maximize profits or the market value of the firm. Because the typical shareholder has her wealth spread out among many firms, she may not care much about the risks incurred by the firm. That is why she simply wants the firm to maximize its profit or market value; and profit-maximizing firms are one of the assumptions of the basic competitive model.

But the shareholders do not themselves make the decisions concerning what the firm does. They must rely on those who manage the firm, and the managers may not do what is in the interests of the shareholders; that is, they may not maximize profits or market value. For instance, a manager's welfare is closely tied with that of the firm. If the firm goes bankrupt, he has a good chance of being out of a job, and other firms may be reluctant to hire him; even if the firm does not go bankrupt, if it does badly, the manager's pay is likely to suffer. Therefore, managers may take too few risks. Another possibility is that they may use their position to enhance their life-style rather than the profits of the firm; they may use corporate jets not so much to improve productivity, but perhaps to fly around to vacation spots also owned by the firm.

There are, in fact, some checks on managerial discretion. A manager who does not take actions that maximize the value of the firm under her charge may find that her firm is threatened with a takeover. Or shareholders may revolt and elect a board that fires the management. But both of these checks provide only imperfect discipline.

Finally, information problems have a major effect on how capital markets work. Chapter 6 took up two ways that firms raise funds: by issuing bonds (or borrowing) and by issuing shares. Bonds are safer from the investors' point of view; they provide a guaranteed return, as long as the firm does not go bankrupt. Because they are safer, they normally pay a lower return.

From a firm's point of view, the issuing of shares has a distinct advantage: firms do not have a fixed obligation to pay. If a firm does badly, it simply pays out less to its shareholders. In effect, the risk is shared. There is no threat of bankruptcy. But in spite of this seeming advantage, firms make little use of equity as a source of new funds raised outside the firm. One of the reasons is that investors find themselves at a disadvantage with regard to information. The original owners of the firm know what they are giving up, and they would not sell shares if they did not think that those buying shares were paying enough—or too much. On the other hand, with bonds, investors have a better idea of what they will be getting.

CLOSE-UP: REFORMING HEALTH CARE

Canada spent about $2,700 per person on health care in 1991. This was about 20 percent more per person than Sweden spent; 35 percent more than Germany; 60 percent more than Japan; and a whopping 100 percent more than the United Kingdom. Only the United States spent more. Moreover, health care expenditures are the most rapidly growing component of government expenditures in Canada. In 1991, health care expenditures by governments in Canada (mainly provincial governments) were 1.5 times as high as they were five years earlier. They had grown from 12.3 percent of total government expenditures to 13.4 percent in just five years. The containment of health care expenditures has become one of the policy priorities of the decade.

Why have health costs increased so rapidly? Economists have offered several explanations, many of which focus on the incentives that exist in the system for using and financing health care, the absence of competitive pressures for economizing, and the role of imperfect information in the provision of health care.

Sick people do not usually act as cautious self-interested consumers, carefully shopping around for different medical care providers and balancing the marginal benefits of various treatments. Most people have incomplete information about what is wrong with them, what treatment might help, and what medical actions are really needed. Moreover, under our system of publicly provided health care, a patient has little reason to care about costs. Her attitude might be that if a trip to the doctor might help, it is worth a try. Unlike with the markets for other goods and services, prices are not used as a rationing device for consumers.

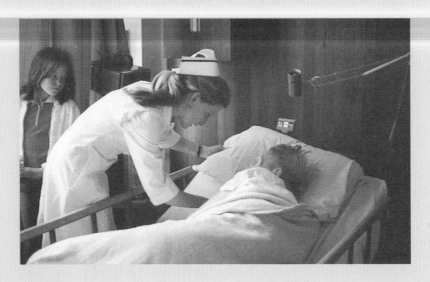

Uncertain information about what health care is truly necessary presents another problem, this one to do with health care professionals. Under our fee-for-service system, doctors are paid for the amount of care they provide, the number of tests they run, and the number of procedures they perform. When patients have both full insurance and incomplete information, they are unlikely to question whether another test or procedure is really necessary. Health care professionals are trained to look after a patient's health. So they face strong economic and professional pressures to try everything, rather than weighing costs of treatment with potential benefits.

If adverse incentives are the problem, it is natural to look for ways in which the system can be changed so as to correct them. Several suggestions have been made. One is simply to institute user fees on patients for the use of health services. Detractors argue that this may have little deterrent effect since it is really the doctor rather than the patient who determines how many services are used. As well, user fees will make health care less accessible to those least able to afford it. Another suggestion is to put doctors on salaries instead of being paid fees for each service performed. After all, other health care workers, such as nurses, are salaried, not to mention other public-sector professionals such as professors and judges. While this would reduce the incentive for doctors to overuse health services, it might also reduce their incentive to take on additional patients and to perform time-consuming procedures.

A more wide-ranging reform would involve changing not only the compensation scheme for doctors but also the organization through which doctors deliver their services. Today many doctors operate their own practices individually. The proposal is that groups of doctors would join together in health maintenance organizations (HMOs) and provide a wide range of medical services to their patients. Patients would be free to join the HMO of their choice, and the HMO would be obliged to accept all patients who selected it. The HMO would receive a specific sum of money per patient (referred to as a "capitation fee") and would be responsible for providing comprehensive health care to each patient. The HMO would pay the health care professionals in their own organization in a manner of their choice. This could be by salary or fee-for-service or some combination of the two.

The use of the HMO for delivering health care is intended to introduce into the system incentives for cost effectiveness as well as competitive pressures. Since patients would be free to shop around, HMOs would effectively compete with each other for patients and would be induced to offer the best mix of services they could. The fact that the payment per patient in the HMO is fixed implies that the HMO would have an incentive to economize on the use of health services. And, each HMO would have to compete for health care professionals, so each would be induced to offer a good working environment with adequate facilities.

The HMO concept is not without difficulties, however. Since the HMO would be obliged to provide services to all patients who choose to join it, there is obviously an advantage to attracting those patients who are less likely to have serious health problems. The HMO might try to do this by putting more effort into providing the sorts of services that attract the healthier elements of the population. It might be difficult for the government to preclude this "cream-skimming" through regulation.

These and other options will undoubtedly be considered as governments try to contain rising health costs.

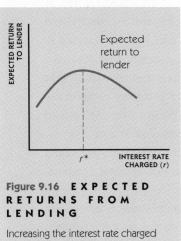

Figure 9.16 EXPECTED RETURNS FROM LENDING

Increasing the interest rate charged may actually lead to lower expected returns, as the best risks decide not to apply for loans and those who do borrow undertake riskier projects.

But while firms find it expensive, and sometimes impossible, to raise funds through equity, sometimes they find that they cannot borrow either. Normally, you might think that if, at the going interest rate, some potential borrower cannot obtain all the funds he wants, all he needs to do is offer to pay a higher interest rate. Lenders would prefer to receive the higher interest rate, and it would seem that no one is precluded from the market. But this does not seem to work, and for a simple reason. Lenders worry that if they charge a higher interest rate, their expected returns will actually decrease because the chance of default will increase. At higher interest rates, safer investors find that it does not pay to borrow. A disproportionate number of those willing to borrow at high rates are high-flyers—people who are undertaking high-risk projects that, if successful, will yield high returns, more than enough to cover the interest charge. But if the projects fail, they simply go bankrupt, and the lender is left "holding the bag."

Thus, the relationship between expected returns to the lender and the interest rate charged may look like the curve in Figure 9.16. In this case, there is an optimal interest rate, r^*, at which the bank's expected return is maximized. If at that interest rate the demand for funds exceeds the supply, lenders will not be willing to lend at a higher interest rate, because they know that their expected returns will actually be lower if they do so. In this situation, economists say there is **credit rationing.** Some borrowers are rationed in the amount of credit they can obtain. The capital market does not clear.

MISSING MARKETS

The basic competitive model assumes that there are competitive markets for all goods and services; the only reason a market for a good might not exist is if, at the minimum cost of producing it, demand is zero. In fact, many markets are missing; among the most important of these are the markets that would provide insurance against the various risks that households and firms face, as was noted in Chapter 6. As a result, government has stepped in to provide a variety of insurance programs, partly because, at least at the time the programs were initiated, the private sector did not.

Sometimes the reason that the private sector does not provide insurance (or that some other market is missing) is related to a problem of information. As Chapter 6 pointed out, those who are most likely to have an accident are most anxious to purchase insurance for the possibility. As the premium rises, there is a process of adverse selection: those least likely to need the insurance decide it is not worth purchasing. Hence, an increase in the price of insurance may not lead to increased profits.

TECHNOLOGICAL CHANGE

The basic competitive model proceeds under the assumption that every firm has a given technology, a given way of converting inputs into outputs. There is a given array of products that are produced. In fact, the development of new products and less expensive ways of producing old products is an essential part of modern industrial economies; the fact that modern economies do these things so well is often cited as one of their greatest virtues.

Because the basic competitive model ignores technological change, it cannot address fundamental issues: Why has productivity increased less rapidly in recent years? Why does productivity seem to increase faster in some countries than in others?

Moreover, in sectors of the economy in which technological change is important, there is a limited number of firms. Each faces a downward-sloping demand curve. It is a price maker, not a price taker. These are the characteristics of imperfect competition. Nevertheless, competition is keen—it involves the race to develop new products and better production methods, so that one company can undercut its rivals.

Government's interest in promoting technological progress often conflicts with its interest in promoting competition. If a firm is to be willing to spend its funds to do research and develop new products, it must be able to get a return from any inventions that are the fruit of that research. Governments therefore grant patents, giving an inventor the exclusive right to an invention for a period of twenty years. The losses from the reduction in competition for this limited period are thought to be outweighed by the gains from the spur to innovation that the patent provides.

Even with a good patent system, there may be insufficient spur to innovation. Firms seldom capture all the benefits that accrue from their inventive activity. Other firms see what they have done, learn from it, and use it as a basis for producing still better products. Customers benefit. Innovation in the computer industry has made faster and faster computers available at lower and lower prices. And in the long run, workers benefit as well, as the improved technology becomes reflected in higher wages. To use the term introduced in Chapter 7, there are *externalities* associated with innovation.

EXTERNALITIES

Whenever there are externalities, markets will not be efficient, since people will not take into account either all the benefits or all the costs of their actions. Externalities arise not only from innovations, or from pollution as discussed in Chapter 7, but in a variety of other circumstances. When a firm decides to undertake a riskier project, which increases the chance of bankruptcy, this action has consequences not only for the firm's shareholders and managers, but also for its bondholders, who may see the value of their bonds decrease. If the firm actually goes bankrupt, both its customers and suppliers may bear costs for which they are not fully compensated; customers may, for instance, find it expensive to switch to other products, which are not perfect substitutes.

ADJUSTMENTS

The basic competitive model focuses on the *equilibrium* of the economy, the state of the economy in which there are no forces for change, where the supply for each good equals the demand—that is, where all markets clear.

Of course, the economy is always changing. One year, the price of oil may rise as a war in the Middle East reduces the supply. Another year, exports may decline as foreign customers face an economic downturn. Technological progress in the Japanese car industry may have a direct and obvious impact on North American producers (and customers). There is a constant need for prices—including the price of labour (the wage) and the price of capital (the interest rate)—to change. Earlier we saw how what happens in one market can, and normally will, have repercussions in other markets.

Imagine that the economy is initially in an equilibrium and then is disturbed, say by a large increase in the price of imported oil. The task of finding the new equilibrium prices for the millions of other goods and services in the economy is an extraordinarily difficult one. The adjustments do not occur overnight; in some cases, they may take weeks, months, perhaps stretch out to years. Meanwhile, some markets may not be in equilibrium: demand may not equal supply (markets may not clear).

INCOME DISTRIBUTION

Even if all the conditions of the basic competitive model were satisfied, this would only mean that the economy was efficient. The resulting distribution of income might be totally unacceptable. Those with few skills might receive a wage that is below what they need to survive.

As was noted in Chapter 8, behind the macroeconomic objectives of stable prices, full employment, and high growth lie other concerns, including the distribution of income. To a large extent, the goals may be complementary. Reducing unemployment is of particular benefit to the poor, since lack of jobs is one of the main causes of poverty. Eliminating those market failures that give rise to unemployment will, at the same time, make the distribution of income more equitable.

While generally, high rates of growth are thought to benefit everyone, this presumption has come to be questioned. Many of the benefits of the long economic expansion that began in 1983 seem to have gone to those in the upper part of the income distribution. Real wages of the unskilled remain unchanged, or actually lower. This experience has convinced many that the government needs to take a more active stance, not only in preventing unemployment, but in ensuring that the fruits of growth will be shared by all.

THE BASIC MODEL COMPARED WITH THE REAL WORLD: A SUMMARY

If the real world matched up to the assumptions of the basic model of perfectly competitive markets, then markets could be given free rein. They would supply efficient outcomes. If an outcome seemed inequitable, society simply would redistribute initial wealth and let markets take care of the rest.

In the two centuries since Adam Smith first enunciated the view that markets ensure economic efficiency, economists have investigated the model with great care. Nothing they have discovered has shaken their belief that markets are, by and large, the most efficient way to coordinate an economy. However, they have found significant departures between modern economies and the competitive model. Few would go so far as to condemn the model totally for its flaws; its insights are simply too powerful. Rather, most economists use the basic competitive model as the starting point for building a richer, more complete model that recognizes the following qualifications.

1. Most markets are not as competitive as those envisioned by the basic model.

2. The basic model simply ignores technological change. It tells us about the striving for efficiency that occurs as consumers and firms meet in competitive markets, but it

assumes that all firms operate with a given technology. Competition in the basic model is over price, yet in the real world, the primary focus of competition is the development of new and better products and the improvements in production, transportation, and marketing that allow products to be brought to customers at lower costs and thus at a lower price. This competition takes place not between the multitude of small producers envisaged in the basic competitive model, but often between industrial giants like Du Pont and Dow Chemical, and between the industrial giants and upstarts, like IBM and a slew of small computer firms that eventually took away a major share of the computer market. Changes in technology lie behind economic growth, one of the principal concerns of macroeconomics.

3. The individuals and firms envisioned in the basic model have easy and inexpensive access to the information they need in order to operate in any market they enter. Buyers know what they are buying, whether it is stocks or bonds, a house, a car, or a refrigerator. Firms know perfectly the productivity of each worker they hire, and when a worker goes to work for a firm, he knows precisely what is expected of him in return for his promised pay.

We have already encountered, in Chapter 6, instances in which information problems are important and may fundamentally affect how markets work. In the following chapters we will see other instances in which imperfect information and the other market imperfections to which imperfect information gives rise help to explain a variety of macroeconomic phenomena. We will see, for instance, in Chapter 11 how lack of information about the quality of people applying for jobs may make firms worry that if they lower the wages they pay, they will obtain a lower-quality work force. In Chapter 16, we will see that lack of information about the consequences of changing prices may result in prices being rigid, which partly explains the slow adjustment of the economy to equilibrium.

4. The basic model assumes that the costs of bringing a good to the market accrue fully and completely to the seller, and that the benefits of consuming a good go fully and completely to the buyer. In Chapter 7, however, we encountered the possibility of externalities, which are extra costs or benefits that do not figure in the market calculation.

5. The basic model answers the question "What goods will be produced, and in what quantities?" by assuming that all desired goods that *can* be brought to market *will* be brought to market. Trees that bloom in gold coins and tablets that guarantee an eternal youth are out of the question. But if customers want to buy green hair colouring, cancer-causing tobacco products, or life insurance policies overladen with extras, then producers can be expected to supply such goods. There are, however, some products consumers would like to buy but cannot that are so similar to existing products that we can expect they *could* be supplied. The most obvious examples are in insurance and capital markets.

Imperfections in the capital market—the inability to obtain funds—play, as we will see, an important role in economic fluctuations. When firms cannot obtain funds to produce or to invest, production, investment, and employment all suffer. And, as in the recession that began in 1990, firms often attribute cutbacks in production and investment to an inability to obtain funds.

6. In the basic model, all markets hover at or near equilibrium. That is, they clear: supply meets demand at the market price. Decades of evidence, however, suggest that labour markets often do not clear. Workers sometimes want to supply their labour services at the market wage, but cannot do so. The Great Depression of the 1930s is the

most dramatic example of large-scale unemployment. During that period, unemployment rates rose to nearly 20 percent of those willing and able to work.

7. Even if markets are efficient, the way they allocate resources may appear to be socially unacceptable; there may be massive pockets of poverty, or other social needs may remain unmet. Income distribution is a major concern of modern societies and their governments.

REVIEW AND PRACTICE

SUMMARY

1. An increase in the price of a good reduces a person's demand for that good both because of the income effect—the higher price makes the individual worse off, and because she is worse off, she reduces her consumption—and because of the substitution effect—the good is now more expensive *relative* to other goods, so she substitutes other goods.

2. An increase in the interest rate has an ambiguous effect on savings and current consumption. The income effect leads to more current consumption (reduced savings), but the substitution effects leads to less current consumption. The net effect on savings is probably slightly positive.

3. An increase in the wage rate has an ambiguous effect on labour supply. Individuals are better off, and so the income effect leads to more leisure (less work). But the substitution effect—the increased consumption from working an additional hour—leads to more work. In practice, the two effects probably just offset each other.

4. The typical firm has a U-shaped average cost curve. It produces at the level where price equals marginal cost, so long as price equals or exceeds average costs. The market supply curve is found by adding the supply curves of each of the firms in an industry. The typical shape is relatively horizontal when output is very low, but close to vertical as capacity is reached.

5. General equilibrium analysis stresses that all markets are interrelated. Equilibrium occurs when demand equals supply for every good and service and every input; the labour, capital, and product markets clear.

6. The circular flow diagram shows the flow of funds among the various parts of the economy.

7. There are some important limitations to the basic competitive model, which explain why sometimes markets fail to produce efficient outcomes. Among these are imperfections of competition, imperfections of information, missing markets, and externalities. Competitive markets may also spend too little on developing new technologies, may be slow in adjusting to new situations, and may fail to distribute income in an egalitarian way.

KEY TERMS

substitution effect	marginal revenue	monopolistic
real income	average costs	competition
income effect	fixed or overhead costs	product differentiation
expected return	variable costs	imperfect information
liquidity	circular flow	efficiency wage theory
real wage	monopoly	credit rationing
marginal cost	oligopoly	

REVIEW QUESTIONS

1. Use the concepts of income and substitution effects to explain why demand curves for goods are normally downward sloping. Why may increases in the interest rate not lead to much more saving? Why may increases in the wage rate not lead to a much greater amount of work done?

2. Why may the price of one good lead to a shift in the demand curve for some goods to the left, and a shift in the demand curve for other goods to the right?

3. What are some of the important factors individuals take into account in deciding how to invest their savings?

4. Why are average cost curves often U-shaped?

5. How is the level of output of a firm determined? What is the effect of an increase in wages on the market supply curve?

6. Why is the demand curve for labour by firms downward sloping?

7. Why may what happens in one market have effects on other markets? Illustrate with an example.

8. What is a circular flow diagram, and what do we learn from it?

9. How is output determined in a monopoly? What are some forms that imperfect competition takes?

10. What are the most important reasons that competitive markets may not yield efficient outcomes?

PROBLEMS

1. Assume Alfred has $10,000, which he can either consume today or save and consume next year. If the interest rate is 10 percent, how much can he consume next year if he consumes nothing now? Draw a budget constraint, with "Consumption today" on the horizontal axis and "Consumption next year" on the vertical. Show

how the budget constraint shifts if the interest rate increases to 20 percent. Use the budget constraint diagram to discuss the income and substitution effects of the increase in the interest rate.

2. Assume now that Alfred has no income this year, but next year will come into an inheritance of $11,000. The bank is willing to lend money to Alfred at a 10 percent interest rate. Draw his budget constraint. Show how the budget constraint shifts if the interest rate the bank charges increases to 20 percent. Why can you be certain that as a result of the higher interest rate, his consumption this year will go down? (Hint: Explain why the income and substitution effects now both work in the same direction.)

3. If Alfred saves an extra dollar today and invests it at 7 percent interest, how much extra consumption can he have in thirty years' time?

4. Draw Alfred's budget constraint between leisure and consumption, assuming he can work 2,000 hours a year and his wage is $10 an hour. Show how his budget constraint changes if his wage increases to $15 an hour. Use the diagram to discuss income and substitution effects.

5. Use demand and supply diagrams for the labour, product, and capital markets to trace out the effects of immigrant workers. Look first at the labour market—what does the increase in the supply of labour do to the equilibrium wage? Explain how the resulting lower wage will shift the demand and supply curves for goods and for capital. Describe how these changes in prices and interest rates will affect the demand and supply curves for labour.

6. Use the extended circular flow diagram, with the foreign sector included, to trace out the possible consequences of the following:
   (a) a law requiring that businesses raise the wages of their employees;
   (b) a decision by consumers to import more and save less;
   (c) an increase in government expenditure financed by a corporate income tax;
   (d) an increase in government expenditure without an accompanying increase in taxes.

7. For each of the programs listed below, discuss what market failures might be given as reasons for implementing the program:
   (a) automobile safety belt requirements;
   (b) regulations on automobile pollution;
   (c) unemployment insurance;
   (d) Medicare (free health care);
   (e) workers compensation (insurance for workers injured on the job);
   (f) federal deposit insurance;
   (g) federally insured mortgages;
   (h) law requiring lenders to disclose the true rate of interest they are charging on loans (truth-in-lending law);
   (i) National Meteorological Service;
   (j) urban renewal.

AN OVERVIEW OF MACROECONOMICS

C hapter 8 described the measures we use for the principal aggregate variables that make up the economy. The challenge of macroeconomics is to explain the movement of these aggregate variables.

In many ways, the explanations lie in the microeconomic principles presented in Chapter 9. If we want to know about output, we certainly want to think about the household's consumption decision and the firm's production decision. Growth rates are connected to the household's savings decision and the firm's investment decision. Explanations of unemployment necessarily involve the household's labour supply decision, and the firm's demand for labour. Inflation is a change in prices, and therefore we want to think about how prices are determined, using the demand and supply analysis presented as far back as Chapter 4.

To a great extent, then, macroeconomics sifts through what we know of microeconomics for its answers. The building blocks are the same, but our perspective will change. The differences between micro- and macroeconomics are striking enough that this chapter is devoted simply to introducing the main analytic issues of the latter. It begins with a brief synopsis of the major schools of macroeconomics. Then it turns to the three major aggregate markets—labour, product, and capital—for an initial look at the issues that will occupy us in the chapters to come.

KEY QUESTIONS

1. How do economists analyze what determines levels of aggregate output, employment, and inflation?

2. What causes shifts in the aggregate demand and supply for labour? Why may unemployment result if wages fail to adjust in response to these shifts?

3. What are the typical shapes of the aggregate demand and supply curves in the product market? What are the consequences of shifts in the aggregate demand and supply curves for output and the price level?

4. What is the effect of an increase in investment on the aggregate demand and supply curves?

5. How can we use the aggregate demand and supply curves to interpret some of the major macroeconomic episodes of the past fifty years?

THE ROOTS OF CONTEMPORARY MACROECONOMICS

Modern macroeconomics traces its origin to that cataclysmic event the Great Depression, which, in Canada, amounted to almost a decade of massive unemployment and underutilization of resources. The dominant group of economists before the Great Depression, referred to as **classical economists,** recognized that the economy might have short periods of unemployment, but believed that market forces would quickly restore the economy to full employment. They believed that the basic competitive model presented in Part One by and large provided a good description of the economy: prices and wages were sufficiently flexible that the product and labour markets were in equilibrium (that is, supply equalled demand) most of the time. The policy prescription of the classical economists was summed up by the phrase *laissez-faire*, French for "let it be." Government intervention was to be avoided; market forces would do the job of guiding the economy.

THE GREAT DEPRESSION: KEYNES

The depth and length of the Great Depression shattered confidence in this view. The British economist John Maynard Keynes launched the modern subdiscipline of macroeconomics with his 1936 book *The General Theory of Employment, Interest, and Money,* in which he explained why the economy could get stuck in a situation where it suffered extended periods of output loss and unemployment. He argued in particular that the labour market might be out of equilibrium for long periods of time—that the supply of labour might exceed the demand, with unemployment as the result. Keynes further maintained that the government should use **fiscal policies,** policies that affect the level of government expenditures and taxes, to bring the economy out of an economic downturn. Keynes was one of the most influential thinkers of the twentieth century, and his work has blossomed into a number of schools of thought that all share the name Keynesian. These schools have in common a belief that the economy may, for a variety of reasons, have unemployed labour and underutilized resources for extended periods of time, and that in these circumstances government action can alleviate the economy's ills.

While World War II brought an economic boom, the aftermath of the war provided an opportunity to test some of Keynes' ideas. Historically, most wars had been followed by economic downturns, as government war expenditures decreased. But by cutting taxes rapidly and stimulating the economy in other ways, the government succeeded in averting a major recession immediately after the war. In the next twenty years, Keynesian theory was applied with greater and greater confidence to help the economy recover. Successive governments in the 1960s and 1970s typically assumed contractionary or (more often) expansionary fiscal policies—raising taxes and cutting expenditures, or vice versa—depending on whether the economy was strong or weak. The year 1963 was regarded by some to be the high-water mark of Keynesian economics: In the United States, President Kennedy, openly espousing Keynesian economics, cut taxes to stimulate the economy. Shortly thereafter, the Canadian government followed suit. With more money in their pockets, people would spend more, and the increased spending, it was hoped, would refuel the economy. Indeed, the predictions of Keynesian economics were borne out.

In the 1950s and 1960s, for the most part periods of high employment and stable prices, attention among macroeconomists shifted to economic growth. The basic theories of growth that we will learn in Chapter 21 were first developed then.

THE 1970S AND 1980S: MONETARIST, NEW CLASSICAL, AND REAL BUSINESS-CYCLE SCHOOLS

In the 1970s, inflation reached double-digit levels, and the economy was faced with a new experience: high inflation accompanied by high unemployment. Out of this experience developed three new schools of thought, all of which held that government intervention was unnecessary and/or undesirable. All three represented modern adaptations of theories that had been prevalent in the years before Keynes and the Great Depression.

The first school tried to explain the causes of inflation by focusing on the government's **monetary policies.** These are the policies that affect the supply of money and credit and the terms on which credit is available to borrowers. Nobel laureate Milton Friedman, then of the University of Chicago, revised and expanded on earlier theories of money, and the modern **monetarist** school of macroeconomics was born.

Keynes had argued that in deep recessions monetary policy was ineffective, but that fiscal policy would stimulate the economy. The monetarists did not deny that fiscal policy could affect the economy, but they argued that the government was more often the problem than the solution; through mistaken monetary and fiscal policies, the government could be the cause of the economy's downturns. Monetarists believed that markets, if left to themselves, had strong forces that ensured that resources would not long be left idle; they favoured sharply restricted limits on fiscal and monetary policy.

While monetarists emphasized the central role of money, they did not have a clearly articulated view of how money affected the economy. Providing such an explanation was a major accomplishment of the **new classical economists,** led by Robert Lucas of the University of Chicago; they were called new classical economists because of the similarity of their views to the old, pre-Keynesian classical economists, who had argued that competitive markets would quickly restore the economy to full employment. In the new classical view, the Great Depression was an aberration. From their 1970s perspective, they pointed out that it had been decades since the economy had experienced a major recession. The new classical economists not only provided a theory of why monetary policy sometimes had major impacts on the economy in the short run, they also explained why the responses of firms and households to government actions—to both fiscal and monetary policies—offset those impacts, with the result that government policy was often ineffective.

By the 1980s, a third school of thought, called the **real business-cycle theory,** had taken the new classical viewpoint even further. Real business-cycle theorists contended that in fact the economy's fluctuations had nothing to do with monetary policy. Money did not matter at all. The state of the economy was determined only by *real* forces—new inventions, droughts, and so on. It was these real shocks to the economy that gave rise to fluctuations.

To real business-cycle theorists, the fact that monetary policy was ineffective was not a problem; they believed even more strongly than the new classical economists that the economy naturally operates at full employment, without any necessity of government intervention. Changes in public financial policy—for instance, raising revenues by taxing as opposed to borrowing—have no real effect. What matters are *real* actions, but even the impact of real actions may be limited. For example, if the government spends more on defence, resources are diverted from other uses. Since the economy is always operating at full employment, decisions concerning government expenditures do not have an effect on unemployment; they only change the composition of output.

THE 1980s: NEW GROWTH AND NEW KEYNESIAN SCHOOLS

Also in the 1980s, North American economists turned once again to growth. The reasons were clear. In the 1970s, the standard of living of the average Canadian or American had risen little if at all. Traditional resource-based sectors, such as mining, agriculture, and fishing, faced weak international markets, and the manufacturing sector that had been the major source of job creation in recent decades saw itself losing in the competition against foreign competitors. Economists sought to understand better the basic forces that led the economy to grow rapidly at one time and slowly at another, or that led some economies to grow faster than others. The result was two additional schools of thought. One of these was the **new growth school,** which built upon the foundations

CLOSE-UP: THE BIRTH OF THE MICRO-MACRO SPLIT

From Adam Smith's time until the 1930s, much of economics focused on what would today be called microeconomics. Economics was about trade and exchange, about rational, well-informed consumers and profit-maximizing firms, about monopoly and new technology. Attention was focused on how different markets worked. But that changed in the 1930s, as the global economy suffered the collapse that became known as the Great Depression. In Canada, the economy shrank 43 percent from 1929 to 1933; the unemployment rate hit almost 20 percent in 1933. Unemployment was still above 11 percent in 1939, before the start of World War II. Attention shifted to what determined aggregate variables like the unemployment rate and GDP.

Today even noneconomists have heard the terms "microeconomics" and "macroeconomics." But economists did not actually begin thinking in those terms until the wrecked economy of the 1930s. In 1933, the famous Norwegian economist Ragnar Frisch clearly had the modern conception of these terms in mind when he wrote: "The micro-dynamic analysis is an analysis by which we try to explain in some detail the behaviour of a certain section of the huge economic mechanism, taking for granted that certain general parameters are given. . . . The macro-dynamic analysis, on the other hand, tries to give an account of the whole economic system taken in its entirety."

John Maynard Keynes also expressed the general idea when he wrote in 1936: "The division of

Economics . . . is, I suggest, between the Theory of the Individual Industry or Firm and of the rewards and the distribution of a given quantity of resources on the one hand, and the Theory of Output and Employment *as a whole* on the other hand."

But neither of these eminent economists actually used the words "microeconomic" and "macroeconomic." The first known written use of the specific terms is by P. de Wolff, a little-known economist at the Netherlands Statistical Institute. In a 1941 article, de Wolff wrote: "The micro-economic interpretation refers to the relation . . . for a single person or family. The macro-economic interpretation is derived from the corresponding relation . . . *for a large group of persons or families (social strata, nations, etc.)*."

In the 1960s and 1970s, many economists became concerned that macroeconomic thinking had strayed too far from its microeconomic roots. Interestingly, some of the most important economic work of the last twenty years—which will be described in the following chapters—has sought to break down that wall and explain how rational, well-informed consumers and profit-maximizing firms can combine in a way that sometimes creates unemployment, inflation, or fluctuations in growth.

Source: Hal R. Varian, "Microeconomics," in Eatwell, Milgate, and Newman, eds., *The New Palgrave: A Dictionary of Economics* (1987) 3:461–63.

of neo-classical growth theory studied a quarter of a century earlier. As with the previous theory, the importance of the rate of savings and investment for growth was emphasized. In both of these, Canada and the United States lagged behind the most rapidly growing economies. In addition, the new growth theories incorporated more recent advances in economic theory, such as the ideas of imperfect competition and technological change, and recognized the importance of international trade and investment.

As in other areas of economics, a controversy developed over the role of government intervention. Noninterventionists saw government expenditures and deficit financing as diverting resources away from the economy's natural tendency towards high growth. Others argued that there were several reasons why government intervention might help the economy. For instance, high-technology firms produced benefits that emanated well beyond those doing the innovating; interventionists believed that government should support similar efforts on the grounds that the benefits were public goods, which would be undersupplied in the absence of such support. Selective and effective government intervention had also played a crucial role in the Asian miracle, the rapid growth experienced by Japan, Korea, Taiwan, and other East Asian economies.

Economic events also turned economists' attention in the 1980s back to unemployment. In the early part of the decade, the Canadian economy experienced the most significant recession since the Great Depression. Some areas of the country seemed economically devastated, with plants shutting down and unemployment rates reaching double digits. Matters were worse elsewhere—in some European countries, as many as one out of five workers could not find a job. And while unemployment decreased slowly in Canada during the remainder of the decade, in several European countries, it persisted. This persistent unemployment again focused economists' attention on disequilibrium, in particular on the possibility that the labour market might have been far out of equilibrium, with wages such that supply greatly exceeded demand. Economists sought explanations for the failure of wages and prices to adjust. Because many of the explanations bore a close affinity to the earlier ideas of Keynes, the new theories were referred to as **new Keynesian.**

The leading schools of macroeconomics today are the new Keynesian and new classical schools. They share one basic premise: unlike their predecessors, both new Keynesian and new classical economists insist on relating macroeconomics to microeconomic principles. Both groups believe an understanding of aggregate behaviour must rest on an analysis of firms, households, and government interacting in the labour, product, and capital markets.

A WORD ABOUT MACROECONOMIC MODELS

This and the next two parts of this book take up the various theories that economists have used to understand the macroeconomy and to devise policies that will improve the economy's performance. As was emphasized in Chapter 2, economists use different models for different purposes, and so it is not surprising that the models most suited for studying, say, an economy whose resources are fully employed and that faces a problem of inflation might differ substantially from models appropriate for studying an economy in the depth of a depression, with no inflation and 15 or 20 percent of its labour force unemployed.

Part One developed a picture of the economy as consisting of three groups of economic agents—households, firms, and government—interacting in three markets. In the labour market, these groups determine levels of employment and the price of labour (the wage). In the product market, they determine output and the price of goods. In the capital market, they determine the availability of funds and their price (the interest rate).

In the basic competitive model, markets always clear. Since there is never any unemployment, if we want to understand unemployment, we will have to make some important changes in the model. Similarly, in the basic model, any firm can sell as much of any good as it wants at the going market price. It never faces a shortage of demand. And any individual can borrow as much as he wants at the going interest rate. But real economies often do not seem to accord well with these features of the basic competitive model, and to understand why we will need to go beyond the basic model.

Macroeconomists want to know, among other things, why the economy fluctuates as much as it does, why some economies grow faster than others, and what causes inflation. These questions also take us beyond the basic competitive model. Even if we believed all of the model's assumptions, we would need to extend and refine it in order to understand these essential macroeconomic questions.

In our study of macroeconomics, we will employ two simplifications. First, we will not (at least initially) try to understand the three major markets simultaneously. In studying unemployment, it is natural to focus on the labour market and the interaction of the demand and supply for labour; Chapter 11 does this. In studying what makes output fluctuate, it is natural to concentrate on the product market, and Chapters 12–16 do this. In studying inflation, it is natural to focus attention on money, credit, and, more broadly, capital markets. This is the aim of Chapters 17–20. Yet, all three markets are interrelated. The demand for and supply of goods affect the labour market, and in particular the demand for workers. The interest rate affects both the product and labour markets. But the world is too complicated to study all of the pieces simultaneously, and that is why we will study only one market at a time. In Part Four, however, which takes up a variety of policy issues, we will explicitly take into account the interactions among the markets.

As we focus on each of the markets, a second simplification will come into play. In focusing on the labour market, for instance, it is natural to ask how wages are determined. As a simplifying assumption, we take the price level as given. In focusing on the product market, it is natural to ask how prices are determined; there, we take wages as given. Are these models—one allowing wages to fluctuate while prices are fixed and the other doing the reverse—inconsistent? Not really. A more complete model would, of course, look at all markets simultaneously, paying careful attention to how changes in one market affect what is going on in the other markets. Such an analysis would take us beyond this elementary course, but the principles derived from our simple model remain valid in these more general models.

We begin our analysis by reviewing the functioning of the labour, product, and capital markets from an aggregate perspective, in order to see how the interaction of demand and supply in these three markets provides insights into the basic macroeconomic issues.

THE LABOUR MARKET

The aggregate labour market includes all the workers in the economy. Macroeconomic analysis usually begins by looking at such figures as total employment or total number of hours worked in the economy, ignoring the fact that there are important differences among skills of different workers. If we were interested in studying other questions, such as the relative wages received by different workers, we would want to use a model that treated skilled and unskilled labourers as operating in separate (but related) markets. Sometimes, even in macroeconomics, we may want to use models that focus on this distinction. If unemployment were concentrated among unskilled workers, for instance, the "problem" with the economy might be not with the labour market as a whole, but with one part of it, the market for unskilled labour.

EQUILIBRIUM IN THE LABOUR MARKET

For now, we focus our attention on the aggregate market for labour, ignoring the differences among workers. Figure 10.1 shows the demand and supply curves for labour. The aggregate demand for labour depends on the wages firms must pay, the prices firms receive for the goods they produce, and the prices they have to pay for other inputs, including raw materials and machines. We assume for simplicity that the prices of all goods—both the goods that are produced and the other inputs of production—are fixed. With fixed prices, a change in nominal (or dollar) wages is equivalent to a change in *real* wages (wages divided by the price level).

As wages fall, the demand for labour increases for two reasons. First, as wages fall relative to the cost of machines, it pays firms to substitute workers for machines. Second, as the wage falls, labour becomes relatively less expensive compared with the price of the goods it produces, and again employers will want to hire more workers. Thus, the demand curve for labour slopes down, as shown in the diagram.

The figure also shows an aggregate labour supply curve. To simplify matters, we assume that labour supply is inelastic; that is, individuals are either in the labour force, working a full (forty-hour) work week, or they are not.[1] They do not enter and exit the market as wages go up and down, nor do they reduce or increase the hours they work in response to such changes. One advantage of making this assumption is that we can put

[1] Recall the definition of elasticity from Chapter 5: the percentage change in quantity divided by the percentage change in price. Thus, an inelastic labour supply means that a 1 percent increase in price results in a small percentage increase in supply. A perfectly inelastic labour supply curve is vertical; that means the labour supply does not change at all when wages increase.

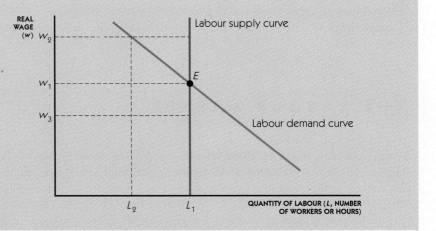

Figure 10.1 THE EFFECTS OF A SHIFT IN THE DEMAND FOR LABOUR

Equilibrium in the labour market is at the intersection of the aggregate demand and supply curves for labour. If the wage is above w_1, where demand equals supply, there will be unemployment, putting pressure on wages to fall as workers compete to offer their services. Below w_1, there will be excess demand for labour, which will put pressure on wages to rise.

either the number of hours worked or the number of workers hired on the horizontal axis of the figure. The demand and supply of labour hours is simply forty times the demand and supply of workers.

Basic supply and demand analysis implies that market equilibrium should occur at the intersection of the demand and supply curves, point E. The reason for this is simple: if the wage happens to be above the equilibrium wage w_1, say at w_2, the demand for labour will be L_2, much less than the supply, L_1. There will be an excess supply of workers. Those without jobs will offer to work for less than the going wage, bidding down the wages of those already working. The process of competition will lead to lower wages, and eventually demand will again equal supply. Likewise, if the wage is lower than w_1, say at w_3, firms in the economy will demand more labour than is supplied. Competing with one another for scarce labour services, they will bid the wage up to w_1.

This is the simple story of the aggregate labour market according to the basic competitive model. New classical economists believe that most of the fluctuations in employment can be explained by a slight variant of such a model, where the labour supply curve is upward sloping and shifts in the demand curve for labour (or the supply curve of labour) will generally result in changes in the equilibrium level of employment. New Keynesians, however, believe that the model has one critical flaw: it does not allow for the kind of persistent unemployment associated with recessions.

ELASTIC LABOUR SUPPLY AND VOLUNTARY UNEMPLOYMENT

The preceding analysis assumed that the supply of workers was inelastic, fixed. It is more realistic to think that as wages rise, the number of people who are willing to work increases. This is a particularly likely possibility for married couples, who may decide that at low enough wages it does not pay for both spouses to work. (Indeed, female labour force participation is quite sensitive to the wage.) Figure 10.2 shows that as wages increase, so do the number of individuals who want to work. The labour supply curve is

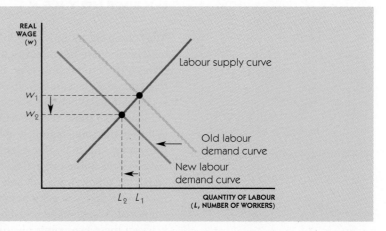

Figure 10.2 THE EFFECTS OF A SHIFT IN THE DEMAND FOR LABOUR: ELASTIC LABOUR SUPPLY

If the supply curve for labour is relatively elastic, then a leftward shift in the demand curve for labour results in a decrease in employment to L_2 and, if wages are flexible, a decrease in real wages to w_2. But so long as wages are sufficiently flexible that they fall to the point where the demand for labour equals the supply, there is no unemployment. Everyone who wishes to work at the (now lower) going wage can get a job.

somewhat elastic (rather than perfectly inelastic, as it was in Figure 10.1). The analysis is little changed: equilibrium in the labour market is still at the intersection of the demand and supply curves.

With workers entering and exiting the market, we have **voluntary unemployment.** That is, if the wage falls, people will drop out of the labour force; they will not be working—they will be unemployed—by choice. Individuals who *choose* not to work are not included in the unemployment statistics. When economists talk about the "unemployed," they do not mean those who have dropped out of the labour force. To economists, if every worker willing to work at the market wage can find a full-time job, there is full employment.

(This seems simple enough in theory. But in practice, as we saw in Chapter 8, matters are more complicated. There is always some frictional unemployment, as workers move from one job to another. Hence, economists say there is full employment even when there are some workers still looking for a job—the "normal" number of people in the process of making a transition. Economists disagree about what that normal number is and about whether the government can do anything to reduce it significantly. For the remainder of this chapter, we ignore these subtleties and simply assume that full employment means what it says, that everyone who wants a job can get one.)

Consider a shift in the demand curve for labour, depicted in Figure 10.2. As a result of the shift, there is a new equilibrium level of employment in the labour market, L_2. We say that even though employment has fallen from L_1 to L_2, there is still full employment. This is because all labour that is available on the market is purchased. The market clears. *By definition*, when the market clears, there is full employment.

When the labour supply curve is not vertical, as in the figure, there is not a single "full employment" level. At the wage w_1, the economy is fully employed when L_1 workers have jobs; at the wage w_2, the economy is fully employed when the smaller number of workers L_2 have jobs. Though the competitive model assumes that wages will be set so that the demand for labour equals the supply, so there is no unemployment, the level of actual *employment* might be quite low. Wages might be so low that many people are unwilling to accept jobs.

WAGE RIGIDITIES AND INVOLUNTARY UNEMPLOYMENT

Most observers are unwilling to accept the possibility that all unemployment is voluntary. Involuntary unemployment occurs when people willing and able to work at the going wage cannot find jobs. Economic explanations of involuntary unemployment focus on wages that are slow to adjust downwards in response to a change in labour market conditions. When this happens, wages are said to be **sticky** downwards.

Figure 10.3 shows the effect of sticky wages. The demand curve for labour has shifted to the left; for some reason, employers now demand less labour at every given wage rate. If the wage falls to w_2, the economy will remain fully employed at L_2. However, if the wage is stuck at the original level, w_1, above the wage at which the demand for labour equals the supply, firms will only hire the amount demanded. More workers will be willing to work than can get jobs at that wage. Those without jobs will be involuntarily unemployed. The demand for labour will only be L_3, while the supply is L_1. The distance between these two points measures the amount of involuntary unemployment. At this high wage, the supply of labour exceeds the demand.

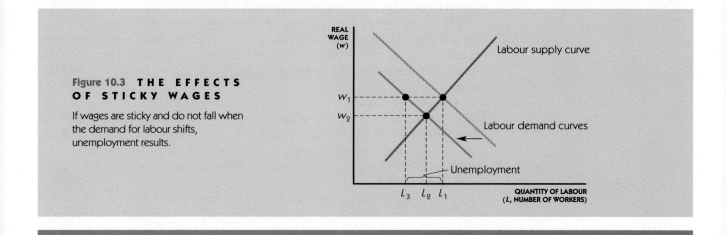

Figure 10.3 THE EFFECTS OF STICKY WAGES

If wages are sticky and do not fall when the demand for labour shifts, unemployment results.

Involuntary unemployment arising from reductions in the demand for labour (combined with wage stickiness) would be much less of a social problem if the impact could be spread over the entire population. Even if the demand for labour were reduced by 10 percent and wages did not fall, the consequences would be limited if each worker worked 10 percent fewer hours. The problem in that case would be **underemployment:** each person in the economy might work only 36 hours per week, when she wished to work 40 hours.

In the modern industrial economy, the problem is different. Most workers continue to work the same, or only a slightly reduced, number of hours when the labour market goes out of equilibrium, but an unfortunate few will find no full-time job at all at the going wage. This is the problem of unemployment. Whenever the supply of labour exceeds the demand at the going wage, there will be "rationing"—some individuals will not be able to sell all the labour they would like. But the impact of this rationing is not evenly spread in the economy; some workers will manage to sell little if any of their labour services, while others will be fully employed. Many of the social problems associated with a reduced demand for labour result from the fact that the economic burden is so concentrated.

SHIFTS IN THE LABOUR DEMAND CURVE, WAGE RIGIDITIES, AND UNEMPLOYMENT

Most economists believe that the labour supply curve, while not perfectly inelastic (or vertical), is relatively inelastic: the supply of labour is relatively unresponsive to wage changes, and the supply curve is *more* like the vertical line in Figure 10.1 than the slanted one in Figure 10.2.

If we look at data on real wages—the wage divided by the price level (the average level of prices of a basket of goods)—we see that wages vary little with economic conditions. Even in the Great Depression, with massive unemployment, they did not fall, or at least did not fall very much. Given the relatively small changes in real wages, the magnitude of the changes in employment that are observed in the economy are greater than can be explained by movements along a fixed, steep labour supply curve. How can we account for such large changes in employment?

There are but two possibilities: either the labour supply curve shifts dramatically or, at least at times, the labour market is not in equilibrium. Because most economists also do not believe that there are sudden dramatic shifts in the labour supply curve, they have focused their attention on the second possibility, that the labour market is not in equilibrium.

Disequilibrium in this case comes about in two steps: a shift in the demand curve for labour, and a failure of wages to adjust. In Figure 10.3, when the demand curve for labour shifts to the left and the wage remains at w_1, firms will employ L_3 units of labour, while workers are still willing to supply L_1. Sticky wages keep the labour market out of equilibrium. At these high wages, the supply of labour exceeds the demand. Workers are involuntarily unemployed.

Most economists believe that a decrease in the demand for labour at each level of wages (a shift in the demand curve for labour) with no corresponding decrease in wages is the primary explanation for an increase in unemployment. This, in turn, focuses attention on two questions: Why do wages not fall? And why would the demand curve for labour shift so suddenly in the first place? Chapter 11 takes up the first question. As for the second, the primary reason for such a shift is a fall in the production of goods by firms, as a result of a decrease in the demand for their products. There is a connection between output levels (as measured, say, by GDP) and the unemployment rate. When output goes up, employment tends to go up as well, and vice versa. Chapters 12–14 will analyze why output might be so variable.

SHIFTS IN THE LABOUR SUPPLY CURVE AND UNEMPLOYMENT

The primary explanation for short-run increases in unemployment is that there is a shift in the demand curve for labour. But there is another possible reason: the supply curve for labour could move to the right, as shown in Figure 10.4, so that more people are

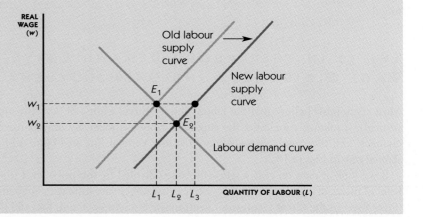

Figure 10.4 A SUPPLY SHIFT IN AGGREGATE LABOUR MARKETS

If the aggregate supply of labour shifts out, and wages change, the new equilibrium (E_2) will be at the lower wage w_2 and higher quantity L_2, and no unemployment will exist. If wages do not change, then demand for labour will not change; L_3 will be the new quantity of labour supplied at the original wage w_1, and there will be unemployed people willing to work at the prevailing wage who cannot find jobs.

willing to work at every given wage rate. Though such shifts in the labour supply curve are unlikely to be important in the short run in explaining recessions, over a period of many years they can play and have played an important role. For example, the birthrate in Canada soared in the years after World War II. Some twenty years later, the number of baby boomers was reflected in an outward shift in the labour supply curve. At the same time, the fraction of women working in the labour force increased, also contributing to the rightward shift in the labour supply curve.

A shift in the labour supply curve, unaccompanied by a change in the demand for labour, results in no unemployment if wages adjust enough. In Figure 10.4, if wages fall to w_2, then everyone wanting to work at that wage will be able to do so and employment will rise to L_2. But if real wages fail to fall, the additional labour supply will be unable to find jobs at the going wage w_1, and unemployment of $L_3 - L_1$ will result.

Although the Canadian economy was able to create an enormous number of new jobs in the 1960s and 1970s, more than had been created in any comparable period, the increase in new jobs was not as great as the increased number of job seekers. There were shifts in the labour demand and supply curves like those shown in Figure 10.5; both shifted to the right, but labour supply shifted more than labour demand.[2] If wages had not changed at all but had remained at w_1, unemployment would have been very large. In fact, wages fell, but not enough. There was considerable unemployment, though not as much as there would have been if wages had remained perfectly rigid. Because wages fell and because the demand for labour increased, employment increased. But so did unemployment; employment did not increase as fast as the supply of labour. The figure shows wages falling to w_3, with employment increasing to L_3. But at this wage, the supply of labour is L_4; there is unemployment in the amount $L_4 - L_3$.

---

[2]When we consider a long-run change, such as here, the assumption of fixed prices is no longer appropriate. With prices freed up, what is relevant for both the demand and supply of labour is the real wage, the wage relative to prices. Thus, it should be understood that this paragraph is referring to real wages.

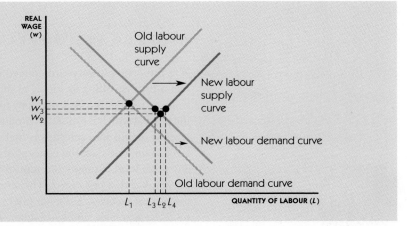

Figure 10.5 DEMAND AND SUPPLY SHIFTS IN THE AGGREGATE LABOUR MARKET

Economic growth in the 1970s caused the demand curve for labour to shift out. The entry of new workers into the labour force caused the supply curve for labour to shift out. Since the supply shift was larger than the demand shift, market forces pushed wages down; however, wages fell only from w_1 to w_3, rather than falling all the way to the new equilibrium wage, w_2. The supply of labour L_4 exceeded the demand for labour L_3, and unemployment was the result.

EXPLANATIONS OF UNEMPLOYMENT

Wages failing to adjust downwards in response to either of the following events:

(a) A shift in the demand curve for labour

(b) A shift in the supply curve for labour
Even if there were large shifts in the demand and supply curves for labour, no unemployment would result if wages adjusted appropriately.

Basic issues:

(a) What causes shifts in the demand and supply curves for labour?

(b) Why do wages fail to adjust?

(c) Why does disequilibrium take the form of unemployment, rather than a proportionate reduction of hours for all workers?

THE PRODUCT MARKET

Economists begin a macroanalysis of the product market by asking how the output (GDP) of the economy is determined. To answer this question, they use concepts analogous to the familiar demand and supply curves for a particular good. Whereas when we focused on the labour market we assumed that wages were free to change but prices were fixed, here we assume that wages are fixed and prices are free to change.

AGGREGATE SUPPLY

The firm's supply curve introduced in Chapter 4 describes the quantities of a product that a firm is willing to supply at different prices. Given the wage the firm has to pay workers and the prices it must pay for other inputs, it will be willing to supply more as the price at which it can sell its product increases. At higher prices, the profit-maximizing level of output for each firm is higher; it pays to produce more. At the economy-wide level, economists use the concept of an **aggregate supply curve.** Aggregate supply at any price level is simply the sum of the quantities supplied by each of the firms in the economy at that price level. The amount that each firm is willing to supply depends on the price it receives. At higher prices, *keeping wages fixed*, each firm is willing to supply more, so aggregate supply is higher. Tracing out the levels of output firms are willing to supply as the price each one receives increases generates the aggregate supply curve depicted in Figure 10.6. As in the case of any supply curve, rather than asking, what will be

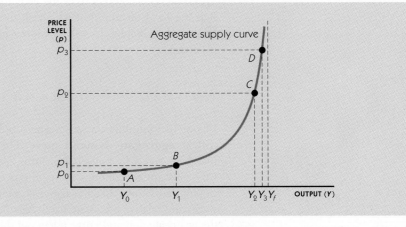

Figure 10.6 THE AGGREGATE SUPPLY CURVE

At higher prices, firms are willing to supply more. When output is low (Y_0), there is excess capacity, and a small increase in price elicits a large increase in supply; the supply curve is relatively flat. When output is high (Y_2), the economy is near full capacity, and it takes a large increase in price to elicit a small increase in supply; the supply curve is relatively steep.

the quantity supplied at each price, we can ask, what will be the price that will elicit a particular supply?

The aggregate supply curve masks underlying microeconomic detail. It ignores questions concerning the composition of output. This is deliberate: the objective of macroeconomics is to focus on the important aggregates that describe the economy, such as the level of output and prices. "Output," or quantity, measured along the horizontal axis, is the sum total of the real value of all goods produced in the economy. The best way of thinking about output here is that it is *real* GDP. The vertical axis shows the "price level." Again, the best way of thinking about this measure is that it represents the average level of prices in the economy, say the GDP deflator, discussed in Chapter 8. If all prices in the economy rise and fall proportionately, then any way of measuring the price level—the consumer price index, the producer price index, the wholesale price index—will give the same result. (In fact, prices of individual goods are constantly changing relative to other goods, and changes in relative prices affect the composition of output. But to focus on aggregate supply, we have to ignore questions concerning the composition of output, and therefore in most of the discussion that follows, we assume that relative prices remain unchanged.)

The aggregate supply curve shown in Figure 10.6 has a typical shape. It is upward sloping, indicating that increases in the price level lead to greater output. Put differently, to elicit increased supply, the price level has to rise. At low levels of output, the aggregate supply curve is relatively flat (or elastic), while at high levels of output, it is relatively steep (or inelastic). The reason for this is as follows. At low levels of output, such as at point A, there is excess capacity in the economy, with underutilized workers and machines. A slight increase in the price level, for instance from p_0 to p_1, would then elicit a very large increase in output, from Y_0 to Y_1.

At very high levels of output, such as at point C, machines and workers are working at close to their capacities, and it is hard to produce much more output. The marginal cost of producing an extra unit may be very large. Accordingly, it takes an enormous increase in the price level, say from p_2 to p_3, to elicit even a small increase in output (from Y_2 to Y_3).

At Y_f, the economy has reached capacity. To produce that level of output with the set of available machines would require everyone in the labour force to be working, and expanding output beyond Y_f would require the addition of more labour or more machines. Y_f is sometimes referred to as the economy's **full-employment** or **potential output.** It is the level of output at which all those who wish to work at the going wage are employed.[3] Chapter 15 will provide a more complete analysis of the aggregate supply curve.

AGGREGATE DEMAND

Figure 10.7 combines an aggregate supply curve, like the one shown in Figure 10.6, with an **aggregate demand curve.** The aggregate demand curve relates the total demand for goods by households, firms, government, and foreigners to the price level. Like most microeconomic demand curves, the aggregate demand curve is downward sloping. This curve, like the aggregate supply curve, is drawn under the assumption that wages and relative prices are fixed. Again, the vertical axis shows a series of price levels; the aggregate demand curve traces out the output that will be demanded at each price level. As prices fall, households can purchase more with the wages they receive; not only can individuals afford more goods, they also feel wealthier. They can purchase more with the money they have. Chapter 15 will also give a more complete derivation of the aggregate demand curve.

AGGREGATE DEMAND AND SUPPLY

Product market equilibrium occurs at the intersection of the aggregate demand and supply curves, point E in Figure 10.7. The argument for why this is the equilibrium should

[3]As a practical matter, things are not so simple, as we saw in Chapter 8. The economy can, at least for short periods of time, have an output greater than Y_f. For instance, during wartime, a country can draw into the labour force people who would not normally be working, or operate machines at full speed without regard to their wear and tear.

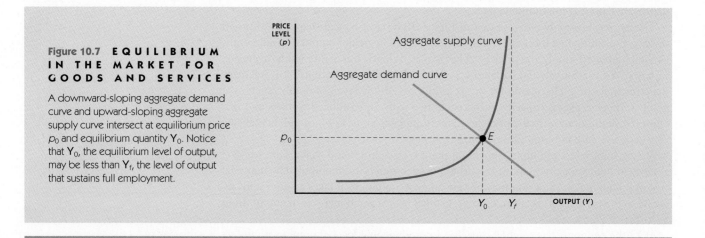

Figure 10.7 EQUILIBRIUM IN THE MARKET FOR GOODS AND SERVICES

A downward-sloping aggregate demand curve and upward-sloping aggregate supply curve intersect at equilibrium price p_0 and equilibrium quantity Y_0. Notice that Y_0, the equilibrium level of output, may be less than Y_f, the level of output that sustains full employment.

by now be familiar. If the price level is greater than that at which aggregate demand equals aggregate supply, firms are willing to supply more goods than are demanded; there is an excess supply of goods, and this excess supply will cause the overall price level to fall. The converse argument holds when the price level is below that at which aggregate demand equals aggregate supply.

Much of the discussion in the chapters that follow will be built on information conveyed by the aggregate supply–aggregate demand diagram. It is, therefore, important to understand how the diagram provides us with information about the major macroeconomic issues. First, when there are large rightward movements in output (measured along the horizontal axis) year after year, the economy will have a high growth rate. A single snapshot cannot show us this—it can only show us the level of output. But the level of output is closely connected to another major macroeconomic issue, unemployment, since the demand for labour normally increases as production increases. Finally, just as growth involves changes in output levels year after year, inflation involves a persistent rise in the price level (measured along the vertical axis). Again, the snapshot given in the aggregate demand–aggregate supply diagram cannot trace persistence. Nevertheless, a movement up the vertical axis is evidence of upward pressure on prices that may well lead to inflation. (Chapter 20 will make these connections clear.)

SHIFTS IN AGGREGATE DEMAND

There are various ways of stimulating aggregate demand. We saw in Chapter 8 that what the economy produces could be divided into consumption, investment, government expenditures, and net exports. The government can stimulate aggregate demand by encouraging spending for any one of these components. But we can already see that the outcome of such efforts depends strongly on where the intersection with aggregate supply lies. Along the flat (elastic) portion of the aggregate supply curve, the economy has excess capacity. A shift in demand, say from AD_1 to AD_2 in panel A of Figure 10.8,

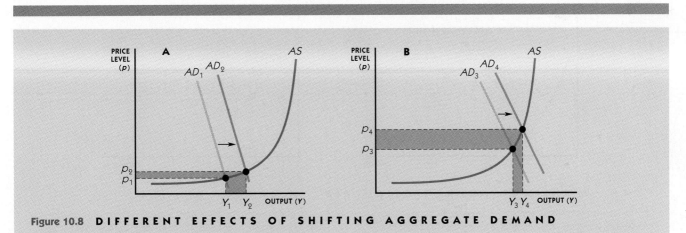

Figure 10.8 **DIFFERENT EFFECTS OF SHIFTING AGGREGATE DEMAND**

The effect of a shift in aggregate demand on the price level and aggregate output depends on where the initial equilibrium occurs. If the initial equilibrium is along the elastic portion of the aggregate supply curve (as in panel A), a rightward shift in aggregate demand increases output substantially and raises prices by only a little. If the initial equilibrium is along the inelastic portion of the aggregate supply curve (as in panel B), a rightward shift in aggregate demand increases prices substantially but leaves output relatively unchanged.

produces a large increase in output with little effect on the price level. Along the steep (inelastic) portion of the aggregate supply curve, the economy is near capacity. A shift in demand, say from AD_3 to AD_4 in panel B, produces little change in output but a great increase in the price level. Such repeated upward shifts in the aggregate demand curve, occurring year after year, leading to increases in the price level, help account for the inflationary bouts the economy has experienced.

SHIFTS IN AGGREGATE SUPPLY

Figure 10.9 illustrates a shift in the aggregate supply curve. There are two possible sources of such a shift. Panel A considers the case of an economy-wide increase in investment in plant and equipment, resulting in greater capacity. The aggregate supply will shift to the right, from AS_0 to AS_1. If the economy is operating initially along the steep portion of the aggregate supply curve and aggregate demand is fairly inelastic, as illustrated by the aggregate demand curve AD_1, then the increase in aggregate supply means that the new equilibrium price level may be substantially below the original. On the other hand, if the economy is operating initially along the flat portion of the aggregate supply curve, as illustrated by the aggregate demand curve AD_0, the shift in that curve has little effect. This is because the flat part of the aggregate supply curve represents excess capacity. The new *extra* excess capacity provides little change in either the equilibrium quantity produced or the equilibrium price level.

The other possible source of such a shift is an increase in the price of some input, such as the price of oil purchased from abroad. For firms to be willing to produce the same amount they produced before, they must receive higher prices. The supply curve

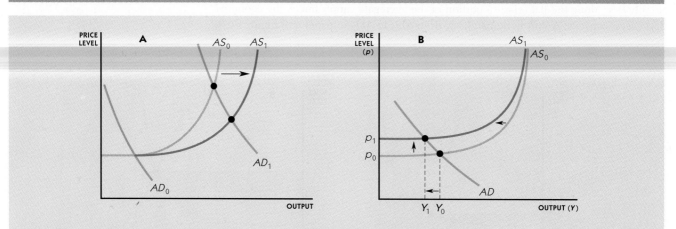

Figure 10.9 A SHIFT IN AGGREGATE SUPPLY

Panel A shows the effect of an increase in capacity. If the economy is operating along the relatively vertical portion of the aggregate supply curve, when the aggregate demand curve is AD_1, equilibrium prices fall and output increases. If the economy is operating along the relatively horizontal portion of the aggregate supply curve, when the aggregate demand curve is AD_0, neither output nor price level is much affected. Panel B shows the effect of an increase in the price of an input purchased from abroad, such as oil. This shifts the aggregate supply curve up, so that the price level increases even if there is excess capacity.

shifts up, as in panel B. Now the shift in the aggregate supply curve has an effect on the equilibrium price level, even when the economy has excess capacity and is operating along the horizontal portion of the aggregate supply curve.

Basic Macroeconomic Issues in the Product Market

1. What are the shapes of the aggregate demand and supply curves?

2. Where does the intersection of the aggregate demand and supply curves occur— along a horizontal portion of the aggregate supply curve, along a vertical portion, or somewhere in between?

3. What causes shifts in the aggregate demand and aggregate supply curves? Is there anything government can do to shift these curves? Can small disturbances to the economy lead to large shifts in these curves? In particular, when the economy is operating along the horizontal portion of the aggregate supply curve, can they lead to large changes in equilibrium output?

Using Aggregate Supply and Demand Analysis

The aggregate demand and aggregate supply framework gives us some insights into a variety of episodes in recent Canadian economic history.[4]

FISCAL EXPANSION IN THE 1960S

Economic policy was distinctly Keynesian in the 1960s, and fiscal policy was used extensively. The alternative policy for managing aggregate demand, as discussed in Chapters 18 and 19, is monetary policy. But it was essentially ruled out by the fact that Canada's currency value was tied to that of the United States through a fixed exchange rate from 1962–1970.

In 1962, Canada was emerging from a two-year recession. Real GDP was growing at the rate of 6.8 percent and unemployment was falling. The federal budgets of 1963 and 1964 raised taxes and effectively erased the budget deficit. But even though real GDP growth remained well above 6 percent in 1965, the government chose to adopt an ex-

---

[4]Some of the following discussion is adopted from John Sargent, *Fiscal and Monetary Policy*, Royal Commission on the Economic Union and Development Prospects for Canada Research Study (Toronto: University of Toronto Press, 1985).

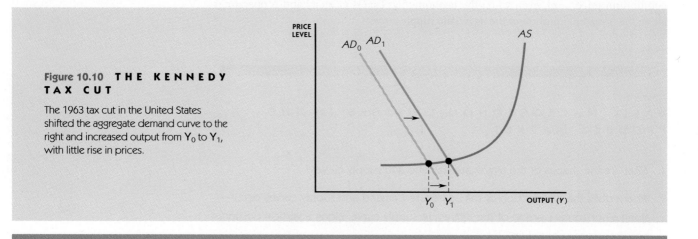

Figure 10.10 THE KENNEDY TAX CUT

The 1963 tax cut in the United States shifted the aggregate demand curve to the right and increased output from Y_0 to Y_1, with little rise in prices.

pansionary fiscal policy. Following the lead of the Kennedy administration in the United States two years earlier, taxes were cut. This made sense in the United States, since in 1963 its unemployment rate was stuck at a relatively high level and its budget was in surplus. The policy of shifting the aggregate demand curve to the right by lowering taxes was successful in the sense that it led to increased output and reduced unemployment without increasing prices. This was because of the excess capacity in the United States. The aggregate supply curve was relatively flat as in Figure 10.10. But when the tax cuts were introduced in Canada, the economy was already operating near capacity and the expansionary policy resulted in inflation that was to persist throughout the 1960s.

Inflationary pressures emerged in the United States in the late 1960s. The U.S. economy was now at an equilibrium along the vertical portion of the aggregate supply curve as in Figure 10.11, but it was faced with the need to undertake large government expenditures, partly to fight the Vietnam War and partly to address pressing domestic issues

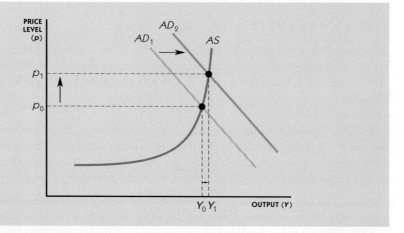

Figure 10.11 THE 1965 TAX CUT IN CANADA

Following the lead of the United States, the federal government cut taxes to stimulate the economy in 1965. The economy was already near full employment. The aggregate demand curve shifted to the right, from AD_1 to AD_2. This raised the price level substantially, from p_0 to p_1, without achieving much increase in output.

with new social programs. President Johnson was unwilling to raise taxes to pay for these expenditures, with the result that aggregate demand shifted to the right and caused inflation. Given the interdependencies of the Canadian and U.S. economies, some of the high demand in the United States spilled over into Canada and increased Canada's levels of output and inflation further.

In response, the 1966 budget reduced government expenditures and raised taxes, with the expected result that output growth slowed down moderately. The government quickly reacted in 1967 with a further expansionary fiscal policy. This was an overreaction since further inflation was induced and remained a problem for the rest of the 1960s. Once again restrictive policies had to be undertaken to combat inflation. Whereas real GDP growth over the early 1960s had averaged 5.2 percent, the anti-inflation policies of the latter half of the decade had reduced it to 2.5 percent by 1970. Given a decade of high growth and inflation, unemployment was low for most of the 1960s.

STAGFLATION IN THE 1970S

Canada recovered from the slowdown of 1970, and real GDP growth reached a decade high of 7.5 percent in 1973. Then a fundamental change in economic conditions worldwide led to a different set of problems in Canada and most other industrialized countries. The main event that precipitated this structural change on the supply side was the so-called *oil price shock*.

The Organization of Petroleum Exporting Countries (OPEC), consisting mainly of nations in the Middle East, decided in 1973 to use its market power to impose an embargo on the shipment of oil to certain Western nations, including Canada and the United States. The original embargo was partially motivated by political concerns, as many OPEC members saw the United States as continually siding with Israel in that country's ongoing dispute with the Arab countries that dominated OPEC. However, they soon realized that they had (at least in the short run) real economic power: the price of oil rose dramatically.

For the Canadian economy as a whole, higher oil prices raised the costs of production in a large number of industries that had come to rely on oil. The result can be viewed as a shift in the aggregate supply curve, as shown in Figure 10.12. Given the higher cost of

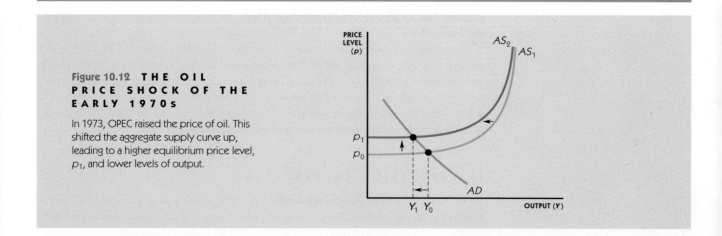

Figure 10.12 THE OIL PRICE SHOCK OF THE EARLY 1970s

In 1973, OPEC raised the price of oil. This shifted the aggregate supply curve up, leading to a higher equilibrium price level, p_1, and lower levels of output.

oil, the amount that firms were willing to produce at each price level was lowered. The shift in the aggregate supply curve gave rise to inflationary pressures. At the original price level, p_0, the shift meant that there was excess demand for goods. Thus, the inflationary episode that had begun with a rightward shift in the aggregate demand curve as a result of the late 1960s inflation was carried forwards with an upward shift in the aggregate supply curve as a result of the oil embargo.

The effect of the upward shift of the aggregate supply curve was that output and employment fell at the same time as the price level rose: a combination referred to as **stagflation.** The federal government focused on the decline in output and misinterpreted the structural change as a recessionary dip (a shift in the aggregate demand curve). The policy response was to cut taxes in the hope of shifting the aggregate demand and restoring output and employment. If the original decline in output and employment had been caused by a leftward shift in the aggregate demand curve instead of the aggregate supply curve, this type of policy might have been appropriate. In the circumstances, however, the expansionary policy served mainly to induce further inflation.

THE EMERGENCE OF MONETARISM IN THE LATE 1970S

The fixed exchange rate regime, begun at the famous Bretton Woods conference at the end of World War II, broke up in 1970. From 1970 to 1975, the Bank of Canada remained committed to maintaining the value of the Canadian dollar at U.S. $1. By 1975, however, the price level began to be seen as a more important monetary policy target than the exchange rate. Keynesian prescriptions were losing credibility because fiscal policy, given the inappropriate way it might have been used in the past, had not been effective in stabilizing prices and generating high output and employment. Inflation had reached double digits in 1974, and many called for a new approach to macroeconomic policy.

The doctrine of monetarism became popular. As mentioned earlier, monetarists believe that the control of the money supply is a more effective way to manage the economy than fiscal policy. In 1975, the Bank of Canada began to announce target rates for the growth of the money supply. This was accompanied by a spell of wage and price controls in 1975, and a reduction in tax rates whose objective was to improve incentives by workers and firms to supply more output. The result was a temporary decline in the inflation rate by almost three percentage points. But the unemployment rate remained stubbornly high.

The effort to stabilize the Canadian economy was further frustrated in 1979 by turmoil in the U.S. economy. Interest rates increased sharply and became more volatile, and Canadian interest rates were forced to comply. Canadian interest rates were allowed to rise somewhat as the Bank of Canada slowed the growth in the money supply. The value of the Canadian dollar was allowed to depreciate relative to the U.S. dollar. By making imports more expensive, this pushed prices upwards.

THE RECESSION OF 1980–1981

By the time President Reagan took office in 1981, there was a widespread view that something had to be done to stop inflation, which was already high and appeared to be

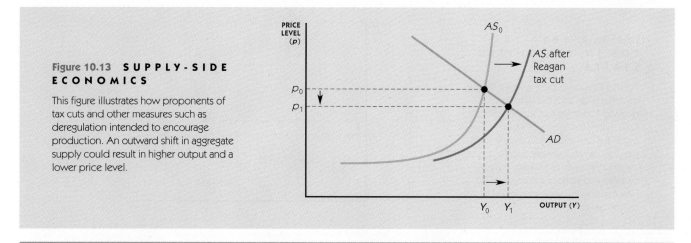

Figure 10.13 SUPPLY-SIDE ECONOMICS

This figure illustrates how proponents of tax cuts and other measures such as deregulation intended to encourage production. An outward shift in aggregate supply could result in higher output and a lower price level.

moving higher.[5] He chose to focus on shifting the supply curve right rather than the traditional approach of shifting the demand curve left. The main policy instrument for doing so was a reduction in marginal tax rates. He believed that this would improve incentives enough that tax revenues would actually rise. Figure 10.13 shows an initial situation where at the given price level p_0 there is an excess demand for goods (and hence inflationary pressures). At p_0, demand is Y_0, which is the steep portion of the aggregate supply curve. Reagan's hope was that the rightward shift in the aggregate supply curve would be large enough to eliminate the excess demand, and thereby stop the inflationary pressures. The emphasis on the importance of supply, as opposed to demand, caused proponents of this view to be called "supply-side economists." Though supply-side economics never caught on in Canada to the same extent, its consequences for the Canadian economy were felt because of the strong interrelationship of the two economies.

Inflation was brought under control, but the evidence suggests that it was because of a leftward shift in the aggregate demand curve rather than a rightward shift in the aggregate supply curve. We can break down this shift in the aggregate demand curve into two steps. First, Reagan's tax cut stimulated spending throughout the economy, thus shifting the aggregate demand curve to the right. It did this at the same time that it shifted the aggregate supply curve *slightly* to the right. Since, at least in the year immediately after the tax cut, the aggregate demand effect exceeded the supply effect, the Reagan tax cut actually raised the equilibrium price level, as shown in Figure 10.14.

The second step was taken when the Federal Reserve Board, or Fed (the counterpart to the Bank of Canada), and particularly its chairman, Paul Volcker, became concerned about these inflationary pressures. The Fed took strong actions to tighten the availability

[5]As we learned earlier, inflation is a persistent increase in prices, occurring month after month. The aggregate demand and supply analysis only shows equilibrium prices and output. Still, shifts in the aggregate demand and supply curves that lead to lower equilibrium price levels usually result in reduced inflation; Chapter 20 will explain why this is so.

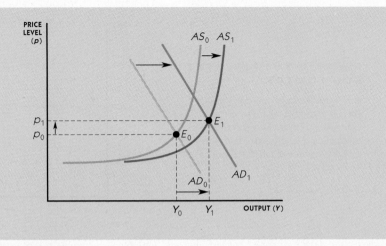

Figure 10.14 1981 TAX CUT IN THE UNITED STATES

The 1981 tax cut under President Reagan had effects on both the aggregate demand and aggregate supply curves. Both shifted to the right. The shift in aggregate demand was probably larger than the shift in aggregate supply, so that the net effect was to increase excess demand and inflationary pressure. The new equilibrium price level, at E_1, is higher than at E_0.

of credit and to raise interest rates—interest rates reached record levels in excess of 20 percent before the Fed deemed inflation defeated. (How the central bank does this and the broader impact of such measures will be the subject of Part Three.) As a result of the Fed's action, firms cut back their investments, and households cut back their purchases of items like cars and houses. This effect far outweighed the effect of the tax cut. Thus, the aggregate demand curve shifted to the left, as shown in Figure 10.15, and the U.S. economy was thrown into a major recession. The national unemployment rate exceeded 11 percent, and climbed as high as 20 percent in certain parts of the country.[6]

[6]However, the recession did have the effect of curbing inflation, which fell from over 13 percent in 1980 to just 3.2 percent in 1983. The relationship between unemployment and inflation rates will be discussed in Chapter 20. In the figure, the new equilibrium entails a lower price level than the old. In fact, prices did not fall. But the downward pressure on prices, reflected in the lower equilibrium level, is what brought inflation under control.

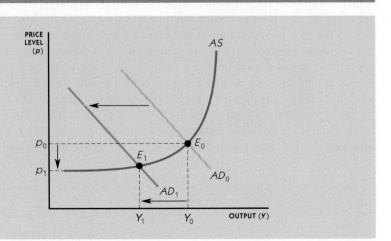

Figure 10.15 MONETARY POLICY CONTROLS INFLATION BUT CAUSES A RECESSION

Beginning in the late 1970s and early 1980s, the Federal Reserve Board in the United States acted to restrict credit, and thus consumption and investment, in an attempt to reduce inflation. The resulting leftward shift in aggregate demand reduced the price level but also caused a recession. The effects were so strong that they more than offset the increased inflationary pressures from the 1981 tax cut.

Note that in the figure, the new equilibrium, E_1, occurs in the horizontal portion of the aggregate supply curve. The recession of 1981, partly induced by the Reagan experiment in supply-side economics, spread into Canada. Both unemployment and inflation rates were running above 11 percent by 1982, and once again the Canadian government was forced to focus on inflation as its immediate policy problem.

THE CAPITAL MARKET

A healthy economy is marked by the full employment of its resources, by price stability, and by sustained economic growth. Unlike the labour or product market, the capital market does not address these goals directly. However, it has a powerful indirect effect on all of them. For example, the availability of credit and the terms on which it is made available have a significant impact on the willingness and ability of firms to invest. Investment in capital goods comprises a major component of the aggregate spending for goods and services, so changes in the capital market affect the aggregate demand curve. We will return to investment spending, and how the capital market influences it, in Chapters 12 and 13. Capital markets are also heavily influenced by monetary policy. In Chapters 17–19, we will see how monetary policy operates, in part at least, by affecting the amount of credit banks make available and the terms on which they make loans.

GROWTH

Macroeconomists are interested not only in the short-run performance of the economy—inflation and unemployment—but also in its long-run performance. In the long run, the capital market has an enormous impact. The cumulative effect of investment spending is a long-term rightward shift in the aggregate supply curve: as the productive capacity of the economy is enhanced by new investment, firms are willing to produce more at any given level of wages and prices. As the economy becomes more productive, the production possibilities curve shifts out. A central question with which we will be concerned is, what determines how rapidly it moves out? One important element is the rate of investment.

Panel A of Figure 10.16 shows the production possibilities of the economy, with investment—the output of capital goods—on the vertical axis and consumption on the horizontal. A key objective of short-run macroeconomic policy is to move the economy closer to the production possibilities curve (which represents the full-employment level of output, or the economy's potential output), from a point such as A to a point such as B. Note that in moving from A to B, the economy has increased both its consumption and its investment. Because resources were not being used efficiently, the economy did not face a trade-off.

Once the economy has reached its production possibilities curve, then hard decisions must be faced. Assume we want to move the curve out to PPC_2, as in panel B. One way to do this is to increase the economy's production potential by investing in more new machines and factories. Investment must be increased; the economy must move along

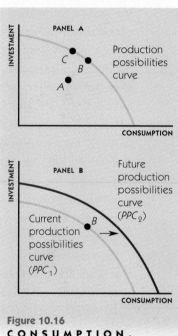

Figure 10.16
CONSUMPTION, INVESTMENT, AND LONG-RUN GROWTH

Short-run macroeconomic policy aims at assuring that the economy uses all its resources. For example, it tries to stimulate a movement from A (below the production possibilities curve) to B (on the curve) in panel A. Long-run policy focuses on making sure that the production possibilities curve shifts out over time. This will involve a shift from consumption to investment, from B to C. The result will be an outward shift from PPC_1 to PPC_2, as shown in panel B.

CLOSE-UP: TRACING THE RECESSION OF 1990–1992 THROUGH THE THREE AGGREGATE MARKETS

Any major macroeconomic event will have ramifications in the aggregate product, labour, and capital markets. The recession of 1990–1992 offers a good example.

Statistics Canada produces quarterly data on GDP. Economic growth since the 1970s has been in the range of 2 or 3 percent annually measured in real terms. In 1989, it was 2.3 percent. But from the second to the third quarter of 1990, the rate of real annual GDP growth was only .1 percent.

Then matters went downhill. From the third to the fourth quarter, real GDP fell by .7 percent. Over the next four quarters real GDP fell at annual rates of 2, 3.6, 1.9, and 1.2 percent. And while the economy began growing again in the first quarter of 1992, the increases were small. By the fourth quarter of 1992, real GDP was still smaller than it had been in the first quarter of 1990. The recession was technically over, but people certainly did not feel that there had been a return to robust economic health.

Economists will study and argue over the precise sequence of events leading up to the recession for years, but it seems clear that factors on both the aggregate demand and supply sides contributed. The world economy was weak heading into the middle of 1990. The rise in oil prices that followed Iraq's invasion of Kuwait in August 1990 helped turn this weakness into a recession; it shifted aggregate supply up for a time. But although oil prices returned to their prewar level by early in 1991, the recessionary threat that they had posed had plunged consumers and businesses into a downward spiral, where low confidence in the future led to reduced spending in Canada and abroad—a shift in the aggregate demand curve. The reduced spending in turn shrank the economy, confirming the gloomy expectations.

The slowdown in the product market reduced the demand for labour, moving the economy away from full employment. Canadian employment peaked in April 1990, when 12.8 million Canadians held jobs, but then sank to 12.2 million by April 1992. The sluggish recovery in early 1992 prevented the number of jobs from declining still further, but since businesses could not be sure whether the recovery was for real, they were not ready to hire many more workers.

Changes in aggregate capital markets were intimately linked to these changes in the product market. As people grew less confident about their jobs and the economic future, their savings increased sharply. Total Canadian personal savings in 1990 were 25 percent higher than the levels in the late 1980s, remaining high in 1991 and 1992.

Higher savings rates, however, meant that consumers were not buying. Businesses, seeing their sales falling, hesitated to invest. Banks, concerned about the ability of borrowers to repay, were reluctant to lend. The low levels of consumer spending and business investment at home and in the United States contributed to the economy's doldrums. Interest rates began falling as inflationary pressures eased in the recession. By mid-1992, the prime rate offered by the banks, the bank rate of the Bank of Canada, and the 90-day Treasury bill rate had dropped to about half of their 1990 levels. Mortgage rates had also fallen significantly. But in tough economic times, like late 1990 and 1991, even these low borrowing rates were not enough to persuade people to buy new homes or businesses to invest in new plant and equipment—at least not enough to restore economic prosperity in short order.

Source: Statistics Canada, *Canadian Economic Observer,* Catalogue Number 11-010, June 1993.

the current production possibilities curve shown in panel A from B to C. In doing so, the level of current consumption will be reduced.

Where along the production possibilities curve the economy operates depends on the capital market—on the interaction of the savings decisions of households and the investment decisions of firms (the demand for capital).[7] Decisions have to be made not only about how much to save and invest, but how to allocate these scarce funds. The investment that determines the economy's long-run growth includes, as well as the investments in buildings and machines, investments in human capital and in research and development.

The consequences for consumption, over time, of how much and how well the economy invests are illustrated in Figure 10.17. The figure shows two different possibilities for the economy's consumption over time. In the first, the pink line, there is a high level of consumption today and little investment. In the second, the red line, the economy sacrifices current consumption—more of today's output is invested; that is why initially consumption is lower. But, assuming that the investment dollars are well spent, the economy will grow faster, and eventually the level of consumption will be higher.

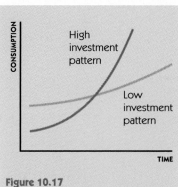

Figure 10.17
INVESTMENT AND GROWTH

If the economy invests a great deal, consumption today will be low, but future output and consumption will be higher.

MAJOR MACROECONOMIC ISSUES IN THE CAPITAL MARKET

1. What goes on in the capital market can have major effects on the economy in both the short run and the long run.

2. In the short run, the capital market particularly affects the level of investment and consumer purchases of durable goods, and therefore the level of output and employment.

   Issues: Can the government, through monetary policy, affect the level of output? If monetary policy can be used to control the economy, how does the policy exercise its influence? Can monetary policy stimulate the economy in a deep recession as effectively as it can bring about a contraction of the economy?

3. In the long run, to the extent that it affects the level of investment, the capital market can lead to increased growth.

   Issues: How effective is monetary policy in stimulating investment? How important is increased investment in stimulating growth? Does Canada invest or save too little? If so, why? And what can be done about it?

[7]See Chapters 9, 13, and 21 for a further analysis of the savings decision and the investment decision.

INTERRELATIONS AMONG MARKETS

Chapter 9 made the point that the three major categories of markets are interrelated. We have just seen another example of this, in the way the capital market affects the aggregate demand curve in the short run and the aggregate supply curve in the long run. Then too the demand curve for labour depends on what happens in the product market; and what happens in the labour market—the level of wages and employment—affects the demand for goods in the product market.

In the analysis of later chapters, we will focus on one market at a time. But the big picture, the fact that what happens in one aggregate market affects the other ones, should be kept in mind. Thus, in Chapter 11, we focus on the labour market; but behind the scenes, we know that the demand for labour depends critically on events in the product market. In Chapters 12–15, we focus on the product market, knowing that one of the reasons we are interested in the product market is that when national output is high, so too is employment.

Not only are the interrelations among the labour, capital, and product markets important, but the interrelations between those markets abroad and those markets in Canada are also important. An increase in the price Canada pays for oil shifts the aggregate supply curve and leads to higher prices and lower output. A recession in the United States reduces Americans' demand for Canadian goods; the resulting shift in the aggregate demand curve leads to lower output in Canada. A fall in prices in the stock market in the United States affects Canadian capital markets, and those effects may reverberate throughout the economy. While we focus on the labour, capital, and product markets within a particular country, again we must keep the bigger picture in mind: Canada is part of a global economy, all the pieces of which are interrelated.

REVIEW AND PRACTICE

SUMMARY

1. Macroeconomics tries to identify the forces that determine the levels of aggregate output, employment, and inflation. It does this by studying what causes changes in the demand and supply curves in the labour, product, and capital markets.

2. To explain unemployment, we need to explain why the aggregate labour market does not clear. If real wages do not adjust to changes in aggregate supply and demand, and either the demand curve for labour shifts to the left or the supply curve for labour shifts to the right, then the quantity of labour supplied will exceed the quantity demanded at the prevailing wage, and unemployment will exist.

3. The demand curve for labour shifts because of a fall in the production of goods by firms, as a result of a decrease in the demand for their products. The supply

curve for labour shifts when many workers enter or exit the labour market, as happened when the baby boom generation and women began to enter the labour force in great numbers.

4. In the product market, the aggregate supply curve is relatively flat (elastic) when output is low and a large fraction of the economy's machines are idle. It is relatively steep (inelastic) when output is high and the economy is operating near capacity.

5. If the initial equilibrium is along the elastic portion of the aggregate supply curve, a rightward shift in aggregate demand increases output substantially and raises price by only a little. If the initial equilibrium is along the inelastic portion of the aggregate supply curve, a rightward shift in aggregate demand increases prices substantially but leaves output relatively unchanged.

6. The capital market has powerful indirect effects on the goals of full employment, price stability, and sustained economic growth. Higher levels of investment lead to a shift in the aggregate demand curve and a long-term shift in the aggregate supply curve; as the productive capacity of the economy is enhanced by new investment, firms are willing to produce more at any given level of wages and prices.

KEY TERMS

classical economists
fiscal policies
monetary policies
monetarists
new classical
   economists
real business-cycle
   theorists

new growth
   economists
new Keynesian
   economists
voluntary
   unemployment
sticky wages

aggregate supply
   curve
full-employment or
   potential output
aggregate demand
   curve
stagflation

REVIEW QUESTIONS

1. What are the three main macroeconomic markets? What is the price called in each market?

2. If the labour market always cleared, would there be any unemployment? What does it mean for the labour market not to clear?

3. If the labour market always cleared, can there be variations in the level of employment?

4. What inferences do you draw from the following two facts?
   (a) The labour supply curve is relatively inelastic.
   (b) Large variations in employment coexist with relatively small variations in real wages.

5. What factors might shift the aggregate demand curve for labour? What factors might shift the aggregate supply curve for labour?

6. Why is the aggregate demand curve downward sloping? Why is the aggregate supply curve upward sloping? What is the characteristic shape of the aggregate supply curve?

7. When will a shift in the aggregate demand curve affect prices little and output a lot? When will the reverse be true?

8. Describe the effects of a shift in the aggregate supply curve.

9. Describe the movement of the economy from a situation where resources are not being fully utilized and unemployment is high to a situation where resources are being fully utilized, in terms of the production possibilities curve. Describe the consequences of an increase in investment when resources are being fully utilized, in terms of a movement along the current production possibilities curve. What does an increase in investment do to next year's production possibilities curve?

10. What is the effect of an increase in investment on the current aggregate demand curve? on the future aggregate supply curve?

PROBLEMS

1. In the 1970s, a large number of new workers entered the Canadian economy from two main sources: the baby boom generation grew to adulthood and the proportion of women working increased substantially. If wages adjust, what effect will these factors have on the equilibrium level of wages and quantity of labour? If wages do not adjust, how does your answer change? In which case will unemployment exist? Draw a diagram to explain your answer.

2. Soon after Iraq invaded Kuwait in August 1990, many firms feared that a recession would occur. They began cutting back on production and employment. If wages adjust, what effect will this cutback have on the equilibrium level of wages and employment? If wages do not adjust, how does your answer change? In which case will unemployment exist?

3. During the 1980s, government spending and budget deficits rose dramatically in Canada. This had the effect of shifting the aggregate demand curve to the right. What effect will this change have on the equilibrium level of prices and national output? Draw a diagram to illustrate your answer.

4. In the early 1980s, some supply-side economists argued that changes in tax rates would cause people to work harder and entrepreneurs to produce more. If this were to occur, what effect would it have on the equilibrium level of prices and output? Does it make a difference if the economy was initially operating with excess capacity?

5. In the late 1970s, the turmoil in the Mideast that followed the fall of the shah of Iran caused oil prices to rise sharply. What effect would this change alone have on the equilibrium level of prices and national output? Draw a diagram to illustrate your answer.

THE AGGREGATE LABOUR MARKET

Large numbers of people collecting unemployment insurance, huge lines at firms that announce they are hiring workers, plants closing down and laying off workers, are all symptoms of an economy in a recession. Though we may regret the loss in output resulting from resources not being fully utilized, and firms will surely miss the loss in profits, the human misery that results from unemployment is far more poignant and underlies the political commitment to limit both the extent and the costs of unemployment in the economy. But if we are to understand how to reduce unemployment, we must first understand its causes.

Since unemployment represents a situation where the supply of labour exceeds the demand, the first place to look when explaining unemployment is at the labour market. We do that in this chapter. The next five chapters take up the product market, which also helps to explain unemployment, because the demand for labour depends in part on the demand and supply for goods.

After an initial look at underlying assumptions, this chapter is divided into four sections. In the first, we address the basic question of whether unemployment is voluntary. This may seem like an odd question, but many economists have suggested that there is at least an element of "voluntariness" in much of unemployment.

Unemployment, as was noted in Chapter 10, is related to the failure of wages to adjust. The second section examines why wages might not adjust quickly to changes either in the demand or supply of labour. The third section argues briefly why unemployment statistics may underestimate the true lack of full utilization of human resources in the economy in periods of recession. The final section considers issues of public policy: if we cannot make wages more flexible, how can we at least reduce the cost of unemployment?

1. What is meant by involuntary unemployment? When does it arise?

2. What are the reasons that wages may not fall even when there is excess supply of labour?

3. What happens to unemployment if a decline in nominal wages is followed by a decrease in prices?

4. What policies might reduce either the extent of unemployment or the costs borne by those who are thrown out of work? What are some of the problems facing the unemployment insurance system?

A WORD ABOUT ASSUMPTIONS

As was noted in Chapter 10, in macroeconomics we are concerned more with the aggregate behaviour of the economy than with the parts, though we cannot ignore the parts. Thus, we focus on total employment and unemployment and, for the most part, do not make distinctions between skills and other differences among individuals. Also, although there are important interactions between the labour, product, and capital markets, we will assume the last two markets are unchanging as we observe changes in the labour market.

Labour is an input to production—often the most important input—so the demand for labour has much to do with the production decision of the firm. The individual firm will normally demand more labour if the price of its product goes up. Its demand for labour will also depend on the prices of the other inputs used in production. In an economy such as Canada's, with thousands of firms, each company, in making decisions about how much to pay its workers, believes that those decisions will have no impact on prices in general and therefore on the price level. A manufacturer of pins is unlikely to worry that because it pays its workers more somehow the price it has to pay for the steel used in the pins, or the price it pays for the electricity required to run its pin-making machines, will be altered. In making wage decisions, it makes sense for the company to take those prices as given. Accordingly, in analyzing the firm's labour demand and deriving the aggregate demand for labour, we take the prices facing the firm and the price level facing the economy as given.

This assumption will also allow us to focus on the relationship between wage changes and employment. In this fixed-price situation, changes in wages are equivalent to changes in *real* wages. Real wages, the cost of labour relative to what it produces and relative to the costs of other inputs, are what firms are concerned with in their employment decisions. Workers too focus on real wages—it is not the dollars that compensate them for working hard, but rather the goods they can buy with those dollars.

As we saw in Chapter 8, prices are not perfectly fixed. While the hiring decision of a single firm is unlikely to affect the price level, the hiring decisions (with the accompanying implications for wages) of all firms may eventually affect the price level. In the Great Depression, the price level fell by an average of about 5 percent per year. In other periods, prices rise. This complicates, but does not alter in any fundamental way, our short-run analysis. Later in the chapter, we will see how price adjustments may be incorporated into the analysis.

Another simplifying assumption that we will employ for most of this chapter is that each and every person who wishes to work wants a full, 40-hour work week. With this assumption, we can express the demand for or supply of labour either in terms of so many (say, 14 million) workers or in terms of so many (say, 14 million × 40 hours = 560 million) work hours. For most of the chapter, our concern is primarily with *unemployment*—with why it is that people who would like to get jobs cannot get them—so it is natural to focus our attention on the demand and supply of workers. Later in the chapter, we will also be concerned with why lower demand for labour results in workers being laid off rather than each employee working shorter work weeks.

Figure 11.1 repeats the demand and supply curves of workers from Chapter 10. There is an equilibrium wage, w^*, at which the demand and supply are equal. Sometimes, however, it seems that the wage gets stuck, at least for a while, at a level above w^*, such as w_0, so that firms hire fewer workers than want jobs at that wage: there is unemployment. The main issue addressed in this chapter is, why do wages get stuck? First, however, we must ask a more fundamental question.

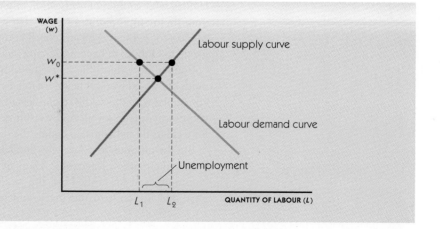

Figure 11.1 INVOLUNTARY UNEMPLOYMENT

The supply of those willing to work, L_2, exceeds the demand for labour, L_1, at the prevailing market wage, w_0. Involuntary unemployment exists.

IS UNEMPLOYMENT VOLUNTARY?

Chapter 8 explained why we do not expect all people to be working all the time: there is seasonal unemployment (gardeners and construction workers in cold climates are likely to be unemployed in the winter) and frictional unemployment (it takes time to move from one job to the next or to get a job when first entering the labour force).

Beyond these two types, there is the unemployment that arises when wages are stuck at a level above that at which the labour market clears. Those who want to work at that higher wage and cannot get employment are said to be involuntarily unemployed. Unemployment is represented in Figure 11.1 by the difference between L_2, the labour supply at wage w_0, and L_1, the labour demand.

The question posed by the classical economists is whether there is really any such thing as involuntary unemployment. In their view, the situation depicted in the figure never arises, or at least arises infrequently and only for brief periods of time. They have advanced two reasons to support their contention.

First, they argue that the unemployed worker could get a job if he would only lower his wage demand to the market-clearing level. By refusing to lower the wage demand, the worker in effect voluntarily makes himself unemployed. The second argument is that there is almost always *some* job a person could get, if he were only willing to make the effort to look for it and then to take it. If the unemployed Halifax welder would move to the Niagara region and pick grapes, he would have a job. (Of course, if *all* the unemployed decided at the same time that they were willing to accept jobs as low-paid dishwashers, grape pickers, or servers in fast-food restaurants, there might not be enough jobs, but the point is that each individual, in deciding *not* to accept these available jobs, has chosen to remain unemployed.)

To most economists, and to almost all noneconomists, pinning the label "voluntary" on unemployment simply because an unemployed worker has forgone the option of moving to Ontario to pick grapes is semantic quibbling. The trained welder living in Halifax who is unemployed, while other welders are working, considers himself involuntarily unemployed as a welder. He would be willing to work at the going wage for welders (or perhaps even at somewhat lower wages). But he is justifiably unwilling to relocate to Ontario to become a grape picker. Other cases are admittedly less clear-cut.

Equally important, there are the same social and economic consequences of thousands of trained workers being unable to find gainful employment at jobs even remotely connected with their skills, regardless of whether we call these workers voluntarily or involuntarily unemployed. And we still need to face the basic problem of why the wages for welders do not adjust to equate the demand and supply for welders.

But the question remains: why don't all workers who are unemployed seek temporary employment at low-wage jobs? Many of them do, but some do not. Several reasons are commonly put forwards. First, the available jobs might be in a different geographical area, and the costs of moving would be significant, particularly if the worker thinks (hopes) his unemployment is only temporary. Second, a low-wage job may convey the wrong kind of information to potential future employers. It may suggest that the individual lacks confidence in his abilities and skills. So long as the unemployed welder believes that accepting a job serving hamburgers at an A & W restaurant conveys a negative signal, he will not do so unless his assets are sufficiently used up that he has no alternative.

THE WAGE-EMPLOYMENT PUZZLE

It turns out to be difficult to reconcile observed changes in employment (or unemployment) and wages with the basic competitive model. If we applied the basic model to the labour market, which is what classical economists did, we would predict that when the demand for labour goes down, as in a recession, the (real) wage also falls, as illustrated in Figure 11.2. A leftward shift in the demand for labour results in lower wages. If the supply of labour is very unresponsive to wage changes (that is, the labour supply curve is inelastic), as depicted by the steepness of the line in the figure, the reduction in the wage may be quite large.

But this does not seem to happen in the real world. In the Great Depression, when the demand for labour fell, real wages in Canada actually rose. Thus, while unemployment rose from about 2.5 percent at the beginning of 1929 to almost 20 percent in 1934, real wages actually *rose* by 8 percent. (In fact, actual wages fell by 14 percent, but the consumer price index fell by 22 percent.) More recently, from 1983 to 1988, real wages fell slightly while the unemployment rate fell from 11.8 percent to 7.8 percent.

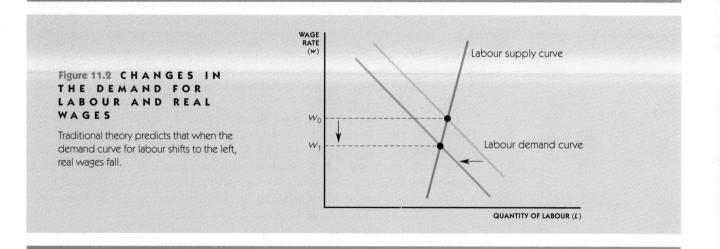

Figure 11.2 CHANGES IN THE DEMAND FOR LABOUR AND REAL WAGES

Traditional theory predicts that when the demand curve for labour shifts to the left, real wages fall.

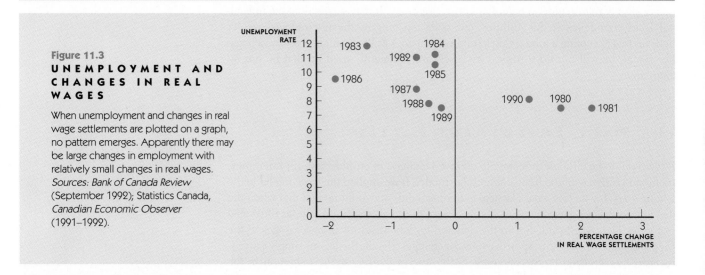

Figure 11.3

UNEMPLOYMENT AND CHANGES IN REAL WAGES

When unemployment and changes in real wage settlements are plotted on a graph, no pattern emerges. Apparently there may be large changes in employment with relatively small changes in real wages. *Sources: Bank of Canada Review* (September 1992); Statistics Canada, *Canadian Economic Observer* (1991–1992).

Figure 11.3 shows real wage rate increases and unemployment rates during the 1980s. It is clear from the diagram that there is no clear relationship between the two; that is, real wage increases have not been determined by changes in the unemployment rate. Despite significant changes in the unemployment rate, real wages changed hardly at all. There are three possible ways to explain the stability of real wages in the face of fluctuating employment levels. The first is that the supply curve for labour is horizontal and the demand curve for labour has shifted, as shown in Figure 11.3A. As demand shifts in, the employment level changes with little change in the (real) wage. In this case, the loss in employment does not represent involuntary unemployment by our definition, because the market winds up at an equilibrium point, with demand equalling supply for labour. The labour market has moved along the labour supply curve to a new point of equilibrium. Almost all economists reject this interpretation, because of the huge amount of evidence suggesting that the labour supply curve is relatively inelastic (steep), not flat.

The second possible interpretation is that there are shifts in the labour supply curve that just offset the shifts in the labour demand curve, as depicted in panel B. The shifting demand and supply curves trace out a pattern of changing employment with little change in the (real) wage. Again, the labour market winds up at an equilibrium point, so by definition there is no involuntary unemployment. The reduced employment in the Great Depression was, in this view, due to a decreased willingness to supply labour—in other words, an increased desire for leisure. As we learned in Chapter 10, there have been marked changes in the supply of labour, as women and baby boomers have joined the labour force. But most economists do not see any persuasive evidence that the supply curve of labour shifts much as the economy goes into or comes out of a recession, let alone to the extent required in Figure 11.3B; and they see no reason why shifts in the demand curve for labour would normally be offset by shifts in the supply curve.

The third interpretation, to which most economists subscribe, is that there has been a

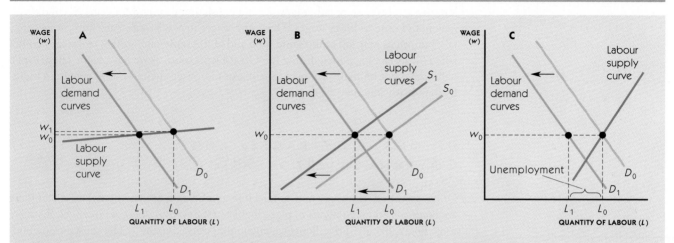

Figure 11.4 **WHY WAGES DO NOT FALL WHEN DEMAND SHIFTS**

Panel A shows a very elastic labour supply curve. A leftward shift in demand for labour from D_0 to D_1 will decrease employment without affecting wages. Panel B shows a shift in both supply and demand curves. Although the shift in demand for labour from D_0 to D_1 would reduce wages by itself, it is offset by a shift in the supply of labour from S_0 to S_1, leaving the wage level unchanged. In panel C, the demand for labour shifts from D_0 to D_1, but wages do not fall for some reason. Involuntary unemployment results.

shift in the demand curve for labour, with no matching shift in the supply curve *and no corresponding change in the wage*, a situation depicted in Figure 11.4C. The labour market is stuck out of equilibrium: at the wage w_0, the amount of labour that workers would like to supply remains at L_0. But as the demand for labour shifts, the number of workers hired at w_0 falls from L_0 to L_1. The difference, $L_0 - L_1$, is the level of unemployment, and it is *involuntary*. The same argument holds even if there is a slight shift in the labour supply curve and a slight change in the wage: the adjustment in the wage is too small to align demand with supply.

The question posed by panel C is fundamental to macroeconomics: how do we explain the apparent fact that wages do not fall in the face of a shift in the demand curve for labour? Good reasons abound, as we will see in the following sections.

EXPLANATIONS OF WAGE RIGIDITIES

When unemployment is related to wages that fail to adjust sufficiently in response to a shift in the demand or supply curve for labour, economists say that wages exhibit **downward rigidity** or stickiness. There are three major explanations for why wages may not fall enough to eliminate unemployment quickly. First, firms may not be allowed to lower wages because of either government legislation or union pressure. Second, firms may not choose to lower wages if lowering wages lowers profits. And third, wages may fall, but prices may fall at the same time and at the same rate, so that *real* wages do not fall. This in fact happened during the Great Depression, as we have seen. These explanations are not mutually exclusive: the reasons for wage stickiness may vary from industry to industry and may overlap.

UNIONS, CONTRACTS, AND GOVERNMENT REGULATIONS

One reason that real wages may not decline much when employment does is that there are contracts and regulations in place that keep them from doing so. In effect, there are wage floors, like the price floors we encountered in Chapter 5. The most conspicuous example is union contracts.

UNION CONTRACTS

Unions typically negotiate nominal wage contracts—i.e., so many dollars per hour. But remember, in this section we are keeping prices constant, so a wage contract translates directly into *real* wages.

In some industries, labour union power explains wage rigidities. High wages in parts of the Canadian manufacturing sector, for example, have undoubtedly contributed to the high costs of production, and to the decline of Canadian companies in world markets. Studies of the impact of unions on wage rates in Canadian industries have shown that unionized workers earn as much as 25 percent more than nonunionized workers, on average. This is especially true for less-skilled workers.[1]

Unions and management share the blame when the high wages called for in their contracts make an industry uncompetitive. In many instances, unions have insisted on high wages even in the face of declining employment. Management has sometimes found it easier to pay the unions what they ask, even if doing so may not be good for the long-term health of the firm, rather than suffer the aggravation of a protracted negotiation or a strike.

Strangely enough, it may be in the interests of those currently employed in unionized industries to make wage demands that significantly reduce the demand for workers. If a union demands ever-higher wages, the employer will have an incentive to reduce the work force. But if the decline in the work force is slow enough, it can be accomplished by natural attrition (that is, by workers who choose to retire or quit). In that case, the job security of those still employed is not threatened, and nonunion workers who would be willing to work for less money are shut out by the union contract and have no way of offering to work for a lower wage.

Unions occasionally accept wage cuts in times of severe economic stress. During the recession of the early 1980s, many companies were faced with bankruptcy or severe cutbacks if they could not reduce their costs. Recognizing this, a number of unions in air-

---

[1] See Wayne Simpson, "The Impact of Unions on the Structure of Canadian Wages: An Empirical Analysis with Microdata," *Canadian Journal of Economics* (February 1985) 18: 164–81.

lines, automobiles, and steel accepted wage cuts. Whether the unions were able to negotiate so that those cuts were smaller than what they would have been in a perfectly competitive labour market is not clear.

WAGE ADJUSTMENTS

Even if unions do not succeed in the long run in obtaining higher wages for their members, they are probably successful in slowing down the process of adjustment of wages to changed economic circumstances. In some industries, it has been the practice to have a three-year contract. If an economic downturn sets in shortly after the contract has been signed, it may be more than two years before the new economic circumstances are reflected in the wages, when the new contract is negotiated. And by then, it is even possible that the economy is on the road to recovery, so that the workers—in the wages they receive—will have been largely insulated from the economic downturn. If the union and management had expected inflation over the next few years, they might even have built in wage increases. When those price increases fail to materialize because of the economic downturn, the built-in wage increases lead to real wage increases even as the unemployment rate is rising.

When inflation rates are moderate to high, contracts frequently do not rely on built-in wage increases. Rather, wages increase with the cost of living. Contract provisions that allow for such increases, called cost-of-living adjustments (COLAs), mean that real wages are relatively unaffected by the level of inflation or unemployment.

In Canada, different contracts expire each month—the contracts are staggered, so a relatively small proportion are up for renegotiation at any time. Thus, adjustments of union wages must be slow; wages do not decline rapidly in response to unemployment, even if the unions were sensitive in their wage bargaining to the unemployment rate.

Union contracts, however, cannot provide the full explanation of rigid wages in Canada. This follows from the simple fact that there was high unemployment before unions became important, and there has been high unemployment recently, despite the long-term decline of unions. As the economy went into the Great Depression in 1929, only 8 percent of the labour force was unionized. In the recession of the early 1980s, unemployment hit over 11 percent, even though the rate of unionization had been virtually unchanged at around 30 percent for the previous thirty years.

Still, while unions cannot be the whole explanation for wage rigidities, it is likely that they have been a contributing factor in particular industries in recent decades. The union membership statistics may understate the influence of unions in determining wages, since many nonunionized firms may base the wages they pay on what unions negotiate for comparable workers. In several European countries wage bargaining occurs at the central level and the fraction of workers belonging to unions is much higher than in North America—45 percent in Italy, 95 percent in Sweden, and 42 percent in Germany. The argument that unions have played an important role in wage rigidities seems more persuasive there than it does in the United States, where unionization covers less than 20 percent of the work force, or in Canada, where only about a third of the workers belong to unions.

IMPLICIT CONTRACTS

Union-contract-style wage rigidities may come about even in the absence of a union or an explicit labour contract. There are economic forces at work that may lead to wage rigidities and limit the extent to which an unemployed worker can hope to get a job by offering to accept a lower wage than employed workers, so that wages would not fall by being "bid down."

The relations between an employer and her employees are governed not just by the formal contract, but by a host of implicit understandings developed over time between the firm and its workers. These implicit understandings are referred to as an **implicit contract.**

Workers are generally risk averse; other things being equal, they would like to avoid fluctuations in their income. Many workers have fixed financial commitments like monthly rent or car payments. They do not want their wages to fluctuate with every change in the demand and supply of labour. Firms can bear these market fluctuations more easily. First, the owners of firms tend to be wealthier, which means that they have a larger cushion for adjusting to variations in income. Second, in the event of a temporary and unexpected shortfall of funds, companies can borrow more easily than can most workers.

Given that firms are less vulnerable to economic fluctuations than individual workers, it pays companies to provide at least some indirect "insurance" to their workers. Workers will be willing to work for a dependable firm that pays a steady wage even if that wage is lower on average than the highly varying wages they could get elsewhere. Such a firm provides a form of insurance to its workers through an implicit contract, an understanding that the wages will not vary with the month-to-month, or even year-to-year, variations in the labour market. That is, the firm behaves *as if* it had a contract with its workers guaranteeing the wage. It is called an implicit contract because it is an understanding, not a formal or explicit contract. The company pays workers a higher wage than it "needs to" in bad periods, but in return workers stay with their firm in good times, even though they are receiving a lower wage than they might obtain elsewhere.

The wage these workers receive can be thought of as consisting of two parts: the "market" wage (the wage the worker could receive elsewhere) plus an adjustment for the implicit insurance component. When the market wage is relatively low, the wage received by the worker may be higher than the market wage; the worker is, in effect, receiving a benefit on the implicit insurance policy. When the market wage is high, the wage received by the worker may be lower than the market wage; the difference is, in effect, the premium the worker pays for keeping wages somewhat more stable.

In many industries in which long-term employment relations are common, implicit contract theory provides a convincing explanation of why wages do not vary much. But while implicit contract theory is useful in explaining why the wages received by workers who are not laid off may not vary much, it does not explain why there are extended layoffs; in fact, the theory predicts that these extended layoffs will not occur. After all, the risk that is of most concern to workers is the complete cessation of their income; this is far more important than a slight reduction in their weekly pay-cheque. Thus, implicit contract theory seems to predict that rather than laying people off, firms will engage in **work sharing;** they will reduce the hours each person works. Some firms have in fact experimented with work sharing, but it is not common. Layoffs are.

Proponents of the implicit contract theory have attempted to explain why firms tend to use layoffs rather than work sharing by focusing on the fixed costs associated with employment and on certain details of the unemployment compensation laws. First, they argue that when the work week is reduced below normal levels, productivity is reduced more than proportionately. For example, if a worker works an eight-hour day, the first hour is spent settling into work, the last hour is spent getting ready to leave; the worker has only six productive hours. If the work day is now reduced to six hours, one hour is still spent getting settled into work and one spent getting ready to leave, and there are only four productive hours. Shortening the work day by 25 percent has reduced the actual number of productive hours by 33 percent. This argument holds that the firm loses more in productivity through work sharing than through layoffs. But the argument only suggests that work sharing should take the form of a three- or four-day work week rather than a shortened workday.

Second, proponents of the implicit contract theory point out that the government encourages layoffs, albeit in an indirect way. In most places, individuals are not eligible for unemployment compensation if they are working part time. So if a company just trims the workday, the worker and the company pay the cost, but if the company lays off a worker, the government picks up part of the cost, by paying the worker unemployment compensation. (Several European countries have been sufficiently concerned about this problem that they have changed their laws to allow for unemployment compensation for those who face reductions in their work week.) But these considerations simply suggest that work sharing should take the form of job rotations. That is, one group of workers might be laid off for two months, then another group laid off for two months, and so on. Firms would then avoid the problems of short work weeks, and workers would be eligible for government unemployment compensation. These job rotations would also reduce the major risks of income variability caused by extended layoffs, and resolve the problems posed by productivity losses from shortened days. Job rotations, however, are almost never observed in the real world.

But the most telling criticism of implicit contract theory is that it does not really explain why wages of job seekers should fail to decline when there is unemployment. Even in the deepest recession, the labour market is like a revolving door, with people quitting jobs and some firms hiring new workers. Even if implicit contract theory could explain why some workers are laid off, it does not explain why employers do not decide to pay lower wages to new employees. If the wages paid to new employees fell sufficiently, presumably there would be no unemployment. Wage systems in which new workers are paid lower wages than current workers are called **two-tier wage systems.**

INSIDER–OUTSIDER THEORY

Seeking an explanation for why firms faced with recessionary conditions do not decide to pay lower wages to new employees, economists have devised what is known as **insider-outsider theory**. Insiders in this case are those with jobs at a particular firm, while outsiders are people who want jobs at that firm. The theory assumes that there are contracts, either explicit or implicit.

Insider-outsider theory focuses on the importance of training costs. Each firm needs a labour force trained in the special ways that it operates. Most of the training is done by current employees, the insiders. The insiders recognize that by training new employees, outsiders, they are reducing their bargaining position with the firm. The company can promise to continue to pay them higher wages than the newcomers, but the insiders know this promise could be broken. After all, they are training their own replacements. In future bargaining situations, the employer can use the availability of these lower-wage workers to exert downward pressure on the wages of the current employees. Knowing this, the insiders refuse to cooperate with training the outsiders, unless the new employees' interests are made coincidental with their own. The firm can accomplish this only by offering similar pay, but this results in wage stickiness: the wages offered new workers cannot be lowered to a level at which the demand for new workers equals the supply. Unemployment persists.

Moreover, insider-outsider theory emphasizes that even if the current employees were so foolish as to train new, lower-paid workers, the firm should not take the new workers' willingness to work at a low wage seriously. For once an outsider has been trained, she becomes a trained insider able to extract from the firm higher wages.

There are, in fact, relatively few exceptions to the general principle that firms do not like two-tier wage systems. Most such experiments—such as the contract between American Motors (Canada) and its workers signed in 1983, which provided that new workers be paid 85 percent of what previously hired workers received—are relatively short-lived. The American Motors (Canada) experiment lasted only for the duration of the three-year contract.

MINIMUM WAGES AND UNEMPLOYMENT INSURANCE

Chapter 5 explained how a minimum wage set by the government could result in unemployment. The minimum wage is a government-enacted price floor. To the extent that workers would accept and firms would offer wages below the minimum if they were allowed to, the minimum wage keeps the demand for labour from equalling supply. Most workers in Canada earn considerably more than the minimum wage, so minimum wage legislation probably has little effect on unemployment for these workers. However, minimum wage legislation probably does contribute *some* to the unemployment of unskilled workers, including teenagers just entering the labour force; how much remains a question of debate. While some provincial governments set a special, lower minimum wage for teenagers, relatively few firms avail themselves of this opportunity. They pay their teenaged employees wages that are in excess of the minimum wage. Still, it is worth noting that in recessions, unemployment rates among unskilled workers and teenagers often increase much more than for the population as a whole.

A policy that is more likely to induce unemployment is the form of unemployment insurance offered by the federal government. Unemployment insurance benefits are payable to workers who are laid off after having worked and contributed premiums to the program for some minimum time, between ten and twenty weeks, depending on the regional unemployment rate. There are various ways in which this scheme can cause unemployment rates to be higher than they otherwise would be. For one thing, unemployment insurance reduces the cost to workers of being laid off temporarily. Therefore firms will be less reluctant to use layoffs in times of low demand as opposed to reducing hours of work or keeping workers employed and building up inventories. For another, given that workers can become eligible for benefits after a relatively short period of contributing to the scheme, there is an incentive for some workers to enter the labour force only long enough to become eligible for benefits. This is especially true for so-called secondary workers (e.g., spouses or dependents of full-time workers) in regions of high unemployment. This increase in temporary labour force participation will cause the observed unemployment rate to rise. Finally, given that the length of time for which laid-off workers can receive benefits is relatively high (up to fifty weeks), workers may spend more time searching for new jobs. This will also increase the observed rate of unemployment. (Of course, if they find jobs that better match their skills and aptitudes as a result of searching longer, the rate of turnover, and therefore the rate of unemployment, in the future may fall.) Empirical studies have tended to support the notion that the generosity of the unemployment insurance system affects the rate of unemployment. It has been estimated that the significant improvements in benefits and reduction in eligibility requirements that were implemented in 1971 caused the rate of unemployment to rise by between 0.5 and 2 percentage points. Similarly, the tightening up of the system in 1979 reduced unemployment rates by about 0.5 percentage points.[2] We return to the policy implications of this later in this chapter.

EFFICIENCY WAGE THEORY

A second reason that wages may not fall enough to eliminate unemployment is that firms may find that they make more profits by paying a wage higher than the one at which the labour market would clear. If paying higher wages leads to higher productivity, then higher wages may improve a firm's profits.

In Chapter 1, we learned that when Henry Ford opened his automobile plant in 1914, he paid his workers the unheard-of wage of $5 per day, more than double the going wage. He wanted his workers to work hard; he knew that with his new technique of production—the assembly line—and hardworking workers, his profits would be higher. Many modern companies apply the same philosophy.

WHY DOES PRODUCTIVITY DEPEND ON WAGES?

Economists have identified three main reasons that firms may benefit if they pay high wages: wages affect the quality of the work force, they affect the level of effort, and they affect the rate of labour turnover. Each of these reasons has been extensively studied in recent years. In each, productivity may depend not just on the wage paid, but also on the wage paid relative to that paid by other firms and on the unemployment rate. The following sections discuss each of the three explanations.

The Quality of the Labour Force   When a firm's demand for workers decreases, it worries that if it cuts wages for all workers, the best employees will be most likely to leave. After all, they will be more confident than their less productive colleagues that they will find a new job at the old (higher) wage. It is all too common for companies to discover after a wage cut that they have lost the best of their workers. Indeed, this is the reason frequently given by firms for not cutting wages. Chapter 6 introduced the concept of adverse selection. The average quality of used cars offered on the markets is affected by the price of cars, the average riskiness of those wishing to buy insurance is affected (adversely) by increases in the premium. The effect just described is an adverse selection effect: the average quality of those offering to work for a firm is affected adversely by a lowering of the wage.[3]

---

[2] These results are summarized in S. Kaliski, "Trends, Changes and Imbalances: A Survey of the Canadian Labour Market," in W. C. Riddell, ed., *Work and Pay: The Canadian Labour Market* (Toronto: University of Toronto Press, 1985), pp. 77–140.

[3] It should be clear that we have now moved away from the assumption that all workers are identical, with which the chapter began.

The Level of Effort   We can easily see that it would not pay any worker to make any effort on the job if all firms paid the market-clearing wage. A worker could reason as follows. "If I shirk—put out a minimal level of effort—I will either be caught or not. If I don't get caught, I get my pay-cheque and have saved the trouble of making an effort. True, if I am unlucky enough to be caught shirking, I risk being fired. But by the terms of the basic competitive model, I can immediately obtain a new job at the same wage. There is, in effect, no penalty for having been caught shirking."

Firms that raise their wages above the market-clearing level will find that they have introduced a penalty for shirking, for two reasons. First, if their workers are caught shirking and are fired, they will have to take the lower wage being offered by other firms. Second, if many firms offer higher-than-market-clearing wages, unemployment will result, since at the higher wages firms as a whole will hire fewer workers. Now a worker who is fired may have to remain unemployed for a time.

Consider the wage that is just high enough that workers are induced not to shirk. We know that this wage must exceed the wage at which the demand for labour equals the supply. If one of the unemployed workers offers to work for a lower wage at a particular firm, he will not be hired. His promise to work is not credible. The firm knows that at the lower wage, it simply does not pay the worker to exert effort.

The no-shirking view of wages also provides a gloomy forecast for the well-intentioned unemployment benefits policy offered by government. Assume the government, concerned about the welfare of the unemployed, increases unemployment benefits. Now the cost of being unemployed is lower, hence the wage a firm must pay to induce workers to work—that is, not to shirk—is higher. As a result, wages are increased, leading in turn to a lower level of employment. The higher unemployment benefits have increased the unemployment rate.

Higher wages may lead to higher levels of effort for another reason: they may lead to improved worker morale. If workers think that the firm is taking advantage of them, they may reciprocate and try to take advantage of the firm. If workers think their boss is treating them well—including paying them good wages—they will reciprocate and go the extra mile. It is not just the threat of being fired that motivates them to work hard.

The Rate of Labour Turnover   Lowering wages increases the rate at which workers quit. Economists refer to this rate as the **labour turnover rate.** It is costly to hire new workers, to find the jobs that best match their talents and interests, and to train them. So firms seek to reduce their labour turnover rate, by paying high wages. The lower the wages, the more likely it is that workers will find another job more to their liking, either because it pays a higher wage or for some other reason. Thus, while firms may save a little on their direct labour costs in the short run if they cut their wages in a recession, these savings will be more than offset by the increased training and hiring costs incurred as demand rises again and they have to replace lost workers. We can think of what workers produce net of the costs of hiring and training them as their *net* productivity. Higher wages, by lowering these turnover costs, lead to higher net productivity.

DETERMINING THE EFFICIENCY WAGE

If, as we have just seen, net productivity increases when a firm pays higher wages, then it may be profitable for an employer not to cut wages even if there is an excess supply of workers. This is because the productivity of the overall work force may decline enough in response to a wage cut that the overall labour costs per unit of production will actually increase.

The employer wants to pay the wage at which total labour costs are minimized; this is called the **efficiency wage.** The wage at which the labour market clears—the wage at which the supply of labour equals the demand for labour—is called the market-clearing wage. There is no reason to expect that the efficiency wage and the market-clearing wage will be the same. **Efficiency wage theory** suggests that labour costs may be minimized by paying a wage higher than the market-clearing wage.

If the efficiency wage is greater than the market-clearing wage, it will still pay each profit-maximizing firm to pay the efficiency wage. There will be unemployed workers who are willing to work at a lower wage, but it simply will not pay firms to hire them. The firms know that at the lower wage, productivity will decline enough to more than offset the lower wage.

In some circumstances, the efficiency wage can also be less than the market-clearing wage. In that case, competition for workers will bid up the wage to the competitive, market-clearing level. Firms would like to pay the lower, efficiency wage, but at that wage they simply cannot hire workers. The market-clearing wage thus forms a floor for wages in efficiency wage theory. If the reason that productivity depends on wages is that effort increases with the wage—the shirking view of wages—then the efficiency wage must exceed the market-clearing level.

The efficiency wage for one firm may differ from that of another. If, for instance, it is easy for a particular company to supervise workers, then workers know that if they shirk, they will quickly be caught, and because the penalty for shirking is fairly certain, the firm may not have to pay a very high wage to persuade workers not to shirk. In general, the efficiency wage for any firm will depend on two factors: the wage paid by other firms and the unemployment rate. The wage paid by other firms matters because if other companies pay a lower wage, a firm will find that it does not have to pay quite as high a wage to elicit a high level of effort. Workers know that if they are fired, the jobs they are likely to find will pay less. Thus, the cost of being fired is increased, and this spurs employees on to working harder.

The unemployment rate also comes into play because as it increases, firms will again find that they do not have to pay quite as high a wage to elicit a high level of effort. The workers know that if they are fired, they will have a harder time getting a new job.

Efficiency wage theory also suggests a slow adjustment process for wages. Each firm is reluctant to lower its wages until others do, for several reasons. The company worries that its best workers will be attracted by other firms. It worries that the morale of its workers, and thus their productivity, will be impaired if they see their wage is below that of similar firms. No company wants to be the leader in wage declines, or at least in significant wage reductions. Each therefore contents itself with reducing its wage slowly, and never much below that of other firms. Gradually, as wages in all firms are lowered, employment is increased and unemployment reduced.

These patterns are in contrast to the basic competitive model, which predicts that with a relatively inelastic supply curve for labour, there will be large and quick changes in wages in response to changes in the demand for labour. It is these wage changes that prevent unemployment.

WHY ARE THERE LAYOFFS?

Efficiency wage theory helps explain why wages do not fall, or fall very much, even when there is an excess supply of labour and why, when wages do fall, they fall slowly. Because productivity depends in part on the wages a firm pays relative to those paid by other firms, each firm is reluctant to lower its wages much until others do.

CLOSE-UP: EFFICIENCY WAGES IN TANZANIA

One of the implications of efficiency wage theory—that employers may be able to get work done more cheaply by increasing wages—can lead to some topsy-turvy implications. Or as Alfred Marshall, a famous economist of the late nineteenth and early twentieth centuries put it: "Highly paid labour is generally efficient and therefore not dear labour; a fact which though it is more full of hope for the future of the human race than any other that is known us, will be found to exercise a very complicating influence." The first chapter of this book gave the example of Henry Ford taking advantage of efficiency wage theory by paying higher wages in the automobile industry. But the theory can have striking implications in less-developed countries too.

Consider the experience of the East African nation of Tanzania, formed by the union of Tanganyika and Zanzibar in 1964. When the area now known as Tanzania achieved independence in 1961, most wage earners worked on large plantations. Most of the workers were migrants, as is commonly the case in Africa, returning from the plantations to their home villages several times each year. The workers had low productivity and were not paid much. After independence, the government decreed that wage rates for the plantation workers would triple. Plantation owners predicted disaster; such a massive increase in the price they paid for labour, they thought, could only drive them out of business. But the government responded with predictions based on efficiency wage theory, that higher wages would lead to a more productive and stable work force.

The government predictions turned out to be correct. Sisal, for example, is a plant cultivated be-cause it produces a strong white fiber that can be used for cord or fiber. Overall production of sisal quadrupled under the efficiency wage policy. This occurred not because of a change in the overall physical capital available, but because more motivated and highly skilled workers were better employed by the plantation owners. Over several years following the wage increase, however, employment in Tanzania's sisal industry fell from 129,000 to 42,000, thus illustrating how efficiency wages can increase unemployment.

Sources: Mrinal Datta-Chaudhuri, *Journal of Economic Perspectives* (Summer 1990): 25–39; Richard Sabot, "Labor Standards in a Small Low-Income Country: Tanzania," Overseas Development Council (1988).

Efficiency wage theory also helps to explain another puzzle of unemployment. If the economy needs a 25 percent reduction in labour supplied, why don't workers simply work thirty hours rather than forty, and save jobs for the 25 percent of their colleagues who otherwise would be laid off? We saw one explanation earlier in this chapter: the fixed costs associated with work. These fixed costs imply that it pays to have workers work a full work day rather than five or six hours. But we also saw that even with fixed costs there can be work sharing, in the form of job rotation. A worker might work one week, his colleague the next, the two of them sharing more fairly the burden of the reduced demand for labour. This does not seem to occur.

According to efficiency wage theory, the reason workers do not just work thirty hours rather than forty is that by reducing work proportionately among its workers, a firm will in effect be reducing overall pay proportionately. The company will fall back into the traps outlined above. If it lowers overall pay, it may lose a disproportionate fraction of its better workers. These workers can obtain offers of full-time work and full-time pay, and they will find this more attractive than a job with 80 percent of full-time work and 80 percent of the pay. They may enjoy the extra leisure, but it will not help meet the mortgage payments. Furthermore, workers now working part time will find that their incentives to exert high levels of effort decline. What they have to lose if they get fired is not so great; losing a part-time job is not as serious as losing a full-time job. This ability to explain concentrated layoffs is one feature that sets efficiency wage theory apart from some of the alternative views of wage rigidity.

THE IMPACT OF UNEMPLOYMENT ON DIFFERENT GROUPS

As noted in Chapter 8, one striking aspect of unemployment in Canada is that it affects different groups in the population very differently. In competitive markets, wages will adjust to reflect productivity; groups with higher productivity will have commensurately higher wage rates, while groups with lower productivity will have lower wage rates. But people in both groups will have jobs. There would be no reason for different groups to have different unemployment rates.

The efficiency wage theory argues that there may be some kinds of labourers, such as part-time workers or those with limited skills, who, at any wage, have sufficiently low productivity that it barely pays a firm to hire them. The labour cost, relative to what the workers produce, is simply too high. These workers are productive, but barely productive enough to offset the wages they receive. Or to put it another way, while these workers may receive a low wage, the wage is low enough only just to offset their low level of productivity. Paying higher wages would not increase productivity enough to offset the wage increase. And paying lower wages would reduce productivity, making that option unworkable as well.

It is these groups, who lie right at the margin of the hiring decision, who will bear the brunt of the fluctuations in the demand for labour. Chapter 8 pointed out, for instance, that teenagers and young workers not only have higher average unemployment rates, they bear more of the burden of variations in employment. We have also noted that in provinces in which the minimum wage for teenagers is lower, most firms continue to pay teenagers more than the minimum wage. Presumably firms are worried that if they cut their wages by 10 percent, productivity will be reduced by more than 10 percent, because they will lose their best teenagers and the remaining workers' effort will be reduced.

LIMITS OF EFFICIENCY WAGE THEORY

Efficiency wage theory may provide a significant part of the explanation for wage rigidities in a number of different situations: where training and turnover costs are high; where monitoring productivity is difficult; and where differences in individuals' productivity are large and important, but it is difficult to ascertain them before hiring and training them. On the other hand, in situations where workers are paid piece rates on the basis of how much they produce, or in situations where training costs are low and monitoring is easy, efficiency wage considerations are likely to be less important. These situations may indeed exhibit greater wage flexibility, or at least they might if there are no union pressures, implicit contracts, or insider-outsider considerations.

CHANGES IN THE PRICE LEVEL

For most of this chapter, we have found it convenient to analyze the labour market assuming that prices of goods are fixed. It is now time to drop that assumption, and discover the consequences. We return to the basic supply and demand model with which we began the chapter. There, the demand and supply for labour depended on the wage paid, under the assumption that the prices of all goods were given. Here, we look at what happens if as wages change, prices change too. Since we are dealing with unemployment, the change we will consider is a decline in wages and the price level.

Lower wages might give rise to more employment *if* that were the end of the story. If workers at a single firm were to agree to a cut in their wages, the firm would have a competitive advantage over its rivals; sales would increase (the firm would cut its prices), and so would employment. But when all firms lower wages, the consequences are different. The lower wages have repercussions on the product market.

This is illustrated in Figure 11.5. Panel A shows the aggregate demand and supply curves for labour, and panel B shows the aggregate demand and supply curves for goods. Remember, each curve in panel A is drawn under the assumption of a particular price level, and each curve in panel B is drawn under the assumption of a particular wage level. Initially, the wage is w_0, with the supply exceeding the demand; the resulting unemployment is U_0. Wages fall to w_1. If nothing else happens, unemployment would fall to U_1. But something else is happening in the product market. Lower wages shift the aggregate supply curve to the right—at each price level, firms are willing to supply more goods because wages are lower. The aggregate demand curve may also shift to the left, since workers have less to spend with the lower wages. In any case, the net effect is that prices fall, to p_2 in the figure.

The fall in prices has further repercussions in the labour market. The amount of labour that firms wish to hire at any (nominal) wage depends on the prices at which they can sell what they produce. At lower prices, they demand less labour at each wage. So the demand curve for labour in panel A shifts to D_1, and at the new level of prices, at the wage w_1, the demand for labour is essentially what it was before. Depending on whether prices fall faster or slower than wages, employment may increase or decrease slightly. The basic point is that wage cuts are often ineffective at reducing unemployment or, at best, work slowly because price changes offset the wage changes.

Some economists believe that if wages and prices fell *enough*, the economy will be restored to full employment. They believe, in other words, that as wages and prices fall,

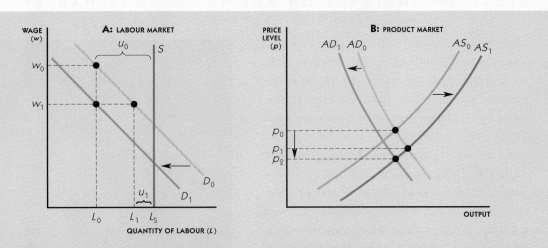

Figure 11.5 PRICE CHANGES OFFSETTING LOWER WAGES

In panel A, the economy begins with wages at w_0, so the supply of labour L_s exceeds the demand for labour L_0, and unemployment exists. The wage begins to decline towards equilibrium and falls to w_1, where firms would be willing to demand L_1. But as panel B shows, the lower wages lead to lower prices. The aggregate supply curve shifts to the right, and the aggregate demand curve shifts to the left; the new equilibrium price level is p_2. This lower price level in turn shifts the demand for labour from D_0 to D_1 in panel A. As a result, the quantity demanded remains at L_0.

the demand curve for labour does not shift down proportionately. One reason it does not is that at very low prices, people feel wealthier; they can buy more with the money they have in the bank. Another reason is that for people to hold the higher *real* supply of money, interest rates must fall, and investment will be stimulated. But during the Great Depression, prices fell by more than 20 percent and wages fell by about 14 percent, and this seemed to make matters worse rather than better. The reasons for this we take up in Chapters 12–19. What seems clear is that if the economy will indeed be restored to full employment when wages and prices fall enough, this process is too slow and too uncertain for governments to rely on. Clamours for the government to do something about the unemployment will be felt long before the process can work itself out.

OKUN'S LAW

As high as the unemployment statistics sometimes climb, they may not fully reflect the underutilization of human resources. Firms find it costly to hire and train workers. Therefore, when they have a temporary lull in demand, they do not immediately fire their workers. They may not even lay them off, for fear that once laid off, the workers will seek employment elsewhere. Firms keep the workers on the job, but they may not fully utilize them. This is referred to as **labour hoarding,** and can be thought of as

CLOSE-UP: IMMIGRATION AND THE LABOUR MARKET

Immigration to Canada has fluctuated widely over time. The high point was in 1913 when 401,000 immigrants entered the country. By the Great Depression, the flow had fallen off considerably, reaching 105,000 by 1930 and still declining. From 1932 to 1944, immigration was so low that net immigration was negative (gross immigration was 13,000 in 1933). From the mid-1940s, it rose steadily to reach a peak in 1957 around 275,000. From 1946 to 1957, 1.7 million immigrants arrived in Canada. In four of those twelve years, the annual rate exceeded 100,000; but since then it has been going through phases of rise and fall.

Immigration policy has always been a contentious issue. Traditionally, immigrants have included mostly low-skilled workers and their families. The Diefenbaker government of 1957 was elected with an immigration policy that shifted the emphasis from a large number of low-skilled immigrants to a small number of high-skilled ones, causing a decline to below 100,000. As the economy strengthened, the number of new arrivals began to rise, reaching 200,000 by 1967. One source of discontent with the new system was its preference for family members and refugees at the expense of independent applicants. In 1967, the Pearson government corrected this with a new selection system for nonfamily, nonrefugee applicants: the point system. This system separated independent applicants from family and refugee applicants and chose the former according to a system of points for a variety of educational and occupational skills. The point system remains the method by which independent immigrants are selected.

The adoption of the point system represented a major innovation in immigration policy, and it has undergone various refinements over the years. The current assignment of points was adopted in 1985 on the basis of a recommendation by the Standing Committee on Labour Employment and Immigration of the House of Commons that immigration should not only be tied to Canada's specific labour-force needs in terms of occupational skills, but also that it should try to smooth out the current age imbalance in the Canadian population, especially to compensate for the fluctuations in domestic fertility rates. Under the point system adopted in 1985, 60 percent of the points were allotted for economic factors (education, training, experience, occupational demand, and arranged employment). The remainder were divided among several other factors, including location, age, knowledge of English or French, and personal suitability. A small bonus was offered for family class or assisted relatives.

A recent study by the Economic Council of Canada analyzed three types of effects of immigration—economic, political, and social. They found that the impact of economic and political effects of immigration was relatively small. The impact on both long-term and short-term unemployment and on filling labour market gaps was negligible. Per capita incomes of Canadians would rise slightly from immigration because of a combination of scale economies from a larger population and contributions of immigrants to tax revenues. Most other economic benefits accrued to the immigrants themselves in the form of higher incomes.

Similarly, the political benefits of having a larger national population or larger populations in some provinces were judged to be small. They argued that the real benefits of immigration were social and humanitarian. The country would benefit from the increased cultural and ethnic diversity. And on humanitarian grounds, immigration was judged to be beneficial since the immigrants would gain a great deal and existing Canadians would not lose. On the basis of this, the council recommended that immigration be raised gradually from the current average of 0.63 percent of the population over the past twenty-five years to 1 percent of the population by 2015; that is, from 168,000 in 1991 to 340,000 in 2015.

Sources: Economic Council of Canada, *Economic and Social Impacts of Immigration* (Ottawa: Minister of Supply and Services Canada, 1991).

a form of disguised unemployment. Employees are not really working, though they are showing up for work. Like open unemployment, it represents a waste of human resources.

The importance of this disguised unemployment was brought home forcefully by a study conducted by the American economist Arthur Okun, chairman of the U.S. Council of Economic Advisers under President Johnson. He showed that as the economy pulls out of a recession, output increases more than proportionately with employment, and as the economy goes into a recession, output decreases more than proportionately with the reduction in employment. This result is sometimes referred to as **Okun's law.** In Okun's study, for every 1 percent increase in employment, output increased by 3 percent. This was a remarkable finding, for it seemed to run contrary to one of the basic principles of economics—the law of diminishing returns, which would have predicted that a 1 percent increase in employment would have less than a proportionate effect on output. The explanation for Okun's law, however, was quite simple: many of those who were "working" in a recession were not really working. They were partially idle. As the economy heated up, they worked more fully, and this is what gave rise to the increased output.

ALTERNATIVE EXPLANATIONS OF WAGE RIGIDITIES

1. Unions with explicit and implicit contracts prevent wages from falling. Insider-outsider theory explains why firms do not pay newly hired workers a lower wage. Minimum wages explain why wages for very low-skilled workers do not fall.

2. Efficiency wage theory suggests that it is profitable for firms to pay above-market wages. This is because wages affect the quality of the labour force, labour turnover rates, and the level of effort exerted by workers.

3. Falling wages may very well be accompanied by falling prices, with the result that there is little change in real wages.

POLICY ISSUES

In this chapter, we have explored a variety of possible reasons why wages do not fall to the market-clearing level, where the demand for labour equals the supply. The truth probably involves a combination of all of these explanations. Minimum wages play a role among very low-skilled workers. Unions play a role in some sectors of the economy. In some jobs, firms do not cut wages because of efficiency wage considerations. Lowering wages actually increases labour costs; the firm will get lower-quality workers, workers will not work as hard, and the firm will face higher turnover rates.

Wages do sometimes fall, as in the Great Depression. But what are important for firm decisions are wages relative to prices. Wages do not fall *fast enough* to equilibrate demand and supply. And all of the reasons given in this chapter play a role in helping us to understand why wages fall slowly or not at all.

When the labour market does not clear and involuntary unemployment is the result, there may be an economic role for government. Government policies that are designed to overcome failures in the labour market have centered on three issues: increasing the demand for labour by lowering (real) wages and otherwise increasing wage flexibility; reducing the costs of unemployment; and increasing the demand for labour by increasing the aggregate demand for the products workers produce. The third of these is the subject of the next three chapters. Here we discuss the first two policies.

INCREASING WAGE FLEXIBILITY

Those who see wage rigidities as a major cause of unemployment and believe that they are created by unions or implicit contracts have sought ways of increasing wage flexibility. In Japan, for example, large companies have long-term (lifetime) implicit contracts with their workers, but workers receive a substantial fraction of their pay in the form of annual bonuses. In effect, this means that the wage a worker receives varies from year to year, depending on the fortunes of the firm. Unemployment in Japan is considerably less variable than in North America, and many economists believe that flexible wages are an important part of the reason. In his book *The Share Economy*, Martin Weitzman of Harvard University has advocated that U.S. firms adopt a similar system.

Two features make wage flexibility unattractive to workers. First, many workers would have to bear more risk in income fluctuations. Under the current system, workers who have considerable seniority, and who often dominate union negotiations, face little risk of being laid off during hard times; their incomes are relatively secure, both from year-to-year variation and from the threat of complete cessation. With the bonus system, however, all employees, including the more senior ones, would face considerable risk. And as the discussion of implicit contracts pointed out, the firm is generally in a better position than the worker to bear the risk of economic fluctuations.

Second, workers worry that the firms most likely to be willing to give large profit shares to their employees in exchange for wage concessions may be those firms that expect the smallest profits; by giving up a share of the profit, they are giving the least away. In effect, when the workers' pay depends on the profits of the firm, workers become much like shareholders—what they receive depends on how well the company does. It does no good to own a large share in the profits of a firm that makes no profits.

This second reason makes it clear why unions do not trust wage flexibility systems. Their concern that only firms without profits will offer to share them with their workers proved justified in 1985, when employees of Eastern Airlines in the United States actually accepted a pay reduction in return for a share of the profits. The share of profits turned out to be worthless when the airline went into bankruptcy soon after.

Still, the fact is that large segments of Japanese industry employ a system with greater wage flexibility, and that system seems to give rise to less variability in employment. Japan appears to have overcome the obstacles to making wages vary with profits. How this happened and whether it is possible for Canada to move to a system with more flexible wages remain questions of debate among economists.

REDUCING THE COSTS OF UNEMPLOYMENT

During the past half century, governments have taken it as their responsibility not only to reduce the level of unemployment, but also to reduce the costs borne by those unfortunate enough not to be able to find a job. The difficulty is, how do we do this without giving rise to further economic problems?

UNEMPLOYMENT INSURANCE

The Unemployment Insurance (UI) program is the most important one for reducing the cost to the individual of being unemployed. It was started by the federal government in 1941 in the wake of the Great Depression. All employed workers must participate in the scheme. The self-employed are generally not eligible, the exception being fishermen. UI is financed by premiums paid by both the employer and the employee, though the employer is responsible for collecting the premiums for Revenue Canada. In 1992, the rate was 3.0 percent for employers and 4.2 percent for employees, up to a maximum amount. Workers who lose their jobs through layoff are eligible for receiving benefits if

CLOSE-UP: UNEMPLOYMENT INSURANCE: A PROBLEM OF DIVIDED JURISDICTION?

The federal government spent close to $19 billion on Unemployment Insurance (UI) in 1992–1993, about 16 percent of its total program expenditures. This has become the largest single category of expenditure, one that has been growing by over 7 percent per year. A large part of this growth can be attributed to the continuing high rates of unemployment facing the Canadian economy in the early 1990s. There are, however, those who would argue that one reason why the system seems to have got out of hand financially is that it tries to accomplish too much, and in so doing makes the matter worse.

There is no doubt that the federal government uses UI as a policy for alleviating regional disparities. Eligibility requirements are considerably lower and the length of benefit payments are considerably higher for depressed regions such as the Atlantic provinces and eastern Quebec. As well, the fishing industry, which is a main source of employment in these areas, is given preferential treatment. UI has become a major source of income to these regions, far greater than the value of premiums paid by them. Why should the federal government use UI, nominally an insurance program, for achieving redistributive goals?

One possible reason is that it is one of the only policy instruments available to it for directing assistance to low-income persons. The provinces retain responsibility for providing services to low-income persons, and they do so mainly through their welfare assistance and services programs. Indeed, the provinces would also have been responsible for UI had it not been for a special amendment to the Canadian Constitution in 1940 turning over exclusive jurisdiction to the federal government. (At the time, the provinces were broke and unable to cope with the consequences of the Great Depression for unemployed workers.)

The fact that UI is delivered by the federal government, while welfare is delivered by the provinces, has given rise both to an uncoordi-

nated system of assistance to low-income persons but also to some adverse incentives for the provinces. An allegedly common practice engaged in by some provinces, especially those in depressed regions, is to arrange to employ workers in the public sector for short periods of time, just enough to make them eligible for UI. This way the workers will be removed from provincial welfare rolls temporarily and will end up being supported for the lengthy benefit period under the federal UI system. The practice has come to be dubbed "Lotto 10-50," a takeoff on the federal government's lottery scheme Lotto 9-49. Here, the 10 refers to the minimum period for which the worker must be employed to become eligible for UI, and the 50 refers to the number of weeks for which benefits will be paid.

For these reasons, many commentators in the ongoing debates over constitutional reform in Canada have argued that UI and welfare assistance should be delivered at the same level of government, most often the provincial level. Note that in Western Europe, where assistance to low-income persons is concentrated at the center, unemployment insurance and welfare assistance tend to be integrated into a single system.

they have worked for a minimum qualifying period. The qualifying period is twenty weeks in areas where the unemployment rate is 6 percent or less, and falls to ten weeks as the area unemployment rate rises to 15 percent. Benefits received depend both upon the number of weeks contributed and upon the earning level when employed. Benefit payments are 60 percent of insurable earnings, and they may be received for up to fifty weeks. There are special benefits for maternity and parental leave and for sickness. Benefits are taxable and are recovered from high-income recipients.

Critics of the program who claim that UI pays too much worry that it reduces the incentive of unemployed workers to search for jobs. There is some evidence for this: the number of people who get jobs just as their unemployment benefits expire is far greater than can be accounted for by chance. Others worry that when high levels of unemployment insurance are available, workers have less incentive to exert effort at any given level of wages and unemployment; after all, given the high level of unemployment compensation, the threat of being fired for shirking is not as fearsome as it would otherwise be. To restore the incentives of efficiency wages, firms must pay higher wages, but when they do, the higher cost of labour induces them to hire fewer workers. By this logic, high unemployment insurance actually contributes to increasing the unemployment rate.

What we have here is another illustration of a familiar basic trade-off—between security (risk) on the one hand and incentives on the other. Economic arrangements that diminish risk also diminish incentives. A person who is guaranteed a job will have little incentive to work. If UI were sufficiently generous that it fully replaced whatever income he lost if he were fired, a worker would not find any economic incentives for working. And a worker who is laid off would have no incentive to look for a new job. Thus, some critics of the current UI system argue that society has chosen the wrong point on the trade-off curve depicted in Figure 11.6; the gain in increased security at point A is not worth the cost in reduced productivity from attenuated incentives relative to B.

Other critics argue that the current Canadian UI system does not provide enough support for either the long-term unemployed or new entrants into the labour force, and

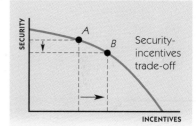

Figure 11.6 TRADE-OFF BETWEEN ECONOMIC SECURITY AND PRODUCTIVITY

Giving workers more job security or better unemployment insurance provides greater economic security but reduces their productivity. There is concern that the present system provides too much security, that it might be possible to get relatively large increases in productivity at the cost of small decreases in security, as shown by the movement from A to B.

provides too much for the short-term unemployed. For a worker who has been employed for a while, insurance for unemployment spells of six or eight weeks may be unnecessary in the eyes of many economists. They argue that people should be able to finance these short-term spells out of savings or by borrowing. There is a waiting period of two weeks before receiving benefits (though it is much longer for those who quit without just cause), but it is argued that this is far too short. These economists believe that in general insurance should be designed to cover *large* losses against which individuals cannot self-insure.

One way to overcome some of these incentive problems, particularly those arising from the alleged overuse of the system to support temporary layoffs, is to introduce insurance principles into the funding of the program. This could be done by making premiums "experience rated," a practice that is followed by some states in the United States. Under experience rating, the premiums paid by a firm and its employees depend upon the amount of benefits that have been claimed in the past. The use of experience rating reduces the incentive for firms to use layoffs to adjust to temporary declines in the demand for their products. It has been frequently advocated in Canada.

There has also been considerable concern with the fact that eligibility criteria and benefit levels are much more favourable in high unemployment regions than elsewhere. In effect, UI is being used both for addressing regional inequalities and for insuring against layoffs. Critics argue that this discourages workers from moving from depressed regions where permanent jobs are scarce to regions where jobs are available, and that it creates an atmosphere of dependency in depressed regions, whereby entire regions come to rely on UI far too much.

REVIEW AND PRACTICE

SUMMARY

1. Involuntary unemployment exists when the supply of labour exceeds the demand for labour at the prevailing market wage. This may happen because demand for labour falls but wages do not decline.

2. It has been argued that all unemployment is voluntary, that workers could always find work at a lower wage or in a different field. But the costs of moving to where jobs are available might be significant, and accepting a low-wage job might send the wrong kind of information to potential future employers.

3. The reasons why firms may be unable to reduce wages and thus unemployment include union contracts, insider-outsider theory, and minimum wage laws.

4. Reducing wages may actually lead to an increase in labour costs, because it may result in a lower average quality of workers as the best workers leave; because it may result in lower effort; and because it may result in higher turnover costs.

5. If a decline in nominal wages causes the overall price level to decline, then a fall in nominal wages may not be translated into a fall in real wages, and may not do much to reduce unemployment.

6. Making wages depend more on firm profits might result in less variability in employment. But workers would risk being laid off in hard times, and would worry that the firms most likely to give large profit shares to employees may expect the smallest profits.

7. Unemployment insurance reduces the costs to workers of being laid off, but it also reduces workers' incentives to work hard or to search for a new job. Firms' responses may lead to higher rather than lower unemployment.

KEY TERMS

involuntary unem-
    ployment
downward rigidity of
    wages

implicit contract
work sharing
insider-outsider
    theory

labour turnover rate
efficiency wage
Okun's law

REVIEW QUESTIONS

1. Under what conditions will economists argue that involuntary unemployment exists? In what sense could unemployment be considered "voluntary"? Discuss the main arguments for this position and the counterarguments.

2. Make a list of reasons that firms may be unable to reduce wages, and a list of reasons that firms may choose not to reduce wages.

3. True or false: "The prevalence of unions and minimum wage laws is the primary reason for wage stickiness, and therefore for unemployment, in the Canadian economy." Discuss your answer.

4. If an implicit contract is not written down, why would a firm abide by it? Why would a worker?

5. Why does implicit contract theory predict that work sharing is more likely than layoffs?

6. Name three reasons why productivity may depend on the level of wages paid.

7. How does an efficiency wage differ from a market-clearing wage?

8. How does efficiency wage theory help to explain the fact that different groups may have very different levels of unemployment?

9. What trade-off does society face when it attempts to expand economic security for workers with higher unemployment benefits or greater job security?

PROBLEMS

1. In 1993, Ontario increased the minimum wage. How will this change affect the stickiness of wages and the level of unemployment? In some provinces, equilibrium wages are above the minimum wage. How would this fact alter your prediction about the effects of the minimum wage in those provinces?

2. Would you be more or less likely to observe implicit contracts in industries where most workers hold their jobs for only a short time? What about industries where most workers hold jobs a long time? Explain.

3. A number of businesses have proposed a two-tier wage scale, in which the wage scale for new employees is lower than the wage scale for current employees. Using the insights of insider-outside theory, would you be more or less likely to observe two-tier wage scales in industries where a lot of on-the-job training is needed? where not much is needed?

4. The following figures represent the relationship between productivity and wages for the Doorware Corporation, which makes hinges.

Wage per hour	$ 8	$10	$12	$14	$16	$18	$20
Hinges produced per hour	20	24	33	42	52	58	60

Graph the productivity-wage relationship. From the graph, how do you determine the efficiency wage? Calculate output per dollar spent on labour for the Doorware Corporation. What is the efficiency wage?

5. Would you be more or less likely to see efficiency wages in the following types of industries?
    (a) industries where training and turnover costs are relatively low;
    (b) industries where it is difficult to monitor individual productivity;
    (c) industries that have many jobs where individual differences in productivity are relatively large.

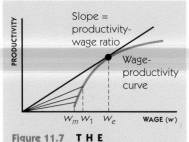

Figure 11.7 THE RELATIONSHIP BETWEEN PRODUCTIVITY AND WAGES

As wages rise, productivity increases, at first quickly and then more slowly. The efficiency wage is the wage at which the ratio of productivity to wage is highest. It is found by drawing a line through the origin tangent to the wage-productivity curve.

APPENDIX: DERIVATION OF THE EFFICIENCY WAGE

Figure 11.7 depicts a curve that represents one possible relationship between productivity and wages. We refer to this curve as the **wage-productivity curve.** Productivity here can be thought of as "the number of pins produced in an hour," or any similar measure of output. There is a minimum wage, w_m, below which the firm will find it difficult, if not impossible, to obtain labour. At a very low wage, w_1, the company can only hire the dregs of the labour market—those who cannot get jobs elsewhere. Worker morale is low, and effort is low. Workers quit as soon as they can get another job, so labour turnover is high.

As the firm raises its wage, productivity increases. The company earns a reputation as a high-wage firm, attracting the best workers. Morale is high, turnover is low, and employees work hard. But eventually, as in so many areas, diminishing returns set in: successive increases in wages have incrementally smaller effects on productivity. The firm is concerned with wage costs per unit of output, not wage costs per employee. Thus, it wishes to minimize not the wage but the wage divided by productivity.

This can be put another way. The company wishes to maximize the output per dollar spent on labour (we are assuming that all the other costs are fixed). Since productivity is defined as the output per unit of time (pins per hour), and the wage is the labour cost per unit of time (dollars per hour), dividing productivity by the wage produces the equation

$$\frac{\text{productivity}}{\text{wage}} = \frac{\text{output/unit of time}}{\text{dollars/unit of time}} = \frac{\text{output}}{\text{dollars spent on labour}}.$$

Thus, a decision to make the ratio of output to dollars spent on labour as high as possible is mathematically equivalent to a decision to make the ratio of productivity to wages as high as possible. To tell what level of wages will accomplish this goal, Figure 11.7 shows the productivity-wage ratio as a line from the origin to a point on the wage-productivity curve. The slope of this line is just the ratio of productivity (the vertical axis) to the wage (the horizontal axis).

As we draw successive lines from the origin to points on the wage-productivity curve with higher wages, the slope first increases and then decreases. The slope is largest for the line through the origin that is just tangent to the wage-productivity curve. The wage at this point of tangency is the wage at which labour costs are minimized: the efficiency wage, w_e.

Changes in unemployment rates may shift the wage-productivity curve, as shown in Figure 11.8. At each wage, the productivity of the labour force is higher at the higher unemployment rate. Also, the efficiency wage—the wage at which the ratio of productivity to the wage is maximized—is lowered slightly: it falls from w_0 to w_1. The change in the efficiency wage may be relatively small, even if the shift in the curve relating productivity to wages is relatively large.

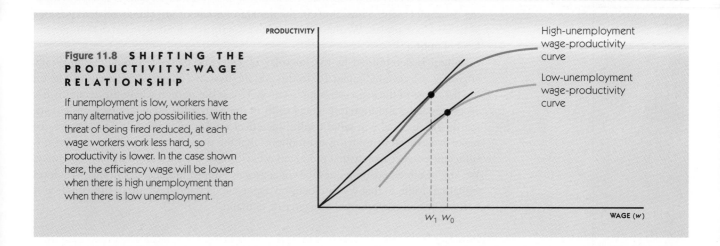

Figure 11.8 SHIFTING THE PRODUCTIVITY-WAGE RELATIONSHIP

If unemployment is low, workers have many alternative job possibilities. With the threat of being fired reduced, at each wage workers work less hard, so productivity is lower. In the case shown here, the efficiency wage will be lower when there is high unemployment than when there is low unemployment.

CHAPTER 12

AGGREGATE DEMAND

n Chapter 11, we focused directly on the labour market. We saw that when the demand for labour decreases, real wages do not fall to allow the labour market to clear, and unemployment is the result. The next question is, what causes the demand curve for labour to shift? The answer lies in the product market. If the level of output (GDP) is high, then employment rates are likely to be high as well. Likewise, declining output is usually accompanied by increasing unemployment. Thus, shifts in the demand for labour are closely related to events in the product market. We therefore need to ask a further question: what determines the level of output?

Output is determined by the interplay of aggregate demand and aggregate supply curves, as we saw in Chapter 10. In this and the next two chapters, our focus will be on the flat range of the aggregate supply curve. This is the portion where the economy has excess capacity, and therefore where shifts in the aggregate demand curve translate primarily into increases in output with little effect on the price level. In this chapter, we make two crucial simplifying assumptions: that the price level is fixed and that there is sufficient excess capacity that producers are willing to produce any output at that price. We are, in effect, pushing questions of aggregate supply and changes in the price level (inflation) aside so that we can focus on aggregate demand. Output, in this simple scenario, is entirely determined by aggregate demand.[1]

[1] The analysis is actually broader than this: it encompasses any situation where the price level is fixed and where, at that price level, firms would be willing to increase output if they were able to sell what they produced.

KEY QUESTIONS

1. When the economy has excess capacity, what determines the aggregate level of output?

2. What are the components of aggregate expenditures?

3. How do consumption and imports increase with income?

4. Why, if investment or government expenditures or exports increase by a dollar, does aggregate output increase by more than a dollar? What determines the amount by which it increases?

INCOME-EXPENDITURE ANALYSIS

Aggregate demand, as we learned in Chapter 10, is the total demand for goods and services produced in the economy. There we got a first look at the aggregate demand curve, which gives the level of aggregate demand at each price level.

To know where this curve comes from, we need to understand a new concept, the **aggregate expenditures schedule.** Aggregate expenditures include the total of what households, firms, and governments, both in Canada and abroad, spend on goods produced in Canada. The aggregate expenditures schedule traces out the relationship, at a fixed price level, between aggregate expenditures and national income. By contrast, the aggregate demand curve traces out the levels of output that are demanded at different price levels.[2]

It is natural to think that as consumers' incomes increase, they will want to spend more. The same pattern holds when all the components of aggregate expenditures are looked at together. Later in the chapter, we will see more precisely how and why increases in income lead to greater expenditure. For now, this rough pattern of aggregate expenditures increasing with income is all we need to form a schedule like the one in Figure 12.1. The vertical axis measures aggregate expenditures, while the horizontal axis shows national income.

There are three critical properties of the aggregate expenditures schedule. First, it is upward sloping—as national income goes up, so do aggregate expenditures. Changes in

[2] In Chapter 15, we will analyze what happens to the aggregate expenditures schedule when the price level changes, and then determine the equilibrium level of aggregate demand at each price level. This will enable us to derive the aggregate demand curve.

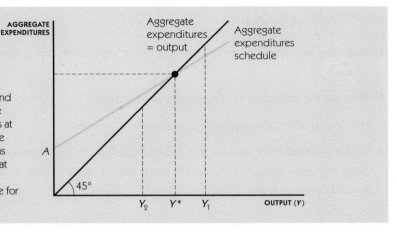

Figure 12.1 THE AGGREGATE EXPENDITURES SCHEDULE AND INCOME-EXPENDITURE ANALYSIS

The aggregate expenditures schedule gives the sum of consumption, investment, government expenditures, and net exports at each level of national income. Aggregate expenditures increase with income. Equilibrium occurs at the intersection of the aggregate expenditures schedule and the 45-degree line. At outputs less than Y^*, such as Y_2, output exceeds aggregate expenditures. Goods are being produced are not being sold; there are unintended inventory accumulations. The reverse is true for outputs greater than Y^*.

other variables (like interest rates, tax rates, and exchange rates) cause the aggregate expenditures schedule to shift up or down, and they may even change the slope.

Second, as income increases by a dollar, aggregate expenditures increase by less than a dollar. The reason for this is that consumers save some of their increased income; they do not spend all of it. Figure 12.1 also shows a line through the origin at a 45-degree angle. The slope of this line is unity. Along the line, as we move to the right on the horizontal axis by a dollar, we move up the vertical axis by a dollar. Since aggregate expenditures increase less than dollar for dollar with increased income, the aggregate expenditures schedule is flatter than the 45-degree line.

Third, even if national income were zero, people would still need to spend money to buy goods; they would pay for the goods by borrowing or out of savings. That is one of the reasons why, even when national income is zero, aggregate expenditures are positive. This is reflected in the figure in the fact that the aggregate expenditures schedule intercepts the vertical axis at a positive level, point A. The facts that (a) the aggregate expenditures schedule is flatter than the 45-degree line through the origin and (b) aggregate expenditures are positive, even when income is zero, imply that the aggregate expenditures schedule intersects the 45-degree line, as seen in the figure.

Our objective is to determine the equilibrium level of output in the economy when there is excess capacity, so that aggregate demand determines the level of output. Besides the aggregate expenditures schedule, there are two more concepts we need for our analysis.

THE NATIONAL INCOME-OUTPUT IDENTITY

Chapter 8 showed that national income is equal to national output. This reflects the fact that when a good is purchased, the money that is paid must eventually wind up in someone's pocket—either as wages, in the pockets of workers in the firm that produced the good (or of workers who produced the intermediate goods that were used in the production of the final good); as interest payments, in the pockets of those who have lent the firm money; or as profits, in the pockets of the owners of the firm. The money eventually must show up as someone's income. For simplicity, we will assume that the residents of the country neither receive money (net) from abroad nor pay money (net) abroad, so GNP and GDP coincide. If Y is used to represent national income, this identity can be written

GDP = national income = Y.

The identity is useful, because it means that we can interpret the horizontal axis in Figure 12.1 in two different ways: we can say the aggregate expenditures schedule gives the level of expenditures at each level of national *income* or that it gives the level of expenditures at each level of national *output*.

EQUILIBRIUM OUTPUT

Normally, firms will only produce what they believe they can sell. This means that the total output produced by all firms will equal the total demand for output. This is our third necessary concept, and it can be put another way: in equilibrium, aggregate expenditures, which we denote by AE, must equal aggregate output (GDP). Since aggregate output equals national income (Y), we have the simple equation

AE = GDP = Y.

In Figure 12.1, the 45-degree line through the origin is labelled "Aggregate expenditures = output." The line traces out all points where the vertical axis (aggregate expenditures) equals the horizontal axis (national income, which equals aggregate output).

Equilibrium lies at the point on the aggregate expenditures schedule that also satisfies the aggregate-expenditures-equal-output condition. That is, equilibrium occurs at the intersection of the aggregate expenditures schedule and the 45-degree line. The corresponding equilibrium value of aggregate output is denoted by Y^*.

The analysis that determines equilibrium output by relating income (output) to aggregate expenditures is called **income-expenditure analysis.** We can see that Y^* is the equilibrium in two different ways. First, it is the only point that satisfies the two conditions for equilibrium. In equilibrium, everything produced must be purchased. Aggregate expenditures must be equal to national output (income), as represented by the 45-degree line. In equilibrium, the level of aggregate expenditures must also be what households, firms, and government want to spend in total at that level of national income, given by the aggregate expenditures schedule.

Second, consider what happens at a level of income Y_1, in excess of Y^*. At that point, the aggregate expenditures schedule lies below the 45-degree line. What households, firms, and government would like to spend at that level of national income, as reflected in the aggregate expenditures schedule, is less than national income (output). More goods are being produced than individuals would like to buy. Some of the goods, like strawberries, cannot be stored. They simply spoil. Other goods can be, and they go into inventories.

Economists distinguish between **planned inventories** and **unplanned inventories.** Planned inventories are inventories firms choose to have on hand because they make business more efficient. They are considered an investment, and their buildup is therefore counted as part of investment spending in the aggregate expenditures schedule. Unplanned inventories come into being simply because firms cannot sell what they are producing. At Y_1, firms find that unplanned inventories are piling up—they are producing goods that cannot be sold, which are either spoiling or increasing inventories beyond the desired level. They respond by cutting back production until they reach Y^*.

Similarly, consider what happens at a level of income Y_2, less than Y^*. At that point, the aggregate expenditures schedule lies above the 45-degree line. At that level of income, households, firms, and government are spending more than national income (output). They are, in other words, purchasing more than the economy is producing. This is possible because firms can sell out of inventories. With planned inventories being depleted, firms increase their production. They continue to do this until equilibrium is restored, with output (income) equal to Y^*.

SHIFTS IN THE AGGREGATE EXPENDITURES SCHEDULE

A variety of changes in the economy could lead households, firms, and government to decide, *at each level of income*, to spend more or less. Such changes give rise to shifts in the aggregate expenditures schedule. Figure 12.2 shows what happens if the level of aggregate expenditures increases at each level of national income by the amount S. The new aggregate expenditures schedule is denoted by AE_1. The equilibrium output increases from Y_0 to Y_1, which is greater than the amount S. How much greater depends on the slope of the aggregate expenditures schedule, as we see in Figure 12.3. Here the aggregate expenditures schedule shifts up by the same amount it did in Figure 12.2. In Figure 12.3, however, the aggregate expenditures schedule is flatter; consequently, the increase in equilibrium output is much smaller.

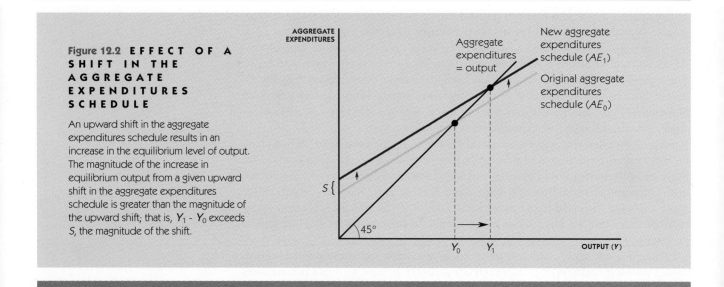

Figure 12.2 EFFECT OF A SHIFT IN THE AGGREGATE EXPENDITURES SCHEDULE

An upward shift in the aggregate expenditures schedule results in an increase in the equilibrium level of output. The magnitude of the increase in equilibrium output from a given upward shift in the aggregate expenditures schedule is greater than the magnitude of the upward shift; that is, $Y_1 - Y_0$ exceeds S, the magnitude of the shift.

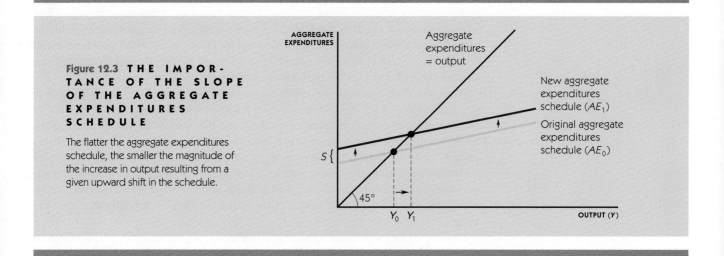

Figure 12.3 THE IMPORTANCE OF THE SLOPE OF THE AGGREGATE EXPENDITURES SCHEDULE

The flatter the aggregate expenditures schedule, the smaller the magnitude of the increase in output resulting from a given upward shift in the schedule.

INCOME-EXPENDITURE ANALYSIS

1. Equilibrium output is at the point where the aggregate expenditures schedule equals output (income).

2. Upward shifts in the aggregate expenditures schedule result in increases in equilibrium output. The increases in equilibrium output are larger than the initial shift in the aggregate expenditures schedule, and become larger when the slope of the aggregate expenditures schedule increases.

We have just learned two of the central principles of macroeconomics: that shifts in the aggregate expenditures schedule determine changes in the equilibrium output of the economy, and that the magnitude of those changes is greater than the magnitude of the shift up or down in the aggregate expenditures schedule and increases with the slope of the aggregate expenditures schedule. The remainder of this chapter, as well as the following two chapters, is devoted to exploring in depth the implications of these principles. Two questions are addressed:

First, what determines the slope of the aggregate expenditures schedule—that is, the extent to which aggregate expenditures increase as income increases? As we have seen, the greater that slope, the larger the increase in output from any upward shift in the schedule.

Second, what causes shifts in the aggregate expenditures schedule? And what, if anything, can the government do to shift the schedule? This is an important question. In the last chapter, we saw that unemployment is created when there is a shift in the demand curve for labour without a corresponding downward adjustment of wages. The primary reason for a shift in the demand curve for labour is a change in the equilibrium level of output: when output is low, the demand for labour is low. If the government can increase the equilibrium level of output by somehow shifting the aggregate expenditures schedule, then it can increase the level of employment.

To answer these questions, we need to take a closer look at each of the components of aggregate expenditures. Recall from Chapter 8 that we can break aggregate expenditures into four components, corresponding to the four final users of the goods produced by the economy: consumption goods, such as food, television sets, or clothes, all of which are purchased by consumers; investment in capital goods, machines or buildings that are bought by firms to help them produce goods; government purchases, goods and services bought either for current use (public consumption) or, like government buildings and roads, for the future benefits they generate (public investment); and net exports.

Exports, the demand by foreigners for Canadian goods, increase the total demand for goods produced in Canada at each level of income. At the same time, we have to remember that some of the demand for goods by consumers, firms, and government is not a demand for goods produced in Canada, but is rather a demand for goods produced abroad. Because we want to know how much will be produced in Canada, we need to subtract off this amount. Thus, in calculating aggregate expenditures we add exports but subtract imports.

Using AE for aggregate expenditures, C for consumption spending, I for investment spending, G for government spending, and E for net exports, we can set out the components of aggregate expenditures in equation form:

$$AE = C + I + G + E.$$

This equation is nothing more than a definition. It says that consumption spending, investment spending, government spending, and net exports add up to aggregate expenditures. Net exports is sometimes written as $X - M$, where X stands for exports and M for imports. These innocuous-looking symbols represent large numbers for the Canadian economy. In 1990, AE was $674 billion, of which C was $400 billion, I was $122 billion, G was $150 billion, X was $169 billion, and M was $167 billion.

We now take a brief look at each of these categories.

Table 12.1 **RELATIONSHIP BETWEEN INCOME AND CONSUMPTION**

Income	Consumption
$ 5,000	$ 6,000
10,000	10,500
20,000	19,500
30,000	28,500

CONSUMPTION

The most important determinant of consumption is income. On average, families with higher incomes spend more. What they do not consume, they save. And on average, families with higher incomes also save more. Someone with an income of $20,000 may save a little; someone with $30,000 will save even more. A person with less than $10,000 is likely to dip into savings or borrow (if she can); she has negative savings.

Table 12.1 shows the relationship between consumption and income for a hypothetical family. The same information is depicted graphically in Figure 12.4A, with the

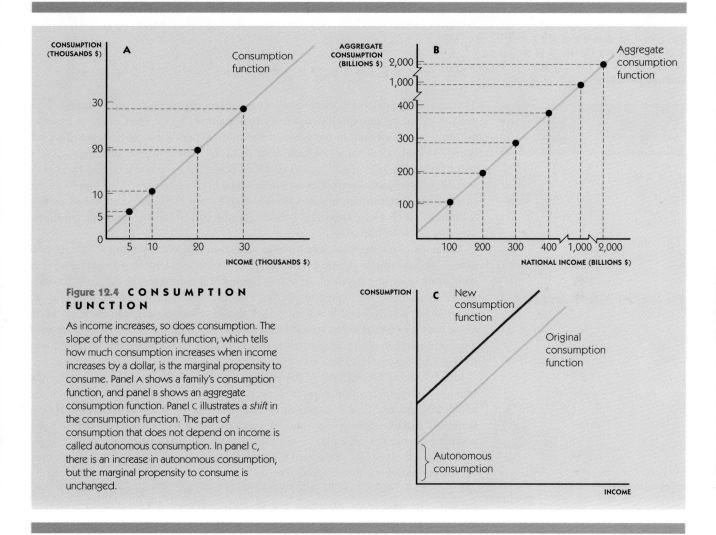

Figure 12.4 CONSUMPTION FUNCTION

As income increases, so does consumption. The slope of the consumption function, which tells how much consumption increases when income increases by a dollar, is the marginal propensity to consume. Panel A shows a family's consumption function, and panel B shows an aggregate consumption function. Panel C illustrates a *shift* in the consumption function. The part of consumption that does not depend on income is called autonomous consumption. In panel C, there is an increase in autonomous consumption, but the marginal propensity to consume is unchanged.

amount of consumption given along the vertical axis and income along the horizontal axis. The upward slope of the line indicates that consumption for this family increases as income does. The relationship between a household's consumption and its income is called its **consumption function.** Every family has different consumption patterns because the tastes and circumstances of families differ, but the pattern shown in Table 12.1 is typical. Aggregate consumption is the sum of the consumption of all the households in the economy. Just as when a typical family's income rises its consumption increases, when the total income of the economy rises, aggregate consumption increases. For purposes of macroeconomics, it is the **aggregate consumption function,** the relationship between aggregate consumption and aggregate income, that is of importance. And the measure of income that is important is disposable income, or what people have after paying taxes.[3] The relationship between aggregate consumption and aggregate income

---

[3] See Chapter 8 for a slightly expanded discussion of disposable income.

Table 12.2 AGGREGATE CONSUMPTION AND NATIONAL INCOME (billions of dollars)

Disposable income	Consumption (C)
$ 100	$ 105
200	195
300	285
400	375
650	600
1,000	915
2,000	1,815

is given in Table 12.2, and the aggregate consumption function is depicted graphically in Figure 12.4B.

THE MARGINAL PROPENSITY TO CONSUME

The amount by which consumption increases when disposable income increases by a dollar is called the **marginal propensity to consume** (*MPC*). For Canada as a whole, the marginal propensity to consume in the postwar period has been somewhere between .85 and .95. That is, of each extra dollar of income households receive, they spend on average between 85 and 95 percent.[4] If aggregate income increases by $10 billion, then aggregate consumption will increase by between $8.5 and $9.5 billion. In the hypothetical consumption function illustrated in Figure 12.4B, the marginal propensity to consume is .9: when disposable income goes up by $10 billion, aggregate consumption goes up by $9 billion.

The slope of the aggregate consumption function conveys important information. It tells us by how much aggregate consumption (measured along the vertical axis) rises with an increase of a dollar of aggregate disposable income (horizontal axis). In other words, the slope of the aggregate consumption function is the marginal propensity to consume. In panels A and B of Figure 12.4, the fact that consumption increases as income rises is reflected in the upward slope of the consumption function, and the marginal propensity to consume is equal to this slope. Flatter slopes would illustrate lower marginal propensities to consume.

John Maynard Keynes stressed the primary role of current disposable income in determining current consumption, and accordingly, the consumption function upon which this chapter focuses is sometimes referred to as the **Keynesian consumption function.** But aggregate consumption depends on the other factors besides current disposable income. For example, higher interest rates might cause people to save more (consume less). If people sense hard times on the horizon, they may cut back their consumption now even if their income goes up.

Figure 12.4C shows a shift in the consumption function. The intercept with the vertical axis—the level of consumption that would prevail even if disposable income were zero—is increased. This part of consumption, which does not depend on the level of income, is sometimes called **autonomous consumption.** With the shift depicted in the figure, the marginal propensity to consume remains unchanged; that is, the slope of the consumption function is the same. Sometimes both autonomous consumption and the marginal propensity to consume change. In the late 1970s, the level of autonomous consumption appeared to be higher and the marginal propensity to consume appeared to be lower than in previous decades.

As usual, we have to be careful to distinguish between changes in consumption that result from *movements along a consumption function*—the increase in consumption that results from higher incomes—and changes in consumption that result from a *shift in the consumption function*. Chapter 13 will discuss some of the factors that lead to shifts in the consumption function.

[4] In the 1970s, consumption was sometimes as high as 95 percent of household income. More recently, consumption has been somewhat lower. These statistics give the *average* ratio of consumption to disposable income. The *marginal* propensity to consume is somewhat smaller.

THE MARGINAL PROPENSITY TO SAVE

Individuals have either to spend or save each extra dollar of disposable income, so savings and consumption are mirror images of each other. The definition income = consumption plus savings tells us that when disposable income rises by a dollar, if aggregate consumption increases by 90 cents, aggregate savings increase by 10 cents. The higher level of savings stemming from an extra dollar of income is called the **marginal propensity to save (MPS).** This is the counterpart to the marginal propensity to consume, and the two must always sum to one:

marginal propensity to save + marginal propensity to consume = 1.

The high marginal propensity to consume today means that there is a low marginal propensity to save. Thirty years ago, the marginal propensity to consume was even larger than it is today, between .9 and .95; of each extra dollar of disposable income, between 90 and 95 cents was spent on consumption. But the marginal propensity to save was smaller; between 5 and 10 cents of each extra dollar of disposable income went into savings.

INVESTMENT

In an exceedingly simply economy—one without government, foreign trade, or investment—the aggregate expenditures schedule would match the consumption function. Aggregate expenditures would consist *only* of consumption, and disposable income would, without taxes, exactly equal total output. The consumption function shown in Figure 12.4B and repeated in Figure 12.5 would then constitute the aggregate expendi-

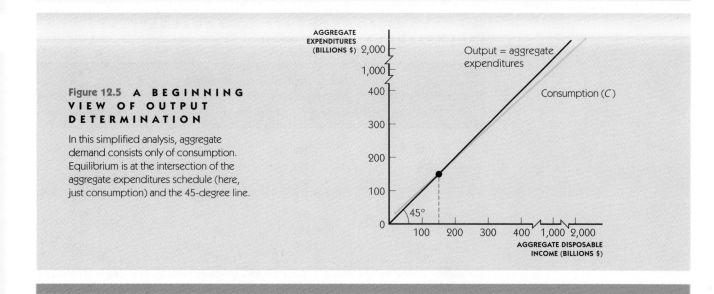

Figure 12.5 A BEGINNING VIEW OF OUTPUT DETERMINATION

In this simplified analysis, aggregate demand consists only of consumption. Equilibrium is at the intersection of the aggregate expenditures schedule (here, just consumption) and the 45-degree line.

tures schedule. In this simple economy, the slope of the aggregate expenditures schedule would be just the slope of the consumption function—the marginal propensity to consume.

To take a more realistic case, let us include some level of investment in the aggregate expenditures schedule; to keep matters simple, we continue to ignore government and net exports.

In Chapter 9, we saw that from the household's perspective, the savings and investment decisions are closely related. But the term "investment" is used in two different ways. Households think of the stocks and bonds they buy as investments—financial investments. These financial investments provide the funds for firms to use to buy capital goods—machines and buildings. The purchases of new machines and buildings represent firms' investments, and we refer to these as *real* investments. In macroeconomics, when we refer to investments, we refer to the real, not the financial, investments. Thus, decisions to invest are made by firms.

Though investment may vary from year to year, we assume the level of investment is (for the moment) unrelated to the level of income this year. This assumption is made largely to simplify the analysis, but it also reflects the view that investment is primarily determined by firms' estimates of the economic prospects over the future. Accordingly, investment levels are not greatly affected by what happens this year and, in particular, not greatly affected by the level of national income.

Table 12.3 combines the information from Table 12.2 with a fixed level of investment, $50 billion. Because we have assumed away government—both taxes and expenditures—disposable income, which we write as Y_d, is the same as national income. The table shows the level of aggregate expenditures for various levels of national income. Now, aggregate expenditures consist of the sum of consumption and investment, shown in the fourth column of the table and plotted in Figure 12.6. Because we assume investment does not depend on current income, the slope of the upper line in the figure is exactly the same as the slope of the consumption function: as income increases, aggregate

Table 12.3 SOME COMPONENTS OF AGGREGATE EXPENDITURES (billions of dollars)

Disposable income (Y_d)	Consumption expenditures (C)	Investment spending (I)	Total aggregate expenditures
$ 100	$ 105	$ 50	$ 155
200	195	50	245
300	285	50	335
400	375	50	425
650	600	50	650
1,000	915	50	965
2,000	1,815	50	1,865

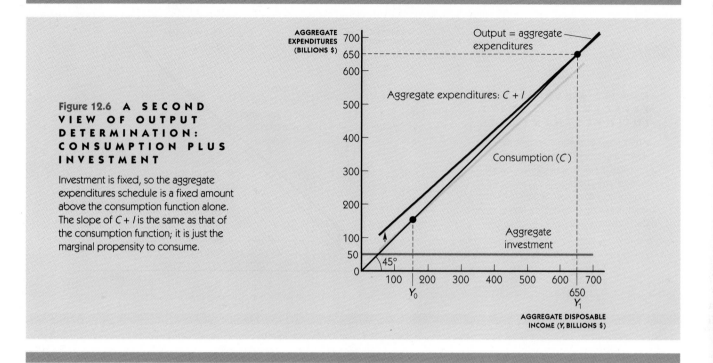

Figure 12.6 A SECOND VIEW OF OUTPUT DETERMINATION: CONSUMPTION PLUS INVESTMENT

Investment is fixed, so the aggregate expenditures schedule is a fixed amount above the consumption function alone. The slope of $C + I$ is the same as that of the consumption function; it is just the marginal propensity to consume.

expenditures increase by the same amount that consumption does, that is, by the marginal propensity to consume. The slope of the aggregate expenditures schedule is still the marginal propensity to consume. The equilibrium—the intersection of the aggregate expenditures schedule and the 45-degree line—is at Y_1 ($650 billion).

THE MULTIPLIER

One of the fundamental insights of income-expenditure analysis is that factors shifting the aggregate expenditures schedule will have a compound effect on output. To see why the equilibrium output increases by more than the direct increase in investment, consider an economy in which there has been a $1 billion increase in investment. We continue to assume that the marginal propensity to consume is .9. The first-round effect of the extra investment spending, shown in Table 12.4, is straightforward: output increases by $1 billion as firms purchase capital goods. This is only the beginning, however. The value of this increased output is distributed to the members of the economy as income, in the form of either higher wages, higher interest payments, or higher profits that become income to the firms' owners. Given that the marginal propensity to consume is .9, this will lead consumption demand to increase by .9 × $1 billion = $900 million. This second-round effect creates a $900 million increase in output and thus income, which in turn brings on a third-round increase of consumption of .9 × $900 million = $810 million. In the next round, output is increased by .9 × $810 million, then by .9 times that amount, then by .9 times that amount, and so on. In this example, when all the increases

Table 12.4 EFFECTS OF AN INCREASE IN INVESTMENT OF $1 BILLION (millions of dollars)

First round	$ 1,000
Second round	900
Third round	810
Fourth round	729
Fifth round	656
Sixth round	590
Seventh round	531
Eighth round	478
Ninth round	430
Tenth round	387
Eleventh round	349
Sum of twelfth and successive rounds	$ 3,140
Total increase	$10,000

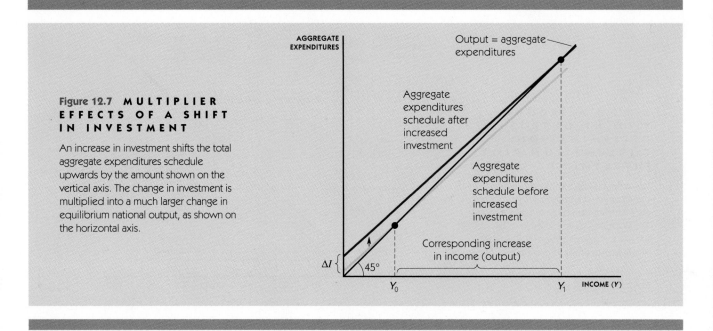

Figure 12.7 MULTIPLIER EFFECTS OF A SHIFT IN INVESTMENT

An increase in investment shifts the total aggregate expenditures schedule upwards by the amount shown on the vertical axis. The change in investment is multiplied into a much larger change in equilibrium national output, as shown on the horizontal axis.

are totalled, a $1 billion increase in investmest will lead to a $10 billion rise in equilibrium output. Figure 12.7 depicts the effect of an increase in investment that shifts up the aggregate expenditures schedule. The change in investment, ΔI, produces a greater change in output, the distance from Y_0 to Y_1.

Unfortunately, the multiplier process also works in reverse. Just as an increase in investment leads to a multiple increase in national output, a decrease in investment leads to a multiple decrease in national output. In our example, with an MPC of .9, if investment decreases by $1 billion, national output will decrease by $10 billion. The relationship between any change in investment expenditures and the resulting eventual change in national output is called the investment multiplier, or just **multiplier** for short. An increase in government expenditures or net exports has a similar multiplier effect.

The multiplier has a simple mathematical form. It is just $1/(1 -$ marginal propensity to consume$)$. In our example, the marginal propensity to consume is .9; the multiplier is therefore $1/(1 - .9) = 1/.1 = 10$. As the MPC increases, $1 - MPC$ gets smaller, and hence the multiplier, $1/(1 - MPC)$, gets larger. Knowing that the marginal propensity to consume is the slope of the consumption function, we can also see that the lesson of Figure 12.3 is borne out by the multiplier: the steeper the aggregate expenditures schedule, the greater the increase in output resulting from a shift in the schedule.

Now consider the denominator of the multiplier, $1 - MPC$. As we learned earlier, any income an individual does not consume is saved, and an increase of income by a dollar must be spent either on consumption or on savings. Therefore,

$1 - MPC = MPS$, the marginal propensity to save.

This result allows us to rewrite the basic formula for the multiplier:

$$\text{multiplier} = \frac{1}{1 - MPC} = \frac{1}{MPS}.$$

The multiplier is the reciprocal of the marginal propensity to save. If the marginal propensity to consume is .9, the marginal propensity to save is $1 - .9 = .1$, and the multiplier is 10.

THE MULTIPLIER

An increase in investment leads to an increase in output that is a multiple of the original increase.

The multiplier equals $1/(1 - MPC)$, or $1/MPS$.

THE FLATTENING EFFECTS OF TAXES AND TRADE

It is time now to bring government and foreign trade back into the analysis. The basic insights remain the same: changes in government expenditure and net exports lead, through a multiplier, to larger changes in equilibrium output. But as we will see, the value of the multiplier is smaller once the effects of government and trade are taken into account.

THE EFFECTS OF TAXES

Government serves as a double-edged sword in the macroeconomy: its spending increases aggregate expenditures at the same time that its taxes reduce the amount of people's income. Since consumption depends on individuals' disposable income, the amount of income they have available to spend after paying taxes, government taxes also reduce consumption.

CLOSE-UP: MULTIPLIER MUSCLE

One lesson the multiplier teaches is that critics should take a second look before condemning government efforts to stimulate the economy as "too small." After all, if the multiplier is large enough, a seemingly small policy may have enough muscle to boost the economy back to full employment.

An expansionary policy that works at one time or in one part of the country, however, may not work in the same way at another time or place. This is because the magnitude of the multiplier, and thus the effectiveness of fiscal policy differs, depending on the propensity to consume rather than save, the amount of income paid in taxes, and the propensity to import.

For instance, though it is doubtful whether Canadians in different regions have noticeably different consumption or saving habits at a given point in time, historically, Canadians have exhibited changing savings rates. High-level consumption was encouraged by the commercialism of the 1980s and was characteristic of the so-called "yuppy" generation. In contrast, children of the Great Depression and of World War II learned to be frugal and grew up to be the high savers of the 1950s and 1960s. Thus, the multiplier would have been higher in the 1980s than in the earlier period, and federal government fiscal policy more effective.

Although consumption behaviour may not differ from one region to another, the size of the multiplier will. For one thing, tax rates can differ significantly across provinces. For example, from 1986 to 1990, personal disposable income as a proportion of Gross Provincial Product (GPP) in Nova Scotia averaged 60.9 percent, while in Manitoba it was 70.1 percent. This indicates that the proportion of income paid as taxes was higher in Nova Scotia over this period. This directly affects the multiplier; the multiplier is smaller in Nova Scotia, so a given amount of provincial government spending in Nova Scotia has less impact there than is the case in Manitoba.

Perhaps more important, the marginal propensity to import into a province is likely to differ considerably across provinces. Some provinces are likely to be more "open" than others in the sense that they rely more on trade with nonresidents, including both foreigners and those in other provinces. As we have seen, a larger marginal

propensity to import gives rise to larger leakages of spending from the economy in question and a smaller multiplier. For example, imports into Ontario make up about 65 percent of its GPP, while for British Columbia it is more like 52 percent. This may seem a bit surprising since one would expect more populous provinces to be more self-sufficient than others. On the other hand, Ontario's population is more concentrated near major U.S. manufacturing areas. In any case, as a consequence the multiplier is much smaller in Ontario than in British Columbia, so a given amount of provincial government expenditure will be less stimulating.

Of course, the multiplier in both British Columbia and Ontario is, by the same reasoning, smaller than the multiplier for all of Canada. This implies that a dollar's worth of federal government spending will have a greater effect on aggregate demand throughout Canada than a dollar's worth of Ontario government spending will have in Ontario. Thus, it is more difficult for Ontario to pursue fiscal policy to affect its level of GPP than for the federal government to do so with GDP in mind. Only if all provinces were to coordinate their fiscal policies would the impact through the multiplier be the same as at the federal level.

Sources: Statistics Canada, CANSIM Database, 1993; John Whalley and Irene Trela, *Regional Aspects of Confederation* (Toronto: University of Toronto Press, 1986), pp. 116–17.

Total income equals total output, denoted by Y. Disposable income is simply total income minus taxes, T:

disposable income $= Y - T$.

Taxes do two things. First, since at each level of national income disposable income is lower with taxes, consumption is lower: taxes shift the aggregate expenditures schedule down. Second, when taxes increase with income, the multiplier is lower (the slope of the aggregate expenditures schedule is smaller). This is because when taxes go up with income, when total income increases by a dollar, consumption increases by less than it otherwise would, since a fraction of the increased income goes to government.

Without taxes, when investment goes up by a dollar, income rises by a dollar, which leads to an increase in consumption determined by the marginal propensity to consume. This increase in consumption then sets off the next round of increases in national income. If when income goes up by a dollar government tax collections increase by 40 cents, then disposable income increases by only 60 cents, so the increase in consumption with taxes is 40 percent smaller than it is without. If the marginal propensity to consume is .9, then taxes mean that when income goes up by a dollar, consumption increases by $.9 \times (1 - .4) = .9 \times 60$ cents $= 54$ cents. Thus, by bringing taxes into the picture, we can see that the consumption function is flatter, as shown in panel A of Figure 12.8.

Because the slope of the aggregate consumption function is flatter, the slope of the aggregate expenditures schedule is flatter, as illustrated in panel B. And because the slope of the aggregate expenditures schedule is flatter, the multiplier is smaller. How much smaller do taxes make the multiplier? With taxes, an increase in before-tax income by a dollar leads to an increase in after-tax income by $(1 - t)$ dollars, where t is the tax rate.

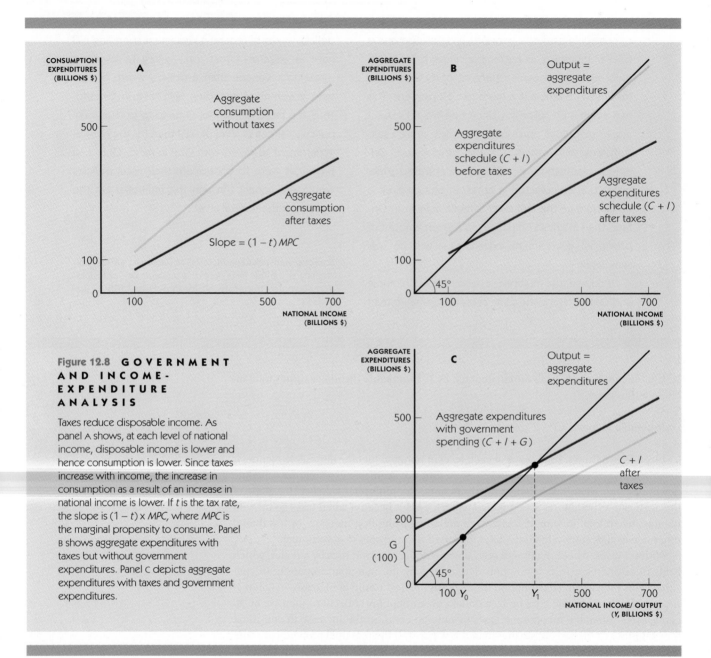

Figure 12.8 GOVERNMENT AND INCOME-EXPENDITURE ANALYSIS

Taxes reduce disposable income. As panel A shows, at each level of national income, disposable income is lower and hence consumption is lower. Since taxes increase with income, the increase in consumption as a result of an increase in national income is lower. If t is the tax rate, the slope is $(1 - t) \times MPC$, where MPC is the marginal propensity to consume. Panel B shows aggregate expenditures with taxes but without government expenditures. Panel C depicts aggregate expenditures with taxes and government expenditures.

An increase in after-tax income increases consumption by the marginal propensity to consume. Hence, the marginal propensity to spend an extra dollar of total income is $(1 - t)\,MPC$, whereas without taxes, the marginal propensity to spend an extra dollar of total income is just MPC. This means that the multiplier is now $1/\{1 - [(1 - t)MPC]\}$; without taxes, it was just $1/(1 - MPC)$. Thus, with $t = .4$ and $MPC = .9$, the multiplier is

$1/[1 - (.6 \times .9)] = 2.17$. By contrast, the multiplier without the income tax is $1/(1 - MPC) = 1/(1 - .9) = 1/.1 = 10$. The difference is significant.

How about government spending? The government's contribution to aggregate expenditures would be much simpler to analyze if its expenditures moved in lockstep with its revenues. We would simply look at the *net* contribution of government to aggregate expenditures, the difference between what it adds as a purchaser of final goods and services and what it subtracts as a consequence of households' reduced consumption. However, the government can spend more than it raises in taxes, by borrowing. When annual government expenditures exceed tax revenues, there is a **deficit,** a commonplace occurrence in Canada in recent years. (When annual government expenditures are less than tax revenues, there is a **surplus.**) There is considerable debate about the effects of deficits, which will be discussed in Chapter 14. For now, we make the simplifying assumption that the deficit has no direct effect on either consumption or investment.

We also assume that government expenditures do not increase automatically with the level of income; they are assumed to be simply fixed, say at $100 billion. Thus, while taxes shift the aggregate expenditures schedule down and flatten it, government expenditures shift the aggregate expenditures schedule up by the amount of those expenditures, as shown in panel C of Figure 12.8. In this panel, the upward shifts in the aggregate expenditures schedule from government expenditures have been superimposed on the downward shifts in the aggregate expenditures schedule from taxes depicted in panel B. Note that the contributions of investment, *I* (which are still assumed to be $50 billion), and government expenditures, G, raise the schedule but do not change its slope. The slope in panel C is the same as in panel B, but it is flatter than in an economy with no taxes: as national income increases, the government takes its share in taxes, dampening the increase in consumption. Equilibrium again occurs at the intersection of the aggregate expenditures schedule and the 45-degree line.

The multiplier means that if the government increases its expenditures (keeping taxes fixed), then the effects on national output will be multiplied. Government expenditures can have a powerful effect in stimulating the economy. But if the economy is in a serious recession and the multiplier is low, the government would have to increase expenditures a great deal to raise output to the full employment level. The multiplier also means that changes in investment, autonomous consumption, or net exports can have a strong effect on the economy. A slight decrease in investment results in a drop in national income by a multiple. A low multiplier means that the level of economic activity will be less sensitive to variations in investment.

MULTIPLIER WITH INCOME-RELATED TAXES

$$\text{Multiplier} = \frac{1}{1 - (1 - t)MPC}, \text{ where } t = \text{tax rate.}$$

THE EFFECTS OF INTERNATIONAL TRADE

The analysis so far has ignored the important role of international trade. This is appropriate for a **closed economy,** an economy that neither exports nor imports, but not for an **open economy,** one actively engaged in international trade. Canada, like most other industrialized countries, is very much an open economy.

International trade can have powerful effects on national output. To begin with, exports expand the market for domestic goods. In recent years, Canada has exported goods amounting to about 25 percent of national output. This is about the same proportion as that for the United Kingdom. Larger, more self-sufficient economies export a much smaller proportion of their output: 7 percent for the United States and 12 percent for Japan.

But just as exports expand the market for domestic goods, so imports decrease it. What matters for aggregate expenditures is net exports, and in recent years these have declined sharply in Canada. Net exports dropped from $11.5 billion in 1985 to less than half that amount in 1986. By 1989, they actually became negative. That is to say, imports exceeded exports. By 1991, net exports amounted to negative 1 percent of GDP. This deterioration in net exports reflects mainly a decline in export growth; the growth rate of imports has stayed at historic levels. This dramatic change in net exports is illustrated in Figure 12.9.

Imports and exports affect the aggregate expenditures schedule in different ways, so it is worth separating them here. First, imports. When households' incomes rise, they not only buy more Canadian-made consumer goods, they also buy more goods from abroad. We can illustrate an **import function** in much the same way that we illustrated a consumption function. (By contrast, we have assumed investment and government expenditures to be fixed, so for now there is no schedule relating either of these to income.) The import function shows the levels of imports corresponding to different levels of income. Table 12.5 shows hypothetical levels of imports for different levels of income. For simplicity, we assume that imports are bought by consumers and that, accordingly, it is

Table 12.5 IMPORTS AND DISPOSABLE INCOME (billions of dollars)

Disposable income	Imports
$ 100	$ 25
200	50
300	75
400	100
500	125
1,000	250
2,000	500

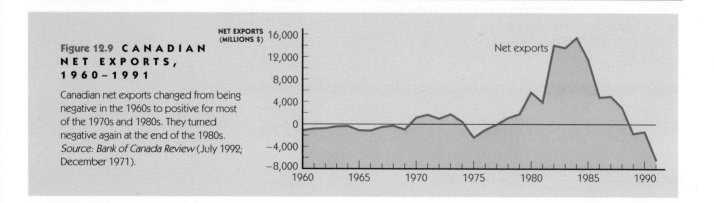

Figure 12.9 CANADIAN NET EXPORTS, 1960–1991

Canadian net exports changed from being negative in the 1960s to positive for most of the 1970s and 1980s. They turned negative again at the end of the 1980s. *Source: Bank of Canada Review* (July 1992; December 1971).

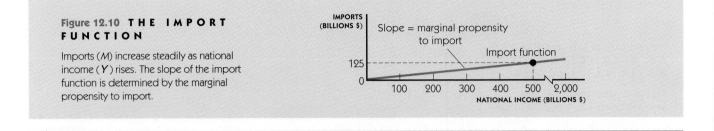

Figure 12.10 THE IMPORT FUNCTION

Imports (*M*) increase steadily as national income (*Y*) rises. The slope of the import function is determined by the marginal propensity to import.

disposable income that determines their level. The import function is depicted in Figure 12.10.

Imports increase with income. The **marginal propensity to import** gives the amount of each extra dollar of income spent on imports. If the marginal propensity to import is .25, then if income goes up by $1,000, imports go up by .25 × $1,000 = $250. In Figure 12.10, the marginal propensity to import is given by the slope of the import function.

As for exports, what foreigners buy from Canada depends on the income of foreigners and not directly on income in Canada. Exports may also depend on other factors, such as the marketing effort of Canadian firms and the prices of Canadian goods relative to those of foreign goods. Our focus here is the determination of output in Canada. For simplicity, we assume that these other factors are fixed and do not depend on what happens in Canada. In particular, we assume that foreigners' incomes do not depend significantly on incomes in Canada. Hence, the level of exports is taken as fixed at $100 billion, and not dependent on the level of income in Canada.

Exports minus imports are sometimes referred to as the **balance of trade.** Net exports at each level of national income are given in Table 12.6 and shown in Figure

Table 12.6 NET EXPORTS (billions of dollars)

Income	Exports	Imports	E (exports – imports)
$ 100	$100	$ 25	$ 75
200	100	50	50
300	100	75	25
400	100	100	0
500	100	125	−25
1,000	100	250	−150
2,000	100	500	−400

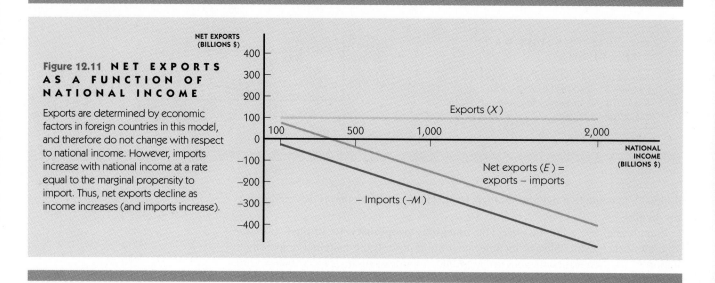

Figure 12.11 NET EXPORTS AS A FUNCTION OF NATIONAL INCOME

Exports are determined by economic factors in foreign countries in this model, and therefore do not change with respect to national income. However, imports increase with national income at a rate equal to the marginal propensity to import. Thus, net exports decline as income increases (and imports increase).

12.11. At very low levels of income, net exports are positive. That is to say, exports exceed imports. As income increases, imports increase, with exports remaining unchanged. Eventually imports exceed exports; the balance of trade becomes negative, as it is now in Canada.

Like taxes, trade has the effect of flattening the aggregate expenditures schedule. This is because as income increases, some of it goes to buy foreign goods rather than domestically produced goods. Hence, aggregate expenditures—spending for goods produced within the country—increase by a smaller amount. When income increases by a dollar in a closed economy, aggregate expenditures increase by the marginal propensity to consume. In an open economy, when income increases by a dollar, aggregate expenditures increase by the marginal propensity to consume *minus* the marginal propensity to import. The difference between the two can be thought of as the marginal propensity to consume domestically produced goods.

This can be seen in Table 12.7, which calculates, for different levels of national income, the level of disposable income, consumption, investment, government expenditures, and net exports. Every time aggregate income increases by $167, disposable income increases by only $100; and while consumption increases by $90, net exports *fall* (because imports increase) by $25, so the net increase in aggregate expenditures is only $65. In a closed economy with government, aggregate expenditures would have increased by $90.

At an income of $667 billion (a disposable income of $400), net exports are zero. At higher levels of income, net exports are negative; at lower levels, they are positive. This means that for lower levels of national income, trade has increased aggregate expenditures, and at higher levels of national income, it has decreased aggregate expenditures. At low levels of income the stimulation provided by exports more than offsets the losses from imports; just the opposite happens at higher levels of income.

In Figure 12.12, the income-expenditure analysis diagram is again used to show how the level of output is determined. As before, the equilibrium condition that output

Table 12.7

AGGREGATE EXPENDITURES SCHEDULE (billions of dollars)

National Income	Disposable income	Consumption	Investment	Government	Net exports	Aggregate expenditures
$ 167	$ 100	$ 105	$50	$100	$ 75	$ 330
333	200	195	50	100	50	395
500	300	285	50	100	25	460
667	400	375	50	100	0	525
1,667	1,000	915	50	100	−150	915
3,333	2,000	1,815	50	100	−400	1,565

Note: The numbers in the table are constructed under the following assumptions: a tax rate of .4, a marginal propensity to consume of .9, and a marginal propensity to import of .25.

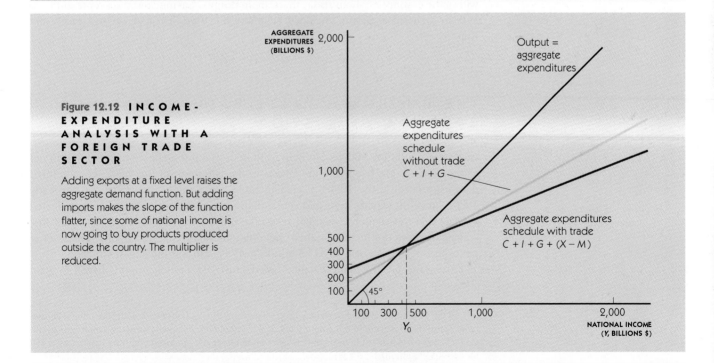

Figure 12.12 INCOME-EXPENDITURE ANALYSIS WITH A FOREIGN TRADE SECTOR

Adding exports at a fixed level raises the aggregate demand function. But adding imports makes the slope of the function flatter, since some of national income is now going to buy products produced outside the country. The multiplier is reduced.

equals aggregate expenditures, $Y = AE$, is represented by the 45-degree line. The aggregate expenditures schedule now sums all of its components: $C + I + G + (X - M)$. The slope of this line is even flatter than in Figure 12.8C, because as income increases, net exports—one of the components of aggregate expenditures—actually decrease. Equilibrium again occurs at the intersection of the aggregate expenditures schedule and the 45-degree line, the output level Y_0 in the figure.

We know that whenever the aggregate expenditures schedule is flattened, the multiplier is lowered. To see precisely how this works in the case of trade, think again about how the multiplier works through various rounds in the economy: the first-round effect of the increase in investment, the second-round effect of the rise in consumption induced by the higher income of those producing the investment goods, the third-round effect of the increase in consumption induced by the higher income of those involved in producing the second round, and so on. But now, when investment rises by 100 million, the second-round effect is only the increase in consumption of domestically produced goods. If the marginal propensity to consume is .9, the tax rate is .4, and the marginal propensity to import is .25, the increase in *domestically produced* consumption goods is $39 million (not $54 million, as it would be without trade, or $90 million, as it would be without taxes or government).[5] Not only is the second-round effect smaller, so is the third-round effect. The increase of $39 million in the second round leads to increased consumption of domestically produced goods of $15.2 million in the third round.

If more of the income generated on each successive round is not spent on goods produced within the country, as is the case here, the multiplier will be smaller. When income generated in one round of production is not used to buy more goods produced within the country, economists say there are **leakages.** Savings and taxes represent leakages in a closed economy. An open economy has three leakages: savings, taxes, and imports.

THE DECLINING TRADE BALANCE OF THE 1980S: A CASE STUDY

Income-expenditure analysis can help us to understand the effect of a reduction in net exports such as has happened in Canada in the latter part of the 1980s. For the three decades preceding the 1980s, Canadian trade was roughly in balance. In the early 1980s, however, exports increased very rapidly, while imports stagnated. This reflected the fact that the economy was in a recession and the slow income growth meant that Canadians were not increasing their spending, including that on imports. The level of net exports reached a peak of $15.4 billion in 1984, and was the largest on record.

This strong positive trade balance lasted until 1985, when imports began to grow

---

[5] Of the $100 million, the government takes 40 percent, leaving households with $60 million. Households consume 90 percent of this amount, but 25 percent of their income is spent on imports; the implication is that 65 percent of their income is spent on domestically produced consumer goods (.65 × $60 million = $39 million).

much more rapidly and net exports began to decline. In 1989, exports were virtually zero, becoming negative two years later. Some of the rise in imports was due to increased income; by this time, the economy was pulling out of the recession, and income was growing rapidly. But some of it was also due to a shift in the import function. At each level of income, Canadians were importing more German and Japanese cars, Japanese electronics, Italian and French designer clothes, and so on.

As a result of this decline in net exports, the aggregate expenditures schedule shifted down, and national output was reduced. With the level of net exports decreasing significantly, there was a large reduction in national output and a correspondingly large reduction in employment.

There are two ways of restoring net exports and thus restoring output and employment: increase exports or reduce imports. While there have been some efforts in Canada to increase exports—for instance, at various times the government has tried to persuade foreign countries to buy more Canadian wheat or countries such as Japan to open their markets to Canadian goods—more attention has focused on reducing imports. There have been many proposals to impose tariffs or to restrict imports in other ways, hoping that this action would shift net exports upwards. Critics of these proposals argue that they are generally ineffective, because other countries may respond by imposing restrictions on Canadian exports.[6] While tariffs may serve to reduce imports, if foreigners retaliate, tariffs may do the same to exports, and *net* exports may remain relatively unaffected or even be reduced.

This is what happened in the Great Depression. Countries, including Canada, and more importantly, the United States, imposed tariffs to reduce their imports in an effort to shift their net export function up. But one country's exports are another country's imports. As other countries responded to the tariffs by imposing retaliatory tariffs, North American exports decreased. These policies aimed at increasing one's national income at the expense of others are often called "beggar thy neighbour" policies. They do not work. The general level of tariffs increases and exports and imports are reduced; however, overall aggregate expenditures are not stimulated and standards of living fall as tariffs stand in the way of each country's taking advantage of its comparative advantage.

There are, however, more constructive ways that governments may try to stimulate net exports; they can, for instance, make their products more competitive. Also, throughout this chapter, we have assumed that prices are fixed. The demand by foreigners for Canadian goods depends, of course, on what they have to pay for those goods. What they have to pay is in turn affected by the exchange rate, how many yen or marks or pounds are exchanged for a dollar. Changes in the exchange rate affect net exports. In later chapters, we will learn in more detail how exchange rates affect net exports, and how government policies can affect the exchange rate.

Governments are often faced with the problem of how to stimulate economic activity without worsening the balance of trade. The government might decide to increase aggregate expenditures by increasing government expenditures. But at the higher level of output, net exports may be negative. This is because exports have not changed (they depend on incomes in other countries), but imports have increased as national income has increased.

---

[6] For a more complete discussion of the objections to proposals to restrict trade, see Chapter 3.

LIMITATIONS OF THE INCOME-EXPENDITURE APPROACH

This chapter has analyzed the determination of national output by focusing exclusively on the aggregate expenditures schedule, which underlies the aggregate demand curve. But what happened to aggregate supply? Isn't that important too?

Recall that aggregate demand rules the roost when there is excess capacity. That is, changes in aggregate demand alone determine what happens to national output when there are idle machines and workers that could be put to work if only there were sufficient demand to purchase the goods they produce. This situation arises when the intersection of the aggregate demand and supply curves occurs along the flat region of the aggregate supply curve. Increases in aggregate demand are translated directly into increases in output, rather than higher prices.[7]

Our analysis has calculated the level of output and aggregate expenditures at a particular price level. This is appropriate, given our assumption that the economy is operating along the horizontal section of the aggregate supply curve. Increases in aggregate expenditures do not lead to changes in prices. More generally, of course, price levels do change, as the record of inflation makes clear, and in a fuller analysis of the product market we need to know the level of aggregate demand at different price levels. This is what is given by the aggregate demand curve, to which we will return in Chapter 15. There we will see how the analysis of this chapter can be used as a basis for deriving that curve. But before doing so, we need to study more fully the components of the aggregate expenditures schedule—consumption, investment, government expenditures, and net exports. This we do in the next two chapters.

REVIEW AND PRACTICE

SUMMARY

1. Income-expenditure analysis shows how the equilibrium level of output in the economy is determined when there is excess capacity (when the economy is operating along the horizontal part of the aggregate supply curve), so that aggregate demand determines the level of output. The price level is taken as fixed.

2. Equilibrium output is determined by the intersection of the 45-degree line and the aggregate expenditures schedule. The aggregate expenditures schedule shows

---

[7] In Chapter 16, we will study another situation in which demand determines output, one involving price rigidities, where the price level is above that at which aggregate demand equals aggregate supply. Firms are willing to produce more, but at the going price level, they cannot sell this increased production. Prices do not decline for some reason, or do not decrease fast enough, so that for a while a situation with excess demand persists. In this situation, too, an increase in aggregate demand leads to an increase in output.

the level of aggregate expenditures at each level of national income, while the 45-degree line represents the points where aggregate expenditures equal output (income).

3. Shifts in the aggregate expenditures schedule give rise to changes in the equilibrium level of output. The magnitude of the increase in output resulting from an upward shift in the aggregate expenditures schedule depends on the slope of the schedule. Much of macroeconomic analysis focuses on the questions of what determines the slope of the aggregate expenditures schedule, what causes shifts in the schedule, and how government can shift the schedule.

4. Aggregate expenditures are the sum of consumption, investment, government expenditures, and net exports. Net exports are the difference between exports and imports.

5. Consumption increases as disposable income increases, and the relationship between income and consumption is called the consumption function. The amount by which consumption increases when disposable income increases by a dollar is called the marginal propensity to consume *(MPC)*. The amount by which savings increase when disposable income increases by a dollar is called the marginal propensity to save *(MPS)*. Since all income must be saved or consumed, the sum of the *MPC* and *MPS* must be 1.

6. The multiplier is the factor by which a change in one of the components of aggregate expenditures must be multiplied to get the resulting change in national output. In a simple model without government spending, taxes, or net exports, the multiplier for changes in investment is $1/(1 - MPC)$, or $1/MPS$.

7. Government spending increases aggregate expenditures, and taxes reduce disposable income and therefore consumption. When taxes increase with income, consumption increases by less than it otherwise would, since a fraction of the increased income goes to government. The aggregate expenditures schedule is flatter, and the multiplier is smaller.

8. Exports increase aggregate demand, and imports reduce aggregate demand. Imports increase with income, but exports are determined by factors in other countries. Trade flattens the aggregate expenditures schedule, because as income increases some of it goes to buy foreign rather than domestic goods. As a result, the multiplier is smaller.

KEY TERMS

aggregate expenditures schedule

planned and unplanned inventories

consumption function

marginal propensity to consume

autonomous consumption

marginal propensity to save

multiplier

deficit

surplus

closed economy

open economy

import function

balance of trade

marginal propensity to import

leakages

REVIEW QUESTIONS

1. What is the aggregate expenditures schedule? How does it differ from the aggregate demand curve? What are the components of aggregate expenditures?

2. How is the equilibrium level of output determined? Why are points on the aggregate expenditures schedule above the 45-degree line not sustainable? Why are points on the aggregate expenditures schedule below the 45-degree line not sustainable?

3. What is a consumption function? What determines its slope? What is an import function? What determines its slope?

4. What is the consequence of a shift in the aggregate expenditures schedule? Give examples of what might give rise to such a shift.

5. Illustrate the difference between a change in consumption resulting from an increase in income with a given consumption function and a change in consumption resulting from a shift in the consumption function.

6. Why is the sum of the marginal propensity to save and the marginal propensity to consume always 1?

7. Show that the magnitude of the effect of a given shift in the aggregate expenditures schedule on equilibrium output depends on the slope of the aggregate expenditures schedule. What determines the slope of the aggregate expenditures schedule? How is it affected by taxes? by imports?

8. How can changes of a certain amount in the level of investment or government spending have a larger effect on national output? What is the multiplier?

PROBLEMS

1. In the economy of Consumerland, national income and consumption are related in this way:

National income	$1,500	$1,600	$1,700	$1,800	$1,900
Consumption	$1,325	$1,420	$1,515	$1,610	$1,705

Calculate national savings at each level of national income. What is the marginal propensity to consume in Consumerland? What is the marginal propensity to save? If national income rose to 2,000, what do you predict consumption and savings would be?

2. To the economy of Consumerland add the fact that investment will be $180 at every level of output. Graph the consumption function and the aggregate expenditures schedule for this simple economy. What determines the slope of the aggregate expenditures schedule? What is the equilibrium?

3. Calculate the first four rounds of the multiplier effect for an increase of $10 billion in investment spending in each of the following cases:

(a) a simple consumption and investment economy where the MPC is .9;

(b) an economy with government but no foreign trade, where the MPC is .9 and the tax rate is .3;

(c) an economy with an MPC of .9, a tax rate of .3, and a marginal propensity to import of .1.

4. If, at each level of disposable income, savings increase, what does this imply about what has happened to the consumption function? What will be the consequences for the equilibrium level of output?

5. Use the income-expenditure analysis diagram to explain why a lower level of investment, government spending, and net exports all have similar effects on the equilibrium level of output.

6. In a more stable economy (where national output is less vulnerable to small changes in, say, exports), government policy is less effective (changes in government expenditures do not do much to stimulate the economy); in a less stable economy, government policy is more effective. Explain why there is a trade-off between the stability of the economy and the power of government policy.

APPENDIX: THE ALGEBRA OF INCOME-EXPENDITURE MODELS

Many of the ideas presented in this chapter can be expressed using simple algebra. In doing so, we will proceed in steps following those of the text. The first step is to derive an explicit expression for the equilibrium level of income for a simplified economy without government and trade. To do this, we first derive the aggregate expenditures schedule. We can write the consumption function algebraically as

$$C = b + (MPC \times Y),$$

where MPC is the marginal propensity to consume; Y is income (without taxes, "income" and "disposable income" are identical); b is what consumption would be if income were zero—it is the intercept of the consumption function with the vertical axis. (As noted in the text, b is sometimes called autonomous consumption.) Adding the fixed level of investment to consumption, we obtain aggregate expenditures, AE:

$$AE = C + I = b + (MPC \times Y) + I.$$

This relationship says that aggregate expenditures increase as national income rises. More precisely, it says that for each extra dollar of income, aggregate expenditures increase by MPC. If MPC is .9, then if national income rises by $1 billion, aggregate expenditures increase by $900 million.

Now we use the national income identity, that income (Y) equals output (GDP), and the equilibrium condition, that aggregate expenditures must equal output (AE = GDP), to obtain

$$Y = b + (MPC \times Y) + I$$
output = aggregate expenditures.

Solving for Y, we obtain

$$Y = \frac{b + I}{1 - MPC} \quad.$$

Notice that for each unit increase in aggregate investment, output will increase by $1/(1 - MPC)$. That is why this figure is called the multiplier.

To see this, let's evaluate Y at two different values of investment, say $10 billion and $11 billion. If Y_0 denotes the first situation and Y_1 the second, we have

$$Y_1 - Y_0 = \frac{b + 11}{1 - MPC} - \frac{b + 10}{1 - MPC} = \frac{1}{1 - MPC} \quad.$$

Next we introduce government. This increases demand by government expenditures, G, but government taxes mean that disposable income is less than GDP. We rewrite the consumption function to remind us that consumption depends on disposable income:

$$C = b + (MPC \times Y_d),$$

where Y_d is disposable income. For simplicity, we assume the government collects a fixed percentage, t, of income as taxes, so

$$Y_d = (1 - t) \times Y.$$

Using the earlier results, we obtain

$$Y = b + [MPC \times (1 - t)Y] + I + G$$
output = aggregate expenditures;

or, solving for Y,

$$Y = \frac{b + I + G}{1 - (1 - t)MPC} \quad.$$

The multiplier is now $1/[1 - (1 - t)MPC]$.

Finally, we bring in international trade, with exports fixed at X and imports increasing with disposable income:

$$M = MPI \times Y_d$$
$$= MPI \times (1 - t)Y,$$

where *MPI* is the marginal propensity to import. Adding these into aggregate expenditures, we now have

$$Y = b + [MPC \times (1-t)Y] + I + G + \{X - [MPI \times (1-t)Y]\}$$

$$= \frac{b + I + G + X}{1 - [(1-t)(MPC - MPI)]} \quad .$$

An increase in I or G or X will increase Y by a multiple amount. The multiplier is now $1/\{1 - [(1-t)(MPC - MPI)]\}$, lower than in the previous cases.

In our example, with $t = .4$, $MPC = .9$, and $MPI = .25$, the multiplier equals $1/[1 - (.6 \times .65)] = 1/(1 - .39) = 1/.61 = 1.64$. The multiplier is now much smaller than in our first example of a closed economy with no taxes, where the multiplier was $1/(1 - MPC) = 1/(1 - .9) = 1/.1 = 10$; it is even much smaller than in a closed economy with taxes, where the multiplier is

$$1/[1 - (1-t)MPC] = 1/[1 - (.6 \times .9)] = 1/(1 - .54) = 1/.46 = 2.17.$$

If the tax rate is zero but there are imports, then using the fact that $1 - MPC$ equals the marginal propensity to save, MPS, the multiplier becomes simply $1/(MPS + MPI)$, the reciprocal of the *sum* of the marginal propensity to save plus the marginal propensity to import. In our example, the multiplier is $1/(.1 + .25) = 1/.35 = 2.86$. Thus, income will rise by $2.86 billion. The multiplier is still large, but smaller than in a closed economy.

13

CONSUMPTION AND INVESTMENT

 ow that we have developed the overall framework of income-expenditure analysis, it is worth taking a closer look at each of the components of aggregate expenditures. Examining them will help us understand both why the level of economic activity fluctuates and what policies the government might pursue to reduce those fluctuations or to stimulate the economy. This chapter takes up consumption and investment; Chapter 14 will consider government spending and net exports.

KEY QUESTIONS

1. Why may current consumption not be very dependent on current income, and how does this affect the use of tax policy to stimulate the economy?

2. What other factors determine the level of aggregate consumption?

3. What are "consumer durables," and why are expenditures on them so volatile?

4. What are the major determinants of the level of investment? What role do variations in real interest rates and the availability of credit play? What role is played by changing perceptions of and the ability and willingness to bear risk?

5. Why is variability in investment and consumer durables expenditures important?

CONSUMPTION

The consumption function presented in Chapter 12 said that the demand for goods and services by households is determined by the level of disposable income: as disposable income goes up, so does consumption. Knowing this year's disposable income, you can use the consumption function to tell you this year's consumption spending.

This simple consumption function is a good starting point, but it is an incomplete model of consumption behaviour. Figure 13.1, which depicts both consumption and in-

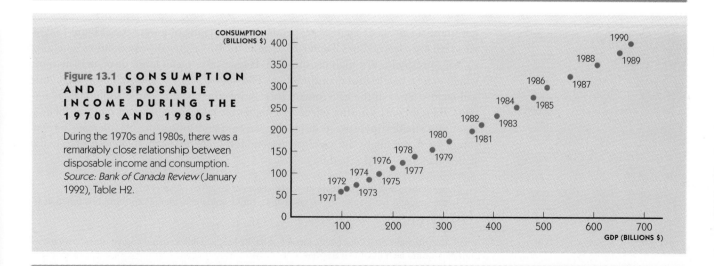

Figure 13.1 CONSUMPTION AND DISPOSABLE INCOME DURING THE 1970s AND 1980s

During the 1970s and 1980s, there was a remarkably close relationship between disposable income and consumption. *Source: Bank of Canada Review* (January 1992), Table H2.

come from 1971 to 1991, shows that the relationship between consumption and income is remarkably strong. Income varies from year to year, and so does consumption. If they moved in lockstep as the simple consumption function predicts, however, a straight line could be drawn through all the points in the figure. Clearly, this is not quite possible; further explanation is necessary. Economists have developed several more elaborate theories to explain and predict more precisely changes in consumption. In all of the theories, consumption depends on income, but the theories differ in the exact definition of income that is relevant for determining consumption. They also differ in what other variables besides income are important in determining aggregate consumption.

THE KEYNESIAN CONSUMPTION FUNCTION

The central feature of the Keynesian consumption function is that current consumption depends on current income. To arrive at this conclusion, Keynes took a back-door approach to the question of how much people consume by asking instead what factors cause people to save money. Since savings are by definition what individuals do not consume, he reasoned, figuring out how savings are determined will also show how consumption is determined.

For the most part, people do not save simply because the act of saving gives them pleasure. They save because they think they will need the money in the future: for an emergency, for retirement, for the down payment on a house, and so on. In short, they save so that they can have more consumption in the future. The decision to save is really a decision of *when* to consume, not whether to consume.

While there are a number of considerations that determine how much an individual saves—whether she is, for instance, saving to send her children through university or to buy a house—in the short run, we can assume that these factors do not change much.[1] Thus, the marginal propensity to save remains constant, which implies that the marginal propensity to consume stays constant as well. To predict changes in consumption from this year to next, we simply need to know the expected change in disposable income, and we multiply this change in disposable income by the marginal propensity to consume.[2]

The Keynesian consumption function suggests a simple mechanism by which the government can affect aggregate expenditures: it can raise or lower taxes. Figure 13.2 reviews what we learned in Chapter 12. One of the two aggregate expenditures schedules shown corresponds to a high-tax situation. Higher taxes mean lower disposable income, which in turn means lower consumption. The high-tax aggregate expenditures schedule is therefore lower. If the government uses an income tax to raise the additional tax revenue, then there is a further effect: at a higher tax rate, an increase in national income leads to a smaller increase in disposable income and thus a smaller increase in consumption. Accordingly, the aggregate expenditures schedule with higher tax rates is also flatter than the low-tax schedule.

---

[1] Some of these considerations are discussed at greater length in Chapter 21.

[2] In the appendix to Chapter 12, we saw that we could write the Keynesian consumption function as

$$C = b + (MPC \times Y_d),$$

where Y_d is the individual's disposable income, what he has available to spend or save, and b is what consumption would be if income were zero.

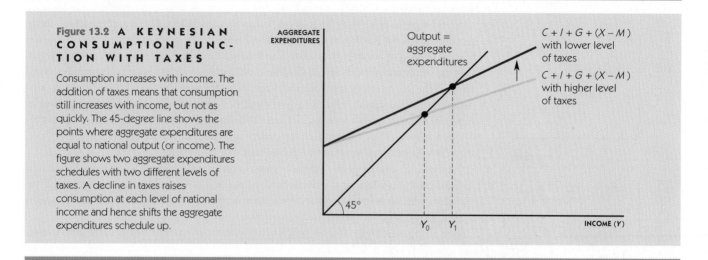

Figure 13.2 A KEYNESIAN CONSUMPTION FUNCTION WITH TAXES

Consumption increases with income. The addition of taxes means that consumption still increases with income, but not as quickly. The 45-degree line shows the points where aggregate expenditures are equal to national output (or income). The figure shows two aggregate expenditures schedules with two different levels of taxes. A decline in taxes raises consumption at each level of national income and hence shifts the aggregate expenditures schedule up.

The figure also shows the 45-degree line. The intersection of the aggregate expenditures schedule with the 45-degree line determines the equilibrium level of output. A reduction in taxes leads to an increase in the equilibrium output level from Y_0 to Y_1.

FUTURE-ORIENTED CONSUMPTION FUNCTIONS

In the decades after Keynes' time, many economists questioned Keynes' notion that current consumption depends primarily on current income. They argued that individuals, in taking consumption decisions, look to the future. Savings that enable a person to take consumption decisions depend not on the vicissitudes of this year's income, but on his total wealth. Wealth here includes not only current capital assets (stocks, bonds, house) but also **human capital,** the present discounted value of expected future wages.

Nobel laureate Franco Modigliani, for instance, emphasized that people save for retirement. He called this motive **life-cycle savings,** a term intended to convey the notion that individuals will save during their working years so that their consumption patterns can remain similar during their retirement years. Milton Friedman, himself a Nobel laureate, also emphasized how the future affects consumption today by pointing out that people save in good years to carry them through bad years. His view is called the **permanent income hypothesis.** Permanent income is a person's average income over her lifetime. Friedman stressed that consumption depends not so much on current income as on total lifetime income, averaging good years with bad. While Modigliani emphasized the role of savings in smoothing consumption between working and retirement years, Friedman emphasized its role in smoothing consumption between good and bad years. Underlying both views is the notion that people do not like consumption to be highly variable.

These future-oriented theories of savings and consumption have a number of differ-

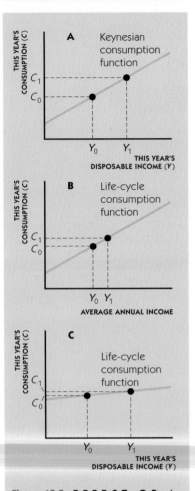

Figure 13.3 EFFECT OF A TEMPORARY INCOME CHANGE IN THE LIFE-CYCLE MODEL

With the Keynesian consumption function, panel A, a temporary change in income results in a large change in consumption. In the life-cycle model, panel B, a temporary change in income has only a small effect on average annual income over a lifetime, and thus leads to only a small change in consumption. Panel C shows how the life-cycle model predicts that consumption will react in response to *this year's income.* Since consumption does not change by much, the life-cycle consumption function is very flat.

ent consequences from the basic Keynesian theory that consumption simply depends on this year's income. Consider an individual who happens to get a windfall gain in income one year—perhaps he wins $1 million in a provincial lottery. If the marginal propensity to consume is .9, the Keynesian consumption function predicts that he will consume $900,000 of his winnings that year. The future-oriented consumption theories suggest that the lucky winner will spread the extra income over a lifetime of consumption. Similarly, if the government temporarily lowers taxes for one year, the future-oriented consumption theories predict that a taxpayer will not dramatically increase consumption in that year but will spread over his lifetime the extra consumption that the one-year tax reduction allows. They suggest that *temporary* tax changes will be much less effective in stimulating consumption than the Keynesian model predicts.

Figure 13.3 compares the future-oriented consumption function and the Keynesian consumption function for the household. Suppose a household were to have a onetime increase in its disposable income. If consumption responds according to the Keynesian consumption function, it will increase from C_0 to C_1 as shown in panel A.

The future-oriented theories predict that consumption will not change very much. We can see this in two different ways. Panel B shows consumption depending on average disposable income over a person's lifetime. Now the change in this year's income from Y_0 to Y_1 has little effect on average disposable income, and hence little effect on consumption. Panel C puts this year's disposable income on the horizontal axis, as does panel A. The difference between the lines in panels A and C is the difference between Keynes' views and those of the future-oriented theorists. Consumption, in the latter view, is not very sensitive to current disposable income, which is why the line is so flat. Rises in income today increase lifetime income and thus lead to an increase in consumption, but that increase is spread over an individual's life. Today's consumption increases relatively little.

The principle that consumption depends not just on income this year but also on longer-run considerations holds at the aggregate level as well as at the level of the individual. Figure 13.4 shows the implications of future-oriented theories for aggregate expenditures and the determination of equilibrium output. Since the relationship between changes in today's income and changes in consumption is weaker than in the Keynesian model, the aggregate expenditures schedule is now much flatter. This in turn has strong implications for the multiplier. An increase in, say, investment, which shifts the aggregate demand curve up, increases equilibrium output by an amount only slightly greater than the original increase in investment. The multiplier is very small.

WEALTH AND CAPITAL GAINS

The future-oriented consumption theories suggest not only that current income is relatively unimportant in determining consumption but also that variables Keynes ignored may be important. For instance, wealthier people consume more (at each level of current income). Since consumption is related to wealth, changes in consumption will be affected by changes in wealth.

The distinction between income and wealth as a determinant of consumption is important. It corresponds to the distinction between flows and stocks. Flows are measured as "rates." Both income and consumption are flow variables. They are measured as dollars *per year.* Wealth is a stock variable.[3] It is measured simply by the total value ("dol-

---

[3] Other stock variables in macroeconomics include capital stock and the national debt; other flow variables include investment and government expenditures.

lars") of one's assets. Future-oriented theories emphasize that there is no reason that an individual's current consumption should be related to his current income. What he consumes should be related to how well off he is, and that is better measured by his wealth.[4] Capital gains, or changes in the value of assets, change an individual's wealth. Thus, these theories predict that when stock or real estate prices rise in value and people expect this change to last for a long time, individuals who own these assets will increase their level of consumption. They will do so because their overall wealth has grown, even if they do not immediately receive any income from the increase in value.

There is some evidence that this is the case. Many economists believe that the stock market crash of 1929, which preceded the Great Depression, contributed to that Depression by generating a downward shift in the consumption function. On the other hand, when the share prices on the Toronto Stock Exchange fell by over 25 percent on a single day in October 1987, consumption did not decline sharply in the way one might have expected; people responded only slightly to this capital loss. One reason for this is that individuals respond to changes in wealth only slowly, and in 1987 their consumption had not yet fully responded to the increases in stock market prices that had occurred during the preceding few years. A prolonged and persistent decline in the stock market might, however, have an extremely depressing effect on consumption.

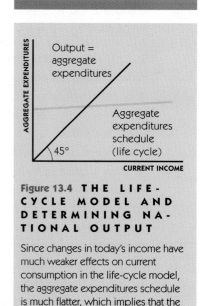

Figure 13.4 THE LIFE-CYCLE MODEL AND DETERMINING NATIONAL OUTPUT

Since changes in today's income have much weaker effects on current consumption in the life-cycle model, the aggregate expenditures schedule is much flatter, which implies that the multiplier is lower.

RECONCILING CONSUMPTION THEORY WITH FACTS

The permanent income and life-cycle hypotheses are convincing theories about how rational households behave. They contain large elements of truth: families do save for their retirement, so life-cycle considerations are important; and households do smooth their consumption between good years and bad, so permanent income considerations are relevant. Nevertheless, household consumption appears to be more dependent on current income than either of these theories would suggest. Two further theories have been advanced to help reconcile the future-oriented hypotheses with the facts. They have to do first with distinguishing the consumption of durable goods from that of nondurable goods, and second with the likelihood that it may not be as easy for an individual to borrow money as the future-oriented theories would have it.

DURABLE GOODS

The discussion so far has not distinguished between different categories of consumption goods—between refrigerators and groceries, between cars and airplane trips, between furniture and dental insurance. However, the distinction between **durable goods,** refrigerators, cars, and furniture, and **nondurable goods,** groceries, airplane trips, and insurance, is an extremely important one. The purchase of durable goods is more in the nature of an *investment* decision than a consumption decision. These goods are bought for the services that they render over a number of years. If you buy groceries, you eat them in a week. But a refrigerator lasts for years.

---

[4] Future-oriented theories take an expansive view of what should be included in wealth: they include *human capital*, the present discounted value of future wage income. (See Chapter 6 for a definition of present discounted value.)

Close-up: An Empirical Puzzle and an Ingenious Theory: Friedman's Permanent Income Hypothesis

The genesis of Milton Friedman's permanent income hypothesis was an empirical puzzle. The story of how he solved it provides a good illustration of insightful economic analysis and the scientific process at work.

When economists plotted aggregate disposable personal income in various years with the corresponding level of aggregate consumption, they obtained a set of points such as those depicted in panel A of the figure. This kind of data suggested a consumption function in which consumption increases roughly proportionately with income. On the other hand, when economists plotted the consumption of different income groups against their current income for any particular year, they obtained a set of points like those depicted in panel B. Households with low incomes consume a much larger fraction of their income than do households with high incomes. This suggests a consumption function in which consumption increases less than proportionately with income. The two kinds of data thus appear to offer quite different views of the relationship between consumption and income. The problem Friedman set for himself was how to reconcile the data.

His ingenious solution was to say that consumption is related to people's long-term or "normal" income, what he called their permanent income. Friedman observed that people with low incomes included a disproportionate number who were

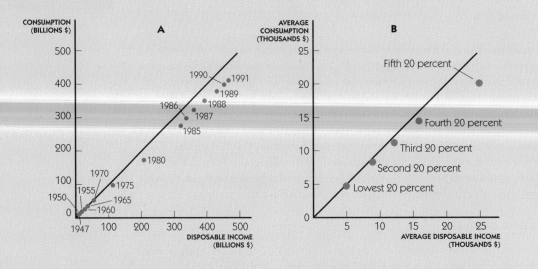

CONSUMPTION FUNCTIONS

Panel A shows that as income has increased over time, consumption has increased almost in proportion. Panel B illustrates the fact that individuals with higher income increase their consumption somewhat less than proportionately, especially at the highest income levels. *Sources:* Statistics Canada, CANSIM Database, 1993; Statistics Canada, 62–555, *Family Expenditure in Canada*, 1992.

having unusually bad years and were consuming more than one would expect from their one-year income; and correspondingly, those with very high incomes included a disproportionate number having unusually good years and consuming less than one would expect. Individuals having a particularly bad year did not reduce their consumption proportionately; those having a particularly good year did not increase their consumption proportionately. Friedman was thus able to explain how, over time, aggregate consumption could rise in proportion to income for the population as a whole even though the consumption of any particular household increased less than proportionately with current income.

Another American economist Robert Hall has pointed out an unsettling consequence of the permanent income hypothesis. Hall noted that the level of consumption a person chooses depends on permanent income, which incorporates all information about what future expected wages and other income will be. Changes in consumption are accordingly related only to *unexpected* changes. By definition, unexpected changes are random and unpredictable. (If they were predictable, they would be part of expected income.) Thus, the permanent income theory predicts that changes in consumption are largely random and unpredictable, which is not good news for economists trying to understand and forecast such patterns.

What people consume each year of a durable good can be described as the services of the good: one year's worth of transportation by car, one year's worth of a place to live, one year's worth of refrigeration for food, and so on. The decision to buy a durable good is thus affected by the kinds of considerations that are part of any investment decision. Three of these considerations are worth noting here.

1. If the real interest rate increases, it becomes more expensive for people to borrow to buy a car (or other durable good), and this discourages car purchases.

2. If credit becomes less available—if banks, for instance, refuse to make car loans to any but those with the best credit history—again, purchases of cars and other big ticket items that many consumers buy on credit will decrease.

3. Uncertainty about future income is also extremely important. If individuals think there is some probability of losing work or being laid off, the uncertainty will cause them to be less likely to take on payments for a new car.

Decisions to postpone purchasing a durable good have quite different consequences from decisions not to buy food or some other nondurable. If you do not buy strawberries today, you will have to do without them. But in most cases, not buying a durable does not mean you will do without the durable. It simply means that you will have to make do with the services provided by an older durable. The costs of postponing the purchase of a new car are often relatively low; you can make do with an old car a little bit longer. However, the benefits of postponing the purchase may be significant.

Given these considerations, it should be no surprise that purchases of durable goods vary a great deal, not only from year to year but also relative to income. Figure 13.5 traces the purchases of durables as a percentage of disposable income during the postwar period. Notice how variable these purchases have been. These fluctuations in purchases of durables, together with the variations in investment, seem to account for much

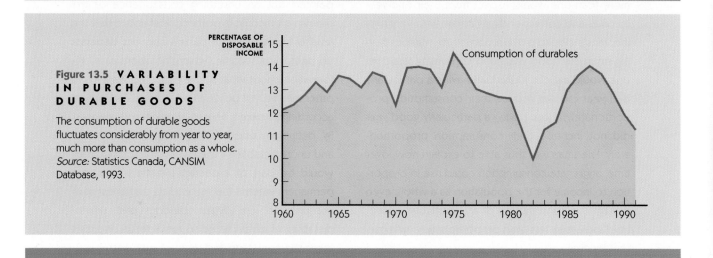

Figure 13.5 VARIABILITY IN PURCHASES OF DURABLE GOODS

The consumption of durable goods fluctuates considerably from year to year, much more than consumption as a whole. *Source:* Statistics Canada, CANSIM Database, 1993.

of the variation in economic activity over the business cycle. Meanwhile, variations in the services provided by durable goods—and hence in true consumption—are much smaller.

Thus, when a household's income is temporarily low, rather than borrowing to maintain a steady pattern of purchases of durables, the household simply postpones the purchase of a durable good. This makes aggregate expenditures depend critically on current income.

CREDIT RATIONING

Empirical studies focusing on nondurables show that even nondurable consumption expenditures seem more dependent on current income than the future-oriented theories suggest. These theories, in particular the permanent income hypothesis, assume that when an individual has a bad year, he can maintain his consumption at a steady level. They assume, in other words, either that the household has a large stock of savings to draw on while its income is temporarily low or that the household can easily borrow.

For many people, neither of these conditions is likely to be true. Most individuals, even in Canada, have few liquid assets upon which they can draw. They may have considerable savings tied up in a pension scheme, but they cannot draw upon these until they retire. They may have some equity in their house, but the last thing they want to do is sell their home. Moreover, it is precisely in times of need, when a person is unemployed or a business is doing badly, that banks are least forthcoming with funds. (As the saying goes, banks only lend to those who don't need the money!)

In short, many individuals are credit rationed, meaning that the unavailability of credit limits their options.[5] When their income declines, they have to reduce their con-

---

[5] Credit rationing occurs when people are unable to obtain funds at the market rate of interest, which reflects the risks associated with lending to them. Frequently there is limited availability of credit through banks; individuals who might be able to obtain credit from a bank at other times, when credit is more readily available, are turned down. Some of these people could obtain funds from other sources at substantially higher interest rates, but this discourages them from borrowing.

sumption. When people have no assets and they are credit rationed, cutting back on consumption when income declines is not a matter of choice. For these individuals, consumption depends heavily on current income.

If people were not credit rationed, short-term unemployment would not be as important a problem as it appears to be. The suffering caused by temporary layoffs would be much less. To see why this is so, we need to look again at the concept of total wealth. Assume, for instance, that a fellow named Evan will work for forty years, that his initial salary is $25,000 per year, that his salary increases in real terms at 5 percent per year, and that 5 percent is the real rate of interest. Then the present discounted value of his lifetime earnings is $1 million. This is his wealth, assuming that he has no unexpected windfall, no inheritance from his great-aunt, and no other assets. Imagine that Evan loses his job and is unemployed for half a year. At first glance, that looks like a personal calamity. But upon closer inspection, we see that it represents a loss of only a bit more than 1 percent of his lifetime wealth.

If Evan could borrow six months' pay, he would have no trouble paying it back, and the period without work would be no tragedy—his life-style would be constrained, but insignificantly. Since he would have to cut expenditures by only a bit more than 1 percent, cutting out a few movies, a fancy restaurant meal or two, and a few other activities would do the trick. However, for most people, losing a job for half a year would in fact be a major disaster, not because of the reduction in total lifetime wealth, but because most individuals face important constraints on the amount they can borrow. Without a job, they cannot obtain loans, except possibly at very high interest rates. Because of these credit constraints, for most lower- and many middle-income individuals, the traditional Keynesian consumption function is all too relevant. When their current income is reduced, their consumption is perforce reduced.

MACROECONOMIC IMPLICATIONS OF CONSUMPTION THEORIES

The alternative theories of consumption we have explored so far have two sets of macroeconomic implications. First, the future-oriented theories of consumption, in arguing that consumption does not depend heavily on current income, maintain that the aggregate expenditures schedule is flat and therefore, as we saw in Chapter 12, the multiplier is low. This is both good news and bad news for the economy. It is good news because the small multiplier means that variations in the level of investment lead to much smaller variations in the level of national income than they would if the multiplier were large. It is bad news because it means that government attempts to stimulate the economy through temporary reductions in taxes, or to dampen an overheated economy through temporary increases in taxes, will not be as effective as they would be if the multiplier were larger.

Second, by identifying other determinants of consumption, future-oriented theories help explain why the ratio of consumption to disposable income may shift from year to year. Expectations concerning future economic conditions, changes in the availability of credit, or variations in the price of houses or shares of stock are among the factors that can give rise to such shifts in the consumption function. These shifts in turn give rise to larger variations in the equilibrium level of national output. Indeed, they help explain how a slight downturn in economic activity can become magnified. With a downturn, consumers may lose confidence in the future. They worry about layoffs, and cut back on purchases of durables. At the same time, banks, nervous about the ability of borrowers to repay loans should the downturn worsen, become more restrictive; even those adventurous souls who are willing to buy a new car in the face of the uncertain future may find it difficult to find a bank willing to lend to them. The net effect is a downward shift in the consumption function, exacerbating the initial decline in national income.

ALTERNATIVE THEORIES OF CONSUMPTION

1. Keynesian consumption function: stresses the dependence of consumption on current income

2. Future-oriented consumption theories: stress the dependence of consumption on total lifetime wealth and the role of savings in smoothing consumption

   a. Life-cycle theory: stresses the importance of savings for retirement
   b. Permanent income theory: stresses the role of savings in smoothing consumption between good and bad years
   c. Implications
      i. Consumption not very dependent on current income: small multipliers
      ii. Consumption sensitive to capital gains and losses

3. Explanations of why consumption seems to be more dependent on current income than future-oriented theories predict

   a. The importance of durable goods
   b. Credit constraints

INVESTMENT

Investment may come second in the $C + I + G + (X - M)$ list of components of the aggregate expenditures schedule, but variations in the level of investment are probably the principal culprit in causing variations in aggregate expenditures, and hence in national output. Just how volatile investment is can be seen in Figure 13.6. In recent years, investment has varied from 16 to 23 percent of GDP.

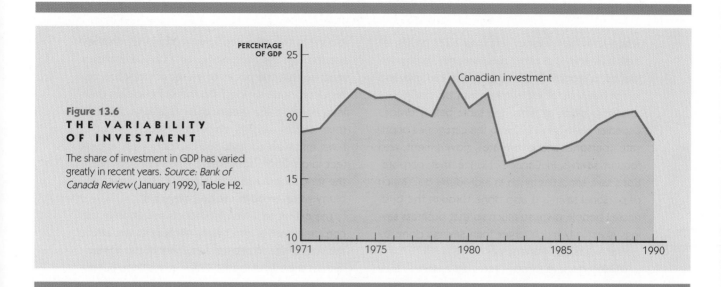

Figure 13.6
**THE VARIABILITY
OF INVESTMENT**

The share of investment in GDP has varied greatly in recent years. *Source: Bank of Canada Review* (January 1992), Table H2.

The investment spending relevant for aggregate expenditures includes three broad categories. The first is firms' purchases of new capital goods, which includes, besides buildings and machines, the automobiles, cash registers, and desks that firms use; these comprise the **plant and equipment** portion of overall investment. Firms also invest in inventories as they store their output in anticipation of sales or store the raw materials they will need to produce more goods. This is the **inventory** portion of investment. The third category consists of households' purchases of new homes. The purchases of previously owned capital goods or houses do not count, because they do not increase output. (Households' financial investments such as stocks and bonds are a related but different concept. Usually when an individual buys, say, a share of stock, she buys it from someone else. She makes an investment, but someone else makes a "disinvestment." There is simply a change in who owns the economy's assets. There is, however, a close relationship between investment in new capital goods and the capital market in general: when firms issue new shares or borrow funds by issuing bonds, they procure the resources with which to purchase new capital goods.

We restrict our focus in this part of the chapter to the two portions of investment done by business firms. Houses can be viewed as very long-lived durable consumption goods—and the principles discussed earlier in the chapter governing the demand for durables apply equally to consumers' demand for new housing.

Business investment is quite volatile. Since decreases in investment are often the source of an economic downturn, it is no surprise that when the government wishes to increase aggregate expenditures to stimulate the economy and reduce unemployment, it often tries to induce increases in business investment. To better understand what determines the level of business investment, why it is so variable, and how the government influences it we will first go into firms' investment in plant and equipment, and then we will discuss firm's investment in inventories.

CLOSE-UP: THE CORPORATE VEIL

When firms have money left over after paying all their bills, they can either use the funds to pay dividends to stockholders or retain the earnings and invest them. Retained earnings can be thought of as savings done by firms. The table below divides Canadian savings in 1990 into the categories of private (personal and corporate), government, and foreign savings in Canada. Notice that corporations save almost as much as individuals do. (Much of personal savings is also done through the businesses people own; so much so that business savings is actually much larger than savings done by persons outside of businesses.)

When firms save through retained earnings, they may invest in new plant and equipment, reduce their indebtedness, or buy government securities and those of other firms. But in each case, the future profits of the firm should be higher as it receives a return from this investment, and anticipation of these higher profits should raise the price of shares of stock in the firm. Strictly rational shareholders will treat this increase in the value of their stock the same as they would if they had saved the money personally.

This line of analysis is plausible enough in theory, but it poses a number of questions. Do people in fact perceive what is happening inside the corporation? In the term economists often use, do they see through the "corporate veil"? Do shareholders react so that the prices of shares of stock fully reflect corporate savings? Do the shareholders then incorporate these wealth changes and savings into their overall savings decisions? Recent theories have emphasized that shareholders have imperfect information concerning what goes on inside the firm, so it is not surprising that they have only blurry vision through the corporate veil.

The extent to which individuals see through the corporate veil is important, because it will affect the size of the multiplier. Assume that the government is successful in stimulating investment. But assume also that firms finance that investment by increasing their retained earnings, forgoing an increase in dividends. If people do not see through the corporate veil, they may only perceive that their dividends have not increased, without fully realizing that the corporation is putting their money into productive investments. If the low dividends lead individuals to reduce their consumption from what it otherwise would have been, then the total increase in aggregate demand resulting from the increase in investment will be much smaller than predicted by traditional Keynesian theory.

Savings by sector in 1990		% of total savings
Gross savings	$137 billion	100
Gross private savings	116 billion	85
Personal savings	67 billion	49
Corporate savings	49 billion	36
Government savings	–6 billion	–4
Foreign savings in Canada	27 billion	20

Source: Statistics Canada, CANSIM Database, 1993.

DETERMINING INVESTMENT IN PLANT AND EQUIPMENT

Firms invest in new plant and equipment because they expect that the future production that will result from the investment will earn them a profit. The fact that investments yield their returns over a long period of time gives rise to two problems in firms' investment decisions. The first is that businesses must make predictions about their products: future prices, future demand, and future production costs. They must try to imagine whether changes such as new inventions or new products will make this investment obsolete too quickly. Would the company be better off buying a computer today or waiting to see if a still better computer is marketed next year? If the new product is one that appeals especially to teenagers or to the elderly, how many people will be in that group in the next ten or fifteen years? Forming these judgments is a central part of the responsibility of the firm's management, though they often rely heavily on economic consultants.

The second problem is that firms must evaluate income and expenses occurring at different dates. Chapter 6 showed how to calculate the present discounted value of a project. A dollar today is worth more than a dollar next year or the year after; firms must discount future receipts and costs in their calculations. They also need to look through the illusions created by inflation and figure *real* profits. Accordingly, we can think of firms proceeding in two steps when evaluating the desirability of a project. First, they convert all future expenditures and receipts into dollars of constant purchasing value. Then they calculate the present discounted value, using the *real* interest rate.[6]

In our analysis, we will begin by assuming the firm has some well-defined projects. It knows how much each costs and what the return each year will be. The critical question is whether the firm can obtain the funds to finance the projects, and what it will have to pay for those refunds. We then turn to factors that determine the company's forecasts of the returns it will receive in coming years.

CHANGES IN THE REAL INTEREST RATE

Keynes first formulated the income-expenditure analysis we are investigating, so it should come as no surprise that we again begin with Keynes' views. While Keynes focused on disposable income as the primary determinant of consumption, he concentrated on interest rates as the primary determinant of investment.

The **investment schedule** describes the total value of investment that firms would like to undertake at each rate of interest. In general, an increase in the real interest rate, the interest rate adjusted for inflation, decreases the level of investment. This is because of present discounted value. The firm invests money today in the expectation of returns in the future. An increase in the real interest rate means that those future profits, valued as of today, are worth less; to put it another way, in calculating the present discounted value of a project, the future profits of the firm must be divided by a larger number. The present discounted value of the project is reduced.

The interest rate represents the "cost" of funds to the firm. When the interest rate is higher, it costs the firm more to borrow. Alternatively, when the interest rate is higher, a

---

[6] Recall that the real interest rate is just the nominal interest rate minus the rate of inflation. If banks charge 10 percent interest on their loans and the rate of inflation is 4 percent, then the real interest rate is 6 percent. See Chapter 6.

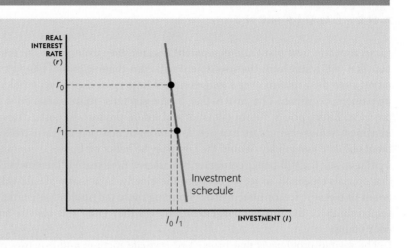

Figure 13.7

THE INVESTMENT SCHEDULE

The number of investment projects that have a positive present discounted value increases as the real rate of interest falls. As the real rate of interest declines from r_0 to r_1, investment increases from I_0 to I_1. However, the relationship is probably inelastic, so that relatively large changes in the real interest rate will have little effect on the level of investment.

firm with funds can obtain a higher return simply by buying a government Treasury bill. A higher interest rate represents a higher opportunity cost of funds. When the cost of funds is higher, only the better projects are worth undertaking. In other words, the higher the interest rate, the fewer the investment projects that are worthwhile.

Figure 13.7 depicts the investment schedule. As the real rate of interest declines from r_0 to r_1, investment increases from I_0 to I_1. The difference in the level of investment represents investment in projects that are profitable at the lower interest rate but not profitable at the higher interest rate. The fact that investment depends on interest rates suggests that government can stimulate the economy by lowering interest rates, thereby increasing investment.

Keynes, having recognized the link between investment and the interest rate, also observed that, at least in recessions and depressions, this may be difficult. There are two reasons. First, it may be difficult to lower the *real* interest rate. And second, because the investment schedule is inelastic—as shown in Figure 13.7, the investment schedule is almost vertical—the interest rate must be lowered a great deal to have a big effect on investment and hence on aggregate expenditures.

While they recognize the overall importance of real interest rates, economists have become increasingly skeptical of their role in explaining many of the short-term variations in investment. Indeed, there is little correspondence between interest rate variation and investment. Figure 13.8A shows the real interest rates during the period from 1954 to 1969 that would have been relevant for a firm borrowing for a ten-year investment. Note that real interest rates varied little, by hardly more than 2 percentage points over this period of sixteen years. In the same figure, we see the fluctuations in investment for the same period. The message of this figure is that investment fluctuations were due to factors *other* than the interest rates.

Looking at real interest rates and investment over a broader span of time, as displayed in panel B, we see that real interest rates have fluctuated much more over the longer run, but again, the fluctuations do not appear to be closely linked with changes in in-

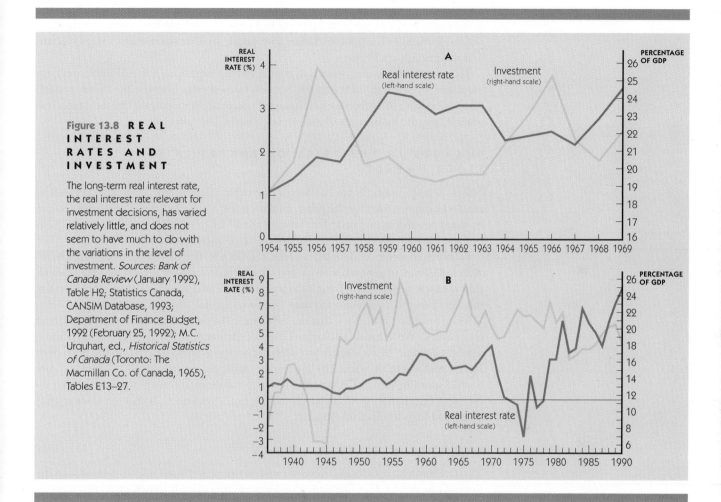

Figure 13.8 **REAL INTEREST RATES AND INVESTMENT**

The long-term real interest rate, the real interest rate relevant for investment decisions, has varied relatively little, and does not seem to have much to do with the variations in the level of investment. *Sources: Bank of Canada Review* (January 1992), Table H2; Statistics Canada, CANSIM Database, 1993; Department of Finance Budget, 1992 (February 25, 1992); M.C. Urquhart, ed., *Historical Statistics of Canada* (Toronto: The Macmillan Co. of Canada, 1965), Tables E13–27.

vestment.[7] Much of the variation in real interest rates falls into three episodes: the late 1940s, the mid-1970s, and the early 1980s. The variations again seem to bear little relationship to the fluctuation in investment. In particular, relatively high levels of real interest rates in the 1980s do not seem to be associated with especially low levels of investment, and the fluctuations in investment are not well accounted for by changes in the real interest rate.

The fact that small variations in real interest rates have relatively little effect on investment is not surprising; given the uncertainty involved in any investment project, a change in the real interest rate from, say, 5 percent to 4 percent will not alter many investment decisions. To be on the safe side, firms typically require that their rough calculations show a 15 to 25 percent (real) return on an investment project before they are willing to undertake it. They know from sad experience that if they insist on this high level of return, they will in fact be fairly certain of actually obtaining a return of only 8 to

---

[7] If we extend the analysis back still further in time, to the nineteenth century, we observe very long periods—decades—with almost no variation in real interest rates.

10 percent, enough to compensate them for their time, effort, and resources. A change in the real rate of interest from 5 percent to 4 percent will have little impact on the decision to go ahead with a project yielding 25 percent; at either interest rate, the project will look enormously profitable.

To make matters worse, what is of concern to the firm is not the real interest rate for borrowers for a month or a quarter, but real interest rates over the life of the project. Thus, even were the government temporarily successful in changing the short-term real interest rate, the long-term real interest rate may be little affected.

CHANGES IN THE PRICE OF SHARES IN THE STOCK MARKET

Nobel laureate James Tobin has argued that what affects a firm's investment is not so much the interest rate, but the price of shares in the stock market relative to the value of its machines and other assets. This ratio is called "Tobin's q." When Tobin's q is high, as in a stock market boom, issuing new shares is an attractive prospect to firms.

In statistical studies conducted over the past decade, this theory has fared only moderately well. True, in general, when Tobin's q is high, investment is high, but the relationship is much weaker than Tobin's theory predicts. Perhaps this is because firms do not rely much on the stock market to raise additional capital.

More troubling is the view that the relationship between share prices and investment is not causal. We learned in Chapter 1 that correlation does not prove causation. Here is a good example. When a firm's prospects are good, investors will bid up the price of its shares. And under the same circumstances, managers are more likely to decide to undertake more investment. Thus, it is not high values of Tobin's q that lead to high investment but, rather, good prospects for the firm that lead to both high stock market prices and high levels of investment.

THE AVAILABILITY OF FUNDS

The fact that changes in real interest rates do not play a large role in determining the level of investment does not mean that government policy is impotent. At times, it can affect the level of investment by varying the availability of funds. Sometimes the government actually gets involved in making loans, for instance to small businesses or to finance housing. Chapter 18 will explore how government monetary policies affect credit availability. For now, we simply observe that to most firms, the availability of funds is often as important as or more important than the interest rate they must pay.

Most firms simply cannot borrow all they want to at the market rate of interest. Credit is rationed. (Appendix B at the end of this chapter explains why this might be the case.) Whether because of credit rationing or for other reasons, most firms rely heavily for their investment capital on retained earnings, the funds left over from sales after paying labour, other production costs, interest on outstanding debt, and dividends to shareholders. If firms have some very promising projects that cannot be financed out of retained earnings, they may turn to the capital market, and in particular to banks, for additional finance. And when firms do turn to banks for funds, they often bump into credit constraints. They have a list of projects that they believe are profitable and that they would undertake if only they could get the necessary funds, but the banks do not share their view. Thus, when firms are credit rationed, making more funds available will lead to increased investment, while making funds less available will lead to decreased investment.

Economic Downturns   When a firm needs money most is often when it finds money least available. In an economic downturn, revenues decrease far more rapidly than expenses, so retained earnings are likely to fall sharply as well even if dividends are cut (and most firms appear very reluctant to cut dividends). In fact, many firms find they cannot even cover costs, let alone meet the interest obligations on their outstanding debt. It is in such circumstances that the company needs most to borrow—its very survival may depend on getting funds—and it is in these circumstances that the bank is most reluctant to lend.

When firms see the possibility of a credit crunch coming up, they may cut back on investment in plant and equipment, and they may also reduce inventories, either of which strategy will have the same negative effect on aggregate expenditures. Their goal is to have funds available for day-to-day expenses; if sales fall short, revenues decline, and with limited availability of credit, they cannot turn to the banks to meet their obligations. If they do not take actions to keep their funds free, without cash to meet their obligations, they may be forced into bankruptcy.

The response of firms to the perception that they may face a shortage of funds can actually help to bring on or aggravate a recession. After all, we saw in Chapter 12 how a decrease in investment spending leads to multiplier effects on national output. Thus, the pessimism of firms can be self-fulfilling. As firm after firm cuts back on investment and reduces inventories, matters turn out every bit as bad as they feared, and they face the shortfall of funds they anticipated. Managers may congratulate themselves on their foresightedness, but in this case their individually rational actions have combined to bring on the very circumstances they hoped to avoid.

The government may recognize this problem and try to encourage banks to make funds more available to firms. But if banks are sufficiently pessimistic—if the reason they are refusing to make funds available is their fear that, with the economic downturn, borrowers will be unable to repay the loans—then the government may be unsuccessful, as we will see in greater detail in Chapter 18.

Stimulating the Economy   We have seen how a reduction in credit availability—or even the anticipation of one—can exacerbate an economic downturn. The bad news does not stop there. In a prolonged economic downturn, firms may become pessimistic about future prospects and be unwilling to undertake many investment projects, even at low real interest rates. An increase in credit availability at this point may be ineffective in stimulating investment. There is an old expression, "You can lead a horse to water, but you can't make him drink." Making more funds available for investment need not lead to more investment, particularly if what is limiting the firm's investment is not the lack of availability of credit but the lack of investment projects that look profitable.

Economic Booms   Just as the lack of credit availability exacerbates economic downturns, economic booms may be sustained in part by the flow of profits (and with them, retained earnings) they generate. There is another old adage, "Nothing succeeds like success." Firms and countries that find themselves in a strong financial position (whether as a result of luck or foresight) will have high levels of investment, which will, at least for a while, sustain and expand the high level of prosperity. In the late 1970s, for example, many oil companies found themselves in a cash-rich position. The price of oil had soared, creating an unexpected bonanza for these firms. Given their high level of retained earnings, they were willing to undertake investments they could not or would not have attempted in leaner days.

THE PROFITABILITY OF PROJECTS

Theories having to do with the cost and availability of funds address one side of the firm's investment decision. On the other side are the expected returns of the projects to which those funds will be applied. We turn now to this side, noting three circumstances in which firms will be induced to invest: if they anticipate that demand for their products will rise, if the investment project will lower the firm's overall costs of production, and if the price of the investment project goes down because of favourable tax treatment.

Demand Forecasts and the Investment Accelerator   If firms believe that the demand for their products will increase in the future, this will heighten their willingness to invest today, so as to be able to meet this expected increase in demand. A major determinant of the level of demand facing any firm is the overall level of national income. Some economists have argued that this relationship gives rise to an investment **accelerator.** That is, investment doubles back: the increased output to which it gives rise produces still more investment. If for some reason, such as a rise in government expenditures, aggregate output increases, firms will increase their investment. This in turn will lead to a further growth in output—and not just via the multiplier.

Since the ratio of capital to annual output in the economy is fairly high (around 2:1), if a firm believes that it faces a level of demand that, valued at today's prices, will be higher by $100,000 per year, it will wish to invest roughly $200,000 more in plant and equipment today in order to meet this expected demand fully. The $200,000 increased investment will lead, through the multiplier, to a much greater increase in output. If the multiplier is 5, then output will rise by $1 million. But if the firm expects this $1 million increase in output to be permanent, it will want to increase investment by $2 million. Through the multiplier, this will lead to a $10 million increase in output, and so on. We now see why the increased investment is called an accelerator: the economy spirals upwards and onwards, like a car going faster and faster, until it eventually runs into constraints—limitations posed by the available labour and capital.

In recent years, however, economists have paid less attention to the investment accelerator. After all, investment decisions are based on long-run considerations, not just on unexpected events of this year. Only the most naive business would simply assume that a change in demand this year will persist forever. Moreover, firms in the simple accelerator model never seem to have anticipated the increase in output; for if they had, they would already have set in place the investment that that higher level of sales called forth.

Increased sales may lead to greater investment for a quite different reason from the accelerator. When sales increase, firms earn more and can therefore retain more earnings for investment. If investment had been limited by the unavailability of funds during a recession, firms will now respond to the wider availability of funds by increasing investment, undertaking some of the investments that were postponed earlier. Moreover, the more favourable financial positions firms find themselves in as a result of the increased sales make them both more willing to undertake the risks associated with investment and more attractive to banks and other lenders. Finally, as the economy recovers from a recession and output increases, the uncertainties associated with how long the recession would last are removed, and this reduction in macroeconomic uncertainty also serves as a stimulus for investment.

Production Costs   A second consideration in the expected-returns calculation is a forecast of costs of production. While all production costs are variable, firms often focus on labour because it represents such a large fraction of total costs. Increases in real wages affect the level of investment, although the effect is ambiguous. Higher (real) wages make it more attractive to use machines rather than labourers, and thus provide an incentive for investing in more machines. On the other hand, higher wages may make some labour-intensive investment projects unprofitable, thus discouraging investment. Finally, higher real wages may reduce the amount of retained earnings that firms have available for investing.

Lowering the Cost of Investment: Taxes   In the past several years, taxes and tax incentives have played a central role in determining the level and timing of firms' investments. The government has encouraged investment at various times by means of an **investment tax credit** (ITC). The ITC works in this way. Firms making long-term investments subtract from their tax bill a specified proportion, say 10 percent, of the value of their investment. The federal government in effect pays 10 percent of the cost of the new machine or project. By reducing the effective costs of investments, the ITC makes more investment projects profitable and thus stimulates investment. But the ITC's effect is even greater when it is temporary. If the government announces that a tax credit will apply only for investments made in one particular year, it encourages firms to invest in that year—to bring forward investments they would have made later and to postpone investments they would have made earlier. The effect is the same as that of a nationwide "sale" on machines, with prices marked down by 10 percent. From 1978 to 1988, the ITC was available to all forms of investment. With the tax reform implemented in 1988, however, it was restricted to some specific types of investment—investments in Atlantic Canada, expenditures on scientific research, and Canadian exploration expenditures.

RISK AND INVESTMENT

Firms do the best they can to forecast sales and costs and thus to determine the profitability of new investments. But try as they might, they can predict the future only imperfectly. Even the best manager's crystal ball is cloudy. There is therefore considerable risk associated with any investment decision. Firms are, for the most part, risk averse; when they perceive the risk associated with an investment project to be particularly high, they will not undertake the project unless the expected returns are sufficiently high to compensate them for bearing the risk. Thus, when the economy goes into a downturn, not only may expected returns decline, the risk associated with investment may increase. This increased risk further discourages investment.

There is another important way that risk enters the firm's investment decision. The issue frequently facing a company is not so much whether to invest but when to invest. An investment opportunity once undertaken cannot be wholly reversed, and investing in even a good project at the wrong time can have disastrous effects. This is because many firms operate on a small margin—costs may be 90 percent or more of revenues. A slight increase in costs or a slight decrease in revenues can have a huge effect on profits, which are the difference between revenues and costs. When costs are 90 percent of revenues, a 1 percent increase in costs can reduce profits by 10 percent. If a firm with such costs should take the risk of investing and a lengthy recession does hit, it may face bankruptcy. Nothing so dire faces the firm if it simply postpones its decision. The company may lose some profits by delaying an investment; it may, for instance, have to get along with an aging machine. But often this possibility of a loss of profit is a small price to pay for the option of waiting to see how economic events unfold.

As firms' perception of risk may change when the economy goes into a downturn, so too may their willingness to bear risk. Firms' willingness to undertake risks depends in part on their financial position. If companies have a strong balance sheet—if they have an ample supply of cash and other liquid assets on hand—then they are more willing to take risks. Even if things turn out badly, they will not go bankrupt. When an economy goes into a downturn, however, firms often face large losses, as sales that had been counted upon fail to materialize. Firms' financial positions deteriorate, making them less willing to undertake the risks associated with investment.

Thus, the risk factor contributes yet another explanation of the volatility of investment. Economic downturns are associated with both a perception of increased risk and a reduced willingness and ability to bear risks. They both contribute to a decline in investment, which, through the multiplier, leads to further declines in national income and exacerbates the economic downturn.

PRINCIPAL DETERMINANTS OF INVESTMENT

1. The cost and availability of funds. Although investment may be influenced by (real) interest rates, it is also influenced more by the availability of funds, both through retained earnings and through capital markets, and both sources may be limited.

2. The expected profitability of the investment project. Firms take into account anticipated future demand for their products, the degree to which the project will reduce their costs of production, and the after-tax cost of the project.

3. Firms' willingness and ability to take on risk. Firms may reduce risk with little effect on expected profitability by delaying an investment project. In an economic downturn, firms' perception of risk increases and their willingness to bear risk decreases, both factors contributing to a downturn in investment.

THEORIES OF INVENTORY INVESTMENT

Investment in plant and equipment, which has been our focus so far, is not the only category of investment. Another category, inventory investment, is a major contributor to fluctuations in aggregate expenditures. To understand inventory investment, we need to understand first the function that inventories serve. Inventories consist of materials that are being held in storage, either awaiting use in production or awaiting sale or delivery to customers.

Inventories are typically very large. In 1991, for example, the value of inventories in manufacturing industries was $41 billion, while the value of final sales of business was only $23.5 billion. In other words, there were about $1.75 worth of goods in storage for every $1 of goods sold.

There is a cost to holding inventories. If firms borrow funds to finance their inventories, planning to pay back the loans after selling the inventoried products, they must pay interest on these funds while the products remain unsold. If a company finances the inventories itself, it faces an opportunity cost: the funds that pay for the inventory could be used for other purposes. Beyond the cost of inventory, storage space costs money, and frequently goods spoil or deteriorate in the process of storage.

Given the costs, why do firms hold so much in inventories? One reason is that inventories on the input side facilitate production. This is called the **production-facilitating function** of inventories. It is very costly, for instance, for a printing plant to run out of paper and have workers and machines standing idle until more arrives. On the output side, customers often rely upon the producer to supply the good to them when they need it. To do that, the producer must maintain inventories sufficient to meet anticipated sales. If there are long delays in fulfilling an order, the customer may well turn elsewhere.

Inventories also enable firms to save money by producing at a steady rate. It is expensive to let sales dictate the level of production. There would be too much variation from day to day or even month to month; workers and machines might be left idle or forced to work overtime. Thus, firms tend to set a steady level of production, which, when combined with the unsteady demand for their products, produces inventory. To smooth production, firms put goods into inventories in slack periods and take them out of inventories in peak times. This is called the **production-smoothing function** of inventories.

In the production-facilitating explanation, inventories are positively correlated with the level of output and aggregate expenditures: inventories increase when the level of output is high. In the production-smoothing explanation, inventories are negatively correlated with aggregate expenditures: they go up when expenditures go down. The latter explanation would seem to suggest that inventories reduce fluctuations in national output, by allowing firms to keep an even level of production.

In fact, inventories vary far more than output, and as was mentioned earlier, they seem to be a major contributing factor to fluctuations in aggregate expenditures. Rather than serving to dampen business fluctuations, they seem to exacerbate them. This is true even for inventories of consumer goods, which should be serving a smoothing role.

One reason for the variability of investment in inventories may again have to do with the risk-averse behaviour of firms and the availability of credit. When the economy enters a recession, firms often find that their net worth is decreased. They are less willing to make any kind of investment. Where possible, they would like to "disinvest," or convert

CAMI of Ingersoll, Ontario, is the newest of three Japanese automobile plants in Canada. (Toyota and Honda are the other two.) It was established in 1986 as a joint venture between Suzuki Motor Corporation, Japan, and General Motors of Canada Limited. CAMI's plant was built in a needlelike shape, called a *nagare* design. *Nagare* is a Japanese term meaning "flowing like a river." The reason? It is a "just-in-time" or *kanban* manufacturing system. Instead of delivering goods from factories to warehouses and then from warehouses to retail stores, the company tries to produce only *after* receiving an order. The needlelike shape facilitates this by allowing delivery ports all along the assembly line so that suppliers can ship goods several times a day to a dock directly adjacent to the appropriate spot on the line—a key part of a just-in-time manufacturing system.

The just-in-time inventory system was pioneered by Toyota in 1972. The idea was to hold inventories to a bare minimum by providing inputs only when they were immediately needed. Toyota, like many large manufacturers, faced a basic inventory dilemma. On the one hand, running out of some input to production could shut down a factory. On the other hand, keeping large stockpiles around means paying for them in advance and maintaining a large storage area. Besides, some products do not keep especially well if stored for too long.

In a just-in-time inventory system, many small deliveries of materials are made throughout a working day, rather than a few large deliveries that need to be stored for days or weeks. The goal is to have supplies arrive just in time to be used, rather than go into storage. At CAMI, for example, each box of inventory parts comes with a kanban card, inserted by the inventory department. Team leaders file the cards in colour-coordinated slots on a kanban board. Inventory workers travel the length of the needlelike plant to collect them. The number of cards filed indicates if a part is running low and should be reordered from the supplier.

Besides saving on the costs of carrying inventory,

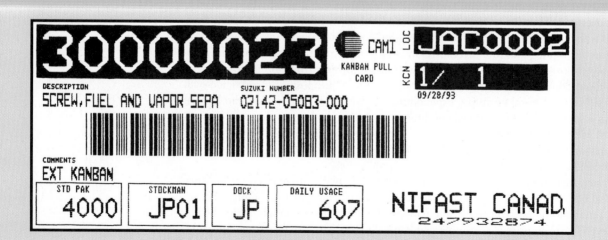

just-in-time systems seem to help companies modernize in many other ways. *The Economist* magazine described it this way: "A favourite analogy is with water in a river. When the level of water falls, rocks start to appear. The rocks can be removed rather than hit." In other words, carrying big inventories can allow a company to cover up a variety of other organizational problems. Thinking about how to organize matters so inventories do not stand around or accumulate can be a powerful tool to thinking about the overall efficiency of the organization.

If just-in-time systems were widely adopted across the entire economy, the overall stability of the economy would tend to be enhanced. When sales dip, a business with large inventories may cut off purchases of inputs altogether for a time, depleting inventories. A business with just-in-time inventories will reduce purchases only a little, and will cut production just by the amount of the reduction in sales.

Sources: The Economist, April 25, 1987; Richard J. Schonberger, "The Transfer of Japanese Manufacturing Management Approaches to U.S. Industry," *Academy of Management Review* (1982) 7:479–87; "Bringing JIT's Benefits to the Bottom Line," *Traffic Management* (November 1991), p. 57; *The Globe and Mail, Report on Business Magazine* (March 1992), pp. 20–21.

their assets back into cash. The easiest way to disinvest is to sell off inventories, rather than, say, a factory. Moreover, when a business faces credit rationing, it may be forced to sell its inventories to raise the requisite capital. And even if it is not yet forced to sell off its inventories, it may fear future credit rationing and, in anticipation, seek to reduce its inventories.

VOLATILITY OF INVESTMENT

Now that we have investigated the main determinants of investment, we can understand better why investment is so volatile. Furthermore, the multiplier explains why the variability of investment translates into even greater volatility in output.

Firms' investments are determined by their ability to raise funds, their perceptions of the profitability of new projects, and their willingness to undertake risks. All of these can change dramatically within a short period of time. An economic decline—or rumors of an economic decline—may lead a firm to be more pessimistic about sales and prices, and therefore about profits. Lower sales or prices may result in losses for the company, thus eroding its net worth and its willingness to undertake risks. The lower flow of funds impairs its ability to finance investment out of retained earnings. Pessimism is contagious; in these same circumstances, banks are reluctant to lend funds (at least on terms that are acceptable to the firm).

The factors that determine investment can be represented as *shifts* in the investment function. Figure 13.9 shows "pessimistic" and "optimistic" versions of the investment schedule first shown in Figure 13.7. Since real interest rates have not varied much, most of the fluctuations in investment are due to shifts of the investment schedule as shown in Figure 13.9, rather than movements along the investment schedule as seen in Figure 13.7.

While the government cannot control all of these determinants, it has a variety of instruments at its disposal that may affect investment. If the business community is con-

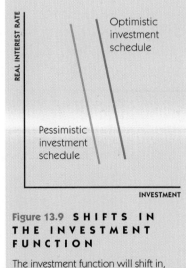

Figure 13.9 SHIFTS IN THE INVESTMENT FUNCTION

The investment function will shift in, resulting in less investment at every level of real interest rates, if firms perceive greater riskiness, if the tax structure is less favourable to investment, and for other reasons.

vinced about the government's commitment to economic stability, businessmen may perceive less risk and be more willing to invest. But predicting, let alone controlling, the psychology of business executives is at best a tricky business.

Temporary tax changes like the investment tax credit are more reliable, but they are a cumbersome tool, because they require action by Parliament. Temporary tax changes may also distort how resources are allocated, though the macroeconomic gains—in higher levels of output—may well be worth the microeconomic losses from these distortions.

For the most part, however, the government relies on monetary policy that affects both the availability of credit and the terms on which firms can borrow. Firms raise funds through the capital market. How and when the government, through the monetary authorities, affects the capital market are questions of sufficient importance and complexity that most of the next part of the book is devoted to exploring them. For now, it is simply worth observing that what goes on in the product market (the determination of the equilibrium level of output) affects the labour market (the level of unemployment in the economy), and what goes on in the capital market (the availability of credit) affects investment and thus the product market.

WAYS OF STIMULATING INVESTMENT

1. Increasing business confidence: government demonstrating a commitment to maintaining high levels of employment and output

2. Lowering the cost of investment: subsidies to investment through the tax system

3. Increasing the availability of credit or making it available on more attractive terms (monetary policy; direct government lending programs)

REVIEW AND PRACTICE

SUMMARY

1. The Keynesian consumption function stresses the importance of current disposable income in determining consumption. In contrast, the life-cycle hypothesis says that people save during their life so that they can spend after retirement. The permanent income hypothesis argues that people save in good years to offset the bad years.

2. In the Keynesian consumption function, the government could manipulate this year's consumption by changing this year's tax rate. In the future-oriented theories, temporary tax reductions would have a limited effect in stimulating consumption, since people are considering a longer horizon than this year for their consumption decisions.

3. Both the life-cycle and permanent income models predict that consumption will depend on lifetime wealth, and that capital gains will therefore affect consumption.

4. Household consumption appears to be more dependent on current income than either the life-cycle or permanent income theory suggests. Consumers can easily postpone the purchase of durables when current income falls. Also, limitations on their ability to borrow (credit rationing) may keep the consumption of many people with little savings close to their current income.

5. Future-oriented theories of consumption suggest that the aggregate expenditures schedule is flat and the multiplier is low; they help explain why the ratio of consumption to disposable income may shift from year to year; and they imply that temporary changes in disposable income may have only a slight effect on consumption.

6. Variations in the level of investment are probably the principal reason for variations in total aggregate expenditures. The three main categories of investment are firms' purchases of plant and equipment, firms' increase or decrease in inventories, and households' purchases of new homes.

7. Historically, short-term variations in real interest rates have proved relatively unimportant in explaining variations in investment.

8. The availability of funds is an important determinant of variations in investment. Most firms finance much of their investment out of retained earnings. They also borrow when possible, although they sometimes face credit constraints. Relatively little use is made of equity markets (selling shares) to finance investments.

9. Firms will be induced to invest if they anticipate that demand for their products will rise, if the investment project will lower the firm's costs of production, or if the price of the investment project goes down, for instance because of favourable tax treatment.

10. In an economic downturn, firms are less willing to bear risk, and this contributes to a downturn in investment.

KEY TERMS

human capital
life-cycle hypothesis
permanent income
 hypothesis
durable goods
plant and equipment
inventory

investment schedule
accelerator
investment tax
 credit (ITC)
production-
 facilitating func-
 tion

production-
 smoothing func-
 tion

REVIEW QUESTIONS

1. What is the difference between the Keynesian model of consumption, the life-cycle model, and the permanent income model?

2. Why do the life-cycle and permanent income hypotheses predict that temporary tax changes will have little effect on current consumption?

3. What factors affect consumer expenditures on durables? Why are these expenditures so volatile?

4. How will the existence of credit rationing make consumption more dependent on current income than the future-oriented consumption theories would suggest?

5. What are the possible sources of funds for firms that wish to invest? Which is used most often, and least often?

6. What is the investment accelerator?

7. Why does an investment tax credit stimulate investment?

8. How might changes in perceptions of economic risk make investment levels more volatile?

9. Why might firms' willingness to bear risk decrease in a recession?

10. Why does holding inventories cost the firm anything extra? Why might inventory investment be as volatile as it is?

PROBLEMS

1. Under which theory of consumption would a temporary tax cut have the largest effect on consumption? Under which theory would a permanent rise in Old Age Security benefits have the largest effect on consumption? Under which theory would permanently higher Unemployment Insurance benefits have the largest effect on consumption? Explain.

2. Which theory of consumption predicts that aggregate savings will depend on the proportion of retired and young people in the population? What is the relationship? Which theories predict that consumption will not vary a great deal according to whether the economy is in a boom or recession? Why?

3. If the government made it easier for people to borrow money, perhaps by enacting programs to help them get loans, would you expect consumption behaviour to become more or less sensitive to current income? Why?

4. How would you predict that a crash in the stock market would affect the relationship between consumption and income? How would you predict that rapidly rising prices for homes would affect the relationship between consumption and income? Draw shifts in the consumption function to illustrate. How do your predictions differ depending on whether the consumer is a Keynesian, life-cycle, or permanent income consumer?

5. A company that expects the long-term real interest rate to be 3 percent is considering a list of projects. Each project costs $10,000, but they vary in the amount of time they will take to pay off, and in how much they will pay off. The first will pay $12,000 in two years; the second, $12,500 in three years; the third, $13,000 in four years. Which projects are worth doing? If the expected interest rate was 5 percent, does your answer change? You may assume that prices are stable.

6. Take the projects in problem #5 and reevaluate them, this time assuming that inflation is at 4 percent per year, and the payoffs are in nominal dollars at the time they occur. Are the projects still worth doing?

7. Draw a diagram to show the direction that the investment function would shift in each of the following situations.
    (a) The government passes an investment tax credit.
    (b) Businesses believe the economic future looks healthier than they had previously thought.
    (c) The government reduces the real interest rate.

8. Imagine that the government raises personal income taxes, but also enacts an investment tax credit for a corresponding amount. Describe under what circumstances this combination of policies would be most effective in stimulating aggregate demand. Consider differing theories of consumption, and the choice between permanent and temporary changes in the tax structure.

APPENDIX A: THE INVESTMENT-SAVINGS IDENTITY

We typically think of savings and investment together. Both are virtues: "A penny saved is a penny earned." Increased investment enhances the future productivity of the economy. In recent years, there has been concern about the level of investment in the Canadian economy. It has frequently been suggested that Canadians should encourage savings, the presumption being that savings are automatically converted into investment.

When the economy is operating along its production possibilities curve, with all resources fully utilized, increased savings—reduced consumption—mean that more capital goods can be produced. But when the economy is operating below its production possibilities curve, increased savings—reduced consumption—may simply push the economy further below the curve.

In *open* economies, savings and investment do not have to change together even when the economy is on its production possibilities curve. The economy can undertake investment, even when there is little domestic saving, by borrowing from abroad. The consequences of this are discussed in later chapters.

The income-expenditure analysis of Chapter 12 focused on the relationship between aggregate expenditures and income. Equilibrium occurs when aggregate expenditures equal national income. An alternative way of describing how national output is determined focuses on savings and investment. We look at a simple model first, in which disposable income equals national income. For this to be the case, we assume that taxes are zero and all of a firm's profits are paid out as dividends. To simplify further, we assume there are no government savings or dissavings, or flow of funds from abroad. Later we will loosen up these assumptions and get a fuller picture.

Individuals can either spend their income today or save it, either to consume later or to leave as a bequest to their children. This is true by definition:

$$\text{income} = \text{consumption} + \text{savings}. \tag{13.1}$$

With no government purchases or net exports, we know from the components of aggregate expenditures that firms can produce only two kinds of goods: consumer goods and investment goods. Thus, output, Y, can be broken into its two components:

$$Y = \text{consumption} + \text{investment}. \tag{13.2}$$

These two identities can be combined to form a new one. Since the value of national output equals national income,

$$Y = \text{income}, \tag{13.3}$$

we can use the right-hand side of (13.1) and (13.2) to get

$$\text{consumption} + \text{savings} = \text{consumption} + \text{investment}. \tag{13.4}$$

Subtracting consumption from both sides of the equation leaves the equation

$$\text{savings} = \text{investment}. \tag{13.5}$$

In short, savings must equal investment. This is a simple matter of definition.

One way to understand this identity is to think of firms as producing a certain amount of goods, the value of which is just equal to the income of the individuals in the economy (because everything firms take in they pay out as income to someone in the economy). The income that is not consumed is, by definition, saved. On the output side, firms either sell the goods they produce or put them into inventory for sale in future years. Some of the inventory buildup is planned, because businesses need inventories to survive. Some of it is unplanned—businesses may be surprised by an economic downturn that spoils their sales projections. Both intended and unintended inventory buildups are considered investment. The goods that are not consumed are, by definition, invested. After all, inventory accumulation consists of goods that are produced not for current consumption but presumably for future consumption.

This identity (13.5) can be transformed into an equation determining national output, once it is recognized that in equilibrium firms will cut back production if there is unintended inventory accumulation. Because firms will cut back, in equilibrium the amount companies invest is the amount they wish to invest (including inventories), given current market conditions. That is, in equilibrium, firms do not suffer unpleasant surprises. The equilibrium condition, then, is that

$$\text{investment} = \text{desired investment}. \tag{13.6}$$

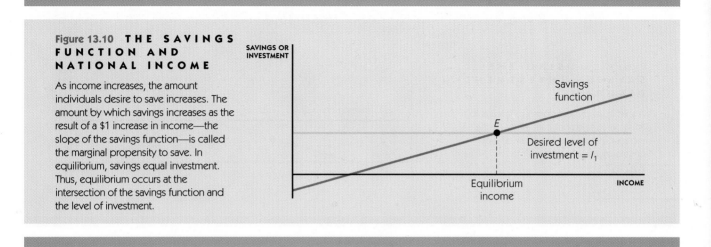

Figure 13.10 THE SAVINGS FUNCTION AND NATIONAL INCOME

As income increases, the amount individuals desire to save increases. The amount by which savings increases as the result of a $1 increase in income—the slope of the savings function—is called the marginal propensity to save. In equilibrium, savings equal investment. Thus, equilibrium occurs at the intersection of the savings function and the level of investment.

Now switch over to the savings side of the identity (13.5). The consumption function presented earlier tells how much people wish to consume at each level of income. But since what is not consumed is saved, the consumption function can easily be transformed into a savings function, giving the level of savings at each level of income. Savings is just income minus consumption:

$$\text{savings} = \text{income } (Y) - \text{consumption}. \tag{13.7}$$

Figure 13.10 shows the savings function. The slope of this curve, the amount by which savings increase with income, is the marginal propensity to save, which is just 1 minus the marginal propensity to consume.

Since savings must equal investment, and in equilibrium investment must equal desired investment, then in equilibrium

$$\text{savings} = \text{desired investment}. \tag{13.8}$$

The figure shows a fixed level of desired investment, I_1. Desired investment is horizontal because investment is assumed to be unaffected by the level of income. Equilibrium occurs at the intersection of the desired investment curve and the savings curve, point E.

As with income-expenditure analysis, savings-investment analysis shows how an increase in investment leads to an increase in output that is a multiple of itself. Figure 13.11 shows that as investment shifts up from I_1 to I_2, the equilibrium shifts from E_1 to E_2, and output increases from Y_1 to Y_2. The change in investment, ΔI, is again smaller than the change in output. This should not surprise us, since income-expenditure analysis and savings-investment analysis are two ways of looking at the same thing.

We can use a similar diagram to illustrate what may seem to be a paradoxical result: when the economy's resources are not fully employed, an increase in thrift—the level of savings at each level of income—may have no effect at all on the equilibrium level of savings or investment. This is called the paradox of thrift. The only effect of greater thrift

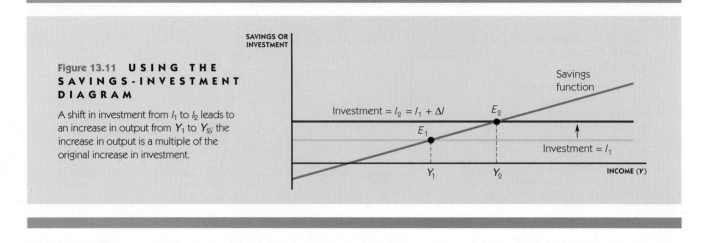

Figure 13.11 USING THE SAVINGS-INVESTMENT DIAGRAM

A shift in investment from I_1 to I_2 leads to an increase in output from Y_1 to Y_2; the increase in output is a multiple of the original increase in investment.

is to lower national income and output. Figure 13.12 shows the effect of an upward shift in the savings function—at each level of income, savings are higher. But in equilibrium, savings equal investment. With investment fixed, savings too, in equilibrium, must be the same; and to attain that level of savings (equal to the level of investment), income must be lowered from Y_1 to Y_2.

What happens when government purchases and net exports are allowed to enter the picture? Again, savings equal investment. Now, however, there are three additional sources of investment funds, along with the household savings we have considered so far (denoted by the symbol S_h). Funds can be obtained from abroad (S_x) or from the government (S_g). Just as household savings are the difference between the household's income and its consumption, government savings are the difference between its income (tax revenues) and its expenditures. In recent years, government savings have been negative—the government has been spending more than its income. Finally, businesses

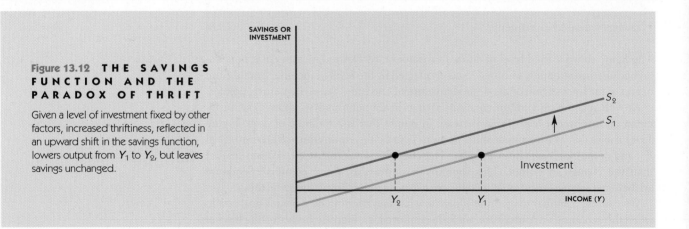

Figure 13.12 THE SAVINGS FUNCTION AND THE PARADOX OF THRIFT

Given a level of investment fixed by other factors, increased thriftiness, reflected in an upward shift in the savings function, lowers output from Y_1 to Y_2, but leaves savings unchanged.

save, too, when their receipts exceed what they pay out as wages, taxes, interest, and dividends,[9] and these savings (S_b) are another source of investment funds. Thus,

$$S_b + S_h + S_g + S_x = I. \tag{13.9}$$

We frequently combine business and household savings together, as private savings (S_p):

$$S_p = S_h + S_b. \tag{13.10}$$

The new savings-investment identity is

$$S_p + S_g + S_x = I. \tag{13.11}$$

Investment must equal the sum of private savings, government savings, and borrowing from abroad.

In the 1980s, the rate of private savings was low and the rate of government savings was actually negative. However, borrowing from abroad increased. Thus, there were large changes in the sources of savings. The explanation for these changes, and their long-run consequences, are questions we will take up in Chapter 22.

APPENDIX B: A CLOSER LOOK AT CREDIT RATIONING

The chapter made the point that firms and individuals may not be able to borrow all they would like at the market rate of interest. There may be credit rationing. To understand credit rationing more fully, picture a medium-sized corporation, Checkout Systems, that produces software that, when used in conjunction with retailers' checkout registers, handles inventory and all other accounting functions as well. The software has been popular, but Checkout Systems realizes that it would be much more successful if it sold the hardware—computer systems, terminals, and cash register drawers—that stores must have in order to use the software. Checkout can get the hardware from a computer manufacturer, but it needs $2 million for warehouse and inventory. The company is fully confident that the $2 million expansion will produce a steady return of at least 30 percent. However, it has no retained earnings with which to pay for the expansion.

This is only the beginning of Checkout's problems. The company has a line of credit, allowing it to borrow up to $400,000 from a local bank at 14 percent interest. It would happily borrow the $2 million at that rate (because the investment will throw off a 30 percent return). But the company's banker refuses to increase the credit limit, because the bank does not share Checkout's optimism. Checkout executives offer to pay a higher price—16 percent interest for the $2 million. Surely the bankers would prefer 16 percent from their loan to 14 percent on someone else's. Indeed, given Checkout's confi-

---

[9] Additions to inventory are included in the firm's books as if they were sales; the firm records a "profit" even though there is no cash to show for it. This profit is saved, and is reflected in statistics on business savings.

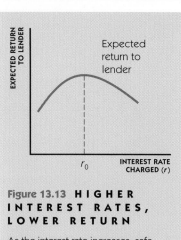

Figure 13.13 HIGHER INTEREST RATES, LOWER RETURN

As the interest rate increases, safe borrowers tend to drop out of the market, and only risky borrowers remain. Beyond some point, rises in the interest rate increase defaults on loans by enough to reduce the expected return to a lender. At higher interest rates, borrowers may also undertake greater risks, again lowering lenders' expected returns.

dence in its returns, it is willing to pay an even higher interest. The bank turns the company down. Is there any interest rate at which the bank would be willing to lend, the Checkout executives ask? The bank replies no.

The bank is aware that some borrowers are more likely to default than others, but it has no way of knowing which ones are most likely to do so. The bank faces an adverse selection problem: as it raises interest rates to accommodate firms like Checkout, its average returns may actually decrease. The reason for this is that at higher interest rates, the "best" borrowers—those with the lowest likelihood of default—decide not to borrow. People willing to take great risks may be willing to borrow even at very high interest rates.

Figure 13.13 shows the return to a lender being maximized at the interest rate r_0. The bank will not raise its interest rates beyond this level, even though at this rate the demand for funds may exceed the supply.

Let's look now at the market for funds for a particular category of loans, say small mortgages (under $100,000) for owner-occupied houses. The supply curve for funds for loans differs from the supply curve depicted in the basic model. Figure 13.14, which is based on the information in Figure 13.13, shows the supply curve for funds as backward bending. This shape reflects the reasonable assumption that as the average return to loans (which should not be confused with the interest rate charged for these loans) increases, the supply of funds increases. The supply curve thus bends backwards beyond r_0. As the interest rate charged rises to this point, average returns increase and so does the supply of funds; but at interest rates beyond this point, average returns decline and so does the supply of funds.

Credit rationing takes three forms. Some borrowers get funds, but less than they would like. Some loan applicants are denied credit, even though similar applicants receive credit. And some whole categories of applicants are simply denied credit. A bank may, for instance, refuse to give loans for vacations or to finance a university education or to buy a house in a particular part of town. In each of these cases, those who have their credit denied or limited will not be any more successful if they offer to pay a higher interest rate.

If lenders had perfect information, there would be no rationing. They would charge higher interest rates to reflect differences in the likelihood of default, but all applicants willing to pay the appropriate rate would get loans. Thus, underlying rationing is a lack of information. No matter how many forms are filled out, how many references are requested, or how many interviews are held, the lenders know there is a residual amount of missing information. They therefore develop rules of thumb for loans: yes to well-run, small businesses; no to vacation loans for university students or to new high-tech computer software firms, both of whom typically have high rates of default.

The lower the interest rate charged, of course, the greater the demand for funds. As the demand curve is drawn in Figure 13.14, average returns are maximized at interest rate r_0, but the supply of funds is less than the demand at this point. There is credit rationing; L_0 loans are actually made, while total demand is L_1. Many qualified borrowers would like to take out loans at the going interest rate but cannot. The magnitude of the credit rationing is measured by the gap between the demand, L_1, and the supply, L_0.

There is a second reason that there may be credit rationing. Let's return to the example of Checkout Systems. The bank knows that Checkout's executives can engage in risky behaviour, some of which the bank will find impossible to monitor. It may worry that the higher the interest rate charged, the more likely that such risk-taking behaviour will occur. And if the firm is near bankruptcy, it will have no chance of survival unless it does take great risks. The bank knows that the higher the interest rate charged, the more likely that the firm will have trouble meeting its obligations and go bankrupt. As we saw in Figure 13.13, expected returns to the bank may actually decrease as the interest rate charged increases, because of this adverse incentive effect.

The arguments used here for credit rationing are similar to those employed in Chapter 11 for efficiency wages. There, we saw that workers' productivity may depend on the wages paid. Just as the expected return to the lender may at first increase and then decrease as the interest rate charged increases, so too a firm's profits may at first increase and then decrease as it raises the wage. When wages are low, the increase in productivity from raising them more than offsets the direct costs. In Chapter 11, we saw that firms will not lower wages below the efficiency wage, even when there is, at the efficiency wage, an excess supply of labour. The same reasoning leads here to the conclusion that firms will not raise interest rates above the level at which the expected return is maximized, even when there is, at that interest rate, an excess demand for funds.

EQUITY RATIONING

We might suppose that firms that are unable to borrow would raise money by issuing more stock. However, established firms seldom raise capital in this way. In recent years, less than a tenth of new financing has occurred through the sale of equity. The reason is not hard to see—when firms issue new equity, the price of existing shares tends to decline, and by more than the amount that one would expect, given the dilution of the ownership of existing shareholders. For example, say that a firm worth $1 million issues $100,000 worth of new shares, and the price of stock falls by 5 percent. The firm's existing shareholders have to give up $50,000 to raise $100,000 in funds from new investors. This is clearly an unattractive deal.

There are several reasons why issuing more equity frequently seems to have such an adverse effect on the price of shares. First, issuing equity adversely affects the market's perception of a firm's value. Investors reason that the firm's original owners and its managers will be most anxious to sell shares when these relatively informed individuals think that the market is overvaluing their shares, and they know that the owners and managers may refuse to issue shares if the shares are undervalued. These concerns are compounded by the fact that firms normally turn first to banks to raise funds. Investors wonder, "Is the reason the firm is trying to issue new shares that banks will not lend to it, or at least not on very favourable terms, or at least not as much as the firm wants? If banks, who have presumably looked closely into the firm and have a fair idea about what is going on, are reluctant to lend, why should I turn over my hard-earned money?" Reasoning this way, they will only invest in the firm if they believe they are getting a good enough deal, that is, if the price of the shares is low enough.

Also, we saw earlier that debt has a positive incentive effect on managers; by the same token, giving the firm more money to play with, without any fixed commitment to repay—which is exactly what equity does—may have an adverse effect on incentives.

For these, and possibly other, reasons, the issue of new shares on average depresses the value of firm shares. Accordingly, only infrequently do established firms raise new capital by issuing shares.

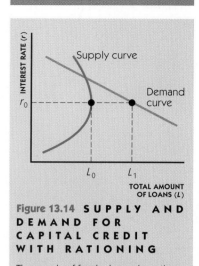

Figure 13.14 SUPPLY AND DEMAND FOR CAPITAL CREDIT WITH RATIONING

The supply of funds depends on the expected return. If that return begins to fall when the interest rate charged gets high, the supply of funds will be backward bending. Even if demand for funds exceeds supply at interest rate r_0, the lender will not raise his interest rate, since that would reduce expected returns. As a result, an excess demand for funds can exist in equilibrium.

GOVERNMENT
EXPENDITURES
AND TRADE

ow we take a closer look at the two other major components of the aggregate expenditures schedule: government expenditures and net exports. As with the study of consumption spending and investment in Chapter 13, our objective here is twofold: to understand why aggregate expenditures fluctuate, and to understand how certain government policies can affect these fluctuations.

1. What is the consequence of an increase in government expenditures matched by an increase in taxes?

2. What is the fiscal deficit? the full-employment deficit? What are the consequences of these deficits?

3. When do government expenditures crowd out private expenditures? Why is crowding out important?

4. How has the role of foreign trade in the economy changed in recent years? What explains the large increase in imports relative to exports?

5. How does the fact that Canada is an open economy affect the conduct of macro-economic policy?

6. Why is protectionism unlikely to be a good solution to the problem of a trade deficit?

GOVERNMENT EXPENDITURES

Like consumers and business firms, the government stimulates the economy when it spends money. Consumers and business firms, however, get the money they spend by selling their services and goods, while government gets most of its money through taxes. Taxes give government funds to spend, but they take an equal amount away from the private sector.

There is one complication to the analysis of fiscal policy that merits a brief mention. While we based the analysis of investment, for instance, on the idea that firms maximize profits or market value, we will not look closely here at the motivations of government officials. For most of this chapter, we simply ask what would happen if the government increased expenditures or reduced taxes. There are economists, however, who believe that the government should be analyzed as an economic organization, like households and firms. They believe that the behaviour of government can (and must) be explained in much the same way that the behaviour of households and firms can be explained, and that the politicians and bureaucrats who make government decisions respond rationally to the incentives they face. Just as changes in economic conditions (an increase in disposable income, for example) lead households to change their consumption decisions or cause firms to change their investments, changes in economic and political

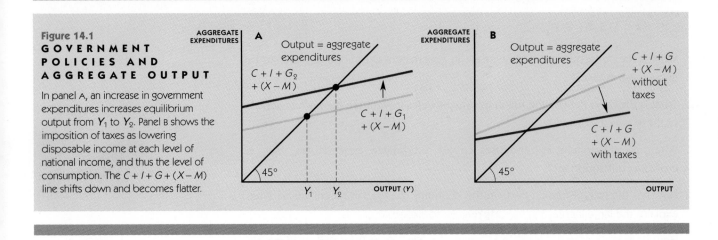

Figure 14.1
GOVERNMENT POLICIES AND AGGREGATE OUTPUT

In panel A, an increase in government expenditures increases equilibrium output from Y_1 to Y_2. Panel B shows the imposition of taxes as lowering disposable income at each level of national income, and thus the level of consumption. The $C + I + G + (X - M)$ line shifts down and becomes flatter.

conditions can, in this view, predictably be related to changes in the behaviour of the government. In some circumstances, the incentives facing politicians may actually lead the government to contribute to the volatility of the economy.

In Chapter 12, we learned that government spending serves to increase aggregate expenditures, shifting the aggregate expenditures schedule up, as in Figure 14.1A. At the same time, taxes reduce disposable income and therefore reduce aggregate expenditures. Moreover, taxes that increase with income make the aggregate expenditures schedule flatter than it is in the absence of government. Thus, government makes the multiplier smaller, as illustrated in panel B. We now take a closer look at the relationship between taxes, government expenditures, and multipliers.

BALANCED BUDGETS

An old-fashioned view of the government (one that is currently enjoying a revival) holds that government should keep its revenues and its expenditures in balance. If Old Age Security, Unemployment Insurance, defence, equalization, and other government programs are going to cost $160 billion this year, then taxes should be set so as to generate $160 billion in revenues.

Even in this simple (simple to explain, not to achieve) scenario, the balanced budget increase in expenditures stimulates output. But the multiplier is greatly reduced; in fact, normally aggregate output and income will go up just by the amount of the increased government expenditures and taxes.

How is it possible that when the government is reducing private income through taxes by the same amount that it increases public spending, aggregate expenditures are nonetheless increased? Assume that some fraction, say 90 percent, of all disposable income is consumed. The remaining 10 percent is saved. If taxes are raised by $1,000, consumption will be reduced by $900. However, government expenditures will have also increased by $1,000, so the first-round effect of the tax rise is to increase overall expenditures (public and private) by $100. This increased expenditures income leads to greater consumption, and then to further increases in income, by the usual multiplier analysis. Thus, the government *can* still play an active role in stabilizing the economy even if it is committed to having balanced budgets. But to stimulate the economy will require much larger variations in government expenditures.

This is illustrated in Figure 14.2, a standard income-expenditure analysis diagram. The initial equilibrium is at Y_0. We can think of a balanced budget increase in expenditures as a two-step process. First, government expenditures are increased from G_0 to G_1. This increases output from Y_0 to Y_1. Then the government raises tax rates to pay for the increased expenditures. The higher tax rates reduce consumption at each level of income, and the aggregate consumption function is flatter. The new equilibrium is at Y_2, much lower than output would have been had taxes not been raised, but still higher than in the initial situation.

A numerical example will help illustrate why this is so. Assume that national output is at $650 billion, and the government calculates that to attain full employment will necessitate increasing national output to $700 billion. That is to say, output is $50 billion short of its full-employment potential. If the multiplier is 5 and the government wants to increase expenditures but leave taxes unchanged, it needs to increase its expenditures by $10 billion ($50 billion ÷ 5)—still a considerable sum, but easier to achieve than $50 billion. If the government is committed to having a balanced budget, however, it will have to increase its expenditures by much more than that amount, as increased taxes offset the effects on consumption of increased income.[1] In effect, the multiplier for an increase in expenditures matched by a corresponding increase in taxes will be small. In-

[1] The exact amount government will have to increase expenditures depends on how it raises the tax revenues. If the government raises the taxes on households, then to raise output by $50 billion, the government would have to raise government expenditures, and taxes, by a full $50 billion. Income after taxes—disposable income—would, accordingly, remain unchanged, so consumption would remain unchanged. Thus, aggregate expenditures—C + I + G (ignoring net exports)—would increase simply by the increase in government expenditures. There is no multiplier at work.

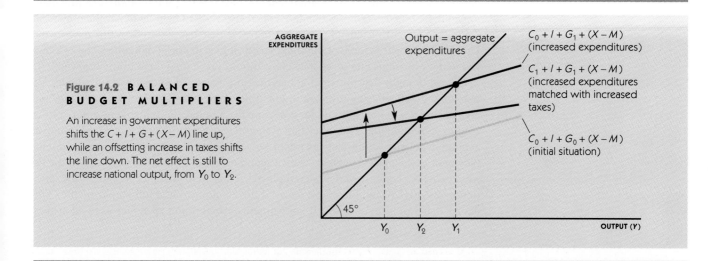

Figure 14.2 BALANCED BUDGET MULTIPLIERS

An increase in government expenditures shifts the $C + I + G + (X - M)$ line up, while an offsetting increase in taxes shifts the line down. The net effect is still to increase national output, from Y_0 to Y_2.

AGGREGATE EXPENDITURES

Output = aggregate expenditures

$C_0 + I + G_1 + (X - M)$ (increased expenditures)

$C_1 + I + G_1 + (X - M)$ (increased expenditures matched with increased taxes)

$C_0 + I + G_0 + (X - M)$ (initial situation)

45°

Y_0 Y_2 Y_1

OUTPUT (Y)

deed, there may be no multiplier, in which case the government would have to increase expenditures by $50 billion. It is unlikely that the government will find good uses for those extra funds, and so it is unlikely that such an increased level of expenditures would be politically acceptable.

The political climate of recent years has called for strict limits on government expenditures, and that attitude, combined with a commitment to a balanced budget, severely limits the scope of the government to use fiscal policy to stabilize the economy. This is a marked reversal of the views of the decades immediately following World War II, when governments were committed to using fiscal policy to stabilize the economy.

THE FULL-EMPLOYMENT DEFICIT

The government can stimulate the economy even more if it increases expenditures without raising taxes at the same time, a situation known as **deficit spending.** Deficit spending requires that the government borrow what it does not raise in taxes. It borrows money by selling Treasury bills and bonds to investors; in effect, the investors are lending the government money it can spend today in exchange for a promise of repayment with interest in the future. Because the stimulus provided by government spending is not offset by the reductions in consumer spending that would result from increased taxes, increases in government expenditures financed by deficits, as opposed to taxes, have multiplier effects.[2]

Budget deficits may seem almost unavoidable today, but the very idea of financing government expenditures through deficits on a regular basis was another of the revolutionary insights produced by John Maynard Keynes. Early in this century, many economists held as a basic tenet that responsible governments should always maintain a balanced budget. Some governments that had borrowed heavily from abroad found themselves unable to pay their debts. They had, in effect, gone bankrupt, an experience that has almost been repeated in the last decade by some governments in Latin America. Within Canada at the time of Confederation, some provinces could not meet their debt payments. Part of the financial arrangements negotiated at the time the first provinces joined the Confederation was that the federal government help them pay the provincial debts by a system of federal-provincial transfers that has survived to this day. In the United States, where some of the states faced similar financial difficulties, the reaction was to put provisions into some state constitutions preventing them from borrowing.

Keynes thought that this rigid adherence to a balanced budget was misguided. He pointed out that an economy sunk in unemployment and stagnation was suffering, and argued that it was irresponsible for governments to allow the valuable resources of the country to remain idle when they had at their disposal instruments that could stimulate economic activity. While deficits might be a problem, there were times when unemployment was a greater problem. Deficit spending could be a useful policy when the resources of the economy were underemployed. Thus, to Keynesian economists, the question to ask was "Would there be a deficit if the economy was at full employment?" The deficit that would have arisen if government revenues and spending were what they

---

[2] Provided, of course, that consumers do not reduce consumption in anticipation of the future taxes they will have to pay to finance the higher government debt.

would have been under full employment (rather than what they actually were) is called a **full-employment deficit.** Most economists believe that a government is fiscally responsible so long as there is no full-employment deficit. But some economists believe that when there is a severe recession, the benefits of stimulating the economy are so great that it may be desirable for the government even to have a full-employment deficit.

Figure 14.3 gives the full-employment and actual deficits since 1955. When the economy is booming, the actual and full-employment deficits are roughly the same, as they were from 1976–1980 and 1985–1987. When the economy is not in a boom, the full-employment deficit is smaller than the actual deficit: for example, in 1982, while the actual deficit was 5.3 percent of GDP, the full-employment deficit was 3.5 percent of GDP. It is even possible for there to be a full-employment surplus and an actual deficit. This happened in 1961 and 1962, and again in 1971. The target of a zero full-employment deficit was approached in the mid-1950s, though there were actual budget surpluses.

The difference between the actual deficit and the full-employment deficit arises because during periods of unemployment, tax revenues are lower and some types of expenditures (such as welfare payments and unemployment insurance) are higher than they would be if the economy were fully employed.

Until 1975 (with the exception of war years), the actual deficits in Canada were always sufficiently small that there was either a full-employment surplus or a negligible full-employment deficit. Since then, the actual deficit has been so massive that there have been substantial full-employment deficits in most years.

Use of the full-employment deficit as a measure of fiscal responsibility is more widespread in the United States than in Canada. In recent legislation aimed at eliminating the huge deficits of the 1980s, the targets that the U.S. Congress has set for itself each year are expressed in terms of a full-employment deficit. The legislation calls for eventually attaining the target of a zero full-employment deficit. But this goal allows for an actual deficit, should the economy be in a recession.

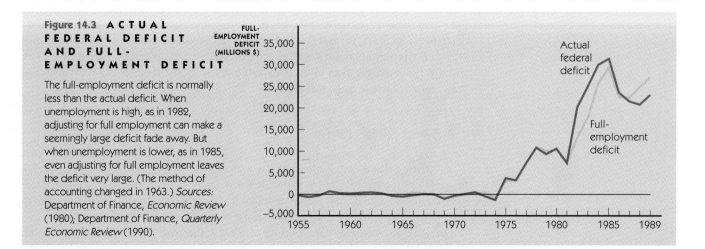

Figure 14.3 ACTUAL FEDERAL DEFICIT AND FULL-EMPLOYMENT DEFICIT

The full-employment deficit is normally less than the actual deficit. When unemployment is high, as in 1982, adjusting for full employment can make a seemingly large deficit fade away. But when unemployment is lower, as in 1985, even adjusting for full employment leaves the deficit very large. (The method of accounting changed in 1963.) *Sources:* Department of Finance, *Economic Review* (1980); Department of Finance, *Quarterly Economic Review* (1990).

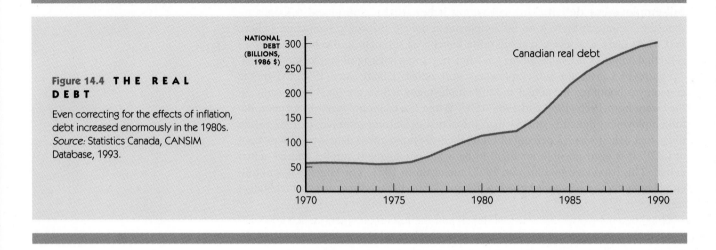

Figure 14.4 THE REAL DEBT

Even correcting for the effects of inflation, debt increased enormously in the 1980s.
Source: Statistics Canada, CANSIM Database, 1993.

THE DEBT AND THE DEFICIT

It is important to distinguish between deficits and government debt. The deficit measures a shortfall in any given year. The debt is the total of unpaid deficits; it measures what the government owes from past years. Figure 14.4 traces the government's debt from 1970 to 1990. Note in particular how it has increased dramatically since 1980. The figures are adjusted for inflation and thus measure the real debt.

The real budget deficit can be defined as the change each year in the real level of total accumulated government debt. If inflation erodes the value of the total debt by more than the government borrows in a particular year, there may be a real budget surplus, even though it may appear to be a nominal dollar deficit. This happened in the early 1970s. The government had incurred a deficit in 1971 and 1972, but inflation was running at about 4 percent as a result of the expansionary policies of the late 1960s and the export demand from the United States during the Vietnam War. As a result, real indebtedness declined; there was a real surplus. It continued to decline for the next two years as the government ran a budget surplus. The budget deficits during the late 1970s and the 1980s appear even more remarkable when we see that the economy switched from real surpluses to huge real deficits.

CROWDING OUT

The analysis behind deficit spending—whatever measure one uses—may overestimate the power of the government to stimulate the economy, because increased government expenditures or deficits may lead to reduced investment. If the government increases its expenditures without at the same time raising taxes, the resulting budget deficit will result in more borrowing by the government. This in turn will reduce the supply of funds available for the private sector to borrow. Economists say that government borrowing will **crowd out** private investment.

Proponents of the crowding out view remind us that government competes with private firms and individuals in the capital market. If there is a fixed amount of funds available, then for the government to obtain more funds (to finance the deficit), firms will have to get less funds. In the extreme case, an increase in government expenditures (with taxes fixed) crowds out investment on a dollar-per-dollar basis: the more deficit spending the government does, the less investing private firms do, and the increase in government expenditures does not stimulate the economy at all.

In fact, the Canadian government is just as likely to do its borrowing from the Americans and Japanese and other lenders from outside the economy as it is from Canadian citizens. The other extreme case is that of an international capital market where the country can borrow as much as it would like at a fixed rate of interest. Then, instead of crowding out domestic investment, government borrowing simply leads to a flow of funds from abroad, as we will see in greater detail in Chapter 22.

Reality lies somewhere in between: as the government tries to get more funds, some additional funds are attracted from abroad and some individuals save more than they otherwise would, and so there is some increase in the total available funds. At the same time, some investment is crowded out, so that the total stimulus provided to the economy by the increased government expenditures is less than the simple model of Chapter 12 would suggest.

The magnitude of crowding out is also likely to depend on whether or not the economy has a lot of excess capacity. In this chapter, as in the preceding two, we are focusing on the situation where the economy is operating along the horizontal part of its aggregate supply curve, as shown in Figure 14.5A. It is in such situations that the actual level of output produced by the economy is determined by aggregate demand. And it is possi-

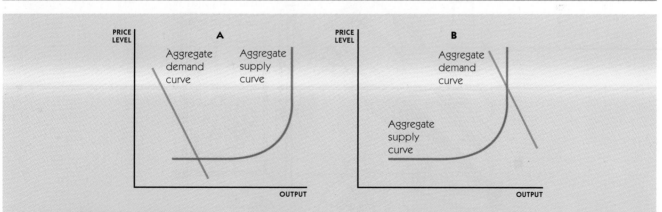

Figure 14.5 **CROWDING OUT**

Panel A shows a situation where initially the economy is operating along the horizontal part of the aggregate supply curve. Increases in government expenditures are likely to increase aggregate demand and thus equilibrium output; there will be at most limited crowding out. Panel B shows a situation where initially the economy is operating along the vertical part of the aggregate supply curve. Since total output cannot increase, increases in government expenditures must come at the expense of some other component of aggregate demand; government expenditures may, for instance, crowd out investment.

CLOSE-UP: THE PUBLIC VEIL

The permanent income and life-cycle theories emphasize that current consumption depends not only on today's income, but also on income that is expected to be received in the future. If disposable income goes up today but is expected to go down next year by a corresponding amount, consumption should remain unchanged. This observation has potentially profound implications for the ability of the government to use tax policy to stabilize the economy.

If the government reduces income taxes this year but keeps expenditures unchanged, the budget deficit will increase. This deficit is a liability for taxpayers; in the future, taxes will have to be increased (from what they otherwise would have been) to pay interest on the debt and to repay the debt. If individuals have their taxes reduced this year but know that they will have to pay for it with higher taxes in the future, their total lifetime income will remain unchanged. In that case, a tax cut—keeping government expenditures fixed—will have no effect on aggregate consumption. Clearly, this view goes beyond the permanent income and life-cycle models introduced earlier, which said a temporary tax cut would have a small effect on total lifetime wealth, and therefore have a small effect on today's aggregate consumption.

The view that whether the government finances a given level of expenditures by taxes or borrowing makes *no* difference to current consumption—the two are perfectly equivalent—is sometimes called the Ricardian equivalence view, in honour

"Papa doesn't want Tsi Tsu in the bedroom while he's hiding his little nest egg."

of David Ricardo, the nineteenth-century English economist who also discovered the principle of comparative advantage. Ricardo described the equivalence theory, then dismissed it as impractical in the real world. In recent years, the view has been resurrected and promoted by Robert Barro of Harvard University.

The theory of Ricardian equivalence suggests that the huge increase in government borrowing in the 1980s should have led to a huge increase in private savings. After all, when people see deficits, they should expect that taxes will increase at some time in the future, and begin setting aside funds to pay the bills. But instead of increasing, private savings rates in Canada continued at about the same level in the 1980s as in the previous decade.

The reasons why Ricardian equivalence does not hold are not completely understood, but they are summarized by the idea of the "public veil." If rational individuals could see through the public veil—that is, if they could look at government borrowing, forecast their future tax liabilities, and act accordingly—then Ricardian equivalence would hold. But people do not seem to see through the public veil, at least not with complete clarity.

Some economists say that this is because most people simply spend most of what they earn and do not adjust to whether the government is saving more or less. Other economists argue that even if taxes do need to be raised in the future, there is uncertainty about when this will happen and who will pay at that time. If the burden of repaying the public debt can be passed on to future generations, as seems likely, and if parents do not fully adjust bequests to their heirs to reflect this, then the tax reduction does represent an increase in the current generation's lifetime wealth, and accordingly aggregate consumption should rise for this generation.

---

ble for the economy to increase government expenditures without reducing the output of other goods. On the other hand, if the economy is operating along the vertical part of the aggregate supply curve, as in panel B, where output cannot be increased by much, increases in government expenditures must be offset by decreases in some other component of national output: there must be some crowding out.

There is an important lesson in all of this: the fact that at times there must be crowding out should not mislead us into thinking that there will always be crowding out. The situations with which we are concerned here, where the economy is not fully utilizing its resources, where some government intervention may be required to restimulate the economy, are precisely those situations in which crowding out is least likely to occur.

AUTOMATIC STABILIZERS

Chapter 12 pointed out that income taxes flatten the aggregate expenditures schedule, thus reducing the multiplier. The fact that the multiplier is smaller has two implications that should be familiar: it means the economy is less sensitive to variations in, say, the level of investment; but it also means that the economy responds less to attempts by the government to stimulate the economy by increasing expenditures.

In effect, the income tax builds a stabilizing mechanism into the economy. As the economy slows down and national income is reduced, the government takes less away from individuals in taxes. Disposable income is reduced by less than total national income. Such mechanisms are called **automatic stabilizers** and are important because they start to work as soon as the economy goes into a downturn. No political debate is required before they can be put to work.

Other government programs in which expenditures increase automatically as national income declines also serve as automatic stabilizers. For example, when incomes decline, Unemployment Insurance benefits increase; Old Age Security benefits tend to rise slightly, as people retire earlier than they otherwise would; and provincial welfare expenditures increase. These government programs are already in place, cushioning the effects of a decline in national income from, say, a decrease in net exports or investment.

By the same token, not only do individual income taxes increase as incomes rise, but so do sales tax revenues, corporate income tax revenues, and excise taxes (taxes on alcoholic beverages, cigarettes, gasoline, and so on). If the economy is growing very rapidly, these mechanisms automatically help to slow it down.

PROVINCIAL AND LOCAL GOVERNMENTS

Though the discussion of government expenditures so far has focused on the taxes and expenditures of the federal government, over one-half of Canadian government expenditures are at the provincial and local levels. These expenditures and the taxes that finance them are governed by quite different considerations from those that prevail at the national level. The provinces do not see stabilizing the economy and maintaining full employment as their responsibility. Indeed, the fluctuations in their expenditures have probably contributed to the fluctuations in the aggregate level of economic activity, as shown in Figure 14.6. The provinces often find it difficult (or at least politically inopportune) to raise tax rates, particularly in bad times. When the economy goes into a recession, they often find their revenues reduced and respond by reducing their expenditures. They are in effect cutting back on the fiscal stimulus at just the time it is most needed. The situation is identical to that of a balanced budget reduction in government expenditures, which leads to reduced national output.

The ability of the provinces to adopt countercyclical fiscal policies is further restricted by the fact that many provincial debt loads are growing to unmanageable proportions. This is partly a result of rapidly increasing expenditure requirements in the areas of education and health care, and partly a result of reductions in the rate of growth of federal-provincial transfers. Total provincial debt is about one-half of the federal debt. This has left the provinces with relatively little room to maneuver in terms of affecting aggregate demand. It has also meant that attempts of the federal government to control the level of debt held by the public sector can only be partially successful. Recent attempts to reduce the debt by restricting transfers to the provinces have led to increased provincial debt. Provinces find it as difficult to reduce their deficits as does the federal government. Some have argued that the provinces should not be allowed to spend beyond their revenues, that is, that they should be required to balance their budgets annually. Some states in the United States are prevented from running deficits by their constitutions.

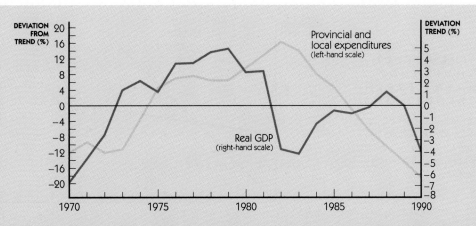

Figure 14.6 EXPENDITURES BY PROVINCIAL AND LOCAL GOVERNMENTS

The figure shows expenditures of provincial and local governments, relative to their trend. These expenditures tend to increase in booms and decrease in recessions, thus contributing to the volatility of the economy. (Provincial and local expenditures have on average been increasing in recent decades. The "trend" is the average rate of increase over a period. The figure shows that in boom years the expenditures are greater than this average, while in recessions they are much less.) *Source:* Statistics Canada, CANSIM Database, 1993.

THE DEFICIT AND STABILIZATION POLICY

The huge deficits of the last decade have placed the subject of deficits at the centre of the stage of political debates. Who is to blame? What are the consequences? What should be done? These are questions we will pursue in greater detail in Chapter 22. Here we ask, what are the implications for government stabilization policy?

In the federal election campaign of 1988, the Conservatives under Prime Minister Mulroney ran on a platform that included reducing the size of the federal debt. Each budget for the next four years included expenditure reduction measures intended to bring the deficit under control. As well, income surtaxes on the well-to-do were maintained and a potentially lucrative source of tax revenue, the Goods and Services Tax, was introduced. Even with these measures in place, the downturn in economic conditions resulted in continuing record deficits, as the automatic stabilizers went to work producing lower tax revenues and higher expenditures. A similar fate befell the provinces.

The expenditure cuts may have had another deleterious effect on the economy. Earlier we distinguished between situations where the economy is at full employment—on the vertical portion of its aggregate supply curve—and where it is in the flat, excess-capacity range. Expenditure cuts shift the aggregate demand curve to the left, reducing national output. In the early 1990s, at the time expenditure cuts were enacted, the economy already appeared to have some excess capacity. There was concern that the expenditure cuts were timed at almost the worst possible moment; rather than offsetting what appeared to be an incipient recession, fiscal policy may have been abetting it. Figure

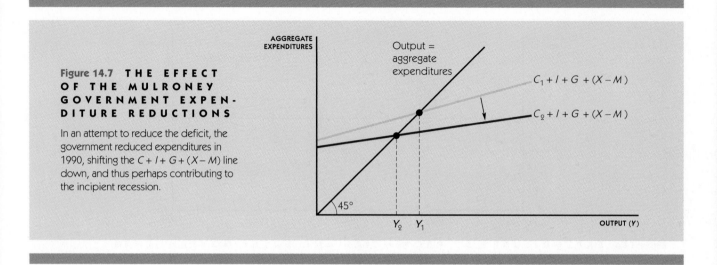

Figure 14.7 THE EFFECT OF THE MULRONEY GOVERNMENT EXPENDITURE REDUCTIONS

In an attempt to reduce the deficit, the government reduced expenditures in 1990, shifting the $C + I + G + (X - M)$ line down, and thus perhaps contributing to the incipient recession.

14.7 shows the downward shift in the $C + I + G + (X - M)$ schedule caused by the expenditure cut, and the resulting reduction in national income from Y_1 to Y_2.

More generally, the large deficits of the 1980s, and the evident difficulty in reducing them, are likely to impair for years to come the government's ability to use fiscal policy to help stabilize the economy.

INTERNATIONAL TRADE

The Canadian economy has always been heavily reliant on foreign trade. Traditionally, we have exported our raw materials and processed natural resources to other countries in return for manufactured goods and foodstuffs from the rest of the world. As a result, Canadians have been referred to as "hewers of wood and drawers of water." Though our menu of exports has been diversified considerably over the years, the extent of our reliance on international trade has remained. This dependence on trade is bound to be an important determinant of the level of economic activity in Canada, as well as tying our fortunes to those of our major trading partners.

Today sales of goods and services to foreigners represent a major proportion of Canadian aggregate demand; about $1 out of every $4 produced by the Canadian economy is exported. The amount of imports that Canada purchases from abroad is of comparable size. The Canadian economy is a highly open one, and the foreign sector is critical to any consideration of policy. The following sections describe the importance of trade in the Canadian economy and how it fits into the macroeconomic analysis presented so far.

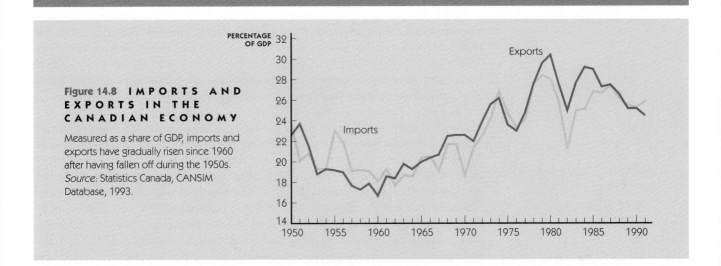

Figure 14.8 IMPORTS AND EXPORTS IN THE CANADIAN ECONOMY

Measured as a share of GDP, imports and exports have gradually risen since 1960 after having fallen off during the 1950s. *Source:* Statistics Canada, CANSIM Database, 1993.

THE EMERGING TRADE DEFICIT

Figure 14.8 shows the continuing significance of imports and exports as a share of GDP in the Canadian economy. Its clear message is that Canada is not self-sufficient; the impact of foreign production cannot be ignored. Figure 14.9 illustrates the fact that Canada's foreign trade looms as large as does foreign trade in the European economies, and much larger than it does in the U.S. economy.

Chapter 3 discussed the reason for all of this trade; it allows each country to make the most of its comparative advantage, to specialize in its strengths. International trade is mutually advantageous—all countries gain.

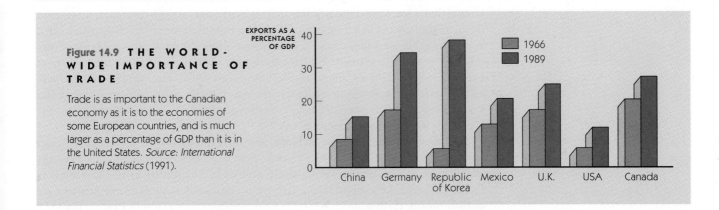

Figure 14.9 THE WORLD-WIDE IMPORTANCE OF TRADE

Trade is as important to the Canadian economy as it is to the economies of some European countries, and is much larger as a percentage of GDP than it is in the United States. *Source: International Financial Statistics* (1991).

But in the midst of these advantages, there is a small dark cloud emerging. As was explained in Chapter 3, when exports exceed imports, there is a trade surplus. Conversely, when exports fall short of imports, there is a trade deficit. Since the early 1980s, a sizable trade surplus has gradually disappeared and been replaced by a growing trade deficit. This trend in international indebtedness has been matched by the advancing federal budget deficits of the same period, and has been the cause for at least as much alarm. The connections between the trade and budget deficits will be discussed in Chapter 22. For now we will examine the trade deficit alone.

One gets a sense of how the Canadian trade situation has changed in the postwar years by noting that prior to the early 1980s, the size of the trade deficit was not an issue. The balance fluctuated between surplus and deficit positions, but it was typically relatively small. Since the early 1980s, when sizable trade surpluses occurred, the trade balance has suffered a continual decline. If we look closely at today's trade deficit, we find that the increase in the aggregate trade deficit is focused primarily on a handful of industries. In the first half of the 1980s, imports of automobile products rose from $13 billion to $31 billion. Machinery imports increased from $19 billion to $28 billion. Imports likewise rose in manufactured consumer goods, like appliances, clothing and textiles, and in industrial goods. Furthermore, some traditional export sectors have stagnated. Agricultural and fish product exports have hardly grown at all, while the exports of other resource-based industries such as forest and energy products have increased at a low rate. As imported products gained market share in Canadian industries and as resource industries found export sales more difficult, regions in Canada where such goods as automobiles and textiles were produced began to suffer unemployment or slower growth. Foreign competition took much of the blame for hard times. While the country as a whole may have benefited from the increase in trade, some regions of the country have been seriously hurt. Similar problems have been faced in the United States, our major trading partner.

PROTECTIONISM, 1990s STYLE

Canada has always used trade protection as a policy device. In recent years, in the face of stiff competition and alleged unfair trade practices from Japan and Europe, the United States has turned increasingly to trade protection as well. Though not necessarily the main target of U.S. protection, Canadian exports to the United States have often been affected by measures intended for other countries. Naturally, this has been of considerable concern to Canada and has contributed to public support for the concept of free trade with the United States, a policy stance that represents a significant break with history. Indeed, the Progressive Conservative party under Brian Mulroney fought and won the 1988 election campaign largely on the issue of free trade after having signed the Canada-U.S. Free Trade Agreement in 1988.

Traditionally, protection was by tariffs. But with the success of the General Agreement on Tariffs and Trade (GATT), tariffs have been reduced gradually since the destructive trade wars of the 1930s. Trade protection has turned to nontariff barriers (NTBs). These take various forms. Two types commonly used in North America are **anti-dumping duties** (preferred by Canada) and **countervailing duties** (preferred by the United States).

Anti-dumping duties arise, as their name indicates, as a penalty for the practice of **dumping,** which refers to a producer selling a product at a lower price in foreign markets than at home and where the price difference is not justified by cost differences. Countries in which products are dumped argue that this represents an unfair trade practice designed to put domestic producers out of business so as to increase the dumping firm's share of the market. According to the rules of GATT, countries may levy anti-dumping duties against foreign firms found to be dumping. It is tempting for a country to use anti-dumping duties as a means of protecting domestic producers against low-cost imports, especially if tariffs are not an option. (Tariffs may be ruled out because of international agreements, or because they cannot be easily applied selectively to particular firms.) It is not a simple matter of distinguishing dumping as a restrictive practice from the acceptable practice of selling at low prices because of excess supply or because of cost conditions. The fact that the decision is in the hands of the government of the importing country makes it tempting to take the side of the domestic firms against the importers. In Canada, the Canadian International Trade Tribunal (CITT), a federal government agency, is responsible for conducting inquiries into whether Canadian producers are injured by imports that are dumped, sold at low cost, or subsidized by the exporting country.

Not surprisingly, the application of anti-dumping duties has varied over the years. A recent report of the CITT found that anti-dumping actions increased rapidly in 1983 after the 1981–1982 recession, then fell off rapidly after 1987, only to increase again in the early 1990s.[3] As well, a large number of existing actions were revoked in the late 1980s. The number of total actions in place peaked at 156 in 1985. On average, about 0.9 percent of domestic manufacturing shipments were covered by anti-dumping actions, with the coverage reaching 1.1 percent in 1983, falling to 0.5 percent in 1990, and rising to 0.9 percent in 1991. One set of industries—footwear, leather, textile, and clothing products—accounted for over 60 percent of the value of goods involved in anti-dumping actions in recent years. In previous years, primary metals tended to be the most affected. Interestingly, coverage of domestic manufacturing shipments arising from anti-dumping actions with the United States averaged only 0.2 percent over the 1980s, though this increased considerably in 1991 as a result of two particular cases, one involving dumping of beer into the British Columbia market and the other involving carpeting. Overall, these findings confirm that anti-dumping duties tend to be used more during recessions and tend to be directed to low-cost countries rather than to the United States, which is by far our largest trading partner.

Another form of NTB is the **countervailing duty,** which is a duty imposed on imports found to have been subsidized in the exporting country. This is the instrument most commonly used by the United States. Its use is triggered when a producer complains about unfair competition resulting from foreign subsidies. Given the extent to which government policies, including general regional subsidies and investment tax credits, impinge upon various industries, the use of countervailing duties is potentially open-ended. For example, the U.S. government found the Canadian softwood lumber industry to have been subsidized by virtue of the fact that the stumpage fees charged by the British Columbia government for the right to cut trees were too low. In other words, low tax rates were deemed to be equivalent to a subsidy.

---

[3] Canadian International Trade Tribunal, *Annual Report*, 1991–1992.

CLOSE-UP: THE CANADA-U.S. FREE TRADE AGREEMENT

To gain easier access to the U.S. market of 250 million persons, the Canadian government negotiated the Free Trade Agreement (FTA) with the U.S. government in 1988. Taking effect on January 1, 1989, it was innovative in several respects. First, it created the largest free-trading bloc in the world. Second, the FTA covered agricultural trade, a sector that had eluded international trade negotiators, such as those of the GATT, in the past. Third, the FTA was also the first trade agreement to address trade in services, business travel, and investment. Finally, the agreement comprised rules and mechanisms for settling disputes between the trading partners.

According to the FTA, virtually all tariff barriers and about one-quarter of the nontariff barriers (such as quotas and administrative procedures) are to be eliminated over a ten-year period. There are two sorts of exceptions to this. The first is that the FTA has adopted the provisions of GATT listing reasons for which import or export control measures can be used to protect national interests. The second sort involves exceptions negotiated specifically for the FTA. Examples of this kind include controls on the export of logs and unprocessed fish, existing practices for the distribution of beer, and cultural policies, such as the Canadian content regulations imposed by the CRTC that stipulate the proportion of television programming and music played on the radio that must be Canadian.

Two important provisions exist to ensure that the elimination of import and export controls between the two countries will actually lead to the freeing of trade. First, so-called "rules of origin" apply, limiting the traded goods that are eligible for free-trade treatment. The rules of origin state that 50 percent of the manufacturing cost of any item must be incurred in either or both of the two countries. Without this provision, other countries could take advantage of the Canada-U.S. free-trade zone. Suppose, for example, that Japanese bicycles are duty-free in Canada but not in the United States. The rules of origin prevent Japan from first moving bicycles duty-free into Canada and from there into the United States to avoid the U.S. tariff.

Second, trade between the two countries is also subject to the principle of "national treatment." This means that each country's domestic policies must apply without discrimination to the producers of the other country. That is, Canada cannot apply taxes or regulations that discourage the consumption of U.S. goods if these do not also apply to domestically produced goods.

Areas covered by the agreement include:

Goods Trade Special attention was devoted to three important sectors—automotive products, agriculture, and energy. Under the FTA, for duty-free trade in cars, trucks, buses, and parts, 50 percent of direct and indirect costs must be incurred in Canada or the United States or both countries. This effectively raises the content requirement to 70 percent of direct costs from 50 percent under the Auto Pact (whose provisions otherwise remain in effect).

The FTA has eliminated export subsidies on agricultural products and is phasing out tariffs over a ten-year period. It allows for the maintenance of import restrictions on fresh fruits, vegetables and grains if the transition to free trade is devastating to these industries.

Virtually all bilateral barriers to trade in energy are eliminated, including import quantity restrictions. The control and licensing of exports is maintained. So is the ability to cut back oil exports in times of tight supply, provided that such restrictions do not reduce the proportion of energy output that is exported to the other party.

Services The FTA is innovative in freeing trade in several service sectors (such as architecture, engineering, tourism, and computing). However, for public policy purposes some services are to be exempt from free trade, including transportation and telecommunications services, doctors, dentists, lawyers, child-care services, and government-provided services (in health, education, social services). National treatment applies to trade in services as well as in goods, though rules of origin do not.

An important component of trade in services involves financial services. Prior to the FTA, the United States Glass-Steagall Act prohibited joint banking and securities firms. Now Canadian banks are allowed to do business in securities in the United States. Similarly, in Canada, some restrictions applying to foreigners regarding ownership of federally regulated financial institutions are removed for U.S. investors.

Investment National treatment is also extended to business investment. This will lead to easier establishment of new firms and acquisition of existing firms in the other country. The energy sector is excluded from this agreement, however, so that the Canadian oil, gas, and uranium industries will remain sovereign. Foreign ownership is also restricted in the telecommunications and transportation sectors, and Crown corporations are in general not up for sale internationally.

Government Procurement For reasons of regional development, government goods and services contracts are often made available only to local or national firms. Under the GATT, federal government goods contracts worth over U.S. $171,000 must be tendered internationally. The FTA lowers this cost threshold for competition between the United States and Canadian suppliers to U.S. $25,000 for most government departments, and sets up a reviewing authority.

Dispute Settlement The FTA defines problem-solving procedures in advance so that the implementation and operation of free trade will be smoother and more assured. A Canada-U.S. Trade Commission, when necessary, will set up panels to resolve different issues, consisting of equal numbers of Canadian and U.S. representatives. A dispute settlement mechanism is also created specifically for cases of anti-dumping and countervailing duties. The FTA does not preclude the use of countervailing and anti-dumping duties as ways of impeding imports into either country. But the two countries have agreed to open negotiations on obtaining a convention on acceptable subsidies so as to reduce the need for such nontariff barriers to trade.

Not surprisingly, given such a wide-ranging agreement, there are those who argue that the FTA will cause harm to Canada. Some focus on the dislocation that the opening of trade will have on domestic manufacturing industries. For example, some firms that produced on a relatively small scale largely for the Canadian market, such as clothing and beer firms, may no longer be able to compete against larger American firms. Others argue that sovereignty over domestic programs will be threatened, especially over social programs and programs to protect cultural industries.

Supporters counter by saying that the benefits from gaining access to the large American market more than outweigh the costs. They argue that Canadian manufacturing firms are too small and inefficient precisely because they have been induced by the protective policies of the past to concentrate on the small domestic market. They also point out that present and future social programs will not be threatened as long as these programs are not designed primarily to protect domestic producers. And they maintain that cultural programs are being provided with all the protection they need.

There are various other ways in which protection can be imposed other than by tariffs, including by subsidies, quotas, voluntary export restraints negotiated with foreign governments, and by straightforward product standard regulation that implicitly discriminates against imports.

The combination of the growth in world trade and the increasing use of restrictive trade policies has led to a recent emphasis on negotiating freer trade internationally. On the one hand, there have been various **bilateral agreements,** such as the 1988 Canada-U.S. Free Trade Agreement, as well as attempts at **multilateral agreements,** such as that among the members of the European Community in 1992 and the so-called Uruguay Round of negotiations under GATT.

While charges of unfair competition and trade practices in the 1980s struck a sympathetic chord with the public, most economists believed that clever or unscrupulous foreign traders were not at the root of North America's trade problems. One can always point to examples of foreign trade practices that seem unfair. But the decline in the trade balances of the 1980s developed rapidly. It is simply not plausible that this happened just because tricky foreigners rapidly increased the extent to which they engaged in unfair practices in those years. Instead, most economists argued that the trade deficit and the resulting economic dislocations were a symptom of a deeper illness in the North American economy. Protectionism was not the appropriate cure; in fact, it was not a cure at all. It might not create jobs, and it would interfere with the ability of the economy to use its comparative advantage, thus making everyone worse off.

An increase in the trade deficit can come about for two reasons. First, with given exports and a given import function, an increase in national income—caused, for example, by an increase in government expenditures or investment—will result in a higher trade deficit. This is simply because as income increases, imports increase, while exports remain unchanged. Second, there could be an upward *shift* in the import function, so that at any given level of income the country imports more. In either case, *net* exports at any given level of income will be lower. Such shifts do put a major drag on the economy, as Figure 14.10 shows. In panel A, an income-expenditure analysis diagram, the initial equilibrium lies at the intersection of the aggregate expenditures schedule with the 45-degree line. If net exports decline to $X_2 - M_2$, national income will decline to Y_2, and employment will also go down.

Figure 14.10 NET EXPORTS AND NATIONAL OUTPUT

In panel A, a reduction in net exports shifts the $C + I + G + (X - M)$ schedule down and lowers national output from Y_1 to Y_2. Panel B shows that trade restrictions may not be effective. While they reduce imports, if foreigners retaliate, exports are also reduced. The net effect may be a reduction in net exports and a further decrease in output from Y_2 to Y_3.

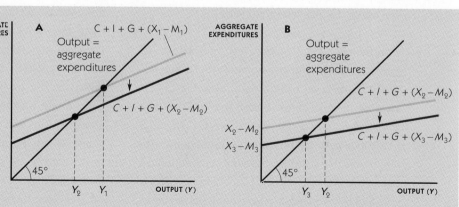

There are several reasons that protectionism may not create jobs. One likely result of protectionism is that foreigners will retaliate against it. If this happens, then while protectionism may reduce Canadian imports, it will also reduce Canadian exports; net exports could therefore be even further reduced, and national output further decreased. Thus, in panel B, the reduction of net exports from $X_2 - M_2$ to $X_3 - M_3$ lowers equilibrium from Y_2 to Y_3, with a corresponding further reduction in employment. As noted earlier, policies that try to increase national income by reducing imports are referred to as beggar-thy-neighbour policies, because one country's economy is helped at the expense of others'.

THE DETERMINANTS OF NET EXPORTS

To understand the marked changes in net exports that have occurred, we need to study more closely the determinants of net exports. Exports are determined by the prices of goods produced by other countries relative to the prices of Canadian goods, as well as the level of incomes abroad and foreigners' tastes for Canadian goods. Imports are also determined by relative prices, as well as the level of income in Canada and Canadians' tastes for foreign goods. The first section below takes up changes in tastes; the second, changes in relative incomes; and the third, changes in relative prices.

CHANGES IN TASTES

In the years following World War II, "Made in America" became a label coveted around the world, as American songs, American dress, and a whole range of American products made great inroads. Many of these products were also made in Canada, often by firms that were subsidiaries of American firms. As a result, at each level of income, net exports increased. This is illustrated in Figure 14.11, which gives the level of net exports at each level of income, by the upward shift from $X_1 - M$ to $X_2 - M$. We refer to this as the **net export function.** An increase in exports leads to an upward shift in the aggregate expenditures schedule, as seen in Figure 14.12—the familiar income-expenditure analysis diagram—increasing national income.

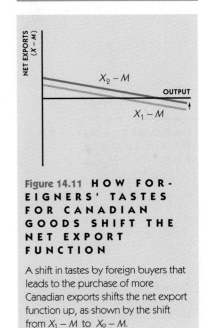

Figure 14.11 HOW FOREIGNERS' TASTES FOR CANADIAN GOODS SHIFT THE NET EXPORT FUNCTION

A shift in tastes by foreign buyers that leads to the purchase of more Canadian exports shifts the net export function up, as shown by the shift from $X_1 - M$ to $X_2 - M$.

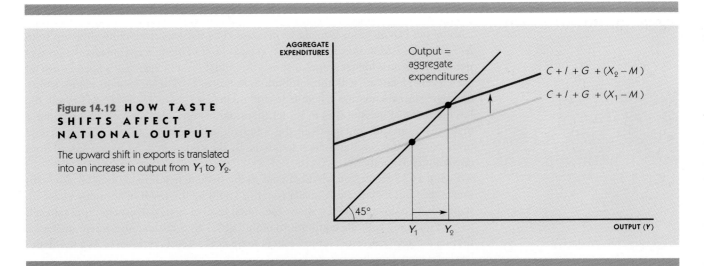

Figure 14.12 HOW TASTE SHIFTS AFFECT NATIONAL OUTPUT

The upward shift in exports is translated into an increase in output from Y_1 to Y_2.

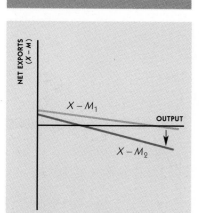

Figure 14.13 HOW TASTES FOR IMPORTS SHIFT THE NET EXPORT FUNCTION

A shift in tastes by Canadian consumers in favour of buying more imports increases the level of imports at each level of income as well as the marginal propensity to import. As a result, the net export function shifts down, from $X - M_1$ to $X - M_2$. Moreover, the larger marginal propensity to import makes the net import function steeper.

Reebok athletic shoes, Christian Dior designer clothes, Mercedes-Benz cars: such high-priced imported goods have long had a certain cachet with Canadian consumers. They have been a symbol of luxury. But in the 1970s and 1980s, middle-class Canadians began buying these brand-name imported goods on a massive scale. Some of the changed demand could be traced to changed economic circumstances: the high price of oil led Canadians to desire the small cars that Japan had learned to produce more efficiently than General Motors Canada or Ford Canada. But some of the changed demand was simply a change in tastes.

The increased level of imports at each level of income reduced net exports at each level of income; this is shown in Figure 14.13 by the reduction from $X - M_1$ to $X - M_2$. The figure assumes not only that Canadians import more at each level of income, but that their **marginal propensity to import** has also increased. Out of each extra dollar of income Canadians have to spend, they spend more of it on imports. That is why the net export function has become steeper. This downward shift in the net export function decreases aggregate expenditures at each level of national output, and as we saw in Chapter 12, the increased marginal propensity to import reduces the multiplier. Increases in government expenditures will be less effective in stimulating the economy than they were when imports were less important.

CHANGES IN RELATIVE INCOMES

Chapter 12 showed how a rise in income in Canada would increase imports. By the same token, higher incomes in foreign countries increase *their* imports—Canadian exports. If incomes in Canada and abroad rise together, then imports increase with exports and trade remains balanced.

The United States began its recovery out of the worldwide recession of the early 1980s around 1983, somewhat earlier than was the case for Canada. The result was a dramatic increase in Canadian exports and the large Canadian trade surplus of the mid-1980s. The subsequent recovery of the European economy contributed to the continuing surplus that lasted for most of the 1980s. But when the United States ceased its rapid growth at the end of the 1980s while the Canadian economy continued to grow, the Canadian demand for imports outpaced the sale of exports, helping to force the trade balance into a deficit position.

Figure 14.14 focuses on what happens to Canadian income if income abroad rises, causing net exports from Canada to increase. The net export function shifts up from $X_1 - M$ to $X_2 - M$ as shown in Panel A: at each level of income in Canada, the level of net exports is now higher. Panel B shows the initial level of aggregate expenditures (at each level of income), with the equilibrium output at Y_1. The increase in exports causes the aggregate expenditures schedule to shift up to $C + I + G + (X_2 - M)$. As a result, the level of national income rises to Y_2, for the usual reasons. One message of the figure is that expansions are contagious in the international economy; an increase in income from one country gets transmitted to others. By the same token, recessions spread from one country to another.

Figure 14.15 focuses on what happens to the trade deficit if incomes abroad remain unchanged but incomes in Canada rise; this could be the result of an increase, for instance, in investment. Panel A shows the initial level of aggregate expenditures (at each level of income), with the equilibrium output at Y_1. Now assume investment increases, shifting the aggregate expenditures schedule up to $C + I_2 + G + (X - M)$. As a result, the level of national income rises to Y_2.

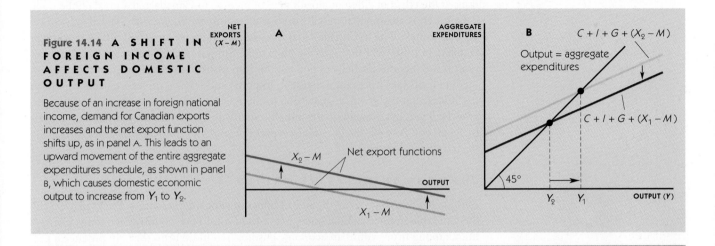

Figure 14.14 A SHIFT IN FOREIGN INCOME AFFECTS DOMESTIC OUTPUT

Because of an increase in foreign national income, demand for Canadian exports increases and the net export function shifts up, as in panel A. This leads to an upward movement of the entire aggregate expenditures schedule, as shown in panel B, which causes domestic economic output to increase from Y_1 to Y_2.

The effect this has on the trade deficit is shown in panel B, which depicts the net export function. (Remember, while exports are assumed not to depend on income, imports are, and that is why net exports decrease as income rises.) In the initial situation, with income (output) equal to Y_1, exports balance imports: net exports are zero. The higher level of income then produces an increase in imports. Incomes abroad remain unchanged, however, so exports remain unchanged.[4] Thus, the higher income produces a trade deficit at Y_2.

[4] Of course, increased Canadian imports mean increased exports for Europe; if not offset by other factors, these increased European exports will raise incomes in Europe. Europe will then import more. Some of those imports will be from Canada. So increased Canadian imports may eventually lead to some increase in Canadian exports.

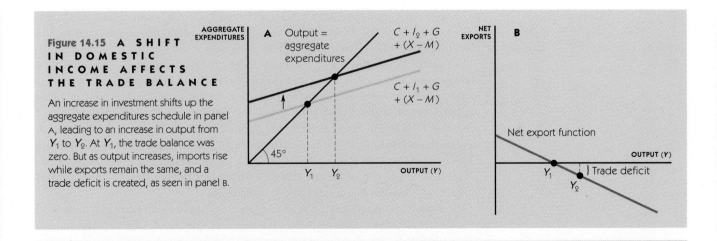

Figure 14.15 A SHIFT IN DOMESTIC INCOME AFFECTS THE TRADE BALANCE

An increase in investment shifts up the aggregate expenditures schedule in panel A, leading to an increase in output from Y_1 to Y_2. At Y_1, the trade balance was zero. But as output increases, imports rise while exports remain the same, and a trade deficit is created, as seen in panel B.

The concept of income elasticity of demand can be used to make very rough calculations of the effect of different growth rates of income in Canada and abroad on the trade deficit. Let us assume that initially exports equal imports in Canada. Now if a major recession comes along in Canada's major trading partners, incomes will still be growing in Canada, but they will stop growing elsewhere. Suppose Canada grows at 5 percent per year. If the income elasticity of demand for imports is 1 (that is, a 1 percent increase in income leads to a 1 percent increase in imports) and relative prices are fixed, exports to the rest of the world will stagnate due to the recession, while imports will continue to grow by 5 percent. Since imports initially equalled exports, now imports exceed exports by 5 percent. As well, the decline in export demand will influence incomes in Canada negatively for that year.

CHANGES IN RELATIVE PRICES

Earlier chapters pointed out the role of prices in allocating resources. Prices play exactly the same role in international trade that they do within one country's economy. Competition among firms within an economy ensures that those firms that can produce a particular good most cheaply will do so. So too within the international setting: competition among international firms ensures that those firms that can produce a particular good most cheaply will do so. If all the low-cost companies in an industry happen to be based in a single country, then that country will dominate the market. As shown in Chapter 3, relative prices reflect comparative advantages, and comparative advantage is the basis of international trade. As the world economy changes, we would expect that comparative advantages change, and accordingly that the relative prices at which different countries can supply different goods change.

If foreign goods become relatively less expensive, then Canadians will import more of them at each level of income just as they did when changing tastes caused Canadians to prefer foreign goods; and the marginal propensity to import will increase as well. The import function, giving the level of imports at each level of income, will shift up, as in Figure 14.16A, and the marginal propensity to import will increase. At the same time, Canadian firms will find it increasingly difficult to sell their goods abroad. As a result, exports will be reduced. Net exports will thus decline from $X_1 - M_1$ to $X_2 - M_2$, as shown in panel B. This in turn means that the aggregate expenditures schedule will drop. Panel C traces out the effect of the shift in the net export function on the level of aggregate expenditures—it shifts down—and hence on the level of equilibrium output, which falls from Y_1 to Y_2. And the flatter slope of the aggregate expenditures schedule means that the multiplier has been reduced as well.

The price of Canadian goods relative to those produced abroad depends on the **exchange rate.** The exchange rate measures the cost of one currency in terms of another, in this case the rate at which Canadian dollars can be exchanged for U.S. dollars, Japanese yen, German marks, British pounds, and other currencies. If a bottle of good French wine costs 80 francs in Paris and if the exchange rate is 4 francs to the dollar, a Canadian can buy the bottle for $20. But if the exchange rate should change, as it did in the early 1980s, so that there are 8 francs to the dollar, a Canadian can buy that same bottle for $10. If Japanese yen become more expensive in terms of dollars, then Japanese goods simultaneously become more expensive to Canadians.

The expression "There are two sides to every coin" applies with particular force to international exchange. A change in the exchange rate—say, from 4 francs to the dollar to 8 francs to the dollar—that makes foreign goods look less expensive to Canadians makes Canadian goods look more expensive to foreigners. This kind of change is called a

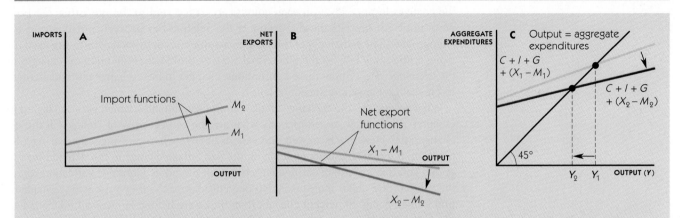

Figure 14.16 CHANGES IN RELATIVE PRICES AFFECT AGGREGATE DEMAND

If foreign goods become less expensive relative to Canadian products, then the import function shifts up, as shown in panel A. Since foreign goods are also now relatively less expensive in their home countries, it becomes more difficult to export, and the net export function shifts down, as in panel B. These combined changes result in a downward shift in the aggregate expenditures schedule and a resulting decrease in the equilibrium level of output, depicted in panel C.

depreciation in the value of the franc (the franc is worth less in terms of dollars) or an **appreciation** in the value of the dollar (the dollar is worth more in terms of francs). When the franc depreciates against the dollar, we say the dollar is stronger and the franc is weaker; conversely, when the franc appreciates against the dollar, we say the dollar is weaker and the franc is stronger.

Changes in exchange rates, like changes in any other relative price, are not necessarily good or bad. It is not necessarily "good" that the dollar becomes stronger or bad that it becomes weaker, though some countries view the strength of their currency as a source of national pride. Like any change in relative prices, some people benefit and some people lose. A strong dollar is good for Canadian consumers, who find they can buy French goods more cheaply, and good for French exporters, who find they can sell their goods more easily. It is bad for Canadian exporters, who find their markets for foreign goods disappearing, and bad for French consumers, who find they can no longer afford Canadian goods. Thus, when the dollar appreciates, Canadian imports increase and exports decrease; when the dollar depreciates, Canadian imports decrease and exports increase.

Relative prices also depend on relative rates of inflation. If Britain has 10 percent inflation while Canada has 5 percent, then even if exchange rates stay the same, last year's British goods will cost 5 percent more in Canada this year. Likewise, the international demand for Canadian goods declines when (at a given exchange rate) inflation in Canada outpaces that in other countries.

Changes in the prices of Canadian goods relative to those produced abroad depend, then, on three factors: changes in the exchange rate; changes in the prices of Canadian goods (in terms of dollars), that is, the rate of inflation in Canada; and changes in the prices of goods produced in foreign countries (in terms of their own currencies), that is, the rate of inflation in each of the producing countries. The exchange rates adjusted for the changes in price levels in each country are called **real exchange rates.** We postpone until Chapter 19 the discussion of the relationship between inflation and exchange rates. The remainder of this chapter assumes prices in each country are fixed (or rising at the same rate, so the differential is zero), and focuses attention on changes in the exchange rate. (Under these assumptions, changes in the exchange rate and changes in the real exchange rate are equivalent.)

What determines the exchange rate is a complicated matter, which we also take up in Chapter 19. For now, we simply ask, what are the *consequences* of changes in the exchange rate? How much imports and exports change when exchange rates change depends on the price elasticity of demand, the percentage change in the demand for imported goods as a result of a 1 percent change in the price. Consider a situation where the value of the dollar increases by 40 percent relative to other currencies: Canadians find foreign goods 40 percent cheaper than they were before; foreigners find Canadian goods 40 percent more expensive than they were before. Assume that the price elasticity of exports is 1.5 and the price elasticity of imports is similarly 1.5; that is, a 1 percent increase in the price results in a 1.5 percent decrease in the quantity demanded. To make the calculations easy, assume that initially there was $200 billion in exports and $200 billion in imports.

Because of the shift in exchange rates, the quantity of Canadian exports demanded by foreigners will decline by 60 percent to $80 billion. At the same time, the *quantity* of imports (at any given level of income in Canada) will increase by 60 percent, but because the dollar is worth 40 percent more, Canadians will only have to spend 20 percent more (in terms of Canadian dollars) to increase their demand by 60 percent.[5] Hence, in terms of dollars, imports will rise to $240 billion. Thanks to the change in exchange rates, the trade deficit will grow from zero to $160 billion. This is a downward shift in the net export function — it is the change in net exports at a particular level of income. The shift in the net export function will, if not offset, give rise to a change in equilibrium output.

SOURCES OF DOWNWARD SHIFTS IN THE NET EXPORT FUNCTION

1. A change in tastes for imported goods

2. An increase in income in Canada relative to incomes abroad

3. An increase in the prices of Canadian goods relative to those of foreigners, caused by either an appreciation of the dollar or a higher rate of inflation in Canada than abroad.

[5] Note that if Canadians' demand for foreign goods is relatively inelastic — say the price elasticity is .2 — then the appreciation of the dollar will actually reduce what Canadians spend abroad. The 40 per-

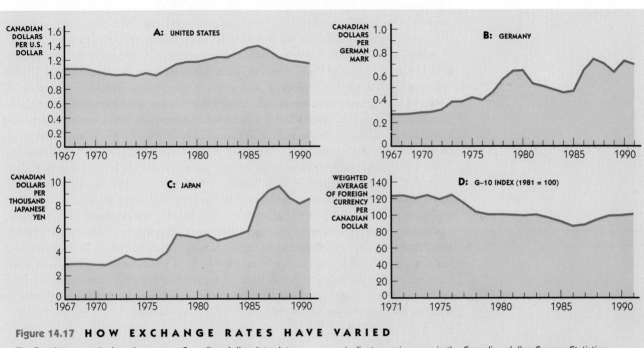

Figure 14.17 **HOW EXCHANGE RATES HAVE VARIED**

The first three panels show how many Canadian dollars it took to buy one U.S. dollar, one German mark, and one thousand Japanese yen. Panel D shows how many units of a mix of currencies of ten trade partners are worth one Canadian dollar; a rise in the index indicates an increase in the Canadian dollar. *Source:* Statistics Canada, *Canadian Economics Observer*, Catalogue No. 11-210, 1991–1992.

Changes in the Exchange Rate in the 1980s   Some of the changes in the Canadian trade balance in the postwar period can be traced to the enormous change in the exchange rates during that period. Figure 14.17 illustrates these changes over the past two decades, showing how much the U.S. dollar, the Japanese yen, and the German mark have been worth in terms of the Canadian dollar. (By comparing the ratios with each other, you can also tell how much one of those currencies is worth in terms of any other one.) Sometimes you may see a reference to one currency, perhaps the dollar, becoming "stronger" or "weaker" with no particular reference to another currency. In that case, the analyst is discussing the dollar in terms of some average of the currencies of Canadian trading partners. These averages are generally weighted to match the trading rela-

cent decline in price will give rise to an 8 percent increase in Canadian imports; so expenditures, measured in dollars, will decline by approximately 32 percent. If foreigners' demand for Canadian goods is inelastic, with a price elasticity of .2, then exports will decline by a relatively small amount—the 40 percent price increase facing foreigners will lead to an 8 percent decrease in Canadian exports. Thus, in this case, imports (measured in dollars) will decrease *more* than exports. The appreciation of the dollar will shift the net export function up. This, however, is not the typical case; normally we expect a dollar appreciation to shift the net export function down, a depreciation to shift it up.

tionships, so that the value of currencies of major trading partners like the United States and Japan receive a greater weight than the currencies of countries that have a smaller amount of trade with Canada. Panel D shows one such weighted average exchange rate, that between the Canadian dollar and an index of ten major foreign currencies.

When the value of the Canadian dollar fell relative to the U.S. dollar by some 30 percent between 1978 and 1985, it was as if Canadian goods were on sale in the United States, marked down by 30 percent, and as if a 30 percent tax had been placed on all American goods imported into Canada. With a sale this big, it is little wonder that Canadian imports from the United States fell, and that Americans found it attractive to buy Canadian products. At the same time as Canada's trade balance was running large surpluses, the U.S. trade deficit was increasing. At the same time, however, the Canadian dollar was rising in value relative to most other major currencies, as indicated by the fall in the G-10 index in Figure 14.17D. While our trade with the United States improved, that with the rest of the world deteriorated. By the latter half of the decade, our currency was rising relative to the U.S. dollar, and our trade balance was beginning to deteriorate.

Canada's trade problems of the late 1980s were primarily macroeconomic, in the sense that they affected all sectors of the economy. Canadian industries that were not keeping up with the foreign competition (that is, firms whose costs of production were, for instance, not declining as fast as those in Japan) had a deeper problem: even if the exchange rates had remained stable, their prices would have risen relative to those of Japanese firms, and their sales would have declined accordingly.

MACROECONOMIC POLICY AND INTERNATIONAL TRADE

Downward shifts in the net export function, whether caused by changes in tastes, shifts in relative income, or shifts in relative prices, can have large effects on output through the multiplier process. Figure 14.18 shows how the government might react to an appre-

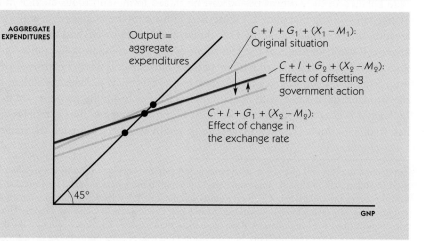

Figure 14.18
MACROECONOMIC POLICY TO OFFSET SHIFTS IN FOREIGN EXCHANGE

Macroeconomic policy can offset changes in exchange rates. If the dollar appreciates, for example, the aggregate expenditures schedule will shift down as imports increase and exports fall. But government policies to stimulate the economy, whether by encouraging consumption or investment or spending more directly, can shift the aggregate expenditures schedule back up again.

ciation of the dollar that has reduced the aggregate demand for Canadian products: the government can stimulate the economy by increasing its own spending, thus at least partially offsetting the original decline in aggregate expenditures.

But although the effect on the aggregate expenditures schedule—and thus on aggregate demand and equilibrium output—can be offset, the shift in the net export curve still affects the composition of output. Firms that sell goods to the government may be doing all right, but firms that are in the business of exporting are still in trouble, as are firms that are in the business of producing goods that directly compete with those produced by foreigners, such as Canadian automakers. Unemployment in industries facing import competition will be high. The fact that somewhere else in the economy someone is doing well provides little solace, particularly to those who find it difficult to move from one job to another. For younger workers and those just entering the labour market, on the other hand, the fact that the overall economy is strong (because the government has taken actions to counteract the effects of the appreciation of the dollar) makes a big difference. They are in a good position to seek out the new jobs being created.

There is another consequence of the government's attempt to restore the economy's output: the trade deficit will increase. Remember, what initiated the problem was a shift in the net export function, so that at each level of income net exports are lower. If the government succeeds in restoring output to the level where it was before the downward shift in the net export function took place, the trade deficit will have increased by the full amount of the downward shift in the net export function (assuming the exchange rate remains unchanged).

LOOKING AHEAD: EXCHANGE RATES AND GOVERNMENT POLICIES

Exchange rates adjust in response to government policies, and how they respond may either decrease or increase the effectiveness of the government policy.

Consider, for instance, the problem posed earlier in this chapter: the effectiveness of protectionism in creating Canadian jobs. If Canada imports less from, say, Japan, as a result of tariffs or other trade barriers, Canadians will demand fewer Japanese goods and therefore fewer yen, since they will need fewer yen to purchase Japanese goods. With less demand for yen, it would not be surprising to see the yen depreciate—become less valuable relative to the dollar. But we have already analyzed the effects of such a change in the exchange rate: an appreciation of the dollar (this corresponds to the depreciation of the yen) shifts the net export function down. Thus, changes in the exchange rate may offset the effect of protectionism. Indeed, these changes may be so powerful that they fully offset the effects of protectionism: imports are not actually reduced in total, and jobs are not created.

Changes in the exchange rate may also offset government attempts to stimulate the economy through increasing government expenditures. In the discussion of government expenditures in the first part of this chapter, we learned that government policies may be less effective in stimulating the economy than was suggested by the basic model of Chapter 12; increased government expenditures may crowd out private investment, and the net effect on the economy may be quite small.

In an open economy, changes in the exchange rate can either dampen or amplify the effectiveness of government attempts to stimulate the economy, depending on whether they lead to an appreciation or depreciation of the dollar. If increased government expenditures lead to an appreciation, then the net export function will shift down, offsetting the stimulating effect of the increased government expenditures. If increased government expenditures lead to a depreciation, just the opposite happens: the upward shift in the net export function reinforces the effectiveness of government policy. Chapter 19 will discuss the circumstances in which increased government expenditures may lead to an appreciation or depreciation of the dollar.

PRINCIPLES OF MACROECONOMIC POLICY IN OPEN ECONOMIES

1. In determining macroeconomic policy in an open economy, the government must pay careful attention to what is happening to the exchange rate, for any changes will not only determine how effective government policy will be, they will also determine how different policies affect different individuals within the economy.

2. In an interconnected world economy, unemployment and recessions are like contagious diseases. Downturns in one economy can spread to others.

3. Upward shifts in the net export function can stimulate the economy, just as downward shifts in the net export function can drag it down.

4. Changes in the exchange rate, by affecting imports, may affect not only the *level* of national income but also the magnitude of the multiplier. This is because changes in the exchange rate affect the fraction of each additional dollar that is spent abroad.

5. Protectionism is not a good solution to macroeconomic problems, even when the unemployment is due to a shift in the net export function. Beggar-thy-neighbour policies may not succeed in restoring net exports, since the reduction in imports is met by retaliation from abroad, which reduces exports; and changes in exchange rates may simply offset any benefits from the protectionist policies. Most important, protectionism is costly because it interferes with countries' ability to use their comparative advantage.

REVIEW AND PRACTICE

SUMMARY

1. If the government simultaneously increases (or decreases) taxes and expenditures by the same amount so that the budget is balanced, aggregate expenditures in the economy still increase.

2. The magnitude of the fiscal stimulus provided by the government is sometimes measured by the full-employment deficit, the deficit that would have arisen if the economy were at full employment. When the economy is below full employment, the full-employment deficit is smaller than the actual deficit.

3. The government debt is the accumulation of annual budget deficits. The real debt takes into account the effects of inflation. The real deficit is the change in the real debt. In some years, while there has been a nominal deficit, real debt has been reduced.

4. If government and private investors are competing for the same fixed pool of capital, then government borrowing to finance the deficit may crowd out private investment. Crowding out is most likely when the economy is near the full-employment level of output, and least likely when the economy has excess capacity.

5. Some government programs act as automatic stabilizers. They increase expenditures and reduce taxes as the economy goes into a recession, and cut expenditures and raise taxes as the economy expands, thus reducing the value of the multiplier and the instability of the economy.

6. Provincial and local governments also tend to increase their spending in booms and reduce it during recessions, thus contributing to the fluctuations of the economy.

7. Foreign trade has always been important to the Canadian economy. About one-quarter of GDP is exported, and about one-quarter of our income is spent on imports. In recent years, the trade balance has deteriorated rapidly as imports have grown more rapidly than exports.

8. Shifts in the net export function, which gives the level of net exports at each level of income, give rise to shifts in the aggregate expenditures schedule and hence to variability in the equilibrium level of output. Possible reasons for these shifts include changes in consumer preferences for imported goods in Canada and abroad, changes in relative incomes in Canada and abroad, and changes in relative prices in Canada and abroad.

9. Such macroeconomic policies as increased government expenditures can offset the effect of changes in the net export function. However, there is no assurance that the government stimulus for the economy will help those who were hurt by declining exports and increased imports.

KEY TERMS

deficit spending
full-employment
  deficit
crowding out
automatic stabilizers
dumping
anti-dumping duties

countervailing
  duties
bilateral agreements
multilateral agree-
  ments
net export function

marginal propensity
  to import
exchange rate
depreciation
appreciation
real exchange rates

REVIEW QUESTIONS

1. Is it possible for the government to stimulate the economy without changing the size of its budget deficit? Explain.

2. How is a full-employment deficit calculated? Will it be higher or lower than the actual deficit? Why?

3. What is the difference between the deficit and the debt?

4. If complete crowding out occurs, how much will running a larger budget deficit stimulate the economy? Explain. What are the factors that make crowding out more likely? less likely?

5. Name at least two automatic stabilizers, and describe how they work.

6. How might the federal government contribute to economic instability? How might provincial and local governments contribute to economic instability?

7. What are the major determinants of shifts in the net export function? Explain how each one can work in each direction.

8. How can recessions be contagious in the world economy?

9. If exchange rates do not change, why is a government stimulus of the economy likely to lead to a trade deficit?

PROBLEMS

1. Suppose that while pursuing your favourite pastime in the dormitory of arguing over economic issues, someone says that the budget deficit rose from $20 billion in 1982 to $30 billion in 1992. How might you adjust these figures to get a more accurate picture of the economic impact of the deficit?

2. Imagine that Japanese products go out of fashion in Canada. How would this affect Japan's net export function and aggregate expenditures schedule? Draw two diagrams to illustrate.

3. Imagine that Canadian consumers begin to believe that imports are often of better quality than Canadian-made products. How will this affect the Canadian net export function and aggregate expenditures schedule? Draw two diagrams to illustrate.

4. Assume that exports equal imports, and both equal $150 billion. Canada's income elasticity for foreign imports is 1.5, while foreigners' income elasticity for Canadian imports is also 1.5. If foreign exchange rates do not change, what happens to Canada's imports if income in Canada increases by 10 percent? What happens to Canadian exports if foreigners' income increases by 10 percent? If both incomes increase, is there a trade deficit? If foreign incomes had increased by only 5 percent (all else remaining the same), what would the trade deficit be? If the income elasticity of demand for Canadian goods was only 1 (all else remaining the same), what would the trade deficit be?

5. Explain whether each of the following would prefer to see the dollar appreciate or depreciate:

    (a) a Canadian tourist in a foreign country;

    (b) a Canadian consumer shopping for a car;

    (c) a European consumer shopping for a car;

    (d) a Japanese consumer electronics business;

    (e) a Canadian steel mill;

    (f) a foreign tourist visiting Canada.

6. Assume initially that exports equal imports, and both equal $100 billion. Suppose that Canada exports goods (like grains) for which the price elasticity is low, say .5, and imports goods (like luxury cars) for which the price elasticity is high, say 2. Assuming that incomes in Canada and abroad do not change, what are the consequences of a 10 percent appreciation of the dollar?

7. Again, begin by assuming that exports equal imports, and both equal $100 billion. Prices in Canada increase by 10 percent, while prices abroad increase by only 5 percent. If the price elasticity of both Canadian and foreign consumers is 2 and the exchange rate does not change, how does the divergence in inflation rates affect exports, imports, and the trade deficit? How large a currency devaluation would be required to restore the trade balance?

8. If foreigners' demand for Canadian exports is inelastic and Canadians' demands for foreigners' goods is inelastic, explain how it is possible that a devaluation could actually make the trade deficit worse.

AGGREGATE DEMAND
AND SUPPLY

e have seen how income-expenditure analysis can be used to show how the equilibrium level of output is determined when there is excess capacity—that is, when the economy is operating along the horizontal portion of the aggregate supply curve. In such a situation, a shift in the aggregate expenditures schedule leads to a higher level of output rather than higher prices.

In wartime and in economic booms, the economy finds itself on the vertical portion of its aggregate supply curve. Here, what limits output is not demand but supply. An increase in aggregate demand simply pushes the economy up the aggregate supply curve. The price level rises, but output does not change much. For output to increase, the aggregate supply curve has to shift; the productive capacity of the economy must increase.

When the economy is operating in between the horizontal and vertical portions of the aggregate supply curve, shifts in the aggregate demand curve have effects on both output (employment) and the price level. In this region, goals of price stability and output (employment) may conflict: if the government can shift the aggregate demand curve up, it can increase output and employment, but only at the expense of a higher price level.

These cases can be illustrated by our familiar aggregate demand and supply diagram. Figure 15.1A shows the situation that was the focus of Chapters 12–14, where the intersection occurs along the horizontal portion of the aggregate supply curve. A rightward shift in the aggregate demand curve simply changes the level of output. In panel B, the intersection is along the vertical portion of the aggregate supply curve, and now the shift in the aggregate demand curve has no effect on output. In panel C, where the intersec-

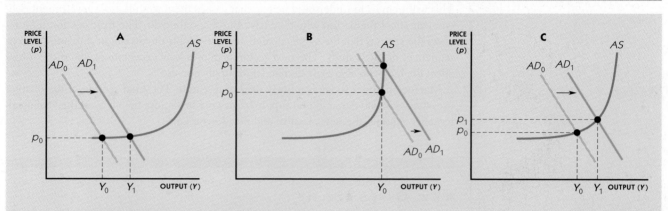

Figure 15.1 PATTERNS OF EQUILIBRIUM

Panel A shows that when the economy is operating along the horizontal portion, a rightward shift in the aggregate demand curve leads to an increase in output with little change in the price level. When the economy is operating along the vertical portion, as in panel B, a rightward shift in the aggregate demand curve leads to an increase in the price level, with little change in output. Panel C shows that in the in-between cases, a shift can lead to some increase in the price level and some increase in output.

tion is between the horizontal and vertical portions, a rightward shift in the aggregate demand curve leads to a higher level of both output and prices.

It is apparent that a fuller analysis of the economy needs to bring in both the aggregate demand and supply curves. We need to know the shape of each of these curves, and what makes them shift. What, for instance, can the government do to shift them? Is the aggregate demand curve relatively steep—do even large changes in the price level have small effects on aggregate demand? Figure 15.2 shows that with an inelastic aggregate demand, a slight leftward movement in the aggregate supply curve results in a large increase in the equilibrium price level.

Figure 15.2 IMPLICATIONS OF AN INELASTIC AGGREGATE DEMAND CURVE

If the aggregate demand curve is relatively inelastic, a leftward shift in the aggregate supply curve results in a large increase in the equilibrium price level.

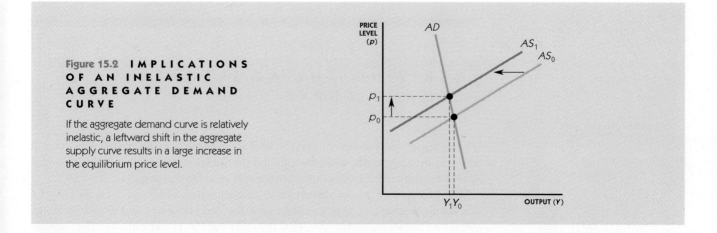

The first two sections show how the aggregate demand and supply curves are derived. This will help us to understand better what causes them to shift, how government policies can affect them, and why they have the shape they do. The third section then reviews the reasons that the aggregate demand and supply curves might shift and the consequences of those shifts. The next section explores how expectations about the future affect the long-run aggregate demand and supply curves.

Macroeconomics today is a lively field of research. The final section of the chapter uses the aggregate demand and supply framework to explore the views of the leading alternative schools: the new classical and new Keynesian.

KEY QUESTIONS

1. How do we use income-expenditure analysis to derive the aggregate demand curve? Why might the aggregate demand curve be inelastic?

2. How do we derive the aggregate supply curve, and what determines its shape?

3. What determines *shifts* in the aggregate demand and supply curves, and how can these lead to a recession?

4. What are the interactions over time between the goods market (aggregate demand and supply) and the labour market (the demand and supply for labour)?

5. What role do expectations play in determining aggregate supply? Why might the aggregate supply curve look different in the long run and in the short run? Why might it appear to be vertical in the long run?

6. What are rational expectations? Why do some economists who believe in rational expectations believe that government policy is ineffective? Why do new Keynesian economists dispute this conclusion?

DERIVING THE AGGREGATE DEMAND CURVE

The aggregate demand curve shows the level of aggregate demand at each price level. It gives us, in other words, what the equilibrium output would be at each price level if there were sufficient capacity in the economy to produce that output.

The objective of income-expenditure analysis, upon which we have focused for the last three chapters, is to calculate what the equilibrium output would be at any price level under the assumption that the economy has excess capacity. The income-expenditure analysis diagram is, accordingly, the basic tool we use in deriving the aggregate demand curve and in understanding its shape. It focuses on the demand side of the economy—what people would like to spend—ignoring all considerations of supply.

Before undertaking the task of using the income-expenditure analysis diagram to construct the aggregate demand curve, we should clarify one further set of assumptions we have been making. In the last three chapters, not only were prices fixed, so were current wages. Expectations about future prices and wages—which form the basis of decisions about consumption and investment—were also given. Likewise, interest rates, the availability of credit, and foreign exchange rates were taken as given. With all these factors fixed, income-expenditure analysis tells us how the components of aggregate expenditures vary with respect to one variable: national income.

To derive the *short-run* aggregate demand curve, which gives the level of aggregate demand at each price level, we loosen up one of these restrictions: we allow prices *today* to vary. We continue for now with the assumption that all other determinants (future prices, interest rates, credit availability, and exchange rates) are unchanged. (These assumptions too will be relaxed in the sections below, when we derive the *long-run* aggregate demand and supply curves; there, expectations of future prices and wages are also allowed to vary, along with current prices and wages.)

At each level of prices, the level of output can be calculated by the techniques set out in Chapter 12. That is, we use the income-expenditure analysis diagram to establish the point on the aggregate expenditures schedule where aggregate expenditures equal the actual level of goods produced: the intersection of the aggregate expenditures schedule and the 45-degree line. Such a calculation is shown in Figure 15.3A. As the price level

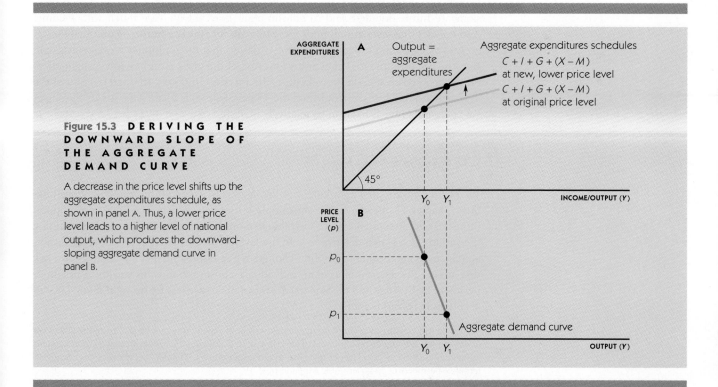

Figure 15.3 DERIVING THE DOWNWARD SLOPE OF THE AGGREGATE DEMAND CURVE

A decrease in the price level shifts up the aggregate expenditures schedule, as shown in panel A. Thus, a lower price level leads to a higher level of national output, which produces the downward-sloping aggregate demand curve in panel B.

decreases, the aggregate expenditures schedule shifts up, for reasons that will be explained shortly. Chapter 12 demonstrated that whenever the aggregate expenditures schedule shifts up, the equilibrium level of output increases. This is true here as well, when the reason for the upward shift in the aggregate expenditures schedule is a fall in the price level.

Thus, we can draw a diagram like the one shown in panel B, which plots for each price level on the vertical axis the corresponding level of output along the horizontal axis. The level of output that we identified as the equilibrium level of output in our income-expenditure analysis (drawn for any particular price level) is the one that, in the aggregate demand curve, corresponds to that particular price level. By using the income-expenditure analysis diagram at a succession of price levels to learn the corresponding outputs, an aggregate demand curve emerges, as shown in panel B. This is the same aggregate demand curve that was originally discussed in Chapter 10.

The aggregate demand curve shown in the diagram is downward sloping. The reason for this becomes clear by looking at what happens to the demand for consumption, investment, and net exports at lower levels of prices. We ask, at each level of income, what happens to consumption, investment, and net exports with a change in the price level.[1] Economists have identified a number of ways in which a change in the price level leads to a change in these components of aggregate expenditures. Here we focus on only the most widely discussed. Other explanations of how price changes affect consumption and investment are presented in the appendix to the chapter.

The net effect of, say, a lowering of the price level is only a slight upward shift in the aggregate expenditures schedule. Any upward shift in the schedule has a larger effect on the change in output because of the multiplier, first introduced in Chapter 12. But as we saw in Chapters 12–14, the multiplier may not be very large—consumption decisions are future-oriented, and so consumption may not increase much with income. And the fact that taxes and imports increase with income is a further reason that the aggregate expenditures schedule is relatively flat, so that the multiplier is relatively small. Because the multiplier is small and a lowering of the price level has only a slight effect on the aggregate expenditures schedule, the increase in output (the intersection of the aggregate expenditures schedule and the 45-degree line) is small. That is why the aggregate demand curve is likely to be relatively inelastic.

CONSUMPTION

We begin with the first component of the aggregate expenditures schedule, consumption. Chapter 12 introduced the consumption function, which shows that consumption increases with income. Chapter 13 elaborated on the consumption function, explaining the various factors that determine both the level of consumption at each level of disposable income and how consumption changes when disposable income changes. We saw that among the determinants of an individual's consumption is his wealth. A wealthier person of a given age and income need, for instance, save less for his retirement. He will accordingly consume more.

[1]We continue with our assumption that *real* government expenditures are fixed. One of the objectives of our inquiry is to understand the role of government in stabilizing the economy; that is, what happens to national income at each level of real government expenditures. Chapter 14 explores more closely alternative perspectives on government expenditures.

More generally, at any given level of income, the higher the level of wealth—not wealth valued in dollars but real wealth, what the individual's bonds and stocks will buy—the higher the level of the consumption function. As prices fall, the *real* value of people's holdings of money (and other assets whose value is fixed in terms of money) increases. People are wealthier. This effect is called the **real balance effect,** because people's financial balances have gone up in real terms, and their increased wealth leads them to consume more. Figure 15.4 shows the real balance effect in action. A fall in the price level has shifted the aggregate consumption function up. This upward shift causes the kind of upward shift in the aggregate expenditures schedule depicted in Figure 15.3A, and this leads in turn to an increase in the equilibrium output.

The real balance effect was stressed by the late British economist A. C. Pigou and continues to be emphasized by Donald Patinkin of Israel. Today most economists believe that, while present, this effect is small at best. Most estimates suggest that a 10 percent increase in overall real wealth increases consumption by around .6 percent. However, only money, government bonds, and other similar dollar-dominated assets are affected by a change in the price level. Such assets represent less than a quarter (25 percent) of overall wealth. Hence, a 10 percent decrease in the price level, which implies the same increase in the value of money and government bonds, represents less than a 2.5 percent increase in the value of total wealth, and leads to an increase in consumption of less than .15 percent (.6 × 2.5 percent). During the Great Depression, the period in this century when prices fell most rapidly, prices fell by about a fifth, inducing an increase in consumption by at most .3 percent—hardly enough to get the economy out of its troubles.

There are several other effects of changes in the price level, involving redistributions of income and wealth and changes in the patterns of consumption over individuals' lives; these are briefly discussed in the appendix to the chapter. The general consensus of most economists, however, is that these effects, while partially offsetting each other, are in total small.

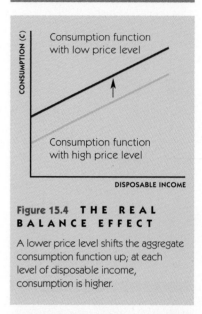

Figure 15.4 THE REAL BALANCE EFFECT

A lower price level shifts the aggregate consumption function up; at each level of disposable income, consumption is higher.

INVESTMENT

Lower prices may lead to higher investment in capital goods primarily through changes in interest rates. Whether, how, and when lower prices lead to lower interest rates is the subject of Part Three. When lower prices do lead to lower interest rates, this results in higher aggregate demand, since at a lower interest rate firms find it more attractive to invest. For simplicity, we refer to this as the **interest rate effect.**

The significance of this effect has been questioned on several grounds, which will be discussed further in Part Three. First, what is relevant for investment is the *real* interest rate (the nominal interest rate minus the rate of inflation), not the nominal interest rate. Many economists question whether lower prices lead to lower *real* interest rates. But even if they do, questions remain about the importance of variations in real interest rates in explaining variations in investment. In recessions, in particular, investment may be relatively insensitive to changes in real interest rates.

There are other reasons that a lower price level, even were it to lead to lower real interest rates, might not result in significant increases in investment. Firms may not be able to increase their investment even if they would like to. We saw in Chapter 13 that many firms may face credit constraints. Hence, for investment funds, these firms must rely on retained earnings. When prices fall, particularly when they fall unexpectedly, the revenue entering a firm goes down, while some of its costs, such as what it owes on money it had previously borrowed, remain unchanged. Then the funds a firm has available for investing decrease, and investment falls. This is the **credit constraint effect.**

Second, even if there are no constraints on the firm's ability to increase investment, it may not be willing to do so. Given the lower level of prices that companies are receiving for their goods, each firm's profits and net worth will fall, especially if the lower prices were not anticipated. If firms are risk averse, then they will be less able to accommodate an economic downturn, and accordingly will be less willing to undertake the risks associated with investment. This effect we refer to as the **firm wealth effect.**

The net result of all this is that investment is probably not stimulated much—and may even be discouraged—by a fall in the price level. For small- and medium-sized firms, the credit constraint and firm wealth effects seem particularly important, and these firms may well decrease their investments. For larger companies, neither the firm wealth effect nor the credit constraint effect may be important, and the interest rate effect may predominate.

NET EXPORTS

We come now to the final component of aggregate expenditures. Lower prices in Canada (at a fixed exchange rate) make Canadian goods more attractive, both to Canadian consumers and to foreign consumers. Hence, exports increase and imports decrease. Net export spending increases.

The net export function, giving the level of net exports at each level of national income, shifts up to the left, as illustrated in Figure 15.5. The shift in net exports shifts up the aggregate expenditures schedule, as in Figure 15.3A, again leading to a higher level of equilibrium output. Thus, at lower prices, aggregate demand is higher.

While the net export function does shift up with a fall in the price level, net exports are a reasonably small fraction of total aggregate expenditures in Canada.[2] Accordingly, even a substantial percentage change in net exports translates into a relatively small upward shift in the aggregate expenditures schedule, and thus into a relatively small shift in the aggregate demand curve.

SUMMING UP

A lower price level causes the aggregate expenditures schedule to shift up slightly, as depicted in Figure 15.3A, but only slightly. Accordingly, even with the multiplier effects taken into account, the equilibrium level of output increases only slightly. Thus, the aggregate demand curve is normally relatively inelastic, or quite steep.

The fact that the aggregate demand curve is relatively inelastic means that when the economy is in the excess capacity range, changes in prices have a relatively small effect on equilibrium output. Though our analysis in Chapters 12–14 focused on calculating the equilibrium output at any particular price level, the equilibrium would not have been much different if we had calculated it at a slightly higher or lower price level.

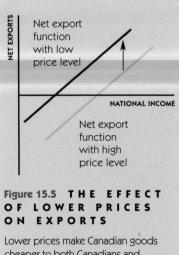

Figure 15.5 THE EFFECT OF LOWER PRICES ON EXPORTS

Lower prices make Canadian goods cheaper to both Canadians and foreigners. Exports increase, and the net export function shifts up.

[2]We are assuming that the exchange rate remains the same. It would be more realistic to assume that it changes in a way that largely reflects the effect of the lower price level.

CLOSE-UP: MEASURING CONSUMER EXPECTATIONS

At an intuitive level, most people find it sensible that consumer expectations about the future rise and fall in response to events. But social scientists insist on having data to test their conjectures. One commonly cited survey of consumer confidence is done by the Forecasting and Analysis Group of the Conference Board, a nonprofit research organization. The survey involves about a thousand interviews with Canadian households each month and includes questions about both the present situation and the future.

Four types of attitudinal questions are posed concerning current and expected financial positions, short-term employment outlook, and major purchases. Some typical questions include whether the consumer plans to buy a new home, car, or other big-ticket items.

A detailed breakdown of the answers to these questions is available, but the number more commonly reported in the newspapers is an index number, which is calculated in relation to an arbitrarily set level of confidence of 100 for 1961. The index is provided nationally, as well as for each province, and each index is seasonally adjusted. As one would expect, the path of consumer expectations varies with the course of the economy.

In June 1990, at the start of the recession, the Index of Consumer Attitudes measured 77, the lowest it has been since the recession of 1981–1982. The index remained at the 80 level for two and one-half years: in December 1992 the level was still 80.4. The only exception in the pattern was a small peak in June 1992 to a level of 90.6. The reasons for that small and brief increase in consumer confidence in the first six months of 1992 are not clear. When the economy performs reasonably well, as during the ten years in between those two recessions, the index ranges around 110.

Changes in consumer confidence are a fairly good predictor that the course of the economy will soon change. When consumer confidence starts turning down, the economy often follows a few months later. When consumer confidence starts turning up, the economy often does the same. One connection may be that businesses watch the survey results closely. When they see that consumers are more likely to spend, they become more willing to invest.

Source: "Index of Consumer Attitudes," The Conference Board of Canada (Winter 1993 and various issues).

THE EFFECT OF LOWER PRICES ON AGGREGATE DEMAND

Consumption

 Real balance effect—positive but small.

Investment

 Interest rate effect (firms' cost of obtaining capital)—positive, but possibly small, particularly in recessions.

 Credit constraint effect (firms' ability to invest)—for small and medium firms, negative.

 Firm wealth effect (firms' desire to bear risks of investing)—for small and medium firms, negative.

Net exports

 With exports a small fraction of GDP, even if exports increase by a large percentage, the percentage increase in aggregate demand may be small.

Overall effect: positive, but small.

DERIVING THE AGGREGATE SUPPLY CURVE

While the construction of the aggregate demand curve was rather complex, that of the aggregate supply curve is more straightforward. The market supply curve was shown there to be the sum of the supply curves of each of the firms in an industry. The supply curve of the typical firm consists of two parts: (1) If the price is too low, it simply does not pay to produce; it is better to shut down. Figure 15.6A denotes this price by p_0. (2) For prices beyond p_0, the higher the price, the more the company produces, up to some capacity level (Q_c in the figure). No matter what the price, the firm cannot produce beyond that capacity level. Since most plants are designed to produce a particular capacity, the firm's supply curve for prices above p_0 is relatively inelastic, as in the figure.

 The market supply curve is formed by adding up the amounts each firm is willing to supply at each price, as in panel B. If all firms had the same supply curves (which they would if they all faced the same technology and costs), then the market supply curve would consist of two parts—a flat portion at p_0 and a rising portion beyond p_0. At p_0, production is increased simply by operating more and more plants.

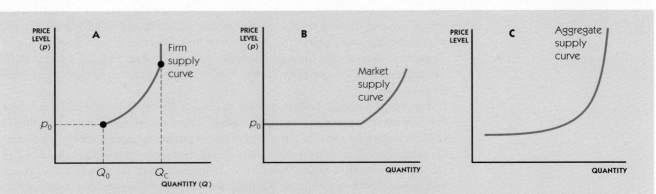

Figure 15.6 DERIVING THE AGGREGATE SUPPLY CURVE

Panel A shows a typical firm supply curve. There is a critical price, p_0, below which the firm will not produce. At that price, there is a minimum scale, Q_0, at which the firm can efficiently operate. At higher prices, output increases until the capacity of the firm, Q_c, is reached. As output gets near Q_c, the firm's supply curve becomes vertical.

Panel B shows a market supply curve, formed by adding up the supply curves of the firms within an industry. At p_0, the curve is flat.

Output is increased by raising the number of firms operating. When all firms are operating, further increases in output require a rise in price. Higher prices elicit greater supply, until the industry capacity is approached.

Panel C shows the aggregate supply curve, whose shape reflects the shape of the market supply curve—a flat portion when there is excess capacity and a vertical portion as the economy approaches full capacity.

The aggregate supply curve can be derived in the same way, and is illustrated in panel C. The output of the economy is nothing more than the sum of the outputs of each of the different industries. And accordingly, the shape of the aggregate supply curve has the same shape we have seen throughout this and earlier chapters: at low levels of output, it is relatively flat; at higher levels of output, relatively steep.

The fact that not all firms are identical means that they do not all shut down their production at exactly the same price. The supply curve, therefore, is not perfectly flat. But still, when the economy is operating with considerable excess capacity, a slight increase in price is much more likely to elicit a considerable increase in production than when the economy is operating at capacity.

We need to note two simplifications in our analysis. The first concerns what we are holding constant in the background. Since our aggregate demand and supply analysis focuses on the market for goods currently being produced, the aggregate demand curve is drawn with the assumption that wages and expectations of future prices and wages are fixed. The aggregate supply curve is drawn under the same assumptions. (This parallels the firm and market supply curves of Chapter 4, where a market supply curve gave the quantity of a good that the industry would supply at each price, taking all other wages and prices, including future wages and prices, as fixed. Later in this chapter, we will see how the long-run supply curve allows expectations of future wages and prices to adjust.)

The second simplification is that this analysis of the aggregate supply curve assumes that product markets are competitive. But as we have seen, many markets are not perfectly competitive. Imperfectly competitive firms face downward-sloping demand curves. They decide at which point along their demand curve to operate, choosing price and output levels. For imperfectly competitive industries and firms, we cannot define a supply curve in the way we did for competitive industries and firms. But we can ask, what is the equilibrium price we will observe firms charging at each level of output? (Imperfectly competitive firms get to *choose* their price.) The resulting curve is called the **aggregate price-quantity curve,** to avoid confusion with competitive aggregate supply curve.

A simple hypothesis about how firms in imperfectly competitive markets behave is that they mark up prices over marginal costs by a fixed percentage. Since where there is considerable excess capacity the marginal cost of producing more is relatively constant, the price charged by firms will be relatively constant within the excess capacity range. On the other hand, as firms reach their capacity constraints, the marginal costs of producing more increase greatly, so that the price charged by firms will rise rapidly. In this range, the aggregate price-quantity curve will accordingly be very steep. Thus, the aggregate price-quantity curve with imperfect competition is the shape we are familiar with: a flat, horizontal portion at high excess capacity and a vertical portion as the economy reaches capacity. The results would be quite similar even if the markup (the relationship between price and marginal cost) was not constant, so long as it did not vary greatly.[3]

SHIFTS IN AGGREGATE DEMAND AND SUPPLY

The economy is characterized by booms and recessions. There are good years and there are bad years. Chapter 8 showed how variable output and employment were in Canada, and similar patterns hold for other countries as well. In recessions, machines and workers remain idle. In booms, they are stretched to capacity. There is real economic waste in leaving resources idle during long recessions. Is there a way of running the economy so that resources are not periodically left idle? To begin to answer this question, we must understand how aggregate demand and aggregate supply curves shift.

---

[3]The markup model (with a constant markup) can be shown to correspond to the profit-maximizing behaviour of an imperfectly competitive firm facing a demand curve with constant elasticity.

An imperfectly competitive firm sets marginal revenue, the extra revenue it receives from selling an extra unit, equal to marginal costs. The exact relationship between price and marginal revenue is described by the equation

marginal revenue = $p[1 - (1/\text{elasticity of demand})]$.

When the elasticity of demand is infinite—that is, when the demand curve is horizontal—marginal revenue equals price, as the equation says. Accordingly, an imperfectly competitive firm sets its price so that

$p[1 - (1/\text{elasticity of demand})]$ = marginal costs,

or

price = marginal cost/$[1 - (1/\text{elasticity of demand})]$.

If the elasticity of demand is constant, then price is a constant markup over marginal cost, where the markup is $1/[1 - (1/\text{elasticity of demand})]$.

SHIFTS IN THE AGGREGATE DEMAND CURVE

We already know why the aggregate demand curve might shift. The reasons were laid out in Chapters 12–14. Anything that makes the aggregate expenditures schedule shift up or down at a given price level also makes the aggregate demand curve shift up or down. The major culprits that give rise to demand volatility are consumer purchases of durable goods, investment demand (particularly inventories and construction), net exports (as a result of changes in the exchange rate), and government expenditures. Usually government expenditures are undertaken in an attempt to stabilize the economy. However, they have not always had a stabilizing effect; the increases in expenditures as the country goes into a war (not offset by tax increases) and the reduction in expenditures as the war ends (not offset by tax decreases) have contributed to the economy's volatility.

The new aggregate demand curve resulting from, say, an increase in real government expenditures is constructed in exactly the same way that the old one was; at each price level, we draw the aggregate expenditures schedule, and then look for the intersection of that schedule with the 45-degree line in the income-expenditure analysis diagram. Figure 15.7 shows an upward shift in the aggregate expenditures schedule. The shift means that at each price level, the level of aggregate demand is higher. In fact, because of the

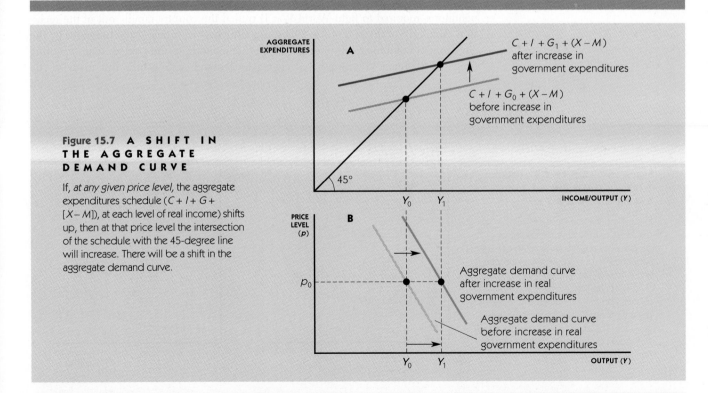

Figure 15.7 A SHIFT IN THE AGGREGATE DEMAND CURVE

If, *at any given price level*, the aggregate expenditures schedule ($C + I + G + [X - M]$), at each level of real income) shifts up, then at that price level the intersection of the schedule with the 45-degree line will increase. There will be a shift in the aggregate demand curve.

multiplier, the increase is a multiple of the initial increase in real government expenditures. Thus, in panel B, the point on the aggregate demand curve corresponding to the initial price level p_0 is shifted to the right.

The consumption, investment, or net export component of aggregate demand can change for any of the reasons discussed in Chapters 12–14—for instance, because of changes in interest rates or the availability of credit—and the consequences can be traced out in exactly the same manner as for a change in government expenditures.

SHIFTS IN THE AGGREGATE SUPPLY CURVE

The explanation of shifts in the aggregate supply curve begins by looking at the underlying supply curves of firms: at any given price level, firms are willing to supply a different quantity of output. A shift in the aggregate supply curve resulting from an increase or decrease in the capacity of the economy has a major impact on the portion of the curve we have been calling the full-capacity range, the vertical portion. For instance, additional capital in the economy will shift the vertical portion of the aggregate supply curve to the right, as in Figure 15.8A.

There are, of course, some circumstances in which the flat portion of the aggregate supply curve may shift. If workers suddenly became more efficient, then firms would be willing to sell their goods at a lower price—even with wages remaining unchanged. The flat portion of the aggregate supply curve would shift down, as in panel B.

Causes of major shifts in aggregate demand are usually easy to see. The military expenditures required to fight World War II pulled the country rapidly out of the recession. Similarly, at the end of the 1960s, spending on major new social programs by the government combined with increased export demand from the United States resulting from the Vietnam War stimulated aggregate demand significantly. But many of the

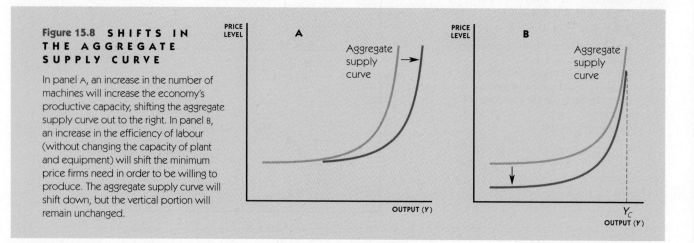

Figure 15.8 SHIFTS IN THE AGGREGATE SUPPLY CURVE

In panel A, an increase in the number of machines will increase the economy's productive capacity, shifting the aggregate supply curve out to the right. In panel B, an increase in the efficiency of labour (without changing the capacity of plant and equipment) will shift the minimum price firms need in order to be willing to produce. The aggregate supply curve will shift down, but the vertical portion will remain unchanged.

shifts in the aggregate supply curve are harder to identify. Five possibilities are worth mentioning. Many of these sources of shifts in aggregate supply correspond to the sources of shifts in market supply curves discussed in Chapter 4.

NATURAL AND MAN-MADE DISASTERS

The most dramatic shifts in aggregate supply result from a natural or man-made disaster. An earthquake or a wartime bombing may greatly reduce the amount of capital in the economy, and as a result, the amount of output that can be produced with any amount of labour will be reduced. This generates a leftward shift in the aggregate supply curve. Natural or other man-made disasters, while they may affect one or another part of the Canadian economy, are usually too small to have much affect on the *aggregate* output. Thus, economists do not spend much of their time studying macroeconomic policies to mitigate the effects of such disasters. Of course, there are a wide variety of natural changes that do change aggregate supplies dramatically over a longer period of time. Demographic changes such as reductions in infant mortality, increases in life expectancy, increased immigration, and changing birth rates as in the early postwar period, all affect the supplies of labour to the economy. But these occur over a long enough period of time to be of little relevance for short-run macroeconomic policy. We return to a discussion of some of these longer-run supply effects in Chapter 21.

TECHNOLOGY SHIFTS

Another possible cause of a shift in the aggregate supply curve might be a change in technology, increasing the amount that could be produced from any given combination of inputs. But although technology does change frequently, these changes are seldom sudden and they take years to disseminate through the economy. Not only must the knowledge diffuse through business, but new machines, making use of the new technology, must be installed. All of this takes more time than can explain one year's recession or boom. Moreover, since technology is almost always improving, the effect of a technological improvement is to move the aggregate supply curve to the right. In studying downturns, economists are interested in shifts of the aggregate supply curve to the left.

CHANGES IN PRICES OF IMPORTED AND EXPORTED GOODS

A more likely cause of a sudden shift in the aggregate supply curve is a change in import and export prices. The amount firms are willing to produce depends on the price they receive relative to the cost of what they must buy in order to produce. Oil is a major input to production in Canada, and most of the oil that is used in eastern Canada is imported. Furthermore, much of the oil produced in western Canada is exported, and its price is essentially determined by the world oil price. An increase in the world price of oil (similar to an increase in real wages) thus decreases the amount of output that Canadian producers (other than oil producers) are willing to produce at a given price. In 1973, the world price of oil rose dramatically, by 45 percent in real terms; in 1979, it increased once again, by an even larger percentage—51 percent in real terms; and then in 1985, it fell in an equally dramatic way, by 47 percent in real terms. Each of these changes can be thought of as inducing shifts in the aggregate supply curve.

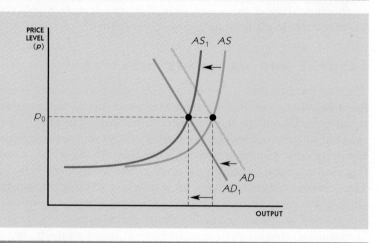

Figure 15.9 THE RISK CONNECTION BETWEEN AGGREGATE DEMAND AND SUPPLY

A shift in the aggregate demand curve from *AD* to AD_1 is accompanied by an increased perception of risk, which can lead aggregate supply to shift from *AS* to AS_1. As drawn here, the result is that the price level remains the same but output is substantially reduced.

CHANGES IN PERCEPTION OF OR WILLINGNESS TO BEAR RISK

There are always risks associated with production. As the economy goes into a recession, these risks increase, and the willingness and ability of firms to bear risks decrease. For instance, the managers of firms do not know how long the recession will last, or if an upturn will restore the demand for the particular goods they produce. If the downturn is unexpected or unexpectedly long, firms will have excess inventories—more reserves than they would like to have. They will have paid their workers to produce these goods, but they will not yet have received any cash in return for their sale. And they still have other obligations to meet—they have to pay interest on their debt, and there may be some loans coming due. If they cannot meet these obligations, they may be forced into bankruptcy. Firms know that if they continue to produce and sales remain at a low level, their cash position will further deteriorate.

Because of these dangers, a general increase in economic uncertainty makes firms more cautious. One way to be more cautious is to cut back on production and inventories—to reduce, in other words, the amount the firm is willing to supply at any price. The amount firms are willing to supply will therefore be reduced as the economy enters a recession.

This has one important implication, illustrated in Figure 15.9. An economic downturn, initiated by a leftward shift in aggregate demand (the shift from *AD* to AD_1), may give rise to a leftward shift in aggregate supply (the movement from *AS* to AS_1), so that there will be relatively little downward pressure on prices. Indeed, in the figure, new aggregate demand equals new aggregate supply at the original price—but output has been greatly reduced.

CHANGES IN WAGE RATES

The aggregate supply curve, like the aggregate demand curve, is drawn under the assumption that wages are given. Changes in wage rates will, accordingly, shift the aggregate supply curve. For example, at lower wages, firms will be willing to supply more of their products at any given price level; lower wages will result in a shift to the right of the aggregate supply curve.

CONSEQUENCES OF SHIFTS IN THE AGGREGATE DEMAND AND SUPPLY CURVES

Shifts in the aggregate demand and aggregate supply curves contribute to the variability in output. Figure 15.10 shows two kinds of shifts that can lead to low levels of output. In both panels A and B, the economy is initially operating along the steep portions of the aggregate supply curve. In panel A, a large leftward shift in the aggregate demand curve results in a new equilibrium in the horizontal portion of the aggregate supply curve. In panel B, a large upward shift in the aggregate supply curve also results in a new equilibrium in the relatively flat portion of the aggregate supply curve. However, of the major downturns that the economy has experienced over the past half century, only two are attributed by general consensus to a shift in the aggregate supply curve: the recessions that took place in the aftermath of the oil price shocks in 1973 and 1979. It is more likely that a shift in the aggregate supply curve will play a role in perpetuating a recession once it begins than that such a shift will set one off in the first place.

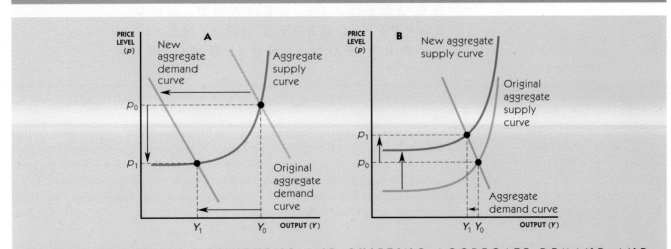

Figure 15.10 **ECONOMIC DOWNTURNS AND SHIFTING AGGREGATE DEMAND AND SUPPLY CURVES**

Shifts in the aggregate demand and supply curves may move the economy from a situation where it is initially operating along the vertical portion of the aggregate supply curve to one where it is operating along the horizontal portion. In panel A, a leftward shift in the aggregate demand curve moves the economy along the aggregate supply curve. In panel B, an upward shift in the aggregate supply curve moves the economy along the aggregate demand curve.

SHIFTS IN THE AGGREGATE DEMAND AND SUPPLY CURVES

Major causes of shifts in the aggregate demand curve
    Changes in consumer purchases of durable goods
    Changes in investment demand (particularly inventories and construction)
    Changes in net exports
    Changes in government expenditures
Major causes of shifts in the aggregate supply curve
    Natural and man-made disasters
    Technology shifts
    Changes in prices of imported goods
    Changes in perception of or willingness to bear risk
    Changes in wage rates

AGGREGATE DEMAND AND SUPPLY CURVES IN THE SHORT RUN AND LONG RUN

The aggregate demand and supply curves analyzed thus far were based upon the assumption that wages today, and expectations of wages and prices in the future, are fixed. These assumptions parallel those we made for the demand and supply curves in Part One, and they are natural simplifying assumptions, given our focus here on the product market. Two variables that have so far been held fixed will now be permitted to move: wages will change, as will expectations about both wages and prices in the future. Keeping them fixed has been a convenient simplifying assumption, but in some cases these assumptions may give misleading results.

SHIFTING AGGREGATE DEMAND AND SUPPLY CURVES

Consider a situation that might describe the Great Depression: initially the economy is at a point where aggregate demand equals aggregate supply, at a point of excess capacity, as depicted in Figure 15.11A. The initial price level is p_0, and the initial output is Y_0. At the same time, in panel B, the wage, w_0, is such that the demand for labour at that wage,

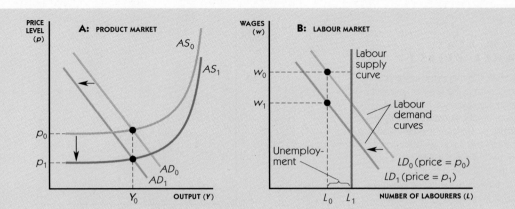

Figure 15.11 OFFSETTING CHANGES IN WAGES AND PRICES

The economy begins in a situation where aggregate demand equals aggregate supply along the horizontal portion of the aggregate supply curve, with price level p_0 and output level Y_0, as shown in panel A. Lower wages shift aggregate demand to the left, to AD_1, and aggregate supply down, to AS_1. As a result of both curves changing, the price level falls to p_1 but output remains at Y_0. In the labour market (panel B), wages are fixed at w_0, with the supply of labour, L_1, exceeding the demand, L_0. The excess supply of labour causes wages to fall from w_0 to w_1. The lower price causes the demand for labour to shift left from LD_0 to LD_1, since firms are receiving lower prices for their output. Although the wage has fallen from w_0 to w_1, unemployment remains the same. Thus, wages and prices have fallen while output and employment are unaffected.

L_0, is less than the supply, L_1; this illustrates the labour market as described in Chapter 11. For simplicity, the labour supply is drawn as a vertical line; it is assumed to be unresponsive to changes in real wages. The results, however, would remain unchanged even if the labour supply responded to changes in real wages.

The excess supply of labour means that wages will fall. As wages fall, income falls; in turn, aggregate demand at any price level falls. This is because consumers can afford to purchase fewer consumption goods.[4] The new aggregate demand curve is to the left of the old, and is labelled AD_1 in panel A. Meanwhile, the aggregate supply curve shifts because firms find their production costs are lower. The amount firms are willing to supply depends on what they get for selling their products—prices—relative to the costs of production. The costs of production are basically wages and the prices of other goods used as inputs. The new aggregate supply curve is labelled AS_1. Panel A shows that even though prices have fallen because of the shifts in the aggregate demand *and* supply curves, the new equilibrium entails the same output at a new, lower price. The fall in prices has failed to stimulate output. At the new price, p_1, output remains Y_0.

Now look again at the demand and supply for labour in panel B. The demand for labour has not received any stimulus from an increase in output. Because prices have fallen, at each wage the demand for labour is lower—the demand curve for labour has

---

[4]At any level of *real* income, a fall in wages implies an increase in profits. This increase may induce more spending, but the spending is still likely to be smaller than the reduced consumption from lower wages, especially during recessions.

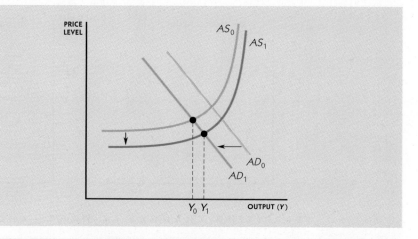

Figure 15.12 REAL BALANCE EFFECTS

As wages fall, the shift in the aggregate demand curve may be less than the shift in the aggregate supply curve, so that equilibrium output increases from Y_0 to Y_1. This may be because the real balance effect—the higher value of consumers' real wealth—induces them to buy more. Still, the net effect on output is small; output is restored to the full-employment level only slowly.

shifted from LD_0 to LD_1. The supply of labour remains unchanged at the same vertical position, so even though the wage has fallen from w_0 to w_1, the gap between labour supply at L_1 and labour demand at L_0 remains unchanged. The level of employment remains virtually unchanged. In this example, the interaction between the product market (aggregate demand and supply) and the labour market is such that as wages and prices fall, output and employment remain relatively unaffected.

Historically, nominal wages and prices have tended to move in tandem. As we have seen, falling wages shift both the aggregate demand and supply curves, leading to lower price levels. Lower price levels shift the demand for labour to the left, thus offsetting the gains from the originally lower wages. In these cases, falling wages and prices do very little to restore the economy to full employment.

Economists who believe that the real balance effect is important believe that the shift in the aggregate demand curve is less than the offsetting shift in the aggregate supply curve, so that there is an increase in the equilibrium output, as illustrated in Figure 15.12 by the movement from Y_0 to Y_1. *Eventually*, they argue, output will be restored to the full-employment output level. Most economists, however, believe that this process is slow; and meanwhile, there is the misery of unemployment and the waste of under-utilized resources.

EXPECTATIONS AND THE LONG-RUN AGGREGATE SUPPLY CURVE

So far, we have seen what happens to the aggregate demand and supply curves when wages fall. We have seen that changes in wages lead to changes in prices. Quite naturally, if this pattern persists, individuals and firms will come to expect future wages and prices to be different from current wages and prices. Such expectations may affect what they are willing to spend or what they are willing to supply at any given level of *current* prices. We focus here, in particular, on how these expectations affect the aggregate supply curve.

When firms expect wages and prices to move together, output will not be very responsive to changes in the price level. And if workers can correctly foresee future prices, it is reasonable to assume that wages will indeed move with prices. If they anticipate prices rising by 10 percent next year, their bargaining position for wages to be paid next year will reflect this. We refer to the aggregate supply curve that has today's wages as well as future wages and prices moving with the current price level as the long-run aggregate supply curve.

If nominal wages move in tandem with prices, the real wages facing firms will remain the same. If the prices of what they sell and the costs of production rise together, firms have no incentive to change their production level. Only if price changes outpace costs will their supply increase. Thus, if every change in the price level is accompanied by an exactly offsetting change in the wage level, the level of output at each price level will be the same. (Remember, wages change because the change in the price level was anticipated.) Under our new assumptions concerning wage and price expectations, the long-run aggregate supply curve will be vertical, as illustrated in Figure 15.13.

The figure illustrates one very strong implication of the vertical long-run aggregate supply curve. Earlier we learned that if the intersection of the aggregate demand and supply curves occurred along a vertical portion of the aggregate supply curve, then a shift in aggregate demand would *only* have an effect on the price level. A vertical long-run aggregate supply curve means that in the long run an increase in aggregate demand from AD to AD_1 has the same result. It has no effect on aggregate output, which remains at Y_0 (and similarly no effect on aggregate employment). It only affects price levels.

It is important to remember that the aggregate demand and supply curves depicted in Figure 15.13 differ from those drawn in Part One, Chapter 10, and earlier in this chapter. The earlier curves were drawn on the assumption that current wages and expected wages and prices were kept fixed. The curves in the figure are drawn on the assumption that all wages and prices (current and future) move together. To remind us of this important difference, the expectations-adjusted aggregate supply curve will always be referred to as the long-run aggregate supply curve.

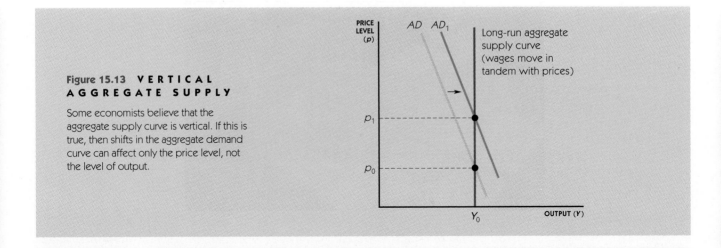

Figure 15.13 VERTICAL AGGREGATE SUPPLY

Some economists believe that the aggregate supply curve is vertical. If this is true, then shifts in the aggregate demand curve can affect only the price level, not the level of output.

CLOSE-UP: COMPUTER TECHNOLOGY AND AGGREGATE SUPPLY

At the start of the 1980s, it was rare for a student to use a computer, at least in any class not related to statistics or computer science itself. Papers for other classes were typed out on typewriters. By the start of the 1990s, however, many university students went off to school with a computer of their own, and instead of running out of typing paper at 3:00 A.M.—the old problem—students panicked at the last minute because their diskette did not seem to work when they tried to print out their papers.

Computers invaded the entire economy, in fact, in industries from manufacturing to banking and finance. Yet even as these technological miracles spread like wildfire to desktops and the inside of machines, productivity growth remained perplexingly low for the North American economy. Robert Solow of MIT once summed up the paradox by saying, "We see computers everywhere except in the productivity statistics."

Has the so-called computer revolution actually contributed little to growth in productivity? If so, how can its seeming failure to spur growth be explained? One set of explanations emphasizes that in many companies, computers may have led to more paperwork rather than more output at lower cost. In this view, too many businesses bought computers because it seemed like the fashionable thing to do, not because they had a real idea of how to use the computers to improve productivity. As a result, computers diverted energy from more productive tasks.

A second explanation, formulated by Paul David of Stanford University, is no less gloomy about the short term, but considerably more optimistic about the long term. David points out that available computer technology is still very young. In the case of the invention of the dynamo, for example, which is used for generating electrical power, it took decades for factories to figure out how to use this new technology and to rebuild their plants and redesign their operations accordingly.

David warns against the impatient belief that a new invention immediately jolts the economy forwards; the diffusion and use of a new invention has always been a process that takes years, if not decades.

A third explanation is that the productivity statistics themselves are misleading. Consider, for example, the case of automatic teller machines at banks, which offer twenty-four-hour access to deposits and allow tellers inside the bank to concentrate more on other services. This new range of services will not necessarily mean an expanded banking industry—they simply will not be captured by the GDP statistics.

There is some evidence that productivity statistics are not especially accurate in many service-related industries, where computer technology is often important in organizing information and customizing service. The underlying problem involves difficulties in measuring output that were introduced back in Chapter 8. It is relatively easy to measure the output of a manufacturing industry by counting the number of cars or tonnes of steel produced. But the output of a service industry such as banking or health care is multidimensional, and harder for statisticians to measure. Making the appropriate adjustments for quality changes may be a close to impossible task.

Sources: Paul David, "General Purpose Engines, Investment, and Productivity Growth: From the Dynamo Revolution to the Computer Revolution," Royal Swedish Academy of Engineering Sciences (January 1990); Ronald H. Schmidt, "Services: A Future of Low Productivity Growth," *Federal Reserve Bank of San Francisco Weekly Letter,* February 14, 1992.

RATIONAL EXPECTATIONS

We have seen that the shape of the long-run aggregate supply curve depends in part on the expectations that firms and individuals have about what will happen in the future.[5] There is some controversy, however, about how individuals form their expectations of future conditions.

One hypothesis is that changes in current prices or wages have no effect on future expected wages and prices. In that case, if prices are lowered today, then today is a good time to buy goods. Under a second hypothesis, households and firms extrapolate any observed price and wage changes and predict that they will continue into the future. The extrapolation principle takes several different forms. In one form, today's lower prices are expected to continue into the future; the change in the price level today makes it neither more nor less attractive to buy today. This is called **static expectations**. In a second form, consumers might extrapolate not the level of prices but the rate of change of prices. Consumers might believe that if prices are lowered today they are going to be even lower in the future. They expect the trend to continue, and accordingly may decide to postpone their consumption. This is called **adaptive expectations**. The difference between the consumer's responses under the static expectations and adaptive expectations hypotheses shows the important role that expectations play in the analysis of how aggregate demand changes with a change in the price level. It plays an equally important role in supply responses.

---

[5]The appendix to the chapter also discusses how aggregate demand may depend on expectations.

Some economists, such as Robert Lucas of the University of Chicago, have argued for another form of expectations. In their view, the static expectations and adaptive expectations hypotheses are naive. Lucas has emphasized that just as people are rational in their decisions concerning what goods to buy, they are rational in forming expectations; that is, they use all the information that is available to them in forming their expectations concerning the future course of events. Expectations formed this way are called **rational expectations**.

Every year, retailers mark down their wares right after New Year's Day. Let's consider how three different consumers, each in the market for a new CD player, respond to these holiday discounts. Marie, who has static expectations, is just as likely to buy in either December or January. Prices, she reasons, will stay the same from December into January. Will, who has adaptive expectations and has already postponed his purchase until January, will be tempted to postpone his consumption until February, thinking that the price decline will continue. But there is a sense in which neither of these ways of forming expectations is fully rational. People know that every year there is a sale in January. It is not rational to ignore this information. Paula has rational expectations; unless she strongly wishes to have the CD player in December (perhaps to give as a Christmas present), she will deliberately postpone the purchase until January because she knows that every year there are holiday season sales.

In a sense, one can say that each of these individuals is extrapolating from the past. Marie's extrapolation assumes that next month is like this month; Will's extrapolation assumes that the change between next month and this month is like the change between this month and last month; and Paula's extrapolation assumes that the pattern of prices over the year will be the same from one year to the next. We say the third method is "rational" because it uses all of the relevant information, whereas the first two methods ignore some of it.

In this example, forming rational expectations was easy. But often it is extremely difficult to know what is relevant when making one's forecast of the future. Events like the Great Depression do not, fortunately, occur every year or even every decade. They are once- or perhaps twice-in-a-lifetime events. If prices start to fall, will consumers extrapolate, believing that they will continue to fall? Do they have any better principle on which to base expectations? These are questions about which there continues to be debate among economists. And as we will see, alternative expectations have very important consequences.[6]

POLICY IMPLICATIONS OF RATIONAL EXPECTATIONS

The principle of rational expectations has some important lessons to teach. If the government announces that in order to reduce the demand for cars it will impose an automobile tax beginning next January, individuals "rationally" know that the cost of purchasing a car will rise next January, and those who were planning to buy a car in January or February will buy it in December. The government, in making its revenue projections, ought to take these responses into account.

---

[6]Many of the simpler rational expectations models have been criticized for their assumption that all individuals are identical and, in particular, have the same expectations. Under the rational expectations assumption, if all individuals had the same information, they would have the same expectations. But, of course, people do not all have the same information, so that the observed differences in opinions may be consistent with the rational expectations view.

The shift in the timing of the purchase of cars from January to December is an unintended but perfectly anticipatable consequence of the government policy. This response will subvert the success of the program in the short run. But in the long run, the tax on cars will indeed reduce car purchases—the government policy will succeed.

Some economists, however, believe that rational expectations responses to government policies frequently subvert those policies, making them almost totally ineffective.

THE NEW CLASSICAL AND NEW KEYNESIAN SCHOOLS OF MACROECONOMICS

Any reader of the newspaper will know that economists do not always agree about what the government should do about the macroeconomic problems facing the economy. Some economists believe that when the economy is facing unemployment, the government should move aggressively to stimulate the economy, and increase aggregate demand by either cutting taxes or increasing government expenditures. Others, more worried about the longer-run consequences of these deficits or about the possible effects that the increased aggregate demand will have on the price level, urge a more cautious course. Later, in Chapter 23, we will look more thoroughly at disagreements about the extent to which government intervention is needed, whether there are any effective tools government can use, and whether government intervention, for the most part, makes matters better or worse.

Underlying these differences in views about government policy are differences in views about the economy. At this point, it will be useful to see how our aggregate demand and supply analysis helps shed light on some of the important differences.

RATIONAL EXPECTATIONS AND POLICY INEFFECTIVENESS

For the most part, economists who study macroeconomic issues today toil either in the classical or in the Keynesian tradition. What distinguishes new classical and new Keynesian economists from their forebears is a common interest in tracing macroeconomic phenomena back to their microeconomic underpinnings, and the explicit attention they pay to the manner in which expectations are formed.

They differ in several respects, which will be discussed in later chapters. But one of the important differences is the extent to which they are willing to push the rational expectations argument. Robert Lucas, one of the leaders in the new classical school of economics, has emphasized the importance to the aggregate supply curve of the relationship between the expected price and the actual price that will be realized in the market in the future. Assume, for instance, that workers make wage agreements with employers based on particular expectations of future prices. If prices are expected to be 10 percent higher, wages are increased in tandem. Once the wage is set, then the higher the price level turns out to be, the larger the amount of goods firms are willing to supply. Higher prices mean lower real wages.

Thus, according to Lucas, the short-run supply curve is upward sloping, as depicted in Figure 15.14. But the real wages are low only because the increase in prices was not fully anticipated. If workers and their employers throughout the economy anticipate price changes correctly, then higher price levels will bring forth only higher wages and no corresponding increase in output. The long-run supply curve, then, is close to vertical. Output will be fixed as Y_L, regardless of the actual level of prices. Lucas argues that normally wages increase in tandem with prices, since with rational expectations workers will anticipate those price increases, and therefore most of the time the relevant supply curve is the vertical one.

Figure 15.14 shows both the long-run and short-run aggregate supply curves. The vertical portion of the short-run aggregate supply curve is drawn slightly to the right of the vertical long-run aggregate supply curve. In Lucas's view, the reason that the short-run aggregate supply curve is upward sloping is that people do not fully anticipate price changes. We saw earlier (in Chapters 8 and 10) that for short periods of time, such as wartime, people can be induced to work more and firms to produce more than they would at other times, so that output can exceed the "normal" capacity of the economy. Similarly, by not fully anticipating price changes, they may be "tricked" into producing more than they would if they had anticipated the changes.

The new classical economists draw a very strong conclusion from the long-run vertical supply curve. Since the long-run level of output in the economy is effectively determined by aggregate supply, which is inelastic, trying to manipulate aggregate demand at most simply changes the price level, as was shown in Figure 15.13. This conclusion, known as the **policy ineffectiveness proposition**, has been criticized by new Keynesian economists. They note that the conclusion that policy is ineffective is a consequence of the vertical supply curve *combined* with the assumption that the economy is operating at the intersection of the aggregate demand and supply curves.

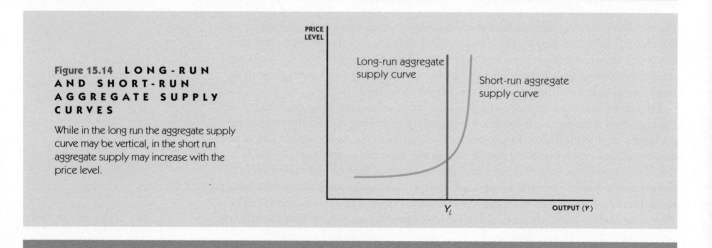

Figure 15.14 LONG-RUN AND SHORT-RUN AGGREGATE SUPPLY CURVES

While in the long run the aggregate supply curve may be vertical, in the short run aggregate supply may increase with the price level.

MARKET CLEARING

A second main difference between the two groups of economists is the assumption of the new classical economists that all markets clear; when applied to the labour market, this assumption precludes the possibility of involuntary unemployment. Changes in the economy can lead to changes in real wages, which affect the level of unemployment (as we saw in Chapters 10 and 11), but in the new classical perspective, involuntary unemployment simply is not a problem. Moreover, the assumption that the product market always clears means that all firms can sell as much as they would like at the going prices, even in the midst of the worst recession. New Keynesians think that wages may be sticky, so that the labour market may not always clear—at times, such as the Great Depression, there really is a problem of involuntary unemployment. And, as we will see in the next chapter, most new Keynesians think that prices may also be sticky, so that the product market too may not clear.

The differences between new classical and new Keynesian economists can be seen as differences in assumptions concerning speeds of adjustment. New classical economists believe that expectations are revised quickly, after making use of all relevant information, and that markets adjust quickly, so that the labour market essentially always clears. New Keynesian economists believe that under certain circumstances, expectations may be slow to be revised and that wages may adjust slowly, so that unemployment may persist for extended periods of time. The new Keynesian economists concede that the new classical economists may be correct in the long run: eventually the economy *may* adjust (but even that is a matter to be established, not assumed), and in the long run it may operate along a vertical supply curve. Thus, shifting the aggregate demand curve may do no good in the long run. The critical question then becomes "How long do we have to wait for the long run?" Keynes dismissed the optimistic assertion that in the long run the economy would restore itself to full employment with the retort "In the long run, we are all dead."

The new Keynesians believe that in the short run, the aggregate supply curve is not vertical, largely because the new classical economists' assumptions of expectations have been questioned. It was the (rational) anticipation of price changes that led wages to change in tandem with prices, so that changes in the price level had no effect on aggregate supply. Many new Keynesians argue that the vagaries of the economy are so great as to make the assumption of rational expectations, in the short run, questionable. As we have seen, it is not clear what it means to have rational expectations concerning events that happen but once or twice in a lifetime. What inferences were to be made about the future consequences of the decline in the stock prices that occurred in October 1987, a larger percentage decline in the value of stocks than had ever occurred? Analogies with earlier periods are at best just that: analogies. There have been enormous changes in the institutions of the economy and its structure since the last major crash of the stock market, in October 1929.

According to new Keynesian economists, even if one believes that firms and households cannot consistently be wrong in their expectations—that eventually expectations become rational—it may take some time for expectations to adjust; and in the interim, the supply curve will be upward sloping.[7] And so long as the short-run aggregate supply

[7]The assumption that rational expectations *necessarily* imply that a fall in the price level must be accompanied by a proportionate fall in wages has also been questioned. The analysis is sufficiently technical to be beyond the scope of this text.

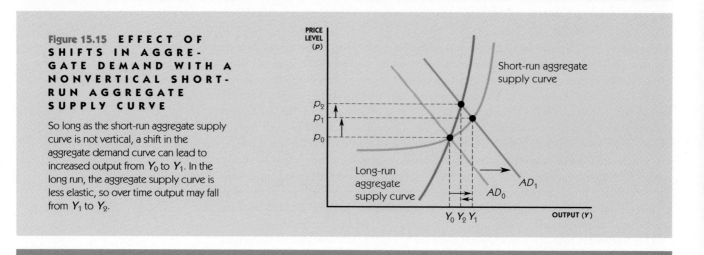

Figure 15.15 EFFECT OF SHIFTS IN AGGREGATE DEMAND WITH A NONVERTICAL SHORT-RUN AGGREGATE SUPPLY CURVE

So long as the short-run aggregate supply curve is not vertical, a shift in the aggregate demand curve can lead to increased output from Y_0 to Y_1. In the long run, the aggregate supply curve is less elastic, so over time output may fall from Y_1 to Y_2.

curve is not vertical, even if prices adjust quickly so that aggregate demand equals aggregate supply, shifting the aggregate demand curve can lead to increased equilibrium output, as illustrated in Figure 15.15. The short-run aggregate supply curve is not vertical; wages are not assumed to move completely in proportion to prices. The intersection is at an output of Y_0 and a price p_0.

NEW CLASSICAL VERSUS NEW KEYNESIAN ECONOMISTS

NEW CLASSICAL ECONOMISTS	NEW KEYNESIAN ECONOMISTS
In the long run, because of rational expectations, the aggregate supply curve is vertical, so that shifts in the aggregate demand curve only affect the price level (policy is ineffective).	In the long run, we are all dead. While rational expectations may be relevant in the long run, they are not in the short run. So for extended periods of time, the aggregate supply curve may be nonvertical, and shifts in the aggregate demand curve have significant effects on output.
The short-run, nonvertical aggregate supply curve, if it applies at all, applies only for very short periods.	There may be extended periods of time during which wages fail to adjust to clear the labour market; unemployment may be persistent.
Equilibrium, in which wages adjust to clear the labour market and there is no involuntary unemployment, is attained very quickly.	

The fact that the aggregate supply curve is less elastic in the long run than in the short run means that the gains to output and employment are less in the long run than in the short run. This is also illustrated in Figure 15.15. The increase in output in the long run, $Y_2 - Y_0$, is smaller than it is in the short run, $Y_1 - Y_0$. The corresponding changes in employment are also smaller in the long run.

The policy ineffectiveness proposition, if confirmed, would be cause for concern to anyone who feels that markets might fail to keep the economy running efficiently and at capacity. But to the new classical economists, who believe that output is determined by aggregate supply, the ineffectiveness of policies attempting to stimulate output by increasing aggregate demand is not much of a worry: they believe that the economy almost always operates efficiently, with labour markets clearing, so there is no unemployment. There is little to be gained from policies aimed at controlling aggregate demand to maintain the economy at full employment. And there is much to be lost: by attempting to stimulate demand, such policies simply induce higher prices.

REVIEW AND PRACTICE

SUMMARY

1. The aggregate demand curve is derived using income-expenditure analysis. The intersection of the 45-degree line with the aggregate expenditures schedule *for a particular price level* determines the point on the aggregate demand curve corresponding to that price level.

2. Lowering the price level shifts the aggregate expenditures schedule up and increases the equilibrium level of output. Accordingly, the aggregate demand curve is downward sloping.

3. Lower prices may lead to a slight upward shift in the aggregate expenditures schedule because consumption increases (the real balance effect), because investment increases (the interest rate effect), or because exports increase. Because the shift is only a small one, the aggregate demand curve may be relatively steep, which means that when the economy is in the excess capacity range (where actual output is determined by aggregate demand), changes in price have a relatively small effect on equilibrium output.

4. The aggregate supply curve is derived from the sum of industry supply curves. At lower levels of output, when there is excess capacity, it is relatively flat; at higher levels of output, it is relatively steep. Causes of shifts in the aggregate supply curve include disasters, technology shifts, changes in import prices, changes in the perception of risk, and changes in wage rates.

5. A decline in prices shifts the demand curve for labour to the left, leading to lower wages. Lower wages may shift the aggregate supply curve to the right and down and the aggregate demand curve to the left, resulting in a new equilibrium with lower prices but relatively unchanged output. If wages and prices fall in tandem, then real

wages will not fall and there will be little change in either the demand for or supply of labour.

6. In the long run, rational expectations of prices and wages mean that higher current prices will be anticipated, followed by higher wages and higher expectations of prices and wages in the future. Then, a rise in prices does not affect aggregate supply, since firms expect that the prices of their inputs—including labour—will rise by the same amount, and the aggregate supply curve is vertical.

7. If the aggregate supply curve is vertical and equilibrium occurs at the intersection of the aggregate demand and supply curves, aggregate demand cannot affect the level of output; rightward shifts in the aggregate demand curve only lead to increases in the price level.

8. New classical economists believe that expectations are rational and therefore the aggregate supply curve is vertical, and that the labour market quickly adjusts so that the economy normally operates at full employment. Policy is ineffective. New Keynesian economists believe that the aggregate supply curve is not vertical and that the labour market may not clear quickly—there may be extended periods of unemployment. Shifts in the aggregate demand curve can have real effects on output and employment.

KEY TERMS

real balance effect
interest rate effect
credit constraint
    effect
firm wealth effect

aggregate price-
    quantity curve
static expectations
adaptive expecta-
    tions

rational expectations
policy ineffective-
    ness proposition

REVIEW QUESTIONS

1. How is income-expenditure analysis used to derive the aggregate demand curve?

2. Why is the aggregate demand curve downward sloping? What are reasons that a lower price level would shift the aggregate expenditures schedule? Why might the aggregate demand curve be relatively inelastic?

3. How is the aggregate supply curve related to the supply curve for a firm? What is the characteristic shape of the aggregate supply curve?

4. What factors can shift the aggregate demand curve? What factors can shift the aggregate supply curve?

5. What effects do lower wages have on aggregate demand and supply? What effects do lower prices have on the demand for and supply of labour? What implications do these interactions have for the adjustment of the economy?

6. What are rational expectations? adaptive expectations? static expectations? What is the role of expectations in determining the slope of an aggregate supply curve?

Why might the aggregate supply curve be vertical in the long run? What are the consequences of a vertical aggregate supply curve?

7. What problems does the rational expectations hypothesis face, particularly in explaining behaviour in the short run?

8. How do the new classical economists and the new Keynesian economists differ in (a) their assumptions about how the economy functions and (b) their views of the need for and effectiveness of government intervention?

PROBLEMS

1. Below are data for aggregate supply and demand curves. The price level is an index number, and aggregate demand and supply are expressed in billions of dollars.

Price level	100	105	110	115	120	125	130
Aggregate demand	640	620	600	580	560	540	520
Aggregate supply	300	400	500	540	560	580	580

Plot the aggregate demand and supply curves, putting *real* output on the horizontal axis.

2. Consider the problem of a firm that has just seen the price of what it produces rise. The firm will reconsider its production plans based on one of the following expectations.
   (a) It expects that the wages it pays and the prices of its inputs will not increase.
   (b) It expects that the wages it pays and the prices of its inputs will increase by the same amount as the rise in price, but this will take several years.
   (c) It expects that the wages it pays and the prices of its inputs will quickly increase by the same amount as the rise in price.
For which set of expectations will the firm make a small change in the amount it supplies? a large change? When will the change be temporary? Explain.

3. Use aggregate demand and supply diagrams to explain why the expansionary fiscal policies of the Liberal government in the mid-1960s, when the Canadian economy was close to full employment, did not have the same effect as the expansionary fiscal policies of the Kennedy administration in the early 1960s in the United States, when there was excess capacity in the American economy.

4. The price of imported oil fell sharply in the early 1980s, from about U.S. $24 a barrel in 1985 to about U.S. $12 a barrel in 1986. Using an aggregate demand and supply diagram, predict how this might affect national output and the price level. Is the effect of the price decrease symmetric with the effect of the rise in oil prices that occurred in 1973 and 1979? (In each case, assume that initially the economy was in equilibrium, at the intersection of the aggregate demand and supply curves. How is your answer affected by whether the economy was operating at first along the horizontal or the vertical portion of the aggregate supply curve?)

APPENDIX: ALTERNATIVE EXPLANATIONS FOR THE DEPENDENCE OF CONSUMPTION AND INVESTMENT ON PRICE

In the text, we learned several of the reasons that a change in the price level may affect consumption or investment. Following are some other reasons economists have given.

EFFECTS OF CURRENT CHANGES ON AGGREGATE DEMAND

What would you do if you saw prices today were very low, but you expected them to be much higher in the future? It would be as if there were an economy-wide sale! You would take advantage of the low prices to buy more consumption goods today. This is called the **intertemporal substitution effect.** "Intertemporal" means over time, and the intertemporal substitution effect is the substitution of consumption at one point in time for consumption at another point. In this case, people substitute consumption when prices are low for consumption when prices are higher.

There is another reason that a decrease in the price level may affect the level of consumption. At any moment, some individuals owe money to other individuals. Some people have borrowed money to buy a variety of consumer goods; others have borrowed money to buy houses. When prices fall, the *real* value of what debtors (those who owe money) owe to creditors (those who lend) has increased. Debtors are worse off; creditors are better off. Debtors will accordingly decrease their demand for consumption goods; creditors will increase their demand. If debtors, on average, respond by decreasing their consumption by more than creditors increase their consumption, aggregate consumption will be reduced. Since debtors are by and large poorer than creditors, one might expect that this in fact happens. This is called the **wealth redistribution effect.** A reduction in the price level shifts wealth in the population, with the ultimate result that aggregate consumption goes down. Thus, the wealth redistribution effect may somewhat offset the real balance and intertemporal substitution effects, both of which lead to higher consumption at lower prices.

Another effect, the **income redistribution effect**, also serves to increase consumption slightly when prices fall (at fixed wages). The increase in real wages lowers profits at the same time that it raises workers' real incomes. Those who depend on profits reduce their consumption, while workers increase theirs. The later consequence is probably greater than the former.

How significant are these effects? Most economists think their significance is relatively small. There is thus some presumption that their net effect combined with the real balance effect is that a reduction in prices does increase consumption, but not by a great deal.

Firms also enjoy the intertemporal substitution effect. When the cost of capital goods has decreased relative to the price of the goods that those machines will produce in the future, firms will want to increase their investment.

EFFECTS OF EXPECTED PRICE CHANGES ON AGGREGATE DEMAND

The impact of a decline in both prices and wages depends on whether households and firms expect such changes to continue. Their expectations are important because they affect the magnitude, and possibly even the direction, of the intertemporal substitution effect. If expectations concerning future prices are fixed, then if the price today is lowered, it is cheaper to buy the good today rather than wait until tomorrow, and this intertemporal substitution effect leads to increased consumption and investment today. But if lowered prices today lead consumers and firms to expect that prices will be even lower tomorrow, then they will postpone their purchases. Lower prices may then actually lead to lower sales.

Thus, as prices fall, if wages fall and expected future prices also fall, aggregate demand is not likely to increase as much as it would have had wages and expected future prices not declined. This weakened intertemporal substitution effect is only one reason. A second reason is that with fixed wages, a decline in prices represents an increase in real wages, and the consequent redistribution of income may slightly increase consumption. With wages falling with prices, there is no income redistribution effect. Third, if the exchange rate changes to offset the change in prices, then there will be no effect on net exports.

Fourth, if the prices at which firms can sell the goods they produce in the future is anticipated to be lower, lower prices of investment goods today will not stimulate more investment; if prices in the future are expected to fall more, investment will be discouraged. Finally, the wealth redistribution effect—the fact that lower prices make creditors better off (since they are being repaid with dollars that are worth more) and debtors worse off—is no longer present, since when the price changes are anticipated, the loan contracts will take these price changes into account. A similar argument holds for what was called the firm wealth effect. Both of these effects depend on the price change being unanticipated.

In short, the main remaining effect on aggregate demand of a decline in prices is the real balance effect, an effect that is at best relatively small. In the text, we saw that the aggregate demand curve is relatively inelastic. When a lower price level is accompanied by a corresponding decline in wages and future expected prices, the aggregate demand curve is even more inelastic. Changes in the price level may do little to restore the economy to full employment. To increase output (and employment), the aggregate demand curve must be shifted.

16

STICKY PRICES*

he discussion of aggregate demand and aggregate supply in Chapter 15 assumes that prices are flexible. When they are, the output of the economy is determined by the intersection of the aggregate demand and supply curves. In Chapter 11, we learned why wages might be rigid, or sticky. The consequence of sticky wages is that the demand for labour might not equal the supply of labour; involuntary unemployment may be the result. It turns out that there are good reasons to think that prices too might not adjust in the speedy way envisioned by the basic competitive model. If they do not, then the economy might get stuck away from the point of intersection of aggregate demand and supply. This has potentially important consequences, for both the behaviour of the economy and the role of government intervention. The objective of this chapter is to explore the causes and consequences of sticky prices.

* This chapter may be omitted without affecting the understanding of later chapters.

KEY QUESTIONS

1. How is output determined when prices are sticky and so do not adjust to the level at which aggregate demand equals aggregate supply?

2. Why might sticky prices give rise to low levels of output, regardless of whether they are stuck at a level that is too low or too high?

3. How does the level at which prices are stuck affect the appropriate remedy for increasing output?

4. How do new classical and new Keynesian economists differ in their views about the importance of sticky prices, and what policy implications follow from these differences in views?

5. What are the principal reasons that prices may be sticky?

DEMAND- AND SUPPLY-CONSTRAINED EQUILIBRIA

In Chapter 5, we studied the effect of price floors (for example, minimum wage legislation) and price ceilings (rent control). Since no firm can be forced to produce more than it wishes, the amount actually produced and consumed when there is a price ceiling, when prices are kept below the market-clearing level, is the quantity firms are willing to supply. Since at the price ceiling demand exceeds supply, after firms produce the amount they are willing to supply, some demand will be left unsatisfied. Likewise for price floors: since no consumer can be forced to consume more than she wishes, the amount actually consumed when prices are above the market-clearing level is just the amount consumers are willing to purchase and lower than the quantity firms are willing to produce. Firms are not irrational. Knowing that demand will be artificially low when there is a price floor, they cut back production. The amount they actually produce then will be less than the amount they would be willing to produce at the given price (and wage), if only there were a demand for their goods.

The same principles apply when the economy gets stuck at a point away from the intersection of aggregate supply and aggregate demand. If the price level is stuck above the level at which aggregate demand equals aggregate supply, so that aggregate demand is less than aggregate supply, then output will be the level of aggregate demand at that price. If the price level is stuck below the intersection of aggregate supply and demand, so that aggregate supply is less than aggregate demand, output will be the level of aggregate supply at that price. The first case is called a **demand-constrained equilibrium,** because what constrains output is demand; the second is called a **supply-constrained equilibrium,** because what constrains output is the amount firms are willing to supply at the given price. Let's look at these equilibria in more detail.

DEMAND-CONSTRAINED EQUILIBRIUM AND KEYNESIAN UNEMPLOYMENT

In Figure 16.1, aggregate demand and supply intersect at a price level p^*. Output at that price level is Y^*. In the diagram, the intersection occurs along the vertical portion of the aggregate supply curve. If prices were flexible and the economy operated at this intersection, it would be operating at full capacity, with all of its resources fully utilized. There would be full employment.

If for some reason prices were stuck at a higher level, say p_0, then the amount produced would only be Y_0, the level of output along the aggregate demand curve corresponding to that price level. It does not pay firms to produce unless there are buyers for their goods, regardless of whether they would make a profit *if* a buyer were available at the going market prices. Firms produce only what they can sell.

Accordingly, when at a given, fixed price level demand is less than the amount firms are willing to supply, the level of output is given by the demand curve. If this level of output is less than that associated with full employment, the resulting unemployment is called **Keynesian unemployment;** it was the great British economist Keynes who first enunciated the idea that what often limits production—and consequently employment— is the demand for output, the willingness of individuals, business firms, and the government to purchase goods.

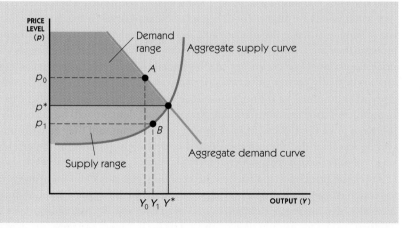

Figure 16.1 DEMAND- AND SUPPLY-CONSTRAINED EQUILIBRIA

If prices are above the intersection of aggregate demand and supply (at p_0), the economy will only produce the amount *demanded*, at point A. If prices are below the intersection of aggregate demand and supply (p_1), the economy will only produce the amount firms are willing to supply, at point B.

SUPPLY-CONSTRAINED EQUILIBRIUM AND CLASSICAL UNEMPLOYMENT

Just as prices might be fixed at a level *above* the point where aggregate demand equals aggregate supply, so too can they be below that point. In this case, when prices are fixed at a point above the intersection of aggregate demand and aggregate supply, firms only produce what they are willing to produce; some customers are left unsatisfied. The reason firms are not willing to produce more is that prices are low relative to wages, and seeing these low prices, firms are unwilling to hire additional workers.

Figure 16.1 illustrates a supply-constrained equilibrium as well. When the price level is stuck at p_1, below the equilibrium price level p^*, the level of output will be Y_1, less than the full-employment level Y^*.

In the 1800s and early 1900s, many economists thought that most of the time the economy operated at full employment. They argued that there were strong economic forces that came into play whenever there was unemployment, which would ensure that the unemployment was only temporary. These economists, as was noted earlier, were referred to as classical economists. In their view, the major cause of unemployment was high real wages (low prices relative to the given level of nominal wages)—the case we have just seen. For this reason, this kind of unemployment is referred to as **classical unemployment.**

In the 1970s, there was a strong revival of this line of thought. The new classical economists, whom we encountered in Chapter 15, while agreeing with the earlier classical economists that most of the time the economy was at full employment, sought explanations of why real wages might temporarily be too high. For instance, if workers and employers had overestimated the rate of increase in prices and workers had succeeded in getting wage increases based on those higher price expectations, then real wages would be (temporarily) high.

CONTRASTING IMPLICATIONS OF DEMAND- AND SUPPLY-CONSTRAINED EQUILIBRIA

Figure 16.1 illustrates the demand- and supply-constrained equilibria. There are two regions: at prices below p^*, output is determined by aggregate supply (the supply-constrained range), and at prices above p^*, output is determined by aggregate demand (the demand-constrained range). The distinction between situations in which demand limits output and those in which supply limits output has important policy implications.

CHANGES IN PRICES AND WAGES

First, consider the effects of an increase in prices (at fixed wages). In the demand-constrained equilibrium (at p_0 in Figure 16.1), as prices rise, output and employment fall because demand falls. This is in spite of the fact that real wages (wages divided by prices) have fallen. At lower real wages—at higher prices—firms are willing to supply more. That is why the aggregate supply curve is upward sloping. But what is limiting output is demand, not supply, and at the higher prices, demand is lower.

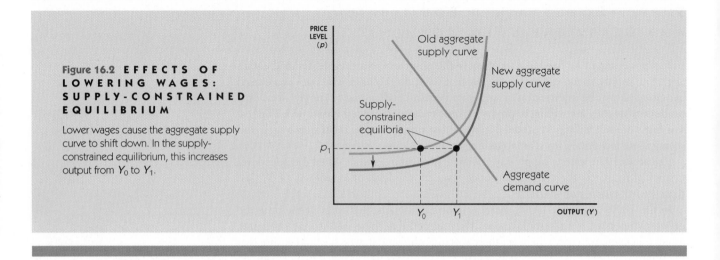

Figure 16.2 EFFECTS OF LOWERING WAGES: SUPPLY-CONSTRAINED EQUILIBRIUM

Lower wages cause the aggregate supply curve to shift down. In the supply-constrained equilibrium, this increases output from Y_0 to Y_1.

By contrast, in the supply-constrained equilibrium (at p_1 in the figure), as prices rise, output and employment rise (again, assuming wages are fixed). The reason that high price levels lead to greater employment is that with fixed wages, at higher prices, firms are willing to produce more; and to produce more, they must hire more labour. In the supply-constrained equilibrium, they can always sell what they produce; what is limiting production is not sales but the profitability of further production.

Classical economists focused on high real wages as the cause of unemployment. Thus, they argued that a lowering of wages would increase the amount that firms are willing to produce at each price level—the aggregate supply curve would shift, as in Figure 16.2. If the economy is in a supply-constrained equilibrium—with the price level at p_1 below that at which demand equals supply—this can have a large effect on the amount produced, increasing production from Y_0 to Y_1.

While the classical economists argued that a (real) wage cut was all that was required to restore full employment, Keynes, focusing on a demand-constrained equilibrium rather than a supply-constrained equilibrium, argued that reductions in wages might actually be harmful; workers, receiving lower wages, would reduce their demand, thus shifting the aggregate demand curve to the left, as illustrated in Figure 16.3. Keynes ignored the effect of wage changes on aggregate supply, because he thought that what limited production was aggregate demand. He thought that typically when there was unemployment, the price level was high, such as p_0 in the figure, above the level at which aggregate demand equalled aggregate supply. The lower wages shift aggregate demand to the left and thus *decrease* output and employment. Keynes argued that the remedy to the problem of low output and high unemployment advocated by the classical economists would actually exacerbate the economy's problems, not alleviate them.

SHIFTS IN THE AGGREGATE DEMAND AND SUPPLY CURVES

Keynes thought that government should respond to economic downturns by stimulating aggregate expenditures somehow. Figure 16.4 reviews how this is done, beginning

Figure 16.3 EFFECTS OF LOWERING WAGES: DEMAND-CONSTRAINED EQUILIBRIUM

In the demand-constrained equilibrium, lowering wages shifts the aggregate demand curve to the left. This lowers national output from Y_0 to Y_1. Though there is also a shift in the aggregate supply curve, this is irrelevant, since what determines output is aggregate demand, not supply.

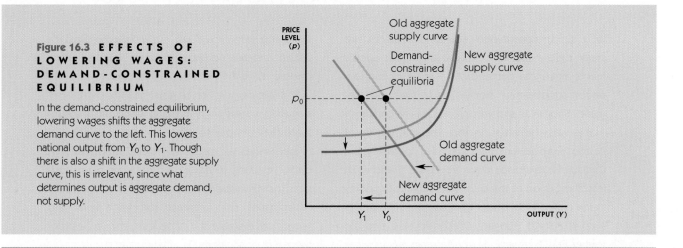

Figure 16.4 EFFECTS OF SHIFTS IN AGGREGATE DEMAND

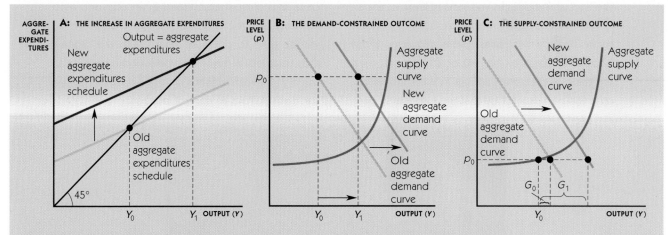

In panel A, an increase in government expenditures shifts the aggregate expenditures schedule up (at any given price level), leading to a higher level of output. As a result, the aggregate demand curve shifts to the right, as depicted in panels B and C. Panel B shows that in the demand-constrained equilibrium, if the government can shift the aggregate demand curve to the right, it can increase output and employment. Panel C shows that in the supply-constrained equilibrium, an increase in aggregate demand has no effect on output; it only increases the gap between aggregate demand and aggregate supply from G_0 to G_1.

Close-up: Supply Constraints in Eastern Europe

In a supply-constrained equilibrium, prices are stuck below the level where aggregate supply meets aggregate demand. As a result of the low prices, suppliers are not willing to meet the demand. Shortages and waiting in lines are common.

This was the situation that the economies of Eastern Europe faced for decades following the Communist takeovers after World War II and even into the period of transition to a market economy in the early 1990s. Under communism, in countries such as Poland, Hungary, Czechoslovakia, and the former East Germany, most consumer prices were fixed by law. Upon winning their political independence in the late 1980s and early 1990s, many of these countries decided to make their producers autonomous and allow them to compete. However, many of the price controls remained in place.

If these nations do not allow prices to move, then suppliers will not expand their production. The lines and shortages will remain. If prices are allowed to increase, then a sizable burst of inflation seems likely, which raises several problems. If the price level jumps by, say, 30 or 40 percent, then the value of everyone's savings in the entire economy will be reduced by that amount. Many pensions and wage levels are not indexed against inflation and are not high to begin with, so many people will suffer from the higher price level.

The natural instinct of governments, when besieged by voters angry at being worse off, is to legislate raises in pay to offset the rise in prices. But higher wages will cause aggregate supply to shift back, resulting in additional pressure from business for still higher prices. If a scenario unfolds in which price rises increase the wage level and wage rises increase the price level, then a destructive cycle of accelerating inflation can begin.

A supply-constrained equilibrium offers no escape from these hard choices. One possible option, the one adopted by Poland and other countries, is to allow a onetime price rise, but then to use fiscal and monetary policy to avoid continuing inflation and to enact social programs to alleviate poverty. Those who find the value of their wages or savings diminished, at least in an economy that has escaped the supply-constrained equilibrium, will be able to purchase goods with the money they have left. A major drawback of this solution is the high unemployment that may (as in Poland) result from policies to control inflation.

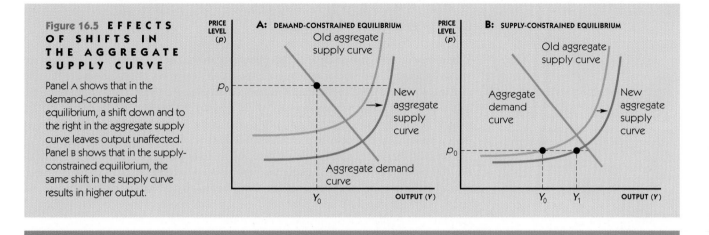

Figure 16.5 EFFECTS OF SHIFTS IN THE AGGREGATE SUPPLY CURVE

Panel A shows that in the demand-constrained equilibrium, a shift down and to the right in the aggregate supply curve leaves output unaffected. Panel B shows that in the supply-constrained equilibrium, the same shift in the supply curve results in higher output.

with the familiar income-expenditure analysis diagram. By lowering taxes, increasing expenditures, or stimulating investment or exports, the government shifts the aggregate expenditures schedule upwards (panel A), so that at each level of income aggregate expenditures are higher. This means that if the economy is in a demand-constrained equilibrium at the given price level, firms are willing to supply more. Thus, an upward shift in the aggregate expenditures schedule means that at the given price level, equilibrium output is higher. The resulting rightward shift in the aggregate demand curve is shown in panel B, with the resulting increase in output (at the given price level) from Y_0 to Y_1.

By contrast, if the economy is in a supply-constrained equilibrium, as in panel C, the shift in the aggregate demand curve is completely irrelevant. What limits production is supply; and the shift in demand does nothing but increase the gap between demand and supply, from G_0 to G_1.

A completely symmetric argument applies to shifts in the aggregate supply curve. Assume somehow the government could, say through a cut in tax rates, engineer a rightward shift in the supply curve, as illustrated in Figure 16.5. In the demand-constrained equilibrium of panel A, this shift in the aggregate supply curve has no effect. In the supply-constrained equilibrium of panel B, the shift leads to increased output.

ECONOMIC POLICY

In effect, Keynes and the classical economists focused on two different sides of the supply and demand scissors. The classical economists ignored the effect of wage changes on aggregate demand, because they thought that what limited production was aggregate supply. Wage changes were, in their view, desirable, because they shifted the aggregate supply curve and led to higher levels of output and employment. Keynes argued that cutting wages was counterproductive because it reduced aggregate demand, and it was aggregate demand that limited output. And since it was aggregate demand that limited output, Keynes thought that government actions to stimulate aggregate demand were effective in increasing national output. The classical economists, focusing on supply-constrained situations, argued that increasing aggregate demand would do no good.

WHO RULES THE ROOST: DEMAND OR SUPPLY?

When we combine the analysis of this chapter with that of the preceding chapters, we see that there are two situations where demand rules the roost: when prices are flexible and the economy finds itself along the horizontal, excess-capacity section of the aggregate supply curve; and when prices are sticky and set at a level above that at which aggregate demand equals aggregate supply. Under either of these circumstances, changes in demand translate directly into changes in output.

Likewise, there are two situations where supply rules the roost: when prices are flexible and the economy operates along the vertical section of the aggregate supply curve; and when prices are sticky and set at a level below that at which aggregate demand equals aggregate supply. Under either of these circumstances, changes in demand are irrelevant, but shifts in the supply curve determine what happens to output.

DEMAND-CONSTRAINED EQUILIBRIUM

In a demand-constrained equilibrium, the price level is above that at which aggregate demand equals aggregate supply. Output is determined by the intersection of the price level and the aggregate demand curve; an increase in aggregate demand is therefore translated directly into an increase in aggregate output. Shifts in the aggregate supply curve have no effect on equilibrium output.

SUPPLY-CONSTRAINED EQUILIBRIUM

In a supply-constrained equilibrium, the price level is below that at which aggregate demand equals aggregate supply. Output is determined by the intersection of the price level and the aggregate supply curve; an increase in aggregate supply is therefore translated directly into an increase in aggregate output. Shifts in the aggregate demand curve have no effect on equilibrium output.

THE SHAPES OF THE CURVES AND THE ROLE OF PRICE RIGIDITIES

In Chapter 15, we saw that the aggregate demand curve is normally fairly inelastic, while the aggregate supply curve has two portions, a relatively flat initial range and a relatively steep range as the economy approaches its capacity. The shape of these curves have some interesting implications.

We have already seen one of these: when the initial equilibrium lies along the almost horizontal portion of the aggregate supply curve, then shifts in the aggregate demand curve have an effect only on output. Figure 16.6A shows the effect of a leftward shift in this situation. If prices are flexible, they fall from p_0 to p_1, and output falls from Y_0 to Y_1. If prices are sticky and remain at p_0, then output falls only slightly more, to Y_2. Whether prices are rigid or not makes little difference.

Now let's look at what happens when the initial equilibrium is in a steeper portion of the aggregate supply curve, as shown in panel B. The shift in the aggregate demand curve leads to a larger reduction in the price level. Because of the large price change, price rigidity now has more important consequences for output. The difference between the output with flexible prices, Y_1, and the output with price rigidities, Y_2, is much larger; price rigidities here are responsible for much of the output decrease.

Thus, the inelasticity of aggregate demand has important consequences for prices but not output when the initial situation occurs in the vertical portion of the aggregate sup-

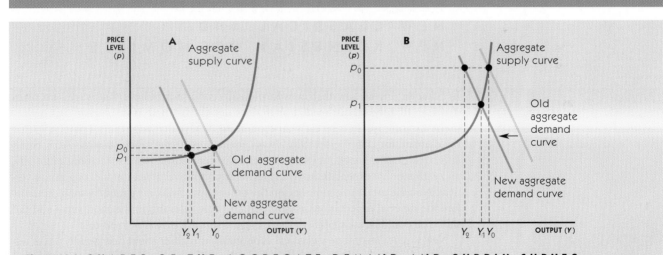

Figure 16.6 SHAPES OF THE AGGREGATE DEMAND AND SUPPLY CURVES AND THE ROLE OF PRICE RIGIDITIES

In panel A, the initial equilibrium is along the relatively horizontal portion of the aggregate supply curve; there is little difference between the effect of a leftward shift in the aggregate demand curve when prices are flexible and when they are sticky. In panel B, where the aggregate supply curve is very inelastic (steep), there is a large difference in the change in the level of output induced by a shift in the aggregate demand curve to the left, depending on whether prices are flexible or sticky.

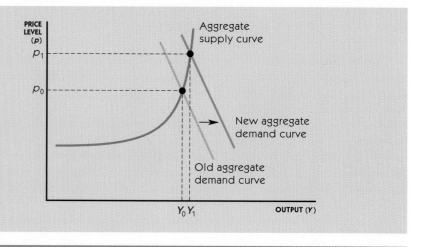

Figure 16.7 VERTICAL AGGREGATE SUPPLY CURVE AND PRICE RIGIDITIES

If the initial equilibrium occurs in the portion of the aggregate supply curve that is nearly vertical, then a rightward shift in the aggregate demand curve will have little effect on output, even if prices are perfectly flexible. The change in the price level, however, may be very large.

ply curve, as Figure 16.7 illustrates. A small shift in the aggregate demand curve to the right can lead to a large increase in the price level but have little effect on output.

PRICE RIGIDITIES AND NEW CLASSICAL AND NEW KEYNESIAN ECONOMISTS

In Chapter 15, we saw that new Keynesian economists believe that wages are often sticky, so that the labour market often does not clear—there is involuntary unemployment. By contrast, the new classical economists believe that wages adjust rapidly, so that the demand for labour essentially always equals supply; the labour market clears. Similarly, new classical economists argue that individuals form their expectations rationally, and with rational expectations the aggregate supply curve, at least in the long run, is vertical. New Keynesian economists, on the other hand, think it might take some time before the rational expectations assumption becomes relevant; in the short run—and the short run could be a long time—the aggregate supply curve is not vertical.

New Keynesian and new classical economists also differ about how rapidly prices adjust. Again, the new Keynesians line up on the side of rigidities, while the new classical economists see rapid price adjustment. If prices are sticky, even if the aggregate supply curve is vertical (as the new classical economists suppose), output may be limited by aggregate demand. If for some reason prices are sufficiently high that aggregate demand is less than aggregate supply, then even with a vertical supply curve a shift in aggregate demand can be effective in increasing output and employment. In Figure 16.8, a rightward shift in the aggregate demand curve at the price p_0 increases output from Y_0 to Y_1.

Our earlier analysis of market equilibrium suggested that when, at the going market price, supply exceeds demand, there are forces at work to lower prices. Firms that would like to supply more but cannot sell their goods try to undercut other firms. The same

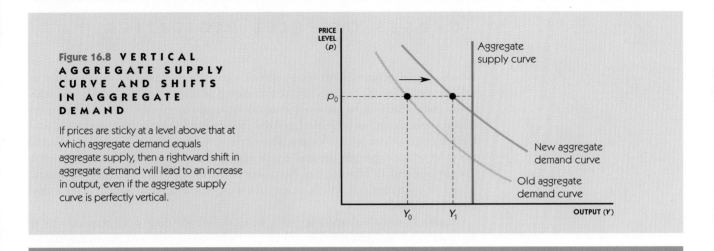

Figure 16.8 VERTICAL AGGREGATE SUPPLY CURVE AND SHIFTS IN AGGREGATE DEMAND

If prices are sticky at a level above that at which aggregate demand equals aggregate supply, then a rightward shift in aggregate demand will lead to an increase in output, even if the aggregate supply curve is perfectly vertical.

principle applies at the aggregate level. When prices are in the demand-constrained range, where supply exceeds demand, there are forces at work to lower prices.

The Keynesian conclusion—that shifting the aggregate demand curve may be an effective way of stimulating the economy—is correct so long as prices do not adjust instantaneously. If prices are slow to adjust, then the government may be able to shift the aggregate demand curve, increasing aggregate output by a considerable amount, before the vertical supply constraints become binding. There is more than just an effect on the price level, even though the aggregate supply curve is vertical: output and employment may be increased.

NEW CLASSICAL AND NEW KEYNESIAN ECONOMISTS AND STICKY PRICES

NEW CLASSICAL ECONOMISTS	NEW KEYNESIAN ECONOMISTS
Prices are flexible, so that equilibrium always occurs at the intersection of the aggregate demand and supply curves. With a vertical aggregate supply curve, output is determined in effect by aggregate supply; shifts in aggregate demand only affect the price level.	Prices are sticky, so that equilibrium may not be at the intersection of the aggregate demand and aggregate supply curves. If the price level is above that at which aggregate demand equals aggregate supply, increases in aggregate demand increase output, even if the aggregate supply curve is vertical.

CAUSES OF PRICE RIGIDITIES

New Keynesian economists disagree with new classical economists on several counts, as we have seen. New Keynesians believe that even if prices are flexible and adjust quickly to the point where aggregate demand equals aggregate supply, the supply curve in the relevant period may not be vertical, and the equilibrium level of output may be less than the full-employment level of output. Price flexibility—the ability of prices to adjust to the point where aggregate demand equals aggregate supply—by itself does not ensure full employment. But further, new Keynesian economists see the existence of significant price and wage rigidities, which, as we have seen, may exacerbate output and employment fluctuations.

Chapter 11 explained why wages may be rigid. But why do prices not quickly fall to the level at which aggregate demand equals aggregate supply? New Keynesian economists have put forward three groups of explanations. All the explanations are based on the hypothesis that at least in the short run, the rules of imperfect competition—in which firms have some control over the prices they charge—rule the economy. That is, if businesses raise their prices a little bit, they will not lose all of their customers, and if they lower their prices a little bit, they will not capture all of the market. Several of the theories are complementary; they emphasize different aspects of the price-setting decision facing firms.

MENU COSTS

The first explanation for price rigidities emphasizes the costs of changing prices. When firms change their prices, they must print new menus and price lists or otherwise convey the change in prices to their customers. Changing prices costs money, and these costs are referred to as **menu costs.** Menu costs may be large, but advocates of the menu-cost explanation of price rigidities, who include Gregory Mankiw of Harvard University and George Akerlof and Janet Yellen of the University of California at Berkeley, point out that even small costs can have big effects.

Let's use an analogy from physics. A ball rolling on a frictionless plane will roll on forever. Just as a small amount of friction has a big effect on how the ball behaves—it eventually will stop—so too if each firm in the economy is slow to adjust its prices because of menu costs, even if these costs are small, the cumulative effects could still be significant. There could be powerful aggregate price rigidities.

RISK AND IMPERFECT INFORMATION

A second explanation has to do with risk. When the economy goes into a downturn, firms face a shift in their demand curve. They must decrease either their price or their output. Businesspeople must make decisions about how much to cut each. In many industries, businesses focus most of their attention on adjusting output rather than price because the uncertainties associated with changing prices may be much greater than those associated with changing output.

CLOSE-UP: MENU COSTS AND MAGAZINES

In January 1982, a copy of *Business Week* cost U.S. $2. In February 1991, it still cost U.S. $2. But during that time, prices in general increased by about 50 percent, which means that the real price of the magazine had actually fallen sharply. Surely *Business Week* knows the rate of inflation. So why was the price of the magazine so sticky? Why didn't it move at all for nine years?

Business Week is not alone in this pattern. One study analyzed price changes of thirty-eight magazines in the United States from 1950 to 1980 and found that magazines allow inflation to erode their cover prices by nearly one-fourth, on average, before raising their price. Over the time of this study, about one-third of all magazines were sold in the form of single copies, rather than by subscription.

This pattern of sticky prices is not unique to magazines, and it makes the point that choosing or changing a price can be among the toughest decisions for a business. In economists' usage, "tough" means costly. As Gregory Mankiw of Harvard University has written, "The act of altering a posed price is certainly costly. These costs include such items as printing new catalogs and informing salesmen of the new price. . . . More metaphorically and more realistically, these menu costs include the time taken to inform customers, the customer annoyance caused by price changes, and the effort required even to think about a price change."

No one denies that menu costs exist or that they provide a reason for individual companies to wait for a time before altering prices, rather than raising prices a bit each year. However, economists remain divided over whether menu costs are a powerful enough factor, taken alone, to explain economy-wide price stickiness.

Sources: N. Gregory Mankiw, "Small Menu Costs and Large Business Cycles: A Macroeconomic Model of Monopoly," *Quarterly Journal of Economics:* 529–37; Mankiw, "A Quick Refresher Course in Macroeconomics," *Journal of Economic Literature* (December 1990): 1645–60; Stephen G. Cecchetti, *Journal of Econometrics* (1986): 255–74.

There are several reasons for this. When a firm lowers its price, whether sales increase or not depends on how other firms in the industry respond and how its customers respond. Customers may think that this is just the first of several price decreases, and decide to postpone purchases until prices get still lower. (In Chapter 15, we saw how expectations of future prices affect households' decisions about when to buy goods.) Customers may simply decide to wait to see how other firms behave. On the other hand, when a firm cuts back on its production, provided it does not cut back too much, its only risk is that its inventories will be depleted below normal levels, and that the firm will have to increase production next period to replace the lost inventories. But if production costs are likely to be approximately the same in both periods, there is little extra cost—and little extra risk—to this strategy.

KINKED DEMAND CURVES

A third group of explanations attribute price rigidities to the shape of demand curves facing firms under imperfect competition. Recall that with perfect competition, a firm faces a horizontal demand curve. With imperfect competition, a firm faces a downward-sloping demand curve; in particular, the demand curve may have a kink, as illustrated in Figure 16.9. The kink means that firms believe that they lose many more sales when they raise prices above p_0 than they gain when they lower prices below p_0.

There are two reasons why the demand curve may be kinked—that is, why there are very different responses to price increases and price decreases. One is that companies believe that if they raise their prices, their own customers will immediately know it and will start searching for stores selling the good at a lower price; but if they lower their prices without heavy expenditures on advertising, customers at other stores may not find out about their lower prices, so they gain few new customers.

Another reason is that firms worry that if they raise their prices their rivals will not match the increase, and hence they will suffer from their relatively uncompetitive

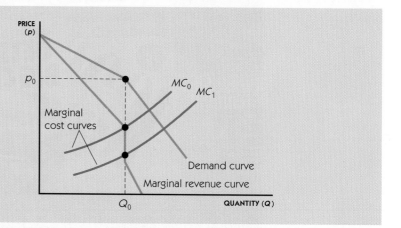

Figure 16.9 KINKED DEMAND CURVES AND PRICE INFLEXIBILITY

If firms lose many more sales from price increases than they gain from price decreases, their demand curve will be kinked. When the demand curve is kinked, the marginal revenue curve has a vertical section, and small changes in marginal cost will not lead to any change in price or output.

prices. But if they lower their prices, rivals will view this as a threat and will match the decrease, and the firm will gain little from its attempt to beat the market.

Kinked demand curves have one dramatic implication: small changes in marginal costs may have no effect on the price firms charge. Even if the company's costs go down, it will continue to charge the price at the kink, p_0 in the Figure 16.9. Firms worry, for instance, that if they cut their price in response to the lower marginal cost, other firms will simply match them and they will be no better off. Thus, kinked demand curves give rise to price rigidities: small changes, perhaps resulting from a fall in wages, have absolutely no effect on either the output or pricing decisions of the firm.[1]

REVIEW AND PRACTICE

SUMMARY

1. If the price level is stuck above the level at which aggregate demand equals aggregate supply, then demand is less than supply, output equals aggregate demand, and the economy is in a demand-constrained equilibrium. If the price level is stuck below the level at which aggregate demand equals aggregate supply, then supply is less than demand, output equals aggregate supply, and the economy is in a supply-constrained equilibrium.

2. Unemployment in the demand-constrained equilibrium, referred to as Keynesian unemployment, is reduced when the aggregate demand curve shifts to the right. Shifts in the supply curve have no effect on output. Unemployment in the supply-constrained equilibrium, referred to as classical unemployment, is reduced when the aggregate supply curve shifts to the right. Shifts in the aggregate demand curve have no effect on output.

3. If the economy is operating in the flat portion of the aggregate supply curve, then shifts in aggregate demand and supply will have approximately the same impact on national output whether prices are flexible or not. When the economy is operating in the upward-sloping portion of the aggregate supply curve, then price rigidity makes a difference: for instance, a rightward shift in the aggregate demand curve has no effect on output if prices are rigid, but a positive effect if prices are flexible.

[1] To see this more formally, we have to look carefully at the marginal revenue curve. Marginal revenue—the extra revenue a firm receives from selling an extra unit—has a jump at the output corresponding to the kink. The firm gains less revenue from lowering its price than it loses when it raises the price. When there is a jump in marginal revenue, we replace the condition that "marginal revenue equals marginal cost" with a new one: marginal revenue from increasing output must be less than marginal cost (it does not pay to expand output); and the marginal revenue from the last unit produced must exceed the marginal cost (it does not pay to reduce output). With the marginal cost curve MC_0, the firm depicted in Figure 16.9 is in equilibrium, producing Q_0 units of the good and selling these units at price p_0. The marginal revenue for increases in output are less than marginal costs: it does not pay to expand production. And for decreases in output, the marginal revenue is greater than marginal costs. It does not pay to reduce production, since the loss in revenue would exceed the reduction in costs. Output remains unchanged even when marginal cost shifts to MC_1.

4. New Keynesian economists believe that prices are sticky, and if they are stuck above the level at which aggregate demand equals aggregate supply, aggregate demand rules the roost. New classical economists believe that prices are flexible and the aggregate supply curve is vertical, so that output is determined by aggregate supply.

5. New Keynesian economists have proposed three reasons why prices may be slow to adjust to the level at which aggregate demand equals aggregate supply. Firms may face menu costs; firms may adjust output rather than prices during a recession because the uncertainties associated with changing prices may be greater; and firms may face kinked demand curves, and with kinked demand curves they may not change prices even when marginal costs change.

KEY TERMS

demand-constrained equilibrium
supply-constrained equilibrium

Keynesian unemployment
classical unemployment

menu costs

REVIEW QUESTIONS

1. What is a demand-constrained equilibrium? a supply-constrained equilibrium? What is Keynesian unemployment? classical unemployment?

2. How do new Keynesian and new classical economists differ in their views about the consequences of changes in prices and wages and shifts in the aggregate demand and aggregate supply curves? How do they differ in their views about policies to help reduce unemployment?

3. What are the two situations in which demand rules the roost? in which supply rules the roost?

4. Under what circumstances does the fact that the aggregate demand curve is inelastic make a difference? Are the consequences of price stickiness different depending on whether the economy is operating along the horizontal or the vertical portion of the aggregate supply curve? Explain.

5. How are the new classical and new Keynesian economists' views about price stickiness different? What are the implications of those differences in views?

6. Name and explain three reasons why prices in the aggregate market for goods and services may be slow to adjust.

PROBLEMS

1. Suppose the economy begins in equilibrium between aggregate demand and supply, but the price level does not change. Illustrate the fact that a rightward shift

and a leftward shift in aggregate demand will not have symmetric effects. Will a rightward shift and a leftward shift in aggregate supply have symmetric effects? Why or why not?

2. There are two ways in which the aggregate supply curve can shift: increased excess capacity can lead to rightward shifts, and reduced wages can lead to downward shifts. Under what circumstances will the consequences of these two forms of shifts be the same? Under what circumstances will they be different?

3. Imagine that the aggregate market for goods and services begins in a demand-constrained equilibrium, but the price level begins to adjust and moves the economy towards equilibrium. Assume that the supply curve for labour is inelastic. Draw a diagram to show what the falling price level does to the demand curve for labour. Why will the fall in prices put downward pressure on the level of wages?

Assume that this change in the price level alters wages by the same amount. Explain how this resulting change in wages will affect aggregate supply and demand, and how it is possible that the economy may end up at the same level of output as when it started.

4. Under what circumstances would you recommend a reduction in wages as a cure for unemployment? When would such a wage reduction be counterproductive? When might it have little if any effect?

5. Compare the discussion of sticky prices in this chapter with the discussion of wage rigidities in Chapter 11. When wages are above the equilibrium level, at which demand equals supply, what determines the employment level? When prices are above the equilibrium level, what determines output? When wages are above the equilibrium level, what are the consequences of a shift in the demand curve for labour? in the supply curve for labour? When prices are above the equilibrium level, what are the consequences of a shift in the aggregate demand curve? of the aggregate supply curve?

PART THREE

Money's Role

One of the lessons we learned earlier is that all of the markets in the economy are interrelated. What goes on in one market can have important effects on other markets. Nonetheless, to develop our understanding of what goes on in the economy, we need to study one market at a time. That is why in Part Two we concentrated on the labour and product markets, making only passing reference to the capital market.

One of the principal determinants of the level of output is the level of investment. This in turn is affected by the capital market, by the availability of funds for investment and the terms (including interest rates) at which firms can obtain those funds. Indeed, one of the main ways by which the government attempts to affect the level of economic activity is through monetary policy, which affects interest rates and the availability of funds.

There is another important reason for focusing attention on the capital market. The central policy concern of Part Two was unemployment. But another major policy concern is inflation, and inflation too is intimately linked to monetary policy.

This part consists of four chapters. Chapter 17 explains what money is, why people hold money, and how the government uses monetary policy to control the money supply. Chapter 18 takes up the question of how and when monetary policy affects the economy in the simple case where the rest of the world can be ignored. Chapter 19 turns to the more realistic situation of monetary policy in an international context. Finally, Chapter 20 focuses on the policy issue of price stability and inflation. It asks, what causes inflation, what are the costs of inflation, and what are the costs of fighting inflation?

MONEY, BANKING, AND CREDIT

S ome say money is the root of all evil. Some say money makes the world go 'round. Actually, in one sense, money does not *do* anything. Money is not a factory or a new invention or a skill that can be taught. While part of the economy is made up of real people working with real machines to make goods that satisfy needs directly, for the most part money is just dumb paper and a ledger mark in a bank account that satisfies needs only indirectly, when it is spent. Yet controlling the supply of money is considered an important function for the government of every industrialized country, and failure to exercise that control has been blamed for inflations and depressions. How can money have such importance? This chapter and the next two will explain what money is from an economist's point of view, why money is important, and why it is sometimes given too much credit or blame for what happens in the economy and in people's lives.

KEY QUESTIONS

1. What *is* money? What economic functions does it serve?

2. What is meant by the money supply, and how is it measured?

3. What institutions in our economy are responsible for controlling the money supply and determining monetary policy?

4. How do modern economies create money through the banking system? How do monetary authorities affect the creation of money and the availability of credit? How do they, in other words, affect the supply of money and credit?

MONEY IS WHAT MONEY DOES

The term "money" is used in a variety of ways, and not just to mean currency and coins. When someone asks you how much money you make, he means what is your income. When someone says, "He has a lot of money," she means he is wealthy, not that he has stashed away lots of currency. When someone accuses corporations of being "interested only in making money," what she really means is that the corporations are interested only in making profits.

Economists use the term "money" in a much narrower sense. Their definition begins with the paper and metal, the currency and coins, that people exchange for goods and services. But these dollar bills and nickels represent only a fraction of what economists call money. They define money by the functions it serves, and it is necessary to look first at these functions before learning a formal definition of money.

MONEY AS A MEDIUM OF EXCHANGE

Trade that occurs without money is called **barter.** Barter involves a simple exchange of one good or service for another. Most examples of barter are fairly simple: two families agree to take turns baby-sitting for each other, or a doctor and a lawyer agree to trade consultations. Nations sometimes sign treaties phrased in barter terms; a certain amount of oil, for example, might be traded for a certain amount of machinery or weapons.

Barter works best in simple economies: one can imagine an old-style farmer bartering with the blacksmith, the tailor, the grocer, and the doctor in his small town. For simple barter to work, however, there must be a **double coincidence of wants.** That is, one individual must have what the other wants, and vice versa. Henry has potatoes and wants shoes, Joshua has an extra pair of shoes and wants potatoes; by bartering they can both be made happier. But if Henry has firewood and Joshua does not need any of that, then bartering for his shoes becomes very difficult, unless Henry and Joshua go searching for more people in the hope that they will be able to make a multilateral exchange. Money provides a way to make multilateral exchange much simpler; Henry sells his firewood to someone else for money and uses the money to buy Joshua's shoes. The convenience of money becomes even clearer when one considers the billions of exchanges that take place in a modern economy. The use of money to facilitate exchange is called the **medium of exchange** function of money.

A wide variety of items have served the medium of exchange function. Indeed, to a large extent, the item chosen as "money" can be thought of as a social convention: the reason that you accept money in payment for what you sell is that others will accept it for things you want to buy. Different cultures in different times have used all sorts of items as money. North American Indians used wampum, and the early settlers used beaver pelts. On some South Sea islands cowrie shells serve as a medium of exchange. In World War II prisoner-of-war camps and in many prisons of today, cigarettes serve as a medium of exchange.

Any easily transportable and storable good could, in principle, be used as a medium of exchange. For a long time, gold was the major medium of exchange. However, gold has some problems. The value of a gold coin depends on its weight and purity, as well as on the supply and demand for gold in the gold market. It would be expensive to weigh and verify the quality of gold every time you engaged in a transaction. So one of the early functions of governments, up until the twentieth century, was to mint gold coins, certifying their weight and quality. But because gold is soft, it wears with usage. Criminals have also profited by shaving the edges off gold coins. The ridges on Canadian dimes and quarters are a carryover from coins developed to deter this practice.

Today all the developed countries of the world use pieces of paper for money. These are printed by the government specially for this purpose. However, most business transactions use not currency but cheques drawn on banks, credit cards whose balances are paid with cheques, or funds wired from one bank to another. Economists consider chequing account balances to be money, just as currency is, because they are accepted as payment at most places and thus serve the medium of exchange function. Since most people have much more money in their chequing account than they do in their wallets, it should be evident that the economists' measure of the money supply is much larger than the amount of coins and currency in circulation.

MONEY AS A STORE OF VALUE

People will only be willing to exchange what they have to sell for money if they believe that they can later exchange the money for the goods or services they wish to purchase. Thus, for money to serve its role as a medium of exchange, it must hold its value, at least for a short while. This function is known as the **store of value** function of money. There was a time when governments feared that paper money by itself would not be accepted at some time in the future and so paper money was not as good a store of value as gold. People had confidence in paper dollars only because they were backed by gold (if you wished, you could exchange your paper dollars for gold).

Today, however, all major economies have **fiat money,** money that has value because the government says it has value and because people are willing to accept it in exchange for goods. The Bank of Canada note (bill) in your wallet recognizes this need for security with its simple message: "This note is legal tender." The fact that it is legal tender means that if you owe someone $100, you have fully discharged that debt if you give her

CLOSE-UP: HISTORICAL PERSPECTIVES ON MONEY CREATION

We have seen that today most money is created within the banking system. But this has not always been the case. When money consisted primarily of gold and silver, the money supply was determined by accidents of fate: the discovery of new sources of these metals. The discovery of the New World, for instance, with its stocks of gold and silver, greatly increased the money supply of Europe in the sixteenth and seventeenth centuries.

With the advent of flat money, expansion of the money supply was a government decision: how fast should the printing presses be run? When the government's revenues fell short of its expenditures and it could not borrow or found borrowing to be too expensive, it paid for expenditures with newly printed money.

In the early days of colonization and settlement of Canada, money consisted of various gold and silver coins, referred to as "specie." Much of it was sent by the imperial government to pay for both the military and the civil administration. Other coins, such as Spanish and American silver dollars,

French louis d'ors, and Johannes from Portugal, were acquired in trade.

The system worked reasonably well in normal times. But sometimes cash flow crises occurred when the coin sent from the imperial government in Europe to the colonial government arrived late or was insufficient to meet extraordinary expenditure requirements, especially during times of war. Two episodes illustrate the problem, one under the French regime and one under the British.

In 1685, the government of the colony of New France did not receive its supply of silver coin from France until September. In order to finance expenditures such as supplies and solders' wages within the colony, the government was forced to be inventive—it issued cut-up playing cards bearing the signatures of senior administrators. These were declared legal tender and redeemable in coin or bills once the shipment came in from France. This playing-card monetary regime was eventually accepted by the colonials, who developed confidence in the government's promise to redeem the

cards and who recognized the convenience and the advantages of the system. The money was light, easy to produce, and less costly than shipping coin. It was also reliable, and it stayed within the colony as it was useless elsewhere. The paper money was supposed to be backed by coins that arrived from France each autumn, but confidence in it was lost when, during the war with the English between 1749 and 1759, more paper money was issued than could be redeemed. When the British took Quebec in 1759, they promptly removed the French paper money from circulation, leaving coins as the only currency.

The British colonial government was reluctant to issue monetary notes, as it viewed the playing-card episode in New France as a failure. But the specie system was unable to cope with the demand for funds to finance its expenditures in the War of 1812. Britain was preoccupied with Napoleon in Europe and could not afford to send to Canada adequate funds to cover soldiers' wages, munitions, and fortifications. The result was a cash-flow crisis in British North America.

At the time, the colonial government did not have seigniorage powers (that is, the power to mint money). Its budget was decided overseas, and the monies were shipped as the imperial government saw fit. Domestic and international capital markets were unsophisticated and were not accessible for borrowing as they are today. The response of Sir Isaac Brock, the colonial administrator and commander of the British forces against the Americans in the War of 1812, was to issue paper money referred to as "army bills" to pay for the war. The money was issued in various denominations, redeemable in coin at the government's discretion. An interest rate of 4 percent was paid on bills of $25 and over. The war was short, so the government did not overextend itself, but redeemed the army bills in 1814 at full value plus interest. The experiment was considered a success since the funds crisis had been resolved and the notes had served as a convenient temporary medium of exchange. Confidence was restored in paper money, paving the way for its issue by the commercial banks shortly after the war ended.

The convenience of note issuance motivated the government to allow private banks to issue their own bank notes, convertible into gold coin. Two of the first to do so, around 1820, were the Bank of Montreal and the Bank of Nova Scotia. Private banks enjoyed sovereignty, as they profited greatly from the practice. The government finally introduced Dominion Notes in 1867. Private bank notes were convertible either into Dominion Notes or directly into specie, and Dominion Notes were convertible into specie.

Convertibility of notes to gold was suspended during World War I, but the gold standard did not break down until 1929. During the years of the Great Depression (1929–1933), Canada, along with most of the nations in the international system, experienced serious deflation. Lenders like deflation: they prefer to be paid back with dollars that are worth more than they were at the time the loan was made. By the same token, debtors dislike deflation, for it means they have to pay off their loans with money that is worth more. Thus farmers and others who are in debt are often at odds with the banks to which they owe money. In deflationary times, this conflict is often resolved in the debtors' favour by printing money and inflating the economy, even when the government cannot afford to convert its entire money supply into its existing stock of gold. Such was the situation during the Great Depression, with the final breakdown of the gold standard occurring in 1929.

Sources: H. H. Binhammer, *Money, Banking and the Canadian Financial System,* 5th ed. (Scarborough, Ontario: Nelson Canada, 1988); Norman E. Cameron, *Money, Financial Markets and Economic Activity,* 2nd ed. (Don Mills, Ontario: Addison-Wesley, 1992).

a hundred-dollar bill. The view that anything, even money, will retain its value just because the government says so flies in the face of the economic theory of demand and supply. One of the important functions of monetary policy, as we will see in Chapter 34, is to maintain the value of fiat money.

There are many other stores of value. Gold, which is no longer "money" because it no longer serves as a medium of exchange, nevertheless continues to serve as a store of value. In India, for instance, people hold much of their savings in the form of gold. The gold in Fort Knox in the United States is still there and worth billions of dollars. Land, corporate stocks and bonds, oil and minerals, are all stores of value. Of course, none of them is perfectly safe, in the sense that you cannot be precisely sure what they can be exchanged for in the future. But currency, chequing account balances, and other forms of money are not perfectly safe stores of value either. If prices change, then the dollars in your pocket or your bank account will be able to buy less or more.

MONEY AS A UNIT OF ACCOUNT

In performing its roles as a medium of exchange and a store of value, money serves a third purpose: it is a way of measuring the relative values of different goods. This is the **unit of account** function of money. If a banana costs 25 cents and a peach 50 cents, then a peach is worth twice as much as a banana. A person who wishes to trade bananas for peaches can do so at the rate of two bananas for one peach. Money thus provides a simple and convenient yardstick for measuring relative market values.

Imagine how difficult it would be for firms to keep track of how well they were doing without such a yardstick. The ledgers might describe how many of each item the firm bought or sold. But the fact that the firm sold more items than it purchased would tell you nothing. You need to know the value of what the firm sells relative to the value of what it purchased; money provides the unit of account, the means by which the firm and others take these measurements.

We are now ready for the economic definition of **money.** Money is anything that is generally accepted as a medium of exchange, a store of value, and a unit of account. Money is, in other words, what money does.

MEASURING THE MONEY SUPPLY

The quantity of money is called the **money supply,** a stock variable like the capital stock. Most of the other variables discussed in this chapter are stock variables as well, but they have important effects on the flow variables (like the level of economic activity, measured as dollars *per year*).

We have already seen that measuring the supply of money is not so simple as counting the number of dollars of currency and coins in circulation. The question is, what should be included in the money supply? A variety of items serve some of the functions of money, but not all of them. For example, the chips issued in casinos for gambling serve as a medium of exchange inside the casino and perhaps even in some nearby

CLOSE-UP: A GLOSSARY OF FINANCIAL TERMS

One of the problems in defining money is that there are many assets that are not directly used as a medium of exchange but can be readily converted into something that could be used as a medium of exchange. Should they be included in the money supply? There is no right or wrong answer. The definition of money is not God-given. Below are definitions of ten terms, some of which were defined in earlier chapters. Each of these assets serves, to some extent, the function of money.

Currency and coins	Two-, five-, ten-, twenty- (and so on) dollar bills, and pennies, nickels, dimes, quarters, and dollar coins.
Traveller's cheques	Cheques issued by a bank or firm, such as American Express, which you can convert into currency on demand.
Demand deposits or chequing accounts	Deposits that you can withdraw upon demand (that is, convert into currency) by simply writing a cheque.
Personal savings deposits	Deposits that technically you can withdraw only upon notice; in practice, banks allow withdrawal upon demand, that is, without notice.
Personal fixed-term deposits	Deposits that are held in specialized forms (for example, Registered Retirement Saving Plans or Quebec Stock Savings Plans), which can offer a higher rate of return or tax advantages and are often designed as personal pension funds and have a penalty for early withdrawal.
Certificates of deposit	Money deposited for a fixed period of time (usually for periods of six months to five years), with a penalty for early withdrawal.
Nonpersonal notice deposits	Deposits that require the depositor to give notice before withdrawing or transferring funds, and that bear higher interest rates than personal savings or demand deposits.
Nonpersonal fixed-term deposits	Similar to nonpersonal notice deposits, except deposited for a fixed term with a penalty for early withdrawal.
Mutual funds in financial institutions	Shares in an investment pool managed by a financial institution comprising such assets as Treasury bills, corporate and public shares and bonds; some financial institutions allow you to convert your shares by writing a cheque.
Eurodollars	U.S. dollar bank accounts in banks outside the United States (mainly in Europe)

stores and restaurants, but no place outside the casino is obligated to take them; they are neither a generally accepted medium of exchange nor a unit of account.

The economists' measure of money begins with the currency and coins that we carry. Economists then expand the measure of money to include anything else that serves the three functions of money as well as they do. Chequing accounts, or

demand deposits, are included in the money supply as are some other forms of accounts in banks and other financial institutions. But if anything that serves the three functions of money is included in the money supply, then what are the limits? There is a continuum here, running from items that everyone would agree should be called money to items that can work as money in many circumstances, to items that can occasionally work as money, to items that would never be considered money.

Economists have thus developed several measures of the money supply. The narrowest, called **M1,** is the total of currency (outside the banks) and demand deposits held in banks. In other words, M1 is currency plus items that through the banking system can be treated like currency. At the end of 1991, M1 totalled $40.5 billion, up from $38.8 billion over the previous year.

A broader measure, **M2,** includes everything that is in M1 plus some items that are *almost* perfect substitutes for M1. Personal savings deposits, daily interest chequing accounts (which combine the features of chequing and savings accounts), and nonpersonal notice deposits are included in M2. At the end of 1991, M2 totalled $279.4 billion, compared with $264 billion a year earlier.

The common characteristic of assets in M2 is that they are very *liquid*, or easily convertible into M1. You cannot just tell a store that the money it requires is in your savings account, but if you have funds in your savings account it is not hard to turn those into something the store will accept. You can transfer funds from your savings account into your chequing account or withdraw them as currency.

A third level of money, **M3,** includes everything that is in M2 (and thus everything that is in M1) plus nonpersonal fixed-term deposits and foreign currency deposits. M3 is just about as liquid as M2. At the end of 1991, M3 totalled $331.2 billion, up from $314 billion at the end of 1990.

In recent years, many other financial institutions have begun to take on some of the traditional roles of banks, including offering both chequing and savings account privileges. This has been a consequence of the rapid change in communications technology as well as lessening of regulation of financial institutions. Since deposits in these nonbank financial institutions fulfill many of the same functions as bank deposits, it is useful to include them in the definition of the money supply. This is done by using an alternative way of expanding M2, referred to as **M2+,** which includes everything in M2 plus deposits in the so-called **near banks.** Near banks include such deposit-taking institutions as trust and mortgage loan companies, credit unions, and caisses populaires, and are discussed further below. At the end of 1991, M2+ totalled $529 billion.

The Bank of Canada regularly publishes the size of M1, M2, M3, and M2+. Figure 17.1 shows the relative magnitude of different measures of the money supply, while Figure 17.2 shows that during the past decade the different measures have grown at different rates.

Recent changes in financial institutions, such as the growth of mutual funds, the more extensive use of credit cards, and home equity loans have made it even more difficult to answer the question of what to include in the money supply. For instance, some asset-trading intermediaries (brokerage firms) such as investment dealers or mutual funds now provide cheque-writing privileges. This makes the investments in these firms as liquid as regular demand deposits, and thus complicates the choice of the appropriate money supply definition.

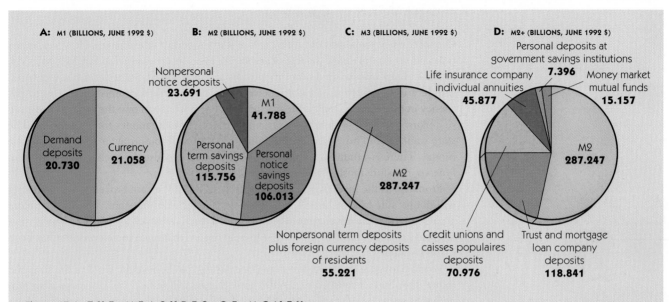

A: M1 (BILLIONS, JUNE 1992 $)   **B:** M2 (BILLIONS, JUNE 1992 $)   **C:** M3 (BILLIONS, JUNE 1992 $)   **D:** M2+ (BILLIONS, JUNE 1992 $)

Demand deposits **20.730**
Currency **21.058**

Nonpersonal notice deposits **23.691**
M1 **41.788**
Personal term savings deposits **115.756**
Personal notice savings deposits **106.013**

M2 **287.247**
Nonpersonal term deposits plus foreign currency deposits of residents **55.221**

Personal deposits at government savings institutions **7.396**
Life insurance company individual annuities **45.877**
Money market mutual funds **15.157**
M2 **287.247**
Credit unions and caisses populaires deposits **70.976**
Trust and mortgage loan company deposits **118.841**

Figure 17.1 THE MEASURES OF MONEY

The money supply can be measured in many ways, including M1, M2, M3, and M2+. *Source: Bank of Canada Review* (Winter 1992–1993), Table E1.

Figure 17.2 GROWTH OF THE MONEY SUPPLY

It makes a difference which measure of the money supply is used. Different measures grew at different rates during the 1980s. *Source: Bank of Canada Review* (various years), Table E1.

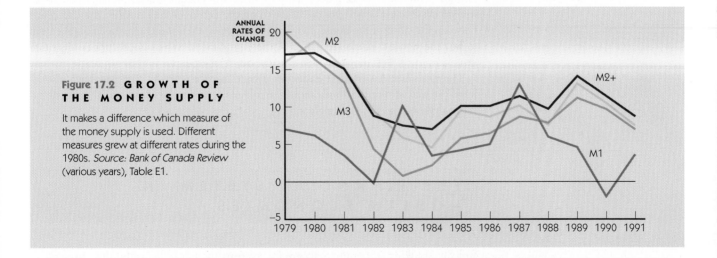

ANNUAL RATES OF CHANGE

M2

M3

M2+

M1

MONEY AND CREDIT

One of the key properties of money is that it is a medium of exchange. However, many transactions do not entail the use of any of the measures presented so far: M1, M2, M3, or M2+. They involve credit, not money. In selling a suit of clothes or a piece of furniture or a car, most stores do not receive money, but rather a promise from you to pay money in the future. Credit is clearly tied to money: what you owe the store is measured in dollars. You want something today, and you will have the money for it tomorrow. The store wants you to buy today and is willing to wait until tomorrow or next week for the money. There is a mutually advantageous trade. But because the exchange is not *simultaneous*, the store must rely on your promise.

Promises, as the saying goes, are often broken. But if they are broken too often, stores will not be able to trust buyers, and credit exchanges will not occur. There is therefore an incentive for the development of institutions, such as banks, to ascertain who is most likely to keep economic promises and to help ensure that once such a promise has been made it is kept.

When banks are involved, the store does not need to believe the word of the shopper; rather, the shopper must convince the bank that he will in fact pay. Consider a car purchase. Suppose a bank agrees to give Luke a loan, and he then buys the car. If he later decides to break his promise and does not pay back the loan, the car dealer is protected. It is the bank that attempts to force Luke to keep his commitment.

As technology has changed, modern economies have increasingly relied on credit as a basis of transactions. Banks have a long tradition of extending **lines of credit** to firms; this means that a bank agrees to lend a business money automatically (up to some limit), as it is needed. With Visa and MasterCard and the variety of other international credit cards that came into widespread use in the 1970s and 1980s, lines of credit have been extended to millions of consumers, who now can purchase goods even when they have no money on hand, in the form of either currency or chequing account balances. Today individuals can also easily get credit based on the equity in their houses (the difference between the value of the house and what they owe on their mortgage, the loan taken out to buy the house). These are called home equity loans. When house prices increased rapidly in the 1980s, they provided a ready source of credit for millions of home owners.

These innovations make it easier for people to obtain credit. But they have also altered the way economists think about the role of money in the economy, blurring definitions that once seemed quite clear.

THE FINANCIAL SYSTEM IN MODERN ECONOMIES

Broadly speaking, a country's **financial system** includes all institutions involved in moving savings from households and firms whose income exceeds their expenditures and transferring it to other households and firms who would like to spend more than their income and liquid assets allow. Here we take a closer look at the most important of these institutions.

FINANCIAL INTERMEDIARIES

The financial system in Canada not only allows consumers to buy cars, televisions, and VCRs even when they do not have the cash to do so, it also enables firms to invest in factories and new machines, to enhance the productivity of the economy and provide jobs for those entering the labour force. Sometimes money goes directly from, say, a household doing some saving to a firm that needs some additional cash. For example, when Ben buys a new bond from Bell Canada promising to pay a fixed amount in 90 or 180 days, or in 5 or 15 years, he is lending money directly to Bell Canada.

But most of the funds flow through **financial intermediaries.** These are firms that stand in between the savers, who have the extra funds, and the borrowers, who need extra funds. The most important group of financial intermediaries is the banks, but there are many other groups of financial intermediaries as well. All are engaged in looking over potential borrowers, ascertaining who are good risks, and monitoring their investments and loans. The intermediaries take "deposits" from consumers and invest them. By putting the funds into many different investments, they diversify and thus reduce the risk. One investment might turn sour, but (with some important exceptions) it is unlikely that many will, and this provides the intermediary with a kind of safety it could not obtain if it put all its eggs in one basket. The different financial institutions differ in who the depositors are, where the funds are invested, and who owns the institutions.

Chartered banks put most of their deposits into loans. Trust companies and mortgage loan companies have traditionally put most of their money into home mortgage lending. Mutual funds put their money into bonds or stocks (or sometimes real estate). Insurance companies put their money into all forms of financial assets. Credit unions and caisses populaires act much like banks, but customers are limited to members; unlike banks, they tend to focus their lending on personal loans, such as financing the purchase of a car or the remodelling of a home. Consumer loan companies provide such loans to the public at large. Retirement funds and pension funds act just like mutual funds, but they hold the funds until individuals retire.

There are also some public institutions that perform some intermediary functions for the public sector. The Bank of Canada acts as the bank for the chartered banks (the "bankers' bank") and also accepts deposits from the federal government. It holds government securities as assets. The Canada Pension Plan is a public pension fund that takes contributions on behalf of all employees outside Quebec and invests them mainly in provincial bonds issued by the remaining nine provinces (and the Territories). The Quebec Pension Plan holds contributions made on behalf of employees in Quebec and invests them in Quebec government bonds and Quebec Crown corporations. There are also federal or provincial public financial institutions that make loans to encourage development of a particular sector of the economy. They raise their funds by issuing shares and bonds as well as accepting deposits.

In Canada, the functions of different types of financial institutions were kept quite separate by restrictive federal and provincial regulation in financial markets, resulting in different types of institutions specializing in different roles. The result was the so-called four-pillar system of financial institutions because it recognized four functions and four types of financial institutions, and assigned one function to each type. Unsecured lending was to be performed by chartered banks and credit unions/caisses populaires; corporate trusteeship by trust companies; securities underwriting and brokerage by invest-

There are a variety of financial intermediaries that take funds from the public and lend them to borrowers or otherwise invest the funds. Though there are many legal differences between these institutions, the principal differences relate to the kinds of loans or investments they make.

Chartered banks	Banks chartered by the federal government under the Bank Act to receive deposits and make loans.
Insurance companies	Companies that collect premiums from policyholders out of which insurance payments are made; they invest in mortgage loans, bonds, and shares.
Trust and mortgage loan companies	Firms that receive deposits and make mostly mortgage loans; trust companies also administer trusteed pension plans on behalf of employees and employers.
Credit unions and caisses populaires	Cooperative (not-for-profit) institutions, originally formed by an occupational group or union, that take deposits or issue shares to members and make loans to members.
Mutual funds	Financial intermediaries that take funds from a group of investors and invest them. They issue shares to invest in a diverse portfolio of common and preferred shares, bonds, and mortgages; they may specialize in one type of financial asset, such as bond mutual funds and stock mutual funds; there can be closed- or open-ended mutual funds.
Sales finance and consumer loan companies	Companies that issue short-term paper and bonds and lend to firms and consumers needing short-term credit.
Investment companies	Companies that issue shares in order to buy long-term into other companies; they may be specialized, such as venture capital companies that lend to promising young firms.
Investment dealers	Retail agents for purchasing financial assets; some (such as brokerage firms) operate cash management accounts that enable people to place stocks, bonds, and other assets into a single account, against which they can write cheques.

ment dealers; and insurance by life or property and casualty insurance companies. These restrictions were argued for not only to limit the power of banks but also to enhance their security, by restricting their participation in the riskier securities industry. But in recent years, the restrictions have come under attack as limiting competition in the securities industry. During the past two decades, a process of deregulation has begun. Not only are the traditional functions of banks being undertaken by other financial institutions, but the banks are also moving into areas, such as dealing in securities, previously restricted to other institutions. In other words, the four pillars are crumbling. Whether the increased competition from deregulation will strengthen the banking industry and thus increase the financial security of the nation's banks, or whether it will lead banks to undertake riskier activities and thus undermine their financial security, remains unclear. Similarly, whether current safeguards against conflicts of interest and other abuses, which originally motivated the regulations, are adequate will become apparent only over time.

THE CENTRAL BANKING SYSTEM

Just as there is a continuum from currency and demand deposits to nonpersonal notice deposits that serve in varying degrees the functions of money, so too is there a continuum of near banks that perform in varying ways the functions that banks perform. For instance, trust companies accept deposits and make loans today in a way that is almost identical to that of banks. Near banks play an important role in our financial system. Their actions affect the supply of money (particularly money in the broader definitions, such as M2, M3, and M2+). Nevertheless, the discussion here focuses on chartered banks and the narrower definition of money, M1. Traditionally, banks have been the most important source of capital for businesses and the focus of government attempts to control the level of investment and hence the level of national economic activity.

Governments today have two objectives in their involvement with the bank portion of the financial system. One objective is to protect consumers: when banks go bankrupt, depositors stand to lose their life's savings. The typical saver is not in a position to audit a bank's books to see whether it is really sound. During the Depression of the 1930s, many banks closed, leaving thousands destitute. Today, banks are more tightly regulated. In addition, depositors are insured by government agencies, to limit their losses should a bankruptcy occur.

The second objective of government involvement in the banking system is to stabilize the level of economic activity. We have seen the important role that the banking system provides in taking funds from savers and providing them to investors. When the banking system collapses, firms cannot obtain funds to make their investments, and the entire economy suffers. More broadly, the banking system, by its actions, affects the level of investment, and this affects the level of economic activity. Sharp declines in investment can throw the economy into a recession; sharp increases can set off an inflationary spiral.

Different economies have developed a variety of institutions and laws for accomplishing these twin objectives. The most important institution in each country is its **central bank.** The central bank is a bank from which other banks can borrow. But it is more than a banker's bank. In each country, the central bank has two main objectives: to stabilize the level of economic activity by controlling the money supply and the availability of credit, and to regulate the banking system to ensure its financial health.

In Canada, the central bank is the **Bank of Canada,** which was established by the Bank of Canada Act of 1934 and nationalized four years later. The Bank is ultimately managed by a Board of Directors consisting of the governor, the senior deputy governor, twelve directors, and the deputy minister of finance (who is a nonvoting member). The directors are appointed by the minister of finance for three-year terms. In turn, the direc-

CLOSE-UP: SHOULD THE BANK OF CANADA ACT BE REFORMED?

Since the formation of the Bank of Canada in the mid-thirties, its mandate and organizational structure have remained largely unchanged. In fact, there has been only one major amendment to the Bank of Canada Act, that of 1967 establishing the right of the minister of finance to issue written directives to the governor, a right that has yet to be exercised. Many would argue that the Bank's mandate, accountability, and governance are badly adapted to the 1990s, given the changes in economic climate as well as the growing importance and needs of regions outside central Canada. Moreover, given that control of Bank policy is in the hands of the governor and a small group of senior officials, there is some feeling that the Bank lacks "legitimacy" and is unresponsive to regional needs.

In recognition of this, in 1991 the federal government proposed a major set of reforms to the Bank of Canada Act. The proposed reforms accompanied a wide-ranging package of proposed changes to the Constitution designed mainly to achieve a lasting agreement with the Quebec government but also to enhance the effectiveness with which the Canadian economic union operated.

The intention of the reforms was to reestablish legitimacy while at the same time respecting the Bank's independence. The proposed changes included four main elements.

The Bank's Mandate The Bank's mandate is currently fairly broad: to protect the external value of currency and to help stabilize the business cycle. The proposed amendment would limit the Bank's mandate to achieving and maintaining price stability. Some monetary policy experts, such as Peter Howitt of the University of Western Ontario, do not agree with this proposal. Howitt argues that while price stability might be rightly considered to be the long-run objective of the Bank, monetary policy does affect more than the price level in the short run. The mandate of the Bank should be broad enough to take account of the short-run effects of monetary policy on real activity as well as the long-run effects on price stability. Others, like David Laidler, also of the University of Western Ontario, favour the federal proposal, but believe that the Bank must also aim at price-level predictability. Laidler would go one step further by recommending a quantitative goal for permissible price-level increases. This is based on the argument that the conduct of monetary policy should be based more on "rules" than on "discretion." The exercise of discretion in monetary policy is said to be as likely to be destabilizing as stabilizing, given the unpredictability of the policy effects and the lags involved before it takes effect.

The Appointment of Directors The Board of Directors includes twelve directors from "diversified occupations" appointed for three-year terms by the minister of finance, a governor and a senior deputy governor appointed for seven-year terms, and the deputy minister of finance. In practice, the Board of Directors has little influence over monetary policy; the operations of the Bank are in the hands of the governor, senior deputy governor, and the Bank's professional staff. The proposal is to amend the act to ensure regional representation on the Board of Directors by requiring the federal government to consult with provincial and territorial governments before appointing directors. Laidler argues that this proposal may only result in an imbalance in representation (for example, by giving

Prince Edward Island and Ontario equal membership) without improving the effectiveness of the Board of Directors. He recommends enhancing the Board of Directors' legitimacy by removing the "diversified occupations" requirement from the act so that more monetary policy experts can serve, and by making the position of directors full time, well paid and of a longer term.

Ratification by the Senate The appointment of the governor would be ratified by the Senate, which under the constitutional reform proposals, would be an elected one. This proposal is intended to improve the legitimacy of the governor and thus of the Bank itself.

Regional Consultative Panels The last reform is to create regional consultative panels so as to ensure that perspectives from all across the country are brought to bear on monetary policy. In these panels, the regional and provincial economic situations would be reviewed, and the reports from the meetings of regional consultative panels would be published as part of the minutes of the Bank of Canada's Board of Directors.

When the federal government sat down with the provincial and territorial governments in 1992 and negotiated a package of constitutional reforms (the so-called Charlottetown Accord), reform of the Bank of Canada Act was dropped from consideration. Whether it will regain urgency in the future remains to be seen.

Sources: David Laidler, *How Shall We Govern the Governor?: A Critique of the Governance of the Bank of Canada* (Toronto: C. D. Howe Institute, 1990); Peter Howitt, "Reform of the Bank of Canada and Harmonization of Macroeconomic Policies," in R. W. Boadway and D. D. Purvis, eds., *Policy Forum on the Economic Aspects of the Federal Government's Constitutional Proposals* (Kingston: John Deutsch Institute for Economic Policy, Queen's University, 1991), pp. 39–59; *Canadian Federalism and Economic Union: Partnership for Prosperity* (Ottawa: Minister of Supply and Services, 1991).

tors appoint the governor and senior deputy governor for seven-year terms. The conduct of monetary policy is the responsibility of the governor (along with the senior deputy governor), with final approval resting with the minister of finance. In practice, the governor has a large degree of independence in the exercise of authority.

The structure of the Bank of Canada is quite different than that of the Federal Reserve, which is the central bank in the United States. The Federal Reserve is organized on a more regional basis and consists of a Board of Governors (the Federal Reserve Board) that supervises a system of twelve regional Federal Reserve banks. The latter in turn monitors the operations of six thousand member banks, very few of which operate on a nationwide basis. The Canadian system is much more centralized. The main chartered banks themselves tend to be national in scope, each with a large number of branches across the country. The Canadian system is referred to as a **branch banking system,** in contrast to the largely **unitary banking system** of the United States. The Bank of Canada also operates as a single national entity. In recent years, there has been some pressure for more explicitly regional input into the central banking structure. Persons in some regions have felt that the priorities of monetary policy were being set with central Canada's interests most in mind. Most suggestions for change, however, do not go as far as proposing to move to a Federal Reserve–like system in Canada. Typically they call for more explicit regional representation on the Bank's Board of Directors.

CONTROLLING THE MONEY SUPPLY

The main function of the Bank of Canada is to control the supply of money in the banking system. The way it does this is by engaging in **open market operations,** so called because the Bank enters the capital market directly much as a private individual or firm would, and buys or sells federal government bonds. At the weekly Treasury bill auctions, the Bank sells or purchases these T-bills in order to influence T-bill prices (and thus interest rates) and the amount of money in the economy. Later in this chapter, we will see exactly how these actions translate into changes in the money supply, and we will look at some other ways in which the Bank can influence the money supply.

REGULATING BANKS

The other primary objective of the central bank is to ensure the financial soundness of banks. In the United States, bank regulation by the Federal Reserve System was originally motivated by the rash of bank failures, about 9,000 in number, during the Great Depression. Canada had much less of a breakdown in the banking system, but enough to help motivate the establishment of the Bank of Canada and its regulatory function.

The Canadian branch banking system is dominated by a few large banks that manage most of the deposits and control most of the assets of the banking system. The chartered banks have 80 percent of the chequable deposits and 35 percent of the total assets held by financial institutions in Canada. By contrast, trust and mortgage companies, life insurance companies, and trusteed pension plans each have between 10 percent and 17 percent of the assets, and the credit unions and caisses populaires have 7 percent.

According to the Bank Act, to open its doors a bank must obtain a federal charter. A charter gives a financial institution the right to call itself a bank and to make an unlimited quantity of unsecured business and personal loans. There are two types of charters. Schedule I charters are granted only to widely held, domestically owned banks, of which there are eight. There are close to sixty Schedule II banks, almost all of them subsidiaries of foreign banks. In the future, they will include subsidiaries of non-bank financial institutions. They face somewhat more restrictions then Schedule I banks.

Chartered banks face a number of regulations and restrictions. Prior to 1992, they were subject to cash reserve requirements against deposits set by the Bank of Canada, though these are to be phased out. Rather than cash reserve requirements, banks will have to keep settlement balances at the Bank of Canada for cheque-clearing purposes and sufficient cash in their vaults for daily operations. They are supervised by the superintendent of financial institutions and must report weekly to the Bank of Canada. There are also certain restrictions on their lending practices and asset holdings. (For example, they cannot acquire more than 10 percent ownership of nonfinancial companies, and their holdings of real estate and shares cannot exceed 70 percent of their equity for each type and 100 percent for both combined.)

Deposits in the banks are insured by the Canada Deposit Insurance Corporation (CDIC) for up to $60,000 per depositor. In return, banks must abide by certain restrictions imposed by the CDIC. As well, the banks belong to the Canadian Payments Association (CPA), which operates an automated clearing and settlement mechanism for clearing cheques written against one bank but deposited in another. Other financial institutions, such as credit unions and caisses populaires, and trust and mortgage loan companies, which are federally or provincially licensed rather than chartered, are also members of the CPA and are able to have their deposits insured by the CDIC.

Thus the chartered banks face three layers of regulation. The superintendent of financial institutions, the Bank of Canada, and the CDIC all share the job of supervision. Nonetheless, in 1985 the major bankruptcies of Canadian Commercial Bank and Northlands Bank both raised questions about the adequacy of bank regulation.

CREATING MONEY IN MODERN ECONOMIES

In order to understand how the Bank of Canada goes about its task of controlling the money supply we need to know more about how a bank runs its business, particularly how banks create money. Surprisingly to many, the money supply of today is created not by a mint or printing press but largely by the banking system. When you put money into the bank, the bank does not simply take the currency down to its vault, put it into a little slot marked with your name, and keep it there until you are ready to take it out. Any bank that did that would be foolish. Instead, banks realize that not all of their thousands of depositors will withdraw their money on any given day. Some will come by next week, some in two weeks, and some not for a year. In the meantime, the bank can lend out the money deposited in the vault and charge interest. The more money the bank can persuade people to deposit, the more can be loaned out and thus the more money the bank will earn. To attract depositors, the bank pays interest on its deposits, effectively passing on (after taking its cut) the interest earned on its loans.

The question is, how much can safely be lent out? Money retained by a bank in case those who have deposited money want it back is called its **reserve.** How much needs to be kept as reserves? Should the bank keep reserves of 5 percent of deposits? 20 percent of deposits? The less it keeps as reserves, the more money it can earn, but the greater the possibility that it will not have enough funds on hand if by chance a large number of depositors should want their deposits back at the same time. To understand how these reserves work and how they affect the supply of money and credit available in the economy, we need to take a close look at a bank's balance sheet.

THE BANK'S BALANCE SHEET

Bankers see the world backwards. Where else would loans be called "assets" and deposits be called "liabilities"? This is the perspective shown on a bank's **balance sheet.** Like any firm's balance sheet, it describes the bank's **assets** and **liabilities.** Assets are what the firm owns, including what is owed to it by others. That is why the bank's loans appear as assets on its balance sheet. Liabilities are what it owes to others. We can think of the bank's depositors as having loaned money to the bank; they can get their money back when they wish. That is why deposits are treated by the bank as liabilities.

Table 17.1 shows the balance sheet of Maple Leaf Bank. Its assets are divided into three categories: loans outstanding, government bonds, and reserves, including cash in the vault. Loans outstanding consist of loans to business firms, real estate loans (mortgages), car loans, house-remodelling loans, and so on. Banks hold some government bonds because they are more secure than loans to households or firms. Most banks' holdings of government bonds are typically concentrated in Treasury bills, short-term bonds maturing in thirty, sixty, or ninety days after the date of issue.[1] Most secure are the cash in the vault and the reserves that are held on deposit at the "banker's bank," the Bank of Canada.

Chapter 13 explained that the amount of money people need to set aside for a rainy day depends (in part) on how easily they can borrow. The same is true for banks. If they can easily borrow from other banks to meet any shortfall of reserves, then they need to keep very little in reserves. In Canada, the Bank of Canada acts as the banker's bank, lending money to other banks when they need it. (Banks do not, however, have an automatic right to borrow; they are rationed in how much they can borrow from the Bank of Canada.) The system of banking in which banks hold a fraction of the amount on deposit in reserves is called the **fractional reserve system.** In determining the amount of reserves to hold, the banks are said to be engaging in **cash reserve management.**

Traditionally, the Bank Act has imposed reserve requirements on banks. Thus, the amount of reserves held was dictated as much by regulations as by the banks' own perceptions of what is prudent. And the level of reserves required by the Bank Act was designed primarily from the perspective of controlling the money supply and thereby the level of economic activity. Under the Bank Act of 1980, cash reserve requirements were 10 percent of Canadian dollar demand deposits, 3 percent of foreign currency deposits held by Canadian residents, 2 percent of term and notice deposits plus 1 percent more for amounts over $500 million. As well, banks were subject to a secondary reserve requirement against Canadian dollar deposits, where secondary reserves include cash, T-bills, and day loans of money market dealers. Secondary reserve requirements were set at the discretion of the Bank of Canada. The Bank Act of 1992 phased out reserve requirements, however, partly because as near banks compete more and more with banks

[1] Long-term bonds are volatile in price, because their price changes with changes in interest rates. Banks hold short-term government bonds because the risk of such changes over a relatively short period of time is low, and the banks wish to avoid risk.

Table 17.1 MAPLE LEAF BANK BALANCE SHEET

Assets		Liabilities	
Loans outstanding	$28 million	Deposits	$30 million
Government bonds	2 million		
Reserves	3 million	Net worth	3 million
Total	33 million	Total	33 million

for deposits, the banks argue that they are placed at a competitive disadvantage by reserve requirements that are not imposed on the near banks. From now on, the level of reserves held by banks will be determined mainly by the bank's own judgment of what is prudent, given that it is costly for the bank to have to borrow if it runs short of cash. But the banks, as well as other direct clearing members of the CPA, will be required to keep settlement balances at the Bank of Canada; the monthly average of such balances must be no less than zero.

The liability side of Maple Leaf Bank's balance sheet consists of two items: deposits and net worth. Deposits can take on a variety of forms: these include chequing accounts, which are technically known as demand deposits, and the variety of forms of savings accounts, which are technically known as time deposits. The bank's net worth is simply the difference between the value of its assets and the value of its liabilities. In other words, if the bank's assets were sold and its depositors paid off, then what remained would equal the net worth of the bank.

Since net worth is *defined* as the difference between the value of the liabilities and the value of the assets, it should be clear that the numbers on both sides of the balance sheet should balance.

How Banks Create Money

Who creates money? Banks do. As we have seen, the coins and currency manufactured by the Royal Canadian Mint are a relatively small part of the money supply.

To see how banks create money, let's figuratively lump all the members of the Canadian Payments Association into a big pile and consider them as one huge superbank. Assume that the banks decide that reserves will be kept at 10 percent of deposits. Now suppose that a wealthy individual deposits $1 billion in currency in his account.

The bank reasons as follows. It wants to keep a reserve-to-deposit ratio of 1 to 10. It has a long line of loan applicants. When the bank makes a loan, it credits the borrower with funds in her chequing account; it does not actually give her currency. What it does is simply place an entry into its books on both the left- and right-hand side of the ledger: there is a loan on the asset side and a deposit on the liability side. If it makes $9 billion worth of loans, its liabilities will have gone up $10 billion (the $1 billion original deposit plus the $9 billion worth of loans). On the asset side, the bank takes the $1 billion in currency to the Bank of Canada and is credited with the amount, so that it now has $1 billion in reserves. Thus, its reserves have increased by $1 billion, its deposits by $10 billion; it has satisfied its desired reserve holdings. Table 17.2 shows both the initial and final balance sheets of the bank.

We can reach the same result by a slower route. The bank might reason, now that its deposits have gone up by $1 billion, that it must send $100 million to the Bank of Canada as a reserve. But it can lend out the remaining $900 million (.9 × $1 billion). This is the first-round balance sheet that appears in the table. Deposits have increased $1 billion (compared with the initial situation), loans have increased $.9 billion, and reserves have increased $.1 billion.

For the sake of argument, let's assume that the loan is all made to one customer: Desktop Publishing borrows $900 million so that it can purchase new computers from Computer Canada. When Desktop pays $900 million for the computers, Computer Canada deposits the money in its account. Thus, the loan of $900 million is reflected in the ad-

Table 17.2 SUPERBANK BALANCE SHEET

Before-deposit equilibrium			
Assets		**Liabilities**	
Loans outstanding	$ 91 billion	Deposits	$100 billion
Government bonds	2 billion		
Reserves	10 billion	Net worth	3 billion
Total	103 billion	Total	103 billion

First round (Add $1 billion deposits, $.9 billion loans)			
Assets		**Liabilities**	
Loans outstanding	$ 91.9 billion	Deposits	$101 billion
Government bonds	2 billion		
Reserves	10.1 billion	Net worth	3 billion
Total	104 billion	Total	104 billion

Second round (Add $.9 billion deposits, $.81 billion loans to previous round*)			
Assets		**Liabilities**	
Loans outstanding	$ 92.71 billion	Deposits	$101.9 billion
Government bonds	2 billion		
Reserves	10.19 billion	Net worth	3 billion
Total	104.9 billion	Total	104.9 billion

Third round (Add $.81 billion deposits, $.73 billion loans to previous round*)			
Assets		**Liabilities**	
Loans outstanding	$ 93.44 billion	Deposits	$102.71 billion
Government bonds	2 billion		
Reserves	10.27 billion	Net worth	3 billion
Total	105.71 billion	Total	105.71 billion

After-deposit equilibrium (Add $10 billion new deposits, $9 billion new loans to original equilibrium)			
Assets		**Liabilities**	
Loans outstanding	$100 billion	Deposits	$110 billion
Government bonds	2 billion		
Reserves	11 billion	Net worth	3 billion
Total	113 billion	Total	113 billion

*In each subsequent round, new deposits equal new loans of the previous round; new loans equal .9 x new deposits.

dition of $900 million in deposits. This is shown on the right-hand side of the second-round balance sheet in the table, where deposits have now risen from $101 billion to $101.9 billion.

But with the $900 million additional deposits, the bank is allowed to increase its lending by .9 × $900 million, or $810 million, putting $90 million into reserves. These changes are shown in the left-hand side of the second-round balance sheet. Assume that all $810 million is lent out to various companies, each of which uses the money to purchase new goods. In each case, some other firm will sell its good and will put these new funds into the superbank. As a result, new deposits at the superbank will again grow by $810 million. As the third round begins, deposits are once again increased.

But the bank is still not in equilibrium. Because of the increase in deposits of $810 million, it can lend out .9 × $810 million = $729 million. And so the process continues. Notice that on each round, the increase in deposits is smaller than in the previous round. In the second round, the increase in deposits was $900 million, in the third round $810 million, and so on. The after-deposit equilibrium balance sheet in the last part of the table shows that the bank has increased its deposits by ten times the original deposit ($100 billion to $110 billion) and increased its lending by nine times the original deposit ($91 billion to $100 billion). The $1 billion injection into the banking system has turned into a $10 billion increase in the money supply.

In the new situation, the banking system is in equilibrium. Its reserves of $11 billion are precisely equal to 10 percent of its $110 billion deposit. It cannot lend out any more without violating its desired reserve requirements.

In this way, any new deposit into the banking system results in a multiple expansion of the number of deposits. This is the "miracle" of the fractional reserve system. Deposits increase by a factor of l/reserve requirement. In the superbank example, the desired reserve requirement was 10 percent; l/reserve requirement is 10. If the desired reserve requirement had been 20 percent, deposits would have increased by 1/.2, or 5. Note that as the deposits increased, so did the supply of outstanding loans.

In this example, there were no "leakages" outside the system. No one decided to hold currency rather than put her money back into the bank. Whenever sellers were paid, they put what they received into the bank. With leakages, the increase in deposits and thus the increase in money will be smaller. These leakages are large; the ratio of M1 to reserves is only around 3, and even for M2 the ratio is only between 11 and 12. Nevertheless, the increase in bank reserves will lead to some multiplied increase in the money supply. This relationship between the change in reserves and the final change in deposits is called the **money multiplier.**[2]

MONEY MULTIPLIERS WITH MANY BANKS

The lesson of the money multiplier works just as well when there is more than one bank involved. Assume that Desktop Publishing and Computer Canada have their bank accounts in two separate banks, Prairie Bank and Maritime Bank, respectively. When Desktop Publishing writes a cheque for $900 million to Computer Canada, $900 million is transferred from Prairie Bank to Maritime Bank. Once that $900 million has been transferred, Maritime Bank will find that it can lend more than it could previously.

---

[2] This multiplier should not be confused with the multiplier introduced in Chapter 12. That multiplier showed that an increase in investment or government expenditures leads to a multiple increase in the equilibrium level of aggregate expenditures. There are clearly some similarities in the way we go about calculating these multipliers.

As a result of the $900 million increase in deposits, it can lend .9 × $900 = $810 million. Suppose it lends the $810 million to the New Telephone Company, which uses the money to buy a machine for making telephones from Equipment Manufacturing. If Equipment Manufacturing has its bank account at Pacific Bank, after Equipment Manufacturing has been paid, Pacific Bank will find that because its deposits have increased by $810 million, it can lend .9 × $810 = $729 million. The process continues, until the new equilibrium is identical to the one described earlier in the superbank example, where there is a $10 billion increase in the money supply. The banking system as a whole will have expanded the money supply by a multiple of the initial deposit, equal to 1/reserve requirement.

It should be clear that when there are many banks, no individual bank can create multiple deposits. Individual banks may not even be aware of the role they play in the process of multiple-deposit creation; all they see is that their reserves have increased and that therefore they are able to make more loans.

The process of multiple-deposit creation may seem somewhat like a magician's pulling rabbits out of a hat: it seems to make something out of nothing. The process of creating deposits is a real physical process. Deposits are created by making entries in records; today electronic impulses create records on computer tapes. The rules of deposit creation are rules specifying when you may make certain entries in the books. It is these rules—in particular, the fractional reserve requirements—that give rise to the ability of the system to create multiple deposits.

MONEY MULTIPLIER

An increase in reserves by a dollar leads to an increase in total deposits by a multiple of the original increase.

THE INSTRUMENTS OF MONETARY POLICY

Most changes in the money supply are not the result of someone depositing a billion dollars of currency in a bank. No longer do they involve someone selling gold to or depositing gold in a bank. Instead, they are the result of actions by the Bank of Canada. The Bank creates reserves. It does so deliberately, in order to increase the supply of money and credit. By such action, the Bank affects the level of economic activity. The connections between the actions the Bank takes and their effect on the level of economic activity are the subject of the next two chapters. Here, our concern is simply with the supply of money and credit. Money and credit, as we have seen, represent the two sides of a bank's balance sheet: when deposits (money) increase, either bank loans (credit) or bank holdings of T-bills must increase. Frequently both will. Though ultimately our concern will be with bank lending, bank lending is not directly under the control of the Bank of Canada. The money supply is more directly under its control.

RESERVE REQUIREMENTS

There are many potential instruments that the Bank of Canada might use to change the money supply, but not all are currently used. For example, the simplest and most direct tool that the Bank of Canada might use is to alter reserve requirements. Since the reserve requirement determines the minimum amount of money each bank is required to hold in reserves as cash plus deposits in the Bank of Canada, changing reserve requirements would give the Bank of Canada a powerful tool with which to influence the amount of money and credit in the economy.

Assume that banks are initially required to maintain reserves equal to 10 percent of deposits, and consider what would happen if reserve requirements were lowered to 5 percent. Each bank would find that it now had **excess reserves** or **free reserves**—reserves in excess of the amount required; that is, each bank would be in a position to lend more. Where a lack of funds might have caused the bank to reject loans to projects it considered worthy, now it would make these loans. The new loans would get spent, creating new deposits and allowing still further loans, and the multiplier process would once again be set in motion.

As powerful as a change in reserve requirements might be as an instrument for changing the money supply, it is a tool that has not been used in recent years. For one thing, it is a tool that is liable to be quite blunt in its effect, and perhaps even disruptive. For another, there are other instruments that can achieve the same results in a more gradual and flexible way. Prior to 1992, reserve ratios were set statutorily by the Bank Act, and were not subject to change by the Bank of Canada. As mentioned above, required reserve ratios for banks were abolished so as not to impose a requirement on the banks that other deposit-taking institutions such as trust companies were not required to satisfy. Instead, the Bank of Canada uses other instruments, and these form the subject of the next three sections.

OPEN MARKET OPERATIONS

Open market operations are the most important instrument the Bank of Canada uses to control the money supply. In open market operations, the Bank enters the market directly to buy or sell government bonds. Imagine that it buys $1 million of government bonds from wealthy Joe Brown (or from a thousand different Joe Brown families), paying him with a $1 million cheque. Joe Brown takes the cheque down to his bank, Maple Leaf Bank, which credits his account with $1 million. Maple Leaf Bank presents the cheque to the Bank of Canada, which credits the bank's account with $1 million. Maple Leaf Bank now has $1 million of new deposits, $1 million in new reserves, and it can accordingly lend out an additional $900,000. A money multiplier goes to work, and the total expansion of the money supply will be equal to a multiple of the initial $1 million increase in deposits. And credit—the amount of outstanding loans—has also increased by a multiple of the initial increase in deposits.

The purchase of bonds from Joe Brown by the Bank of Canada has a quite different effect from a purchase of the same bonds by a private citizen, Jill White. In the latter case, Jill White's deposit account goes down by $1 million, and Joe Brown's deposit account goes up by $1 million. The funds available in the system as a whole remain unchanged. The money multiplier goes to work only when funds enter from "outside," and in particular from the Bank of Canada.

There is an equivalent and related way for the Bank of Canada to obtain the same effect as open market operations on the reserves of the banking system, and that is to shift Government of Canada deposits between itself and the chartered banks. In addition to operating as the banker to the banks, the Bank of Canada also is a banker for the federal government. That is, the federal government holds some of its accounts in the Bank of Canada as well as in the chartered banks. The Bank can affect the level of reserves in the banks by shifting federal government deposits between itself and the chartered banks. For example, to increase the reserves in the banking system, the Bank simply transfers some federal funds from an account in the Bank to an account in a chartered bank. This has the same effect on the banking system as an open market purchase of government securities. The banks are able to expand their deposits by a multiple of the amount of the transfer. Alternatively, a transfer of federal government deposits from a chartered bank to an account in the Bank of Canada is equivalent in its effect to an open market sale of government securities.

THE BANK RATE

A second tool of monetary policy is a change in the **bank rate.** As explained earlier in this chapter, the Bank of Canada is called the banker's bank because it holds banks' deposits and banks can borrow from it. The interest rate the banks pay when they borrow from the Bank of Canada is called the **bank rate.** When the bank rate is high, it is more expensive for the banks to borrow from the Bank of Canada. It might be expected in turn that the interest charged by the banks would be high, and banks would make fewer loans available.

Consider an aggressive bank that always keeps a given ratio of reserves to deposits, and no more. It lends out all the funds that are not kept in reserves. If a major depositor suddenly wishes to withdraw funds, the bank is forced to borrow funds, either from other banks or from the Bank of Canada. When the bank rate increases, the interest rate the bank must pay for borrowing from other banks increases in tandem. The bank rate affects this bank as a direct cost of doing business. If it has to pay the Bank of Canada more to borrow itself, it must charge its own customers more.

If the bank pursues a less aggressive policy and holds more funds in the form of Treasury bills or other liquid assets, a large deposit withdrawal causes only a minor adjustment: the bank simply sells some of its liquid assets. Raising the bank rate makes it more expensive to call upon the Bank of Canada in the event of a shortfall of funds, and this induces banks to hold more liquid assets, which in turn means that the bank will be lending less. In fact, bank borrowing from the Bank of Canada is used only as a last resort and is virtually never done. When they are short of reserves, the banks tend to borrow directly from the money market. The bank rate therefore does not serve as a constraint on the banks. Its role in monetary policy is a less direct one.

Prior to 1980, the Bank of Canada set the bank rate and changed it periodically as a signal or "announcement" of its monetary policy stance. Since then, the bank rate has been pegged by the Bank of Canada at 25 basis points (that is, one-quarter of a percentage point) above the average yield of three-month Treasury bills at the weekly auction. The bank rate therefore follows the market closely. Because the Bank can influence the price of Treasury bills through open market operations, however, it maintains some control over the bank rate. That rate is seen by banks and other financial institutions (and the financial press) as an economic signal of the Bank of Canada's monetary policy.

MORAL SUASION

One final instrument that can be used by the Bank of Canada to influence monetary policy is referred to as **moral suasion.** In fact, moral suasion has little to do with morality as such. It is simply a term that refers to the fact that the Bank of Canada is able to persuade the banks to take certain actions that the Bank thinks would further the objectives of monetary policy at a given point in time. Moral suasion is possible because there are a relatively small number of banks in Canada, and the banks are constantly in communication with the Bank of Canada; the Bank of Canada wields a certain amount of implicit authority over the banks through its role as a regulator; and the Bank can ultimately engage in open market operations to achieve its objectives.

The object of the moral suasion can take a variety of forms. At one extreme it may simply involve the Bank of Canada discussing with the banks its current monetary policy objectives. At the other, the Bank may wish the banks to take some specific action, such as changing the composition or size of their liabilities (deposits), or restricting some forms of lending. Given that moral suasion is not done publicly, it is not easy to assess how important or successful it has been in the past. Some have suggested that it might assume more importance in the future as the banks no longer have to maintain fixed reserve requirements, but instead are simply monitored by the Bank of Canada.

Thus the Bank of Canada has three indirect ways in which it controls the money supply and credit-creating activities of the banks. Through open market operations (and transfers of government deposits), it affects the supply of reserves. Through the bank rate, its current monetary policy stance is signalled. And through moral suasion, it elicits the cooperation of the banks in pursuing the objectives of monetary policy. The result of all these activities is to influence the amount of loans the banks can make and on what terms.

SELECTING THE APPROPRIATE INSTRUMENT

Of the three instruments, open market operations are the most effective. Changes in bank rates and moral suasion are viewed to be blunt tools, compared with the fine-tuning that open market operations make possible. Changes in the bank rate, however, are used to announce major shifts in monetary policy, but not on a regular basis. Such changes signal tighter credit (that is, changes in monetary policy that entail higher interest rates and reduced credit availability) or looser credit (that is, changes in monetary policy that have the reverse effect). They can be quite effective: for instance, banks, foreseeing a tightening of credit, may cut back their lending, and firms may put plans for investment onto the shelf.

INSTRUMENTS OF MONETARY POLICY

1. Open market operations—by buying and selling government securities, the Bank of Canada changes the supply of reserves and thus the money supply. It can also affect the supply of reserves by transferring Government of Canada accounts between itself and the chartered banks.

2. Bank rate announcements—by setting its bank rate at 25 basis points above the T-bill rate each week, it signals its current monetary policy stance.

3. Moral suasion—by communicating directly to the banks, it elicits their cooperation in achieving monetary policy objectives.

THE STABILITY OF THE CANADIAN BANKING SYSTEM

The fractional reserve system explains how banks create money, and it also explains how, without the Bank of Canada, banks can get into trouble. Well-managed banks, even before the advent of the Bank of Canada, kept reserves equal to some average expectation of day-to-day needs. A bank could get into trouble in a hurry if one day's needs exceeded its reserves.

If (for good reasons or bad) many depositors lose confidence in a bank at the same time, they will attempt to withdraw their funds all at once. The bank simply will not have the money available, since most of the money will have been lent out in loans that cannot be called in instantaneously. This situation is called a **bank run.** Bank runs were as common in nineteenth-century America as they were in the old Western movies, where customers in a small town would line up at the bank while it paid out what reserves it had on a first-come, first-served basis. People who showed up and asked for their money got it until there was no more left. Even if a bank was fairly healthy, such a run could quickly drive it out of business. After all, if a rumor spread that a bank was in trouble and a few savers ran to the bank to clean out their accounts, then other investors would feel they were foolish to sit back and wait. Only by running down to the bank themselves could they protect their deposits. Rumors could easily snowball into panic, and other banks could also be drawn into a run. As a result, one vicious rumor could lead to a healthy bank's having to shut down, thus destabilizing the banking system and the local economy.

REDUCING THE THREAT OF BANK RUNS

Bank runs and panics have periodically afflicted the banking system. They have been much more prevalent in the United States than in Canada, largely because of the branch banking system that exists in Canada. Large banks with many branches are able to share reserves and pool their risks more readily. Nonetheless, bank failures can occur, and when they do they can be quite traumatic both for the depositors and for the economy as a whole. As mentioned, one of the reasons why the Bank of Canada was set up was to make them less likely. The modern banking system has evolved a number of safeguards that have ended, or at least reduced, the threat of bank runs for most banks. There are three levels of protection.

First, the Bank of Canada serves as a banker's bank, as we have seen. If the only problem facing the bank is one of short-term liquidity—having the cash on hand to meet depositors' demands—it can now borrow from the Bank of Canada. The Bank is therefore referred to as "the lender of last resort." In fact, the banks rarely have to resort to loans from the Bank of Canada. If another Great Depression came along, however, that safeguard would always exist.

The second level of protection is provided by the owners of the bank. Most banks are started by investors who put up a certain amount of money in exchange for a share of ownership. The net worth of the firm—the difference between the bank's assets and its liabilities—is this initial investment, augmented or decreased over time by the bank's profits or losses. If the bank makes bad investment decisions, then these shareholders can be forced to bear the cost, not the depositors. This cushion provided by shareholders not only protects depositors, it also encourages the bank to be more prudent in its loans. If the bank makes bad loans, the owners risk their entire investment. If the owners' net worth in the bank is too small, the owners may see themselves in a "Heads I win, tails you lose" situation: if risky investments turn out well, the extra profits accrue to the bank; if they turn out badly, the bank goes bankrupt, but since the owners had little at stake, they have little to lose. Thus, the government through the Bank Act has imposed **capital adequacy requirements** on banks: banks are subject to limits on their ratio of assets to equity. Capital adequacy requirements protect against insolvency; they mean that if the bank invests badly and many of its loans default, the bank will still be able to pay back depositors. (By contrast, reserves and the ability to borrow from the Bank protect against illiquidity; they ensure that if depositors want cash, they can get it.)

As a third and final backstop, the banks are required to insure their depositors for up to $60,000 with the Canada Deposit Insurance Corporation. In fact, the CDIC insures all deposit-taking institutions in Canada. Since deposits are guaranteed by their CDIC, depositors fearing the collapse of a financial institution have no need to rush to it. They can walk to the financial institution rather than run. The deposit insurance thus not only protects depositors, it has an enormous impact in increasing the stability of the financial system. The beauty of deposit insurance lies in the fact that because it exists, the threat against which it insures is much less likely to occur. It is as if life insurance somehow prolonged life dramatically.

Critics of deposit insurance point to an offsetting disadvantage: depositors no longer have any incentive to monitor financial institutions, to make sure that they are investing the funds safely. Regardless of what the institution does with their funds, they are protected. While many economists are not convinced that depositors themselves could effectively monitor banks, the system of deposit insurance creates some peculiar incentives. Depositors have an incentive to put their money with whatever institution offers the highest returns. To earn high returns requires the financial institution to undertake greater risk. But greater risks make it more likely that the institution will fail and need to call on its CDIC guarantees. The fact the depositors are protected against the risk of an institution becoming insolvent makes it more likely that bankruptcy will occur. This is an application of the notion of moral hazard in insurance discussed in Chapter 6. Some economists have suggested that the deposit insurance offered by the CDIC should conform more closely with insurance, or actuarial, principles. That is, they believe that the premiums paid by various financial institutions to insure their depositors should reflect the riskiness of the assets the institution holds and therefore the probability of going bankrupt.

Since depositors have no incentive to monitor the financial institutions—and might not do a very effective job even if their incentives had not been removed by depositor insurance—the burden of monitoring them rests on the Bank of Canada and other government agencies. This regulation goes beyond just capital requirements: it limits the kinds of investments that banks can make.

REVIEW AND PRACTICE

SUMMARY

1. Money is anything that is generally accepted in a given society as a medium of exchange, store of value, and unit of account.

2. There are many ways of measuring the money supply, with names like M1, M2, M3, and M2+. All include both currency and chequing accounts. They differ in what they include as assets that are close substitutes to currency and chequing accounts.

3. A buyer does not need money to purchase a good, at least not right away, if the seller or a financial institution is willing to extend credit.

4. Financial intermediaries, which include banks, trust and mortgage loan companies, credit unions and caisses populaires, insurance companies, and others, all have in common that they form the link between savers who have extra funds and borrowers who desire extra funds.

5. Government is involved with the banking industry for two reasons. First, by regulating the activities banks can undertake and providing deposit insurance, government seeks to protect depositors and ensure the stability of the financial system. Second, by influencing the willingness of banks to make loans, government attempts to influence the level of investment and overall economic activity.

6. By making loans, banks can create an increase in the supply of money that is a multiple of an initial increase in the banks' deposits. If every bank loans all the money it can and every dollar lent is spent to buy goods from other firms that deposit the cheque in their account, the money multiplier is 1/the reserve requirement chosen by the banks. In practice, the money multiplier is considerably smaller.

7. The Bank of Canada can affect the money supply by open market operations or transferring federal government deposits between itself and the chartered banks. It can also influence the behaviour of banks by moral suasion and by changing the bank rate.

8. The Bank acts as a lender of last resort, imposes capital adequacy requirements, and provides deposit insurance, all of which have made bank runs rare. But the structure of deposit insurance can encourage financial institutions to take more risks than they might otherwise.

KEY TERMS

medium of exchange	financial intermediaries	fractional reserve system
store of value	central bank	cash reserve management
fiat money	branch banking system	money multiplier
unit of account	unitary banking system	bank rate
money	open market operations	moral suasion
money supply	reserve	bank run
demand deposits		capital adequacy requirements
M1, M2, M3, M2+		
near banks		
lines of credit		

REVIEW QUESTIONS

1. What are the three characteristics that define money?

2. What are the differences between M1, M2, M3, and M2+?

3. When consumers or businesses desire to make a large purchase, are they limited to spending only as much as the M1 money that they have on hand? Explain.

4. What is the Bank of Canada?

5. What are the two main reasons for government involvement in the banking system?

6. What are the ways for the Bank of Canada to reduce the money supply?

7. What has the government done to make bank runs less likely?

PROBLEMS

1. Identify which of money's three traits each of the following assets shares, and which traits it does not share:
  (a) a house;
  (b) a day pass for an amusement park;
  (c) German marks held by a resident of Montreal;
  (d) a painting;
  (e) gold.

2. How might bank depositors be protected by legal prohibitions on banks' entering businesses like insurance, or selling and investing in stocks or venture capital? What are the possible costs and benefits of such prohibitions for depositors and for the government?

3. Down Home Trust Company has the following assets and liabilities: $6 million in government bonds and reserves; $40 million in deposits; $36 million in outstanding loans. Draw up a balance sheet for the bank. What is its net worth?

4. What factors might affect the value of a bank's loan portfolio? If these factors are changing, explain how this would complicate the job of a bank examiner trying to ascertain the magnitude of the bank's net worth. Why would the bank examiner be concerned about the value of the net worth?

5. While gardening in his backyard, Lucky Bob finds a mason jar containing $100,000 in currency. After he deposits the money in his lucky bank, where the reserve requirement is .05, how much will the money supply eventually increase?

6. Why is it that if the Bank of Canada sells government bonds the money supply changes, but if a big company sells government bonds (to anyone other than the Fed) the money supply does not change?

7. "So long as the Bank of Canada stands ready to lend to any bank with a positive net worth, reserve requirements are unnecessary. What underlies the stability of the banking system is the central bank's role as a lender of last resort, combined with policies aimed at ensuring the financial viability of the banks—for instance, the net worth requirements." Comment.

MONETARY THEORY AND POLICY

I n Chapter 17, we saw the close link between the creation of money and credit (loans). This chapter explains why the money supply and the availability of credit are important to the economy. Knowing this, we can interpret monetary policy, the collection of policies aimed at affecting the money supply and the availability of credit. As was pointed out in Chapter 10, monetary and fiscal policy are the two main instruments the government uses to pursue its goals of economic growth, stable prices, and full employment.

In Chapter 17, we saw how the Bank of Canada through open market operations, moral suasion, and changes in the bank rate can affect both the supply of money and the amount of credit (loans) that banks make available to borrowers. This chapter addresses the questions of *how* and *when* the Bank's actions have significant effects on the level of economic activity.

Changes in the money supply and changes in the availability of credit are two sides of the same coin. Different economists have focused on each side. We begin by looking at the Bank of Canada's direct effects on the money supply, then turn to its effects on credit availability.

KEY QUESTIONS

1. What determines the demand for money? How and why does it depend on the interest rate and the level of income?

2. How is the demand for money equilibrated to the supply of money?

3. What are the consequences of changes in the supply of money? Under what circumstances will a change in the money supply simply lead to a change in the price level? When will it lead to a change in real output? When will it largely lead to a change in the amount of money that individuals are willing to hold?

4. What are the channels through which monetary policy affects the economy? What role is played by changes in the real interest rate? the availability of credit?

5. What are the different schools of thought concerning the extent to which monetary policy affects the economy? What are the underlying sources of their disagreements? What are some of the important ways that they differ in their policy recommendations?

MONEY SUPPLY AND ECONOMIC ACTIVITY

If the Bank of Canada causes the money supply to increase, three different results are possible. First, people who get the additional money could just hold on to it. Nothing would happen to the rest of the economy, only these people's bank balances would be increased. This outcome is most likely when the economy is in a deep recession, such as the Great Depression, in which case monetary policy will be relatively ineffective.

Second, those who get the additional money could try to spend it. By bringing that new money to the market, they might increase aggregate expenditures and shift the aggregate demand curve to an intersection with aggregate supply at a higher output level, as seen in Figure 18.1A. This is more likely to occur if initially there was considerable excess capacity.

The third result is that those who get the additional money also spend it, but this time the economy is originally in a situation where there is no excess capacity, as in panel B. The initial intersection of the aggregate demand and aggregate supply curves occurs along the vertical portion of the aggregate supply curve. Instead of output increasing, only prices increase.

What actually happens when the money supply is increased is some combination of the three possibilities—changed holdings of money, changed output, and changed

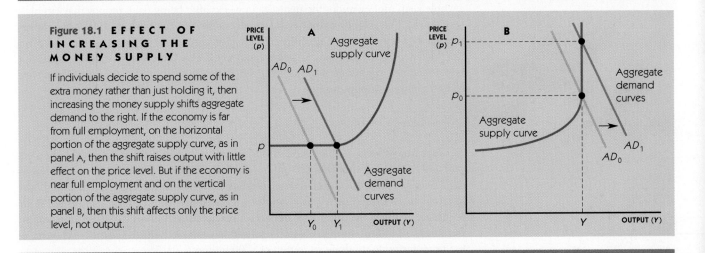

Figure 18.1 EFFECT OF INCREASING THE MONEY SUPPLY

If individuals decide to spend some of the extra money rather than just holding it, then increasing the money supply shifts aggregate demand to the right. If the economy is far from full employment, on the horizontal portion of the aggregate supply curve, as in panel A, then the shift raises output with little effect on the price level. But if the economy is near full employment and on the vertical portion of the aggregate supply curve, as in panel B, then this shift affects only the price level, not output.

prices. Which outcome is more likely to occur depends, as noted, on economic circumstances.

What policies the government wishes to pursue will also depend on economic circumstances. When the economy is in a recession and has excess capacity, the government wants to stimulate the economy. In this case, the question is whether or under what circumstances monetary policy can be used to stimulate the economy. On the other hand, when all of the resources of the economy are fully utilized, attention is switched to the problem of inflation and the role of monetary policy in reducing aggregate demand and thus reducing those inflationary pressures.

In Chapter 17, we learned several different ways of measuring the money supply—M1, M2, M3, and M2+. For much of our discussion, we do not have to be very precise about which supply of money we have in mind. But it is natural to focus our attention on M1, for two reasons. First, M1 is the supply of money most directly under the control of the Bank of Canada. Second, the key attribute of money upon which we will focus is its role as a medium of exchange; money facilitates transactions. And M1, which includes chequing accounts and currency, is the definition of money most directly related to its use as a medium of exchange.

Within M1, we will focus on the portion most directly under the Bank's control: the demand and other chequing-account deposits. This is also appropriate because they are more important—they comprise over half of the M1 total.

THE VELOCITY OF MONEY

As important to monetary policy as the money supply itself is its **velocity,** the speed with which money circulates in the economy. In a bustling city, money changes hands quickly, and thus a given money supply supports many more transactions there than it would in a depressed city where people do not make exchanges as often. If individuals as a whole keep money under the mattress for weeks after being paid, money may circulate very slowly. The velocity of money is formally defined as the ratio of GDP to the money supply. If Q represents the quantity of final goods produced in the economy and p is a weighted average of their prices, pQ is equal to GDP (which, you will recall, equals national income), represented by the symbol Y. Using the symbol V to denote velocity and M as the money supply, we get

$$V = pQ/M = Y/M.$$

To see how velocity is calculated using this equation, assume that Y is $700 billion per year and the money supply is $70 billion; the velocity would be 10 (per year). If producing a dollar of output required only one transaction, then the average dollar would have to circulate 10 times every year to produce an output of $700 billion—or, to put it another way, to allow the amount of dollars to "service" the economy. If the money supply were only $7 billion, then every dollar would have to circulate 100 times each year, or ten times faster, to produce an output of $700 billion.

The variable p was called a weighted average of prices. This is the same as calling p the price level. Let's use the velocity equation to look again at what happens when the money supply increases. If M increases, either V must be lowered, Q must increase, or p must increase. This result matches the three possible consequences of an increase in the money supply with which we began the chapter: individuals could simply hold the extra money, which would decrease velocity; the amount bought, Q, may increase; or the price level, p, may rise.

The essential problem of monetary theory is to understand when each of these outcomes will result. While the extreme cases, where only one of the three possibilities occurs, are instructive for understanding what is going on, they can be misleading. When the *only* effect is on prices or on money holdings, monetary policy is completely ineffective in stimulating aggregate output and employment. But if there is *some* effect on output as well, then monetary policy can be a useful instrument in stimulating the economy. It may take a larger dose of the medicine—a larger increase in the money supply—to achieve any desired goal.

POSSIBLE CONSEQUENCES OF INCREASED MONEY SUPPLY

Increased money holdings (decreased velocity)

Changes in quantities produced and sold

Changes in prices

To solve this problem, we need to ask two questions. First, to what extent will a change in the money supply lead to a change in velocity or a change in income, pQ? And second, how will any change in pQ be divided into a change in price level, p, and change in output, Q?

The second question is easy to answer, given what we have already learned about aggregate demand and supply curves. If the economy is operating along the horizontal portion of the aggregate supply curve, with excess capacity, then the price level will be unaffected when aggregate demand increases; only output will change. But if the economy is operating along the vertical portion of the aggregate supply curve, where output cannot change, then only the price level will be affected when aggregate demand increases.

We now turn to the first question. To keep the discussion simple, we focus on the situation where the economy is in the excess-capacity region, so that the price level is fixed.

THE DEMAND FOR MONEY

The velocity of money—how fast money circulates through the system—depends on how willing people are to hold, or keep, money. You may remember the game of hot potato, in which a hot potato is passed rapidly among people in a group. In a way, money is like a hot potato. Currency is an asset that bears no interest. Since people would usually prefer to earn interest, they have an incentive to pass their currency along to someone else, exchanging it for either goods or an interest-bearing asset like a Treasury bill. Why do they hold money at all? Because it is convenient. You can buy groceries with currency. You cannot buy groceries with a T-bill; you would have to convert your T-bill back into currency, and there are costs (transactions costs) of doing so.

Thus, people's willingness to hold money is a result of their balancing the benefits of holding money—the convenience—against the *opportunity* cost, the forgone interest. The benefits of holding money are related to money's use as a medium of exchange. The more transactions people engage in, the more money they will want to hold. The demand for money arising from its use in facilitating transactions is called the **transactions demand for money.** This demand for money rises with *nominal* income: higher incomes mean that the value of goods bought will be greater, which implies that the value of transactions will be greater. In fact, the demand for money increases proportionately with the nominal value of output, pQ; if prices double, then other things being equal, people will need to have twice the amount of money to engage in the same transactions.

The basic elements of monetary economics we have learned so far are agreed upon by most economists: the Bank of Canada controls (or at least affects) the money supply—through open market operations—and the demand for money increases with the level of nominal income. But there is some disagreement about whether the ratio of money demand to income—the velocity of circulation—is constant, or even predictable; and the extent to which the demand for money, at any income level, depends on the interest rate. We will now explore the reasons for these differences in views, and their consequences.

COMMONLY ACCEPTED INGREDIENTS OF MONETARY THEORIES

1. The Bank of Canada controls (or affects) the money supply through open market operations.

2. Money demand depends on nominal income.

KEYNESIAN MONETARY THEORY

Keynesians have traditionally emphasized that the demand for money may be dependent on the rate of interest. The cost of holding money is the interest that could have been earned if the money in your chequing account (or in your pocket) had been invested in some other asset. If chequing deposits pay interest of 0 percent and very short-term government bonds (Treasury bills) pay 4 percent, then the cost of holding money is 4 percent per year. Today some chequing accounts pay interest, so the opportunity cost of holding funds in them is lower than it used to be. Nevertheless, the difference between the interest paid on chequing accounts and the return to other assets deters people from holding money. We focus on the interest rate paid on T-bills for a simple reason: they are just as safe as money. The only difference is that T-bills yield a higher interest rate, but money is better as a medium of exchange.

The demand for money is much like the demand for any other good; it depends on the price and on people's incomes. The price of a good tells us what a person has to give up of other goods to get an additional unit of this good. This price also measures the opportunity cost of consuming an additional unit of the good. The interest rate (r) the individual could have earned on a government bond can be thought of as the price of money, since it measures the opportunity cost of holding money. As the interest rate rises, the amount of money demanded declines.

Another way to think about this is to remember that the velocity of circulation measures how fast money moves through the economy—that is, how frequently a given dollar bill circulates. The lower the interest rate, the lower the velocity of circulation. It is costly to hold on to money—people must forgo interest that they could otherwise be earning. The higher the interest rate, the more costly and therefore the more quickly they pass it on to someone else after receiving it, by buying goods or investing it in an asset yielding a higher return.

Table 18.1 DEMAND FOR MONEY

Nominal interest rate	Money demand for income of	
	$600 billion	$1,200 billion
2%	$124	$248
4%	121	242
6%	118	236
8%	115	230
10%	112	224

To see how the demand for money depends on people's incomes, consider Table 18.1, which shows a hypothetical example. These are the numbers plotted in Figure 18.2. With an income level of $600 billion, the demand for money is given by the curve on the left. The table and figure illustrate the two basic properties of the demand for money: it decreases as the interest rate rises, and increases, at a fixed interest rate, in proportion to income. Doubling the income level to $1,200 billion at any fixed interest rate shifts the demand curve for money out.

In equilibrium, the interest rate adjusts to make the demand for money equal the sup-

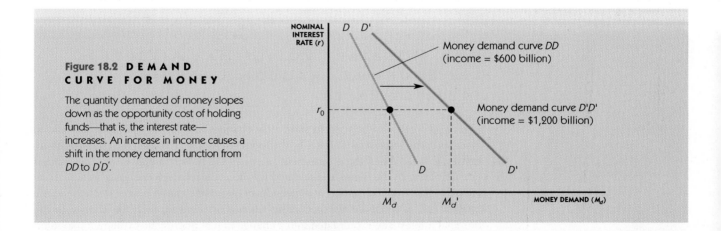

Figure 18.2 DEMAND CURVE FOR MONEY

The quantity demanded of money slopes down as the opportunity cost of holding funds—that is, the interest rate—increases. An increase in income causes a shift in the money demand function from *DD* to *D'D'*.

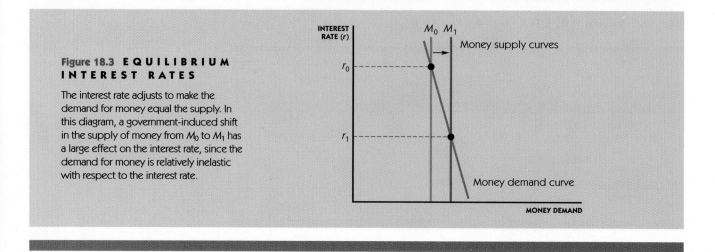

Figure 18.3 EQUILIBRIUM INTEREST RATES

The interest rate adjusts to make the demand for money equal the supply. In this diagram, a government-induced shift in the supply of money from M_0 to M_1 has a large effect on the interest rate, since the demand for money is relatively inelastic with respect to the interest rate.

ply. Figure 18.3 shows supply curves for money as well as a demand curve. The supply of money is controlled by the government (the Bank of Canada), through the instruments described in Chapter 17. The amount of money the Bank makes available does not depend at all on the interest rate. That is why the supply curves are vertical. The equilibrium interest rate with money supply M_0 is r_0.

The principles described in this section—that the nominal interest rate is the opportunity cost of holding money, the demand for money decreases as the interest rate rises, and the interest rate is determined to equate the demand and supply of money—are together called **Keynesian monetary theory.** Keynes used this theory to explain how monetary policy works when it works, and why it sometimes does not work. To do this, he traced out the effects of a change in the supply of money on the interest rate, the effects of a change in the interest rate on investment, and the effects of a change in investment on the level of national income. We now take a closer look at each of these steps.

HOW MONETARY POLICY MAY AFFECT THE ECONOMY THROUGH CHANGING INTEREST RATES

Figure 18.3 can also be used to show how changes in the money supply can lead to changes in the interest rates. Initially, the money supply is at M_0 and the equilibrium interest rate is r_0. When the government increases the money supply to M_1, the interest rate falls to r_1. In the figure, the demand for money is relatively inelastic, so that an increase in the supply of money at a given level of income causes a large decrease in the interest rate. If inflationary expectations remain unchanged, then the change in the nominal interest rate is translated into a change in real interest rates (the nominal interest rate minus the rate of inflation). As interest rates fall, investment rises. As investment spending increases, income (which is the same as output) rises via the multiplier.

The increase in investment shifts the aggregate expenditures schedule up, as depicted

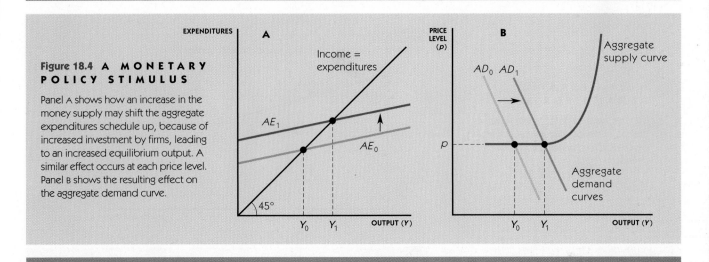

Figure 18.4 A MONETARY POLICY STIMULUS

Panel A shows how an increase in the money supply may shift the aggregate expenditures schedule up, because of increased investment by firms, leading to an increased equilibrium output. A similar effect occurs at each price level. Panel B shows the resulting effect on the aggregate demand curve.

in Figure 18.4A, and results in a higher equilibrium level of output. Output increases from Y_0 to Y_1.

The aggregate expenditures schedule assumes a particular price level. A similar effect occurs at each price level. Accordingly, the aggregate demand curve shifts to the right, as shown in Figure 18.4B. Here in the initial equilibrium there is excess capacity; that is, the intersection of the aggregate demand and aggregate supply curves occurs along the horizontal portion of the aggregate supply curve. Thus, the effect of the shift in the aggregate demand curve is to increase output, with no change in prices.

When income increases, the money demand curve shifts to the right, as is shown in Figure 18.5. Thus, the eventual equilibrium attained will involve a smaller decrease in the rate of interest than r_1. The new equilibrium interest rate will lie somewhere between r_0 and r_1; in the figure, it is r_2.

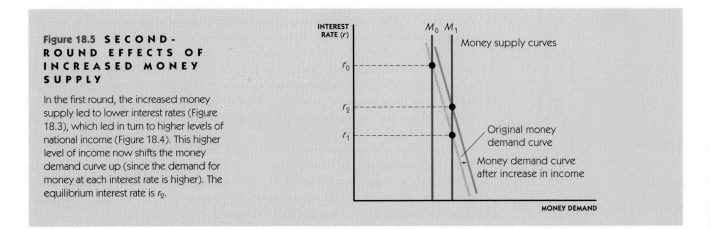

Figure 18.5 SECOND-ROUND EFFECTS OF INCREASED MONEY SUPPLY

In the first round, the increased money supply led to lower interest rates (Figure 18.3), which led in turn to higher levels of national income (Figure 18.4). This higher level of income now shifts the money demand curve up (since the demand for money at each interest rate is higher). The equilibrium interest rate is r_2.

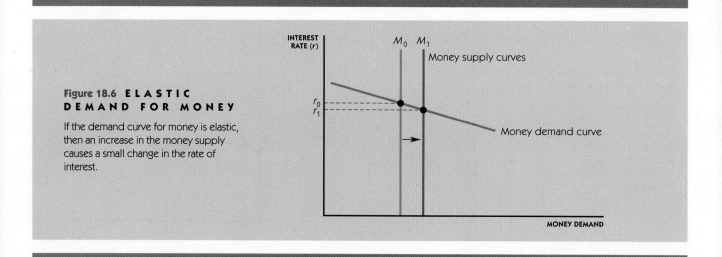

Figure 18.6 ELASTIC DEMAND FOR MONEY

If the demand curve for money is elastic, then an increase in the money supply causes a small change in the rate of interest.

MONETARY POLICY IN DEEP RECESSIONS AND IN PERIODS OF FULL EMPLOYMENT

Figure 18.6 illustrates a situation that Keynes thought was prevalent in an economy suffering from deep recession: the demand curve for money is relatively elastic, so that changes in the supply of money have a negligible effect on the interest rate. In an extreme case, the demand curve for money would be perfectly horizontal. Then the only effect of an increase in the money supply would be that people would hold more money. Although this extreme case is not likely to occur, in deep recessions even large changes in the supply of money may induce relatively small changes in the interest rate.

Not only did Keynes think increasing the money supply would have little effect on interest rates, he also thought that in a recession any changes in the interest rate that did occur would have little effect on aggregate expenditures, since investment would be relatively unresponsive to changes in interest rates. Consumers would also respond little to reductions in the interest rate. Hence, in Keynes' view, increases in the money supply did not cause increases in output when they were most needed. Money supply changes did not move the aggregate expenditures schedule upward by much, and as a result they did not induce much of a change in the aggregate demand curve. They mostly changed the velocity of circulation.

Keynes' theory of monetary policy can easily be extended to situations where the economy is not in a recession but is operating along the vertical portion of the aggregate supply curve, as depicted in Figure 18.7A. The lower interest rate shifts the aggregate demand curve to the right, as we have seen before. But now the shift only results in an increase in the price level. It has no effect on output.

In between the two extremes are cases where the economy is operating along the

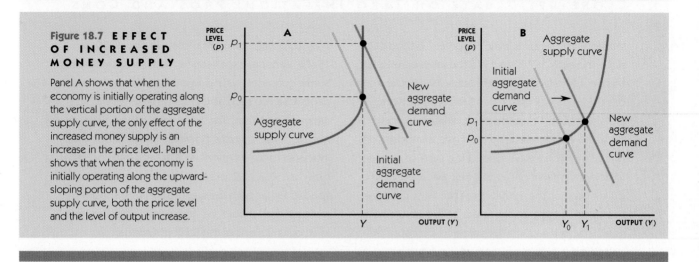

Figure 18.7 EFFECT OF INCREASED MONEY SUPPLY

Panel A shows that when the economy is initially operating along the vertical portion of the aggregate supply curve, the only effect of the increased money supply is an increase in the price level. Panel B shows that when the economy is initially operating along the upward-sloping portion of the aggregate supply curve, both the price level and the level of output increase.

upward-sloping portion of the aggregate supply curve, seen in panel B. Then the increase in money supply will lower interest rates, shift the aggregate demand curve, and result in both a higher output and a higher price level.

KEYNESIAN MONETARY THEORY

The nominal interest rate is the opportunity cost of holding money.
The demand for money decreases as the interest rate rises.
The interest rate equates the demand and supply for money.

KEYNESIAN THEORY OF MONETARY POLICY

When monetary policy is effective in generating increased output, it is because the policy induces a lower interest rate.

Monetary policy is ineffective in deep recessions, because

1. the money demand curve is elastic, so changes in the money supply induce only small changes in interest rates; and

2. even large changes in the interest rate induce little change in investment and hence in aggregate demand.

CLOSE-UP: DEBATE ON ZERO INFLATION: PROS AND CONS

Inflation has been a major problem periodically since the early 1970s. In 1975 the inflation rate hit the double digits, and in the early 1980s it did so once again. Since then it has fluctuated between 3 and 6 percent. The persistence of inflation, its tendency to accelerate, and the costs it imposes on the economy have persuaded the Bank of Canada to focus on inflation as the key macroeconomic policy issue of the 1990s. Most recently, the Bank has taken a zero-inflation rate to be its ultimate goal. Is zero inflation a feasible and desirable policy objective? Here are some of the arguments:

Con: Short–Term Costs Deflationary monetary policy has negative effects on the economy. If the federal government cannot print money to finance its expenditures, it must either cut spending, which depresses income and employment; sell in the bond market, which adds to the debt; or raise taxes, which reduces Canadians' disposable income and consumption. In the process of reducing inflation, short-term interest rates must rise. This discourages investment and causes the exchange rate to appreciate, hurting Canadian exporters.

Pro: Long–Term Benefits Efficiency gains are associated with a stable price level. Increased certainty about the economy and lower long–term nominal interest rates lead to higher industrial and consumer durables investment.

Con: Zero Inflation Is Neither Achievable Nor Sustainable The Bank of Canada cannot unilaterally impose zero inflation, especially when it is unclear which definition of the money supply should be controlled, M1, M2, or M3. The generation of money substitutes by financial institutions, as well as the expectations and behaviour of product pricers and wage earners, would have to be in line with the objectives of the monetary authority.

Pro: Zero Inflation Is Feasible In the 1950s and 1960s Canada experienced near–zero inflation. Some countries with powerful and independent central banks, such as Germany, have very low inflation rates today. The term zero inflation should not be taken literally, however. Most economists interpret "zero inflation" as a steady inflation rate between 0 and 2 percent. Some suggest that a specific target path for the inflation rate should be defined and should be the prime directive and legal commitment of the Bank of Canada.

Con: Inflation Is Not the Most Pressing Economic Problem A country with a major debt and deficit problem should concentrate its efforts on maintaining the exchange rate and lowering interest rates rather than lowering inflation. A country with high unemployment should not take further contractionary measures in an attempt to control the price level.

Pro: Response Globalization and innovations in financial markets have meant increased access to global markets in goods, services, and capital. Central banks in small open economies such as Canada can influence real interest rates and the real exchange rate to a limited extent in the short term, and not at all in the long term. Thus, the Bank of Canada can influence only the nominal interest rate and the nominal exchange rate, reducing their level and volatility only by lowering inflation.

Some economists believe that the pros of a zero-inflation policy outweigh the cons; some believe the opposite.

Sources: Richard G. Lipsey, ed., *Zero Inflation: The Goal of Price Stability* (Toronto: C. D. Howe Institute, 1990); Robert C. York, ed., *Taking Aim: The Debate on Zero Inflation* (Toronto: C.D. Howe Institute, 1990).

CRITICISMS OF THE KEYNESIAN THEORY OF THE DEMAND FOR MONEY

In the Keynesian monetary theory, there is a simple mechanism by which monetary policy affects the economy: when the government increases the supply of money, interest rates must fall in order for the demand for money to equal the supply; and lower interest rates induce more investment and consumer purchases of durables, stimulating aggregate demand. In recent years, changes in the financial system have led to a reexamination of this theory. Both its premises and its conclusions about the mechanisms by which monetary policy affects the economy have been questioned.

RELATIONSHIP BETWEEN MONEY AND INCOME

Economists have raised several questions concerning the demand function for money underlying the theory. Some questions focus on the relationship between the demand for money and income, others on the effect of interest rates on the demand for money.

Earlier we saw that what particularly distinguishes money from other assets such as government Treasury bills is its role as a medium of exchange in facilitating transactions. The Keynesian monetary theory implies that the higher their income, the more money people will want to hold. There is a simple relationship between the volume of transactions and the level of income. This would be the case if most transactions were directly related to output—employers paying wages and buying goods from suppliers, customers buying goods from firms, and so on.

But in fact, in terms of their dollar value, most transactions are for exchanges of financial assets, not the purchase of goods and services. One individual thinks Canadian Pacific stock is going to go down, and so he sells his shares. Another person thinks it is going up, and so she buys shares. The relationship between the volume of these financial transactions has virtually no direct bearing on national output and income. Indeed, the *ratio* of these transactions to national income may change markedly with economic conditions. When there is greater uncertainty and change, there may be more financial exchange, as people take differing views of what the future holds and as individual circumstances change rapidly.

In the longer run, there are a number of other factors that affect the relationship between money and income. For instance, not all transactions require payment by cash or cheque; today most transactions are made with credit. You need neither to have money in a bank account nor currency in your pocket to buy a car or a vacation in Banff, so long as you can get credit. You can pay with a credit card or write a cheque against your trust company account. Of course, some kinds of transactions are not easily done with credit; in Canada, you still have to pay for taxis and groceries with cash. But in Australia, taxis accept Visa, MasterCard, and American Express, and in the United States some grocery stores accept them as well. The transactions that require money at the point of sale represent a relatively small and shrinking proportion of all transactions in the modern economy.

Similarly, technology has altered the whole idea of the velocity of money. With electronic fund transfers, in which computers can transfer funds from bank to bank or from account to account almost instantaneously, the velocity of circulation can become extremely high, even close to infinite for a few moments.

One might have thought that the increased use of credit and new technologies would have led to a higher velocity, a reduced ratio of money to income. In fact, the upward trend of velocity in the previous forty years has been reversed since 1980. There are no widely accepted explanations for these changes, and they appear to have had little effect on the economy.[1] Nevertheless, to the extent that they indicate that the money demand curve moves in ways that are not totally predictable, the ability to rely on monetary policy has been thrown into doubt.

RELATIONSHIP BETWEEN INTEREST RATES AND THE DEMAND FOR MONEY

Another set of criticisms of Keynesian monetary theory relates to the relationship between interest rates and the demand for money. Today some demand deposits, which constitute the bulk of the money supply, pay interest. Thus, the opportunity cost of holding money is now the *difference* between the return to holding a government bond, for example, and the return to keeping one's money in a chequing account; and that difference is small and may relate primarily to the bank's cost of running the chequing account. Interest-bearing chequing accounts were largely unavailable in the early part of this century, when the Keynesian theory of money demand was set forth. Their existence today calls into question the extent to which the demand for money will rise or fall in response to changes in interest rates.

But the Keynesian version of monetary theory has been criticized, not only because the underlying assumptions concerning the demand for money are unpersuasive, but also because of questions about its conclusion that monetary policy operates through changes in the interest rate. It is the real interest rate that matters most to firms, but it is the nominal interest rate that the Bank of Canada controls. The link between nominal and real interest rates may be tenuous. Changes in nominal interest rates translate directly into changes in real interest rates only if they produce no change in inflationary expectations. However, this is unlikely. By and large, higher nominal interest rates are associated with higher rates of inflation. And the data discussed in Chapter 13 showed that for long periods of time real interest rates varied relatively little.

Not only has the link between monetary policy and real interest rates been questioned, so has the link between real interest rates and investment. The data presented in Chapter 13, showing little relationship between changes in real interest rates and investment, suggest that much of the time the interest rate is not the only or primary mechanism through which monetary policy operates.

---

[1] One hypothesis is that there is a growing "underground" economy—drug dealers and others wishing to avoid paying income taxes. These individuals hold money as a store of value. But many observers think that the magnitude of the shift is too large to be simply accounted for by the development of the underground economy.

MONEY AND KEYNESIAN MONETARY THEORY: SOME PROBLEMS

There is no simple relationship between the demand for money and income.

> Most transactions involve not goods and services (output) but the exchange of assets. The connection between transactions related to output and those related to exchange may not be stable.
>
> Transactions do not necessarily need money; credit will do.
>
> Changes in technology have allowed more extensive use of credit and make possible much higher velocities.

Real interest rates may not be directly affected by monetary policy.

> Today most money takes the form of demand deposits and is interest-bearing. Thus, the opportunity cost of holding money is low and is not directly related to the nominal interest rate.
>
> The opportunity cost is the nominal interest rate; investment is affected by real interest rates.
>
> Fluctuations in investment are not closely linked with changes in real interest rates.

ALTERNATIVE WAYS THAT MONETARY POLICY WORKS

Economists dissatisfied with the interest rate links between money supply and output, but nonetheless convinced that there *is* a link between money and output, have looked for alternative ways that monetary policy exerts its effects. One important channel, through exports and imports, will be discussed in Chapter 19. Here we look at three other theories.

The first theory argues that investment is affected not so much because monetary policy changes the interest rate, but rather because it changes the prices of shares. The second extends this argument and maintains that as monetary policy increases the prices of shares and long-term bonds, people feel wealthier and are induced to consume more. The third provides an alternative explanation for why interest rates may fall when the government engages in open market operations; it focuses not on households' demand for money but on the behaviour of banks.

INVESTMENT AND PORTFOLIO THEORY

Portfolio theories, which draw attention to stock market prices, focus on the store of value role of money. Individuals, in deciding on their portfolios, look at the returns afforded by different assets—by Treasury bills, long-term government and corporate bonds, and stocks. Money is an asset that has similar properties to Treasury bills, except that it is also a medium of exchange and yields a lower return.

Nobel laureate James Tobin, of Yale University, focuses on the fact that when interest rates are low, individuals will shift their wealth towards stocks. This will drive the price of stocks up. At the higher price of shares, firms will engage in more investment. This theory is important in that it emphasizes the fact that firms do not look solely at the rate of interest on government bonds in deciding their investment. But it probably overemphasizes the role of the price of shares in determining firms' investment decisions, particularly since even in the best of times new equity issues finance a relatively small proportion of all investment.[2]

CONSUMPTION AND WEALTH EFFECTS

Another theory points out that the higher prices of shares and long-term bonds resulting from lower interest rates may make people feel wealthier. And when they feel wealthier, they consume more. It is not clear, however, how significant this wealth effect is in the short run. As we saw in Chapter 13, individuals do not adjust their consumption quickly to changes in market values of their stocks and bonds, and even when they do, the increase in consumption is limited.

Still another set of theories pays less attention to households and firms and more attention to banks, but with much the same result in terms of national output. Open market operations result in banks' having more reserves. Earlier we saw how non-interest-bearing money is like a hot potato: it yields a zero return, so that apart from any convenience it might yield in facilitating transactions, you would like to get rid of it as fast as you can, to get an asset that yields a return. Today, since money yields a return, it is less like a hot potato. But to banks, reserves are really like hot potatoes, since they do not yield a return.[3] In our system, where banks manage their own reserves, they hold cash reserves mainly for transactions purposes. The reserves are not required for "safety," since holding Treasury bills is as safe as holding reserves.

Consider what happens when the Bank of Canada creates some reserves through open market operations. Suppose the bank buys a $10,000 Treasury bill from Rose Smith, who takes her cheque drawn against the Bank down to her local bank and deposits it. The Bank credits the bank with additional reserves. Reserves have gone up by $10,000 and so have deposits. The bank now has excess reserves and wants to invest them. It lowers its interest rates to attract more loan applicants, or it buys Treasury bills. As it tries to

---

[2] Moreover, empirical studies show the relationship between investment and the price of shares to be much weaker than Tobin's theory suggests. See Chapter 13 for a fuller discussion, including why even the weak relationship that has been observed can be interpreted in a quite different way.

[3] In some European countries, reserves do yield a return.

buy T-bills, the price of T-bills goes up, and again the interest rate falls. And as the interest rate falls, stock and bond prices rise, and investment may increase because of either the lower interest rates or higher stock market prices. But, as we have seen, many economists are skeptical about the significance of these effects, and they look to an alternative mechanism, the availability of credit.

ALTERNATIVE MECHANISMS BY WHICH MONETARY POLICY MAY WORK

1. An increased money supply leads to lower interest rates and may also lead to higher prices of shares, which induces greater investment.

2. Higher prices of shares and long-term bonds may result in more consumption because consumers feel wealthier.

3. Open market operations may lead to lower interest rates and higher prices of shares and bonds because of the way banks respond to increased reserves.

MONETARISTS

One group of economists who were particularly influential in the late 1970s and early 1980s are the monetarists, whom we first encountered in Chapter 10; Nobel laureate Milton Friedman is perhaps the best known. Monetarists emphasize that what is important is not *how* monetary policy exerts its effects, but the simple fact that it *does* exert effects—that there is a systematic and predictable relationship between the money supply and the level of national income, or output.

The simplest version of this theory returns to the basic definition of velocity:

$$V = pQ/M.$$

Now let's assume that velocity is constant and use an asterisk to signify this. We can rewrite the equation as

$$MV^* = pQ.$$

If V^* is a constant and M doubles, pQ, the value of income, must also double. The theory that holds that velocity is constant so that increases in the money supply are reflected simply in proportionate increases in income is called the **quantity theory of money.**

We have repeatedly seen that whether p increases or Q increases, or a combination of both, depends on whether the economy is initially operating along the horizontal, vertical, or upward-sloping portion of the aggregate supply curve. Consider, in particular, what happens if the economy is operating along the vertical portion, so that output cannot change. Then if M increases, the price level must increase proportionately. Consider what would happen if one night an elf went around doubling the money in everyone's pocket. Stores, acting perfectly efficiently, knowing that there is a fixed supply of goods available and knowing that the money supply had doubled, would immediately double their prices. Nothing *real* would happen.

How does an increase in the money supply have this effect on the price level? How does it lead to a shift in the aggregate demand curve? Some monetarists believe the answer is very simple: with more money chasing the same number of goods, prices must rise, just as though there were an elf. Others think the process may be more complicated. But monetarists all agree on the outcome: if money supply goes up and the economy is at full capacity, the price level must go up proportionately.

A MONEY DEMAND CURVE INTERPRETATION

The fact that velocity is constant means that individuals' willingness to hold money is not sensitive to the interest rate. That is, the demand curve for money is perfectly inelastic, as depicted in Figure 18.8. The demand for money, M_d, is simply proportional to income:

$$M_d = k(pQ),$$

where k is a proportionality constant. In equilibrium, the demand for money must equal the supply, M_s:

$$M_s = M_d = k(pQ).$$

Note that by comparing this expression with the definition of the velocity of circulation above, we see that the proportion k is simply the reciprocal of the velocity of circulation; or, $k = 1/V$.

When velocity is constant, changes in the interest rate cannot balance the demand and supply of money. The only way that the demand and supply of money can be in equilibrium is through changes in the level of income. The demand for money is simply proportional to income, so that if the supply of money is increased by 10 percent, for the demand for money to equal supply, national income must rise by 10 percent. If the supply of money is decreased by 10 percent, then national income must fall by 10 percent.

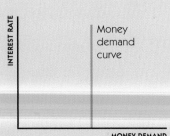

Figure 18.8 INELASTIC DEMAND CURVE FOR MONEY

Monetarists believe that the interest elasticity of the demand curve for money is essentially zero, which means that it is a vertical line.

MONETARISM AND MONETARY POLICY

Monetarists see a clear prescription for economy policy: let the money supply grow at the rate of growth of full-employment output. When the economy is operating along the vertical portion of the aggregate supply curve (there is no excess capacity), then such a policy ensures that prices will be stable. If output grows by 3 percent and the Bank of Canada increases the money supply by 3 percent, the price level will remain unchanged. At a faster rate of growth of the money supply, the price level will have to increase.

When the economy is operating along the horizontal portion of the aggregate supply curve, a decrease in the money supply can have devastating effects on the level of national income. In situations with excess capacity, we can take the price level as fixed. Thus, changes in the money supply result in proportionate changes in output. Monetarists like Milton Friedman believe that contractions of the money supply are largely responsible for many of the major downturns in the economy, including the Great Depression.

While Keynes focused on one extreme case, where the demand for money is highly sensitive to the interest rate, the monetarists focus on the other extreme, where the demand for money does not depend at all on the interest rate. More generally, the effectiveness of monetary policy depends on two variables: the elasticity of the demand curve for money (how sensitive the demand for money is to interest rates) and the interest elasticity of investment (how sensitive investment is to interest rates). Both of these elasticities can change with economic circumstances. Except in the extreme cases upon which Keynes focused, we would expect to see some relationship between the money supply and the level of economic activity, and there clearly is such a relationship. Figure 18.9 shows the rate of growth of the money supply. The shaded areas represent recessions. It is apparent that every major recession has been preceded by a decline in the rate of growth of the money supply (though there have been instances where the rate of growth of money has declined and the economy has not gone into a recession).

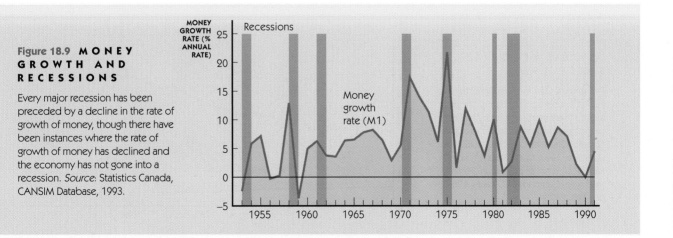

Figure 18.9 MONEY GROWTH AND RECESSIONS

Every major recession has been preceded by a decline in the rate of growth of money, though there have been instances where the rate of growth of money has declined and the economy has not gone into a recession. *Source*: Statistics Canada, CANSIM Database, 1993.

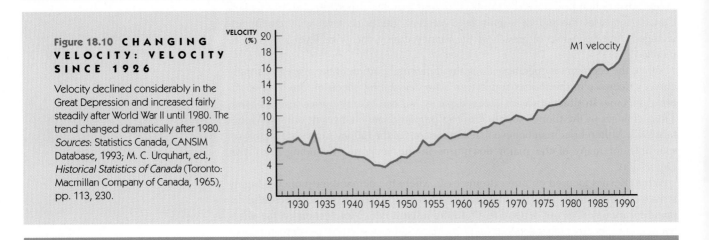

Figure 18.10 CHANGING VELOCITY: VELOCITY SINCE 1926

Velocity declined considerably in the Great Depression and increased fairly steadily after World War II until 1980. The trend changed dramatically after 1980. *Sources*: Statistics Canada, CANSIM Database, 1993; M. C. Urquhart, ed., *Historical Statistics of Canada* (Toronto: Macmillan Company of Canada, 1965), pp. 113, 230.

VARIATIONS IN VELOCITY

A closer look at the data helps us see more clearly the nature of the money-income relationship. Figure 18.10 shows the velocity since 1926, and Figure 18.11 shows a close-up of the patterns since 1968. Three conclusions emerge.

First, in the one major economic downturn of this century, the Great Depression, velocity changed significantly.

Second, in the post–World War II period until the 1980s, the dominant feature of velocity was its steady upward trend. This steady upward trend was slowed down in reces-

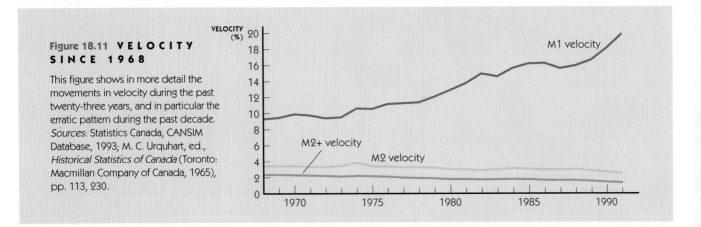

Figure 18.11 VELOCITY SINCE 1968

This figure shows in more detail the movements in velocity during the past twenty-three years, and in particular the erratic pattern during the past decade. *Sources*: Statistics Canada, CANSIM Database, 1993; M. C. Urquhart, ed., *Historical Statistics of Canada* (Toronto: Macmillan Company of Canada, 1965), pp. 113, 230.

sions. The relatively slight effect of these recessions on velocity could be for two reasons. One is that nominal interest rates in fact changed relatively little—that after an initial downturn they quickly returned to their previous level. The other reason is that the demand for money is relatively insensitive to changes in nominal interest rates.

The third conclusion is that since 1980, the behaviour of velocity has been somewhat erratic. It declined at the start of the second half of the decade, only to pick up again at the end. At the very least, the monetarist idea of a constant or predictable money-income relationship has to be looked at with suspicion.

MONEY AND CREDIT AVAILABILITY

As economists have sought alternative explanations for why monetary policy works when it does and why it does not work in deep recessions, they have focused attention on the availability of credit (the availability of loans). We saw in Chapter 17 that when the money supply is increased (deposits appear on the right-hand side of a bank's balance sheet), reserves are increased and the bank's assets—its holdings of Treasury bills and its loan portfolio—are increased. Thus, money and credit are two sides of the same coin, or two sides of the same balance sheet. But money and credit do not have to move perfectly in tandem, because banks can decide to increase their holdings of Treasury bills rather than making additional loans.

The credit availability theories focus on how and when the Bank of Canada's actions induce banks to make more or fewer loans or make loans available on easier or more restrictive terms. These changes in credit availability have a direct effect on economic activity: if credit is more available, or available at better terms, firms will undertake more investments and consumers may buy more goods, particularly durables. There is an important proviso, however: the Bank's credit-making powers will only be effective in stimulating the economy when firms' investment and household purchases are limited only by the availability of credit or the terms at which credit is available.

We saw earlier that changes in the interest rate may not induce much additional investment. Even if banks announced that they were willing to lend money at a zero interest rate to any project that could persuade the loan officers that the loan had at least a 95 percent chance of being repaid, few additional loans might be made: if prices were falling at the rate of 10 percent a year (as they did at times in the Great Depression), the real interest rate would be 10 percent, and given the terrible economic conditions, firms might not be willing to undertake much investment at that high real interest rate.

INDUCING BANKS TO LEND MORE

The first question in the credit availability approach to monetary policy is, how does the Bank induce banks to lend more? One way is to engage in open market operations. That is, the Bank buys Treasury bills. We saw in Chapter 17 that when the cheque the Bank uses to buy the Treasury bills is deposited in a bank, the deposits in the banking system increase, as do the reserves. Banks then want to invest more either in Treasury bills or in loans. If there are good loan opportunities, banks will lend more.

It may take banks a while before they can lend out additional funds, however. Meanwhile, they will invest funds in Treasury bills. Thus, in the short run, the demand for Treasury bills will increase, raising their price and lowering the rate of interest. In the longer run, the interest rate effect on T-bills will be reduced as banks find good loan opportunities and buy fewer T-bills; but banks may still decide to hold some of their increased assets in the form of T-bills, so that even in the longer run interest rates on T-bills may be slightly lower.

Bank of Canada policies affect the banks' ability to lend. As the expression goes, however, you can lead a horse to water, but you cannot make it drink. The Bank of Canada cannot *force* banks to lend. Banks decide whether to lend more or to buy Treasury bills. And there are three problems banks might have with lending. First, when default rates are high, banks are more likely to be content with a low but safe return on Treasury bills rather than risk a loss on a loan. Second, their ability and willingness to bear these risks depend on their financial positions. If their net worth has been greatly reduced by defaults on earlier loans, then they will be less willing to make loans. They have no cushion to absorb any further losses. Third, the capacity and willingness of the banking system as a whole to make loans may be adversely affected when some financial institutions have gone bankrupt. Each institution has specialized information about those firms to which it normally lends money. It has information about the prospects of these firms, and knows how much it can safely lend. If one financial institution fails, others, including banks, lacking this information, will be reluctant to step in.

All three of these problems were present to some extent in the Great Depression: the high default rate made lending seem particularly risky; the huge losses banks had experienced meant that many of them had no cushion to bear further losses; and the bankruptcy rates among banks further diminished the system's capacity to make loans.

Some of these problems appeared again in somewhat muted form in the recession that began in 1991. While banks were well protected against bankruptcy, the banking system itself was not in great shape. Banks had encountered huge losses in real estate loans, including quite dramatic ones like those to the massive developer Olympia and York. The decrease in the price of oil in the mid-1980s had led to large defaults on oil and gas loans made by some banks. Finally, the banks had lent billions of dollars to less-developed countries such as those in Latin America, and several of these countries found their debt burdens beyond their capacity to repay. In the United States, there were some major bankruptcies. Many of the so-called savings and loan banks (which are similar to trust and mortgage loan companies in Canada) went bankrupt as did the Bank of New England, the largest bank in the U.S. Northeast, mainly as a result of real estate losses. The Canadian banking system was spared major bankruptcies this time around, partly because bank supervision had been extended somewhat after the failure of Northlands and CCB (discussed in Chapter 6). Nonetheless, the banking system as a whole seemed reluctant to make loans.

LENDING RATES AND CREDIT RATIONING

While the Treasury bill rate is important to banks and may be an important determinant of the demand for money, firms are concerned with the interest rates they have to pay to borrow funds. Sometimes the same forces that cause the Treasury bill rate to fall also cause the rate on private loans to fall. If the Bank of Canada reduces the rate on Treasury bills by increasing the money supply through open market operations, the increased ability of banks to lend drives down the interest rate charged to borrowers, as banks compete for borrowers. At the lower interest rates, more investment projects are undertaken. The economy is stimulated, much as Keynesian monetary theory suggests. In some cases, however, banks may not change their interest rates very much in response to the change in the Treasury bill rate.

Appendix B in Chapter 13 explained why this might be so. As interest rates rise, the best borrowers, those most likely to repay their loans, decide not to borrow. And those who do borrow attempt to offset the effect of higher interest rates by getting a higher return, but to do that, they must undertake greater risks. As a result, there is a greater chance that they will be unable to meet their commitments to repay. Increased interest rates have an adverse selection effect on the mix of those taking loans and an adverse effect on incentives (from the banks' perspective).

Figure 18.12 shows the result of both of these effects. The expected return to the bank—which takes into account the increased rate of default—may actually decline as the interest rate charged by the bank increases beyond r^*. Therefore, banks do not raise the rate of interest they charge beyond r^*, even if there is an excess demand for credit at that interest rate. They simply ration credit. By the same token, when banks are in a credit rationing situation, a fall in the interest rate on Treasury bills induced by the Bank of Canada may not be successful at lowering interest rates on loans.

The prevalence of credit rationing has serious implications for monetary policy. Consider a situation where at r^* there is an excess demand for loans. But banks do not respond by raising the interest rate, since doing so would only reduce the expected returns to the loans. Now, assume that the Bank of Canada engages in open market operations, making it possible for banks to lend more. More loans are made, at the same interest rate. Monetary policy has its effects, not because it leads to a large change in the real interest rate charged on loans, but because it leads to changes in the availability of credit. The same process works in reverse. If the Bank tightens credit by engaging in open market operations, banks reduce the number of loans; they may not raise the interest rate, or may raise it only a little.

Whether or not credit rationing is in effect depends upon the circumstances of the time, such as business confidence and the availability of good investment projects. It does not appear to have been a factor in the most recent recession. When the T-bill rate rose from 12.05 to 12.81 percent over 1989–1990, the rate on 90-day commercial paper rose from 12.21 to 13.03 percent and that on long-term bonds rose from 9.92 to 10.85 percent. The Bank of Canada was successful in reducing both rates by inducing a substantial fall in the T-bill rate by mid-1992 to 6.72 percent. The interest rate on 90-day commercial paper fell to 6.78 percent and the long-term bond rate fell to 9.51 percent.

When banks tighten or loosen credit, with minimal changes in interest rates, they may nonetheless alter other terms of the credit contract. They may, for instance, increase their collateral requirements, the assets that borrowers have to put up when they take a loan and that will be forfeited in the event of a default. Higher collateral requirements both preclude some borrowers from borrowing—those with insufficient collateral to get loans—and make borrowing less attractive to other borrowers, who now have more to lose.

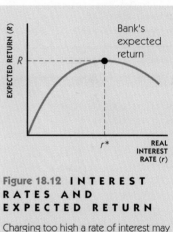

Figure 18.12 INTEREST RATES AND EXPECTED RETURN

Charging too high a rate of interest may actually lower the expected return, because the higher interest rate will tend to drive away prudent borrowers who would have been careful to repay. The bank's expected return is maximized at r^*, and charging a higher interest rate would reduce the bank's return.

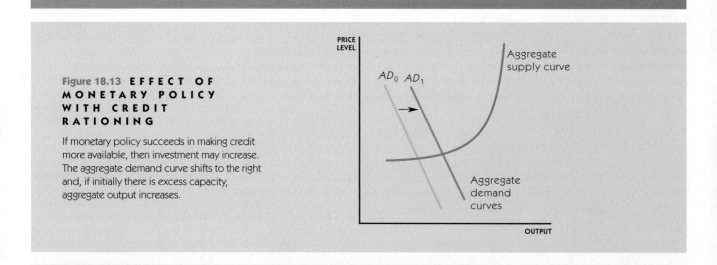

Figure 18.13 EFFECT OF MONETARY POLICY WITH CREDIT RATIONING

If monetary policy succeeds in making credit more available, then investment may increase. The aggregate demand curve shifts to the right and, if initially there is excess capacity, aggregate output increases.

Figure 18.13 shows the effect of monetary policy. As banks make credit more available, investment increases. The aggregate demand curve therefore shifts to the right, and equilibrium output increases.

OTHER CREDIT AVAILABILITY INSIGHTS

Credit availability theory provides several explanations other than credit rationing for why monetary policy is sometimes effective and sometimes not. Monetary policy will be ineffective under two circumstances. First, even if banks are willing (at the initial interest rates) to lend more, it may be hard to induce firms to borrow more. Firms may have an inelastic investment curve, as was pointed out in Chapter 13; as banks compete for borrowers, interest rates fall but little additional investment results. Second, the Bank of Canada may have difficulty inducing additional lending.

Thus, those holding credit availability theories come to much the same conclusion as Keynes did: in severe recessions, monetary policy may be of limited effectiveness. Keynes and the credit availability theorists only partially agree on the reasons. Both believe that it may be hard to get firms to invest more or consumers to purchase more through monetary policy. Both believe that there may be small changes in the interest rate. In Keynes' theory, the small change in the interest rate is caused by an elastic demand for money. In the credit availability theories, the small change in the interest rate is caused by the fact that it does not pay banks to lower the interest rate they charge on loans. Both believe that small—or, in a depression, even large—changes in interest rates may have only small effects. In the prolonged recession that began in 1990, all of these results were observed. While the Bank succeeded in lowering interest rates on Treasury bills, the effect on lending rates and credit availability was small; and what changes in interest rates did occur did not stimulate much additional investment.

At the same time, credit availability theorists believe that in mild recessions, monetary policy may stimulate the economy by increasing the availability of credit. Conversely, and more important, monetary policy may lead to a contraction of the economy, by reducing the availability of credit. These expansions or contractions may or may not be accompanied by changes in interest rates. There may well be changes in Treasury bill rates, which are much larger than changes in lending rates. But the credit availability approach stresses that while interest rate changes may frequently accompany monetary policy changes, monetary policy works largely through effects on the availability of credit.

Proponents of the credit availability approach warn, further, that the Bank's ability to restrict credit in the longer run may be limited: it can reduce the amount of credit that banks can extend, but borrowers can find substitute sources of credit. Some big firms, like Bell Canada, can borrow directly by issuing what is called commercial paper; they do not have to use banks or any other financial intermediaries. Other borrowers can switch from banks to one of the other financial intermediaries discussed in Chapter 17. In the longer run, the net contraction in credit may be less than the contraction in bank credit. Still, at least in the short run, borrowers cannot quickly find substitute sources of finance, so that credit restrictions take their toll.

CREDIT AVAILABILITY THEORIES

1. The role of credit availability should be the focus rather than money supply directly or interest rates.

2. Increases in money supply may not lead to increases in credit, particularly in severe recessions, if financial institutions decide to invest in government bonds.

   Increased financial-institution lending is likely to be limited if
   a. financial institutions are pessimistic about returns on loans and view them as particularly risky;
   b. financial institutions have lost a substantial amount of their net worth as a result of defaults, and so are unwilling or unable to bear high risks;
   c. many financial institutions have gone into default.

3. Interest rates charged borrowers may not change much in response to credit availability; other terms of credit may adjust.

MONEY AND CREDIT: COMPETING OR COMPLEMENTARY THEORIES?

Money affects the economy for a variety of reasons and in a variety of ways. Advocates of different monetary theories argue not that theirs is the only way that money affects the economy, but that focusing on their particular approach provides a best "first picture" of what is going on. As we have seen, money and credit are two sides of the same coin, or of a bank's balance sheet.

The different theories provide a simple and intuitive explanation not only for why there should be a relationship between credit or money and output, but also for the fact that increases in credit or money occur before increases in production. When firms plan to expand their production and sales, they take out loans, which increase the measures of both credit and money. That is why measures of credit increase before Christmas, just as does the money supply.

This example provides another dramatic illustration of the difference between correlation and causation. The fact that the money supply or credit increases before the huge increases in sales at Christmastime would not fool many people into thinking that the money supply *causes* the increased sales at this time. On the contrary, it is the huge anticipated increases in sales at Christmas that lead merchants to borrow more to buy goods to stock their shelves. But while the increased credit does not cause the rise in sales, if the Bank of Canada were to try to contract credit before December, it could have a disastrous effect on Christmas sales.

For many purposes, the exact mechanism by which monetary policy affects the economy may make little difference. In fact, since increases in the money supply and bank loans are closely connected, changes in the money supply may provide a good measure of the tightness of credit. Indeed, they may provide a better measure than looking at the interest rates at which banks make loans. Interest rates, as the credit availability theories emphasize, may not change much even when credit is significantly tightened.

There are situations where the different theories have different implications: credit availability theories suggest that changes in the credit institutions of the economy may alter earlier stable relationships between income and credit, and may even affect the efficacy of monetary policy. If many or most borrowers can easily find close substitutes for banks for raising capital, attempts by the Bank of Canada to restrict credit may have limited effects. On the other hand, the theories that focus on the role of money in transactions suggest that changes in the institutions by which transactions are conducted (like credit cards) may have large effects on the relationship between money and income.

DIFFERING VIEWS ON THE ROLE AND MECHANISMS OF MONETARY POLICY

We have seen in this chapter the different effects that monetary policy may have and the different channels through which it may operate. In spite of a variety of sources of disagreement, today most economists would agree with the following conclusions.

1. When the economy is operating close to capacity, looser monetary policy is likely to lead to increased prices.

2. A major tightening of money and credit may so reduce aggregate demand, as illustrated in Figure 18.14, that the economy shifts from being close to full employment to having substantial unemployment. This is the common interpretation of what happened in the early 1980s. (See Chapter 10.)

3. When the economy has excess capacity, a loosening of credit may shift the aggregate demand curve out, leading to an increase in output (not in prices).

4. When the economy is in a deep recession, monetary policy may be relatively ineffective. Drastic actions may be required to stimulate the economy. (Economists disagree whether even then monetary policy will be effective.)

This is a good time to ask how the different schools of thought we have encountered in this book—real business-cycle theorists, new classical economists, new Keynesians, and monetarists—view the role of monetary policy.

For real business-cycle theorists, the answer is easiest: they believe that monetary policy has no effect on the level of economic activity. Real variables such as real output and real wages are, in their view, determined by real forces like changes in technology, not by money. Monetary policy affects the price level, but nothing more. In effect, with a vertical aggregate supply curve, all that monetary policy can do is change the level of prices or the rate of inflation. At the same time, monetary policy is not responsible for recessions. The lack of effectiveness of monetary policy is of no great concern to real business-cycle theorists. They believe that the competitive model described in Part Two provides a good description of the economy. Accordingly, they believe that markets are efficient without government intervention. They do not believe that unemployment is a serious economic problem.

Monetarists tend to agree with real business-cycle theorists that in the long run the main impact of monetary policy is on the price level. However, for monetarists, money can have real effects on output in the short run. They believe that velocity is not very

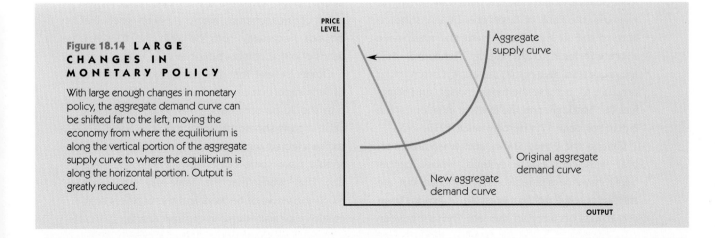

Figure 18.14 LARGE CHANGES IN MONETARY POLICY

With large enough changes in monetary policy, the aggregate demand curve can be shifted far to the left, moving the economy from where the equilibrium is along the vertical portion of the aggregate supply curve to where the equilibrium is along the horizontal portion. Output is greatly reduced.

CLOSE-UP: WHO SHOULD CONTROL MONETARY POLICY?

There are many possible answers to the question of who should control monetary policy. At one extreme, the monetary authorities may be given a single goal, like controlling inflation, and then be given the authority to pursue that goal with minimal political interference. At the other extreme, monetary authorities may be subject to considerable political control and thus come under pressure to stimulate the economy, even if it means allowing greater inflationary pressure.

Germany and Switzerland have exceptionally independent central banks. In Germany, the law explicitly states that the central bank has the "assigned task of preserving monetary stability" and "shall be independent of instructions from the federal government." Perhaps not surprisingly, both countries have had relatively low rates of inflation—about 3.5 percent since 1975 (though even the German inflation rate has proven to be difficult to hold down since reunification and the conversion of the former East German currency into West German marks). The flip side is that monetary policy is not often used to stimulate the economy in the face of an economic downturn.

In the United Kingdom and Italy, the monetary authorities have relatively little independence from political control. In the United Kingdom, for example, the Bank of England is by law subordinate to the Treasury Department and must make short-term loans to the Treasury whenever they are requested. As a result, the bank is often under pressure to increase the money supply and stimulate the economy, and the average inflation rate in Britain has been 12.4 percent since 1975.

Canada, the United States, and Japan are countries with intermediate systems, whose central banks have considerable independence but are still under some political pressure. A famous sparring match occurred in the late 1950s between Governor of the Bank of Canada James Coyne and Finance Minister Donald Fleming. Coyne refused to go along with the expansionary policies advocated by the government, and the government responded by introducing a bill declaring the position of governor vacant. Though the bill never passed, Coyne resigned anyway. As a result of the "Coyne Affair," a mechanism of consultation and directive was developed that was ultimately put into the Bank Act in 1967. Under the mechanism, the governor and the minister of finance consult regularly on monetary policy. In the event of disagreement, the act empowers the minister of finance to issue a written directive overriding the Bank's monetary policy decisions for a fixed period of time. The directive power gives the government ultimate responsibility for monetary policy, but in its absence the Bank has immediate responsibility. No directive has ever been issued, though if one were issued, a likely outcome would be the resignation of the governor.

Whether the central bank should be less accountable to the government is an ongoing political issue. Many observers believe that the questions of monetary policy are better kept out of the political process. The goals of monetary policy, especially price stability and the maintenance of the value of the currency, are longer-term goals that do not necessarily coincide with the four–year terms of office of most politicians.

Others believe that in a democracy, any matter of such importance to the functioning of the economy should be controlled by Parliament. That is, a central bank should be accountable in some way to the elected representatives of the people and should have some reasonably clear responsibilities. They worry that the Bank may reflect too much the views of bankers and the business community, especially those in central Canada.

sensitive to changes in the interest rate, so that changes in the money supply will be reflected in changes in nominal national income. Recall the basic quantity theory equation: $MV = PQ$. The right-hand side, PQ, is the nominal value of national income. With V fixed, an increase in M is immediately translated into a corresponding increase in PQ. Unlike real business-cycle theorists, monetarists believe that the price level may not immediately adjust downwards in response to a decrease in the money supply. If prices do not immediately adjust downwards, the only way that national income can fall is for output to fall. Monetarists are not specific about the mechanism by which a change in the money supply is translated into a change in nominal income, nor about why prices do not quickly adjust.

New classical economists also believe that in the long run monetary policy can only affect the price level. Their major contribution has been their emphasis on rational expectations: in the long run, firms and consumers understand exactly what the government is doing with the money supply and therefore translate money supply changes into price level changes. In some cases, firms and consumers may see straight through a policy change, and the price adjustment may be instantaneous. In other cases, however, firms or consumers may have difficulty distinguishing between real and nominal changes, and so in the short run prices may not adjust fully to an increase or decrease in the money supply.

While monetarists and new classical economists thus believe that monetary policy can affect the economy in the short run, they are not in favour of government intervention, for two reasons. First, the short run is short: an increase in output induced by an expansionary monetary policy quickly leads to price increases. The reductions in unemployment resulting from an expansionary monetary policy are thus short-lived in their view, but the price increases to which it gives rise may be persistent.

Second, the two schools emphasize that bad government policy can cause a recession. In fact, they see the major fluctuations in the economy as being caused by bad monetary policy. As a result, they prefer the government to follow simple rules, like expanding the money supply at a constant rate. While such rules preclude the government from taking an active role in stabilizing the economy, they serve the more important function of preventing the government from messing things up.

Finally, new Keynesians take an eclectic view. They too believe that money is a central factor in the determination of national income. They share Keynes' view that the economy adjusts slowly, so that there may be extended periods with unemployment. Most share Keynes' conclusions about monetary policy being ineffective in deep recessions, either because it is difficult to get banks to lend more or because it is difficult to persuade firms to invest more. But they differ in their views about how monetary policy may succeed at other times in stimulating output. Some believe that the interest-rate mechanism is central, others emphasize the portfolio theories, while still others stress the role of credit availability. Indeed, there is no reason that monetary policy needs to work through any single channel; it may work through many different mechanisms. When monetary policy is ineffective, all of the mechanisms become weak.

Monetary policy is only one of the instruments that the government has at its disposal, and to understand more fully the appropriate role of monetary policy, we have to consider it together with government's other principal set of tools, fiscal policy. This we do in Chapter 23. But first we need to see how monetary policy operates in a world in which Canadians can borrow not only from Canadian banks, but also from American and other foreign sources (Chapter 19). And second, we need to complete our discussion of the major objectives of macroeconomic policy, price stability (preventing inflation) and growth, to which we turn in Chapters 20 and 21.

ALTERNATIVE VIEWS OF MONETARY POLICY

SCHOOL	EFFECT OF MONETARY POLICY	DESIRABILITY OF ACTIVE MONETARY POLICY
Real business cycle	Unemployment is not a serious economic problem. Money only has an effect on the price level, and no effect on output.	Monetary policy is largely irrelevant, other than for determining the price level. Monetary policy is not responsible for recessions.
Monetarist	Money is central to the determination of national income. In the short run, money can affect the level of output. In the long run, it affects mainly the price level.	Misguided monetary policies are largely responsible for recessions. Policy should be limited to a simple rule such as a constant rate of increase in the money supply.
New classical	Firms and consumers with rational expectations see through monetary policy, at least in the long run, and translate money supply changes into price level changes.	Same as monetarists.
New Keynesian	Money is one of the central factors in the determination of national income. The economy may be at less than full employment for extended periods of time.	Monetary policy may exercise its effects through a variety of channels: the interest rate, credit availability, and portfolio effects. When the economy is in a deep recession, monetary policy is ineffective, either because it is difficult to induce banks to lend more or because it is difficult to persuade firms to invest more.

REVIEW AND PRACTICE

SUMMARY

1. Theories concerning the effect of monetary policy on the economy focus on the two sides of the banks' balance sheet, on money and on credit.

2. Changes in the supply of money can cause some combination of three effects: changes in holdings of money, changes in output, or changes in prices. When the economy is at full capacity, then an increased supply of money will affect mainly the price level. When the economy has considerable excess capacity, normally output will increase; in deep recessions, the effect on output may be minimal.

3. Keynesian theories of the demand for money focused on its dependence on the (nominal) rate of interest and on the level of income. Equilibrium required the demand for money to be equal to the supply. Changes in the supply of money resulted in changes in the interest rate and, through changes in the interest rate, in the level of aggregate expenditures and equilibrium output.

4. Keynes argued that in severe recessions, the interest elasticity of the demand for money was high and the interest elasticity of investment was low, so monetary policy was ineffective.

5. The quantity theory of money holds that the demand for money does not depend on the interest rate, and accordingly that the velocity of money is constant. Increases in money supply then result in proportionate increases in national income.

6. There are many difficulties with traditional monetary theory. Money is not used for many transactions, and many transactions involve exchanges of assets, which have little to do with income generation. Changes in technology and the structure of the economy may alter the money-income relationship. Most money bears interest, and the opportunity cost is only the difference between the interest rate it pays and the interest rate on government Treasury bills. Finally, the link between changes in the nominal interest rate and the real interest rate is tenuous, and depends on inflationary expectations; and the link between real interest rates and investment appears weak. In recent years, velocity has changed in relatively unpredictable ways.

6. Portfolio theories stress the effect of changes in monetary policy on the demand and supply of various assets and the resulting effect on prices of assets.

7. Credit availability theories stress the effects of monetary policy on the availability of credit by banks. The Bank of Canada may, in some recessions, have a hard time inducing the banking system to lend more if banks view commercial loans as highly risky, if as a result of previous defaults banks' net worth and thus their ability to bear risk has been eroded, or if financial institutions have gone into bankruptcy.

KEY TERMS

velocity

transactions demand
  for money

portfolio theories

quantity theory of
  money

REVIEW QUESTIONS

1. What are the three things that might happen in response to a change in the money supply?

2. Is it possible for a change in the money supply to affect neither the price level nor the output level in the economy? Explain.

3. What is the most likely effect of an increase in the supply of money when the economy is at full capacity?

4. Why does demand for money fall as the interest rate rises? What is the opportunity cost of holding money that pays interest (such as demand deposits)?

5. What might cause changes in the relationship between the demand for money and income besides changes in the interest rate?

6. Why might changes in the money supply not lead to increases in the level of investment in a severe recession?

7. What assumptions are involved in the quantity theory of money? What conclusion can be drawn on the basis of those assumptions? What is the evidence concerning the constancy of the velocity of circulation?

8. What are the mechanisms by which portfolio theories suggest that monetary policy affects the economy?

9. Describe how monetary policy might affect investment or consumption, *even if monetary policy has no effect at all on interest rates.*

10. Why might a bank refuse to charge the interest rate determined by the intersection of supply and demand for credit, and instead insist on offering loans only at a lower interest rate?

11. Why might the Bank of Canada have a hard time expanding credit?

PROBLEMS

1. If GDP is $600 billion and the money supply is $40 billion, what is velocity? How does your answer change if GDP rises to $700 billion while the money supply remains the same? If GDP remains at $600 billion while the money supply increases to $50 billion, how does velocity change?

2. Graph the money demand curve from the following data, with quantity of money demanded given in billions of dollars.

Interest rate	7%	8%	9%	10%	11%	12%
Money demanded	45	44	43	42	41	40.5

How do changes in national income affect the demand curve?

3. Using money supply and demand diagrams, explain how the elasticity of the money demand curve determines whether monetary policy can have a substantial effect on the interest rate.

4. Explain how the elasticity of investment with respect to interest rates determines whether monetary policy can have a substantial effect on aggregate demand.

5. Explain how each of the following might affect the demand for money:
    (a) interest is paid on chequing accounts;
    (b) credit cards become more readily available;
    (c) electronic fund transfers become common.
Would the changes in the demand for money necessarily reduce the ability of the Bank of Canada to use monetary policy to affect the economy?

6. Explain how the Bank of Canada can reduce the amount of credit in an economy where credit rationing is common without affecting the interest rate.

APPENDIX: AN ALGEBRAIC DERIVATION OF EQUILIBRIUM IN THE MONEY MARKET

The money demand equation can be written

$$M_d = M_d(r, Y),$$

where M_d is the demand for money and $Y = pQ$, the value of national income. If M_s is the money supply, then the equilibrium condition that the demand for money equals the supply can be written

$$M_s = M_d(r, Y). \tag{18.1}$$

From Chapter 12, we know that

$$Y = C + I + G + (X - M),$$

where I (investment) depends on the interest rate, r, and G (government expenditures), X (exports), and M (imports) are assumed to be fixed. If consumption is just $(1 - s)$ times income, Y, then

$$Y = (1 - s)Y + I(r) + G + (X - M),$$

or

$$Y = [I(r) + G + (X - M)]/s. \tag{18.2}$$

Equations (18.1) and (18.2) provide us two equations in two unknowns. The solution gives us the equilibrium income and interest rate. An increase in the money supply results in a new solution, with a lower interest rate and a higher level of national income.

MONETARY POLICY: THE INTERNATIONAL SIDE

 n economies such as Canada's that are open to international trade, monetary policy may induce changes in the exchange rate and in the flow of capital from abroad. Thus, the channels by which monetary policy affects the
economy in an international setting may be quite different from those in an
economy closed to international trade and capital movements. This
chapter traces out the channels by which monetary policy affects exchange rates, capital
flows, and ultimately the level of economic activity in an open economy.

1. Increasingly, we live in a world in which all economies are interrelated. How does this fact affect the workings of monetary policy?

2. What determines the exchange rate? And how does monetary policy affect the exchange rate?

DETERMINING THE EXCHANGE RATE

To understand how monetary policy works in an open economy, it is essential to understand what determines the exchange rate, the rate at which dollars are exchanged for yen, or marks for pounds. The **foreign exchange market** is the market in which currencies are bought and sold. When the Japanese yen becomes more valuable relative to the Canadian dollar, then we say that the yen has appreciated and the dollar has depreciated. If there used to be 200 yen to the dollar and now there are 125 yen to the dollar, the yen has appreciated; you need fewer of them to get a dollar now than you did before.

Systems in which exchange rates are determined by the law of supply and demand, without government interference, are called **flexible** or **floating exchange rate systems.** Governments often do intervene in foreign exchange markets, and later in the chapter we will look at the different forms government intervention takes. But first we need to learn what determines the exchange rate in flexible exchange rate systems.

Consider a world consisting of only two countries, Canada and another country we will call Europa, whose currency is called the Euro. Canadians and Europans exchange dollars for Euros. There are three reasons that Europans might want dollars, and might therefore supply Euros to the foreign exchange market: to buy Canadian goods (Canadian exports, or imports into Europa), to make investments in Canada, or for speculative purposes—that is, if Europans think the dollar is going to become more valuable relative to the Euro, they might want to hold dollars in order to reap that increase in value, called a capital gain. Similarly, there are three reasons that Canadians might want Euros, and might accordingly supply dollars to the foreign exchange market: to buy Europan goods, to make investments in Europa, and for speculative purposes, if they think that the Euro is going to become more valuable relative to the dollar. The question is, how many Euros will a Canadian get in exchange for a dollar, or equivalently, how many dollars will a Europan get in exchange for her Euros? The exchange rate can be thought of as nothing more than the *relative price* of dollars and Euros.

In competitive markets, prices are determined by demand and supply. We can view the exchange rate in this two-country example as being determined from the perspective of either the demand and supply of dollars or the demand and supply of Euros. The two are equivalent. The Europan supply of Euros on the foreign exchange market is equivalent to Europans' demand for dollars. The Canadian supply of dollars is equivalent to Canadians' demand for Euros.

The three reasons why Europans might want dollars and that Canadians might want Euros are the three main factors that determine the exchange rate. The first factor is the demand and supply of exports and imports, to which we now turn.

EXPORTS AND IMPORTS

Figure 19.1A shows a demand and supply diagram for Canadian dollars. The vertical axis is the exchange rate, the "price" of dollars, expressed in this example as Euro/dollar. When the exchange rate is 1,000 Euros to the dollar, the dollar is very expensive; when it is 300 Euros to the dollar, the dollar is relatively cheap. The figure shows a downward-sloping demand curve and an upward-sloping supply curve, and the intersection represents the equilibrium exchange rate. A rightward shift in the supply curve (panel B) or a leftward shift in the demand curve (panel C) leads to a depreciation of the dollar. The value of the dollar relative to Euros is then lower.

While thinking about exchange rates in terms of demand and supply is helpful, it pushes the question back still one more step. Why do demand and supply curves for foreign exchange have the shape they do? What might cause them to shift and thus the exchange rate to change?

EXCHANGE RATES WITH NO BORROWING

Let's return to our two-country example. Suppose Europa was a country that trusted no one and that no one trusted. No Europan would be allowed to borrow abroad, because potential lenders would fear that the loan would not be repaid. Similarly, the country would refuse to loan out any money to foreigners. Europa's exports must precisely equal its imports.

When Canadian producers sell products in Europa, they receive Euros, and they want to convert those Euros immediately into dollars. After all, if they do not convert the Euros into dollars, they will have to deposit them in a bank or investment in Europa—they will have to *lend* the Euros to Europa—and they do not trust Europa enough to do that. Similarly, when producers from Europa sell in Canada, they receive Canadian dollars, and they want to exchange those dollars immediately into Euros. In short, this situation has parties who want to trade Euros for dollars and parties who want to trade dollars for Euros. Clearly, there are possibilities for mutually beneficial exchange. At a low exchange rate, like e_1 in Figure 19.2, the demand for dollars exceeds the supply. At a high exchange rate, like e_2, the supply of dollars exceeds the demand. The point at which the demand for dollars equals the supply is the equilibrium exchange rate. In the figure, this point is e_0.

We can also see how the exchange rate is determined by focusing directly on exports and imports. In the absence of borrowing or lending, the value of exports must equal the value of imports. Canadians might like to import more from Europa than they export, but unless they sell goods to Europa, they will not have the money (the Euros) with which to buy Europan goods. And since Europans are skeptical about whether Canadians will repay any loans, they will not deliver the goods without receiving the money first. There are no credit sales.

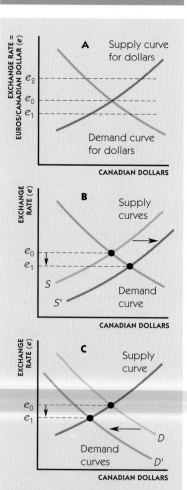

Figure 19.1 THE EXCHANGE RATE

In equilibrium, the exchange rate is determined where the demand for dollars equals the supply, as in panel A. A rightward shift in the supply curve of dollars (panel B) or a leftward shift in the demand curve for dollars (panel C) results in a lower exchange rate; that is, the dollar depreciates.

At a high value of the dollar, Canadian exports will be low. Europans must give up a lot of their currency to buy Canadian goods. Europans' demand for imports will translate directly into a supply of dollars. A high value of the dollar is equivalent to a low value of the foreign currency (here, Euros). From the perspective of Canadians, foreign goods are cheap, and Canadians will want to buy them. Their demand for imports will be high. To buy these goods, they have to pay the Europans in their own currency, Euros. So Canadian importers supply dollars to be exchanged for Euros on the foreign exchange market.

Figure 19.3A and B shows how imports increase and exports decrease as the exchange rate increases (as the dollar becomes "more expensive"). The exchange rate at which exports equal imports is the equilibrium exchange rate. In the Canada–Europa example, a decrease in the exchange rate has one of two causes: either a reduction in the demand for Canadian exports *at any exchange rate*, which will translate into a leftward shift in the demand curve for dollars, or an increased Canadian demand for imports *at any exchange rate*, which will translate into a rightward shift in the supply of dollars. These are illustrated in panel C.

In this simple model, changes in the exchange rate can be related to shifts in the Canadian demand for imports (at any exchange rate) or in foreigners' demand for Canadian goods. For instance, shifts in the demand curves for imports and exports played a

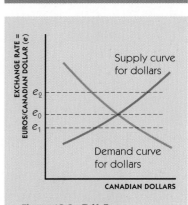

Figure 19.2 THE EQUILIBRIUM EXCHANGE RATE

At the exchange rate e_2, supply exceeds demand. At e_1, demand exceeds supply. At e_0, equilibrium is achieved.

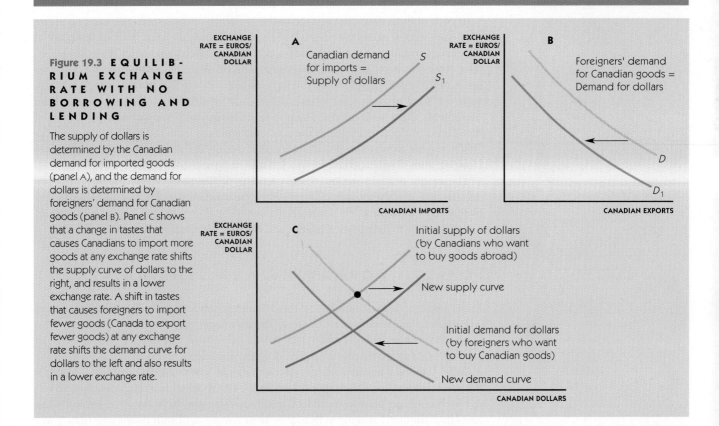

Figure 19.3 EQUILIBRIUM EXCHANGE RATE WITH NO BORROWING AND LENDING

The supply of dollars is determined by the Canadian demand for imported goods (panel A), and the demand for dollars is determined by foreigners' demand for Canadian goods (panel B). Panel C shows that a change in tastes that causes Canadians to import more goods at any exchange rate shifts the supply curve of dollars to the right, and results in a lower exchange rate. A shift in tastes that causes foreigners to import fewer goods (Canada to export fewer goods) at any exchange rate shifts the demand curve for dollars to the left and also results in a lower exchange rate.

role in the recession of the early 1980s. For one thing, the shift of Canadian tastes to smaller, foreign-made cars can be thought of as an increase in the demand for imports (a rightward shift in the supply curve for dollars), at each level of income. Figure 19.3A illustrates this shift in the demand for imports. Panel C shows how the shift in the demand curve for imports translates into a shift in the supply curve of dollars for foreigners. The increased supply of dollars would, if nothing else had happened, have led to a depreciation of the dollar—that is, to a lower exchange rate—as illustrated in the figure. By the same token, the recession in the United States caused Americans to spend less on our exports, thereby shifting the demand curve for our exports to the left as in panel B. This, in turn, translates into a shift in the demand curve for dollars to the left as in panel C and leads to a further reduction in the exchange rate. The depreciation of the dollar means that foreign imports would be smaller and exports larger than they would have been had exchange rates remained fixed. Thus, with flexible exchange rates, the decline in net exports at each level of national income was *smaller* than it would have been if exchange rates had not changed. The adjustments in the exchange rate helped to stabilize the economy.

As the economy recovers from a recession (as it did in the period after 1983), incomes in Canada rise, and at any exchange rate the demand for imports increases. Exports at any exchange rate are unaffected, since they depend on the incomes of foreigners. Thus, higher levels of income induce a shift in the demand curve for imports, or equivalently a shift in the supply curve of dollars. Again, this leads to a depreciation of the dollar, the effect of which is to *enhance* the recovery.

In each of these cases, the change in the exchange rate dampens the increase in imports from what it would have been had exchange rates been fixed. That is, as a result of the change in tastes or change in national income, imports are higher than they would have otherwise been *at any exchange rate*. The resulting devaluation of the dollar reduces imports, although they are still larger than they were in the initial situation. As always, we have to be careful to distinguish shifts in demand and supply curves from movements along those curves. These sorts of changes help to explain why the value of the Canadian dollar declined as the economy emerged from the recession in the mid-1980s, as well as why the dollar appreciated during the recession of the early 1990s. However, they do not account for the dollar's fall since then.

The model of trade without foreign lending or borrowing made more sense a few decades ago, when international financial markets were not widely developed and so exchange rates were primarily shaped by the supply and demand for imports and exports. Today we need to look beyond exports and imports to capital markets.

FOREIGN BORROWING AND LENDING

In the world of Europa and Euros, there is never a trade deficit. The values of exports and imports, when compared by using the exchange rate, are always the same. This means that the problem of trade deficits will never arise. Likewise, a trade deficit can only occur if foreign borrowing and lending are possible.

Today there is a massive amount of international borrowing and lending, and this is the second factor that determines the exchange rate. Capital markets today, the markets in which funds are borrowed and lent, are global. Investors in Japan, Europe, and North America, constantly seeking to maximize their returns, will shift their funds from Japan or Europe to Canada if returns there are highest. When investors respond quickly and shift their funds in response to slight differences in expected returns, economists say that capital is **perfectly mobile.** In today's world, capital is highly but not perfectly mobile. Canadian investors may still feel slightly more comfortable keeping their money within Canada than sending it abroad; they may feel relatively uninformed about changes in economic conditions or tax conditions that could quickly and adversely affect their investments. Foreign investors may feel the same way about keeping their funds within their own country. The more stable the political and economic environment of the world, the more mobile capital becomes across countries.

Determining the exchange rate becomes considerably more complicated when foreign borrowing and lending are introduced. Now the equilibrium exchange rate is not just a matter of balancing imports and exports as they occur; it is affected by borrowing and lending decisions as well. Figure 19.2 can be modified to incorporate these effects. Foreigners who want to invest in Canada will want dollars to make their purchases of Canadian assets. This increases the demand for dollars. On the other hand, some Canadians may want to make investments abroad. They want to sell dollars to get foreign currency with which to make these investments. How these investments affect the exchange rate depends on whether foreigners want to invest more in Canada than Canadians want to invest abroad.

Figure 19.4 shows the demand and supply curves for dollars both with and without foreign borrowing and lending. Some Canadians want to invest abroad, and hence the supply of dollars at any exchange rate is greater than it would have been without foreign investment; and some foreigners want to invest in Canada, and so the demand for dollars is greater than it otherwise would have been. In this example, however, the amount foreigners want to invest in Canada is much greater than the amount Canadians want to invest abroad. The demand curve for dollars shifts more to the right than does the supply curve for dollars. As a result, the exchange rate increases.

Normally, if investments in Canada become more attractive, Canadians will decide to leave more of their wealth at home rather than investing abroad. Then the supply of

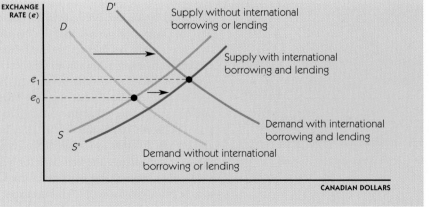

Figure 19.4 **EQUILIBRIUM EXCHANGE RATE WITH BORROWING AND LENDING**

When Canadians want to invest abroad and foreigners want to invest in Canada, the supply of and demand for dollars are greater than they otherwise would have been. In the figure, more foreigners want to invest in Canada than Canadians want to invest abroad, so the demand curve for dollars shifts more to the right than does the supply curve for dollars. As a result the exchange rate increases.

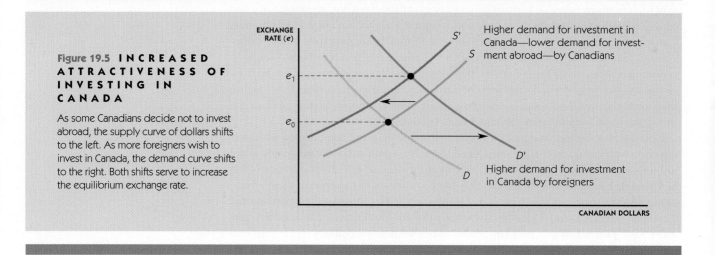

Figure 19.5 INCREASED ATTRACTIVENESS OF INVESTING IN CANADA

As some Canadians decide not to invest abroad, the supply curve of dollars shifts to the left. As more foreigners wish to invest in Canada, the demand curve shifts to the right. Both shifts serve to increase the equilibrium exchange rate.

dollars will shift to the left, as in Figure 19.5. At the same time, foreigners will decide to invest more in Canada, shifting the demand for dollars to the right. Both of these effects work to increase the value of the dollar relative to other currencies.

This helps to explain some of the movements of the exchange rate in the 1980s. Foreign investment into Canada fell dramatically in 1981 and 1982, and the exchange rate depreciated rapidly. It continued to depreciate until the second half of the decade when foreign investment began to surge upwards. Direct investment doubled in 1987, and in the same year the exchange rate began to appreciate. The appreciation continued until the end of the decade as foreign investment continued to rise.

SPECULATION

The third factor that is important in determining the exchange rates today is speculation. In Chapter 6, we saw that the demand for any asset depends on beliefs about what that asset could be sold for in the future; it depends on expectations. Money in any country is an asset, as we saw in Chapter 18. If Canadians believe that the Japanese yen is going to increase in value relative to the dollar, they may want to hold Japanese yen. For instance, consider what happens if the current exchange rate is 200 yen to the dollar and investors believe that the yen is going to appreciate, so that by the end of the month it will be worth 100 to the dollar. They believe, in other words, that if they took $1,000 and bought 200,000 yen (each dollar is exchanged for 200 yen), at the end of the month they could exchange the yen back for $2,000. By holding yen for a month, they would earn a phenomenal 100 percent return. Canadian investors with such a belief will want to hold more yen today. This is how expectations about future changes in exchange rates are translated immediately into increased exchange rates today.

Demanding currency for the possible gains from the appreciation of the currency is called **foreign exchange speculation.** With speculation, exchange rates in the market depend not only on the demand for and supply of exports and imports and investment today but on expectations concerning those factors in the future.

EXPECTATIONS

Expectations about changes in the exchange rate in fact play a role in all overseas investments. Consider the Japanese investor who is planning to convert his yen into dollars and invest it in Canada. He will want to bring his profits back to Japan, and he may even decide eventually to sell his investment and bring his money back home. In either case, he will have to convert his dollars back into yen at some later date. The question is, how many yen will he get for his dollars? If he believes that the dollar is going to become weaker, then he believes that he will get fewer yen when he exchanges his dollars in the foreign exchange market. If he thinks that the dollar will become stronger in the future, investment in Canada appears more attractive.

Canadian investors thinking about investing abroad will be equally concerned about changes in exchange rates. But for Canadians, expectations that the dollar will become *weaker* in the future make investment abroad more attractive.

Now let's suppose our Japanese investor is thinking about buying a Canadian government Treasury bill. He will not want to put his money in a T-bill that yields a 10 percent return, even if bonds issued by the Japanese government yield only 5 percent, if he believes that the dollar is going to decrease in value by more than 5 percent during the year. To see why this is so, suppose he has 300,000 yen to invest, and assume the current exchange rate is 300 yen to the dollar. If he invests the 300,000 yen in a Japanese government bond, he will have 315,000 at the end of the year. But if he takes the 300,000 yen to his banker, his banker will give him $1,000. With that $1,000, he buys a Treasury bill. At the end of the year, he has $1,100. He now takes this $1,100 back to his banker, who tells him that because the dollar has depreciated in value, each dollar is worth, say, 250 yen. Thus, at the end of the year, he has only 275,000 yen, fewer yen than at the beginning of the year. The Japanese investor's expectations can be summed up in a formula:

rate of return in yen = dollar interest rate − expected rate of change in exchange rate.

Over the long run, expectations of changes in the exchange rate are linked to changes in price levels across countries. To see how this works, we focus on the case of two countries, Canada and Japan, in which the rates of inflation differ.

INFLATION

If two countries differ in their rates of inflation, over the long run there will be changes in exchange rates that offset those inflation rates. For example, if the rate of inflation in Canada is 3 percent and there is no inflation in Japan, the dollar is becoming less valuable—each year people can purchase 3 percent fewer goods with a dollar bill—while the value of the yen is unchanged. Thus, the exchange rate might be expected to change; the dollar will depreciate 3 percent against the yen each year.

In a world with perfect capital mobility, interest rates will have to adjust quickly to reflect differences in inflation rates and changing exchange rates. If the interest rate in Japan is 5 percent, the interest rate in Canada should be 8 percent; the extra 3 percent reflects the higher rate of inflation. Notice that if this is the case, the *real* interest rate in Japan and Canada will be the same (5 percent). Moreover, a Japanese investor will be indifferent between investing in Canada or in Japan; his real return will be the same, even though he earns a higher nominal return in Canada.

These adjustments in interest rates and exchange rates just offset the effects of inflation: they mean that Canadians find Japanese products become no more or less attractive over time, and Japan's consumers find Canadian products become no more or less attractive over time. Like the real wages and real interest rates, economists use the term **real exchange rate** to indicate the exchange rate adjusted for changes in the relative price levels in two countries. That is, if the inflation rate is 3 percent higher in Canada than in Japan and the nominal exchange rate has changed so that the dollar is worth 3 percent less relative to the yen, the real exchange rate has remained unchanged; the changes in the nominal exchange rate are just those required to offset the changes in relative price levels. Similarly, in spite of differences in nominal returns, investors find real returns to be the same. Figure 19.6 contrasts movements in the real and nominal exchange rates between Canada and Japan during the 1980s.

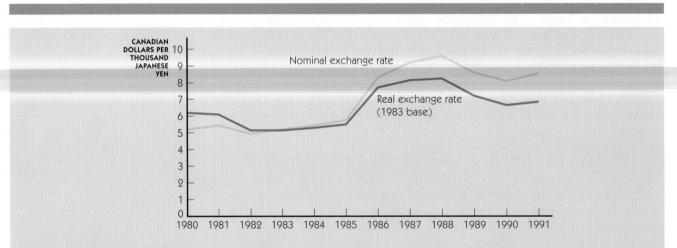

Figure 19.6 REAL VERSUS NOMINAL EXCHANGE RATES

Real exchange rates vary from nominal exchange rates because they take account of changes in price levels. In the case of the Canadian dollar/yen exchange rate, the widened difference between the two in the late 1980s reflects larger differences than in the rates of inflation. *Sources:* Statistics Canada, *Canadian Economic Observer,* Catalogue No. 11-210, 1991–1992; *Economic Report of the President* (January 1993), Tables B-105 and B-107.

WHAT DETERMINES THE EXCHANGE RATE?

The Canadian exchange rate today is determined by supply and demand for dollars. Foreigners' demand for Canadian dollars and Canadians' supply of dollars is determined by

1. underlying trade factors: the demand for Canadian goods (Canadian exports) and Canadians' demand for foreign goods (imports);
2. underlying investment factors: the returns to investments in Canada and abroad;
3. speculation based on expectations concerning future changes in the exchange rate.

A shift in tastes for foreign goods or an increase in income in Canada will lead to a depreciation of the Canadian dollar.

Improved attractiveness of investment in Canada will lead to an appreciation of the dollar.

MONETARY POLICY IN AN OPEN ECONOMY

The global capital market makes the Bank of Canada's job of controlling the economy much more difficult. The total supply of funds is much broader than the supply of funds from Canadian sources. Today it is not uncommon for Canadian firms to borrow funds from banks in the United States and other countries. Indeed, many foreign banks even have branches within Canada. Attempts by the Bank of Canada to change the interest rate or total credit availability are hampered because it can focus only on domestic banks. If it tries to raise interest rates as part of a campaign against inflation, for example, Canadians will simply borrow abroad, and the impact of the Bank's action will be dramatically dampened.

SUBSTITUTABILITY AND THE EFFECTIVENESS OF MONETARY POLICY

The Bank of Canada exercises control only over the banking system. Through open market operations and changes in the bank rate, it affects the money supply and the availability of bank credit. But its actions touch other financial institutions and eventually reverberate throughout the entire economy. The extent of the effects of monetary policy depends largely on whether there are substitutes for the credit, transaction, and other services provided by the banking system. If there are, monetary policy may have limited effects.

As we have seen, Canadians can borrow abroad if the Bank reduces the availability of credit. Not everyone has easy access to foreign credit, but large Canadian firms like Noranda and Ford Canada, which operate in countries around the world, can easily obtain funds elsewhere. This alone is enough seriously to weaken the effectiveness of monetary policy. If enough firms borrow abroad, then it will take an enormous reduction in credit availability in Canada to have significant effects on spending by firms and individuals.

In Chapter 18, we observed two other examples of substitution: other sources of credit are a substitute for bank credit; and credit and other financial institutions provide close substitutes for money.

The fact that monetary policy may be less effective in the context of global capital markets in limiting credit availability or changing the interest rate does not mean that monetary policy is completely ineffective. This is because, in practice, international capital markets are far from perfect. Accordingly, when the Bank acts to tighten monetary policy through open market operations, interest rates within Canada may indeed rise and credit may become less available. Investment and purchases of consumer durables are likely to be dampened.

To some extent, the global situation today mirrors the relationship among the individual provinces of Canada. It is difficult to conceive of a small province like Prince Edward Island or Saskatchewan having an independent monetary policy. Any attempt at a change in the availability of credit or interest rates in P.E.I. would be quickly dampened as funds flowed in from the rest of the country. As Canada becomes part of a larger international community, with countries lending to and borrowing from each other, it may be increasingly difficult for Canada to change interest rates or credit availability within the country.

There is, however, one important difference between the relationship of Canada with other countries and the relationships of the different provinces with one another: there is a common currency within Canada, while different countries have different currencies. With different currencies, exchange rates can change, and these changes in the exchange rate can have large, real effects.

CHANGES IN EXCHANGE RATES

Assume that the Bank of Canada succeeds in increasing interest rates in Canada, and the United States and other countries do not match the interest rate changes. Then the higher yields in bonds in Canada make these more attractive to both foreigners and Canadians. The result can be seen in Figure 19.7. Canadians' supply of dollars (at any exchange rate) shifts to the left, and foreigners' demand for dollars shifts to the right; there is a new, higher equilibrium exchange rate.

The higher exchange rate discourages exports and encourages imports. The aggregate expenditures schedule shifts down, as in Figure 19.8A, yielding (at any price level) a lower level of output. Correspondingly, the aggregate demand curve shifts to the left, as illustrated in panel B. Thus, monetary policy succeeds in dampening aggregate de-

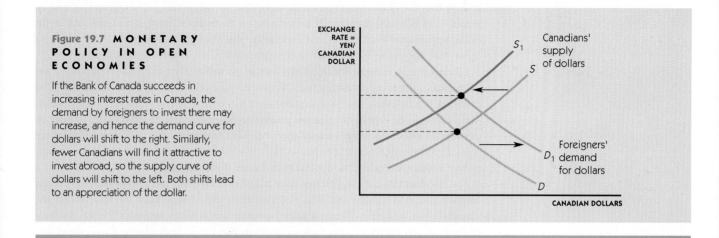

Figure 19.7 MONETARY POLICY IN OPEN ECONOMIES

If the Bank of Canada succeeds in increasing interest rates in Canada, the demand by foreigners to invest there may increase, and hence the demand curve for dollars will shift to the right. Similarly, fewer Canadians will find it attractive to invest abroad, so the supply curve of dollars will shift to the left. Both shifts lead to an appreciation of the dollar.

mand, not so much by restricting credit availability and reducing investment as by discouraging exports and encouraging imports.

Monetary policy may also affect expectations concerning future exchange rates. Changes in those expectations may either reinforce or dampen the effects described so far. How expectations are formed and how they are affected by monetary policy are complicated matters, and it may therefore be difficult to predict the precise effect of monetary policy.

Earlier, we saw that one ingredient in determining expectations of changes in the exchange rate are expectations concerning inflation. If tighter monetary policy leads investors to believe that inflation will be reduced (that is, if investors believe that monetary

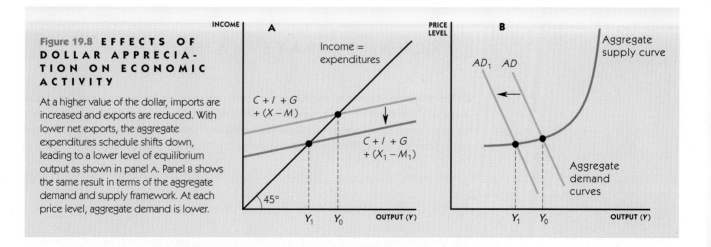

Figure 19.8 EFFECTS OF DOLLAR APPRECIATION ON ECONOMIC ACTIVITY

At a higher value of the dollar, imports are increased and exports are reduced. With lower net exports, the aggregate expenditures schedule shifts down, leading to a lower level of equilibrium output as shown in panel A. Panel B shows the same result in terms of the aggregate demand and supply framework. At each price level, aggregate demand is lower.

policy actually works to shift the aggregate demand curve to the right), then they may believe that the dollar will become stronger (the exchange rate higher) than it otherwise would have been. In that case, it becomes even more attractive to invest in Canada, the dollar appreciates even more, and exports are discouraged and imports are encouraged more than they would have been in the absence of these changed expectations.

Changed expectations induced by changes in monetary policy may have large and immediate effects on exchange rates. If investors believe that the Bank will succeed in lowering the inflation rate by 2 percent over the course of the next year and therefore the dollar will be 2 percent stronger relative to other currencies, then that will have an immediate effect on today's exchange rate. The reason for this is simple. If investors think that the dollar is going to be worth 2 percent more tomorrow, then they will want to buy it today, to realize the capital gain; hence it will go up 2 percent today.

But the fact that exchange rates may adjust quickly does not mean that exports and imports adjust as rapidly and thus that monetary policy has quick effects through this channel. For instance, German and Japanese automakers responded very slowly to changes in the exchange rate that occurred in the 1980s; they changed the prices they charged in Canada only gradually, so automobile imports decreased slowly as the dollar depreciated.

MONETARY POLICY IN AN OPEN ECONOMY

In an open economy, the effect of monetary policy on domestic spending is dampened by the ability of Canadians to borrow abroad. But it is strengthened because it may affect exchange rates and, through exchange rates, the level of economic activity.

EXCHANGE RATE MANAGEMENT

As the link between monetary policy and exchange rates has become increasingly clear, monetary authorities in many countries have attempted to "manage" the exchange rate. In some cases, they have simply tried to smooth out day-to-day fluctuations in exchange rates. In other cases, they have tried to move the exchange rate permanently higher or lower.

FIXED EXCHANGE RATE SYSTEM

The current international system of flexible exchange rates, in which exchange rates are determined by demand and supply, has been in practice for only two decades. Previously, the world had a **fixed exchange rate system,** in which exchange rates were

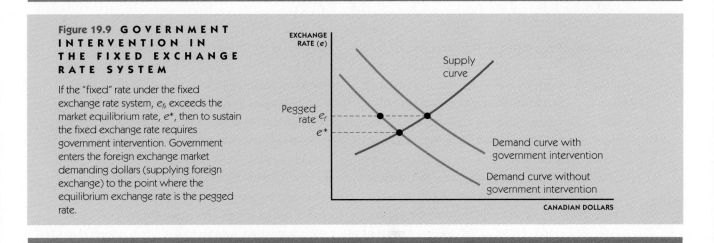

Figure 19.9 GOVERNMENT INTERVENTION IN THE FIXED EXCHANGE RATE SYSTEM

If the "fixed" rate under the fixed exchange rate system, e_f, exceeds the market equilibrium rate, e^*, then to sustain the fixed exchange rate requires government intervention. Government enters the foreign exchange market demanding dollars (supplying foreign exchange) to the point where the equilibrium exchange rate is the pegged rate.

pegged at a particular level. If, as in Figure 19.9, the market equilibrium exchange rate (e^*) was below the pegged level (e_f), then the government intervened; it bought dollars, selling gold or foreign currencies that it held in reserve, shifting the demand curve up.

Sometimes government intervention was not needed. If investors believed that the government was going to succeed in sustaining the pegged rate, they helped the government. If the exchange rate drifted slightly below the pegged rate, they knew that sooner or later the government would intervene and increase the exchange rate. Hence, foreign speculators believed that if they bought dollars they would reap a capital gain. These expectations led them to demand dollars, to the point where the exchange rate was driven up to the pegged level.

The problem arose when investors believed that the equilibrium exchange rate was far different from the pegged rate. Recall that the way the government attempted to sustain the exchange rate was to buy dollars, selling gold or foreign currencies. But if the government had insufficient gold or foreign currencies and investors believed that the government could not or would not sustain the exchange rate at the pegged level, the results were disastrous.

When the government announces that there will be a new, lower exchange rate under the fixed exchange rate system in order to stimulate exports and help industries that face competition from foreign imports, then it is said to **devalue** the currency. When investors believe that the dollar is about to be devalued, they will not want to hold dollars. Canadians, by holding foreign currencies, can reap large capital gains. As we saw in an earlier example (p. 536), they can convert their dollars to a foreign currency and then reconvert to dollars the next day. The result is that the supply of dollars increases enormously. The gap between supply and demand at the original pegged exchange rate becomes enormous. The task of the government in sustaining the exchange rate becomes impossible.

Many governments have attempted to maintain the exchange rate at a rate higher than what would have prevailed in a free market; in such cases, the currency is said to be **overvalued.** The government may take such action for a variety of reasons. In some cases, the exchange rate is a source of pride. A depreciation of the currency is taken to reflect negatively on the country or the government's ability to manage its economic af-

CLOSE-UP: BRITAIN AND THE EMS

In October 1990, after an acrimonious debate between and within its political parties, Great Britain joined the European Monetary System. In joining, Britain promised to stabilize the foreign exchange value of the pound relative to the average of the other European currencies, limiting fluctuations to 3 percent, plus or minus. The primary controversy was whether Britain had surrendered control over its own monetary policy. To some extent, it had.

Here's why. To stabilize the value of the pound, the Bank of England must avoid extremes of inflation (which would depreciate the currency) and high real interest rates (which would tend to appreciate the currency). Either too loose or too tight a monetary policy could easily push exchange rates out of their agreed-upon range. Thus, unless all the rest of Europe decides to pursue a loose monetary policy, Britain will not be able to do so. And since Germany, the largest European economy, has traditionally held inflation in check by running a tight monetary policy, Britain will be compelled to do the same.

But those who favoured joining the EMS argued that limiting the power of the central bank was a good thing. They argued, for instance, that the promise of a relatively stable currency would allow British businesses to make long-term plans for investing in the rest of Europe, and European businesses to make long-term plans for investing in Britain.

During August and September 1992, with Germany maintaining high interest rates to combat inflation and Britain trying to keep interest rates low to stimulate its sluggish economy, the high demand for German marks relative to the British pound led to a higher "equilibrium" exchange rate. To maintain the exchange rate within the agreed-upon limits required more government intervention, to buy pounds and sell marks. As speculators and investors became convinced that the exchange rate could not be maintained, the demand for marks and the supply of pounds became still greater, requiring further intervention. Finally, the week of September 14, the pound fell, and Britain withdrew, at least temporarily, from the EMS.

Source: "Going for It," *The Economist,* October 13, 1990, pp. 14–15.

fairs. Sometimes the government attempts to keep a high exchange rate to enable it to buy foreign goods such as expensive luxury imports for the ruling elites or expensive machines for new factories at a lower cost in terms of domestic currency.

GOVERNMENT INTERVENTION IN FLEXIBLE EXCHANGE RATE SYSTEMS

Today, while governments do not peg the exchange rate at a particular value, they frequently intervene in the foreign exchange markets, buying and selling currencies, in an attempt to reduce the day-to-day variability in exchange rates. Economists sometimes refer to this as a **dirty float system**. As we will see, this variability itself may have a dampening effect on the economy, exposing both export and import sectors to considerable risk.

VOLATILITY OF EXPECTATIONS

Many economists have been concerned with the high degree of volatility in exchange rate markets. Exchange rates have fluctuated greatly, both on a day-to-day and on a longer-term basis, as illustrated in Figure 19.10. The American dollar went from 1.17 Canadian dollars in 1980 to 1.39 Canadian dollars in 1986, and back to 1.18 Canadian dollars in 1989. Our dollar has experienced rapid depreciations against other currencies, in response to changed political and economic circumstances. The night before Finance Minister Michael Wilson's budget announcement in April 1989, information about the new Goods and Services Tax was leaked. Overnight, the American dollar rose by a full cent to 1.20 Canadian dollars, as financial markets in Japan and other Far Eastern countries responded to the news. Luckily, activity in North American markets the next day was more positive, and the cost of American dollars fell back by more than one cent to 1.189 Canadian dollars. The initial rise of 1¢ was an increase of more than .8 percent. If this does not seem large, imagine if our dollar lost .8 percent to the American

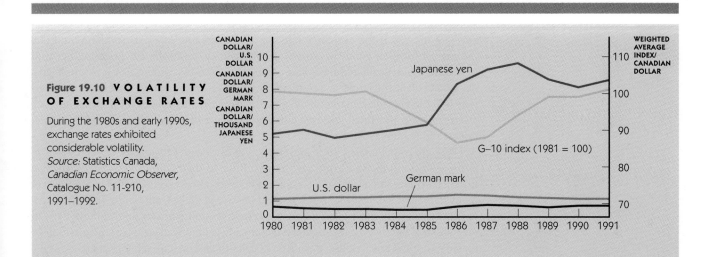

Figure 19.10 VOLATILITY OF EXCHANGE RATES

During the 1980s and early 1990s, exchange rates exhibited considerable volatility.
Source: Statistics Canada, *Canadian Economic Observer*, Catalogue No. 11-210, 1991–1992.

dollar every business day for a year. This would amount to a loss of approximately 200 percent. Many of these gyrations, particularly the ones that happen from day to day, cannot be explained by any correspondingly large changes in the real economy. They only seem explainable in terms of large shifts in expectations.

As was noted above, dollars or yen are assets. That is why the value of the exchange rate today depends on what they expect the exchange rate will be next year. Thus, the stability of the exchange rate depends on the stability of the expectations of investors. For instance, when the dollar is lower, foreign investors might expect it to rise again. In that case, as the value of the dollar declines, the expected return to holding dollars increases because investors believe that it is likely to appreciate and that they will benefit from a capital gain when the dollar does appreciate. In this case, expectations help stabilize the market, since foreign investors may help to limit any decline in the dollar by buying it as it falls.

But if as the dollar depreciates foreign investors expect further depreciation, then their willingness to lend may actually decrease as the dollar falls in value. In that case, an initial decline in the value of the dollar in effect shifts the demand curve for dollars down, leading to further decreases in the value of the dollar.

Economists have noted that prices of assets move like a "random walk." A random walk corresponds to how a drunken person moves, lurching first one way, then another, in a totally unpredictable manner. If there were predictable patterns, investors would discover them and, by their resulting bidding actions, eliminate them. Dollars, pounds, yen, francs, marks, are all assets. If it were the case that normally when the dollar depreciated with respect to the yen, it recovered, then investors would know that under these circumstances the dollar was a good buy. They would bid for dollars, driving up the exchange rate. In equilibrium, then, investors must believe that whatever the exchange rate is today, it must have a roughly equal chance of going up or down. Exchange rates that do not move this way cannot be consistent with rational expectations. While the empirical evidence casts some doubt on whether foreign exchange markets are well described by a random walk, it is nonetheless clear that it is extremely difficult to predict how exchange rates will move.

Whatever their cause and whatever the nature of expectations concerning future movements, these huge swings in exchange rates add to the risk of doing business in the world market and thus discourage businesses and countries from pursuing their comparative advantages. If the exchange rate appreciates greatly, exporters suddenly find that the market for their goods has dried up, unless they drastically cut prices; either way, profits are dramatically reduced. Even Canadian firms that produce only for the Canadian market face huge risks as a result of exchange rate fluctuations. Shoe manufacturers may find the Canadian market flooded with cheap Brazilian shoes if the dollar appreciates relative to the Brazilian cruzado; again, they either lose sales or must cut their prices, and in either case, profits fall.

There are ways that exporting and importing firms can mitigate the effects of foreign exchange risks in the short run, say the next three to six months. Consider a Canadian firm that exports abroad. It has a contract to deliver so many ball bearings to France at so many francs per ball bearing. But it pays its workers in dollars, not francs. If the franc depreciates, when the firm takes the francs it receives and converts them into dollars, its revenues will fall short of the dollars it has already paid to workers. It can insure itself by making a contract (with either a bank or a dealer in the foreign exchange market) for the future delivery or sale of those francs at a price agreed upon today. It can thus avoid the risk of a change in the foreign exchange rate. However, firms cannot easily buy or sell foreign exchange for delivery two or three years into the future. Since many investment projects have a planning horizon of years or even decades, investors are exposed to foreign exchange risks against which they cannot get insurance. But even firms that do not buy or sell in foreign markets are exposed to risks from foreign exchange rate fluctuations: Canadian firms cannot buy insurance against the longer-term risk that the Canadian market will be flooded with cheap imports as a result of an appreciation of the Canadian dollar.

STABILIZING THE EXCHANGE RATE

Given the costs of exchange rate instability, there have been demands that the government should actively try to stabilize the exchange rate. What producers are particularly concerned with is stabilizing the real exchange rate, so that if inflation in Canada is higher than in foreign countries, Canadian exporters can still sell their goods abroad. As Figure 19.11 shows, there have been large movements in real exchange rates between Canadian and U.S. dollars, just as there have been in nominal exchange rates.[1]

A number of different strategies have been suggested to stabilize the real exchange rate. These can involve Bank of Canada intervention in the foreign exchange market, international governmental cooperation, or basing exchange rate policy on other macroeconomic policy goals. In recent years, the Bank of Canada has followed the third approach. The Bank believes that its primary objective is to keep the rate of inflation as low as possible, and achieving and maintaining confidence in the value of the Canadian dollar makes an important contribution to that objective. Imported goods make up one-quarter of domestic incomes, and changes in the price of imports contribute significantly to changes in the consumer price index. Therefore, keeping the exchange rate stable has an important effect on keeping the domestic price level stable by preventing fluctuations in the price of imports to Canadians. In turn, if the price level is relatively

---

[1] The figure shows the trade-weighted value of Canadian dollars, with (real) and without (nominal) adjustments for inflation in different countries.

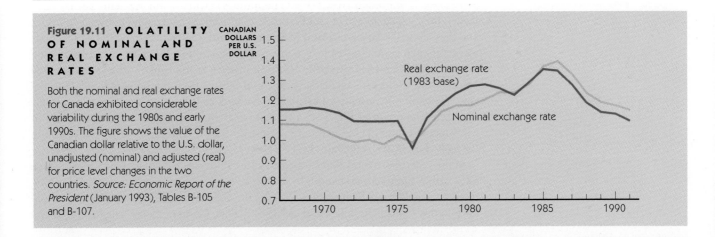

Figure 19.11 VOLATILITY OF NOMINAL AND REAL EXCHANGE RATES

Both the nominal and real exchange rates for Canada exhibited considerable variability during the 1980s and early 1990s. The figure shows the value of the Canadian dollar relative to the U.S. dollar, unadjusted (nominal) and adjusted (real) for price level changes in the two countries. *Source: Economic Report of the President* (January 1993), Tables B-105 and B-107.

stable, then the real exchange rate, which depends on the rate of change of domestic prices, will not be subject to major or unexpected fluctuations. Thus, despite the recession of the early 1990s, the Bank of Canada has been adopting a policy of monetary stringency to prevent the value of the dollar from depreciating and causing a bout of inflation. Critics have argued that this focus by the Bank on the importance of fighting inflation by tight monetary policy has come at the expense of prolonging the recession.

In intervening in the foreign exchange market to stabilize the real exchange rate, the Bank must follow a few necessary steps. First, it must choose what the exchange rate should be. Second, it must have a mechanism for keeping the real exchange rate at that value. For example, if the Canadian dollar seems to be climbing too high against the U.S. dollar, a plan might propose that the Bank sell Canadian dollars and buy U.S. dollars, thus pushing up the demand for U.S. dollars and increasing the supply of Canadian dollars. Producers in Canada may be delighted by this move; demand for exports will increase, as will demand for goods that compete closely with imports. But producers in the United States will feel just the opposite. If the American government, responding to these pressures, were to intervene simultaneously and start selling U.S. dollars and buying Canadian dollars, the two efforts would offset each other. In effect, it would be as if the Canadian government sold Canadian dollars in exchange for U.S. dollars directly to the American government, with private markets unaffected.

This brings up a third step for stabilizing the real exchange rate: ensuring some degree of cooperation among countries. This is particularly true in the modern world economy, where no single country is dominant. There are several big players—Japan, Germany, and the United States—along with other medium-sized ones, including Canada, and setting exchange rates requires these governments to work together.

INTERNATIONAL COOPERATION

Following World War II, the major countries, including Britain, France, the United States, and Canada, recognized their economic interdependence and the importance of orderly foreign exchange markets for the conduct of international trade. In a famous 1944 meeting at Bretton Woods, New Hampshire, at which John Maynard Keynes was a leader, they signed an agreement that called for fixed exchange rates between countries and that set up the **International Monetary Fund** (IMF). Just as the Bank of Canada was set up as a central or bankers' bank, providing a source that Canadian banks could borrow from in times of need, the IMF was to serve as the bank for the various central banks of the world. In Canada, a bank could borrow from the Bank of Canada in the case of a bank run, and the knowledge that a bank could do so was supposed to reduce the likelihood of a run. Likewise, a central bank could borrow from the IMF, and this was supposed to protect the country against runs on its currency and help it maintain the agreed-upon exchange rate.

In the years after World War II, the countries of the world tried to maintain exchange rates within fairly narrow bands. To do this required governments' buying and selling money and gold out of their reserves. To keep the dollar at the desired level, Canada would have to buy Canadian dollars and sell U.S. dollars, German marks, Japanese yen, and whatever other currencies were gaining strength against the dollar. During the first two decades after the war, the American economy dominated the world scene, and it was easy for the United States to take on the responsibility of stabilizing exchange rates— buying and selling U.S. dollars, foreign currencies, and gold to do so. Everyone wanted American goods, and the United States exported much more than it imported. The U.S. Federal Reserve System (the Fed) accumulated vast amounts of foreign currency. Thus, if it looked like the demand for marks at the fixed exchange rate exceeded the supply, the Fed would simply sell some of the marks out of its horde. But what happens when the Fed runs out of its reserves, when it has no more marks or yen to sell?

If the demand for U.S. dollars is weak, the dollar's exchange rate will not be able to be sustained at the desired value. Foreign central banks could intervene. The German Bundesbank might, for instance, buy U.S. dollars and sell marks, and the increased demand for U.S. dollars would allow the exchange rate to be maintained. But the German bank might not want to do this. If it believes that the U.S. dollar cannot be sustained at the pegged value, then the Germans will be left holding U.S. dollars that are about to decrease in value. This seems like bad business. Why should they pay the price of America's problems?

Although the Fed could borrow from the IMF, this may only postpone the eventual day of reckoning. Try as they might, governments cannot support forever an exchange rate that differs from the one that would have emerged without government intervention in the market. Under the Bretton Woods system, Britain, France, and other countries found from time to time that they simply had to devalue their currencies.

The end of the system of fixed exchange rates can probably be dated to 1971, when the United States, which had been the pillar of the system, found it increasingly difficult to support the value of the U.S. dollar. The United States (with the rest of the world quickly following) switched to a system of flexible exchange rates. Advocates of flexible exchange rates say that it is better to have frequent small changes in response to market forces rather than the large, disruptive changes that characterize a fixed exchange rate regime. Even with flexible exchange rates, however, there are still heavy doses of government intervention, requiring continuing cooperation among the countries of the world. Every year there is an economic summit of the leaders of the major industrialized countries, referred to as the G-7 countries, and one of the topics frequently discussed is exchange rate management. Canada has been concerned with not only the volatility of the dollar, but also its level.

Especially in the late 1980s and early 1990s when the Canadian dollar was flying high, it was often argued that the dollar is overvalued, making it difficult for Canada to export and for Canadian producers to compete with foreign imports. Most of the leaders of the other countries have been only mildly sympathetic. They believe that in the long run the exchange rate is determined by basic economic forces. Most economists share this view. The high value of the dollar in the early 1990s was caused by the huge flow of capital to Canada; this in turn was caused by the high interest rates paid in Canada, which in turn was related to the huge amount of borrowing on the part of the federal and provincial governments as well as the restrictive monetary policies of the Bank of Canada. The governments of Canada's major economic partners have contended that there is little that can be done about the overall level of the exchange rate unless Canada first takes serious steps to cut its budget deficit. Cooperation may still have a role in maintaining short-run stability in exchange rates.

Close-up: Predicting Exchange Rates

Investors face two major problems in forming expectations about what exchange rates will be in the future. One problem is that even if an investor can make a reasonably confident prediction about what the exchange rate ought to be, she cannot be sure of how long it will take the market to reach that particular value. Thus, an investor might have said in 1984: "Look, the dollar has depreciated against the American dollar by 10¢ since 1980; $1.29 per U.S. dollar is the lowest it's ever been, and our economy is improving. I'm sure it will go up." By 1990, the dollar was back to its 1980 value, but it had declined to $1.41 per U.S. dollar in 1986 before it began to rise. An investor who had bought other currencies, planning to cash them back into dollars when the dollar fell, could easily have gone broke during this time. Investors cannot always wait for the long run; they have to worry about the short run too.

The second problem investors face is even more fundamental. How can they tell what the equilibrium exchange rate will be? Any government that decides its currency is too high or too low and wants to alter its value will face a similar problem of deciding what the "correct" value should be.

The purchasing power parity theorem offers a way of tackling this question. This theorem holds that in equilibrium, the value of different currencies should be such that one could purchase a roughly equivalent bundle of goods for the same amount of money in different countries. For example, consider a bundle of goods made up of wheat, oil, steel, cars, computers, and other internationally traded goods. If it costs $1 million to purchase this bundle in Canada, then the purchasing power parity exchange rate will be determined by how many yen or marks or pounds or francs it takes to buy that same bundle in another country.

The theorem does *not* say that the price of individual goods must be the same in different countries, only that the price level of internationally traded goods, taken as a group, should be equal. After all, if all tradable goods were, on average, much more expensive in one country than another, then that country would have a very difficult time exporting at all! The purchasing power parity theorem is thus based on the premise that in the long run, countries will not continually be borrowers or lenders.

Tourists travelling in other countries may feel that purchasing power parity cannot be right since hotels, meals, and trips often are either cheaper or more expensive in other countries. But most of what tourists buy when they visit a country are goods and services that are not internationally traded, like a hotel room, and the purchasing power parity theorem has nothing to say about such prices.

Businesspeople and investors concerned with the currency market usually keep the purchasing power parity exchange rate in their peripheral vision. But they know that the economy may take years to converge to that rate. In the meantime, they tend to focus their attention on trying to understand and predict the short-term determinants of exchange rates, like government actions, the course of inflation, and the expectations of other investors.

CAN EXCHANGE RATES BE STABILIZED?

Some economists are skeptical about the ability of the government to stabilize the exchange rate even in the short run. If the current exchange rate between the franc and the dollar is 6 francs to the dollar, and if the market knows that the exchange rate must change in the near future to 6.6 francs to the dollar, it will be futile for the government to try, in the short run, to maintain the current exchange rate. French investors, believing that there will be a devaluation of the franc, know that the return to holding assets in dollars will be enormous. By converting their francs to dollars and holding them for the short period until the franc is devalued, they obtain a large return.

There will be what is referred to as a run on the franc, as those holding assets denominated in francs seek to sell them now. This run will be too large for the French government to stop by buying francs and selling dollars. There are more private individuals willing to sell francs and buy dollars than the French government has resources to cope with. The government may be successful in postponing the fall of the franc for a few days, but to do that it must pay a huge price. It would have obtained the capital gain on the dollars that it held if it did not sell dollars for francs; instead, the capital gain is earned by private individuals. If the government spends $1 billion trying to support the franc and the franc goes down 10 percent (as in our example), the cost of the short-run support is more that $100 million.

Critics of government stabilization programs make several other points. First, they stress the difficulties in determining the equilibrium exchange rate that is supposed to be stabilized. Is there any reason, they ask, to believe that government bureaucrats are in a better position to make judgments about the equilibrium exchange rate than the thousands of investors who buy and sell foreign exchange every day? If the government makes mistakes, as it is almost bound to do, it can actually contribute to destabilizing the exchange rate rather than stabilizing it. Exchange rates often need to change. For example, if one economy grows faster than another or has higher inflation than another, the exchange rate will have to compensate. How will a scheme for stabilizing exchange rates let them adjust naturally while controlling them at the same time?

Second, critics of government stabilization programs question whether international economic cooperation is achievable. Running domestic economic policy is difficult enough. For example, to keep a political agreement with foreign countries, will a country take steps to raise its exchange rate and thus hurt its exporters?

Thus, there are questions about whether stabilizing the currency is possible either economically or politically.

REVIEW AND PRACTICE

SUMMARY

1. Exchange rates are determined by the forces of demand and supply. The demand and supply for dollars is determined by exports and imports, foreigners' demand for investment in Canada and Canadians' demand for investment abroad,

and by speculators, whose demands for various currencies are based on expectations concerning changes in exchange rates.

2. In an open economy, government monetary policy is likely to have a smaller effect on interest rates and credit availability than it otherwise would. If the Bank of Canada attempts to restrict credit or raise interest rates, capital can flow in from abroad.

3. To the extent that monetary policy leads to flows of capital into the country, it also normally leads to an appreciation of the dollar, reducing exports and increasing imports.

4. It may not be possible for the government to stabilize exchange rates effectively. It is difficult to determine the equilibrium exchange rate that is supposed to be stabilized, and international economic cooperation may not be achievable.

KEY TERMS

flexible or floating exchange rate system

perfectly mobile capital
real exchange rates

fixed exchange rate system
devaluation

REVIEW QUESTIONS

1. Why is monetary policy, whether tight or loose, likely to have less of an effect on interest rates or on the supply of credit in an open economy?

2. Name three factors that cause exchange rates to shift.

3. How does monetary policy affect output in an open economy?

4. Why are expectations concerning changes in the exchange rate important? How do relative rates of inflation affect those expectations?

5. What are the costs of exchange rate stability? How might the government attempt to reduce instability in exchange rates? What are the obstacles to doing so? Why is international coordination important? What problems might result from government attempts to stabilize the exchange rate at a nonequilibrium level?

6. Why would you be surprised to find obvious patterns in movements of foreign exchange markets?

PROBLEMS

1. Tell whether each of the economic actors in the following list would be suppliers or demanders in the foreign exchange market for Canadian dollars:
    (a) a Canadian tourist in Europe;
    (b) a Japanese firm exporting to Canada;
    (c) a British investor who wants to buy Canadian stocks;

(d) a Brazilian tourist in Canada;

(e) a German firm importing from Canada;

(f) a Canadian investor who wants to buy real estate in Australia;

(g) an American corporation in Canada that sends dividends home to its shareholders.

2. Explain whether each of the following changes would tend to appreciate or depreciate the Canadian dollar, using supply and demand curves for the foreign exchange market to illustrate your answers:

(a) higher interest rates in Japan;

(b) faster economic growth in Germany;

(c) a higher Canadian rate of inflation;

(d) a tight Canadian monetary policy;

(e) an expansionary Canadian fiscal policy.

3. Suppose that at the start of 1991, a Canadian investor put $10,000 into a one-year German investment. If the exchange rate was 1.5 marks per dollar, how much was this in marks? Over the course of the year, the German investment paid 10 percent interest. But when the investor switched back to dollars at the end of the year, the exchange rate was now 2 marks per dollar. Did the change in exchange rates earn the investor more or less money? How much? How does your analysis change if the mark had fallen to 1 per dollar?

4. If the government wanted to reduce its trade deficit by altering the exchange rate, what sort of monetary policy should it employ? Explain.

5. If the government succeeds in raising the exchange rate, who benefits and who is injured?

CHAPTER 20

PRICE STABILITY

It is an axiom of political rhetoric that inflation is bad. Popular sentiment runs so strongly against inflation that it is usually taken for granted that the government should do something about it. This is especially true when, for example, the price level doubles every month; no one would then dispute the view that the economy is in some way sick. Such extremely high rates of inflation, called **hyperinflation,** have plagued many countries in recent years, including Brazil, Argentina, Bolivia, and Israel. With these rates of inflation, money no longer serves its primary functions very well; it is no longer a good store of value or a unit of account, and it may not even be used widely as a medium of exchange. In certain Latin American countries, the rate of inflation has been so high at times that people have preferred not to use their own national currency; instead, they often use U.S. dollars, whose value is relatively stable.

For the past two centuries, Canada has been spared these extremes of inflation. But even far lower inflation rates have given rise to concern, as when the inflation rate soared in the late 1970s and early 1980s, climbing as high as 1 percent per month in 1981. It is less clear that these relatively low rates of inflation portend any serious problems for the economy. If incomes go up as rapidly as prices do, then the family's opportunity set remains the same. Under these circumstances, is there any harm in (moderate) inflation? More generally, what causes inflation and what can or should be done about it? No inflation may be preferable to even moderate inflation, but with a better understanding of the causes and remedies, we will see that the cure may be as bad as or worse than the disease.

KEY QUESTIONS

1. What are the "costs" of inflation? How have modern countries been able to reduce those costs? Why does it make a difference whether inflation is anticipated or not? Who today is most adversely affected by inflation?

2. What causes inflation? What keeps it going?

3. What is the cost of fighting inflation? Is there a trade-off between inflation and unemployment, so that when inflation is reduced, unemployment is increased? What factors might cause the relationship between inflation and unemployment to change? Why are inflationary expectations so important?

4. What are the various methods that governments have employed to fight inflation?

LIVING WITH MODERATE INFLATION

Inflation is much maligned, but most of the economic costs of inflation disappear when it is anticipated. Workers who know that the consumer price index will be rising by 10 percent this year may negotiate wages that rise fast enough to offset the inflation. If inflation drives up a producer's costs but boosts the price he receives for his product by a similar amount, then the producer is no worse off (and no better off) on account of inflation.

The formal linking of any payment to some measure of inflation is called **indexing.** To see how indexing works, consider the provisions called **cost-of-living adjustments,** or COLAs, that appear in many labour contracts. Collective bargaining agreements (the contract) often cover three years or so. To be sure that the wages negotiated today for three years from now will have the purchasing power agreed to, a COLA is often added. This provision contains a formula that will further increase the (nominal) wage if inflation has occurred. Thus, a worker with a COLA is relatively immune to the effects of inflation (but she should also remember that a COLA raise will not buy her more groceries or a larger car). Likewise, Old Age Security payments, interest rates, and tax rates have been indexed in recent years, and this has eased the economic cost of inflation throughout the economy.

THE EFFECTS OF INFLATION

While indexing goes a long way towards softening the effects of inflation, it is far from complete. So what are the effects of inflation, both on individuals and on the economy as a whole?

WHO SUFFERS FROM INFLATION?

Many people may suffer a little from inflation, since indexing does not fully protect them, but some are more likely to suffer than others. Among the groups most imperfectly protected are lenders, taxpayers, and holders of currency.

Lenders   Since most loans are not fully indexed, increases in inflation mean that the dollars that lenders receive back from borrowers are worth less than what they lent out. We often think of bankers as the country's major lenders, and making bankers worse off is hardly likely to evoke an outpouring of sympathy. But many people put a large part of their savings for their retirement into bonds or other fixed-income securities. These people will suffer if an inflationary bout comes between them and their nest eggs. The extent to which they will suffer depends in large measure on whether the price changes were anticipated. After World War II, many people bought bonds yielding a 3 or 4 percent annual return. They did not anticipate much inflation. When inflation reached double-digit levels in the late 1970s, they were badly hurt; the rate of interest they received did not even come close to compensating them for the reduced value of the dollars. In real terms, they received a negative return on their savings. If the inflation had been anticipated, the interest rate would have reflected this.

Taxpayers   Our tax system is only partially indexed, and inflation frequently hurts investors badly. All returns to investment are taxed, including those that do nothing more than offset inflation. Consequently, real after-tax returns are often negative. Consider a rate of inflation of 10 percent and an asset that yields a return of 12 percent before tax. If the individual has to pay a 33 percent tax on the return, his after-tax yield is 9 percent—not enough to compensate him for inflation. His after-tax real return is minus 1 percent.

Holders of Currency   Inflation also makes it expensive for people to hold currency because as they hold it, the currency loses its value. Since currency facilitates a variety of transactions, inflation interferes with the efficiency of the economy by discouraging the holding of currency. The fact that inflation takes away the value of money means that inflation acts as a tax on holding money. Consequently, economists refer to this distortionary effect as an **inflation tax.**

This distortion is not as important in modern economies, where even transactions that use money more frequently entail the use of chequing accounts, and chequing accounts typically pay interest. As the rate of inflation increases, the interest rate they pay normally increases. Even in Argentina in the 1970s, when prices were rising at 800 percent a month, bank accounts yielded more than 800 percent a month. Still, poorer individuals who do not have chequing accounts and therefore must hold much of what little wealth they have in the form of currency are adversely affected.

THE EFFECTS OF INFLATION ON THE ECONOMY

The economy as a whole suffers from inflation for two reasons. The first has to do with relative prices. Normally increases in the rate of inflation lead to a greater variability of relative prices. If the shoe industry makes price adjustments only every three months, then in the third month, right before its price increase, shoes may be relatively cheap, while right after the price increase, shoes may be relatively expensive. On the other hand, the prices of groceries might change continually throughout the three-month period. Therefore, the ratio of the price of groceries to the price of shoes will continually

Close-up: Hyperinflation in Germany in the 1920s

Following World War I, Germany was required by the victorious Allied nations to make substantial "reparation" payments. But the sheer size of the reparations, combined with the wartime devastation of German industry, made payment nearly impossible. John Maynard Keynes, then an economic adviser to the British government, was among those who warned that the reparations were too large. To finance some of Germany's financial obligations, the German government started simply printing money.

The resulting increases in both the amount of circulating currency and the price level can be seen in the figure. From January 1922 to November 1923, the average price level increased by a factor of almost 20 billion. People made desperate attempts to spend their currency as soon as they received it, since the value of currency was declining so rapidly. One story often told by Keynes was how Germans would buy two beers at once, even though one was likely to get warm, for fear that otherwise, when it came time to buy the second beer, the price would have risen.

At an annual inflation rate of 100 percent, money loses half its value every year. If you save $100 today, in five years it will have buying power equal to only 3 current dollars. It is possible for

nominal interest rates to adjust even to very high inflation rates. But when those high inflation rates fluctuate in unanticipated ways, the effects can be disastrous.

Periods of hyperinflation create a massive redistribution of wealth. If an individual is smart or lucky enough to hold assets in a form such as foreign funds or land, then the hyperinflation will do little to reduce that person's actual wealth. Those who cannot avail themselves of these "inflation-proof" assets will see their wealth fall.

Source: Thomas Sargent, "The Ends of Four Big Inflations," in Robert Hall, ed., *Inflation* (Chicago: University of Chicago Press, 1982), pp. 74–75.

THE GERMAN HYPERINFLATION

Inflation in Germany during the 1920s reached levels that may seem unbelievably high. At the end of 1923, prices were 10 billion times higher than they were two years earlier.

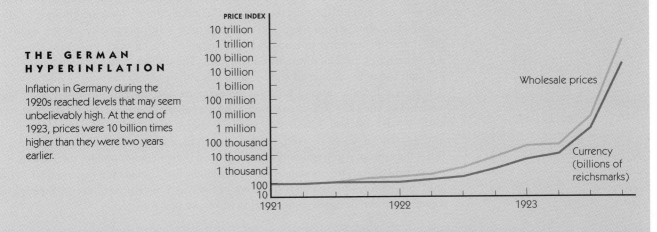

be changing. Price increases are never perfectly coordinated. When the average rate of inflation is only 2 or 3 percent per year, this does not cause much of a problem. But when the average rate of inflation is 10 percent per month, this can be serious. At rates this high, inflation causes real distortions in how society allocates its resources.

The second economy-wide cost of inflation arises from the risk and uncertainty that inflation generates. If there were perfect indexing, the uncertainty about the rate of inflation would be unimportant. But indexing is, as has been noted, far from perfect, and the resulting uncertainty makes it difficult to plan. Lenders cannot charge interest rates that would take into account fully the fact that the dollars paid back will be worth less than the dollars lent. People saving for their retirements cannot know what to put aside. Business firms borrowing money are uncertain about the price they will receive for the goods they produce. Firms are also hurt when they build wage increases into multiyear contracts to reflect anticipated inflation. If for any reason a firm finds that the prices it can charge increase less rapidly than what was anticipated in the contract, the employer suffers.

PERCEIVED COSTS OF INFLATION

Before leaving the subject of inflation's costs, we would do well to review some of the perceived costs, and how economists weigh them. While some people gain from inflation and some lose, more individuals *perceive* that they are losers. If a poll were conducted asking people whether they were hurt or helped by inflation, most would say they were hurt. Much of this is simply perception. People "feel" price increases much more vividly than they do the corresponding income increases. They "feel" the higher interest rates they have to pay on loans more than they do the decrease in the value of the dollars with which they repay lenders. A closer look at who benefits and who loses from unanticipated inflation suggests that there are probably more gainers than there are losers. This is simply because there are probably more debtors than lenders, and debtors benefit from unanticipated inflation.

In many inflationary episodes, many individuals not only *feel* worse off, they *are* worse off—but inflation itself is not the culprit. The oil price increases of 1973 set off a widespread inflation in Canada. The higher price of oil also made eastern Canada poorer than it had previously been, because it was an oil importer. Someone's standard of living had to be cut, and inflation did the cutting. Frequently those whose incomes were cut—unskilled workers, whose wages did not keep pace with prices—cited as the *cause* of their lower incomes the inflation that accompanied the oil price increases. However, generalized price inflation was only a symptom. The underlying cause of that particular inflation and of the decreased real incomes was a sharp rise in the price of oil.

It is clear that the costs of inflation are different, and undoubtedly lower, than they were before indexing was so extensive. Today economists are not agreed on how seriously to take inflation. Given the popular concern about inflation, most economists would say that it would be worth reducing inflation, if it were relatively costless to do so. But if the costs of fighting inflation are high and if the benefits are low, then it may not pay to fight at least the moderate kind of inflation that Canada has experienced in the past half century. To ascertain the costs of fighting inflation, we have to understand something about its causes, a question to which we now turn.

WHY THE PRICE LEVEL CHANGES

The discussion of the goods market in Part Two focused on situations where there is excess capacity, where the intersection of the aggregate demand and supply curves occurs along the horizontal portion of the aggregate supply curve. In such cases, changes in aggregate demand lead to changes in output levels, with no change in the price level. Here, we focus on situations where there is no excess capacity, where the intersection of the aggregate demand and supply curves occurs along the vertical portion of the aggregate supply curve; this is the condition in which inflation most frequently occurs. Because inflation is the process of prices rising over an extended period of time, not a once-and-for-all change in the price level, we break the analysis of inflation down into two parts: what causes the inflation, and what perpetuates it. This section is concerned with the first part.

Figure 20.1 shows an economy initially in equilibrium, with aggregate demand equal to aggregate supply, at a point where the economy is operating at capacity. The machines are all humming at top speed, and workers are all employed. Panel A shows a cause of inflation known as a **demand shock.** In a full-capacity economy, if there is a rightward shift in the aggregate demand curve, from AD_0 to AD_1, then at the initial price level p_0 there is excess demand. We say there is "inflationary pressure." With the demand for goods exceeding the supply, prices tend to rise, in this case to p_1.

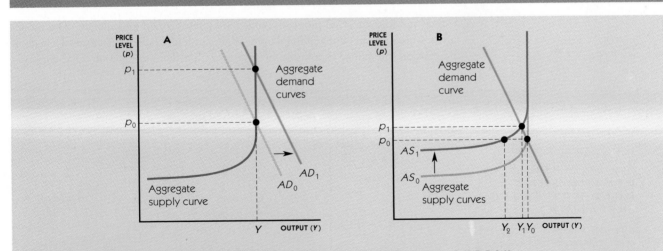

Figure 20.1 HOW SHIFTS IN AGGREGATE DEMAND AND SUPPLY CAN CAUSE INFLATION

In panel A, a rightward shift in the aggregate demand curve from AD_0 to AD_1 leads to an increase in the equilibrium price level when the equilibrium is already near full employment. Panel B shows that an upward shift in the aggregate supply curve from AS_0 to AS_1 leads to an increase in the equilibrium price level. At the original price level, p_0, aggregate demand, Y_0, exceeds the level of aggregate supply, Y_2.

Panel B shows another cause of inflation, called a **supply shock.** Here, it is the aggregate supply curve that shifts. This upward shift leaves capacity unchanged—that is why the vertical portions of the two curves coincide. But firms require higher prices to be willing to supply any given level of output. Again, there is excess demand at the original price level p_0. Like demand shocks, supply shocks introduce inflationary pressure.

AGGREGATE DEMAND SHOCKS

What might cause the aggregate demand curve to shift? We know that aggregate demand is the sum of consumption, investment, government expenditures, and exports minus imports; it can shift because of an increase in any one of these four components. For example, an inflationary episode began in the United States in 1966 due to increased government expenditures for the Vietnam War. These expenditures spilled over into Canada in the form of increased export demand. Thus Canada experienced inflation along with the United States.

Increases in aggregate demand do not always cause inflation. When the economy is operating in the flat portion of its aggregate supply curve, as in Figure 20.2, increases in aggregate demand can be an important tool for stimulating the economy—increasing output without necessarily increasing prices. However, when the economy is operating close to full capacity, in the vertical portion of its aggregate supply curve, an increase in demand will simply increase prices, leaving output unchanged.

TRACING OUT MONETARY POLICY THROUGH THE AGGREGATE DEMAND CURVE

Money and misconceived monetary policy are often blamed for inflation. The monetarists, whom we encountered in Chapter 18, in particular believe that excessively rapid increases in the money supply are the primary culprit behind inflation. One common

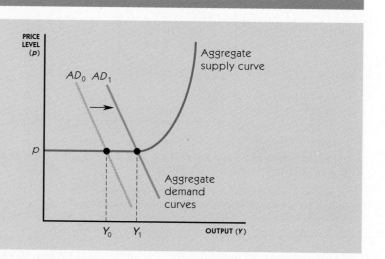

Figure 20.2 WHEN A DEMAND SHIFT DOES NOT CAUSE INFLATION

If the economy initially has considerable unemployment, so that it is operating along the horizontal section of the aggregate supply curve, shifts in aggregate demand lead to increases in output but no inflation.

description of inflation is "too much money chasing too few goods." It is natural that money should be the focus of attention: after all, prices simply tell us how much money must be exchanged for each product. When there is inflation, you have to give up more dollar bills to buy a soft drink. From the point of view of the seller, inflation means giving up fewer soft drinks to receive a dollar.

Just as an increase in the supply of fruit juices relative to that of soft drinks will lead to an increase in the price of soft drinks relative to the price of fruit juices, an increase in the supply of money relative to that of soft drinks will result in an increase in the price of soft drinks relative to money; soft drinks become more expensive.

To take an example from an earlier period, the influx of gold from the New World in the sixteenth century increased the money supply in Europe and set off an inflationary episode. Those who brought the gold to Europe wanted to exchange it for goods. And with only a given supply of goods, the amount of gold required to obtain any item increased—the price of goods in terms of gold increased. The increase of aggregate demand as a result of an increase in the money supply is a particular example of a demand shock, and is referred to as a **monetary shock.**

Likewise, in wartime, governments often simply print money to make up for the gap between what they want to spend and what taxes bring in. Though we can look at the resulting inflation as too much money chasing too few goods—we can say the inflation was due to a monetary shock—we can also look at inflation as simply a problem of excess aggregate demand: the combination of households' demand for consumer goods, firms' demand for investment, governments' demands for goods and services (including those required to fight the war), and foreigners' demand for net exports simply exceeds the available supply of goods.

In modern economies, governments usually do not simply print money. But they can have the same effect on aggregate demand through their monetary policies. If the monetary authorities pursue a loose monetary policy and lower interest rates, banks find it easier and more attractive to make loans; credit becomes more readily available on easier terms, so investment and consumer purchases of durables are stimulated. Lower interest rates also lead to an outflow of funds from Canada to abroad, resulting in a lower value of the Canadian dollar, higher exports, and lower imports. Aggregate demand will shift up, and if the economy is operating along the vertical portion of its aggregate supply curve, near full capacity, the price level will rise, as illustrated earlier in Figure 20.1A.[1]

Monetarists place particular stress on the role of the monetary authorities in causing inflation. The monetarists, you will recall, typically believe that the economy is close to full employment—on the vertical section of the aggregate supply curve—and that velocity is close to constant, so that increases in the money supply in excess of the growth in output must necessarily be translated into higher prices.[2] In their view, the exact channel by which the increased money supply raises prices—whether the shift in aggregate demand is a result of increased investment, increased exports, or increased consumption—is not so important as the fact that inevitably prices must rise.

[1] The increased investment *eventually* may choke off the rise in the price level through its impact on the aggregate supply curve, as the economy's productive potential increases. However, the effects on aggregate demand come first.

[2] On the other hand, most monetarists believe that large *negative* shocks to the money supply can move the aggregate demand curve down so much that they can, in the short run, induce substantial unemployment.

AGGREGATE SUPPLY SHOCKS

Other inflationary episodes have been attributed to supply curve shifts, or supply shocks. In 1973 as a result of the Arab oil embargo, the world price of oil increased almost fourfold. The increase in the cost of any important input will result in an upward shift in the supply curve, as illustrated earlier in Figure 20.1B. This is because the price firms must receive to make them willing to supply any given quantity is increased. At the old price level, p_0, there is a gap between aggregate demand, Y_0, and the new level of aggregate supply, Y_2; the excess of aggregate demand over aggregate supply gives rise to inflationary pressures. The price level at which aggregate demand equals aggregate supply, p_1, is higher than the initial level, p_0.

WHY INFLATION PERSISTS

The analysis so far has sketched how a shock to the economy can shift the aggregate demand or supply curve, leading to a new, higher equilibrium price level. But inflation is not a onetime change in the price level; it is a persistent increase in the price level, month after month. In most modern industrialized economies, inflation tends to have inertia. Much like a skater, who will continue to glide on the ice after an initial push, an economy that has an inflation rate of 5 percent will continue to experience an inflation rate of 5 percent unless something dramatic happens.

The reason for this is that if most people in the economy expect the same rate of inflation, then these inflationary expectations will be built in to the economy's institutional practices. We then say that the economy has entered into an **inflationary spiral.** Labourers bargaining with managers will make sure that their wages keep pace with price increases so that their *real* wages will not fall. Bankers, in giving out loans, will want to guarantee themselves a certain *real* rate of return, and accordingly will demand interest rates that take into account the fact that the dollars they will receive at the end of the year will be worth less than the dollars they lend out at the beginning. These expectations are self-fulfilling. And because they are realized, there is no reason for anyone to revise them.

The essential property of an inflationary spiral is that it is self-perpetuating. It matters little what causes the inflation. It could be initiated by an increase in aggregate demand. For example, there could be an increase in government expenditures to fight a war when the economy is already at full employment; as a result, the price level rises, and this in turn leads workers to negotiate wage increases simply to keep up with changes in the price level. This kind of inflation is referred to as **demand-pull.**

On the other hand, there are situations in which wage increases and other higher costs of production can be thought of as a cause of inflation. For example, strong unions sometimes demand wage increases that are far in excess of productivity or price level increases. These higher wages induce an upward shift in the aggregate supply curve; automobile firms will be willing to supply a given quantity only if they receive a higher price.[3] The effect of this shift in the supply curve is exactly the same as a shift in the supply curve caused by any other increase in cost. If the economy is initially in equilibrium, then after the supply shift at the old level of prices, there will be an excess demand for goods. This will lead to higher prices, which may in turn create another increase in wage demands and upward shift in the aggregate supply curve, and the inflationary spiral is perpetuated. When increases in wages or other costs of production, such as the price of oil, are the initial cause of the inflation, the inflation is known as **cost-push** inflation, which refers to the increased production costs that push up prices.[4]

Unfortunately, it is difficult to tell in many circumstances whether the inflation is cost-push or demand-pull. It is like asking which came first, the chicken or the egg. Price levels rise because wages increase; and wages increase because price levels are rising.

Once the inflation starts, the two processes (demand-pull and cost-push) look essentially the same. And the inflation can perpetuate itself even after the initial cause of the inflation, whether it was demand or costs, has disappeared. When workers expect prices to go up, they will insist on higher wages, which increase firms' costs, and these in fact lead to higher prices.

ACCOMMODATING INFLATION

As price levels rise, firms will need to have access to more credit to finance the same level of real investment. The demand for money and credit, in nominal terms, by both households and firms will rise with the price level. The Bank of Canada then must decide whether to allow an expansion of money and credit to "accommodate" the inflation. If it does not, then credit, in real terms, will become tighter, real interest rates may rise, investment will be discouraged, and aggregate demand will decrease. The decrease in aggregate demand will reduce inflationary pressures. But at the same time, the decrease in aggregate demand may reduce the *real* level of output and employment if the decrease is large enough to move the aggregate demand curve far enough to the left so that the new intersection of the aggregate demand and supply curves is *not* on the vertical portion of the aggregate supply curve.

The Bank of Canada is often blamed for causing inflation. But just as it is difficult to distinguish cost-push from demand-pull inflation, it is often difficult to distinguish situations where excessively loose credit starts an inflationary episode from those in which monetary policy simply accommodates the inflation. In the latter cases, when the inflation results from, for instance, a demand shock from higher government spending or a

---

[3] It is no coincidence that many of the industries that decide to pay large wage increases are far from competitive. They are price makers, rather than price takers. When they set their price to maximize their profits, they will raise prices to offset cost increases, thus passing on part of the wage increases to their customers.

[4] Remember that the aggregate demand and supply curves give the levels of aggregate demand and supply at each price level *given* the level of wages. An increase in wages shifts the aggregate supply curve up; to elicit the same aggregate supply, prices have to be higher. It also typically shifts the aggregate demand curve to the right; because workers have higher incomes, the amount they are willing to spend, at each price level, is increased. (Higher wages, at any price level, imply that profits are lower; this may reduce the consumption level of owners of firms and may even reduce investment, but it is usually thought that this effect is smaller than the stimulation to workers' consumption.)

INITIATING AND PERPETUATING INFLATION

Initiating inflation

> Shift in aggregate demand (up and to the right) when the economy's resources are already fully employed, from an increase in consumption, investment, government expenditures, or net exports: demand-pull
>> May be induced by monetary policy
> Upward shift in aggregate supply from an increase in wages or the price of imports (e.g., oil): cost-push

Perpetuating inflation

> Price increases lead to wage increases, which lead to further price increases: inflationary spiral

Role of monetary policy

> May initiate inflation by causing a shift in the aggregate demand curve
> May perpetuate inflation by increasing the money and credit supply—accommodating inflation
> May choke off inflation by refusing to accommodate, shifting the aggregate demand curve to the left

supply shock from oil prices, the Bank simply lets money and credit expand with the price level.

While inflation can be fought by identifying and attacking its cause, inflation from any cause can often be checked by a sufficiently large decrease in aggregate demand, whether that happens through a decrease in government expenditure, an increase in taxes, or a tightening of monetary policy. While several factors may have contributed to the high rates of inflation of the 1970s (the oil price shock, increased export demand, excessive union wage increases), the extremely tight monetary policy of the Bank of Canada in the early 1980s was successful in reining in inflation. The rate of inflation fell from over 12 percent in 1981 to less than 4 percent four years later.

The process of reining in inflation is illustrated in Figure 20.3. Initially the economy is in equilibrium at price level p_0 and output Y. Then there is a shift in aggregate demand, caused, for example, by increased exports to the United States. This is reflected in the rightward shift in aggregate demand to AD_1. At the initial price level, there is excess demand; there are inflationary pressures to drive the price level up to p_1. Then the Bank of Canada steps in, tightening monetary policy. This reduces investment and consumer purchases of durables, and aggregate demand shifts back to AD_0. The inflationary

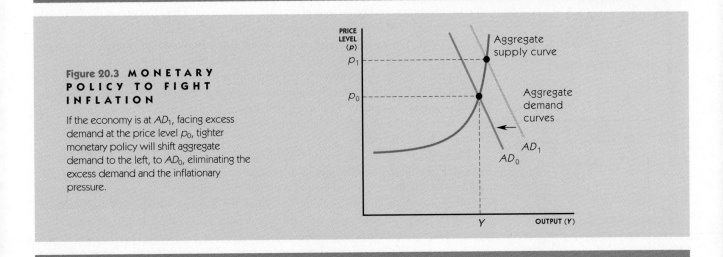

Figure 20.3 MONETARY POLICY TO FIGHT INFLATION

If the economy is at AD_1, facing excess demand at the price level p_0, tighter monetary policy will shift aggregate demand to the left, to AD_0, eliminating the excess demand and the inflationary pressure.

pressure has been eliminated. The original source of the inflationary pressure has not been eliminated; but the higher level of exports is balanced by a lower level of investment and consumer purchases of durables.

THE COSTS OF FIGHTING INFLATION

The Bank of Canada began to have some success reining in inflation in 1982, but this came at the cost of a major recession. The restrictive monetary policy of the late 1970s and early 1980s designed to curb inflation and expectations of inflation kept interest rates high and discouraged private spending and investment. Combined with the restrictive monetary policies being undertaken in the United States, which reduced export demand, employment and the rate of growth of the economy suffered. Thus, while inflation certainly causes problems in a world of uncertainty and imperfect indexing, taming inflation often has costs too. To get less inflation, an economy may have to take on more unemployment; and to get less unemployment, the economy may have to take on more inflation.

THE PHILLIPS CURVE AND THE UNEMPLOYMENT-INFLATION TRADE-OFF

To fight unemployment, the government often seeks to stimulate the economy. As it reduces unemployment towards the full-employment level, the labour market becomes

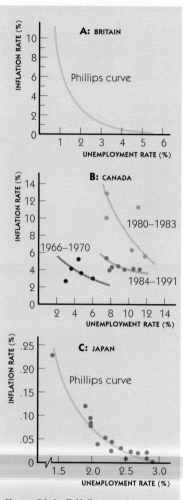

Figure 20.4 THE PHILLIPS CURVE

The Phillips curve shows that as the level of unemployment falls, the rate of inflation rises. The intercept of the curve with the horizontal axis gives the unemployment rate at which inflation is zero, which is called the natural rate. Panel A shows the curve A. W. Phillips actually plotted in 1958 for the British economy. Panel B depicts the Phillips curve relationship for Canadian data in the late 1960s, early 1980s, and late 1980s. Panel C gives the Phillips curve for Japan. Source: *Economic Report of the President* (1992), Tables B-37, B-59, B-105, B-106; Statistics Canada, Catalogues 62-010 and 71-001.

tighter. More and more firms find it difficult to obtain the labour they want, and so as they compete for workers, wages get bid up. Conversely, when the unemployment rate is very high, there are many more job seekers than jobs, and there is little pressure to increase wages. Accordingly, less unemployment results in more rapid increases in wages, which in turn result through the inflationary spiral in more rapid increases in prices.

There is thus a trade-off between unemployment and inflation: lower levels of unemployment will be associated with higher levels of inflation. This relationship is called the **Phillips curve,** after A. W. Phillips, a New Zealander teaching in England in the 1950s who discovered the historical relationship between the unemployment and inflation statistics for Great Britain.

Figure 20.4A depicts the curve that Phillips fitted to British data. Since Phillips was focusing his attention on the labour market, he put the unemployment rate on the horizontal axis and the rate of increase in wages on the vertical axis. Because wage increases implied price level increases, there was a link between unemployment and inflation. His study suggested that lower inflation rates could be achieved, but there would be a cost: higher unemployment rates.

In the data Phillips analyzed, wages (and hence the price level) were stable when there was 5.5 percent unemployment. When the unemployment rate is anywhere near 0 percent, the inflation rate is very high. The rate of unemployment at which inflation is zero has come to be called the **natural rate,** but the name should not confuse you; just as natural foods may or may not be good for you, the natural rate of unemployment may or may not be good for the economy. All the natural rate signifies is that wages and therefore the price level are stable at that rate of unemployment.[5] With less unemployment, the price level would rise; with more, the price level would decline. Whether it is desirable to attain the natural rate depends on how much extra inflation results if unemployment is reduced below the natural rate, on who bears the costs of the inflation or unemployment, and on how one weighs these various costs.

THE PHILLIPS CURVE

1. There is a trade-off between inflation and unemployment.

2. When the rate of inflation is zero, the rate of unemployment is greater than zero. This rate is called the natural rate of unemployment.

[5] That the natural rate of unemployment is not zero but rather some positive amount may seem to contradict the model of how labour markets clear. After all, if there are unemployed workers, won't wages be bid *down?* In the real economy, however, not every worker is qualified to do every job. There may be unemployment in Saint John and vacancies in Oshawa, but unemployed shipbuilders in Saint John cannot simply walk into jobs making automobiles in Oshawa.

Policymakers weighing these costs need to know the shape and position of the Phillips curve. They need to know the unemployment-inflation trade-off—how much *extra* unemployment they must absorb if they want to reduce inflation by 1 percent, and how much inflation will increase if they want to reduce unemployment. If the Phillips curve is very steep, then the cost is high; that is, reducing the unemployment rate a little results in a large increase in the inflation rate, and, conversely, a government decision to fight inflation may lead to a higher rate of unemployment. A comparison of panels A, B, and C of Figure 20.4 shows that the shape and position of the Phillips curve can vary in different countries and within the same country at different times.

SHIFTS IN THE PHILLIPS CURVE

Chapter 4 distinguished between movements along a curve and shifts in the curve. We saw how the demand curve gives the quantity demanded at each price; but that when incomes, tastes, or a variety of other circumstances change, the demand curve shifts. The same basic principle applies to the Phillips curve. The curve gives the rate of inflation corresponding to any level of unemployment, but there are a number of changes in economic circumstances that lead to shifts in this relationship.

The distinction between shifts in and movements along the Phillips curve is important. Figure 20.5A shows a movement from point A on an old Phillips curve to point *B* on a new Phillips curve. Because the Phillips curve has shifted up, at *B* there is more unemployment and more inflation that at A. It appears as if there is a perverse trade-off. But that is wrong. If, at the later date, unemployment had been reduced to the level that it was at A (to point C), inflation would have been even higher.

In the 1970s, the Phillips curve shifted considerably. Panel B contains the data for this period, which by themselves show no evidence of a systematic trade-off. There was more inflation along with more unemployment, a situation that was dubbed **stagflation.** By

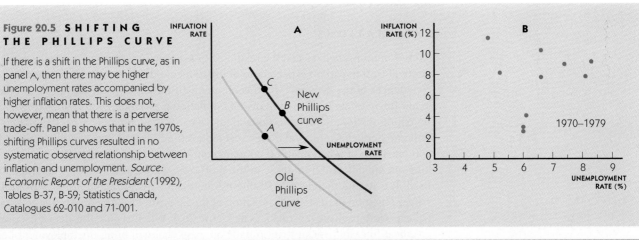

Figure 20.5 SHIFTING THE PHILLIPS CURVE

If there is a shift in the Phillips curve, as in panel A, then there may be higher unemployment rates accompanied by higher inflation rates. This does not, however, mean that there is a perverse trade-off. Panel B shows that in the 1970s, shifting Phillips curves resulted in no systematic observed relationship between inflation and unemployment. *Source: Economic Report of the President* (1992), Tables B-37, B-59; Statistics Canada, Catalogues 62-010 and 71-001.

the mid to late 1980s, a more stable relationship seems to have emerged, as illustrated earlier in panel B of Figure 20.4.

What causes the Phillips curve to shift? And what, in particular, happened in the 1970s to lead to such decisive shifts? The two most important causes are changes in the structure of the labour market, referred to as *real* factors, and expectations.

REAL FACTORS

One real factor that can shift the Phillips curve is the size and composition of the labour force. In the 1970s, the number of workers expanded dramatically, for two reasons. First, the working-age population soared as the post–World War II baby boomers (born between 1945 and 1960) entered the labour force. Second, the percentage of working women rose dramatically as several thousands more women entered the labour force than had previously done so. Younger workers change jobs more frequently than older workers do. So do new entrants to the labour force, as they explore various jobs to find out what they like and what they are well suited for. Thus, if the fraction of workers that are young or that are new entrants increases, as it did in the 1970s, the level of frictional unemployment may increase. This shifts the Phillips curve and raises the natural rate of unemployment, as we saw in Figure 20.5A.

A second factor is how fast individuals move between jobs, which also affects the level of frictional unemployment. If workers receive generous unemployment compensation, this may reduce their incentives to search for a job or accept a job, and thus extend the length of time during which they remain unemployed. Also, if there are laws that make it more difficult or costly for firms to lay off or fire workers, then firms will be reluctant to hire new workers. The effect will be to slow down the process of workers moving from areas where there is an excess supply to areas where there is an excess demand, and the natural rate of unemployment will shift. Finally, as a third factor, if skills become more specialized through advances in technology, it will be more difficult to substitute those workers who are in excess supply for those who are in excess demand, and the natural rate of unemployment will again rise.

These changes in the size of the labour force, in government programs that reduce the cost of being unemployed, and in technology probably contributed to the increase in the natural rate of unemployment and the kind of shift in the Phillips curve depicted in Figure 20.5A.

EXPECTATIONS

Most economists believe that the relationship between inflation and unemployment depends at least in part on expectations of inflation, and these expectations depend on the experiences of the economy. If an economy with unemployment operates at any level below the natural rate of unemployment, inflation is engendered. It is not rational to ignore this inflation. Rather, it is rational for everyone to incorporate expectations of inflation into her behaviour. And these expectations themselves shift the Phillips curve. The combinations of inflation and unemployment that are available to the economy in the long run are different from those in the short run, when expectations are assumed to be fixed. It is useful, therefore, to distinguish between a long-run and a short-run Phillips curve. The most dramatic interpretation of the long-run Phillips curve is that fully rational expectations make it vertical, as in Figure 20.6. When economists draw the curve as a vertical line, they mean that no trade-off exists that will bring unemployment below

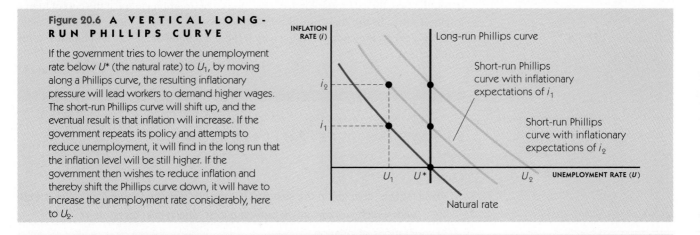

Figure 20.6 A VERTICAL LONG-RUN PHILLIPS CURVE

If the government tries to lower the unemployment rate below U^* (the natural rate) to U_1, by moving along a Phillips curve, the resulting inflationary pressure will lead workers to demand higher wages. The short-run Phillips curve will shift up, and the eventual result is that inflation will increase. If the government repeats its policy and attempts to reduce unemployment, it will find in the long run that the inflation level will be still higher. If the government then wishes to reduce inflation and thereby shift the Phillips curve down, it will have to increase the unemployment rate considerably, here to U_2.

the natural rate. The so-called **natural-rate proposition** argues that if the government attempts to reduce unemployment below the natural rate, it simply induces an increase in the inflation rate. At best, reductions in unemployment are only temporary.

To see how shifting expectations can give rise to a vertical long-run Phillips curve, consider what happens if the government attempts to lower the unemployment rate below the natural rate, from U^* to U_1 in the figure. The inflation rate rises to i_1. But if workers come to believe that this new inflation rate will persist, then the Phillips curve will shift upwards. This is because all workers insist on wage increases just to offset the effects of inflation, so that the inflation rate at U^* is not zero but the rate that the economy has been experiencing, i_1. The inflation rate corresponding to U_1 is now even higher at i_2. But if the government persists in maintaining the low unemployment rate and workers believe that this new, higher rate of unemployment will persist, the Phillips curve will shift up even more.

The government faces an uphill battle. It can, in the short run, get the economy to an unemployment rate below the natural rate, but it can do so for an extended period only at the cost of higher and higher rates of inflation. And the economy may pay a very high price, even for a short-run reduction in unemployment. This is because inflationary expectations may be stuck even if the government decides to abandon its policy of trying to force an unemployment rate below the natural rate. The economy will have purchased a low level of unemployment for one period at the price of a persistent rate of inflation. If the economy then wants to restore price stability, it again has to pay a high price: it must increase unemployment to a level high enough to bring inflation down and thus inflationary expectations down. If inflationary expectations are at i_2, unemployment must increase up to U_2. Given the shape of the Phillips curve, the increase in unemployment required to wring out inflationary expectations may be much larger than the initial decrease in unemployment.

In the late 1970s, many economists became convinced that the long-run Phillips curve was, if not vertical, in any case quite steep. The evidence of the 1980s was different, however. Higher unemployment rates coincided with lower inflation rates. This restored the faith of many economists not only in the existence of a trade-off relationship between unemployment and inflation, but even in the stability of the relationship between the two: the economy can have lower rates of unemployment at the cost of higher inflation rates. In the long run, the Phillips curve might be vertical. But nonetheless, there may exist a long period during which there is a trade-off between inflation and unemployment.

SHIFTS IN THE PHILLIPS CURVE

Causes
    Real factors: changes in the size and composition of the labour force, the speed
        with which workers move between jobs, changes in technology
    Expectations of inflation

Consequences
    There may be stagflation, with higher unemployment *and* inflation.
    The long-run Phillips curve may be essentially vertical; there may be no trade-off
        between inflation and unemployment in the long run.
    There may still be a short-run trade-off.

GOVERNMENT POLICIES TOWARDS INFLATION

Governments have long sought to control the rate of inflation. In the late Middle Ages in Europe, there was an episode in which several governments attempted to limit inflation by imposing price and wage controls; these were enforced in one instance by the threat of having one's ears cut off. Today there are two major differences in perspectives about how important it is to fight inflation, and how best to go about it. For simplicity, we can group these different views into those of the monetarists and those of the Keynesians and new Keynesians.

THE MONETARIST PERSPECTIVE

The monetarists stress the cost of inflation, particularly the uncertainty it induces and the distortions to the economy that result from the inflation tax. Perhaps most important, they believe in a vertical Phillips curve, at least in the long run, so that any gains that come from pushing unemployment below the natural rate are only temporary. With a vertical Phillips curve, there is no trade-off: one does not purchase less unemployment with a higher inflation rate. Thus, while there are costs in *attempting* to lower the unemployment rate below the natural rate, the benefits, if any, are but temporary.

For fighting inflation, the monetarists have a simple prescription: the Bank of Canada should simply increase the money supply at a constant rate, the rate chosen to ensure that in the long run prices will be stable. If real output is increasing on average at 3 percent per year and if the money supply is increasing at 3 percent and velocity is constant, then prices will be stable. If real output is increasing at 3 percent per year and changes in technology enable velocity to increase at 1 percent per year, then the monetary authorities should ensure that the money supply increases at a steady 2 percent per year.

Monetarists believe that this prescription will ensure that monetary shocks will not initiate an inflationary episode, and that monetary policy will not accommodate an inflationary episode. Whatever the source of the inflation, such a policy will choke the inflationary pressures off.

THE MONETARIST PERSPECTIVE

1. Inflation is costly.

2. The Phillips curve is vertical.

3. The best way to fight inflation is to control the money supply.

THE KEYNESIAN CRITIQUE OF THE MONETARIST PERSPECTIVE

Keynesians and new Keynesians believe that monetarists overemphasize the costs of inflation, particularly in modern economies with extensive indexing. And they believe that monetarists, by assuming a vertical Phillips curve, underestimate the costs of *fighting* inflation. With a vertical Phillips curve, there is no trade-off; fighting inflation does not give rise to increased unemployment, since no matter what the government does, the unemployment rate will be stuck at the natural unemployment rate. But Keynesians believe that there are real costs, in terms of increased unemployment, to fighting inflation and that at least in the short run, the Phillips curve is not vertical.

Keynesians also point out that the burden of fighting inflation is concentrated among those who are thrown out of work rather than spread among the population as a whole. Furthermore, those who lose their jobs are disproportionately the unskilled, whose income in any case is low and whose ability to bear the burden of even temporary unemployment is limited. By contrast, inflation for the most part hurts lenders, who are repaid with dollars that are worth less. Thus, fighting inflation benefits disproportionately the rich.

As for the monetarist prescription for fighting inflation, Keynesians have three objections. The first is the focus on monetary policy. Keynesians believe that the government needs to make use of all the instruments in its arsenal, not just monetary policy. The second objection is that the reliance on a rule—such as the expansion of the money supply at a fixed rate—amounts to the abandonment of the use of **discretionary policy,** the ability to use monetary policy to respond to economic circumstances.

The third source of dispute is the particular rule that monetarists tend to advocate, which is a constant expansion of the money supply. Such policies, called **money target policies,** were widely adopted towards the end of the 1970s and early 1980s. These policies led to extremely volatile and at times extremely high interest rates. Part of the difficulty with such policies is the instability in velocity during the past decade. With velocity being unstable, the effect of a constant rate of change in the money supply on inflation is uncertain. Thus, money target policies may actually contribute to uncertainty rather than reduce it. Today almost all governments that adopted these simple policies have abandoned them. Still, monetary authorities continue to eye closely the rate of increase of money and credit, and they have become more sensitive to their role in perpetuating inflation by accommodating to it.

THE KEYNESIAN POLICY PRESCRIPTION

Keynesian policies for fighting inflation can be grouped into two categories, those intended to move the economy along the Phillips curve and those intended to shift the Phillips curve.

MOVING ALONG THE PHILLIPS CURVE

To move the economy down along the Phillips curve requires reducing aggregate demand, so that the aggregate demand curve shifts to the left. The government can accomplish this through tight monetary policy, through a decrease in its level of expenditures, or through an increase in taxes, which leads consumers to spend less. One way of thinking about these choices in reducing aggregate demand is that the sum of claims on national output—by consumers, firms, foreigners, and government—exceeds the output that is available. These three methods, in effect, attempt to reduce the claims of one or more of the claimants. The difficulty for government is to decide who should receive less—those who benefit from government spending (by reducing government expenditures), consumers (by increasing taxes, reducing after-tax income), or future generations (whose incomes will be lower as a result of reduced investment).

Reductions in aggregate demand lessen inflationary pressure because they reduce the gap between the demand and supply of goods. But they also lead to reductions in the demand for labour and thus more unemployment. And when the level of unemployment rises, the pressure for wage increases is reduced. Thus, whether one believes in demand-pull or cost-push inflation, reductions in aggregate demand may be an effective instrument in fighting the inflation.

SHIFTING THE PHILLIPS CURVE

When the economy fights inflation by moving along the Phillips curve, it pays a high price: increased unemployment. But if government policy can shift the Phillips curve, then it can achieve lower inflation without increasing unemployment. The government can attempt to do this by affecting real factors, using wage and price controls, using moral suasion, or changing expectations.

Real Factors   One of the reasons that the natural unemployment rate may be high is that it takes time to find a new job. Government has an ambiguous effect on job mobility: while government job-placement services facilitate labour mobility, unemployment insurance may actually encourage people to search longer for a job after they are thrown out of work. In Europe, where unemployment rates remained persistently high through the 1980s, there is concern that legislation that was intended to increase workers' job security (by making it more difficult for employers to fire them) has had the side effect of making employers more reluctant to hire new workers, and has thus impeded the process of job transition. Changing these laws may shift the Phillips curve.

An alternative way of shifting the Phillips curve, in the short run at least, is to shift the aggregate supply curve down and out, as illustrated in Figure 20.7. This increases output and the employment level, and thus reduces inflationary pressure. One way of shifting the aggregate supply curve is to reduce regulation. Deregulating railroads, trucks, and domestic oil and gas prices, for example, leads to lower prices as competitive forces come into play. And these lower prices have a ripple effect as they spread their way throughout the economy; industries that use rail transport and natural gas as inputs lower their prices, and sectors that use those industries' products in turn are able to lower their own prices. This improvement in supply-side efficiency has been the main argument for deregulation introduced by the successive Conservative governments under Prime Minister Mulroney in such sectors as transportation, energy, and telecommunications. Privatization of Crown corporations is often rationalized on the same grounds.

Deregulation was a major component of U.S. economic policy in the early 1980s. Most economists applauded the deregulatory initiatives of Presidents Carter, Reagan, and Bush because they would increase the efficiency of the economy. However, skeptics questioned both the magnitude of the effects and the speed with which they would come into play. Many economists think that the time it takes for supply reactions to occur, if they do occur, is far too long to make supply-side policies effective instruments for short-term inflation control. Thus, it appears that the government has a very limited ability to shift the Phillips curve through real factors.

Wage and Price Controls   Perhaps the most direct, but by no means the best, response to inflation is simply to outlaw price (and wage) increases. This amounts to attempting to legislate a shift in the Phillips curve. Governments often resort to **wage and price controls,** as such policies are known, during periods of war. Such controls have been tried only rarely in peacetime in Canada. An exception is the wage and price control regime imposed by the Trudeau government in 1975. Inflation had become a concern in the early 1960s, when the consumer price index (CPI) began to increase at a rate of more than 1 percent per year. By 1969, the rate had risen to 4.5 percent, which was high by postwar standards. Inflation abated in 1970–1971, after the Bretton Woods fixed exchange rate system broke down, but picked up again in 1972, and continued to grow to double digits in 1974. In that year alone, the CPI rose by 13 percentage points. As mentioned earlier, one major reason for the price increase in 1974 was the rapid rise in oil prices that resulted from the OPEC oil embargo initiated a year earlier. The combination of a high and rapidly rising inflation rate was seen to be unacceptable.

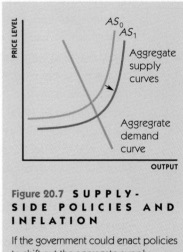

Figure 20.7 SUPPLY-SIDE POLICIES AND INFLATION

If the government could enact policies to shift out the aggregate supply curve, this would be a practical method of fighting inflation.

CLOSE-UP: INFLATION AND GROWTH EFFECTS OF SUPPLY-SIDE ECONOMICS

The supply-siders of the Reagan administration in the United States were neo-conservatives who practiced a new economic philosophy: they focused on the aggregate supply curve. President Reagan's economic advisers argued that the tax system weakened economic incentives. They claimed that cutting corporate taxes would induce firms to expand investment and the supply of goods, and that households would respond to personal income tax cuts by increasing their savings and their supply of labour. These supply increases would exert downward pressure on the price level, and output and employment would increase as the aggregate supply curve shifted to the right. Inflation in the United States was in fact curbed initially in 1982, but this was more due to the Fed's tight monetary policy and the recession of the early 1980s. Output and employment soon fell off due to the recession.

Grant Devine, premier of Saskatchewan from 1982–1991, experimented with supply-side economics after its apparent failure in the United States. In 1982, Devine announced that "Saskatchewan has decided not to participate in the recession," and he proceeded to stimulate the economy in a supply-side manner by removing the gasoline tax and declaring a one-year tax holiday for oil drillers and investors. In addition, the government reformed the personal income tax. The progressive tax, which charged higher-income earners a higher tax rate,

was partially replaced by a flat tax, where a lower rate was applied to all incomes. The reasoning was that higher-income earners would work and invest more when faced with a smaller tax burden. Total production would rise and so would tax revenues, despite the lower tax rates.

Premier Devine's tax reforms did not have the intended incentive effects. For example, the increase in disposable income to households from the gasoline tax cut went towards consumer spending and not savings. Investment, on the whole, declined (although the oil industry was prospering in all three Prairie provinces at this time). Instead of an expansion of labour and goods supply, Saskatchewan experienced more unemployment and output loss than the national average during the recession. Inflation in Saskatchewan matched the nationwide double-digit rates in 1982, and the provincial budget was in deficit, partly because of lower tax revenues. Thus, the remedies espoused by the supply-side economists did not work in Saskatchewan. Apparently, successful policies for shifting the aggregate supply curve would have to involve more than simply removing disincentives from the tax system.

Source: James M. Pitsula and Ken Rasmussen, *Privatizing a Province—The New Right in Saskatchewan* (Vancouver: New Star Books Ltd., 1990), pp. 56–60.

In response, the government established a program of wage and price controls, referred to as an **incomes policy.** Wages and salaries were not permitted to increase by more than 10 percent in the first year, and that figure was to be gradually reduced in the following three years of the program. Price increases by firms were not to exceed the increase in their costs of production. The program was administered by the Anti-Inflation

Board (AIB), which would monitor growth rates of wages and profit margins of private firms with 500 plus employees. The wages of all public-sector employees as well as workers in firms regulated by the federal government were controlled directly. On the monetary side, the Bank of Canada cooperated in the attempt to reduce inflation by embarking on a gradually contracting monetary policy.

The wage and price control program remained in effect until 1978. The government had some success in halting inflation: by the second quarter of 1978, the rate of increase of the CPI (excluding food, whose prices were not controlled by the AIB) had fallen to 6 percent. Wage settlements fell from a nearly 20 percent per year increase to a less than 7 percent increase in 1978. Unfortunately, the unemployment rate over the period of late 1974 to 1978 rose from 5.3 percent to more than 8 percent. A rise in unemployment in a time of declining inflation is not unexpected since it is consistent with the predictions of the Phillips curve analysis.

But the wage and price control program was a temporary one. While it may have succeeded in bottling up inflationary pressures in the short run, it could not hold them back indefinitely. In the three years after the end of the controls, inflation rose 4 percentage points, reaching 12.4 percent in 1981. Double-digit inflation had reappeared. It took a major recession to bring inflation back under control.

Most economists oppose price controls because they do not attack the underlying problems, such as the excess demand for goods. Also, such controls are difficult to administer and frequently result in a variety of inefficiencies. For instance, when wage controls are imposed, employers can get around them by reclassifying jobs. It may be illegal to increase the salary of a secretary, but it is not illegal to promote the secretary to a "new" job, perhaps administrative assistant, and pay a new wage. Similarly, a firm may not be able to increase the price it charges for its washing machine model 70237, but it can phase out that model, introduce "new" model 70238 with some minor variations, and increase the price. Or the firm could keep the price the same but strip some features from the model, providing in effect a lower-quality machine at the same price. The manufacturer may claim, of course, that it has increased the quality by improving the design. The sheer weight of bureaucracy makes it virtually impossible for the government to rule on each of the myriad of resulting cases.

There is another difficulty with enforcing price controls. Inflation, remember, is the price of all goods taken together, not the price of each good separately. Even when there is little or no inflation in the overall price level, relative prices of different goods are constantly changing. The prices of computers have declined and the prices of haircuts have increased over the last twenty years. If price controls are to remain in force for any extended period of time, they must allow for these changes in relative prices. If they do not, shortages will develop of those goods whose prices are kept below their equilibrium level.

This happened with the price controls imposed in the United States in the early 1970s, when there was suddenly a shortage of chickens. Price controls were more effective in limiting the prices chicken producers could charge than in limiting the prices they had to pay for their inputs, such as feed. As a result, at the fixed prices that they were able to sell their chickens, it simply did not pay them to produce the quantity of chickens that consumers demanded at that price. Socialist economies, where price controls are universal, are constantly experiencing shortages and surpluses of one good or another. In short, the price controller simply cannot make allowances for all the needed changes in relative prices.

Moral Suasion   Another way that governments have fought inflation is through informal wage and price controls. Rather than controlling prices and wages directly, the government might use **moral suasion.** As with the Bank of Canada's use of this tactic with banks, the government tries to *persuade* firms and workers not to raise prices and wages. The government sets wage and price guidelines, with which it hopes workers and firms will comply. The government often has considerable leverage beyond its appeal to moral rectitude because it can threaten not to buy from firms that violate its suggestions. There have been two episodes of moral suasion in the postwar period. In 1969, when the inflation rate increased to what was then considered a high rate of 5.2 percent, the federal government instituted a set of voluntary wage and price guidelines. A Prices and Incomes Commission was established to monitor the guidelines and to advise the government. But the influence of the commission was clearly limited by the fact that the program was voluntary. In 1983, with inflation having persisted in the double digits for three years, the federal government introduced the so-called 6 & 5 Restraint Program, according to which they combined restraint in the public sector with exhortation to the private sector. The government limited the indexation of the income tax system and of the various transfers it made to individuals (such as family allowances, Old Age Security, and public-sector pensions) and to the provinces (such as Established Program Financing) to 6 percent in 1983 and 5 percent in 1984. Likewise pay increases for federal government employees and price increases in federally regulated agencies were also limited to 6 percent in 1983 and 5 percent in 1984. The federal finance minister expressed the hope that not only would provincial governments follow these guidelines but also that the program would spill over to the private sector. As an inducement, government contracts were restricted to those firms that abided by the 6 & 5 guidelines. As it turned out, the rate of inflation fell from over 11 percent in 1982 to half that amount in 1983.

Changing Expectations   When moral suasion has worked, it has been largely because this method served to break the inflationary psychology, the expectations that can play such an important role in perpetuating inflation. If unions and firms believe that everyone else will comply, they will be willing to moderate their wage demands and price increases. But that is precisely why moral suasion is an unreliable instrument: it is difficult to predict the market psychology reaction.

Some economists think that a major role of monetary policy is also persuasion, as when the Bank of Canada attempts to convince everyone that it will be tough on inflation. If the Bank is successful, inflationary expectations are broken, wage increases are lowered, and the wage-price spiral may be broken. The Bank's success is self-confirming: given that inflation has been broken, it does not have to take actions like tightening credit, which would have adverse effects on output and employment.

If people believe that any of the actions government takes to break inflation will be successful, these expectations themselves will help dampen inflation. On the other hand, if they do not believe the policy is going to work, inflationary expectations will not be broken and inflation is likely to persist.

How sensitive the rate of inflation and people's expectations are to government policy is the subject of considerable debate among economists. If there is a shock to the economy, such as a change in government policy, and individuals continue to base their inflationary expectations on past inflation rates, then the economy will be stuck with its inflation rate for a long time. Severe, protracted shocks to the economy will be required to change people's inflationary expectations.

With slowly changing expectations, there will be a trade-off between unemployment and inflation, extending over a long time. Slowly changing expectations make it relatively easy for the government to reduce unemployment without setting off rapid inflation. But once inflationary expectations have been developed, it is difficult to stop inflation. Even if the unemployment rate is high, the rate of inflation will be high. To break the back of inflation will require high unemployment rates over long periods of time.

But with rapidly adapting expectations, the Phillips curve will be close to vertical, even in the short run. This has both its positive and negative sides. If individuals react to certain changes in government policy by immediately changing their expectations of future inflation, inflation's back can be quickly broken. The costs of fighting inflation will be quite small, only requiring an appropriate government policy. On the negative side, rapidly changing expectations make it relatively easy to set off an inflationary spiral if an attempt is made to reduce unemployment below the natural rate.

Economists who believe that expectations adapt slowly point to the difficulty involved in reducing the high inflation rates of the 1970s. Those who believe that expectations adapt quickly concentrate their attention on historical periods of extremely high inflation, like the German hyperinflation of the 1920s, when phenomenally high rates of inflation were brought quickly under control. Both views may be right: whether expectations adapt slowly or quickly depends on the situation.

THE KEYNESIAN PRESCRIPTION FOR FIGHTING INFLATION

Movements along the Phillips curve
    Limiting aggregate demand by tightening monetary policy, decreasing government expenditures, or increasing taxes

Shifts in the Phillips curve
    Changing real factors
        Facilitating job mobility
        Shifting the aggregate supply curve
    Wage and price controls
    Moral suasion
    Changing expectations
        Any policy that is believed to be effective may be effective.
        Slowly adjusting expectations mean that there is a short-run unemployment-inflation trade-off, but inflationary expectations, once built in, are hard to reverse.
    Quickly adjusting expectations mean that the Phillips curve may be close to vertical even in the short run, but inflation is easy to reverse because inflationary expectations are easy to reverse.

REVIEW AND PRACTICE

SUMMARY

1. Most of inflation's effects can be lessened through indexing—adjustments in wages, Old Age Security payments, interest rates, and tax rates—to changes in the price level. Unanticipated inflation without indexing tends to injure lenders, taxpayers, and holders of currency.

2. Inflation can be caused either by a demand shock—excess demand for goods shifting the aggregate demand curve to the right—or by a supply shock—sharp increases in costs shifting the aggregate supply curve upwards. Regardless of the initial cause, a spiral of higher wages and prices may be created.

3. Monetary policy may increase the supply of money and credit, thereby accommodating the inflation, or it may refuse to accommodate the inflation and thus shift the aggregate demand curve to the left.

4. Lower levels of unemployment are associated with higher levels of inflation, a trade-off depicted by the Phillips curve. The Phillips curve can shift because of real factors (changes in the structure of the labour market) and expectations.

5. Monetarists contend that the costs of inflation are high, that the Phillips curve is vertical (so that any *attempt* to reduce unemployment below the natural rate will lead to higher inflation), and that the best method of fighting inflation is limiting the growth of the money supply.

6. Keynesians contend that with indexing, the costs of inflation are not that high; that for an extended period of time, at least, the Phillips curve is not vertical, and fighting inflation results in higher unemployment; and that those who lose their jobs are disproportionately the unskilled.

7. Keynesians believe that the government can limit aggregate demand and move down along the Phillips curve by tightening monetary policy, decreasing government expenditures, or increasing taxes. The government can attempt to shift the Phillips curve by changing real factors, using wage and price controls, using moral suasion, or changing expectations.

KEY TERMS

hyperinflation
indexing
cost of living adjustments
inflation tax
demand shock
supply shock
monetary shock

inflationary spiral
demand-pull inflation
cost-push inflation
Phillips curve
natural rate of unemployment
stagflation

wage and price controls
incomes policy
moral suasion

REVIEW QUESTIONS

1. What difference does it make whether inflation is anticipated or unanticipated? What difference does it make whether there is indexing or not?

2. How do lenders, taxpayers, and holders of currency suffer from inflation? To what extent are retired individuals hurt by inflation today? How is the economy as a whole adversely affected by inflation?

3. How does an inflationary spiral perpetuate itself?

4. What is the difference between cost-push and demand-pull inflation?

5. What is the relationship between monetary policy and inflation?

6. What is a Phillips curve?

7. What are the reasons that a short-term Phillips curve might shift? When the Phillips curve shifts, what might be the observed patterns of unemployment and inflation?

8. Why might the long-run Phillips curve be vertical?

9. What are the principal differences between monetarists and Keynesians over the costs of inflation, the costs of fighting inflation, and how best to fight it?

10. What are the various policies that might induce a movement along the Phillips curve? a shift in the Phillips curve?

11. What are the costs of using wage and price controls to fight inflation? How might companies circumvent such controls?

PROBLEMS

1. Priscilla earns $40,000 per year, but her wages are not indexed to inflation. If over a period of three years inflation is at 5 percent and Priscilla receives raises of 2 percent, how much has the actual buying power of her income changed over that time?

2. Patrick receives a gift of two $100 bills for his birthday. Because he likes having the bills around to admire, he does not spend them for a year. With an inflation rate of 6 percent, what inflation tax does he pay?

3. "It is unfair to tax capital gains—the increases in the value of stocks and bonds—at the same rate as ordinary income in inflationary situations." Discuss.

4. There have been proposals to increase Old Age Security benefits with the wages received by current workers, so that retired individuals do not fall behind those who are employed. What would be the consequences of increasing Old Age Security benefits *both* to compensate for increases in the price level and to match salary increases of the currently employed?

5. Use aggregate supply and demand curves to explain whether (and when) the following events are likely to trigger inflation:

(a) an increase in business confidence;
(b) an increase in the discount rate;
(c) the development of important new technologies;
(d) an increase in the price of imports;
(e) an increase in government spending.

6. What would be the effect on the Phillips curve of falling oil prices?

7. While playing around with old economics data in your spare time, you find that in 1966, unemployment was 3.4 percent and inflation was 1.7 percent; in 1972, unemployment was 6.2 percent and inflation was 3.5 percent; in 1979, unemployment was 7.4 percent and inflation 9.1 percent; in 1988, unemployment was 7.8 percent and inflation was 4.0 percent. Does this evidence necessarily imply anything about the shape of the short-run or long-run Phillips curve? How might you interpret this data?

APPENDIX: THE INFLATIONARY SPIRAL: A DIAGRAMMATIC ANALYSIS

The inflationary spiral can be illustrated in diagrams describing demand and supply in the labour market and the product market. In Figure 20.8A, initially the economy is in equilibrium at point E on the relatively steep portion of the aggregate supply curve. Now consider a shift in the aggregate demand curve from AD_0 to AD_1. This shift leads to excess demand at the initial price level p_0, and prices consequently rise to p_1.

Panel B shows the implications of these changes for the labour market. For simplicity, we assume that the supply of labour is inelastic. The number of people who wish to work remains unchanged, at least with small changes in wages and prices. Firms are willing to employ workers as long as the real wage they pay is less than or equal to the marginal output new workers produce. Given that the labour market was initially in equilibrium at wage rate w_0, with this new increase in the price level and no change (yet) in the wage rate, the real wage falls and employers demand more labour at this wage. The labour demand curve shifts to the right, to L_2. The new equilibrium wage, w_1, is higher.

To see what this implies, let's return to the goods market in panel C. The aggregate demand and supply curves are drawn on the basis of a given level of wages. The higher wage rate means that people have more income, leading to greater consumption and hence increased aggregate demand, and the aggregate demand curve shifts from AD_1 to AD_2. At each price level, aggregate demand is higher. Similarly, the aggregate supply curve shifts up from AS_1 to AS_2 because the higher wages mean that firms must receive a higher price to induce them to supply any given quantity. At the new price level p_1, the gap between the new aggregate demand curve AD_2 and the new aggregate supply

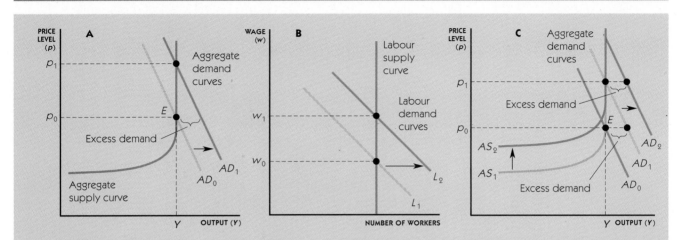

Figure 20.8 AN INFLATIONARY SPIRAL

In panel A, the shift in aggregate demand from AD_0 to AD_1 increases the price level from p_0 to p_1. This causes an increase in nominal wages, shown in panel B, because the increase in the price level shifts the demand for labour to the right. In panel C,

higher wages then shift the aggregate supply curve up from AS_1 to AS_2, while also shifting the aggregate demand curve to the right from AD_1 to AD_2. Again there is excess demand for goods. The resulting higher prices will again lead to higher wages.

curve AS_2 remains. Again we are left with excess demand for goods, leading to further price increases, setting off another increase in wages, and so on.[6] The inflationary pressure keeps cycling through the economy.

It makes little difference to this analysis whether the initial disturbance that set off the inflationary episode was an increase in aggregate demand or a decrease in aggregate supply. Both will result in an excess demand for goods at the original price level. Once inflationary expectations are built in to wage- and price-setting behaviour, inflation may persist. Note too that the story of the inflationary spiral would have been exactly the same if the initial impetus to the inflation had occurred in the labour market.

---

[6] Some economists argue that this process could not go on indefinitely. They point to the real balance effect described in Chapter 15. With these increased prices, the government bonds that individuals hold would be worth less; people would experience a decline in their wealth and would consequently cut back on their demand, shifting back the aggregate demand curve. The effect of real balances in modern economies is empirically small and is therefore unlikely to make much of a difference at low levels of inflation.

PART FOUR

Policies for Growth and Stability

U nemployment and inflation, the subjects of Parts Two and Three, are not the only economic concerns that make the news. Deficits in Canada, starvation in Ethiopia, the economic crises in the formerly Communist countries of the Soviet Union and Eastern Europe, are among other events that have grabbed headlines in the past decade. In this part of the book, we use the principles and insights developed in the preceding chapters to take a look at these and other current public-policy issues.

Chapter 21 discusses a major problem facing Canada: the slowdown in its rate of economic growth. The country is growing neither as fast as it did in earlier decades nor as fast as some of its major economic rivals. We ask, what causes economic growth, and what can be done to stimulate it?

Chapter 22 focuses on two deficits. The fiscal deficit has been at the center of public concern now for almost a decade, and has persisted despite seeming efforts to reduce it. The current-account deficit—the excess of interest and dividend payments to foreigners over net exports of goods and services—has also persisted since the mid-1980s.

The economy seems to have its ups and downs. There are boom years and bust years. Having developed an understanding of what causes unemployment and inflation, we ask, is there a reason that the economy fluctuates so greatly? Is there no way of maintaining a more even course? As we will see in Chapter 23, the various macroeconomic schools we have encountered look at this question from different perspectives and provide different answers about what the government should do.

The collapse of the Soviet empire is undoubtedly one of the biggest events of the twentieth century, just as its rise was, in the aftermath of World War I. The Soviets established an alternative economic system that they believed would eventually dominate capitalism. In Chapter 24, we look at what the system's basic tenets were, why it failed, and the problems these countries face today in making a transition to capitalism.

Most of the world lives in countries where incomes are but a fraction of those in Canada, the United States, Western Europe, Japan, and the other developed countries. By the standards in these less-developed countries, referred to as the Third World, most people who consider themselves poor in the more-developed countries are indeed well off. In Chapter 25, we learn some of the major differences between the developed and less-developed countries. We also ask, what are some of the major issues facing these poorer countries as they struggle to grow and raise themselves out of the mire of poverty in which they have remained for centuries?

CHAPTER 21

GROWTH AND PRODUCTIVITY

I t is hard to comprehend fully the changes that have taken place in the standard of living during the past century. In 1900, Canadians' level of consumption was little higher than that of the average citizen in Mexico or the Philippines today. Life expectancy was low, in part because diseases like smallpox, diphtheria, typhoid fever, and whooping cough were still common. You were fifteen times more likely to catch measles in 1900 than you would be today. Though the abundance of land in Canada meant that relatively few Canadians were starving, luxuries were scarce. People worked as long as they could, and when they could no longer work, they became the responsibility of their children; there was no easy period of retirement.

During the nineteenth century, the standard of living in England and a few other European countries was comparable, perhaps slightly higher than that of Canada; for the time, these countries' standard of living was the highest in the world. But even within Europe, there were periodic famines. In the most famous of these, the Irish potato famine of 1845–1848, more than a tenth of the population is estimated to have died, and more than another tenth migrated to Canada and the United States. And for those living in Asia, Africa, and Latin America, as the vast majority of people did then and do now, life was even harder.

Chapter 8 set out the various ways in which increased standards of living could be measured, such as higher per capita incomes and longer life expectancy. But higher standards of living are also reflected in shorter working hours and higher levels of education. The improved education is both a benefit of a higher standard of living and one of its causes. Table 21.1 sets forth a comparison between Canada today and in 1926.

Table 21.1 CANADA IN 1926 AND 1990

	1926	1990
Population	9.5 million	26.6 million
Life expectancy	61 years	77 years
GDP (in 1990 dollars)	$42 billion	$672 billion
GDP per capita (in 1990 dollars)	$4,427	$25,237
Consumer purchasing power per dollar (in 1990 dollars)	$8.51	$1.00
Average hours worked each week in manufacturing industry	50 hours	38 hours
Average hourly pay in manufacturing industry (in 1990 dollars)	$3.41	$15.39
Total telephones in country	1.2 million	14.5 million
Total bachelor's degrees conferred	4,319	106,430
Total doctoral degrees conferred	28	2,700
Percentage of those age 5–19 enrolled in school	64.3 percent	91 percent

Source: *Canada Year Book 1992*; Statistics Canada, CANSIM Database, 1993; M. C. Urquhart and K. A. H. Buckley, eds., *Historical Statistics of Canada* (Toronto: Macmillan Co. of Canada, 1965); Statistics Canada, *Advance Statistics of Education* (1990–1991), Catalogue No. 81-220.

Underlying all of these changes is an increase in the output of each hour worked, what Chapter 8 identified as productivity. A major concern of this chapter is to understand what causes productivity to increase.

There is a second objective. In the last two decades, confidence in North America's technological leadership has declined. Canadians are no longer certain that their wages and standard of living will continue to rise as they have for over a century. Behind these concerns is the sudden slowdown in the rate of increase of productivity during the past two decades. What caused this sudden slowdown, and what can be done to reverse it?

KEY QUESTIONS

1. What are the principal determinants of the growth of the economy?

2. What factors might account for the slowdown of growth in Canada? What, for instance, might explain the decline in productivity?

3. Are there any policies available to the government that might stimulate the country's economic growth?

THE PRODUCTIVITY SLOWDOWN

For almost a century, the United States has been at the center of the technological advances that have changed the face of the world. Canada has benefited from our proximity to the United States and from the relatively open border that has allowed goods, capital, labour, and knowledge to flow freely back and forth. Though the automobile was not actually invented in the United States, the techniques of mass production (like the assembly line) that made the car almost universally affordable were developed in the United States. The airplane, from its inception at the hands of the Wright brothers to the development of the jet engine and the modern commercial aircraft, has a "Made in the USA" stamp on it. The telegraph, atomic energy, the laser, the transistor . . . the list of America's technological achievements goes on and on. Canada's contributions, though much more modest in absolute terms, were nonetheless far-reaching, as the example of the telephone shows. This is not meant to deny the importance of technological developments that happened in other parts of the world—for example, Italy's Guglielmo Marconi and the radio or Britain's Sir Alexander Fleming and penicillin— nor the importance that foreigners have played in America's breakthroughs. The team that developed atomic energy, for instance, was based in the United States but it was truly international. All told, however, it is fair to say that America has been on the technological frontier during the twentieth century, and the country has reaped a huge reward: levels of productivity and thus living standards increased continually, so that by the end of World War II they were among the highest in the world. And Canada was always close behind.

Today that leadership in technology and growth is being challenged. As the twentieth century draws towards its close, productivity levels and living standards in the United States and Canada are still among the highest in the world, as shown in Figure 21.1. The figure also shows, however, that other countries also enjoy comparable living stan-

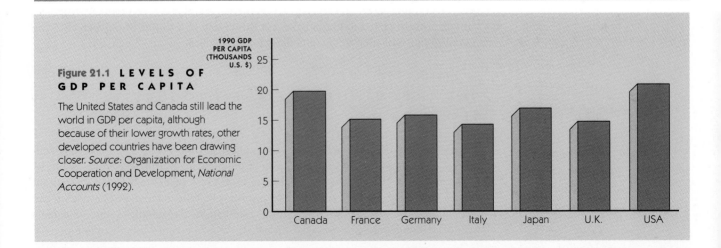

1990 GDP PER CAPITA (THOUSANDS U.S. $)

Figure 21.1 LEVELS OF GDP PER CAPITA

The United States and Canada still lead the world in GDP per capita, although because of their lower growth rates, other developed countries have been drawing closer. *Source*: Organization for Economic Cooperation and Development, *National Accounts* (1992).

Canada | France | Germany | Italy | Japan | U.K. | USA

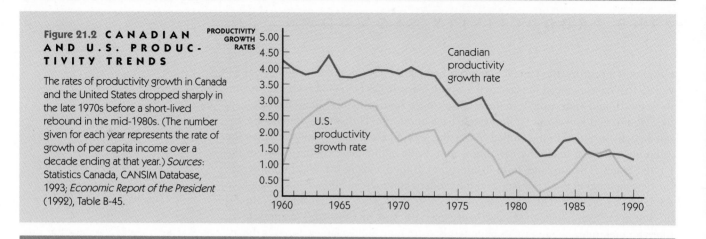

Figure 21.2 CANADIAN AND U.S. PRODUCTIVITY TRENDS

The rates of productivity growth in Canada and the United States dropped sharply in the late 1970s before a short-lived rebound in the mid-1980s. (The number given for each year represents the rate of growth of per capita income over a decade ending at that year.) *Sources*: Statistics Canada, CANSIM Database, 1993; *Economic Report of the President* (1992), Table B-45.

dards and productivity. And in several key industries, the formerly dominant North American position seems to be slipping. This is true not only in the heavy industries like steel, cars, and shipbuilding, but in more technologically oriented industries such as electronics and computers. For instance, though the United States has continued to be in the forefront in developing new and better computers and computer chips, most of the personal computers (whether assembled in the United States or not) consist mostly of foreign-made parts.

The U.S. and Canadian rates of growth of productivity have followed remarkably similar patterns as shown in Figure 21.2. The rates slowed considerably in the late 1960s and early 1970s. By the late 1970s, the rate of growth of productivity was less than half of what it was in the 1950s and 1960s. There appears to have been a small rebound in the 1980s, but nothing like a return to the earlier levels. Clearly, similar influences seem to have operated in Canada as in the United States. But the magnitude of the decline has been much more severe in Canada than in the United States. Our productivity growth has fallen from a rate of almost 5 percent thirty years ago to just over 1 percent. The American rate has fallen to the same level but from a peak of only 3 percent.

THE IMPORTANCE OF THE PRODUCTIVITY SLOWDOWN

A skeptic might question whether the percentages shown in Figure 21.2 make much difference. Fifteen years ago the average rate of productivity growth used to be slightly in excess of 2 percent, and now it is slightly in excess of 1 percent—what's so important about a difference of only 1 percent? The answer is that the percentage point difference compounds over time. Consider this simple calculation. Two countries start out equally wealthy, but one grows at an average annual rate of 2.5 percent while the other grows at

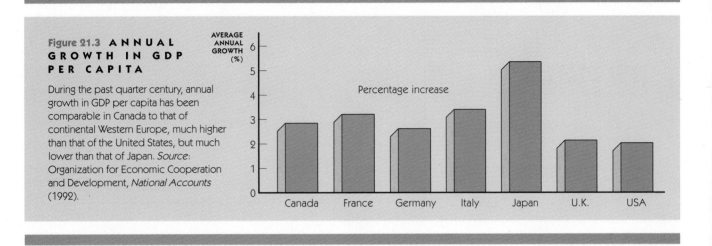

Figure 21.3 ANNUAL GROWTH IN GDP PER CAPITA

During the past quarter century, annual growth in GDP per capita has been comparable in Canada to that of continental Western Europe, much higher than that of the United States, but much lower than that of Japan. *Source*: Organization for Economic Cooperation and Development, *National Accounts* (1992).

an average annual rate of 3.5 percent. The difference would be barely perceptible for a few years. But after thirty years, the slower-growing country would be only three-quarters as wealthy as the faster-growing one. Slow growth can move a country from relative wealth to relative poverty in a few generations. Some argue that North America, after more than a decade of slow growth, may be locked into this low-growth pattern. America's lower growth compared with the growth of other developed countries in the last two decades, shown in Figure 21.3, explains why many countries, including Canada, have almost caught up to the United States. This figure is a twenty-year average and hides the fact that Canada's rate of productivity growth has now declined to the American rate.

Lower growth in productivity means lower growth (on average) in standards of living. Incomes will be lower than they would have been had productivity grown more rapidly. On average, people will have less of everything—not only fewer consumer goods, but also less medical care, less education, less travel, and fewer government services for the poor. If North America's rate of growth of productivity remains below that of other countries, other countries will eventually catch up to and outstrip the United States and Canada in their standard of living, which means that the middle class in other countries will be able to afford new products and services that only wealthy Canadian citizens can now afford.

The symptoms of the productivity slowdown are already showing. Over the long run, wage rates tend to change with productivity increases. Unless productivity continues to grow, wages cannot continue to grow. From this perspective, the last decade has been a real disappointment: real wages have hardly changed at all, especially for the service industries. Figure 21.4 illustrates the movement of real wages in manufacturing and service industries since 1961. While they increased dramatically in the 1960s, the rate of increase has slowed down considerably since then. (However, the *incomes* of Canadian families rose much more, mainly because as women became more active in the labour force, the total number of hours worked by members of each household increased.)

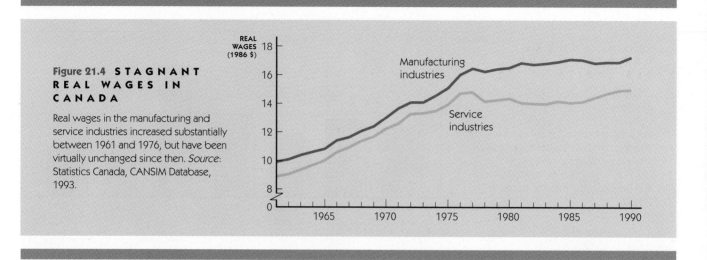

Figure 21.4 STAGNANT REAL WAGES IN CANADA

Real wages in the manufacturing and service industries increased substantially between 1961 and 1976, but have been virtually unchanged since then. *Source*: Statistics Canada, CANSIM Database, 1993.

Some economists believe that measurement problems exaggerate the magnitude of the slowdown in productivity, for the reasons discussed in Chapter 8. For instance, the measure of output ignores the improvement in the quality of the air and water during the past two decades, and the degradation of the environment that occurred in earlier decades. Still, even when account of these measurement problems is taken, there is a general consensus that there has been some slowdown in productivity.

The question is, what is the prognosis for the future? To answer this question, we need to know what causes growth and increases in productivity, and to see what factors can account for the productivity slowdown.

THE SOURCES OF PRODUCTIVITY GROWTH

Economists have studied the sources of economic growth for a variety of reasons. One reason is historical, to understand what changes in the latter half of the nineteenth century allowed for the remarkable increase in productivity that began then. Another reason is to understand why different countries have had different rates of growth. A third reason is to help in formulating policies to encourage growth. Economists have found that there are four major causes of increases in productivity: increases in the accumulation of capital goods (investment), a higher quality of the labour force, greater efficiency in allocating resources, and technological change.

INCREASES IN THE ACCUMULATION OF CAPITAL GOODS (INVESTMENT)

If workers in one country have more capital goods with which to work than do their counterparts in other countries, their productivity will normally be higher. Even a relatively simple device like an electric screwdriver has increased the productivity of workers in the construction industry enormously. As agriculture became more mechanized, beginning in the late nineteenth century, productivity soared. In the less-developed economies, farmers often grow barely enough to support their own families, while in Canada the 3 percent of the population currently employed in agriculture produce more than Canadians can eat. Even after Canada has exported a large share of its agricultural production, there are still surpluses of major crops. Much of this increase in productivity is due to the mechanization of Canadian agriculture. Tractors, combines, and other equipment allow Canadian farm workers today to do in an hour what might have taken them a week fifty or seventy-five years ago.

Economists dispute exactly how important the accumulation of capital goods is, but there is no disagreement about two simpler propositions: no country has gone from being less developed to more developed without the accumulation of a considerable amount of capital goods, and countries that fail to maintain their level of capital goods per worker suffer decreases in productivity. Thus, countries that have rapidly growing populations must invest a great deal just to provide new entrants to the labour force with the machines required to sustain their productivity. Canada does not have a rapidly growing population, but during the 1970s it had a rapidly growing labour force, as more and more women decided to work outside the home. Given that the rate of accumulation of capital goods did not increase during the 1970s, this entry of new workers is one reason that measured productivity slowed down at about this time. Investment is also required to implement new technologies. Without high rates of investment, North American industry will fall behind technologically.

WHY INVESTMENT (CAPITAL GOODS) IS IMPORTANT

1. It provides new entrants into the labour force with machines to make them productive.

2. It provides existing workers with more machines, to increase their productivity.

3. It implements new technologies.

HOW IMPORTANT ARE DIMINISHING RETURNS?

The effect of an increase in capital goods per worker is shown in Figure 21.5. The level of output depends on the level of inputs (capital goods, labour, and raw materials). More inputs obviously imply greater output. By the same token, the more capital goods *per worker*, the greater the output *per worker*, as depicted in the figure. But while output per worker increases with capital goods per worker, the law of diminishing returns also applies. Successive increments in capital lead to smaller and smaller increments in output per worker.

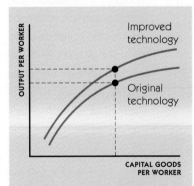

Figure 21.5 CAPITAL GOODS AND PRODUCTIVITY

As the amount of capital goods available to each worker increases, output per worker increases. But the existence of diminishing returns means that each successive increment to capital goods adds less and less to output per worker. An improvement in technology would shift the entire production function upwards.

CLOSE-UP: THE PRODUCTIVITY SLOWDOWN AND INCREASED INEQUALITY

The years following 1970 were marked not only by a slowdown in the rate of growth of productivity, but also by an increase in income inequality. The strongest evidence for this has come from studies in the United States. Between 1970 and 1989, real hourly wages for the lowest paid 10 percent of American prime-aged male workers had fallen by 30 percent, while those for the top 40 percent had increased slightly. One consequence of this wage gap was a significant increase in inequality. The top 20 percent of income earners in the United States increased their share of national income from slightly more than 40 percent in 1970 to about 45 percent today. At the same time, the share of the poorest 20 percent had decreased from around 5.6 percent in 1970 to 4.6 percent today.

The increase in inequality has not been as pronounced in Canada. Here, the top 20 percent of income earners increased their share of national income from just over 41 percent in 1965 to almost 44 percent in 1991. At the same time, the bottom 20 percent changed hardly at all, rising slightly from 4.4 to 4.7 percent. This does not mean that wage inequality has not increased in

Canada as well. Our relatively generous system of transfers to low-income persons (welfare, unemployment insurance, public pensions) helps prevent a wage gap being translated into an income gap. Data on the wage gap have not been compiled for Canada, but given the degree of integration of our economy with that of the United States, we might expect the same phenomena to be at work.

Economists have speculated about whether, and in what ways, the decline in productivity growth and the increase in inequality are interrelated. Some look to supply-side explanations, particularly for the decrease in real wages among the lowest decile. They see the "television era" in particular, and the decreased quality of education in general, as having increased the number of functionally illiterate and semiliterate workers. They also see life-style changes—the drug culture, the larger number of broken homes, the increased fraction of homes in which both parents are out working—as having played some role.

Other economists focus on demand-side explanations. They see technological change as having decreased the demand for unskilled workers and

INCREASING INCOME INEQUALITY

Increasing wage inequality has contributed to greater income inequality. Today the share of national income going to the richest 20 percent is much higher than it was a quarter century ago, and the share of national income going to the poorest 20 percent is lower.

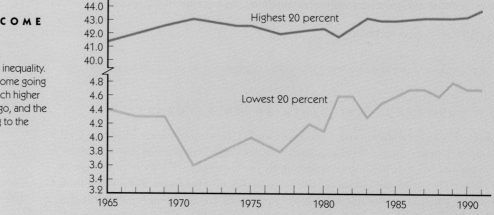

increased the demand for highly skilled workers, such as those who work with computers. While immigration of unskilled workers, particularly from Latin America, may also have driven down the wages of unskilled workers in the United States, that has not likely been a factor in Canada where immigration has been much more oriented to those with skills needed here. Instead, the increased flow of imports from low-wage countries may have had important effects. To compete with these cheap imports, workers in some industries had to accept wage cuts or be content with smaller than usual wage increases. Meanwhile, high-wage industries like steel and autos faced a decline in employment, as they modernized—or faced rapid decline—in the face of the competition.

As international trade becomes more liberalized and low-wage countries continue to grow rapidly, this pressure is likely to continue to be present. This is one reason why some labour leaders express concern about the North America Free Trade Agreement with Mexico and the United States.

Source: C. John, K. Murphy, and R. Topel, "Why Has the Natural Rate of Unemployment Increased over Time?," *Brookings Papers on Economic Activity* (1991); Statistics Canada, *Income Distribution by Size in Canada,* various years, Catalogue No. 13-207.

An important implication of diminishing returns is that higher investment rates (that is, the fraction of national output that is invested) cannot sustain higher *rates of growth* in the economy forever, though they can lead to a sustained increase in the *level* of per capita income. As the economy's per capita capital goods stock increases, a higher investment rate is required simply to sustain that higher level, to give new workers the machines with which to work and to replace old machines as they wear out. Higher investment rates can help provide a short-term spur to the economy.

If increases in the amount of capital goods per worker were the only, or primary, source of increases in productivity—in output per worker—then we would expect diminishing returns eventually to set in, no matter how high the investment rate. The higher *rates of growth* of productivity could only be sustained by higher and higher investment rates. From the late 1950s the rate of growth of productivity increased—during a period in which there was an enormous accumulation of capital goods. Canada was able to sustain a high and in fact increasing rate of productivity growth for long periods of time without diminishing returns seeming to set in.

Similar patterns have been observed elsewhere. Japan, for the past quarter century, has had huge investment rates, resulting in large increases in capital goods per worker. Yet the rate of productivity growth has not decreased in the way that one would have expected on the basis of diminishing returns.

The reason that diminishing returns did not seem to set in in these instances is that the technological change more than offset the effects of diminishing returns. The high rate of technological progress accompanying the high rate of investment may not have been a mere accident. There is, in fact, a double link between investment and technological change. Higher rates of technological change increase investment, because the new technologies provide better investment opportunities; at the same time, higher rates of investment provide manufacturers of machines greater incentives to develop new, improved machines. The consequences of investment accompanied by technological

Figure 21.6 EXPLAINING THE FAILURE TO OBSERVE DIMINISHING RETURNS

With a given production function, the increase in capital goods per worker from C_2 to C_3 would result in a smaller increase in productivity than the corresponding increase from C_1 to C_2. But as the economy increases its capital goods per worker, the production function shifts. Rather than moving from B to C, the economy moves from B to D. The proportionate increase in output per worker may be as large as or even larger than the movement from A to B.

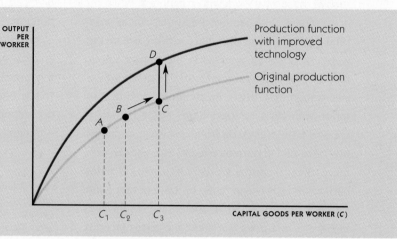

change can be seen in Figure 21.6. As the economy invests more, the production function shifts up enough to offset the effects of diminishing returns. Thus, the output per worker increases proportionately as capital goods per worker increase.

THE LINK BETWEEN SAVINGS AND INVESTMENT: CLOSED VERSUS OPEN ECONOMIES

In a closed economy, the level of investment is determined by the domestic level of savings. Investment equals savings, and investment cannot be increased without greater savings. In an open economy, the link between the two is severed, since a country can borrow from abroad to finance its investment. Chapter 22 will explore the enormous amount of foreign borrowing that Canada has done during the 1980s. But by and large, it remains true that savings and investment within a country have tended to move together, as shown by data for Canada in Figure 21.7.[1]

This might be so for a number of reasons. One possibility is that so much of investment in modern economies is done within large corporations, which finance much of their investment out of retained earnings, and which save more when they see better investment opportunities.

[1] The close link between savings and investment even for economies that are supposedly open was noted in a famous paper by Martin Feldstein and Charles Horioka in the *Economic Journal* (June 1980), Vol. 90, No. 358. There is by now a large literature that tries to explain this puzzling finding.

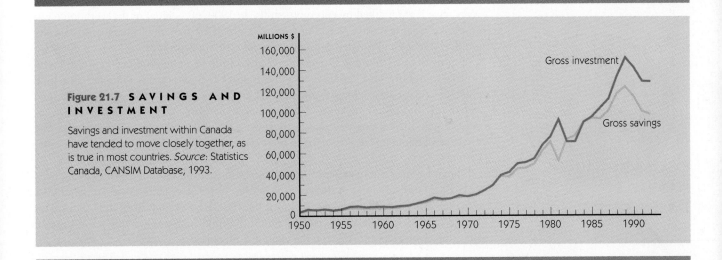

Figure 21.7 SAVINGS AND INVESTMENT

Savings and investment within Canada have tended to move closely together, as is true in most countries. *Source*: Statistics Canada, CANSIM Database, 1993.

HIGHER QUALITY OF THE LABOUR FORCE

A second source of productivity growth is the quality of the labour force. If workers become more efficient, so that a worker can do in one hour what used to take two, productivity will increase. Many factors contribute to the productivity of labour. Good nutrition and health are obviously important, and the last century has made great strides in this direction. Shorter work weeks may enable workers to be more productive while they are working, and thus may contribute not only to the quality of life but also to the quality of work. In 1947, the typical work week was 43 hours; by 1990, it was 38 hours.

Recent discussions of the quality of the labour force have focused on workers' skills. The more skilled the labour force, the higher will be the economy's productivity. There is a general consensus that it would be difficult if not impossible to run a modern industrial economy without a well-educated labour force. In addition, an economy on the cutting edge of technological change needs trained engineers and scientists to discover and shape those innovations. Canada invests, publicly and privately, over $50 billion each year in the formal education of its youth. Investments in individuals are referred to as investments in human capital. A more educated work force is an important element contributing to the increase in productivity. But there is concern that Canada has been falling behind both in providing a basic core education to everyone and in training enough engineers and scientists.

REALLOCATING RESOURCES FROM LOW- TO HIGH-PRODUCTIVITY SECTORS

As the economy shifts resources such as labour from sectors in which they are less productive (like traditional agriculture) to modern manufacturing industries in which they

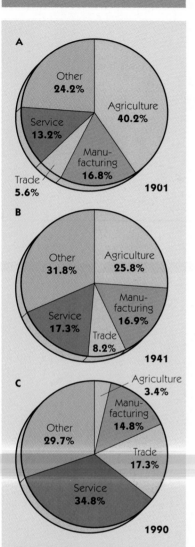

Figure 21.8 SECTORAL SHIFTS

Employment in the Canadian economy shifted out of agriculture to all other industries in the first half of this century, and from agriculture and manufacturing to trade and services in the second half. *Sources*: M. C. Urquhart and K. A. H. Buckley, eds., *Historical Statistics of Canada* (Toronto: Macmillan Co. of Canada, 1965); Statistics Canada, CANSIM Database, 1993.

are more productive, the *average* productivity of the economy goes up. The last hundred years have been marked by enormous shifts. In 1900, 40 percent of the work force was employed in agriculture. As recently as 1960, about 10 percent of the labour force was employed in agriculture; today the share is one-third that amount.

During the past century, Canada has evolved from an agricultural economy to an industrial economy to a service economy. Figure 21.8 shows this dramatic structural change. The service sector, broadly defined, includes not only traditional services such as haircuts and restaurant meals but also the services provided by doctors and lawyers, educational institutions, secretaries, accountants, and computer programmers. The medical sector alone has grown to the point where today it accounts for more than 9 percent of GDP.

The movement out of agriculture and into industry explains much of the productivity increase in the early part of the century. While the level of productivity in agriculture was increasing rapidly, it remained lower than the level in industry. Thus, as workers shifted out of low-productivity jobs in agriculture into high-productivity jobs in manufacturing, average productivity in the economy increased.

TECHNOLOGICAL CHANGE

This final source of productivity growth may be the most important. One of the major ways that the economy today is different from what it was at the start of this century is that the modern economy has made change routine: it has created systematic processes by which knowledge is acquired, translated into uses, and applied. Technological change shifts the production function, meaning that at each level of inputs, more output can be produced. In particular, at each level of capital goods per worker, output per worker is increased, as illustrated in Figure 21.5. The upper line represents the higher level of productivity at each capital goods–labour ratio resulting from technological change.

The prototype of the nineteenth- and early twentieth-century inventors were men like Thomas Edison and Alexander Graham Bell—lone individuals, working by themselves or with a small number of collaborators. By contrast, the prototype of a modern research effort might be something like the U.S. program to put a man on the moon, in which thousands of scientists worked together to accomplish in the space of a few short years what would have been almost unimaginable a short time before. Modern research is centered in huge laboratories, some of them employing thousands of people. While some of these laboratories are run by the government, such as the National Research Centre, which carries out research in basic science, many are private, like Connaught Laboratories, where insulin was developed. Indeed, most major firms have research departments and spend approximately 3 percent of their gross revenues on research and development.

Although much of the research today requires capital expenditures that far exceed the means of any individual, small entrepreneurs and innovators do continue to play a role in developing new products. The computer industry in particular has been marked by a disproportionate number of major innovations created by relatively small firms, as compared with those developed by the industry leader, IBM.

The current level of technological progress has become so expected that it is hard to believe how different the view of reputable economists was in the early 1800s. After all, by then the real wages of workers were little higher than they had been five hundred years earlier, when the bubonic plague destroyed a large part of the population of Europe and thereby created a great scarcity of labour. After half a millennium of at best slow progress, it is no wonder that economists writing in the early nineteenth century had such a gloomy view of the future! Thomas Malthus, one of the greatest economists of that time, saw population expanding more rapidly than the capacity of the economy to support it. What was missing from these dismal forecasts was technological change.

SOURCES OF TECHNOLOGICAL PROGRESS

While technological progress in modern industrialized society is largely the result of searches for new ideas, new products, and better ways of producing, some of it happens through experience. This is called learning by doing: in the process of production, firms learn how to produce their goods more efficiently. The learning curve describes how costs come down with experience. Figure 21.9 shows the learning curve for building air frames (the basic bodies of airplanes) during World War II. As more and more air frames were constructed, better and better ways of organizing the production were discovered, and costs of production fell dramatically.

There is often an intimate connection between progress resulting from R & D expenditures and progress resulting from learning by doing. Firms learn more if they systematically study their production experiences. For instance, they can experiment with different ways of organizing a production process, or give some employees the primary responsibility of thinking about how productivity can be improved. In Japan, about 10 percent of the labour force in manufacturing consists of engineers who are directly involved in production and whose task is to make constant incremental improvements in production processes.

While discussions of technological progress often focus on manufacturing, and particularly on dramatic inventions such as transistors and lasers, no less important are those smaller innovations that year by year lead to steadily higher levels of productivity. This

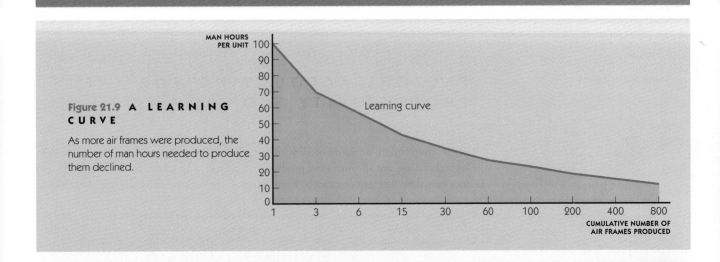

Figure 21.9 A LEARNING CURVE

As more air frames were produced, the number of man hours needed to produce them declined.

has been particularly evident in agriculture. The output of Canadian farms per worker has increased eightfold in the last forty years. Productivity increases like these have enabled a relatively small fraction of the population to provide all the food requirements for the whole country. Various government programs prohibit or discourage farmers from producing all they can, but even so, Canada exports roughly three-quarters of its agricultural produce. These rapid advances in agricultural productivity have resulted from mechanization (the use of the tractor), the development of better fertilizers, new techniques of planting, new seeds, and a better adaptation of seeds, fertilizers, crops, and farming patterns to local conditions.

INTERRELATION OF SOURCES OF PRODUCTIVITY

These four sources of productivity growth are interrelated. For example, the invention of a new machine (technological change) may also require new investment (increases in capital goods) in order to enter the economy. The idea of a jet engine does not increase productivity until the new jet engines are actually produced. New ideas do not simply happen: it takes researchers, engineers, and good managers to bring them about. This in turn requires a high level of human capital. Though the movement from agriculture to industry was reflected in an increase in average productivity, that movement would not have been possible without the innovations that increased productivity in agriculture so enormously.

Though all four factors are important and intertwined, economists have tried to measure their relative importance. The classic study in this area is by Robert Solow of MIT, who received the Nobel Prize for his work on growth theory. He estimated that increases in the supply of capital goods have accounted for approximately one-eighth of the increases in productivity. The rest of the growth was due to the other three factors. Edward Denison of the Brookings Institution has concluded that while human capital is important, technological change has played the predominant role.[2] The sections that follow take a closer look at how declines in these sources of productivity growth may lead to a productivity slowdown.

FACTORS ACCOUNTING FOR THE PRODUCTIVITY SLOWDOWN

Whereas investment, a higher-quality labour force, reallocation of resources, and technological change are all sources of productivity growth, a breakdown in any one of these factors can slow the rate of growth. Economists have focused primarily on shortfalls in

---

[2] Just as measurement problems make it difficult to obtain a precise estimate of the rate of growth of productivity, they also make it difficult to obtain a good estimate of the relative importance of various sources of economic growth. Dale Jorgenson of Harvard University, for instance, claims that most of the increase in productivity can be attributed to increases in capital goods.

investment, labour force quality, and technological progress in explaining the productivity slowdown.

LOW RATE OF ACCUMULATION OF CAPITAL GOODS

Investment in capital goods is necessary both to provide the machines to employ the rapidly growing labour force and to implement technological innovations. The level of investment is influenced jointly by the supply of savings and the demand for capital goods. Both sides of the market can contribute to the low level of investment.

Although savings and investment do tend to move together, each one responds to different stimuli; and understanding the spurs to each will help policymakers in their goal of improving productivity.

WHY HAVE SAVINGS RATES FALLEN?

There are three sources of savings: personal (or household) savings, corporate savings, and government savings (the fiscal surplus or deficit). Figure 21.10 shows how each of these, as well as total savings, has changed over time. These show gross savings. About half of gross savings go for depreciation, or the replacement of worn-out capital. The other half constitutes net savings, what is available for purchasing additional capital stock. Total Canadian savings were relatively low in the 1980s. We can see this in Figure

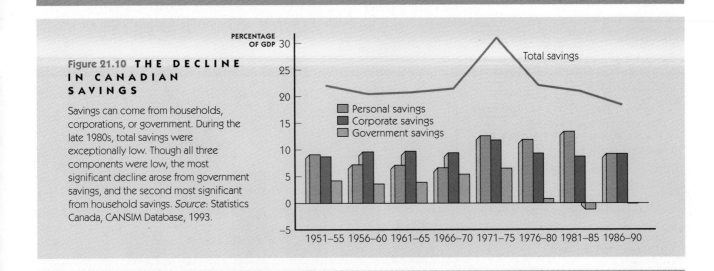

Figure 21.10 THE DECLINE IN CANADIAN SAVINGS

Savings can come from households, corporations, or government. During the late 1980s, total savings were exceptionally low. Though all three components were low, the most significant decline arose from government savings, and the second most significant from household savings. *Source*: Statistics Canada, CANSIM Database, 1993.

21.11, which compares net savings in Canada with those of other countries. The Canadian savings rate is about one-third that of Japan, but twice the American rate.

Figure 21.10 makes clear that much of the decline in saving is due to the huge government deficits in recent years. But both household and corporate savings rates have also fallen. What gave rise to the government deficits will be discussed in Chapter 22. Here, the focus is on private-sector savings.

The decline of private savings in recent years is partially explainable in terms of the motives for saving and changes in the Canadian economy in recent decades, though the extent of the decline is both disturbing and puzzling. Chapter 13 identified several motives for saving: people save for retirement (life-cycle savings) and to buy a home, to pay for their children's university education or to meet certain other needs (target savings); people save for emergencies, for a rainy day, for periods in which their incomes may be low either because they are laid off from their job or because they are sick (precautionary savings); and people save to leave something to their children (bequest savings). Furthermore, we saw that savings can be analyzed like any other consumption choice. The price (with savings, this is the interest rate) and the public's "taste" for savings—their attitudes about the future—also influence rates of saving.

During the past two decades, many of the motives and incentives for saving changed in a way to discourage saving. Improved public pensions and retirement savings programs (particularly during the 1970s) reduced the need for savings for retirement; improved capital markets and insurance—provided by both government and employers—meant that people did not have to save as much for emergencies; improved capital markets also meant that people did not have to save as much for a down payment for a house; and improved government student-loan programs meant that parents did not have to save as much for their children's education.

On the other hand, there were some changes that should have stimulated savings. What is relevant for savings is the real after-tax return. This return can increase if either tax rates are lowered (so that the individual gets to keep more of the return) or real before-tax returns rise. In the 1980s, taxes on the return to capital, particularly for upper-income levels fell, and real before-tax returns increased. Nevertheless, savings fell. This should not come as too much of a surprise: we learned in Chapter 9 that the effect of

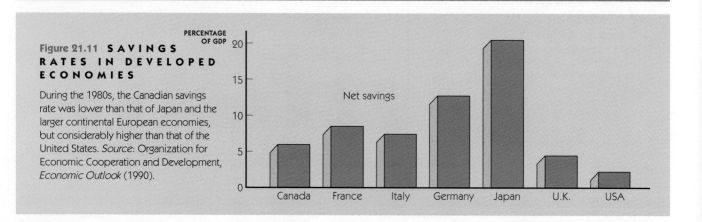

Figure 21.11 SAVINGS RATES IN DEVELOPED ECONOMIES

During the 1980s, the Canadian savings rate was lower than that of Japan and the larger continental European economies, but considerably higher than that of the United States. *Source*: Organization for Economic Cooperation and Development, *Economic Outlook* (1990).

changes in real after-tax interest rates on savings, while positive, is probably small.[3]

But the changes discussed so far, by themselves, do not seem to account fully for the reduced levels of savings. Accordingly, economists have looked elsewhere for an explanation.

Changes in Age Profile of Population   The life-cycle theory of savings suggests that people save in the period of life when their earnings are relatively high (ages 45–65) to accumulate wealth for consumption in their retirement, when earnings are low. Also, people borrow in their youth when earnings are still low (ages 21–44), yet their demands for expensive consumption goods such as cars and houses are high. This means that the age profile of the population affects total savings. Since the middle 1970s, the 45–65 age group has grown relatively smaller and the ratio of prime savers to prime borrowers has decreased, with a pattern very similar to the decline in the personal savings rate. But there is also cause for optimism: in the 1990s, the ratio of prime savers to prime borrowers is likely to recover, and personal savings may also increase.

Changes in Personal Values   Many economists believe that changes in attitudes and values are more responsible for the decline in the savings rate in North America than the changes in economic conditions and institutions. What is sometimes referred to as the "Me" generation wants immediate gratification; its willingness to defer consumption to a later date is very low. In nineteenth-century discussions of the rise of capitalism, writers like Max Weber placed considerable stress on the importance of the "work ethic" and savings, with these values being particularly associated with certain religious beliefs. The weakening of religious beliefs during recent decades may have been accompanied by a corresponding weakening in these values.

Other changes in cultural patterns have reduced the level of bequest motive savings. Social changes have loosened the links among family members. Just as public pensions have meant that children take less responsibility for their parents as they age, parents may increasingly feel that aside from being entitled to a good education, children should be responsible for themselves. Such changes in cultural attitudes would be reflected in a lower level of bequests.

Statistical Confusion   Another view is that the statistics underestimate savings and thus overestimate the extent of the savings problem. From the perspective of the individual, savings can be thought of as an increase in wealth. Income and savings, in this view, should include not only wages and interest, but also capital gains. After all, people care about the total return they get from an asset, the capital gain plus the dividend or interest, and accordingly both should be treated as part of income, and any capital gains that are not "realized" by selling the asset should be treated as part of savings.

During the 1970s and 1980s, the price of houses increased enormously. In effect, individuals were increasing their wealth simply by holding on to their houses; they were saving, not by taking a part of their pay cheque down to the bank, but simply by letting their houses appreciate in value. They could, of course, have tried to borrow against their houses. They could have consumed more than their wages and interest income. But they chose not to; they chose to save their capital gains. Conventional statistics mea-

---

[3] There, we saw that while the *substitution* effect leads to increased savings, the *income* effect results in reduced savings. While on theoretical grounds the *net* effect is ambiguous, the evidence supports a small positive effect.

suring savings as a fraction of national income or GDP do not include capital gains. In this view, then, Canada does not have a problem with the *level* of savings, but with the form these savings take. Savings are largely in the form of capital gains for housing, which do not allow for a flow of resources into manufacturing and production.

This problem has plagued many poorer countries, where savings have gone into purchases of land or holdings of gold rather than uses that would have a greater effect on increasing productivity. Those who believe that most savings are in the form of capital gains put some of the blame on government: tax policies have encouraged investment in housing; removing these tax preferences would induce a flow of resources elsewhere.

Still, while the capital gains on housing may provide part of the explanation of the reduced savings rate (as conventionally measured), it probably does not account for all of it. And it does not resolve the basic problem: how to increase the flow of funds available to be invested in the new machines and new enterprises that would increase the productivity of the economy.

Stymied by a Low Savings Rate   All in all, both government officials and economists feel somewhat stymied by the low level of savings. The price-related tools that economists like to work with best, like changes in real after-tax interest rates, are not likely by themselves to prove effective. Savings do not seem to be very sensitive to real after-tax interest rates.[4] It would prove difficult, to say the least, to substantially reduce Old Age Security or medical insurance or to make it more difficult for people to borrow, all in the name of increasing the savings rate! In fact, few people advocate such steps.

Thus, microeconomic instruments to stimulate household savings are likely, at best, to have small effects. The other major reason for low national savings is the huge government deficit. While the government may be ineffective in stimulating private savings, it might be able to get its own house in order. But doing that, as we will see in the next chapter, is perhaps easier said than done.

THE PUZZLE OF THE LOW CANADIAN SAVINGS RATE

Factor that increases the savings rate
> High real after-tax interest rates

Factors that decrease the savings rate
> Reduced need for life-cycle savings: improved Old Age Security
>
> Reduced need for precautionary savings: better insurance and easier access to the capital market
>
> Reduced bequest motive savings: changes in social attitudes
>
> Changes in age profile of the population
>
> Underestimates of savings due to unrealized capital gains from home ownership

---

[4] As noted earlier, income and substitution effects work in opposite directions.

THE LEVEL AND ALLOCATION OF INVESTMENT

There are two concerns about investment in Canada: that the level of investment is too low, and that too much investment has gone into areas—like real estate—that do not contribute much to long-run productivity growth.

A Bad Investment Climate: High Risk and Problems in Obtaining Finance A number of factors contributed to the relatively low level of investment in the 1980s, including high costs of capital, a heightened sense of uncertainty, and increased government regulations.

The cost of obtaining funds in Canada was higher than in the United States, and was substantially higher than in Japan. Real interest rates in Canada during the 1980s were very high, and highly variable, by historical standards. By the same token, funds for investment in new machines, new ventures, and research and development seemed to be less available, as both Bay Street and Wall Street focused their energies on high-profile takeovers and corporate reorganizations. Funds became even less available in the late 1980s and early 1990s; as their real estate and other loans went sour, many financial institutions responded to severe economic problems by tightening credit standards, and as many of the supposedly great deals of the early and mid-1980s wound up in insolvency, many investors became more skeptical of new security issues.

Frequent changes in tax laws, highly variable interest rates, and extreme fluctuations of exchange rates all contributed to a sense of business uncertainty. As we learned in Chapter 19, exchange rate volatility, for instance, means that exporters do not know whether they will be able to sell their goods abroad (at a price at which they can recover their costs), and domestic producers worry about the threat of foreign competition. This uncertainty has discouraged firms from making the long-term commitments that are associated with investment.

The Effect of Rules and Regulations on Investment Government rules and regulations can affect investment too. Changes in regulations during the past two decades may have contributed to the productivity slowdown, by both discouraging investment and forcing investment to take forms that do not show up in the national income statistics.

There is concern, for instance, that laws aimed at protecting the environment force businesses to put too much of their money into clean air rather than into more efficient methods of production. The improved quality of air benefits the standard of living, of course, but is not reflected in GDP statistics or hence in productivity measures. Investment in the electric power industry, particularly investment in hydroelectric power plants, has been dominated by environmental concerns. Similarly, investments in forestry, pulp and paper, and other resource-based industries have come under increasing scrutiny as the public becomes more aware of the effects of some of these activities on the quality of air and water, as well as on neighbouring communities and on the wildlife habitat. The uncertainties involved in obtaining approval, however, often from two levels of government, add greatly to the costs and discourage potential investors who can often take their funds to jurisdictions with laxer environmental standards.

People in the construction industry often point to the myriad of regulations that raise their costs and decrease their productivity. For instance, obtaining approval of plans leads to delays, and these delays bring large costs. In some places where the delays may be particularly long, like large urban areas, those in the industry claim that they raise the cost of construction by as much as a third.

Misallocating Investment   Taxes affect both the level of investment and its allocation. In the early 1980s, the tax laws gave extremely favourable tax treatment to commercial real estate such as office buildings. These laws, combined with a widespread belief that they were too generous to be permanent, spurred a boom in commercial real estate, which by the mid-1980s had resulted in oversupply. Vacancy rates for commercial real estate were as high as 20–30 percent in many urban areas. As anticipated, the income tax reform of 1988 took most of the special treatment away.

Prior to 1987, the corporate tax system also contained special provisions intended to encourage investment, especially in the manufacturing and processing industries. These included accelerated depreciation of machinery and equipment in the latter industries, and generous investment tax credits, especially for investments in depressed regions. The provisions were successful in some cases; with these tax breaks and additional indirect subsidies from trade protectionism, the automobile industry retooled and once again became competitive and the steel industry held its own despite a glut on world steel markets. However, for other industries, such as textiles, even the combination of tax breaks and trade protectionism were not enough.

The broad intent of the corporate tax reform of 1988 was to provide a more "level" playing field, so that scarce investment resources would be used where productivity was highest, not where tax benefits were the greatest. In this it was only partially successful. For instance, the special favourable treatment of the resource industries consisting of rapid write-offs of exploration and development expenses was retained. Similarly, manufacturing industries continued to benefit from lower tax rates and from relatively generous depreciation allowances. And the investment tax credit was retained for firms operating in high-unemployment regions. But the size of the differential advantage was reduced. Furthermore, as the tax base was broadened, rates could be lowered, reducing the extent to which the tax system interfered with investment decisions in general.

Investment in Infrastructure   The vast system of roads and highways is showing increasing signs of wear and tear. This system together with others such as airports, bridges, and sewer lines form an infrastructure that allows the economy to operate. These physical investments are of real importance to the sustained productivity of the economy. There is a growing concern that the government's failure to maintain this infrastructure at an adequate level, and to improve it to keep pace with the potential growth of the economy, will act as a dampening force on future economic growth. For instance, the nation's airports have not been able to keep up with the increase in air traffic; and the Trans-Canada highway system that was created in the 1950s is, at critical points, not up to the burden of the 1990s.

Encouraging Investment   Encouraging investment is not much easier and may be more problematic than encouraging savings. Most economists would agree that government should provide more of the basic infrastructure, such as roads and airports, which are its responsibility, and reduce unnecessary regulatory interference. The disagreement arises in trying to figure out which of the regulations could be eliminated or simplified without serious harm to the objectives for which the regulations were adopted. Though few would advocate stripping away all environmental and safety regulations, many economists think that some of the regulations yield at best marginal benefits at huge costs.

The government can use tax policy to encourage investment—for instance, by providing investment tax credits (see Chapter 13). But in the past, at least, its policies have led as much to a misallocation of investment, by stimulating tax-favoured investments at the expense of others, as they have to an overall increase in the level of investment.

Looser monetary policies (lower interest rates) can encourage investment. To offset the inflationary pressures to which such policies may give rise, government may need to have tighter fiscal policies—it may have to limit government expenditures and increase taxes on households. In fact, during the 1980s and early 1990s, the government pursued exactly the opposite pair of policies: tight monetary policies combined with large government deficits. Only the huge inflow of funds from abroad prevented this combination of policies from having disastrous effects on Canadian investment.

THE QUALITY OF THE LABOUR FORCE

In order to exploit the advantages of modern technology and to implement the most modern techniques of production, a highly skilled labour force is needed. This, in turn, is dependent on an effective education system.

THE SYMPTOMS OF A HUMAN CAPITAL PROBLEM

It is increasingly common to read in the newspapers about the shortcomings of Canada's educational system. The symptoms are well-publicized: the high school dropout rate is close to 20 percent; the level of literacy is lower in the 16–24 age bracket than in the 35–44 bracket; the proportion of students enrolled in postsecondary institutions who actually graduate is relatively low; and enrollment in science-oriented programs falls well below the international average. Thus, despite the enormous resources put into education and the fact that, along with the United States, the average number of years of schooling is among the highest, there is concern that we are not getting value for money in our schools and postsecondary institutions.

Some indication of the problem with the educational system can be seen by examining the results of standardized testing. Figure 21.12 shows how Canadian thirteen-year-

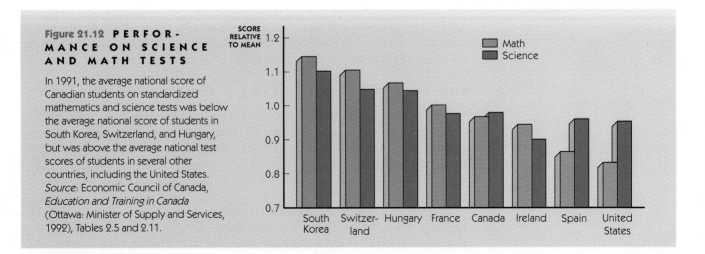

Figure 21.12 PERFORMANCE ON SCIENCE AND MATH TESTS

In 1991, the average national score of Canadian students on standardized mathematics and science tests was below the average national score of students in South Korea, Switzerland, and Hungary, but was above the average national test scores of students in several other countries, including the United States. *Source*: Economic Council of Canada, *Education and Training in Canada* (Ottawa: Minister of Supply and Services, 1992), Tables 2.5 and 2.11.

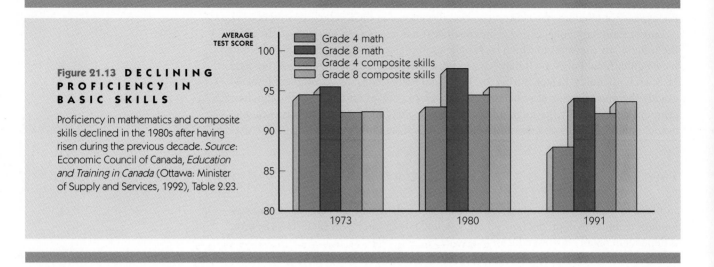

Figure 21.13 DECLINING PROFICIENCY IN BASIC SKILLS

Proficiency in mathematics and composite skills declined in the 1980s after having risen during the previous decade. *Source:* Economic Council of Canada, *Education and Training in Canada* (Ottawa: Minister of Supply and Services, 1992), Table 2.23.

olds fared in tests of mathematics and science performance relative to those of other countries. In both cases, the average score for Canadian students was well below the average score for students from countries such as South Korea, Switzerland, and Hungary, and matched the average score of students from France. Interestingly, U.S. students did far worse than ours, as did students from Ireland and Spain. On the other hand, student performance also varied across provinces, as might be expected. Average scores for students from the Atlantic provinces, Ontario, and Manitoba fell below the international average score, while average scores for students from Alberta, Quebec, and British Columbia were above. Indeed, average science scores for students from Ontario, Newfoundland, and New Brunswick were below the average scores of American students.

A greater cause for concern is that skills learned in school seem to be declining in recent years. Figure 21.13 shows that over the last decade both grade four and grade eight student skills in mathematics and in a composite of subjects have fallen after having risen during the 1970s. Of course, these standardized tests are imperfect and limited; one of many problems with them is that they do not measure creativity. But the tests do measure success in certain objectives of education, such as mastery over basic skills, and the mediocre performance of Canadian students is accordingly disturbing.

THE STRENGTHS OF CANADA'S EDUCATIONAL SYSTEM

While Canada's elementary and secondary schooling has come under extensive criticism, its educational system as a whole has some distinct strengths. One is the greater commitment to egalitarianism. For instance, young children are not assigned particular schools that will determine whether or not they can go on to college. Early "tracking" of this sort, based on test scores, gives a distinct advantage to children with more educated parents.

Another great strength is the Canadian system of community colleges and universities, many of which provide a high-quality education to those who could not afford to go to private schools or who may not have performed well in high school. In many countries, such students would have been precluded from further education. Ironically, while in many respects the Canadian educational system is more egalitarian than those of other developed countries, in one respect it is less so: most European countries charge virtually no tuition to students who are admitted to their universities, and some actually pay all or part of students' living costs.

A third strength is Canada's universities overall, which provide a uniformly high level of postsecondary education. Students from virtually every other country come to Canada to study, as both undergraduates and graduate students. The discoveries and innovations flowing out of the universities' research laboratories have been an important basis of Canada's technological success. Indeed, the success of the universities, in light of the problems at the elementary and high school levels, appears almost paradoxical.

ADDRESSING CANADA'S EDUCATIONAL DEFICIENCIES

What are the sources of Canada's educational deficiencies, and what can be done about them? To some, the sources lie not so much in the educational system itself as in society more broadly. Some observers have, for instance, expressed concern that with fewer women staying at home with children, there is less education going on at home; and this home education has been shown to be an important complement to what schools provide. As well, children of families with both parents present in the home have been shown to achieve higher academic results than those from single-parent families.

Other changes in society have increased the challenges facing elementary and secondary schools. It has been documented, for example, that educational achievement declines proportionately with the amount of television viewing. There is also strong evidence of a decline in the quality of teachers, particularly in the sciences. One reason is that as job opportunities for women have increased, many of the able women who formerly would have gone into teaching because of the circumscribed opportunities elsewhere are now seeking employment in higher-paying jobs.

One of the educational system's great strengths—its commitment to egalitarian education—may impair one of its basic objectives, to provide the most able students with the skills required to help the country sustain technological excellence. An increasing commitment to egalitarianism means that a larger proportion of the available resources go into raising slower learners up to a minimal level than into helping faster learners cover as much material as they can.

While there is a consensus that Canada's educational system has its problems, there is no consensus on what should be done. It is not clear that more resources would help. Expenditures per pupil increased significantly over the past fifteen years, and they are considerably higher in Canada than in other countries whose students seem consistently to outperform Canadian students. There is a general view that money is not the only solution. In any case, in the prevailing mood of financial stringency, substantial expenditure increases seem unlikely.

Recent discussions have focused on reorganizing the educational system, in ways that would elicit more involvement from parents and more commitment from teachers. One proposal would decentralize public schools, giving more discretion to the principal in the running of her school. Another advocates more competition between private and public schools. In one widely discussed plan, the government would provide educational vouchers that parents could use to enroll their children at either public or private schools. Advocates of proposals like these believe that competition among schools will improve their quality, and the process of choice will enhance commitment and involvement of all participants in the educational process.

THE CHANGING MIX OF THE WORK FORCE

The productivity of the work force is affected by the mix of workers of which it is composed. Very young workers, for instance, are less productive, because they have not yet acquired the range of skills that can only be obtained by experience. And very old workers are often less productive, both because the skills they have acquired may have become obsolete and because of health problems. Historically, women have been less educated and have remained out of the labour force during their childbearing years; they therefore lacked the productivity-enhancing job experiences of their male counterparts. Today these differences have become much less important.

As we have seen, there were important changes in the composition of the labour force in the 1970s and 1980s, from the influx of baby boomers who reached working age and the dramatic increase in the fraction of women who sought employment outside the home. To the extent that new workers in the labour force are actually less productive than those already *in* the labour force, the new workers will tend to bring down the average productivity as measured by standard productivity statistics. However, if new workers are nonetheless more productive in the job market than they used to be when they were not in the job market, then the true productivity of the economy will increase. This increase, however, will not be captured in the productivity statistics.

By the same token, early retirement has become much more of a possibility in recent years. In 1921, 71 percent of men over age sixty-five were holding jobs or looking for jobs, while in 1990, the figure had fallen to 11.4 percent. However, these late working years that have been cut off are (on average) among a worker's least productive years, and thus early retirement has probably helped create a work force that is *more* productive on average.

Finally, it appears that unemployment may have a long-term effect on the quality of the labour force. In general, sustained work experience makes workers more productive over time. In a deep recession, though, when unemployment climbs near 10 percent or even higher, a large number of workers are not adding any experience. In fact, some of their work skills may atrophy. In this way, a deep recession can mean a reduction not only in current output but in the growth of future output as well.

The changing composition of the labour force and periods of unemployment, while they play an important role in determining changes in productivity in the long run, are probably not that important in explaining the productivity slowdown. On the other hand, a deterioration in the quality of schools—a lower level of human capital—may play a role, the quantitative significance of which is hard to ascertain.

LIMITS TO TECHNOLOGICAL CHANGE

While we have come to expect technological progress, confidence in North America's technological superiority has eroded during the past two decades. *Some* of the observed decline in the rate of productivity growth is related to the changes in the composition of output noted earlier.

Some economists contend that the decline in heavy industry—in steel, automobiles, and manufacturing in general—and relative growth in the service sector help explain the recent slowdown in productivity growth. They worry that the opportunities for innovation in the service sector are lower than in manufacturing or agriculture. They cite

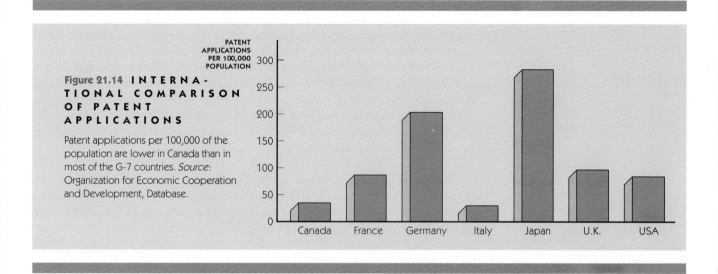

Figure 21.14 INTERNATIONAL COMPARISON OF PATENT APPLICATIONS

Patent applications per 100,000 of the population are lower in Canada than in most of the G-7 countries. *Source*: Organization for Economic Cooperation and Development, Database.

haircutting as an example: the only major innovation in this field in the past hundred years has been the electric hair clipper. Other economists are more hopeful. They cite the development by McDonald's of more efficient ways of delivering "fast food" and improvements by many of the country's major retailers that have reduced the markup of retail prices over wholesale costs. In addition, the computer revolution continues to open up new technological possibilities in service industries such as banking, insurance, accounting, and design.

But there is more to the productivity slowdown than just the change in the composition of output. One indicator of technological leadership is the number of patents. Figure 21.14 shows that today, relative to the size of the population, both Canada and the United States are performing more poorly (by this indicator) than Japan, the United Kingdom, and Germany.

POLICIES TO INCREASE THE RATE OF TECHNOLOGICAL CHANGE

There are some important connections between government programs to stabilize the economy and the economy's rate of technological progress. If the government is successful in sustaining the economy near full employment, it will at the same time stimulate productivity growth. In a recession, national economic output actually declines, which means that the amount of "doing," and hence the amount of learning by doing, in the economy falls as well. Furthermore, when profit margins are squeezed to the bone in a recession, firms are less likely to take the risk of trying out slightly new production processes or undertaking the risks of research and development expenditures. These are among the first expenditures to be cut in an economic downturn. Macroeconomic policies that maintain the economy at a high level of output and employment are therefore one important way that the government can help promote growth.

There are also a variety of "microeconomic" government policies that affect the rate of technological progress. Unfortunately, the link between these policies and technological progress is often difficult to perceive, since the benefits from increased productivity may be felt only years later. Because the consequences of cutbacks in R & D are not felt immediately, they are an obvious target when either the government or private firms are in a period of financial stringency. By the same token, it may be years before the effects of the cutbacks of the 1980s show in the productivity statistics. To the extent that the productivity slowdown in the 1970s was due to decreased expenditures on research, it would have been due to a decrease in expenditures in the 1950s and 1960s. But the 1960s in particular were a period of high spending on research; some economists are therefore skeptical about the role of the levels of expenditures on research in explaining the *current* productivity slowdown.

Direct Expenditures: Government versus Private Sector   Not only may there be a long and variable lag between R & D expenditures and productivity, but the connection between different types of R & D and productivity may be tenuous. The private sector has an interest in investing in R & D that is likely to generate financial rewards for the firm incurring the expense. This may include process innovations or discoveries that can be patented. Many types of invention or discovery, however, yield returns that cannot be appropriated by the discoverer. Such, for example, is the case with the findings of basic scientific research. Funding for this type of R & D must come from the government.[5]

The government does provide considerable direct support for R & D, much of it for research in the basic principles of science, what can be thought of as the underlying intellectual infrastructure. As Figure 21.15 shows, however, federal government expenditures on R & D have actually declined as a percent of GDP in the past two decades, de-

---

[5] Basic research is normally the responsibility of government. It is a public good, the benefits of which accrue to many firms, often in many different industries, and to their consumers. Research also has large positive externalities. If the responsibility was left to the private sector, there would be too little research.

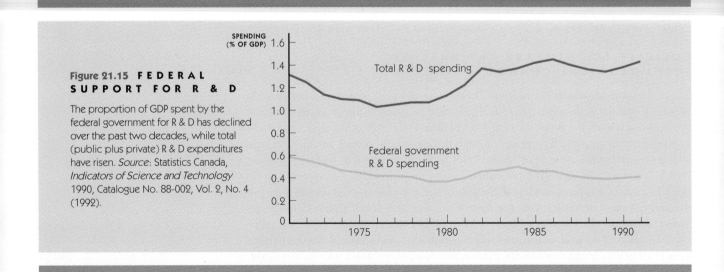

Figure 21.15 FEDERAL SUPPORT FOR R & D

The proportion of GDP spent by the federal government for R & D has declined over the past two decades, while total (public plus private) R & D expenditures have risen. *Source*: Statistics Canada, *Indicators of Science and Technology* 1990, Catalogue No. 88-002, Vol. 2, No. 4 (1992).

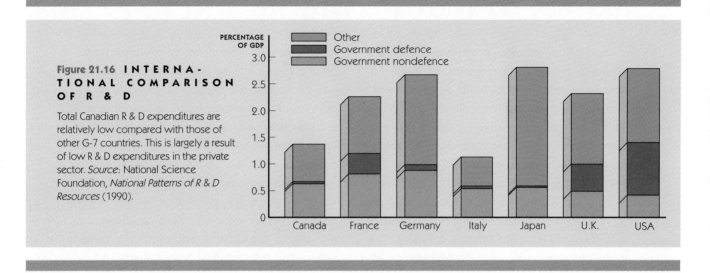

Figure 21.16 INTERNA-TIONAL COMPARISON OF R & D

Total Canadian R & D expenditures are relatively low compared with those of other G-7 countries. This is largely a result of low R & D expenditures in the private sector. *Source*: National Science Foundation, *National Patterns of R & D Resources* (1990).

spite the fact that total public plus private R & D expenditures as a proportion of GDP have risen. Indeed, the fall in federal spending on R & D has been dramatic: as a proportion of GDP it was a third smaller in 1991 than it was in 1971.

Furthermore, Figure 21.16 shows that in terms of total R & D (relative to the size of the economy) Canada fares badly among the G-7 industrialized countries—only Italy fares worse. On the other hand, much of our standing is due to low private-sector R & D spending rather than low public-sector spending. It is also noteworthy that hardly any of our R & D effort takes place in the defence sector unlike, say, in the United States or the United Kingdom.

Taxes   Taxes that reduce the return to investments in general also reduce the return to investments in research and development and thus discourage R & D. The income tax reforms of 1988 included higher taxes on capital gains. Since a large part of the return obtained by entrepreneurs takes the forms of capital gains—when a high-tech company is successful, its shares soar in value—there was considerable concern that this tax increase would discourage R & D.

Many government policies to encourage R & D are similar to those used to encourage other forms of investment. The government has one tax program directed specifically at research and development: R & D tax credits. Through these credits, the government in effect pays part of the costs of R & D.

The Legal and Regulatory Environment   There has been concern that changes in the legal environment have had an adverse effect on innovation. When a firm develops a new product, there is always some danger that even after it has been well tested, there may be some adverse effects. For example, some drugs may have unanticipated side effects that show up only years later. Courts in recent years, especially in the United States, have provided huge awards to compensate victims of such drugs. While these

CLOSE-UP: THE PROSPERITY INITIATIVE

In response to growing concerns that Canada's prosperity was being threatened by a fiercely competitive global economy, the federal government launched the Prosperity Initiative in 1991. It formed an independent Steering Group on Prosperity consisting of twenty Canadians (all volunteers) from a wide range of backgrounds. The Steering Group produced an Action Plan in October of 1992. It reflected the views of thousands of Canadians who had participated in community talks, roundtables, conferences, and forums. The Action Plan set forth a total of fifty-four specific actions, indicated who should be responsible for them, and even set target dates for undertaking the actions.

The Action Plan consists of three parts. The first part involves creating a growing economy, able to compete in a global economy. The keys to achieving this are an emphasis on innovation and quality along with technological mastery and productivity growth. Nearly half of the actions in the plan concern these achievements. Among the main recommendations are the formation of a National Quality Institute and the introduction of consumer education courses in schools and adult education centres. To reduce the burden of government, the plan calls for an independent review of federal and provincial taxes and expenditures, a competitiveness impact assessment for existing and proposed laws and regulations, a regulatory budget to review the economic impact of regulations, and a tough performance review of the number of government departments. The plan recommends a high-speed, broad-band electronic "information highway" to link Canadians to one another and to the world of ideas, and to encourage greater use of existing technologies and development of new ones. As well, tax incentives would be given for the use of innovative equipment and technologies, and more dynamic and innovative capital markets would be encouraged to help create new firms and aid small firms to grow larger. A coordinated private-sector strategy would have as its objective a doubling of the number of firms that export. A Centre of Excellence for Sustainable Development would be created to help achieve

environmental goals and to enable Canadians to compete in the market for "green" products. And a nationwide approach to worker adjustment would be used to prepare the work force to take on new jobs.

The second part of the strategy would improve education and training systems. While Canada spends 7.2 percent of its gross domestic product on education, the highest percentage of any developed country, we are not getting value for our investment. To remedy this, the plan calls for a Canadian forum on learning whose purpose is to define goals and to promote innovation and partnerships for excellence in learning. It calls for competence-based systems for all levels of education and training, where success is defined by measurable skills. A concerted effort would be made to build stronger links between schools and the world of work, and to ensure that all young people complete secondary school. Employer-led training should be increased to be equal to 2 percent of working time. Finally, there should be a 30 percent per year increase in the availability of computers and software in schools.

The third part of the plan aims to make Canada a truly inclusive society in which all persons have the opportunity to achieve their full potential and to share the opportunities that innovation brings. This is important because women, immigrants, and visible minorities will constitute an increasing proportion of Canada's labour force. Key recommendations include an integrated approach to income security that enhances the ability of these groups to find work, while reducing disincentives to work; a restructuring of the work place to accommodate family and other social pressures; and a new set of training programs for aboriginal managers at institutions of higher learning.

The Action Plan represents a far-reaching and inclusive set of proposals meant to address the economic and social challenges of the twenty-first century. As the plan says: "The time for action is now. Let's get going! Allons-y!"

Source: Inventing Our Future: An Action Plan for Canada's Prosperity, The Steering Group on Prosperity, Ottawa, 1992.

suits have encouraged producers to be more careful, they have also made them more reluctant to bring out new products. Valuable new drugs have been developed that no manufacturer is willing to sell. As a result, there are currently proposals to limit **product liability** (the obligation of a producer to compensate victims of a defective product that has injured them) in the case of new drugs.

Other aspects of the regulatory environment may also affect the pace of R & D. The long and extensive testing of drugs and the long delays in gaining approval for their production undoubtedly have a dampening effect. There is clearly a problem of weighing and balancing costs and benefits.

Patent and Anti-Combines Policies   Patent policies, which enable an inventor to appropriate the returns to his innovative activity, are another major aspect of government policies affecting R & D. By and large, "stronger" patents—patents that are broader in coverage and longer in duration—provide greater incentives for R & D. Anti-combines policies, which prohibit firms from colluding, also impede them from cooperating in research ventures, though recent legislation has made such ventures easier than previously. Here too, the government must balance the losses from reduced competition with the gains from increased innovation.

Foreign Investment and R & D   In one important sense, the shortfall of R & D expenditures in Canada gives a misleading impression as to the extent to which innovations are available to Canadian firms. A high proportion of firms operating in high-tech and innovative sectors in Canada are actually subsidiaries of multinational corporations based elsewhere. These companies tend to do a disproportionate amount of the R & D in the home country, especially the United States. On the one hand, this should be of limited concern since the discoveries become available to Canadian subsidiaries (and any tax credits are borne by the home country). On the other hand, the fact that R & D takes place elsewhere implies that Canadian scientists may be lured abroad rather than working at home.

THE COSTS OF ECONOMIC GROWTH

There is a widespread faith in the virtues of economic progress. Even among people who have serious doubts about certain technologies, few will openly embrace the alternatives of economic stagnation and a relatively lower standard of living for Canada in comparison with other developed countries. However, this acceptance of technological progress should not blind anyone to its real costs.

In the early 1800s, English workmen sometimes destroyed labour-saving machinery rather than see it take over their jobs. They were referred to as **Luddites,** after their leader Ned Ludd. (Ludd's role may have been largely mythical, but the term still bears his name.) Concerns about workers who are thrown out of their jobs as a result of some innovation are no less real today, although those fighting against technological change today have their unions to help, and they are more successful than the Luddites were. For example, plumbers' unions got many communities to forbid the use of plastic pipes, which, while cheaper and better for some uses than metal pipes, require less skill to install. Similarly, pilots' unions have insisted on crews of three even for planes designed for crews of two.

Technological progress creates jobs as it destroys them. Earlier this century, jobs for blacksmiths were replaced by jobs for automobile mechanics. Today a computerized "brain" in a machine may mean that fewer automobile workers are needed on the assembly line, but new jobs are created in the computing industry. The adjustment of the economy, however, is more complicated than the simple conversion of an assembly-line worker into a computer programmer. It is better to think of the new computer-programming job as setting off a chain. Had the new job not come along, the computer programmer would have taken a slightly less skilled job; by taking this new position, he frees up the less skilled job. This less skilled job is grabbed by a worker who otherwise would have had a still less skilled job—say, a semiskilled job. But this creates a vacancy at the semiskilled job, and so on down the chain. The assembly-line worker may find that there is thus a job requiring only slightly more skills than he presently has, skills that, with an appropriate job-training program, he can readily acquire.

Of course, it can be hard to teach an old dog new tricks, so a middle-aged or older worker who loses her job may have real difficulty in getting another that is even nearly as good. She may have to content herself with taking an unskilled job, with a commensurately lower wage. How much sympathy this displaced worker should receive is a matter on which reasonable people can disagree. Does a worker who is used to a certain wage deserve not to have it changed? Should we pay more attention to the costs to the worker who loses a job than to the benefits to a worker in the new industry who gets a better job.

Not surprisingly, then, technological progress frequently meets with resistance. The loss of any jobs as a result of technological progress gives rise to fear and insecurity, even among people who are not immediately threatened with losing their own jobs. The pleas of those affected to "stop" or at least slow down the pace of innovation strikes a concordant note in others, and the government often responds positively to the pleas for its intervention. We have already noted the sometimes successful attempt by plumbers to incorporate into building codes restrictions against plastic piping. There are many more instances throughout the economy.

Most economists believe that these self-serving restrictions are harmful when judged from an overall perspective. The cost to society exceeds the gains to the protected groups. On the other hand, the concerns of the displaced cannot simply be ignored. The objective of the government should be to design programs that assist in the transition of people displaced by technological change. Such programs can be thought of as a form of insurance. Most workers face the possibility that their job will be made technologically obsolete. Knowing that if they are thrown out of work for this reason they will be at least partially protected adds to a sense of security, something most risk-averse workers value highly. In the long run, such programs actually help increase the rate at which technological changes are adopted by making job loss a less fearful prospect.

ARE THERE LIMITS TO ECONOMIC GROWTH?

As we learned earlier, technological progress was not taken for granted in the early 1800s as it is today. Thomas Malthus envisioned the future as one in which more and more workers would crowd themselves into a fixed supply of land. The ever-increasing labour force would push wages down to the subsistence level, or even lower. Any technological progress that occurred would, in his view, raise wages only temporarily; as the labour supply increased, wages would eventually fall back to the subsistence level. The capitalists, who owned the land and factories and machines, would eventually receive any gains from technological improvements.

Over the past century, there has been a decrease in the rate of population growth, and this phenomenon, which was also unforeseen, is perhaps as remarkable as the increase in the rate of technological progress. One might have thought that improved medicine and health conditions would have led to a population explosion, but the spread of birth control and family planning has had the opposite effect, at least in the more-developed countries. Today family size has decreased to the point where in many countries population growth (apart from migration) has almost halted. Those who worry about the limits to growth today usually describe the future not as a case of more and more people crowding onto a plot of land, but rather a case of some natural resource such as oil, natural gas, phosphorus, or potassium running out. They believe that *exhaustible* natural resources like these may pose a limit to economic growth as they are used up in the ordinary course of production.

However, most economists believe that markets do provide incentives for wise use of most resources. They believe that as any good becomes more scarce and its price rises, the search for substitutes will be stimulated. Thus, the rise in the price of oil led to smaller, more efficient cars, cooler but better-insulated houses, and a search for alternative sources of energy like geothermal and synthetic fuels, all of which resulted in a decline in the consumption of oil.

Since the time of Malthus, an unending string of doomsayers have worried that the world was about to run out of something or other. There were predictions that when the world ran out of oil, economic growth would stop. Someday these dire predictions may come true. But for now, the prospects look about as good as they always have. There appears to be a sufficient supply of fossil fuels for decades to come. As these fuels become more scarce and thus more expensive, perhaps new technologies like solar power or nuclear fusion will provide an almost limitless supply of cleanly produced energy. This argument, that rising prices encourage both greater conservation and a search for substitutes, applies to other exhaustible natural resources as well.

Still, there is one area in which the price system does not work well—the area of externalities. Without government intervention, producers do not have incentives to worry about air and water pollution. And in our globally connected world, what one country does results in externalities for other. Cutting down the rain forest in Brazil, for example, may have worldwide climatic consequences. The less-developed countries feel that they can ill afford the costs of pollution control, when they can barely pay the price of any industrialization. They feel it is unfair to ask them to pay the price of maintaining the environment, when the major industrialized economies are the major source of the environmental degradation. Environmentalists argue that we are all in the same boat together. And if global warming occurs, it could have disastrous effects on all of us, in both the less- and more-developed countries. While the scientific community is not in agreement about the significance of these concerns, most economists do not believe that we face an either/or choice: we do not have to abandon growth to preserve our environment. Nevertheless, a sensitivity to the quality of our environment may affect how we go about growing.

THE PROGNOSIS

It is too soon for any final judgment as to whether the productivity slowdown in North America is permanent or only a temporary aberration. Though this century has been marked by large increases in productivity, the rate of productivity growth has not been steady. There have been periods of relative stagnation as well as periods in which the economy has burst forth with energy and growth. The hopeful interpretation of the decline in productivity growth is that it is just a passing phase.

A less optimistic view is that the high rates of productivity growth experienced during the 1950s and 1960s were the aberration. Some economists believe that various possibilities for economic growth were bottled up during the Great Depression of the 1930s and World War II in the early 1940s, and the realization of those postponed opportunities resulted in the productivity boom of the 1950s and 1960s. From this point of view, the loss in North America's dominant technological position is not surprising. After all, North America has no monopoly on ideas or on the ability to do research, and it was only a matter of time before some countries would catch up.

The analysis of this chapter suggests that there are grounds for both pessimism and optimism. There is no quick or easy reversal of many of the factors hampering productivity growth, such as the low rate of savings; the failure of the Canadian educational system to provide the kind of education required in a competitive, technologically oriented world; and the changing structure of the Canadian economy, with the low-productivity service sector growing more rapidly than other parts of the economy.

Some of the factors hampering productivity growth could more easily be altered. These include the failure of government to improve the economy's infrastructure; the distortion of taxes and regulations; and the low level of expenditures on research and development, at least expenditures on basic research.

Thus, while most economists think it unlikely that North America will ever again be in the position of technological superiority that it held for so long, there is widespread optimism that the Canadian economy can return to a higher level of productivity growth, provided the right government policies are pursued.

An Agenda for Economic Growth

Factors that stimulate savings
   Lower federal government budgetary deficits
   Tax breaks for savers
Factors that stimulate investment
   Improved economic environment: less regulation, lower cost of capital, less risk
      with stable economy operating at full employment
   Tax breaks for firms that invest
Factors that improve human capital
   Reorganization of education—more decentralization, more competition, more
      choice
Factors that stimulate technological change
   Tax breaks—reducing capital gains taxation for R & D projects
   More funds for training scientists and engineers
   More support for basic research
   Improved economic environment
      Reduced regulation
      Reduced legal barriers
   Ensuring that anti-combines policies do not act as impediments

REVIEW AND PRACTICE

SUMMARY

1. Canada and the United States experienced a marked slowdown in the rate of productivity growth in the late 1960s and early 1970s. Even seemingly small declines in the rate of increase in productivity will have a powerful adverse effect on the standard of living over a generation or two.

2. There are four major sources of productivity growth: increases in the accumulation of capital goods (investment); a higher quality of the labour force; greater efficiency in allocating resources; and technological change.

3. The rate of savings in Canada has declined in recent years. Some of the reasons are improved government retirement programs, more extensive insurance coverage and greater ease in borrowing, changes in social attitudes, the fact that the proportion of the population in their prime savings years during the 1980s was relatively low, and the fact that people are choosing to save by building up equity in houses, rather than by setting aside income.

4. The most plausible way to achieve an immediate increase in overall national savings would be to reduce the government deficits.

5. Investment levels were relatively low during the 1980s. Possible reasons include the high costs of capital, the impact of government rules and regulations, and uncertainty about the future, including changes in taxes and interest rates.

6. The government has several policies available to stimulate investment: spending money on infrastructure projects like roads and bridges, monetary and fiscal policies to keep credit available and interest rates low, and incentives like the investment tax credit.

7. There are serious concerns about the quality of education Canadian students are receiving in preparation for the labour force and about the number of scientists and engineers being trained. Allocating more money to training and education alone may not help. Educational reorganization may also be needed.

8. The twentieth century has been marked by shifts in the Canadian economy from an agricultural base to an industrial base and more recently to a service base. Some economists think that the potential for technological progress is less in the service sector than in the industrial sector, and this accounts for part of the productivity slowdown.

9. Government supports R & D through both direct spending and tax incentives, though direct support for R & D has actually declined as a share of GDP during the past two decades.

10. There has long been concern that certain natural resources (like oil) will someday run out, causing economic growth to halt. However, most economists would argue that the price of resources will increase as they become more scarce, and this will encourage both greater conservation and a search for substitutes.

KEY TERMS

product liability   Luddites

REVIEW QUESTIONS

1. True or false: "Since growth-oriented policies might have an effect of only a percent or two per year, they are not worth worrying much about." Explain.

2. What are the four possible sources of productivity growth?

3. What are the components of overall Canadian savings, and how did they change in the 1980s?

4. What are some reasons for the decrease in savings during the 1980s?

5. Will government policies to raise the rate of return on savings necessarily lead to increased savings?

6. What are the factors that contribute to a low level of investment?

7. How might a recession contribute to a slowdown in productivity several years later?

8. What policies might the government use to increase investment in R & D?

9. What are some costs of economic growth? Short of seeking to restrain growth, how might government deal with these costs?

PROBLEMS

1. Will the following changes increase or decrease the rate of household savings.
    (a) The proportion of people in the 45–64 age bracket increases.
    (b) Government programs provide secure retirement benefits.
    (c) Credit cards become much more prevalent.
    (d) The proportion of people in the 21–45 age bracket increases.
    (e) Government programs to guarantee student loans are enacted.

2. Explain how the following factors would increase or decrease the average productivity of labour:
    (a) successful reforms of the education system;
    (b) the entry of new workers into the economy;
    (c) earlier retirement;
    (d) high unemployment rates during a recession.

3. Suppose a firm is considering spending $1 million on R & D projects, which it believes will translate into patents that it will be able to sell for $2.5 million in ten years. Assume that the firm ignores risk. If the interest rate is 10 percent, is the firm likely to attempt these R & D projects? If the government offers a 20 percent R & D tax credit, how does the firm's calculation change?

4. Explain why a rapid influx of workers would result in a lower output per worker (a reduction in productivity). Would the effect on productivity depend on the skill level of the new workers?

5. Explain, using supply and demand diagrams, how a technological change such as computerization could lead to lower wages of unskilled workers and higher wages of skilled workers.

6. Consider the growth agenda set forth on page 615. Discuss the relative importance of the various items. Which are most likely to have a significant effect on growth?

THE PROBLEM OF THE TWIN DEFICITS

ach decade seems to have particular economic themes. The major economic phenomenon of the 1960s, for example, is generally taken to be the decision of the Canadian government to follow the United States in pursuing expansionary policies. In the United States, this took the form of a "guns and butter" economic policy involving fighting the war in Vietnam at the same time as introducing major social spending to fight a War on Poverty. This spilled into Canada as increased export demand at the same time that our government was undertaking substantial expenditures, especially on new social programs. The result, as explained in Chapter 8, was a surge of inflation. The major economic events of the 1970s were the dramatic increases in the price of oil in 1973 and 1979.

In the 1980s, the most prominent economic themes were several: the lagging growth in productivity discussed in Chapter 21; the huge fiscal, or budget, deficit of the federal government, with spending far exceeding tax revenues; and the huge deficit in the current account of the balance of payments, with the net payment of interest and dividends to foreigners far exceeding net exports. Both deficits set new records and became a cause for concern.

This chapter inquires into the causes and consequences of the twin deficits. How might they be related? And are they a genuine cause for alarm?

KEY QUESTIONS

1. What gave rise to the fiscal deficit? And why is it so difficult to reduce?

2. What gave rise to the current-account deficit in the balance of payments? What is the relationship between the fiscal deficit and the current-account deficit? Why is it so difficult to reduce the current-account deficit? Why are protectionist policies aimed at keeping out foreign imports unlikely to reduce the current-account deficit, and why are they likely to have harmful effects?

THE MAGNITUDE OF THE TWO DEFICITS

The combination of the tax and spending policies pursued by a succession of federal governments in the 1980s was extraordinary. Government spending rose during the 1980s from 21.3 percent of GDP in 1981 to 23.1 percent of GDP in 1991. But taxes failed to rise to match this boost in spending and, as a result, the government had to borrow increasingly large sums of money. While taxes were 17 percent of GDP in 1981, by 1991 they had risen only to 18.4 percent of GDP, far less than was required to finance expenditures. The annual deficit, that is, the amount by which expenditures exceeded tax revenues, was enormous, whether measured in real terms, as a ratio of GDP, or as a percentage of government expenditures.[1] The total federal debt, which is the accumulated sum of the deficits, was also huge, no matter how it was measured.

Figures 22.1 and 22.2 show this impressive increase in deficit and debt. Figure 22.1, which expresses the annual budget deficit, makes clear why there is concern about the deficit: it skyrocketed in the 1980s and early 1990s. Figure 22.2 shows how the debt measured in real dollars has varied for most of the postwar period. Much of World War II was financed by borrowing. By the late 1940s, the size of the debt began to fall and continued to do so for most of the 1950s. The size of the real debt then seemed to stabilize until the late 1970s, when it began to increase rapidly. What was remarkable about the deficits of the 1980s was that they occurred in peacetime, and indeed in a period in which the economy was experiencing relative prosperity. Large deficits had previously only arisen in times of war and depression. The federal debt as a percentage of GDP

[1] Chapter 14 noted two other ways of measuring the deficit that make the *change* in the deficit appear to be even more dramatic. One measure is defined as the difference between the real value of the outstanding deficit at the beginning of the year and at the end; it takes account of the change in the real value of the outstanding debt as a result of inflation. The other, the full-employment deficit, takes account of the level of economic activity in the economy; that is, it asks what the actual deficit would have been had the economy been operating at full employment.

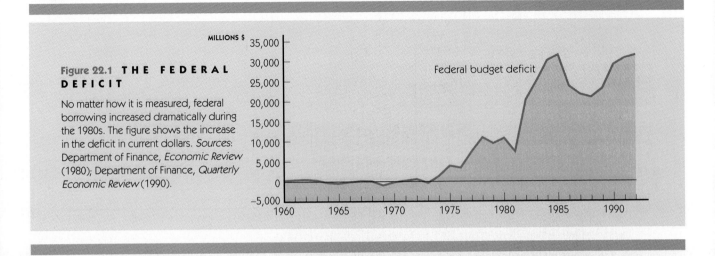

Figure 22.1 THE FEDERAL DEFICIT

No matter how it is measured, federal borrowing increased dramatically during the 1980s. The figure shows the increase in the deficit in current dollars. *Sources*: Department of Finance, *Economic Review* (1980); Department of Finance, *Quarterly Economic Review* (1990).

rose from about 18 percent in 1974–1975, which was the postwar low, to a record high of almost 60 percent by 1992.

The deficit in the current account of the balance of payments rose to prominence in the latter half of the 1980s, roughly at the same time as the budget deficit. The current account includes the net exports of merchandise and of services, and the net inflow of investment income and transfers. The current account was on average in balance until 1985. Surpluses on the merchandise trade account tended to offset the combined deficits in services trade and investment income. A modest current-account surplus of $1.7 billion in 1984 turned into a modest deficit of $3 billion in 1985, and then exploded to a deficit of over $11 billion in 1986. The deficit then almost tripled by 1991. This happened despite a surge in the merchandise trade surplus from $7 billion in 1982

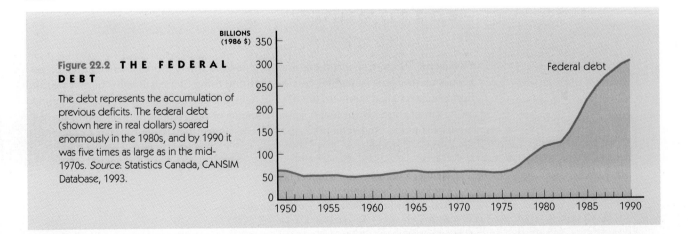

Figure 22.2 THE FEDERAL DEBT

The debt represents the accumulation of previous deficits. The federal debt (shown here in real dollars) soared enormously in the 1980s, and by 1990 it was five times as large as in the mid-1970s. *Source*: Statistics Canada, CANSIM Database, 1993.

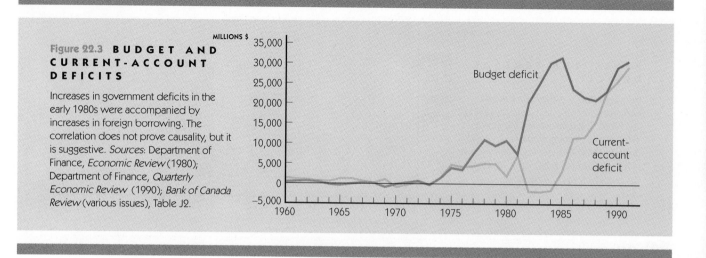

Figure 22.3 BUDGET AND CURRENT-ACCOUNT DEFICITS

Increases in government deficits in the early 1980s were accompanied by increases in foreign borrowing. The correlation does not prove causality, but it is suggestive. *Sources*: Department of Finance, *Economic Review* (1980); Department of Finance, *Quarterly Economic Review* (1990); Bank of Canada Review (various issues), Table J2.

to $11 billion in 1990. The deficit in services trade increased from over $4 billion in 1984 to almost $9 billion in 1990. More importantly, the outflow of net investment income, mostly interest and dividend payments, rose from $13 billion in 1984 to about $24 billion in 1990. Figure 22.3 depicts graphically the dramatic rise in the current-account deficit in the 1980s.

Figure 22.3 also shows the fiscal deficit. We can see that both deficits increased during the 1980s, with the current-account deficit following the fiscal deficit. This is no accident; the fiscal deficit and the current-account deficit are in fact closely related.

THE BURDEN OF GOVERNMENT BORROWING

During the 1980s, Canadians consistently rated the federal budget deficit as the biggest economic problem facing the country. For one thing, deficits involve borrowing, and borrowing has a bad name. In the Middle Ages, the payment of interest was condemned as the sin of usury. Even today, some segments of the Islamic religion forbid the payment of interest. And remember the fatherly advice that Polonius gives to Laertes in Shakespeare's *Hamlet*:

> Neither a borrower nor a lender be;
> For loan oft loses both itself and friend,
> And borrowing dulls the edge of husbandry.

Economists have traditionally argued that government borrowing, just like individual borrowing, makes sense or does not make sense according to the purpose for which the money is used. It makes some sense to borrow to buy a house that you will live in for many years or a car that you will drive for a few years. In that way, you spread out paying for the item as you use it. It makes economic sense to borrow money for an educational degree that will lead to a higher-paying job in the future. But if you are paying this year for the vacation that you took two years ago, maybe you should think about chopping up your credit cards!

Countries are in a similar situation. Borrowing to finance a road or a school or an industrial project that will be used for many years may be quite appropriate. Borrowing to pay for projects that are never completed (or perhaps are never even started) or borrowing to finance this year's government salaries poses real problems. Over time, many governments have taken one more debt than they could comfortably pay off. Many countries have had to raise taxes sharply and reduce their standard of living to pay off their debts. Others have simply failed to repay, jeopardizing their ability to borrow in the future. Mexico, Brazil, Argentina, the Philippines, and several other countries faced this harsh choice in the 1980s.

How Future Generations Are Affected by the Deficits

Government debt does differ from private debt in some ways. A child generally has no legal obligation to repay the debts of a parent, but the obligation to repay government debt rests on everyone in the country, including future generations. There are three distinct ways that the debt produced by federal fiscal deficits imposes a burden on future generations.

DIRECT SHIFTING

First, when resources are devoted to public expenditures (to fight a war, for example), resources have to be diverted away from other uses, from private consumption in particular. The question is, whose private consumption is reduced? By borrowing, the government places the burden of this reduced consumption on future generations. The Canadian government partly financed World War II by borrowing rather than raising taxes. Though the resources were indeed spent during the war, those who had to forgo consumption to pay the bill were not (only) those working at that time.

Typically, governments borrow by issuing bonds. Suppose that the government decides to issue bonds to finance a war and these bonds are purchased by forty-year-old workers. Thirty years later, as these forty-year-olds retire, the government decides to pay off the bonds by raising taxes on those who are then in the labour force. In effect, the government is transferring funds from these younger workers to those who *were* the workers during the war, who are now seventy and retired. Thus, part of the cost of the war is borne by the generation who entered the work force after the war. The lifetime consumption of the original forty-year-olds is little affected. They might otherwise have put their savings into stocks or bonds issued by firms; the war (to the extent it is financed by debt, or bonds) affects the form of their savings, but not the total amount they have to spend over their lifetime.

DECLINE IN INVESTMENT

The burden of government debt also affects future generations by leading to a decline in investment in capital goods. As we have just seen, when the government borrows, the current generation puts their savings into government bonds rather than leaving the funds available for private companies to borrow for productive investments. In effect, the government borrowing crowds out private investment (see Chapter 14). If the government invests the money itself (perhaps in schools, research and development activities, or highways and bridges), then the government debt may not affect future levels of economic output. However, if the government spends or invests the money in ill-conceived projects, the result will be less human and physical capital in the economy, which in turn means that output and wages in future years will be lower than they might otherwise have been.

FOREIGN INDEBTEDNESS

In Chapter 14, we saw that as the world economy has become more open, concerns about government borrowing crowding out investment have become less acute. Rather than reducing investment, the government simply borrows from abroad. Instead of selling bonds to Canadian citizens, the government has increasingly financed its budget deficits by selling some of them to foreign investors. When it comes time to repay these bonds, the buying power will be transferred out of the country. An ever-increasing fraction of national output will have to be sent overseas to pay interest on what is owed to foreigners. The net income levels, what is left over after paying foreigners interest on their capital, of future generations will be lower.

If we look at who has bought the additional bonds the government has been issuing in recent years, we note that some but not all of the higher deficit has been financed by foreigners. But the consequences are equally or even more disturbing if they do not *directly* finance the deficit. The government can increase foreign debt directly by borrowing directly from abroad, or it can increase foreign debt indirectly by sopping up available domestic savings so that Canadians no longer have the money to invest in Canadian businesses and foreigners come in to fill the gap. Some economists have described the latter situation by saying that government borrowing can "crowd in" foreign investment. In either case, whether the foreigners' funds have gone directly to finance the debt or have gone to buy Canadian stocks and real estate, releasing funds for Canadians to finance the deficit, the aggregate indebtedness of the country to foreigners has increased. Canadians, in total, will be making payments to foreigners for some time, reducing future standards of living.

THE "DEBT DOES NOT MATTER BECAUSE WE OWE IT TO OURSELVES" ARGUMENT

It used to be argued that the fiscal deficit does not matter because we simply owe the money to ourselves. The budget deficit was compared to the effect of one brother borrowing from another on the total welfare of the family. One member of the family may be better off, another worse off, but the indebtedness does not really matter much to the family as a whole. Financing government expenditures by debt, it was argued, clearly could lead to a transfer of resources between generations, but this transfer would still keep all the buying power in the hands of Canadian citizens.

We now recognize that this argument is wrong on two counts. First, even if we owe the money to ourselves, the debt affects investment and thus future wages and productivity, as noted. And second, we do not in fact owe the money to ourselves: Canada is borrowing abroad. It is becoming more indebted to foreigners. The consequences of the country spending beyond its means are no different from those of a family spending beyond its means: eventually it has to pay the price of the consumption binge. In the case of a national consumption binge, it is future generations that may have to pay the price.

CONSEQUENCES OF GOVERNMENT FISCAL DEFICITS

1. Some of the burden of current expenditures is shifted to future generations directly.

2. Issuing bonds may decrease investment and thus make future generations worse off indirectly.

3. Foreign indebtedness may increase, reducing future standards of living.

THE SOURCE OF THE GROWING BUDGET DEFICIT

Isolating the cause of the explosive increase in the budget deficits during the 1980s and early 1990s is a tricky business, because most analysts have an axe to grind. If people believe that taxes should be raised to reduce the budget deficit, they tend to argue that the failure to raise taxes created the deficit. If they believe social spending should be cut to reduce the deficit, they tend to emphasize how increases in some social programs caused the deficit to occur. But there is no reason why the solutions to the deficit problem should match up neatly with the causes. After all, the causes are rooted in the political and economic climate of the late 1970s and early 1980s, but the solutions will have to be rooted in the political and economic climate of the 1990s and the twenty-first century.

CHANGES LEADING TO THE HIGHER DEFICIT

One way of posing the question of what caused the budget deficit is to ask, what changed between the 1970s (and earlier decades) and the 1980s? There are four main answers to this question.

HIGHER PAYMENTS TO THE ELDERLY

As the number of elderly people in Canada has grown, federal expenditures on programs like Old Age Security and the Guaranteed Income Supplement have expanded rapidly as well. While the proportion of the federal budget devoted to payments to the elderly has stayed around 12 percent since the late 1970s, as a proportion of GDP they have risen from 2.5 percent in 1981 to over 2.7 percent a decade later. Given the gradual aging of the population, this proportion will increase even further in the 1990s since all persons sixty-five years of age and over have access to these programs.

HIGHER SPENDING ON UNEMPLOYMENT INSURANCE BENEFITS

As discussed in Chapter 11, UI was liberalized considerably in 1970. Coverage was expanded to a wide variety of persons, and eligibility requirements for receiving benefits were eased. As long as unemployment rates remained relatively low, as they did in the 1970s, the costs of the program were contained. With the dramatic rise of unemployment rates into double digit figures in the 1980s, however, expenditures on UI benefits escalated rapidly, more than tripling between 1982 and 1992. As a proportion of the federal budget, UI payments almost doubled between these two years. The Mulroney government was finally forced to act by announcing in early 1993 that persons who voluntarily left their jobs would no longer be eligible to receive UI benefits.

HIGHER TRANSFERS TO THE PROVINCES

Transfers to the provinces have always been an important component of federal expenditures. Traditionally, the federal government has made equalizing transfers to the less well-off provinces (essentially all except Alberta, British Columbia, and Ontario). But with the implementation of major shared-cost programs in the areas of health, welfare, and postsecondary education in the 1950s and 1960s, the importance of transfers to the provinces as a federal budgetary expense increased markedly. In the early 1950s, federal transfers to the provinces amounted to under 1.5 percent of GDP. This rose to 3.2 percent by the end of the 1960s, and to over 4 percent by the beginning of the 1980s. It remained at those levels for most of the decade, despite the fact that the federal government periodically introduced measures to contain it.

HIGHER INTEREST PAYMENTS

Like any other borrower, the federal government has to pay interest. During the 1970s, federal government interest payments were about 1.5 percent of GDP (or 12 percent of government expenditures). From 1983 to 1990, however, interest payments exceeded 4.5 percent of GDP. By 1991, they had reached 6.3 percent of GDP and made up over a third of federal government expenditures.

GOVERNMENT POLICY RESPONSES

Federal tax receipts as a percentage of GDP have been increasing slightly since 1981, rising from 14.6 percent of GDP in that year to 16.7 percent at the start of the 1990s, but there is strong political resistance against raising taxes sharply. Indeed, the Conservative government elected in 1988 took the view that the deficit should largely be re-

CLOSE-UP: MEASURING THE BUDGET DEFICIT

There is no doubt that the deficits in the 1980s and early 1990s are huge, though exactly how huge is a matter of some dispute. The official federal deficit reached a peak of 8.7 percent of GDP in 1984–1985 ($38.5 billion), and then began to decline over the latter part of the 1980s. It has been increasing rapidly since 1989–1990. By 1992–1993, the official federal budget deficit reached $35.5 billion, or 6.4 percent of GDP.

One of the problems in evaluating the deficit is that there are a variety of ways of measuring it. One could measure the federal government's deficit alone, or the deficit of the consolidated government sector, which includes the federal, provincial, municipal, and hospital sectors. Regardless of the level of the consolidation, there are numerous bases for deficit measurement.

The measure used by the federal government and reported in its budget is calculated on a "public-accounts" basis. Its purpose is to provide Parliament with information on the government's tax and expenditure transactions. It excludes non-budgetary items, such as loans and advances by the government, and transactions on special accounts like the Canada Pension Plan and the Unemployment Insurance account.

Adding the non-budgetary items to the public-accounts deficit yields the "financial-requirements" deficit, which measures the amount that the government must borrow by selling bonds. Since receipts have outweighed payments on these items, the financial-requirements deficit is smaller than the reported deficit. Thus, in 1984–1985, the financial-requirements deficit was only $23 billion compared with the reported deficit of $38.5 billion. By 1992–1993, the financial-requirements deficit was $31.8 billion for 1991–1992 compared with a reported deficit of $34.6 billion.

Accounting for the effects of inflation on the value of the government's debt will also reduce the value of the deficit. The existence of inflation means that the real value of outstanding debt is smaller. Since the government is a net debtor, inflation makes the government better off in the sense that the real value of its liabilities are less, and the amount of resources that must be transferred from the private sector in the future to repay the debt is reduced. Economists refer to this as an "inflation tax." It has been estimated that inflation adjustment would reduce the federal deficit by about one-half in the mid-1980s.

Other adjustments are possible. For example, in times of high unemployment, the reported deficit is likely to be much higher than when there is full employment. The so-called full-employment deficit, which we encountered in Chapter 14, was as much as $5 billion less than the actual deficit in the early 1980s. Also, some part of government expenditures represents net investment, including investment in human capital, and this is equivalent to reducing the net debt of the government. Making adjustments for these sorts of things could actually turn a reported deficit into a surplus!

The budget deficit may look worse than it really is. Nonetheless, the numbers are still large and troublesome. The losses from having the economy run below full employment are enormous. These are real costs, and they bring real suffering. The existence of a large deficit constrains the ability of the government to use fiscal policy to reduce unemployment.

Sources: N. Bruce and D. Purvis, *Evaluating the Deficit: The Case for Budget Cuts* (Toronto: C.D. Howe Institute, 1984); *The Deficit in Perspective* (Ottawa: Department of Finance, April 1983).

duced by using expenditure reductions rather than tax increases. Furthermore, it ruled out transfers to persons (which comprise over one-third of program spending) as an instrument as well. This left expenditures on goods and services, transfers to businesses, and transfers to the provinces as the main potential sources of expenditure reduction. Expenditures on all three of these categories fell as a percent of GDP between 1985 and 1992—goods and services from 0.6 to 0.4 percent, transfers to business from 2.4 to 1.3 percent, and transfers to the provinces from 4.5 percent to 4.0 percent. The result was that federal government program expenditures (expenditures net of interest on the public debt) actually fell from 19.6 percent of GDP in 1985 to 16.0 percent by the end of the decade.

The efforts to reduce the government deficit succeeded in reducing program expenditures below tax revenues; the entire deficit could be accounted for by interest on the debt. But the deficit control program suffered a setback with the recession of 1991, which reduced government revenues and increased public expenditures for such programs as Unemployment Insurance; in fact, a new record for the deficit was set. But even without the recession, the slightly higher taxes and decreased program spending would not have helped enough to bring the government budget into balance. Unless something dramatic happens, large deficits loom for the foreseeable future.

Another source of budget deficit problems are the deficits of the provinces and their municipalities. Just as the federal deficit has been increasing since the early 1980s, so have the deficits of the provinces. For example, in 1982, the combined deficit of all provinces and their municipalities stood at $1.3 billion. By 1992, it had risen to over $15 billion, about half the federal deficit. Given that provincial expenditure responsibilities in the areas of health and education are among the most rapidly growing areas, the pressures on the expenditure side are likely to continue for some time. As well, the use of reductions in transfers to the provinces as a way of fighting the federal deficit is likely simply to transfer the federal deficit problem to the provinces. The provinces may be no better able to bring these deficits under control than the federal government.

DEALING WITH THE BUDGET DEFICIT

During the 1960s and 1970s, most economists focused their attention on the trade-off between unemployment and inflation as reflected in the Phillips curve. At the time, many would have predicted that if the federal government chose to run extraordinarily large budget deficits, the result would be higher employment (if only in the short run) followed by higher inflation. In effect, the huge deficits would shift the aggregate demand curve to the point where it intersected the aggregate supply curve on the steep upward-sloping portion, illustrated in Figure 22.4A. The rightward shift in the aggregate demand curve from AD_0 to AD_1 would result in a significant increase in the equilibrium price level, and many economists would have predicted that this would set off an inflationary spiral.

As the experience of the 1980s has made clear, that view of government budget deficits ignored the fact that the economy was largely open to foreign capital and foreign goods. In the 1980s, the economy was able to consume more without moving past the

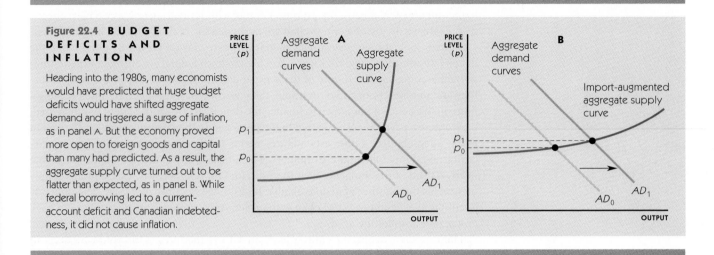

Figure 22.4 BUDGET DEFICITS AND INFLATION

Heading into the 1980s, many economists would have predicted that huge budget deficits would have shifted aggregate demand and triggered a surge of inflation, as in panel A. But the economy proved more open to foreign goods and capital than many had predicted. As a result, the aggregate supply curve turned out to be flatter than expected, as in panel B. While federal borrowing led to a current-account deficit and Canadian indebtedness, it did not cause inflation.

full-employment portion of the aggregate supply curve to where inflation would be increasing sharply. Thus, an open economy appears more able to absorb an increase in aggregate demand without inducing inflation. In effect, the import-augmented aggregate supply curve—the total supply of goods available to the economy, produced both at home and abroad—is relatively flat, as illustrated in panel B. Therefore, the shift in the aggregate demand curve need not give rise to much inflationary pressure.

However, avoiding one trade-off led to another in the 1980s. The accelerating inflow of foreign capital and the Canadian status as a debtor nation means that a share of Canadian output must be repaid to foreign investors, with interest. In effect, the money borrowed from abroad during the 1980s was not invested in projects that will yield greater economic growth in the future, but rather went to finance increased government expenditures on social programs, unemployment insurance, and subsidies to businesses while keeping tax burdens largely unchanged. As desirable as any of these expenditures may have been, they are not like expenditures on new factories: they do not themselves generate the returns that will pay back these loans with interest.

This means that it will not be possible to repay the foreign borrowing with a portion of the fruits of economic growth; instead, repayment will require Canadians to have a lower standard of living than they otherwise would have. Even if the standard of living is only a few tenths of a percent lower, that accumulates in a generation into a heavy burden. The fact that for a decade, beginning around 1973, real wages did not rise at all, and even since then real wages have increased but slowly, has shaken the long-standing confidence that come what may, incomes and living standards will always be rising. If an increasing proportion of these slowly rising incomes has to go abroad to repay the debts of the 1980s and 1990s, then living standards may indeed have to fall.

POLICY OPTIONS

When the Mulroney government ran for re-election in 1988, it did so partly on a promise to eliminate the fiscal deficit over a period of time. Despite reducing program expenditures in everything from defence to family allowances, and imposing surtaxes on higher-income Canadians, the promise has met with limited success as we have already seen. Here we discuss the options that are now open for dealing with the budget deficit.

A closer look at how government spends its money makes clear why eliminating the deficit has proved so difficult. Figure 22.5 breaks down federal government expenditures into different categories. Some of these expenditures cannot be cut in the short run—they are nondiscretionary. For example, the government must meet the interest obligations on the bonds it has issued to finance the deficit; as government debt has increased, these interest payments have soared to the point where they now account for 28 percent of the federal budget. Other expenditures are for entitlement programs like Old Age Security and Unemployment Insurance. These social insurance programs constitute nearly a third of the budget. Given the rules for Old Age Security, expenditures simply increase as the number of people eligible for Old Age Security increases. The only way to cut these expenditures is to change the rules. And no one seems to want to cut back on the programs for the aged.

There is some scope for cutting back on UI expenditures. This could be done in a variety of ways, such as reducing the size of the benefit or the length of the period over which payments are made; relating benefits more closely to some measure of need, such as family income; tightening up eligibility requirements, as the Mulroney government did by making persons ineligible who quit voluntarily, or increasing the number of working weeks required before a worker becomes eligible; or making the program more like a true insurance scheme by introducing experience rating into the premiums (a firm's premiums would vary according to its track record with layoffs). Such savings will only make a small dent in the deficit as long as unemployment rates remain high. Furthermore, it is very difficult politically to implement such changes. All of the above-mentioned remedies have been advocated at one time or an-

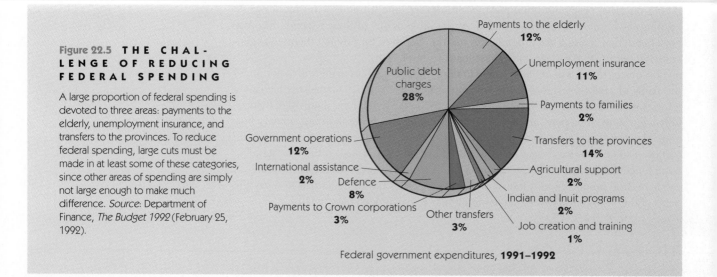

Figure 22.5 THE CHALLENGE OF REDUCING FEDERAL SPENDING

A large proportion of federal spending is devoted to three areas: payments to the elderly, unemployment insurance, and transfers to the provinces. To reduce federal spending, large cuts must be made in at least some of these categories, since other areas of spending are simply not large enough to make much difference. *Source*: Department of Finance, *The Budget 1992* (February 25, 1992).

Payments to the elderly
12%

Unemployment insurance
11%

Public debt charges
28%

Payments to families
2%

Transfers to the provinces
14%

Government operations
12%

Agricultural support
2%

International assistance
2%

Indian and Inuit programs
2%

Defence
8%

Payments to Crown corporations
3%

Other transfers
3%

Job creation and training
1%

Federal government expenditures, **1991–1992**

other in the past, yet few have been acted on. Not only that, but tightening up UI might only cause persons to go on welfare instead of unemployment insurance. In this case, the cost will simply be shifted from the federal government to the provinces. The overall public-sector budget deficit will hardly be affected.

Nor is there much more scope for cutting back on expenditures on goods and services. Government operations have been pared to the bone. The major category of these expenditures is for defence, and these expenditures have already been cut drastically at a time when the Canadian Armed Forces are being called upon to engage in an increasing number of international peacekeeping missions.

The largest single component of federal government program expenditures is for transfer payments to the provinces. This category has already been asked to bear a disproportionate share of the costs of deficit reduction. Moreover, in a sense, such reductions by themselves do nothing to address the public-sector deficit problem; they simply transfer it from the federal government to the provinces. This will only help solve the problem if the provinces are better able to find ways to cut expenditures than the federal government. Given that the most rapidly growing categories of expenditures, namely health and education, are at the provincial level, this may be possible. So far, however, the provinces have been unable to contain their expenditures either.

Though the Mulroney government pledged to attack the deficit largely on the expenditure side of the budget, and by exempting transfer payments as well, the circumstances are now such that tax increases and transfer reductions cannot be ruled out as alternative ways of reducing the federal deficit. The government now has in place a potentially lucrative source of tax revenues in the GST, a tax that has been referred to as a "cash cow." Despite a pledge to the contrary, it will be very tempting to milk it as a revenue-raising device for deficit-reduction purposes. And the government has already shown its willingness to use at least one form of transfer payment, unemployment insurance. Those who see the budget deficit as a serious threat to Canada's long-run economic strength want more of both: more temporary tax increases and more cutbacks in transfer programs. Without these, there seems to be no possibility of making serious inroads into a problem that has plagued the country for more than a decade.

REDUCING THE BUDGET DEFICIT

Basic problem: large fraction of total expenditures that are nondiscretionary, such as interest payments

Three major alternatives

1. Increase taxes.

2. Reduce transfer payments.

3. Contain costs of other government programs.

THE GROWTH OF THE CURRENT-ACCOUNT DEFICIT

A deficit (or surplus) on the current account is the aggregate of a variety of types of transactions between Canadians and foreigners. One component is the merchandise trade balance, that is, the difference between imports and exports of goods. Another is the net import of services, including such things as travel, insurance, and transportation costs. Yet another is the balance of investment income, such as interest and dividends, paid to foreigners and received from foreign sources. A final component includes net transfers to and from foreigners. This includes such things as remittances sent home by persons who have immigrated to Canada and inheritances received from or sent abroad. The movements in the components of the current account since 1975 are shown in Figure 22.6. As we have seen in earlier chapters, the merchandise trade balance has typically been in a surplus position, while the services trade and investment-income accounts have been in deficit. But after having risen to record levels in the mid-1980s, the surplus on the merchandise trade account has gradually deteriorated. This deterioration has been matched by a substantial erosion of the services trade account. This account has been in deficit continually for the last two decades, but the deficit has increased at alarming rates since the mid-1980s. The same might be said of the investment-income account.

EXCHANGE RATE EFFECTS

Much of the movement of the merchandise trade account and services trade account can be attributed to movements in the exchange rate. While the Canadian dollar was depreciating in the early 1980s, the overall trade account was improving. Once the

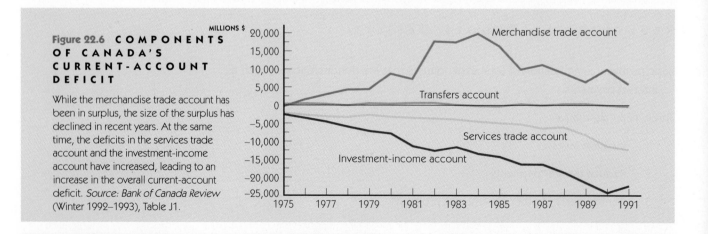

Figure 22.6 COMPONENTS OF CANADA'S CURRENT-ACCOUNT DEFICIT

While the merchandise trade account has been in surplus, the size of the surplus has declined in recent years. At the same time, the deficits in the services trade account and the investment-income account have increased, leading to an increase in the overall current-account deficit. *Source: Bank of Canada Review* (Winter 1992–1993), Table J1.

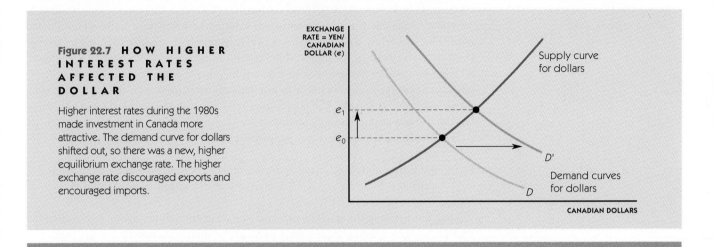

Figure 22.7 HOW HIGHER INTEREST RATES AFFECTED THE DOLLAR

Higher interest rates during the 1980s made investment in Canada more attractive. The demand curve for dollars shifted out, so there was a new, higher equilibrium exchange rate. The higher exchange rate discouraged exports and encouraged imports.

value of the Canadian dollar began to improve in the mid-1980s, both the merchandise trade and the services trade accounts began to deteriorate rapidly. This rapid decline, accompanied by a simultaneous decline in the investment-income balance, has spelled real trouble for the current account.

But why did the dollar appreciate? Largely because of the fact that, to keep inflation in check, the Bank of Canada was implementing a tight monetary policy that kept rates of interest high in Canada compared with abroad, especially compared with those in the United States. Investors base their investment decisions on relative returns. If the returns to investing in Canada rise, relative to returns to investing elsewhere, capital will flow to Canada from foreign investors, and the value of the dollar will rise. In the international capital markets of the modern economy, investors are willing to shift their investments from country to country in response to relatively small changes in returns. Such shifts are particularly attractive if a country with high interest rates also has a stable government. Thus, the relatively small increase in the return to investing in Canada that occurred in the late 1980s induced fairly large capital flows, explaining the change in the value of the dollar and the resulting trade deficit.

Figure 22.7 depicts demand and supply curves for dollars that depend on the exchange rate between dollars and yen. The initial exchange rate is e_0. The shift in the demand curve for dollars, caused by foreigners wishing to invest in Canada, results in the exchange rate rising to e_1. The dollar is worth more yen. This means that a Japanese firm wanting to buy, say, a computer in Canada for $10,000 must give up more yen. In terms of the foreign country's currency, the computer is more expensive. Not surprisingly, the demand for Canadian products decreases.

CAPITAL FLOWS

The fact that capital flows to Canada accompanied the current-account deficit is no accident or coincidence; in fact, it is a matter of definition. Let's trace what happens when a Canadian decides to buy a German car. To buy the car, he needs German marks. So he goes to a German bank and exchanges his dollars for marks. But the bank is not simply going to hold those dollars. It will eventually sell them, either to someone wanting to purchase Canadian goods or to someone wanting to invest in a dollar-denominated asset. The same story will apply when Canadians purchase services supplied by foreign firms or pay interest or dividends to foreigners. Thus, every dollar paid to a foreigner, whether for goods, services, or as investment income, eventually comes back, either to pay Canadians for similar items or to purchase an investment in Canada. By the same token, every dollar used by Canadians to purchase investments abroad must also come back to Canada as purchases by foreigners.

We can express this relation by a simple equation:

$$\text{Current payments by Canadians} = \text{current receipts by Canadians} + \text{net foreign investment in Canada, or net capital flows.}$$

If foreigners invest nothing in Canada and vice versa, then this equation tells us that the current account must balance. But if some of the money earned by foreign producers goes to buy investments in Canada, then the equation shows that the value of Canadian purchases from abroad will exceed the value of Canadian receipts. This is by definition a current-account deficit. The magnitude of the deficit will be exactly equal to the amount invested in Canada. A current-account deficit and an inflow of foreign capital are really two ways of saying the same thing. This can be put another way: the only way that Canadian consumers and businesses can import more from abroad than they export abroad is if foreigners are willing to make up the difference by lending to or investing in Canada.

This international borrowing and lending often takes place through financial intermediaries. For example, Toyota might accept payment for its cars in dollars, knowing that a Japanese businessman who is interested in buying an apartment building in Vancouver, an office building in Toronto, shares in a Canadian company, or an Ontario government bond is willing to trade his yen to Toyota for Toyota's dollars. Although the two might make the exchange directly, it is more likely that Toyota will exchange its dollars for yen at the bank (or equivalently, Toyota might insist on being paid in yen, in which case the Canadian buyer would take her dollars to the bank to buy yen) and that the Japanese businessman will go to the same bank and exchange his yen for Toyota's dollars. And then the businessman will return his dollars to Canada as he makes his investment there.

In a world of multilateral trade, the accounts between any particular company or country and Canada do not have to balance. Toyota may sell the dollars it earns, not to a Japanese businessman, but to a German or French investor. But what must be true for any country is that the current-account deficit equals capital inflows. What are important are *net* capital inflows, the difference between what foreigners invest in Canada and what Canadians invest abroad. This is the capital-account balance. Moreover, the basic balance-of-payments identity can be expressed as follows:

$$\text{current-account deficit} = \text{capital-account surplus.}[2]$$

---

[2] This equation is exactly the same as the equation given earlier; simply subtract current receipts by Canadians from both sides of the earlier equation.

Capital flows are a shorthand way of summarizing all the borrowing and lending that goes on. Canadian firms invest in Japan; Japanese firms invest in Canada. To calculate the net capital flows between Canada and Japan, we add up all the dollars lent by Japan to Canada, all the investment by Japan in Canada, all the Japanese purchases of bonds, and the increase in Japanese holdings of Canadian dollars, and then subtract the corresponding numbers on the Canadian side.

As noted earlier, since we live in a world of multilateral trade, a Canadian current-account deficit with Japan does not necessarily have to equal capital inflows from Japan. Assume Japan and the United States are in current-account balance and Canada and the United States are in current-account balance, but Japanese investors like to put their money into the United States and Americans like to invest in Canada. The United States has zero net capital inflows, with a positive capital flow from Japan offset by a capital flow to Canada. In this situation, the Canadian current-account deficit with Japan is offset by a capital flow from the United States.

The basic identity could describe a capital outflow as well as a capital inflow. For example, in the 1950s, the United States had a substantial trade surplus, as the country exported more than it imported. This was offset by a capital outflow from the United States. The United States has since gone into a current-account deficit position and is a net capital importer. Japan is now in a situation analogous to that of the United States in the 1950s.

Canada has typically been a net capital importer, first from Great Britain, then from the United States, and more recently also from Japan and Hong Kong. This in itself has implications for the current account. Capital inflows today give rise to interest and dividend payments in the future. Thus, the investment-income portion of the current account is in a deficit position. The extent of the deficit in investment income depends upon whether foreign asset owners "repatriate" their capital income or reinvest it in Canada. If the foreign capital inflow takes the form of direct investment by foreign firms operating in Canada, the profit earned from such investments may simply be retained and reinvested in Canada, in which case they do not give rise to investment income outflows. Much investment by foreign firms in Canada takes the form of retained earnings. But if the capital inflow takes the form of a purchase of interest-bearing assets such as bonds, the interest earned is more likely to be repatriated when received. In fact, almost all of the deterioration of the investment-account balance since the mid-1980s can be attributed to an increase in interest payments to foreigners, especially interest accruing on debt issued by the government to finance its deficit. We return to this relationship between the budget deficit and the current-account deficit below.

The basic balance-of-payments identity is *only* an identity: it only provides a framework for looking for an explanation. It says that if we observe a change in one part of the identity, we will always see corresponding changes in some other part. But the identity alone does not allow us to differentiate between explanations. It does not explain whether the Canadian current-account deficit was caused by an increase in the demand for imports, with foreign firms accommodating that increase by lending Canadians the money to buy those goods; whether the foreign taste for Canadian exports suddenly declined; or whether there was an increase in the amount foreigners wanted to invest in Canada, which led to an exchange rate (dollar) appreciation, which in turn resulted in the current-account deficit. To determine what actually happened in the late 1980s, it is necessary to look more closely at how the deficits developed.

While it is theoretically possible that the current-account deficits developed because

Close-up: The Canadian Dollar and the Current-Account Deficit with the United States

The United States is by far Canada's largest trading partner; over three-quarters of our trade is with Americans. Because such a large volume of both our merchandise and non-merchandise (services) trade is with the United States, our current account is greatly influenced by the Canada-U.S. exchange rate. Indeed, we are accustomed to thinking of the value of our dollars in terms of U.S. dollars. In the same way, the Irish relate the value of their pound to the British pound, and the Danes their kroner to the German mark

Generally one expects a currency depreciation to result in an improvement in the current account as imports fall and exports rise, and vice versa for an appreciation. And indeed, this pattern seems to have been borne out in our transactions with the United States during the 1980s. During the first half of the decade, the Canadian dollar depreciated against the U.S. dollar, and our current account with the United States went from a deficit of $7.9 billion in 1980 to a surplus of $8.3 billion in

1985. Then, while the Canadian dollar appreciated by about 20 percent in the late 1980s, the current account fell to a deficit of $2.7 billion with the United States by 1990.

But focusing on movements in the overall current account turns out to be a bit misleading since the components of this account behaved in somewhat contradictory ways. For example, while the merchandise trade account with the United States improved in the early 1980s with the depreciation of the currency, it was virtually the same in 1990 as in 1986 despite the appreciation of the Canadian dollar. The non-merchandise account, on the other hand, declined rapidly in the late 1980s, accounting for the decline in the overall current account. How do we explain this anomalous behaviour in the second half of the decade?

One explanation for the fact that the merchandise trade account failed to deteriorate with the currency appreciation of 1986–1991 emphasizes lags in the response of exporters and importers, or

a low short-run elasticity of demand for exports and imports. Most international trade is in manufactured goods, which differ in characteristics and qualities. A Citroën is not just like a Chevy, and a British Shetland sweater is different from a Bretton sweater. Markets for these goods have to be cultivated, and this takes time. When the Canadian dollar rose, Canadian consumers did not immediately shift to foreign goods, nor did foreign buyers shift away from Canadian goods. Many exports are intermediate goods that are used to produce final goods. These intermediate goods must be manufactured to exact specifications, and it takes time to find alternative sources of supply. Even in the case of goods like oil and wheat, much trade occurs under long-term contracts, slowing down the process of adjustment.

In this view, then, had the dollar not appreciated, the current-account deficit would have improved even more as these adjustments continued. The appreciation of the dollar prevented any additional improvement. Support for the importance of the lag in adjustment may be found by noting that the merchandise trade account with the United States began to deteriorate sharply in the early 1990s, five years after the currency began appreciating.

To explain the decline in the non-merchandise trade account from 1986 to 1990, we must turn to the role of the national income identity as a determinant of exchange rates. If Canada as a whole saves less and spends more—whether because of higher government borrowing or a low level of individual saving—then the nation must borrow from abroad. From this point of view, exchange rates will adjust to reflect the underlying balance between sectional savings and investment. The capital inflow, which causes the exchange rate to appreciate, will itself induce a deterioration of the non-merchandise account. Payments of interest and dividends to foreigners will rise to compensate them for the capital they have lent to Canada. This is precisely what happened in the late 1980s as Canadian borrowing, especially by the government, rose rapidly and the Canadian dollar appreciated.

of a substantial shift in the Canadian demand curve for imports or a shift in the foreign demand curve for Canadian exports, the much likelier reason is higher interest rates in Canada, which attracted foreign investment, raised the value of the dollar, and thus made imports appear cheaper and exports more expensive. That is, as Figure 22.7 showed, there was a shift in the demand for dollars, which led to an appreciation of the dollar; this was caused not by a change in tastes but by a demand for funds to invest in Canada.

Foreigners wanted to invest in Canada because the returns to their investments were relatively higher. But the cause of these higher returns does not seem to have been the prosperity of the country. Although Canada was growing faster than most European countries, it was not doing any better than Japan or the United States. Rather, the high interest rate reflected the high demand for borrowed funds in Canada. The demand for borrowing increased sharply in the mid-1980s largely as a result of the increase in federal government borrowing. The one really large change between the 1980s and the preceding years was the federal budget deficits. The fact that the current-account and budget deficits have increased together is no accident: large fiscal deficits lead to higher exchange rates, which lead to current-account deficits. In this sense, the fiscal deficit is responsible for the current-account deficit. We can see this more clearly if we take a closer look at savings and investment in the Canadian economy.

THE SAVINGS-INVESTMENT IDENTITY FOR AN OPEN ECONOMY

In an economy without trade, where government does not borrow or lend, private (household and business) savings must equal private investment, as we learned in Chapter 13. However, in an economy with international borrowing and lending, private savings might be loaned out abroad and foreign savings might be borrowed to finance private investment. Private savings need not equal private borrowing. These considerations lead to an expanded formulation of the savings-investment identity:

$$\begin{matrix} \text{private (household and business) savings} \\ + \text{ capital flows (borrowing) from abroad} \end{matrix} = \begin{matrix} \text{investment in machines and equipment} \\ + \text{ federal budget deficit.} \end{matrix}$$

Private savings and capital flows from abroad can be thought of as the "sources" of funds; and investment and budget deficits can be thought of as the uses of funds. A slightly different approach is to think of the fiscal deficit as dissaving, or negative savings. Just as when a household spends less than its income it is saving, and when it spends more than its income it is dissaving, so too with government. The savings-investment identity can thus be rewritten:

$$\text{private savings} + \text{government savings} + \text{capital flows from abroad} = \text{investment.}$$

In the latter half of the 1970s, gross private savings were about normal at around 21 percent of GDP.[3] Gross private investment was also about normal by historical standards, at about 20 percent of GDP in 1978 and 1979. There was a moderate federal budget deficit matched by a moderate current-account deficit (capital flows from abroad). But then the budget deficits exploded, and their increase meant that at least one of four things had to happen. Either private savings or borrowing from abroad had to increase to provide more money; or either investment or the deficit had to be reduced. This is what the basic identity tells us. The identity does not tell us which of these four possibilities will occur. As it happened, the main factor that adjusted was foreign capital flows.

The savings-investment identity says that if there is an increase in the deficit and if private savings and investment are unchanged, capital flows from abroad must increase and foreigners must end up holding more Canadian assets. But the identity does not specify which assets they will hold. It does *not* say, for example, that the link between the current-account deficit and the fiscal deficit is that foreign investors are buying Canadian government bonds. That is true, but it is only part of the story. Foreign investors may be buying Canadian companies, and Canadians may be holding Canadian government bonds.

---

[3] Remember that gross private savings include not only savings by households but also savings by firms. Household savings were much smaller, in the range of 3 to 6 percent.

REVERSING THE CURRENT-ACCOUNT DEFICIT

Some of the complaints about the current-account deficit are self-interested, coming from producers who are forced to compete with imports and would like protection or from those in the export sector who would like government subsidies. But there is also genuine reason to be concerned that huge current-account deficits are not in the long-run interests of Canada.

WHY THE CURRENT-ACCOUNT DEFICITS ARE A PROBLEM

Throughout its history, Canada has borrowed heavily from abroad. Eventually, however, one would expect that to be reversed. A typical pattern would be: in the early stages of development, countries borrow, use the money to build up their economies, and repay the loans with a portion of their economic gains. More mature economies, on the other hand, typically lend capital.

To some extent this has happened in Canada. For most of the 1980s, direct investment by Canadians abroad has exceeded foreign direct investment in Canada. But this has been more than offset by the rapid escalation of other forms of borrowing from abroad, reflected in the current-account deficit. Just as when the government borrows year after year the cumulative budget deficits lead to a high level of government debt, when the country borrows from abroad year after year, the cumulative current-account deficits (cumulative capital inflows) also lead to a high level of debt to foreigners.

The effect of the large current-account deficits of the 1980s was to cause the level of Canadian indebtedness to foreigners to escalate rapidly. Figure 22.8 shows the extent of

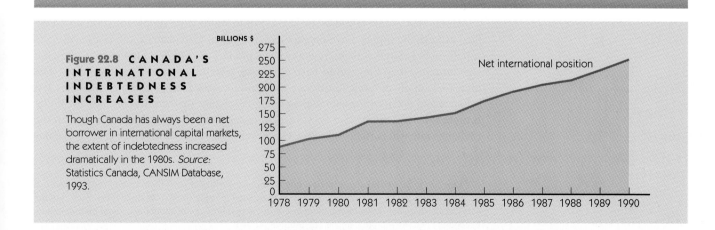

Figure 22.8 CANADA'S INTERNATIONAL INDEBTEDNESS INCREASES

Though Canada has always been a net borrower in international capital markets, the extent of indebtedness increased dramatically in the 1980s. *Source:* Statistics Canada, CANSIM Database, 1993.

BILLIONS $

Net international position

this increase. The level of indebtedness virtually tripled between 1978 and 1990.[4] The effect of this has been to increase the amount of interest and dividend payments to foreigners each year. This is reflected in the rapid deterioration of the investment-income part of the current account.

The consequences for the nation are little different from those you would experience as an individual if you borrowed a large amount from the bank. In the future, unless you used the borrowed funds to make an investment that yielded a return at least equal to the interest you had to pay, you would be unable to consume as much as you would otherwise; your consumption must be less than your income, as you must pay the bank interest as well as the principal. Consider this rough calculation: if the nation's debt to foreign investors reaches $300 billion by the mid-1990s and the average rate of interest is 6 percent, the interest payments alone work out to over $600 for every man, woman, and child in Canada *every year*.

In a world of international trade, the fiscal deficit is a problem because unless private savings increase commensurately or private investment decreases commensurately, it leads to a current-account deficit and foreign borrowing. The current-account deficit in turn means that in the future, the Canadian economy will have to send abroad a part of what it produces at home to pay off this debt.

The balance-of-payments identity and the savings-investment identity provide a framework for thinking about what might be done about the current-account deficit. One policy option is to try to affect trade directly, by stimulating exports or decreasing imports; another option is to try to affect the capital flows, by making capital flows to Canada less attractive. We now take a closer look at these options, to see if either is viable.

TRADE POLICIES

Surely, by subsidizing exports and imposing tariffs on imports, it is possible to increase exports and reduce imports. Isn't that the basic lesson of economics—that markets respond to prices? But this situation is complicated by an important factor: the exchange rate.

Assume that export subsidies are successful in shifting the supply function for Canadian exports; the supply curve for exports shifts out, as Canadian exporters are willing to supply more goods to foreigners at any given price. The exporters then receive more foreign currency than they would have otherwise, which they try to trade for dollars. The increased supply of foreign currency will tend to make foreign currency relatively less valuable and dollars more valuable on foreign exchange markets. But because the dollar is more valuable, the market for Canadian exports will be reduced; the changes in the exchange rate will partially offset the export subsidies. Subsidies do distort the efficiency

---

[4] One has to be careful about interpreting the figures. Critics of such figures point out that many of the assets that Canada owns abroad have greatly increased in value since it obtained those assets, but the data do not adequately reflect these increases. Still, there is little doubt about the general picture—there is a definite deterioration in Canada's investment position.

of the economy. The export industries that are lucky or powerful enough to get government subsidies will be a little better off; the export industries that do not get subsidized will be hurt by the increased exchange rate.

The same story will hold, in reverse, for attempts to restrict imports. The exchange rate will change in a way that offsets at least part of the import restriction.

It may seem paradoxical to say that policies intended to restrict imports or subsidies to encourage exports will be offset by changes in the exchange rate. But remember the lesson of the basic trade identity, which says that capital inflows equal the current-account deficit as a matter of definition. If it proves impossible to reduce Canada's foreign borrowing, since those funds are needed to finance the budget deficit, then it immediately follows from the basic balance-of-payments identity that no measures for promoting exports or reducing imports will be successful in reducing the current-account deficit. If capital flows cannot be changed, then the current-account deficit cannot be changed. Attempts to deal with the goods and services side of international trade while ignoring the capital side are likely to have little effect in reducing the current-account deficit; what they will do is interfere with the efficiency of the economy.

PROTECTIONISM IN NORTH AMERICA

Canada is no stranger to protectionism. Tariffs were used as long ago as the 1870s as an explicit policy to protect manufacturing industries from foreign competition. Since then, they have been supplemented by a variety of other instruments designed to give Canadian firms a leg up on potential foreign competitors in the Canadian market. These include quotas on imports, subsidies and special tax breaks for manufacturing industries, restrictions on foreign investment, and cheap energy pricing. Protectionism was initially directed primarily at the United States, our largest trading partner. Great Britain was spared to some extent by a mutual system of preferential treatment that existed among Commonwealth countries.

This long-standing policy of protectionism against foreign imports has come to be questioned in recent years for a number of reasons. Within Canada, primary producers, especially those in the West, have complained because the tariff served largely to protect manufacturing industries located in central Canada. Thus, they were forced to purchase their machinery and equipment at protected prices rather than importing them from lower-cost sources. As well, although the protective tariff certainly encouraged the growth of a large manufacturing sector, it was argued that the result was a series of manufacturing industries that consisted of too many small-scale firms designed to serve the relatively small domestic market. Studies showed that a more competitive and open environment that forced the manufacturing industries to operate more efficiently and take advantage of larger-scale production could cause GDP to be as much as 10 percent higher.

Finally, and perhaps most influentially, it was argued that Canadian exporters had more to lose than import industries had to gain by a policy of protecting the latter. The reasoning was as follows. Tariffs are largely applied to merchandise imports. But Canada's merchandise trade balance has been in surplus for several years. Not only that, but the merchandise trade balance with the United States has been largely responsible for that. For example, since the mid-1980s, merchandise trade with the United States has shown an average surplus of about $16 billion per year, while that with the rest of the world has been in deficit by about $5 billion per year. Over the same period, the U.S. trade deficit has been increasing at an alarming rate, resulting in soaring protectionist policies in the United States, despite the talk about free trade by the Reagan administration.

The threat of American protectionism against Canadian products was seen by many as more than compensating for any benefits that might accrue to Canadian producers from domestic protectionism. This recognition led the Royal Commission on the Economic Union and Development Prospects for Canada—better known as the Macdonald Royal Commission after its chairman, former Finance Minister Donald Macdonald—to recommend in 1985 a system of free trade with the United States. As we have seen in Chapter 14, this recommendation led to the Canada-U.S. Free Trade Agreement (FTA) being negotiated two years later and signed in 1988.

While the FTA removes more trade barriers between Canada and the United States, a trade deficit of increasing size remains with the rest of the world. Imports from overseas, especially from countries with low wage costs, are seen as taking away jobs from Canadian workers. Not surprisingly, protectionism retains some popular support as a way of dealing with the problem.

Economists have long waged a battle against protectionism on the grounds that (1) such policies do not in general succeed in creating jobs and (2) such policies interfere with the efficiency of the economy; when they do create jobs, they create them at a high cost.

Protectionist policies can ultimately have negative effects on jobs in Canada. When Canada acts to shut out imports from other countries, those other countries often retaliate by shutting out Canadian exports. For example, if Canada limits automobiles and electronics products from Korea, Korea might act to shut out Canadian farm exports. In trying to save jobs in one industry, protectionism often creates a reaction that makes other Canadian workers worse off. Industries (like automobiles) that have strong competition from imports might well benefit from a ban on imports, but industries (like farming) that rely on exports would suffer considerably.

Economists' second objection is that when protectionism does save jobs, the evidence suggests it does so at a high cost. Consider what happened in the automobile industry. Threatened by Japanese imports, North American car producers in 1981 persuaded the Canadian and U.S. governments to negotiate what were called "voluntary export restraints." Under these restraints, the Japanese "voluntarily" agreed to reduce their auto sales in North America (with the knowledge that if they did not agree Canada and the United States would impose them anyway). Shutting out less expensive imports of cars will certainly help workers in the North American automobile industry. But limiting the competition from imports forces Canadian consumers to pay higher prices for a car that would perhaps have been only their second choice. And the reduction in competition means that Canadians pay more for domestic cars as well as imported cars. Import restrictions have imposed costs on consumers that amount to as much as $100,000 or more in higher prices for every job saved in the protected industry.

More generally, protectionism results in the Canadian economy becoming less efficient. There is a loss of gains from trade: less specialization, less ability to take advantage of comparative advantage, and less competition. With less competition, not only can Canadian producers charge higher prices, firms have a reduced incentive to be efficient and become more productive and competitive. In the long run, these factors can also lead to slower growth of productivity. Most economists would argue that the negative effects of trade, such as putting people or businesses out of work, should be countered directly by helping businesses become more productive and helping workers find new jobs, not by trying to freeze the economy in one place.

EXPORT SUBSIDIES

Besides restricting imports, another way of reducing the current-account deficit is to increase exports. Firms in exporting industries often argue that the government should subsidize them, to enable them to sell more abroad. The government does provide direct subsidies for agricultural exports and hidden subsidies, through loan guarantees and favourable credit terms, to a variety of other industries.

But export subsidies suffer from the same problems that protectionist policies do. Changes in the exchange rate reduce their effectiveness. Foreign governments frequently match whatever export subsidies are being offered. Canadian producers thus do not gain at the expense of foreign producers, though more of the subsidized product will be purchased than would have been the case if it were not subsidized. Finally, even when such policies do create jobs, the cost of creating them is extremely high. The whole economy pays a high price for the inefficiencies these policies induce.

Of course, people in the export industry and in industries that compete with imports see things differently. There is little doubt that many individual industries and workers could benefit, at the expense of the rest of the Canadian economy, from export subsidies. Industries asking for protection often talk about the pain they are suffering, but downplay or ignore the costs that protectionism would impose on the rest of the economy. Those in the export industry see the extra profits they obtain if they can sell more exports, possibly with the help of government subsidies, and it is natural for them to feel that it is important to the country that their particular business do well. They too often fail to account for the costs that these subsidies impose on the nation as a whole.

The case for free trade is not that it is a favour Canada does for foreign countries. Trade is not aid; it is not a giveaway. Even from the point of view of Canada's own narrow self-interest, free trade is a favour Canada can do for itself.

CHANGING THE EXCHANGE RATE

There is one other way that the government may attempt to reduce the current-account deficit, a way that does not discriminate against or favour particular industries: it can try to change the exchange rate. If the government can do something that leads to a depreciation of the dollar, imports will be more expensive and foreigners will view Canadian goods as less expensive, so that exports will increase.

Sometimes monetary policy can achieve this effect, at least in the short run. Monetary policy can drive down interest rates, making it less attractive for foreigners to invest in Canada. The demand curve for dollars (to be used to purchase investments in Canada) shifts down, and this in turn leads to a depreciation of the dollar. In the longer run, however, changes in the exchange rate will be related to the magnitude of underlying capital flows, to which we now turn.

WHY TRADE RESTRICTIONS ARE INEFFECTIVE AND UNDESIRABLE

1. The exchange rate adjusts in such a way as to offset the effects of export subsidies and import duties.

2. They may lead to retaliation from other countries, so that Canada loses exports as it reduces imports.

3. They succeed in shutting out particular imports, but the country loses its gains from trade, the ability to take advantage of specialization, comparative advantage, and competition.

4. The insulation of Canadian producers from foreign competition may reduce the efficiency of Canadian firms.

REDUCING CAPITAL FLOWS

If trying to affect imports and exports will not succeed in reducing the current-account deficit, what will? The basic balance-of-payments identity provides another answer: reducing capital flows. The savings-investment identity suggests how this might be done. In an open economy, capital flows equal investment plus the fiscal deficit minus private savings. So to decrease capital flows, it is necessary either to reduce the budget deficit, to increase private savings, or to decrease investment in machines and equipment by Canadian firms. Some of these possibilities are self-evidently bad policy. For example, decreasing investment would have terrible consequences for the growth of the economy. Indeed, an objective of growth-oriented policies is to *increase* the rate of investment.

What about increasing household savings? For savings to be increased, consumption must be reduced. In a sense, this is the nub of the problem: Canada has been living beyond its means.

If it were possible to stimulate household savings, there is general agreement that it would be desirable to do so. Canadian savings rates are lower than those of many other industrialized countries and much lower than Japan's. But as we saw in Chapter 21, experts in savings behaviour are generally pessimistic concerning the government's capacity to stimulate the savings rate in the near future.

Business savings might be increased if after-tax corporate profits were higher. (Indeed, the extra funds would likely stimulate further firm investment as well.) But beyond increasing the general level of economic activity (when the economy is operating at a high level, profits tend to be high), the only way to increase after-tax corporate profits is to lower the tax rate on corporations, and doing so would only add to the federal budget deficit. Thus, while business savings would be increased, government savings would be reduced and the overall picture would remain unchanged.

The only remaining way—the only practical way—to decrease capital flows and reduce the current-account deficit is to reduce the government's fiscal deficit. The twin deficits are indeed intimately interlinked.

REDUCING THE CURRENT-ACCOUNT DEFICIT, USING THE SAVINGS-INVESTMENT IDENTITY

1. Reduce investment.

2. Increase household savings.

3. Increase business savings.

4. Reduce the federal budget deficit.

REVIEW AND PRACTICE

SUMMARY

1. The early 1980s were marked by a surge in the size of federal budget deficits. There appear to be four main causes of the increase: higher unemployment insurance spending, higher spending on support for the elderly, higher transfer payments to the provinces, and higher interest payments.

2. The 1980s were also marked by a large increase in the Canadian current-account deficit, and by a sharp increase in Canadian borrowing from abroad. Since the mid-1980s Canadian net foreign indebtedness has increased rapidly.

3. Government borrowing can be an economic burden for future generations in several ways. First, future generations may have to bear the burden of paying off the borrowing; there is a transfer from one generation to another. Second, government borrowing can crowd out investment, which will reduce future output and wages. Third, when the money is borrowed from foreign investors, then Canadians as a whole must pay some of their national income each year to foreigners just for interest, resulting in lower standards of living.

4. Reducing the federal budget deficit has proved to be politically difficult. Two-thirds of federal spending goes to transfers to individuals, transfers to provinces, and

interest payments. Without tax increases or large cuts in these areas, the deficit cannot be easily reduced.

5. A country's current-account deficit is equal to the difference between its payments to foreigners for imports, investment income, and transfers, and its receipts from export sales, investment income, and transfers, which is also equal to its net capital inflow. Thus, a current-account deficit and borrowing from abroad are two ways of describing the same pattern.

6. The savings-investment identity for an open economy says that the sum of private savings, capital flows from abroad, and government savings are equal to investment. This identity implies that a change in any one factor must also involve offsetting changes in the other factors.

7. Policies that aim to reduce the current-account deficit and foreign borrowing by blocking imports or subsidizing exports encounter several problems: the exchange rate will adjust in a way that offsets the policy; other countries are likely to retaliate; restricting imports means that foreigners will buy less from Canadian exporters; the economy loses its gains from trade.

8. Other policy options for reducing the current-account deficit and foreign borrowing include decreasing investment (a bad idea for long-term growth), increasing household and business savings (a good idea if the government could do it), or reducing the federal budget deficit.

REVIEW QUESTIONS

1. What happened to the size of the budget deficits in the 1980s? Had there ever been such large deficits in peacetime?

2. Name four fiscal changes that contributed to the large budget deficits of the 1980s.

3. What is the relationship between the deficits and the federal government debt?

4. How can borrowing from abroad affect future generations for the better? How can it affect future generations for the worse?

5. What is the argument that "the debt doesn't matter, since we owe it to ourselves"? What is wrong with this argument?

6. Since it is politically or legally difficult to cut transfers to individuals and interest payments, why can't federal spending be cut substantially by focusing on all the other federal programs?

7. What happened to the current-account deficit during the 1980s? How did the foreign indebtedness of the Canadian economy change during the 1980s? What is the relationship between these two changes? What is the relationship between the current-account deficit and an inflow of foreign capital?

8. What is the savings-investment identity for an open economy?

9. Why may protectionism fail to save jobs? Why is protectionism costly?

10. Using the savings-investment identity for an open economy, list the various ways that capital flows from abroad might be reduced. Evaluate each of these alternatives.

PROBLEMS

1. Canadian foreign indebtedness is comparable to that of Mexico. But does this necessarily mean that Canada has a similar debt problem as Mexico? Why or why not? Can you think of a situation in which an individual with debts of larger value may actually have less of a debt problem?

2. True or false: "Government borrowing can transfer resources from future generations to the present, but it cannot affect the overall wealth of the country." Discuss.

3. If Parliament were to pass a law prohibiting foreigners from buying Canadian Treasury bills, would this prevent government borrowing from leading to capital inflows? Discuss.

4. Japan had large trade surpluses during the 1980s. Would this cause Japan to be a borrower or a lender in international capital markets?

5. If a nation borrowed $20 billion from abroad one year and its imports were worth $300 billion, what would be the value of its exports? How does your answer change if, instead of borrowing, the nation loaned $10 billion abroad?

6. Suppose a certain country has private savings of 6 percent of GDP, foreign borrowing of 1 percent of GDP, and a balanced budget. What is its level of investment? If the budget deficit is 1.5 percent of GDP, how does your answer change?

7. Imagine that a nation's budget deficit increases while its foreign borrowing remains unchanged. What factors would you expect to change in this situation?

8. Since other countries benefit from exporting their products to Canada, why shouldn't the Canadian government charge them for the privilege of selling in Canada?

9. Explain how reducing the budget deficit would contribute to long-term growth, using the savings-investment identity.

23

DIFFERING APPROACHES TO MACROECONOMIC POLICY

 he making of government economic policy often seems like walking a tightrope. Lean too far to one side, and the economy faces growing unemployment. Lean too far to the other, and there is inflation. While it may be difficult to reach the best of all possible worlds, it does seem possible to have the worst of all worlds: simultaneous inflation, unemployment, and slow growth.

Many of the basic macroeconomic problems arise out of the variability in the level of economic activity. When the economy seems to be dragging along, a jump start may be required to reignite it. But when the economy is racing along, unless something is done to slow it down, inflation may loom ahead. Both unemployment and inflation cause economic hardship to large segments of the population. Unemployment particularly affects the young, who have no cushion of accumulated savings to fall back upon, as well as secondary and unskilled workers. Inflation takes its toll among retired individuals, who may suffer because their incomes do not rise commensurately with inflation.

It should come as no surprise that with a subject as vital as the economic health of the nation, there is much disagreement even among experts. This chapter begins by reviewing the evidence concerning economic fluctuations and how that evidence has been interpreted. We then look at the related question of what government can do about economic fluctuations. We will see that the major macroeconomic schools can be divided into two categories: those who favour government intervention and those who do not. For economists who favour intervention, the question becomes how best to do so, and the final section of the chapter reviews the major policy instruments and the criteria that should be used in choosing among them.

KEY QUESTIONS

1. What are the alternative explanations of the pronounced fluctuations in the level of economic activity in the economy? Why does the economy periodically experience a downturn in which unemployment is high, growth slows down, and output actually falls?

2. Why do some economists believe that the government should not intervene to stabilize the economy? Why do they believe that such intervention is unnecessary, ineffective, or more likely to do harm than good? And why do other economists believe that intervention can at times be helpful?

3. If intervention is desirable, what are the different instruments that are available to government? What are their different impacts? What are the criteria for choosing among them?

BUSINESS FLUCTUATIONS

The recession that began in 1990 closed the door on the longest peacetime expansion in Canadian history. There had been seven years of uninterrupted economic growth, 1983–1989. Some of the growth was simply the recovery from the worst recession since World War II, which had gripped the economy in the years immediately prior to 1983. But even taking that into account, the record was impressive. Most economists believed the expansion would not continue forever, and they were right; the economy went into a downturn in the fall of 1990.

All modern economies experience ups and downs in the level of economic activity. There are periods of faster growth and higher employment, followed by periods of slower growth. Figure 23.1A shows the movement of Canadian economic output over the postwar years. A smooth line has been drawn through the data, tracing out the path that the economy might have taken had it grown at a steady rate. This line represents the economy's **long-term trend.** The figure makes clear that while the long-term trend is upwards, the economy is sometimes above the trend line and sometimes below. Panel B shows the percentage by which the economy has been below or above that trend line. It

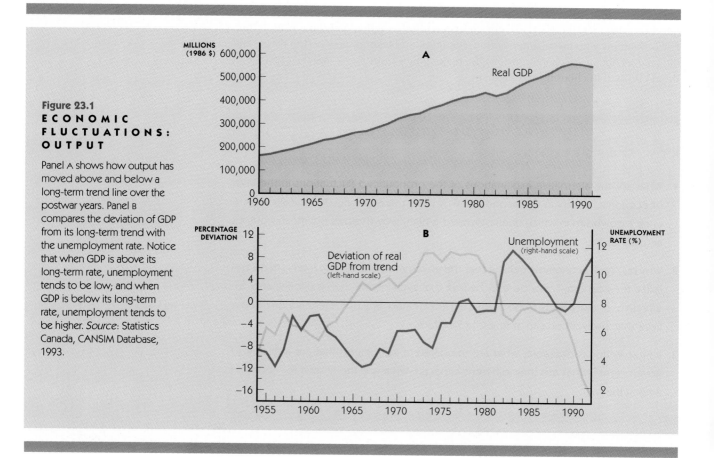

Figure 23.1
ECONOMIC FLUCTUATIONS: OUTPUT

Panel A shows how output has moved above and below a long-term trend line over the postwar years. Panel B compares the deviation of GDP from its long-term trend with the unemployment rate. Notice that when GDP is above its long-term rate, unemployment tends to be low; and when GDP is below its long-term rate, unemployment tends to be higher. *Source:* Statistics Canada, CANSIM Database, 1993.

also shows the unemployment rate, to illustrate the inverse correlation between these deviations of output from trend and unemployment.

It is apparent from the figure that the economy fluctuates. Sometimes it grows faster than at other times. The term "recession" is reserved for periods in which output actually declines, but even growth at a substantially lower rate represents an economic slowdown, with significant consequences. To take one important example, jobs will likely not be created at a rate that will allow new workers to be absorbed into the labour force, so unemployment will rise.

There are four principal views on the nature of these fluctuations in the level of economic activity, often referred to as business cycles. The traditional business-cycle theory argues that there are built-in forces within the economy that give rise to fluctuations. The real business-cycle theory argues that the fluctuations are nothing more than the result of random and unpredictable shocks. Monetarists and new classical economists see the fluctuations as largely the consequence of misguided monetary policy. And new Keynesians see the fluctuations as originating from a variety of sources both inside and outside the economy, but believe that built-in characteristics of modern economies amplify some of the disturbances and make their effects persist.

CLOSE-UP: ASSIGNING BLAME FOR BUSINESS CYCLES

Deciding when a recession begins is a tricky business with potential political consequences. The typical definition of a recession is two successive quarters in which GDP does not rise. By this definition, there were two recessions in the early 1980s. One started in January 1980 and ended in July 1980. The other began in July 1981 and ended in October 1992. Many people (including many economists) merge the two into a single downturn with a plateau in the middle. Some call it a "double dip" recession.

Considerable politicking has surrounded this dating question. If the two recessions are considered as one, then a mega-recession could be viewed as being a consequence of Joe Clark's brief term (1979–1980) as Conservative prime minister, with the nation pulling out of it when the Liberals under Pierre Trudeau came back to power (1980–1984). According to this view, the Trudeau government could be credited with bringing on a decade of economic growth. On the other hand, if a brand-new recession began in July 1981, Conservatives can blame it on the turbulence and uncertainty caused by the return to office of the Trudeau Liberals.

While a stable political environment may be conducive to a healthy economy, there are more powerful explanatory factors behind the 1980–1982 recession than the rapid turnover of governments. The main cause of the downturn in 1980 was the increase in oil prices that followed the collapse of the Iranian government in 1979. In mid-1981, GDP dropped for a second time because of a decline in the demand for exports, investment, and consumer durables, which was a direct result of the lower demand for Canadian products in the United States resulting from the U.S. recession. This led to a lower demand for investment in consumer durables as investor confidence waned, and Canada followed the United States into a recession, despite the thrust of Canadian monetary policy, which was to keep interest rates artificially low. Rather than stimulating demand, this caused the Canadian dollar to remain weak; imports remained expensive and inflation continued at a high level (above 12 percent until 1982 and above 10 percent even at the end of 1982).

Ten years later, another recession provoked political debate. Real GDP fell during the third quarter of 1990. If the beginning of the recession was the month of August rather than July, then the likely trigger was Saddam Hussein's invasion of Kuwait in August, which caused oil prices to skyrocket for several months. The rise in oil prices led to a decline in consumer and business confidence that fed on itself and became a recession. Again, the economic downturn was an international experience, so lower export demand, especially from the United States, was largely responsible for the reduction in aggregate demand.

This explanation for the recession implies that the federal government could have done nothing to prevent it. But real GDP did not bottom out until the first quarter of 1991, by which time it could be argued that federal government policies had exacerbated the recession. Federal sales tax reform (the introduction of the GST) had been implemented in January 1991, and the adjustment to it had been costly in terms of consumer confidence and price realignments. Moreover, both the federal and provincial governments were showing fiscal restraint, cutting expenditures and increasing taxes, in an attempt to moderate their deficits and thus their debt levels. Thus, domestic policy along with international events both exerted negative pressures on the economy in this as well as the previous recession.

Source: Bank of Canada, *Annual Reports*, 1982, 1991, 1992.

THE TRADITIONAL BUSINESS-CYCLE VIEW

The traditional view of business cycles held that there are regular and predictable fluctuations in economic output, and it is the structure of the economy that gives rise to them. In this view, the source of the fluctuations is **endogenous**, that is, within the economy itself; if this is the case, then the upswings and downswings of the economy are to a large extent predictable.

THE MULTIPLIER-ACCELERATOR

To see how internal forces cause fluctuations, assume that the economy is initially in a recession but output begins to increase, as it did in 1983. Suppose the upturn is initiated by an additional $100 million of exports, and the multiplier is 2.5. Then national income increases by $250 million. With higher sales of $250 million, firms believe that they need to install additional capacity, or capital goods. If the accelerator is 2 (the accelerator is the increase in capital goods—the investment required to produce greater output), then the increased sales of $250 million lead to increased investment of $500 million. Now, the increased investment of $500 million leads, through the multiplier process, to a greater output of $1.25 billion ($500 million × 2.5). The higher sales reinforce firms' optimism. Wanting to keep pace with their sales, they increase investment by $2.5 billion (output is now up by an additional $1.25 billion, so they think they need $2.5 billion of new capital goods). And this greater investment leads to a still larger output.

Eventually the economy hits constraints; for example, shortages of labour may impose a limit on the expansion of the economy. Once these constraints are hit, the economy stops expanding, or at least stops expanding as fast. But when the economy expands at a slower rate, the demand for investment decreases. And because of the multiplier effects, this reduces aggregate demand. A downturn in the economy thus begins. As output declines, investment drops lower, further accentuating the decline. Investment comes to a standstill. But eventually the old machines wear out or become obsolete. Even to produce the low level of output associated with the recession, new investment is required. This new investment stimulates demand, which in turn stimulates investment; the economy turns up.

This way of relating business cycles to the internal working of the economy is called the **multiplier-accelerator model** and was first developed by Nobel laureate Paul Samuelson of MIT. The term reflects the model's two major ingredients: the multiplier discussed in Chapter 12 and the accelerator, based on the relationship between capital and output, discussed in Chapter 13.

THE REAL BUSINESS-CYCLE VIEW

By contrast with the traditional business-cycle theory, which sees cycles as regular and predictable, the real business-cycle view considers fluctuations in economic output to be random and unpredictable. In this view, if the economy has been growing by 4 percent, it is as likely to grow by 5 percent next year as it is to grow by 3 percent. If the economy is growing at 2 percent, it is as likely to decline to 1 percent next year as it is to grow by 3 percent. Where the traditional business-cycle school finds the cause for fluctuations in the internal forces of the economy, such as the working of the multiplier and accelerator, this school pins the blame on real, external events such as a change in the price of an important input like oil, natural disasters, and especially shocks to technology such as new inventions. These shocks all come from outside the economy, or at least outside the part of the economy upon which we are focusing; they are **exogenous** events. Because they are exogenous, they are outside the control of policymakers.

The shocks real business-cycle theorists focus on are those to the supply side of the economy, to what all firms are willing to produce at any given set of wages and prices. Real business-cycle theorists thus stand in stark contrast to the other economic schools, which emphasize the importance of shocks to aggregate demand as being a major source of disturbances to the economy. Real business-cycle theorists also tend to believe that markets respond quickly and efficiently to these supply-side shocks, so they do not see economic fluctuations as a major problem.

"Cycle" is something of a misnomer here, since the real business-cycle school sees nothing as predictable as a cycle in its observation of economic fluctuations. But what about the patterns that we saw in Figure 23.1, the ups and downs that look like cycles? Real business-cycle proponents see these as illusions. They observe that when someone flips a coin several hundred times, she may come up with some streaks of heads or tails just by blind chance. Some fifty years ago, the great Russian mathematical economist Eugene Slutsky demonstrated that what might appear to be regular cycles could have been generated simply from random events. Figure 23.2A shows how totally random oc-

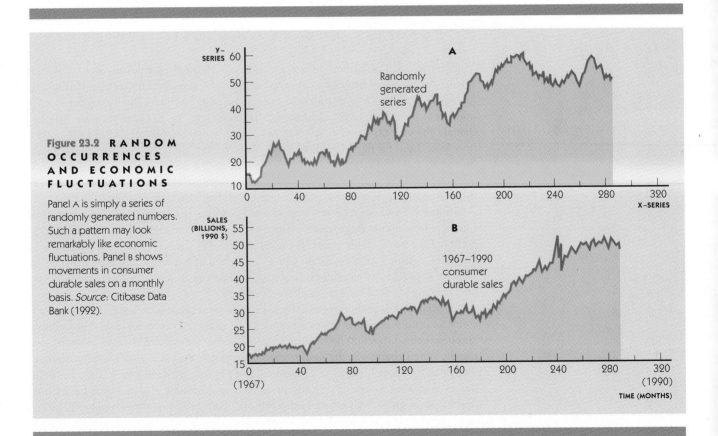

Figure 23.2 RANDOM OCCURRENCES AND ECONOMIC FLUCTUATIONS

Panel A is simply a series of randomly generated numbers. Such a pattern may look remarkably like economic fluctuations. Panel B shows movements in consumer durable sales on a monthly basis. *Source*: Citibase Data Bank (1992).

currences can add up to a picture that looks remarkably like the cyclical fluctuation of consumer durable sales shown in panel B.

Some economists have criticized real business-cycle theories because of their failure to identify the large exogenous disturbances that could account for the magnitude of the fluctuations the economy has experienced. Even the largest shocks in recent decades, such as the increase in the price of oil in the 1970s, are quite small when viewed from the perspective of the economy as a whole. For example, oil imports account for a fairly small share of GDP. If the cost of oil doubled and nothing else happened, the effect would be the same as a reduction in aggregate income of a commensurately small amount. When the world price of oil increased sharply in the early 1970s, the total value of Canadian oil imports climbed from $0.7 billion in 1973 to $3.3 billion in 1975. A large increase to be sure, but since the increase of $2.6 billion was only about 1.5 percent of 1975 GDP, one might think it would have only a small effect.

Critics also maintain that supply-side shocks do not have immediate effects. It takes years for a major new innovation like computers or lasers or transistors to be absorbed into the economy. Equally important, real business-cycle theory has failed to explain the major downturns in the economy. There has been no convincing interpretation of the large negative shocks that real business-cycle theorists claim are responsible for economic fluctuations: what set off the Great Depression or, even more recently, the recession that began in 1990?

MONETARIST AND NEW CLASSICAL VIEWS

Monetarists such as Milton Friedman and new classical economists such as Robert Lucas share the real business-cycle view that for the most part the economy responds quickly and efficiently to disturbances, which are unpredictable. But they differ in their opinion of the source of the disturbances. In their view, it is not changes in technology that are the culprits; there simply are not large enough exogenous shocks to the economy to account for the magnitude of the observed variations. Indeed, these economists believe that if left to itself, the economy would not be highly variable. People smooth consumption over time. Investors look to the long run. These and other factors imply that the economy does a good job of smoothing what little bumps might buffet it.

Monetarists and new classical economists blame the big bumps that give rise to most significant economic fluctuations on the government. For example, when the government fights a war but fails to raise the taxes to pay for it, the increased aggregate demand gives rise to strong inflationary pressures; and when after the war the government cuts back on expenditures without cutting back on taxes to stimulate consumption, the reduced aggregate demand can set off a recession.

But beyond this, both monetarists and new classical economists see much of the variability in output as arising out of misguided monetary policy. New classical economists emphasize the distinction between anticipated and unanticipated changes in the money supply. When changes in the money supply are anticipated, the price level can change; the real money supply remains unchanged, and nothing "real" happens. Changes in the money supply cause changes in the price level and nothing else; policy is ineffective. And in the long run, with rational expectations, changes in the money supply will be anticipated. But in the short run, monetary authorities can act in ways that are unanticipated. When firms do not know that the money supply has been reduced, they do not reduce the price level proportionately.

The important point both schools make is that government is not the solution, it is the problem; it is the unpredictable actions of government, and monetary authorities in particular, that give rise to economic fluctuations and interfere in the normal functioning of the market economy.

In fact, the money supply does tend to decrease as the economy goes into a recession, as the monetarists and new classical economists claim. Indeed, as the economy entered the Great Depression, the money supply decreased faster than prices, so that the real money supply (the money divided by the price level) did decrease. But as we learned earlier, one has to be careful in distinguishing between causality and correlation. The real money supply always increases before Christmas, yet few would claim that the higher sales at Christmas are due to the larger money supply; rather the larger money supply is a response to the anticipated increase in sales. Critics of the monetarist analysis of the Depression suggest that a similar argument applies here: the lower money supply was not the cause but the consequence of the Depression. (Even the somewhat weaker contention, that while the Bank of Canada may not have caused the Depression it should have done more to reverse it, is disputed; as we have seen, there are reasons to believe that in a deep recession monetary policy may be relatively ineffective.)

NEW KEYNESIAN VIEWS

Between the traditional business-cycle theory and the real business-cycle theory is a view held by new Keynesians that there are processes in the economy that amplify a variety of small- and medium-sized external, unpredictable shocks and transform them into large fluctuations. And the economy not only amplifies the shocks, it makes their effects persist long after the initial disturbance has disappeared. In this view, the sources of the disturbances are exogenous, but there are endogenous forces that make the fluctuations significant and make the effects of disturbances persist.

New Keynesians include as possible sources of disturbances to the economy both the kinds of supply-side disturbances emphasized by the real business-cycle theorists and the monetary disturbances emphasized by the monetarists and new classical economists. They differ from these groups in that they do not believe that the market economy is *always* able to absorb and respond to shocks so that full employment is maintained. On the contrary, they believe that there are times in which the economy actually amplifies a shock and makes its effects persist.

To new Keynesians, what is important is not so much the source of shocks—the economy is frequently disturbed, sometimes from the demand side, sometimes from the supply side—but how the economy responds to them. Historically, the length and depth of the Great Depression in Canada provided the strongest evidence of the weak nature of the economy's restorative forces; further evidence has been provided more recently by the persistently high levels of unemployment in many European countries. Critics of this perspective argue either that these are exceptions and that economics should focus on the normal case, or that in these cases government policy interfered with the normal restorative process of the market—for instance, by repeatedly reducing the real money supply during the Great Depression.

AMPLIFICATION

To understand the new Keynesian perspective, we need to understand how the economic system can amplify disturbances. The model of the economy analyzed in Parts Two and Three shows how this can occur. Any change in investment has a multiplier effect on national output. In a credit-constrained economy, reduced sales and lower prices eat up firms' cash reserves and reduce their ability to fund investment projects and their willingness to undertake the risks associated with investment. Hence, a reduction in a firm's sales today, for any reason, may lead to a more than corresponding reduction in investment, and this, through the multiplier process, has an even larger effect on national output.

The same process works in reverse. A positive shock to the economy—for example, an increase in the demand for exports—results in higher profits, allowing firms to increase their investment and stimulating the economy further. This view of a positive shock is similar to the multiplier-accelerator approach of traditional business-cycle theory, with one important difference. While that theory emphasizes the fact that a positive shock to the economy leads to more optimistic expectations for the future, and thus to increased demand for machines and buildings and to higher levels of investment, the new Keynesian theories emphasize the effect of positive shocks on the availability of funds for investment (profits). In reality, both effects undoubtedly play a role.

PERSISTENCE

Not only might the economy amplify external shocks, but it might respond only slowly to the economic forces that restore it to health. As recession-mired firms pursue their conservative production and investment strategy, their financial position improves, but only gradually. As machines wear out, it becomes more and more expensive to postpone making new investments. Eventually investment starts to recuperate. As this happens, output increases. As output increases, investor confidence is restored, and firms' financial position improves further and faster. The economy does recover, but the process of recovery may take months or years.

Recessions also sometimes seem to have long-lasting effects on the rate of economic growth, with the economy taking years to get to where it would have been in the absence of the recession. Two recent recessions, one in 1973–1974 and the other in the early 1980s, are cases in point. They pushed the economy down to the point that even by 1990, when the most recent expansion ended, the economy did not seem to have bounced back to what would have been expected by extrapolating the trend of growth that existed in the late 1960s and early 1970s. In this new Keynesian view, the costs of the economic downturn are not just the lost output from the idle resources, shown in Figure 23.3A as the shaded area, but also the lower output that the economy experiences from then on, shown as the shaded area in panel B.

One possible reason for these long-run effects is that workers who are thrown out of work or do not manage to get jobs in the several years of a deep recession may lose experience and job skills so that they are less productive for the rest of their working lives. A second reason is that in recessions, firms not only invest less in machines and factories, they also invest less in R & D.

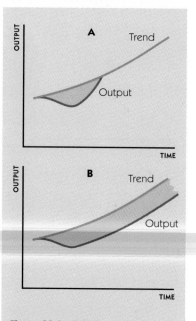

Figure 23.3 THE LINGERING COSTS OF A DOWNTURN

A downturn pushes the economy off its trend line, as shown in panel A. Even when resources are put back to work at the end of the recession, however, the economy may find itself on a new trend line, as shown in panel B. In this interpretation, the costs of the original recession are much larger, as we can see by comparing the shaded areas in the two panels.

DIFFERING VIEWS OF BUSINESS FLUCTUATIONS

SCHOOL	REGULARITY OF FLUCTUATIONS	SOURCE OF FLUCTUATIONS
Traditional business cycle	Fluctuations are regular and predictable.	Arise from endogenous forces as exemplified by the multiplier-accelerator process.
Real business cycle	Fluctuations are largely irregular and unpredictable.	Arise from exogenous shocks, mainly on the supply side, and there mainly through changes in technology.
Monetarist/New classical	Fluctuations are largely irregular and unpredictable.	Arise mainly from shocks to aggregate demand that result from changes in monetary policy.
New Keynesian	Fluctuations are largely irregular and unpredictable.	Arise from shocks to both aggregate demand and aggregate supply; the effect of exogenous shocks are amplified and persist as a result of the structure of the economy.

DIFFERING APPROACHES TO ECONOMIC POLICY

The alternative views described in this chapter of the source of the economy's fluctuations are important because they have different implications for government policy. If the source of fluctuations is exogenous disturbances to which the economy quickly adapts, as the real business-cycle theorists claim, there is no role for government; the market will provide the best possible solution to any change in the economic environment. If, on the other hand, as the new Keynesian theories contend, the economy amplifies disturbances, allowing them to have large and persistent effects, then there is a *potential* role for the government: it *might* be able either to offset the initial disturbance, or to alter the structure of the economy in such a way that the effects of the disturbance are less amplified, less persistent. If the government is the cause of the problem, as the monetarists and new classical economists argue, then one really needs to rethink the whole question of the role of government in stabilizing the economy.

We can oversimplify matters slightly and group economists into two categories: those who believe in strong discretionary government intervention to regulate the macroeconomy (the "interventionists") and those who believe that by and large discretionary government intervention should not be allowed (the "noninterventionists"). The noninterventionists include real business-cycle theorists, who view government intervention as futile; and monetarists and new classical economists, who feel that policy does have effects but mainly negative ones, and that government should therefore be bound by policy rules. The interventionists consist largely of traditional business-cycle theorists and new Keynesian economists. We now take a closer look at what these different schools have to say about economic policy.

THE REAL BUSINESS-CYCLE APPROACH

The position of the real business-cycle theorists is the easiest to explain. As has been pointed out, they believe that the source of economic fluctuations is exogenous shocks to the economy, to which the economy quickly and efficiently responds. The fluctuations do not require government intervention because the market economy will give the best possible solution. Even the variability in income to which fluctuations give rise is not a problem; people acting rationally will have put aside savings to protect themselves against hard times. And unemployment, according to real business-cycle theorists, is more apparent than real. Individuals who want jobs could get them if only they lowered their expectations as to wage and nonpecuniary remuneration. It is better to encourage them to do this and move quickly to new jobs than to prolong the agony by allowing them not to face the facts.

While monetary policy is unnecessary to real business-cycle economists, it is also largely ineffective. If firms see that the government has increased the money supply, they simply increase prices proportionately. And individuals and firms protect themselves against the effects of change in the price level through indexing. There are no *real* effects. The real money supply and the real credit supply are unchanged. A distinctive lesson of the real business-cycle view is that while the government can offer no relief, it can also do no harm.

In the form just presented, the real business-cycle theory may seem too extreme—monetary policy has no effect, inflation has no consequences, unemployment is not important. Still, many economists believe that its basic lesson is still correct: by and large, economic fluctuations are a result of real disturbances, to which the economy adjusts relatively efficiently, and government policy is unlikely to speed or improve the adjustment.

While monetary policy has no effect according to the real business-cycle theory, fiscal policy does. The effect is simple and straightforward: government expenditures divert resources from private consumption to the government. But fiscal policy does not have any effect on the real unemployment rate since there is, in real business-cycle theorists' perspective, no unemployment.

This view of fiscal policy is different from that found in traditional Keynesian analysis. To Keynesians, the government expenditure level has a direct effect in stimulating the economy. Taxes have exactly the opposite effect, and much of their focus is on the difference between expenditures and revenues—the deficits. Deficits stimulate the economy. Real business-cycle theorists deny this. They believe that only the expenditures matter; deficits are as irrelevant as monetary policy. If the government borrows to pay for current expenditures (deficit spending), taxpayers know that eventually they will have to pay, so they set aside the appropriate amount. Savings rise to match the deficit. The failure of household savings to rise in response to the huge government deficits of the past decade has provided the most telling criticism of this aspect of real business-cycle theory.

THE NEW CLASSICAL AND MONETARIST APPROACH

The new classical and monetarist theories have much in common with real business-cycle theories. All three believe that markets respond quickly to changes in the economy. To a great extent, all three agree that the economy adjusts quickly enough to government policy to make it *largely* ineffective. The view that government policy is largely ineffective has been a long-standing one among monetarists and classical (old and new) economists. They believe that private actions may offset government actions, thus impairing the effectiveness of policy instruments.

This view, most effectively articulated by the new classical economists, is known as the policy ineffectiveness proposition. Its adherents hold, with Abraham Lincoln, that while you can fool all the people some of the time and some of the people all the time, you can't fool all the people all the time. The market learns what the government is doing and "undoes" it. If the government attempts to stimulate the economy by monetary policy, the market, with its rational expectations of government policy, figures this out and raises prices. There will then be no real effects—no effects on the amount of goods produced or on the level of employment.

MONETARY POLICY AND INFLATION

Monetarists and new classical economists believe that expansionary monetary policy can cause inflation. They do not consider inflation as innocuous as real business-cycle theorists or many new Keynesian economists do. The economy is only partially indexed against inflation, as we saw in Chapter 20; and so long as this is the case, inflation can take its toll. They believe, moreover, that the uncertainty to which inflation gives rise has further debilitating effects on the economy. They also believe that the Phillips curve is vertical, so that when the government attempts to stimulate the economy by monetary policy, *all* it does is increase the price level—it gets nothing in return. The policy prescription is clear. Do not try to use monetary policy to stimulate the economy; use it only to maintain a stable price level.

FISCAL POLICY

New classical economists and monetarists agree for the most part with real business-cycle theorists that the main effect of fiscal policy—of an increase in government expenditures—is to divert resources away from the private sector and towards the public sector. Since most of the time the economy's resources are fully employed, only movements along the production possibilities curve are possible: more of one good can be produced only by producing less of another; more public goods can be produced only by producing fewer private goods.

This conclusion is not affected by the presence of some unemployment. To new classical economists and monetarists, there is a *natural* rate of unemployment—a level of unemployment that arises as workers move between jobs and as new jobs are created, replacing old jobs that are destroyed as new technologies develop. In Chapter 20, we saw how some economists, such as new classical economists, believe the long-run Phillips curve is vertical at the natural rate of unemployment. In their view, it is not possible for the unemployment rate to be lowered permanently below this level. Attempts to do so simply lead to higher and higher rates of inflation.

The conclusions of new classical economists and monetarists concerning the use of fiscal policy to stabilize the economy parallel their conclusions concerning monetary policy. At most, the government might be able to reduce the unemployment rate below the natural rate for a short period of time. But the cost in terms of increased inflation may be enormous, and in all likelihood the government will mess up in its timing and stimulate the economy precisely at the time when it should be doing the reverse.

PERVERSE EFFECTS OF GOVERNMENT INTERVENTION

The new classical and monetarist economists depart from the real business-cycle theorists in one important way. For the new classical and monetarist economists government policy is not *completely* ineffective. Government policy, particularly its monetary policy, has at times had large *real* effects on output and employment. The trouble is that well-intentioned government policy is just as likely to do harm as to do good. In the view of one monetarist, Milton Friedman, monetary authorities were the primary culprit in causing the Great Depression. They contracted the money supply too much. More recently, monetarists have blamed contractionary monetary policy for the downturns of 1979 and 1982.

Friedman's reason for why monetary policy has real effects on output and employment is that the price level does not adjust instantaneously to undo the effect of decreases in the money supply. The new classical economist Robert Lucas provides one explanation for why prices do not adjust. In Lucas' theory, producers are unable to distinguish whether a decrease in demand is the result of monetary policy—to which the appropriate response would be an equal offsetting decrease in prices—or the result of a shift in demand towards the particular products they produce. And because of these limitations on their information, producers tend not to offset fully changes in the money supply. Because prices do not adjust fully to changes in the money supply, these changes can have real effects. They can affect the level of aggregate demand; a decrease in the money supply can cause an economic downturn.

While monetarists and new classical economists thus contend that monetary policy may have real effects, they believe there are innate reasons why government cannot use

CLOSE-UP: THE POLITICAL BUSINESS CYCLE

Several economists, such as Bruno Frey of the University of Zurich and William Nordhaus of Yale University, have argued that there is an intimate connection between the electoral process and the economy's fluctuations.

First, they note that the electorate is very sensitive to economic conditions. When unemployment is high, people tend to vote against the incumbents, blaming them for the bad economic conditions. Political scientists and economists have done a remarkably accurate job using these economic factors to predict, for instance, the fraction of seats in Parliament that will change. Second, politicians are aware of this. Since politicians like to get re-elected, they plan for economic policies to be favourable at the time of election.

The third part of the theory maintains that the electorate is short-sighted. The economists argue that it pays politicians to overstimulate the economy as elections approach, even though this may (and systematically does) have adverse effects after the election. The overheated economy generates inflation; to quell the inflation, after the election, the government slows down the economy, causing unemployment. But voters' memories are limited. They do not hold grudges. So long as the economy has recovered by the time of the next election, they are forgiving. In this view, then, the electoral process is a primary source of economic fluctuations.

Some would argue that the Conservative party paid the political price in the 1993 federal election for resisting the temptation to stimulate the economy prior to the election campaign despite the fact that unemployment was sitting at over 11 percent.

these powers to stabilize the economy. The first is that government has only a limited ability to forecast accurately, and there are long lags in implementing policies and in policies having effects. Thus, it is impossible for the government to intervene in a timely way. By the time the government has recognized a problem and taken an action and the action has had time to have its effects, it is likely that what is required is something quite different. For instance, if the government finally sees the economy in a recession, by the time it acts to stimulate the economy and that action has had time to have its effects fully felt, the economy may be well on the way to recovery on its own. The main effect of the government stimulation may then simply be to bring on inflationary pressures.

The interplay between politics and economics, with governments excessively stimulating the economy shortly before an election in order to win more votes, also results in government destabilizing the economy rather than stabilizing it.

RULES VERSUS DISCRETION

Monetarists such as Milton Friedman who have grave doubts about the government's ability to stabilize the economy argue that the government should not have discretion in setting economic policy. It should be bound by policy rules. For instance, the money supply should increase at a fixed rate per year, or at a rate proportional to the increase in last year's income. Such rules, they contend, would allow the economy to grow, fully utilizing its resources, without inflation.[1]

Government expenditures should likewise be limited to a fixed proportion of national income. Deficits should be zero or limited to some share of GDP. Those who advocate the use of policy rules argue further that implementing such rules will eliminate a major source of uncertainty in the economy; the future course of policy would be known.

NEW KEYNESIAN AND TRADITIONAL BUSINESS-CYCLE THEORIES

New Keynesians as well as traditional business-cycle theorists disagree with virtually every one of the presumptions underlying the noninterventionist theories, with the new Keynesians taking the lead in recent debates. First, they believe that markets often do not adjust quickly, so that there may be periods of extended unemployment. As evidence, they cite the Great Depression in North America and the extended period of high unemployment in Canada and Europe during the 1980s. The economic misery of recessions cannot be ignored. Government can and should do something about it.

POLICY EFFECTIVENESS

New Keynesians also believe that even with rational expectations, some government policies can have large effects. For instance, there is strong evidence that the effects of

---

[1] Recall that the relationship between velocity, V, money supply, M, the price level, p, and output, Q, is given by $MV = pQ$. Thus, if velocity is increasing at a steady rate of 3 percent and the full-employment output of the economy is increasing on average at 4 percent, then if money supply increases at the rate of 1 percent, the price level can remain on average constant.

monetary policies have not always been offset by changes in the price level. The recession of the late 1970s, generally attributed to the tight monetary policy pursued by both the Bank of Canada and the U.S. Federal Reserve, persuaded most economists that monetary policy can have large real effects (see Chapter 10). More recently, the monetary restraint adopted by the Bank in the early 1990s to protect the value of the Canadian dollar seems to have perpetuated the recession. And the effects of the increased government deficits during the 1980s certainly did not seem to be offset by *increases* in private savings.

New Keynesians agree that the new classical and monetarist economists have made an important contribution in emphasizing that private actions may offset public policies. Government needs to take into account the responses of the private sector to its actions. Frequently the reactions of private individuals, who have rational expectations, do partially offset the government actions. Occasionally they might even fully offset government actions. But to new Keynesians, the contention that they always will do so seems incorrect.

For one thing, theories that the private sector will always offset public-sector actions assume that prices and wages are more flexible than they really are (recall the discussion of price rigidities in Chapter 16). For another, some of the assumptions underlying the rational expectations theories, that households and firms will quickly respond to any government action by undoing it, are, to say the least, questionable. Most observers are skeptical that people can quickly learn what the government has done, know enough about the structure of the economy to be able to undo government policy, and believe that everyone else will behave similarly.

Even if there are some policies for which the private sector can and will take offsetting actions, there are other policies for which this is not true. Tax policies affect the prices individuals and firms face. Investment tax credits affect the cost of investment. Changes in the tax rate on interest income or on capital gains affect the incentives to save. The responses of households and firms to these policies may just as well augment as offset them. An increase in the interest income tax may not only induce more consumption directly, but will produce more government revenue and thus reduce the deficit. This in turn may stimulate consumption as well, as taxpayers realize that their future tax liabilities for paying off the deficit are reduced. Similarly, consumers, knowing that their future incomes will be higher as a result of the investment stimulated by an investment tax credit, may, with these rational expectations, decide to enjoy some of these future benefits today; they may increase consumption today, further stimulating the economy.

POLICY SUCCESSES

Finally, new Keynesians believe that on balance the government has done more to stabilize the economy than to destabilize it. They point to successes like the expansionary fiscal policy in 1974 and the Kennedy tax cut in the United States in 1963, which did exactly what macroeconomic theory said it should to stimulate the economy.

New Keynesians disagree with those who assign to the government the blame for many downturns. For instance, while they agree that the real money supply decreased in the Great Depression, they believe that the underlying source of the economic downturn lay elsewhere. Indeed, the decrease in the real money supply was largely a consequence of the low levels of economic and lending activity, rather than a cause. The

Bank of Canada and the U.S. Federal Reserve System tried to increase lending activity but met with only limited success. Perhaps they should have tried harder, but there is no reason to believe that there was much they could do. Unfortunately, the historical evidence is sufficiently ambiguous that in many cases the debates will continue indefinitely.

RULES VERSUS DISCRETION: THE NEW KEYNESIAN PERSPECTIVE

Thus, new Keynesians see a need for government action because of the failure of markets to adjust by themselves sufficiently rapidly to maintain full employment, and they believe that government action can be and has been effective. They also believe that government should not bind itself to fixed rules, such as increasing the money supply at a fixed rate, but should use discretionary policies. Changing economic circumstances require changes in economic policy, and it is impossible to prescribe ahead of time what policies would be appropriate. While there are common patterns to all economic downturns, most have distinctive characteristics. The 1973 recession was initially the result of an increase in the price of oil. The fall in real estate prices in the late 1980s and the precarious position of many banks and trust companies posed their own particular problems in the recession that began in 1990.

New Keynesians not only argue that discretionary policies can be helpful and effective, they question whether the government could really commit itself to following a set of rules. It is all well and good, they point out, for academics to talk about the government pursuing noninterventionist policies. The reality is that no government can stand idly by as 10, 15, or 20 percent of its workers face unemployment.

Accordingly, there is no way really to remove the uncertainty associated with changes in government policy. Even if lawmakers and policymakers say they will follow a particular rule, such as expanding the money supply at a constant rate, what is to prevent them from altering their behaviour should it prove desirable to do so? In 1984, the Mulroney government was elected on a promise to bring the federal budget deficit under control. By 1987, it became apparent that that goal could not be attained; although the annual deficit had fallen from $30 billion to $21 billion, the stock of debt increased from $180 billion to $264 billion. The government was re-elected in 1988, and once again made deficit reduction its main budgetary policy objective. By 1992, it was clear that the deficit was continuing to get worse rather than better, despite the fact that virtually every budget since 1988 predicted a fall in the deficit.

The problem of whether the government will actually carry out a promised course of action is called the problem of **dynamic consistency.** The government may announce that a particular tax change is permanent—and it might even deceive itself into believing that the tax change *is* permanent. But when circumstances change, policies will change. And the fact that policies will change (or that individuals and firms expect them to change) has enormous consequences for the behaviour of individuals and firms. In 1985, for instance, the federal government introduced a generous tax exemption for capital gains earned by Canadians. All capital gains up to a lifetime limit of $500,000 were to be made exempt from taxation. These breaks were intended to be permanent and were intended to encourage savings in equities. In the next couple of years, many persons who had already owned shares whose values had increased considerably decided to cash them in. They figured, correctly as it turned out, that this policy would not last. In fact, only two years later the lifetime exemption was reduced to $100,000 and the rate of tax on capital gains was increased. All the initial exemption did was induce persons to sell their existing shares rather than to invest in new ones.

The new Keynesians' conclusion is that if the unemployment rate becomes high, government must and will do something, regardless of what it has said. The role of economists is to advise the government on the policies most likely to be effective.

New Keynesian economists also believe that it is virtually impossible to design rules that are appropriate in the face of a rapidly changing economy. When velocity fell unexpectedly in the 1980s, the rule of expanding the money supply at a constant rate, had it been adopted, might well have gotten the economy into serious trouble. If the monetary authorities had restricted the increase of the money supply to, say, 3 percent, with the associated increase in credit, the economy might have been thrown into a major recession.[2]

The argument of the monetarists and new classical economists that the government has at times contributed to the economy's fluctuations has had a profound effect on new Keynesian views concerning the scope of government intervention. New Keynesians believe that society can learn from these historical experiences how to improve the effectiveness of fiscal and monetary policy. Most new Keynesians are not as optimistic as their Keynesian forebears about the ability of the government to "fine tune" the economy, keeping the economy humming along with full employment and no inflation. They tend to agree with monetarists and new classical economists that by attempting to do too much, the government may do worse than it would if it were less ambitious.

AUTOMATIC STABILIZERS

At the same time, new Keynesians and traditional business-cycle theorists believe that there are some policies or rules that will enhance the stability of the economy and make it more likely that shocks to the economy will have less adverse effects. Indeed, one of the major objectives of traditional business-cycle theory, which emphasizes the endogenous nature of cyclical fluctuations, is to find policies that will reduce the endogenous forces that give rise to cycles. These policies are called automatic stabilizers, and were discussed in Chapter 14. Unemployment insurance payments, for example, automatically increase when unemployment rises; and when income falls, the average tax rate drops because of the progressive tax structure in Canada.[3]

---

[2] Note 1 recalled the basic relationship between M, the money supply, V, velocity, p, the price level, and Q, aggregate output: $MV = pQ$. This implies that if the government anticipates an increase in velocity of 3 percent per year and an increase in full-employment output of 4 percent per year, then the appropriate rule for stabilizing the price level is a 1 percent annual increase in the money supply. But in the 1980s, velocity suddenly started to decrease. If, instead of the 3 percent increase in velocity that had been anticipated, velocity fell 3 percent, prices would have to fall 6 percent if output was to continue to grow at the desired rate. If prices did not fall, output would have to fall.

[3] The tax system is supposed to be an automatic stabilizer, but in periods of stagflation, when prices rise though unemployment is high, it contributes to the downturn. Prior to 1974, the tax system was not indexed; that is, the income levels at which various tax rates came into play were not adjusted for changes in price levels. With stagflation, there was unemployment as well as inflation. Though "real" output and employment were declining, "nominal" output (measured in terms of dollars) was increasing, and hence the tax system imposed higher and higher taxes, further depressing the economy. Today, the tax system is indexed, but only at 3 percent less than the inflation rate.

DIFFERING VIEWS OF ECONOMIC POLICY

NONINTERVENTIONIST THEORIES

Markets respond quickly to economic disturbances, so that resources are fully and efficiently utilized almost all the time. Actions of households and firms negate any effect the government may have. Government expenditures displace private expenditures, making fiscal policy ineffective except insofar as it diverts resources from private to public uses. Deficit financing has no effect, as increased private savings have an exactly offsetting effect. When government does affect the economy, it more often makes matters worse than better. The prescription: the government should stop mucking around in the economy. It should adopt rules, rather than use discretionary policy.

Real business-cycle theorists	There is no role for government in stabilizing the economy. Monetary policy has no effect, but does no harm.
Monetarists/New classical economists	Because of the sluggish adjustment of prices, in the short run monetary policy can have real effects. Government does more harm than good; it has been responsible (particularly through monetary policy) for major economic downturns.

INTERVENTIONIST THEORIES

Markets often respond slowly, so there may be extended periods of unemployment. Some government instruments are effective. While the government makes mistakes, on balance government policy is beneficial and is becoming increasingly so as we learn more about how the economy functions.

New Keynesians	Government should use discretionary policy to offset forces of economic shocks rather than binding itself to fixed rules; changing economic circumstances require changes in economic policy.
Traditional business-cycle theorists	Government should design built-in stabilizers to make the economy more stable, reducing the endogenous forces that give rise to cycles.

EVALUATING ALTERNATIVE INSTRUMENTS

For new Keynesians and others favouring government intervention in the macroeconomy, the various noninterventionist schools have served an important function in addition to their contributions to macroeconomic analysis. They have taught that government intervention should not blithely be thought of as cost-free or necessarily effective. If undertaken at all, it should be undertaken with care. We now look at the different policy options the government has at its disposal.

THE POLICY INSTRUMENTS

If the government is to intervene in the economy, the question remains, how should it do so? The term "instrument" is used here to mean a way in which the government affects the economy. Fiscal policy instruments include the cutting (or raising) of taxes or the increasing (or decreasing) of government expenditures. A tax cut could be a lowering of the taxes faced by individuals, which might stimulate consumption, or a tax break for corporations, which may stimulate investment. It can be temporary or permanent. Each policy has effects that go beyond macroeconomics; for instance, lowering taxes on the poor more than on the rich may have the combined effect of increasing equality while at the same time stimulating consumption more than if taxes were lowered uniformly. A decrease in government expenditures could be for welfare or for an investment like road construction, to take two examples. In one case, the poor are adversely affected; in the other, future generations.

The government can also try to target particular sectors of the economy. For example, it can provide investment tax credits to stimulate investment in manufacturing industries, or it can provide export subsidies to stimulate exports. Parts Four and Five showed how each of these instruments works.

Monetary policy instruments include open market operations and moral suasion. Monetary policies lowering interest rates, as we have seen, may stimulate investment by firms, exports, and household purchases of durables. Higher rates have the opposite effect and thus dampen the economy.

Unfortunately, the fiscal or monetary instruments do not match up neatly with the principal goals of macroeconomic policy: full employment, high growth, and stable prices. There is no "growth" instrument, "employment" instrument, or "inflation" instrument. Many instruments simultaneously affect all three goals. Nor does using one instrument preclude using others. Choosing the best set of policy instruments is thus an important job for policymakers. The sections that follow explore the major considerations for choosing among them.

INSTRUMENTS OF GOVERNMENT POLICY

Fiscal instruments
   Changes in tax rates facing consumers and/or business firms
   Changes in levels of expenditures

Monetary instruments
   Open market operations
   Moral suasion

EFFECTIVENESS IN ATTAINING OBJECTIVES

The single most important criterion in choosing an instrument is the likelihood that it will be successful in attaining the desired objectives. Consider, for instance, the situation where the country is in a recession and policymakers want to stimulate the economy. Experts often question whether monetary instruments will work. Chapter 18 explained why in deep recessions the Bank of Canada may be relatively ineffective in encouraging banks to make more loans to increase investment. The banks see few good loan prospects. And even if banks were willing to lend more, firms might not be willing to undertake the risks of additional investment without a dramatic change in interest rates.

There is also a debate about whether fiscal instruments like tax cuts will stimulate the economy. Individuals might simply decide to put away much of their increased income rather than spend it. This may be especially true if they are nervous about the future, as they often are when the economy goes into a recession. In such a situation, a tax cut or transfer payment increase aimed directly at the poor may be the most effective option. In a prolonged recession, the poor have used up their savings and spend whatever income they can get. Increased government expenditures financed by borrowing may also successfully stimulate the economy. Particularly when there is access to foreign borrowing, such expenditures are unlikely to crowd out much investment.

Those who subscribe to the policy ineffectiveness proposition, as we learned earlier, argue that particularly with rational expectations, individuals will undertake actions that offset the government's actions. The effect of an increase in the money supply will be offset by an increase in prices. An increase in deficit spending will be offset by an increase in private savings. While new Keynesians are aware that private actions do offset some government actions, they believe that other government policies do not bring offsetting actions; these policies are, accordingly, more likely to be effective. For instance, when the government makes it cheaper to invest by increasing the investment tax credit, it stimulates investment; for such policies, there is no offsetting private action.

EFFECT ON THE COMPOSITION OF OUTPUT

One particularly important consideration in choosing among instruments is the effect the instrument will have on the composition of national output. Chapter 12 identified four components of aggregate demand: consumption, investment, net exports, and government expenditures. Government policymakers can stimulate aggregate demand in a recession by increasing any one (or more) of these, and they can dampen aggregate demand in an inflationary boom by contracting any one. The different instruments available to the government determine whether consumption, investment, net exports, or government expenditures are expanded or contracted; they therefore affect the extent to which other objectives, such as high growth, are achieved. Instruments that stimulate the economy by encouraging investment are especially likely to be conducive to growth.

One way to encourage investment is through monetary policy, though as we have seen, in an open economy the effects of loose monetary policy may be felt more through an increase in exports, as a result of a depreciation of the domestic currency. Loose monetary policy may also encourage the purchase of consumer durables, thus increasing the production of automobiles, refrigerators, and other major purchases.

Another policy for stimulating investment is a reduction in the taxation of businesses, particularly reductions such as investment tax credits. Not only do appropriately designed tax cuts stimulate investment by increasing the after-tax return to investing, they also provide firms with additional resources for investing.

Some policies may stimulate the economy but have a much more limited effect in encouraging investment. For example, the first-round effect of cuts in the individual income tax is to stimulate consumption; investment will only increase as a by-product of greater business optimism. Other policies may actually decrease investment. When a country has limited access to foreign borrowing, an increase in government expenditures, financed by government borrowing, may raise interest rates and thus crowd out investment. The net effect may be positive—the increase in government expenditures may well exceed the reduction in investment. Even so, such a policy results in a higher current output at the price of a lower future capital stock. With a highly open international capital market, this effect has become much less important, as Canada borrows abroad to finance its deficit.

The crowding out of investment is an indirect effect of government expenditures. The direct effect depends on how the money is spent. An increase in government expenditures to build roads or schools or otherwise improve the infrastructure may make future generations better off and stimulate economic growth. On the other hand, if government spends more on Old Age Security payments or higher welfare payments, then only current consumption is increased.

BREADTH OF IMPACTS

Some economic policies have a large effect on a few narrowly defined sectors of the economy, with the repercussions spreading out from these points of impact. For instance, tight monetary policy has particularly strong and direct effects on those who depend on banks for credit or whose customers depend on credit. Small businesses and the consumer durable industries thus feel the brunt of tight monetary policy.

In today's increasingly integrated international economy, tight monetary policy often has particularly large effects on export and import competing industries. For example, Canada competes to export farm products, and Canadian automakers face stiff competition from imports. High interest rates lead to an influx of foreign capital, bidding up the value of the dollar and making it more difficult for Canadian firms to export their products and for Canadian automobile firms to compete against overseas imports. Assume the government wants to reduce total aggregate demand by 5 percent. If the government limits itself to policies that affect, say, only a quarter of the economy, aggregate demand in those sectors would have to be reduced by four times as much, or by 20 percent.

On the other hand, dampening the economy by increasing the individual income tax decreases demand for a broad spectrum of consumer goods. These broader impacts reduce the economic dislocations associated with policies with more narrowly focused impacts. Many economists believe that it is undesirable to have too high a reliance on monetary policy for stabilizing the economy, because the first-round impacts are fairly narrow.

In another dimension, monetary policy can have too broad an impact. In a country as expansive and diverse as Canada, different regions may be in different phases of the business cycle. A case in point is the 1988–1989 period. The central Canadian economy was overheating as a result partly of a construction boom in southern Ontario. Real estate prices were rising rapidly, and labour markets were tight. At the same time, in other parts of the country, especially the Atlantic provinces, unemployment rates remained stubbornly high due to a continued depressed state of many markets for natural resources. The Bank of Canada, concerned primarily with the possibility of a surge of inflation being set off in Ontario, adopted a restrictive monetary policy. Not surprisingly, this led to complaints from many persons in the East, some of whom called for more regional input into monetary policy decisions. But given the speed with which capital can flow among regions, it is not possible to conduct monetary policy on a regional basis. On the other hand, fiscal instruments, like investment tax credits, can be differentiated across regions.

FLEXIBILITY AND SPEED OF ADJUSTMENT

Different instruments differ in the speed with which they can be implemented. In many industrialized countries, including Canada, monetary and fiscal policies are set in different parts of government. In Canada, the Bank of Canada sets monetary policy virtually independently, while fiscal policy is set by Parliament. Furthermore, the provincial legislatures legislate their own fiscal measures, and often do so after the federal government. Coordination is therefore difficult to start with. In addition, there are lags in the government's ability to recognize a downturn in economic activity, design a program to combat it, implement the program, and then allow the program to have its effects. Each of these steps takes time. And by the time the effects of the policy have begun to be felt, economic conditions may have changed again.

These delays may be more important for fiscal than for monetary policy since fiscal policy measures have to be legislated by Parliament. But the process allows tax adjustments to be implemented considerably more quickly than expenditure measures, and for that reason they are used frequently as policy measures. In March or April of each year, the minister of finance announces his government's budget for the coming fiscal year. The budget will contain both tax and expenditure changes. The tax measures can be put into effect very quickly, though they technically need to be ratified by Parliament. Indirect tax changes apply immediately, whereas income tax changes typically begin within months. Expenditure measures usually take longer to apply. Very few budgets go by without some change in taxes. If the need is particularly urgent, the finance minister may choose not to wait until the regular annual budget time to make fiscal changes, but may bring forth a "mini-budget," say, in the fall, which contains changes in the budget for the current year. For example, the mini-budget of October 1975 was introduced to deal with accelerating inflation. It was this budget that set up the Anti-Inflation Board discussed in Chapter 20. In November 1978, the mini-budget was used to introduce a reduction in the federal sales tax and an increase in the rate of investment tax credit to stimulate the economy.

Although fiscal policy changes take some time to implement through the budgetary process, they can be done much more quickly in a parliamentary system like that of Canada or Great Britain than in a system like that of the United States. There, the president proposes budgetary changes to the Congress, but there is no guarantee that they will be passed. The process of persuading Congress to enact budgetary measures involves seemingly endless haggling, with a large number of persons representing a wide variety of interests involved in the process. It takes at least six months for a change in individual income tax rates to make their way through the system. As a result tax changes are an especially clumsy instrument for stabilizing the U.S. economy. There have been two such changes in recent decades: a permanent tax reduction under President Kennedy to stimulate the economy in 1963, and a temporary tax increase in 1968 under President Johnson to reduce aggregate demand, to offset partially the increased expenditures on the Vietnam War.

The lags in fiscal policy go beyond decision making. After a decision is made, the policy must be implemented. If the government decides to spend more to build additional roads, engineers must draw up plans before the contracts can be let. After a tax reduction is enacted and takes effect, it may take consumers a while to respond fully. Responses to an investment tax credit are likely to be even slower, as firms must draw up new investment plans and obtain the required capital.

One of the major advantages of monetary instruments over fiscal instruments in Canada is their greater flexibility. It is relatively easy for the Bank of Canada to change course, to decide this week to make credit more available and next week to make it less so. The Bank holds a weekly meeting to make these decisions; at this time, it takes the pulse of the economy and makes a judgment about the dose of medicine that is required.

Once implemented, monetary policy suffers such lags as well. The banking system responds to the Bank's actions by making credit more or less available; this is usually a fairly short lag, of a few weeks. And then firms must respond to the actions of the banking system, increasing or decreasing investment; this often takes considerably longer.

CERTAINTY OF CONSEQUENCES

The effect of most government programs depends in part on how consumers and firms respond. Will consumers spend most of a tax reduction, believing that it is permanent, or will they squirrel away the extra funds? Will firms increase investment in response to a reduction in the interest rate, or will they wait, hoping for still further reductions? Because of these questions and because the responses depend on expectations of future government actions, there is inevitably considerable uncertainty about the effects of many policy changes.

Even so, the effects of some policy instruments are more predictable than others. In a recession, there is much uncertainty about the effectiveness of monetary policy. For example, it may be uncertain whether an increase in bank reserves through open-market operations will lead to a significant amount of increased lending and investment by firms.

There is also considerable uncertainty associated with the effects of changes in income tax rates. If a tax reduction is taken to be temporary, people will treat it as a "windfall"—a onetime increase in spendable income. Individuals tend to save a large fraction of windfall gains, as the theories of consumption described in Chapter 13 suggest. If, however, the change is taken to be permanent, people may increase their consumption substantially. Announcements by the government are not always believed, largely because the government finds it difficult to commit itself. The government might announce that a tax change is temporary, yet taxpayers believe that political forces will make it permanent. Or the government might announce that a tax reduction is permanent, and taxpayers, seeing future government deficits, expect the "permanent" change to be quickly repealed.

The uncertainties about the consequences of policy changes extend to questions of how markets perform. If the government borrows more to finance increased government expenditures, will private investment be crowded out? This depends on the flow of funds from abroad. If the supply curve of funds from abroad is very elastic, then increased government borrowing will have little effect on interest rates or the availability of credit.

Another uncertainty involves how well monetary and fiscal policies mesh. A crucial determinant of the extent to which government expenditures crowd out private investment is the response of the Bank of Canada. If the Bank believes that there are inflationary pressures, it may respond to increased government expenditures by tightening monetary policy, making credit less available. Then the increased government expenditures may have little *net* effect on aggregate demand; they only change the demand's composition, with a larger proportion of the nation's output going into the public sector and a smaller proportion into investment.

These uncertainties have two important implications for economic policy. First, at any given time, the uncertainties associated with some instrument are likely to be greater than the uncertainties with other instruments. As the economy seems to be plunging headlong into a recession, the government may want to reverse quickly the recessionary psychology. If the data indicate that many consumers are spending what they can get hold of and are saving little, then a tax reduction may have more certain effects than monetary policy and therefore be the instrument of choice. While the government can be fairly confident that consumers will spend a large part of the extra money in their pockets, it may be quite uncertain whether, given the bad business climate, banks will be willing to lend much more or firms will be willing to invest much more in response to lower interest rates resulting from open market operations.

Second, in some cases, the uncertainties can be quickly resolved, and government actions can be modified accordingly. In other cases, it will take a long time to resolve the uncertainties. Consumers, for instance, are more likely to respond quickly to a tax rate change, particularly if they see an immediate change in their take-home pay. The government can see how workers are responding, and then determine whether or how much further action is required. On the other hand, it may take firms months or in some cases years to change their investment plans.

There have been periods, particularly in the 1960s, when macroeconomists hoped to understand policy instruments well enough to "fine tune" the economy; that is, to make sure that the economy was kept constantly at the lowest unemployment rate consistent with stable prices. The long delays associated with many government instruments combined with the uncertainty as to their consequences imply that it is extremely difficult for the government to do this. Still, when the economy is in a prolonged downturn, when unemployment rates have persisted at high rates as they did through the 1980s and in the Great Depression, there will be loud calls for some form of macroeconomic intervention.

CRITERIA FOR EVALUATING POLICY INSTRUMENTS

Effectiveness of instrument: Some policies may be more effective than others; in some cases, actions of the private sector may offset the effects of policy instruments.

Effect on composition of output: Among policies with similar effects on aggregate demand, some increase the relative size of the public sector, some increase current consumption, and some increase the future growth of the economy by stimulating investment.

Breadth of impact: Some policies, such as monetary policy, have narrow impacts; others, fiscal instruments like tax reductions, have more broadly based impacts.

Flexibility and speed of implementation: Some policies, such as monetary policy, are more flexible than others, and their impacts are felt more quickly.

Certainty of consequences: At any given time, the impact of some policies is more certain than that of others.

Presence of unintended side effects: Some policies have significant unintended (and often negative) side effects.

UNINTENDED SIDE EFFECTS

In choosing which instruments to use, the government wants to avoid unintended negative side effects. For instance, in 1991 the federal government increased the tax on cigarettes by 3 cents per cigarette expecting that this would reduce cigarette consumption. Though it did succeed to some extent, it also induced a significant increase in smuggling activities. Canadian cigarettes could be purchased in the United States at prices

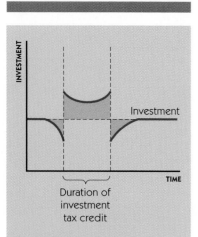

Figure 23.4 EFFECT OF TEMPORARY INVESTMENT TAX CREDIT OVER TIME

Temporary taxes and tax credits do not merely increase investment while they are in effect. They also decrease investment just before they go into effect, as firms reduce investment in anticipation of the taxes, and reduce investment just after they end. Firms modify investment timing to take advantage of the tax credit. The result may be that total investment is much the same over the longer period, but the pattern of investment is disrupted.

that were significantly below Canadian prices, making it profitable for persons to import and sell Canadian cigarettes illicitly. In addition to costing the federal government revenues, this partly foiled the attempt to reduce cigarette consumption.

Temporary programs also often have such side effects. Consider the effect of a temporary investment tax credit, such as the one that was offered to businesses who invested in Cape Breton between 1985 and 1988. In effect, the credit reduces the costs of making investments during a certain period. The effects are illustrated in Figure 23.4. There is reduced investment right before the investment tax credit goes into effect and reduced investment right after it is removed, as investors try to shift their investment to the period in which it is being subsidized.

These effects may be undesirable for two reasons. First, the intent of the investment tax credit may be to stimulate investment, not to change the date at which investments are made. The temporary tax credit may have little effect on total investment. Second, the government may not want to reduce investment immediately after the removal of the tax credit or immediately before it goes into effect, for these decreases in demand may exacerbate recessionary pressures at those times.

REVIEW AND PRACTICE

SUMMARY

1. Traditional business-cycle theorists believe economic fluctuations are caused by endogenous forces in the economy. Real business-cycle theorists believe fluctuations are the result of exogenous shocks to the economy, and the economy efficiently adapts to these shocks. Monetarists and new classical economists see government in general, and monetary policy in particular, as the source of the shocks. New Keynesians also believe that the shocks are exogenous but that the economy contains forces that amplify these shocks and make their effects persist.

2. Traditional business-cycle theory sees economic fluctuations as regular and predictable; the other theories see fluctuations as induced by randomly occurring shocks and thus largely unpredictable.

3. Noninterventionists, which include real business-cycle theorists, new classical economists, and monetarists, believe that the economy operates efficiently, at or near full employment, and that it responds quickly to external shocks. Government intervention is thus unnecessary.

4. Interventionists, which include new Keynesians, believe that periods of persistent unemployment are evidence that the economy sometimes does not adjust quickly and that at least in severe recessions, government policy can and should be used to stimulate the economy.

5. Real business-cycle theorists hold that monetary policy has no effect, but that does not matter, since the economy is generally near full employment. Monetarists and new classical economists believe the economy would be better off if the gov-

ernment stuck to simple rules, like expanding the money supply at a constant rate. New Keynesians believe that government can use both fiscal and monetary policy to stabilize the economy effectively.

6. In deciding which policy instrument to use, the government looks at several criteria: the effectiveness of the instrument, its effect on the composition of output, the breadth of its impact, the flexibility and speed of its implementation, the certainty of the consequences, and the possibility of unintended side effects.

KEY TERMS

multiplier-accelerator   **exogenous effects**
  model   **dynamic consistency**
endogenous effects

REVIEW QUESTIONS

1. What are the alternative explanations of the sources of the economy's fluctuations? What is the relationship between views about the nature of these fluctuations and views about the role of government?

2. What is the multiplier-accelerator model?

3. Describe the rules versus discretion debate.

4. Why do some economists believe that active government intervention in an attempt to stabilize the economy is either unnecessary or undesirable? What are the counterarguments?

5. What are the relative advantages and disadvantages of the use of monetary versus fiscal instruments?

6. What is the problem of dynamic inconsistency? Give an example of dynamic inconsistency.

7. Provide some examples of how different policies or instruments affect different groups in society.

8. What are the principal criteria for evaluating alternative instruments?

PROBLEMS

1. Is fiscal or monetary policy more likely to affect consumption? investment? home buyers? exports? imports? Explain your answers.

2. If the income tax schedule has been changing every year, would you expect consumer spending to decrease substantially when the government announces a "permanent" income tax increase? Explain. Why, under the same circumstances, might you expect consumer purchases of automobiles to decrease substantially when the government announces a "permanent" tax on the purchase of automobiles?

3. Use the concepts of income and substitution effects to explain the differences in effects of a temporary income tax and a temporary tax on consumer durables.

4. Assume that the government increases its spending by $10 billion, while the multiplier is 4 and the accelerator is 2. How much will the original increase in government spending increase national output? How much investment will result from that increase in output? How much will the increase in investment increase national output?

5. If the economy is in a boom, why might a multiplier-accelerator model predict that it will eventually slow down? If the economy is in a recession, why might the multiplier-accelerator model predict that it will eventually speed up?

6. What are some ways the government can use automatic stabilizers to help stabilize the economy?

7. If the economy is in a recession and the government wants to stimulate output in a way that will promote long-run growth, what instruments might the government favour to stimulate the economy?

8. If the economy is in a recession and the government is particularly concerned about how the rich have suffered during recent years, what instruments might the government favour to stimulate the economy?

9. Describe the effect on the composition of output of combining a tax cut with a tighter monetary policy.

CHAPTER 24

ALTERNATIVE ECONOMIC SYSTEMS

More than thirty years ago while giving a speech at the United Nations, Nikita Khrushchev pounded his shoe on the table and declared, "We will bury you!" Khrushchev, president of the Soviet Union, was referring to the rivalry between his country's communist economy and the mixed capitalist economies of Western Europe and North America. Indeed, a number of reputable Western economists agreed with him then that it was only a matter of time before the Soviet Union caught up with and surpassed the United States.

Today most of the former communist countries are seeking to restructure their economies. Countries like Poland, Hungary, the Czech Republic, and Slovakia look at their Western European neighbours, Germany, Italy, and the Scandinavian countries, and see higher standards of living. In a few momentous months in 1989, most of the Eastern European countries began to overhaul their systems into economies based on the market. In 1990, even Albania, the country seemingly most committed to communism, began to make market reforms. Events in the Soviet Union in 1991—including the attempted overthrow of President Gorbachev, the attainment of independence by the Baltic republics, and finally the breakup of the Union itself—set the stage for similar reforms there.

Nevertheless, the most populous country in the world, China, remains committed to some version of communism, though there is an ongoing debate in the country about how most effectively to improve its economy.

KEY QUESTIONS

1. What were the economic conditions that gave rise to the socialist idea?

2. What were the central characteristics of Soviet-style socialism? How did it differ from the market system in the way it allocated resources?

3. Why did it fail?

4. What are some of the principal reforms of Soviet-style socialism that have been tried, and how have they fared?

5. What problems do the former socialist economies face in the process of transition to a market economy?

SOCIALIST AND COMMUNIST ECONOMIC SYSTEMS

A variety of terms are used to describe the alternative economic systems used in various parts of the world. Under **socialism,** the government owns and operates the basic means of production—the factories that make cars and steel, the mines, the railroads, the telephone system, and so on. Under **communism,** the government essentially owns all property—not only the factories, but also the houses and the land. In practice, no government has abolished all private property; people still own the clothes they wear, and if they are well enough off, they might even own cars and television sets.

The term "communism" is used to describe the economic system in the countries that came under the domination of the Soviet Union and China in the years after World War II, though there were in fact considerable variations in economic practices. In Poland, for instance, most land remained in the hands of the farmers who worked it. But by and large, these countries shared an economic system that involved not only state ownership of assets but also considerable central control of economic decisions, or **central planning,** and a political system that did not allow free elections, free speech, or the multitude of other rights found in democracies. Because of the important role played by central planning, these economies are sometimes referred to as planned economies or centrally planned economies. For simplicity, we will refer to the kind of economic system that evolved in the Soviet Union, Eastern Europe, and China as "Soviet-style socialist economies."

This chapter contrasts the Soviet-style economies with those of North America and Western Europe. Because of the important role played by private capital in the latter economies, they are commonly referred to as capitalist economies; further, since government plays a large role, they are often called mixed economies; and because of their heavy reliance on firms and households interacting in markets, they are also referred to as market economies. Again, there are considerable variations among these economies: for example, government plays a more important role in Sweden than it does in Switzerland. Yet they share much in common. The objective of this chapter is to enhance our understanding of the major differences between the market economies and the Soviet-style economies. Towards the end of the chapter, we will learn about the two major versions of socialism that differed from that of the Soviet Union: the worker cooperatives of the former Yugoslavia and the attempts by Hungary and China to incorporate some elements of a market into socialism.

Table 24.1 provides some data comparing living standards in the Soviet-style economies just before the revolutionary events of 1989–1991 with those in the rest of the world.

Table 24.1 COMPARISON OF LIVING STANDARDS BETWEEN PLANNED AND MARKET ECONOMIES

	GDP per capita (1988 U.S. $)	Annual GDP growth rate (%) 1965–1988	Life expectancy at birth	Adult illiteracy (%)
Soviet-style economies:				
USSR	2,660	4.0	70	< 5
China	330	5.4	70	31
Hungary	2,460	5.1	71	< 5
Market economies:				
Canada	16,960	2.3	77	< 5
USA	19,840	1.6	76	< 5
India	340	1.8	58	57
Italy	13,330	3.0	77	< 5
Egypt	660	3.6	63	56
Sweden	19,300	1.8	77	< 5

Source: World Bank, *World Development Report* (1990).

THE ORIGINS OF SOCIALISM AND COMMUNISM

The eighteenth and nineteenth centuries produced the Industrial Revolution, and with it a dramatic change in the structures of the economies and societies it touched. The new technologies of the Industrial Revolution resulted in the development of the factory system and an increased movement of workers from rural to urban areas. In the fast-growing cities, workers often lived in squalid conditions. In order for families to eke out a living, children went alongside their parents to work in the factories, where they all

CLOSE-UP: MARXIST ECONOMICS

While there were many writers in the nineteenth century who advocated socialism, none was more influential than Karl Marx. His ideas not only influenced how socialism developed within the Soviet Union, they have given rise to a school of economics called the Marxist school. Like any major school, there is an evolution of ideas and disagreements among its members.

One important idea concerns what determines, or should determine, prices. The answer given by the basic economic model is the law of supply and demand. Marx, by contrast, made use of what was called the labour theory of value, a set of ideas developed earlier by the British economist David Ricardo. The labour theory of value argued that the value of any good should be attributed to the workers who made it; a good that required more labour should be valued more highly, and vice versa. Marx considered the difference between what a good was sold for and the labour costs that went into making the good, the profits of the firm and the return to capital, as an exploitation of workers. By contrast, in market economies profits are viewed as providing firms with incentives, and capital is seen as a scarce factor—like any other scarce factor, such as land or labour—that will be efficiently allocated only when it fetches a return.

Another important strand in Marxist thought is that the economic system affects the nature of individuals and the evolution of technology. Many Marxists believe that under a different social system, people would behave differently. They would be less materialistic, more concerned about helping one another, more committed to their jobs. During wartime, we often see changes in attitudes and behaviour. Whether human nature is sufficiently mutable that some social system might achieve these idealistic goals over long periods of time remains debatable; what is clear is that none

of the Soviet-style economies, during their decades-long experiments, have succeeded.

A third strand of Marxist thought emphasizes the link between politics and economics. Marxists claim that the answer to the question of "for whom" is provided not just by the impersonal workings of the law of supply and demand in competitive markets, but by power—the economic power of monopolies and the political power of the wealthy. The wealthy use the government to gain for themselves what they cannot achieve in the marketplace. Marxists cite instances of Western governments spending hundreds of billions of dollars to fight a war to preserve business interests—as some allege was an important part of the motivation for the war in the Persian Gulf in 1990–1991—while claiming it has insufficient money to eradicate poverty at home or to feed the starving millions in Africa.

Marx stressed the importance of economic factors in determining the entire structure of society. Changes in technology bring about concomitant changes in economic relations. Such changes in the past had led the economy from feudalism to capitalism, and would lead from capitalism to socialism and on to communism. While Marx peered into the future with what from hindsight looks like a very cloudy crystal ball, he may have been correct in his emphasis on the importance of economic factors in determining the evolution of society. In an ironic twist of history, though, economic forces appear to have injured socialism more than capitalism. After all, it is the economic successes of the capitalist systems of the world's industrialized countries, combined with the economic failures of the Soviet-style socialist economies, that have led to the reaction against socialism in Eastern Europe and the Soviet Union, and to the ongoing changes in their political systems.

worked long hours in unhealthy conditions. Periodically economies faced a recession or depression, and the workers were thrown out of their jobs and forced to beg, steal, or starve. Life for the unlanded peasants in the rural sectors was hardly more idyllic: in Ireland in the 1840s, for instance, a fifth of the population (half a million people) starved to death.

While the vast majority of people thus lived on the edge of survival, a few individuals had considerable wealth, often inherited. Between the very wealthy and the poor was a small but growing middle class, mainly commercial and professional. (By contrast, today in Europe and America, it is the middle class, consisting of professionals, businesspeople, and high-wage workers, that is dominant.)

Were these conditions inevitable? Could they be changed? If so, how? These questions were raised by numerous social thinkers from the late eighteenth century on. Many saw the culprit in the capitalist economic system. The most influential critic of the capitalist system was a German living in London, England, Karl Marx.

Marx, like many of the other critics, was concerned with both the efficiency and equity of the capitalist system, to use the terms that we would use today. He saw people working hard and long, but the fruits of their labour seemed to accrue largely to the owners of the firm. He spoke of the exploitation of the workers. Marx was concerned not just with the abject living standards of workers, but with the conditions in which they worked. While people spent most of their time sweating in workshops, the work was not a meaningful part of their lives; they were alienated from their work. The political process provided no relief, for Marx saw the government, consisting of individuals drawn from the upper and middle classes, as pursuing what he referred to as class interests, which were antagonistic to the interests of the workers and peasants.

Marx's prognosis for capitalism as an economic structure was bleak. He believed that wages would remain at a bare subsistence level; if they should happen to rise above this level, the population would increase fast enough that the greater supply of labour would drive wages back down. But capitalists—owners of firms, or those who supplied firms with the funds they needed— would not fare well either in the long run, in Marx's view. He saw capitalists as having an uncontrollable urge to accumulate capital, to save. They would run out of investment opportunities, and thus the return to capital would decline. Moreover, the goods produced in their factories would go unsold, and workers would be paid so little they would be able to do no more than survive. To put this last insight in modern terms, Marx saw a persistent deficiency in aggregate demand.

According to Marx, the only way out of this morass was a change in the economic system, a change that he thought was inevitable. Just as the force of history had led the economy to evolve from medieval feudalism to capitalism, he believed that the economy would evolve from capitalism to socialism and eventually to communism. Not only would there be no private property, the state would make all allocation decisions: "From each according to his ability," wrote Marx, "and to each according to his needs."[1] Clearly Marx's vision of socialism provided different answers than the market economy to the basic economic questions of what to produce and in what quantities, how to produce it, for whom it should be produced, and who makes the decisions. The state, not the market, would decide what, how, and for whom.[2]

---

[1] Karl Marx, *Critique of the Gotha Program* (1875).

[2] In Marx's view, socialism itself was a transitional stage to an eventual time when the state would wither away. How production would be organized—how the basic decisions of what to produce, how to produce it, and for whom it should be produced would be made—in this eventual period was left unclear.

Among those who found Marx's ideas particularly attractive was a Russian revolutionary, Vladimir Ilyich Lenin. In the early years of the twentieth century, Russia was among the most backward of the countries of Europe. Peasants lived in a close-to-feudal relationship with their landlords. The Industrial Revolution had hardly touched the country. The poor conditions became even worse during World War I, when millions of Russian soldiers were killed. As the war dragged on, the military became increasingly unhappy with the support it was receiving from the government. The country was ripe for a revolution, and toward the war's end in February 1917, the czar was overthrown. A democratic coalition of parties took over, but it was short-lived. In October 1917, the Bolsheviks—the party of Lenin, with Marxism as its official ideology—seized the government. The first "communist" government was established.

There is considerable debate over whether the Russian version of communism matched Marx's incompletely sketched vision. In fact, Marx's primary concern was not detailing a plan for an alternative economic system. Rather, he was more concerned with studying capitalism, both its origins and its future.

Translating Marx's ideology into a program for running a populous, poor, and largely undeveloped and rural country was no easy task. To a great extent, it was ironic that Russia, hardly touched by capitalism at the time of the revolution, became the first to try to implement Marx's ideas. Marx had predicted that countries would have to pass through the capitalist phase on the way to socialism, and he had therefore expected socialism to arise first in countries such as Britain or France.

Indeed, the economic system that we know today as communism is as much due to how Lenin and his successor, Joseph Stalin, adapted Marx's ideas to the situation they found in Russia as it is to Marx's original ideas. What Marx's reaction would be to what evolved there one can only guess, but a hint is provided by his comment on the ideas of the French Marxists: "As for me, I am not a Marxist."

THE DISILLUSIONMENT WITH MARKETS

It is difficult today to understand how viable an alternative communism seemed to be in the 1920s and 1930s. In Canada and other developed countries today, there is widespread confidence in markets and in the efficiency with which they allocate resources. To be sure, there are problems; there are market failures, periods of unemployment, and pockets of poverty. But we have seen in this book how markets by and large allocate resources efficiently. We have seen as well how selective government interventions can remedy the market failures and, if there is the political will, at least partially address the problem of the inequality of income generated by the market. Confidence in market-based economic systems is built on more than just economic theory: in market economies, living standards have soared well beyond the imagination of anyone living a century ago.

But this confidence has not always been present; neither is it universal now. When North America went into the Great Depression in 1929, not to recover fully until World War II, hundreds of thousands of Canadians were thrown out of jobs. The capitalist economic system did not seem to be functioning well. Today, to the billions of people still living in abject poverty in India, elsewhere in Asia, and in Africa and South America, markets have failed to meet their rising aspirations. And even within the industrialized countries, there are many who have not partaken of the general prosperity; in their eyes, the market system has not worked.

It is not surprising, then, that many have sought an alternative economic system, which would be able at the same time to generate faster sustained economic growth and promote greater equality. Throughout the first half of this century, many saw socialism as the answer. They believed that if the government controlled the economy, not only would recessions be eliminated, so too would what they saw as the chaos of the marketplace, for instance the excess expansion of capacity in one industry accompanied by shortages in another industry.

HOW SOVIET-STYLE SOCIALIST ECONOMIES WORK

With its complete control over the economy, the government of a Soviet-style socialist economy has to provide all the answers to the basic economic questions—what is to be produced and in what quantities, how it is to be produced, for whom it is to be produced, and who makes the decisions. We saw in Chapter 2 the central role that private property, prices, and the profit incentive play in market economies. If these are to be abandoned, what is to replace them?

First, in Soviet-style economies, the coordination of economic activity was to be done by government ministries, through central planning. The government would make the decisions. Major decision making did not occur at the level of the plant, and at times not even in the ministry in charge of agriculture or mining or steel, but in a single ministry responsible for directing the economy. Five-year plans were drawn up, with well-defined targets—how much steel production was to be increased, how much food production, and so on. Individual plant managers were told not only what they were to produce, but how they were to produce it—what technologies to use, how much labour they would have, how much coal, and so forth.

Second, market incentive schemes were sometimes replaced by force. We saw in earlier chapters that some incentive schemes take the form of the carrot, some of the stick. The Soviet Union under Joseph Stalin preferred the stick: those who did not meet their targets were rewarded with a sojourn in Siberia.

Third, political controls and rewards also helped replace the lack of economic incentives. Key positions in the economy went to faithful members of the Communist party. In the early days of the revolution, these included many who really believed in socialism as an alternative, superior form of economic organization. Given their ideological commitment, economic incentives to work hard to meet the goals were relatively unimportant; and to the extent that incentives were important, they were provided by the potential for promotion. But as the years went by, membership in the party came to be seen as the vehicle for getting ahead. People joined the party, but not because they believed in anything it might have once stood for. Under Leonid Brezhnev, who was the first secretary of the Communist party (1964–1982), a term used to describe the actual head of the party, this cynical attitude spread; the party faithful not only received good jobs but enjoyed other benefits, including access to special stores at which goods not generally available could be acquired.

Another basic aspect of market economies, competition, was also shunned. Just as the Communist party had a monopoly in the political sphere, no competition with government enterprises was allowed, and the government enterprises did not compete with one another. The Soviet-style socialist governments failed to recognize the importance of competition in providing incentives and in deciding who was best suited to fulfill various roles in the economy. They did not, of course, eliminate all competition: there was still competition to be promoted to top positions and thus receive higher incomes and access to desirable goods. But success in this competition was not based on how efficiently you produced the goods that consumers wanted, or how innovative you were in devising new products. Rather, success was measured by how well you complied with the bureaucratic targets and requirements and how well you performed in the politics of the bureaucracy and party.

How well did central planning succeed in replacing markets? To answer that question, we need to take a closer look at each of the three principal markets.

THE LABOUR MARKET

Canada is noted for its labour mobility. Young people try one job, then another, until they find a job for which they are well suited. As technology and market conditions change, firms are born and die, and jobs are born and die with them. When some skills, such as computer programming, are in short supply, programmers' wages are bid up. This scarce resource goes to where it is most needed, and the high wage attracts more people to computer programming. Job mobility is an important part of the capitalist economy's incentive structure. Those who perform well are rewarded with better jobs; those who perform badly will not be promoted and may even be fired.

Under Soviet-style socialism, there was little job mobility. A worker was assigned to a firm early in life and often stayed with it until retirement. If by bad luck you were assigned a job you did not like, you might have been stuck with it for life. Under Stalin, the Soviet government ordered thousands of people to take jobs in distant parts of the Soviet Union. Some workers from Moscow were assigned to the Baltic republics, others to the far eastern regions of the Union. With the government controlling the labour market, there was little choice; you could not decline the offer. Control of the labour market provided the government with enormous political control.

The system supplied some countervailing advantages, however. There was little evidence of unemployment, although there may have been high levels of "disguised" unemployment. In a capitalist economy, if a firm finds it no longer needs a worker, it lets the worker go. Competition forces it to do this. When markets work well, the worker laid off by one firm finds a job at another where she is needed. This continual reallocation of labour is essential for economic efficiency. In the Soviet-socialist economies, however, firms had little incentive to lay off workers, since they could run losses with impunity. There were no incentives to maximize profits, and strong incentives to avoid "causing trouble." Laying off workers would be viewed as causing trouble. Moreover, in some countries, laying off workers was simply not allowed. In China, this has been colourfully referred to as the "iron rice bowl" policy. For the system, the gains in job security were purchased at the price of a loss in economic efficiency, a trade-off depicted in Figure 24.1. Socialist economies choose a point such as A in the figure, with far more security and far less efficiency than the capitalist economies, which choose point B.

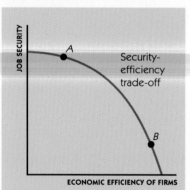

Figure 24.1 **THE SECURITY-EFFICIENCY TRADE-OFF**

Socialist countries have usually chosen a point like A, with far more security and far less efficiency, than the capitalist economies, which have chosen points more like B.

THE CAPITAL MARKET

Lenin, and Stalin after him, considered modernizing the economy the first task of the socialist system. If the country was to industrialize, it needed capital. Many developing countries, like Canada in the nineteenth century, have used foreign capital markets in the early stages of growth. This option was not available to the USSR, for two reasons. First, the new government faced an immediate hostile reaction from almost all the industrialized countries. Second, the new government refused to honour the debts incurred by the czarist government. Not surprisingly, then, it was cut off from credit and most trade. If capital was to be raised, it had to be raised internally.

There had been great inequality in czarist days, with a few individuals having much more wealth than others. But even after seizing what wealth it could, the new Communist government had insufficient capital to finance a development program. Furthermore, realizing its base of support was among the urban workers, the government was loath to tax them much to raise the funds. The only option was to raise funds from the peasants who lived in the rural sector, and who comprised the vast majority of the population at the time.

From the perspective of the peasants, all that had happened was that the exploitive landlords were replaced by an even more exploitive government. As the government attempted to tax them more, they produced less and less for the market. The resulting crisis persuaded Stalin that there was only one way out: to take control of the farms, to "collectivize" agriculture, in effect to organize agriculture more along the lines of a factory system. Rather than allowing a worker to run his own farm, the worker was made a state employee. The nationalization of the land accorded well with the general ideological commitment against private property. But in the process of the forced collectivization of agriculture, there were huge famines. Millions of people starved to death in Ukraine, a now independent republic known as the country's "bread basket" for its fertile land, while output was being forcibly removed to feed people in the cities.

In private markets, investment funds go to where the marginal returns are highest. Interest rates are the "price" of capital; they measure its scarcity value. In the Soviet-style socialist economies, it was the government that decided where scarce investment funds went. But how did these governments decide where funds should go? How did they decide how much should go to each sector?

To a large extent, these decisions were based on a belief about the "correct" path of development. Stalin had two basic ideas. First, he recognized that resources that were not allocated to consumption could be given to investment. He was aware of the production possibilities curve, depicted in Figure 24.2, entailing a trade-off between consumption and investment. Thus, his first objective was to reduce consumption, and move the economy from a point such as E_0 to E_1. One of the aims of the collectivization of agriculture was to do just that, to squeeze the farmers as much as possible. But urban workers' wages were also kept low. By keeping wages low and the supply of consumer goods limited, the Soviet planners in effect "forced" the economy to have high savings.

The second idea was to focus investment on heavy industry. Stalin considered huge factories, such as steel mills, the central symbol of modern economies, which distinguished them from less-developed, agrarian economies. He therefore invested primarily in heavy industry, providing little support for agriculture, consumer goods, or housing. The two ideas were in a sense intertwined: with low wages and low consumption, there was little need to invest in industries to provide consumption goods.

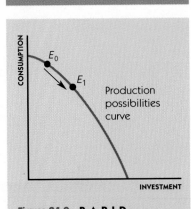

Figure 24.2 RAPID INDUSTRIALIZATION: MOVEMENTS ALONG THE PRODUCTION POSSIBILITIES CURVE

Soviet-style socialists believed that rapid growth of heavy industry was desirable, so they increased investment. But as the production possibilities curve shows, this can only be done at the expense of consumption. Central planners tried to move the economy towards a point such as E_1, with a high output of investment goods and a low output of consumption goods.

Thus, the central aspect of the Soviet-style socialist version of the capital market was low consumption, allowing the country as a whole to have a high savings rate, and heavy industrialization. The patterns initiated by the Soviet Union, including the collectivization of agriculture, were imitated by the other Communist governments.[3]

THE PRODUCT MARKET

In the USSR, government ministries decided what goods should be produced and how they should be produced. To a great extent, they also decided to whom goods were to be distributed. Many of the essentials of life, such as medical care and housing, were provided freely or at a modest price, though the individual had little choice about what she got. But not even the most enthusiastic government planner thought it was feasible for the government to decide how much each individual should receive of each good. Some discretion was left to the family. They could decide which foods or what clothing to purchase; to this extent, a market system was used to distribute goods. But even here, the government did not really rely on the price system. It set prices, but they were substantially below the market-clearing level, as illustrated in Figure 24.3, so there were shortages.

In Chapter 5, we learned what happens if prices are fixed at a level below market-clearing: there is excess demand. Shortages are pervasive. People have to wait in long

[3] With some minor exceptions. Poland never collectivized its agriculture.

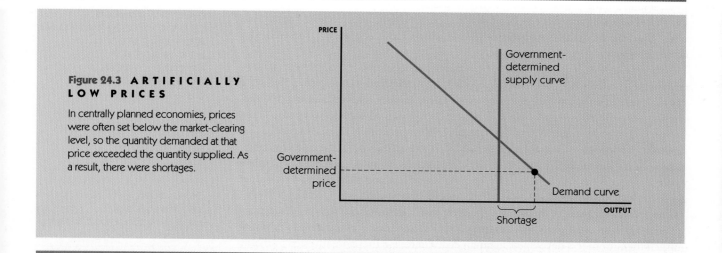

Figure 24.3 ARTIFICIALLY LOW PRICES

In centrally planned economies, prices were often set below the market-clearing level, so the quantity demanded at that price exceeded the quantity supplied. As a result, there were shortages.

lines to get the limited supply of goods. For durables like cars, shortages mean waiting for months, sometimes years, to get the goods, even if one has the cash. Shortages give enormous power to those who have discretion about who gets the goods in short supply. Thus, managers in the USSR were reputed to exchange "favours" with one another. For a manager to sell goods at a price higher than the official price would be a crime; but for the manager of a firm that manufactures television sets to allow the manager of a car plant to jump to the head of the line and get his TV, with the favour reciprocated, seemed not only acceptable but commonplace.

When prices are not set at their market-clearing levels and are not responsive to changes in economic circumstances, it is clear that they will not serve the role in allocating resources that they do in market economies.

While in market economies prices guide firms in making decisions about how their goods are to be produced—prices signal the relative scarcity of different inputs—in the socialist economy, prices could not perform that role. Ideology was important in two ways. First, government ministries associated the charging of interest with capitalism. They did not understand the important role that interest rates play in allocating one of society's scarce resources, capital. Second, as we have seen, they thought of heavy industrialization as the hallmark of a successful economy. Thus, Soviet-style economies tended to use very capital-intensive methods of production, and because of their failure to charge interest, they never realized how high the costs of these methods were.

By the same token, profits and losses did not serve the role in Soviet-style economies that they did in market economies. The quest for profits in market economies provides the incentive for entrepreneurs; equally important, losses are a signal for firms to close down. Returns to investment are the signals that determine how capital should be allocated. In socialist economies, with the state owning all firms and therefore all profits, profits provide little incentive; and losses are seldom used as a basis for shutting down establishments. If a firm makes a loss, the government meets the deficit. János Kornai, a Hungarian economist, refers to this phenomenon as **soft budget constraints,** to contrast them with the harsh reality of budget constraints facing firms in a market economy. For the firm in a socialist system, there is no penalty for making losses and no incentive to conserve on resources.

In a way, it made sense for the Soviet government not to pay too much attention to profits, since the prices firms received for what they produced and the prices they paid for the inputs they used (including labour and capital) were not market-clearing prices; they did not represent the scarcity value of the resources used or of the goods produced. Thus, the profits were not a good measure of the benefits or costs of the firm's production. By the same token, since prices were not set at market-clearing levels, they did not reflect true scarcity, and hence returns to investment—measured in rubles—were not a sound guide for allocating investments. Prices and wages provided little guidance for whether firms should try to economize more on labour or capital or other inputs. There is an important lesson here: failure to use the market in one area (for example, the product market) makes it virtually impossible to rely on the market in other areas (for example, the capital market).

It is perhaps no accident that the fields in which the Soviet Union was able to achieve its greatest successes—for example, military research, space technology, and mathematics and physics—were all fields in which markets play a limited role in capitalist economies.

THE THREE MARKETS, SOVIET STYLE

LABOUR MARKET

    There was no labour mobility.

    Government assigned individuals to jobs.

    There was no unemployment.

    Incentives were low.

CAPITAL MARKET

    Government owned all capital.

    Government determined the savings rate.

        High savings, low consumption

    Government allocated all investment.

        Emphasis on heavy industry

PRODUCT MARKET

    Markets were used to distribute goods.

    Government kept prices below market-clearing levels.

        Pervasive shortages, long queues

        Prices failing to serve their allocative role

SOVIET-STYLE SOCIALISM AND INEQUALITY

The Soviet government, through its planning ministry, not only decided what was to be produced and how, it also provided the answer to the "for whom" question. In answering this question, three aspects of Soviet ideology played an important role. First, Soviet-style economies were committed to heavy industrialization and a de-emphasis on agriculture. Not surprisingly, then, a large part of the burden of the costs was borne by agriculture. Forced collectivization in agriculture kept agriculture wages low. In effect, there were high taxes on agriculture.

Second, the program of high savings and low consumption could be interpreted as putting an emphasis on the consumption of future generations at the expense of the consumption of the current generation.

Third, an attempt was made to reduce the inequality in society, or at least that is what leaders' rhetoric said. The government determined everyone's wages. It decided how much more a skilled worker got than an unskilled worker. Some goods it allocated directly, such as markets for housing and medical care. Whether or to what extent Soviet-style socialist systems were successful in reducing inequality remains debatable. On the one hand, after confiscating all land and other property, there were no longer any very rich people. Also, free medicine and highly subsidized food and apartments provided what was referred to as a "safety net" for the poor.

But on the other hand, differences in life-style between the worst-off members of society and high party officials remained enormous. Among those who were not high party officials, whole families lived crowded together in one room. Though no one starved, long hours were spent in lines trying to obtain the barest necessities of life. By contrast, high party officials enjoyed vacations along the beaches of the Black Sea, could buy goods unavailable elsewhere at stores reserved for party members, and had chauffeur-driven cars and other powers and perquisites enjoyed by relatively few within the capitalist world. Among workers, there existed large wage differentials, commensurate with those observed in capitalist economies; though since so many things were provided cheaply by the state, the wage differentials translated into perhaps smaller differences in living standards.

Even the most vaunted achievements of socialism, the prevention of the abject extremes of poverty, have in recent years been thrown into doubt. In the period of 1960–1961 in China, demographers now estimate that as many as 20 million Chinese starved to death. In the democracies, a free press would have presumably ensured that a calamity like this simply could not have occurred. Something would have been done. In China, it went almost unnoticed.

THE BASIC ECONOMIC QUESTIONS UNDER SOVIET-STYLE SOCIALISM

1. What is produced?
   Heavy industrial goods
   Other goods as the state sees fit

2. How are goods produced?
   With technologies and inputs decided upon by the state (often capital-intensive technologies)

3. For whom are they produced?
   For future generations (high forced savings rates)
   For present generations according to the wages set by government (high "taxes" on agriculture)
   For government officials, who get high rewards

4. Who makes the decisions?
   Central planners

THE FAILURE OF SOCIALISM

For several decades, Stalin's program appeared to enjoy a modicum of success. He was able to force net investment rates up to almost unprecedented levels of more than 23 percent of net national product in 1937. Many factories were built. The official statistics suggested that the high savings rates had spearheaded a path of rapid industrialization and growth. Though there is growing doubt about the reliability of the statistics, there is little doubt that what gains were made were accompanied by a high level of political repression. The USSR's economic progress was interrupted by World War II, in which 20 million Russians are believed to have died, and the economy was greatly disrupted.

The period after World War II saw the spread of Soviet-style socialism to Eastern Europe—Poland, Czechoslovakia, East Germany, Hungary, Romania, Bulgaria, Yugoslavia, and Albania—and, in 1949, to China.[4] In the case of the Eastern European countries, at least, the spread was hardly voluntary; it was the price they paid for being liberated from the Germans by Soviet troops at the end of the war. Before the war, some of the Eastern European countries had enjoyed reasonably high standards of living. Others, such as Albania, had been extremely poor and backwards.

The ensuing decades witnessed several changes in attitudes towards the Soviet-style socialist experiment. At first, the "efficiency" virtues of the system were lauded. The planning mechanism replaced the perceived chaos of the marketplace. Investment could be directed in a rational way. Resources could be quickly mobilized. Moreover, the government could force the high levels of savings required for a successful development program. Textbooks as well as popular writings talked about a trade-off between growth and development on the one hand and freedom on the other. Strong central control was thought to be necessary for rapid growth. Moreover, it was thought that Soviet-style socialism could make possible a level of equality that the market economy had not been able to attain. Basic human services like health and education could be brought to the masses.

But economies like Czechoslovakia and Hungary, which had been prosperous before the war, fell behind other European countries; when this happened, concerns about the efficiency of the system began to be raised. Such systems could force their citizens to save more because they could repress consumption, but could they allocate resources efficiently? It became increasingly clear that the countries were not growing as fast as one would have thought. The higher savings rates did little more than offset the higher levels of inefficiency.

By the mid-1970s, inklings of an impending economic crisis became more and more apparent. While agricultural productivity in North America and Western Europe had boomed, in the Soviet-style socialist countries it had stagnated. Nikita Khrushchev, who led the Soviet Union from the death of Stalin until he was replaced by Brezhnev in 1964, recognized the problems in agriculture and directed more of the country's investment there. But in 1973, the Soviet Union began buying massive amounts of wheat from Canada, the United States, and other Western countries to feed its people. Mean-

---

[4] Mongolia had adopted Soviet-style socialism much earlier, in 1924. Cuba adopted a variant much later under Castro, in 1959. North Korea and North Vietnam both adopted Soviet-style socialism as soon as their governments were established.

CLOSE-UP: ENVIRONMENTAL DAMAGE IN THE SOVIET UNION

One of the alleged advantages of centrally controlled economies was that unlike ruthless capitalists, socialist firms would take into account the costs and benefits to all members of society. In the area of environmental protection, that promise was not kept. In fact, in the words of one recent study, "When historians finally conduct an autopsy on the Soviet Union and Soviet Communism, they may reach the verdict of death by ecocide."

Market economies may often have difficulty dealing with pollution externalities. But in attempting to stimulate their economy, Soviet central planners often made pollution problems worse. For example, oil and energy prices were held deliberately low, as a form of assistance to manufacturers who used oil as an input. But lower prices encouraged wasteful use of energy, and when combined with a lack of antipollution measures, this produced a literally sickening air pollution. Today in the industrial center of what was called Industrial Magniogorsk, nine out of ten children become ill with pollution-related diseases like bronchitis, asthma, and cancer.

Highly intensive farming, in a situation where no one had a property right to the land and an incentive to protect it, led to massive pesticide use and soil erosion. Three-quarters of the surface water in what used to be the Soviet Union is now badly polluted, whether from industrial or agricultural sources.

Perhaps the most publicized result of all was the explosion at the Chernobyl nuclear power station in 1986, which exposed perhaps 20 million Soviet citizens to excessive levels of radiation. If that nuclear power plant had been forced to use high-priced safety equipment to avoid that externality, it might well have been shut down years earlier.

In many cities and republics, a protest against this environmental destruction formed the base of the popular movements that rebelled against the Soviet Union in the early 1990s. Rather than correcting the market failures that led to pollution, Soviet central planners had magnified them into ecological disasters.

Sources: "Rubbishing of a Superpower," *The Economist,* April 25, 1992, pp. 99–100; Murray Feshbach and Alfred Friendly, *Ecocide in the USSR* (New York: Basic Books, 1992).

while, the Eastern European countries' reputation for low-quality workmanship was underscored when a nuclear power plant at Chernobyl, in Ukraine, suffered a melt-down in 1986, releasing radiation across much of Europe.

As Mikhail Gorbachev, who came to power in 1985, attempted to introduce reforms to make the economy more efficient, the magnitude of the problems the country faced became clearer: it became evident that many of the statistics on industrial production had been more exaggerated than even many skeptics had thought. Indicators of well-being, such as infant mortality statistics, had similarly been spun out of thin air. Inadequate hospitals with substandard equipment had not only failed to keep pace with developments in the West, but may actually have become worse during recent decades.

The final verdict on the Soviet-style socialist experiment, in most economists' judgment, is that it has been a failure. Today, more than seventy years after the socialist experiment began in the Soviet Union, income per capita is a tenth of what it is in Canada and the United States. Far from having buried the United States, the Soviet Union finds its standard of living to be close to that of Brazil, Argentina, and other countries considered to be underdeveloped, as illustrated in Figure 24.4. The socialist experiment in the Soviet Union has had some remarkable achievements, like the Sputnik satellite, but a productive and growing economy is not among them.

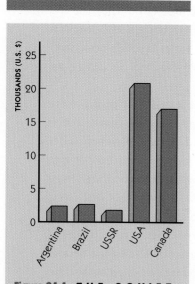

Figure 24.4 THE SOVIET STANDARD OF LIVING

After decades of socialism, the average standard of living in the former Soviet Union was close to that of Brazil, Argentina, and other less-developed nations. Sources: World Development Report (1991), Table 1; World Bank, World Tables (1991).

REASONS FOR THE FAILURE

The continued success of the capitalist system and the failure of Soviet-style socialist economies can be attributed to incentives and markets, or the lack of them.

The socialists failed to recognize the importance of incentives. Workers, both in collective farms and in manufacturing firms, had no incentive to do more than was required. Managers similarly had no incentives. Firms could not keep any profits they made, and managerial pay in any case did not depend on the profitability of the enterprise. There was no competition, and the soft budget constraints—the fact that losses would be made up by the government—further attenuated managerial incentives.

Equally important, there was no incentive for innovation and growth. The increases in productivity of the labour force in capitalist economies over the past century, with the concomitant increases in wages, are in no small measure the result of the innovative efforts of entrepreneurs. These entrepreneurs almost surely did not succeed out of the desire to enhance the welfare of their workers; they were motivated by the lust for profits and the desire for returns to their savings. But as Adam Smith said, such motives provide a far surer guide to the enhancement of a nation's wealth than any other.

Socialists wanted to replace the market mechanism for allocating resources with central planning. But they encountered two further problems. First, the bureaucrats did not have the requisite information to know how to allocate resources efficiently. Managers of firms had no incentive to tell the central planners what the minimum inputs required to meet their production goals were. Rather, they had every incentive to claim they needed more than they really did. This made their job easier. And they had no incentive to exceed their goals; for if they did, the planners would raise their targets for the next year.

Second, planners could not perfectly monitor the various firms in the economy, to ensure that resources were used in the way intended. And firms had only limited incentives to comply with the planners' directives. They were not rewarded, and they knew they were only imperfectly monitored. Sometimes the managers could divert resources meant for the firm to their own private use. Their disdain for the planners was enhanced by the fact that the planners often put impossible demands on them, such as asking them to produce outputs without providing them the requisite inputs. To fulfill their quota, firms had to acquire the inputs from a "gray" market outside the planning system.

The socialists did not understand the importance of capital markets, interest rates, and profits. As this text has emphasized, capital is a scarce resource. It must be allocated efficiently. Prices provide the signals that make this possible. Because the Soviet-style socialist economies set prices by command rather than through markets, prices did not provide the necessary signals. Try as they might to use the planning mechanism to replace the market mechanism, socialist government planning boards simply did not have the requisite information to allocate investment efficiently.

Given the scarcity of capital, the Soviet strategy of heavy industrialization probably did not make much sense. It would have made more sense to focus attention on industries that require less capital.

The failure of worker incentives, the failure of planners to allocate resources efficiently, and the failure of firms to use resources efficiently largely accounted for the inefficiency of the system. But there were other factors as well. The drabness of life, the lack of opportunity afforded by the system, the long hours spent in lines trying to get rotten vegetables or a small portion of meat, all contributed to a social malaise, evidenced by a high incidence of alcoholism, which impaired worker productivity. The worker under Soviet-style socialism seemed truly alienated from his work.

CAUSES OF THE FAILURE OF SOVIET-STYLE SOCIALISM

1. Failure to provide adequate incentives to workers and managers
   A lack of competition, soft budget constraints, and a lack of incentives to stimulate innovation and growth were major factors.

2. Failure of planning mechanism to replace markets
   Planners lacked the requisite information to allocate resources efficiently.
   Planners lacked the ability to monitor firms and make sure resources were used in the ways intended.

REFORMS IN THE SOVIET-STYLE SOCIALIST ECONOMIES

As the failures of Soviet-style socialism became more evident, a variety of reforms were discussed. There were three possible tacks: try harder to make the socialist system work; give up on socialism and move to a market-based system; or find a third way, which would be neither capitalism nor socialism. For three decades, beginning with Khrushchev, the Soviet Union tried the first strategy. Workers were exhorted to work harder. Money poured into agriculture but seemed to disappear, leaving little traces of enhanced productivity. Anti-vodka campaigns were launched to increase worker productivity.

During 1990 and 1991, there was much debate over whether or not the first strategy should be abandoned. In October of 1990, Gorbachev announced that the Soviet Union would be converted to capitalism in five hundred days; but he soon dropped this program, whereupon the economists who had been advising him on the market strategy resigned and it appeared as if there would be another attempt to make socialism work. But then, following the attempted coup in August 1991 and the dissolution of the Soviet Union, directions were changed again: most of the newly created republics seemed committed to adopting some form of market system.

People who looked for a third solution sought ways of combining what they saw as the strengths of capitalism with those of socialism. While Hungary made some attempt to do this, perhaps the most successful experiment along these lines was performed in China, where the so-called responsibility system in agriculture essentially allowed farmers to sell most of what they produced in markets and to keep the proceeds. As a result, agricultural production skyrocketed during the late 1970s and early 1980s. The annual growth rate of grain production in the six years after the responsibility system was adopted (1978–1984) was 5 percent, compared with 3.5 percent in the thirteen years before the new system (1965–1978).

MARKET SOCIALISM

An important idea lying behind several of the reform movements was that of market socialism, which argued that an economy could combine the advantages of market mechanisms with public ownership of the means of production. Oskar Lange, who was a professor of economics at the University of Chicago before returning to Poland after World War II, eventually to become a vice-president of that country's Communist government, was a leading advocate of this concept.

Under market socialism, prices would serve the same allocative role that they do in capitalist economies. Prices would be set so that demand equalled supply. Firms would act like competitive price takers. They would maximize their profits at the prices they faced. They would produce up to the point where price equalled marginal cost. They would hire labour up to the point where the value of the marginal product of labour was equal to the wage. Since the government owned all machines and buildings, it would have to take responsibility for all investment decisions. These decisions would be made according to a national plan, which defined the nation's priorities. The planning process would entail a close interaction between the government planners and the firms, with the firms informing the planners of what was required to meet various production goals.

In the 1930s, there was a great debate between the advocates of market socialism, including Oskar Lange and the American economist Abba Lerner, and a group of Austrian economists, including Ludwig von Mises and Nobel laureate Friedrich von Hayek. The Austrians did not believe that the government would have the information required to allocate investment efficiently. They thought that the task of allocating resources, or even setting market-clearing prices, was simply too complicated to be done by a government bureau. (As it turned out, they were largely correct.) And they did not believe that government-owned firms would act like private firms. In their view, market socialism was doomed to failure.

The advocates of market socialism emphasized the fact that there were, in modern terms, pervasive market failures. Capital and risk markets were imperfect. There were externalities. Competition was imperfect. The market gave rise to great inequality. And capitalist economies seemed prone to periodic chronic illnesses—to recessions and depressions.

PROBLEMS WITH MARKET SOCIALISM

Market socialism faces two key problems: obtaining the requisite information to set prices and providing managers with incentives.

First, in order to set prices at market-clearing levels, planners have to know, in effect, demand and supply curves; they have to know an enormous amount about what consumers want as well as firms' capabilities. They seldom have this information, partly, as has been noted, because firms have no incentive to tell planners what their capabilities are. Even with good information, it is extraordinarily difficult for a government bureaucracy to set prices at market-clearing levels. Lange hoped that with better computers the task could be done quickly, but as better and better computers have been developed, it has become increasingly clear that the problems of setting simultaneously the prices of the millions of goods produced in a modern market economy cannot be solved by a computer, however advanced.

Indeed, it has become clear that while prices play a central role in how the market economy functions, they are only part of the market's incentive systems. Customers care about the quality of the goods they purchase. For instance, for firms, having inputs delivered on time is essential. Consider the simple problem of producing nails in a socialist economy. Given a directive to produce so many nails, the nail factory produces short, stubby nails. When the directive is modified to include a specification for a longer nail, the factory responds by producing a nail with the cheapest steel it can get hold of; the result is that the nail splits when hit too hard. When told that the steel should not be too brittle, the firm finds a steel that bends too easily to make it useful for many purposes.

In market economies, firms will not produce at the market price unless they know they can sell the goods. In a socialist economy, the producer simply delivers the goods to another government enterprise, whose problem it is to sell the goods. When China set too high a price for fans, for example, the factories produced more fans than could be sold. Meanwhile, there were huge shortages of most other consumer goods.

While setting prices wrong for consumer goods causes inconvenience, setting prices wrong for producer goods causes further inefficiencies and dislocations. Shortages of inputs impair the entire production process. If a firm producing an intermediate good cannot get some input it needs, it will not be able to provide its product to the firms that need it. A shortage at one critical point can thus have reverberations through other parts of the economy.

A second problem with market socialism is that managers often lack incentives. When the enterprise makes a profit, they cannot keep the profit. And when the enterprise makes a loss, the government makes up the deficit. Market socialism therefore does not resolve the problem of soft budget constraints. Furthermore, competition, which lies at the heart of the market's incentive system, is absent, and this lack of competition is reflected in all aspects of behaviour, including the incentive to produce goods that reflect what customers want.

Market socialists thought the central control of prices had one distinct advantage: the government could remedy some of the market failures that arise in capitalist economies. If a particular industry polluted the air, production of that industry's good would be limited and higher prices would be charged to reflect the externality. In principle, if there is an externality associated with burning coal, that it contributes to global warming, the socialist planner would let that be reflected in the price it announced for the use of coal.

But socialism, including market socialism, turned out far less willing to face up to these externalities than did capitalist economies. Each of the socialist countries has reported disastrous levels of air and water pollution: huge lakes that are being drained of life, smog rivalling anything seen in the West, rivers that have become chemical sewers. Evidently those in the economic ministries saw their responsibility as increasing production as fast as possible, regardless of the environmental cost; rather than raising the price of coal to discourage its use, they kept its price low as a means of encouraging production. Furthermore, the absence of democracy meant there was no forum in which those who had to suffer could register their protest.

Parts of the experiment with market socialism have been an unambiguous success, at least as compared with Soviet-style socialism. As was noted, the responsibility system of agriculture in China has resulted in huge increases in agricultural productivity. But other parts of the experiment are more debated. To some, market socialism lacks the best features of both capitalism and socialism: it lacks the market's incentive structure and traditional socialism's other mechanisms of economic control. Thus, within Hungary, which had gone the farthest along the road to market socialism before 1989, a consensus seems to have developed against market socialism.

WORKERS' COOPERATIVES IN YUGOSLAVIA

Yet another type of socialist experiment occurred in Yugoslavia. Marshal Tito, a Communist who led the fight against the Nazis in Yugoslavia and became the country's leader after World War II, broke with Stalin in 1948. In the ensuing years, a new form of socialism evolved in which decentralization and decision making by firms played a much larger role. In effect, ownership of firms was turned over to the workers, who were responsible for choosing their own managers. In practice, the Communist party exercised considerable influence both in the choice of managers and in the decisions made.

The idea of worker-owned and -managed firms—cooperatives—has had a long history, with a variety of experiments performed throughout Europe and North America. Even today in the United States, there are some enormously successful worker-owned firms—Amana, which makes refrigerators, Avis, the car rental company, and W. W. Norton, the publisher of this book. Ulgar, a successful household appliances firm, began as a worker cooperative in Mondragón, Spain. Today, with thousands of workers located in many separate plants, it is still run as a cooperative.

Cooperatives have the advantage that because the worker is also a part owner, she has a greater commitment to the firm and more incentive to work hard. While this argument seems valid for cooperatives involving relatively few workers, it does not apply as well to large enterprises, and this proved to be a problem in Yugoslavia. Managers elected by a vote of the workers may be as remote as managers chosen by a board of directors. In cooperatives with thousands of workers, each worker gets back a negligible amount of any extra profits that result from anything she does. The most successful cooperatives thus are often the smaller ones.

In Yugoslavia, the cooperatives encountered another problem. What is the incentive to hire new workers? If new workers have the same rights as old workers, the profits of the enterprise must be divided more ways. Whether for this or another reason, Yugoslavia was plagued with high unemployment rates.

Investment posed still a third problem. When Yugoslavian workers left their cooperative, they received nothing. There was therefore little interest in investing, at least in the long term, or otherwise increasing the market value of the enterprise. Workers did not have an incentive to make investments that yielded returns beyond the date of their retirement. The investment problem was exacerbated by the employment problem: the reluctance to hire new workers resulted in an aging work force, and as the work force aged, incentives to invest were diminished. There was every incentive to pay high wages and to borrow to pay for any needed investment. Not surprisingly, the cooperatives' economic condition deteriorated steadily.[5]

Some of these problems are not *inherent* in cooperatives. For instance, in cooperatives in North America and Europe, when a person retires or leaves the cooperative for any other reason, he takes his capital out. That is, he is viewed as a part owner of the enterprise; the share he owns depends on the rules of the cooperative, typically how long he has been with the cooperative and in what positions he has served. By the same token, when a worker joins a cooperative, she has in effect to buy a share. (The company may loan her the money, so her take-home pay may be reduced until she has contributed her capital share.) The better the cooperative does, the more valuable it is, the more she will be able to receive when she leaves. This provides an obvious incentive for the cooperative to make good investment decisions.

THE TRANSITION TO MARKET ECONOMIES

Today many of the former socialist countries, including Hungary, the Czech Republic, Slovakia, and Poland, are committed to transforming their economies into market economies. Others, such as Bulgaria, Romania, and Albania, want *some* market reforms, but how many and how fast remains uncertain. The following paragraphs describe some of the key problems facing those countries that are attempting to make the transition to a market economy. Studying these transition problems has enhanced economists' understanding of modern market economies.

The problems of transition faced by the Eastern European countries have been exacerbated by the economic chaos in the former Soviet Union. The Soviet Union was the main trading partner of the Eastern European countries. Thus, as they face the problem

---

[5] This list of problems that Yugoslavia faced is not meant to be exhaustive. There were others: lack of competition among people who purchased farmers' produce, for instance, meant that farmers received lower prices for their goods, and this discouraged farmers' production.

of making the transition to a market economy, they face the additional burden of finding new markets to replace sales to the republics of the former Soviet Union, which have plummeted. To make matters worse, the kinds of goods they produced for the Soviet Union are not the kinds of high-quality goods consumers in Western Europe, Japan, and North America want. Not only must they find new markets, they must reorient their production.

MACROECONOMIC PROBLEMS

The first hurdle Eastern European economies face in making a transition to markets is a period of disruption in which living standards, at least for some, fall below even the low level that they had been under socialism.

A central problem with socialism was that resources were inefficiently allocated. If the economy is to move from a point inside its production possibilities curve such as A in Figure 24.5 to a point on the curve, resources will have to be reallocated. Factories will have to be shut down. Workers will have to be let go. These disruptions will be reflected in high unemployment. Transitional unemployment is like frictional unemployment, the unemployment that occurs as workers move between jobs, just magnified many times over. Poland, the first country to attempt the transition, experienced unemployment rates variously estimated at between 25 and 33 percent. In Romania, miners, seeing their real wages cut by a third, rioted and succeeded in bringing down the market-oriented prime minister; the new prime minister, however, was an economist even more committed to market reforms.

Unemployment is particularly serious in Eastern European countries, because they do not have in place the same kinds of safety nets to protect people forced out of jobs as are found in Canada and other Western countries. This is not surprising, since under the previous regime unemployment was not a problem; firms retained workers even when they were no longer needed. They had no profit motive, no budget constraint. But now, in the transition, firms do face budget constraints. Moreover, capital markets are not yet working well, and new firms are not being created and old firms are not expanding production to absorb the workers who have been laid off.

Inflation receives considerable attention in Eastern European countries these days, partly because it is felt by everyone, partly because typically wages do not keep pace with prices, so that living standards fall. But the fall in living standards is not really caused by the inflation; it is caused by the economic disruption of the transition process, which simultaneously reduces output, leads to inflation, and lowers living standards.

The reason that inflation always seems to arise in the transition is easy to see. The Soviet-style economies were run with prices below market-clearing levels; shortages were endemic. Hence, once prices were freed, an increase in prices was inevitable. One-time price increases, particularly of necessities like bread, which had been heavily subsidized (so much so that it was cheaper for farmers to buy bread to feed to their pigs than to buy grain), cause political problems: such price increases led to the downfall of the Polish government in 1989. But what also worries governments in most of these countries is the likelihood of the onset of inflation. Chapter 20 explained one reason for their worry: that inflationary expectations, once established, may perpetuate inflation.

Many of these countries, especially Russia and Poland, face another problem: the shortage of consumer goods has resulted in the accumulation of large holdings of

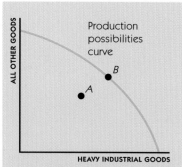

Figure 24.5
INEFFICIENCIES UNDER SOCIALISM

The Soviet-style socialist economies seemed to use their resources inefficiently, so that they operated substantially below the production possibilities curve, such as at point A. Moving the economy from A to a point like B, on the production possibilities curve, will entail substantial improvements in efficiency.

money. This is referred to as the problem of **monetary overhang,** and it contributes to the inflationary pressures. The Soviet Union attempted to deal with this problem by calling in all notes of 50 rubles or more. (Before the economic crisis, the ruble was worth $2 at the official exchange rate; for the average Soviet citizen, 50 rubles was a substantial amount of money. By mid-1992, there were 200 rubles to the dollar, so 50 rubles amounted to a quarter.) Each individual was allowed to exchange a few old 50-ruble notes for new ones, but any excess was in effect confiscated by the government. This seemingly capricious action, while it did reduce the monetary overhang, increased the disaffection of the people towards their government.

Huge government deficits have also contributed to inflationary pressures. As the government's control over the economy weakens, its revenue sources also diminish. Under socialism, it could simply seize corporate profits; if it wanted to increase profits and thus its revenues, it could just increase the prices charged or reduce the wages paid. As the government abandoned its role in wage and price setting, it lost its ability to collect revenues in this way. But cutting back on expenditures seems no easier in Eastern Europe than elsewhere. Food subsidies are a major drain on the budget, but government threats to reduce them have met with stiff opposition. In the Soviet Union, the government deficit had reached 10 percent of GDP by 1990.

As the crisis in the Soviet economy unfolded in the late 1980s and early 1990s, inflation—and the threat of further inflation—and the unavailability of goods proved extremely disruptive to what remained of the old economic structure. Farmers, for instance, did not want to deliver food to the city in return for rubles that were constantly falling in value; and even if the rubles did not fall in value, people could not obtain goods with them. All the transition governments are committed to doing something about inflation. The range of instruments that a transition government has to control inflation, having abandoned direct price controls, are those discussed in Parts Four, Five, and earlier chapters in Six: cutting government expenditures, raising taxes, and restricting credit. But controlling the credit supply has proved both important and difficult in several of the countries in transition, such as Hungary. There are often several different lending institutions, with no central bank able to control the overall level of credit. Moreover, there is often considerable interfirm lending, so that firms that have access to credit extend it to others. Without any controls on the level of credit, it is easy to arrive at a situation in which there is excess demand for goods.

Poland did succeed in gaining control over credit, but with mixed effects on the economy; while aggregate demand was checked, the lack of credit impaired many firms' ability to produce. Firms need to have access to credit to purchase their inputs. Thus, the credit contraction not only decreased aggregate demand, it also decreased aggregate supply. Nonetheless, inflationary pressures were abated in Poland; other countries may not be so lucky.

PRIVATIZATION AND COMPETITION

Private property and competition are at the centre of the market economy. *Allowing* competition is easy. The government can simply say that anyone who wants to set up a firm and has the necessary resources can do so. Generating and sustaining competition are more difficult.

One important way for Eastern European countries to promote competition is through trade liberalization—opening up the economy to competition from abroad.

But while most economists believe that trade liberalization will enhance economic efficiency in the long run, some are concerned about those who lose out in the competition, including people who lose their jobs. They give a variant of the infant industry argument, which goes like this. Enterprises in the former socialist economies have been insulated from competition for decades. It is unfair suddenly to subject them to competition and make their survival depend on this market test. They need time to learn how to compete.

Another way to promote competition is to sell off different parts of existing state enterprises to private entrepreneurs. There are few problems in selling off small businesses—barbershops, retail stores, restaurants. The real difficulties come in selling large enterprises like automobile or cement factories. Selling them to foreigners raises a host of thorny problems. No country likes to see its factories owned by foreigners. And if a country sells the factories to buyers abroad at too low a price, it is as if the country is giving away its hard-earned savings to foreigners. In Eastern Europe, there is a further problem: people within these countries who have the most money include former party bosses. There is a bitter irony in seeing those who exploited the system under the Communist government for their own advantage retain their advantageous position, this time as capitalist bosses.

How the different countries will resolve these seeming dilemmas remains to be seen. Czechoslovakia (now divided into the Czech Republic and Slovakia), for one, first privatized stores, restricted purchases of the stores to citizens of the country (and prohibited their resale to foreigners for two years), and accepted the grim fact that many of the hated Communist bosses would now become capitalist bosses. Economic efficiency, in the minds of Czech reformers, was more important than revenge. The country distributed vouchers to all citizens, which the citizens used to bid for shares in the larger, privatized firms. Thus, in one stroke, the Czechs hope both to privatize and to establish a viable stock market. With the widely distributed ownership of firms, they planned to establish a people's capitalism. The next problem the Czechs face is the fact that with no shareholders having a large stake in a firm, managers will run the firm with little outside check on their behaviour. There have been proposals to deal with this problem, such as the establishment of holding companies or investment banks, but no consensus has emerged.

By contrast, Hungary has taken the view that the advantages of foreign ownership—in particular, the advantage of foreigners' expertise—outweigh the disadvantages. Government officials point out that almost 40 percent of Belgian firms are foreign owned, with no adverse effects. They envisage a similar role for foreign ownership within their own economy.

While many of the countries have waited to figure out the best way of privatizing, they have broken up the large state enterprises into competing units, thus hoping to enjoy some of the benefits of competition. But in the absence of competition policies—policies designed to promote competition and prohibit restrictive trade practices—there is a natural tendency for these separate enterprises to work together (as they put it) or to collude (perhaps a more apt description of what they are doing). The heads of the different companies had worked closely together in the years before the breakup, and it seems natural for them to work closely afterwards.

The lack of competition has particularly harmful effects on agriculture. In Poland and what was formerly Yugoslavia, for instance, agriculture is now largely in private hands. The farmers used to have to sell their produce to state enterprises and buy their inputs (seeds, fertilizers, and tractors) from state enterprises. Now they find that they get equally low prices for their produce and pay equally high prices for their inputs; the prices are set not by the government but by the "new" noncompeting enterprises. If entry into the industries that supply inputs to farmers were easy, the high prices would attract competition that would drive prices down. But entry is not so easy. Most important, the uncertain economic environment makes foreigners less willing to make investments, and the small number of entrepreneurs within the country and their lack of access to capital impede entry. But even if foreigners are reluctant to invest, they are willing to trade, and the actual and potential competition from foreign firms may eventually provide a good substitute for the limited levels of domestic competition.

PRIVATIZATION OF LAND

In Hungary and the former Czechoslovakia, where memories are long and land is held in cooperatives and state farms, land privatization has proved controversial. One problem is how to treat old claims. The Communist government took away land without compensation. The original owners argue that if land is to become private, it should go to the person who owned it before the Communist regime. But in Hungary, there were **land reforms,** in which land was taken away from the large landowners and given to the peasants who actually worked the land, before the Communists took over. The Small Landowners party of Hungary wants the land returned to those who received it as part of the land reform. But others ask, why stop there? Why not undo the land reform itself, if private property is sacrosanct?

In the Czech Republic and Slovakia, there are many farm cooperatives, which means in principle that farmers "voluntarily" contribute their land. If the cooperatives were dissolved, the land would return to its original owners. In both countries, four decades have left much changed; the original owners have died, most of the children have left the farms, others may have moved in. There is a general consensus among economists, but less so in the political sphere, that to sort out the old claims would be impossible. Let bygones be bygones.

SPEED OF TRANSITION

The former Soviet-style socialist economies face a difficult problem in deciding how fast to make the transition to capitalism. One approach is called "cold turkey": make the plunge, live through a short nightmarish period, and then enjoy a future prosperity. The other approach calls for a more gradual transition and considers political as well as economic issues. For instance, will the pain caused by the cold turkey approach be so great that support for the market will erode?

Poland tried the cold turkey approach, at least with respect to its macroeconomic adjustment. Inflation was brought under control, but at the expense of a drastic drop in output and employment and the defeat of the government that undertook the plan. And even after the macroadjustments are made, the microeconomic problems—for instance, making factories more efficient, reallocating labour and capital—remain. Most of the other countries have moved more cautiously.

The problem is that the success of market economies depends on a host of long-established institutions, not just on the abstract concept of markets. And all of these institutions have to be functioning reasonably well if the economy is to prosper. There must be credit institutions to sort out potential loan applicants, to monitor the loans, and to see that funds go where they are most productive and are used in the way promised. There must be a legal structure that ensures that contracts will be enforced, and that determines what happens when one party cannot fulfill its contract (bankruptcy). There must be a competition policy that ensures that firms compete against one another.

Beyond that, the more advanced developed countries have developed a set of safety nets to help certain segments of society, such as the unemployed. Since unemployment was not a problem in the socialist economies, these societies do not have such safety nets. There may be a huge human toll if the transition, with its attendant unemployment, proceeds before the safety nets are in place. Yet the budgetary problems facing all of these governments make it hard to institute such programs quickly.

Those who advocate a more gradual transition to market economies believe that the long-run success of these economies will be enhanced by thinking through each of the components, trying to design the best possible institutions, adapting to the particular situations in which they find themselves, and borrowing where appropriate from North America, Western Europe, and Japan.

Whether slow or fast, the problems of the transition to a market economy are likely to be enormous. Yet Poland, the Czech Republic, Slovakia, and Hungary, upon whom the Soviet-style socialist system was imposed by brute force, seem committed to making the transition. There are disagreements about how and how fast to get there, but not on the ultimate destination.

Within the republics of the former Soviet Union, where by now several generations have grown up under, been taught, and come to believe the Communist ideology, the debate about the destination—a reformed socialism, a humane capitalism, or a third system—goes on. There, a slow transition faces a major hurdle: for market reforms to work, market attitudes must be created. Those who make profits have to feel that they can keep them and that they will not be branded antisocial speculators. The government must be committed to enforcing contracts and must not interfere with wages and prices. Firms have to believe that budget constraints are firm, that they will not be bailed out if they make losses and threaten to close down. The great Harvard economist Joseph Schumpeter described the essence of capitalism as "creative destruction," a process of constant turmoil as old jobs and firms are eliminated and new, improved ones are created. There has to be general willingness to accept this creative destruction.

Today, the republics of the former Soviet Union stand in limbo. The failure of the coup attempt in August 1991, followed by the banning of the Communist party, seemed to many a liberation from oppression much like the liberation of the countries of Eastern Europe. Their citizens wanted to obtain all the fruits of this liberation: not only a democratic political system but also a market-oriented economic system. But old ideas die slowly. Both the political and economic systems are unsettled, and there is not a universal consensus on the desirability of all the features of capitalism. Without the commitment to a market economy, few entrepreneurs are coming forth, and the private economy is not getting off the ground. The planning apparatus, while it may have been inefficient, worked when accompanied by the strong system of political control. Today the planning apparatus seems to have largely broken down. Which way the republics will turn remains unclear.

REVIEW AND PRACTICE

SUMMARY

1. Socialism grew out of the grave economic problems that characterized nineteenth-century industrial economies—severe recessions and depressions, unemployment, and bad working and living conditions.

2. Soviet-style socialism used central planning, under which government bureaucrats made all major decisions about what would be produced, how it would be produced, and for whom it would be produced. Competition was banned. Prices, set by the government, often did not reflect relative scarcities. Private property was restricted.

3. Socialism protected workers against layoffs. The trade-off was that this greater security created a lesser incentive for efficiency.

4. In Soviet-style economies, the government decided where investment funds went. The major Soviet aims in the capital market were a high savings rate (which meant low consumption) and heavy industrialization.

5. In socialist economies, firms had little incentive to make profits since profits went to the state, and little incentive to avoid losses since the government would meet any deficits. Firms thus faced "soft" budget constraints.

6. The Soviet-style socialist experiment is today considered a failure by most economists. The Soviet Union's standard of living is no higher than that of many underdeveloped countries.

7. Three possible reforms have been proposed for Soviet-style socialist economies: try harder to make socialism work; give up on socialism and move to a market-based system; find a third alternative between socialism and markets.

8. Among the problems faced by the countries of Eastern Europe and the former Soviet Union in their transition to a market economy are unemployment and inflation. These countries also do not have in place a safety net to protect those who are hurt in the transition process.

9. Privatizing state-controlled firms and land has proved difficult in practice. For instance, no one wants to sell factories to foreigners or former party bosses; the absence of anti-combines policies makes colluding among firms easy; and it is difficult to sort out old claims on land.

KEY TERMS

socialism

communism

central planning

soft budget constraints

land reform

REVIEW QUESTIONS

1. What were some of the problems that motivated Karl Marx's criticism of capitalism?

2. What are some of the central characteristics of Soviet-style socialism?

3. How is the rate of national savings determined in a socialist economy, as opposed to a capitalist economy? How is the allocation of capital determined in a socialist economy, as opposed to a capitalist economy? Who determines what goods are produced in a socialist economy?

4. Why are budget constraints "soft" in socialist countries and "hard" in market economies?

5. What effect do the job-security policies of Soviet-style socialism have on the incentives of workers to put forward their strongest effort?

6. What is market socialism? What did its advocates claim? What are the main problems it faces?

7. What are worker cooperatives? What did its advocates claim for them? What were the problems of worker cooperatives in Yugoslavia?

8. What are the central problems facing countries trying to move from Soviet-style socialism to market economies? Why are inflationary pressures common in a socialist country that is moving towards a market economy? Why is rising unemployment common?

9. What benefits do socialist economies hope to gain from privatization? What are some of the problems facing privatization programs?

10. What are the advantages and disadvantages of the "cold turkey" approach for a socialist economy in transition?

PROBLEMS

1. Explain how the incentives of each of the following people are different in a socialist and a market economy:
    (a) the incentive of a manager to make wise decisions;
    (b) the incentive of workers to exert their best effort;
    (c) the incentive of a bank manager to screen prospective borrowers carefully.

2. Queues form when there is a shortage of goods. Use a supply and demand diagram to explain why socialist price controls tend to lead to queues.

3. Are the problems of soft budget constraints unique to socialist economies?

4. Why did the Soviet-style socialist economies have almost no safety nets of unemployment and welfare benefits?

5. In the Soviet-style socialist economies, there was a great scarcity of housing, and much of the housing was controlled by various firms. What consequences might this have for labour mobility?

6. If you were a top official in a country that practiced Soviet-style socialism, would you rather have a very high income or access to a special store where all items are guaranteed to be in stock? Why?

7. Imagine that you are sixty years old and you work for a worker cooperative in Yugoslavia. If you consider only your own self-interest, are you likely to support hiring more workers? Would you support long-term investments in capital?

CHAPTER 25

DEVELOPMENT

hree-quarters of the world's population live in what are often referred to as **less-developed countries,** or **LDCs.** In Canada, one of the world's wealthiest nations, the idea of "less developed" is often applied to rural areas, or to urban areas where the houses and businesses are dingy and run down. The problem of life in the LDCs is far more serious. It is not that houses are run down, but that a large percentage of the population may have no housing at all; not that people's diet is limited, but that they are starving to death; not that medical care is far off or costly, but that it may simply be unavailable. The contrast between life in some LDCs and life in Canada is significantly larger than the contrast between life in Canada today and two centuries ago.

The LDCs pose some of the most poignant problems in economics. There are no simple answers, no easy formulas that, if followed, will ensure successful solutions. Still, economists have learned a lot about the process of economic development during recent decades. This chapter discusses some of the more important theories that have been formulated as a result of this new knowledge.

KEY QUESTIONS

1. In what ways, besides their grinding poverty, do the developing countries differ from the countries of North America, Japan, and Western Europe?

2. What are the impediments to the growth of developing countries?

3. What policies can these countries pursue to improve their standards of living? In particular, why have most of the success stories involved policies encouraging exports?

SOME BACKGROUND

Statistics cannot convey the full measure of what it means to live in a less-developed country, but they can provide a start. In Canada, life expectancy at birth is about 77 years. In Peru, it is 62 years; in India, 58 years; in Nigeria and Bangladesh, 51 years. In Canada, 7 infants die for every 1,000 live births; in Brazil, 61; in Pakistan, 107; in Nepal, 126. The average Canadian completes 12 years of schooling, while the average African gets only 5 years. India, with a population of 815 million, has a GDP roughly one-half that of Canada, which has a population of about 28 million. This means that per capita income in India is less than 2 percent of that in Canada. The industrial output of India is comparable to the output of the Netherlands, but the Netherlands has a population of less than 15 million, less than 2 percent of India's.

The statistics connect to one another in a vicious cycle. A lack of schools leads to widespread illiteracy; a lack of food brings malnutrition, starvation, and death; a lack of doctors and hospitals and clean water leads to more sickness and death. Life is hard in LDCs, and there is little hope that it will get better. In recent decades, many African countries, whose standards of living were already low enough, have had populations growing faster than national income, so that per capita income is falling; life is getting worse, not better.

The United Nations and the World Bank (a bank established by the major industrialized countries after World War II that provides loans to less-developed countries) group countries into three categories: low-income countries are those with a GDP per capita of U.S. $580 or less in 1989; high-income countries have a GDP per capita in excess of U.S. $6,000; and middle-income countries are those in between. The low-income countries are less-developed countries, while the high-income countries are sometimes simply referred to as the **developed countries.** Because the basis of their higher level of income is their higher level of industrialization, they are also often referred to as the

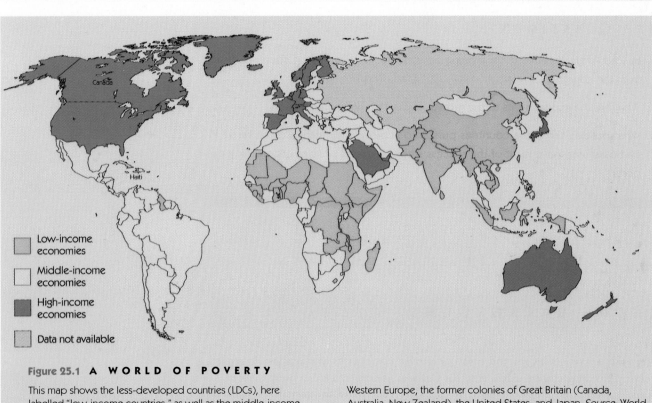

Figure 25.1 A WORLD OF POVERTY

This map shows the less-developed countries (LDCs), here labelled "low-income countries," as well as the middle-income and developed countries. Most of the world lives in low-income countries. The developed countries consist mainly of those in Western Europe, the former colonies of Great Britain (Canada, Australia, New Zealand), the United States, and Japan. *Source*: World Bank, *World Development Report* (1990).

Low-income economies

Middle-income economies

High-income economies

Data not available

industrialized countries. Figure 25.1 is a map of the world showing the countries in their different categories. In the Western Hemisphere lie two of the richest countries, the United States, with a per capita income of U.S. $22,000 in 1990, and Canada, with a per capita income of U.S. $21,600; and one of the poorest, Haiti, with a per capita income of U.S. $360. Table 25.1 compares some of the relevant statistics for Canada and its neighbours, the United States and Mexico.

The income gap among the more high-income countries, including the countries of Western Europe, the United States, Canada, Japan, Australia, and New Zealand, has narrowed considerably over the past hundred years, but the gap between the high-income countries and the low-income countries has not. Figure 25.2 shows per capita income in several different LDCs, ranging from U.S. $120 in Ethiopia to U.S. $370 in Pakistan. By way of comparison, note that the Canadian per capita income in 1990 was U.S. $21,600, 180 and 58 times as large, respectively. However, there are signs that change is possible. Some countries have made notable progress in recent years.

First, several countries have moved from the circle of the LDCs to the ranks of the middle-income countries. These are sometimes referred to collectively as **newly industrialized countries,** or **NICs** for short. These success stories include the "gang of four": South Korea, Taiwan, Singapore, and Hong Kong. Just thirty years after the devas-

Table 25.1 **STANDARD OF LIVING MEASUREMENTS IN CANADA, THE UNITED STATES, AND MEXICO**

Category	Canada	U.S.	Mexico
GDP per capita (U.S.$)	$19,030	$20,910	$2,010
Life expectancy	77	76	69
Agriculture as % of GDP	2	2	9
Energy consumption per capita (kilograms of oil equivalent)	9,959	7,794	1,288
Food as % of total household consumption	11	13	35
Medical care as % of total household consumption	5	14	5
Average annual inflation (GNP deflator) 1980–1989*	4.6	3.9	72.8
Average annual growth of population (%): 1980–1989	0.9	1	2.1
Infant mortality rate (per 1,000 live births)	7	10	40
Population per physician	510	470	1,242
Population in cities of 1 million or more as % of total population	30	36	32

* Like the GDP deflator discussed in Chapter 8, the GNP deflator is the measure of the price level used to adjust GNP for inflation.
Source: World Bank, *World Development Report* (1991). Data are for the most recent years available, in most cases 1989.

Figure 25.2
DIFFERENCES IN PER CAPITA INCOME

Some middle-income countries such as Egypt and Costa Rica have per capita incomes up to ten times those of the world's poorest nations and yet their per capita incomes are up to ten times smaller than those of the world's wealthiest nations. For high-income countries, the conversion uses purchasing power parity; for other countries, the conversion uses the exchange rate. *Sources*: Organization for Economic Cooperation and Development, *National Accounts* (1991); World Bank, *World Development Report* (1991), Table 1.

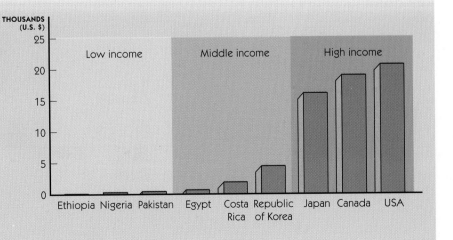

tating Korean War, for instance, South Korea has moved from the category of backward country to that of major producer, not just of simple products such as textiles but of automobiles (the Hyundai) and computers (many of the IBM clones are made in South Korea), which require a reasonably high level of technological expertise. Even more impressive, Japan has moved from the ranks of middle-income countries to the position of one of the most prosperous countries in the world.

Second, there have been pockets of remarkable progress within the less-developed countries. In the early 1960s, agricultural research centres around the world funded largely by the Rockefeller Foundation developed new kinds of seeds, which under the correct conditions increase the yields per hectare enormously. The introduction and dissemination of these new seeds, accompanied by enormous improvements in agricultural practices—known as the **green revolution**—led to huge increases in output. India, for example, finally managed to produce enough food to feed its burgeoning population, and now sometimes can export wheat to other countries.

Third, even the grim statistics for life expectancy and infant mortality represent improvements for many countries. But these improvements have a darker side in some countries—a population explosion that is reminiscent of the Malthusian nightmare. Malthus, you will recall from Chapter 21, envisioned a world in which population growth outpaced increases in the food supply. In Kenya during the early 1980s, for instance, improved health conditions enabled the population to grow at the remarkable rate of 4.1 percent a year, implying a doubling of the population every eighteen years, while output increased only at the rate of 1.9 percent a year. Output increases do nothing to improve per capita income when the population grows at a faster rate.

The 1980s proved to be a particularly hard decade for some of the poorest countries, as Figure 25.3 shows. While sub-Saharan Africa (all of Africa south of the Sahara except South Africa) has basically stagnated for the past quarter century, during the 1980s per capita income actually fell at the rate of 2.4 percent per year. Latin America has grown an average of a little more than 2 percent a year in per capita income for a quarter century, but during the 1980s per capita income fell at the rate of .7 percent a year.

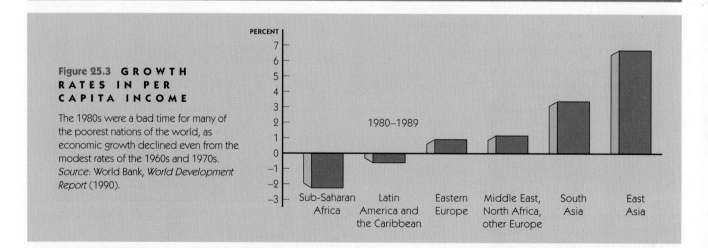

Figure 25.3 GROWTH RATES IN PER CAPITA INCOME

The 1980s were a bad time for many of the poorest nations of the world, as economic growth declined even from the modest rates of the 1960s and 1970s. *Source*: World Bank, *World Development Report* (1990).

LIFE IN AN LDC

Just as there are large differences between the LDCs and the industrialized countries, so too are there large differences among the LDCs. The largest of them all, China, has a Communist government; the second largest, India, has an avowedly Socialist government, but also functions as the world's largest democracy. Literacy standards and life spans in Costa Rica rank with those of the industrialized countries, while more than half of the adult population in sub-Saharan Africa is illiterate and the expected life span is roughly two-thirds that of the industrialized countries. Accordingly, one must be careful in generalizing about the less-developed countries. Still, certain observations are true for *most* of these countries.

AGRICULTURE

Agriculture plays a much more important role in LDCs than in the more-developed countries; we can see this in Figure 25.4. In wealthy countries like the United States

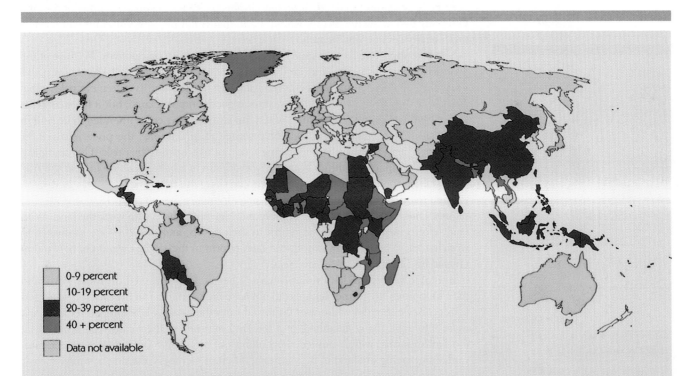

0-9 percent
10-19 percent
20-39 percent
40 + percent
Data not available

Figure 25.4 AGRICULTURE AS A SHARE OF GDP

Agriculture is a much larger share of the economy in LDCs than in the industrialized nations of the world. *Source*: World Bank, *World Development Report* (1990).

and Canada, agriculture is generally 5 percent or less of the total gross domestic product. In poor countries, agriculture is often 40 percent or more of GDP.

Farms in less-developed countries tend to be much smaller than in Canada—less than a hectare on average compared with more than 200 hectares in Canada. The number of people working on each hectare in LDCs is higher, but even so, output per worker is much, much lower. That is because these countries use less-advanced farming techniques and less fertilizer. Developed countries use roughly twice as much fertilizer per hectare of land as do less-developed countries. They employ tractors, combines, and other equipment, while in LDCs a wealthy farmer may use oxen to plow his fields and a poor one may have nothing but a hand plow. The lack of productivity is not a result of lack of hard work; human and animal labour must substitute for a lack of fertilizer and machinery.

Some of the institutional arrangements in LDCs may also contribute to the lack of productivity. Much of the land in less-developed countries is farmed under a sharecropping arrangement, in which the landlord takes a share of the output, usually between a third and a half. Sharecropping reduces tenant farmers' incentives to work—if they work harder, they receive only one-half to two-thirds of the extra output, with the rest going to the landlord. In addition, since the workers do not own the land, they may not be as careful to maintain its quality, for instance by using the right kind and amount of fertilizer, by ensuring that drainage is proper, and so on. Absentee landlords do not, perhaps because they cannot, make their tenant farmers maintain the quality of the land in the same way that an owner-farmer would. Land that is not properly cared for can have its productivity decline significantly.

Sharecropping survives, in spite of its negative effects on productivity, because of the great inequality in wealth and land ownership prevalent in many LDCs. Given this inequality, sharecropping has certain advantages. Agriculture is extremely risky, especially in poor countries. When the weather is good, output is large; but if the weather is bad, output can drop dramatically. When the farmer grows crops intended to be sold in the world market, there is an additional source of uncertainty: the price received for crops may vary enormously. Poor farmers do not like bearing this risk. The landlords, who are often much wealthier than the workers, are in a better position to bear the risk. With sharecropping, landlord and workers can share the risk.

Land reforms may have an enormous effect in increasing output in LDCs. With land reform, land is broken into smaller plots and is given to those who work the land. With land reform, workers get all the return to their efforts, and thus they are motivated to work harder. When Taiwan introduced land reform in the 1950s, output per hectare increased by 22 percent in only five years.

But to be successful, land reforms have to be carefully designed. In India, Peru, and the Philippines, the former tenants did not have the capital to run the farm or to buy fertilizer. They either did without or borrowed from the wealthy landlord. As tenants sank more into debt, many defaulted, and the land returned to the wealthy. In other cases, the land reforms, which limited the holdings of any single individual, were circumvented by placing the land in the names of different members of a single family.

THE DUAL ECONOMY: LIFE IN THE CITIES

Today in the more-developed countries, 60 percent or more of the population live in urban centres, as Figure 25.5 shows. For Canada, the figure is 77 percent. In the LDCs,

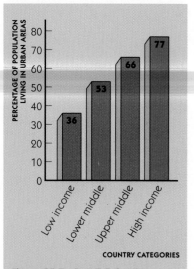

Figure 25.5 RATES OF URBANIZATION

The percentage of the population living in urban areas tends to be higher in developed countries than in LDCs. *Source*: World Bank, *World Development Report* (1990).

the figure is commonly around 30 to 40 percent. Though these urban areas represent a small fraction of the population, they are often responsible for a large fraction of national output. Thus, productivity in LDCs, measured in output per worker, is often considerably higher in urban areas. Cities may employ relatively modern manufacturing techniques, and the level of education, while still lower than in the developed economies, is typically far higher than in the rural sector. There is a marked contrast between the urban and rural sectors of the economy, a disparity known as the **dual economy.**

One aspect of these dual economies has been a particular source of concern—the high levels of urban unemployment. Wages in the urban sector are frequently far higher than in the rural sector, higher than can be accounted for by the differences in cost of living. The higher wages have an important and obvious consequence: workers migrate from the low-wage rural sector to the urban sector even if they are not sure of obtaining a job. Because of the lure of higher wages, they are willing to spend a considerable length of time looking for a job in the city. In some LDCs, unemployment has risen to as high as 20 percent or more of the urban labour force. These unemployed are of concern not only because they represent underutilized human resources, but also because they may be a source of political unrest.

Visitors to LDCs do not see a pretty sight; they see rural poverty and urban squalor. While average incomes of those employed may be far higher in the urban sector, visitors cannot help but notice the homeless sleeping in the streets, the shantytowns with cardboard houses and open sewers that house the recent migrants, the children begging in tattered clothes. It is hard not to want to do something. But to know what to do, we must understand the causes of the predicament in which these countries find themselves.

SOME IMPORTANT DIFFERENCES BETWEEN DEVELOPED AND LESS-DEVELOPED COUNTRIES

	DEVELOPED COUNTRIES	LDCs
Per capita income	Over U.S. $6,000	Less than U.S. $580 per year
Production/Employment	Less than 10% of the work force is in agriculture	More than 70% of the work force is in agriculture
Urbanization	Less than 30% live in rural areas	More than 60% live in rural areas
Population growth rate	Less than 1.0%	Often more than 3.0%

EXPLANATIONS OF UNDERDEVELOPMENT

Chapter 21 related growth to increases in physical capital (machines, plants) and human capital (education), to the efficiency with which resources are used, and to technological progress. Similarly, the lack of development in LDCs is related to the lack of machines and equipment and an educated labour force, the failure to use resources efficiently, and the failure to take full advantage of technological progress.

But while there are some similarities between the problems of growth in developed countries and in LDCs, there are some important differences. The essential problem can be stated simply: the institutions and structure of less-developed economies do not facilitate growth. For instance, not only is there a shortage of capital, but capital markets do not function well, so capital is often not allocated wisely. The following paragraphs examine this and other major impediments to development.

CAPITAL

The description of economic growth in Chapter 21 emphasized the importance of capital. The less-developed countries have much less capital per capita. The low capital is not for want of trying: as Figure 25.6 shows, savings rates in most LDCs are comparable to that of Canada, though not so high as in Japan and Korea. Indonesia, which has been growing rapidly, is an exception. The accumulation of capital has been an important component of virtually all successful development programs. But incomes are so low that even a high savings rate does not permit a rapid increase in the capital stock.

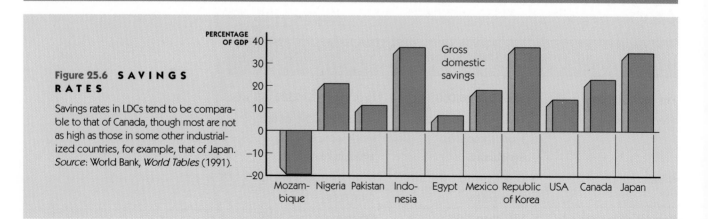

Figure 25.6 SAVINGS RATES

Savings rates in LDCs tend to be comparable to that of Canada, though most are not as high as those in some other industrialized countries, for example, that of Japan. *Source*: World Bank, *World Tables* (1991).

FOREIGN AID AS A REMEDY

Those who hold the view that the major problem in less-developed economies is a shortage of capital have emphasized the importance of extending loans (or grants) to the LDCs. Canada and several other industrialized countries provide foreign aid to the LDCs to help build their roads and ports, to assist in the construction of new factories, and to help develop educational and health systems. Total aid in recent years from the developed to the less-developed countries has exceeded U.S. $50 billion per year. Canada's contribution to foreign aid, most of it financed by a government agency called the Canadian International Development Agency, is about average for industrialized countries. At 0.4 percent of GDP, it is comparable to that of Germany (0.42 percent) and France (0.52 percent), and much higher than Japan (0.31 percent), Great Britain (0.27 percent), and especially the United States (0.19 percent). But it remains well below the target of 1 percent of GDP set by the United Nations, and less than that of the most generous countries, the Netherlands and Denmark (both at 0.93 percent) and Sweden (0.9 percent). Moreover Canada's contribution rate has fallen from a peak of 0.5 percent and is predicted to continue falling as the aid budget falls victim to the federal government's deficit reduction program discussed in Chapter 22.

Today much of the aid from the more-advanced countries to the LDCs is channelled through multilateral international agencies in which the donor countries work together. The most important of these agencies is the World Bank, which currently lends over U.S. $10 billion a year to the less-developed countries. But loans from the World Bank or elsewhere eventually lead to an improvement in the standard of living only if they yield returns in excess of the interest the countries must pay. Many LDCs have faced financial crises as they have found it increasingly difficult to make the required interest payments, let alone the repayment of the principal.

OTHER SOURCES OF CAPITAL

Another source of capital is direct foreign investment, which has one major advantage over loans. The foreign companies making the investment risk their own capital; if the investment fails to yield a return, they, not the country, suffer the loss. And the fact that they bear this risk provides them with greater incentive to make sure the investment pays off. Foreign investment may also facilitate the transfer of modern technology and know-how. But in spite of these advantages, many countries have resisted foreign investment from fear that somehow it compromises their sovereignty or that the foreign companies will take advantage of them. In some cases, for instance when a foreign company is extracting the country's natural resources, there may be legitimate cause for concern; the country may be receiving less for the natural resources than they are really worth. Or the company may convince the country to provide trade protection, which amounts to a hidden subsidy to the firm paid by consumers within the country.

For foreign companies to be willing to invest, they must feel that the political environment is stable and conducive to business. When it is not, they can run up against a host of problems. In the past, LDCs have nationalized foreign-owned companies, paying them inadequate compensation for their investments; they have imposed taxes that effectively confiscate most of the profits; they have imposed foreign exchange restrictions that make it difficult for companies to obtain needed inputs; or they have imposed licensing requirements that make it difficult for foreign firms to operate. The governments of Canada, the United States, and many European countries provide insurance

CLOSE-UP: TRANSNATIONAL CORPORATIONS AS A SOURCE OF CAPITAL

Less-developed countries have all the unskilled labour they need. What they lack is investment capital, both to build the physical tools needed for greater production and to increase the human capital of their population. But where is that capital to come from?

LDCs can, through savings, provide some capital themselves. Countries like Mexico, Brazil, and South Korea have shown a capacity to save more than 20 percent of GDP per year. By world standards, those countries are fairly well off. The poorest countries save only about 7 percent of GDP.

The other alternatives all involve investment capital coming in from abroad, whether it is through foreign aid, private bank loans, or direct foreign investment. The problem with depending on foreign aid is that there is not enough of it. For example, in one recent year the total foreign aid received by all less-developed nations was perhaps 1 percent of their combined GDP.

Another possibility is private financial capital, commonly in the form of bank loans. This method of sending capital to LDCs was tried with a vengeance in the 1970s. But after the experience of countries like Brazil, Argentina, and Mexico not being able to repay their loans on time in the 1980s, Western banks are not eager to plunge into a massive new round of lending.

The final possibility is direct foreign investment, more commonly known as investment by multinational or transnational corporations. This method has some obvious advantages. The transnational company has an interest in looking after its investment and managing it carefully, which means that the money is less likely to be spent inefficiently, such as on a grandiose project. In addition, direct investment is not a loan; the country need not repay it. Finally, the company doing the investment will often send new technology to the LDC and train workers there.

The main disadvantage of direct investment is political. The governments of LDCs generally prefer loans or grants that they can spend as they wish over investment controlled by foreign business executives. LDCs have often passed laws that discouraged foreign companies from investing. But as the options for obtaining capital from other sources are dwindling, transnational corporations are looking better and better as an alternative. The current level of direct foreign investment in LDCs is only about U.S. $10 billion now. However, according to a recent United Nations report:

> The revision by a large number of developing countries of their laws and regulations in the area of foreign direct investment is part and parcel of [a] broader process. There has been a marked decline in the incidence of nationalization and an increase in the arbitration of disputes between transnational corporations and host country Governments. To be sure, the straitened economic circumstances that many countries are facing has left them with no other option. But, generally, foreign investment and transnational corporations have come to be seen in a more favourable—and more technical and less political—light. . . .
>
> In an era of large international capital flows and rapid technological change, developing countries will increasingly look to transnational corporations for economic stimulation. For their part, transnational corporations will frequently be in a position to provide significant long-term benefits to many developing countries. An important component in the next generation of development policies is that this mutuality of interest continues to grow.

Source: United Nations Center on Transnational Corporations, *Transnational Corporations in World Development* (New York: United Nations, 1988), pp. 10–11.

for their companies investing in LDCs against the risk of nationalization, but there remain many other risks. Providing a politically stable environment has proved a difficult problem for many LDCs.

IMPORTANCE OF CAPITAL

How much of the difference between developed and less-developed countries can actually be attributed to lack of capital? If a shortage of capital in LDCs were the major difference between the developed and less-developed countries, then the law of diminishing returns would predict that the return to capital in the industrialized countries would be much lower than the return in LDCs. The more capital a country has relative to the size of its population, the lower is the output per machine and the lower is the marginal return to capital. In other words, the shortage of capital should make the return to capital greater. This difference in returns would naturally result in a movement of capital from the more-developed to the less-developed countries, as business firms searched out profitable investment opportunities.

While the evidence does show some differences in the return to capital, they are too small to demonstrate that a capital shortage is the major problem faced by the LDCs. Moreover, if a capital shortage were the major problem, the LDCs would use what capital they have very intensively. But this does not seem to happen; for example, factories run extra daily shifts more often in developed countries than in LDCs.

MISALLOCATION OF CAPITAL

An important impediment to growth in many less-developed countries is the lack of efficiency in how the scarce funds that are available are used. In Venezuela, which tried to invest its oil dollars as fast as they came in during the 1970s, output increased by 10 cents for every dollar invested in capital equipment. In contrast, in Canada and other developed countries, each extra dollar of investment results on average in an increase of output of between 30 and 50 cents—three to five times higher. In many LDCs, greater investment simply does not lead to much increased output.

There are a number of reasons for this. Some economists have argued that at any moment a country has only a limited absorptive capacity for more capital. It lacks the human capital, the experience, and technological know-how to pursue many projects simultaneously. The absorptive capacity is most limited in the poorest countries. When investments are pushed beyond the absorptive capacity, they yield very low returns.

As we will see below, in many LDCs governments have taken a strong role in allocating capital, partly because capital markets are underdeveloped. But by taking a strong role, the government may have hindered the development of capital markets. In many cases, governments have not proved adept at allocating capital efficiently, and have invested in enterprises that do not reflect the economy's comparative advantage.

More generally, the lack of developed capital markets to facilitate the allocation of capital to its most productive uses and the lack of entrepreneurs who could find new projects well suited for the particular conditions of the LDCs have together contributed to the low returns obtained on capital in many LDCs.

POPULATION GROWTH AND LABOUR SUPPLY

A second explanation for the predicament of the LDCs is that while their overall population is growing too rapidly, they have an inadequate supply of trained workers. There is

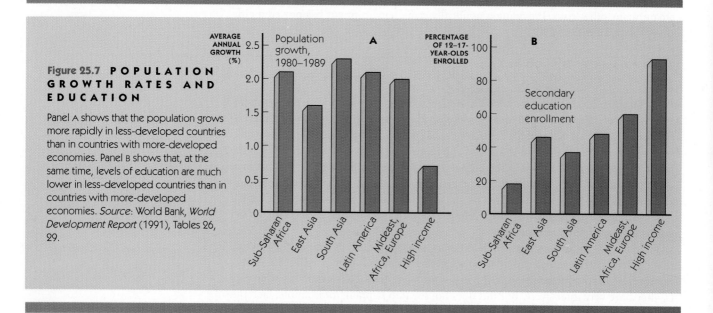

Figure 25.7 POPULATION GROWTH RATES AND EDUCATION

Panel A shows that the population grows more rapidly in less-developed countries than in countries with more-developed economies. Panel B shows that, at the same time, levels of education are much lower in less-developed countries than in countries with more-developed economies. *Source*: World Bank, *World Development Report* (1991), Tables 26, 29.

a shortage of human capital. Figure 25.7A shows the growth rate of the population in the less-developed regions of the world in comparison with that of high-income countries; panel B shows the levels of education. The populations in LDCs are growing more rapidly, but they have a much lower level of education.

In the developed countries, the Malthusian forecast has not been realized. Food production has increased more rapidly than Malthus anticipated because of technological change, and population has grown less rapidly. Higher living standards and improved medicine have resulted in greater longevity, lower infant mortality, and a lower incidence of sterility. These factors might have contributed to the growth of the population, but at the same time, family planning has become widely accepted; as a result, population sizes have stabilized.

The LDCs have benefited from the improved medicine, but in most of these countries family planning has not yet taken hold to the extent necessary to offset its effects. Families are still large. One reason is lack of information. Another has to do with economic forces: in agricultural societies without public pension programs, children provide both a source of labour and a source of support in old age. In developed countries, children have become more of an economic liability than an asset.

Whatever the reason, populations in LDCs are burgeoning. This presents several problems. First, the higher population growth rate leads to an increase in the fraction of the population in childhood years who have to be supported by others. In sub-Saharan Africa, almost half the population is under fourteen years old, as seen in Figure 25.8, while in the typical developed country, one in four is under fourteen. When the ratio of dependents to working adults is high, per capita incomes and savings will be lower. Moreover, as these children grow up and enter the labour force, the stock of capital goods available for each worker will suffer. Just to provide the new entrants with the additional capital goods required to sustain a given level of capital goods per worker requires high savings rates, higher than many LDCs can manage.

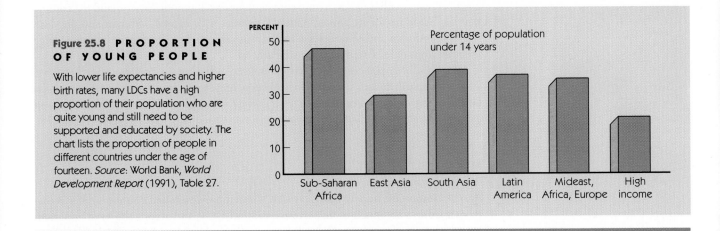

Figure 25.8 PROPORTION OF YOUNG PEOPLE

With lower life expectancies and higher birth rates, many LDCs have a high proportion of their population who are quite young and still need to be supported and educated by society. The chart lists the proportion of people in different countries under the age of fourteen. *Source*: World Bank, *World Development Report* (1991), Table 27.

In many ways, then, rapid population growth impairs the development prospects for LDCs. Therefore, one of the most effective forms of aid that the industrialized countries can provide to these countries is assistance with their family planning programs. But in the United States, one of the largest donor countries, such programs touch upon politically divisive issues, and aid for family planning has itself become highly controversial.

Another way to help the LDCs is to offer education to their citizens, in the form of fellowships to their students to study in Canada or another developed country, or funds to assist in the development of their educational systems. Care must be taken in educational aid as well, however. While the lack of skilled workers is an important problem in some LDCs, others, such as India and Kenya, have the opposite problem. They cannot seem to generate enough jobs that will use the skills of their high school graduates. In some instances, the problem is that the skills for which individuals are trained are not the skills the economy needs. Many of the LDCs have educational systems inherited from their colonial past. Students may be able to recite the list of the kings and queens of England, but do not get the vocational skills required for a modern industrialized society. Cultural attitudes and values may reinforce these problems; students may aspire to be a government bureaucrat rather than an engineer or an entrepreneur (though in many cases the high pay of government jobs combined with the security of employment provide a simple economic rationale for these aspirations).

Furthermore, at the same time as aid budgets are being used to provide higher education to students from LDCs, some of the brightest and best educated of them are being accepted as immigrants to Canada and the United States. For example, the Canadian immigration system rewards highly skilled persons such as doctors, dentists, and engineers, professions that are also in short supply at home.

LACK OF NATURAL RESOURCES AND TECHNOLOGY

Some of the poorest of the LDCs are poor simply by virtue of a lack of natural resources. The countries that border on the Sahara Desert, with little land that is suitable for farming and, so far, no mineral wealth, are the most dramatic examples. Natural resources are, of course, neither necessary nor sufficient for development. Switzerland is a country that has made up for its limited natural resources with capital—human and physical. And some African and Middle Eastern countries remain less developed, in spite of large incomes from natural resources, particularly oil.

Also, less-developed countries often do not use well what limited resources they have. This is due partly to lack of technological know-how, really another manifestation of the lack of human capital. For instance, by training farmers to use better techniques, as well as providing them with better seeds, agricultural productivity may be greatly enhanced.

MARKET FAILURES

Another important respect in which LDCs and more-developed countries differ is that market failures are much more pervasive within LDCs. And among the most important is the *absence* of markets. As we have seen throughout this book, markets serve an important function in helping ensure that resources are allocated efficiently. When markets are absent or do not work well, as is so often the case in LDCs, then resources are not efficiently allocated. Thus, not only do LDCs face a scarcity of capital and trained labour, what human and physical capital they have may not be put to its best use.

We get a picture of how underdeveloped capital markets are in LDCs by considering the ratio of net financial assets (bank accounts, stocks, etc.) to GDP. This is an indicator of the strength of the financial institutions. In most LDCs, this ratio is about one-third of the ratio in developed countries.

Labour markets also do not work well—they do not allow individuals to move easily from one employer to another or from one city to another. Ethnic divisions and language barriers divide many LDCs into small labour markets, with limited flows between them.

UNEMPLOYMENT

Among the most important aspects of market failure in LDCs is the pervasive unemployment. Unemployment, a major cause of the extremes of poverty, is concentrated in cities. In rural areas, the problem is underemployment; families may have more than enough labour to work their farms. This underemployment is best considered as disguised unemployment. In his classic 1954 study of the development process, Nobel laureate Arthur Lewis emphasized the importance of this ready supply of labour, which he called **surplus labour,** for the development process. The migration of surplus labour to the cities made industrialization possible with very little rise in wages, and this in turn enabled a flow of profits to be generated and capital to be accumulated. In the 1960s, a darker side of this rural to urban migration became apparent: urban centers faced unemployment rates of 15, 20, or 25 percent.

Because of the massive and conspicuous unemployment in many cities in LDCs, it is safe to assume that wages there are higher than they would be in a competitive equilibrium, in which wages are set at market-clearing levels. Because wages do not reflect the true scarcity value of labour, many LDCs have encouraged public enterprises to choose techniques that require more labour than more advanced techniques that are designed to save on the use of labour. Economists sometimes refer to the true social value of a resource as its **shadow price.** For example, when there is unemployment, the shadow wage may be below the market wage. Thus, to encourage the use of more labour-intensive techniques, many LDCs have instructed their public enterprises to use shadow prices and wages rather than market prices and wages when choosing techniques of production.

LACK OF ENTREPRENEURSHIP

A critical problem in many LDCs is the lack of entrepreneurs. Entrepreneurs can be thought of as the individuals who have the ability and the incentive to recognize ways in which markets are not supplying needed products and to undertake new enterprises that will supply these products. Not only is there a lack of entrepreneurs, but what limited entrepreneurial talent that is available is often not well used, at least from a social perspective. For instance, entrepreneurs may spend their time dealing with the obstacles that government bureaucrats impose on private firms.

Economists do not know why there is a lack of entrepreneurs. Economic historians and psychologists have also tried to explain the lack, without any clear answers. In some cases, as in West Africa, there is considerable evidence of some forms of entrepreneurship, such as small-scale marketing, but this is seldom translated into larger-scale enterprises. Lack of capital and imperfectly functioning capital markets that prevent entrepreneurs from obtaining capital are obvious hindrances. The colonial experience, in which foreigners dominated the nonagricultural sector, may be another. Even today in many LDCs, foreign firms predominate in the industrial sector. These firms may fail to train the indigenous population in entrepreneurship, and the indigenous population may think of entrepreneurship as foreign to their culture. Governments provide a variety of additional obstacles, including bureaucratic delays in obtaining permits, licences, and foreign exchange; sometimes entrepreneurs are required to pay bribes to obtain them.

EXTERNALITIES

Another problem with markets in LDCs is externalities. Chapter 7 showed that when there are important externalities, markets will not work well. One of the problems facing many firms in the early stages of development is finding workers who work effectively within large organizations. In developed countries, employers are lucky in being able to draw upon a well-educated labour pool (educated largely in public schools) for skilled labour. In LDCs, more of the burden of training falls upon firms. Firms, in hiring and training workers with little previous experience, contribute to the pool of individuals with manufacturing skills. Once trained, a worker may move on to another company, which will benefit from the skills the worker acquired in the first firm. There is thus an externality. Firms collectively will not hire and train as many workers as society would like them to because they cannot capture this externality.

INEQUALITY

Visitors to many LDCs are struck by the extremes in inequality, such as homeless people sleeping in the streets along which the wealthy travel in Mercedes cars. Politicians in LDCs find it popular to attack the wealthy, suggesting that if only their wealth could be directed away from conspicuous consumption and towards productive uses, the country's development problems would be solved. Unfortunately, as much money as the

CLOSE-UP: THE INTERNATIONAL DEBT CRISIS

Borrowing from abroad can make sound economic sense. For instance, much of the development of the Canadian transcontinental railway in the nineteenth century was financed by bonds issued in Europe. Over the past two decades, many firms and governments of less-developed countries borrowed billions of dollars from banks in Canada, the United States, and other developed countries, as the table here shows. But while the nineteenth-century railroad companies were able to repay investments, it became apparent in the 1980s that some of the countries that had borrowed heavily—particularly Brazil, Argentina, and Mexico—could not repay what they owed. The resulting crisis threatened the economic prospects of the LDCs and the financial viability of many Western banks. How the problem arose and what should be done about it remain hotly debated questions.

The immediate cause of the problem was apparent. In the 1970s, real interest rates were low, and banks were flush with "petro dollars"—dollars that oil producers, particularly in the Middle East, had earned from selling their oil at the high prices that prevailed beginning in 1973—and wanted to invest or deposit abroad. Both borrowers and lenders were optimistic that the loans would create economic growth, and repayment would be an easy matter.

Then three things happened. First, nominal and real interest rates soared in the late 1970s, and since most of the loans had adjustable rates, the interest payments rose far beyond any level that the borrowers had imagined. Second, the world entered a recession in the early 1980s, and the worldwide slowdown in growth made it more difficult for the LDCs to pay back what they owed. Third, oil prices fell in the early 1980s. Some of the largest borrowers had been oil producers, like Mexico and Indonesia, and they had intended to repay their loans by selling oil.

But bad luck is not the only culprit; the banks are also to blame for failing to take into account the risks associated with the loans they were making. They should have realized, for instance, that prices for goods like oil are volatile. They did not take into account the fact that when foreign borrowers refuse to pay, Canadian lenders cannot sue to recover some of their losses, as they can when the borrower is Canadian. And they failed to learn the lesson of diversification: they put too many of their eggs in the same basket.

The banks also seem to have placed too much trust in the assurance of foreign governments that the loans would be invested productively. At least some of the funds were siphoned off from the investment projects for which they were intended and, it is claimed, used by wealthy Argentineans, Mexicans, and Brazillians to purchase real estate in the United States. Moreover, much of the money was invested in projects that were probably not economically viable from the start. By contrast, some better-managed countries like the Republic of Korea borrowed heavily but invested the money in sound projects and have been able to repay it.

Finally, some economists believe that deposit insurance is partly responsible: since depositors knew they would get their money back no matter how risky the loans made by their banks, they had no reason to monitor their banks and raise warning flags when the banks made the more risky loans to LDCs.

So far, massive defaults on loans have been avoided by debt rescheduling, which means that as a payment comes due, the banks lend the country more money, in effect postponing the date at which repayment is to occur. As a condition for this rescheduling, the lenders have insisted that the borrowers "put their houses in order," cutting back, for instance, on their huge budget deficits. But this strategy of squeezing the LDCs to pay does not seem likely to work; they simply do not have the money, and pressuring them can destabilize their economies and governments. An alternative strategy would be to help the countries grow, so they could afford to repay at least some of their debt. But growth may require additional capital, which foreign lenders are reluctant to provide. The only way out may be to forgive some of the debt and then count on the rest being repaid.

Debt forgiveness, which amounts to a gift to the debtor countries, has its own problems. If banks are forced to forgive the debts, they will suffer financially. Moreover, many worry about the incentives and fairness of forgiving debt. Will forgiveness encourage countries to borrow more in the future than they have the capacity to repay? Is Brazil more deserving of such a multibillion-dollar gift than many poorer countries in Latin America or Africa, just because it borrowed more?

Country	Public or publicly guaranteed external debt in 1989 (U.S. $)
Brazil	$84 billion
Mexico	$76 billion
India	$54 billion
Argentina	$51 billion
Indonesia	$41 billion
Egypt	$40 billion
China	$37 billion
Poland	$35 billion
Turkey	$35 billion
Nigeria	$32 billion
Venezuela	$25 billion
Algeria	$24 billion
Philippines	$23 billion
Morocco	$19 billion
Korea	$17 billion

Source: World Bank, World Development Report (1991), Table 21.

wealthy may have, even if all their wealth were confiscated and invested, it would only make a small dent in the problems these countries face.

Programs of redistribution, if well designed, can still play a positive role in the development effort. Earlier we saw how sharecropping attenuated workers' incentives. Land reforms such as that of Taiwan can have a large effect on agricultural productivity. The use of excessively high income tax rates to redistribute wealth, however, can have a deleterious effect. They reduce the incentives for entrepreneurship, and within the urban sector they may reduce the funds available for reinvestment by successful enterprises. Many LDCs have imposed tax rates on upper-income groups in excess of 80 or even 90 percent. These rates, however, turn out to be more statements of ideology; the taxes are seldom effectively enforced.

The magnitude of the inequality colours all aspects of development policy. A policy is evaluated not only in terms of its effect on national output, but in terms of its impact on unemployment and, more generally, on what the policy will do to inequality. The grinding poverty in which so much of the population lives often makes it impossible to pursue policies that would maximize the rate of growth. Governments often feel themselves forced to spend much of their scarce revenues on food subsidies rather than on investments; and when governments have attempted to cut back on these food subsidies, as happened in the Dominican Republic or Morocco, there are riots.

Perhaps the way in which great inequality most impairs development is through its effects on the political process: inequality frequently gives rise to political instability, and political instability has strong adverse effects on the economic climate. In such an atmosphere, both domestic and foreign firms will feel reluctant to invest.

IMPEDIMENTS TO DEVELOPMENT

Capital
    Insufficient supply
    Absence of capital markets, leading to inefficient allocation
Population/Labour
    High population growth rates
    Insufficient number of trained individuals
Lack of natural resources and technology
Market failures
    Imperfect labour and capital markets
    Unemployment
    Lack of entrepreneurs
    Externalities, such as are associated with the development of a pool of educated
        workers
Inequality
    Direct effects, such as attenuation of incentives in sharecropping
    Indirect effects, like the possibility of political instability, which creates an unfa-
        vourable investment climate

SHOULD GOVERNMENT MAKE THE BASIC ECONOMIC DECISIONS?

How can less-developed countries find their way to sustained economic growth? Economists break this question down into two issues. Who should make and carry out the decisions about resource allocation, government or markets? And, assuming the government does intervene in resource allocation, in which direction should it push (or pull) the economy? We now look at each of these issues in turn.

A QUESTIONABLE ROLE: PLANNING

A popular view among development economists in the 1960s was that governments in the LDCs should take a central role in planning the growth of the economy, to avoid market failures. A "Ministry of Planning" would draw up a detailed plan, perhaps for five years, specifying how much each sector of the economy would grow, how much investment would occur in each sector, where the output of each sector would go, and where each sector would receive its inputs. The Ministry of Planning would have enormous powers, among them allocating investment funds and the foreign exchange required to import raw materials from abroad.

The spread of the planning model was greatly influenced by the seeming success of the Soviet Union in the early stages of its industrialization program. In most LDCs that used the planning approach, such as India, the government did not have the all-pervasive role that it did in the Soviet Union, where not only did the government plan the investment, but government enterprises actually undertook the investment. In India and other LDCs, the government did undertake some of the investments itself, but it also gave powerful inducements to private firms to conform to the dictates of the government's plan—for example, by restricting access to needed foreign exchange only to approved investment projects or by making credit more readily available for approved investment projects.

DISILLUSIONMENT WITH PLANNING

In the last decade, there has been considerable disillusionment with planning. This disillusionment set in even before the failures of the Soviet-style system became widely evident. Planned economies like India have not done better than unplanned economies like Hong Kong and Taiwan—in fact, in most cases they have done worse. There are good reasons for this. The 1960s views on the need for planning ignored the extensive planning that goes on in all economies. For example, when Stelco decided to build a steel mill on the western shores of Lake Ontario, it made sure that there were sources of inputs and the transportation facilities to deliver these inputs—electricity from Ontario Hydro, shipping along the St. Lawrence Seaway, and iron ore from Quebec. It also made sure that there was a source of demand. The issue is not whether planning is needed—it surely is—but whether the most effective place to do the planning is in a government centralized bureau or at the level of the firm. Today most economists are skeptical about the ability of a centralized bureau to do effective planning.

One of the main arguments for centralized planning was its presumed greater ability to coordinate. But the experience of the past quarter century has shown that centralized planning offices generally do not do a good job at coordination. One reason is that they often do not have the requisite information. Another is that the details of investment projects—deciding what kind of plant to construct, how to construct it, making sure that it is constructed in an efficient way, and so on—are details firms can more easily deal with than government bureaucrats, and these details, more than anything else, determine the success of the projects.

WHEN GOVERNMENT BECOMES THE PROBLEM

Sometimes government has actually impeded the development process. It has done this both by allocating inefficiently those resources over which it has direct control and by interfering in the function of markets so that *they* could not efficiently allocate resources. Countries following the Soviet model attempted to imitate not only its reliance on planning, but also its pattern of development, with heavy emphasis on industries such as steel, whether such a pattern of industrialization was appropriate for those countries or not.

When Mao Tse-tung decided that China should grow more wheat, perhaps because he saw that wheat was the predominant grain consumed in the more-developed countries, he directed that vast areas be converted from rice to wheat. This land was not suited for wheat growing, and agricultural productivity suffered. Moreover, the conversion to wheat fields depleted the land of its fertility, so that when it was eventually returned to growing rice, productivity was lower.

Of course, private firms make mistakes as well. There are flops, like the Edsel or the nicotine-free cigarette, mistakes that cost the companies making them hundreds of millions of dollars. But the firm (its owners) bears the costs of these mistakes, and when this is the case, these kinds of mistakes seem to get made less often. The firm has a strong incentive to avoid making them. A company that makes a mistake cannot finance itself for a long time. When the Ford Motor Company discovered that the Edsel was a mistake, it quickly discontinued production, cutting its losses; it knew, and acted upon, the basic lesson that such costs should be treated as bygones.

The government, by contrast, can support an unprofitable firm for many years. Also, the scale of the mistakes that governments sometimes make sets them apart from the mistakes of private firms. If a single farmer mistakenly decides to grow wheat rather than rice, the costs he faces are not comparable to the costs borne by China when Mao made his mistaken judgment.

Mao's mistake was an honest one; it was a mistake of judgment, not a consequence of his pursuit of private interests. But some of the problems facing the LDCs arise from governmental corruption, and here private interests conflict with public ones. Corruption is often associated with the large role that government plays in an LDC, particularly in restricting foreign trade. When the government imposes a high tariff or otherwise protects an industry, the protected firms can raise their prices and thereby increase their profits. If there are only one or two such firms, they will be tempted to share some of the resulting profits with the government official responsible for the protection. And the government official, knowing this, has a strong incentive to ask the private firms to share some of the profits.

In those countries where the government controls foreign exchange, manufacturers needing inputs from abroad can also find themselves at the whim of a foreign exchange official. The refusal to provide the foreign exchange required to purchase inputs can be disastrous for a manufacturer, and delays in granting the import permits can be costly. There is a clear incentive for corrupt behaviour. By the same token, whenever there are government regulations that must be satisfied, government officials almost always have some discretion in implementing the regulations. They may not be able to prohibit the planned activity, such as a new plant or product, but they may be able to delay the approvals, and the delays can be costly. Again, the economic incentives to bribe a quick approval from the appropriate government officials are frequently overwhelming.

These problems arise in all countries: the building inspectors in New York have periodically been charged with accepting bribes to speed approvals, for instance. However, these problems are more likely to arise in countries such as LDCs, where government salaries are low relative to the size of the bribes being offered, where institutions like a free press that might closely monitor this kind of corruption do not exist, and where government regulations are more pervasive.

Between honest mistakes and corruption lies a third category, which economists label **rent seeking** activities. If the government has the power to confer special benefits, people will seek those benefits for themselves. Firms will try to persuade government that they deserve protection from foreign competition, knowing that such protection will increase their profits. They may give outright bribes, or they may simply spend funds to help elect officials who are sympathetic to their views.

Critics of an activist role for government in development, such as the American economist Anne Krueger, formerly vice-president of the World Bank, thus argue that while we might *imagine* a government's improving on the market, if we look more closely at how governments actually behave, and take into account the natural incentives for counterproductive behaviour on the part of government bureaucrats as opposed to the incentives for efficiency on the part of private firms, we see that government activity can and often does impede development.

A CLEAR ROLE: PROVIDING INFRASTRUCTURE

The debate about the role of government in developing countries is a long-standing one, but most economists agree that there are certain things government must do if there is to be a successful development program. Government must provide the necessary economic **infrastructure**—the roads, bridges, and ports—without which no economy can function well. In recent years, economists have extended the concept of infrastructure to include the legal system, specifically the set of property rights that can be enforced. If Harry has a painting to sell, Maria will be willing to buy it only if she can be sure that Harry actually owns the painting and that after she buys it she will really own it. If Amy lends Adam money, it is useful to have a legal system that will require Adam to repay the money; otherwise Amy will be less willing to lend.

If property rights are not well defined by the legal system, economic efficiency may suffer. If title to land is not clear, so that disputes can easily arise about who really owns a particular piece of real estate, the capital market will be impaired. Individuals will find it difficult to borrow using land as collateral; and "owners" of land will have an insufficient incentive to maintain it (making sure, for instance, that its fertility is not damaged), since they may not be able to bear the fruits of these efforts.

Although economists agree that government should establish and maintain the economic and legal infrastructure, they disagree about what form government intervention should take and how extensive it should be. Those who see the government as a major hindrance in development think that the best policy is to stop meddling: without government interference, markets could forward the development effort enormously. But others, noting widespread market failures, including important externalities, call for government direction, albeit in a more limited form than what the planning boards would provide. In Japan, for instance, the Ministry for International Trade and Industry (MITI) has played an active role in coordinating public- and private-sector activities in many industries. In Korea and other successful Asian countries, governments have tried to tilt the economy in certain directions, as we will now see.

Close-up: Zambia and Malawi

Zambia and Malawi are two African countries that sit side by side. Each won independence from Britain in 1963, and each has a population of about 7 million. Both countries are dreadfully poor. In 1989, GDP per capita in Zambia was only U.S. $390 per person; in Malawi, it was a mere U.S. $180. But although the two countries are similar in the extent of their poverty, the economy in Malawi has grown up to its present poverty level, while the economy in Zambia has shrunk down. In 1965, for example, per capita income in Malawi was only U.S. $117, but per capita income in Zambia was about U.S. $430.

How did this happen? Clearly, changes in per capita income involve two factors: economic growth and population growth. Population growth in Zambia was about .2 percent faster each year than in Malawi over those two decades, so the Zambian economy would have had to grow .2 percent faster a year just to keep its edge in per capita income. However, economic growth in Zambia was actually much slower. The economy in Malawi grew at an annual rate of 5.5 percent a year from 1965 to 1980, but then slowed to a growth rate of 2.7 percent a year in the 1980s. The economy in Zambia, by comparison, grew at only 2.0 percent a year from 1965 to 1980, and only .8 percent a year in the 1980s.

These differences in economic growth are not accidental. Zambia's economic errors consisted of printing extra money to finance its budget deficits, thus fueling inflation; keeping farm prices low to benefit consumers, thus damaging its agricultural sector; going deeply into debt without investing the money in economically profitable ventures; and persistent incompetence and corruption, particularly in the important copper mining industry. Copper reserves are likely to be exhausted within a few years, and much of the population today is heavily infected with AIDS.

Malawi, on the other hand, has focused on building rural roads and railways and on subsidizing fertilizer so farmers could expand their production. The government has imposed some price and production controls, but has adjusted those controls to compensate for market realities. Although a war in neighbouring Mozambique has been flooding Malawi with refugees, the short-term outlook for Malawi is not as bleak as that for Zambia.

Both countries remain desperately poor. The poor in Malawi complain that their relatively laissez-faire government has not done more to subsidize lower prices for food and medical care. The poor in Zambia have gotten steadily poorer over the last two decades, and they did not have much to start with. Clearly, the governments of such countries face heart-wrenching choices; just as clearly, those choices make a major difference to their people.

Sources: World Bank, *World Development Report* (1991), various charts; *The Economist,* February 18-24, 1989, pp. 88–89.

WHO SHOULD MAKE THE DECISIONS?

Questionable role for government: Planning
> Planning goes on in economies anyway
> Governments lack requisite information to do a good job at planning

Government misdirects resources
> From misguided theories
> Because of corruption
> Because of rent-seeking behaviour

Clear role for government
> Providing economic infrastructure
> Providing legal infrastructure (property rights)

TILTING THE ECONOMY

If there is to be government intervention, the question is, what should the governments in LDCs try to encourage? There are several directions in which the government can attempt to tilt the economy. It can try either to encourage exports or encourage domestically produced goods in place of imports. Or it can try to promote either agriculture or industry. Both of these policy issues have been the subject of much discussion in recent years.

EXPORT-LED GROWTH

Most economists who see a role for government in LDCs in tilting the direction of the market believe the government should encourage the production and export of goods in which the country has a comparative advantage. This strategy is referred to as **export-led growth,** and is closely tied to the belief that there is a well-developed international market for goods. With exports, the demand for the goods produced by LDCs is not limited by the low incomes of their citizens.

Advocates of export-led growth also believe that the high level of competition provided by the export market is an important stimulus to efficiency and modernization. The only way a firm can succeed in the face of keen international competition is to produce what consumers want, at the quality they want, and at the lowest possible costs. This keen competition forces specialization in areas where low-wage, less-developed countries have a comparative advantage, such as labour-intensive products. It also forces firms to look for the best ways of producing. International firms often take a role in helping to enhance efficiency. For instance, the clothing store chain Benetton has developed production techniques that combine large production runs with rapid adaptability in style and color. In this way, the firm has been able to take advantage of low-wage LDCs by producing most of what it sells in these countries.

Another advantage of export-led growth is that there is a natural test of its success: can the country compete effectively with foreign producers?

While some economists believe that no government intervention is required for export-led growth—that firms on their own will find it profitable to export the goods in which the country has a comparative advantage—some of the most notable success stories entail active government encouragement. For example, as part of the successful development programs in both Japan and Korea, the government provided export subsidies and the credit necessary for the expansion of the export sectors. Japan's development efforts were spurred and coordinated by its powerful Ministry for International Trade and Industry. Within the space of less than two decades, it reversed its image from a producer of cheap, low-quality products to a manufacturer of quality high-tech products, including cameras, automobiles, and electronic equipment. Korea's success is no less notable, though since it started at a much lower level, it still has a long way to go to catch up to the more-developed countries.

Critics of export-led growth cite three main problems with this approach. First, they worry that if countries simply play to their current comparative advantage, they will specialize in cheap, labour-intensive goods and in agricultural products like coffee, cocoa, and bananas, for which they have a comparative advantage based on climate. Their incomes may rise slightly, but they will not become developed.

Second, critics do not believe that it is as easy (or profitable) to export as those in favour of the export-led growth approach believe. The world market runs not just on price, but on trade patterns that have been established over long periods of time. The success of many products is based on reputations, which are not easy to establish. Developing export markets may be difficult even for products for which one might think there was a well-developed international market, like rice. Different countries come to rely on different sources of rice; there are variations in the quality of rice about which some consumers feel quite strongly. And a rice-growing country like Thailand, which is dependent on exports, puts itself at the mercy of others' foreign trade policies. Thus, when the U.S. government increased its protection of American rice farmers in 1986, Thailand saw an important part of its market disappear, and the price Thai farmers received fell by a third.

Third, critics are concerned that export-led growth has helped to perpetuate the dual structure of many LDCs, in which some parts of the economy are quite advanced but others remain at much lower stages of development. Export-led growth may create only isolated pockets of development, loosely connected with the rest of the economy. This may not pose a problem for small islands, like Hong Kong, Taiwan, and Singapore, but it does for the larger developing economies.

Supporters of export-led growth agree that there have been instances in which these concerns are valid. But they also point out that the most important such instances either are special cases—such as used to be the case in Malaysia, with its rubber plantation enclaves—or involve export industries that have developed as a result of government protection, with little relation to the rest of the country. When the exports are based on the country's comparative advantages, when they are labour intensive and have strong links with the rest of the economy, then the growth in the export industries will inevitably spill over to other sectors.

IMPORT SUBSTITUTION

A contrasting strategy, known as **import substitution,** stresses the development of a domestic market, by substituting domestically produced goods for goods that were previously imported. In this view, the hallmark of a developed country is modern industry. Rather than importing steel, automobiles, TV sets, computers, and other such products, a nation should produce them itself in order to develop the skills necessary for modernization. It should produce, in other words, all the goods that it had previously imported from the industrialized economies. This is the road to development that most of the larger LDCs, including India, China, and Brazil, undertook in the years after World War II. At times, each of these countries has taken import substitution to extremes, insisting, for example, on domestically produced computers even when they might not be able to perform the functions of imported computers.

India, like many other LDCs, has also placed a heavy emphasis on domestically owned businesses. At least 50 percent of each company must be owned by Indians. When Coca-Cola refused to disclose the secret of its closely guarded formula to its Indian-controlled subsidiary, the government shut down Coca-Cola. At times, it seemed as if "Indian-made cola for Indians" would become a rallying point for Indian nationalism, just as "Buy American" campaigns have been a rallying point for protectionism in the United States.

But the import substitution approach has disadvantages of its own. Trade barriers set up to protect domestic firms can end up protecting inefficient producers. The absence of competition means that there is an insufficient spur to innovation and efficiency. The profits to which trade barriers frequently give rise provide a source of government corruption. And unfortunately, the trade barriers remain years after they are introduced.

In some cases, the value added of the protected industry is actually negative. Consider an Indian car producer. Many of the car parts have to be imported. The value added of the car manufacturer is not the total value of the car, but only the difference between the value of the car and the value of the imported components. Assume that because of sloppy manufacturing, a significant fraction of the imported parts are damaged. It might be cheaper for the country to import the entire car than import the components and assemble the car. Of course, with protection, the Indian car manufacturer may still be making profits. Consumers suffer, because they have to pay higher prices.

The problems are even worse when the protected industry is one like steel, whose product is used in other industries. An Indian car manufacturer might be profitable if it could only purchase steel at international prices. But if it is forced to pay inflated prices to buy Indian steel, it cannot compete with foreign producers. The government might try to offset this by subsidizing the car manufacturers. A subsidy or trade protection in one sector thus grows into a complex of subsidies and trade protection in other sectors.

While in general trade protection to stimulate import substitution seems to lead to massive inefficiencies, it has proved successful for a time in some countries such as Brazil, which enjoyed several decades of rapid growth before the debt crisis of the 1980s tainted that picture somewhat. Also, supporters of import substitution note that many of the most rapid bursts of growth of the current developed countries occurred in wartimes, when the economy was inwardly directed, not export oriented. These same supporters, looking at the experience of Japan, argue that at least for industrial goods, import substitution—the development of a domestic market—must precede exports. Before Japan was able successfully to sell cars abroad, it first had to develop a market for Japanese cars at home.

Choosing between Export-Led and Import Substitution Policies

There is one respect in which those who advocate government intervention to stimulate export-led growth and those who advocate government intervention to stimulate import substitution agree: *current* comparative advantage is not the appropriate basis for the design of a development strategy. In the modern economy, a dynamic comparative advantage is what is important, one based not so much on current resource endowments as on acquired skills. Chapter 21 stressed the importance of learning by doing, of the improvement in skills and productivity that comes from the experience of production. Twenty years ago, Japan could not compete with the United States in the production of computer chips. Then the Japanese government subsidized the chip industry, and as the nation's firms gained experience, they became effective competitors, to the point where government subsidies were no longer needed. This is the infant industry argument for government assistance.

Today the question of export-led growth versus import substitution is viewed as one of balance. A competitive export sector is essential for a successful development program. A highly protected domestic import substitution sector can be an important barrier to development, but limited forms of government encouragement—for both exports and import substitution—may play an important positive role. And the more-developed countries can provide effective assistance to LDCs by encouraging their firms to trade with these countries. At the very least, they should not construct trade barriers that keep products of LDCs out.

EXPORT-LED GROWTH VERSUS IMPORT SUBSTITUTION

General principles:

    Resources should be allocated on the basis of dynamic comparative advantage rather than current comparative advantage.

Export-led growth

    Strengths:

        The demand for goods is not limited by the income of the country.

        High levels of competition stimulate efficiency and modernization.

        The ability to compete with foreign producers provides a strong market test.

    Problems:

        May lead countries to specialize in cheap, labour-intensive goods and agriculture with little long-run growth potential.

        It may not be easy to develop export markets.

        May lead to an economy with a developed export sector and the rest of the economy remaining less developed.

Import substitution

    Strength:

        Helps country develop broad range of skills necessary for modernization.

    Problems:

        Trade barriers can discourage innovation and efficiency and encourage corruption.

        It is often difficult to remove trade barriers once imposed.

        When a protected industry makes goods used as inputs for firms in other sectors, this raises costs and lowers the competitiveness of these other sectors.

AGRICULTURE VERSUS INDUSTRY

A debate much like the one between export-led growth and import substitution concerns the role of agriculture versus industry in the development process. Many LDCs decided that growth must be based on the development of the industrialized sector. They therefore taxed the agriculture sector to provide the revenues required to support industrialization and to provide food subsidies to people living in the urban sector. This strategy has been criticized on the grounds of both efficiency and equity.

    The comparative advantage of many LDCs lies in agriculture. While development may entail the growth of the urban sector, that growth in turn is based on a prosperous and productive rural sector. In the last decade, there has been a shift in development strategies to limit the taxes imposed on agriculture. The World Bank has focused much of its efforts on agriculture, aiding, for instance, the development of irrigation systems. China has returned control of much of the agricultural land to families, and has realized that the taxes it had been imposing on agriculture were so severe that production was badly discouraged. Placing the burden for raising resources for development on the rural sector through higher taxes is often viewed as inequitable, since those in the rural sector are poorer on average than those in the urban sector.

The agriculture-industry conflict has long played a role in Canada's history. Shortly after Confederation, the Conservative government of Sir John A. Macdonald instituted its National Policy. It consisted of three elements—import tariffs to protect the fledgling manufacturing industries of central Canada against foreign competition, an active immigration policy to populate the fertile farm lands of the Prairie provinces, and a subsidized transportation system connecting one end of the country to the other. The effect of the National Policy was to perpetuate a system of east-west trade in defiance of the geographically more natural north-south movement. The primary beneficiaries of this system were seen to be central Canadians whose manufacturing industries were protected from American competition. Westerners, whose livelihood relied mostly on the export of agricultural products, were forced to pay artificially high prices for goods that could have been imported more cheaply from the United States. As long as the population in the West was relatively small and engaged mostly in agriculture production, their dissatisfaction could be kept in check. After all, they did benefit from subsidized railway prices in getting their products to market. As well, they benefited from federal government equalization payments to their provincial governments. But as their populations grew and as their wealth increased with the exploitation of timber and the discovery of oil, gas, and other natural resources, they became more forceful in expressing their dissatisfaction with what they saw as central government exploitation of the West. The term "western alienation" graphically described their discontent, a discontent that came to a head with the National Energy Policy of the Trudeau government. This policy artificially held the price of oil produced in Canada below the world price and deprived western producers and governments of what they saw as their rightful share of the wealth. As a consequence, western Canadians became among the most ardent supporters of the Canada-U.S. Free Trade Agreement discussed in Chapter 14. More recently, they became strong advocates of the institution of a Senate with equal representation of all provinces and greater decentralization of economic power from the federal government to the provinces. Both of these ideas came to be components of the constitutional proposals agreed to by the prime minister and the provincial premiers in 1992. This agreement, known as the Charlottetown Accord, was subsequently defeated in a national referendum in June 1992.

THE PROSPECTS

The Bible says, "The poor ye always have with you" (Matthew 26:11). For centuries, people seemed engaged in a race between population and the economy's ability to support that population. The industrial and scientific revolutions of the past two centuries, and the enhanced means of production that resulted, have meant ever-rising living standards for most of those lucky enough to live in the developed countries of Europe and North America. And the past fifty years have extended the benefits to an increasing number of countries—to Japan in full measure, and to a lesser extent to a number of middle-income countries such as Singapore, Korea, and Taiwan.

Elsewhere, there are pockets of success—the area around São Paulo in Brazil has the look and feel of prosperity. India, as noted above, has become self-sufficient with regard to food. Thailand has been having a boom. But their success is precarious; the debt crisis of the 1980s represented a major setback for many of these countries, including Mexico. Still, the outstanding lesson of recent decades is that success is possible: there is the real prospect that more and more of these countries, if they pursue wise policies and enjoy political stability, will be able to pull themselves out of the cycle of poverty in which they have lived for centuries.

But for the most unfortunate countries, such as sub-Saharan Africa, which lack human and physical resources and have burgeoning populations that consume much of whatever gains they are able to obtain, the prospects are less optimistic. And the lack of hope contributes to political instability, making economic progress all the more difficult.

AN AGENDA FOR DEVELOPMENT

How the developed countries can help
    Reduce trade barriers
    Increase foreign aid
    Facilitate foreign investment
Growth-oriented policies for LDCs
    Reduce rates of growth of the population
    Increase quantity and quality of education
    Provide a basic infrastructure (roads, ports, a legal system)
    Provide a favourable climate for investment, including foreign investment
    Facilitate the development of capital markets (financial intermediaries)
    Spend more of government revenues on investment rather than consumption, such as food subsidies
    Develop a competitive export sector
Policies that may inhibit growth
    Trade protection
    Regulations, licensing

REVIEW AND PRACTICE

SUMMARY

1. In less-developed countries, or LDCs, life expectancies are usually shorter, infant mortality is higher, and people are less educated than in developed countries. Also, a larger fraction of the population lives in the rural sector, and population growth rates are higher.

2. In recent years, newly industrialized countries such as South Korea, Singapore, Hong Kong, and Taiwan have managed to improve their economic status dramatically. Other LDCs, like India, have expanded food production considerably. But the standard of living in some of the poorest LDCs, such as many African nations, has actually been declining, as population growth has outstripped economic growth.

3. Among the factors contributing to underdevelopment are a rapidly growing population, a lack of educated workers, market failures such as the absence of markets to allocate capital efficiently, a lack of entrepreneurs, and extremes of inequality.

4. Central planning has not been effective in LDCs. Governments lack the requisite information and often misdirect resources. On the other hand, governments have played an important role in providing an economic and legal infrastructure.

5. Some economists believe LDCs should tilt the economy by pursuing export-led economic growth. Others advocate a strategy of import substitution, where the goal is to develop skills and self-sufficiency by replacing imports. Both groups agree that resources should be allocated on the basis of dynamic comparative advantage.

6. Most LDCs have a comparative advantage in agriculture, but governments have often attempted to tilt the economy more towards industry. More recent development strategies have focused on improving productivity in the rural sector.

KEY TERMS

less-developed countries (LDCs)
developed or industrialized countries

newly industrialized countries (NICs)
green revolution
dual economy
surplus labour

shadow price
rent seeking
infrastructure
export-led growth
import substitution

REVIEW QUESTIONS

1. List some of the important ways in which LDCs differ from more-developed countries.

2. Why may a land reform increase agricultural output? What factors would hinder the success of a land reform?

3. What does it mean to say that less-developed countries have a dual economy?

4. What are the most important factors inhibiting growth in the LDCs?

5. What can be done to help overcome the problem of capital shortage?

6. Why is capital often inefficiently allocated in LDCs?

7. How does rapid population growth make it more difficult to increase a country's standard of living?

8. What are the important instances of market failures in LDCs? In what ways are market failures more pervasive in LDCs than in developed countries? What are the consequences of market failures in LDCs?

9. Why has government planning failed?

10. Why have governments in LDCs put more emphasis on agriculture in recent years?

PROBLEMS

1. In Canada, the economy grew by 3.3 percent per year (in real terms) during the 1980s. In India, the economy grew by 5.3 percent during the 1980s. However, population growth in Canada was .8 percent annually, while population growth in India was 2.1 percent annually. Which country increased its standard of living faster for the average citizen? By how much?

2. Nominal GDP in Kenya was 9 billion shillings in 1967 and 135 billion shillings in 1987. The price level in Kenya (using 1980 as a base year) rose from 40 in 1967 to 200 in 1987. And the population of Kenya increased from 10 million to 22 million in those twenty years. What was the total percentage change in real GDP per capita in Kenya from 1967 to 1987?

3. True or false: "LDCs do not have much capital because their rates of saving are low. If they saved more or received more foreign aid, they could rapidly expand their economic growth." Discuss.

4. How might each of the following hinder entrepreneurs in LDCs?
    (a) a lack of functioning capital markets;
    (b) pervasive government control of the economy;
    (c) a lack of companies that offer business services;
    (d) a tradition of substantial foreign control of large enterprises.

5. What is the economist's case for having the government be responsible for providing infrastructure? (Hint: You may wish to review the concept of a public good from Chapter 7.)

6. If many LDCs simultaneously attempted to pursue export-led growth, what would be the effect in world markets on the quantities and prices of products

mainly sold by LDCs, like minerals, agricultural goods, and textiles? What effect might these quantities and prices have on the success of such export-led growth policies?

7. Explain how the idea of import substitution conflicts in the short run with the idea of comparative advantage. Need the two ideas conflict in the long run? Why or why not?

8. Why does sharecropping reduce a farmer's incentive to work hard? Why is sharecropping nonetheless so prevalent in LDCs?

9. Why might a family in an LDC have an economic pressure towards having more children than a family in a developed country?

GLOSSARY

absolute advantage: a country has an absolute advantage over another country in the production of a good if it can produce that good more efficiently (with fewer inputs)

accelerator: the effect on GDP of the increase in investment that results from an increase in output. For instance, the greater output leads a firm to believe the demand for its products will rise in the future; the resulting increase in investment leads to growth in output and still further increases in investment, accelerating the expansion of the economy

acquired endowments: resources a country builds for itself, like a network of roads or an educated population

actuarially fair: pricing insurance programs according to the expected cost of paying out insurance so that the insurer just breaks even

adaptive expectations: expectations based on the extrapolation of events in the recent past into the future

adverse selection: principle that says that those who most want to buy insurance tend to be those most at risk, so charging a high price for insurance (to cover those at high risk) will discourage those at less risk from buying insurance at all; similar phenomena occur in credit, labour, and product markets

affirmative action: the requirement that employers seek out or promote persons from designated groups

aggregate demand curve: a curve relating the total demand for the economy's goods and services at each price level, given the level of wages

aggregate price-quantity curve: a curve showing the equilibrium price that imperfectly competitive firms will charge at each level of output

aggregate supply curve: a curve relating the total supply of the economy's goods and services at each price level, given the level of wages

aggregate expenditures schedule: a curve that traces out the relationship between expenditures—the sum of consumption, investment, government expenditures, and net exports—and national income, at a fixed price level

annuity: an asset whose return takes the form of a fixed annual payment for as long as the owner lives

anti-combines laws: laws that discourage monopoly and restrictive practices and encourage greater competition

anti-dumping duties: penalties imposed by importing countries on producers who sell a product at a lower price abroad than in their home economy

appreciation: a change in the exchange rate that enables a unit of currency to buy more units of foreign currencies

arbitrage: the process by which assets with comparable risk, liquidity, and tax treatment are priced to yield comparable expected returns

asset: any item that is long-lived, purchased for the service it renders over its life and for what one will receive when one sells it

assistance in kind: public assistance that provides particular goods and services, like housing or medical care, rather than cash

asymmetric information: a situation in which the parties to a transaction have different information, as when the seller of a used car has more information about its quality than the buyer

automatic stabilizers: mechanisms that automatically take money out of the economy when the economy is booming and put money in when it is slowing down

autonomous consumption: that part of consumption that does not depend on income

average costs: the total costs divided by the total output

average productivity: the total quantity of output divided by the total quantity of input

average tax rate: the ratio of taxes payable to total income

average variable costs: the total variable costs divided by the total output

backward-bending labour supply curve: the tendency at high wage rates for further increases in wages to cause labour supply to decrease

balance of payments: the summary of transactions of all types between Canadians and foreigners, comprised of the sum of the current and the capital accounts

balance of trade: the difference between the value of exports and the value of imports in a given year

bank rate: the interest rate paid by chartered banks on loans from the Bank of Canada

bank run: the attempt by a large number of depositors to withdraw money from a bank in which they have lost confidence

barriers to entry: factors that prevent firms from entering a market, such as government rules or patents

basic competitive model: the model of the economy that pulls together the assumptions of self-interested consumers, profit-maximizing firms, and perfectly competitive markets

benefits in kind: provision by the government of goods and services to individuals rather than cash

bequest savings motive: people save so that they can leave an inheritance to their children

Bertrand competition: an oligopoly in which each firm believes that its rivals are committed to keeping their prices fixed and that customers can be lured away by offering lower prices

bilateral agreements: agreements between two countries to reduce trade barriers, such as the Canada-U.S. Free Trade Agreement

bilateral trade: trade between two parties

bonds: promises by a borrower to repay a certain amount in a given number of years in the future to a lender, and to make fixed interest payments periodically on the amount borrowed

boom: a period of time when resources are being fully used and GDP is growing steadily

branch banking system: a banking system with national banks that have a large number of branches across the country

breach of contract: when a party to an agreement (such as a supplier of products to another firm) decides not to abide by the terms of the contract

budget constraints: opportunity sets whose constraints are imposed by money

business cycle: fluctuations up and down in economic activity that occur with some regularity

capital-account surplus: net borrowing (borrowing less lending) by Canadians from foreigners

capital adequacy requirements: limits placed by the Bank Act on the ratio of assets to equity of chartered banks

capital gain: the increase in the value of an asset between the time it is purchased and the time it is sold

capital goods: the machines and buildings firms invest in with funds obtained in the capital market

capital market: the market in which savings are made available to those who need additional funds, such as firms that wish to invest, and in which ownership claims on different assets and their associated risks are exchanged

cartel: a group of producers with an agreement to collude in setting prices and output

cash reserve management: the determination by banks of the amount of reserves to hold

categorical assistance: public assistance aimed at a particular category of people, like the elderly or the disabled

causation: the relationship that results when a change in one variable is not only correlated with but actually causes a change in another variable; the change in the second variable is a consequence of the change in the first variable, rather than both changes being a consequence of a change in a third variable

central bank: the bank (Bank of Canada) that oversees and monitors the rest of the banking system and serves as the bankers' bank

central planning: the system in which central government bureaucrats (as opposed to private entrepreneurs or even local government bureaucrats) determine what will be produced and how it will be produced

centralization: organizational structure in which decision making is concentrated at the top

centrally planned economy: an economy in which most decisions about resource allocation are made by the central government

certificate of deposit (CD): an account in which money is deposited for a preset length of time, that yields a slightly higher return to compensate for the reduced liquidity

circular flow: the way in which funds move through the capital, labour, and product markets between households, firms, the government, and the foreign sector

classical economists: economists prevalent before the Great Depression who believed that the basic competitive model provided a good description of the economy and that if short periods of unemployment did occur, market forces would quickly restore the economy to full employment

classical unemployment: unemployment that occurs as a result of too-high real wages; it occurs in the supply-constrained equilibrium, so that rightward shifts in aggregate supply reduce the level of unemployment

closed economy: an economy that neither exports nor imports

Coase theorem: the assertion that if property rights are properly defined, then people will be forced to pay for any negative externalities they impose on others, and market transactions will produce efficient outcomes

co-insurance: the requirement for an insured individual to pay a share of the costs of an accident along with the insurance company

common property resource: a natural resource that is collectively owned rather than privately owned and that is treated as being freely accessible to the users rather than being scarce

common share: a normal share of ownership with full voting rights in a firm and a right to a share of the profits

communism: an economic system in which the government owns and controls virtually all property except personal property

comparative advantage: a country has a comparative advantage over another country in one good as opposed to another good if its *relative* efficiency in the production of the first good is higher than the other country's

compensating wage differentials: differences in wages that can be traced to nonpecuniary attributes of a job, such as the degree of autonomy and risk

competitive equilibrium price: the price at which the quantity supplied and the quantity demanded are equal to each other

complement: two goods are complements if the demand for one (at a given price) decreases as the price of the other increases

compound interest: interest earned on interest previously earned and saved

consumer price index (CPI): a price index in which the basket of goods is defined by what a typical consumer purchases

consumer protection legislation: laws aimed at protecting consumers, for instance by assuring that consumers have more complete information about items they are considering buying

consumer surplus: the difference between what a person would be willing to pay and what he actually has to pay to buy a certain amount of a good

consumption function: the relationship between disposable income and consumption

contestable markets: markets in which the potential entry of competitors keeps prices near their competitive levels

contingency clauses: statements within a contract that make the level of payment or the work to be performed conditional upon various factors

corporate finance: the study of how firms raise financial capital

corporate income tax: a tax based on the income, or profit, received by a corporation

corporation: a firm with limited liability, owned by shareholders, who elect a board of directors that chooses the top executives

correlation: the relationship that results when a change in one variable is consistently associated with a change in another variable

cost-of-living adjustments (COLAs): provisions in wage contracts for wages to rise automatically with inflation

cost-push inflation: inflation whose initial cause is a rise in production costs

Cournot competition: an oligopoly in which each firm believes that its rivals are committed to a certain level of production and that rivals will reduce their prices as needed to sell that amount

countervailing duties: duties imposed on imports that are found to have been subsidized in the exporting country

credentials competition: the trend in which prospective workers acquire higher educational credentials, not so much because of anything they actually learn in the process but to convince potential employers to hire them by signalling that they will be more productive employees than those with weaker credentials

credit constraint effect: when prices fall, firms' revenues also fall, but the money they owe creditors remains unchanged; as a result, firms have fewer funds of their own to invest. Because of credit rationing, firms cannot make up the difference; accordingly, investment decreases

credit rationing: credit is rationed when no lender is willing to make a loan to a borrower or the amount lenders are willing to lend to borrowers is limited, even if the borrower is willing to pay more than other borrowers of comparable risk who are getting loans

cross subsidization: the practice of charging higher prices to one group of consumers in order to subsidize lower prices for another group

crowding out: a decrease in private investment resulting from an increase in government expenditures

Crown corporations: firms that are owned by the federal or provincial governments

current account: the sum of the merchandise trade, invisibles, and investment income accounts

cyclical unemployment: unemployment that increases with a downtown in the economy and decreases with a boom

debt: capital, such as bonds and bank loans, supplied to a firm by lenders; the firm promises to repay the amount borrowed plus interest

decentralization: organizational structure in which many individuals or subunits can make decisions

decision tree: a device for structured decision making that spells out the choices and possible consequences of alternative actions

deductible: the requirement for a insured person to pay a fixed amount of the costs of an accident before the insurance policy covers the rest

default: failure to make a promised repayment of a loan

deficit: when government expenditures exceed tax revenues in a given year

deficit spending: the situation that exists when government expenditures are greater than revenues

deflation: a persistent decrease in the general level of prices

demand curve: the relationship between the quantity demanded of a good and the price, whether for an individual or for the market (all individuals) as a whole

demand-constrained equilibrium: the equilibrium that occurs when prices are stuck at a level above that at which aggregate demand equals aggregate supply; output is equal to aggregate demand

demand deposits: deposits that can be drawn upon instantly, like chequing accounts

demand-pull inflation: inflation whose initial cause is aggregate demand exceeding aggregate supply at the current price level

demand shock: a rightward shift in the aggregate demand curve, which will initiate inflation in an economy operating at full capacity

demographic effects: effects that arise from changes in characteristics of the population such as age, birthrates, and location

depreciation: (a) the decrease in the value of an asset; in particular, the amount that capital goods decrease in value as they are used and become old; (b) a change in the exchange rate that enables a unit of one currency to buy fewer units of foreign currencies

deregulation: the lifting of government regulations to allow the market to function more freely

devaluation: a reduction in the rate of exchange between one currency and other currencies under a fixed exchange rate system

developed or **industrialized countries:** the wealthiest nations in the world, including Western Europe, the United States, Canada, Japan, Australia, and New Zealand

diminishing marginal utility: the principle that says that as an individual consumes more and more of a good, each successive unit increases her utility, or enjoyment, less and less

diminishing returns: the principle that says that as one input increases, with other inputs fixed, the resulting increase in output tends to be smaller and smaller

discouraged workers: workers who would be willing to work but have given up looking for jobs, and thus are not officially counted as unemployed

disposable income: what households have available to spend out of their incomes after paying income taxes (income less income taxes)

dividends: that portion of corporate profits paid out to shareholders

downward rigidity of wages: the situation that exists when wages do not fall quickly in response to a shift in the demand or supply curve for labour, resulting in an excess supply of labour

dual economy: the separation in many LDCs between an impoverished rural sector and an urban sector that has higher wages and more advanced technology

dumping: the sale of a product abroad at a price less than the cost of production

duopoly: an industry with only two firms

durable goods: goods that provide a service over a number of years, such as cars, major appliances, and furniture

dynamic consistency: a policy is said to have dynamic consistency when government announces a course of action and then has the incentives to actually carry out that policy

economic rents: payments made to a factor of production that are in excess of what is required to elicit the supply of that factor

economies of scope: the situation that exists when it is less expensive to produce two products together than it would be to produce each one separately

efficiency wage: the wage at which total labour costs are minimized

efficiency wage theory: the theory that paying higher wages (up to a point) lowers total production costs, for instance by leading to a more productive labour force

efficient market theory: the theory that all available information is reflected in the current price of an asset

elasticity of labour supply: the percentage change in labour supplied resulting from a 1 percent change in wages

elasticity of supply: see **price elasticity of supply**

eminent domain: the right to seize private property for public use with fair compensation

employment equity: the principle that all types of persons should have equal access to employment opportunities

endogenous effects: sources of business cycle fluctuations that originate within the workings of the market economy

entrepreneurs: individuals who create new businesses and introduce innovations in products and processes

equalization payments: transfers paid by the federal government to the provinces whose tax capacities are below average and designed to equalize their ability to provide public service to their residents; currently paid to all provinces except Alberta, British Columbia, and Ontario

equilibrium price: see **competitive equilibrium price**

equilibrium quantity: the amount demanded and supplied when a market is in equilibrium

equity, shares, stock: terms that indicate part ownership of a firm; the firm sells these in order to raise money, or capital

excess capacity: production capacity that is greater than that currently needed

excess demand: the situation in which the quantity demanded at a given price exceeds the quantity supplied

excess supply: the situation in which the quantity supplied at a given price exceeds the quantity demanded

exchange efficiency: the condition in which whatever the economy produces is distributed among people in such a way that there are no gains to further trade

exchange rate: the rate at which one currency (such as dollars) can be exchanged for another (such as marks, yen, or pounds)

excise tax or **duty:** a tax on a particular good or service

exclusive dealing: when a producer insists that firms selling its products not sell those of its rivals

exogenous effects: sources of business cycle fluctuations that originate in events outside the economy, such as an oil price shock

expected return: the average return—a single number that combines the various possible returns per dollar invested with the chances that each of these returns will actually be paid

export-led growth: the strategy that government should encourage exports in which the country has a comparative advantage to stimulate growth

exports: goods produced domestically but sold abroad

externality: a phenomenon that arises when an individual or firm takes an action but does not bear all the costs (negative externality) or receive all the benefits (positive externality)

extraterritoriality: the requirement that firms operating abroad abide by the laws of their home country

factor demand: the amount of an input (factor of production) demanded by a firm, given the price of the input and the quantity of output being produced; in a competitive market, an input will be demanded up to the point where the value of the marginal product of that input equals the price of the input

federal governmental structure: a system in which government activity takes place at several levels—national, provincial, municipal

fiat money: money that the government creates and declares to have value

final goods: products that are sold to final users (such as consumers) rather than being used as inputs into further production processes

financial intermediaries: institutions that form the link between savers who have extra funds and borrowers who desire extra funds

firm wealth effect: lower prices or lower demand cause

firms' profits and net worth to fall, and this makes them less willing to undertake the risks involved with investment

fiscal policies: policies that affect the level of government expenditures and taxes

fixed costs: the costs resulting from fixed inputs, sometimes called **overhead costs**

fixed exchange rate system: an exchange rate system in which the value of each currency is fixed in relationship to other currencies

fixed or **overhead inputs:** (a) inputs that do not change depending on the quantity of output; (b) fixed inputs also sometimes refer to inputs that are fixed in the short run—that is, they do not depend on *current* output—but may depend on output in the long run

flexible or **floating exchange rate system:** a system in which exchange rates are determined by market forces, the law of supply and demand, without government interference

flow statistics: measurements of a certain rate or quantity per period of time, such as GDP, which measures output per year

four-firm concentration ratio: the fraction of an industry's output produced by the top four firms

fractional reserve system: a banking system in which banks hold a fraction of the amount of deposits as reserves

free-market economists: those who have strong faith in unfettered markets as being necessary for economic efficiency

free-rider problem: the problem that occurs when someone thinks he may be able to enjoy something without paying for it, and so fails to contribute to the cost; free-rider problems arise in the provision of public goods

frictional unemployment: unemployment that reflects workers moving between jobs

full-employment deficit: the budget deficit that would have prevailed if the economy were at full employment, thus with higher tax revenues and lower unemployment insurance expenditures

full-employment or **potential output:** the level of output that would prevail if labour were fully employed (output may exceed that level if workers work more than the normal level of overtime)

funded pensions: pension schemes in which payments to retirees are from a fund accumulated on their behalf during their working lives

gains from trade: the benefits that each side enjoys from a trade

GDP deflator: a weighted average of the prices of different goods and services, where the weights represent the importance of each of the goods and services in GDP

GDP per capita: the value of all final goods and services produced in the economy divided by the population

general equilibrium analysis: a simultaneous analysis of all capital, product, and labour markets throughout the economy; it shows, for instance, the impact on all prices and quantities of immigration or a change in taxes

Giffen goods: goods whose demand falls when their price falls in the lower part of their price range

Gini coefficient: a measure of inequality (equal to twice the area between the 45-degree line and the Lorenz curve)

Goods and Services Tax (GST): a tax levied by the federal government on the purchases of almost all goods and services in Canada

green revolution: the invention and dissemination of new seeds and agricultural practices that led to vast increases in agricultural output in less-developed countries during the 1960s and 1970s

gross domestic product (GDP): the total money value of all final goods and services produced by the residents of a nation during a specified period

gross national product (GNP): a measure of the incomes of residents of a country, including income they receive from abroad but subtracting similar payments made to those abroad

horizontal equity: the principle that says that those who are in identical or similar circumstances should pay identical or similar amounts in taxes

horizontal merger or **integration:** a merger between two firms that produce the same goods

horizontal restraints or **agreements:** restrictive practices, such as price fixing or collusion, engaged in by two or more firms selling in a given market

human capital: the stock of accumulated skills and experience that make workers more productive

hyperinflation: extremely high rates of inflation

imperfect competition: any market structure in which there is some competition but firms face downward-sloping demand curves

imperfect information: a situation in which market participants lack information (such as information about prices or characteristics of goods and services) important for their decision making

imperfect-market economists: those who question the efficiency of markets that are left to operate on their own

imperfect substitutes: goods sufficiently similar that they can be used for many of the same purposes

implicit contract: an unwritten understanding between two groups involved in an exchange, such as an understanding between employer and employees that employees will receive a stable wage throughout fluctuating economic conditions

import function: the relationship between imports and national income

import substitution: the strategy that focuses on the substitution of domestic goods for goods that were previously imported

imports: goods produced abroad but bought domestically

imputed rent: the consumption services obtained by owning one's house rather than having to pay rent

income effect: the reduced consumption of a good whose price has increased that is due to the reduction in a person's buying power, or "real" income; when a person's real income is lower, normally she will consume less of all goods, including the higher-priced good

income elasticity of demand: the percentage change in quantity demanded of a good as the result of a 1 percent change in income (the percentage change in quantity demanded divided by the percentage change in income)

incomes policy: a government-mandated program of constraints on wage and price increases

incomplete markets: situations in which no market may exist for some good or for some risk, or in which some individuals cannot borrow for some purposes

increasing, constant, or **diminishing returns to scale:** when all inputs are increased by a certain proportion, output increases by a greater, equal, or smaller proportion, respectively; increasing returns to scale are also called **economies of scale**

indexed funds: mutual funds that are made up of a representative mix of assets on the stock market, such as the Toronto Stock Exchange 35 Index

indexing: the formal linking of any payment to a price index

individual income tax: a tax based on the income received by an individual or household

infant industry argument for protection: the argument that industries must be protected from foreign competition while they are young, until they have a chance to acquire the skills to enable them to compete on equal terms

inferior good: a good the consumption of which falls as income rises

infinite elasticity of demand: the situation that exists when any amount will be demanded at a particular price, but nothing will be demanded if the price increases even a small amount

infinite elasticity of supply: the situation that exists when any amount will be supplied at a particular price, but nothing will be supplied if the price declines even a small amount.

inflation: the general upward movement of the average of all prices

inflation rate: the percentage increase in the general level of prices

inflation tax: the decrease in buying power (wealth) that inflation imposes on those who hold currency (and other assets, like bonds, the payments for which are fixed in terms of dollars)

inflationary spiral: a self-perpetuating system in which price increases lead to higher wages, which lead to further price increases

information-based wage differentials: wage differentials that exist because workers do not know about higher-paying jobs elsewhere

infrastructure: the roads, ports, bridges, and legal system that provide the necessary basis for a working economy

insider-outsider theory: the theory that firms are reluctant to pay new workers (outsiders) a lower wage than current workers (insiders), because current workers will fear being replaced by the new, low-wage workers and will not participate in cooperating with and training them

insider trading: trading in a firm's shares by persons who have inside information, such as the firm's managers

interest: the return a saver receives in addition to the original amount she deposited (loaned), and the amount a borrower must pay in addition to the original amount he borrowed

interest rate effect: the situation that exists when lower interest rates (resulting from an increase in the money supply or a fall in the price level) induce firms to invest more

intermediate goods: goods produced in one firm that are used as inputs by other firms

inventory: goods that a firm stores in anticipation of its use later on as a product for sale or an input to production

investment: the purchase of an asset that will provide a return over a long period of time

investment schedule: the relationship between the level of investment and the (real) rate of interest

investment tax credit (ITC): a provision of the tax law in which the government reduces a company's tax bill by an amount equal to a percentage of its spending on investment

invisible account: the difference between exports and imports of services

involuntary unemployment: the situation that occurs when the supply of those willing to work at the going market wage exceeds the demand for labour

job discrimination: when disadvantaged groups have limited access to better-paying jobs

Keynesian unemployment: unemployment that occurs as a result of insufficient aggregate demand; it arises in the demand-constrained equilibrium (where aggregate demand is less than aggregate supply), so that rightward shifts in aggregate demand reduce the level of unemployment

kinked demand curve: the demand curve perceived by an oligopolist who believes that rivals will match any price cuts but will not match price increases

labour force participation rate: the fraction of the working-age population that is employed or seeking employment

labour market: the market in which labour services are bought and sold

labour turnover rate: the rate at which workers leave jobs

land reform: the redistribution of land by the government to those who actually work the land

law of supply and demand: the observation that actual prices tend to be equilibrium prices at which demand equals supply

leakages: income generated but not spent within the economy, such as imports, savings, or taxes

learning by doing: the increase in productivity that occurs as a firm gains experience from producing, and that results in a decrease in the firm's production costs

learning curve: the curve describing how costs of production decline as cumulative output increases over time

less-developed countries (LDCs): the poorest nations of the world, including much of Africa, Latin America, and Asia

licences and user fees: charges imposed by governments for specific types of activities, such as driving an automobile, hunting, fishing, etc.

licensing agreement: an agreement under which a firm makes payments to a patent-holder for the right to produce goods that are under patent

life-cycle hypothesis: the theory that individuals typically save when they are young and working and spend their savings as they age and retire

life-cycle savings motive: people save during their working lives so that they can consume more during retirement

limited liability: the fact that the owner of a corporation can lose all the money he invests in the shares of the corporation, but no more

limit pricing: the practice of charging a lower price than the level at which marginal revenue equals marginal cost, as a way of deterring entry by persuading potential competitors that their profits from entering are likely to be limited

lines of credit: agreements by banks to lend businesses money automatically up to some limit

liquidity: the ease with which an asset can be sold

long-term bonds: bonds that mature in ten years or more

Lorenz curve: a curve that shows the cumulative proportion of income that goes to each cumulative proportion of the population, starting with the lowest income group

loss: a situation in which costs exceed revenues so profits are negative

Luddites: early nineteenth-century workmen who destroyed labour-saving machinery rather than see it take over their jobs

lump-sum taxes: taxes that are fixed in amount for an individual and do not depend upon any actions taken by the individual

M1, M2, M3, M2+: measures of the money supply: M1 includes currency and demand deposits; M2 includes M1 plus savings deposits, daily interest chequing accounts, and nonpersonal notice deposits; M3 includes M2 plus nonpersonal fixed-term deposits and foreign currency deposits; M2+ includes M2 plus deposits in near banks

macroeconomics: the top-down view of the economy, focusing on aggregate characteristics

managerial slack: the lack of managerial efficiency (for instance, in cutting costs) that occurs when firms are insulated from competition

marginal cost: the additional cost corresponding to an additional unit of output produced

marginal costs and benefits: the extra costs and benefits that result from choosing a little bit more of one thing

marginal product: the amount output increases with the addition of one unit of an input

marginal propensity to consume: the amount by which consumption increases when disposable income increases by a dollar

marginal propensity to import: the amount by which imports increase when disposable income increases by a dollar

marginal propensity to save: the amount by which savings increase when disposable income increases by a dollar

marginal revenue: the extra revenue received by a firm for selling one additional unit of a good

marginal tax rate: the tax paid on the last increment of income obtained

marginal utility: the extra utility, or enjoyment, a person receives from the consumption of one additional unit of a good

market clearing: the situation that exists when supply equals demand, so there is neither excess supply nor excess demand

market demand curve: total quantity of a good demanded by all individuals at each price

market economy: an economy that allocates resources primarily through the interaction of individuals (households) and private firms

market equilibrium: a situation in which the market price has settled where market demand equals market supply

market failure: the situation in which a market economy fails to attain economic efficiency

market failures approach: the argument that government may have an economic role to play when markets fail to produce efficient outcomes

market labour supply curve: the relationship between the wage paid and the amount of labour willingly supplied, found by adding up the labour supply curves of all the individuals in the economy

market power: the ability of a firm to affect the market price by changing its output

market restrictions or **exclusive territories:** exclusive rights to sell a product within a given region given by a producer to wholesalers or retailers

market supply curve: total quantity of a good supplied by all firms at each price.

market value of the firm: the sum of the value of the firm's debt and equity

marketable permits: permits for the right to emit a given quantity of pollutants; these permits are issued by the government and tradable among firms

median voter: the voter such that half the population have preferences on one side of this voter (for instance, they want higher government expenditures and taxes), while the other half of the population have preferences on the other side of this voter (they want lower taxes and expenditures)

medium of exchange: any item that can be commonly exchanged for goods and services throughout the economy

menu costs: the costs to firms of changing their prices

merit goods and bads: goods that are determined by government to be good or bad for people, regardless of whether people desire them for themselves or not

microeconomics: the bottom-up view of the economy, focusing on individual households and firms

mixed economy: an economy that allocates resources through a mixture of public (governmental) and private decision making

model: a set of assumptions and data used by economists to study an aspect of the economy and make predictions about the future or about the consequences of various policy changes

Modigliani-Miller theorem: the theorem that says that under a simplified set of conditions, the manner in which a firm finances itself does not matter

monetarists: economists who emphasize the importance of money in the economy; they tend to believe that an appropriate monetary policy is all the economy needs from government, and market forces will otherwise solve any macroeconomic problems

monetary policies: policies that affect the supply of money and credit and the terms on which credit is available to borrowers

monetary shock: an increase in aggregate demand as a result of an increase in the money supply

money: any item that serves as a medium of exchange, a store of value, and a unit of account

money market asset: highly marketable debt instruments typically of less than one year's maturity

money multiplier: the amount by which a new deposit into the banking system (from the outside) is multiplied as it is loaned out, redeposited, reloaned, etc., by banks

money supply: the quantity of money in the economy

monopolistic competition: the form of imperfect competition in which the market has sufficiently few firms that each one faces a downward-sloping demand curve, but enough that each can ignore the reactions of rivals to what it does

monopoly: a market consisting of only one firm

moral hazard: the principle that says that those who purchase insurance have a reduced incentive to avoid what they are insured against

moral suasion: attempts by the Bank of Canada to persuade chartered banks to take certain actions to achieve monetary policy objectives

multilateral agreements: agreements among more than two countries to reduce barriers to trade, such as the General Agreement on Tariffs and Trade

multilateral trade: trade among more than two parties

multiplier: the factor by which a change in a component of aggregate demand, like investment or government spending, is multiplied to lead to a larger change in equilibrium national output

multiplier-accelerator model: a model that relates business cycles to the internal working of the economy, showing how changes in investment and output reinforce each other; the central ingredients of the model are the multiplier and the accelerator

mutual fund: a fund that gathers money from different investors and purchases a range of assets; each investor then owns a portion of the entire fund

nationalization: the process whereby a private industry is taken over by the government, whether by buying it or simply seizing it

natural endowments: a country's natural resources, such as good climate, fertile land, or minerals

natural monopoly: a monopoly that exists because average costs of production are declining beyond the level of output demanded in the market, thus making entry unprofitable and making it efficient for there to be only a single firm

natural rate of unemployment: the rate of unemployment at which the rate of inflation is zero

near banks: financial institutions that take deposits and make loans in much the same way as banks

net domestic product (NDP): GDP minus the value of the depreciation of the country's capital goods

net export function: a curve that gives the level of net exports at each level of income

net exports: the difference between exports and imports

new classical economists: economists who, beginning in the 1970s, built on the tradition of classical economists and believed that by and large, market forces, if left to themselves, would solve the problems of unemployment and recessions

new growth economists: economists who, beginning in the 1980s, sought to understand better the basic forces that led the economy to grow fast at one time and slow at another, or some countries to grow faster than others

new Keynesian economists: economists who, beginning in the 1980s, built on the tradition of Keynesian economists and focused attention on unemployment; they sought explanations for the failure of wages and prices to adjust to make labour markets and possibly other markets clear

newly industrialized countries (NICs): nations that have recently moved from being quite poor to being middle-income countries, including South Korea, Taiwan, Singapore, Malaysia, and Hong Kong

nominal GDP: gross domestic prices measured in current prices and not adjusted for inflation

nominal interest rate: the interest rate actually paid on a loan in dollar terms, uncorrected for inflation

non-renewable resources: natural resources that are fixed in supply, such as oil and gas and minerals

normal good: a good the consumption of which rises as income rises

normative economics: economics in which judgments about the desirability of various policies are made; the conclusions rest on value judgments as well as facts and theories

Okun's law: the observation that as the economy pulls out of a recession, output increases more than proportionately to increases in employment

oligopoly: the form of imperfect competition in which the market has several firms, but sufficiently few that each one must take into account the reactions of rivals to what it does

open economy: an economy that is actively engaged in international trade

open market operations: central bank's purchase or sale of government bonds in the open market

opportunity cost: the cost of a resource, measured by the value of the next-best, alternative use of that resource

opportunity sets: a summary of the choices available to individuals, as defined by budget constraints and time constraints

options: an asset that gives the holder the right to buy a given number of shares at a given price at any time within a fixed period of time

Pareto-efficient allocations: resource allocations such that one person cannot be made better off without making someone else worse off

partial equilibrium analysis: an analysis that focuses on only one or a few markets at a time

partnership: a business owned by two or more individuals, who share the profits and are jointly liable for any losses

patent: a government decree giving an inventor the exclusive right to produce, use, or sell an invention

paternalism: the making of judgments by government about what is good for people to have, rather than letting people choose on their own

pay-as-you-go system: public pensions whose benefits are paid by a tax on the current working population rather than from a fund accumulated from past contributions

pay equity: the principle that comparable jobs should receive comparable pay no matter what type of persons hold them

payroll tax: a tax based on payroll (wages) that is used to finance programs like Unemployment Insurance and the Canada Pension Plan

perfect competition: a situation in which each firm is a price taker—it cannot influence the market price; at the market price, the firm can sell as much as it wishes, but if it raises its price, it loses all sales

perfectly mobile capital: capital that responds quickly to changes in returns in different countries

permanent income hypothesis: the theory that individuals base their current consumption levels on their permanent (long-run average) incomes

permanent-income savings motive: people save in good years to tide them over in bad years; they choose their pattern of saving and spending year by year to average, or smooth, their consumption over good years and bad

Phillips curve: the trade-off between unemployment and inflation such that a lower level of unemployment is associated with a higher level of inflation

piece-rate system: a compensation system in which workers are paid according to the amount they produce

planned and **unplanned inventories:** planned inventories are those that firms choose to have on hand because they make business more efficient; unplanned inventories result when firms cannot sell what they produce

plant and equipment: buildings and machines that a firm uses to produce its output

policy ineffectiveness proposition: the proposition that government policies are ineffective—policies aimed at stimulating aggregate demand at most change the price level

portfolio theories of monetary policy: theories that argue that monetary policy affects output through its effect on various asset prices, in particular the prices of stocks

portfolio: an investor's entire collection of assets and liabilities

positive economics: economics that describes how the economy behaves and predicts how it might change—for instance, in response to some policy change

potential GDP: a measure of what the value of GDP would be if the economy's resources were fully employed

poverty line: the income level below which persons are deemed to be living in poverty; defined differently by different organizations

precautionary savings motive: people save so that they will be able to meet the costs of an unexpected illness, accident, or other emergency

predatory pricing: the practice of cutting prices below the marginal cost of production to drive out a new firm (or to deter future entry), at which point prices can be raised again

preferred share: a share that includes a promise to pay a given amount to the shareholder before common shareholders receive anything

present discounted value: how much an amount of money to be received in the future is worth right now

price ceiling: a maximum price above which a market's price is not legally allowed to rise

price discrimination: the practice of a firm charging different prices to different customers or in different markets

price dispersion: a situation that occurs when the same item is sold for different prices by different firms

price elasticity of demand: the percentage change in quantity demanded of a good as the result of a 1 percent change in price (the percentage change in quantity demanded divided by the percentage change in price)

price elasticity of supply: the percentage change in quantity supplied of a good as the result of a 1 percent change in price (the percentage change in quantity supplied divided by the percentage change in price)

price floor: a minimum price below which a market's price is not legally allowed to fall

price index: a measure of the level of prices found by comparing the cost of a certain basket of goods in one year with the cost in a base year

price leader: the dominant firm in an industry that sets prices for others to follow

principal: the original amount a saver lends or a borrower borrows

principal-agent problem: any situation in which one party (the principal) needs to delegate actions to another party (the agent), and thus wishes to provide the agent with incentives to work hard and make decisions about risk that reflect the interests of the principal

principle of consumer sovereignty: the principle that holds that each individual is the best judge of what makes him better off

principle of minimum differentiation: the tendency of political parties to bunch around the middle position in order to maximize their votes; also used to explain why firms tend to produce similar types of certain products

Prisoner's Dilemma: a situation in which the noncooperative pursuit of self-interest by two parties makes them both worse off

private corporations: corporations whose shares are not traded publicly and that tend to be owned by a small number of persons

private marginal cost: the marginal cost of production borne by the producer of a good; when there is a negative externality, such as air pollution, private marginal cost is less than social marginal cost

privatization: the process whereby functions that were formerly undertaken by government are delegated instead to the private sector

procyclical stocks: stocks whose value increases when the economy is up, and whose value decreases when the economy is down

producer price index: a price index that measures the average level of producers' prices

product differentiation: the fact that similar products (like breakfast cereals or soft drinks) are perceived to differ from one another and thus are imperfect substitutes

product liability: the obligation of a producer to compensate victims of a defective product that has injured them

product market: the market in which goods and services are bought and sold

product-mix efficiency: the condition in which the mix of goods produced by the economy reflects the preferences of consumers

production efficiency: the condition in which firms cannot produce more of some goods without producing less of other goods; the economy is on its production possibilities curve

production-facilitating function: the holding of inventories of inputs to facilitate production

production function: the relationship between the inputs used in production and the level of output

production possibilities curve: a curve that defines the opportunity set for a firm or an entire economy and gives the possible combinations of goods (outputs) that can be produced from a given level of inputs

production-smoothing function: the holding of inventories of outputs to smooth production between peak and slack selling periods

productivity, or **GDP per hour worked:** how much an average worker produces per hour, calculated by dividing real GDP by hours worked in the economy

productivity wage differentials: wage differences accounted for by differences in the productivity of workers

profit-and-loss statement: a table summarizing all the revenues and costs of a firm over the year

profits: total revenues minus total costs

progressive tax: a tax in which the rich pay a larger fraction of their income than the poor

property tax: a tax based on the value of property

proprietorship: a business owned by a single person, usually a small business

protectionism: the policy of protecting domestic industries from the competition of foreign-made goods

public corporations: corporations whose shares are traded publicly

public good: a good, such as national defence, that costs little or nothing for an extra individual to enjoy, and for which the costs of preventing any individual from enjoying them are high; public goods have the properties of nonrivalrous consumption and nonexcludability

pure profit or **monopoly rents:** the profit earned by a monopolist that results from its reducing output and increasing the price from the level at which price equals marginal cost

quantity theory of money: the theory that velocity is constant, so that changes in the money supply lead to proportionate changes in nominal income

random walk: a term used to describe the way the prices of stocks move; the next movement cannot be predicted on the basis of previous movements

rational expectations: the expectations of individuals that are formed by using all available information

rationing systems: ways of distributing goods that do not rely on prices, such as queues, lotteries, or coupons

real balance effect: as prices fall, the real value of people's money holdings increases, and they consume more

real business-cycle theorists: economists who contend that the economy's fluctuations have nothing to do with monetary policy but are determined by real forces

real exchange rates: exchange rates adjusted for changes in the relative price levels in different countries

real GDP: the real value of all final goods and services produced in the economy, measured in dollars adjusted for inflation

real income: income measured by what it can actually buy, rather than by the amount of money

real interest rate: the real return to saving, equal to the nominal interest rate minus the rate of inflation

real product wage: the wage divided by the price of the good being produced

recession: two consecutive three-month periods (quarters) during which GDP falls

Registered Retirement Savings Plans: savings by individuals for their retirement that are deductible up to a prescribed limit from income tax when paid into the plan, but taxable when taken out in retirement

Registered Pension Plans: pension plans operated by firms for their employees in which contributions up to a prescribed limit are deductible from income tax when paid into the plan, but taxable when taken out in retirement as a pension

regressive tax: a tax in which the poor pay a larger fraction of their income than the rich

regulatory capture: a term used to describe a situation in which regulators serve the interests of the regulated rather than the interests of consumers

relative performance compensation: pay based on performance on the job relative to others who have similar responsibilities and authority

relative price: the ratio of the prices of two goods, reflecting how much of one must be given up to get more of the other

renewable resources: natural resources that have the capacity to regenerate themselves, such as forests and fisheries

rent: see **economic rent**

rent seeking: the name given to behaviour that seeks to obtain benefits from favourable government decisions, such as protection from foreign competition

reputation rents: returns that firms earn on the basis of their good reputations

resale price maintenance: when a producer insists that a retailer selling its product do so at a prescribed price

reserves: money kept on hand by a bank in the event that some of those who have made deposits wish to withdraw their money

retail sales tax: a tax levied by all provinces and territories except Alberta on the sale of most goods by retailers in their jurisdictions

retained earnings: income that a firm earns that is not paid as dividends but is retained for investment by the firm

revenue curve: the relationship between a firm's total output and its revenues

revenues: the amount a firm receives for selling its products, equal to the price received multiplied by the quantity sold

risk averse, risk loving, risk neutral: given equal expected returns and different risks, risk-averse people will choose assets with lower risk, risk-loving people will choose assets with higher risk, and risk-neutral individuals will not care about differences in risk

risk premium: the additional interest required by lenders as compensation for the risk that a borrower may default; more generally, the extra return required to compensate an investor for bearing risk

savings account: a bank account that pays interest, that can be withdrawn at any time, and against which cheques typically cannot be written

screening: the process of differentiating among job candidates when there is incomplete information to determine who will be the most productive

seasonal unemployment: unemployment that results from seasonal variations

sectoral free trade: free trade between countries in the products of a particular industry, such as automobiles

self-selection device: a mechanism by which individuals are confronted with choices that will induce them to reveal something about themselves

service economy: the part of the economy that produces services rather than goods

shadow price: the true social value of a resource

shortage: when people would like to buy something, but it is not available at the going price

short-term bonds: bonds that mature within a few years

signalling: conveying information to persuade an employer that a prospective employee has desirable characteristics that will enhance his productivity—for example, a prospective worker's earning a university degree

simple interest: interest that is paid on the principal but not on interest previously earned

slope: the amount by which the value along the vertical axis increases as the result of a change in one unit along the horizontal axis; the slope is calculated by dividing the change in the vertical axis (the "rise") by the change in the horizontal axis (the "run")

Smith's "invisible hand": the idea that if people act in their own self-interest, they will often also be acting in a broader social interest, as if they had been directed by an "invisible hand"

smoothing consumption: consuming similar amounts in the present and future, rather than letting year-to-year income dictate consumption

social marginal cost: the marginal cost of production, including the cost of any negative externality, such as air pollution, borne by individuals in the economy other than the producer

socialism: an economic system in which the means of production are owned and controlled by the state

soft budget constraints: budget constraints facing a firm in which the government subsidizes any losses

stagflation: a situation in which high inflation exists alongside high unemployment

static expectations: the belief of individuals that today's prices and wages are likely to continue into the future

statistical discrimination: discriminating among persons in employment and wages according to characteristics they have that, on average, reflect differing productivities

sticky prices: prices that do not adjust or adjust only slowly towards a new equilibrium

sticky wages: wages that are slow to adjust in response to a change in labour market conditions

stock options: the option offered to a firm's executives to purchase a specified number of shares at a specified price and open for a specified period of time

stock statistics: measurements of the quantity of a certain item at a certain point in time, such as capital stock, the total value of buildings and machines

store of value: something that can be accepted as payment in the present and exchanged for items of value in the future

structural unemployment: long-term unemployment resulting from structural changes in the economy, such as changes in the composition of industrial output

substitute: two goods are substitutes if the demand for one increases when the price of the other increases

substitution effect: the reduced consumption of a good whose price has increased that is due to the changed trade-off, the fact that one has to give up more of other goods to get one more unit of the high-priced good; the substitution effect is associated with a change in the slope of the budget constraint

sunk cost: a cost that has been incurred and cannot be recovered

supply curve: the relationship between the quantity supplied of a good and its price, whether for a single firm or the market (all firms) as a whole

supply-constrained equilibrium: the equilibrium that occurs when prices are stuck at a level below that at which aggregate demand equals aggregate supply; in a supply-constrained equilibrium, output is equal to aggregate supply but less than aggregate demand

supply shock: an upward shift in the aggregate supply curve which can initiate an inflationary episode

surplus: when tax revenues exceed government expenditures in a given year

surplus labour: a great deal of unemployed or underemployed labour, readily available to potential employers

tacit collusion: an implicit understanding by firms not to compete too vigorously and to avoid price cutting

target savings motive: people save for a particular target, for example to make a down payment on a house or to pay for a future vacation

tariffs: charges levied by the federal government on the importation of certain goods and services from abroad

tax collection agreements: agreements between the federal government and individual provinces under which the federal government agrees to collect income taxes on behalf of a province provided the province abides by the federal tax base and rate structure

tax credit: the ability of a firm to reduce its taxes payable if it engages in certain activities, such as research and development or investment

tax expenditures: the name given to tax revenues lost to the government as a result of special tax concessions or tax breaks that are given to encourage certain types of activities or to achieve certain social objectives

tax incidence: the description of how the burden of taxes is ultimately borne by various income groups

theory: a set of assumptions and the conclusions derived from those assumptions put forward as an explanation for some phenomena

thin markets: markets with relatively few buyers and sellers

tie-ins or **tied selling:** when a firm that buys one product from another firm is obliged also to buy another product

time constraints: opportunity sets whose constraints are imposed by time

time value of money: the value attached to receiving a dollar now rather than some time in the future

total costs: the sum of all fixed costs and variable costs

trade deficit: the excess of imports over exports

trade secret: an innovation or knowledge of a production process that a firm does not disclose to others

trade-offs: the need to give up some of one item to get more of another

trade surplus: the excess of exports over imports

transactions costs: the extra costs (beyond the price of the purchase) of conducting a transaction, whether those costs are money, time, or inconvenience

transactions demand for money: the demand for money arising from its use in buying goods and services

transfer programs: programs directly concerned with redistribution, such as welfare assistance, that move money from one group in society to another

Treasury bills (T-bills): bills the government sells in return for a promise to pay a certain amount in a short period, usually less than 180 days

unemployment rate: the fraction of the labour force (those unemployed *plus* those seeking jobs) who are seeking jobs but are unable to find them

unitary banking system: a banking system with a large number of banks operating mainly on a regional basis

unit of account: something that provides a way of measuring and comparing the relative values of different goods

utility: the level of enjoyment an individual attains from choosing a certain combination of goods

utility possibilities curve: a curve showing the maximum level of utility that one individual can attain, given the level of utility attained by others

value added: the difference between the value of a firm's output and the cost of its intermediate inputs

variable costs: the costs resulting from variable inputs

variable inputs: inputs that rise and fall with the quantity of output

velocity: the speed with which money circulates in the economy, defined as the ratio of income to the money supply

vertical equity: the principle that says that people who are better off should pay more taxes

vertical merger or **integration:** a merger between two firms, one of which is a supplier or distributor for the other

vertical restraints or **agreements:** restrictions placed by a firm on the purchase or sale of its products by other firms; examples include resale price maintenance, tied selling, and market restrictions

voluntary unemployment: a situation in which workers voluntarily drop out of the labour force when the wage level falls

voting paradox: the fact that under some circumstances there may be no determinate outcome with majority voting: choice A wins a majority over B, B wins over C, and C wins over A

wage and price controls: government-imposed restrictions on wage and price increases

wholesale price index: a price index that measures the average level of wholesale prices

workfare programs: welfare programs that provide support on the condition that recipients work or engage in training or education

work sharing: reducing all employees' hours by equal amounts rather than firing some workers

zero elasticity of demand: the situation that exists when the quantity demanded will not change, regardless of changes in price

zero elasticity of supply: the situation that exists when the quantity supplied will not change, regardless of changes in price

CREDITS

Index